THEGREENGUIDE
Japan

Mount Fuji with tea plantations, Shizuoka Prefecture © Aflo/hemis.fr

THEGREENGUIDE **JAPAN**

Special thanks goes to the Visit Japan Campaign of the Japan National Tourism Organization (JNTO) and the Regional Offices of the Department of Transportation for their help in the creation of this guide. Thanks also goes to Akihiro Nishida, Mayuko Shimazaki, Sakiko Ishibashi, Takayasu Ito, Tetsushi Morita, Maria Gaspar, Didier Broussard.

Editoral Director	Cynthia Clayton Ochterbeck
Editor	Sophie Friedman
Editorial	Rebecca Hallett, Jackie Strachan, Yoshimi Kanazawa, Catherine Guégan, Geneviève Clastres, Floriane Charron, Akihiro Nishida
Principal Writers	JMS Books LLP (Howard Curtis, Barbara Beeby, Elsi Pichel-Juan, Simon Knight, Malcolm Garrard, Jenni Davis, Sheila Murphy)
Special Features Writers	*Understanding Japan*: P. Pons (Journalist); J.-M. Butel (Senior Lecturer, INALCO); P. Pataud Célérier (Journalist); É. Barral (Journalist); J-L. Toula-Breysse (Journalist); Ch. Polak (Historian); B. Delmas (Michelin Japan); Ch. Vendredi-Auzanneau (Assistant Professor of History of Architecture, Keio University, Tokyo); M. Tardits (Architect, Mikan group); C. Brisset (Senior Lecturer, University of Paris Diderot-Paris 7); M. Lucken (INALCO); M. Inoue (Journalist); H. Kelmachter (Cultural Attachée, French Embassy, Tokyo); S. Sarrazin (Journalist); P. Duval (Journalist); M. Wasserman (Professor at Ritsumeikan University, Kyoto); F. Moréchand (Lifestyle Journalist); J-F. Mesplède (Michelin); G. Maucout (Michelin), G. Clastres (journalist) *Discovering Japan*: P. Pataud Célérier (Tokyo and surroundings, Kyoto, Tohoku, and Hokkaido); J. Saglio (Kansai, Chugoku, Shikoku, Kyushu, Okinawa, and Chubu); S. Guillot (Kansai); Ph. Orain (Hokkaido); M. Fonovich, F. Sichet, L. Crooson, G. Battistella
Production Manager	Natasha George
Cartography	©2015 Cartographic data Shobunsha/Michelin, © Tokyo Metro Co., Ltd .Approved (Approval Number 26-A051), Peter Wrenn, Thierry Lemasson, Evelyne Girard, Denis Rasse
Picture Editor	Yoshimi Kanazawa
Interior Design	Chris Bell
Cover Design	Chris Bell, Christelle Le Déan
Layout	Natasha George
Contact Us	Michelin Travel and Lifestyle North America One Parkway South, Greenville, SC 29615 USA travel.lifestyle@us.michelin.com Michelin Travel Partner Hannay House, 39 Clarendon Road, Watford, Herts WD17 1JA UK ☎01923 205240 travelpubsales@uk.michelin.com www.viamichelin.co.uk
Special Sales	For information regarding bulk sales, customized editions and premium sales, please contact us at: travel.lifestyle@us.michelin.com

HOW TO USE THIS GUIDE

PLANNING YOUR TRIP

The blue-tabbed PLANNING YOUR TRIP section at the front of the guide gives you **ideas for your trip** and **practical information** to help you organize it. You'll find tours, a host of outdoor activities, a calendar of events, useful information on shopping, sightseeing, children's activities, and more.

INTRODUCTION

The orange-tabbed INTRODUCTION section explores Japan's **Nature**, geography, and geology. The **History** section spans the Jomon era through to today. The **Art and Culture** sections explore Japan's architecture, the visual arts, literature, and music, while **A Way of Life** delves into modern Japanese lifestyle and culture.

DISCOVERING

The green-tabbed DISCOVERING section features Principal Sights by region, including the most interesting local **Sights** and **Walking Tours**. Note that the admission prices shown are normally for a single adult.

ADDRESSES

We've selected the best hotels, restaurants, cafes, shops, nightlife, and entertainment to fit all budgets. See page 45 for an explanation of the price categories (or the Legend p651). See the back of the guide for an index of where to find hotels and restaurants.

Sidebars

Throughout the guide you will find blue, orange and green-colored text boxes with lively anecdotes, detailed history, and background information.

😊 A Bit of Advice 😊

Green advice boxes found in this guide contain practical tips and handy information relevant to your visit or to a sight in the Discovering section.

STAR RATINGS★★★

Michelin has given star ratings for more than 100 years. If you're pressed for time, we recommend you visit the ★★★, or ★★ sights first:

★★★ **Worth a special journey**

★★ **Worth a detour**

★ **Interesting**

MAPS

🗺 Regions of Japan in the guide

🗺 Regional maps

🗺 Maps of towns and cities

🗺 Maps of national parks

🗺 Subway map

All maps in this guide are oriented north, unless otherwise indicated by a directional arrow. The term "Regional Map" refers to a map at the beginning of a Tourism Region. A complete list of the maps found in the guide appears at the back of this book. In the guide, some subway station names spelt with an "n" before consonants (e.g. Jinbocho) are spelt with an "m" on the subway map (e.g. Jimbocho).

PLANNING YOUR TRIP

© Joe Carini/age fotostock

INTRODUCTION TO JAPAN

CONTENTS

© prasit chansarekorn/iStock

DISCOVERING JAPAN

Welcome to Japan

Japan's popular image is often limited to its hypermodern cities, bustling consumerism, and packed trains. Explore beyond the stereotype, though, and you'll find a complex, contradictory country. While on the surface it's dominated by bright neon and shiny plastic, Japanese culture finds beauty in impermanence, celebrating the fleeting cherry blossom and creating the aesthetic ideas of *wabi sabi* and *mono no aware*. As architect Tadao Ando said: "In Japan a temple is made of wood. The divine spirit inside the building is eternal, so the enclosure doesn't have to be." In other words, a visit to Japan will be more than just an interesting trip to another country; you may also learn to see past the clichés to the quiet beauty within.

TOKYO AND SURROUNDINGS
(pp130–251)

Multifaceted Tokyo never ceases to amaze—each of its 23 wards has a different atmosphere and personality. In the capital, the traditions of imperial Japan are juxtaposed with the ultra-modern. Akihabara is overflowing with the latest electronic gadgets, and Ginza with high-end boutiques, while the bright lights of Shinjuku beckon visitors to sample Japanese nightlife. Yet there is another side to Tokyo: incense-scented Asakusa temples, old bookstores in Jinbocho and a cup of sake that a fellow patron in a Shibuya bar pours you in friendship.

CENTRAL HONSHU (CHUBU)
(pp252–307)

Chubu, the central section of Honshu island, is where you will discover old Japan. Takayama, built by the carpenters who made Kyoto, brightens up the dark wood of its streets at festival time with colorful banners. In the Japan Alps deep gorges are lined with thick, fir-scented forests. Warm up after a glorious, crisp day on the pistes at a hot spring, soaking in waters which long ago soothed the aching muscles of monks and nobles. Feudal Japan lives on in this region: 16C Matsumoto Castle is one of the finest in the country, while Ise Shrine is Japan's most holy site; yet you may dine simply, at the hearth of a centuries-old inn, to the sound of frogs croaking in the night.

KYOTO AND KANSAI
(pp308–421)

For some 11 centuries the Kyoto aristocracy developed their cultural pursuits to the highest possible degree of refinement and sophistication. Today, almost a quarter of Japan's National Treasures can be found here, in temples, shrines, and museums. You can still glimpse this Golden Age in the dainty gait of a young trainee geisha, known as a maiko, and in Nara, where sacred deer wander freely among temples and eat from your hand. Yet a contemporary world welcomes you warmly in Osaka, Kansai's economic capital.

WESTERN HONSHU (CHUGOKU) *(pp422–461)*

In Chugoku you can visit Japan's second-most important shrine, Izumo Taisha, also said to be the oldest. This is where young women who wish to get married pray to Okuninushi, who is believed to bring joyous harmony to marriage. In Hiroshima there is remembrance of things past, but also hope, echoed in the peacefulness of Koraku-en, one of Japan's loveliest gardens. Enjoy a cup of *matcha* in its teahouse . Isukushima Shrine (often called Miyajima) is where the goddess of the sea is worshipped; you can access the celebrated vermillion-lacquered "floating torii" by waiting for low tide. It's at its most enchanting at dusk, when lanterns illuminate one of Japan's most iconic views.

NORTHERN HONSHU (TOHOKU) *(pp462–511)*

Tohoku is Japan's largest region after Hokkaido and one of the Ainu people's original homelands. The view from the rugged coastline out over the 260 pine-clad islands in the deep blue of Matsushima Bay is considered one of the country's most beautiful. From here you can follow the trail to Mount Haguro for a temple stay. Take a flat-bottomed boat through Genbikei Gorge, explore the ancient Buddhist temple of Chuson-ji in Hiraizumi and wander the samurai district of Kakunodate. Or take the waters in one of the man *onsen* around Yamagata.

HOKKAIDO *(pp512–545)*

Hokkaido is Japan's northernmost and largest region. The Ainu people settled here before the Jomon era (10,000–300 BC). Visit in February to see the celebrated Snow Festival and marvel at the talent of the artists who create gigantic ice sculptures in the open air. A "Genghis Khan" dinner of barbecued mutton and vegetables will ward off the deep chill or winter, while a foaming Sapporo beer from the local brewery cheers the soul. Even in the depths of winter, the hot water of Lake Shikotsu never freezes; it was formed around 40,000 years agoin the crater of a volcano.

SHIKOKU *(pp546–574)*

The smallest and least-populated of Japan's four main islands is Shikoku. Its tranquillity has long been a source of comfort and inspiration, with 17C Kikugetsu-tei an evocative spot to experience a tea ceremony. In the surrounding garden of Ritsurin-koen, twisted black pines have been shaped over five generations to suggest dragons or cranes in flight. Before leaving to hike the wild countryside of the Iya Valley or watch the 100,000 dancers of the Awa Odori festival, take time out with a visit to Dogo Onsen,

Kabira Bay, Ishigaki-jima, Okinawa Archipelago

© paprikaworks/iStock

one of the longest-used hot springs in Japan, with a history stretching back over 3,000 years, and a special bath reserved for the sole use of the Imperial Family.

KYUSHU *(pp575–623)*

With its intense volcanic activity, Kyushu, "land of fire," was long Japan's main point of contact with other cultures. Learn about Japan's fine ceramic tradition in the "ceramic cities" of Imari, Arita, and Okawachiyama. In dynamic Fukuoka, you can see contemporary works of art at the Asian Art Museum, followed by an evening in lively Nakasu; dinner may be on the wooden bench of a street stand (*yatai*), eating noodles in thick pork broth. When you're ready for a different pace, explore mist-shrouded Yakushima's rainforest, or try a volcanic-sand bath in Ibusuki.

OKINAWA ARCHIPELAGO *(pp624–635)*

Some 60 islands stretch in an arc across the East China Sea, each a subtropical paradise of its own. On Okinawa-honto, head to the covered market to see exotic fruits and fish sold by spry old ladies, then take a boat trip to spot humpback whales. After a short plane ride to Ishigaki-jima, you can dive the coral reefs and see manta rays, before heading to a small inn on the beach for dinner overlooking the blue-green sea.

Shinkansen Hayabusa and Kagayaki at Tokyo Station
© Didier Zylberyng/hemis.fr

When and Where to Go

WHEN TO GO

Spring (*Mar–May*) and **fall** (*Sept–Nov*) are the best seasons to visit Japan: the temperatures are mild and constant, and the countryside looks beautiful. Spring is famous for the luxuriant cherry blossom trees, which burst into flower first on Kyushu in the south in March, and then farther north across Honshu and Hokkaido throughout April. In the fall, the forests and gardens are ablaze with magnificent gold and purple hues. The humid heat of summer (*Jun–Aug*) can be hard to take, accompanied as it is by incessant rain and sometimes even typhoons (*end Aug*). But it is the ideal season for enjoying the beaches, hiking on Hokkaido or in the mountains of Honshu, and attending the festivals and firework displays that are held in these regions. In winter (*Dec–Feb*), on Hokkaido, and on the coasts of the Sea of Japan, traveling can be difficult, as the roads and railways are sometimes blocked by snow. The cold is not all that severe, however, and is often interspersed with fine sunny days that are perfect for skiing at the winter sports resorts on Hokkaido and in the Japan Alps. In addition, some towns and regions offer special deals to attract winter visitors.
In contrast to the cold weather of Honshu, beach lovers and diving enthusiasts will find October to April the best time to visit the subtropical islands of Okinawa.

SEASONS

Generally speaking, whichever region you decide to visit, watch out for the tourist **high seasons**, which coincide with the Japanese public holidays. During New Year (*Dec 29–Jan 3*), Golden Week (*late Apr–early May*), and the Bon Festival (*around Aug 15*), the temples and most famous places of interest are overwhelmed by vast crowds of visitors. Buying a ticket for a train or plane and finding a hotel to stay at becomes problematic, the more so because the prices increase significantly during these periods.
See Making Reservations p35.

WHAT TO PACK
CLOTHES

In spring (*Mar–May*) and in the fall (*Sept–Nov*), take lightweight jackets and sweaters. In summer (*Jun–Aug*), choose loose, light clothes, and be prepared for the downpours of *tsuyu* (rainy season). In winter (*Dec–Mar*), pack coats, fleeces, or warm sweaters, and thick socks, plus snow shoes and other specialist equipment if heading to ski area. Your choice of clothing should also take account the region you are visiting: in spring it is still cold in Sapporo and Sendai, mild in Tokyo, Kyoto, and Fukuoka, and quite hot on Okinawa. Whenever you travel, it is advisable to pack warm clothes for the evenings and in mountainous areas. Take also a light raincoat or an umbrella and comfortable shoes that are easily removed (shoes need to be constantly taken off in Japan).

OTHER ITEMS

A small compass is helpful to help orient yourself in large towns, particularly when coming out of the subway and in districts where signs are only written in Japanese, and of course in wilderness areas. A suitcase on wheels saves unnecessary effort and a small knapsack for excursions is a must. A plug adapter is vital, but can be bought cheaply in Japan. Avoid taking a very large suitcase, as baggage racks in trains, coin lockers and hotel rooms can be small. If you need a large bag, look into *takkyubin* (luggage forwarding) services like the one provided by Yamato Transport (*www.kuronekoyamato.co.jp/ytc/en/send/services/takkyubin*). Bring all necessary medications; Japanese pharmacies rarely dispense them without prescriptions. A dictionary or offline translator is a good idea, as English is not widely spoken.

WHERE TO GO

This multifacted country is so rich and offers so much to discover it can feel overwhelming when organizing your trip. How can you decide where to go, to feel you have seen the essential, especially if your time there is limited? It seems modern Japan cannot be experienced without its ancient traditions; city life takes on meaning when contrasted with life in the villages; even Tokyo seems to need to be offset by the Kyoto experience. First let your budget, energy level, and available time define the limits on your plans; then let your curiosity take you where it will. Even a small taste of Japan's complexity will give you some understanding of it as a whole.

CHOOSE YOUR ROUTE

On the inside front cover, the **Regions of Japan map** gives a general picture of the places featured and the star-rated areas.

The beginning of the section for **each Japanese region** includes a detailed map to help you get your bearings, a description of the places of interest, what to do with children, and advice on how best to organize your time and plan your trip.

IDEAS FOR YOUR VISIT

Most tourists begin with the vast and varied city of Tokyo; if your time is limited, don't miss Asakusa's temples, Akihabara's electronics shopping, Jinbocho's bookselling district, and Shinjuku's nightlife. With more time you can make day trips to Nikko, Kamakura, or Yokohama, of overnight in Hakone. If you have a few more days, take the bullet train from Tokyo to make a combined trip to Kyoto, Nara, and Mount Fuji.

Hiroshima is an important destination not only for its Peace Park and Memorial Museum, but also for its castle, art museum, and gardens; while there, visit nearby Miyajima (properly called Itsukushima), which is considered one of the most beautiful places in Japan.

GUIDED TOURS

Several Japanese agencies organize guided tours for visitors. Package tours, including transport, hotels, meals, and visits, are often good value and offer a speedy trip to a town or region. Another option is the "free plan" – a little more flexible for those who prefer not to be part of a group.

JTB Sunrise Tours – ℘03-5796-5454 in Tokyo, japanican.com/en/tour. For visits to Tokyo, Nikko, Ise, Kyoto, Nara, and Hiroshima, this reliable and reputable agency offers a wide range of tours lasting 2–3 days or longer at attractive prices. For something a little different, try the **Sumo Tour** in Tokyo during the Sumo Championships. Half-day excursions are also available.

Inside Japan Tours – ℘0117-244-3380, insidejapantours.com. This UK-based agency organizes individual and group tours, either self-guided or with expert guides, with an emphasis on balancing major sights with off-the-beaten-track destinations.

NATIONAL PARKS

Visitors to Japan often think first of its cities, but nature lovers will also find a plethora of extraordinary sites to be enjoyed in every season. Serene lakes reflect ancient temples; craggy ravines become dramatic when dressed in autumnal color; tropical fish dart by coral reefs, and lofty peaks are snow-capped against ice-blue winter skies. Japan has 34 national parks, overseen by the Ministry of the Environment (env. go.jp/en/nature/nps/park), with a view to preserving these superb examples of the natural beauty the country has to offer for the enjoyment of those who take the trouble to seek them out. The Kanto national parks are Chichibu-Tama-Kai (*natural forests, mountains and gorges*); Fuji-Hakone-Izu (*Mt. Fuji, Fuji Five Lakes, woodland*); Minami Alps (*including Kita-dake, Japan's second-highest peak*); Nikko (*Toshogu and other important shrines and temples*); Ogasawara (*over 30 subtropical islands*); and Oze (*mountains surrounding one of Japan's largest moors*).

On Hokkaido, there are the parks of Akan-Mashu (*volcanoes and one of the world's clearest lakes*); Daisetsuzan (*the Roof of Hokkaido, Japan's largest park*); Kushiroshitsugen (*the country's largest marshland*); Rishiri-Rebun-Sarobetsu (*Japan's northernmost park*); Shikotsu-Toya (*two large lakes and active volcanoes*); and Shiretoko (*mountains, lakes and wilderness*).

The national parks on and around Kyushu are Aso-Kuju (*many volcanoes and the world's largest caldera basin*); Kirishima-Kinkowan (*several volcanoes, and cedars over 1,000 years old*); Saikai (*over 400 islands*); Unzen-Amakusa (*with a resort around the active volcano of Fugen-dake*); and Yakushima (*a forest-covered volcanic island, with some trees over a millennium old*).

The southern islands of Okinawa are home to the national parks of Amamigunto (*diverse ecosystem and unique island culture*); Iriomote-Ishigaki (*subtropical forests and Japan's largest coral reef*); Keramashoto (*mostly ocean, with excellent diving and whale-watching*); and Yambaru (*dense subtropical forest and varied wildlife*).

In the Tohoku area lie the national parks of Bandai-Asahi (*lakes, forest, and peaks, including Dewa-sanzan*); Sanriku Fukko (*rugged coastline of sharp cliffs, known as the Sea Alps*); and Towada-Hachimantai (*Lake Towada and the Oirase River, as well as hot springs and volcanoes*).

In Chubu you'll find Joshin'etsukogen (*Japan's second-largest national park, with famous peaks including Mt. Asama*); Chubusangaku (*ravines and mountain streams, and an important ptarmigan habitat*); Hakusan (*along with Mt. Fuji and Mt. Tateyama, one of Japan's three sacred mountains*); Ise-Shima (*islets, deep coves and the famous Ise-jingu*); and Myoko-Togakushi renzan (*diverse mountains, including Mt. Myoko, and a history of mountain worship*).

In the Kansai region are the national parks of Yoshino-Kumano (*Mt. Yoshino, noted for its cherry blossoms, and Mt.*

Omine, worshipped by ascetics) and San'inkaigan (*a marine park extending to the sand dunes of Tottori*).

The national parks around the Chugoku region and Shikoku island are Ashizuri-Uwakai (*includes the Ashizuri Promontory and Tatsukushi Marine Park*); Daisen-Oki (*the site of Mt. Daisen and the Oki Archipelago*); and Setonaikai (*the varied islands of the inland sea between the Chugoku and Kansai regions, Shikoku and Kyushu*). ⓒ*See Discovering Japan section.*

TEMPLES AND SHRINES

Temples are Buddhist places of worship and are for quiet reflection. Show respect by putting a coin in the offering box before a brief prayer. If you buy incense, light it and let it burn a few seconds, extinguishing the flame by waving your hand rather than blowing it out. Then place the incense in the burner and fan the smoke toward yourself – it is believed to have healing powers. If you are asked to take off your shoes, leave them on the shelves at the entrance or take them with you if bags are provided. Be sure to wear socks! Shrines are places of worship and the dwellings of the *kami*, or Shinto gods. People visit to pay their respects to the *kami* or to pray for good fortune, coming especially during festivals, to present new babies, or to hold wedding ceremonies. Traditionally, those ill or with an open wound or those in mourning may not visit, as these are considered causes of impurity. At the purification fountain at the entrance, use a ladle to rinse your left then right hands, then transfer some water into your cupped left hand and rinse off your lips, before once more rinsing the left hand and tipping any remaining water back over the ladle's handle. You are not supposed to drink from the ladle or to swallow the water. Once inside, throw a coin in the offering box, ring the bell (if there is one), bow deeply twice, clap twice, and then pray for a few seconds. Bow once again when finished.

What to See and Do

OUTDOOR FUN
AND SPECTATOR SPORTS
Martial arts and sumo

Japan is well known for its martial arts such as judo, aikido, karate, kendo (two-handed sword-fighting), and kyudo (Japanese archery), which are all widely practiced across the country. Sports enthusiasts will find plenty of opportunities to see martial arts demonstrations and to watch contests while in Japan, though visitors are unlikely to be able to take part in training sessions.

Sumo tournaments last 15 days and are held six times a year: in January, May, and September in Tokyo; in March in Osaka; in July in Nagoya; and in November in Fukuoka. It's best to book tickets in advance (*see sumo.or.jp/En for information on where you can buy them*). Bouts are normally televized, often in the late afternoon, but the atmosphere of a is best experienced in person if possible.

For more information, contact the following sports federations:

Akikai Foundation, Aikido World Headquarters – *℘03-3203-9236, aikikai.or.jp/eng.*

All Japan Judo Federation – *℘03-3818-4199, judo.or.jp/english.*

All Japan Kendo Federation – *℘03-3234-6271, kendo.or.jp/en.*

All Nippon Kyudo Federation – *℘03-3481-2387, kyudo.jp/info/ english.html.*

Nihon Sumo Kyokai – *℘03-3623-5111, www.sumo.or.jp/En. See also Martial Arts and Sumo p118.*

Baseball

Introduced to Japan during the Meiji era and known as *yakyu* in Japanese, baseball is extremely popular in Japan. The championships take place between April and October. There are two professional leagues, the **Central League** and the **Pacific League**, with six teams in each. Matches are transmitted live on television. The university championships also have a considerable following. In Tokyo, the giant Tokyo Dome on the site of the old Koraku-en Stadium is home to the famous Yomiuri Giants baseball team. The historic Koshien stadium, home of the Hanshin Tigers, is located between Osaka and Kobe and inspires the dreams of young players in the high school baseball championships.

Watching a professional league match is a great experience. You can get tickets from the stadium or ahead from terminals at convenience stores (or *conbini*), such as 7-Eleven and Lawson. *Dates, results and further information are on npb.jp/eng.*

Yomiuri Giants playing Hiroshima Toyo Carp at Tokyo Dome

Golf

Some 17 million Japanese people play golf, but the number of golf courses is limited (even so, there are almost 2,400) and green fees are consequently high (*around ¥10,000*). However, you can keep your handicap up by playing on one of the urban driving ranges, often found on the top of multistory buildings, and surrounded by protective netting. *For a complete list of golf courses in Japan, with descriptions, prices, and addresses, go to* golf-in-japan.com.

Hiking

The many footpaths crisscrossing the valleys and mountainous regions of Japan lead through some exceptionally beautiful countryside and are accessible and well signposted. The Japan Alps around Nagano and Kamikochi, the pilgrimage to the 88 temples of Shikoku, the national parks of Hokkaido, the walk up Mount Fuji, trails around Kyoto, Nara, or Nikko … the choice for walkers is wide and varied. Paths are generally well marked and frequently pass campsites, refuges, temples, and places where you can spend the night. *(Information and suggestions for itineraries can be found at* www.outdoorjapan.com *or* japanhike.wordpress.com.*) Hiking in Japan,* published by Kodansha, also gives detailed descriptions of many routes. Avoid hiking in the rainy season when paths are particularly slippery.

Skiing

Japan boasts several ski slopes, all well equipped with ski lifts. The resorts of Hokkaido, Tohoku, and those in the center of Honshu are best for powder snow. Niseko, also on Hokkaido, has some superb pistes and is very lively in the evenings. Hakuba (*see p282*), near Nagano, hosted a number of events during the Winter Olympics of 1998. Gala Yuzawa, near Niigata, is just 90 minutes from Tokyo by shinkansen. During vacation periods and winter weekends, the resorts are packed, so it is best to reserve accommodation in advance. The Japanese ski slopes are neither steep nor long, but many of the hotels include *onsen* (hot springs), which are pleasant and relaxing after a day's skiing. (*Expect to pay from around ¥4,500 for use of the ski lift and ¥5,000 for equipment rental*). *You will find more information on* snowjapan.com, *an excellent source of information for skiers and snowboarders. To organize a ski tour (accommodation, ski rental, etc.),* see also skijapan.com.

Water sports

The most popular area for **diving** is among the splendid coral reefs off Okinawa (*see p624*), and in the clear, temperate waters of the islands of the Izu Peninsula. Expert and more intrepid divers can dive under the midwinter ice in the Sea of Okhotsk, off Hokkaido. The choice of dives available is wide, but prices are high. Two dives, plus boat and equipment rental, can easily cost ¥20,000. *For information,* see divejapan.com.
Bathing at the beaches, however, costs nothing. The beaches at Chiba, near Tokyo, those between Kobe and Himeji in the Kansai area, at Kamakura, on the Izu Peninsula (*see p246*), and those on Okinawa, with their superb white sand, attract large summer crowds. Some offer excellent conditions for surfing and **windsurfing**. But, apart from Okinawa, a few protected areas of Izu, and the south of Shikoku and Kyushu, the Japanese coastline rarely comes up to expectations; the detractions include polluted seawater near towns, swarms of jellyfish from mid-August onward, beaches piled with concrete tetrapods, and large blocks designed to prevent coastal erosion. *For surfing and windsurfing information,* see outdoorjapan.com *and* japansurf.com. Many beaches prohibit visitors with tattoos, so if you have one it may be simplest to keep it covered. *There's a (not exhaustive) list of beaches which allow tattoos on* tattoo-friendly.jp.

ENTERTAINMENT

THEME PARKS

Japan is crazy about theme parks, which have sprung up all over the country. **History theme parks**, built to resemble villages from the samurai era; parks containing **models** of monuments from the world's great cities; **leisure parks**, such as Disneyland or Sanrio Puroland in Tokyo, and Fuji-Q Highland near Mount Fuji; **science parks** like Space World at Fukuoka; **water parks** such as Ocean Dome in Miyazaki, DisneySea in Tokyo, or Hakkeijima Sea Paradise at Yokohama, etc. For many Japanese people, these parks have become substitutes for the long-haul vacations that they can no longer afford.

ONSEN, SENTO AND SUPER SENTO

Hot springs of volcanic origin are found in many parts of the Japanese archipelago. They are visited as much for rest and relaxation as for health reasons (see The Onsen Ritual p112). The various types of onsen are differentiated by the mineral composition of the water; the size, number and types of bath provided and whether they are made of wood or stone; also whether the baths are indoor or outdoor (rotenburo). "Wild" outdor onsen are often found in mountainous areas and river valleys or along the coast, but most now have facilities such as changing rooms and are part of a bathhouse, ryokan (traditional Japanese inns) or hotel complex.

In areas without an abundance of naturally heated spring water, often in the heart of big towns or cities, you'll find sento. The water here comes from the normal supply, and the bathhouse is seen as a local amenity rather than relaxing treat. Many sento are decorated with beautiful tiling and murals, and different baths may have medicinal or aromatic herbs added (or even a light electric current).

Super sento differ from regular sento in size and facilities, offering a number of (sometimes themed) pools, jacuzzis, and saunas, along with restaurants, gyms, and massage facilities. The largest are like theme parks, and may include swimming pools and water slides for kids. Those interested in experiencing one in Tokyo could try Oedo Onsen Monogatari (see p174) or LaQua at Tokyo Dome City (laqua. jp/en). Unless you have good reason to think otherwise, you should assume that onsen and sento will be separated by gender, will not allow clothes (even swimsuits or towels) in the pools, and will not allow guests with tattoos. There's a (not exhaustive) list of onsen and sento which allow tattoos on tattoo-friendly.jp.

SHOWS, CINEMAS, AND CONCERTS

Despite the language barrier, a visit to a classic Japanese theater is recommended. Kabuki, bunraku, and Noh theater productions are performed regularly in the large theaters in Tokyo, Kyoto, and Osaka. For opera, dance, musical comedies, concerts, and cinema, consult local magazines such as Metropolis (metropolisjapan.com) for Tokyo. Reduced rate tickets for shows (and also train and plane journeys) are offered by **discount ticket shops** (kinken shoppu). These small stores are found just about everywhere in the big towns, but the vendors rarely speak any English.

PACHINKO

Pachinko is a flourishing industry that arouses deep passions in many Japanese people. The popular pachinko parlors (gaming halls), with endless rows of machines and flashing lights, are wreathed in clouds of smoke and ring to the cacophony of the metal balls dropping down through the machines. Pachinko is a cross between a pinball and a slot machine. By pressing a lever, a steel ball shoots upward and then drops down the machine, passing through an array of pins. If a ball falls into a "gate", the payout is in the form of more metal balls, which can be exchanged for small prizes or tokens. Gambling is forbidden by law in Japan, but by happy coincidence, *pachinko* prizes can be sold in a nearby shop. The real pros spend their days combing the parlors, trying to identify the machines that pay out most often.

KARAOKE

If a Japanese person should invite you out for the evening, there is little hope of avoiding karaoke at some stage in the proceedings, where amateurs sing along to a musical backing track, following the lyrics flashed up on a screen. In Japan, this far outstrips clubbing as the nighttime entertainment of choice.
A symbol of Japanese pop culture, karaoke (meaning "empty orchestra") was invented in 1971 and since then has spread throughout the world. The karaoke halls in Japan are made up of a series of little rooms ("boxes"), furnished with couches and a television set, that may be reserved by the half-hour or the night (*from around ¥100 for 30min off-peak, or ¥2,000 for the night*), so it's a popular choice if you miss the last train. Drinks and food can be ordered, and many establishments offer a *nomihoudai* (all you can drink) deal. Karaoke catalogs offer thousands of songs, many in English, so pick your number and Broadway, here you come!

ACTIVITIES FOR KIDS 👪👤

Japan is an ideal place for a vacation with children, with its reputation for cleanliness and for being relatively crime-free. Jars of baby and toddler food, milk formula for infants, and diapers are readily available in *depato* (department stores) and *conbini* (convenience stores). Most public places, such as big stores, railway stations, and trains, have restrooms with changing areas for babies. The majority of most hotels have cribs for small children and some offer a baby-sitting service.

In terms of activities for children—apart from discovering the natural world and a new culture—Japan offers a wide range of attractions, including theme parks (*such as Universal Studios in Osaka*), excellent interactive museums (*like Tokyo's Ghibli Museum*), shops selling toys and electronic games, zoos, aquaria, etc. Children under 6 years old travel free on public transport, while those aged 6–11 pay half the adult tariff.
We have made a selection of activities and places to visit that might appeal to children in each of Japan's regions (👪*see Family Activities below*). You will more information on them in the *Discovering Japan* section, identified by this symbol 👪👤.

FAMILY ACTIVITIES

(In order of appearance in the guide)
Tokyo: Ghibli Museum; Harajuku Bridge; Yoyogi Park; a monorail trip to Odaiba and Decks shopping mall; Inokashira Park; Oedo Onsen Monogatari; teamLab Borderless; National Musem of Emerging Science and Innovation; Tokyo Skytree.
Yokohama: Chinatown; Landmark Tower; the *Nippon Maru*.
Miura Peninsula: walking in Arasaki Park or on Jogashima; Miura Beach.
Nikko: *Yabusame* archery contests May 17–18; the avenue lined with *Jizo* statues.
Mount Fuji: Tenzan Onsen; Museum of the Little Prince; old Hakone Checkpoint.
Izu Peninsula: A walk from Wakano-Ura to Shimoda or from Chikurin no Komichi to Shuzenji.
Nagoya: The port area; Karakuri-kan puppet museum; Meiji-mura open-air museum.
Japan Alps: Seeing the snow monkeys at Jigokudani Yaen-koen; Nozawa Onsen; the Ninja Village at Togakushi Folk Museum.
Sado Island: A *Bunya Ningyo* puppet show; a tub boat ride; a Kodo drummer performance.
Kyoto: Kyoto International Manga Museum; watch an *odori* show; a

stroll through the Gion district; Toei Studio Park; take a boat down the Hozu River to Arashiyama.
Nara: Feed the deer in the park.
Koya-san: A stay in a *shukubo* (temple lodging).
Kumano Kodo: Shirahama Onsen; Nachi waterfall; the pilgrimage route around Yunomine Onsen.
Osaka: Spa World; Osaka Bay; the storks at Toyooka .
Kobe: Kobe Maritime Museum; the Tetsujin 28 robot; Suma Beach; Himeji Castle.
San'yo Coast, Okayama: Japan Rural Toy Museum at Kurashiki.
San'yo Coast, Hiroshima: Miyajima Island; the Peace Memorial Museum (for older children).
San'in Coast: The Tottori Sand Dunes; Yonago Waterbird Sanctuary; Matsue Vogel Park; a boat trip around Matsue Castle moat.
Sendai and around: Date Masamune's armor in Sendai City Museum; Shiogama fish market; a boat trip in Matsushima Bay; Ishinomori Manga Museum.
Hiraizumi and around: A boat ride down Genbikei Gorge.
Tsuruoka and around: The monk mummy at Churen-ji; Mount Haguro and its *shukubo*.
Akita and around: The samurai district at Kakunodate; a boat trip on Lake Tazawa.
Hirosaki: The crafts complex Neputa-mura; Oirase Gorge; Shirakami-sanchi forest.
Sapporo: Dai-ichi Takimoto-kan at Noboribetsu Onsen; the Snow Festival (*Feb*); the Volcano Science Museum.
Daisetsuzan National Park: An excursion to Mount Asahi; the cable car to Mount Kuro.
Shiretoko National Park: a boat trip by the cliffs.
Hakodate and around: Museum of Northern Peoples.
Akan National Park: fishing at Lake Akan; the Akan International Crane Center.
Inland Sea: Nao-shima's beaches and public art exhibits.

Matsuyama: A trip on the small steam train *Botchan Ressha* from Dogo Onsen.
The Iya Valley: A boat trip through Oboke Gorge.
Kochi and the Pacific Coast: The beach at Katsurahama; whale watching; Makino Botanical Garden.
Fukuoka: Hakata Machiya Folk Museum; Kyushu National Museum; Sky Dream giant wheel and Robosquare; Canal City.
Saga and around: Saga Castle; the Prefectural Space & Science Museum.
Kumamoto and Mount Aso: watching dolphins at Tsuji-shima; a pony-ride at Mount Aso.
Kagoshima: The beach at Ibusuki.
Okinawa: The beach at Minna-jima; whale-spotting at Zamami-jima; a ride in a buffalo-drawn cart on Iriomote-jima or Taketomi-jima.

SHOPPING
CRAFT ITEMS AND ANTIQUES
Prices shown in store often do not include consumption tax (10 percent).

Amulets
Shops and stands selling good-luck charms and *ema* (wooden votive plaques) abound at the entrances to temples and shrines.

Prints and engravings
Original engravings are sold in specialist shops (*see Asakusa and Ueno Addresses p184*). Prices depend on their rarity and quality. You may be able to find a beautiful old *ukiyo-e* for less than ¥15,000, but if your budget is limited, there are some good-quality reproductions available.

Lacquerware, wood, bamboo
There is a vast range of goods on sale made of these materials, from useful everyday items (bowls, chopsticks, trays, combs) to decorative ones (statuettes, dolls, boxes). Prices are generally affordable for small items, but for larger or superior-quality lacquerware or antique wood furniture, the cost can be pretty extortionate.

Paper and calligraphy

Handmade Japanese paper (*washi*) is of excellent quality. It is often brightly colored and sometimes speckled or encrusted with flower petals. *Washi* is used to make many items, such as notebooks and exercise books, boxes, and fans, and is also used in origami. Stores specializing in paper often sell incense, too, along with necessary materials for calligraphy: brushes, ink, and ink-stones.

Umbrellas

Made from bamboo and oiled paper, highly decorative traditional umbrellas are often sold in craft shops.

Pottery and ceramics

There are many potters working in Japan. Stores selling bowls, plates, cups, and bottles can be found in all villages, while ceramics may be found in department stores and craft centers in towns. Each region has its own style of earthenware or porcelain and its own specialties. The finest examples of Bizen, Arita, or Imari can cost millions of yen. However, pieces at a reduced price and cheaper items suitable for gifts can often be found in the big stores.

Dolls

Japanese dolls (*ningyo*) are beautifully made, and as such are less toys than collectable pieces. During the Hina Matsuri (*Mar 3*), dolls are given to girls and on Children's Day (*May 5*), boys receive samurai dolls. There are also *kokeshi*, stylised wooden dolls often with hand-painted decoration. They all make interesting gifts and souvenirs.

Swords

The elegant Japanese swords (*katana*) carried by the samurai of the past now command colossal prices due to the amount of work that goes into making them. If an original, authentic sword from an antique shop is out of the question, you can still find good-quality modern versions for a reasonable price in the big stores, or buy directly from the producer.

OTHER PURCHASES

Foodstuffs

Candy and cakes – These are bought as much for their containers— delightful little boxes and colored packaging that make perfect gifts—as for their contents. You'll find local variations on all the major types throughout the country.

Sake – There are hundreds of types of sake, some with labels written in ornate calligraphy. If you are not sure which to choose or have a particular budget, just ask in any big store and they'll help you pick. Alternatively, go on a brewery tour and buy your favorite after the tasting.

Tea – Since you are in the kingdom of green tea and the formal tea ceremony, taking a small box or two home with you is a must. You may like to buy a teapot too, but the cast-iron ones are rather heavy to carry.

ELECTRONIC AND PHOTOGRAPHIC EQUIPMENT

In the cities, the stores selling electronic goods tend to be grouped together in certain districts, such as Akihabara in Tokyo (see p148) and Den Den Town in Osaka, where the prices are often quite reasonable. Big chains such as Bic Camera or Yodobashi Camera also offer a wide choice at **fairly competitive prices**. The prices are much the same as those charged in Hong Kong or Singapore, but you are more likely to get a genuine deal. Japan being a world leader in cutting-edge technology, it's no surprise that Japanese stores stock the very latest in electronic novelties and high-tech gadgets. It is worth asking for a discount; some stores will respond and you might be able to knock down the price by as much as 10 percent. Be careful to check for compatibility—in particular with regard to software and voltage—before buying a product, though, and make sure that a user manual in English is included. If you have the choice, buy models made for export.

Nakabashi Bridge

Higashiyama Temple Area

Shinhotaka Ropeway

Hida Folk Village

TAKAYAMA
TOKYO
KYOTO

HIDA-TAKAYAMA
https://www.hida.jp/english/

MUSIC AND VIDEOS

Hard copies of music and films are still big business in Japan, so you'll find chains such as HMV and Tower Records represented in the cities, offering a good choice of foreign CDs and DVDs. There are also a number of shops that sell them secondhand. Remember, however, if you are tempted to buy secondhand DVDs, that the onscreen menu will be in Japanese.

COOL JAPAN

Kawaii fashion and accessories, along with J-pop, manga, *anime*, and video game merchandise, are widely available in stores in most districts, including those of the Anime chain, and are a big draw for locals and tourists alike. The popular Totoro stores (and Studio Ghibli merchandise in all its forms) are just as tempting, along with Hello Kitty, Kapibarasan, Pokémon, and others.

CLOTHES AND TEXTILES

The big stores offer a wide range of superb silk kimono, but often at prohibitive prices. Better deals can be obtained from secondhand shops, where kimono are generally between ¥5,000 and ¥20,000. New *yukata* (light cotton kimonos) are cheaper, at around ¥4,000. For Western-style clothing, chains like Uniqlo have moderate prices, while many stores offer local and international labels. Stores selling secondhand casual clothes and sometimes upcycled versions of secondhand items are increasing in number and offer some great bargains. The top Japanese fashion houses (Yamamoto, Miyake) on the other hand are very expensive, but prices do fall during the **sales**, generally held in January and July.

WHERE TO SHOP

Department stores

The big department store (*depato*) chains such as Daimaru, Takashimaya, Seibu, Mitsukoshi, and Isetan are all crammed with a wide variety of high-quality goods, whether clothing and accessories or food. If time is tight, they offer an excellent, practical solution. The service is uniformly good, many of the staff speak English, and most of them accept credit cards. On the whole, however, they tend to be quite expensive.

Shopping arcades

Most towns have at least one long covered arcade, often downtown or near the train station, and sometimes undergound. They feature all kinds of shops: local chains selling clothes, shoes and accessories, specialty shops and cafes. There is something to suit every shopper and budget!

Conbini

You will find *conbini* (convenience stores) on every street corner, with main chains including Lawson, FamilyMart and 7-Eleven. Open 24 hours, these handy minisupermarkets stock an amazing range and quality of products, from underwear to food, alongside magazines, cosmetics, batteries, etc. They are practical for everyday items and small impulse buys, but are not usually a particularly good source for gifts and souvenirs beyond interesting flavors of candy.

100 Yen shops

Hyaku-en shoppu are everywhere, particularly near railway stations, in shopping arcades, and in malls. As the name implies, they sell all kinds of goods for just ¥100 per item (plus tax). Among the household and everyday goods, you will find a number of typical Japanese items such as chopsticks, toys, fans, dishes, etc.

Specialist stores

Specialist stores and craft workshops may be found in the shopping districts of larger towns. They sell high-quality items, including the rare and unusual. If you are pressed for time, however, visit one of the big craft centers aimed at tourists, such as the Oriental Bazaar in Tokyo (*see p171*) or the Kyoto Antiques Center (*see p360*).

Flea markets

Called *nomi-no-ichi* in Japanese, flea markets are lively affairs, generally held in the mornings in the grounds of temples and shrines, such as at Hanazono Jinja on Sundays in Tokyo (*see p193*). It is usually possible to find something interesting to take home, such as a secondhand kimono, and inexpensive souvenirs.

TAX REFUNDS

A consumption tax of 10 percent is levied on every purchase and is not always included in the marked price. However, visitors from abroad can obtain a tax refund on purchases over ¥5,000. The tax can either be deducted at the point of sale or refunded on completion of a form in the same store. In either case a passport must be produced. The tax refund applies notably to clothes, electronics and photographic equipment, but also to everyday items like food and cosmetics. There are duty-free counters in most big stores, and tax-free stores are marked with the logo "tax free". However, prices in the latter are often high. In practice, any shop selling electronic items can process a tax refund on request. *See tax-freeshop. jnto.go.jp/eng/shopping-guide.php.*

MAILING YOUR PURCHASES

If you want to send a package home by mail, try to go for the Express Mail Service **(EMS)** rather than the cheaper, slower Economy Air (SAL) Service. EMS offers better insurance terms *(you can track the item on post.japanpost.jp/ index_ en.html).*

BOOKS
CIVILIZATION AND SOCIETY

CRAIG, Albert M., *The Heritage of Japanese Civilization,* Prentice Hall, 2002. A short survey of Japan's rich and long history.

GOLDEN, Arthur, *Memoirs of a Geisha,* Knopf, 1997. Bestselling novel following the life of Sayuri, the most celebrated geisha in Gion, before and after World War II.

KOMOMO (author) and OGINO, Naoyuki (photographer), *A Geisha's Journey: My Life as a Kyoto Apprentice,* Kodansha International, 2008. Illustrated autobiography of a Japanese teen's seven-year apprenticeship to become a geisha.

KURE, Mitsuo, *Samurai: An Illustrated History,* Tuttle, 2002. A chronological account of samurai history.

KUSHNER, Barak, *Slurp! A Social and Culinary History of Ramen – Japan's Favorite Noodle Soup,* Global Oriental, 2012. An entertaining yet academic look at Japan's history with China, through the lens of ramen.

MACKIE, Vera, *Feminism in Modern Japan,* Cambridge University Press, 2003. An account of the history of feminism in Japan from the end of the 19C to the present day.

NENZI, Laura, *Excursions in Identity: Travel and the Intersection of Place, Gender, and Status in Edo Japan,* University of Hawaii Press, 2008. An account of how travel changed the lives of people, in particular women, in the Edo period, 1603–1868.

SCHIROKAUER, Conrad, LURIE, David, and GAY, Suzanne, *A Brief History of Japanese Civilization,* Wadsworth, 2006. A clear and accessible overview of all aspects of Japanese history.

SUZUKI, Shogo, *Civilization and Empire: China and Japan's Encounter with European International Society,* Routledge, 2009. A critical examination of international society's attempts to introduce civilization to "barbarous" polities of East Asia in the 19C.

DETECTIVE NOVELS

HIGASHINO Keigo, *The Devotion of Suspect X*. An award-winning tale of love and murder.

ISHIDA Ira, *Ikebukuro West Gate Park (IWGP)*. A collection of short stories about teen gangs in Tokyo's Ikebukuro district.

KIRINO Natsuo, *Out*, *Grotesque*, and *Real World*. Three of the prolific crime writer's best works.

NAKAMURA Fuminori, *The Thief*. Philosophical thriller by a popular writer of Tokyo noir.

HISTORY

BEASLEY, W.G., *The Japanese Experience: A Short History of Japan*, University of California Press, 2000. A concise but comprehensive and authoritative history of Japan.

HARTSHORNE, Anna, *Japan and Her People,* Jetlag Press, 2007. Written in 1902 and republished, this book describes life in late-19C Japan.

HENSHALL, Kenneth G., *A History of Japan: From Stone Age to Superpower,* Palgrave Macmillan, 2001. A well-balanced overview of pre-modern and modern Japan.

HERSEY, John, *Hiroshima*, Vintage, 1989. First-hand accounts from those who survived the Hiroshima bomb.

HOTTA, Eri, *Japan 1941: Countdown to Infamy,* Penguin Random House, 2014. An analysis of the attack on Pearl Harbor from the Japanese perspective.

NISHIMURA, Shigeo, *Illustrated History of Japan,* Tuttle, 2005. Aimed at children, this book highlights events in Japanese history through panoramic paintings with brief captions.

MORTON, W. Scott and OLENIK, J. Kenneth, *Japan: Its History and Culture,* McGraw-Hill, 2004. The history of Japan from its earliest-known civilization to the present day.

TOLAND, John, *The Rising Sun: The Decline and Fall of the Japanese Empire, 1936–1945*, Modern Library, 2003. An accessible, informative account of the Pacific War.

ART, CULTURE, AND RELIGION

BEIDAS, Elspeth and MOUL, Robin (editors), *Be More Japan: the Art of Japanese Living*, Dorling Kindersley, 2019. A richly illustrated overview of modern Japanese culture.

DAVIES, Roger J. and IKENO Osamu, *The Japanese Mind: Understanding Contemporary Japanese Culture*, Tuttle, 2002. An exploration of the unique aspects of Japanese culture and what makes the Japanese tick.

DE WAAL, Edmund, *The Hare with Amber Eyes: A Hidden Inheritance,* Farrar, Straus and Giroux, 2010. A memoir based on a collection of *netsuke* (small Japanese carvings).

EARLE, Joe (editor), *Japanese Art and Design,* V&A Publishing, 2009. An illustrated overview of Japanese art from the last four centuries.

HERRIGEL, Eugen, *Zen in the Art of Archery: Training the Mind and body to Become One*, Vintage, 1999. An absorbing personal tale of understanding Zen through *kyudo*, Japanese archery.

HIBI Sadao, *Japanese Detail: Architecture*, Chronicle Books, 2002. An exploration of the essential elements of the Japanese architectural aesthetic.

JESPERSEN, Bo M. and ALEXANDER, George W., *Dictionary of Japanese Martial Arts*, Yamazato, 2002. A guide to martial arts and weaponry.

KASAHARA Kazuo, *A History of Japanese Religion*, Kosei, 2002. An overview of the history and development of Japan's major spiritual traditions.

MENEGAZZO, Rossella and PIOTTI, Stefania, *WA: The Essence of Japanese Design*, Phaidon Press, 2014. An exploration of the beauty and essence of Japanese design.

OKAKURA, Kakuzo, *The Book of Tea: The Classic Work on the Japanese Tea Ceremony and the Value of Beauty*, Kodansha, 2006. The history and rules of the Japanese tea ceremony.

POPP, Daniel John, *The Floating Brush: Learning Japanese Shodo from a Kendo Master*, Kamel Press, 2014. An introduction to the ancient art of Japanese calligraphy.

SOSNOSKI, Daniel, *Introduction to Japanese Culture*, Tuttle, 1996. Illustrated guide to the country's customs and culture.

TANIZAKI, Jun'ichiro, *In Praise of Shadows*, Vintage, 2001. Classic essay on traditional Japanese aesthetics.

YOUNG, David, YOUNG, Michico, and YEW, Tan Hong, *The Art of the Japanese Garden*, Tuttle, 2005. The philosophy behind the various styles of Japanese garden.

TRAVEL WRITING

BEATON, Hamish, *Under the Osakan Sun*, Awa Press, 2008. An account of traveling and teaching in Japan.

BOOTH, Alan, *Looking for the Lost*, Kodansha, 1996; *The Roads to Sata*, Kodansha, 1997. Two beautifully written accounts of walking the length and breadth of Japan.

CLANCY, Judith, *Exploring Kyoto: On Foot in the Ancient Capital*, Stone Bridge Press, 2008. Thirty routes around Kyoto.

DE MENTE, Boyé Lafayette, *The Dining Guide to Japan*, Tuttle, 2007. What to expect, what to order, what to eat, and dining etiquette in Japan.

FERGUSON, Will, *Hokkaido Highway Blues*, 1998. Irreverent, funny tales of hitchhiking the length of Japan, chasing the cherry blossoms.

KAJIYAMA, Sumiko, *Cool Japan*, Museyon Inc, 2018. A guide to Japan's must-see places from the perspective of a local expert.

REYNOLDS, Betty, *Clueless in Tokyo*, Weatherhill 1997; *Still Clueless in Tokyo*, Weatherhill, 2003. The quirks of Tokyo life, lovingly illustrated.

ROSCOE, Bruce, *Windows on Japan: A Walk through Place and Perception*, Algora, 2007. An account of a walk through rural Japan.

WILLIAMSON, Kate T., *A Year in Japan*, Princeton Architectural Press, 2006. Journal with watercolor illustrations by the author.

ZARIFEH, Ramsey and UDAGAWA, Anna, *Japan by Rail*, Trailblazer, 2016. A guide to exploring Japan with the Japan Rail Pass.

JAPANESE LITERATURE

ABE Kobo, *The Woman in the Dunes*, Vintage, 1962.

DAZAI Osamu, *The Setting Sun,* New Directions, 1947.

ENDO Shusaku, *Silence,* Tuttle, 1966.

IBUSE Masuji, *Black Rain: A Novel,* Kodansha, 1965.

INOUE Hisashi, *Tales from a Mountain Cave*, Thames River Press, 1976.

INOUE Yasushi, *The Hunting Gun*, Peter Owen, 1961.

KAWABATA Yasunari, *The Master of Go*, Vintage, Kodansha, 1951; *Thousand Cranes*, Vintage, Kodansha 1952; *House of the Sleeping Beauties*, Kodansha, 1961.

KEENE, Donald (editor), *Anthology of Japanese Literature*, Grove Press, 1955.

McALPINE, Helen and William, *Tales from Japan*, Oxford University Press, 2002.

MISHIMA Yukio, *Confessions of a Mask*, New Directions, 1949; *The Sailor Who Fell From Grace with the Sea*, Vintage, 1963; *Spring Snow*, Vintage, 1969.

MURAKAMI Haruki, *A Wild Sheep Chase*, Vintage, 1982; *The Wind-up Bird Chronicle*, Vintage, 1994; *What I Talk About When I Talk About Running*, Vintage, 2007; *IQ84*, Knopf, 2009; *Colorless Tsukuru Tazaki and His Years of Pilgrimage*, Knopf, 2013.

MURAKAMI Ryu, *Coin Locker Babies*, Kodansha, 1980; *Piercing*, Penguin, 1994; *In the Miso Soup*, Penguin, 1997.

MURASAKI Shikibu, *The Tale of Genji*, c. 1008, W. W. Norton, 2017.

MURATA SAYAKA, *Convenience Store Woman*, Grove Atlantic, 2016.

NAGAI Kafu, *American Stories*, Columbia University Press, 1908; *Geisha in Rivalry*, Columbia University Press, 1916.

OE Kenzaburo, *Nip the Buds, Shoot the Kids*, Grove Press, 1958; *A Personal Matter*, Grove Cross, 1964.

OGAWA Yoko, *The Diving Pool: Three Novellas*, Picador, 1991; *The Housekeeper and the Professor*, Picador, 2003.

OOKA Shohei, *Taken Captive: A Japanese POW's Story,* Wiley, 1948.

OZEKI Ruth, *A-Tale-for-the Time-Being*, Viking, 2013.

SOSEKI Natsume, *I Am a Cat,* Tuttle, 1905; *Botchan,* Kodansha, 1906; *Kusamakura,* Penguin, 1906; *Kokoro,* Dover, 1914.

TANIZAKI Jun'ichiro, *Naomi*, Vintage, 1924; *The Key & Diary of a Mad Old Man*, Vintage, 1961.

YOSHIMOTO Banana, *Kitchen*, Grove Press, 1988; *Goodbye Tsugumi*, Grove Press, 1989; *Hardboiled and Hard Luck*, Grove Press, 1999.

YOSHIMURA Akira, *Shipwrecks*, Harvest Books, 1996.

MANGA

For the latest manga, check out the main publishers' websites, or to read manga online or on your device, subscribe to services like Crunchyroll (*crunchyroll.com*).

JOSO, Estudio and CASAUS, Fernando, *The Monster Book of Manga: Draw Like the Experts*, Collins Design, 2006. Step-by-step instructions on creating manga illustrations.

TAKARI Saori, *Manga Moods*, Japanime, 2006. How to transform the mood of a manga character in a stroke.

TSUKAMOTO Hiroyoshi, *Manga Matrix: Create Unique Characters Using the Japanese Matrix System*, Collins Design, 2006. Drawing manga with the grid method.

PHOTOGRAPHY

MARCH, Philipp and DELANK, Claudia (editors), *The Adventure of Japanese Photography 1860–1890*, Kehrer Verlag, 2003. Images of Japan by the pioneering photographers Felice Beato and Adolpho Fasari.

MORIYAMA Daido, *How I Take Photographs*, Laurence King, 2019. An introduction to the legendary Japanese street photographer and his process.

NAKANO Masataka, *Tokyo Nobody*, Trucatriche, 2000. A collection of photographs taken in and around Tokyo.

RUBINFIEN, Leo, PHILLIPS, Sandra S., DOWER, John W. and TOMATSU Shomei, *Skin of the Nation*, Yale University Press, 2004. The career of the photographer Tomatsu Shomei.

TUCKER, Anne, *The History of Japanese Photography*, Yale University Press, 2003. Collection of photographs, including rare vintage images.

FILMS
FOREIGN DIRECTORS

COPPOLA, Sofia, *Lost in Translation*, 2003.

ESTENBERG, Erik, *Monster,* 2008.

KRAWCZYK, Gérard, *Wasabi*, 2001.

MARSHALL, Rob, *Memoirs of a Geisha*, 2005.

MORRISON, Christopher, *Into the Sun*, 2005.

SCORSESE, Martin, *Silence,* 2016.

YONG-HI, Yang, *Our Homeland,* 2012.

ZWICK, Edward, *The Last Samurai,* 2003.

JAPANESE DIRECTORS

FUKASAKU Kinji, *Battle Royale,* 2000.

IMAMURA Shohei, *The Ballad of Narayama*, 1983; *The Eel*, 1997.

ITAMI Juzo, *Tampopo*, 1987.

KAWASE Naomi, *Suzaku*, 1997; *The Mourning Forest*, 2007.

KITANO Takeshi, *Hana-bi*, 1997.

KOBAYASHI Masaki, *Human Condition*, 1959; *Hara Kiri*, 1963.

KOIZUMI Takashi, *After the Rain*, 2000.

KON Satoshi, *Perfect Blue*, 1997; *Paprika*, 2006.

KOREEDA Hirokazu, *Nobody Knows*, 2004; *Our Little Sister,* 2016.

KUROSAWA Akira,*The Seven Samurai,* 1954; *Ran*, 1985.

MIIKE Takashi, *Audition*, 1999.

MIYAZAKI Hayao, *My Neighbor Totoro*, 1988; *Spirited Away*, 2002.

MIZOGUCHI Kenji, *Sisters of the Gion*, 1936; *The Crucified Lovers*, 1954.

NARUSE Mikio, *When a Woman Ascends the Stairs*, 1960.

NARUSHIMA Izuru, *Rebirth* 2011; *Solomon's Perjury,* 2015.

NISHIKAWA Miwa, *Sway*, 2006.

OSHIMA Nagisa, *Cruel Story of Youth*, 1960; *Taboo*, 2000.

OTOMO Katsuhiro, *Metropolis*, 2001
   Metropolis, 2001; *Steamboy*, 2004.
OZU Yasujiro, *I Was born, But...*, 1932;
   Tokyo Story, 1953.
SHIMIZU Takashi, *The Grudge,* 2004.
SHINKAI Makoto, *The Place Promised in
   Our Early Days*, 2004; *Your Name*,
   2016.
TAKITA Yojiro, *Departures*, 2008.
TANADA Yuki, *One Million Yen Girl*,
   2008.
TESHIGARA Hiroshi, *Woman in the
   Dunes*, 1963; *The Face of Another*,
   1966.
YANG Yong-Hi, *Dear Pyongyang*, 2005;
   Our Homeland, 2012.
YOSHIDA Kiju, *Akitsu Springs*, 1962;
   Impasse, 1967.

MUSIC
TRADITIONAL
Flower Dance: Japanese Folk Melodies,
   Explorer series: East Asia/Japan,
   Nonesuch, 2008.
Move, Yoshida Brothers, Domo
   Records, 2000.
The Very Best of Japanese Music,
   various artists, Arc Music, 2004.
Traditional Japanese Music, various
   artists, Nippon Colombia, 2015.

J-POP AND J-ROCK
AKB48, *Kamiyokutachi*, 2010.
AMURO, Namie, *Queen of the
   Hip-hop*, 2006.
ARASHI, *Boku no Miteiru Fukei*, 2010.
ASIAN KUN FU GENERATION,
   Fan Club, 2006.
B'Z, *The Best Pleasure,* 1998; *Circle*,
   2005.
EVERY LITTLE THING, *4 force*, 2001.
GLAY, *Pure Soul*, 1999; *The Frustrated*,
   2006.
KYARY PAMYU PAMYU, *Japamyu*, 2018.
HAMASAKI, Ayumi, *Miss-Understood*,
   2006.
HIRAI, Ken, *Fakin' Pop,* 2008.
OOMORI, Seiko, *Brainwashing*, 2014.
SAZAN ALL STARS, *Dirty Old Man*,
   2006.
SMAP, *Shake*, 1996; *Pop up Smap*, 2006.
UTADA, Hikaru, *Ultra Blue*,
   2006.

JAPANESE CULTURE OVERSEAS
CULTURAL CENTERS
Japan Society
333 East 47th Street
New York, NY 10017
☎212-715-1258; japansociety.org
*Popular culture, performances,
exhibitions, lectures, language center,
gallery, and shop.*

**Japanese American Cultural &
Community Center**
244 S. San Pedro Street
Los Angeles, CA 90012
☎213-628-2725; jaccc.org
*Exhibitions, film screenings,
conferences, and culinary center.*

**Japanese Canadian
Cultural Centre**
6 Garamond Court
Toronto, ON M3C 1Z5
☎416-441-2345; jccc.on.ca
*Cultural and martial arts classes and
workshops; festivals.*

The Japan Foundation
101-111 Kensington High Street
London, W8 5SA
☎020-7492-6570; jpf.org.uk

Level 4, Central Park
28 Broadway
Chippendale, NSW 2008
☎02-8239-0055; jpf.org.au
*Arts and culture, Japanese studies,
language department, and cinema.*

Asia New Zealand Foundation
Level 16, Fujitsu Tower
141 The Terrace
Wellington 6143
☎04-471-2320; asianz.org.nz
*Programs to promote Asian culture;
movie screenings.*

MUSEUMS
**Japanese American
National Museum**
100 North Central Avenue
Los Angeles, CA 90012
☎213-625-0414; janm.org

Permanent and temporary exhibitions; literary and film festivals; family festivals, workshops, and guided walks.

Japanese Canadian National Museum
6688 Southoaks Crescent
Burnaby, BC V5E 4M7
📞604-777-7000; jcnm.ca
Permanent and temporary exhibitions; lectures, workshops, and concerts.

V&A South Kensington
Cromwell Road
London SW7 2RL
📞020-7942-2000; vam.ac.uk
Art and artifacts from the 6C to the present day in the Japan gallery.

FESTIVALS

Japanese Street Festival
Annual celebration of Japanese culture, held by the Japan-America Society of Washington.
sakuramatsuri.org

Japanese Summer Festival
Festival held annually in Melbourne, with performances, displays, demonstrations, and stands.
jcjsm.org.au/fest

Powell Street Festival
Yearly Vancouver festival of Japanese-Canadian arts, culture, and heritage.
powellstreetfestival.com

Calendar of Events

Japan has three main holiday seasons: the first is Shogatsu, the New Year period from Jan 1–3; the second is Golden Week, grouping four national holidays into one week in late April and early May; and the third is Obon, a Buddhist event during which families gather together as it is believed ancestors' spirits return to visit. Obon is in mid-August in many regions, mid-July in others. Try to avoid these periods, or book well in advance.
Also see Gion Matsuri p336.

JANUARY
Jan 1 – National holiday of Shogatsu. Family celebrations and visits to temples or shrines; the most important holiday in Japan.
Jan 6 – Tokyo (Kanto). Dezomeshiki. Big parade with firefighting demonstrations, put on by the Tokyo Fire Department.
Jan 9–11 – Osaka (Kansai). Ebisu Festival. People pray to the god of business and good fortune.
Mid-Jan – Tokyo (Kanto). First sumo Tournament, lasting for 15 days.
2nd Mon in Jan – National holiday of Seijin No Hi, Coming of Age Day. People turning 20 turn out in formal dress for town celebrations.
Jan 14 – Sendai (Tohoku). Hachiman Matsuri. New Year parade to the Hachiman Shrine.
3rd or 4th Sat in month – Nara (Kansai). Yamayaki. Dry grass on the Wakakusa hill is set on fire.

FEBRUARY
Beginning of Feb – Sapporo (Hokkaido). Yuki Matsuri (Snow Festival), lasting 7 days.
Feb 3 – Throughout Japan. Setsubun. Festival during which beans are scattered in the temples.
Feb 3 – Nara (Kansai). Lantern Festival at the Kasuga Shrine. It also takes place on Aug 14–15.
Feb 11 – National holiday of Kenkoku Kinenbi, National Foundation Day. First Japanese emperor said to be crowned on this day in 660 BC.
Feb 15–16 – Yokote (Akita). Kamakura Festival. Igloo-like structures are built around town.

MARCH

Mar 1–14 – Nara (Kansai). Omizutori (Water-drawing Festival) at the temple of Todai-ji.

Mar 3 – Throughout Japan. Hina Matsuri (Doll Festival) for young girls. Also called Girls' Day.

Mid-Mar – Osaka (Kansai). Second sumo tournament, lasting 15 days.

About Mar 20 – National holiday of Shunbun No Hi, the Spring Equinox. Visits to family graves.

APRIL

End Mar–beg April – Throughout Japan. *Hanami* (cherry blossom viewing) picnics and parties held under the blooms.

Apr 1–30 – Kyoto (Kansai). Miyako Odori (Spring Dance Festival). Dance performances by apprentice geishas.

Apr 8 – Throughout Japan. Hana Matsuri (Flower Festival) in the temples, for Buddha's birthday.

Apr 14–15 – Takayama (Chubu). Sanno Matsuri. Parade of *yatai* (floats) dedicated to Hie Shrine.

Apr 16–17 – Nikko (Kanto). Yayoi Matsuri in Futarasan Shrine.

Apr 29 – National holiday of Showa No Hi, birthday of former Emperor Showa.

MAY

May 3 – National holiday of Kenpo Kinenbi, Constitution Day. Remembrance of the new constitution put into effect following World War II.

May 4 – National holiday of Midori No Hi, Greenery Day, celebrating former Emperor Showa's love of plants and nature.

May 5 – National holiday of Kodomo No Hi, Children's or Boys' Day. Colorful banners in the shape of carp *(koi nobori)*, made of paper or fabric, are hung everywhere.

May 15 – Kyoto (Kansai). Aoi Matsuri. Grand parade in costumes of the Heian era.

Mid-May – Tokyo (Kanto). Third sumo tournament, lasting 15 days.

May 17–18 – Nikko (Kanto). Grand Festival of Tosho-gu shrine. Spectacular parade.

3rd weekend in May – Tokyo (Kanto). Sanja Matsuri. Religious festival held at Asakusa Shrine.

JUNE

Jun 1–2 – Kyoto (Kansai). Open-air Noh theater performance lit by lanterns at Heian Shrine.

JULY

Jul 1–15 – Fukuoka (Kyushu). The largest of Fukuoka's summer *matsuri*, the Yamagasa Festival, sets out from Kushida Shrine.

Mid-Jul – Nagoya (Chubu). Fourth sumo tournament, lasting 15 days.

Jul 14 – Nachi (Kansai). Nachi no Ogi Matsuri (Fire Festival) staged at Nachi Shrine.

3rd Mon of Jul – National holiday of Umi No Hi, Ocean Day. Marks return of Emperor Meiji from 1876 boat trip to Hokkaido.

Jul 16–17 – Kyoto (Kansai). Gion Matsuri. Parade of floats from Yasaka Shrine.

AUGUST

Aug 1–7 – Hirosaki (Tohoku). Neputa Matsuri. Parade of floats decorated with enormous papier mâché figures.

Aug 2–7 – Aomori (Tohoku). Nebuta Matsuri. Parade of huge papier mâché floats, accompanied by complex music and dancing.

Aug 3–6 – Akita (Tohoku). Kanto Matsuri. Parade with tall bamboo lanterns balanced on participants' hands, hips or even heads.

Aug 6–8 – Sendai (Tohoku). The Tanabata Matsuri celebrates summer with colorful streamers.

Mid-Aug – Throughout Japan. Obon (Festival of the Dead). It takes place in mid-July in some areas.

Mid-Aug – Sado Island. Earth Celebration, a global festival featuring the Kodo drummers.

Aug 12–15 – Tokushima (Shikoku). Awa Odori. Largest parade of popular dance in Japan, held during Obon (see pp61 & 518).

SEPTEMBER

Mid-Sept – Tokyo (Kanto). Fifth sumo tournament, lasting 15 days.

Sep 16 – Kamakura (Kanto). Tournament and displays of archery on horseback at Hachiman-gu Shrine.

3rd Mon of Sep – National holiday of Keiro No Hi, Respect for the Aged Day, celebrating age and longevity.

About Sept 23 – National holiday of Shubun No Hi, Fall Equinox Day. Family graves visited.

OCTOBER

Oct 9–10 – Takayama (Chubu). Hachiman Matsuri. Parade of *yatai* (giant floats) in honor of Sakurayama, divine guardian of the northern part of the town.

2nd Mon of Oct – National holiday of Taiiku No Hi, Health and Sports day.

Mid-Oct – Nagoya (Chubu). Nagoya Matsuri. Town festival with processions of people dressed in feudal costume.

Oct 17 – Nikko (Kanto). Fall Festival at Tosho-gu Shrine.

Oct 22 – Kyoto (Kansai). Jidai Matsuri (Festival of the Ages). Historical parade with people dressed in the costumes of various eras.

NOVEMBER

Nov 3 – National holiday of Bunka No Hi, Culture Day.

Nov 15 – Shichi-go-San. Children aged 3, 5 and 7 are taken to visit shrines in traditional dress.

Mid-Nov – Fukuoka (Kyushu). Sixth sumo tournament, lasting 15 days.

Nov 23 – National holiday of Kinro Kansha No Hi, Labour Thanksgiving Day.

DECEMBER

Dec 15–18 – Nara (Kansai). Kasuga Wakamiya On-Matsuri held at the grand shrine of Kasuga Taisha. Festival, including a procession of characters in historical costumes from 9C to 19C.

Dec 31 – Kyoto (Kansai). Okera Mairi ceremony (the lighting of a sacred fire) at Yasaka Shrine.

Know Before You Go

USEFUL WEBSITES

jnto.go.jp – The official site of the Japan National Tourism Organization, providing comprehensive information on all aspects of the country, including transport, accommodation, sport, and leisure activities.

jnto.org.au – The JNTO's site for visitors from Australia and New Zealand.

seejapan.co.uk – The JNTO's site for UK visitors.

us.jnto.go.jp – The JNTO's site for US visitors.

ilovejapan.ca – The JTNO's site for Canadian visitors.

gotokyo.org – The capital's official Tourist Office site.

fco.gov.uk – The British government's Foreign and Commonwealth Office website provides up-to-date travel and safety information.

japan-guide.com – Excellent source of regularly updated travel information, including a cherry blossom forecast .

state.gov – American visitors may check the US State Department website for travel advice.

smartraveller.gov.au – Australian Government website with information and advice on travel.

UPOPOY
NATIONAL AINU MUSEUM and PARK

The Story Behind the Name UPOPOY : In the Ainu language, the word "upopoy" means "many people singing together."

The Ainu are the indigenous people of Japan, with most of the population inhabiting the northernmost island of Hokkaido.
The Japanese government actively promotes various activities and measures that aim to preserve, revive, disseminate and raise awareness about the unique culture of the Ainu people.

In the town of Shiraoi in Hokkaido, a new facility for the dissemination of Ainu culture, UPOPOY, will open its doors in April of 2020.
Combining a newly established National Ainu Museum and National Ainu Park, UPOPOY will serve as a location that symbolizes harmonious coexistence among people of different ethnic groups.

UPOPOY is Japan's first-ever national museum and park built around the theme of the Ainu people.

HOKKAIDO
SHIRAOI

https://ainu-upopoy.jp/

SAPPORO

SHIRAOI

TOKYO
KYOTO

www.govt.nz – NZ Government website, with information and advice on travel.
japantimes.co.jp – News and useful information.
jma.go.jp – The Japanese weather service website, with an English link for forecasts.
web-japan.org – The Japanese Ministry of Foreign Affairs' "Introduction to Japan" website.
kunaicho.go.jp/eindex.html – Website of the Imperial Household Agency, giving information on visiting royal palaces and public events.

JNTO TOURIST OFFICES

THE JAPAN NATIONAL TOURISM ORGANIZATION (JNTO)

- ◆ **JNTO London**
  32 Queensway,
  Bayswater,
  London, W2 3RX
  ✆020-7398-5670

- ◆ **JNTO New York**
  One Grand Central Place
  60 East 42nd Street
  Suite 448
  New York, NY 10165
  ✆212-757-5640

- ◆ **JNTO Los Angeles**
  707 Wilshire Boulevard,
  Suite 4325,
  Los Angeles, CA 90017
  ✆213-623-6301

- ◆ **JNTO Toronto**
  481 University Avenue,
  Suite 711,
  Toronto, ON M5G 2E9
  ✆416-366-7140

INTERNATIONAL VISITORS

EMBASSIES AND CONSULATES
US Embassy
1-10-5 Akasaka, Minato-ku,
Tokyo, 107-8420
✆03-3224-5000; jp.usembassy.gov

US Consulate, Osaka
2-11-5 Nishitenma, Kita-ku,
Osaka 530-8543
✆06-6315-5900; jp.usembassy.gov/
   embassy-consulates/osaka

US Consulate, Nagoya
Nagoya International Center Bldg.
6th floor, 1-47-1 Nagono,
Nakamura-ku,
Nagoya, 450-0001
✆052-581-4501; jp.usembassy.gov/
embassy-consulates/nagoya

US Consulate, Fukuoka
5-26, Ohori 2-chome, Chuo-ku
Fukuoka, Japan 810-0052
✆03-3224-5000; jp.usembassy.gov/
   embassy-consulates/fukuoka

US Consulate, Sapporo
Kita 1-jo Nishi 28-chome, Chuo-ku,
Sapporo, 064-0821
✆011-641-1115; jp.usembassy.gov/
   embassy-consulates/sapporo

US Consulate, Naha
2-1-1 Toyama, Urasoe City,
Okinawa 901-2104
✆098-876-4211; jp.usembassy.
   gov/embassy-consulates/naha

Australian Embassy
2-1-14 Mita, Minato-ku,
Tokyo, 108-8361
✆03-5232-4111; japan.embassy.
   gov.au

Australian Consulate, Osaka
16F Twin 21 MID Tower,
2-1-61 Shiromi, Chuo-ku,
Osaka, 540-6116
✆06-6941-9271; japan.embassy.
   gov.au/tkyo/location_osaka.html

Australian Consulate, Fukuoka
7th Floor, Tenjin Twin Building,
1-6-8 Tenjin, Chuo-ku,
Fukuoka, 810-0001
✆092-734-5055; japan.embassy.
   gov.au/tkyo/location_fukuoka.
   html

Australian Consulate, Sapporo

17th Floor, Sapporo Centre Building,
North 5, West 6-2, Chuo-ku,
Sapporo, 060-0005

🖉011-242-4381; japan.embassy.gov.
au/tkyo/location_sapporo.html

British Embassy

1 Ichiban-cho, Chiyoda-ku,
Tokyo, 102-8381

🖉03-5211-1100; www.gov.uk/
world/organisations/british-
embassy-tokyo

British Consulate, Osaka

3-5-1 Bakuro-machi, Chuo-ku,
Osaka, 541-0059.

🖉06-6120-5600; www.gov.uk/world/
organisations/british-consulate-
general-osaka

Canadian Embassy

7-3-38 Akasaka, Minato-ku,
Tokyo, 107-8503

🖉03-5412-6200; canadainternational.
gc.ca/japan-japon/offices-
bureaux/tokyo.aspx?lang=eng

Canadian Consulate, Nagoya

Nakato Marunouchi Bldg., 6F,
3-17-6 Marunouchi, Naka-ku,
Nagoya, 460-0002

🖉052-972-0450; canadainternational.
gc.ca/japan-japon/offices-
bureaux/nagoya.aspx?lang=eng

Embassy of Ireland

Ireland House,
2-10-7 Kojimachi, Chiyoda-ku,
Tokyo, 102-0083

🖉03-3263-0695 ; dfa.ie/irish-
embassy/japan

Honorary Irish Consulate, Sapporo

2-23, East 17, North 46,
Higashi-ku
Sapporo, 007-0846

🖉011-783-8011; dfa.ie/embassies/
irish-embassies-abroad/asia-and-
oceania/japan

TOURIST OFFICES

The **Tourist Information Centers** (TIC) in Tokyo and at the airports of Narita and Kansai have a wealth of information and will suggest itineraries for traveling around the country. They give out free brochures in English published by the Japan National Tourism Organization (JNTO) and can help you to reserve a room in a network of reliable hotels, inns and reasonably priced *ryokan*. Most towns and villages have local **Tourist Offices**, generally situated in or near to the railway station, which will also be able to help with local attractions, passes and accommodation.
Many of them have multilingual staff and booklets in English, but in rural areas and small locations, you shopuldn't count on this. The best policy is to be patient and courteous, as the staff will still bend over backwards to help you. You can ask the Tourist Offices to put you in contact with the local **Goodwill Guides**, volunteer bilingual guides who will take you to the places you wish to see. This is a free service, apart from the cost of transport, meals, and entry to sites.

ENTRY REQUIREMENTS
PASSPORTS AND VISAS

A valid passport is essential for entry into Japan. Citizens of the UK, US, Canada, Australia, New Zealand, and the Republic of Ireland do not need a visa for a stay of up to 90 days. They are automatically given a temporary visa for this period of time upon arrival in Japan. Visitors from the UK, Ireland and some other European countries can also apply to extend this stay for a further 90 days at the Tokyo Regional Immigration Bureau (*www.immi-moj. go.jp*). Proof of onward travel may be required.

CUSTOMS REGULATIONS

Those over 20 years of age may import, tax-free, 400 cigarettes or 100 cigars, 3 bottles of alcohol of 25fl oz/76cl, 2fl oz/60ml of perfume, and gifts and souvenirs to a total value not exceeding ¥200,000. Amounts of foreign currency/traveler's cheques equivalent to over ¥1 million must be declared.

VACCINATIONS

No vaccination certificate is required.

HEALTH

All the usual medicines are sold in Japanese pharmacies, but take the precaution of packing a small first-aid kit: aspirin or paracetamol, anti-inflammatory remedies, dressings, antiseptic, anti-diarrhea products, sunscreen, and mosquito repellent if heading for rural areas in summer. *See also Basic Information p53.*

INSURANCE

Before taking out insurance, check whether there is an aid and repatriation policy included in the price of your ticket. This is often the case if travel is booked through a tour operator or paid for using certain credit or bank cards. However, it is advisable to examine the clauses of any contract to check their contents and for any possible exclusions.

If necessary, take out a travel policy that covers the cost of canceling the trip, sickness, repatriation in case of accident, and loss or theft of baggage. Keep the details of your insurer and the reference number of the policy with you during the trip.

Travel Guard – 📞1-800-826-4919 (US toll free) or 📞1-715-345-0505 (international collect), travelguard.com.

Travelex – 📞1-800-228-9792, travelexinsurance.com.

Alliance Global Assistance – 📞020-8686-1666, allianz-assistance.co.uk.

BUDGET

To help plan your trip, you will find below, as a rough guide, four examples of a daily budget. The price has been calculated for one person, based on two people staying together in low season. It does not include flights or Japan Rail Passes. Local

transportation is generally expensive, as are some tickets to visit attractions such as museums, temples or shrines, especially if seeing several of them in one day.

It's easy to travel on a shoestring or in luxury in Japan, but planning your accommodation and transport ahead of time (and avoiding major holiday priods, *see calendar p27*) is essential if you have a budget to stick to.

Mini budget with accommodation in a youth hostel dormitory or a bed in a *minshuku* or business hotel, shared travel and transportation, a bowl of noodles or a *bento* (lunch box) at noon, a low-priced menu at dinner, and two visits to temples or museums: allow ¥7000 per day.

Low budget with accommodation at a modest hotel or *ryokan*, shared travel and transportation, low-priced or set menu at lunch, dinner in a small restaurant, four cultural visits, and a coffee: allow ¥12,000 per day.

Average budget with accommodation in a comfortable hotel or *ryokan*, shared transport and a taxi in the evening, two restaurants each day, one purchase, one coffee, and either four cultural visits or an outing to a couple of bars: allow ¥22,000 per day.

High budget with accommodation in luxury hotels or very sophisticated *ryokan*, travel by taxi or rental car, meals in fashionable or gastronomic restaurants, and shopping or attractions to fill the afternoon: allow around ¥35,000 per day.

😊 Remember that the overall cost of your stay in Japan will depend upon the exchange rate, which can fluctuate significantly. You should also be sure to check whether consumption tax is included in quoted prices.

😊 Some popular destination such as Tokyo, Kyoto and Osaka also apply a per-night accommodation tax. This varies depending on the cost of your room, ranging from ¥100 (for Osaka or Tokyo rooms under ¥15,000 per night) to ¥1000 (for Kyoto rooms over ¥50,000 per night).

DISCOUNT CARDS

The **ISIC** (**International Identity Card**), for full-time students at school, college or university, is a passport to good discounts on museum entrance and transport tickets, etc. (*apply online at isic.org or get it issued at various venues, listed online*). For those under 31, students or not, the **IYTC** (**International Youth Travel Card**) offers similar but not quite as advantageous discounts (*apply online at isic.org or at listed venues*).

Over 65s can enjoy discounts on transport along with tickets to monuments, museums, and events. In addition to various transport passes, discounts on travel are available from *kinken shoppu* (discount ticket shops) located near main train stations and in major shopping areas. You can get discounts on tickets for train and air travel, movies, shows, and even coffee at reduced prices.

MONEY
CURRENCY

The Japanese unit of currency is the yen, written in Japanese as 円 (¥ or international code JPY). It comes in bills of ¥1000, ¥5000, and ¥10,000. Coins are valued at ¥1, 5, 10, 50, 100, or 500.

EXCHANGE RATE

At the time of publication of this guide the exchange rate is approximately $1 = ¥106, £1 = ¥129, and ¥100 = around $0.93 (0.77 GBP; 0.85 EUR; 1.39 AUD; 1.48 NZD; 1.24 CAD). It could be useful to buy a small quantity of yen from a bank or foreign exchange office before your trip. During your stay in Japan, yen can be withdrawn and foreign money can be changed in banks, foreign exchange offices, main post offices, and some hotels and department stores. Bear in mind, however, that many Japanese banks will only change US dollars, and that these operations can be lengthy. To avoid this, or to exchange other currencies, go to foreign exchange offices, located in large towns or at airports. Especially if you are likely to visit rural areas, it is advisable to change a substantial amount of money in advance.

TRAVELER'S CHECKS

These are not widely used in Japan. Banks, foreign exchange offices, main post offices, and large hotels should be able to change them (though they prefer those made out in dollars), but it is simpler and cheaper to pay cash.

CREDIT CARDS

Despite its level of technological advancement, in Japan cash is still king, and you should always be prepared for the possibility that you won't be able to pay by card. Luckily, Japan is also one of the safest countries in the world, and you run almost no risk of being robbed. That said, international credit cards are very useful in Japan, especially for large purchases. The most readily accepted is Visa, followed by MasterCard. Payment by credit card is becoming more widely accepted in large towns, where many hotels, restaurants, and shops accept them. But in small establishments and rural areas, you are unlikely to find many places able to process card payments.

WITHDRAWING MONEY

It is possible to withdraw money on international debit/credit cards everywhere in Japan, thanks to a network of 24,000 **post offices** (*global.map.japanpost.jp/p/en/search*) with ATMs. Many only operate until 5pm or 7pm during the week (from 8am), and on Saturday in some large towns, and are closed Sundays. Some ATMS at Sumitomo Mitsui, Shinsei Banks and Prestia/SMBC Trust Bank (previously Citibank) ATMs accept foreign cards; those in large towns are available 24 hours (*see www.smbctb.co.jp/en/banking/branch_atm/search/index.html*). Please note that the ATMs of other Japanese banks do not accept foreign cards, even foreign Visa cards. If a card is refused, do not try again:

after three attempts the card will be retained. You can also withdraw money with international credit cards (Visa or MasterCard) from the ATMs in the Japanese **7-Eleven** convenience stores, which are open 24 hours (*over 20,000 shops throughout the country, including more than 2700 in Tokyo*); this is often the cheapest and most convenient option for withdrawing cash using a foreign card.

Generally speaking, you can only withdraw a certain amount daily (*e.g. around ¥30,000 at a 7-Eleven ATM, using a card with a magnetic stripe*). Check this amount with your bank, and if necessary, ask for an increase for the duration of your stay; otherwise bring an adequate cash reserve.

Contactless is not yet widely used in Japan. In most places, you will either need to insert your card and use your PIN, or the establishment will swipe the card and ask for your signature.

MAKING RESERVATIONS

A few of the key venues require reservations as far ahead as possible. This is the case in Tokyo for the Imperial Palace (♿ *see p149*) and the Ghibli Museum (♿ *see p177*); in Kyoto for the Imperial Palace (♿ *see p323*), Shugaku-in Imperial Villa (♿ *see p330*), Katsura Rikyu(♿ *see p343*) and Koke-dera/Saiho-ji (♿ *see p343*), along with Kinza on Nao-shima (♿ *see p556*).

You need to book ahead for tickets to sumo tournaments or matches in the final rounds of baseball championships.

😊 If traveling during the 3 weeks of **high season** (*Dec 27–Jan 4, Apr 29–May 5, and the week of Aug 15*), or during the preceding or following weekends, it is essential to reserve hotels and transportation **at least one month in advance**. The period when the cherry trees are in bloom (*late March to eary April*) is also very busy and much more expensive, especially in Kyoto. ♿*See also Where to Stay p45.*

ACCESSIBILITY ♿

Since Japan's enactment of the Fundamental Law for Disabled Persons in 1993, there has been a real efforts to facilitate daily life for those with disabilities, and the ageing population has helped to sharpen the focus on making access easier for everyone. At major stations, hotels, airports, most new shopping centers and theaters and on city buses, disabled travelers should have little trouble. About 35 percent of Japan's train stations are accessible and barrier-free toilets are in half of all stations and most newer buildings, with many places also offering ostomy toilets. Smaller business hotels and more traditional Japanese-style inns may not be accessible.

If you have special needs, check with your travel agent or directly with the facility before making reservations.

♿ accessible-japan .com.
♿ accessible.jp.org/tokyo.

MANNERS
BASIC PRINCIPLES

Japanese people attach great importance to etiquette and convention, which they regard as indispensable for maintaining a harmonious and peaceful society. The group takes precedence over the individual, imposing on everyone the correct attitude to be observed. It is good manners to use respectful language and show politeness and humility; to dress smartly; to observe strict punctuality when keeping appointments; to take care never to express opinions or feelings openly; and to apologize repeatedly should a problem arise. Don't be surprised therefore if, in the course of discussions with Japanese people, they express what appear to be banal or conformist ideas: these are not necessarily a true reflection of what they actually think.

Japanese politeness is very subtle and codified. In order to refuse something, a Japanese person will never say "no," which would be terribly crass. Instead, they will say in a seemingly embarrassed way, "I'm sorry, it is difficult" or "I will think about it." In public, the Japanese behave discreetly and disapprove of such ostentatious behavior as shouting, laughing out loud, or, in the case of couples, kissing. These rules, however, are not absolutely inflexible and are often broken, notably in the course of an evening of drinking or at a festival. *See p16 & p111 for information about onsen (hot spring bath) sento (public bath) and ryokan o-furo (communal bath) etiquette.*

WHEN MEETING SOMEONE
Greeting

It is not customary in Japan to make any physical contact when meeting someone, such as shaking hands or kissing. However, some Japanese people will offer their hand when meeting a foreigner, in an effort to make them feel more comfortable. The traditional Japanese form of greeting is to bow from the waist, keeping the arms down beside the body, or held forward in the case of a woman. The depth of the bow and the length of time it is held should be judged according to the age and hierarchical position of the person being greeted. The bow is also used to express thanks, an apology, to ask for help or a favor, and to say "goodbye."

Names and courtesies

In Japan, the family name is normally placed before the given name, but many Japanese reverse the order when making introductions to foreigners. Check if possible, if you are not sure. People are normally addressed by their surname, with the addition of the word *san* as the equivalent of Mr. or Mrs. (for example, Smith-*san*, meaning Mr. Smith). The title of *sensei* (Master) is reserved for professors, doctors, and other professional people.

Visiting cards

On a business trip to Japan a good supply of business cards *(meishi)* is a must, as these are essential for establishing credibility. To give or receive a card, use two hand, or if not, the right hand only. A person's card should always be accepted respectfully, read attentively, then placed face up on the table beside you. When the meeting is over, don't fold it or slip it into the rear pocket of your pants—place it in your wallet or somewhere equally respectful.

Gifts

It is customary for the Japanese to give each other small gifts when meeting or visiting. If invited to a Japanese home, always take a gift. This does not need to be expensive, but it must be beautifully wrapped. Wine, small cakes, or chocolates are all suitable offerings. Never take four gifts at the same time, because the figure 4 symbolizes death for those who are superstitious.

Offer the gift with both hands, while making light of it, uttering the time-honored formula that "it is nothing of consequence,"("*Tsumaranai monodesu ga...*"), but always give profuse thanks for any gifts that you receive.

Shoes and Japanese interiors

The rule is not to contaminate a clean interior with dirt that may be brought in from outside. Before entering a house, temple, *ryokan*, traditional restaurant, or often even the changing rooms in a store, remove your shoes and leave them on the rack that is normally by the door. Put on any slippers that are provided or, if there are none, just wear socks (it isn't exactly rude to go barefoot, but it is a little unusual, and some places will offer you socks to avoid awkwardness). Never walk on *tatami* wearing slippers and remember, also, to take them off when entering the bathroom. Even if you are already wearing slippers, they should be exchanged for the provided bathroom slippers upon entering and then changed back again afterwards. Umbrellas should also be left at the entrance to houses, temples, museums, hotels, and stores, or slipped into a plastic case so they do not drip on the floor.

BEHAVIOR AT TABLE

Before the meal

When taking a meal or tea on a *tatami* mat, the ideal posture is to kneel (*seiza* position), but even on a pillow this soon becomes uncomfortable. Instead, men may sit cross-legged and women with their legs folded to one side. Before eating, guests say: "*Itadakimasu*" ("Thank you for the meal"), and after, "*Gochisosama deshita!*" ("That was a real feast!") If offered a small, wet towel (*oshibori*) before the meal, remember it is intended strictly for wiping the hands, not the face or neck.

Chopstick taboos

Using chopsticks (*hashi*) correctly requires some practice and a degree of dexterity. Nevertheless, there are certain faux pas that must be avoided at all costs. For instance, do not stand chopsticks upright in a bowl of rice, as this forms part of a funeral rite. Never pass food from your chopsticks onto those of someone else, never use your chopsticks to point at something or someone, and never play with them. Separate, usually longer, chopsticks are normally provided for picking up food from serving plates; if not, you can flip your chopsticks upside down and use the other end to serve yourself, so you don't contaminate the communal dishes. Finally, when you have finished eating, place the chopsticks on the holder provided, or side by side on the table, but not on the plate or in the bowl.

Other good and bad manners

Blowing one's nose at table is considered impolite, while it is good manners to slurp soup or noodles noisily. Never sprinkle soy sauce on a bowl of rice. When drinking alcohol, serve others but not yourself, say "*kampai!*" for "cheers", and try to keep your glass lower than other' to signal humility while clinking glasses.

Getting There and Getting Around

GETTING THERE

BY PLANE

Regular airlines – Direct flights

- **Air Canada** – ✆1-888-247-2262, aircanada.com.
- **Air New Zealand** – ✆0800-028-4149, airnewzealand.co.nz.
- **All Nippon Airways (ANA)** – ✆800-235-9262, ana.co.jp.
- **American Airlines** – ✆800-433-7300, aa.com.
- **British Airways** – ✆0344-493-0787, britishairways.com.
- **Japan Airlines (JAL)** – 0570-025-121, jal.com.
- **Qantas** – ✆0845-774-7767, qantas.com.

Most travelers opt to fly to Tokyo, but there are plenty of flights available to other major airports such as Kansai Interational (Osaka). A direct New York–Tokyo flight lasts about 13 hours. Ticket prices vary according to the airline, time you fly, and day of the week, and many of the cheapest options will include a layover.

Airports

Flights for Tokyo land at Narita (NRT) and Haneda (HND) International Airports. Flights to Osaka usually land at Kansai (KIX) International. Some airlines, mainly Asian, also serve the international airports at Nagoya (Honshu), Fukuoka (Kyushu), Naha (Okinawa), and Sapporo (Hokkaido). Airport taxes should be included in the price of your ticket.

GETTING AROUND

Japan undoubtedly possesses the finest public transport network in the world, being both extensive and well organized. The rail network alone covers almost every possible destination. The speed, punctuality, and frequency of the trains make it the best method of traveling throughout most of the country. Bus and boat travel should not be discounted, though; they may take longer, but are sometimes more economical, and they fill in the few gaps. Air travel is used widely (the leg between Tokyo and Sapporo is one of the busiest in the world) and is a good way of covering the long distances between the islands. 🐢 While traveling in Japan, try making use of that inspired Japanese invention, the express delivery service for baggage, or **takkyubin**. Check in cases the evening before your departure and, for about ¥1,500–3,000 per item, the express delivery service undertakes to deliver them the next day to the hotel or *ryokan* at your next stopover, whatever the distance. Avoiding the need to carry heavy cases around, this is particularly useful if you are moving from place to place. *Takkyubin* offices are found at airports and in most *conbini* (convenience stores). You can also ask the hotel receptionist to take care of it.

INTERNAL FLIGHTS
Airlines
JAL and **ANA** airlines cover the essential internal services, but they have competition from low-cost airlines This fierce competition has done much to lower prices. Thanks to discounts and special offers, some flights cost less than making the same journey by Shinkansen. All have websites in English.

Passes and reduced fares
JAL and ANA both offer useful **passes**, out of which the best value are the ANA Experience Japan Fare and JAL Explorer Pass. With these, particular domestic flights cost ¥5400, ¥7560 or ¥10,800. Both must be bought through the airline's website, and can only be purchased by foreign visitors to Japan who have proof of onward travel. Between them they cover most parts of the counttry, but they may not be valid during certain holiday periods, notably at Christmas and New Year. Aside from passes, JAL and ANA both offer multiple **reduction** options on flights reserved in advance (*25–70 percent for a reservation made more than one month in advance*). Low-cost airlines also make similar reductions but at even lower prices, their normal fares being in general 20 percent lower than those of JAL and ANA.

- **JAL** – ☎0344-856-9778, jal.co.jp; world.jal.co.jp/world/en/japan_explorer_pass/lp.
- **ANA** – ☎0570-029-767, ana.co.jp; ana.co.jp/en/gb/promotions/share/experience_jp.

Low-cost airlines:
- **Peach** – ☎03-6731-9241 flypeach.com (main hub Osaka, but operates throughout Japan and some other Asian destinations). **Skymark** – ☎0570-039-283, smart.skymark.jp/en (mainly flies from Tokyo Haneda and Kobe).
- **Air Do** – ☎0120-057-333, airdo.jp/en (connects Hokkaido and Honshu). **Jetstar Japan** – ☎0570-550 538, jetstar.com/jp/en. **Solaseed Air** – ☎0570-037-283 or 06-7637-8817, solaseedair.jp/en (links Tokyo, Kyushu and Okinawa).
- **IBEX** – ☎0120-686-009 or 03-6741-6688, ibexair.co.jp/en (Honshu, Hokkaido, Kyushu and Shikoku).
- **Starflyer** – ☎0570-07-3200, starflyer.jp/en (hub in KitaKyushu, but operates throughout Japan).

BY TRAIN
Rapid, frequent, punctual, reliable, clean, and comfortable, Japanese trains are great. The national company **Japan Railways** (**JR**) runs about 70 percent of the rail network, including almost all of

the long-distance lines; various private companies run the rest, operating above all in large urban areas and on some tourist lines. Japan Railways (JR) is divided into six main networks: JR East, JR West, JR Hokkaido, JR Kyushu, JR Shikoku, and JR Central.

Using the trains
There are several categories of trains, listed here from fastest to slowest. The **shinkansen**, or super-express trains, operate on the fastest lines. They run especially on the Tokaido (Tokyo to Osaka), San'yo (Osaka to Fukuoka), Joetsu (Tokyo to Niigata), Hokuriku (Tokyo-Nagano-Kanazawa), Yamagata (Tokyo to Shinjo), Tohoku (Tokyo to Shin-Aomori), Akita (Tokyo to Akita), and Kyushu (Fukuoka to Kagoshima) lines.
The Hokuriku Line will extend to Fukui, Tsuruga by 2025, and will terminate at Shin-Osaka. The Hokkaido Line between Shin-Aomori and Shin-Hakodate should extend to Sapporo in 2030.
A shinkansen supplement *(¥800–8000 depending on the train, the most expensive being the Nozomi)* is added to the ticket price. The price is determined also by the distance, with the tariff always remaining the same for any given route, no matter when you travel or buy the ticket (in advance or on the day of travel).
Limited express trains (*tokkyu* or *shinkaisoku*) are fast trains stopping only at main stations. The supplement is between ¥500 and ¥4000, again depending on distance traveled.
Express trains (*kyuko*) stop only at some stations and also carry a supplement.
Rapid trains (*kaisoku*) stop a bit more often than the expresses and there are no supplements.
Local trains (*futsu* or *kakueki-teisha*) stop at all stations, with no supplement. Shinkansens and limited express trains consist of ordinary and green (first class) cars, with green cars costing more. Some shinkansen also have gran class cars, which is the highest

level (and highest supplement). Seat reservations (*shitei-seki*) require supplements too, but all trains have cars with nonreserved seats (*jiyu-seki*) avaiable. Night trains also include sleeping cars with couchettes, also with a supplement. If you don't have a pass (JR Pass, Suica, or other pass) buy your tickets from the automatic ticket machines (for short distances) or from station ticket offices, writing down in English anything you want to tell or ask the vendor. If you cannot find the exact fare listed on the machines, take the next cheapest. You can always pay the supplement to the train inspector with no penalty or extra cost. If necessary, pay the difference at the *fare adjustment machine* or at the window located near the platform exits. As for the subway and bus, you must keep your ticket with you until you exit at your arrival station or stop. Note that while unfailingly punctual, the trains only stop briefly in stations. Be there well in advance to find your platform and your car's position, marked on the ground. The JR Company publishes a useful booklet in English, the **Railway Timetable**, with all main journey times and costs. You can get it free in all main stations. *For all kinds of information (times, fares, etc.),* ✆*see hyperdia.com/ en orjorudan.co.jp/english*.

The Japan Rail Pass
Reserved for foreign visitors, the JR Pass is a real bargain that greatly simplifies life. Valid on the JR network, except for the shinkansen Nozomi and Mizuho trains, it allows travel anywhere without having to buy a ticket over a period of 7, 14, or 21 days. The JR Pass should be bought outside Japan from specialist tour operators. When purchasing, you will be given a reservation voucher. On arrival in Japan the voucher can be exchanged for a pass in one of the JR Travel Service Centers, which can be found in all main stations and at Narita, Haneda, and Kansai airports.

あんしんを羽ばたく力に ──京急グループ

Ginza

Asakusa

Shinjuku

Welcome to Tokyo!

The Keikyu Line offers convenient access
in every direction from Haneda Airport.

Yokosuka

Yokohama

Miura

Hayama

Tokyo Sky Tree

Use the Keikyu Line to get where you're going.

Take the Keikyu Line
to Yokohama, Yokosuka,
and Miura.

The Keikyu Line connects directly
with the Keisei Line and the Toei Subway.

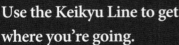

Oshiage (Sky Tree Mae)
35min

To Narita Airport

Higashi-ginza
24min

Asakusa
32min

JR Line

Tokyo

Shinjuku
30min

Shimbashi

Toei Subway

Tokaido Shinkansen

To Osaka and Kyoto

Keikyu Line

Shinagawa
11min ¥300

Misakiguchi
76min

Yokosuka-chuo
54min

Yokohama
24min

Haneda Airport

KEIKYU
京急電鉄

The pass should be marked with the date on which you intend to begin using it. There is no point in starting it immediately if, for example, you will be staying for a few days in Tokyo first. The initial outlay is easily covered: with the 7-day pass *(¥29,650)*, if you make a round trip Tokyo to Kyoto on a shinkansen *(over ¥27,000 with reserved seats)* and add one transfer between Tokyo and Narita Airport *(around ¥3000)*, you will have paid for your pass. The 14-day pass costs ¥47,250 and the 21-day pass ¥60,450; children under 11 travel half-fare. *see japanrailpass.net/en.*

Other passes and reductions

Depending on your itinerary, other, cheaper regional passes may be better for your needs; many of these can be bought in Japan for a little extra. We've outlined some of the most useful options below. *A full, up-to-date list of regional rail passes is maintained at japan-guide.com/e/e2357.html.*
JR East offers various passes (note than none of them covers the Tokaido line, which connects Tokyo and Kyoto). The **JR East South Hokkaido Pass** *(¥26,000)* is valid in Kanto, Tohoku, and southern Hokkaido for any 6 days in a 14-day period; the **Tohoku South Hokkaido Pass** *(¥19,000)* covers the same area minus Kanto, for 5 out of 14 days. The **Tohoku Area Pass** *(¥19,000)* covers Kanto and Tohoku for 5 out of 14 days. Again applying to 5 out of 14 days, the **Nagano Niigata Area Pass** *(¥17,000)* covers Kanto and Koshintetsu and makes you eligible for the good-value Sado-Niigata Pass *(¥4000)*. The **Tokyo Wide Pass** *(¥10,000)* covers the Kanto region for 3 days, while the **Hokuriku Arch Pass** *(¥24,000)* links Tokyo and Osaka via Chubu over 7 days. *see jreast.co.jp/e.*
The **JR Hokkaido Pass** gives access to the whole of the JR network on Hokkaido, excluding the Hokkaido shinkansen, for 3 *(¥16,500)*, 5 *(¥22,000)* or 7 consecutive days *(¥24,000)*, or any 4 days in a 10-day period *(¥22,000)*. *see www2.jrhokkaido.co.jp/global.*

JR Central has the **Takayama-Hokuriku Tourist Pass** *(5 days, ¥14,000)* linking Nagoya with Osaka via Chubu, plus the **Ise Kumano Tourist Pass** *(5 days, ¥14,000)*, which connects Nagoya and Osaka with Ise and the Kumano region, and the **Fuji Shizuoka Tourist Pass** *(3 days, ¥4500)*. *see global.jr-central.co.jp/en.*
JR West offers the **Kansai Area Pass** for the whole JR Kansai network, from 1 day *(¥2200)* to 4 days *(¥6300)*, plus the **Kansai Wide Area Pass**, which covers a wider area *(5 days, ¥9000)*. JR West also has the **San'yo-San'in Area Pass**, which covers the Osaka region and the Sanyo Line as far as Fukuoka *(7 days, ¥19,000);* the **San'yo-San'in Northern Kyushu Pass** extends further into Kyushu *(¥22,000)*. The **Setouchi Area Pass** is also helpful, covering the whole Inland Sea area *(7 days, ¥17,000)*. *see westjr.co.jp/english.*
JR Kyushu offers the All Kyushu Area Pass *(3 days ¥15,000, 5 days ¥18,000)*, North Kyushu Pass *(3 days ¥8500, 5 days ¥10,000)* and South Kyushu Pass *(3 days, ¥7000)*. *see jrkyushu.co.jp/english.*
The **All Shikoku Rail Pass** is valid for the whole of the island of Shikoku, both JR and private lines, for 3 days *(¥9000)* to 7 days *(¥13,000)*. *see jr-shikoku.co.jp/global/en.*
There are also options beyond the regional JR passes. The **JR Seishun Juhachi Kippu**, on sale in most stations, allows unlimited travel on the JR network for 5 days *(¥11,850)*. However, it is only valid for local and rapid trains (not on the limited express and shinkansen), and only during school holiday periods. *see jreast. co.jp/e/pass/seishun18.html.*
The **Kansai Thru Pass** *(2 days ¥4300, 3 days ¥5300)* covers non-JR travel around the Kansai region *(surutto.com/tickets/ kansai_thru_english.html)*, while the **Kintetsu Rail Pass** *(from 1 day for ¥1500)* is valid for Kintetsu trains in Kansai *(kintetsu.co.jp/foreign/english/ index.html)*. The **Platt Kodama Economy Plan** from JR Tokai Tours is a great option for a one-way trip on the Tokaido shinkansen *(e.g. Tokyo to*

Kyoto for ¥10,300, or ¥11,800 for green car; jrtours.co.jp/kodama/english).
🕭*For passes specific to certain towns and regions, see the Transport section in the Addresses sections in each Discovering Japan chapter.*

BY BUS

Many tourists are unaware of the **long-distance buses** that cross Japan, but they are a cheap way of traveling. **Night buses**, for the most part with comfortable reclining seats, also save the cost of a night in a hotel, though journeys take much longer than by train. Seats must be reserved in advance at bus stations, local travel agencies or (for JR buses) station ticket offices. Tickets for large companies like Willer Express (*willerexpress. com/en*) can be reserved online. There's basic information about some 1500 long-distance bus lines on **highway-bus.jnto.go.jp/en**, with links to English-language booking sites and to the (many) bus companies. 🚌Be wary of low tariffs that seem too good to be true from some low-cost companies, some of whose vehicles have been involved in accidents.

The Japan Bus Pass

This pass must be purchased outside Japan and permits travel anywhere on the Willer Express long-distance bus network, starting at ¥10,000 for a 3-day pass valid Mondays through Thursdays. A maximum of 3 trips may be reserved per day; days of use need not be consecutive. The pass is valid for 2 months (not valid at certain times, e.g. during Golden Week and beginning January). *Information, reservations, and sample itineraries at willerexpress.com/st/3/en/pc/buspass.*

BY BOAT

🕭*Routes described by region in Discovering Japan.*
An armada of ferries links the islands of Japan, especially the smallest ones, which can often only be reached by sea. While the large islands of Hokkaido, Honshu, Kyushu, and Shikoku are linked by tunnels and bridges, traveling by boat is a good option both to keep costs down and to enjoy pleasant **views** of coastal scenery. The large long-distance ferries can take passengers, vehicles, and goods. They have various facilities on board, such as restaurants, boutiques, casinos, and bathing facilities. Cheaper tickets give access to a communal room, where you can put down your sleeping bag. Dormitory beds in second class cost a little more (*20–40 percent extra*), while first-class cabins cost around double the basic fare. Reserve a ticket at the ferry terminals, or better still online or through a hotel, travel agency, or the local Tourist Office, as shipping company personnel rarely speak English. The **Japan Long Course Ferry Service Association** publishes a free brochure in English with ferry line timetables and prices (in most Tourist Offices). 🕭*See also jlc-ferry.jp/en.* Ferry routes are not covered by the JR pass, except for the JR Miyajima ferry near Hiroshima, though some regional passes cover specific ones. Boats in Japan are above all a means of transport; for the moment there are few cruises, just a few boat trips lasting a few hours.

BY CAR

The efficient public transport system means car rental in large towns is unnecessary, as it is for taking major routes such as the Tokyo–Nagoya–Kyoto–Osaka–Hiroshima roads. Yet a car is a very practical way of seeing rural or mountainous areas, or remote islands, where public transport is often limited. This also applies to the center of Japan and in the east of Shikoku, the south of Kyushu, the mountains of Tohoku, and Hokkaido. A good compromise is to travel by train to your destination and rent a car locally.

Road network

There is no problem about driving in Japan: the roads are reliable, the signs are clear (on major roads the signs carry a translation in the Roman alphabet), and Japanese drivers tend to be prudent and respectful. In Japan they drive on the **left**. The speed limit is 18–25mph/30–40kph in towns and 37mph/60kph on country roads; 50–62mph/80–100kph on freeways and expressways. Freeways and expressways are **toll** roads, and the cost can add up fast; consider an Expressway Pass if you're not going to be able to avoid them. There are plenty of gas stations (*Esso, Jomo, etc.*) and gas costs about ¥525 per gal or ¥140 per liter. Large towns are often congested, so prepare the route in advance, noting street names and road numbers. Towns charge for parking (expensive, at parking meters or car parks), but hotels offer free or reduced-rate (*¥1,000*) parking to guests. You may find a bilingual road atlas useful, the most complete being the *Japan Road Atlas* from Shobunsha. Less specific for roads but with good town plans, train lines, and subway details is the *Japan Atlas* from Kodansha. Or choose a rental car with vocal GPS in English. If you need breakdown assistance, ring the **Japan Automobile Federation's 24-hour emergency line**, in English (*📞0570-00-8139, www.jaf.or.jp/e*).

Driving license

Citizens from English-speaking countries who intend to drive in Japan must carry an **international driving permit** (issued by your national automobile association) as well as a **national driving license**.
Japan Automobile Federation – 2-2-17 Shiba, Minato-ku, Tokyo 105-8562, 📞03-6833-9100. *A list of offices is at www.jaf.or.jp/e.*

Car rental

Car rental agencies, mostly near railway stations and in airports, rent by the half-day, day, or week, often inclusive of unlimited mileage and insurance. An excess must be deposited in case of accident. There is also a mileage supplement if vehicles are returned at a different location.

Prices vary little between small and large agencies. That said, international companies such as Avis, Hertz, or Budget are generally more expensive than national ones like Nissan Rent-A-Car, Toyota Rent-A-Car, Nippon Rent-A-Car, Eki Rent-A-Car, or Orix Rent-A-Car. For an economy-class car, the price is around ¥7500 per day and around ¥50,000 for a week. Japanese car rental agencies do not generally have English websites and in most agencies the personnel do not speak English. Based in Tokyo and accustomed to foreign travelers, the ToCoo! Agency (*📞03-5333-0246, www2.tocoo.jp/en*) offers cheap rates right across Japan. Reserve online.
Child car seats – Japanese legislation requires car rental agencies to offer child car seats, but some have very few; check availability beforehand.

GPS – While all Japanese cars come with GPS, very few of them have it in English. Reserve your English-language GPS in advance to be sure of having one. The great innovation of Japanese GPS is the option of choosing your destination by telephone number. To be sure, ask the agency personnel to show you how the GPS works; you can also operate a Japanese GPS, which has road and motorway numbers in Roman numerals with a good road atlas.

ON TWO WHEELS

You can rent small 50cc scooters at most places of interest, but you may not use them on the roads. Very few car rental agencies offer motorcycles larger than 125cc for hire and those that do rarely have English-speakers on their staff. As for touring Japan by bicycle, it is possible, but only if you are very fit and have plenty of time as the roads involve a lot of climbs. Take a good road atlas to discover small, secondary roads and know enough Japanese to be able to read the key road sign *kanji* (chinese ideograms). The regions best for cycling excursions are the center of Honshu, the islands

43

of the Inland Sea, Hokkaido, Shikoku, and the south of Kyushu. Good cycling trails have been built on the Kibi Plain (👢see p428) and the bridges linking Onomichi and Shikoku (👢see Shimanami Kaido p562). Exploring Kyoto, Kanazawa, Hagi, and Tono is also very enjoyable by bike.

To avoid the difficult exit from large towns, take the train. Bikes must be put in special bags (rinko baggu) to go on trains; these are sold in cycle accessory shops. For more details, 👢see cyclingjapan.jp, japancycling.org, kancycling.com and outdoorjapan.com. (👢See also Bicycles.)

IN TOWNS

Subways and trains

Big cities such as Tokyo, Yokohama, Kyoto, Osaka, Fukuoka, or Sapporo have a network of subways, privately owned railways, and, in some cities, monorails, independent of the JR network. These are often the fastest means of urban transport. Buy your ticket from the automated ticket machines after checking the price for your destination on the information board, posted high for visibility; press the corresponding machine button and insert the money. If the exact fare is not indicated on the board, take a cheaper ticket and pay the balance when you leave at the fare adjustment machine, near the exit gates. Keep your ticket until you exit at your station. Alternatively, get an IC card such as Suica or Pasmo; these are especially convenient as you can also use them in many shops, such as conbini. One-day subway passes are also good value.

Buses and trams

Trams are easy to use and still run in many cities, including Hiroshima, Matsuyama, Okayama, and Nagasaki. Like buses, they are usually boarded at the back (at the front in Tokyo); then, you take a ticket from the machine indicating the number of your boarding zone. At each stop a sign lights at the front with the cost for

each route section; you pay into the small machine near the driver when you get off. There are also day passes, which will need to be stamped by the driver on your first journey. The Tokyo and Kyoto buses charge a flat fare whatever the distance covered.

Taxis

Taxis are expensive in Japan, but trains and subways stop after midnight and bus service is limited in small towns. The big taxi stands are near railway stations and you can expect to pay ¥650–750 for the first 1.2mi/2km, and then ¥100 per 1,640ft/500m. It costs extra to take a taxi at night or to phone for one. Available taxis have a red light behind the windshield; a green light means the taxi is taken. Don't touch the taxi doors, which open and close automatically. Drivers are smartly dressed and wear white gloves but generally don't speak English. Show where you want to go on a map or by indicating the kanji for your destination (like those in this guide). Tips are unnecessary, being included in the fare.

Bicycles

Japanese people cycle everywhere and tourists can easily rent bikes for a day near tourist sites for about ¥1000. Many places now offer electric bike rental, too, which can be especially handy in mountainous areas. Alternatively, think about buying a used bike at the start of your stay; prices are usually fairly reasonable. Remember to lock bikes up, though, as theft does occur. Cyclists should ride on the road and park in special parking lots, but in practice they often ride on sidewalks and park anywhere. The police tolerate this, but a badly parked bike can be impounded, resulting in a heavy fine.

Where to Stay and Eat

WHERE TO STAY
ADDRESSES IN THE GUIDE

In the Discovery section, the **Address Books** list a selection of accommodation addresses in or near the town or places of interest. To make it easy for you to find these addresses on the town maps (where given), we have marked each hotel (and restaurant) with a colored number.

Price categories

We have given a **range of prices**: for accommodation; the prices indicated are calculated for **two people excluding meals** in high season (outside Golden Week, Obon and New Year, when prices are often much higher); for dormitories, prices indicate the cost per person.

For restaurants, the prices are based on a standard menu or an à la carte meal consisting of two dishes (starter and main course), but do not include drinks. The addresses are classed according to four price categories to meet all budgets:

◯ **Lowest price** – These include *minshuku* (◯ *see p47*), business hotels, and, in some regions, youth hostels.
Hotels: ¥10,000 and under
Restaurants: ¥1500 and under

◯◯ **Average price** – Includes *ryokan*, hotels noted for their charm and atmosphere (often offering a choice of Japanese or Western-style rooms), and small specialty restaurants.
Hotels: ¥10,000–20,000
Restaurants: ¥1500–3000

◯◯◯ **Splashing out** –
Hotels: ¥20,000–30,000
Restaurants: ¥3000–8000

◯◯◯◯ **Top of the range** –
To spoil yourself, try one of the historic *ryokan*, contemporary hotels, or a *kaiseki* meal (◯ *see p49 & p120*).

Hotels: ¥30,000 and over
Restaurants: ¥8,000 and over
(◯ *See also guide.michelin.co.jp for addresses in Tokyo, Kyoto, and Osaka.*)

CAMPSITES

Camping is popular and the most economical form of accommodation (*allow ¥400–4000 per night; there is no charge for some sites*), and also a good way of visiting the national parks (◯ *see p12*), but camping in the wild in the national parks is strictly forbidden. Unfortunately, most of the 3000 or so campsites are difficult to access if you are not in a car, and are only open July/ August. They get extremely crowded. Equipment available on site is often limited, so it is advisable to take your own tent, etc. The JNTO provides up-to-date information at *japan.travel/ en/guide/camping*, and the **Outdoor Japan** website (*outdoorjapan.com*) is also a useful reference.

YOUTH HOSTELS

There are almost 360 youth hostels in Japan, offering clean, cheap dormitories and sometimes a few individual rooms as well. A night in a dormitory costs around ¥3000, breakfast is about ¥600, and dinner roughly ¥1000. The appeal of these hostels varies greatly. Some are housed in ugly, downtown buildings; others are found in smart areas or idyllic rural settings. Most are equipped with a communal kitchen, internet access, and laundry facilities. There is no age limit for access to youth hostels, but the rather strict regulations and boarding-school atmosphere which prevail in many of the older ones are not to everybody's taste. Not all hostels in Japan are affiliated with Hostelling International, but if planning to stay in hostels which are, it is a good idea to get a membership card before traveling as nonmembers are charged a nightly supplement. The prices quoted in this guide are those payable by nonmembers. The website of the **Japan Youth Hostel Association** *(jyh.or.jp/e/index.php)* lists all the youth hostels in Japan by region. During the high season and summer vacation it is essential to book well in advance. The rest of the time, make reservations at least 2 days before. You can book many hostels online through the HI website (*hihostels. com),* and the JNTO publishes a free *Japan Youth Hostel Map,* available in the main Tourist Offices. In addition to hostels under the management of regional governments, there are increasing numbers of private hostels, offering a slightly warmer welcome at the same price and without the need for membership. Most also have a few basic private rooms on the premesis.

CAPSULE HOTELS

A typical Japanese invention, *capsule hotels* were originally created for office workers who, having missed the last train home, or finding themselves too tired or drunk to go back to their suburban homes, need an **inexpensive place** *(averaging ¥4000 per capsule)* in which to spend the night. Most still cater to this group; these capsule hotels are usually located close to railway stations or in districts filled with bars and clubs, and rarely admit women (unless there is an area especially reserved for them). However, as foreign visitors have become more interested, more have been established for that market; these are more welcoming to women, and are often well-designed with attractive communal areas
The capsules are set in rows along corridors, one above the other, like tiny cabins on a ship. Measuring around 6.6ft/2m by 3.3ft/1m wide and 2.6ft/80cm high, they only contain a bed, but are well equipped with air-conditioning, television, radio, alarm clock, and bedside lamp. Lockers, automatic dispensers (razors, drinks), showers and occasionally a communal lounge are provided. Visitors to Japan may find a night in a capsule hotel an interesting experience, but only if they do not suffer from claustrophobia.

LOVE HOTELS

Another Japanese curiosity, *love hotels* welcome couples wishing to spend time together in discreet anonymity. They sometimes have outrageously kitsch façades, and themed rooms: jungle, science fiction, dolls' house, Parisian, even prison cell... not forgetting the mirrored ceilings, soft lighting and choice of music, movies, and other accessories on demand. Rooms are rented for a 2- to 3-hour period during the day *(around ¥4000)* or for the whole night *(around ¥8000).* Though an outlandish choice on the surface, they're often a fun and well-priced place for a night or two.

BUSINESS HOTELS

These Western-style hotels, often located near railway stations and sometimes part of a chain, are intended for travelers on a reduced budget. For tourists, they have the advantage of providing **comfort at a modest price**. Rooms are similar to those in an American motel, with molded plastic bathroom fittings and simple but functional equipment, but smaller. Despite their size, they are always clean and well equipped (air-conditioning, small refrigerator, television, kettle, hairdryer, *yukata* [loose cotton robe], razor, toothbrush, etc.). In the lowest-priced ones *(¥6000–10,000 for a double room),* the minimal service is taken care of by a range of vending machines. Washing machines and dryers are available. The quality of the breakfast, which may cost extra, varies enormously from simple snacks to a Japanese buffet. You can book rooms ahead online on the websites of large business hotel chains, where you can see the different prices for each day and take advantage of good discounts on Sunday evenings. Some of the best major chains (many of which also run other, non-business hotels) include: *toyoko-inn.com superhoteljapan.com/en tokyuhotelsjapan.com/global route-inn.co.jp.*

CLASSIC WESTERN HOTELS

There are a great many Western-style hotels in the large towns, belonging to Japanese (Nikko, JAL, Granvia, Tokyu, etc.) or international chains. They are generally high-capacity (more than 100 rooms), with extensive facilities (parking, restaurants, bars, boutiques). Most of them also have a few Japanese-style rooms, with *tatami* and futons, but the bulk of the accommodation is in wall-to-wall carpeted rooms with Western-style beds. The degree of luxury varies, ranging from middle-category hotels (*¥12,000–18,000 for a double room*) to luxurious four-star hotels (*¥30,000–60,000 for a double room*). Staff generally speak impeccable English. A tax of 10–15 percent is added for service, while a buffet-style breakfast costs ¥1000–2500. ☺ Double rooms are often less expensive than twin rooms. Prices vary daily and are at their lowest on Sunday nights. *You can reserve rooms ahead on the hotel's own website, the chain's general website, booking sites or apps like booking.com, or via rakuten. com or japanican.com/en.*

MINSHUKU 民宿

These **family-run** bed-and-breakfast style guesthouses are found all over Japan, but mostly in rural areas. As in *ryokan*, guests sleep in Japanese *tatami* rooms. Accommodation in a *minshuku* is usually a little simpler than in a *ryokan,* but the price is correspondingly cheaper. Guests unroll and arrange the futons themselves, share a communal bathroom, and a supplement is sometimes charged for towels. As is the case in all traditional Japanese accommodation, the prices are usually quoted per person. You can generally expect to pay around ¥6,000–8,000 per night, with breakfast and dinner.

SHUKUBO 宿坊

Certain Buddhist **temples** also offer accommodation, which is known as a *shukubo* (temple stay).

They traditionally offered bed and board to passing pilgrims, but some now take in travelers. For tourists it is a great opportunity to discover something of Japanese monastic life by joining in the morning prayers and meditation sessions. Most of the temples serve delicious vegetarian cuisine *(shojin ryori)*. Japan's most famous *shukubo* are found in the Koya-san area of Kansai (see p382; eng.shukubo.net). The average price is around ¥10,000 per person, including meals. Couples or families may normally stay together in a *shukubo* (*children's price sometimes 30 to 50 percent less*), but it is wise to check with the temple beforehand.

RYOKAN 旅館

Ryokan are **traditional Japanese inns**, where meals are served and guests sleep in *tatami* rooms. There is a wide range, from the traditional to the modern, and from modest, family-run establishments to the more luxurious. They all offer an elegant but relaxing atmosphere. To experience authentic Japanese-style accommodation, visitors should spend at least one night in a *ryokan*. Entered via sliding partitions, the furnishings are minimal: a low table, a few cushions, and a *tokonoma* – an alcove decorated with flowers or calligraphy (do not walk or stow suitcases in these alcoves). A futon (a mattress and a quilt) is rolled out on the floor for the night and then put away in a cupboard by the staff next morning. A *yukata* (light cotton kimono) is also supplied for guests and may be worn anywhere within the *ryokan*. Apart from in the most modest *ryokan*, all rooms have a bathroom, but there is always a communal bathroom for the hot bath (*o-furo*), sometimes fed by a thermal spring, with separate access for men and women. Some *ryokan* also allow the reservation of the *o-furo* for private use for an hour or so.

Ryokan prices are per person, including meals (breakfast and dinner), served in the dining room or sometimes in your room. It is generally not possible to rent a room without also taking meals. Expect to pay ¥6000 per person for the most basic *ryokan*, ¥15,000–20,000 for one that is middle of the range, and ¥30,000–80,000 for top of the range. The **Japan Ryokan Association's website**, (*ryokan.or.jp/english*), provides a long list of *ryokan*, classified by region, with addresses and phone numbers. Some *ryokan* can be booked online, but most cannot.

LONG-TERM ACCOMMODATION

If you are staying for some time in Japan, the most economical way is to rent a **gaijin house**. These are fully-equipped studios or apartments found in the major cities such as Tokyo or Kyoto, which foreign visitors may rent in their entirety or just by the room *(about ¥50,000 per month);* in the latter case the communal parts of the apartment etc. are shared with the other occupants. Addresses of *gaijin* (foreigner) houses can be found online, in magazines such as **Tokyo Classified** or through agencies such as **Sakura House** (*sakura-house.com*).

RESERVATIONS ONLINE

Apart from the websites already indicated, here are a few more useful links to consult:
jnto.go.jp/ja-search/eng/index.php – Research hotels and *ryokan* by region.
japaneseinngroup.com – The Japanese Inn network includes a hundred or so inexpensive small *ryokan* and *minshuku* throughout Japan.
j-hotel.or.jp/en – The Japan Hotel Association groups together good-quality hotels, most of which are Western-style.
japanhotel.net – A wide choice of various categories of hotels and *ryokan*, classified by region and described in detail.
travel.rakuten.com – Rakuten Travel is the biggest agency for online hotel reservations in Japan, sometimes offering reductions on the price of the rooms.
japanican.com/en – Reservations per night with reductions, for all types of accommodation.
japaneseguesthouses.com – Almost 500 traditional *ryokan*, classified by region, with descriptive information for each. Many of the *ryokan* listed are in hot spring areas.
toho.net/english – A network of small rural hotels, notably on Hokkaido, which charge low prices (*about ¥5000–6000 per person, including two meals*).

WHERE TO EAT

♿*Also see Gastronomy p120. Price categories, see p45.*
Restaurants in Japan may not have a menu in English, nor any English-speaking staff, but you can often make yourself understood by pointing at the wax models of dishes displayed in the window or menus with photos. Apart from in the large towns, meals are usually served from 11.30am to 2pm and from 6 to 8.30/9pm, although many nevertheless stay open later. Wherever you go you will be greeted by a resounding "*Irasshaimase!*" ("Welcome!") before being seated at a table or a counter. The majority of restaurants specialize in a **single type of cuisine**: skewers, noodles, sushi, etc. Many offer a cheap lunchtime menu (*teishoku*), with the evening menu often more expensive. There is no service charge—other than in the grander restaurants, where a supplement of 10–15 percent is added to the bill—and there is no need to tip (♿*see p59*). Take the check to the cash desk and pay (usually in cash) when you leave.

INFORMATION AND SPECIALIST RESTAURANTS

Kare-ya – Restaurants serving curry and rice (*kare raisu*), often at unbeatably low prices, and generally located near railway stations.
Kushikatsu-ya and kushiage-ya – Eateries serving deep-fried skewers

of meat and vegetables, covered in batter and panko breadcrumbs.

Okonomiyaki-ya – Inexpensive cafes where *okonomiyaki* (savory pancake) is prepared on a griddle.

Ramen-ya – Restaurants serving low-priced *ramen* dishes.

Soba-ya – Restaurants specializing in *soba* and sometimes *udon*, types of Japanese noodles.

Sukiyaki-ya – Chic and usually expensive restaurants, since good beef is a luxury in Japan. *Sukiyaki* is a dish containing meat and vegetables cooked on a griddle.

Sushi-ya – Restaurants serving *sushi* and *sashimi*, often in bars where you sit at a counter and watch the chef preparing the food. A good sushi restaurant can be expensive, but there are many low-priced versions, *kaiten-zushi-ya*, where the plates of sushi are set out on a rotating belt and you help yourself as the dishes pass in front of you. Price is usually indicated by the color of the plate.

Tempura-ya – Sometimes very expensive, these serve an assortment of tempura.

Tonkatsu-ya – These restaurants serve *tonkatsu* and *korokke* (potato croquettes), both popular breaded and deep-fried items.

Unagi-ya – Restaurants specializing in grilled eel *(unagi)*, which is carefully prepared and usually served on top of rice.

Yakiniku-ya – Generally quite low-priced, these restaurants specialize in Korean-style barbecues, where diners grill strips of marinated meat and shellfish at the table.

Yakitori-ya – Restaurants serving *yakitori* (chicken skewers).

OTHER TYPES OF RESTAURANT

Izakaya, a type of very popular bar or pub serving small dishes and light snacks such as pickles, salads, sashimi and grilled meat for snacking with drinks, though some have more of a focus on food. Most offer **nomihoudai,** an attractive all-you-can-drink happy hour fixed price *(about ¥2500)*

appreciated by businessmen and students.

Shokudo and **famiresu** (family restaurants) are low-priced and near railway stations, universities or in the basements of large buildings. They offer various dishes, sometimes Western food, and cheap set menus *(teishoku)*. They're often open 24hr.

Kaiseki ryori is the best Japanese haute cuisine. Some places offer *kaiseki* menus for tourists at affordable prices *(¥5000–8000)*, but the best of the best is to be found in the *ryotei* in Kyoto, restaurants with wonderful gardens. The prices can be colossal.

Temple restaurants, especially in Kyoto, produce traditional vegetarian cuisine *(shojin ryori)*, often based on tofu and *yuba* (skin of boiled soy milk).

Western cuisine (*yoshoku*), usually strongly influenced and altered by Japanese tastes, has a clear presence in the large towns, often in the form of mediocre Italian restaurants and the ever-present American fast-food outlets. French cuisine, which takes pride of place in large hotels, is often both meager and rather pretentious. It is often better to choose restaurants serving the food of **other Asian countries**, such as Chinese, Thai, Indonesian, and Vietnamese, which is often good value.

Coffee shops (*kissaten*) often serve a Western-style breakfast *(morning set)* consisting of toast, fried eggs, salad, and coffee, for about ¥800. Some of them also offer a cheap breakfast menu *(around ¥1000)*, consisting of one dish, a salad, a bowl of rice, and a drink. If you are on a tight budget, go for a *bento* (lunch box) from a *conbini*. In the shopping streets in the evenings, the *yatai* (food stands) offer quick snacks such as *ramen* and *takoyaki*. In Tokyo, Kyoto, Osaka, or Sapporo, some *sushi-ya*, *yakiniku-ya*, and *kushikatsu-ya* will display a tempting **tabehoudai** (all you can eat) sign from time to time. You'll have 90 minutes in which to eat as much as you want, usually for around ¥2500.

Bitchu-Matsuyama Castle/Takahashi

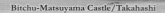
Kurashiki Bikan Historical Quarter

Okayama Koraku-en, one of the three great gardens of Japan

Okayama
http://okayama-japan.jp/en/

Kagawa
http://www.my-kagawa.jp/eg/

Okayama
Tokyo
Hiroshima
Kyoto
Kagawa

Ritsurin Garden/Takamatsu

"Red Pumpkin" Yayoi Kusama,
2006 Naoshima Miyanoura Port Square
Photo/Daisuke Aochi

Mt.Shiudeyama/Mitoyo

Useful Words and Phrases

Written Japanese is a combination of *kanji* (Chinese ideograms) and two alphabets, *hiragana* (for Japanese words) and *katakana* (usually for words of foreign origin). You'll also see some text in *romaji* (Roman alphabet). Pronunciation is much the same as in English. Diphthongs are pronounced separately, so "ai" is pronounced "aï" as in "high." "U" is pronounced either as "oo" or as a short and barely audible "ew," as in "few." The letter "e" is pronounced "eh," and is always pronounced, even at the end of a word, and "i" is "ee" as in "see." "G" is hard, as in "goose" and the "j" as in "judge." "Ch" is pronounced as in "church." "R" is pronounced wit a mouth position somewhere between the English "r" and "l", ending up sounding almost like "d." "S" is pronounced as in "hiss." "W" is the same as in English.

Glossary of Place Names

	Translation
bridge	-bashi or -hashi
district	-chome
peak	-dake or -take
waterfall	-daki or -taki
valley	-dani or -tani
temple	-dera, -tera, -in, or -ji
hall in a temple	-do
street	-dori or -tori
garden	-en
river	-gawa or -kawa
beach	-hama
peninsula	-hanto
east	-higashi
rock	-iwa
island	-jima or -shima
Shinto shrine	-jinja, -jingu, or -taisha
castle	-jo
sea	-kai
coast	-kaigan
prefecture	-ken
north	-kita
lake	-ko
park, garden	-koen
ward (subdivision of a department)	-ku
district, town	-machi
south	-minami
port	-minato or -ko
gate	-mon
village	-mura
west	-nishi
thermal spring	-onsen
slope	-saka or -zaka
town, city	-shi
pagoda/tower	-to
shrine gate	-torii
bay, creek	-ura or -wan
mountain	-yama, -zan or -san

BASIC CONVERSATION

Yes/no hai/iie
Good morning ohayo gozaimasu
Good day konnichiwa
Good evening konban wa
Good night oyasumi nasai
Goodbye sayonara
How are you? ogenki desuka?
Very well, thank you hai, genki desu
Thank you very much (domo) arigato (gozaimasu)
No, thank you iie, kekko desu
Don't mention it do itashimashite
Please (come in, help yourself) dozo
Excuse me sumimasen/gomen nasai
If you please onegai shimasu
Delighted to meet you
　hajime mashite
What is your name?
　o namae wa nan desu ka?
My name is … watashi wa … desu
What is your nationality?
　nani jin desuka?
I am American/English watashi wa amerika-jin/igirisu-jin desu
Do you speak English? eigo ga hanasemasuka?
I understand/don't understand
　wakarimasu/wakarimasen
Please repeat that
　mo ichido itte kudasai
What is the Japanese for …?
　nihongo de … wa nan to iimasuka?

Please write it in English eigo de kaite kudasai
Please give me a moment chotto matte kudasai
I like/do not like …
… ga suki desu/… ga kirai desu

Orienting Yourself
Right/to the right migi/migi ni
Left/to the left hidari/hidari ni
Straight on massugu
In front/behind mae/ushiro
I want to go to … … ni ikitai desu
Whereabouts is …?
… wa doko desu ka?
Where is it?/Is it here?
doko desu ka?/koko desu ka?
Is it near?/Is it far?
chikai desu ka?/toi desu ka?
Can I get there on foot?
aruite wa ikemasu ka?
Please draw me a map
chizu o kaite kudasai
I am lost mayoimashita

MONEY AND PURCHASES
Bank ginko
Could you change some money?
ryogae ga dekimasu ka?
How much is it? ikura desu ka?
Do you take credit cards? kurejitto kado wa tsukaemasu ka?
Expensive/cheap takai/yasui
Do you have …? … wa arimasu ka?
What is this? kore wa nan desu ka?
Can I try this on? kite mite mo ii desu ka?
Small/large chiisai/okii
I'll take this kore o kudasai

AT THE HOTEL
Have you a room available?
heya wa arimasuka?
I would like to reserve a room
heya o yoyaku shitai desu
I have a reservation yoyaku o shimashita
I have not made a reservation
yoyaku wa shite imasen
Single room/double/twin
shinguru/daburu/tsuin
Japanese room/Western-type room
washitsu/yoshitsu
Room with bathroom
ofuro tsuki no heya

What does it cost per night?
ippaku ikura desu ka?
I will stay for 1/2/3 nights
ippaku/nihaku/sanpaku tomarimasu
Do you have wifi? wai fai wa arimasu ka?
May I leave my baggage?
nimotsu o azukatte moraemasu ka?
I will be leaving the hotel tomorrow
ashita shuppatsu shimasu
Please call me a taxi
takushii o yonde kudasai
Key/passport/reception
kagi/pasupoto/furonto

IN A RESTAURANT
A table for two, please
futari onegaishimasu
Have you a menu in English?
eigo no menu wa arimasu ka?
Give me … please … o kudasai
The same thing as my neighbor
tonari no hito to onaji mono o kudasai
Breakfast/lunch/dinner
choshoku/chushoku/yushoku [or] asagohan/hirugohan/bangohan
Hot/cold atsui/tsumetai
I'm hungry/I'm not hungry onaka ga suite imasu/onaka ga suite imasen
It's delicious oishii desu
Waiter, the check please! sumimasen, okanjo onegai shimasu!

How to order in a sushi-ya
Abalone:	awabi
Bonito:	katsuo
Bream:	tai
Crab:	kani
Cuttlefish:	ika
Eel:	anago (sea), unagi (freshwater)
Ginger:	gari
Mackerel:	saba
Octopus:	tako
Omelet:	tamago
Raw shrimp:	nama ebi
Salmon roe:	ikura
Sardine:	iwashi
Scallop:	hotate
Sea bass:	suzuki
Sea urchin:	uni
Shrimp:	ebi
Soy sauce:	shoyu
Tuna belly:	toro
Tuna:	maguro

EMERGENCIES AND HEALTH

I have a headache/stomachache/toothache atama/onaka/ha ga itai desu
Help! tasukete!
Call an ambulance kyukyusha o yonde kudasai
Call the police keisatsu o yonde kudasai
I need a doctor isha ga hitsuyo desu
Where is the hospital? byoin wa doko ni arimasu ka?
I've lost my passport pasupoto o nakushimashita
Embassy taishi kan
Police booth koban
Drugstore kusuriya

TRANSPORTATION

Aircraft/airport hikoki/kuko
Station/train eki/densha
Subway/tram chikatetsu/romen densha
Boat fune, boto
Bus/bus stop basu/basu-tei
Bicycle/rental bicycle jitensha/kashi-jitensha [or] renta-saikuru
Car/driver's license kuruma/unten-menkyo
Taxi stand takushii noriba
Stop here, please koko de tomatte kudasai
A ticket to … please … yuki no kippu o kudasai
One-way/return trip katamichi kippu/ofuku kippu
Reserved seat/non-reserved seat shitei seki/jiyu seki
Second class/first class nito/itto
Ticket office/baggage room kippu uriba/nimotsu azukarijo
What time does the bus for … leave? … iki no basu wa nanji ni demasu ka?
What time do we arrive? nanji ni tsukimasu ka?

How long does it take? dono gurai kakarimasu ka?
Which platform does the train for … leave from? … yuki wa nanban no homu desu ka?
Is this the train for …? … yuki no densha wa kore desu ka?
Which station is this? kono eki wa doko desu ka?
Let me know when we arrive at … … ni tsuitara oshiete kudasai

FIGURES AND NUMBERS

	Translation
0	zero, rei
1	ichi
2	ni
3	san
4	yon, shi
5	go
6	roku
7	nana, shichi
8	hachi
9	kyu
10	ju
11	ju-ichi
100	hyaku
200	ni-hyaku
1,000	sen
10,000	ichi-man
100,000	ju-man
1 million	hyaku-man
1 person	hitori
2 people	futari
3 people	sannin
4 people	yonin

Basic Information

DRINKING WATER

It is safe to drink the tap water throughout the whole of Japan. Mineral water can be bought from vending machines or in *conbini* and other stores.

ELECTRICITY

The electrical current is 100V, 50 to 60Hz AC. Japanese plugs generally have two flat pins, like American ones; occasionally they have three pins (two flat and one rounded). Though the two-pin plugs look very similar to American plugs, visitors from North America may need an adapter. Adapters are available cheaply in Japan, or may even be hired in some hotels. North American visitors may also need a converter for larger appliances such as irons and hairdryers, but should have no problem with cell phones and digital cameras. Visitors from other countries may need a converter for devices that are not 100–200V, such as kettles or hairdryers, or, if there is no battery adapter or dual voltage AC charger available, a transformer may be needed for devices such as computers.

IN CASE OF EMERGENCY
Police: ✆110.
Fire brigade or ambulance: ✆119.
Japan Helpline: ✆0570-000-911 (jhelp.com/en/jhlp.html). There is no charge for assistance in English, 24hr.

HEALTH
ILLNESSES
The high standard of hygiene in Japan makes the risk of contracting an illness fairly small. Some precautions should be taken: there are many mosquitoes, so packing some insect repellent would not go amiss, but it's also readily available in drugstores.

MEDICAL SERVICES
Japan has good hospitals and clinics (at least in large towns), but they are expensive. You are strongly advised to take out an insurance policy covering medical care abroad in case a problem occurs. In an **emergency** (fire or ambulance), dial 119. Ask your hotel to call a doctor or an ambulance, or tourist information centers may have a list of English-speaking doctors. To find an English-speaking doctor, you can also contact the **Amda** International Medical Information Center in Tokyo (eng.amda-imic.com). A list of general hospitals in Tokyo with English-speaking staff available appears on the website of the US Embassy, (jp.usembassy.gov), under US Citizen Services: Medical Assistance. ⬥See also Health p33.

INTERNET
Japan is one of the most connected countries in the world, and at high speed. One particularly inspired Japanese invention is the **manga cafe** (manga kissa); these cafes offer unlimited manga comics and drinks, plus booths or small rooms equipped with high-speed internet and sometimes video game consoles. Some also have showers and sofas, so you can even spend the night. There are many manga cafes in big towns (prices are around ¥600 per hour), but they are not always easy to find as their signs are generally written in kanji. Staff may not speak English. Manga cafes usually also offer packages for 3 hours, 5 hours (around ¥1200), or even a whole night.
Computer keyboards have both kana (Japanese script) and Roman letters arranged in the QWERTY layout. One key normally switches between the Roman and Japanese characters.
There are also many other places where the internet can be accessed **at no cost** to check e-mails: in some youth hostels and ryokan, most hotels, cafes and bars (customers only); in public libraries, town halls, and Tourist Offices; and also in large computer stores (Bic Camera, Yodobashi), where computers are used for demonstration purposes.
😊 Most hotels have wifi at reception, but not necessarily in the rooms, especially in older or more traditional hotels. Mobile wi-fi routers can be hired from companies such as Pupuru (pupuruwifi.com/en) and on arrival at Narita or Haneda airport, and are provided in some hotels and apartment rentals.

LAUNDRY
Coin-operated laundrettes are often located in or near sento, the local public baths, and dry cleaners are often located in shopping centers. Otherwise, hotels generally offer a laundry service (prices correspond to

the class of hotel, but tend to be high). Youth hostels, *ryokan*, and business hotels normally provide washing machines for customers to use. *(Expect to pay around ¥300 to use the washing machine, ¥50 for the detergent, and ¥100 to use a dryer for 10min.)*

MAIL/POST

The Japanese mail service *(post. japanpost.jp/int/index_en.html)* is efficient, reliable, and fast, with little risk of an item going astray, whether sent for delivery locally or abroad. The cost of mailing a postcard to the USA, Canada, the UK, Australia, and New Zealand is ¥70; for a letter ¥110. Post offices are recognizable by their logo, a red-orange T topped by a horizontal bar (〒). They also sell boxes and bags for mailing parcels.

If you need to forward your luggage in Japan, *takkyubin* is your best bet. The main company is Yamato Transport *(kuronekoyamato.co.jp/en)*, also called *kuro neko* (black cat) for their logo.

MEDIA
NEWSPAPERS AND MAGAZINES

The Japanese press is noted for the huge circulation figures of its daily newspapers: 9 million for the *Yomiuri Shimbun*, 6.4 million for the *Asahi Shimbun*. English versions of these papers, as well as the *Japan Times,* are sold in bookshops in the larger towns and from kiosks at railway stations. They are also available online in English *(asahi.com/ajw and japantimes.co.jp)*. The *International Herald Tribune* is also widely available. A list of magazines published monthly or weekly runs to some 3000, including journals in English, such as *Newsweek* and *Time*.

TELEVISION AND RADIO

Even with some grasp of the language, watching Japanese television can be very baffling in terms of sound, pace, and content. Talk shows and cooking shows featuring the preparation and tasting of regional specialities play a big role in the scheduling. Apart from the public television channels of NHK

(the main state broadcaster), many commercial channels are also available *(NTV, TBS, Fuji-TV, TV-Asahi, TV-Tokyo)*, with regional and specialist versions. Some films and imported programs are broadcast in the original versions. It's also possible to tune in to an English language commentary for the NHK evening news on some TVs, and you may be able to access a bilingual soundtrack for other shows. CNN, BBC, or BS1 are normally received in the large hotels. You can hear the news in English on the radio via InterFM *(76.1)* broadcast from Tokyo and FM Cocolo *(76.5)* from Kansai. The BBC World Service is broadcast throughout Japan *(bbc.co.uk/worldserviceradio)* and the AFN-TOKYO *(American Forces Network)* provides 24-hour radio services to its principal military audience across Japan *(afnpacific.net/Local-Stations/ Tokyo)*. AFN's Eagle 810 broadcasts throughout the Kanto Plain on 90.3 FM.

MUSEUM, MONUMENT, AND SITE TARIFFS

Entry charges vary according to the nature and importance of the attraction or site. The cost of entry to most temples ranges from ¥200 to ¥800, and for museums from ¥300 to ¥1000, or ¥1500 for some temporary exhibitions.

NAMES OF STREETS

Finding an address in large towns can sometimes prove difficult, for the Japanese inhabitants as well as for visitors, as most of the streets do not display a name. To make it even more complicated, the numbers of the buildings are not consecutive, but allocated according to the date they were built. Instead of indicating the street, addresses generally include the area *(ku)* and the district *(cho* or *machi)*, accompanied by a series of three figures indicating the number of the ward, the number of the block, and the number of the building. For example: Sony Building, 8F, 3-6-2 Tenjin-cho, Chuo-ku. 8F indicates the *floor*, with the ground floor labeled 1F.

OPENING HOURS
BANKS

Banks are usually open 9am–3pm Monday to Friday. Foreign exchange offices keep more flexible hours. ATMs in banks and post offices are almost always inaccessible in the evening and at weekends.

OFFICES, GOVERNMENT OFFICES, AND POST OFFICES

Offices and government offices open 9am–5pm, except at weekends. Small post offices open 9am–5pm, Monday to Friday, and large post offices 9am–7pm during the week and up to 3pm on Saturdays. Only the main post offices in very large towns and cities have a counter open on Sundays.

STORES

Shops and department stores are usually open 10am–7pm or 8pm, every day (or Tuesday to Sunday). Some stores, including *conbini*, stay open 24 hours a day, 7 days a week.

MUSEUMS, MONUMENTS, AND SITES

Museums generally open 10am–5pm, except on Monday. When Monday falls on a public holiday, they close on the following Tuesday. Temples and castles tend to open daily 9am–5pm. In most cases last admissions are 30min before closing time. Many sites are closed from Dec 28 to Jan 3.

RESTAURANTS

Restaurants open every day, usually 11.30am–10.30pm (some may be 24hr). Some restaurants close 2.30– 6pm. Last orders are generally around 8.30/9pm, sometimes indicated by the letters LO.

PHOTOGRAPHY

Memory cards, camera batteries, lenses and camera accessoriesare widely available and prices are reasonable, as you would expect in a country where photography is so popular. Bic Camera and Yodobashi Camera should have everything you need. Shops that develop and print photos *(minilabs)* can still be found in most towns, and automatic machines print digital photos in next to no time. Traditional photographic film is also widely available.

PUBLIC HOLIDAYS

When a public holiday falls on a Sunday, it is celebrated on the following day.
Jan 1: New Year's Day
2nd Mon in Jan: Coming of Age Day
Feb 11: National Foundation Day
Around Mar 21: Spring Equinox
Apr 29: Showa Day
May 3: Constitution Memorial Day
May 4: Greenery Day
May 5: Children's Day
3rd Mon in Jul: Marine Day
Aug 11: Mountain Day
3rd Mon in Sept: Respect for the Aged Day
Around Sept 23: Fall Equinox
2nd Mon in Oct: Health and Sports Day
Nov 3: Culture Day
Nov 23: Labor Thanksgiving Day
Dec 23: The Emperor's Birthday

PUBLIC TOILETS

There are public toilets everywhere in Japan—in places of interest, train stations, the subway, department stores—that are free to use and usually clean. The most common are the traditional squat toilets, normally found in public places; there's usually at least one Western toilet available, though, which should be marked on the stall door. Slippers are sometimes left by the door in restaurants or hotels; these must be put on before entering and removed on leaving. The toilets in hotels and private homes are generally modern and very high-tech, with heated seats, illuminated push buttons, discreet background music, and extra fittings such as bidets.

SECURITY

While muggings and crime in general are pretty rare, theft does sometimes occur, especially in big cities and in busy areas such as railway stations. If you are in any kind of difficulty, or are simply lost and looking for an address, the easiest solution is to go to the nearest **koban**, the local police booth. They are recognizable by the small red lamp at the front.

EARTHQUAKES AND NATURAL DISASTERS

Earthquakes are quite frequent in Japan. Fortunately most of them are minor and cause minimal damage since buildings are designed to resist tremors. Should an earthquake occur when you are inside a building, keep away from windows, furniture and anything that is likely to topple over, and take shelter under a solid table or stand under a door frame. If out in the open, find a clear place well away from debris and dangerous objects (signboards, electric cables) that could fall. Don't panic, and follow the evacuation instructions given by the person responsible for security. Alerts are put out for **tidal waves** *(tsunami)*. In the event of an alert, if you are on a beach, leave immediately and take refuge on high ground. Don't panic and, if necessary, get in contact with your embassy or consulate. The **typhoon** season occurs between the end of August and October. The impending arrival of these violent tropical storms is announced in warning bulletins on radio and television. Trains may be stopped and some sites and stores may be closed. They are not dangerous provided you keep under cover in some form of strong and durable shelter until they pass.

SMOKING

Cigarettes may be bought from *conbini* or from the cigarette vending machines that are located more or less everywhere in the streets, stores, bars, and hotels. However, to buy cigarettes from a vending machine, the consumer needs a Taspo card. Since this is only available to residents, short-term visitors will have to rely on the other outlets. Both Japanese and American brands sell for around ¥270–300 a packet.

Many Japanese people are heavy smokers. Nevertheless, for some years now laws protecting nonsmokers in public places have been applied with increasing strictness. As a result, smokers now congregate in spaces reserved for them, in stations and on the streets. In Tokyo smoking in the street is now banned in some districts, and towns such as Kobe, Kyoto, and Hiroshima are following suit. In places where there is a ban it is clearly marked. By contrast, most bars still allow smoking indoors, and it's common for cafes and restaurants to have a designated smoking area. Japan has been slower to take up vaping than in much of the rest of the developed world, so refills may be harder to find in some districts.

TELEPHONES

CALLING JAPAN FROM ABROAD

To call Japan from the USA/Canada, dial 011 + 81 + the regional code, omitting the first 0, + the number; from the UK/Ireland/New Zealand, dial 00 + 81, etc.; from Australia dial 0011 + 81 etc.

INTERNATIONAL CALLS FROM JAPAN

International calls can be made directly *(with ¥100 coins)* from public telephones marked International & Domestic Card/Coin Phone. Unfortunately there are not many of them. They can usually be found in the lobbies of big hotels, airports, large railway stations, and some city centers. For international calls from Japan, dial 010, then dial the country code *(1 for the US and Canada, 44 for the UK, 353 for Ireland, 61 for Australia, 64 for New Zealand)*, followed by the area code *(minus the first 0, if the number starts with one)*, and then the number. Tariffs vary depending on the operating company.

LOCAL CALLS WITHIN JAPAN

Even though there are fewer of them than there used to be, the gray or green **public telephones**

are still fairly ubiquitous. They take ¥10 and ¥100 coins as well as prepaid telephone cards. A local call costs ¥10 per minute. They will not, however, give change for ¥100 coins. To avoid a constant search for the necessary coins, buy a **telephone card** if you plan to use these phones regularly. Cards with a value of ¥500 or ¥1000 are sold from kiosks in railway stations, in *conbini,* and from automatic machines; they are often beautifully decorated.

To call a number within the town or region in which you are located, dial the number omitting the regional code that is shown in brackets. To telephone from one town or region to another, dial the number preceded by the regional code.

Free Numbers – There is no charge for numbers that begin with 0120.

Directory Information – For national information, dial 104.

CELL PHONES/MOBILE PHONES

Japan is *the* country of the cell phone, (*keitai denwa, or sumatofon for smartphones*). But only European 4G cell phones and smartphones (or last generation 3G) will work on the Japanese network (where the operators do not use GSM). If your phone is not compatible, there is no point in bringing it, nor in buying one in Japan that you could then not use back home.

It is possible, however, to **rent** a cell phone during your stay from a number of private telecommunications companies and insert your SIM card, if it is compatible. Similarly, you can rent a Japanese SIM (usually with data) if your phone is unlocked. Data-only cards are also available for smartphones, laptops, and tablets. Most companies have a counter at Narita or Kansai airports, or can deliver direct to your hotel. NTT Docomo, the biggest Japanese cell phone company, offers numerous services and products (*nttdocomo.co.jp/english*). Before deciding, compare the offers (price of rental, cost of calls, amount of data) on the following websites: *softbank-rental.jp/en, cellularabroad.com, rentafonejapan.com, telecomsquare. co.jp,* and *mobal.com.*

If you have an unlocked smartphone, you may be able to rent a SIM card *(¥110 per day)* with a Japanese number from the Softbank counters in the airports, making it a convenient option. Be sure to disconnect access to the internet to avoid prohibitive costs.

TIME DIFFERENCE

Compared to the US East Coast, the time difference in Japan is +13 hours (i.e., when it is 11am in New York, it is midnight in Tokyo); US West Coast: +16 hours; UK/Ireland: +9 hours; Eastern Australia: -1 hour; Western Australia: +1 hour; New Zealand: -3 hours. Time differences vary when DST is in operation.

TIPPING

Tipping is not customary in Japan, and in some cases is offensive, tantamount to saying that the establishment does not properly pay their staff. However, a service charge is automatically added to the bill by the main hotels and *ryokan,* and in luxury restaurants (10–15 percent).

WEATHER

Weather forecasts are given on television and in the newspapers. For a forecast in English by phone, dial **177** *(for local forecasts, dial the code for the region – such as 03 for Tokyo – then 177).* For the **weather forecast in English** *see jnto.go.jp/weather/eng/index.php.* See also When to Go p11.

Okinawan dancers
© Joe Carini/age fotostock

Understanding Japan

At the end of the 19C, Lafcadio Hearn (1871–1904), one of the first Westerners to write about Japan, said: "One must learn how to understand," which is the best advice that can be given to any new visitor. But "learning how to understand" takes time—time to get to know both the people and the country at first hand, and not simply through books—and for the traveler, time is something that is often in short supply. However, awareness of what lies beneath the surface will enable foreigners to avoid basing their views of Japan on the usual clichés, and on Japan's reputation for being "Westernized." Japan has its own rich history—it cannot be understood simply by reference to the culture of the West. The WW II period (and its string of atrocities) aside, Westerners have generally formed their view of Japan from a cultural angle—usually by focusing on the stereotypes of the samurai and the geisha at the expense of ordinary Japanese people. Consequently, Western ideas of the "Japanese spirit" tend to ignore the country's complex history, its social structures, and the values and traditions of the majority of the population. With images of the samurai and geisha to the fore, and the popularity of anime and manga, many people's concept of Japan fluctuates confusedly between the mawkish and twee, an aggressive nation, and a highly technologically productive country.

A CONFUSING MODERNITY

Japan's modern society is not just a simple carbon copy of the West's. Japanese democracy is not an American import. The Occupation (1945–52, see p80) facilitated democratization but by the end of the 19C, liberal, even socialist ideas, had already begun to take root and despite the drift toward militarism, political thinking continued to evolve. This is why the Japanese "embraced" their defeat in World War II so well, to paraphrase the title of one of the most enlightening books on the Japanese postwar recovery, *Embracing Defeat*, by the American historian John Dower. And, though Japan was in ruins in 1945, it had been a world power: in 1905, the Japanese Navy sank the Russian fleet, a victory that gave it a place among the world's great powers less than 50 years after the Meiji reforms.

Contact with the West was the spur to modernize, but it was not the only stimulus. When Japan abandoned its isolationist policy in the middle of the 19C, it was regarded by the West as being politically and economically "backward" in comparison to Europe, though not in terms of its "civilization." Urban culture (popular literature, the press), the development of cities, and the standard of literacy were all on a par with Europe. With a population of 1 million, Edo—as Tokyo was then known—was as densely populated as London.

The modernization of Japan was therefore the outcome of Japanese heritage coming into contact with more foreign countries, with mutually beneficial and productive results.

If visitors can successfully distance themselves from the cliché that within every Japanese man lurks a potential samurai, that every Japanese woman is a submissive housewife waiting hand and foot on her "captain of industry" husband, the reality of Japanese culture will become apparent. In the end, the best way to gain an understanding of Japan is to explore it, and the best place to start is with its cities.

ON FOOT IN THE CITY

In a city such as Tokyo, the real Japan can be discovered in small, everyday things just as much as in its wealth of cultural heritage or ultramodern architecture. A stroll around the urban landscape of Japan's capital city will reveal a vast architectural collage in a fascinating patchwork of styles. By Western standards of urbanization,

People appreciateing the cherry blossoms, Shinjuku Gyoen National Garden, Tokyo

© Jon Arnold Images/hemis.fr

however, the large Japanese cities might be regarded as "ugly" and lacking in the harmony that gives European cities their beauty, even a city such as Kyoto. Unlike Florence, Kyoto's beauty is not immediately on show, but rather hidden in its temples and gardens, and in the old districts that lie sandwiched between a grid of wide, bland highways. With its jumble of highrise buildings, architectural styles, and power lines, confusion seems to reign supreme in Tokyo. Due to the earthquake of 1923, the firebombing of World War II, and the financial speculation of the 1980s, its historic legacy is not as rich as Kyoto's. And yet, take a detour into a small street squeezed in between two apartment blocks and you will soon find another side to the city: suddenly the tempo shifts from the throbbing pulse of a metropolis to the peace and quiet of a village.

The charm of a Japanese city, especially Tokyo, lies in its network of little streets and one-way alleys. It's a way of life that owes less to materialism than to the neighborliness of its inhabitants. Here, cars are an intrusion and pedestrians and bicycles rule. Individual houses, little gardens, and small shops—nothing that is architecturally striking, but a genuine sense of community prevails in these urban villages.

So, where are these "urban villages"? The answer is almost everywhere—in the Hongo, Ueno, Uguisudani, and Yanaka districts, in the area that used to be called the "town below" (*shitamachi*) or "downtown," where the ordinary city folk lived. But this dual urban identity, which encompasses a whole galaxy of universes that coexist and interweave with each other, can also be found in the wealthier districts, where a certain social fluidity still exists.

Potted plants, flowering shrubs, and bamboos proliferate in the small streets, and this patchwork of traditional greenery lends a particular gaiety. Paradoxically, in the middle of the city it's a glimpse of the unsual relationship that Japan has with nature, a relationship that has been raised to a high aesthetic level, though it did not prevent the city from being ravaged during the period of huge economic growth from 1960 to 1980.

Attuned to the cycles of nature, Japanese culture is highly aware of the fragility of the natural world, and being in such a seismically active area, it also respects its power. The result is a unique mix of venerating the natural world and seeking to control it, visiting shrines of water deities while damming most of the country's rivers to control their flow. Ravaged by earthquakes and fires, Tokyo is a city aware of the power of nature, but still celebrating the beauty to be found in blooming cherry trees and hidden gardens.

Philippe Pons

Japan Today

Japan is often considered to be the non-Western country whose practices and institutions are closest to those of the West. The quality of its products and services is admired, as is its creativity in the areas of art, science and technology. Its youth have embraced Western street culture, turning it into something unique of their own. However, Japan's originality or idiosyncrasy tends to be too readily explained by reference to its religious system. In the following portrait of a young couple and a brief survey of Japan's religions, we aim to show Japan as it is today: resolutely modern, but in its own way.

WORK, LIFE AND LOVE IN MODERN JAPAN

Eiko closes her laptop. She has just finished speaking with her boyfriend, Taka. While she works in Tokyo, he's posted in Kobe; they talk regularly, and plan to get engaged once he's secured a transfer to his company's head office. For now, though, at an early stage in their careers, they live separately and focus on work.

THE WOMAN'S WORLD

In her mid-20s, Eiko's life looks quite different to how her mother's did. During Eiko's childhood her mother did not work, focusing instead on raising her children, maintaining her home, and supporting her husband's career. This was made possible by his steady wages and "job for life". Since the economic downturn of the 1990s, most of these jobs have dried up, and fewer and fewer couples have found a single-income household feasible. However, Eiko enjoys her job; though she would like to marry someday, and maybe have kids, she feels no pressure from her peers to hurry up; they, too, are dealing firstly with their uncertain economic future. After four years at university and starting in a low-level role at her company, she feels she is finally gaining some responsibility at work—though she and her female colleagues are still the ones asked to make tea, copy docu-

ments and do tedious data entry tasks, even when there are male employees in positions junior to them.

THE MAN'S WORLD

Taka is mostly enjoying his time in Kobe. Like Eiko, he works very long hours, with no extra pay for ovetime, and is often expected to go for drinks with colleagues. He spends little time in his apartment due to this, usually eating on the go from a *conbini* or in a stand-up noodle bar by the station. All of the senior figures at work are men, and especially at *nomikai* (after-work drinks) they tease their young employees, asking when the men are going to find a nice wife to cook for them, and when the women are going to get married and retire. Though he's tired of these jokes, Taka does feel lucky to have met Eiko at university: many of his colleagues find it incredibly difficult to meet potential romantic partners, which is unsurprising as they have to devote all of their time to their work.

HOME AND ITS CHOICES

While they're apart, Eiko and Taka are both living alone in small apartments. Despite working in similar fields, and despite Eiko living in the more expensive city, she is paid slightly less than Taka; the gender pay gap remains around 25 percent. As such, around a third of her salary goes on her apartment.

Eiko and Taka know their marriage will look different to their parents', but there are some topics neither has felt comfortable talking about. The average married Japanese man spends just 26 minutes a day on household tasks, and numerous surveys show that women spend several times longer on domestic tasks than their male partners, even when both of them have jobs. Will Taka expect a similar balance of household responsibility?

If they have a child, it's financially unlikely Eiko will be able to quit her job to raise them, but with under 1 percent of men taking paternity leave, she fears Taka's company will not allow him to contribute any time to childcare. And will Eiko's own promotion prospects be limited if her bosses think she wants to have child-

Japan's declining birth rate

At 1.42 children per woman (2018), Japan's fertility rate is one of the lowest in the world, and it's likely to drop still further. Only around 920,000 children were born in 2018 (a low not seen since 1899, the year births were first registered). The population has been stagnant or declining since 2005, with 200,000 fewer Japanese people every year. The reasons are legion, and complex to tackle. Most couples find that, especially with the rising cost of living, it's no longer economically feasible for one partner to leave their job to focus on childcare— and the onus is almost always on the woman to do this. However, the root of the problem goes deeper, to the declining marriage rate: having a child out of wedlock is deeply taboo in Japan, with 98% of children born within marriage. Many women in particular are less keen to get married, as it limits their career prospects (the term *kotobuki taisha* is used specifically to describe a woman quitting her job to get married). So far, government efforts to encourage marriage, thereby tackling the population problem, have had little effect.

ren? Domestic duties like housework, plus child-rearing and helping to care for elderly parents, still tend to fall on women's shoulders, and Eiko worries how she'll handle this "second shift".

Currently Eiko and Taka are discussing what they'll do when he is transferred to Tokyo. Will they live separately until they marry, as is still the cultural norm? Or will they cohabit for a while first, as more young people are now doing, to help them save money for the wedding?

THE ROLE OF MARRIAGE

The average age to get married in Japan is 30, a number which has steadily risen since the 1990s. The marriage rate has decreased over the same period, with around 580,000 weddings in 2018. However, it's still the norm to marry, and Taka and Eiko look forward to it—though they're less excited about the cost, which averages over 3 million yen.

It's still frowned upon to have children out of wedlock, which makes it especially important while the population is declining. However, this has little to do with Taka and Eiko's desire to marry; rather, it simply feels like the next natural step in legitimizing their relationship. They've been in a relationship for several years, but neither of them has told their parents, feeling that until they're engaged it will not seem serious to their families.

Having attended a few weddings, Taka and Eiko have some idea of what they would like their own wedding to look

like. It's a lucrative industry offering an overwhelming array of choices, but over 60 percent of couples opt for a Western-style wedding with a chapel, a bride in a white dress and a groom in a suit. Taka recently attended the traditional Japanese wedding of his sister and her American husband, though, and is leaning toward that option. Mixed marriages are still unusual in Japan, only around 1 percent of total marriages, and the traditional style of the wedding, held at a Shinto shrine in Taka's hometown, showed the groom's commitment to integrating into the family's culture.

A friend of Eiko's recently held a same-sex marriage ceremony at a temple in Kyoto, Shunko-in. The union is not legally recognized as a marriage, though, and Kyoto is not one of the (as of 2019) 25 municipalities and 1 prefecture (Ibaraki) offering "partnership certificates," which grant some rights to same-sex couples. The number of places issuing these certificates is rapidly increasing, thugh, doubling in the first half of 2019 alone.

RELIGION OR SPIRITUALITY

It soon becomes apparent to Western visitors that just below the surface of this modern, materialistic society, Japan is a deeply spiritual nation. After all, this is the country that gave us Zen meditation, the haiku (a strictly defined form of Japanese poetry which distills scenes down to their essence), and the martial arts.

This is not how Japanese people tend to see themselves, however. Surveys conducted in Japan confirm that many people are not religious, are not interested in religion, and even distrust religion. This conviction has been reinforced by the criminal acivitities of some cult movements, such as the sarin gas attack carried out by Aum Shinrikyo in the Tokyo subway on March 20, 1995 (12 dead and more than 5000 injured). Though exceptional, this attack was a shock that saw a hardening of public opinion and later the law with regard to religion. Even before that, over 80 percent of Japanese people claimed to distrust religious organizations, barely 10 percent of parents considered that religion was an important aspect of education, and religion was ranked ninth in a list of the ten "most important elements in life." Perhaps more astonishingly to visitors from very religious countries, under 40 percent of Japanese people said in 2008 that they believed in "spiritual things" like life after death. As a result, people rarely have conversations about their religious convictions, differentiating Japan from many Western countries. Tourists who take the time to talk with a monk or priest may come away with the impression that theirs is a lonely life. Although Japan has not developed a tradition of militant atheism, the country is overall deeply irreligious.

The official figures

For all that, most Japanese people are in some way engaged with religious practices. In a 2008 NHK survey, around

Kanda Matsuri at Kanda Myojin, Kanda, Tokyo

© JTB Photo/UIG via Getty Images

Matsuri

The term *matsuri* ("festival") comes from the verb *matsuru*, which means "respecting and invoking the gods." The origins of the *matsuri* are essentially religious, a way of pacifying the *kami*, omnipresent divinities that make their presence felt through volcanic eruptions, earthquakes, or tidal waves. To ensure good harvests and therefore the survival of a community, the *matsuri* originally coincided with the two most important times of the agricultural year: sowing in spring and the harvest in the fall. Since the *kami* are very demanding, other rites were added: the Festival of the New Year Fire (Hi-no-Matsuri), the essential period of purification during which the year's impurities are symbolically burned, and the Buddhist Festival of the Dead (Bon), celebrated throughout the country in July and August. Matsuri evolved over the centuries as festivals, adapting and acquiring new elements to suit individual communities. For the Japanese, there is always an excuse for a good-humored festival and for revisiting one's *furusato* (village or place of origin).

🕭 *Also see Aoi Matsuri p329, Yamagasa Matsuri p578, and Awa Odori p568.*

half of respondents said they had drawn *o-mikuji* (fortunes) or owned good luck charms. A similar number take part in *hatsumode* (the first shrine visit of the new year) and/or visit graves, while 90 percent have done one or the other at some point. Only 39 percent identified with a religion (34% Buddhist, 3% Shinto, 1% Christian, 1% other), while 49 percent said they did not adhere to a religion. However, the ambiguity of the words used in relation to religion and belief may contribute to this high number. Many Japanese people do not view Shintoism as a religion per se (unless they are a member of a particular Shinto organization), interpreting the word used for religion (*shukyo*) as indicating a specific group of which you either are or aren't a member. By this definition, engaging in Shinto rituals and practices, even if you feel an affiliation to the philosophy and mythology behind them, does not make you a "religious" person. Daily worship is often more concerned with going through the motions of a ritual correctly than it is with deep spiritual reflection.

The right ritual at the right time

Japanese people visit their ancestral tombs on certain days of the year and especially during **Bon, The Festival of the Dead,** usually held around August 15. Due to the large numbers of people traveling on such days, the roads and railways get very busy (it is wise to avoid traveling then if possible).

The summer is also when many festivals (*matsuri, see box opposite*) are held. For the 60 percent of Japanese people who take advantage of high-summer public holidays to honor the spirits of their ancestors, it means a return to their roots, as well as cheerful reunions with family and friends, dances that can take a year to organize, meals with plenty of liquor and food that harks back to childhood, the exchange of gifts, fireworks, and lanterns swaying in the wind. No one gives a thought to the history of Bon with its Indian origins, or to its religious roots (it is strongly Buddhist in character), or even really to the festival's implication that the dead live on in another world.

Bon is an extreme example, perhaps, and its religious aspect is quite prominent, but a quick run through the year's other major festivals illustrates that Japanese life is organized along largely secular lines. Experts have suggested the term "communal religion" to describe the collection of miscellaneous rites that mark the Japanese calendar and cannot be classified within any one existing system, but this is just another attempt to construct a framework where one does not exist, and indeed does not seem particularly necessary.

Many Japanese people will cheerfully admit **"In Japan, you are born Shinto, married Christian, and die Buddhist,"** as principal birth ceremonies take place in Shinto shrines, two-thirds of marriages are celebrated in Christian-style chapels, and funeral rites are generally organized by Buddhist monks. In addition, social ties such as those in business or at school have long been based on Confucian principles; the organization of time (the horoscope or almanacs) and space (the construction of houses) is often based on Taoist wisdom; and politics is conducted along democratic, atheist principles. Although there have been tensions, in general this easygoing syncretism can be explained by a generalized refusal to accept exclusive faith systems, allied to a belief in the efficacy of the right gesture made at the right moment and according to the right protocol, regardless of the religion that generated it.

SHINTO

Shinto, "the way of the gods," is often held as Japan's indigenous religion. The preceding paragraph shows why it is wrong to see it as the Japanese religion as religious practice here often combines many beliefs. Nevertheless, over 90 percent of the 81,500 shrines in the country belong to the same Association of Shinto Shrines. All Shinto priests train in one of two Shinto study centers, and practices differ little from one shrine to another: they chiefly honor a local divinity who also has national status, give thanks on behalf of the community, and submit requests for the future.

Shinto and Buddhism

These two religious movements are so inextricably intertwined in Japan that it may seem arbitrary to use a separate vocabulary when speaking of either, but some usages are now well established in Japan and elsewhere. In the context of Shinto, followers worship at a "shrine" (*jinja*, "pavilion of the gods," of which there are more than 80,000); it is a "priest" or "shrine priest" (*kan-nushi*, who serves the divinities—there are nearly 60,000 priests) or a "head priest" *(guji)* who officiates. Buddhist worship takes place at a "temple" (*o-tera*, of which there are around 80,000); the temples are staffed by "monks" (*o-bo-san*— nearly 300,000, including just under 100,000 women) and a "superior" (*hoshi*, "master of the law"). The functions of Shinto priests and Buddhist monks are hereditary, some of them claiming descent through 74 generations.

As meditation does not feature strongly in Shinto practices, there are no monasteries. New converts who wish to become priests (the figures have increased recently) are brought into the administation of a shrine, where they are often confined to humble tasks, like sweeping the courtyard. In contrast, Buddhism has many institutions for monks and nuns.

This homogenized Shintoism is, however, fairly recent and in fact results from a late 19C move to harmonize religion in Japan. Intellectuals and politicians then came to the fore with the restoration of Imperial power in lieu of the shogunate (1867), and sought to establish a nationalistic religion (State Shinto, *Kokka Shinto*). This was seen as an essential component of a strong state capable of rivaling Western empires. Shinto and Buddhism, which had previously coexisted, were forceably separated; cult objects thought to encourage popular superstition or to offend public morals (especially phallic objects) were destroyed, shrines reorganized, and some temples demolished. As a result, Buddhism was suppressed and Shinto became the official religion of Japan. Promoting veneration of the emperor and valuing loyalty, inner strength, and self-denial, it was taught in schools and became a model for its Asiatic neighbors (shrines were built in the new colonies, starting with Taiwan). The suppression of Buddhism finally ended in 1946 when the Allies ordered the Japanese government to adopt a new constitution incorporating religious freedom and the separation of state and religion.

Despite this period of enforced homogenization lasting nearly 60 years, Shintoism remains diverse, encompassing beliefs and customs derived from tradition and different social strata. **"Primitive Shinto"** is an all-purpose term for religious practices from prehistory (i.e. before the 6C) identified through archeology and some Chinese writings. **"Folk Shinto"** derives from traditional peasant-class customs still practised widely at the beginning of the 1970s, and is based on annual observances involving respect for the earth's fertility, the sea, and the fecundity of women. While Folk Shinto can be seen as deriving from Primitive Shinto, it shows that recent schisms in belief systems in Japan are nothing new. The **"Shinto of myths"** deals with the representation of the world as revealed in the divine saga *Kojiki (The Records of Ancient Matters)*, written in the 8C by members of the elite who sought to preserve knowledge threatened by the introduction of Chinese culture. **"Schools Shinto"** is a syncretic merging of teachings by one master, which developed chiefly between the 15C and 19C, while **"Shrine Shinto"** focuses on worship in important public shrines (from the 14C missionaries traveled through Japan praising the magical power of the divinity venerated in their sanctuary). Finally, **Imperial Household Shinto** is performed by the emperor at shrines in the grounds of the Imperial Palace.

Row of Jizo (boddhisatva) statues, Kanman-ga-fuchi Walk, Nikko
© PobladuraFCG/iStock

Shinto is therefore a general term covering a range of different concepts, practices, outlooks, and perspectives linked only in that they were developed in the same part of the world, initially existing before Buddhism and subsequently refined in reaction to it. It is therefore difficult to define Shinto in precise and concise terms. It applies to a series of places, rites, and attitudes that Japanese people hold specific to their culture and which they are delighted to display to visitors as evidence of their profound and distinctive cultural identity.

Though Shinto has left relatively few traces in art history, it is recognizable in the architecture of its shrines and in the joyful dynamism of its festivals. The discovery of this deep-rooted, many-faceted religion is one of the great pleasures of traveling in Japan.

BUDDHISM

Mahayana ("Great Vehicle") Buddhism arrived in Japan in the 6C, along with writing, science, the practice of divination, the structuring of the state around a system of codes, and the existence of an elite class.

Over 14 centuries, it formed part of the iconographic, literary, and philosophical advances made in Japan. When, in the 19C, it was necessary to understand Western concepts, they were explained in terms of the Buddhist vocabulary.

Buddhism developed in many forms, often in different but concurrent schools, which variously emphasized esoteric learning and a complex liturgy (Tendai, Shingon), an ascetic, mountain-dwelling lifestyle (the syncretic Buddhism of Shugendo), salvation for all (Pure Land), or meditation (chiefly Zen schools). To some degree Buddhism's worldview penetra-

Words of the religions

The literal meaning of *Bukkyo*, or Buddhism, is "the teaching *(kyo)* of the Buddha *(butsu)."*
The concept of religion as wisdom passed from master to disciple can also be found in the names of other movements in Japan: "teaching of the man of good will" (*jukyo*, Confucianism), "teaching of the way" (*dokyo*, Taoism), "the teaching of Christ" (*kurisuto-kyo*, Christianity), etc. Shinto constitutes a special case as the term, first used in the 15C, means the "way of the gods" (*to*, another pronunciation of the Taoist *do*; *shin* for "gods," though *kami* is used when singular). This use of *do* is not unique to religion—*on-myo-do* is the "way of yin and yang," *ju-do* is "the way of suppleness," and *ken-do* "the way of the sword."

Young People in Japan Today

Faced with social pressures that expect them to get into the best schools and find a prestigious job, to study hard and find a spouse suitable to their family, young people in Japan often seek ways to quietly resist, to free themselves, indeed simply to escape for a while from a system that is all too rigid. Today, it seems, anything goes for the young, from extreme clothing styles to the virtual bubble that makes it possible to live life in front of a screen or console, or immersed in the worlds of manga and anime.

The School Marathon

The entire school career of Japanese children has one sole objective – to get into the best university possible, with a view to getting a "proper" job afterward. To stack the cards in their favor, parents take care to be selective in choosing schools, right from kindergarten. For those with the financial means, the answer is private schools (whose intake is not determined by place of residence, unlike public schools), but some families go as far as moving house in order to live close to the best state-run schools. In this way pupils can be followed—in other words "coached"—by their families throughout their entire school careers, with compulsory evening classes and extra tuition at *juku* ("cram schools") to ensure they will be ready for the infamous university entrance exams; those who fail sign up for private lessons in order to try their luck again. Leading up to graduation, another marathon begins with attempts to get into the most prestigious company they can. *Shushoku katsudo* ("job hunting") tends to be done en masse at one time in the spring and summer before graduation, meaning that students who fail to find a job (sometimes 50% in a year) often choose to retake an education year, creating a situation where students who have finished their courses find themselves forced to pay for a year of study perhaps costing US$30,000 in order to stay in the system. It is therefore no surprise that the spirit of competition is born extremely early. Under such pressure throughout their school career, some begin to struggle, or search for other ways to bring some color into their daily lives.

Fashion Exerts Its Power

In order to escape school, some young people develop images for themselves through uniforms or carefully created looks, while others take to the streets having adopted outlandish styles. While the super-weird might be in a minority and even looked at askance by the majority of young people, who are often more discreet and conventional, this by no means suggests that there is not a whole gallery of "looks" to be seen at certain locations, such as Harajuku Jingu-Bashi (bridge), where adolescents converge to show off their extravagant get-ups (see p169).

The fashions seem to change by the week, and often feature an elevated or unusual take on a global fashion trend, and usually a mix of high-end and affordable fashion with vintage and DIY elements. There are of course plenty of styles which are unique to Japan, or originated here, the most famous of which is the Lolita look. This is actually a varied collection of styles, including Gothic Lolitas with their lace skirts and "coffin bags," Sweet Lolitas, childish and smiling with puffball sleeves, pastel colors and Mary Jane shoes, Industrial Lolitas in Japanese punk styles, and more besides. The men are not be outdone, from Gothic to grotesque, including Cybers, fans of electronica who favour latex and plastic clothes, and Koadana (or Oji), who go for a "little prince" or young boy look.

As is the way with fashions, they rise and fall, changing rules, style, and district over the seasons. But there's always a place for kimono and *yukata* (a light kimono made of cotton), whether worn in traditional style or with a twist.

The effect of the whole fashion fad scene is something of a throwback to a precise dress code of years gone by, but also illustrates the trends of the moment and the personalities of the figures that the wearers hope to embody, much like the fans of cosplay, who buy or make their own costumes (depicting manga, *anime* or video game characters) in a fashion that started in the USA and has since been embraced in Japan. Cosplay addicts also have their own hang-outs, such as the alleys of Akihabara and

Computer game and comic shop in Akihabara

© Markus Schilder/hemis.fr

the Nakano Broadway district, where the eponymous shopping mall can supply every accessory imaginable, spread over several floors. Dressed as their favorite characters, they attend fairs, clubs, and other events dedicated to manga and anime, such as Comiket or the Wonder Festival.

A Superficial World To Escape Everyday Life?

The brief window of opportunity offered by youth, a special time in Japan, has also given rise to childish fashions that echo this need to escape from a reality that is often hard to bear. From stationery to hair accessories, phone charms to cookware, you can make every area of your life *kawaii* if you so desire.

The immense Animate store at Ikebukuro sells hundreds of items to tempt young *otaku*, including branded products featuring cute animals, collections of "garage kit" figurines representing cartoon heroes, and "cells," drawings on celluloid taken from cult animation films. Even those people who aren't big fans of manga and *anime* are likely to enjoy cute animated fashion accessories, whether a Totoro backpack or Pokémon purse. Disneyland is considered a prime date spot, and Hello Kitty is perhaps more popular with adults than children.

Even with the dominance of Instagam *purikura* remain popular. At these photo booths, you can sit with your friends and choose color schemes, backgrounds, and filters for the self-adhesive stickers they produce. Though the booth does much of the work for you, if you want to be *kawaii* yourself there's still a lot you'll need to do. Some young women adopt a pigeon-toed gait, turning in their feet in the imitation of babies, and speak in a high-pitched voice. Most fashions and make-up trends (such as having round points of blush high on the cheeks, or the "puppy eyes" style of eyeliner) prioritise a youthful, cute look over anything sexy or grown-up.

While these trends come and go, the need from the earliest age to seek refuge in a metaphorical cocoon of cotton wool appears to remain a constant, a super-soft buttress against the demanding world that is slowly taking shape around young people. However, the recent popularity of Sanrio's Gudetama (a sardonic, depressed egg) and Aggretsuko (an animated Netflix comedy about the indignities of being a young professional in Japan) indicates a growing taste for media which takes a wry look at the less sunny side of adult life, albeit through a cartoon lens

Continued overleaf

A Sense of Isolation

Perhaps it's because they're used to being spoon-fed at school and in the many clubs and associations they have access to, but young people in Japan today seem largely uninterested in the world outside. Often this manifests as a preference for spending time online, with their cellphone, or reading manga. The general lack of face-to-face communication has an isolating effect, and some young people are finding it hard to control their emotions.

It can be difficult to be yourself and stand out from the crowd in Japan; as the famous saying goes, "the nail that sticks out gets hammered down" (*deru kugi wa utareru*). This traditionally conformist view combined with modern technology which makes it easy to isolate yourself means that many young people feel like outcasts, unable to express themselves or find like-minded friends offline. Those unlucky enough to look or feel different, or to struggle with Japan's highly competitive education system, can easily find themselves ostracized, and the result can be exclusion from their peer group, name calling and bullying by classmates, or even fights.

At the extreme end, these social pressures and technological escapes can push someone into becoming a *hikikomori* (shut-in). Though the numbers of *hikikomori* remain low, they get a lot of media coverage in Japan and overseas, as they're the most sensational expression of how isolated many young people feel, and how afraid of the unpredictibility and responsibility of the outside world.

Given the sharp focus on academics, and the high levels of stress that causes, it's perhaps no wonder that the preoccupations of young Japanese people generally remain focused more on fun and escapism than any major issues. Few young people read a daily newspaper, and the most popular programs on television are entertainment shows. There are, of course, young Japanese people who do get involved in politics and activism, but they remain a minority. However, the growth of the *hikikomori*, NEET (someone "Not in Education, Employment or Training") and *freeter* (someone who is temporarily unemployed or working low-paid, part-time jobs) demographics may represent a rejection of traditional Japanese values, and the salaryman life path—a political statement in itself.

Geneviève Clastres

Otaku, A World Apart

The *otaku* emerged in the early 1980s from a reaction to a conformist society that criticized its manga and video-game loving young people for their "frivolous" pastimes. The *otaku* deliberately refrain from making too many social links. This Japanese term is a kind of impersonal honorific implying zero personal contact and used among themselves by young people within this community. Disenchanted by their surroundings, they sought refuge on the screens that were ubiquitous in their daily lives (cell phone, games console, computer) and found it easier to forge friendships with virtual avatars than with their classmates.

While there are still many young people cut off from their peers who prefer sitting at screens to direct contact with people, many *otaku* develop truly creative talents and have become very successful, such as Tajiri Satoshi, a gamer who dreamed up the famous Pokémon series that has generated sales of more than US$95 billion around the world. The *otaku* subculture has spread far beyond the borders of Japan and is now present on every continent, with millions of new enthusiasts bewitched in their turn by their virtual heroes.

Étienne Barral

ted every level and aspect of society, from the warrior elite to peasants and merchants, and from court poetry to street shows. It was strictly monitored by the ruling class who, when necessary, moved temples to more easily controlled localities. Buddhism was a network that reached throughout the whole country, playing a defining role in the creation of a national culture.

It's no surprise, then, that today a large part of Japan's national heritage can be found in the treasuries and storehouses of Buddhist temples.

THE NEW RELIGIONS

The freedom of worship imposed by the Americans following World War II sparked the blossoming of a multitude of religious organizations of every kind. Some 180,000 groups are legally recognized, of which over 500 are considered "new religions" (*shin-shukyo*). They claim more than 30 million adherents and some have spread overseas, with branches in Europe and the US, such as **Soka Gakkai** or **Tenri-kyo**, both founded before the war.

The 1970s saw the emergence of new religions, energetically proselytizing sects capable of recruiting thousands in a short time. They generally focused on mystical experiences and an exaggerated apocalyptic vision laid over previously distinct religious traditions. These sects, which in the view of many are simple cults, tend to exacerbate the distrust with which most Japanese people regard "religious institutions."

Jean-Michel Butel

Administration and Economy

Japan was shaped by a long tradition of monarchy and strict hierarchies. After WW II, however, remarkable and lengthy political stability followed with the conservative Liberal Democratic Party majority. The bursting of the financial bubble in the early 1990s ended rapid economic growth, resulting in a restructured economy as well as recast political and social realms. More recently, the reduction in population (since 2005), the world economic crisis following the collapse of Lehman Brothers (2008), the Tohoku earthquake and tsunami and the nuclear accident at Fukushima (2011), and the increase in national debt are all new challenges, to which Prime Minister Abe's government has responded by the putting into place of an ambitious economic policy known as Abenomics, aimed at pulling Japan out of deflation.

POLITICS
THE POLITICAL SYSTEM

Japan's parliamentary system is similar to that of the UK, with a two-chamber National Diet. The **1946 Constitution** is based on the principles of pacifism and the separation of power, giving sovereignty to the people, as opposed to the emperor, who is "the symbol of the State and of the unity of the people," but with no political power. Article 9 of the Constitution forbids any acts of war by the State but authorizes the maintenance of a professional army for self-defense. It is 250,000-strong and very well equipped. Faced with the bellicose attitude of North Korea and the might of China, Abe Shinzo's government have made their first encroachment on Article 9; new legislation, passed in 2015, allows Japan to send troops abroad to aid an ally who is under attack. The emperor has no political power but remains a symbol of the state and the unity of the nation. Legislative authority is vested in the two houses of the **Diet**, which are elected by universal suffrage. There are 480 representatives (House of Repre-

Political parties

Japan has a wide spectrum of political parties ranging from the Communist Party (Kyosanto) to the Nationalist Party (Kokuminto), by way of New Komeito, a center-right party associated with the Buddhist organization Soka Gakkai. Today's power politics mostly involve two large parties: the **Liberal Democratic Party** (LDP, Jiminto), which has been in power almost without interruption since 1955, (under Abe Shinzo, who now has a mandate until 2021) and the **Democratic Party of Japan** (DPJ, Minshuto), formed in 1996 by the merger between the New Party for Progress (NPP) and elements of the Socialist Party (SPJ). The issues at the heart of modern political debate revolve around reinforcing the executive authority of the government, the decline in the administration's power, and greater autonomy for the regions.

sentatives), who are elected for a four-year term, and 250 senators (House of Councillors), half of whose membership is re-elected every three years. Executive power is devolved to the Cabinet chosen by the **prime minister**, who is selected from members of the Diet. The prime minister has authority to dissolve assemblies but it is difficult to govern without political control over both Houses.

Judicial authority is independent of both Houses and controlled by a Supreme Court, whose role is to protect the Constitution and exercise judicial review over tribunals and Courts of Appeal. Japanese people tend to make relatively little recourse to the law, and the judicial system is underdeveloped. The death penalty is still in force.

A CHANGING ADMINISTRATION

The administration consists of agencies and ministries, of which METI (the Ministry of Economy, Trade, and Industry), as leader in economic development, plays a central role in the Japanese state. The ineffectual but powerful central administration largely relies on local authorities to implement its policies and is heavily dependent on the private sector.

The substantial police force is supervised by the NPA, the National Police Agency. A network of community police units operating from local substations *(koban)* ensures excellent neighborhood security.

ECONOMY

Japan is the third-largest economic power in the world by GDP, which rose to USD 5807 billion in 2019, according to IMF figures (the USA was in first place and the UK in fifth) and an unemployment rate around 2.5%. However, the country has recently suffered two major crises, firstly with the 1973 oil crisis and then the collapse of the "speculative bubble" in the early 1990s.

In order to reboot the economy and adapt to global developments (especially given its heavy reliance on exports), in the 2010s the Japanese state instigated a policy of extremely low interest rates and major construction projects financed by the national debt, which is mostly held by the Japanese themselves, thus protecting the country from any incursion by speculators. In 2016, the national debt amounted to 246.6% of GDP in 2016 according to the OECD, making it the highest in the world.

Businesses have had to work on some radical changes, including questioning the concept of a "jobs for life," key industrial structural reform and delocalization outside Japan, as well as a shift of focus toward high-tech products. Intended to pull the country up out of deflation, this set of policies (collectively known as Abenomics) is based upon three key pillars, or "three arrows". Firstly, intervention by the Bank of Japan to monetize sovereign debt, which has translated into a significant devaluation of the yen. Secondly, state budgetary intervention, particularly in the reconstruction and revitalization of Tohoku after the earthquake of 2011. And thirdly, economic reform and expansion (encouraging women to join the workforce, developing economic partnerships with other countries, stimulating local investment, etc.).

Specifically looking at improving workplace gender parity, Abenomics has been a qualified success, with 48.2% of women aged 15+ in the labor market in 2012, and 52.5% in 2018 (ILO statistics). However, despite comparable educational outcomes to men, women tend to be employed in part-time or low-wage work, and the gender pay gap remains significant at 25.7%, the third-worst in the OECD.

ENERGY DEPENDENCE

Japan's fishing industry is one of the world's largest, its plentiful rivers are used to irrigate the rice fields and to produce hydroelectricity, and its large and varied forests supply timber for construction. However, the country is heavily dependent on **imports of essential raw materials** and the energy needed for its development. The proportion of electric energy generated by nuclear power was about 30% in 2010 (in the USA around 20% and in the UK around 17%), but this percentage has fallen drastically since the Fukushima nuclear disaster. In response to a population ill-disposed toward atomic power, Japan revised its energy policy: a possible shut down of its nuclear program by 2030, ramping up renewable energy sources, and promoting energy-saving measures at every level of society. However, it seems unlikely that the country will meet its climate targets without the use of nuclear power, so at present, the government is aiming for around 20% of Japan's electricity to be generated by nuclear power by 2030.

RICE AND FISH

The scarcity of arable land suitable for large-scale crop growing has been compensated by the mastery of irrigation techniques developed over the centuries. Rice is the basis of the Japanese diet and **riziculture** still the major crop in half the cultivated land of the alluvial plains; the rest is devoted to high-value crops like flowers, fruits, or vegetables. The size of agricultural plots is very small, 3.2 acres (1.3h) on average. About 4% of the working population in the primary sector (1.2% of GDP) only make a living thanks to significant subsidies from the state.

Fish and seafood form a vital element of the Japanese diet. Japan has developed a strong fishing industry, both coastal and offshore, thanks to the country's fleet of processing vessels. Aquaculture is a growth sector.

However, **Japan is only 38 percent self-sufficient in its dietary requirements**, representing a real threat in the event of international crisis.

A GLOBAL ECONOMY

Industry (28 percent of GDP) is Japan's strong point and it leads the world in many sectors: shipbuilding, automotive, robotics, electronics, semiconductors, bio-industries, and new materials. Japan is **the world's fourth largest exporter**, almost exclusively in the areas of high value-added products or cultural products such as manga, while importing cheaper products in return. The Japanese economy also benefits from the rapid growth in other Asian economies, especially that of China, which has become a major economic partner.

Thanks to a large balance of payments surpluses, Japan has made significant overseas investments, so becoming a **major financial power**. Today, the country seeks to exploit its **capacity for innovation**. The government has focused on robotics, nanotechnologies, information and environmental technology, and Japan's expenditure on research represents 3.1% of GDP (US around 2.7%, UK around 1.7%), with 70% coming from the private sector. Japan remains no less vulnerable because of this and will have to pursue its attempts to adapt to fluctuations in the world economy, in the face of its energy dependency, shrinking population, and sovereign debt.

Bernard Delmas, Philippe Pataud Célérier

History

With its position on the western edge of the Pacific Ocean, beyond mainland Asia, Japan's history is marked by insularity. In spite of centuries of tumult and strong regional contrasts, the archipelago has largely remained united. Apart from a few years at the end of WW II, it has never been colonized or occupied. This innovative and pragmatic civilization of extremes has been influenced by other countries, however, and now as a modern, industrialized country Japan is resolutely open to the rest of the world.

THE MAJOR ERAS

PREHISTORY

The earliest signs of civilization in Japan date from the **Jomon** era, a period that lasted from around 14,000 to 300 BC. Its people were hunter-gatherers, fishers, and weavers. The development of bartering led to settlement in villages and pottery making. Even before it was applied to the whole period, the term *jomon*, meaning "cord pattern," was used to describe the decoration of the first pots discovered Jars, statuettes, figurines, generally female and often with a swelling belly, are evidence of the role of pottery in ritual practices and daily life. The exuberance of the forms and motifs in those prehistoric times, which vary depending on period and region, reveal remarkable artistry.

During the **Yayoi** era (300 BC–AD 300), named after a site near Tokyo, the first wheel-turned pottery was found. This period is also notable for the development of irrigated wet-rice cultivation and cereal culture, while bronze and iron work also became widespread.

THE KOFUN ERA (3–7C)

The term *kofun* describes the burial mounds raised for members of the ruling class, in which furniture, weapons, and jewelry were buried with the deceased. Outside the tomb, *haniwa* (cylindrical pottery and hollow clay statues) guarded the funerary monuments. The era of these great tumuli marks the beginning of political centralization with the emergence of a state in the Yamato region and the emergence of the clan system *(uji)*. This powerful Yamato polity, south of Nara, would come to dominate nearly all the country—with the exception of the north of the archipelago, home of the Ainu, and the far southern Ryukyu Islands—creating an imperial dynasty whose authority could not be questioned as it was claimed to be of divine origin (☞*see box left*).

THE ASUKA ERA (592–710)

The dynasty established at Asuka during the Yamato period introduced reforms to Japan, which was transformed by the arrival of Korean and Chinese immigrants to the country, the introduction of new techniques such as the adoption of Chinese written characters, and the domestication of horses. When Buddhism was introduced in the 6C, Japan assimilated Sino-Indian culture. The Empress Suiko (593–628) laid the foundations of an imperial administration based on the Chinese model. Her nephew and heir, the Prince Regent

Mythical origins

The earliest Japanese literary work still in existence, the *Kojiki* (712), gives an account of the history of Japan and its mythological origins. One of the primary Shinto sources, it recounts the creation of Heaven and Earth. According to Shinto myth, the imperial dynasty that founded the Japanese nation was descended from the radiant sun goddess **Amaterasu**, daughter of Izanagi, who was held to be the direct ancestor of **Jinmu**, first emperor of Japan. Subsequent emperors claimed to be descended from Jinmu, attributing divine origins to the Imperial Dynasty. The myth consecrated the imperial line and gave it political legitimacy.

© DEA/G DAGLI ORTI/age fotostock

12C illustration from the Tales of Genji scroll (Genji monogatari emaki)

Shotoku Taishi (574–622), proclaimed Buddhism to be the state religion, built temples dedicated to the Enlightened One, and promulgated a "17 Article Constitution." During the reign of Emperor Kotoku (645–54), power was centralized in a series of administrative measures known as the **Taika reforms**, based on the example of China's Tang dynasty. Peasants and their lands were placed under the authority of the Imperial Court. In 663, under the guise of an alliance with the Korean kingdom of Paekche, soldiers of the Yamato empire invaded the Korean kingdoms of Koguryo and Silla, but were wiped out.

THE NARA ERA (710–94)

In 710, Empress Genmei established a permanent capital at Nara (**Heijo-kyo**), abandoning the custom of changing the location of the Imperial residence after the death of each emperor. Administrative and penal codes were enacted, which were to remain in place for over a thousand years. Techniques learned from Korean craftsmen brought the arts of ceramics, bronze, silk, and architecture to a high level and they were developed into a specifically Japanese art. Imposing Buddhist monasteries such as Horyu-ji, Kofuku-ji, and Todai-ji were also built.

THE HEIAN ERA (794–1185)

Founded in 794, **Heian-kyo** ("capital of peace and tranquility"), present-day **Kyoto**, became the seat of the Imperial Court in preference to Nara. Emperor Kanmu (737–806) ordered this transfer to escape the influence of the Buddhist schools installed at Nara, which, instead of devoting themselves to spiritual matters, too often interfered with political issues. The new capital would remain the heart of Japan for more than a thousand years.

Japan now developed its own writing systems (*hiragana* and *katakana*), and this was a golden age for literature. The work of women predominated, particularly in literature. With *The Tale of Genji (Genji monogatari)*, Murasaki Shikibu (973–1016; see p348) wrote the world's first known novel. During the same period, the poet Sei Shonagon wrote *The Pillow Book (Makura no soshi)*, intimate observations on the lives of her contemporaries.

In this "Florence of the Far East," the emperor appointed *kanpaku* (senior advisors) responsible for government business, who soon managed to arrogate imperial power to themselves and effectively ruled the country. Chief among the holders of this almost hereditary office were the **Fujiwara** clan, which led to many feuds among the aristocracy while the great landowning monasteries armed themselves to defend both their lands and status.

THE KAMAKURA ERA (1185–1333)

A troubled period followed. Far from the influence of the court, principalities emerged under the protection of local chieftains. For centuries local warlords struggled for power, weakening central rule. During this period Japan became the battleground for a succession of military conflicts. The powerful chief **Minamoto no Yoritomo** defeated the warrior **Taira clan**, consolidating the supremacy of the Minamoto family. The emperor in Kyoto awarded Yoritomo the title of **shogun** (military governor), and he settled at Kamakura in modern-day Kanagawa prefecture. During these years new Buddhist trends emerged, including the Zen school of meditation.

The **powerful military caste** owes its fame to *bushido* (the way of the samurai), a chivalrous code of honor and loyalty marked by the practical application of Zen and neo-Confucian ideals such as fidelity to duty and respect for the clan. The warrior class became dominant to the detriment of the Imperial Court, which lost its influence in state affairs.

At the end of the 13C the Mongols stepped up their conquest of Asia and Kublai Khan, grandson of Genghis Khan, called on Japan to pay tribute to China, threatening reprisals if they failed to do so. His ultimatum was rejected, so he launched an expeditionary force in 1274. This attempt failed, so a second invasion was launched in 1281. A fleet of warships carrying over 100,000 men tried to land in Japan. Repulsed from the Kyushu coastline, the Mongol fleet was caught in a typhoon and destroyed. The Japanese call this wind that saved them *kamikaze*, literally "divine wind."

THE MUROMACHI ERA (1336–1573)

The history of this unstable period is complex and characterized by internal struggles. It began in 1336 with the short-lived restoration of Imperial power initiated by Emperor Go-Daigo, who tried to undermine the Kamakura regime with the help of powerful warlord Ashikaga Takauji (1305–58), a direct descendant of the Minamoto family. Takauji subsequently turned against Go-Daigo in favor of another emperor (Komyo), who awarded him the title of shogun in 1338. Go-Daigo fled to Yoshino, near Nara, while Komyo set up his court in the Muromachi district of Kyoto. There were therefore **two Imperial Courts**: Go-Daigo's, known as the Southern Court, in Yoshino; and that of Komyo, known as the Northern Court, in Kyoto. The rivalry lasted nearly 60 years. While the first Portuguese and Spanish traders imported gunpowder, the missionaries following in their wake preached the Gospel. In 1549, the Jesuit Francis Xavier introduced **Christianity** to Japan.

THE AZUCHI–MOMOYAMA ERA (1573–1603)

In this transitional period, **Toyotomi Hideyoshi** (1536–98) completed the unification of the country initiated by Oda Nobunaga (1534–82) and sought to consolidate his power by conquering the Korean peninsula and thereafter China. In 1592 and 1597, he sent expeditionary forces to Korea. The Chinese army repulsed the attackers and the Koreans rose against the occupation troops, refusing to accept Japanese sovereignty. Hostilities finally ceased with the death of Hideyoshi, which precipitated a succession crisis that ended with the accession of **Tokugawa Ieyasu** (1542–1616). His ascendency marked the close of Japan's long Sengoku (Warring States) period, which started in 1467 and ended with the establishment of the Tokugawa shogunate.

THE EDO ERA (1603–1867)

Although the emperor nominally ruled from Kyoto, the **Tokugawa Shogunate** established its administrative capital in **Edo** (present-day Tokyo), seat of the military government. Tokugawa Ieyasu consolidated his power by eliminating his rivals, the supporters of the Toyotomi clan. The Tokugawas ruled without interruption for more than 250 years, controlling all aspects of political and social life. In 1613, Christianity was banned, Japanese converts persecuted, and missionaries expelled. Fearing European expansionism, the authorities **closed the country to foreigners**, with the exception of some Korean diplomats, a few Chinese merchants, and small numbers of Dutch traders of the East India Company, who were allowed to operate in the Nagasaki harbor area alone. No Japanese person was permitted to travel outside the empire. This policy of isolationism was known as *sakoku*; the country turned in upon itself, but trade was not totally suppressed and this was an era of peace and security, synonymous with **urban expansion** and **tremendous cultural development**. Merchants and craftsmen flourished, while many samurai were now out of work, facing a period of peace in which warriors were not so in demand, and so becoming *ronin* (masterless samurai). Japan underwent a demographic explosion.

Then Western expansionism threw everything into turmoil. In 1853, a fleet of "black ships" commanded by American Commodore Matthew Perry anchored in the bay of Edo and demanded the relaxation of trade restrictions. Fearing a naval bombardment, Japan was obliged to abandon isolationism; the shogunate was forced to sign a treaty of friendship with the Americans, followed by a commercial treaty. Russia, Britain, France, and The Netherlands rushed into the breach and similar agreements, known in Japan as **"unequal treaties,"** were signed, granting foreign traders exorbitant customs privileges (from 1895 they were revised after lengthy representation from Japanese diplomats). This coup led to a wave of national protest that was to prove fatal for the Tokugawa regime.

THE MEIJI ERA (1868–1912)

Forced to abandon its isolation under pressure from Western powers, Japan now moved toward modernization with startling speed. Industrial, political, social, and cultural upheavals swept away the shoguns' power. The **restoration of imperial power** signaled the end of the regime of clans and fiefs. The feudal system was abolished. A **Constitution** was adopted in 1889 and, while it acknowledged the emperor's supreme power and divine right, it also established a parliamentary system with elected representatives. Shinto became the state religion and Buddhism was disestablished. Japan's former ruling elite abandoned their status as warlords to go into battle on the economic front, and the yen became the national currency. In under 30 years Japan became a great power and joined the ranks of capitalist countries with the watchwords "rich country, strong military."

This era aso saw the start of Japanese expansionism, modelled on the empires of foreign powers like the UK. They began by incorporating Ezo, the land of the Ainu people, into Japan in 1869, renaming it Hokkaido. In 1879, the Ryukyu Kingdom was annexed and renamed Okinawa, its king Sho Tai deposed and made to relocate to Tokyo. In both cases, Japan then forced the local population to assimilate, dispossessing indigenous populations of their land, customs, languages and religions and decalaring that they were now *wajin* (people of Japan). Following these early successes Japan looked further afield, annexing Formosa (now Taiwan) 1895 and Korea in 1910.

THE TAISHO ERA (1912–26)

The initial euphoria following the democratization of politics and society gradually faded but the island empire felt it was on the right track. For many Japanese, the Taisho period also brought changes in their way of life with the development of a popular and urban culture, the opening of leisure parks, and the growth of cinema, radio, and liberal publishing houses. All this continued until the terrible earthquake of 1923, which destroyed much of Tokyo.

THE SHOWA ERA (1926–89)

In 1926, Hirohito succeeded the Imperial throne. Japan, now recognized as a great power by the West, pursued its policy of colonial expansion to the extent of occupying Manchuria (1931) in northeastern

China, hungry for its mineral and agricultural wealth. During the 1930s militarists seized control of the government with the aim of making Japan master of Asia. Criticized on the international stage, Japan left the League of Nations in 1933 and a few years later formed an alliance with the fascist regimes of the German–Italian Axis, confident the Soviet Union would remain neutral. **Militarism** and **ultranationalism** led to repression, while propaganda was used to justify expansionism. In 1937, Japan invaded China, launching the second Sino-Japanese War, which merged into the **Pacific War** when the bombing of Pearl Harbor on December 7, 1941 prompted the United States to declare war on Japan. Although Japan dominated Asia and the Pacific, their defeat by American naval forces at the Battle of Midway in June 1942 changed the course of the war.

Following massive incendiary bombing of Tokyo, and alongside the USSR's successful invasion of Manchuria and the Japanese archipelago's nothernmost territories, the President of the United States, Harry Truman, decided to unleash atomic power against Japan. The first atomic bomb was dropped over Hiroshima on August 6, 1945, killing 140,000 people. Three days later, a second bomb was dropped on Nagasaki, killing 70,000 civilians. These tragedies brought Japan to its knees.

Jean-Luc Toula-Breysse

POSTWAR JAPAN

Few would have guessed that a country with a lower per capita rate of income than Malaya at the end of World War II would have the highest standard of living in the world within 45 years. Yet Japan's postwar trajectory was meteoric, transforming it from a nation in defeat to one of the most successful economic forces on earth. Japan regained its poise and dug deep to find the resources and national strength to catapult itself to the status of a world economic power. In 1951, Japan's GNP was US$14.2 billion—half of West Germany, three times less than Britain and only 4.2% of the USA. By 1970, Japan had overtaken every economy in Europe to represent over 20% of the US's GNP. In 1975, it was double that of the UK, and in 1980, reached US$1040 billion—around 40% of that of the US. Yet Japan's postwar era is testament to more than just an ability to conjure up impressive digits: it demonstrates a resolute determination to rebuild—in social and economic terms. Few countries have experienced such extraordinary and rapid changes in daily life, material culture, and pecuniary fortunes as it sought to redefine its role in the world.

The Aftermath of War

After yielding to **American occupation** and a program of demilitarization and democratization, Japan conceded many US demands. This brought significant legal changes to the Japanese family system, providing a woman with legal rights equal to those of her husband in terms of property and divorce. Daughters gained the right to inherit the same property as sons. Males at the age of 18 and females at the age of 16 were also now able to marry without parental consent. Suffrage proved a popular move, and won widespread support. Japan, in turn, negotiated the retention of the Imperial Family. Japan's postwar occupation by the US-led Allied Powers began in August 1945 and ended in April 1952, with American general **Douglas MacArthur** its first Supreme Commander. After dismantling the remains of Japan's war machine, the US general held trials. Over 500 military officers committed suicide straight after Japan surrendered, and hundreds more were executed after being found guilty of war crimes. In 1947, a new constitution took effect with MacArthur intent on decentralization and widespread land reform. During the occupation, Japan's media was subject to rigid censorship. Despite this, the transition period was relatively smooth, with good levels of Japanese cooperation with the Allied Powers. In 1952, the **1951 San Francisco Peace Treaty** took effect and occupation ended. Japan was once again an independent state, regaining its sovereignty, having pledged concord with 48 nations.

TIME LINE

14,000–300 BC – Jomon era. Sedentarism.
660 BC Mythical founding of Japan by Emperor Jinmu, descended from goddess Amaterasu.
300 BC–AD 300 Yayoi era.
3–7C Kofun era, burial mounds.
592–710 Asuka era. Introduction of Buddhism. 1st Constitution.
710–94 Nara era. Introduction of legal codes.
794–1185 Heian era. Foundation of the Rinzai Zen school by Eisai (12C).
1185–1333 Kamakura era.
1336–1573 Muromachi era. Civil wars and peasant revolts. Catholicism preached by the Jesuit Francis Xavier (1549).
1573–1603 Momoyama era. Reunification of the country.
1603–1867 Edo or Tokugawa era. Japan's ancien régime is at its peak; Christianity banned. The country turns in on itself.
1853–67 Bakumatsu period. The end of the shogunate. Commodore Perry's American fleet forces the country to open to the West (1853).
1868 Start of the Meiji era. Restoration of Imperial rule.
1889 Promulgation of the Constitution.
1894–5 First Sino-Japanese war.
1904–5 Russo–Japanese war. Japanese victory in Manchuria.
1910 Japan annexes Korea.
1912–26 Taisho era. Tentative democratic advances.
1914 Japan declares war on Germany.
1919 Treaty of Versailles: Japan seizes German territories in the Pacific and China. It joins the League of Nations.
1923 Great Kanto Earthquake (see p133).
1931 Occupation of Manchuria.

1945 US drops atomic bombs on Hiroshima (August 6) and Nagasaki (August 9). Japan capitulates unconditionally on August 15, surrenders on September 2.
1947 New Constitution.
1952 End of Allied occupation of Japan.
1956 Japan joins the United Nations.
1964 First Asian Olympic Games held in Tokyo.
1972 US restores control of the Okinawa archipelago to Japan.
1989 Death of Emperor Hirohito. Prince Akihito becomes Emperor of Japan.
1995 Kobe earthquake (Jan 17). Sarin gas attack in Tokyo (March 20).
1991 The collapse of Japan's asset price bubble causes an economic downturn. The following 10 years are known as the Lost Decade (with some including the following several years into the Lost Score, ending around 2010).
2004 Japanese troops are sent to aid US forces in Iraq.
2005 Aichi International Exhibition.
2006 Princess Kiko gives birth to Prince Hisahito, third in line to the throne. Abe Shinzo is elected prime minister.
2009 For the first time, the DPJ (Democratic Party) wins a victory over the LDP (Liberal Democratic Party). Hatoyama Yukio becomes prime minister.
2010 Hatoyama is the fourth prime minister to resign in four years. The DPJ's Kan Naoto succeeds him.
2011 March 11, a magnitude 9 earthquake resulting tsunami hit Tohoku, causing 18,000 deaths and widespread destruction and damage to Fukushima Daiichi nuclear power plant. Over 125,000 people have to leave the area.

	Unpopular due to his handling of the crisis, Kan resigns and is succeeded by Noda Yoshihiko as prime minister.
2012	The LPD wins the elections and Abe Shinzo becomes prime minister for the second time, launching a strategy to boost the economy, encourage a spirit of nationalism, and reaffirm political and military confidence, collectively known as "Abenomics."
2013	Tokyo wins the bid to host the 2020 Olympic Games. Crisis with China over the Senkaku islands in the East China Sea.
2014	For the first time since 2011, despite popular opposition, a nuclear power plant is restarted. In its third quarter, the Japanese economy falls into recession. Abe Shinzo wins a third term with a new two-thirds majority in December.
2015	For the first time the census shows a drop in population (-0.8%), highlighting the *shoushi-koureika* (declining birth rate and ageing population) problem.
2016	At the end of 2016, Japan recorded its first trade surplus since 2011, but growth remains sluggish. The cost of the catastrophe at Fukushisma is revised upwards to more than US$187 billion . These outgoings are joined by the estimated US$25 billion for the 2020 Olympics (six times the budget originally proposed).
2017	Special legislation is passed to allow Emperor Akihito (aged 83) to abdicate in favour of Crown Prince Naruhito.
2019	Emperor Akihito abdicates and Naruhito ascends to the Chrysanthemum Throne, ushering in the Reiwa era.

Cultural and Societal Shifts

During the American occupation, Japan's various segments of society had sought ways to bolster their own cultural identity against the constantly shifting political and economic contexts of the transition. Postwar demographic shifts brought great change to the composition of Japanese communities amid the immense material influences of Westernization. Faced with the diluting effect of large-scale migration and social transformation, Japan fought hard to retain its own identity in the face of tremendous cultural change, shunning many outside influences.

Political Reformation

Rumbles of political wrangling reached boiling point in 1960, prompting a major sea-change in the Japanese political system. The merging of the socialist parties was the catalyst for the joining together of the conservative prewar Liberal and Democratic parties to secure a majority of legislative seats and create the one-and-a-half-party system that dominated Japanese politics for over 30 years. It prompted widespread unrest and resistance in 1960 with the Liberal Democratic Party (LDP) making numerous high-profile bids to undo occupation-era reforms. Protests against the renewal of the US–Japan Security Treaty (Anpo) followed, along with a labor strike at the Miike coal mines in Kyushu. As a result, the LDP sacked its party leader and promoted an economic "income-doubling" plan—a highly successful initiative with the Japanese populace.

Facing the World

Winning the bid to host the **Olympics** in 1964 prompted a much-needed construction boom across the country. Redevelopment significantly reshaped not only the landscape but also, in many ways, the psyche and outlook of its people, spawning the famous **bullet train** (shinkansen), emblematic of Japan's high-tech capabilities and push for modernization. Japan's sleek, high-speed rail system grabbed headlines across the world in the run-up to the Games. The spectacle of the Olympiad presented the Japanese government with a vehicle to showcase its revitalized postwar image as a peaceful, democratic, and unified nation. Cultural virtues figured prominently in Japan's Olympic publicity package for the Olympics, an ostensibly safe theme that nevertheless was shaped by and contributed to political forces of the time.

The Games showed Japan's remarkable postwar economic development to the world, in a glittering event that consigned Tokyo's withdrawal as host of the 1940 Games due to the outbreak of war to history. The 1964 Tokyo Games cost over US$3 billion, with 93 participating nations (5151 athletes). To underline Japan's emergence as a major political and economic force worldwide, the final torchbearer was **Sakai Yoshinori**, who was born in Hiroshima the day the city was destroyed by an atomic bomb. The Games passed without controversy, heralding Japan's new era of technology-led prosperity. Cutting-edge architecture won considerable praise from Olympic organizers, in particular the **Budokan**, modeled on age-old Japanese temple traditions, and a magnificent futuristic swimming venue that was hailed "the cathedral of sports" by IOC chiefs. Japan's standing in the world community was further enhanced when Sapporo hosted the 1972 Winter Olympic Games.

Economic Climb

Japan's postwar economy is characterized by a 15-year period of high growth, beginning in the mid-1950s, that allowed it to catch up with the developed economies of the USA and Europe. In many ways Japan was haunted by its bilateral agreement as it allowed detractors to suggest that the country's postwar economic climb owed much to the efforts of its former enemy. Certainly, the US did not require Japan to pay war reparations. In fact, by 1951, the US had poured over US$2 billion into the Japanese economy. Japan's renouncement of militarism meant that it need only spend a minimal amount on defense (around 1% of its GNP), allowing the government to invest more public funds into programs for developing the nation's industries. However, other social scientists point to the tremendous stress this "US help" placed on the Japanese economy. Postwar **inflation** resulted in a total augmentation of 15,000% from 1945 through 1949, with the US imposing three harsh measures: a balanced budget, the suspension of all state loans to industry, and the abolition of all state subsidies. The Yen was set to a favorable rate of 360 for 1 US$ to stimulate export. What is certain, politics aside, is that Japan was in a severely weakened and exhausted state in the aftermath of World War II and that to revive itself as a nation, and to revamp its political and social infrastructure, it required assistance. Most of its cities had been devastated by attack, with 60% of Tokyo razed to the ground by Allied firebombing raids. Air attacks had destroyed 30% of Japan's industrial capacity.

Bolstered by high rates of personal savings, healthy private-sector facilities' investment, a committed labor force with a strong work ethic, plentiful supplies of cheap oil, innovative technology, and effective government intervention in private-sector industries, Japan reaped the rewards of its swift-growing postwar thrust and cut. It fine-tuned its competitive strength and achieved economic growth based on exports, private-sector facilities' investment, and the successful stimulation of strong domestic demand that powered an industrial explosion in cities nationwide. By 1965 manufacturing had quadrupled in terms of output compared with prewar figures. Dominating the industrial sector were iron and steel, ship building, machine tools, motor vehicles, and electronics. However, this strong and rapid economic growth did take its toll on the environment.

Much like China today, Japan suffered a significant environmental backlash as a result of its rush to industrialization, sparking strong opposition and protest across the world. As a nation which considers itself instinctively in tune with its natural landscape—Japan has a strongly held traditional ethos that balance is achieved in harmony with the cycles of nature—the strength of this ecological criticism came as a shock. Yet, the Japanese government eventually conceded its mushrooming cities had grown at the expense of natural habitats and clean air.

International Relations

Despite its wealth and position in the world economy, Japan had little influence in global politics for much of the postwar period. A dispute over the Soviet occupation of what Japan calls its Northern Territories (the two most southerly islands in the Kurils, plus Shikotan and the Habomai Islands northeast of Hokkaido, all seized by the USSR at the end of World War II) saw Japanese residents deported to Japan, leaving 30,000 Russians on the isles. Although this dispute remains unresolved, in 1956 the **Japan–Soviet Joint Declaration** restored diplomatic ties between the nations; a formal peace deal remained out of reach due to the dispute. In 1972, Prime Minister **Tanaka Kakuei** visited the Republic of China, where he expressed a keen consciousness of Japan's responsibility in the war, and its intent to realize normal relations between the two countries. The 1980s saw Japan experience its history textbook controversy, in which elements of a "regrettable" past were erased from official memory. Notably, at the time of the death of **Hirohito** (the emperor whose reign spanned wartime and postwar Japan) in 1989, neither the State nor the emperor had uttered a clear public apology to other Asian countries for colonial rule and wartime aggression. Events during the mid- and late-1990s, such as difficult relations between Beijing and Taipei, and the 1998 North Korea missile launch, forced Japan to begin taking security issues more seriously. Japan sought to strengthen its military might, participating (albeit in a carefully limited manner) in the Gulf War in 1991—just as the country was about to come down from the dizzying heights of an unprecedented economic boom-time.

Oil Shock

Just as Japan settled into an easy economic rhythm in the 1970s, President Richard Nixon's decision to unilaterally end fixed currency exchange rates brought with it a reminder of the country's economic vulnerability and dependency on the US market. In 1971, the American administration imposed a 10% surcharge on Japanese imports and pressurized the Japanese government to revalue the yen upward—much to Japan's chagrin. With over 30% of its exports going to the US, Japan faced an acute economic crisis. The surcharge prompted rapid contingency planning that saw major state projects, such as the new Tokyo airport at Sanrizuka, pushed to the fore. As the country's main source of energy, oil import supply was a priority for the Japanese government. However, oil increased in price from US$2 a barrel to US$11 in 1973, then to US$24 a barrel in 1974, and to US$35 a barrel in late 1979—a nightmare scenario for the energy-strapped nation. This situation prompted strenuous energy-saving efforts and technological innovations during crises commonly remembered as "oil shock" by the Japanese people. As a result, Japan now only requires 12,098gal/55kl of crude oil—nearly half the 23,317gal/106kl it once did—to generate 100 million yen in GDP.

Technological and Agriculture

Pressures regarding environmental pollution also sparked a shift toward high-tech and service-sector business as Japan moved its heavy and chemical industries offshore.

In 1982, under the leadership of **Prime Minister Nakasone Yasuhiro**, the privatization of certain state-run enterprises was undertaken, with some success. Combined with the rapid rate of industrialization in the shift to high-tech and service-sector businesses, this led to only 18% of Japan's labor force being employed in the agricultural sector compared with 50% in the 1930s

The shift away from agriculture as the heart of the economy began around 1961, the year in which the **Agricultural**

Basic Law came into force with the aim of structurally reforming the agricultural sector. The changes, however, ended up being for the worse, not the better, pushing far more people out of the agricultural sector than was useful. Between 1960 and 2005 agricultural production's share of GDP fell from 9% to just 1%, the agricultural working population from 11.96 million to 2.52 million, the proportion of the total working population employed in agriculture from 26.6% to 4%, and the number of farming households from 6.06 million to 2.85 million. These demographic issues in farming have continued to worsen as the Japanese population has aged; the percentage of elderly workers in the farming community increased to over 50 percent by the early twenty-first century, and there's little incentive for younger people to move into jobs in the agricultural sector.

Today, Japan's food self-sufficiency—once a proud boast of the nation—has dropped below 40%. In 2008, the head of Japan's National Agriculture and Food Research Organization launched a slew of new agricultural concepts and technologies aimed at turning round Japan's agricultural fortunes in conjunction with its consumption-based society. Despite this, however, whole sectors of Japanese agriculture remain viable largely because of government protectionism.

To some extent, programs to revitalize country life in the late-1980s and 1990s rejuvenated Japan's love affair with its rural regions, but there is still a strong desire within many Japanese people to be viewed as thoroughly urban and modern, not rural and old-fashioned.

Banking Woes

During the late-1980s, East Asia accounted for nearly half of the world's expansion, so when the full force of Japan's banking crisis dealt its body-blow, the nation was sent reeling into a deep, painful, and prolonged recession. Japan's accelerated program of deregulation and deepening of capital markets without an appropriate adjustment in the regulatory framework were blamed, together with its weak corporate governance and regulatory forbearance. Rapid credit expansion during the 1980s had placed Japan in a fragile position: the bubble had well and truly burst.

The 1995 Kobe earthquake and sarin gas attack by religious cult Aum Shinrikyo in Tokyo's subway system compounded the country's woes. Both events presented challenges to the Japanese government, and all this against a backdrop of a fast-growing population that had seen over 50 million added to the Japanese roll-call since the end of World War II.

Population Growth

Japan's population density rapidly became a drain on residential space in major cities, with over 330 people per sq km—a figure that quintuples in the context of habitable land, resulting in overcrowding in Japanese cities. As the urban sprawl continued to grow, Japan's rural areas suffered depopulation as workers abandoned jobs in farming, fishing, and forestry for the bright lights and salaries of the cities.

Japan also began to emerge as an exporter of culture during the 1980s, as a cult audience around the world began to develop for manga (comic books), *kaiju* (monster) movies, *anime* (cartoons), and other products of modern Japanese culture. In the early 1950s, US soldiers returning from the occupation had become the first exporters of Japanese storybooks, drawings, and artifacts. Subsequently, US troops based in Japan further played their part in sending a steady stream of cartoons and comics back to friends and family at home. In Japan itself, contemporary forms of popular culture became a form of escape from the problems of an industrial world during the 1990s. Around this, the annual **Japan Fantasy Novel Award** was launched in acknowledgment of the rising popularity of this genre.

Japan's overpopulation crisis had been mooted in the 1930s, prompting a series of **eugenics laws** which culminated in the 1948 legalization of abortion based on economic necessity, among other potential reasons—though doctors were able to decide this themselves, without consulting the parents. This law was revised in 1993 to become the Maternal Protection Law, requiring the consent of the pregnant person. Some victims of unwanted abortions in previous years were offered compensation.

As a result of the 1948 law, the fertility rate temporarily dropped by around a half. But in recent years, the opposite problem to overpopulation has emerged: a decreasing population, due to a declining birth rate. Despite generous tax breaks for married couples and a series of pro-natal laws being passed, Japan's population looks set to keep declining; it peaked at 128 million in 2008, and the National Institute for Population and Social Security Research estimeates it will fall below 100 million around 2050. Life expectancy in Japan continues to rise. At the end of World War II it was 50 for men and 54 for women; in 2018, it was 81 and 87. Infant mortality has dropped to one of the lowest in the world, while maternal mortality is now virtually zero. Japan's postwar demographics also bear testament to the mass migration from the countryside to the cities with over half of the nation's residents living in Tokyo, the Nagoya region, and the Osaka–Kobe area by the mid-1980s.

Following the destruction of large parts of these cities in World War II, notably the fire-bombing of Tokyo, vast housing projects known as *danchi* were built around this trio of key metropolitan areas. Soon becoming middle-class enclaves, the *danchi* helped to ease urban overcrowding. These neat, modern residential zones epitomized the Japanese postwar dream of family prosperity and mirrored the surge in domestic consumer demand for high-tech goods and labor-saving devices.

Consumerism Takes Hold

By the mid-1960s refrigerators, washing machines, and TVs had all become must-have items, with demand for cars and air-conditioning high. At staggering speed, "ordinary" Japanese people were able to buy these goods, not just long for them, following Prime Minister Ikeda Hayato's pledge to double the average Japanese income within a decade. The average Japanese family consumed 75% more in goods and services than their counterparts in the mid-1930s. As society became more affluent, parents began to invest more in their children's education. University became the norm, with over 90% of Japanese children graduating from high school by the mid-1970s; by now it's 97%, while in the US it's 83%. Japanese students now attend school on average 5.5 days a week, 240 days a year. By the 1980s, Japan's new postwar generation was growing up knowing only affluence and social unity. Today, over 90% of Japanese people describe themselves as "middle class", with the gap between rich and poor much less than that of the USA. By 1981, Japan was the world's largest producer of motor vehicles, and by 1983 the country produced nearly 30% of all motor vehicles. By 1985, Japan had also cornered the world market in cameras, radios, quartz watches, TVs, calculators, VCRs, stereos, computers, silicon memory chips, and genetic engineering. In 1982, 90% of all VCRs were made in Japan, and 70% of all computers.

Technology companies continue to invest massively in research and development to stay ahead of the world's great innovating nations and modernize their products and production techniques. Furthermore, a combination of demanding consumers and prolonged economic hard times has also taught Japanese companies how to adapt—quickly. As markets ebb and flow, Japan's leading companies have turned understanding consumer habits—and their changes—into a science. Few nations are as precise in anticipating consumer trends as Japan, where new products are created, distribution channels altered, and the basis of competition redefined at the same time as cost-cutting is evaluated. Accounting for 80% of consumers' financial assets and income, this segment has continued to grow in one of the most rapidly aging countries, where a more frugal mindset remains a legacy of the prewar era.

The Post Postwar Era

Despite a government proclamation in its 1956 Economic White Paper that the "postwar era was over" *(mo haya sengo de wa nai)*, many social scientists, including within Japan itself, questioned if that was the case for many more decades. However, on the 60th anniversary of the end of World War II in 2005, Japan could finally lay this period to rest. It was a fundamental watershed in modern Japanese history, signifying the "final end" of the postwar era.

Yet the 21C has been tough for Japan, with political turmoil, economic squeezes, and the March 2011 earthquake and tsunami, not to mention the ticking time-bomb of its aging population. Government ministers were forced to admit that the country faced a potential shortfall of funds necessary to meet the nation's senior citizens' basic needs. Critics slammed Japan's public works projects as an inefficient use of hard-earned tax revenue, while the economy struggled to rise after a decade-long slump. Protestors demanded an end to the immense powers of bureaucrats in favor of a more democratic political system capable of meeting the nation's challenges, citing the 1990s as "Japan's Lost Decade," in reference to its economic underperformance.

Though the Japanese government responded to these unprecedented difficulties by introducing wide-ranging reforms, such as non-profit organizations, information disclosure, and judicial reform legislation, there has been widespread call for more.

Also notable is a strong nostalgia for the feudal **Edo Era**. Now perceived by many to have offered stability and greater cultural vitality against a modern backdrop of overcrowding, work-related stress, fragmented family structures, and a continued economic slump, this yearning for the past has garnered a bigger voice in recent years. In 2008, Japan headed toward its worst postwar recession as factory output slumped an unprecedented 9.6% during the last quarter—the biggest fall since figures were first compiled in 1953. Unemployment surged and households cut spending as the global financial crisis took hold.

This nostalgia for the era of *sakoku* (isolation) may seem at odds with Japan's global culture and economy, especially the image presented at events like the 2019 Rugby World Cup and 2020 Olympics, but xenophobia remains a deep-rooted issue. There is little political will to discuss raising immigration quotas, despite the growing need for elderly care and the lack of progress in increasing the birth rate. However, there are some signs of progress: in 2015, **Miyamoto Ariana** was named Miss Japan, the first Japanese person of mixed ehtnic heritage to win the title, sparking debate about what it means to be "Japanese" in the modern era; while in April 2019, the **Ainu** were formally recognized as an indigenous people of Japan.

Though low by European and US standards, rising crime rates are the subject of much debate on Japanese TV and in newspapers. A series of high-profile murders and the increase in juvenile delinquency, which has grown by 80% since 1972, have further eroded the image of a crime-free Japan. However, Japanese cities routinely rank among the world's safest (Tokyo and Osaka were first and third on the 2019 Safe Cities List). Japan also tends to sit high on the Global Peace Index, ranking ninth in 2019.

Despite the challenges of a difficult global economy, Japan continues to face the future with the efficiency and forward-thinking characteristic of a country that has traditionally shown great resilience. It serves as a world leader in environmental awareness and high-tech research and development. Japanese automotive manufacturers are known worldwide not only for producing comparatively environmentally friendly cars, but also for producing them in a way that is ecologically friendly. Pioneering research ranging from high-speed transportation systems to nanotechnologies exemplifies the country's dedication to continuing its global competitiveness.

Art and Culture

Japan's geographical situation at the "Terminus of the Silk Road," as described by French orientalist René Grousset, also made this the end of the road for the ideas, styles, and techniques that, originating in the West, Central Asia, and China, made their way east.

Although sometimes sought out and valued by the Japanese for their intrinsic qualities, these imported cultural influences also evolved into their own unique and complex forms, particularly in the visual arts. From earliest forays into cinema to the enormous popularity of manga today, Japan's creativity never ceases to surprise.

PAINTING AND SCULPTURE
PREHISTORY

Although there is evidence of figurative representation dating back to the Paleolithic era, the most impressive examples come from the neolithic or **Jomon era,** noted for its spectacular ritual vases and richly expressive terracotta figurines, which probably represent the goddesses of a fertility cult.

During the Chalcolithic or **Yayoi era**, the arrival of metalworking from the Asian continent coincided with the appearance of bronze ritual bells, generally decorated with animal motifs or scenes of daily life.

The protohistoric **Kofun era** saw a unique phenomenon in the centralization of political power. Built to receive the bodies of great clan chiefs, including those of the future Imperial Family, the often huge tombs of the era provide lasting evidence of this centralization. The importance of the burial mounds is such that the era is named after them; "kofun" means "ancient grave."

They contain mortuary chambers, sometimes sumptuously decorated with wall paintings and quantities of burial goods, as well as skillfully worked terracotta figures, arranged above or around the mounds, apparently in order to protect the deceased.

THE ARRIVAL OF BUDDHISM

Archeological remains and early written sources indicate that cultural exchanges between Japan and the Asian mainland took place from the Yayoi period onward, but it was not until a centralized state emerged toward the **end of the 6C**, coinciding with the adoption of Buddhism, that the **Chinese influence** became significant. The Chinese system became the model for the organization of the Japanese administration, and the Imperial Court and many aspects of its culture. Chinese and Korean influences can be seen in **Buddhist art**, both in architecture and in the layout of monasteries, as well as the statuary that began to flourish from the beginning of the **Asuka era**.

Notable among the works of this rich period is Nara's Horyu-ji (7C), the oldest monastery in Japan, which contains the gilded bronze triad of the Buddha Shakyamuni, cast in 623 by the sculptor Tori. In contrast to the severe hieratic style of this early work, the rounded sweetness of the sculpture of the **Hakuho period** reached its apogee with the Miroku Buddha, carved in lacquered wood, in Chugu-ji, Nara, whose expression of gentle contemplation is a high point in Japanese art.

The **Nara era** (also known as Tenpyo in art history) is characterized by the use of new techniques, while the costly dry lacquer technique was abandoned. This era gave rise to some spectacular creations such as Toshodai-ji's bodhisattva, the Fukukenjaku ("thousand-handed") Kannon, more than 16ft/5m high (second half of 8C). The use of clay enabled sculptors to achieve finer, more accentuated modeling, as can be seen in the guardian gods of the gates of Horyu-ji (added in 711), whose imposing stature (12.5ft/4m), ferocious expressions, and impressive musculature were designed to protect the monastery from evil demons. Shoso-in, situated in the compound of the "Great Eastern Temple," Todai-ji (751), the construction of which was the most important religious event to take place during the Nara era, was used to house the collection of Emperor Shomu (701–56). It contained more than 4000 objects brought to Japan from Constantinople, Persia, India, and China via the Silk Road. The Nara era also saw the beginning of the adaptation of Chinese characters to express the sounds of Japanese, which would lead two centuries later to the invention of the Japanese syllabic notation system and the birth of a calligraphic tradition that is now over a thousand years old.

THE GOLDEN AGE OF CLASSICAL ART

At the end of the 8C, the Imperial capital was established at Heian (Kyoto). Liberated from the cultural influence of China, with which the court had broken off all official relations in 894, during the course of the following centuries Japanese culture would distance itself by degrees from Chinese influence to produce an art that was wholly original. This first "golden age" of Japanese art that constituted the **Heian era** was itself subdivided into smaller periods. Until the mid-10C, the large, powerful but severe statues of the Jogan period showed the still-prevalent influence of Tang Chinese art; conversely, the statuary of the **Fujiwara era** is characterized by sweetness of expression and a lightness of touch. This new, specifically Japanese trend would reach its height with the Amida Buddha carved by the sculptor **Jocho**, housed in the temple of Byodo-in (1053) at Uji, near Kyoto.

The Heian period was also a rich one in terms of painting; the mandalas and other works created in an esoteric Buddhist framework are noteworthy. However, it was the emergence of **secular narrative painting** in the 12C that was to be the most important development in pictorial art during this period, a fine example being the illustration of Murasaki Shikibu's famous *Tale of Genji* (Genji monogatari 🔖). In the 11C, the climate of religious uncertainty that surrounded the beginning of the "Last Era of Buddhist Law," (the Japanese preoccupation with *mappo*, the pre-ordained collapse of Buddhist Law),

gave rise to many devotional practices, including the illumination of copies of canonical texts (sutra), executed with the greatest of care. This decorative trend would culminate the following century in the creation of sumptuous ensembles of scrolls such as the Lotus Sutra (Heike nokyo), donated by the Heike clan to the Itsukushima Shrine, on the island of Miyajima.

THE MEDIEVAL PERIOD

During the **Middle Ages,** the emperor remained at Kyoto while the military government established itself first at Kamakura (1185–1333), and then Muromachi (1333–1573). It was a split that was both symbolic and cultural, stimulating the appearance of new genres and styles that were different from the formalized aesthetic of courtly art, and challenging the Imperial Court's role as arbiter of taste. Influenced by Zen Buddhism, this new art found its most typical expression in portraiture, which may have developed at the Court but was immediately adopted by the ruling clans, who adapted it to their own preference for simple, realistic monochrome painting. A good example is the portrait presumed to be of Minamoto no Yoritomo (1147–99), founder of the Kamakura Shogunate. Attributed to **Fujiwara no Takanobu** (1142–1205) but probably dating from the 13C, this scroll painting is now at Jingo-ji, Kyoto, where it is one of three hanging scrolls designated National Treasures.

During this period, portrait painting was also developed by Zen Buddhist monks but the **Kei school**'s revival of Buddhist sculpture is most typical of the period, notably the work of the sculptor **Unkei**, whose painted-wood sculptures of **Muchaku** and **Seshin**, two Indian monks who lived in the 4/5C, can be seen at Kofuku-ji in Nara (1212). There is no attempt at idealization in these portraits, but instead a new, more realistic style is used to convey inner intensity and spirituality.

Although dominated by a total fragmentation of political power and constant wars, the **Muromachi** period was artistically fruitful. The **shoguns of the Ashikaga dynasty** were great patrons who collected Chinese art and encouraged painting, which achieved an artistic highpoint in Zen monasteries.

It was in this troubled period that the famous Japanese dry landscape gardens first appeared, Ryoan-ji in Kyoto being the best-known example (late 15C). At the end of the 14C, the shogun Ashikaga Yoshimitsu ordered the construction of Kyoto's Golden Pavilion, the ultimate expression of the aesthetic ideal of the time. A century later, the shogun Ashikaga Yoshimasa built the Silver Pavilion as a refuge where he could enjoy moments of calm while the country was being ravaged by brutal civil wars. Yoshimasa also encouraged the development of the tea ceremony, a new social ritual that was both spiritual and aesthetic (♨ see p125). Influenced by the Song dynasty in China, painting also underwent a revival, notably monochrome landscape painting. Works imported from the mainland produced a fruitful Japanese reinterpretation by great painters such as **Sesshu** (1420–1506).

The new Japanese works were displayed on large-scale decorative supports, such as screens and sliding panels, in monasteries and the houses of the aristocracy. Large-scale works in monochrome or color followed, illustrating themes such as *Landscapes of Four Seasons* or *Famous Landscapes* and, especially popular, *Views of the Capital and its Districts*, along with the classics of Japanese literature. Coinciding with the use of humorous subject matter in the first popular art form, an ancient precursor of today's manga, painting was elevated to the status of a profession with the success of the **Tosa and Kano Schools** of painting.

THE MODERN ERA: POPULAR ART AT ITS PEAK

At the beginning of the modern era, the brief **Azuchi-Momoyama period** saw the trend for large decorative works that had begun in the preceding era reach a highpoint with the emergence of great artists such as **Kano Eitoku** (1543–90) and **Hasegawa Tohaku** (1539–1610). The stability of the **Edo era** that followed gave rise to an amazingly rich urban culture. New forms of artistic expression developed simultaneously with the emergence of an urban bourgeoisie.

The leisured merchant classes of the central regions encouraged the growth of the **Rinpa School**, whose greatest exponents, **Honami Koetsu** (1558–1637), **Tawaraya Sotatsu** (c. 1570–1640), **Ogata Korin** (1658–1716), and his brother **Kenzan** (1663–1743), revolutionized the interpretation of Heian artistic themes. The bourgeoisie in the new cities supported the creation of a **popular art** of great vitality, which made use of new printing techniques.

This well-known style of **woodblock prints** known as *ukiyo-e* ("images of the floating world") focused on three principal areas: portraits of actors and courtesans, landscapes, and the famous "images of spring," which combined social irony with praise of earthly love. Great artists working in this medium included **Suzuki Harunobu** (active 1756–70), **Kitagawa Utamaro** (1753–1806), **Sharaku** (active 1794–95), **Katsushika Hokusai** (1760–1849), and **Ando Hiroshige** (1797–1858).

Finding its way into Japan via the Dutch merchants who, from 1641, were the only Westerners allowed to live in Japan, European art aroused the interest of some Japanese painters, such as **Maruyama Okyo** (1733–95), whose experiments in the field heralded the coming of a new era.

MODERNIZATION AND IDEALISM

The ending of Tokugawa domination saw a gradual decline in *ukiyo-e* and the popular culture of Edo, while Buddhist art, lacking its usual supporters, also lost impetus.

Western-style painting (*yoga*) began to develop in 1876 with the support of the Meiji government. The fresh approach of **Takahashi Yuichi** was typical of this new period. Around 1900, **Asai Chu** and **Kuroda Seiki** popularized a style inspired by the French open-air painters, while bronze commemorative sculpture began to appear in public spaces, significantly transforming the appearance of big cities. However, in reaction to this Westernization, the critic and art scholar **Okakura Tenshin** revitalized Japanese art by advocating a fusion of traditional Japanese and Chinese styles, stimulating the emergence around 1890 of the Nihonga painters, whose most famous exponents were **Yokoyama Taikan** and **Hishida Shunso**. Calligraphy, pottery, and *ikebana* all struggled to find a place in this new artistic era.

THE TWENTIETH CENTURY
An age of choice
The period between 1912 and 1941 was marked by a succession of European-inspired movements: Post-Impressionism with **Yorozu Tetsugoro** and **Kishida Ryusei**, Dadaism with the **Mavo group**, Proletarian Realism, the Surrealism of **Koga Harue** and **Kitawaki Noboru**. On the other hand, Cubism and Constructivism made little impact, demonstrating that Japanese assimilation could be selective.

During the 1930s, many forms of creative and artistic expression such as gardening, architecture, and *ikebana* (thanks to **Teshigahara Sofu**, founder of the **Sogetsu School**) underwent a revival, reinventing Japanese traditions in a dialogue with Modernism. **Yanagi Soetsu** led the movement for the recognition of folk art or *mingei* ("handicraft art of the ordinary people"), restoring the connections between Buddhism and crafts.

War and its consequences
World War II saw a period of intense, state-controlled artistic activity. Although creativity was stimulated, the wartime government's need for propaganda created a demand for realistic paintings celebrating Japan's military triumphs. **Foujita ("Leonard") Tsuguharu** painted many patriotic battle scenes, some of which were seized by the US in 1946.

Memory of the conflict remained vivid for many years. Thousands of funerary or peace monuments and statues of the bodhisattva Kannon, the incarnation of compassion, were erected throughout Japan. The Hiroshima Panels (1950–82), a series depicting the atomic explosions painted by the husband-and-wife team of **Maruki Iri** and **Maruki Toshi**, graphically illustrate the tragedies of Hiroshima and Nagasaki.

In the mid-1950s the **Gutai group** (Yoshihara Jiro, Shiraga Kazuo, Murakami Saburo, and others), pioneered striking works in the Osaka region that broke with tradition by playing with materials and forms in ways that anticipated later happenings, performance, and conceptual art.

Toward the future
In the 1950s there was a vogue for abstract art in Japan, although the works of **Okamoto Taro** and **Saito Yoshishige** demonstrated that its challenges were as much social or formal as expressionist.

In the 1960s, Pop Art rediscovered Edo culture, thanks to the painter and graphic artist **Yokoo Tadanori**, while groups like **Hi-Red Center** (founded in 1963) staged performances critical of the consumer society.

Around 1970 the **Mono-ha movement** (Lee Ufan and Sekine Nobuo) used installations in earth, wood, and rock to "bring things together," allowing the materials to create their own ecology by establishing a relationship between them with little artistic intervention.

Michael Lucken

CONTEMPORARY ART
After a period during which external influences and styles were absorbed into the homegrown scene, the 1980s marked the arrival of Japanese artists internationally. With a surprising freedom of expression, Japanese art moved easily back and forth between the traditional and the invention of a new artistic language.

There are no barriers between culture and subculture, as **Murakami Takashi** (1962–) demonstrates, producing works inspired by manga and the world of the

© Naoharu Obayashi/Benesse Art Site Naoshima

Benesse House Museum

Where to see contemporary art in Japan

In Tokyo, galleries in Roppongi, such as the Mori Arts Center and 21–21 Design Sight, or the Museum of Contemporary Art in Kiyosumi-Shirakawa—where some of the city's most dynamic and innovative galleries are found—put on exhibitions sure to please the most demanding contemporary art lover. Japan also offers many different ways of experiencing contemporary art. Kanazawa's **21st Century Museum of Contemporary Art**, designed by Sejima Kazuyo and Nishizawa Ryue, exhibits the work of acclaimed artists from Japan and all over the world. Also designed by Nishizawa, **Towada Art Center** shows contemporary Japanese and international artists creating innovative, often interactive pieces. Several regions mount **triennial art exhibitions**, much of the work remaining in place afterwards. Created for a 2006 triennial, James Turrell's House of Light (in Niigata prefecture) is unlike any other in Japan. You can stay in the traditional-style house to experience light in a variety of conditions centered around a sky-viewing room where an aperture in the roof can be opened and closed.

Equally magical is a stay on the island of **Nao-shima** (🍃 *see p554*). Here, the Benesse Art Site displays site-specific works on permanent exhibition, not only inside in the formal exhibition spaces, but outside in the natural surroundings of Nao-shima. Opened in the early 1990s by the Benesse Foundation, the facilities include the **Benesse House** (designed by architect Ando Tadao), the Chichu Art Museum, the Art House Project, and Honmura Lounge & Archive.

Hélène Kelmachter

---

otaku (🍃 *see p72*), as well as a range of mass-market objects.

Tradition vs modernity
Kimono vs street fashion, wooden temples vs high-tech structures of glass and steel: tradition and modernity rub together on a daily basis in urban Japan.

Some artists have appropriated age-old traditions by reinventing them, like **Nakagawa Yukio** (1918–2012) and **Suda Yoshihiro** (1969–), who have reinvented *ikebana* in a radical way.
The work of **Yamaguchi Akira** (1969–) is inspired by the pale colors and flat perspective of Edo-era prints, as are those of

Takano Aya (1976–), depicting modern teens often caught in erotic poses.

"Kawaii!" Cute or weird?

As in everyday life, the fad for all things *kawaii* (cute or childish) also appears in art. The sulky faces of little girls painted by **Nara Yoshitomo** (1959–) present a sweet-sour image of childhood. This "disturbing strangeness" is also found in the doll paintings of **Kato Mika** (1975–), where the precise detail provokes unease. The bright, digital work of **Aoshima Chiho** (1974–) is populated with young women, often shown tied up or as skeletons, evoking a response torn between the appeal of the sparkling colors and the violence represented.

Japan at bay

A great power whose world image has long been that of a country at the forefront of technology, Japan's experience of the collapse of the "bubble economy" in the 1990s, and the unemployment and insecurity that accompanied it, has been painful. The provocative work of **Aida Makoto** (1965–) reveals the darkest aspects of Japan; his *Shinjuku Castle*, a cardboard palace for the homeless, is a comment on the economic crisis but also an expression of his taste for the absurd. Inspired by clips from newspapers and television programs, the installations and animations of **Tabaimo** (1975–) glide from an ordinary situation into an enigmatic and disturbing event to reveal the dark side of modern Japanese society.

The menace of catastrophe

The post-World War II generation grew up in a society marked by technological innovation but also by the experience of the atomic bomb. This dual memory is present in the works of **Yanobe Kenji** (1965–), whose *Radiation Suit Uran,* incorporating a shower unit to wash out contaminants, projects us into a sci-fi world inspired by the 1970 Osaka World's Fair. Another collective fear runs through contemporary art, as depicted in the lithographs of **Motoda Hisaharu** (1973–), where earthquakes evoke apocalyptic visions of Tokyo in ruins, or the installations of **Kawamata Tadashi** (1953–), with monumental, ephemeral projects in wood created on sites under repair or awaiting destruction.

The poetry of the imaginary

Kusama Yayoi (1928–), a member of the postwar Japanese avant-garde noted for her obsessional, hallucinatory art, has profoundly influenced many younger artists. **Nawa Kohei** (1975–) creates extraordinary objects by covering them with glass beads or by filling a space with giant molecular shapes. A dreamlike quality can also be found in the works of **Mori Mariko** (1967–), who combines the technology of three-dimensional images with references to Buddhism. The same blend of technology and Japanese philosophy is employed by **Miyajima Tatsuo** (1957–), whose digital counters tick off the seconds as they pass, evoking the passage of time and the continuity and interconnectedness of the human life-cycle. The work of **Ishigami Junya** (1974–), a mixture of design, aarchitecture, and installation, testifies to the originality, daring, and renewal of this generation of Japanese artists.

Hélène Kelmachter

CINEMA

The people of Japan were instantly fascinated by early cinema tecchnology. 1898 saw their first forays into narrative films, with adaptations of ghost stories such as *Bake-jizo (Jizo the Ghost)* and *Shinin no sosei (Resurrection of a Corpse).*

THE GREAT DIRECTORS

Japanese cinema is firmly tied to notions of the auteur, art, and the essay. By the outbreak of World War II, the first great directors, **Mizoguchi Kenji** (1898–1956) and **Ozu Yasujiro** (1903–63), had produced several major works, including *Sisters of Gion* (Mizoguchi, 1936) and *An Inn in Tokyo* (Ozu, 1935).

In the 1950s, Japan made an impression on the international film scene with the arrival of **Kurosawa Akira** (1910–98), the first Japanese film director to win a European award, for *Rashomon* (1950), the story of the same crime reported

Still from Seven Samurai *(1954) by Kurosawa Akira, with Mifune Toshiro*

from the differing points of view of the chief participants. The film also took the Golden Lion at the Venice Film Festival and made actor **Mifune Toshiro** Japan's first global film star. Despite his epic tales of samurai, Kurosawa was considered the most "Western" of the Japanese directors, drawing inspiration from the western movies of John Ford and the works of Shakespeare and the great Russian writers.

Mizoguchi often revisited subjects dealing with the plight of Japanese women and also triumphed at Venice with *Ugetsu* (1953), the story of a potter seduced by the ghost of a noblewoman; it won Venice's Silver Lion for Best Direction. Mizoguchi also helped Japan's first female director to get a foothold in the industry, working with **Sakane Tazuko** at Nikkatsu Studio in the 1930s; she even assisted him on his first talkie, *Hometown* (1930).

Ozu Yasujiro had been dead for some years before his work finally became available and recognized outside Japan. His masterpiece, *Tokyo Story* (1953), is the portrait of a widow played by Hara Setsuko, who retains her sense of duty while Tokyo changes all around her.

Naruse Mikio (1905–69) was one of the most prominent directors of his time, though his work is the least known outside Japan. Like those of Ozu, his films deal primarily with the postwar role of women and feature many of Japan's great actresses. Among these was **Tanaka Kinuyo** (who also worked with Kurosawa, Mizoguchi and Ozu), who alongside her acclaimed acting career became Japan's second female film director.

GENRE MOVIES

Some Japanese studios concentrate on genre cinema. **Toei** specializes in films about yakuza (gangsters), the best-known being those by **Fukasaku Kinji** (1930–2003), especially his *Battles without Honor and Humanity* series (1973–4). Toei also acquired an animation studio that has created a large number of TV series and movies, and adapted Japanese comics into animated series, becoming one of the mainstays of *anime* today.

The **Nikkatsu** studio produced the films of **Suzuki Seijun** (1923–2017), a visually extravagant filmmaker who was eventually dismissed because of his increasingly surreal style. Both Fukasaku and Suzuki have influenced many US filmmakers, from Jim Jarmusch to Quentin Tarantino. It's also worth mentioning that director Tim Burton, who is passionate about *kaiju* (monster movies), is a big fan of the **Toho** studios, producer of the Godzilla series, which launched atomic-trauma science fiction, the best films being directed by **Honda Ishiro** (1911–93), a close friend of Kurosawa Akira.

Nikkatsu was also responsible for a genre called "**roman porno,**" a brand of erotic movies that saved the studio from going under and produced some major directors: **Konuma Masaru** (1937–), **Kumashiro Tatsumi** (1927–95), and **Tanaka Noboru** (1937–2006). This genre was a training ground for several young filmmakers, including **Somai Shinji** (1948–2001) and **Kurosawa Kiyoshi** (1955–), before they moved on to more mainstream cinema.

Following a similar trajectory, **Hamano Sachi** has not only focused mostly on "pink films" in her career, but has enjoyed international critical success with them. Her 2001 *Lily Festival*, about sexuality in a senior citizens' home, won Best Feature at the Philadelphia International Gay & Lesbian Film Festival.

INDEPENDENT FILM

Wakamatsu Koji pioneered independent Japanese film production by creating his own studio in the 1960s. He inspired other filmmakers under contract with the big studios, including **Oshima Nagisa** (1932–2013) and **Yoshida Yoshishige** (1933–), who were with Shochiku, and **Imamura Shohei** (1926–2006), who worked for Nikkatsu. Along with **Shinoda Masahiro** (1931–), they constituted Japan's New Wave, creating a stir on the international circuit with the political and erotic content of their movies. Imamura was twice awarded Cannes' Palme d'or, for *The Ballad of Narayama* (1983) and *The Eel* (1997). A number of Oshima Nagisa's films were successful abroad, notably *In the Realm of the Senses* (1976) and *Merry Christmas, Mr Lawrence* (1983), which starred musicians David Bowie and Sakamoto Ryuichi.

In 1984, **Miyazaki Hayao** (1941–) wrote and directed *Nausicaä of the Valley of the Wind*, adapting it from his manga series of the same title, and turned the world of animation upside down. Together with **Takahata Isao** (1935–2018), who directed *Grave of the Fireflies* (1988), he set up his own animated production company, Studio Ghibli. Other successful directors include **Oshii Mamoru** (1951–), creator of Ghost in the Shell (1995), with Production I.G, and **Kon Satoshi** (1963–2010), director of *Paprika* (2006), with Madhouse. All these directors have shown at Berlin, Cannes, and Venice, while Miyazaki's *Spirited Away* was the first anime film to win an Academy Award, only the second Oscar ever awarded for Best Animated Feature.

Tsukamoto Shin'ya (1960–) launched the cyberpunk wave with *Tetsuo: The Iron Man* in 1989, while the actor **Kitano Takeshi** (1947–) replaced Fukasaku Kinji as director of *Violent Cop*, in which he also starred (under the name Beat Takeshi). Kitano has directed and starred in most of his movies, often writing and/or editing them as well. *Hana-Bi* (*Fireworks*, 1997) won the Golden Lion at the Venice Film Festival.

The 1990s and early 2000s saw another upsurge of Japanese cinematic talent with the arrival of **Kurosawa Kiyoshi** (1955–), **Aoyama Shinji** (1964–), **Kawase Naomi** (1969–), **Ogigami Naoko** (1972–), **Kore'eda Hirokazu** (1962–), **Miike Takashi** (1960–), **Nishikawa Miwa** (1974–), and **Nakata Hideo** (1961–), all of whose work has been distributed internationally.

In 2002 **Shinkai Makoto** (1973–) released the beautiful, moving short *Voices of a Distant Star*, which he wrote and animated alone in 7 months. He was soon producing feature-length films, with 2016's *Your Name* the second highest-grossing *anime* film ever, after Ghibli's *Spirited Away*. Also in this period, **Hosoda Mamoru** (1967–) directed *The Girl Who Leapt Through Time* and *Summer Wars* at Madhouse, before setting up his own animation studio. Here, he continued creating playful, nostalgic films like 2018's *Mirai* (nominated for Best Animated Feature at the 2019 Academy Awards).

In 2004, **Ishii Katsuhito** (1966–) made *The Taste of Tea*, launching a wave of movies drawing on both Japan's traditional culture, and the world of manga and *anime*, including *Memories of Matsuko* by **Nakashima Tetsuya** (1959–).

2005 saw the release of *Dear Pyongyang*, a documentary by **Yang Yong-hi**, a Japanese-North Korean filmmaker. In the following years she continued to highlight issues faced by this little-known community in her work, with her first feature film (*Our Homeland*) released in 2012.

Stephen Sarrazin

PHOTOGRAPHY

Japan is a world leader in camera manufacture and technology, and Japanese people tend to enjoy taking photos, especially in cherry blossom season. *Purikura* photo booths, with their array of cute and flattering editing options, still feature in young people's days out, but there's an increasing tendency to simply use smartphone apps to acheive the same effect.

THE FIRST PHOTOGRAPHERS

Fukuhara Shinzo (1883–1948) and his brother **Roso** (1892–1946) pioneered photography in Japan and, in 1924, founded the Japanese Photographic Society. The brothers were famous for their pictures of landscapes and flowers, hand-tinted in gentle sepia tones. In the 1920s and 1930s, curiosity about Western ideas stimulated experimentation, inspired by avant-garde Europeans such as the Surrealists. During World War II, Japanese photographers worked largely for the imperial government, and in the immediate postwar years, for press and publishing companies. The US-born **Ishimoto Yasuhiro** (1921–2012) introduced American theories and technology to Japan in 1953.

THE GREAT PHOTOGRAPHERS

One of the witnesses to the spectacular changes undergone by post-war Japan was the avant-garde photographic magazine "**Provoke**," whose three editions (1968–9) shook the foundations of practical photography, and could be summed up in three words: grainy, blurred, out-of-focus *(are, bure, boke)*. These innovative perspectives came from the likes of **Takuma Nakahira** (1938–2015), **Masahisa Fukase** (1934–2012), **Hosoe Eikoh** (1933–), **Shomei Tomatsu** (1930–2012) and of course **Moriyama Daido** (1938–), with his bizarrely disjointed, grainy shots.

His friend **Nobuyoshi Araki** (1940–) tends to produce sharp, precise images of young women in erotic poses and shackled postures, while another master of the nude, **Shinoyama Kishin** (1940–), stylizes bodies to the point of abstraction. In the decade after *Provoke* was published, **Kai Fusayoshi** (1949–) began capturing scenes of Kyoto life, from the countercultural movements to beautiful women, kids to street cats.

CAPTURING A MOMENT IN TIME

For **Sugimoto Hiroshi** (1948–), photography is an almost Zen-like act of meditation. The formal beauty and classical perfection of his work, taken in series, is based on concepts of time, the transience of life, and the conflict between life and death.

Hatakeyama Naoya (1958–) defies the passage of time in his work by capturing the arrested moment in his photographs of explosions taken in quarries. The poetic style of **Kawauchi Rinko** (1972–), capturing the small, beautiful details of everyday life, is a meditation on the fleeting wonders of the world.

PHOTO ID

In work that is as surprising as it is original, **Morimura Yasumasa** (1951–) uses photography as a homage to painting. He recreates the works of Western artists such as Manet and Rembrandt by substituting his own face for those of the original subjects. Following in his wake, several young Japanese photographers have explored the theme of identity through self-portraits or by playing with the photographic image.

Sawada Tomoko (1977–) puts herself in the picture in school photographs, substituting her own face for every uniformed schoolgirl, or recreates her image *ad infinitum* in photo booth portraits, or photographs herself dressed in costume against different backgrounds. **Yanagi Miwa** (1967–) photographs staged scenes and uses computer manipulation to produce images of places that are at once familiar and unreal. Artifice and reality merge in her work to give a surreal view of the 21C city.

Japanese galleries specializing in photography include **Taka Ishii** and **MEM** in Tokyo, and **Foil** in Kyoto.

Hélène Kelmachter,
Philippe Pataud Célérier

MANGA

Manga has become increasingly popular worldwide since the international publication of **Otomo Katsuhiro**'s *Akira* in the 1990s. Despite its image as a contemporary phenomenon, a type of manga has existed in Japan since the Middle Ages. The Muromachi era (1336–1573) saw the appearance of the first painted scrolls with pictures and calligraphic text. They sometimes featured humorous drawings and caricatures of people and animals engaged in human activity.

The term *manga* itself, which means disorderly or clumsy *(man)* drawing *(ga)*, was not coined until much later, when **Katsushika Hokusai**, a master engraver, called the series of grimacing faces which he published between 1814 and 1834, *Hokusai Manga*. There is now a museum dedicated to Hokusai's work in Tokyo (*see p142*).

EARLY MANGA

It was Western illustrators working in Japan at the end of the 19C, such as English artist and cartoonist Charles Wirgman and French cartoonist and illustrator Georges Ferdinand Bigot, who acted as the springboard for the early modern manga. Wirgman launched the satirical magazine *Japan Punch* and Bigot's work appeared in *Toba-e*.

The first modern Japanese manga, by **Kitazawa Rakuten** (Kitazawa Yasuji), appeared in 1902 in the newspaper *Jiji Shinpo*'s Sunday supplement. It was influenced by the European style, echoing the subject of one of the Lumière brothers' earliest films. A sign of things to come, Japanese cartoon styles would borrow heavily from the cinema for their scenarios, as well as the way their stories were framed.

© Manakin/iStock

Comic books for sale in Tokyo

MODERN MANGA

Manga became very popular in Japan in the interwar period, and nearly every newspaper and magazine featured it. Soon, however, the military regime clam-

---

Mangamania

Japanese manga has spread far beyond the realm of the comic book superhero to deal with almost every subject, from war to cookery, polar exploration to porn, and of course science fiction. As a marketing tool, manga is also a way of targeting readers at specific ages; the *shojo* genre, aimed exclusively at young girls, is divided into two main subgenres: "Magical Girl," where the heroines use supernatural powers to combat evil; and "Romance," usually involving stories about Prince Charming. Aimed at boys, in the *nekketsu* genre (literally meaning "hot blood"), action characters attempt to outdo each other's exploits, promoting the values of bravery and loyalty. Adult manga and the soft porn *pantsu* genre mean that, once hooked, the publishers are able to hold onto their audience for life.

ped down, censoring all forms of caricature, using the new medium of comic strips to distribute its own propaganda instead, especially to young people.

Manga did not recover until the early 1960s, this time influenced by American comics brought to Japan by the GIs of the occupying Allied forces. One artist in particular played a leading part in this renaissance: **Tezuka Osamu** (1928–89). Trained as a doctor (although he never practiced), he devoted himself to manga, single-handedly inventing almost all the characteristics of the modern idiom: cinematic framing, big round eyes for hero and heroine, the use of written onomatopoeia to describe sounds, etc.

A big fan of Walt Disney (he was said to have seen *Bambi* over 80 times), Tezuka was equally at home with a camera as with a pencil, and in 1963, he created the first real hero of Japanese manga, **Tetsuwan Atomu** ("Mighty Atom") known internationally as **Astro Boy**. The character was phenomenally successful, both on television and in print.

During his prolific career, Tezuka published more than 700 works, though it was not until 1990 that his status as an artist was officially recognized with a major retrospective organized by Tokyo's National Museum of Modern Art.

POST TEZUKA

The illustrators now following in Tezuka's footsteps work in both manga and *anime*. **Miyazaki Hayao** (*My Neighbor Totoro, Princess Mononoke,* etc.) has been successful in both genres and is known internationally for his films. On the manga side, new heroes succeeded Astro Boy in the 1970s and 1980s, the best known being **Goldorak** and **Candy**. Both have been hugely successful not only in Japan but worldwide.

Creators of manga for adults such as **Otomo Katsuhiro** (*Akira*) or **Taniguchi Jiro** (1947–2017; *Haruka na Machi e, Icaro,* etc.) now reach a discerning audience that values manga as a literary and illustrative art form. **Kazuto Tatsuta** (1965–) produced a formidable graphic memoir of the workers who performed the clean-up operation at Fukushima, *Ichi-F.*

But it was the arrival of **Toriyama Akira**'s manga series *Dragon Ball* that really launched "mangamania" internationally. More than 250 million copies were sold in less than ten years after its release, smashing the record held by *Tintin*, which has sold "only" 200 million over more than 40 years. Manga reaches a wide audience in France, now the biggest consumer of manga after Japan, with more than ten million volumes sold every year.

Patrick Duval

ARCHITECTURE

For many centuries Japan's architecture owed much to foreign influences. While the Kingdom of Paekche (Korea) played a central role, notably with the introduction of Buddhism and the temples associated with it, China provided the initial inspiration for the layout of towns and palaces. Likewise, the architecture of the temples used in Zen Buddhism, introduced in the 12C, was inspired by those created during the Song dynasty. However, Japanese architects subsequently devoted centuries to creating their own styles, generally by reworking existing ones to reveal the essence of Japanese culture. This process of assimilation, well known in Japanese postwar industry, marks the whole of Japan's cultural history. In the 20C, however, this system of appropriating elements from other cultures largely faded out, leaving to the Meiji government the distinction of having presided over the last period during which Japan looked largely toward Europe and America for inspiration for its architecture. By the second half of the 20C, it was the West that looked to Japan, which enjoyed international acclaim for its modern architecture.

STAGES OF DEVELOPMENT

As early as the **Yayoi period** (500–300 BC), Japanese architecture made ingenious use of wood. Timber was readily available and was used for Buddhist temples, Shinto shrines, and houses for both the elite and ordinary people.

Designed to house a spiritual presence *(kami)*, **Shinto shrines** (*see illustration p102*) recreated the physical isolation of

Tokyo Station

© coward_lion/iStock

the early places of worship using a series of compounds preceded by tall gateways *(torii)*. The innermost sanctuaries are reached after cleansing the hands and mouth at a purification font *(temizuya)*. Shrines are notable for their simplicity of line and the natural materials used. The colors too are usually simple and natural, with the exception of vermilion red (thought to repel evil spirits, but also to preserve wood). Secondary structures have double roofs supported by a succession of posts. Only the innermost part of the shrine where the *kami* resides *(honden)*, raised on pillars, is partitioned off. Shrine architecture reached an unparalleled degree of complexity when shrines began to be dedicated to national heroes like Tokugawa Ieyasu, whose remains are entombed in the highly elaborate 17C Tosho-gu at Nikko. In **Buddhist architecture** building complexes were enclosed by walls, into which were set monumental gates *(chumon)*. Buddhist temples consisted of a main building *(kondo)* housing an image of the Buddha, and depending on the size of the temple, a series of auxiliary buildings, including pagodas, inspired by the Indian stupa. Buddhist temples (⊚ *see illustration p103)* are differentiated from Shinto shrines not only by their roofs with upturned corners, made from tiles or copper rather than thatch or bark,

but also through their use of colored lacquer. Despite the major earthquakes suffered over the centuries, some very fine Buddhist temples remain in the oldest Japanese cities.

For obvious reasons, stone came to replace wood in **defensive architecture**: it was used for the vast foundations surmounted by spiraling walled ramps and keeps, built in a mixture of stone and earth. Himeji Castle in Hyogo prefecture (⊚ *see illustration p104 and photograph p417)* is a fine example of a Japanese castle, with many defensive structures and features.

The Birth Of Modern Architecture

The **Meiji Restoration** marks a turning point in Japanese architecture, when Japan began to adopt Western architectural concepts.

It was a new era of architectural thinking, which led to the spread of a "hard" architecture and the start of new building programs. British architect **Josiah Conder** was appointed by the Meiji government to take up a teaching position, and in less than 20 years, he and his students had designed the buildings that would reflect the status of the new Meiji state (university buildings, ministries, museums) in a wide variety of styles. They included Tatsuno Kingo's Tokyo Station and Bank of Japan,

Conder's Iwasaki House (Tokyo), Thomas Waters' Japanese Mint (Osaka), and Katayama Tokuma's National Museums in Kyoto and Nara. All were demonstrably a reprise of all the "neos" once fashionable in Europe.

In continuing its program of modernization during the first third of the 20C, Japan looked toward continental Europe, considered the world leader in Modernist construction techniques and styles. An exception was **Frank Lloyd Wright**, whose Imperial Hotel (1917–22) is partially preserved at Meiji-mura near-Nagoya. Unlike in the 19C, this was not a "top-down" import from abroad, with study missions or official invitations to foreign professionals (though in 1941, French architect/designer **Charlotte Perriand** was officially invited to advise on industrial design). In general, Japan's acclimatization to the international style came about quite informally, through contact with European architects working in Japan, such as **Bruno Taut** or **Antonin Raymond**, or through Japanese architects making the reverse journey to train at leading European architectural schools and practices During the 1930s, rampant nationalism led to official rejection of the Modernism introduced by, among others, **Maekawa Kunio** and **Sakakura Junzo**, two former associates of Le Corbusier. The authorities preferred constructions that had no hint of the modern about them apart from their building materials, and the recreation of traditional styles, as in **Watanabe Jin**'s redesign of the Toyko National Museum or the Kabuki-za theater by **Okada Shinichiro**, which are typical of the "imperial crown style."

A few Modernist buildings that escaped destruction have been relocated to Tokyo's open-air **Museum of Architecture**; they include the house of Maekawa Kunio, who worked in the Tokyo office of Antonin Raymond (St Paul Chapel, Karuizawa), where Modernist principles are translated into wood, and the Koide house by **Sutemi Horiguchi**, combining a thatched roof and Western living spaces.

Kansai International: An Airport in the Sea

Owing to the respective problems of land purchase issues and noise pollution at Narita and Osaka Airports, the Japanese had the astounding idea of building Kansai International Airport on water. This technological exploit called for 20 years of study before the actual works began in 1984 in Osaka Bay. A wall was to be first built on the ocean floor to delineate the future artificial island, reinforced from the outside by a sea wall, to protect the island against typhoons and other natural disasters. Sixty-nine steel chambers were therefore sunk into the ocean floor to form the perimeter of the island, and then, protected by the sea wall, the ground of the future island was built with a layer of fill 98ft/30m thick. Six years later, in 1990, the building of the artificial island 2.5mi/4km long and 6mi/1km wide was completed with another exploit: constructing a bridge 1.9mi/3km long to link the airport to the coast. Then came a major problem: during construction, the embankment had compressed 27ft/8m, significantly more than the experts had estimated. Unruffled, the Japanese engineers simply came up with another innovation: that of adjustable steel columns to support the terminal building, which could be extended by inserting thick metal plates into their bases. Designed by the Italian Renzo Piano, Kansai International Airport, 1mi/1.7km in length, was on completion the longest airport terminal in the world. From 1994, flights from the world over began landing on its single runway. The airport emerged unscathed from the Kobe earthquake, a victory for its builders, and in 2002 a second runway was added, followed by a second terminal building in 2012.

National Art Center designed by Kurokawa Kisho

© Iain Masterton/age fotostock

The Emergence of Modern Japanese Architecture

The Czech architect **Antonin Raymond,** who had worked in Japan before World War II, was the first Western architect authorized to build during the American Occupation. When he reopened his Tokyo practice in 1948, he introduced new technology developed in the US, and used *ashiba maruta* (wood scaffolding blocks) to reconstruct buildings destroyed by bombs (the Inoue House, Takasaki; Meguro Catholic Church). This inexpensive construction system offered an alternative to **Seike Kiyoshi**'s prefabricated housing. Raymond was also noted for his passion for reinforced concrete, which influenced **Tange Kenzo** via Maekawa, his one-time collaborator. Some of Raymond's buildings can be seen at Takasaki (Gunma Music Center), Nagoya (Nanzan University), and Tokyo (Meguro Catholic Church).

The traditional vs modern debate that began before World War II still revolves around Tange Kenzo. As his Hiroshima Peace Memorial Park (see p441) demonstrates, Tange was influenced by Le Corbusier and identified with the Modernists, translating materials and building techniques into structures to which he gave a rare, powerful expressiveness, such as the Yoyogi Stadium for the 1964 Olympic Games, Tokyo.

The break with the tutelary figures of Modernist architecture came with the generation that included **Kurokawa Kisho, Kikutake Kiyonori, Isozaki Arata**, and **Maki Fumihiko**, who were still students when Le Corbusier visited Japan in 1955 (and delivered the drawings for the National Museum of Western Art in Tokyo). It was this generation who, during the 1960 International Design Conference held in Tokyo, redefined Japanese architecture with designs that, like those of the avant-garde British group Archigram, broke with the usual concepts relating to infrastructure and architecture. They believed that the city of the future should seem as natural as possible, and its architecture should evolve organically following the cycles of urban growth and decline.

The aim of this **Metabolist movement** (named from the title of a manifesto signed by several of the architects) was the renewal of urban society through its architecture. Few examples were built, however; they include the headquarters of Shizuoka Press (Tange Kenzo) and the Nakagin Capsule Tower (Kurokawa Kisho) in Tokyo, and the Tokoen Hotel and Sado Grand Hotel (Kikutake Kiyonori) at Yonago and Sado.

101

Shinto shrine (Nagare/Honden style)

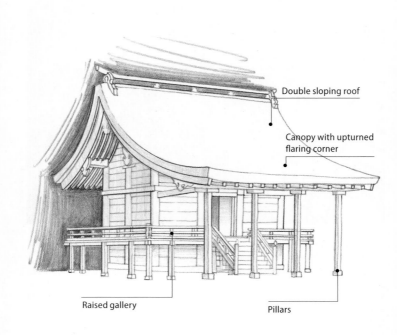

Double sloping roof

Canopy with upturned flaring corner

Raised gallery

Pillars

Shinto complex

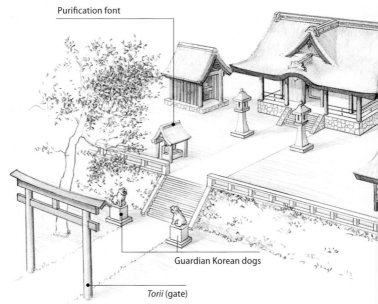

Purification font

Guardian Korean dogs

Torii (gate)

Zen Buddhist temple

Facade

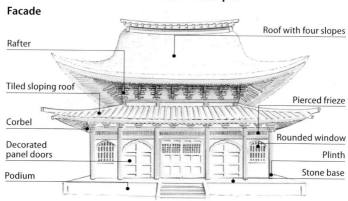

Rafter

Tiled sloping roof

Corbel

Decorated panel doors

Podium

Roof with four slopes

Pierced frieze

Rounded window

Plinth

Stone base

Cross section

Cross strut

Hidden rafter

Central ceiling

Tie beam

Exposed rafter

Main beam

Inner sanctum

Posts supporting ceiling at the rear

Altar

Outer section

Five-story Pagoda

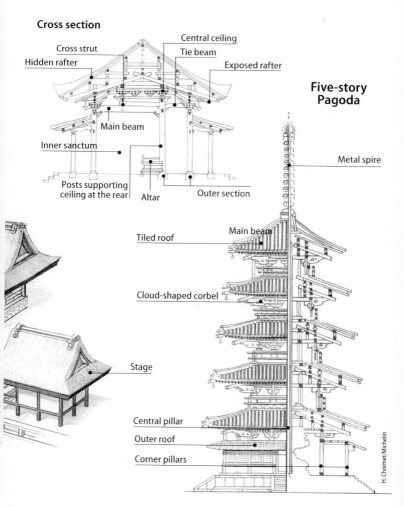

Metal spire

Main beam

Tiled roof

Cloud-shaped corbel

Stage

Central pillar

Outer roof

Corner pillars

H. Choimet/Michelin

The Old Eri Family Residence (late-17C)
Kagawa Prefecture (Shikoku)

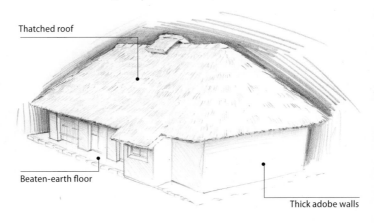

Thatched roof

Beaten-earth floor

Thick adobe walls

Himeji Castle (early 17th century)

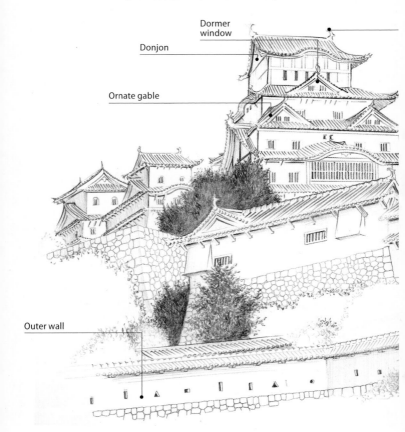

Dormer window

Donjon

Ornate gable

Outer wall

Shoin-style interior (late-16C)

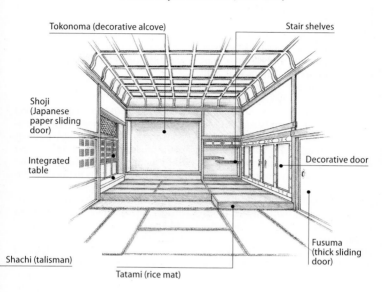

Tokonoma (decorative alcove)

Stair shelves

Shoji (Japanese paper sliding door)

Integrated table

Decorative door

Shachi (talisman)

Fusuma (thick sliding door)

Tatami (rice mat)

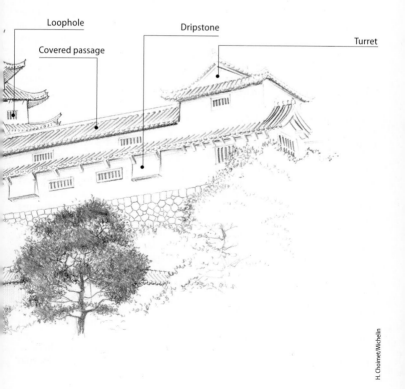

Loophole

Dripstone

Turret

Covered passage

H. Choimet/Michelin

Postmodern Metaphors
In the early 1970s, **Isozaki Arata** and **Hara Hiroshi** radically challenged all-out modernization and Japan's unequivocal relationship with the West. Their Postmodernist works offer erudite metaphors for various eras and places that question Japanese identity. While Isozaki wittily combines "collisions" (Ledoux, Michelangelo, and contemporary forms in Tsukuba's Civic Center), Hara builds "multilayered structures" or "atmospheres" influenced by his research into village communities around the world (Kyoto station).

A New Japanism
The economic growth of the 1960s and 1970s was accompanied by violent destruction of the environment and chaotic expansion of cities. Two masters of residential architecture, **Shinohara Kazuo** and **Ando Tadao,** attempted a spiritual realignment through the domestic environment.
Influenced by *minka*, traditional private residences, Shinohara embraced Japan's chaotic urban condition at the end of the 1970s as a design theme. As carefully conceived works of art, his buildings successively explored tradition and the "savagery of contemporary architecture" (House In Uehara, Tokyo; Tokyo Institute of Technology's Centennial Hall).
Ando creates simple, introverted geometric shapes in cast concrete, usually facing toward inner courtyards, using enclosure to establish a human zone and to deflect the surrounding urban chaos. In his own words, "Such things as light and wind only have meaning when they are introduced inside a house in a form cut off from the outside world." His buildings are true acts of "urban guerrillaism," rejecting all contact with an aggressive context (Row House in Sumiyoshi, Osaka). His public buildings are equally noted for this approach (Church of the Light, Kobe; Time's Building, Kyoto).
The 1990s work of **Kuma Kengo** (Hiroshige Museum, Tochigi) and **Aoki Jun** (Vuitton store, Tokyo) experimented with materials and techniques in the mannerist style, arguing for a new Japanism which reinterpreted the traditions of Japanese buildings. Architectural historian **Fujimori Terunobu** (Jinchokan Moriya Museum, Chino) designs quirky buildings which glorify the human touch and delight in natural building materials.

Other View of The Urban Environment
During the 1980s and 1990s, the period of the "bubble" economy, new generations of architects offered other readings of the urban environment. **Takamatsu Shin** suggested the only appropriate response was a highly extrovert architecture (Kirin Plaza, Osaka) marked by mechanical and anthropomorphic imagery. In the same mode, **Yamamoto Riken** created rational fragments to house micro communities (Saitama University). In step with this logic of affirmative identity, **Hasegawa Itsuko** designed artificial landscapes (Shonandai Cultural Center, Fujisawa) while, by contrast, **Ito Toyo** aimed to combine the physical and virtual worlds of the city in transparent, light, and ephemeral architecture (the Sendai Mediatheque). For **Sejima Kazuyo**, the city-dweller is an urban nomad wandering an ever-changing environment (21st Century Museum of Contemporary Art, Kanazawa), as it is for her collaborator **Nishizawa Ryue** (Towada Art Center).

Urban Subculture
Other talented architects appeared during the 1990s, often noted for their interest in the manifestations of the contemporary urban environment. They include **Atelier Bow-wow** (established by Kaijima Momoyo and Tsukamoto Yoshiharu), **Ban Shigeru**, **Chiba Manabu**, **Coelacanth** (Horiba Hiroshi and Kudo Kazumi), **Mikan** (Kamo Kiwako, Sogabe Masashi, Takeuchi MAsayoshi, Manuel Tardits), **Nishizawa Taira**, **Tezuka Yui** and **Tezuka Takahara** in the Kanto region; **Abe Hitoshi** in Sendai; **Endo Shuhei** and **Miyamoto Yoshiaki** in the Kansai region; **Murakami Toru** and **Sanbuichi Hiroshi** in Hiroshima; and **Arima Hiroyuki** in Fukuoka.

Thanks to Japan's growing internationalization, its architects increasingly work abroad. **Ban Shigeru** designed the antenna for the Pompidou Center, Metz, France, while **Sejima Kazuyo** worked on the Louvre Lens, also in France. **Kuma Kengo** (who won the commission for the 2020 Tokyo Olympic Stadium, after Zaha Hadid's previously accepted design was declared too expensive) designed the V&A Dundee in Scotland.

At the same time, many **Western architects** have contributed to Japan's urban landscape. In the twenty-first century, these have included the Swiss firm Herzog & de Meuron (Prada Building, Tokyo), the Netherlands-based MVRDV (Gyre Shopping Center, Tokyo), the French architect Jean Nouvel (Dentsu Building, Tokyo), and the Italian Renzo Piano (Kansai Airport, Osaka).

Christine Vendredi-Auzanneau
Manuel Tardits

LITERATURE AND THE PERFORMING ARTS

Japanese literature, far from being stuck in the groove of age-old tradition, is constantly renewed by young literary talents. In the performing arts, Noh and Kabuki actors are stars who are adored throughout the whole country, while Japanese music is open to all influences.

LITERATURE

The oldest Japanese works of literature still in existence are the *Kojiki (The Records of Ancient Matters)* and the *Nihon shoki (Chronicles of Japan)*, written in 712 and 720 respectively. Commissioned by the Court, these texts were the basis for the mythology that grew up around the Imperial Family, who, until 1945, were presented as being the direct descendents of the sun goddess Amaterasu (see also p76).

The rules of Japanese poetry were also established in the 8C, in particular the **tanka**, with lines of 5, 7, then 5 syllables (from which **haiku** developed), followd by two lines of 7 syllables each.

The *Man'yoshu (Collection of Ten Thousand Leaves)* is an anthology of 4500 poems written between the 7C and 8C, which gives a fascinating glimpse of life during the Nara era. It contains poems and prose writings reflecting on war, lifestyle, and small domestic dramas. The authors, nearly all anonymous, come from every strand of society.

The First Novel

An exclusively Japanese literature did not evolve until the Heian period. Until the 9C the Japanese language was written with Chinese characters in a complex system accessible to only a few intellectuals. Around the 900s, the invention of *kana*, a form of syllabic writing, made it possible to write Japanese phonetically; this did much to democratize literature, especially by enabling women to express themselves in writing (many women were barred from learning Chinese).

Around the beginning of the 11C, **Murasaki Shikibu,** lady-in-waiting at the Imperial Court, wrote **Genji monogatari** *(The Tale of Genji)*, the first true work of fiction in Japanese, and quite possibly the first novel in the world. It skillfully relates the tale of the life and loves of Genji, a charming, cultivated prince who is nevertheless relatively indifferent to the unhappiness he creates around him. Now considered *the* masterpiece of Japanese literature, it celebrated its millennium in 2008, sparking off various exhibitions and new editions worldwide.

The Battle Recitals of Medieval Times

Over the following centuries literary output was colored by the interminable clash between two rival clans, the Minamoto and the Taira. This gave rise to many tales of war, generally oral works carried from village to village by blind monks, who sang them, accompanying themselves on the *biwa*, a lute. Chief among these is the *Heike monogatari (Tale of the Heike)*, recounting the defeat of the Taira in the Genpei War.

The Refined Literature of the Edo Era

In 1603, the dominance of the Tokugawa Shogunate brought an end to a long, troubled period, bringing a remarkable stability to the country that was to last for nearly three centuries. The themes of war gradually faded from literature, being replaced by those of love and the pleasures of the "floating world" (the urban lifestyle), which also featured prominently in woodblock prints (&see p90). **Ihara Saikaku** (1642–93) is unquestionably the greatest novelist of the 17C. His racy, lively style was largely due to his mastery of the *haikai* form of linked-verse poetry, and although he began his career as a novelist with *buke mono* (warrior stories) or *chonin mono* (tales of townspeople), he quickly discovered that demand for his work was much greater when he wrote *koshoku mono* (amorous or erotic stories) with titillating titles. *The Man Who Lived Only for Love* and *The Life of an Amorous Woman* were huge commercial successes—the first Japanese bestsellers.

The haiku

During this period of peace when Japan, although closed to the outside world, developed its own artistic rules, poetry—especially the haiku—became a ruling passion. A haiku (or *hokku* as it was often called at the time) is a short poem in three metrical phrases of 5, 7, and 5 sound units that, by its brevity, evokes the evanescence of things. **Matsuo Basho** (1644–94) excelled in this deceptively simple art. Born into a samurai family, Basho (real name Matsuo Munefusa) quickly renounced a life in the military to devote himself to religion and literature. The power of his poems always relies on suggestion rather than description. Emotion comes from the observation of the most ordinary of things, as in this famous haiku (here translated by Robert Aitken):

> The old pond;
> A frog jumps in—
> The sound of the water

When composing his poems, Basho was guided by two concepts: *wabi*, the notion of simplicity and asymmetry, with a touch of melancholy, and *sabi*, evoking the quest for simplicity and the beauty of things altered by time. In literature as in the other arts, the concept of *wabi-sabi* would become the basis of Japanese aesthetics.

The great novelists of the 18C

Many talented writers of fiction emerged in the 18C, of whom the greatest is probably **Ueda Akinari** (1734–1809). His masterpiece, *Tales of Moonlight and Rain (Ugetsu monogatari)*, was brought to the screen by Mizoguchi Kenji.

Meiji: the Encounter with the West

Japan's opening-up to Western culture toward the end of the 19C, which paradoxically coincided with the emperor's regaining of power after the 15th Tokugawa Shogun Tokugawa Yoshinobu resigned his position, exerted a profound influence on literature. It ushered in several trends "imported" from the West, such as the introspective, autobiographical novels of **Shiga Naoya** (1883–1925) or the naturalism inspired by Émile Zola, of which **Shimazaki Toson** (1872–1943) is undoubtedly the best representative.

Short stories in the style of Chekhov, Edgar Allan Poe, or Guy de Maupassant were also popular, with **Akutagawa Ryunosuke** (1892–1927) being the most impressive in this genre. His best-known short story, *Rashomon*, written in 1915, would provide the film director Kurosawa Akira with the theme of one of his greatest masterpieces (though most of the film's plot actually came from another Akutagawa story, *In a Grove*). The Akutagawa Prize, Japan's most prestigious literary award for promising new writers, is awarded annually in his honor. Three Meiji period novelists won international acclaim: **Natsume Soseki** (1867–1916), **Mori Ogai** (1862–1922), and **Nagai Kafu** (1879–1959).

The works of Natsume Soseki (pen name of Natsume Kin'nosuke), such as *I am a Cat* and *Botchan*, deal with many of the very Japanese themes of shame and culpability, the "hero" inevitably being driven to suicide (another major Japanese theme).

Mori Ogai's style is even more austere, probably influenced by the author's long sojourn in Germany. Hints of burgeoning patriotism can be detected, together with a strong strain of pessimism. Nagai Kafu is the only writer not to embrace this tendency, preferring to use themes from the "floating world" of the Edo period in his fiction (*A Strange Tale from East of the River*, *The Dancer*, etc.)

From the Postwar Period to Contemporary Literature

During the postwar period, some fine novelists emerged into international literary prominence. Deeply scarred by Japan's military defeat, they were often nostalgic for the tradition of *bushido*, which they saw as threatened by increasing Westernization. Chief among them was **Dazai Osamu** (1909–48), who published *The Setting Sun* in 1946, and **Tanizaki Jun'ichiro** (1886–1965), whose works, including *Diary of a Mad Old Man* and *In Praise of Shadows*, are classics of Japanese literature.

The first Japanese writer to win the Nobel Prize for Literature was **Kawabata Yasunari** (1899–1972), whose works include *Snow Country*, *The Sound of the Mountain*, and *The Dancing Girl of Izu*. Another fine writer was **Inoue Yasushi** (1907–91), author of *The Hunting Gun* and *Journey Beyond Samarkand*, while the exceptional talent of **Mishima Yukio** (1925–70) is often eclipsed by his right-wing politics and death by *seppuku*.

The most prominent intellectual figure among contemporary writers is **Oe Kenzaburo** (1935–). His Nobel Prize-winning body of work, which includes *The Silent Cry* (1967) and *Hiroshima Notes* (1965), interrogates the history of Japan with great moral urgency. His writing has also been profoundly influenced by the birth of his son Hikari, who has Down's Syndrome and to whom he has dedicated several of his works.

While **Murakami Haruki** (1949–) is one of the best-known modern writers (*Kafka on the Shore*; *What I Talk About When I Talk About Running*), a new generation is emerging, dominated by female voices. Among the many exceptional writers are **Yoshimoto Banana** (1964–), who prefers a light tone and direct approach

---

The influence of Japanese theater abroad

American avante-garde director and playwright **Robert Wilson** respects and admires Japan's classical theater and the visual language of the Noh plays, drawing upon it for his own work. Eckhard Roelcke described his Tamino in *The Magic Flute* as "a disciplined, Oriental bundle of energy." The robe, painted eyes, and statuesque posture of Wilson's Gurnemanz in *Parsifal* were highly reminiscent of Japanese theatrical figures. English composer **Benjamin Britten** visited Japan in 1956 and was fascinated by Noh theater, which inspired his three Church Parables. The first of these, *Curlew River*, is based on a Noh play, *Sumidagawa (Sumida River)* by Juro Motomasa, although Britten gave it a Christian context and transposed the setting to medieval England.

---

to deal with often dark subjects; **Yoko Tawada** (1960–), whose challenging work is marked by linguistic inventiveness; and **Murata Sayaka** (1979–), whose breakout novel *Convenience Store Woman* explores themes of nonconformity and isolation in modern life.

Patrick Duval,
Philippe Pataud Célérier

THE PERFORMING ARTS

Classical theater in Japan is no dusty relic of the past. Performers of traditional Japanese theatrical arts such as Noh, *kyogen*, *bunraku*, and Kabuki are stars today and maintain a vibrant artistic spirit, often handed down through generations, while contemporary innovations such as *butoh*, an avant-garde dance form, often incorporate influences from the traditional performing arts.

Noh

The classical theater of Japan, combining dance, singing, and music, Noh (also spelled No) is characterized by its subtlety and restraint.

Kabuki performance of Yoshitsune Senbon Zakura

It is performed on a square stage with no decor save for a painted backdrop. Actors (all-male in most troupes) are accompanied by a chorus and musicians. The basic form of Noh was established by the playwright **Zeami** (1363–1443), who codified the rules and revised texts by his father **Kanami** to create the essence of the genre as it is known today. The repertoire overflows with tales of ghosts and demons, warriors and abandoned maidens in epic dramas. The art of Noh has held a fascination for many creative Westerners, including Bertolt Brecht, W.B. Yeats, Samuel Beckett, Benjamin Britten, Peter Brook, Ariane Mnouchkine, and Robert Wilson. *Kyogen* ("mad words") is traditionally performed as an interlude between Noh plays as a counterpoint to the dramatic intensity of the latter. These comic sketches, often containing elements of slapstick or satire, are designed to make the audience laugh about the problems of everyday life.

Bunraku

Puppet theater, *bunraku,* originated in Osaka during the 17C. It uses stylized puppets to enact stories, the main repertoire being historic sagas, peasant dramas, and legends. Three puppeteers manipulate each large puppet, while the dramatic action is narrated by a chanter accompanied by musicians. The strength of the emotions that the puppeteers manage to convey via these wooden dolls is remarkable.

Kabuki

Kabuki, the popular, highly stylized form of dance-drama derived from traditional religious and popular dancing styles, was developed in Kyoto in 1603. Created by a priestess and dancer, **Okuni**, it was first performed exclusively by women. The authorities soon found their choreography too erotic and in 1629 they were banned and replaced by boys. They too caused scandal and in 1652, the shogunate decreed that only older actors could perform Kabuki. To this day, women's roles are usually played by men known as *onnagata* (*onna* meaning "woman", and *gata* "form"), who evoke a traditional and stylized image of womanhood. Performance skills and secrets are often handed down from father to son, or to a nephew or adopted son, if there is no direct male descendant. Kabuki includes partly chanted speeches and naturalistic sound effects. Wooden clappers signal the opening and closing of the play and cue the actors. Many famous playwrights, including **Chikamatsu Monzaemon**,

(1653–1724), have written masterpieces for Kabuki actors, with plots borrowed from *bunraku*, Noh, and *kyogen*. An ancestor of musical comedy, with its blend of realism, illusion, and symbolism, Kabuki flourished in the second half of the 18C and revolutionized Japanese theater. The three characters that make up the word *kabuki* mean singing (*ka*), dancing (*bu*), and art or skill (*ki*), but it can also mean "extravagant" or "the height of fashion."

Butoh

Long marginalized in Japan, *butoh* is strongly influenced by German Expressionism, the writings of Antonin Artaud ("Theater of Cruelty"), and Georges Bataille. It draws on the depths of the Japanese soul following the traumas of Hiroshima and Nagasaki, combining eroticism and violence, emptiness, and silence in a "dance of darkness." Creator **Hijikata Tatsumi** (1926–86) scandalized with the first performances in the late 1950s. Brought to the West by Ohno Kazuo and the Sankai Juku company, *butoh* is normally performed in white body makeup, with extremely slow and precise movements.

Takarazuka Revue

Established in 1913 in Takarazuka near Osaka, this troupe is a nationwide phenomenon. In response to what he saw as the old-fashioned, elitist Kabuki—and to increase use of the Hankyu railway, which he owned—industrialist Kobayashi Ichizo founded this all-female theater, which produces Japanese and foreign musicals with lavish costumes and make-up. Performers follow a strict training regimen, and specialize in either female roles (*musumeyaku*) or male roles (*otokoyaku*). Kobayashi stated that the troupe aimed to produce "good wives and wise mothers", and there have been numerous efforts to limit accusations that the revue "encourages" lesbianism. Nonetheless, it is necessarily somewhat radical in terms of gender. Many performers decide to prioritise their careers, going against Kobayashi's wish that they retire to marry, and attraction to the performers (especially *otokoyaku*) is clear among many in their legions of female fans.

Jean-Luc Toula-Breyss

MUSIC

The Imperial Court's *gagaku* orchestra, a wind, string, and percussion ensemble, plays in connection with Imperial household duties or rituals, giving only rare public performances. This is Japan's oldest music, descended from 8C and 9C Chinese and Korean culture, giving today a glimpse of the early court's extreme refinement. Japanese music evolved with the rise of the aristocracy, with roots also in the spoken word and theater.

Heian era (794–1185) courtly life gave way to the 13C–16C feudal culture favoring epic recitation performed by monks wandering from village to village, like European medieval minstrels, accompanying themselves on a **five-stringed lute** or **biwa**. The military elite fostered the birth of Noh (*see p109*), patronizing it until Japan's late-19C modernization.

In the mid-19C, the West forced Japan to open its frontiers and traditional music lost ground in the Western educational system Japan adopted, and lost even more with the resulting huge demand for Western music. Contemporary Japan, with its many auditoriums with excellent acoustics, is an essential stop on international concert or opera company tours. Today an impressive wealth of Western classical music is on offer in Tokyo, and top Japanese musicians, conductors, and composers such as **Takemitsu Toru** (1930–96), **Hisaishi Joe** (1950–), and **Sakamoto Ryuichi** (1952–) have successfully breathed new life into both traditions. Amateurs in Japan have a musical literacy that is quite probably-unequaled in the world, while there is also a flourishing instrument-making industry, notably of pianos.

Michel Wasserman

A Way of Life

One of the great pleasures of visiting Japan is the discovery of the unique aesthetic that infuses daily life. It touches everything, from gardening to bathing, gastronomy to the formal tea ceremony, and the mundane to the highly intellectual—testament to a centuries-old tradition.

BATHING

The bath (*o-furo*) and the ritual of bathing are absolutely integral to Japanese culture. Japanese people enjoy bathing not simply as a means of relaxation and for the feelings of **wellbeing** that it stimulates, but also because it perpetuates an age-old tradition.

The Japanese passion for cleanliness is also an important factor. The origins of bathing lie in the **Shinto** religion, the animist faith that venerates nature. Before entering the bath, it is important to observe certain rituals, **purifying the body**, in a reminder never to soil the waters dispensed by the gods.

THE PLEASURE OF THE BATH

Bathing used to be a mixed-gender activity, but when Japan started to open up to the West in the Meiji era, Anglo-American prudishness began to prevail. During the military occupation (1945–52), the Western Allied Powers ordered the segregation of the sexes in baths, in an attempt to modernize and, as they saw it, counter decadence. The owners of some *onsen* (hot springs) had the bright idea of running a cord across the baths in order to keep the sexes apart and respect the new regulations. A small number of *onsen* still have mixed-gender pools, and it's often possible to to reserve an unsegregated private bath for family and friends, while fathers sometimes bring their small daughters to baths reserved for men, and mothers may bring their young sons to the women's baths.

© kuppa_rock/iStock

The *Onsen* Ritual

The ritual in an *onsen* (hot spring) at a thermal spa is the same as in the city *sento* (public baths). Everyone undresses completely, stowing their clothes in the changing room. They then sit on a small stool under a shower head and wash thoroughly with a small cloth before entering the bath. Wearing a bathing suit is not permitted, but the more self-conscious can hide behind the small towel provided on entry (not the large one used for drying yourself off, which is left in the changing area). It is bad form to enter the water while still dirty, or with soap on the body. If bathing in someone's home or a guesthouse, never empty the bath on leaving as others will use it after you.

In Japan, the bath is not for washing; it is a place for relaxing, relieving stress, and enjoying a moment of quiet repose: never use soap in a bath, make sure you leave it clean, and never allow your towel to drop into the water. Japanese people visit *onsen* and *sento* with their family or friends, or sometimes with work colleagues, since they can talk peacefully and even drink a cold beer or sake in the hot water. Often the water temperature is more than 104°F/40°C and can exceed 122°F/50°C, so it's advisable to test the temperature before entering.

Macaques in hot springs, Jigokudani Yaen-koen
© undercrimson/iStock

In practice, the intimacy of nudity abolishes social barriers, although bathers still observe some tacit rules of modesty, such as covering their genitals with a small towel when outside the bath.

Wash thoroughly under the showers provided before entering the water, making sure to rinse away all soap. Soap should never be used in the baths themselves and long hair must be tied back.

HOT SPRINGS

From the smallest and most picturesque to the most visited, *onsen* attract more than 151 million people every year. They can be found throughout Japan, situated by the sea, in the mountains, and in both town and country. Thanks to the volcanic nature of the landscape, springs well up from the earth in many places (*℄ see p112*), some renowned for their healing powers. In 2006, the Ministry of the Environment officially recorded 3157 *onsen* resorts and 28,154 springs.

According to a law passed in 1948, to qualify as an *onsen*, the water temperature must be at least 77°F/25°C at its source and contain at least one of 19 minerals designated by the public authorities. Many *ryokan* pride themselves on having their own springs, and *onsen* are a big draw for Japanese tourists as well as for foreign visitors.

One of the oldest and best known is **Arima Onsen**, north of Kobe (*℄ see p413*). Said to date back to the 7C, this is where the shogun Toyotomi Hideyoshi (1537–98), accompanied by the distinguished tea master Sen no Rikyu (1522–91), came to recharge his batteries during Japan's feudal era. Arima attracts many people who appreciate the beauty and tranquility of its natural surroundings, which are nevertheless within easy reach of the city.

Onsen are currently experiencing a boom, but it's not only humans who enjoy bathing in them. In Tokyo, a large *onsen*/leisure park has a pool reserved for dogs, which is sometimes also used for racehorses. There are stories of wounded birds being cured, thanks to the healing waters of the onsen, while Japan's macaque monkeys also enjoy relaxing in hot springs, notably at Jigokudani (near Nagano) in winter.

Jean-Luc Toula-Breysse

GARDENS

Japanese culture is closely tied to the natural world, a relationship which is clear in traditional gardens. These have more in common with the natural-looking, carefully planned estates of Capability Brown than any other element of the Western garden tradition, viewing nature not as something which you can subdue and impose order upon, but as something you can shape and work in harmony with, to create an even more perfect scene. In the Shinto tradition, the natural world is populated by a whole host of spirits (*kami*), who must be treated with reverence and respect. This tradition, as well Buddhism (chiefly the Pure Land and Zen schools), shaped Japanese garden design for centuries.

THE ART OF GARDENS

Japanese master gardeners prefer to suggest rather than represent. Working in harmony with the rhythms of seasonal flowering and the color variations of leaves, they respect the impermanence of nature, creating gardens that offer a balance between space and content. Like painters, they recompose the reality of the world, the rake across gravel replacing a brush across a canvas.

Inspired by Chinese and Korean gardens, the garden as an artform first appeared in the 6C, its popularity spreading during the Heian period, promoted by the aristocracy. The classic manual on the art of the garden, the *Sakutei-ki (Records of Garden-Making)*, thought to have been written during the second half of the 11C, is an invaluable source of information on the principles of the Japanese garden.

Many of these gardens are designed to integrate the exterior landscape, seen over a wall or hedge, into the design. As the name suggests, this **shakkei** or **"borrowed landscape"** style seeks to incorporate the background landscape into the garden itself, as if there were no boundary between them. The gardens of the Katsura Imperial Villa in Kyoto are a perfect example of this technique.

In the **paradise garden**, the paradise in question is that of Amida, the Japanese name for Amitabha, the principle Buddha of the Pure Land sect of Buddhism. They were a means of visualizing Amida's paradise here on Earth. Typical features are pools dotted with tranquil islets, or encircling a larger island symbolizing man's inner nature. The gardens of Byodo-in at Uji, near Kyoto, are a fine example.

The **tea garden** (*chatei*) is laid out around a pavilion dedicated to the tea ceremony (see p125). Tea gardens make use of the understated colors of foliage plants and the shade that they create. The rustic character of these small gardens offers an insight into the values of the tea masters, often excellent gardeners, and the concept of *wabi sabi* (simplicity, imperfection and impermanence) valued so highly by many of them.

The dry landscape (*kare-sansui*), commonly known as a **Zen garden**, signals a major stage in the evolution of the Japanese garden, following the principles of Zen art: serenity, austerity, asymmetry, simplicity, subtlety, naturalness, and freedom. Zen practitioners used abstract representation to grasp the quintessence of nature. To follow the path of spiritual enlightenment, the gardener-monks freed themselves from all formalism. Hence these gardens reproduce natural landscapes in an abstract way, using rocks, raked sand and gravel, moss, and small shrubs. Water is suggested by the sand and gravel, and the rocks and moss form the landscape features.

A fine example of this genre is attributed to the monk **Muso Soseki** (1275–1351). Tucked away in the northern part of the grounds of the Saiho-ji (also called Koke-dera, or "Moss Temple", for its lush, moss-covered garden) in western Kyoto, is an arrangement of rocks in the shape of a waterfall. The most famous of the dry landscape gardens is **the garden of Ryoan-ji** (Temple of the Peaceful Dragon) in Kyoto, designed in the 15C. It consists of a sea of white sand and 15 rocks arranged in such a way that only 14 are visible at a glance, something that has given rise to many interpretations. To some, it evokes ocean waves surrounding small islands; others see the rocks as mountains peaks floating in mist and cloud. There is no pathway through the stone; it is the ultimate expression of the garden conceived for meditation.

Fashionable during the Edo period, the **stroll garden**, where pools or streams wend their way through a planted landscape, is designed for walking. Paths lead the visitor to discover previously hidden viewpoints, walkways lead over artificial hillocks, while bridges span water. The landscaping frequently echoes celebra-

Dry landscape garden, Ryoan-ji, Kyoto

© SeanPavonePhoto/iStock

...ted Japanese and Chinese scenery, both real and imagined.

In addition to the outstanding gardens in Kyoto are three famous landscape gardens, often described as "The Three Great Gardens of Japan." They are **Kenroku-en** in Kanazawa (see p296), containing more than 12,000 trees of 150 different species; **Koraku-en** in Okayama (see p425), with maples, cherry trees, bamboos, and Japanese apricots; and **Kairaku-en** in Mito, resplendent in March when the plum trees are in bloom. All three gardens showcase the essentials of Japanesese garden design: a sense of space, formality, serenity, artifice, decorative beauty, and water in abundance. Whatever its style, the Japanese garden is a unique representation of life in miniature beneath an open sky.

Jean-Luc Toula-Breysse

Japan's National Treasures

With its focus on mastery, it's no surprise that Japanese culture holds exceptional and unusual objects and people in particularly high regard. This covers not only works of art or items with great historical value, but pieces and people which represent the peak of achievement in crafts, architecture or performance. It also applies to objects originating outside of Japan, such as the finely crafted Chinese tea bowl subsequently used by the shoguns. Because of their history, quality, and rarity, such objects and performances have been classified as "National Treasures" if they are unique, or as "Important Cultural Properties" if only a few examples exist in Japan or elsewhere. The Agency for Cultural Affairs (*Bunkacho*) currently lists almost 900 works as National Treasures (*kokuho*), about twenty percent of which are structures such as shrines or castles.

The same honors are extended to exceptional human beings (*Ningen Kokuho*, Living National Treasures) who are considered masters in their field. Currently Japan has 141 Living National Treasures: 57 individuals and 12 groups in the performing arts (*gagaku*, Noh, *bunraku*, Kabuki, music, etc.), and 59 individuals and 13 groups in arts and crafts (ceramics, textiles, lacquer, metal, bamboo, dolls, paper, etc.).

Gilles Maucout

Elaborately decorated geta (wooden clogs)

© Jon Arnold Images/hemis.fr

HANDICRAFTS

Japanese folk art is known as *mingei*, from the words *minshu* (people) and *kogei* (craft). Late in gaining recognition in Japan, it was not until the 1920s that, influenced by the distinguished intellectual **Yanagi Soetsu** (1889–1961), folk art took its place alongside the fine arts, which until then were the only arts considered worthy of attention.

Soetsu sparked off the *mingei* movement through his influential book, *The Unknown Craftsman*, encouraging the appreciation of everyday objects whose function may be mundane, but which have a simple beauty.

BEAUTY IN THE ORDINARY

In *mingei*, the classic distinction that is made between the decorative arts, fine arts, and popular art is no longer valid. The beautiful can be everyday, functional, and anonymous, whatever the material from which it is made.

Japanese craftsmen often work in paper, silk, and wood, as well as in metal, bamboo, hemp, rice-straw, clay … a wealth of natural materials with their own intrinsic beauty that the talent of the Japanese artist, respectful of the *kami* living in all natural things, brings out. In the same way, the Japanese style of flower arranging, *ikebana* ("the way of flowers"), aims to pay tribute to nature through its strict rules.

ARTISTS OR ARTISANS?

In Japan the artist is a craftsman who, rather than attempting to rival the beauty of nature, instead transcribes its beauty into the objects they produce. A good example of this is *washi*, the Japanese paper originally used for Buddhist calligraphy, since only its purity was worthy of holy texts. Given the care that goes into the making of a paper initially created to honor first the gods and then the emperors, no Japanese craftspeople working in paper would ever treat it with anything other than the utmost respect. In lanterns, umbrellas, fans, windows, and room dividers, paper plays with light and shadows. It's no accident that it was the Japanese who developed **origami**, the art of folding paper into objects and designs without the use of scissors. Japanese people tend to take great care when unfolding wrapping paper from around a gift, as much care as the person who wrapped it.

HARD-WON EXPERTISE

Craftspeople reach the pinnacle of their professions only after years or decades of practice, improving upon and handing down their techniques to succeeding generations, frequently within the same family. In **pottery**, for example, the techniques for the famous *raku* (hands-shaped stoneware often used in the tea ceremony, fired at low temperatures) have been handed down through 15 generations. Japanese pottery (terracotta or glazed stoneware) was initially designed exclusively for domestic use, but toward the end of the High Middle Ages (16C), it was adopted by the tea masters, who found sophistication in its extreme simplicity, paying tribute to the honest clay that produced it.

Less fragile than pottery, **wood** is one of the most commonly used materials in Japan. Available in quantity (see Nature p126), its association with the deities of the forest makes it doubly precious. **Lacquer** has been used since the Nara period to decorate and protect the most precious woods against humidity. In the maki-e technique developed in the Heian era, gold or silver powder is used as decoration.

Other popular materials include bamboo and **silk**, which replaced the material made from the inner bark fiber of the mulberry, from which Japanese garments were made in ancient times. In the Nara era, wearing silk was the privilege of the aristocracy and highly sophisticated techniques were employed in weaving and coloring it; in kasuri, for example, the threads are dyed in the right places to form patterns before the fabric is woven.

Finally, **stone**, the most basic of materials, can be carved into lanterns, basins, and sculptures. When patinated by time and eroded by wind and rain, nature adds its own simple finishing touches.

Philippe Pataud Célérier

FASHION
FROM THE KIMONO ...

The history of the kimono stretches back a thousand years, reflecting changes in lifestyle and culture, and technical developments in textiles and production. Though kimono simply means "thing to wear," it's now viewed as a fairly formal item, especially overseas. The kimono is famous for the elegant simplicity of its shape (formed from six bands of silk, traditionally hand-painted and of the very highest quality), its flexibility, and the fact that it suits all sizes, as well as for its sophisticated weaves and rich decoration.

Despite its long history and symbolic role, sales of the kimono declined dramatically after World War II. Women adopted Western dress for everyday life, reserving the traditional costume for cultural or family occasions, such as the hatsumode (first shrine visit of the New Year), the Shichi-Go-San ceremony for children of three, five, and seven on November 15 (when families visit the shrine with children wearing colored kimonos to pray to the gods to keep them safe), graduation ceremonies, weddings, and the Coming of Age ceremony (20 is the age of majority in Japan) on the second Monday in January.

But appreciation of the kimono seems to have recently undergone a transformation, with a rise in demand from 20–30-year-olds. Many people in this age group seem to feel saturated with Western culture, and are seeking ways to incorporate their traditional culture into their modern livesmodern livesmodern livesmodern lives. This new interest is well catered for by websites dedicated to the pleasures and ways of wearing the kimono, and designers seeking innovative ways to use centuries-old Japanese fabrics and dyeing techniques.

In response to the demand, **kimono shops**, selling secondhand, vintage and reworked kimonos at often low prices, have sprung up around the country. They are patronized by foreigners as well as Japanese shoppers because, thanks to its super-simple cut, the kimono can be adapted to fit many styles. Kimono accoutrements, such as the haori and happi coats, can slot even more easily into a modern Western wardrobe.

Traditionally, **the cut, colors, and fabric** of the kimono vary according to the occasion, the season, and the age, sex, and marital status of the wearer. If you're aiming for a traditional look, the garment should be tied with an obi (a stiff silk belt, thick and worn at the waist for women, narrower and worn on the hips for men) and worn with geta (wooden clogs) or zori (leather sandals). In cooler weather you can add tabi (split-toed cotton socks, which also add more formality) and various styles of coat.

In contrast to this traditional approach, **younger wearers of the kimono** often combine it with Western accessories like necklaces, earrings, designer handbags, and sometimes even high heels. Some young women have gone so far as to wear the kimono with jeans or boots, a style that, admittedly, may horrify some in the older generation for whom this modern interpretation represents an unacceptable break with tradition.

This **mixture of styles**, traditional and contemporary, is particularly noticeable in the fashionable Tokyo districts of Harajuku and Shibuya, although high-end Ginza remains traditional. A sign of the times, however, is that you can find clothes and accessories made from kimono fabric even here. All these trends reflect the evolution of traditional costume and confirm that the "spirit of kimono" remains deeply anchored in Japanese culture, and constantly evolving.

... TO "STREET FASHION"

In accordance with their fresh attitude toward the kimono, many young Japanese people wear Western clothing with flair and great creativity. While the previous generation tended to followed the rules of French-style fashion to the letter, wearing the classic two-piece suit that was adopted by some as an alternative to the kimono, today's young people seem to be much more adventurous overall. They have succeeded in inventing a distinctly Japanese version of street fashion, which some foreign designers have reappropriated for their own collections. During the 1970s and 1980s, the celebrated designs of **Issey Miyake** (considered the first Japanese designer to combine Japanese and Western style, in 1974) helped liberate young women from a completely Western style. Ten years later, **Yamamoto Yohji** and **Kawakubo Rei** (Comme des Garçons) challenged Western ideas about the use of color, the construction of garments, body shape, and even the sexism inherent in much high fashion. These two designers revolutionized fashion, championing conceptual shapes, plainness, and dark colors in place of the "pink, frilly, flowery" trend in vogue during the 1960s. Kawakubo Rei in particular specializes in "anti-fashion" with austere, asymmetrical shapes.

In reaction to this trend, however, many young Japanese people rediscovered color, frills, and sexy clothing. A feminine, decidedly Japanese style now takes up the majority of space in clothing stores aimed at young women. The **Lolita style**, at the extreme end of that trend, emerged in the 1980s on the streets of Tokyo with a whole range of specific types. "Gothic Lolitas" wear black lace frills and heavy makeup; "Punk Lolitas" sport the same frills but decorated with chains and skulls; "Eros Lolitas" are in lingerie, laced corsets, and boots; "Hime (princess) Lolitas," wear tiaras and layered skirts decorated with roses.

But, despite this exuberance of dress for the young, fashion is still structured in a typically Japanese way, and university is effectively the only time in most Japanese people's lives that they can dress as they like, every day. There is also still a sense that, in order to look successful, you need to wear designer brands, as in the bubble era. If you follow the expected life path as a young Japanese woman, then after graduating from university your *kawaii* (*see p92*) bag is swapped for a Chanel; once established in your corporate career, the Armani skirt suit makes an appearance; and so on.

A whole range of Japanese designers, including anti-brand **Muji** (**Mujirushi**) and **Uniqlo**, two fashion retailers now branching out worldwide, have made Japan a melting pot in which traditional Japanese attention to detail and technique is allied to cutting-edge technological innovation. In their wide variety of styles, ranging from the extreme to the classic, designers are responding not just to the demands of a population that no longer wants one-style-fits-all fashion, but also to the broader quest for freedom that has infused postwar Japan.

Françoise Moréchand

Sumo match at Ryogoku Kokugikan, Tokyo

© Sylvain Grandadam/age fotostock

MARTIAL ARTS AND SUMO

Unlike the Chinese martial arts that developed in villages as a defense against attack, the Japanese martial arts are closely linked to the history of samurai, or *bushi*, whose exclusive preserve they were for centuries. When it first appeared in the 8C, the word *samurai* was still pronounced *saburai*, from the verb *saburau*, to serve one's master. This ideal of following a code of honor called *bushido* (the way of the samurai; this term only became common in the 20C, to describe an earlier phenomenon) would endure among the warrior class until it disappeared at the end of the 19C.

THE ORIGIN OF MARTIAL ARTS

The traditional Japanese martial arts developed during the Edo period comprise seven principal skills: the art of the sword (*kenjutsu*), the art of the spear (*sojutsu*), the art of using a bow (*kyujutsu*), combat on horseback (*bajutsu*), unarmed combat (*jujutsu*), the use of firearms (*hojutsu*), and strategy (*hyoho*). The art of the sword is considered the noblest technique, and in the Edo period, the warrior elite of Japanese society had the right to strike down anyone of a lower class who compromised their honor with no fear of punishment (*kirisute gomen*). This warrior mentality remained the ideological basis for the military regime that existed from 1930–45, for whom the practice of martial arts was primarily a way of "serving the emperor"

and defending the country. This belief was dramatically illustrated in 1945 at Okinawa (where karate originated) when the inhabitants, short of arms and ammunition, attempted to repulse the US Army with their bare hands.

Following the Occupation, the Allied forces discouraged the teaching of most martial arts and it was not until 1949 that judo, for example, was again permitted, provided that it was run purely on the basis of a democratic sport, having been purged of all references to war and violence. After this, martial arts became divorced from the cult of the emperor

The rules of sumo

Sumo rules are simple: it involves pushing an opponent out of the *dohyo*, a clay circle 15ft/4.5m in diameter surrounded by a rope, or unbalancing him so that some part of his body other than the bottom of his feet touches the ground. There are 70 winning techniques but in general around 30 are used. The size of the wrestlers is one of the unusual elements of the sport: to compete more effectively, they pack on the weight until they sometimes weigh over 441lb/200kg. However, this does not prevent them being both supple and fast. In the ring they wear only a *mawashi*, a band of cloth wrapped around the waist and between the legs.

and the domination of one social class. Instead, they became popular sporting disciplines, with an emphasis placed on courtesy and respect for the adversary. Martial arts demand patience and humility, with the learning process often involving endless repetitions of **kata** ("forms," choreographed patterns of movement) until they can be performed to perfection. Rankings (*dan*), generally denoted by differently colored belts, classify practitioners according to their skill level. In their still relatively new guise as sports, several martial arts have undergone a real renaissance and some (including judo) are now Olympic events.

There are **dozens of martial arts** ranging from *jo-jutsu* (combat with a short staff) to *ju-jutsu* (combat with bare hands), along with *tessen-jutsu* (fighting with a war-fan—a fan made of iron) or *yabusame* (archery on horseback). The most popular, in Japan as in the rest of the world, are judo, karate, and aikido, which have existed for less than a century in their modern forms.

Judo

Derived from *ju-jutsu*, judo (the way of gentleness), was founded by Kano Jigoro in 1882. It is based on a series of throws, rolls, falls, choking techniques, arm locks, and groundwork (changing the position of the body and limbs to gain advantage and control), all designed to immobilize an opponent. Judo became a fully-fledged Olympic sport for men at the Tokyo Olympics in 1964 and for women in 1992.

Karate

Karate-do (the way of the "empty hand") originated in China at the Shaolin Temple toward the end of the 5C. In the 15C, it was adapted and developed by the people of the Ryukyu Islands (Okinawa) as a response to a decree banning them from carrying weapons. It was popularized by Funakoshi Gichin, himself a native of Okinawa and founder of the Shotokan school of karate in 1938. Modern karate is based on punching, kicking, knee or elbow strikes, and techniques using the flat hand.

Aikido

Aikido is among the more recent martial arts. It was developed between 1930 and 1960 by Ueshiba Morihei, who derived it from ancient *ju-jutsu* techniques. In contrast to judo and karate, aikido (the way of vital energy, the *ki*) is not based on attack but on controlling an opponent by utilizing their energy against them. As such, it does not focus on physical strength, and is increasingly popular with women.

SUMO

Sumo is not considered a martial art and is practiced by only a relatively small number of wrestlers (*rikishi*). However, along with baseball, it is one of the most popular sports in Japan, where champions (*yokozuna*) are treated like movie stars. Only outstanding wrestlers achieve this status, and it is extremely difficult to make it into the top two divisions (*juryo* and *makuuchi*) that regularly appear in tournaments (*basho*), and to receive a salary (other wrestlers merely get an allowance and have to act as personal attendants to the top wrestlers). These high-ranked wrestlers (*sekitori*) are also the only ones allowed to wear the *o-icho-mage* hairstyle, a fanlike topknot said to resemble a gingko leaf; it is finally cut off in a ceremony at the end of their career. The **origins of sumo** are almost as old as those of Japan itself, with many of its rituals deriving from Shintoism, such as the throwing of salt into the ring for purification before each bout, the referee's elaborate costume, etc.

Although long the exclusive preserve of Japanese wrestlers, sumo is gradually opening up to foreigners. Hawaiians were the first to break through, during the 1960s and 1970s, and their most famous wrestler Takamiyama even became the first foreign *yokozuna* in the history of sumo. More recently, several Mongolian wrestlers (notably Asashoryu, Harumafuji, Hakuho, and Rikisaburo) have held the title.

Patrick Duval

GASTRONOMY
THE ART OF LIVING

In Japan, you say *"Itadakimasu!"* when you sit down to eat. It's often translated as "bon appétit" but in fact means "I humbly receive it" and is an expression of gratitude toward everything that has contributed to the meal. It is addressed firstly to the gods (this is a Shinto custom), then to the animals and plants who gave their lives for the meal, and finally to the cook who has assembled all these ingredients in a nourishing, appetizing dish. *"Itadakimasu"* also recalls the old expression *"inochi o itadakimasu"* ("I take your honorable life), used by samurai exercising their grisly right of *kirisute gomen* (✎see p118).

Now, however, although they continue to pronounce this formula three times daily, most Japanese people give little thought to its etymology. Nevertheless, it demonstrates a special relationship with food, with particular attention paid to the products and labor that have gone into the meal.

In fact, Japanese cuisine could be viewed as quite unassuming, rather more moderate or indeed ascetic than indulgent. For instance, consider the meaning of the word *kaiseki*. Initially a simple hot stone that monks applied to their stomachs to calm hunger pangs, *kaiseki* then came to signify a light repast served before the tea ceremony. Today it is used to describe the most sophisticated kind of multi-course Japanese banquet.

"Good cooking," said French food writer Curnonsky, "is when things taste of what they are." No definition can better apply to Japanese cooking, in which cooks seek not to make foods tasty by adding sauces or combining them with other ingredients, but to bring out the flavor of each ingredient by different cooking processes. Another challenge is to get the most out of every ingredient so as to limit the waste of resources. Japanese cooking is a digestible and **well-balanced** cuisine that seems to aid good health and long life; for the past 20 years Japan has held the world record for **longevity**.

A LONG HISTORY

The history of Japanese cookery goes back to the Yayoi era (300 BC–AD 300), during which **rice** cultivation was developed, new styles of pottery and bronze appeared, and conservation techniques of drying or fermentation evolved, leading to the brewing of **sake** and later, the making of **miso**.

During the Nara (8C) and Heian (8–12C) periods, Japan came under Chinese influence. The first dairy products appeared, such as **raku**, a sharp, liquid, cheese-like nutrient. Use of vinegar and salt also date from this period. Zen Buddhism was introduced in the Kamakura era (12–14C) and its influence was significant: *shojin* is a Buddhist term meaning "to distance oneself from distractions, purify the body, and prepare oneself with ardor."

Shojin cuisine became popular and remains one of the key styles of Japanese cuisine. The Muromachi and Momoyama periods (14–16C) saw the appearance of **soy sauce, sugar**, and **konbu** (seaweed), three elements essential to the "Japanese taste." Then, owing to the development of a technique for drying bonito (skipjack tuna; *katsuo bushi)*, the **dashi** style of fish stock was invented, which still features prominently in Japanese gastronomy.

During the same period, the *Nanban* (literally "Southern barbarians," in this case meaning the Portuguese) introduced fried food into Japan, which soon developed into **tempura** (meat, fish, or vegetables deep-fried in batter). At the end of the 16C, the tea ceremony had reached such a pitch of sophistication (inspired by the master Sen no Rikyu) that a special cuisine, **kaiseki ryori**, was created to go with it. Under the influence of Buddhism (the monks of that time were essentially vegetarian), meat consumption was in theory punishable by death.

Later on, from the beginning of the Meiji era (1868), many dietary prohibitions disappeared. The emperor publicly praised the benefits of red meat and Western influence led to an influx of new products. They remain well segregated, however, and restaurants often specialize in one type of cooking:

sushi, *tonkatsu* (breaded pork), tempura, *yakitori*, and so on.

TYPES OF CUISINE

Nabemono: Japanese fondue
Nabemono means "cooking pot" and **sukiyaki** is the best-known dish in this style of cooking. It consists of thinly sliced beef cooked in a broth called *warishita*, a mixture of mirin, sake, soy sauce, and sugar. Each mouthful is then dipped in raw egg and eaten with accompaniments such as shiitake and enoki mushrooms, Chinese cabbage, chrysanthemum leaves, tofu, and, finally, thin transparent noodles called shirataki. **Shabu-shabu** is another dish made with the same basic ingredients, but with a different broth.

Sashimi, sushi: raw fish
As Japan is surrounded by sea, fish has always played a big part in the national diet, even if the consumption of meat has nowadays overtaken it for some people. On the other hand, eating raw fish has now become popular in many other countries, with **sushi** bars springing up everywhere. For example, in 2008 there were more than 800 sushi bars in Paris, and its popularity shows no signs of abating.

If you're presented with a plate of raw fish, this is not sushi but **sashimi**, usually served simply sliced and dipped in *shoyu* (soy sauce). Sushi must contain rice dressed with a mix of vinegar, salt and sugar alongside the raw fish (or other ingredients). It's commonly served as *nigiri zushi*, in which a slice of fish is placed on a small ball of seasoned rice, or as *maki zushi*, in which the fish or other filling is placed on a bed of rice laid over *nori* (seaweed), rolled into a cylinder, and then sliced in pieces. Between bites, the palate is cleansed with strips of pickled ginger. You may also see *temaki*, where you roll rice and toppings in a cone of *nori*, or *chirashi*, where it's served on a bed of seasoned rice.

Sushi and sashimi are often served in *moriawase*, or recommended assortments. These generally comprise one or two red fish such as tuna or bonito; white fish such as sea bass or bream; raw or cooked shrimp; cuttlefish; mackerel; and Japanese omelet.

Seasonal fish or shellfish, sea urchins, or eel may also be ordered, and the selection can be varied not only according to the season but also to the appetite and budget of the client. A good choice is an *omakase* menu, the chef's selection of the best of the day's products. The platter will also come with a small mound of wasabi, a fiery grated green root similar in flavor to horseradish. This is usually already added to *nigiri* and *maki*, so be sure to ask for them without wasabi if you're not keen on the taste.

Monks' cookery
Shojin cuisine, introduced to Japan in the Edo period, originated with the meager meals of Zen Buddhist monks and from Chinese *fucha* cooking. It uses only vegetables, seaweed, miso and other non-animal foodstuffs. Some temples, notably in Kyoto and Kamakura, offer visitors the chance to experience it, and there are also restaurants dedicated to it. **Kaiseki** is a branch of *shojin* cuisine adapted at the end of the 16C to accompany the tea ceremony, and is not necessarily vegetarian. It involves a succession of elaborately arranged small dishes, whose formal beauty is an aesthetic experience. It is served in *ryotei* (luxury restaurants) or *ryokan* (traditional inns).

The way of the noodle
Noodles originated in China and are now one of the most popular dishes in Japan, both as gourmet meals and int he form form of the Cup Noodle (instant noodles, which were invented in Japan).

There are three main kinds of noodles: **soba**, made with buckwheat flour and eaten hot or cold, also have a symbolic value as *soba* means "nearby." It is the custom for those who move house to offer a packet to their new neighbors.

A specialty of the island of Shikoku, **udon** are thick wheat noodles, served in a broth, usually with beef, pork, fried tofu or tempura shrimp. **Ramen** are also wheat noodles, thinner than udon and served in big bowls of stock with similar toppings. You can also find sautéed wheat noodles (yakisoba), served with pork, squid or vegetables.

Tempura: fritters

This dish of Portuguese origin is a variant of the fritters cooked in Mediterranean regions. Vegetables, shrimp, or fish are dipped in a batter of water, egg, and flour, then dropped in boiling oil. The chef's skill lies in making a crispy, non-greasy coating and retaining the product's taste and a warm center. **Tempura** is served immediately and eaten hot. A tempura set menu consists of several batches, eaten with a pinch of salt (sometimes mixed with powdered matcha), lightly dipped in a sauce of soy and grated white radish (daikon), or sprinkled with lemon juice. At the end of the meal a large *kakiage* fritter made with vegetables, shrimp, scallops, and herbs is served with rice, accompanied by a broth, miso soup, or tea.

Hot-plate cuisine

Hot-plate cooking or **teppanyaki** is popular in the US, which is why chefs who specialize in it are sometimes called Japanese "cowboys," especially since a well-known chain, *Benihana*, has popularized this kind of cooking by adding more than a touch of showmanship. In Japan, usually the cook simply grills pieces of beef, shrimp, scallops, or vegetables in front of the client, then sprinkles them with lemon juice or flambées them (sometimes with sake).

Another hot-plate specialty, **okonomi-yaki**, originates in the Kansai region. *Okonomi* means "as you like it" and *yaki* means "grilled," and as the name implies there are endless variations. The standard version, though, involves a pancake filled with a cabbage and a choice of meat, vegetables, or seafood. The cooked pancake is then coated with a sweet brown sauce to which mayonnaise, dried seaweed and a *katsuo bushi* may be added.

Breaded dishes

Tonkatsu, breaded deep-fried pork, is the Japanese interpretation of a Western

Grilled eel

© kuppa_rock/iStock

dish, the cutlet; pronounced Japanese-style this first became *katsu-retsu*, then *ton* (pork) *katsu*. Introduced into Japan around 1890, it has been popular since the 1930s. Pork fillets or sirloin are dipped into an egg and flour batter, then coated with breadcrumbs and fried. The dish is served with a finely chopped cabbage, white rice, and a *tonkatsu* sauce, which can be either mild (*amakuchi*) or a bit spicier (*karakuchi*). The pork and rice may also come in a bowl, with egg and grilled onions (**katsudon**). Alternative versions are made with shrimp (**ebifurai**) or oysters (**kakifurai**).

Unagi: grilled eel

Rich in proteins, vitamin A, and calcium, eel is usually eaten in summer. In specialist restaurants, recognizable by the character "う" (u), they are delivered live. The chef arranges them on little bamboo skewers before barbecuing or steaming them, or both methods successively. Presented on white rice in a lacquered box, the eel is anointed with a sweet sauce, the recipe for which (always a secret) varies from one restaurant to another. It can be spiced up to taste with a pinch of *sansho* pepper.

Skewered chicken

Yakitori (literally "grilled bird") consists of bite-sized pieces of chicken glazed with a soy-based sauce sweetened with sugar and *mirin*, then grilled on skewers. Salt and sauce can be added, if desired. Prepared in front of the client, the skewers are served when ready and may be seasoned with *shichimi togarashi* (a citrussy spice mix with seven ingredients). *Yakitori* originated in the Meiji period, when it was made from restaurant leftovers recovered by small traders and sold from street stands. Much later, during the 1960s, the importation of chicken from America made *yakitori* one of Japan's most popular dishes.

Along with sushi, it is also among the most widely exported. In Japan a *yakitori* meal may also include vegetables and sometimes even beef or pork, while rice is served at the end of the meal, shaped into a ball and grilled *(yaki onigiri)*, sometimes wrapped in *nori* (seaweed).

Patrick Duval

WARRIORS AND SCHOLAR MONKS

In the Edo period (17–19C), the Tokugawa shogunate applied a policy known as *sakoku* which closed Japan off almost entirely from the rest of the world. In this time, Shintoism and Buddhism formed the main basis of Japan's unique and complex cultural development.

Japan's samurai class adopted Zen Buddhism because of the moral virtues it espoused. The tea pavilion became a sacred place to the warrior elite, encouraged in this by the Zen monks who gravitated to them. So, we read about the general **Kawamori Yoshishige**: "He defended the castle of Kishikawa and personally decapitated 208 persons … He was also an excellent tea master …" In due course three important people departed from Chinese influence to make the tea ceremony distinctly Japanese. **Murata Shuko** (1422–1502) reduced the size of the pavilion, creating the *soan* style: a room spread with four or five tatami mats, where objects of varying origins combined in a purely Japanese style. The tea ceremony accordingly became more intimate, moving from its conventional hierarchic framework.

A century later, **Takeno Joo** (1504–55) returned to Zen basics by introducing greater austerity in space and materials used.

Finally, **Sen no Rikyu** (1522–91) determined the context of the ceremony, including the passage of guests via the *roji* (a garden marking the transition from the external world to the pure world of the tea pavilion) and the symbolic purification on the *tsukubai* (a stone basin in which to rinse fingers and mouth). He also separated the tea pavilion from the main residence, obliging guests to crouch to enter through the *nijiriguchi,* a small opening that compelled the greatest lord to humility.

Through the tea ceremony, the esthetic of *wabi* (simplicity) was defined: it would mark the Japanese psyche forever.

Tetsubin and kama

Tetsubin are cast-iron pots, used in feudal times to boil water for tea. There is a distinction to be made between the kettle with a handle, which was set on the fire or hung above it, and the *kama*, a round pot, generally without handles but with a lug on each side into which a metal handle can be inserted, used exclusively to heat the water in tea ceremonies. In each case these utensils were not used as teapots in the way they are used in Europe. In Japan, teapots are generally made of porcelain, even today.

The Tea Pavilion

While the Chinese tea pavilion (four pillars supporting a roof) is largely open, the Japanese pavilion is hermetically closed in upon itself. All the elements—the morning-gathered flower arrangement *(chabana)*, the filtered light on the *shoji,* and the utensils necessary for the ceremony—give the impression of a microcosm where emptiness gives meaning to fullness.

In this setting, the master can prepare tea for their guests, their measured movements showing the degree of expertise and precision that they have attained. To achieve this, the brain, breath, and abdomen (the *hara*) need to be perfectly coordinated in a discipline common to all the martial arts

© Francisco Po Egea/AGE/Photononstop

The Tea Ceremony

The Tea Ceremony *(cha-no-yu)*, or way of tea *(sado)*, is sometimes wrongly seen in the West as a simple pastime, and one limited to women, like one of those cultural activities adopted by geishas for tourists in search of the exotic, but not overly concerned with the authentic. This is a complete mis-interpretation of an activity that for centuries was a spiritual discipline central to the warrior class that ruled the country. Today it remains an important element of Japanese culture, practised across age and gender lines.

Origin and context

Between the 10C and the 14C, China's intellectual and artistic influence radiated throughout Asia. Buddhism, calligraphy, painting, poetry, pottery, architecture, the cultivation of bonsai, and flower arranging were all taken up by the Japanese aristocracy. The cultivation and culture of tea were imported by the monk **Eisai** (1141–1215) and a brew of powdered dried leaves *(matcha)*, used to banish sleepiness during meditation sessions in Zen temples.

Next, the monk **Ikkyu** (1394–1481) brought to Japan the already established Chinese custom of serving notable guests with bowls of green tea in the temple's ceremonial halls. Tea leaves were ground to a fine green powder, placed in a bowl (the *chawan*) into which hot water was poured, then the brew was mixed with the aid of a small bamboo whisk (the *chasen*). The tea ceremony became the prerogative of the ruling classes and remained so until the end of the 19C and the fall of the feudal regime.

(from which comes the term *sado* or "the way of tea").

The Japanese spirit

Harmony, respect, purity, and serenity are the four fundamental principles involved in the tea ceremony. Nevertheless, while developing the modest tea pavilion, the samurai went much further, forging throughout more than four centuries what would become Japan's great strength: study, concentration, continuous practice, precision of gestures, a sense of detail, determination, and abnegation. All qualities that the Japanese would subsequently put to use in many other situations far removed from the context of the tea ceremony.

Gilles Maucout

Nature

The Japanese archipelago's geography is one of the world's most varied, shaping the character of its inhabitants, who have had to adjust to the challenging but beautiful environment. It consists of about 3500 islands and islets lying in a long chain which extends over 1864mi/3000km between the latitudes 45° and 25° north.

A GREAT SEAFARING COUNTRY

Japan's landmass is modest: 95 percent of its 146,000sq mi/378,000sq km is taken up by the four main islands of Kyushu, Shikoku, Honshu, and Hokkaido. However, if territorial seas are included—the Exclusive Economic Zones (EEZ) that extend 200 nautical miles (230mi/370.4km) out from the coastline—the country achieves an area of 1.7 million sq mi/4.5 million sq km. As such, with Japan's 20,500mi/33,000km of coastline taken into account, its world ranking for area jumps from fiftieth to sixth.

A MOUNTAINOUS REGION

Between its northern and southern poles (Hokkaido and Okinawa), Japan's climatic and environmental range varies from the subtropical mangrove region to the resinous subpolar tip, passing through innumerable zones of broad-leaved trees (oak, beech, dog-wood, magnolia, maple), resinous trees (*Cryptomeria japonica*), and cherry trees (*Prunus*) of the temperate zones of Honshu, the large central island.

The sea gives the archipelago its heavy rainfall, two-thirds of the country getting about 5ft/1.5m of rain annually. Around two-thirds of the Japanese landmass is forested (186 tree types and 4500 plant varieties), but only one-fifth is habitable because about 70 percent is mountainous. In fact, slopes with an incline of 15 percent or greater form three-quarters of the country.

THE PLAINS

Japan has very little arable land (only 16 percent of the territory), but the rich, cultivable plains benefit from their volcanic origins. The plain of Kanto, in the Tokyo region, once the largest in Japan (around 5800sq mi/15,000sq km), is now the world's largest conurbation, with around 30 million inhabitants. Urban development and hyper-industrialization have progressively encroached on these plains.

NATURAL DANGERS

In addition to its many mountains, Japan also has numerous volcanoes. The country's highest mountain, the celebrated Mount Fuji, is in fact a volcanic cone 12,388ft/3776m high, which has been dormant since the 18C. More than 260 volcanoes have been identified

Japan Alps in autumn, Nagano, Honshu

© nevermode/iStock

in Japan, of which around a hundred are active—about 10 percent of the world's active volcanoes. This volcanic activity is due to the fact that Japan sits directly on the "Pacific ring of fire." The Japanese archipelago, situated at the confluence of the Eurasian, North American, Pacific, and Philippine Plates, is regularly shaken by these tectonic forces, leading to often devastating earthquakes. The most disastrous killed 140,000 people in 1923, more than 5500 were killed in Kobe in 1995; then the 2008 earthquakes in Iwate and Miyagi fortunately claimed only a few victims in these less-populated regions, although on a scale comparable to that of Kobe. In 2011, though, the same region was badly hit by the Great East Japan Earthquake: 9.0 on the Richter scale, it unleashed a huge tsunami on Japan's eastern coastline. It was the most powerful earthquake to ever hit Japan and one of the five most powerful earthquakes recorded worldwide, leaving over 15,000 dead and 2500 missing across 20 prefectures.

AN UNFRIENDLY HABITAT

Japanese peope have adapted to this often unfavorable natural habitat: the inhospitable slopes mean using irrigated rice cultivation, divided into plots to employ the rural population. Livestock farming is proscribed for lack of pasture, harmonizing with Buddhist principles forbidding slaughter of animals.

For heavy, humid seasons, Japanese architecture has sliding doors to permit currents of air. Faced with earthquakes or heavy snowfalls in the north, building in wood was commonplace: abundant, flexible, and lighter than stone, and more resistant to frost. They have learned how to draw hot-water springs (*onsen*) from boiling, menacing volcanoes, facilitating hygiene, moments of serenity, a place for sociability, and union with nature. And, to combat the lack of usable space, they have enlarged the coastal strips. Conversely, multiple techniques have been developed to control and circulate or dam their plentiful water supply.

The "back of Japan" and the "front of Japan"

Although Japan's central region is situated in a temperate zone, the mountainous spine that divides it in two along almost its entire length experiences some striking contrasts. In winter cold, damp winds blow from the northwest, bringing heavy snowfall on the side facing the Sea of Japan, known as the "back of Japan" (Ura Nihon). On the other side of the Japan Alps, the Pacific coastline, or "front of Japan" (Omote Nihon), is much sunnier in winter but rainy in summer. Tropical air masses from the southwest mount toward the north, bringing monsoon rains (*tsuyu*) in June, followed by tropical cyclones in September.

A RURAL EXODUS

This mastery of Japan's weather and limited space has downsides, with coastlines overdeveloped in many areas. Urban modernity has accelerated the rural exodus. Today three-quarters of the Japanese population lives in towns and cities rather than in the countryside. A quarter of the population lives in the Tokyo region alone, which is only 2 percent of the territory. High-tech infrastructure sometimes overlooks the natural dangers, though there is also great innovation in construction and architecture which can withstand earthquakes.

As a result of the many perils Japan have long had to face, there is still a great emphasis upon collective functioning and coordination, and upon efficiency and exactitude. The animistic beliefs of the Shinto faith remain, perhaps in part because because no matter how sophisticated the technological world of modern Japan becomes, it will never measure up to the power, beauty and chaos which underlies it.

Philippe Pataud-Célérier

Mount Fuji and Lake Kawaguchi in autumn, Yamanashi
© prasit chansarekorn/iStock

TOKYO AND SURROUNDINGS

Much has been written about this enormous metropolis and its sprawling suburbs, its inhabitants sometimes likened to ants scurrying around a vast nest. Tokyo is much more than this, however, even if it is slowly but surely encroaching upon the outskirts of other towns, just as it did upon Yokohama, the country's second city, only 15.5mi/25km from the capital. Including the city center, the suburbs, and the agglomeration of neighboring towns that have also been absorbed, Tokyo is in fact the largest conurbation in the world, extending across Japan's largest plain (2703sq mi/7000sq km), in the heart of the Kanto region.

Highlights

1 The superb collection of **Tokyo National Museum** (p143)

2 The breathtaking view from Roppongi's **Mori Arts Center Gallery** atop the Mori Tower (p159)

3 People watching on **Harajuku Jingu-bashi** (bridge) on a shopping trip (p169)

4 The tranquil shrine of **Meiji-jingu** (p169)

5 Day trips to historic **Nikko** (p217) and cosmopolitan **Yokohama** (p197)

The region today

The Kanto region is Japan's most densely populated, with 43.5 million inhabitants. With seven prefectures on only 8.6 percent of Japan's total surface area, it holds a third of the country's population and the seat of the central government as well; it is no surprise that is also the nation's most economically productive. With good infrastructure and a large workforce, supported by the best universities in the country funded by financial institutions ever keen to establish their headquarters close to the seat of power, Kanto additionally has the highest regional GDP in Japan. Perhaps more surprising is that less than an hour's train ride from this hyper-industrialized area are regions with very different identities, whether it be Kamakura (Kanagawa prefecture), the great city of temples and gardens, the glittering lakes of the Izu Peninsula (Shizuoka prefecture), or Nikko (Tochigi prefecture), the sepulchral beauty of which shimmers under a lofty canopy of ancient Japanese cedars.

▶ **Population:** 48 million.

Michelin Map: Tokyo & Surroundings, opposite; Regions of Japan Map 1.

Location: Situated on Honshu, the largest of the archipelago's islands, **Kanto** now includes the metropolitan prefecture *(to)* of Tokyo (13.9 million inhabitants), plus six other prefectures *(ken)*: Chiba (6.3 million inhabitants), Ibaraki (2.9 million), Tochigi (2 million), Gunma (2 million), Saitama (7.3 million), and Kanagawa (9.1 million). In the neighboring region of Chubu are the prefectures of Shizuoka (*see Izu Peninsula p246*) and Yamanashi (*see Mount Fuji p232*).

Kids: An afternoon in the futuristic port of Yokohama; the Izu Peninsula's trails; session in an *onsen*; Miura beach; a stroll among cedars in Nikko.

Timing: If you have two weeks, a good balance would be to spend a week in Tokyo, plus one day in Yokohama; then two days in Kamakura; one day each for the Miura peninsula and Hakone, or two days on the Izu Peninsula; and finally two days around Mount Fuji or in Nikko.

Don't miss: Nikko, Kamakura, Shuzenji.

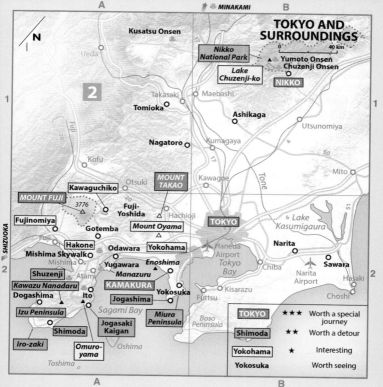

TOKYO AND SURROUNDINGS

0 — 40 km

N

SHIZUOKA

MINAKAMI

Kusatsu Onsen

Nikko National Park

Lake Chuzenji-ko

Yumoto Onsen
Chuzenji Onsen

NIKKO

Ueda

Takasaki   Maebashi

Tomioka

Ashikaga

Utsunomiya

Nagatoro

Kumagaya

Kofu   Otsuki   Kawagoe   Mito

MOUNT TAKAO

Kawaguchiko

MOUNT FUJI   3776

Fuji-Yoshida   Hachioji

Lake Kasumigaura

Fujinomiya

Mount Oyama

TOKYO

Gotemba

Hakone   Odawara   Yokohama

Haneda Airport

Narita

Mishima Skywalk   Mishima

Tokyo Bay

Chiba

Sawara

Narita Airport

Hasaki

Shuzenji   Atami

Yugawara   Enoshima   Manazuru

KAMAKURA

Kisarazu

Choshi

Kawazu Nanadaru

Dogashima   Ito

Jogashima

Yokosuka

Sagami Bay

Futtsu

Izu Peninsula

Miura Peninsula

Boso Peninsula

Jogasaki Kaigan

Shimoda

Iro-zaki

Omuro-yama

Oshima

Toshima

TOKYO	★★★	Worth a special journey
Shimoda	★★	Worth a detour
Yokohama	★	Interesting
Yokosuka		Worth seeing

Shinjuku skyline

Administrative organization

The Japanese archipelago is made up of eight regions. From north to south they are: Hokkaido (30,500sq mi/79,000sq km); the regions of Tohoku, Kanto, Chubu, Kansai (or Kinki), and Chugoku on the main central island of Honshu (87,645sq mi/227,000sq km); Shikoku (6,949.8sq mi/18,000sq km); and Kyushu (15,080sq mi/39,000sq km), which includes the Okinawan archipelago. These regions are themselves divided into 47 prefectures.

Tokyo★★★ 東京

Vast, sprawling, overpopulated... there's no shortage of adjectives to describe the largest metropolis in the world. But there is far more to Tokyo than its size, although the city's character is not so easy to pin down, as it needs redefining every time you set foot in a new neighborhood. Despite its disparate nature, however, Tokyo's inhabitants are united in the energy they devote to building and rebuilding their city, as if intent upon keeping it constantly on its toes.

A BIT OF HISTORY

A CASTLE FOR THE VILLAGE OF EDO

Tokyo didn't really put itself on the map until the end of the 15C, when Ota Dokan built the first Edo Castle (1457); until then, Edo (the old name for modern-day Tokyo, meaning "mouth of the estuary") had been a fishing village. While almost certainly occupied since ancient times—the name of one of its districts, Yayoi-cho, has come to denote the period 3C BC–AD 3C—it had no autonomy, existing first in the shadow of Nara and then of Kyoto. Following the assassination of Ota Dokan, the castle took on new significance.

Toyotomi Hideyoshi (1536–98), having just brought peace to Kanto, entrusted the province to his chief lieutenant, **Tokugawa Ieyasu** (1542–1616). Ieyasu chose Dokan's castle as his residence, continuing its fortification as the region was still unstable. Victory at Sekigahara (1600) assured him of total supremacy over a Japan that was still in the process of unification.

THE SHOGUNATE MILITARY GOVERNMENT AND THE *DAIMYO*

Three years later, Edo became the seat of the shogun's military government (*bakufu*). A town grew up beneath the castle (*jokamachi*), gravitating toward Ieyasu's centralized power base. The *daimyo* (feudal lords) were obliged to

▶ **Population:** 9.3 million in 23 wards of Tokyo, 13.9 million in prefecture.

Michelin Map: Regions of Japan map 1, Tokyo & Surroundings p131.

Tokyo city has 23 districts (wards), but the Tokyo administrative region includes 26 cities plus several small towns. To these must be added the Izu and Ogasawara islands, though the latter are 620 miles/1000 km to the south in the Pacific Ocean. The Tokyo region is the most populated of Japan's prefectures, and the metropolitan area is the world's most populous.

Kids: Ghibli Museum; Yoyogi Park; the futuristic town of Odaiba.

Don't miss: The temple of Senso-ji and Kappabashi-dori; Ameyoko Market; the Yanaka district; Chuo-dori; an evening at the Kabuki; Shibuya shopping and nightlife; Akihabara ("Electric Town"); Jinbocho, the book-selling district; Harajuku Bridge and Yoyogi Park; Shibuya crossing; a bar crawl in Golden Gai. **Shrine**: Meiji-jingu. **Architecture**: The skyscrapers of Nishi-Shinjuku; Tokyo International Forum; the National Art Center; haute couture and prêt-à-porter houses of Omotesando. **Museum**: Tokyo National Museum; Yayoi Kusama Museum; Edo-Tokyo Museum; National Museum of Modern Art; 21–21 Design Sight; Mori Art Museum; Metropolitan Museum of Photography.

SUGGESTED INTINERARIES

IN THREE DAYS:

Day 1: The temple of Senso-ji (Kaminari-mon, Nakamise-dori); sumo if a tournament is on; Ueno Park picnic lunch; Edo-Tokyo Museum; evening Kabuki performance.

Day 2: Ginza food and shopping; Imperial Palace (East Garden); Shinjuku (Shinjuku Gyoen); Golden Gai for drinks; Tokyo Metropolitan Government Building for night view of the city;

Day 3: Omotesando and Harajuku for people-watching; Meiji-jingu; Shibuya crossing, lunch and shopping; Roppongi Hills early evening; night view from Tokyo Tower.

IN SEVEN DAYS:

Day 1: Morning in Asakusa; Ueno Park picnic lunch; Tokyo Dome City late afternoon. **Day 2:** Morning at Ryogoku Kokugikan, Kiyosumi-teien; sumo if a turnament is on; afternoon in Edo-Tokyo Museum, Hokusai Museum or Tokyo National Museum; Kabuki performance. **Day 3:** Breakfast at Tsukiji outer Market; day trip to Yokohama. **Day 4:** Imperial Palace East Garden; Shinjuku; Golden Gai.

Day 5: Kamakura day trip. **Day 6:** Omotesando, Harajuku, Meiji-jingu; Shibuya crossing; Roppongi Hills early evening; Mori Tower night view.

Day 7: For kids: Ghibli Museum and Inokashira-koen or Odaiba (can replace Yokohama day), or Miura beaches.

live for half the time in Edo due to the system of *sankin kotai* (📖 *see box p134*), a relationship to the shogunate that shaped the town.

A CONTINUALLY GROWING SEAT OF POWER

The way towns and cities were organized in Japan thus started to change.

The city began to develop its structure from the **center** outward, with the *bakufu* organizing and allocating districts by social class, according to their relationship with the central power: great lords were located closest to the shogunate, followed by warriors, clerics, merchants, etc. As the elected representatives were not great in number,

the center of the city was considerably less populated than the **outlying areas**, which were packed with people from all social levels.

This distribution of people, which reflected a political and later a social order but did not take into account the criteria of town planning, had many consequences that are still visible today. Diverse urban areas formed in the outskirts, as lively as they were distant from a centralized authority, which was strict, discriminatory, and moralizing. These new suburbs, called Shinjuku, Asakusa, and Ryogoku, prospered.

From that time onward, far from both the seat of power and residential districts (like Yamanote on the slopes of

Earthquakes and violence

One hundred and forty thousand people missing, 300,000 houses destroyed ... at the time of the Great Kanto Earthquake in 1923, fire was the main scourge. It was all the more destructive because it struck at lunchtime, just as food braziers were glowing red in the streets. The lower part of town, with its densely packed wooden buildings, was reduced to ashes. Fire broke out in hundreds of places across the city and rumors began to circulate: the Koreans living in Tokyo were accused of trying to take revenge on Japan for the occupation of their country. Vigilante groups were formed and 6000 Koreans disappeared. Whether this was due to the earthquake or the ensuing violence that followed it, the exact cause of many of the deaths was never clearly established.

GETTING AROUND ON THE SUBWAY

The network has 13 lines: nine managed by **Tokyo Metro** and four by **Toei Subway**. The entrance to the first nine is indicated by a white M against a blue background; the other four can be recognized by a stylized green gingko leaf on a white background. For a station that has both lines, the panel is rectangular and shows the front view of a train.

The alpha-numeric signs combine color coding with letters and numbers. Each station is identified by two pieces of information in addition to its name and color: a **letter** that corresponds to the first letter of the name of the line (apart from in exceptional circumstances) and a **number** identifying its position between the point of departure and the terminus. "Change at Shirokane-Takanawa and then alight at Tameike-Sanno" becomes "Change at I03, then alight at N06." In addition to the fact that this information is easier to spot than the names of the stations when you're in the subway, this allows you to work out how much of your journey remains, by referring to the ascending or descending order of the numbers. A voice also announces the upcoming station and all connections in English. A subway map is available at all stations.

Websites: tokyometro.jp/en (Tokyo Metro network) and kotsu.metro.tokyo.jp/eng (Toei network). The Tokyo Metro app enables you to plan an itinerary and calculate the price and journey time (it covers Toei lines, too).

The addresses in the guide give details of the nearest station, to enable you to quickly find your bearings on the subway map.

Note: in the guide, subway station names spelt with an "n" before consonants (e.g. Jinbocho) may be spelled with an "m" on the map (e.g. Jimbocho).

For price information about tickets and passes, see Practical Information p179.

Musashino Terrace in Western Tokyo) the lower part of the city, Shitamachi, expanded to incorporate sprawling "pleasure districts" (Yoshiwara, north of Asakusa, was then the largest in Asia). With such attractions, the city grew. Large numbers of unaffiliated samurai *(ronin)* mingled with merchants and craftsmen. Despite the disasters that regularly afflicted it—the terrible fire of Meireki destroyed 60 percent of the city in 1657—by the time of eighth shogun Tokugawa Yoshimune (1684–1751), Edo already had almost a million inhabitants.

THE MEIJI ERA TO WORLD WAR II
The opening of diplomatic and commercial relations with the United States precipitated the fall of the Tokugawa shogunate. On September 13, 1868 the

---

Expenditure and revenues

Under the Tokugawa shogunate, the *daimyo* had to spend about half their time in Edo and build a residence near the castle in proportion to their status, as well as mantaining a home in their own fief. This system was known as *sankin kotai*, alternate attendance. When the *daimyo* left Edo, their families remained there, effectively as hostages. In this way the shogunate could keep the power and finances of the *daimyo*, who became indebted to Edo's merchants, in check. Rice formed the basis of the economy, with a *koku* of rice (the amount judged sufficient to feed one person for a year) being the equivalent of 5 bushels (around 50 gallons/185 liters). Samurai in the service of the shogun received a wage calculated in *koku*. Rice brokers, the *fudasashi*, stored rice belonging to the *daimyo* for a fee and also provided loans, often at very high interest rates.

Yoshiwara

North of Asakusa, Yoshiwara (now called Senzoku), was a pleasure district for three centuries (1657–1957). Unable to ban sex work and related trades (collectively known as the *mizu shobai*, or water trade), the shogun decided to contain it. The red-light district developed its brothels into premises where pleasure was elevated to an art form, depending on the status of the courtesans. Etiquette was to be obeyed and this evolved its own rules; for instance, samurai were welcome, so long as they left their weapons at the gates. Although people of all genders worked in Yoshiwara, the majority were female, and most had been indentured to a brothel at a young age due to the poverty of their family. Sex work was not the only trade plied in Yoshiwara; the whole life of the area became known as the *ukiyo* (floating world) and immortalised in *ukiyo-e* prints.

Meiji era began and Edo was renamed Tokyo (literally, "the capital of the east"). Influenced by the West, Tokyo underwent a process of modernization and rationalization. The residences of the *daimyo* were pulled down and replaced with the official buildings required by the emperor for the new Imperial Palace. Ginza was the first district to be Westernized.

The earthquake of 1923 flattened Tokyo (𝒸 *see box p133*), and it had only just been rebuilt when a quarter of the city was razed to the ground by the bombing raids of World War II (102 air raids were recorded). By the end of the war, the population of Tokyo had fallen to 3.5 million (half as many as in 1940).

TOKYO TODAY, BOTH MODERN AND TRADITIONAL

The time for reconstruction had come. With no historical constraints, the city fired the imagination of architects the world over. The 1964 Olympic Games provided the first boost, but funds were still lacking. During the 1980s, when Japan became the world's second-largest economy, the capital had a ringside seat. Every district wanted a landmark of its own: a skyscraper. Thirty percent of Tokyo's buildings date back no further than 1985 and some of the most ambitious projects were completed in less than a year.

There are some fine examples of modern architecture in Tokyo, but the impact of these is often compromised by the surrounding identikit "temples to consumption" built by renowned international companies. Despite this flurry of real estate expansion, which threatened to push ordinary people to the outskirts of Tokyo, a number of areas with a strong identity and a maze of streets lined with low-roofed houses and small gardens remain. Golden Gai is an example of gritty "old Tokyo" sitting right alongside the shining skyscrapers of Shinjuku. But however much Tokyo adorns itself with dazzling masterpieces, what continues to fascinate is its energy; the city's propensity for constantly reconstructing itself, as if to limit the impact of future disasters.

ASAKUSA ★★ 浅草
𝒸*Map IV, p138.*

Crowds have been flocking to Asakusa ever since the Tokugawa (Edo) period (1603–1867). Lying northeast of Edo, the district developed around Senso-ji, the oldest Buddhist temple in the town. In those days, life was particularly hard and paying a visit to the temple of Kannon, the most altruistic of the deities associated with mercy and compassion (𝒸*see box p139*), was a wise course of action. However, Kannon would not have proven so popular had it not been for some other factors: first, Asakusa was on the route to Yoshiwara, the famous red-light district (𝒸*see box above*), and secondly, in the mid-19C the shogun authorities had driven Kabuki, a form of theater they considered too outrageous to be performed in the center of the city, to the outskirts of town. The result was that the actors who were to play the roles of women (*onnagata*) invaded

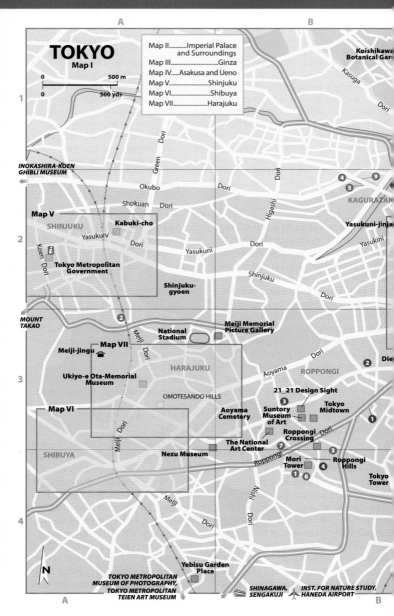

TOKYO
Map I

Map II	Imperial Palace and Surroundings
Map III	Ginza
Map IV	Asakusa and Ueno
Map V	Shinjuku
Map VI	Shibuya
Map VII	Harajuku

0 ___ 500 m
0 ___ 500 yds

Koishikawa Botanical Gardens

Kasuga Dori

INOKASHIRA-KOEN GHIBLI MUSEUM

Okubo Dori

Shokuan Dori

KAGURAZAK

Map V
SHINJUKU
Kabuki-cho

Yasukuni Dori

Yasukuni-jinja

Tokyo Metropolitan Government

Koen Dori

Yasukuni

Shinjuku Dori

Shinjuku-gyoen

Higashi Dori

MOUNT TAKAO

Meiji Dori

National Stadium

Meiji Memorial Picture Gallery

Meiji-jingu

Map VII

Aoyama Dori

ROPPONGI

Die

Ukiyo-e Ota-Memorial Museum

HARAJUKU

21_21 Design Sight

OMOTESANDO HILLS

Tokyo Midtown

Map VI

Aoyama Cemetery

Suntory Museum of Art

Roppongi Crossing

SHIBUYA

Nezu Museum

The National Art Center

Roppongi Dori

Mori Tower

Roppongi Hills

Tokyo Tower

Meiji Dori

Nishi Dori

N

TOKYO METROPOLITAN MUSEUM OF PHOTOGRAPHY, TOKYO METROPOLITAN TEIEN ART MUSEUM

Yebisu Garden Place

SHINAGAWA, SENGAKUJI

INST. FOR NATURE STUDY, HANEDA AIRPORT

Asakusa to learn their trade from the courtesans of Yoshiwara. The range of pleasures on offer changed with the times. Cinemas, funfairs, archery ranges (which sometimes became brothels), theaters, striptease joints, and cafes—Asakusa was quick to learn new ways of keeping customers happy. In the Meiji era Asakusa even became one of the famous *sakariba*, entertainment districts that gave the Japanese some respite from the rigid and class-divided strait-jacket of society. Artists, intellectuals, and writers (Kawabata wrote his *Chronicles of Asakusa* in 1929) strolled happily through the crowded district where

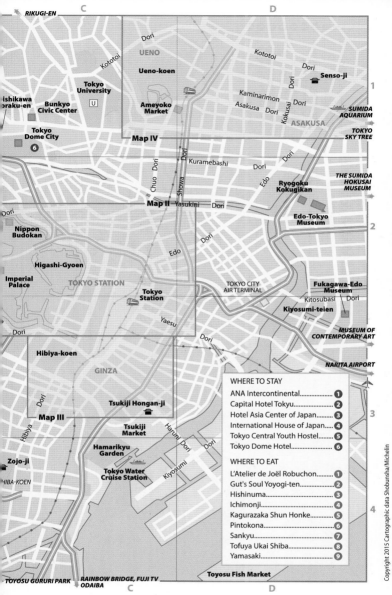

WHERE TO STAY

ANA Intercontinental	①
Capital Hotel Tokyu	②
Hotel Asia Center of Japan	③
International House of Japan	④
Tokyo Central Youth Hostel	⑤
Tokyo Dome Hotel	⑥

WHERE TO EAT

L'Atelier de Joël Robuchon	①
Gut's Soul Yoyogi-ten	②
Hishinuma	③
Ichimonji	④
Kagurazaka Shun Honke	⑤
Pintokona	⑥
Sankyu	⑦
Tofuya Ukai Shiba	⑧
Yamasaki	⑨

"all trembling desires are laid bare," regardless of class.

The bombing of World War II reduced Asakusa to ashes. The district was rebuilt, but still with narrow streets and low-roofed houses huddled around the temple, and the same daily influx of crowds still hungered for pleasure.

Twenty million people now visit Senso-ji every year. Worshippers and tourists rub shoulders with children brought here on school trips. The smallest children wear colourful round hats or baseball caps, their brass-buttoned uniforms often speckled with the crumbs of *sembei* (crunchy rice crackers) or the sugar of

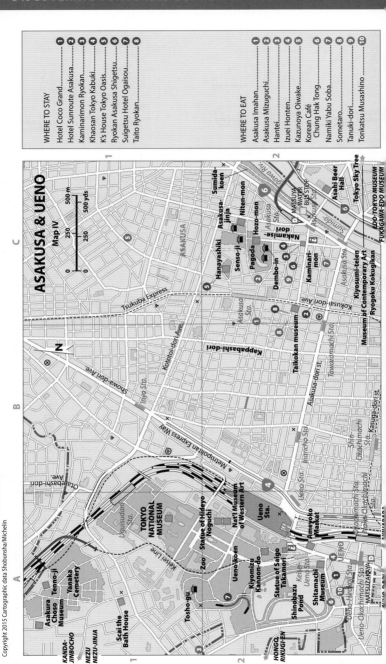

ASAKUSA & UENO

Map IV

WHERE TO STAY
Hotel Coco Grand..........❶
Hotel Sunroute Asakusa...❷
Kaminarimon Ryokan........❸
Khaosan Tokyo Kabuki......❹
K's House Tokyo Oasis......❺
Ryokan Asakusa Shigetsu...❻
Suigetsu Hotel Ogaisou.....❼
Taito Ryokan................❽

WHERE TO EAT
Asakusa Imahan...........❶
Asakusa Mizuguchi........❷
Hantei...................❸
Izuei Honten.............❹
Kazunoya Oiwake..........❺
Korean Café
Chung Hak Tong..........❻
Namiki Yabu Soba.........❼
Sometaro.................❽
Tanuki-dori..............❾
Tonkatsu Musashino.......❿

kaminari-okoshi (Japanese sweet crackers). In the evening, visitors may catch a glimpse of an elegantly attired geisha on her way to an appointment among the narrow maze of streets.

Asakusa Culture and Tourism Center ★ 浅草文化観光センター
Map IV, C2. 2-18-9 Kaminari-mon, Taito-ku. Subway A18, G19, TS01 or TX03, Asakusa, Ginza, Tobu Skytree or Tsukuba Express lines, Asakusa station. Open daily 9am–8pm. ☎03-3842-5566. ☐. The Tsukuba Express station building is less convenient.
This Kengo Kuma design in concrete, wood and glass is a modern take on a pagoda. Each of the eight floors making up the building has a different shape, lending the silhouette real movement, and each floor is ringed with variously spaced wooden slats. The center provides tourist information and you will also find exhibitions, a ticket office and a cafe here. There is a superb panoramic **view ★★** from the top floor.

Kaminari-mon ★ 雷門
The huge red paper lantern bears the Japanese characters for the imposing "Thunder Gate" and leads the way to the Senso-ji. Flanking its two red pillars, the gods of thunder *(Raijin, on the left)* and wind *(Fujin, on the right)* are charged with frightening away demons *(kimon)*.

Nakamise-dori ★ 仲見世通り
Once through the gate, this pedestrian avenue awaits, covered with paper lanterns and lined with stalls selling *omiyage* (small gifts), originally sold by priests to fund the restoration of their temple. Visitors can choose from combs, *yukata*, fans, and papier mâché masks *(see Addresses, Shopping p187)*. On the left, just before a second large gate *(Hozo-mon)* leading to Senso-ji, overlooked by a five-story **pagoda ★** (rebuilt in 1973), is the hiding place of the very secret garden of **Denbo-in ★**, attributed to Kobori Enshu, great master gardener of the 17C *(open one day a year, usually in early spring; otherwise visit by appointment only; ☎03-3842-0181).*

Heads – Kannon
Kannon is the androgynous manifestation of the Hindu god Avalokitesvara, whose name means "Lord who looks from on high," that is, who looks down with compassion. And this god is not short of pity, pausing on the path of enlightenment before becoming a Buddha to give aid to others. Kannon is often represented with 10 heads on top of her own (she is all seeing) and a body covered in 1000 hands to illustrate her infinitely welcoming nature. In China, Kannon is Guang Yin, goddess of pity and fertility. She even went on to become a famous brand name: Canon.

Senso-ji ★★ 浅草寺
Map IV, C2. Subway A18, G19, TS01 or TX03, Asakusa line, Ginza line, Tobu Skytree line, or Tsukuba Express, Asakusa station. Open daily 24hr. No charge. The Tsukuba Express station building is closer to the temple, but will not take you via Nakamise-dori.
This temple, the oldest one in the city, was founded in the 7C by two fishermen who, according to legend, happened to net a small golden statue of Kannon that had been lying in the Sumida River. Few parts of the 17C central building escaped destruction in World War II. The building you see now is a reconstruction dating from 1958. It's worth visiting to see people at prayer by the incense burner, and for the bustle of the temple precincts, but the inside of Senso-ji is of little interest. To the right of the **main temple ★** stands the Shinto shrine **Asakusa-jinja**, erected in 1649 and also known as Sanja-sama (Shrine of the Three Guardians), dedicated to the two fishermen.
The **Sanja Matsuri**, one of the most popular festivals in the city, takes place here every year in the third weekend of May. Two million people join the crowd of around a hundred *mikoshi* (portable shrines) paraded through the streets.

Taikokan (Drum Museum) ★★
太鼓館

🕭Map IV, C2. 4F 2-1-1 Nishiasakusa, Taito-ku. Access to the museum is through Miyamoto Unosuke Shoten, famous Japanese drum makers since 1861. ○Open Wed–Sun 10am–5pm. ∞¥500. ℘03-3842-5622. miyamoto-unosuke.co.jp/taikokan.

Opened in 1988, this small, very educational museum has hundreds of percussion instruments on display from around the world: from New Guinea (Asmat) and Vanuatu, to Africa. Some of the drums can be played.

All types of Japanese drum are represented, from the *tsuzumi* (a small hand drum shaped like an hour-glass) to the *oke-daiko* with a shell made of strips of wood joined together and covered with hide and fastened with ropes.

Kappabashi-dori ★ かっぱ橋通り
🕭Map IV, B2.

A street of specialist kitchenware, from ovens to those famous plastic plates of food (*mihon*) that customers drool over in Japanese restaurants. There's a large choice of items at very low prices.

Sumida-koen ★★ 隅田公園
🕭Map IV, C2.

On either side of the Sumida River, between the Azuma and Sakura bridges, Sumida Park comes to life when the cherry blossom trees are in flower, and for the annual firework display (*hanabi taikai*) on the last Saturday in July. One of the most spectacular in Tokyo, the display has been held since the Edo period.

▶ Head toward the bank of the Sumida River.

Dealing with fate

Leaning over the huge bronze censer, passers-by try to waft the healing virtues of the incense fumes toward them, even if it might sting their eyes a little. Students write their wishes for success on little wooden plaques, and give small offerings (*ema*) signifying "horse image" (the preferred mount of the gods). Businessmen attach small stickers (*senjafuda*) with their own name or their company's onto the columns of the shrine, while schoolchildren take small pieces of paper (*omikuji*) out of a wooden box and impatiently unfold them to read their fortune. The luckiest ones will find the *daikichi* (extremely lucky) or *kichi* (very lucky) characters written there. Those not so lucky will have *shokichi* (a bit lucky), or worse, *kyo* (bad luck). In the latter case the paper will be tied up in the temple grounds to be soaked by the rain and battered by the wind.

Asahi Beer Hall ★
スーパードライホール

Map IV, C2. 1-23-1 Azumabashi, Sumida-ku.

Located on the banks of the Sumida River, the Asahi Beer Hall is easily identified: a large golden flame sculpture "flickers" above its opaque black tomb-like walls. The "flame" is intended to evoke the light, golden head of Asahi beer just after it's been poured. Weighing no less than 300 tons, buikders had to use cutting-edge naval construction techniques to construct it. No one really calls it The Asahi Flame; instead it's known as *kin no unko*, the golden turd, and it's hard to deny the resemblance.

Tokyo Skytree ★★
東京スカイツリー

Map I, D1. 1-1-2 Oshiage, Sumida-ku. Subway TS02, Tobu Skytree line, Tokyo Skytree station; or TS03, A20, Z14 or KS45, Tobu Skytree, Asakusa, Hanzomon Keisei Oshiage lines, Oshiage Skytree station. Open daily 8am–10pm *(last admission 9pm).* ¥1000–¥4200 *(children from ¥550). tokyo-skytree.jp.*

At a height of 2080ft (634m), with 31 floors, Tokyo Skytree is the world's tallest tower. It was inspired by 8C Japanese building techniques. A steel mesh frame sourrounds a central pillar to which it is connected by dampers. Two elevators speed you up to the observation decks, Tembo Deck at 1150ft (350m) and Tembo Galleria at 1480ft (450m), from where you can enjoy a dizzying panorama over Tokyo and to Mount Fuji on a clear day.

Sumida Aquarium ★
すみだ水族館

Map I, D1. 5–6F Tokyo Skytree Town Solamachi, 1-1-2 Oshiage, Sumida-ku. Subway TS02, Tobu Skytree line, Tokyo Skytree station; or TS03, A20, Z14 or KS45, Oshiage Skytree station. Open daily 9am–9pm. ¥2050 *(children ¥600–¥1500). sumida-aquarium.com/en. Allow 1hr.*

👥 A collection of tropical fish, penguins and seals on two floors, much of it designed to look like the depths of the ocean around the Ogasawara Islands.

RYOGOKU ★ 両国
Map I; D2–3, p136.

Cross the Ryogoku Bridge over the **Sumida River** to reach the district of Ryogoku. Famous in the Edo period as one of the city's largest entertainment areas (the artist Hokusai regularly made sketches of what went on), nowadays it attracts visitors to the sumo wrestling tournaments held over a period of two weeks, three times a year in January, May, and September (*see Addresses p188*).

Ryogoku Kokugikan ★
両国国技館

Map I, D2. 1-3-28 Yokohami, Sumida-ku. Subway E12 or JB21, Oedo line or JR Chuo-Sobu line, Ryogoku station. Museum open Mon–Fri 10am–4.30pm. Closed during tournaments. *No charge. sumo.or.jp*

The sport of sumo wrestling (*see p118*) was awarded the largest sports stadium in the whole of Asia in 1909: the Kokugikan or National Sports Stadium. It's well worth attending a few bouts if you can (they take place over the course of a day, with the best wrestlers, or *rikishi*, on last), but it's often difficult to get tickets (*¥1000–¥50,000*). There's a small museum next to the stadium, which merits a quick look.

See also p188.

Edo-Tokyo Museum ★★
江戸東京博物館

Map I, D2. 1-4-1 Yokoami, Sumida-ku. Subway E12 or JB21, Oedo line or JR Chuo-Sobu line, Ryogoku station, exit A4. Open Tue–Sun 9.30am–5.30pm *(Sat 7.30pm).* ¥600 *(excludes special exhibitions).* 03-3626-9974. *edo-tokyo-museum.or.jp.* ✉. *English tours available 10am–3pm, book ahead.*

The style of this imposing building, erected on pillars, brings to mind both a traditional rice loft and a pair of *geta* (wooden clogs). It houses a fascinating museum that tells the history of the city from the Edo period to modern-day Tokyo (*allow at least 2hr to visit its 323,000sq ft/30,000sq m space, which starts on the 6th floor*).

The full-scale replica of **Nihonbashi** (**Bridge of Japan**; ☝see p153) leads into the colorful world of the Edo period. Models (like the one of the impressive residence of the *daimyo* Matsudaira Tadamasa) and full-scale reconstructions of districts, commercial buildings, a printing workshop, and a Kabuki theater show how the city planned by Tokugawa Ieyasu (1542–1616) evolved. By the 18C it already contained around a million inhabitants, 60 percent of them men.

Museum of Contemporary Art Tokyo ★★
東京都現代美術館

☝*Map I; D3, off map. 4-1-1 Miyoshi, Koto-ku. 10min walk from Kiyosumi-Shirakawa subway station, exit B2 (Hanzomon line) or 15min from Kiba subway station, exit 3 (Tozai line).* ◷*Open Tue–Sun 10am–6pm.* ◷*Closed twice a year for change of exhibition, so it's advisable to check.* ⚏*¥500 (excluding special exhibitions).* ✆*03-5245-4111. mot-art-museum.jp/en.* ⌐.

As well as holding excellent special exhibitions, MCAT has a permanent collection covering the last 50 years of 20C art: Gerhard Richter, Roy Lichtenstein, David Hockney, Frank Stella, Julian Schnabel, and many Japanese artists such as Jiro Yoshihara, Katsura Funakoshi, and Kusama Yayoi.

Sumida Hokusai Museum ★
すみだ北斎美術館

☝*Map I; D2, off map. 2-7-2 Kamezawa, Sumida-ku. 10min walk from the Museum of Contemporary Art.* ◷*Open Tue–Sun 9.30am–5.30pm.* ⚏*¥400 (excludes special exhibitions). hokusai-museum.jp.*

This museum, which opened its doors in November 2016, is housed in a superb contemporary building designed by Sejima Kazuyo. The museum's temporary exhibitions and (very informative) permanent collection showcase every aspect of the inspired and extremely prolific work of Katsushika Hokusai (1760–1849), the most famous woodcut artist of the Edo period, who was born in the Sumida ward.

Fukagawa-Edo Museum ★
深川江戸資料館

☝*Map I, D3. 1-3-28 Shirakawa, Koto-ku. Subway Z11 or E14, Hanzomon or Oedo lines, Kiyosumi-Shirakawa subway station, exit A3. kcf.or.jp/fukagawa.* ◷*Open daily 9.30am–5pm.* ◷*Closed 2nd & 4th Mon of the month.* ⚏*¥400.*

A fine reconstruction of the Fukagawa district, a network of wooden workshops, warehouses, and dwellings that flanked the left bank of the Sumida River in the 19C. One of its streets leads down to the port.

Kiyosumi-teien★   清澄庭園

☝*Map I, D3. 3-3-9 Kiyosumi, Koto-ku. Subway Z11 or E14, Hanzomon or Oedo lines, Kiyosumi-Shirakawa subway station, exit A3.* ◷*Open 9am–5pm (last entry 4.30pm).* ⚏*¥150.*

This magnificent, little-known garden from the Edo period is worth a detour, particularly in spring when the azaleas create a blaze of color on the little hill overlooking the pond. Its banks are dotted with beautiful stones from all four corners of Japan. There's also an excellent *ryotei* (traditional restaurant) on site, which requires reservations well in advance.

UENO AND SURROUNDINGS
★★★ 上野

☝*Map IV, p138.*

Ueno district is famous for its park. Built on a plain and slightly elevated, it was the object of many a *daimyo's* desires in the past. When the Tokugawa family took control, some fine buildings were constructed, such as the temple of Kan'ei-ji built by Tenkai, advisor to the first Tokugawa shogun.

Only the beautiful five-story pagoda remains today; the rest were destroyed during the Meiji Restoration, when the emperor and the Tokugawa clan struggled for power. If today Ueno is visited for its museums, it really is a must in April for the traditional *hanami*, the viewing and enjoyment of the hundreds of cherry blossoms here.

Ueno-koen in spring

© idmanjoe/iStock

Ueno-koen ★ 上野公園

🕭*Map IV, A1/2. Subway G16, H17, JK30 or JY05, Ginza, Hibiya, JR Yamanote and JR Keihin-Tohoku lines, Ueno Station, Koen exit ("Park Exit"); subway KS01, Keisei main line, Keisei-Ueno Station.*

The biggest park in Tokyo (210 acres/ 85ha) is the oldest public garden in Japan. The tour begins with the museums by JR Ueno Station and finishes at the statue of Saigo Takamori, near Keisei-Ueno Station. If you're short of time, make a point of seeing the **Honkan** and the **Gallery of Horyu-ji Treasures** in the Tokyo National Museum.

National Museum of Western Art ★ 国立西洋美術館

🕭*Map IV, A2.* ◷*Open Tue–Sun 9.30am–5.30pm (Fri & Sat 8pm).* ☺*¥500 (no charge 2nd & 4th Sat each month; excludes special exhibitions). nmwa. go.jp/en.* 🖃.

Designed by Le Corbusier, this museum was opened in 1959 to house the collection of Kojiro Matsukata (1865–1950), a naval construction entrepreneur who made his fortune during World War I. He assembled an exceptional collection of Impressionist art, much of it acquired in Paris. Sadly, a great deal was destroyed during World War II, when works stored in Britain were destroyed by fire and those left in Japan by Allied bombing. A few pieces remain, including some of the most important: Rodin sculptures, paintings by Monet, Gauguin, Denis

(Young Girl with a Hen), and Gustave Moreau's magnificent *pietà*. Following its 50th anniversary, the museum now houses an expanded collection from the Renaissance to World War II, but the Impressionist paintings remain the keystone of this collection.

Tokyo National Museum★★★ 東京国立博物館

🕭*Map IV, A1.* ◷*Open Tue–Sun 9.30am–5pm (Fri & Sat 9pm), last admission 30min before closing.* ☺*¥620 (excludes special exhibtions). tnm.jp/?lang=en.* 🖃.

Opened in 1872, the oldest and largest museum in Japan *(around 110,000 pieces, 87 National Treasures)* is housed in five main buildings.

Hon-kan ★★★ – The central building, which is also called the Japanese Gallery, is as well stocked as a miniature Smithsonian or Tate: 23 galleries are located on two floors, covering the Jomon period to World War II. Begin on the **second floor** with the Jomon culture and move on to an introduction to Buddhism in Japan (6C), painting and calligraphy from the National Treasures, art of the Court (Heian era), Zen art (Kamakura and Muromachi periods), tea ceremony art, samurai armor, everyday objects, etc. The galleries with paintings and some of the major works are particularly worth visiting: **Akasagarbha ★★★**, *the Peacock King*, **the Sixteen Arhats** of the Heian era, **Bodhidharma beneath a pine**

Haniwa, Tokyo National Museum

tree from the Kamakura era, the **Jigoku Zoshi** ★★, the *Handscroll of Buddhist Hells*. The **Gaki Zoshi** ★★★, the *Scroll of the Hungry Ghosts* (Heian era), is particularly unmissable, a mythical Asian counterpart to the works of Bosch or Bruegel. Ike no Taiga's **Chinese landscape** ★★★ (18C) is delightful. Room 8 looks at the two main movements in calligraphy: **Oieryu** (used by the court nobles), a traditional Japanese movement that developed independently from the Heian era onward, and **Karayo**, which was initially linked to Chinese ideograms but then evolved, developing a formal, more abstract, and creative approach better enabling it to reflect the personality and creativity of the calligrapher. Karayo became very popular among followers of Confucianism, Zen priests, poets, and artists. Rooms 9 and 10, devoted to Noh and Kabuki masks, *ukiyo-e*, and the fashion of the Edo period, are a welcome digression into the world of Japanese art. Ceramic items, sabers, and lacquerware complete this vast collection.
Heisei-kan ★ – *Located behind the Hon-kan and linked to it by a corridor.* Displayed on the ground floor is a large array of archeological objects, mainly proto-Japanese, from 30,000 BC to the 19C. It includes superb **Dotaku** ★★★ (Yayoi period) bronze bells decorated in relief with scenes of everyday life,

magnificent **Haniwa** ★★★ terracotta funeral figurines (Kofun period, 6C) and the famous **dogu** ★★★, terracotta "clay dolls," probably linked to the cult of fertility (late Jomon, 1000–300 BC). Special exhibitions are held on the floor above.

▶ As you retrace your steps toward the main door you cross the **Hyokei-kan** (open only for special exhibitions).

Gallery of Horyu-ji Treasures ★★★ – *Just behind the Hyokei-kan.* In 1878 the temple of Horyu-ji in Nara, a masterpiece of the Asuka era, donated more than 300 objects to the Imperial Household. Since 1999, these pieces—most of which date from the 7C—have been displayed in a building worthy of their splendor, designed by the architect Yoshio Taniguchi (1937–), who is best known for his redesign of New York's Museum of Modern Art (MoMA).
At the entrance you can admire one of the most remarkable objects in the collection: the **kanjoban** ★★★ (7C). This openwork gilt bronze banner was once used for Buddhist ceremonies. In the second gallery there is a beautifully presented group of 48 bronze statues of the Buddha (7C). The **Seated Nyorai** ★★★ and the **Bodhisattva in half-lotus position** ★★★ (Asuka period) are exceptionally delicate.

A number of these pieces, such as the magnificent **Buddha Triad ★★★** (6C), were produced in Korea during the period of the Three Kingdoms and then imported into Japan. These pieces had a determining influence on the Japanese imagination, which at the time—the Buddha was not long known in Japan—was searching for a way to depict Buddhist iconography.

Each Buddha has a fine *kohai*, halo, encircling the head. The third gallery contains **gigaku ★★★** masks (among the oldest in Japan) made of camphor wood, paulownia, or painted ramie. They are said to have been used during the spectacles that preceded the Buddhist ceremonies copied from the Korean kingdom of Paekche during the first half of the 7C.

Galleries 4 and 5 contain wooden, lacquer, and metal objects (shrines, sutra boxes, bows, and *inro*, small medicine boxes). In the last room (6) there is a very valuable **illustrated biography ★★★** of Shotoku (574–622), the Prince Regent who turned Japan into a Buddhist state. These 10 screen paintings by Hatano Chitei (1069, Heian period) depict episodes from the Prince's life and were originally in the *Eden* (Hall of Paintings), in the *To-in*, the eastern precinct of Nara's Horyu-ji. In the interests of preservation they are not on permanent display.

Toyo-kan – The Asian Gallery (excluding Japanese art), displayed over three floors, is devoted to art and archeology from Egypt to China. **First floor:** sculptures from India (Mathura Head of Buddha, 2C), Pakistan (Gandara Seated Buddha), and China; Egyptian and South east Asian archeology. **Second floor:** Chinese archeology. **Third floor:** Korean and Central Asian archeology.

Ueno Tosho-gu ★★
上野東照宮

Map IV, A1. In Ueno Park, at the end of the main avenue joining the National Museum of Western Art. Open 9am–5.30pm Mar–Sept; 9am–4.30pm Oct–Feb. ¥500 (with winter peony garden, ¥1100). uenotoshogu.com/en.
This Shinto shrine was established by Tokugawa Iemitsu in memory of his grandfather **Tokugawa Ieyasu** (1542–1616), founder of the Tokugawa dynasty. Built in 1627 and enlarged in 1651 to house shogun relics, it has miraculously escaped the various natural and man-made disasters that have afflicted Tokyo. Don't miss the magnificent Chinese-style gate *(kara-mon)*. The two dragons on either side are the work of the great left-handed sculptor **Hidari Jingoro** (1594–1634; see Nikko p221). The doors and columns are entirely covered in gold leaf. Inside there are beautiful sculpted ceilings above painted walls, the work of **Kano Tanyu** (1602–74), the most distinguished painter of the Kano School.

From the preceding temple, take the Aesop footbridge. You will see a five-story pagoda, the last trace of the Kan'ei-ji temple built for the Tokugawa family, burned down during the Meiji Restoration, moved here in 1957.

Ueno Zoo ★ 上野動物園
Map IV, A1. Open Tue–Sun 9.30am–5pm (last entry 4pm). ¥600 (children up to 12 no charge). tokyo-zoo.net/english/ueno/index.html.
Japan's oldest zoo (1882) is still open for business, although a sad episode during World War II nearly put an end to it.

Figuring that the zoo would be bombed, releasing the animals into the streets to terrorize the inhabitants, the Japanese army demanded that they all be killed. The staff begged for a reprieve or to be allowed to relocate the animals, but were refused, and so the animals were poisoned (the elephants refused their food and died of starvation).

The zoo currently has 2600 animals across 464 species, including its star attractions: giant pandas and a Sumatran tiger. Unsurprisingly for such a venerable zoo, while the enclosures seem sufficient for the smaller animals, they're far too small to give the larger animals enough room and stimulation.

Shinobazu Pond ★★ 不忍池
Map IV, A2.

A wildlife protection area that is part of Ueno Park actually consisting of three ponds. A strip of land forms a causeway across the lotus beds for which Shinobazu Pond is famous to a tiny man-made island on which sits **Benten-do**, a 17C temple (rebuilt in 1958) dedicated to Benten, goddess of the arts, the sciences, and wisdom.

Kiyomizu Kannon-do ★
清水観音堂

Map IV, A2. South of the Shinobazu Pond (with Hasu Pond on the right), heading toward Kiyomizu.

A pale imitation of Kiyomizu-dera in Kyoto (*see p333*), though still lovely, this temple, also called Kan'ei-ji in reference to the Kan'ei period (1624–44) in which it was built, was initially constructed in 1631 at the highest point of Ueno Park (Suribachi-yama). Its founder, the high priest Tenkai, superintendent of the Tendai Buddhist school, intended it to protect the northern gate of Edo Castle (now the Imperial Palace), a key point vulnerable to attack.

At the end of the 17C, however, it was transferred to its current location and dedicated to **Senju Kannon**, the deity with a thousand arms, whose statue can only be seen in February. The faithful also pray to **Kosodate Kannon**, protector of childbearing women. Women whose prayers for fertility have been granted must offer a doll to the goddess to compensate for the real child that they have taken from her. These dolls are cremated on September 25 every year in a special ceremony.

Statue of Saigo Takamori ★
西郷隆盛像

Map IV, A2. About 110yd/100m SW of Kiyomizu Kannon-do. Call in at the Ueno Royal Museum to check on the special exhibitions program.

Saigo Takamori (1828–77) was the last of the true samurai warriors. At first a fervent advocate of the Meiji revolution, he distanced himself from it once he realized that the emperor's modernization plans deprived the samurai of their status. He committed *seppuku* (ritual suicide) after defeat at the famous "Satsuma Rebellion" in 1877 (*see p599*), but was rehabilitated by the emperor in 1891. His statue shows him wearing a traditional *yukata* and carrying his sword. In 2003, a Hollywood version of his story was told in Edward Zwick's film *The Last Samurai* (with Tom Cruise).

Shitamachi Museum ★★
下町風俗資料館

Map IV, A2. At the southeast corner of Shinobazu Pond. Subway: Ueno or Ueno-Okachimachi (E09). Open Tue–Sun 9.30am–4.30pm. ¥300. taitocity. net/zaidan/shitamachi.

This fascinating museum recreates the district of Shitamachi as it was from the end of the Edo period to the Taisho era, before it was destroyed in the 1923 earthquake (*see box p133*) and World War II bombing raids. The ground floor is the old house of a manufacturer of *hanao*, cloth straps that fastened *zori* (sandals) and *geta* (wooden clogs). In the 1920s it was common practice to change the color and design every season, and *hanao* workshops lined the banks of the Sumida River, each selling around 1000

Nagaya

Nagaya, literally "long, narrow houses," gave structure to the lower town of Shitamachi, and particularly to the narrow streets and alleyways *(roji)* that fed into its main thoroughfares. There were two kinds of row house, those which faced the street *(omote nagaya: front nagaya)* or those with a small interior courtyard *(ura nagaya: back nagaya)*. As the latter could not be used for commerce they were occupied mainly by poor tenants, whose main activity, as Philippe Pons recounts in his book *From Edo to Tokyo*, was "selling the tenants' excrement to local peasant farmers for use as fertilizer."

Ameyoko Market

straps per day. The shoes were so ubiquitous there's a specific term for the sound they make on the ground: *kara-koro*. There is also a shop that sold *dagashi* candies, literally "second-class candies," and a workshop manufacturing *dayoka* copper, essential for making and repairing teapots, water containers, and gutters. The pieces of orange peel hanging on the walls dispelled bad smells from the drains, which at that time ran down the center of the street. On the first floor are some historical documents and an array of traditional toys.

Ameyoko Market ★
アメヤ横丁

Map IV, A2. The market runs along the train tracks between Ueno and Okachimachi stations. ⏱ *Open daily 10am–7pm (times vary between the stalls). ameyoko.net.*

Opened in 1883 and reconstructed after the 1923 earthquake, today Ueno Station is a major Tokyo rail hub. In the years immediately after the Second World War, it became a big center for the black market. When stalls began to appear in the streets and beneath bridges, what is now the fascinating maze of Ameya Yokocho market was born. Farmers made candies *(ame)* from sweet potatoes, a rare but inexpensive commodity, to sell to passers-by and "Ameya-yokocho" ("candy sellers' alley") eventually became "Ameyokocho."

YANAKA DISTRICT ★★ 谷中
Map IV, A1. Subway C15, JR/Keisei Line, Nippori Station.

Nature manages to triumph over the concrete of the city in this peaceful district, where it's pleasant to stroll among temples and wooden houses surrounded by wild grasses. This well-preserved and tranquil environment (there are few cars) escaped the flames of the Great Fire of Meireki in 1657, the earthquake of 1923, and the bombing raids of 1945.

▶ To explore Yanaka, from Nippori Station (Yamanote Line) either take Yanaka Ginza street (west exit), full of stands selling *senbei,* tofu, and other treats, or head for Tenno-ji (south exit) and cross the small Yanaka Cemetery.

Yanaka Cemetery ★★ 谷中霊園
Map IV, A1.

A vast cemetery lined with gravestones polished like pebbles on the seashore. Famous for its cherry blossom in April, it has a section dedicated to the Tokugawa clan; the last of the shoguns, **Tokugawa Yoshinobu** (1837–1913) is buried here.

Asakura Museum of Sculpture
★★ 朝倉彫塑館
Map IV, A1. 7-18-10 Yanaka, Taito-ku. Subway JY07, JK32, JJ02, KS02 or NT01, with JR, Keisei and Toei lines, Nippori Station. ⏱ *Open Tue, Wed & Fri –Sun*

*9.30am–4.30pm (last admission 4pm).
¥500. taitocity.net/zaidan/asakura.*
The building housing this museum
was the studio and residence of sculptor **Asakura Fumio** (1883–1964), the
father of modern Japanese sculpture.
His bronzes, particularly, studies of cats,
have a feline fluidity. There's a fine **view**
of the district from the rooftop garden
and a charming small Japanese garden
in the central courtyard. Note that you'll
need to remove your shoes when entering, and should wear socks.

Scai the Bathhouse ★★
スカイ・ザ・バスハウス
*Map IV, A1. Kashiwayu-ato, 6-1-23
Yanaka, Taito-ku. 10min walk from
Nippori or Nezu stations. Open Tue–
Sat noon–6pm. Closed public hols.
No charge. scaithebathhouse.com/en.*
This ancient public bathhouse has been
turned into a leading contemporary art
gallery, which displays often quite dar-
ing works that are changed regularly.
Around 110yd/100m away is the **Shita-
machi Museum Annex** (*open Tue–
Sun 9.30am–4.30pm; no charge*), with
displays on the traditional culture of the
Shitamachi, a working-class neighbor-
hood, where you can also see inside an
early 20C liquor house.

Rikugi-en ★★ 六義園
*Map I; C1, off map. 6-16-3 Honkoma-
gome, Bunkyo-ku. Subway N14 or
JY10, Namboku or JR Yamanote lines,
Komagome Station. Open daily
9am–5pm (last entry 4.30pm). ¥300.
tokyo-park.or.jp/teien/en/rikugien*
A gorgeous garden created in 1702 by
Yanagisawa Yoshiyasu, a *daimyo* and
official of the fifth shogun. A cultured
man of letters, he designed the garden
to evoke 88 scenes from classical Japanese poetry.

AKIHABARA DISTRICT ★
秋葉原
*Map IV; A2, off map. Subway H15,
JK28, JY03, JB19 or TX01, Hibiya line, JR
Keihin-Tohoku, Yamanote or Chuo-Sobu
lines, Tsukuba Express line, Akihabara
Station.*

From the southern point of Ueno Park
Chuo-dori drops down to Ginza. On the
way it crosses more than 0.6mi/1km of
Akihabara, an electronic paradise nicknamed "Electric Town," which attracts
technology, video gaming and *anime*
fans— indeed, *otaku* of all stripes. The
fashion here is for maid cafes and butler
cafes, and the *cosplay* girls of Harajuku
(*see p169*) come to strut their stuff here
each week, on the district's main street
of Showa-dori. Even if you're not into
Japan's booming geek culture, it can be
an eye-opening place to wander around
for an afternoon

KANDA-JINBOCHO DISTRICT★
神田神保町
*Map IV; A1, off map. Subway I10,
S06 or Z07, Toei Mita, Toei Shinjuku
and Hanzomon lines, Jinbocho
Station, exit A2.*
The *Jinbocho* district, known as the
"book town" of Japan, has around 160
bookshops and stands selling some 10
million books on every subject under
the sun. It's not all in Japanese, either:
foreign literature, including some out-
of-print material, can also be found here.
For even the slightest of bookworms,
nosing around here is a real pleasure,
despite or perhaps even because of the
casual disorder.

IMPERIAL PALACE AND
SURROUNDINGS ★★ 皇居
Map II, p150.
The Imperial residence has been here
for nearly three centuries. The old Edo
Castle was destroyed to make way for
this park of 250 acres (101ha). It is closed
to the public except on February 23,
the emperor's birthday, and New Year's
Day. The palace remains the primary
residence of the emperor and his family. The park is virtually empty except for
the palace buildings in the west part of
the grounds. The space here is a luxury
in a city where buildings are crammed in
together, and a haven for nature.

Imperial Palace ★ 皇居
*Map II, A2 & A3. Subway C10, Chiyoda
Line, Nijubashimae Station, exit 6.*

Niju-bashi, Imperial Palace

© golaizola/iStock

Surrounded by outer walls, ramparts, and moats, the first Edo Castle was built in 1457 by Ota Dokan (1432–86) to dominate the Bay of Tokyo and the Kanto plain. When Tokugawa Ieyasu took over the castle, which had fallen into ruin after the assassination of Ota, he took on the task of enlarging it.

With its sturdy keep looking down on the city, the castle was tangible evidence of the shogun's power. The city's increasing need for defenses (waterways, levees, urban fortifications, strengthening of the estuary bank below the castle, etc.) became the driving force behind its construction and development (*see A Bit of History p132*). With the Meiji Restoration (1868) and the removal of the Imperial Court from Kyoto to Tokyo, the castle was transformed into the Imperial Palace. The bombing raids of World War II reduced it to rubble, but in 1968, it was rebuilt exactly as before. In the 1990s further Imperial residences were added.

Imperial Palace visit ★

⏱*Two tour slots per day Tues–Sat: 9am–11.15am & 12.30–2.45pm.*

⏱*Closed Sun & Mon; Dec 28–Jan 4; afternoons of Jul 21–Aug 31; public hols.* ⚲*No charge. Reservations required at least four days in advance via sankan. kunaicho.go.jp/english/guide/koukyo. html or ☎03-5223-8071. Limited number*

of same-day tickets available from Kikyo-mon (distributed 1hr before tour). Persons under 18 must be accompanied by an adult. A passport and permit (print out, or request by phone and collect from the Imperial Household Agency) are required. Arrive at Kikyo-mon 10min before start of tour (subway Nijubashi-mae Station, exit 6; 5min walk). Audio-guide and brochures in English.

The only way to see inside the place is on one of these (quite informative) guided tours, although the areas open to the public are still very restricted. The elegant **Nijubashi** area with its two bridges across the moat is accessible.

Higashi-gyoen (East Garden) ★
皇居東御苑

♿*Map II, B2. Subway C11, M18, I09, T09 or Z08, Otemachi Station, exit C10 or C13.* ⏱*Open Tue–Thu & Sat–Sun 9am–4/5pm (6pm mid-Apr–Aug).* ⚲*No charge.*

The East Garden was opened to the public in 1968, and with its fine lawns and 250,000 trees, it's a pleasant place to stroll. Also here are the remains of Edo Castle (outer walls of imposing square blocks of stone). The best way to enter is through the main gate (**Ote-mon**), which was an integral part of the castle. Just inside is the **Sannomaru Shozo-kan**, the Museum of the Imperial Col-

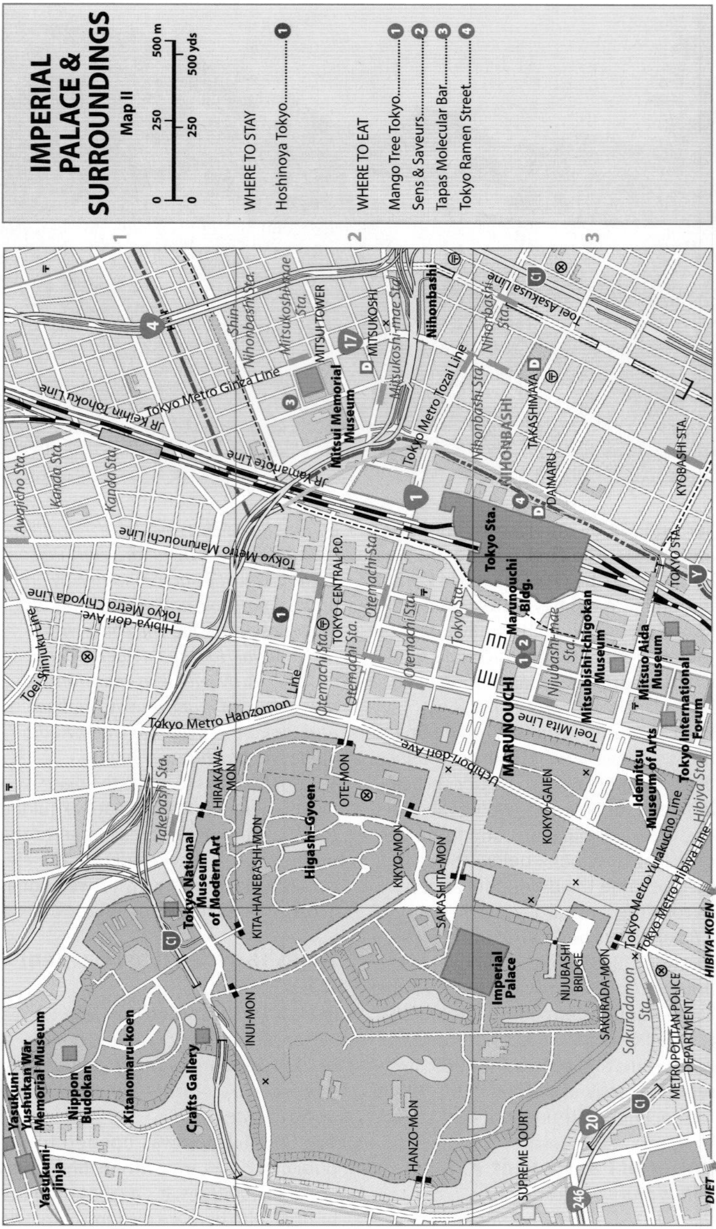

IMPERIAL PALACE & SURROUNDINGS

Map II

0   250   500 m
0   250   500 yds

WHERE TO STAY

Hoshinoya Tokyo................ ❶

WHERE TO EAT

Mango Tree Tokyo................ ❶
Sens & Saveurs.................... ❷
Tapas Molecular Bar........... ❸
Tokyo Ramen Street........... ❹

Copyright 2015 Cartographic data Shobunsha/Michelin

Yasukuni-Jinja
Yasukuni War Memorial Museum
Yushukan Museum
Nippon Budokan
Kitanomaru-koen
Crafts Gallery
Tokyo National Museum of Modern Art
SUPREME COURT
HANZO-MON
INUI-MON
KITA-HANEBASHI-MON
HIRAKAWA-MON
TAKEBASHI Sta.
Higashi-Gyoen
OTE-MON
KIKYO-MON
SAKASHITA-MON
KOKYO-GAIEN
Imperial Palace
NIJUBASHI BRIDGE
NIJUBASHI-MON
SAKURADA-MON
Sakuradamon Sta.
METROPOLITAN POLICE DEPARTMENT
246
20
DIET
HIBIYA-KOEN
HIBIYA-KOEN
Tokyo Metro Yurakucho Line
Tokyo Metro Hibiya Line
Hibiya Sta.
Tokyo International Forum
Idemitsu Museum of Arts
Mitsuo Aida Museum
Mitsubishi Ichigokan Museum
MARUNOUCHI
Marunouchi Bldg.
Uchibori-dori Ave
Toei Mita Line
Nijubashi-mae Sta.
Tokyo Sta.
TOKYO STA.
KYOBASHI STA.
Tokyo Sta.
Marunouchi Line
TOKYO CENTRAL P.O.
Otemachi Sta.
Otemachi Sta.
Otemachi Sta.
Tokyo Metro Chiyoda Line
Toei Shinjuku Line
Hibiya-dori Ave
Tokyo Metro Hanzomon Line
Tokyo Metro Marunouchi Line
Awajicho Sta.
Kanda Sta.
Kanda Sta.
JR Yamanote Line
JR Keihin Tohoku Line
Tokyo Metro Ginza Line
Mitsui Memorial Museum
MITSUI TOWER
MITSUKOSHI
Mitsukoshi-mae Sta.
Shin-Nihonbashi Sta.
Nihonbashi
Tokyo Metro Tozai Line
Nihonbashi Sta.
Toei Asakusa Line
NIHONBASHI
TAKASHIMAYA
DAIMARU
Tokyo Metro Tozai Line

lections (*no charge*), which exhibits only a tiny portion of the Imperial family's 8000 works of art. On leaving the museum, take the southwest path to the **Fujimi-Yagura** watchtower (1659), one of the finest buildings in the garden. Its name indicates that, from the top, Mount Fuji can be seen in the distance.

▶ Arrive at Kitahanebashi-mon (*northwest gate*), which leads to Kitanomaru-koen.

Kitanomaru-koen ★ 北の丸公園
Map II, A1. Subway T08, Tozai Line, Takebashi Station, exit 1A or 1B.
The most notable feature of this park is that it is home to a number of excellent museums.

Tokyo National Museum of Modern Art★★
東京国立近代美術館
Map II, A–B1. 3-1 Kitanomaru-koen, Chiyoda-ku. ○*Open Tue–Sun 10am–5pm (museum Fri & Sat 8pm; last admission 30min before closing). Museum ¥500, Crafts Gallery ¥210 (1st Sun every month no charge; excludes special exhibitions). momat.go.jp.* ☕.
This museum houses a good round-up of Japanese art from the Meiji period to the 1980s. Of the 9000 pieces, 300 are displayed at any one time. A few artists are worthy of special attention: Tomioka Tessai (1836–1924), Yorozu Tetsugoro (1885–1927), Kishida Ryusei (1891–1929), and Kitaoka Fumio (1918–2007).
A few hundred yards away the **Crafts Gallery** contains craft exhibitions of limited interest except for the red-brick building itself (1910, former headquarters of the Imperial Guard).

Nippon Budokan ★ 日本武道館
Map II, A1. Subways S05, Z06, T07.
This Japanese martial arts hall, inspired by Horyu-ji temple in Nara, was built for the 1964 Olympic Games. It also serves as a venue for large music concerts. The Beatles taped *Live at Budokan* in 1966, Deep Purple recorded here for *Made in Japan* in 1972, and *Bob Dylan at Budokan* was released in 1978.

Yasukuni-jinja ★ 靖國神社
Map II, A1. 3-1-1 Kudankita, Chiyoda-ku. Subway S05, Z06, T07, Kudanshita Station. ○*Open daily 6am–6pm (5pm Nov–Feb). No charge. yasukuni.or.jp/english.*
Past the statue of Masujiro Omura (1824–69), founder of the modern Japanese army, an avenue lined with gingko trees and stone lanterns leads to a door *(Shin-mon)* made of cypress wood, decorated with 16-petal chrysanthemums, the Imperial family's emblem. Founded in 1869, the Yasukuni ("Restful country") **shrine complex** contains the Yushukan War Memorial Museum. Behind the central hall *(haiden)* is the principal shrine *(honden)*, and behind this is the Reijibo Hoan-den, where the names of those who have died fighting on behalf of the emperor, and to whom the shrine is dedicated, are inscribed by hand on Japanese paper.

Yasukuni Yushukan War Memorial Museum ★ 靖国遊就館
Map II, A1. ○*Open daily 9am–4.30pm (last admission 30min before closing). ¥1000. yasukuni.or.jp/english/yushukan.*
Japan's oldest museum (founded in 1882, rebuilt and renovated in 2002) is dedicated to a conservative telling of Japan's military history. Its 20 or so rooms are spread over two floors, and the museum is easily identifiable by the Zero fighter plane on display.
The first room evokes the spirit of the samurai, while in the rest souvenirs and photos of the war dead honored here *(see box above)* are displayed. Many visitors find the World War II displays, which present the narrative that Japan was simply defending its interests and was forced into war by the West, overly selective.

SURROUNDING AREA
MARANOUCHI DISTRICT ★
丸の内
Map II, B3.
As you leave Tokyo Station and head west *(toward Miyuki-dori)*, you are immediately confronted with numerous tower blocks.

The Shrine of Discord

Every year on August 15, the anniversary of Japan's capitulation in World War II, the controversy reignites: will the Japanese prime minister go to Yasukuni to pay tribute to the memory of the 2.5 million Japanese soldiers who have given their lives since the Meiji era? The question is of great importance and the response is nervously awaited by the principal victims of the Japanese empire, such as China and Korea. In 1978, 14 war criminals were enshrined at Yasukuni. "We must accept all who have died in the service of Japan," is the monks' comment, adding that a "dead soul that does not rest in peace may seriously disturb the world of the living." This argument may have persuaded (prime minister 2001–6), who visited on many occasions, but most of his successors (bar Abe Shinzo, who went once as prime minister in 2013) have preferred to align themselves with the emperor. Emperor Hirohito had put a stop to the pilgrimages in 1978, as soon as he learned that war criminals who had claimed to be acting in the name of the emperor had been enshrined, and his successors maintained this stance. Despite this, in 2012 two members of the government decided to visit, though in a private capacity rather than an official one so the constitutionally mandated separation of church and state was still, technically, maintained. Their initiative revived, despite the disapproval of the vast majority of the Japanese public, a dispute from times gone by, which soured diplomatic relations between Japan and her neighbors.

Most of these buildings bear the name Marunouchi ("within the castle walls"), which refers to a space historically reserved for the most powerful *daimyo*. Since then, automotive manufacturer Mitsubishi has developed the area, shaping it with new constructions like the Marunouchi Building, or "Maru-Biru." Of the recent arrivals, 2012's **JP Tower** deserves a mention. The headquarters of Japan Post, it towers 656ft/200m over the Tokyo Central Post Office (built 1931). There is also a vast, luxurious shopping mall called **KITTE** next door, on the second floor of which you'll find **Intermediatheque ★**, a fascinating museum that houses exhibits from the collection built up since 1877 by the University of Tokyo. In this vast cabinet of curiosities, you will pass from giant leaves through flocks of stuffed birds and maps from distant eras to colorful mineral samples as you stroll through a beautiful space where rough concrete rubs shoulders with lacquered wood display cases (🕐 *open Tue–Sun 11am–6pm, Fri & Sat to 8pm;* 🎫 *no charge; intermediatheque.jp/en*).

Tokyo Station ★ 東京駅
🕐 *Map II, B3–C3.*
Modeled on Amsterdam Centraal with its red brick façade, the station was built in 1914 and meticulously reconstructed after bomb damage in 1945, with the addition of two elegant cupolas. The eastern part (on the Yaesu/ Nihonbashi side) has a glass façade extended by "wings." Between the two domes, there are 28 platforms for 17 rail lines (6 are reserved for shinkansen). Which makes it only… Tokyo's fourth-largest station! Beneath the rails is a vast network of passageways lined with restaurants and shops, a veritable underground city.

Mitsubishi Ichigokan Museum ★ 三菱一号館美術館
🕐 *Map II, B3. 2-6-2 Marunouchi, Chiyoda-ku. Subway M17, Marunouchi Line, Tokyo Station, Marunouchi exit; or JK25, JY30 or Y18, Yurakucho Station.*
🕐 *Open Tue–Sun 10am–6pm (Fri & 2nd Wed of month 9pm).* 🎫 *Charge varies by exhibition. mimt.jp/english.* 💬.
This museum is housed in building that is a copy of the first red-brick building to be constructed in the district (in 1894,

by the British architect **Josiah Conder,** (🕯*see p99),* but which was demolished in 1968. Under the aegis of its director Akiya Takahashi, a specialist in French art, it is dedicated to 18–20C modern art.

Tokyo International Forum ★★
東京国際フォーラム

🕯*Map II, B3. 3-5-1 Marunouchi, Chiyoda-ku. Subway JK25, JY30 or Y18, Yurakucho Station, exit D5.* 🕐*Open daily 7am–11.30pm.* ⬚*No charge. t-i-forum.co.jp.* ⬚.

This arts and conference center, opened in 1997, is notable for its long, flowing lines. The 226,042sq ft/21,000sq m atrium is topped by a **huge glass roof** shaped like an inverted ship. At a height of almost 197ft/60m, linked iron arches repeat across its 738ft/225m length with the regularity of waves on water. The "hull," ribbed with cables and crossed by slightly sloping, tensioned walkways, is supported by just two columns, one at either end. This billion-dollar gem, built at a time when the yen was advantageously low, was designed by Rafael Viñoly, an American architect of Uruguayan origin, born in 1941.

The Forum has seven auditoriums of different sizes *(Hall A has 5000 seats)* and 34 conference rooms. It also houses the Oedo Antique Market every first and third Sunday in the month. Every year, it receives more than 20 million visitors. At first basement level *(Forum B1),* the **Mitsuo Aida Museum ★** (🕐*open Tue–Sun 10am–5.30pm;* ⬚*¥800; mitsuo.co.jp/ museum/foreign)* has been exhibiting the calligraphy of the poet Aida Mitsuo (1924–91) since 2003. His work was influenced by a philosophy stamped with great humanity, learned from his mentor Tetsuo, a Zen monk of the Soto sect.

Idemitsu Museum of Arts★★
出光美術館

🕯*Map II, B3. 9F Teigeki Bldg, 3-1-1 Marunouchi, Chiyoda-ku. Subway Yurakucho (JK25, JY30, Y18) or Hibiya (C09, H07, I08) stations, exit D1.* 🕐*Open Tue–Sun 10am–5pm (Fri 7pm).* ⬚*¥1000. idemitsu- museum.or.jp/en.* ⬚.

This museum, created in 1966 by the founder of the Idemitsu oil company, is known for its temporary exhibits. The main collection includes some fine pieces of Japanese and Western art, including porcelain from the Hizen area of Kyushu, masterpieces by Sengai, and the world's largest private **Georges Rouault** collection, with over 400 works.

Hibiya-koen ★ 日比谷公園

🕯*Map III, A1. Subway C09, H07 or I08, Hibiya Station.*

Japan's first Western-style garden, opened in 1903, covers the site of an ancient *daimyo* residence close to Edo Castle. Renowned for its tulips, in September it also has displays of chrysanthemums, the Imperial family's emblem. East of the garden, on the other side of the administrative district *(Kasumigaseki),* is the **Diet** *(Kokkai)* or Japanese Parliament *(Subway: Kokkaigijido-mae).*

Nihonbashi ★ 日本橋

🕯*Map II, C2–3. Subway G12 or Z09, Mitsukoshimae Station.*

Nihonbashi, the "Bridge of Japan," the point zero from which all distances in the country are measured, was built of wood in 1603 by Tokugawa Ieyasu. The current version (1911) has been trapped beneath an expressway since the 1960s.

Mitsui Memorial Museum ★
三井記念美術館

🕯*Map II, C2. 7F Mitsui Main Building, 2-1-1 Nihonbashi Muromachi, Chuo-ku. Subway G12 or Z09, Mitsukoshimae Station.* 🕐*Open Tue–Sun 10am–5pm.* ⬚*¥1000 (excludes special exhibitions). mitsui-museum.jp.* ⬚.

This museum, entered through the atrium of the Nihonbashi Mitsui Tower, displays in rotation items accumulated by the Mitsui family over 400 years: tea containers, kimonos, etc. Six of the 3700 objects are National Treasures.

👁*Visit the Mandarin Oriental Hotel, in the same building, before you leave. Its glass lobby on the 38th floor is amazing.*

In the footlights

During the Edo era (1603–1867), many theaters staged Kabuki performances, the largest being in Ginza. But the art, which was very popular for its frequent caricatures of the shogun, endured varying fortunes. Never entirely prohibited, it was still moved out of Ginza toward Asakusa in 1841 before it returned, updated and refined by the official canons, in the Meiji era. Thus in 1899 the National Theatre (*Kabuki-za*) opened its doors in what is now Ginza 4-chome. The venue dominated Japanese theater for 20 years before a devastating fire in 1921, after which it was rebuilt and destroyed three separate times before its modern incarnation (*kabuki-za.co.jp*) was unveiled in 2013. Today the theater is overlooked by a 29-storey skyscraper, which curiously enhances its presence.

Artizon museum ★
アーティゾン美術館
Map II, C3. Museum Tower Kyobashi, 1-7-2 Kyobashi, Chuo-ku. Subway G10, Ginza Line, Kyobashi Station. Open Tue–Sun 10am–5pm (8pm Fri). ¥1000 (excludes special exhibitions). artizon. museum/en.

Previously known as the Bridgestone Museum, the Artizon opened in a brand new building in 2020. It still contains the impressive collection of the founder of the Bridgestone tire company, Ishibashi Shojiro—which covers Western and Japanese work from the Meiji period onward—but also acquired several more important works during the changeover. On display are some fine sculptures (Rodin, Bourdelle, Despiau) and paintings (Manet, Van Gogh) in a chic, welcoming new home.

GINZA ★★ 銀座
Map III, p 155. Subway G09, H08 or M16, Ginza, Hibiya and Marunouchi lines, Ginza Station.

The "place where silver is minted" (a mint was established here in the time of Tokugawa Ieyasu) is now where it is spent, as is clear from a brief walk down the main shopping street, **Chuo-dori**. Just as on Fifth Avenue or Bond Street, it is lined with the biggest names in fashion and luxury goods—Armani, Louis Vuitton, Cartier, Chanel, etc. Ginza was ravaged by fire in 1872, the earthquake of 1923, then twenty years later World War II bombs, but he constant rebuilding kept the district ahead of the times (first paved roads, first street lighting,

first department stores, first brick buildings). Today the architecture is diverse, from brick, stone, and concrete to iron and glass, all appearing gradually as the fashions changed with the decades.

CHUO-DORI AND HARUMI-DORI
中央通り・晴海通り
Map III, B1/2

Ginza Crossing ★★ 銀座4丁目
交差点
Map III, B1. Subway G09, H08 or M16.
You can't miss this famous intersection where the busy thoroughfares of **Chuo-dori**, also called **Ginza-dori** (*running north–south*) and **Harumi-dori** (*east–west*) cross. There's a large building on every corner of Chuo-dori. **Wako★** (*Map III, B1*), one of the oldest *depato* (a term derived from "department stores") in Ginza, occupies one of the corners. Its clock tower is a landmark; the first was erected in 1894 but was destroyed in the 1923 earthquake, and ilts clock has been telling the time since 1898. Close by, the entrance to the prestigious **Mitsukoshi** department store is via the basement, where the excellent food hall is located; the store entrance is directly connected to the subway. The upper floors are filled with expensive, high-quality goods. Towering over the Ginza intersection is the tall, cylindrical **San'ai** building, whose every neon-lit floor offers a different cocktail of cultures and fashion. The elegant **Ginza Place** building (2016), with its white lattice cladding and Nissan and Sony showrooms, is on the opposite corner. In a strange juxtaposition of

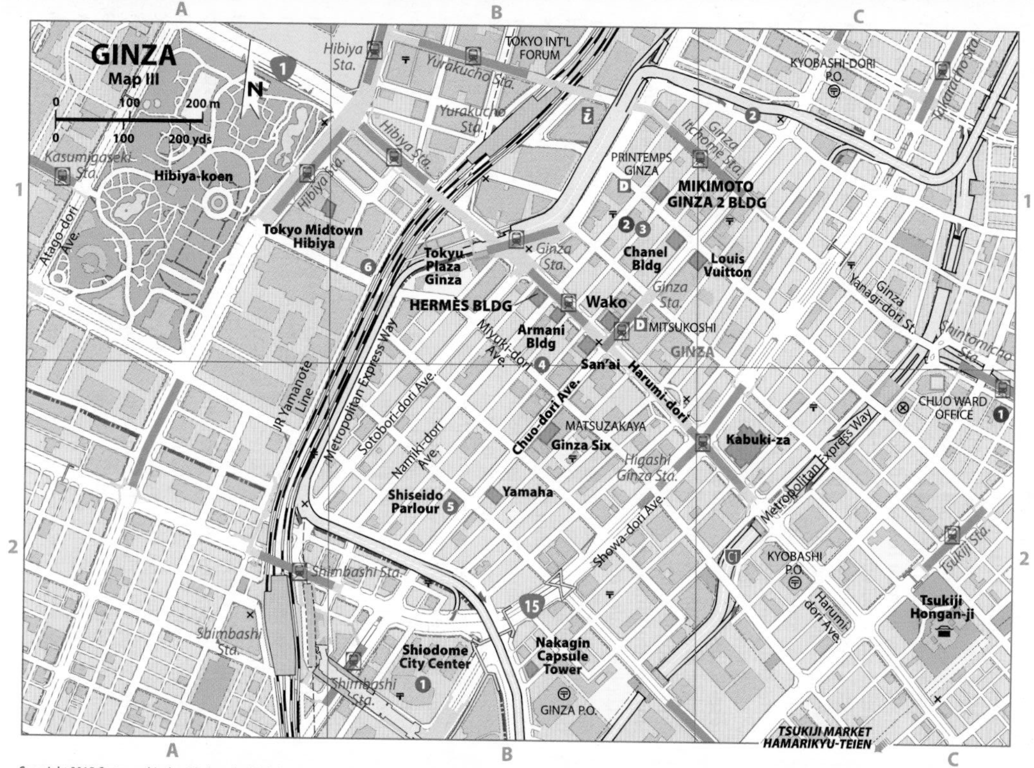

WHERE TO STAY

Hotel Gracery Ginza.......... ❶
MUJI Hotel Ginza............... ❷

WHERE TO EAT

Fish Bank Tokyo................. ❶
Gonpachi G-Zone.............. ❷
Restaurant Dazzle............. ❸
Sakura Suisan Ginza
Sanchome-ten................. ❹
Shiseido Parlour
Ginza Honten................... ❺
Sushizanmai
Yurakucho-ten................. ❻

GINZA
Map III

0   100   200 m
0   100   200 yds

Kasumigaseki Sta.
Atago-dori Ave.
Hibiya-koen
Hibiya Sta.
Tokyo Midtown Hibiya
Yurakucho Sta.
Hibiya Sta.
TOKYO INTL FORUM
PRINTEMPS GINZA
Ginza Itchome Sta.
KYOBASHI-DORI
Ginza Yanagi-dori St.
KYOBASHI P.O.
CHUO WARD OFFICE
Shintomi-cho
Tsukiji Sta.
Tsukiji Hongan-ji
MIKIMOTO
GINZA 2 BLDG
Louis Vuitton
Chanel Bldg
Wako
San'ai
Harumi-dori
MITSUKOSHI
Ginza Sta.
GINZA
Kabuki-za
Metropolitan Express Way
KYOBASHI P.O.
Harumi-dori Ave.
Tokyu Plaza Ginza
HERMES BLDG
Armani Bldg
Chuo-dori Ave.
MATSUZAKAWA
Ginza Six
Yamaha
Higashi Ginza Sta.
Showa-dori Ave.
GINZA P.O.
Sukiyabashi
Miyuki-dori Ave.
Sotobori-dori Ave.
Namiki-dori Ave.
Shiseido Parlour
Shiodome City Center
Nakagin Capsule Tower
JR Yamanote Line
Shimbashi Sta.
Shimbashi Sta.
Shiodome Sta.

TSUKIJI MARKET
HAMARIKYU-TEIEN

Copyright 2015 Cartographic data Shobunsha/Michelin

155

styles, just 300yd from Ginza Crossing is the **Kabuki-za** ★★ (*kabuki-za.co.jp*), Japan's leading traditional kabuki theater venue (&*see box p154*).

▶ Take Harumi-dori going west and toward Hibiya Park.

The **Dior Building** ★★ (&*Map III, B1*), designed by award-winning architects Sejima and Nishizawa working jointly as SANAA, has a smooth façade illuminated with thousands of fiber-optic lights at night. The highest tower in the district is the 12-story **Armani Tower** ★, designed by the Italian couturier in 2007 in collaboration with the architect Massimiliano Fuksas. Its glass frontage refects the sky and the surrounding buildings. Lights in the shape of leaves positioned along vertical strips of light cascade down it, resembling bamboo. Inside is a bar-lounge, a restaurant, and the world's first Armani Spa. A short distance away, the **Hermès Building** ★★★ (&*Map III, B1*) occupies an area of 64,584sq ft/6000sq m on 15 floors. The mosaic-style exterior, designed by Renzo Piano, is made up of 13,000 glass blocks (four together are exactly the same size as a Hermès headscarf), creating a "magic lantern" inspired by the glass house built by Pierre Chareau in Paris in the 1920s. On the top floor contemporary art exhibitions provide a pleasant contrast to the building's clean lines (&*no charge*). There's even a small Japanese-style roof garden, though it is closed to the public.

The imposing **Tokyu Plaza Ginza** (&*Map III, B1; ginza.tokyu-plaza.com/en*), built in 2016 and featuring an elegant cut-glass design inspired by traditional Edo Kiriko art, houses more than 120 shops arranged around a monumental atrium. There is a cluster of restaurants just around the corner, beneath the rail tracks linking Yurakucho and Shimbashi stations (&*see Addresses p189*).

▶ Head northeast up Chuo-dori, toward Kyobashi.

On the right-hand sidewalk, you will see the **Louis Vuitton store** ★, a Jun Aoki design featuring illuminated apertures and doors which bring to mind the fashion house's iconic monogrammed designs. On the sidewalk opposite, the **Chanel Building** ★ (&*Map III, B1*) is the first to catch the eye. The largest store on the Chuo-dori, with 10 floors, its double walls of dark glass produce a quilted effect suggestive of the brand's signature bags. When night falls, it lights up with 700,000 LEDs. The tenth floor is occupied by Alain Ducasse's restaurant **Beige** (Coco Chanel's favorite color).

On the opposite side of Ginza-Maronie-dori is the **De Beers Ginza Building** ★★ (which no longer contains the jewelers). Designed by Japanese architect Jun Mitsui, the twisted curve of the front of the building gives the appearance of being caught in time, as it undulates like seaweed with the ebb and flow of the tide. Nearby, the iconic façade of the **Mikimoto Ginza 2 Building** ★★★ (&*Map III, B1*), designed by Toyo Ito, is clad in pink-tinted steel, with windows of an irregular shape. The company's founder, Kokichi Mikimoto, produced cultured pearls (&*see p267*). The sumptuous interior houses a restaurant named Dazzle (&*see Addresses p190*), and a tearoom.

▶ On Chuo-dori going south toward Shiodome.

The **Shiseido Building** ★★ (&*Map III, B2*), was designed by Catalan architect Ricardo Bofill on the site of the giant Japanese cosmetics company's original headquarters. The red-brick-colored building also contains two restaurants (&*see Addresses p190*) and a bar on the upper floors, with fine panoramic views, plus an art gallery in the basement (◷*open Tue–Sat 11am–7pm, Sun to 6pm*). Just up Chuo-dori, the **Yamaha** ★ (2010) façade is a checkerboard of gold, bronze, and white diamonds.

At the south end of Chuo-dori, head left along the expressway and you will see the **Nakagin Capsule Tower** ★★ (&*Map III, B2*). Built in 1972 by Kisho

© José Fuste Raga/age fotostock

Hamarikyu Garden

Kurokawa (1934–2007), it is made up of modules of prefabricated concrete that form two interconnected towers (☞ *not open to the public*). Each module, whether studio apartment or office, measures 7.5 x 12.5 x 6.9ft/2.3m x 3.8m x 2.1m, and the result is impressive. A prime example of Japan's Metabolist architectural movement (ⓒ *see p101*).

Tsukiji Outer Market ★
築地場外市場

ⓒ *Map I, C3. 5-2-1 Tsukiji, Chuo-ku. Subway E18, Oedo Line, Tsukijishijo Station; or H10, Hibiya Line, Tsukiji Station.* ⏰ *Open Mon–Sat 5am–2pm (varies by shop).* ⊗ *No charge. tsukiji.or.jp/english.*
In 2018, the inner market at Tsukiji was relocated to Toyosu, after years of discussions. Though visitors can no longer see the early-morning bustle of the world's largest fish market at this site, it's still worth a visit for the outer market. This is the cluster of shops, restaurants and food stands which sprung up around Tsukiji, and it's still one of the best bets for a super-fresh plate of sushi. The outer market is made up of an atmospheric network of narrow alleyways lined with restaurants—some of which are tiny—and shops selling seafood (such as bonito and dried seaweed) to eat in or take away, as well as crockery, knives and other kitchen utensils, and even rubber boots!

Hamarikyu Garden ★★
浜離宮恩賜庭園

ⓒ *Map I, C4. 1-1 Hamarikyu-teien, Chuo-ku. Subway E19 or U02, Toei Oedo or Yurikamome lines, Shiodome Station. The garden is also connected to Asakusa by water bus.* ⏰ *Open daily 9am–5pm (last admission 4.30pm).* ⊗ *¥300. tokyo-park.or.jp/teien/en/hama-rikyu.* ☕.
Situated beside Tokyo Bay, the distinctive characteristic of this garden is that the lake and moat surrounding the park are filled with seawater, so the level fluctuates with the tide. There is a scenic teahouse, Nakajima-no-ochaya, where you can stop for a cup of matcha (⏰ *open 9am–4.30pm,* ⊗ *¥510*). It is a typical example of a *daimyo* garden from the Edo era, now in pleasing contrast with the surrounding skyscrapers.

▷ You now have the option to go straight to Tokyo Bay (Odaiba), if you wish (ⓒ *see p172*). You can also easily access Odaiba from Toyosu Market.

Toyosu Market ★ 豊洲市場

ⓒ *Map I, D4. 6-6-1 Toyosu, Koto-ku. Subway U14, Yurikamome Line, Shijomae Station (connected to the arket buildings).* ⏰ *Open Mon–Sat 5am–5pm (varies by area).* ⏰ *Closed some Wed, check online.* ⊗ *No charge. toyosu-market.or.jp.*
In 2018, operations from Tsukiji Inner Market were controversially moved to

this new site at Toyosu. Though they lack the grimy glamour of Tsukiji, the shiny new buildings do provide plenty of space for auctions, and have also been constructed with tourism in mind. Visitors are corralled into certain areas form where they can see all the action without getting in the traders' way.

The most famous event is the 5.30am **tuna auction**, which you can watch from two areas. The open-access Tuna Auction Observation Windows give a view from one floor up; as they're double-glazed, you won't hear anything going on. The Tuna Auction Observation Deck is on the same floor as the auction, and has thinner glass, so you'll be able to feel the cold, smell the fish and hear the bids. It's much more atmospheric, but also harder to get into: you need to apply for the ticket lottery about a month in advance, then if you're successful, you'll get a 10min slot between 5.45am and 6.15am.

Toyosu also has plenty of restaurants—a bowl of rice topped with the freshest sashimi makes a great breakfast after an early-morning auction—and a large roof garden with excellent **views** of the bay.

ROPPONGI ★ 六本木
🕭*Map I, p136.*

The name Roppongi ("six trees") comes from the tree ideogram in the name of each of the six *daimyo* who used to live here. The area has had a bad reputation, not least because of its nightlife, also associated with the American base established here after World War II, and it's still one of Tokyo's most famous enter-

tainment areas. The main street, Gaien Higashi-dori, is lined with neon signs and patrolled by touts intent on dragging you into their bar. It's disorienting, perhaps even more so for Japanese visitors than for the Westerners who come here in droves. Architecturally, the tale of woe is less comprehensive, though the main street is still dominated by uninspired concrete and overshadowed by an expressway. With new buildings in the 21C came a fresh focus, with the National Art Center and 21_21 Design Sight developed around conceptually bold spaces. Now Roppongi is praised as the Art Triangle as often as it's decried as a den of iniquity—and it's probably more fun for being both.

ROPPONGI HILLS ★★ 六本木ヒルズ
🕭*Map I, B4. 6-10-1 Roppongi, Minato-ku. Subway H04, exit 1C; or E23, exit 3. Stores:* 🕐*open 11am–9pm with exceptions. roppongihills.com/en.*

The inventory of this vast complex, 17 years in the making, is rather conventional: offices, shops, gardens, walkways, movie theaters, etc. That said, it does house a great selection of art.

The actual hills of Roppongi offer some perspective, as does the giant spider bestriding Roku-Roku plaza by Franco-American sculptor Louise Bourgeois.

Mori Tower ★★ 森タワー
🕭*Map I, B4.*

It's hard to miss the Mori Tower's 54 floors, designed by American archi-

---

Mr Satoh's Formula

Mr Satoh, who runs the Shigeyoshi restaurant (🕭*see Addresses p195*), develops a mischievous twinkle in his eye when you ask to see the following day's menu. He has no idea what it will be and says: "It's been the same thing every morning for years" until he comes back from the fish market, where he's known as the "white wolf", who wanted to be a sea fish. "What I cook depends on what I find, but I only find what I'm looking for." And what Mr Satoh is looking for is very simple: "The best seafood. Quality is not just about the freshness of the fish, it's about what's in season. You can't just fish for anything, anywhere, and at any time. This morning, for example, they put some turtles they'd caught off Kyushu on one side for me. They're only available for about two weeks in the year. I took four, which will make a tasty soup for four people, no more."

Tokyo City View, Mori Tower, Roppongi Hills

tects Kohn Pedersen Fox. The unusual entrance, called the Metro Hat, funnels you through two turns of a spiral staircase to the actual tower entrance.

Tokyo City View ★★

52F Mori Tower. ⏱*Open daily 10am–11pm (Fri–Sat 1am; last entry 30min–1hr before closing).* 🎟*¥1800 including Mori Art Museum, ¥2000 with entry to Mori Arts Center Gallery. tcv.roppongihills. com/en.* ♿

On the 52nd floor a circular atrium, 984ft/300m around and 36ft/11m high, provides a jaw-dropping 360-degree **view** over Tokyo. It is magical by day (with Mount Fuji visible on a clear day), and stunning at night. in good weather, you may be able to head out onto the Skydeck (⏱*Open Mon–Sun 11am–8pm).* On the same floor is the **Mori Arts Center Gallery** (*opening times and entry charge vary with exhibition*) and on the floor above, the **Mori Art Museum ★★** (⏱*open Wed–Mon 10am–10pm, Tue 10pm–5pm*). Temporary exhibitions based on the current issues of contemporary art follow each other in rapid succession.

Tokyo Tower ★ 東京タワー

♿*Map I, B4. 4-2-8 Shibakoen, Minato-ku. Subway E21, Toei Oedo Line, Akabanebashi Station; or H05, Hibiya Line, Kamiyacho Station.* ⏱*Open daily 9am–11pm (top deck 10.45pm).* 🎟*Main deck ¥900, top & main decks ¥2800. tokyotower.co.jp/en.html.*

Built in 1958 and 1093ft/333m high, Tokyo Tower resembles the Eiffel Tower but painted red and white (to be visible from the air). The tower is a relay station for the transmission of more than 20 television channels and includes, among other things, restaurants, shops, and excellent observation decks.

Zojo-ji ★ 増上寺

♿*Map I, C4. 4-7-35 Shibakoen. Subway E21. www.zojoji.or.jp/en/index.html.*

The temple of Zojo-ji lies in Shiba Park, west of Tokyo Tower. Founded in 1393 and transferred to this site in 1598, when shogun Tokugawa Ieyasu settled in Edo, it contains the tombs of no fewer than six Tokugawa shoguns.

After wartime bombing, Zojo-ji was rebuilt in the 1970s; only the entrance Gate of Triple Deliverance (from anger, stupidity, and greed), **Sangedatsu-mon ★**, had escaped the bombs. Dating from 1622, the gate is the oldest wooden structure in Tokyo.

TOKYO MIDTOWN ★
東京ミッドタウン

♿*Map I, B3. 9-7-1 Akasaka, Minato-ku. Subway E23 or H04, Toei Oedo or Hibiya lines, Roppongi Station, exit 7.* ⏱*Open*

daily: shops 11am–9pm; restaurants 11am–midnight. tokyo-midtown.com.
Lawns, gingko biloba, and camphor trees wend their way through this complex of six buildings dominated by **Midtown Tower**, which at 814ft/248m is Tokyo's second-tallest building. With a huge glass-and-steel canopy outside and gently sloping ramps in greenery-filled spaces inside, four floors of luxury goods and 50 or so bars, cafes, and restaurants are waiting to be explored.

Suntory Museum of Art ★★
サントリー美術館
Map I, B3. 3F Tokyo Midtown Galleria. Subway E23 or H04, exit 7. Open Wed–Mon 10am–6pm (Fri & Sat 8pm). Varies by exhibition. suntory.com/sma.
Remodeled in April 2007 by Kengo Kuma, the museum houses a permanent collection of 3000 exhibits (lacquerware, Satsuma ceramics, textiles, and Noh costumes), displayed alongside temporary exhibitions organized in association with the major museums of the world. Themes of the temporary exhibitions range from the relationship between French and Japanese art to haute couture (Kosode kimonos) in the Edo era.

Turn right on leaving the museum for an excellent view over Hinokicho Park and 21_21 Design Sight.

21_21 Design Sight★★
トゥーワン・トゥーワン・デザインサイト
Map I, B3. 9-7-6 Akasaka, Minato-ku. Subway E23 or H04, exit 7. Open Wed–Mon 10am–7pm. ¥1100. 2121designsight.jp/en.
Built in 2007 and designed by Ando Tadao, the high priest of modern architecture, this building squats on the ground like a crumpled origami insect. The aim of the design center (*18,300sq ft/1700sq m on two levels*) is to rediscover and reinterpret the objects and events of everyday life through a prism of highly innovative design (the name is a play on 20/20 vision) via thought-provoking exhibitions (four annually). Fashion designer Issey Miyake is one of its directors.

National Art Center ★★
国立新美術館
Map I, B3. 7-22-2 Roppongi, Minato-ku. Subway C05, Chiyoda Line, Nogizaka Station, exit 6. Open Wed–Mon 10am–6pm (Fri & Sat 8pm). Varies by exhibition. nact.jp/english.
The National Art Center's 525ft/160m-long façade of undulating glass is one of the last works of Kisho Kurokawa (1934–2007), who was at the forefront of Japan's architectural renaissance. He also designed the famous Nakagin capsule tower in Ginza (*see p158*). The center opened in 2007 and has 150,695sq ft/14,000sq m of exhibition space; the Ueno museums sometimes use it for major exhibitions. Inside are 12 rooms of at least 10,765sq ft/1000sq m (and two of 21,528sq ft/2000sq m), three conference areas, an art library, three cafes, shops, and the Paul Bocuse brasserie at the top of one of the two inverted cones that give the building's glass frontage its unusual shape. The National Art Center is a powerful tool in the service of culture and contemporary art, a jewel of a building that cost millions of dollars.

SHINJUKU ★★ 新宿
Map V, p162.
In the midst of all the skyscrapers, it's difficult to imagine the "new villages" *(shin juku)* that once stood on this marshy ground and profited from merchants on their way to Koshu *(now Yamanashi prefecture)*. The popular tearooms at staging posts along the road offered a range of illicit pleasures. As the district grew, so too did its houses of ill repute, until the 1970s when it was radically redeveloped due to the demand for land. This thriving street life was pushed into the area on either side of Shinjuku Station, with its small street traders and the odours of grilling food from the *yatai* (food stands) tempting passersby in their lunch break. To the west, **Nishi-Shinjuku** is a forest of skyscrapers housing some 300,000 salarymen, while to the east is **Higashi-Shinjuku**, and the legendary Kabuki-cho and Golden Gai nightlife districts.

NISHI-SHINKUKU 西新宿

Around 30 of the buildings in this forest of skyscrapers are more than 328ft/100m high, most with an observation deck.

Seiji Togo Memorial Sonpo Japan Museum of Art ★

損保ジャパン東郷青児美術館

📍*Map V, B1. Sonpo Japan Building, 1-26-1 Nishi-Shinjuku. Subway E01 or M07, Toei Oedo or Marunouchi lines, Nishi-Shinjuku or Shinjuku-Nishiguchi stations.* ⏱*Open Tue–Sun 10am–6pm.* 🎫*Entry charge varies with exhibition. sjnk-museum.org/en.* 💬*.*

This museum belongs to the Yasuda insurance company, renamed Sonpo in 2002. If you're not familiar with the name, think back to the record auction price achieved at Christie's in 1987, when the Yasuda Fire & Marine Insurance Co. bought Vincent Van Gogh's *Sunflowers* for ¥5.3 billion. In so doing the company created for itself a worldwide "low budget" publicity campaign.

Today the foundation has 650 pieces, including many masterpieces, displayed in rotation: *Sunflowers* (1888), *L'Allée des Alyscamps* (1888) by Gauguin, *Pommes et Serviette* (1879) by Cézanne, and *Nostalgia* (1959) by Togo Seiji (1897–1978), an important Japanese artist, whose own works *(around 200)* feature in the foundation's permanent display.

Tokyo Metropolitan Government building ★★★

東京都庁

📍*Map V, A2. 2-8-1 Nishi-Shinjuku. Subway E28, Toei Oedo Line, Tochomae Station. North Tower observatory:* ⏱*Open daily 9.30am–5.30pm (11pm when South Tower closed).* ⏱*Closed 2nd & 4th Mon of the month. South Tower observatory:* ⏱*Open daily 9.30am–11pm.* ⏱*Closed 1st & 3rd Tue of the month.* 🎫*No charge. Large Tourist Information Center on first (ground) floor.*

This building, designed by Japanese architect **Tange Kenzo** (📍*see box p172*), has the look of a Western-style Gothic cathedral and stands out among the other skyscrapers. The observatories sit-

uated in its towers (797ft/243m) provide excellent **views** over Shinjuku (accessible by elevator in just 45 seconds!). This austere building clad in granite is not the most hospitable looking, but its vast dimensions accommodate some 1300 white collar workers.

A short distance south is the **Shinjuku Park Tower** (771ft/235m). The deluxe **Park Hyatt Hotel** occupies floors 39–52. with the famous New York Bar on floor 52 (📍*see Addresses p193*).

Sumitomo Building ★

新宿住友ビルディング

📍*Map V, A2. 2-6-1 Nishi-Shinjuku. Subway E28, Tochomae Station.* 🎫*No charge.*

Rising 689ft/210m, the Sumitomo Building has an atrium running its entire height. A number of relatively inexpensive restaurants are on the floors 49–52, most with a beautiful **view** of Tokyo and the neighbouring skyscrapers. There is also a curious WWII history museum on the 33rd floor, and a free observation deck on the 51st.

Mode Gakuen Cocoon Tower ★★ モード学園コクーンタワー

📍*Map V B1. 1-7-2 Nishi-Shinjuku. Subway E28, Tochomae Station.* 🎫*No charge.*

This eye-catching 2008 skyscraper is, at 669ft/204m, the world's second-tallest building for education after the University of Moscow. It contains a fashion school, a technology college and a medical college. Its unusual white aluminum and blue glass design with an immense crisscross pattern recalls a cocoon, hence the name.

Tokyo Opera City Tower

東京オペラシティタワー

📍*Map V; A2, off map. 3-20-2 Nishi-Shinjuku. Subway KO02, Keio New Line, Hatsudai Station. operacity.jp/en.*

Ten minutes or so to the southwest is Shinjuku's third-highest tower *(768ft/234m)*. This 54-floor multiplex contains offices, restaurants, and shops, as well as six theaters, the magnificent **Tokyo Opera City Concert Hall**, a contem-

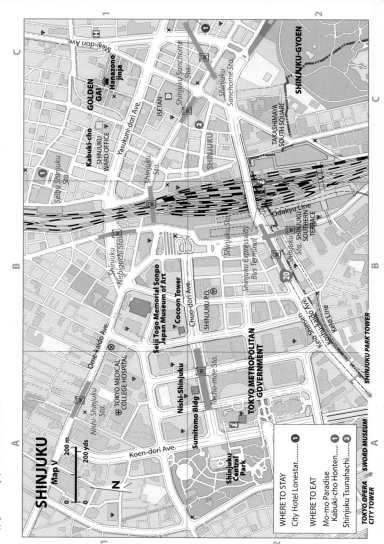

SHINJUKU
Map V

Copyright 2015 Cartographic data Shobunsha/Michelin

WHERE TO STAY
City Hotel Lonestar........ **1**

WHERE TO EAT
Mo-mo Paradise
Kabuki-cho Honten....... **1**
Shinjuku Tsunahachi....... **2**

Shinjuku Station

Three and a half million passengers travel on Shinjuku Station's 5000 trains every day, making it the world's busiest station. Many stations *(run by different companies)* and lines *(both subway and overland)* feed into this dizzying whirl, "where people scurry backward and forward on a thousand practical errands, from the train to the store, from clothes to food, and where a train can run right up to a shoe store" wrote Roland Barthes *(Empire of Signs*, Éditions Skira, 1970). The phenomenon has its roots in the numerous black market centers that flourished in the stations of Tokyo after the war; Shinjuku was the first of these.

Golden Gai, "Streets of Gold"

In postwar Shinjuku, which had been completely razed to the ground, a small district sprung up, constructed from recycled material supplied partly by GIs, who were all the more eager to help since these little shacks provided shelter for Japanese girls who acted as both concubines and madams. When the Treaty of San Francisco ended the American occupation in 1952, the district went into decline, and the 1958 law prohibiting sex work changed things further. Modest rents attracted unconventional figures (artists, cross-dressers, etc.), who were aware of the irony in naming this poverty-ridden district "Streets of Gold." Filmmakers, photographers, and writers (Oshima Nagisa, Imamura Shohei, Araki Nobuyoshi, Tanaka Komimasa) all came to recharge their batteries in its 300 bars. Today, no more than 50 of these establishments remain, far fewer than the legions of developers with plenty of ideas for the real estate.

porary art gallery (*open Tue–Sun 11am–7pm, Fri & Sat 8pm; ¥1200*), and the highly innovative **NTT Intercommunication Center** (*open Tue–Sun 11am–6pm; tariff varies with exhibition, www.ntticc.or.jp*) displaying works combining robotics and new technology. The **New National Theatre** (*behind the tower*) stages opera, ballet, and modern dance performances.

HIGASHI-SHINJUKU 東新宿

From JR Shinjuku Station, east Kabuki-cho exit, take Yasukuni-dori.

Kabuki-cho ★ 歌舞伎町
Map V, C1. Subway JR lines, Shinjuku Station, east exit.

In the early 1950s, an association campaigning for the reconstruction of Shinjuku, which had been largely destroyed by World War II bombs, wanted to build a theater for Kabuki performances. Although the project failed for financial reasons, the district adopted the name, along with the uninhibited character of the sort historically associated with actors. Today, neon signs invite you into a shady world of massage parlors, gaming rooms, saunas, host and hostess clubs, and karaoke bars. Japanese white-collar workers in particular appreciate the social interludes that these venues provide, where nothing is taboo and they can discuss any subject with both colleagues and their superiors.

Golden Gai ★★ 新宿ゴールデン街
Map V, C1. Subway JR lines, Shinjuku Station, east exit.

Sandwiched between Kabuki-cho and Hanazono shrine, Golden Gai is a small, compact area lined with bars, best visited at night. Squeezed in on top of one another, some of the bars can barely accommodate a dozen people. Generally the best plan is to wader about and see which bars take your fancy, but there are some standouts like *La Jetée*, a bar named after the 1962 French short film and owned by a movie fan.

Neighboring **Hanazono-jinja** is a fitting place to come and pray to the god of business, no matter what that business may be. Every year, the **Tori no ichi Festival** is held here. Dating back to the Edo era, it takes place in November on the day of the Rooster *(tori)* in accordance with the old Chinese lunar calendar. You can buy lucky charms called *kumade* ("bamboo rakes") to help bring good fortune in the year to come. A **flea market** is held the first Saturday and third Sunday of the month.

Shinjuku Gyoen National Garden ★★★ 新宿御苑
Map V, C2. 11 Naito-cho, Shinjuku-ku. Subway M10, Marunouchi Line, Shinjuku-gyoen-mae Station; or Shinjuku Station. Open Tue–Sun 9am–4.30pm (March–June & Sept 6pm, July & Aug 7pm). ¥500. env.go.jp/ garden/shinjukugyoen/english.

Yayoi Kusama Museum

This garden (*1433 acre/58ha*), once owned by the *daimyo* Naito, has been managed by the Imperial Household Agency since 1906. Next to a Japanese stroll garden is a landscaped English garden and, in the southeastern corner, a French-style garden with an avenue of plane trees. Farther north, near the Okido Gate (you can also enter the garden via the Sendagaya or Shinjuku gates), a tropical greenhouse shelters 2000 plants. During the Meiji era, it was in this garden that experiments were made with fruit imported from the West. Shinjuku Gyoen is also where the prime minister holds his *hanami* each year, a garden party to view (*mi*) the blossom (*hana*) of the cherry trees (*sakura*) in spring. In the fall, the chrysanthemums are in bloom and the maple trees blaze a glorious scarlet.

▶ Head north up Gaien Higashi-dori.

Yayoi Kusama Museum ★★
草間彌生美術館

⌖*Map I, A1. 107 Benten-cho, Shinjuku-ku. Subway E04 or T04, Toei Oedo or Tozai lines, Ushigome-Yanagicho or Waseda stations.* ⏱*Open Thu–Sun 11am–5pm.* 💳*¥1000. Tickets must be booked in advance for specific time slots (6 per day, 1hr 30min each). yayoikusamamuseum.jp.* This sleek, simple white building in Kagurazaka is the perfect backdrop for Kusama Yayoi's riotously bright, colorful and inventive work. Exhibitions change twice per year, and might include one of her mirror rooms, densely packed dot paintings, or large-scale sculptures.

▶ Walk north; cross the Kanda River.

The rise of the host club

In the early evening, men and women may go looking for a little company in one of Kabuki-cho's 150 hostess or host clubs. Women-only clubs are rapidly growing in popularity, a response to Japanese society's chauvinistic side. The young men, or hosts, charged with entertaining them can usually be spotted by their elaborate outfits, pointed shoes and gravity-defying hairstyles. Their pictures are displayed in the front window or outside by touts, or the men themselves approach passers-by. The reputation of a host rests on his kindness, consideration, and humor, everything a client may need after a stressful day at work. Of course, the more his female client drinks, the more the host earns. The whole setup bears more than a passing resemblance to the tea houses where Kabuki actors used to charge rich women for their company.

While you're in the area, it's worth visiting the stunning, brutalist **St Mary's Cathedral ★** (open daily 9am–5pm; no charge), a dramatic concrete building designed by Tange Kenzo. Just across the road but feeling like a world apart is **Chinzan-so** (attached to a hotel, but open to the public; no charge), a traditional Japanese garden. Both make a pleasant escape from the tourist trail.

SHIBUYA ★★ 渋谷
 Map VI, p166.

At the heart of Shibuya is an enormous scramble crossing lined with giant screens, beneath which hundreds of thousands of people scurry backward and forward, somehow seeming never to bump into each other. Here, courtesy is perhaps less a demonstration of mutual respect than a practical way of making sure you don't hit someone. Shibuya owes this frenetic activity to the fact that its two private rail companies, Tokyu and Seibu, create a particularly high footfall around the station: this district of southwest Tokyo can easily play host to 750,000 people a day. Each corporation owns several buildings in the area. While teens head for Shibuya 109 department store, the 200 or so shops of Hikarie tower, and the movie theaters in the Bunkamura arts complex owned by Tokyu, older visitors prefer the Parco and Seibu department stores of its competitor. Both companies also own offices, restaurants, cafes, hotels, etc.

Shibuya Station
 Map VI, B2.

Nine rail lines run by four companies converge at Shibuya. The area is in the midst of a protracted metamorphosis which will see it transformed into a vast complex of skyscrapers, walkways, and gardens by 2027, the first stage of which was the Hikarie tower (see p167).

The most popular place to meet in Shibuya is near the statue of the dog **Hachiko ★**, to whom there is a sad story attached. Every evening, Hachiko would wait for his master, a professor at the University of Tokyo, at the station exit.

One day the professor didn't return, having died of a heart attack. The dog returned to the station every day to wait for his master until he himself died some 10 years later. The tale of Hachiko's loyalty spread throughout Japan. A bronze statue was erected in his memory, though the yakitori vendors, who befriended the dog and fed him every day, were soon forgotten.

Shibuya Crossing ★
 Map VI, B2.

Surrounded by tall buildings festooned with screens, all throwing out a stream of images and decibels, this is the most photographed crossing in the world. The **multidirectional pedestrian crossing** turning into a flood of people crossing in all directions but never colliding is a true example of Japanese discipline!

Center Gai ★ センター街
 Map VI, B2. Shibuya-ku, 3min walk from Shibuya Station (Hachiko exit).

Beyond the crossing, there is a network of more or less pedestrianized streets, of which the largest is Center Gai. All of them are lined with stores selling fashion, cheap goods, and cultural artefacts, as well as restaurants and karaoke clubs, the walls plastered with neon signs announcing them.

If you're not sure where to go, head for one of the major stores: in Loft and Tokyu Hands you'll find everything you need (or almost), while Q Front is the place for music and Shibuya 109 for all the latest (and the next) fashions. The streets here are a real labyrinth, horizontally and vertically, and they get particularly packed at the weekend with crowds of teenagers on the hunt for the latest craze.

Around Dogenzaka 道玄坂
 Map VI, A2.

Just behind the Tokyu department store, at the end of Kamura-dori, is **Bunka-mura ★** (2-24-1 Dogenzaka, bunkamura. co.jp/english, open daily 10am–7pm, Fri–Sat 9pm). This vast arts center displays a relaxed eclecticism: concert hall, theater (Cocoon), opera house (Orchard

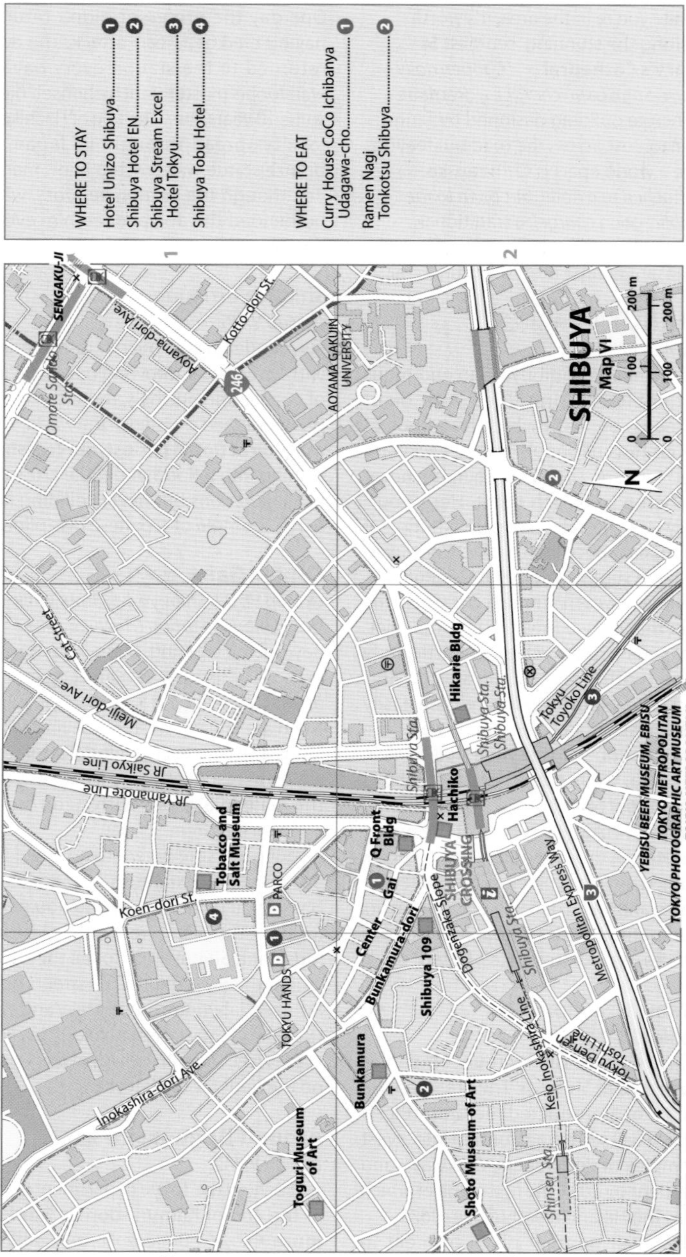

WHERE TO STAY

Hotel Unizo Shibuya............ ❶
Shibuya Hotel EN................ ❷
Shibuya Stream Excel
Hotel Tokyu......................... ❸
Shibuya Tobu Hotel............. ❹

WHERE TO EAT

Curry House CoCo Ichibanya
Udagawa-cho....................... ❶
Ramen Nagi
Tonkotsu Shibuya............... ❷

Copyright 2015 Cartographic data Shobunsha/Michelin

SHIBUYA
Map VI

N

0   100   200 m
0   100   200 m

SENGAKU-JI

Omote Sando St.
Aoyama-dori Ave.
Kotto-dori St.
246
AOYAMA GAKUIN
UNIVERSITY

Meiji-dori Ave.
Cat Street
JR Saikyo Line
JR Yamanote Line

Hikarie Bldg
Shibuya Sta.
Shibuya Sta.
Tokyu
Toyoko Line

Koen-dori St.
Tobacco and
Salt Museum
PARCO
Q Front
Bldg
Center
Gai
Bunkamura-dori
Shibuya 109
Dogenzaka Slope
SHIBUYA
CROSSING
Hachiko
Shibuya Sta.
Metropolitan Express Way
Shibuya Sta.

TOKYU HANDS

Inokashira-dori Ave.
Bunkamura
Shoto Museum of Art
Toguri Museum
of Art

Keio Inokashira Line
Tokyu Den-en
Toshi Line
Shinsen Sta.

YEBISU BEER MUSEUM, EBISU,
TOKYO METROPOLITAN
TOKYO PHOTOGRAPHIC ART MUSEUM
TOKYO METROPOLITAN
TEIEN ART MUSEUM

On Harajuku Bridge

For years, Harajuku Bridge has been a place for young people (usually between the ages of 15 and 20) to gather, dressed up according to whichever particular subculture they're part of. The styles change year by year, but some of the most iconic have been *visual-kei* (an androgynous rock group look), *cosplay* (manga or *anime* character costumes), *Gothic Lolita* (frills, flounces and a flair for the macabre), and *Kogal* (shiny blondes with school-uniform miniskirts and fake lashes). Their motivations vary—some do it for fun, others to be seen without being recognized (makeup and masks confer relative anonymity), and some just to break the strict social and dress codes they have to abide by otherwise. Some do it to look like their avatars, their self-representations online. Some also stroll up and down the main street in Akihabara, another Tokyo district with the nickname "Electric Town" (see p148).

Hall), and movie theater follow on from each other on six floors.

An excellent art gallery and some temporary exhibits complete the picture. You can also enjoy a coffee at Les Deux Magots (open daily 11.30am–10.30pm); every year since 1991 the cafe has awarded a literary prize to a promising young writer, just like its namesake in Paris.

If you walk up Dogenzaka, you'll find yourself in an area full of love hotels and some of the hippest clubs in town.

Shibuya Hikarie
Map VI, B2.
The first building to shoot up in the station area as part of its transformation, this tower (2012) looms over the (extremely futuristic) Fukutoshin Line station. Its 34 floors house 200 stores, 26 restaurants, art galleries, offices, and a 2000-seat concert hall that extends over four floors—not to mention its "switch rooms" (large, elaborately furnished restrooms designed to "switch" your mood) and the **Sky Lobby** on the 11th floor, with its beautiful panoramic view.

HARAJUKU AND AROUND ★ 原宿
Map VII, p168.
A mash-up of all the most eccentric things you are likely to run into in Tokyo, these areas have something to beguile everyone: roads both great and small, peppered with interesting buildings;

cultural and social customs that draw tourists and sociologists from all over the world to the area around Harajuku Bridge; and, as the profane rarely exists without the sacred, adjoining the bridge there is the imperial shrine of Meiji-jingu, one of the most venerated in Tokyo. For those in need of some solitude, there are two options close by: the large Yoyogi Park and Aoyama Cemetery.

HARAJUKU

Leaving Harajuku Station, you have a choice between Takeshita-dori and Harajuku bridge.

Takeshita-dori ★ 竹下通り
Subway JY19, JR Yamanote Line, Harajuku Station, Takeshita exit.
The bustling pedestrian street opposite is **Takeshita-dori**. This is to Tokyo what Carnaby Street once was to London. The outfits hanging on mannequins outside the shops seem to change outfits multiple times a day to keep up with the trends. Black leather with studs, white blouses with high collars, worn over tiny, checked skirts. This is a fashion world for adolescents, from out and out "gothic" to little pink boots, skintight athleisure outfits and pastel-coloured Lolita dresses. Continuing beyond Meiji-dori, you will come across a maze of quieter streets, where a riot of explosive colors radiates across four walls at the **Design Festa Gallery**. Nearby is **Cat Street**, which,

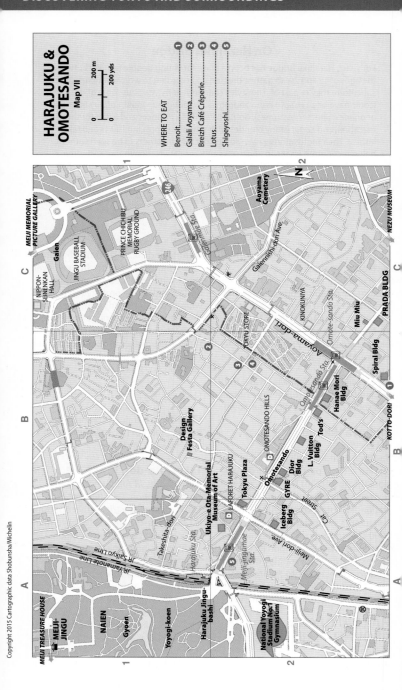

HARAJUKU & OMOTESANDO

Map VII

0   200 m
0   200 yds

WHERE TO EAT

Benoit............................. 1
Galali Aoyama................. 2
Breizh Café Crêperie....... 3
Lotus.............................. 4
Shigeyoshi...................... 5

Politics and religion

The founder of the shogunate, Tokugawa Ieyasu, is honored in a syncretic Shinto-Buddhist shrine, while Emperor Meiji has a purely Shinto shrine. Does this represent a difference of nature or just of extent? The man who led the modernization of Japan between 1868 and 1912 decreed Buddhism and Shintoism should be officially separated. His intention was that Shinto, the only indigenous religion, should once again be the only religion of the Japanese people. When this shrine was dedicated to the emperor eight years after his death, Shintoism became the state religion. The emperor was the sovereign leader of Japan and also the living representation of the descendants of the Shinto gods who created the country. However, in 1945 the defeat of Japan sounded the death knell for Shintoism as the state religion. The emperor, whom the Japanese still call *Tenno*, he "who comes from above," also lost his divine origins—but not his popularity. To get an idea of how beloved the emperor still is, you need only join the crowds visiting the shrine around New Year.

with its hip boutiques and independent cafes, has become the new center of cool in Harajuku as Takeshita-dori has grown more touristy.

▶ Turn right on leaving the station to head to the shrine via Harajuku Bridge.

Meiji-jingu ★★★ 明治神宮
Map VII, A1. No charge.
www.meijijingu.or.jp/english.
The Meiji emperor Mutsuhito and his wife, the empress Shoken, are honored at this Shinto shrine, in recognition of the emperor's role in the Meiji Restoration, which restored imperial rule to Japan. Although recent, dating from the early 1920s, it is one of the holiest shrines in the country, and one of the most popular, welcoming 3 million visitors each New Year for *hatsumode* (the first shrine visit).
The 173-acre/70ha park around the shrine is divided into two estates about 0.6mi/1km apart: the inner estate in the east (Naien), which is by far the more interesting, and the outer estate in the west (Gaien), which can also be accessed from the north side of Aoyama Cemetery at the end of the round trip.

Naien★★★ 内苑
Map VII, A1. Subway C03 or F15, Chiyoda and Fukotoshin lines, Meiji-jingumae Station; or JY19, JR Yamanote Line, Harajuku Station.

At the end of a wide avenue through the trees, you'll see a vast (40ft/12m) gate carved out of 1500-year-old cypress trees. Before you enter the sacred area of the shrine, make your way along the narrow path on the left through a cluster of trees to the beautiful and fertile **Inner Garden** (open daily 9am–4.30pm, Nov–Feb 4pm; ¥500). There's an iris garden at one end of a pond designed by the emperor for his wife.
The shrine was built with public funds in memory of the emperor, and Japanese people from every province donated 130,000 trees to the enterprise. Destroyed in World War II, it was rebuilt in 1958 according to the original plans. Sparseness and simplicity turn the shrine, with its copper-tiled roof, into a striking homage to the surrounding natural world, a world to which the emperor was not insensitive, as is evident in the short poems *(waka)* he used to write: "Look and learn from the rocks, hollowed out by drops of water." *(They are recorded on tiny scrolls, around ¥100.)* Farther north, the **Meiji Treasure House** exhibits family objects in rotation.

Gaien 外苑
Map VII, C1. Subway JB12, JR Chuo-Sobu Line, Sendagaya Station.
An avenue lined with gingko trees leads to the **Meiji Memorial Picture Gallery** (open daily 9am–5pm; ¥500). The different stages of the Emperor's life are

Naien, Meiji-jingu

© BirgerNiss/iStock

displayed in 80 wall paintings (mainly of historical interest). Beyond the gallery, the Gaien is popular for picnics, jogging and informal sports games.

Yoyogi-koen ★ 代々木公園
Map VII, A1/2. Subway JY19, JR Yamanote Line, Harajuku Station.

One of the biggest parks in Tokyo is also one of the most original in terms of both the informal and formal activities that take place here: sports competitions, festivals, rock concerts, both improvised and planned, dance displays of all kinds, etc. They turn the area into a highly colorful space that is rendered deafening by police sirens, rockers, and *takenokozuku* (literally "young bamboo shoots," meaning street dancers), particularly on Sundays. The two **Olympic stadiums** of the Yoyogi National Stadium, designed in 1964 by Tange Kenzo, are at the edge of the park. The National Gymnasium is famous for its suspended roof design and housed the swimming and diving events at the 1964 Summer Olympics.

OMOTESANDO ★ 表参道
Map VII, B2.
Omotesando literally means "the main road leading to the shrine," and this wide, leafy street lined with designer stores does indeed lead right to Meiji-

jingu. Before heading into the iconic **Laforet ★** store on the corner with Meiji-dori, take a detour via the Ota Museum.

Ukiyo-e Ota Memorial Museum of Art ★ 太田記念美術館
Map VII, A2. 1-10-10 Jingumae, Shibuya-ku. Subway C03 or F15, exit 5; or JY19, Omotesando-guchi exit. ☉Open Tue–Sun 10.30am–5.30pm. ☞Entry charge varies with exhibition. ukiyoe-ota-muse.jp/eng.

More than 12,000 woodblock prints *(ukiyo-e)* spanning the Edo era form the basic collection of this small museum established by Ota Seizo (1893–1977), a former insurance company director. All the great masters are here: Utamaro, Hokusai, Hiroshige, Toyoyuni, Toyaharu, Monorobu, and Harunobu.

▶ Continue down Omotesando-dori, heading away from Meiji-jingu.

Past the Laforet crossroad, the commercial center **Tokyu Plaza ★** and the architecturally audacious buildings of some of the world's biggest luxury brand names (**Dior★** in a light, multi-layered treasure box of a building, and **Tod's★★** looking like a white metal tree has grown up over it) jostle for space on the sidewalk of this wide avenue shaded by zelkova trees. To the left, near the top of the road, is the property developer Mori's complex, **Omotesando Hills**. Designed by Ando Tadao, it includes a shopping mall, some stylish apartments, and boutiques, all made up of Ando's clean lines. On the other side of the road are six floors of paradise for children, **Kiddyland** 👫 (6-1-9 Jingumae) and the **Oriental Bazaar** (🕐 open Fri–Wed 10am–7pm, orientalbazaar.co.jp), which overflows with Japanese souvenirs and antiques. At the end of Omotesando-dori you'll see the glass cubes of the **Hanae Mori Building ★**, named after the fashion designer Hanae Mori, and designed by Tange Kenzo in 1978.

AOYAMA ★ 青山
🕐 Map VII, B2–C2.
Ready-to-wear and haute couture stores line the sidewalks of **Aoyama-dori** with their amazing buildings, such as the **Spiral Building ★** by Maki Fumihiko (🕐 Map VII, B2). The exterior is asymmetrical, and a huge spiral ramp winds around inside. On Minami Aoyama-dori the stores of powerhouse Japanese brands Issey Miyake, Comme des Garçons (Rei Kawakubo), Yohji Yamamoto (5-3-6 Minami Aoyama) and international favorites like Prada and Cartier (Bruno Moinard) follow one after the other.
The most remarkable of these is the **Prada Building ★★★** (🕐 Map VII, C2), designed by the Swiss architects Herzog & de Meuron, who also designed the famous Bird's Nest stadium for the Beijing Olympic Games. The walls of its six floors are made up of diamond-shaped panes of glass supported in a framework of steel, giving the appearance of quilted fabric. It's particularly worth seeing by night.
The same architects also designed the **Miu Miu ★★** store, the understated design of which looks like a box with one flap slightly open to form a metallic awning, and copper-colored surfaces inside.

Nezu Museum ★★★ 根津美術館
🕐 Map VII, C2, off map. 6-5-1 Minami-Aoyama, Minato-ku. Subway C04, G02 or Z02, Chiyoda, Ginza and Hanzomon lines, Omotesando Station.

🕐 Open Tue–Sun 10am–5pm. 🎫 ¥1100 (excluding special exhibitions). www.nezu-muse.or.jp/en. ☕.
The museum was established over 40 years ago by Nezu Kaichiro, who had spent a lifetime collecting calligraphy, sculptures, ceramics, textiles, and archeological materials from Asia. Today housed in a warm, Kuma Kengo-designed building, the collection contains over 1000 works, including 87 Important Cultural Properties. The Chinese bronzes dating from the Shang (1700 BC–1050/25 BC) and Zhou (1050/25 BC–256 BC) dynasties are among the highlights. In the superb Japanese garden, bamboo conceals tea houses and a charming café (tea ceremonies on certain dates, reservation required). A real haven of peace.

Aoyama Cemetery ★★ 青山霊園
🕐 Map VII, C2. Subway G03, Ginza Line, Gaienmae Station.
More than 100,000 tombs fill the Aoyama (Japanese for "blue mountain") Cemetery. Opened in 1872, it covers an area of some 279,862sq ft/26,000sq m. Its prestigious occupants include Inukai Tsuyoshi, a prime minister assassinated in 1932, and Shiga Naoya (1883–1971), a modern novelist known for writing stories in the first person, inserting material from his personal life into a fictional framework. The ashes of the famous dog **Hachiko** (🕐 see p165) are also buried here next to his master, Professor Ueno Eisaburo.
Also worth a look is the section designated as a historic gaikokujin bochi, or cemetery for foreigners.

ODAIBA ★ お台場
🕐 Map I; C4, off map, p136.
The name of this **artificial island** in Tokyo Bay comes from the "cannon batteries" (odaiba) that the shogun installed in the 19C as protection against foreign invasion. However, this defense didn't prevent the American Commodore Perry's "black ships" from mooring in the bay in 1853 to request and require that the country be opened up to them. Since then, the batteries have made way for entertainment, with museums, parks, luxury hotels... There's not a part

of Odaiba that isn't dedicated to some form of leisure activity in some outlandish structure. And all served by monorail. From Shinbashi an automated train, the **👥 Yurikamome monorail ★★** *(every 5min)*, loops round the seafront buildings before disappearing over Rainbow Bridge. It then goes on to serve most of the sites described below. *(If you want to stop off at several places it's better to get a 1-day Open Pass for ¥820.)* You can also take the Rinkai Line.

Rainbow Bridge ★
レインボーブリッジ

A stroll across Rainbow Bridge, almost 2618ft/798m long and 417ft/127m at its highest point, is the best way to approach this futuristic district. Access (◑open Apr–Oct 9am–9pm, Nov–Mar 10am–6pm; ◑closed 3rd Mon of the month; ⚏no charge) is via elevators near Shibaura-Futo monorail station. You can either walk on the bridge's north side (views towards Tokyo) or its south side (views over Odaiba).

Fuji TV Building ★★
フジテレビ本社ビル

Subway U07, Yurikamome, Daiba stop; or R04, Rinkai Line, Tokyo Teleport stop. ◑*Open Tue–Sun 10am–6pm. Viewing deck:* ⚏*¥700. fujitv.com/visit_fujitv.*
This building, which looks as though it's made out of a giant children's construction set, was designed by **Tange Kenzo** (◖*see box below*) in 1996. It includes, in the sphere on the 25th floor, an observation deck. Nearby, on the river bank, is a replica of the **Statue of Liberty**, which has been in position since 1998.

Museum of Maritime Science
★ 船の科学館

3-1 Higashi-Yashio, Shinagawa-ku. Subway U08, Yurikamome, International Cruise Terminal Station. ◑*Open Tue–Sun 10am–5pm.* ⚏*No charge. funenokagakukan.or.jp.*
This museum, shaped like a cruise ship, has excellent models *(level 3F)* and a life-size ship's bridge replica *(level 6)*. At the quayside are the *Yotei Maru*, a ferry which plied the route between Aomori and Hokkaido until a tunnel was built

Fuji TV Building

© Darren Anderson/MICHELIN

Architecture in evolution

Tange Kenzo (1913–2005) graduated from Tokyo University with a degree in architecture and engineering. When he joined the practice of Maekawa Kunio, a pupil of the great master Le Corbusier, Tange was influenced by the use of reinforced concrete, a material particularly appropriate in the reconstruction of postwar Japan, where the use of flammable wood was severely restricted. In 1949, he won a competition to design the Peace Memorial Park and Atomic Bomb Museum in Hiroshima, launching his career. He was one of several architects to join the Metabolist movement (◖*see p101*), which aimed to lay the foundations of an architecture that could adapt to a permanently growing urban organism, even if it meant creating sprawling structures that encroached on both sky and sea. His projects flourished in the "Tokyo 1960" development plan, and in 1987, his reputation was sealed when he won the Pritzker Architecture Prize.

Rainbow Bridge at night

in 1988, and the *Soya*, an Antarctic ice-breaker and scientific observation ship.

National Museum of Emerging Science and Innovation (Miraikan) ★ 日本科学未来館

2-3-6 Aomi, Koto-ku. Subway U09, Yurikamome, Telecom Center Station. ◐*Open Wed–Mon 10am–5pm.* ⊜*¥620 (under-19s ¥210). www.miraikan.jst. go.jp/en.* ☕.

👥 This fine structure is as well thought-out as its exhibits. The highly educational 3F exhibitions show robotics (you can even meet Asimo the robot), nano-technology, and superconductivity; particle acceleration and general science are on 5F; and 6F houses the Dome Theater. The museum presents a broad, involved overview that is never dull.

Oedo Onsen Monogatari ★
大江戸温泉物語

2-6-3 Aomi, Koto-ku. Subway U09, Yurikamome, Telecom Center Station. ◐*Open daily 10am–9am.* ⊜*¥2720 (Sat–Sun ¥2936, public hols ¥3044); after 6pm ¥2180 (Sat–Sun ¥2396, public hols ¥2504). daiba.ooedoonsen.jp/en.* ☕.

👥 Oedo Onsen Monogatari's numerous well-kept baths (indoor, outdoor, sand baths, etc.) are designed to transport you back to the Edo period, complete with colorful cotton yukata to wear while you stroll around. The huge complex feels like a hot spring theme park, and has plenty to keep kids happy. Note that Oedo Onsen Monogatari will refuse entry to anyone with a tattoo.

Tokyo Olympics 2020

Having been selected to organise the 1940 Games—which were cancelled because of the Second World War—Tokyo finally made it in 1964, the first Asian city to host the event. It then managed to win the bid for the 2020 Games, too, becoming the first city in Asia to host the Summer Olympics twice. New structures like the Olympic Village, built to be a model of sustainable urban design, have added to the Tokyo cityscape, leaving an architectural legacy just as 1964 did. But infrastructure from the previous Games was not wasted, with the artificial islands in the bay playing host to events such as canoeing, rowing and beach volleyball—though the area was not suitable for surfing, a new addition for 2020, which was held in neighboring Chiba prefecture.

Palette Town ★ パレットタウン

1-3-15 Aomi, Koto-ku. Subway U10, Yurikamome, Aomi Station.

👥This multifaceted amusement complex includes a **giant Ferris wheel** 328ft/100m in diameter (🕐*open 10am–10pm, Fri & Sat 10.40pm*; ✆¥1000), the Zepp Tokyo concert hall, and a shopping mall, **Venus Fort,** designed like an 18C European city. In this rather kitsch setting (🕐*open 11am–11pm, venusfort.co.jp*), 170 shops (outlet mall 3F) and restaurants beckon under an artifical sky whose color changes by the hour. At **Toyota Mega Web ★** (🕐*open 11am–9pm*; ✆*no charge; megaweb.gr.jp*) you can visit the Ride One test drive area (✆¥300; *reservation required, yoyaku.megaweb.gr.jp/reserve/index.html*). The History Garage displays classic cars and an array of model cars.

Accessible on the 2F (by the ferris wheel entrance) is the **teamLab Borderless Digital Art Museum ★★** at the Mori Building (🕐*open Mon–Fri 10am–7pm, Sat & Sun 10am–9pm*; 🕐*closed 2nd & 4th Tue of month*; ✆¥3200, *under-15s ¥1000; borderless.teamlab.art*). In this interactive, immersive digital art exhibition you stand in bright projections which change as you touch them, wander through rooms of softly glowing balloons, and relax in a tearoom where digital flowers bloom in your cup.

Decks Tokyo Beach
デックス東京ビーチ

1-6-1 Daiba, Monato-ku. Subway U06, Yurikamome, Odaiba-kaihinkoen Station. odaiba-decks.com.

On the 4th floor of the Seaside Mall is the **Takoyaki Museum,** where you can sample as many of these delicious snacks (octopus dumplings) as you can eat. On the same floor is the **Daiba Ichome Shotengai,** which takes you back to Japan in the 1960s. Re-created home interiors, a kindergarten, and even a subway station await, with streets of traditional shops lit by paper lanterns. Video gamers will love **Joypolis** (entrance Seaside Mall 3F); the Sega amusement park is on three levels (🕐*open daily 10am–10pm; unlimited pass* ✆*¥4500 for adults, ¥3500*

for under-18s; tokyo-joypolis.com), and is Japan's largest indoor indoor amusement park.

Tokyo Big Sight 東京ビックサイト (東京国際展示場)

3-11-1 Ariake, Koto-ku. Subway U11, Yurikamome, Tokyo Big Sight Station. bigsight.jp/english.

Japan's largest exhibition center stands on four enormous feet shaped like inverted pyramids. At the entrance is a giant steel-and-plastic sculpture of a red-handled saw, buried in the ground as if cutting through it, byAmerican artist Claes Oldenburg.

Panasonic Center Tokyo
パナソニックセンター東京

3-5-1 Ariake, Koto-ku. Subway Ariake Station. 🕐*Open Tue–Sun 10am–6pm.* ✆*No charge. www.panasonic.com/global/corporate/center/tokyo.html.*

A four-story technological showcase for the company, often featuring special exhibitions relating to Japanese culture and technology.

KAGURAZAKA★ 神楽坂 AND KORAKU-EN 後楽園

📍*Map I, B2–C2, p136.*

Kagura is northwest of the gardens of the Imperial Palace. An ancient entertainment district, renowned in the Edo period, it has been spared the developers to date and is particularly lively as night falls thanks to its many restaurants (📖*see Addresses p196*). Over on the other side of the Kanda River is Koraku-en, an area dedicated to sport and leisure.

Kagurazaka-dori ★
神楽坂通り

Kagurazaka was once Edo's primary geish district, but today you're less likely to hear the clatter of wooden-soled *geta* than you are too overhear a conversation in French. The Institut Français is just around the corner from this maze of little lanes, and the area has become known for its blend of traditional Japanese and European influences; it's home to a number of French restaurants, bakeries, wine bars, and bookshops.

Koishikawa Koraku-en,
Tokyo Dome City in the background

© Gargolas/iStock

Tokyo Dome City ★
東京ドームシティ

Map I, C1. 1-3-61 Koraku, Bunkyo-ku. Subway M22 or N11, Marunouchi or Nanboku lines, Korakuen Station. www.tokyo-dome.co.jp/e.

This entertainment complex is centered on a **baseball stadium** (*sometimes nicknamed "Big Egg"*), which opened in 1988 with a capacity of 55,000 and is home to the Yomiuri Giants baseball team. There's also the interactive, kid-friendly **TeNQ Space Museum** (*open Mon–Fri 11am–8pm, Sat & Sun 10am–8pm; ¥1800, under-16s ¥1200*); the *onsen* at **Spa LaQua** (*open 11am– 9am; from ¥2850*); and an **amusement park** (*hours vary; one-day pass ¥4200, under-18s ¥3700*) with hair-raising rides not for the faint-hearted! You'll also find restaurants, shops, sports facilities, a gallery and a bowling alley.

Bunkyo Civic Center
文京シビックセンター

Map I, C1. 1-16-21 Kasuga, Bunkyo-ku. Subway JB17 or I11, JR Chuo-Sobu or Toei Mita lines, Suidobashi Station. Open Mon–Fri 9am–8.30pm.

This building, which looks like nothing so much as a giant Pez dispenser, has a 330-degree observation deck on the 25th floor (*no charge*), and a number of restaurants with panoramic views.

Koishikawa Koraku-en ★★
小石川後楽園

Map I, C1. 1-6-6 Koraku, Bunkyo-ku. Subway JB16, T06, Y13, N10 or E06, Iidabashi Station. Open daily 9am–5pm (last entry 30min before closing). ¥300.

Created in the early Edo era, this Japanese garden is one of the oldest in Tokyo. It's a stroll garden, reproducing in miniature well-known Chinese and Japanese landscapes. Dotted with waterfalls and stone bridges, it is particularly beautiful when the plum trees are in blossom (*mid-Feb–Mar*), and in cherry blossom season immediately afterwards.

EBISU DISTRICT 恵比寿

Map I, A4. Subway JA09, JS18, JY21 or H02, JR Saikyo, Shonan-Shinjuku and Yamanote lines or Hibiya Line, Ebisu Station, east exit.

A moving walkway several hundred feet long leads from the station to **Yebisu Garden Place** and, rather incongruously, a Louis XIII-style château, one of the many extravagant constructions to come out of the bubble economy era. Inside is a Joël Robuchon restaurant and store. Left of the château is **Yebisu Beer Museum** (*4-20-1 Ebisu, Shibuya-ku, Ebisu Station; open Tue–Sun 11am–7pm; no charge*), which offers free guided tours and ¥400 tastings.

Theme Parks in Japan

Japan has so enthusiastically embraced *tema paku* (theme parks) that it now boasts dozens of superb examples. An established form of entertainment in Japan today, they can make for a fantastic day out. Some of the best-known are:

Tokyo Disneyland Resort, comprised of Tokyo Disneyland and DisneySea (*Urayasu City, Chiba, just outside Tokyo; www.tokyodisneyresort.jp/en*). **Tokyo Disneyland** is huge (115 acres/46ha) and easy to explore with its circular plan, internal train, and Fastpass to avoid lines. Main Street is roofed for year-round temperature control. Dining establishments tend to favor classic American fast-food, while souvenir shops focus on Mickey. **DisneySea** is next door, its seven themed "ports of call" presenting tales of the sea around the central Mount Prometheus landmark. There are rides, shops, restaurants, live shows and the Fastpass, but since the target audience includes adults as well as children, alcohol is available; illuminations make it romantic by night.

Sanrio Puroland (*Tama City, west of Tokyo; en.puroland.jp*) is a fairly small indoor theme park featuring Hello Kitty and friends. The nine main attractions, five themed eateries and Japan's largest Sanrio store guarantee total immersion in *kawaii*! There is plenty of information in English. A good choice for small children, while adults will particularly enjoy the Gudetama section. A full-scale outdoor version of Sanrio Puroland, **Harmonyland**, has been opened near Beppu in Oita City, on the southern island of Kyushu (*harmonyland.jp*). It has fourteen main attractions, and four eateries ranging from fast food to a more formal restaurant.

Universal Studios Japan (*Osaka; www.usj.co.jp/e*) brings movie magic to life. Resembling the Orlando version, its nine areas contain nineteen attractions, 45 themed restaurants and shops. The Wizarding World of Harry Potter is a popular section, while the ultra-cute Universal Wonderland is great for kids. There are many attractions indoors as well as outdoors, and an Express Pass system to avoid lines. Particularly popular with Asian visitors.

Opening hours and entrance fees vary, so plan your visit in advance by checking the theme parks' websites before you set off.

Tokyo Photographic Art Museum ★★ 東京都写真美術館

Map I, A4. Yebisu Garden Place, 1-13-3 Mita, Meguro-ku. 7min walk from Ebisu Station. Open Tue–Sun 10am–6pm (Thu–Fri 8pm). Entry charge varies with exhibition. topmuseum.jp/e/contents/index.html.

One of the most outstanding museums of photography in the country, exploring Japan's rich photographic tradition, and showing the work of promising global photographers.

Tokyo Metropolitan Teien Art Museum ★ 東京都庭園美術館

Map I; A4, off map. 5-21-9 Shirokanedai, Minato-ku. Subway JY22, N01, I01, or MG01, Meguro Station, east exit or main gate. Open daily 10am–6pm. Closed 2nd & 4th Wed of the month. Entry charge varies with exhibition; garden ¥200. www.teien-art-museum.ne.jp/en.

Completed in 1933, the former residence of Prince Asaka (who studied in France), the husband of Emperor Meiji's eighth daughter, is stamped with early-20C European artistic influences. This Art Deco mini-palace (entirely renovated and extended in 2014) is a small jewel of a building where the works of French designers such as René Lalique, Raymond Subes, Léon Blanchot, and Henri Rapin are exhibited beside contemporary Japanese artists. The attractive garden, too, has both European and Japanese sections.

Institute for Nature Study ★★
附属自然教育園

Map I; B4, off map. 5-21-5 Shirokanedai, Minato-ku. 10min walk from Meguro Station, east exit. Open daily 9am–5pm (Sept–Apr 4.30pm; last entry 1hr before closing). ¥310. ins.kahaku.go.jp/english. Though it seems impossible now, the land where Tokyo stands was originally thick forest and marshland. At the Institute for Nature Study, a small slice of this landscape is preserved, an oasis of calm right in the middle of the metropolis.

Sengaku-ji ★ 泉岳寺

Map I; B4, off map. 2-11-1 Takanawa, Minato-ku. Subway A07, Toei Asakusa and Keikyu Main lines, Sengakuji Station. Temple: open daily Apr–Sept 7am–6pm (Oct–Mar 5pm). No charge. Museum: open daily 9am–4pm. ¥500. sengakuji.or.jp.

This temple, founded by Tokugawa Ieyasu in 1612, gives an introduction to one of the best-known historical events of 18C Japan, the suicide by *seppuku* of the **47 ronin**. The *ronin* (samurai who had lost their leader) avenged the death of their master, the Lord of Ako. After they executed their master's opponent they gave themselves up to the authorities. The sentence was pronounced and they were condemned to *seppuku*, a sentence they carried out one after the other without blinking.

The name and age of each *ronin* is written on their grave; the youngest was just 16 years old, while the oldest was 77. On December 14, the anniversary of the event, people flock here in large numbers to pay tribute to this extraordinary sacrificial act.

EXCURSIONS

KICHIJOJI ★ 吉祥寺

Map I; A2, off map. Subway IN17, JC11 or JB02, Keio Inokashira, JR Chuo or JR Chuo-Sobu lines, Kichijoji Station.
Often called Tokyo's most livable area, Kichijoji is known for its welcoming atmosphere, attractive stores, beautiful park and excellent museum.

Inokashira-koen ★ 井の頭公園

Map I; A2, off map. 1-18-31 Gotenyama, Musashino-shi. Subway Kichijoji Station, or IN16, Keio Inokashira Line, Inokashira-koen Station. Open daily 24hr. No charge.

At over 100 years old, Inokashira-koen has been one of Tokyo's best-loved parks for a long time. The walks around the lake are very pleasant, especially when the water is dotted with springtime cherry blossoms or the scarlet foliage of fall. A small temple in the depths of the large park is dedicated to Benzaiken, goddess of love and waterways, who is said to have enchanted the lake so that lovers crossing it will separate. Peddlars sell crafts on the shores at weekends.

Take kids out on a swan-shaped pedal boat or rowing boat, and don't forget to treat them to a traditional *kaki-gori* (shaved ice with syrup) at the park's entrance in summer.

Ghibli Museum ★★
三鷹の森ジブリ美術館

Map I; A2, off map. 1-1-83 Shimorenjaku, Mitaka-shi. Subway JC12 or JB01, JR Chuo or Chuo-Sobu lines, Mitaka Station, south exit; then 15min walk or 5min bus (¥300 round trip). Open Wed–Mon 10am–6pm. ¥1000, under-19s ¥700. Admission by timed ticket, which must be reserved well in advance (full details on website). www.ghibli-museum.jp/en.

This whimsical museum, located in the far southwest of Inokashira-koen, is truly delightful. While kids will find plenty to marvel at, adults who have an interest in Japanese culture and animation in general, or Studio Ghibli in particular, will also be enchanted. Highlights include the full-size Cat Bus and the re-creation of Miyazaki's studio. The talented animator **Hayao Miyazaki** co-founded Studio Ghibli after the successful film adaptation of his manga *Nausicaa of the Valley of the Wind* (1984). Others followed including *Princess Mononoke* (1997), *Spirited Away* (2001, the first non-English-language movie to win the Best Animated Feature Oscar), and *The Wind Rises* (2013).

Mount Fuji viewed from Mount Takao

© Dick Thomas Johnson/Getty Images

Mount Takao ★★★ 高尾山

♿ *Map I; A3, off map. Subway KO53, Keio Takao Line, Takaosanguchi Station (55min from Shinjuku). www.keio.co.jp/ english/local/takao.html. Allow at least half a day.*

🚶 Mount Takao, 1,965ft/599m high, is in Hachioji city, southeast of the Kanto foothills, and is technically part of the Tokyo urban area. The forested areas are right on the border between Japan's subtropical and temperate zones, with trees representative of both types of vegetation forming a real paradise for flora and fauna.

There are seven different hiking trails. No.1, the Pilgrim Trail, takes you to the summit *(allow 1hr 40min for 2.4mi/3.8km)* past the temple of Yakuo-in. The chairlift (Sanroku Station) or cable car (Kiyotaki Station) shortens the distance by about a third *(🚠¥930 round trip)*. You'll pass forests of 100-year-old cedars, beech trees, and wildflowers on the ascent, and can enjoy a fine **view** of Tokyo, and of Mt. Fuji in good weather.

Ogasawara – a tropical paradise in Tokyo

Did you know that Tokyo has an exceptionally high number of endemic animal species? Or that Tokyo has large expanses of tropical humid forests? Or that there are thousands of palm trees lining its long beaches of white sand, where startlingly blue waters gently lap? The Tokyo metropolitan area's administrative territory includes the archipelago of the **Ogasawara Islands**, a tropical paradise inhabited by fewer than 3000 islanders and located 620 miles/1000km from the heart of the Japanese capital.

The archipelago's fantastically varied scenery is home to a rich diversity of animal life, including a very rare bat, the Bonin flying fox. With 441 indigenous plants, the islands' vegetation reflects the evolutionary processes that once combined the plant species of Southeast Asia with others from Northeastern Asia. The hot springs of these Eden-like islands have attracted extraordinary aquatic life. The store of natural riches is so great that the islands have been designated a UNESCO World Heritage site.

To access the islands you need to take a 24-hour boat trip (some islanders have been lobbying for an airport for years), and all accommodation should be booked in advance. More details at www.ogasawaramura.com.

USEFUL INFORMATION
TOKYO

Tourist Offices – Tokyo Tourist Information Center, *1F Metropolitan Government Bldg no. 1, 2-8-1 Nishishinjuku, Shinjuku-ku. Subway E28, JR Shinjuku Station, west exit. Map V, A2. Open daily 9.30am–6.30pm. ℘03-5321-3078. www.tokyotouristinfo.com/en.*

JTO Tourist Information Center, *1F Shin Tokyo Building, 3-3-1 Marunouchi, Chiyoda-ku. 5min walk from Yurakucho Station (subway Y18 or JR Yamanote Line). Map III, B1. Open daily 9am–5pm. Closed Jan 1. ℘03-3201-3331. www.japan.travel/en/plan/tic/tic-tokyo.*

Go Tokyo – Tokyo city's official tourism site, informative and updated regularly: www.gotokyo.org/en/index.html.

⊛ If you're planning to visit several museums, save money by purchasing a **Grutt Pass** (¥2000), which gives free or discounted entry to 68 museums, art galleries, zoos and aquariums in Tokyo. Inquire at the ticket office of one of the participating museums, which includes all the largest ones.

Bank/Foreign Exchange – Prestia/SMBC Trust Bank, *1F Ote Center Bldg, 1-1-3 Otemachi, Chiyoda-ku. Subway M18, exit C9. Open Mon–Fri 9am–3pm. Closed public holidays. ATM approx 24hr. ℘03-3215-0051.* Prestia ATMs (was Citibank) accept Western cards. There are branches in Ginza, Shibuya, Aoyama, Shinjuku, etc. You will also find ATMs that accept foreign cards in most post offices and 7-Eleven stores *(open 24hr).*

Post Office – Tokyo Central Post Office, *JP Tower Bldg, 2-7-2 Marunouchi, Chiyoda-ku, Subay M17 or C10. Map II, B2. Open Mon–Fri 9am–9pm, Sat–Sun & public holidays 9am–7pm. ℘03-3217-5231.*

Emergency Services/Health – **Fire Service and ambulance** ℘119 *(24hr)* or 03-3212-2111. **Police** ℘110 *(24hr).*

Information in English: the Tokyo government's **Himawari hospitals information service** offers a foreign language information service for the capital's medical services *(daily 9am–8pm; ℘03-5285-8181; www.himawari.metro. tokyo.jp)* and also an emergency translation service for difficulties in comprehension on admission to hospital. The **Amda Service International**

Medical Information Center provides the addresses of multilingual doctors throughout the whole of Japan. *Open Mon–Fri 9am–5pm (℘03-5285-8088. eng. amda-imic.com).*

Pharmacy – American Pharmacy, *B1F Marunouchi Bldg, 2-4-1 Marunouchi, Chiyoda-ku. Subway M17, C10. ℘03-5220-7716. www.marunouchi. com/e/shop/detail/1002. Shop open 9am–9pm (Sat 10am–9pm, Sun & public holidays 10am–8pm); pharmacy open 10.30am–7.30pm.*

TRANSPORTATION
BY PLANE –

Narita International Airport, *www.narita-airport.jp/en.* Located almost 43.5mi/70km east of Tokyo, Narita has three terminals, with a free transfer shuttle between them. Terminal 1 Tourist Information Center: *1F Central Bldg (open daily 8am–8pm, ℘0476-30-3383).* Terminal 2 Tourist Information Center: *1F Main Bldg (open 8am–8pm; ℘0476-34-5877).*

Haneda Airport, *www.tokyo-airport-bldg.co.jp/en.* Haneda airport is located 12.5mi/20km south of Tokyo on an island facing the bay at the mouth of the Tama River *(Map I; B4, off map).* Most domestic flights arrive at Terminals 1 and 2. Flights from Paris, Seoul, Hong Kong, Beijing, and Shanghai arrive at the International Terminal, Terminal 1. There are several Tourist Information Centers in each terminal building.

⊛ Trains run between Narita and Haneda *(1hr 30min ¥3080, or 2hr ¥1760).* The same journey costs ¥3100 by Limousine Bus and takes about 1hr15min.

From Narita Airport to central Tokyo: From Narita, the **Narita Express** (N'EX) run by JR East leaves almost every 30min (7:30am–7pm) or every hour (8pm and 9pm). It connects to Tokyo Station (1hr journey), Shibuya (1hr 20min)), Shinjuku (1hr 25min)), and Ikebukuro (1hr 30min), all around ¥3100.

⊛ Save money with a **N'EX pass** (¥4000), valid for a round trip between Narita and several major urban stations (Shinagawa, Shibuya, Shinjuku, Ikebukuro; www.jreast. co.jp/e/nex). The **Suica** prepaid card can be used on the subway and Tokyo buses as well as JR lines. You can buy passes and cards from the JR East Travel Service Centers at Narita.

If you have time and want to save money, choose the **rapid train** that goes to Tokyo Station (1hr 30min, ¥1320).

The **Skyliner Airport Express** run by Keisei (*www.keisei.co.jp*) stops at Nippori Station (36min, ¥2470), Keisei-Ueno Station (41min, ¥2470), Shinjuku (56min, ¥2670), and Shibuya (63min, ¥2,670). Departurtes nearly every 40min. This is the fastest and most practical way to travel if staying in the Ueno Park area. Slower but also cheaper (¥1030), the **Limited Express**, also run by Keisei, takes 1hr13min to Nippori and 1hr16min to Ueno; departures roughly every 20min.

Remember, if you take the train, you will probably need to add the price of a taxi fare, or at least a subway ticket, to get to your exact destination.

The Limousine Bus Company (*www.limousinebus.co.jp/en*) takes passengers from the arrivals hall to a number of (mostly high-end, well-established) hotels in central Tokyo. Tickets (about ¥3100, round-trip ticket available for ¥4500; departures every 15–30min) can be purchased from desks at the passport control exit. Bags are labeled and stowed by an efficient member of staff. The Limousine Bus is good for travelers with heavy suitcases who are staying in a hotel on the bus route, or one situated within a short walking distance.

The Limousine Bus also goes to Shinjuku Station (minimum journey time 1hr 30min, ¥3100) and Tokyo City Air Terminal (T-CAT; *www.tcat-hakozaki.co.jp/en*)**,** northeast of downtown Tokyo (around 1hr, ¥3000), which connects to Suitengumae station on the Hanzomon Line (subway Z10). The steady traffic between the airport and the T-CAT ensures that timetables can generally be met (it can get more difficult after the T-CAT). Departures every 10min.

A journey from the airport to the wards of Bunkyo, Chiyoda, and Chuo **by taxi** costs around ¥20,000, and ¥21,500 to Shinjuku, Shibuya, or Minato, six times as much as a Limousine Bus and no faster!

From Haneda to downtown Tokyo:
The **Tokyo Monorail** departs every 5–10min (*www.tokyo-monorail.co.jp/english*) for Hamamatsucho Station on the JR Yamanote Line (13min, ¥490).
🐾 If you're planning to transfer at Hamamatsucho, get the Monorail and Yamanote Line discount Ticket (¥500) which covers you from Haneda to any Yamanote Line station.

The **Keikyu Airport Line** (*Keikyu Tourist Information Center: arrivals hall 2F, daily 7am–10pm*) runs to Shinagawa Station (20min, ¥410).

A **Limousine Bus** to Tokyo Station costs about ¥930, taking around 45min, and a **taxi** to downtown Tokyo about ¥8000.

BY TRAIN –

The **Shinkansen** from the west of Japan (Osaka, Kyoto) and from the north (Nagano, Akita, etc.) generally arrives at Tokyo Station, downtown (Map II, C3), or at Shinagawa, near Tokyo Bay (Map I; B4, off map). Some trains go on as far as Ueno, in the north of the city (Map I, C1).

Any **JR Pass** which covers the JR East routes will cover unlimited journeys on Japan Rail lines (within the allotted timeframe) in and around Tokyo, including Mount Fuji, Izu and Nikko.
The **JR Tokyo Wide Pass** (*3 days; ¥10,000, children ¥5000*) is an economical option if you plan on doing a few day trips back to back. Passports need to be shown when buying the pass. For sales points see *www.jreast.co.jp/e/tokyowidepass.*

BY BUS –

Long-distance buses (**Highway Buses**, in Japanese *Kosoku Basu*) arrive at the major stations on the Yamanote Line (Tokyo, Shinagawa, Shibuya, Shinjuku, and Ikebukuro). They are 20–50 percent cheaper than the train. Prices can vary significantly between companies.
For Nagoya, there are several buses a day with **Keio** (*www.highway-buses.jp*), **Meitetsu** (*www.meitetsu-bus.co.jp/english/index.html*)**,** **JR Tokai Bus** (*www.jrtbinm.co.jp*) and **Willer Express** (*willerexpress.com/en*). All take around 6hr 30min/7hr, and cost ¥4000–7500.
For Kyoto, there are several departures a day (and overnight) with **JR Bus Kanto** (*www.jrbuskanto.co.jp*) and **JR Bus West Japan** (*www.nishinihonjrbus.co.jp/en*). All around 8hr, ¥5000–8500.
For Osaka, departures with several companies such as **JR Bus Kanto, JR Bus West Japan, Seibu** (*www.seibubus.co.jp/sp/english_information*) and **Kintetsu** (*www.kintetsu-bus.co.jp/en*). All about 8hr, ¥5600–8900.

For Hiroshima, departures with companies including **JR Bus Chugoku** (www.chugoku-jrbus.co.jp), and **Willer Express**. All around 12hr, ¥5000 –12,000.

⊘ For more information, visit www.bus. or.jp/en/index.html.

BY BOAT –

Ocean Tokyu Ferry company (✆03-5148-0109, www.otf.jp/English_page.html) boats for Tokyo regularly set off from Tokushima in Shikoku (9am–5pm, 1 boat per day, 18hr crossing, shared cabin from ¥12,180, 2-bed cabin ¥10,000), or from Kitakyushu (1 boat per day, 34hr, shared cabin from ¥17,080, 2-bed cabin ¥15,000). Boats land at the port of Ariake in Odaiba. From there, buses run to the Shin-Kiba Station (subway JE05, Y24, R01). Alternatively, the Yurikamome Line (nearest station Tokyo Big Sight) runs over the Rainbow Bridge and stops at Shinbashi (subway JK24, JT02, JY29, JO18, G08, A10, U01). Another alternative is the Rinkai Line from Kokusai-Tenjijo Station, which runs to Osaki (subway JY24, JS17, JA08, R08).

NAVIGATING IN TOKYO

It's unwise to try to navigate Tokyo by street name. Unlike the Western system where a street has either a name or a number, the streets here, with the exception of a few large avenues (dori) remain nameless.

So, how do the people of Tokyo get about and orient themselves in such a huge, densely populated, and complicated city? It would appear to be impossible and yet it works quite well, thanks to a naming system based on the land registry. In addition to the name of the ward, to which the suffix -ku and the district are added, **the address is usually made up of a string of three numbers** (2-11-3 Ginza, Chuo-ku): the first number corresponds to that of a *chome*, the subdivision of a district with several blocks; the second refers to the block; the third relates to the construction date of the building, not its position in relation to the buildings in front of, or behind it on the site. Therefore no. 3, for example, can be next to no. 17 or no. 8. So, the same address can also be written *11-3 Ginza, 2-chome, Chuo-ku*. On most buildings a metal plate inscribed with the numbers (all three or just the last two) is fixed to the street light.

Although postal workers and the police are able to find their way around easily, when Tokyo residents venture into unknown territory they can find orienting themselves almost as difficult as foreigners do. And although armed with street plans and GPS navigation devices, taxi drivers don't always arrive at their destinations. Visitors may therefore find themselves hopelessly lost, in which case the best advice is to approach a friendly policeman installed in one of the many police substations (koban), often found in strategic positions.

HOW TO GET AROUND

BY SUBWAY – Although it's easy to get lost in the streets of Tokyo, everything is simpler below ground, thanks to the impeccable alpha-numeric signs that combine color coding with letters and numbers. These coordinates make it easy to work out how much of your journey remains, depending on whether the numbers are in ascending or descending order. A voice also announces the next station and all connections in English. Admiration for the subway system only increases upon the discovery that almost all stations are equipped with immaculately clean, free toilets and coin lockers. (🕐 See also p134 for tips.)

The network has 13 lines, **Tokyo Metro** (www.tokyometro.jp) running nine of them, **Toei Subway** (www.kotsu.metro.tokyo.jp) the remaining four (see map inside back cover). The entrance to the first nine is indicated by a panel with a white "M" against a blue background; the other four can be recognized by a white panel with a stylized green gingko leaf in the center. For a station served by both lines, a rectangular panel shows the front view of a train. A **subway map** is available at all stations.

⊘ To work out an itinerary and calculate the price and journey time visit the website www.tokyometro.jp; it includes Toei lines.

A **day ticket** on the nine Tokyo Metro lines costs around *¥600 (children ¥300)*, while for the Toei lines it's *¥700 (children ¥350)*; it's better value to buy a **Tokyo Subway Ticket** (only available to foreign tourists) to cover both, plus the tram and city buses, for *¥800 (children ¥400)*.

To buy a ticket for each journey there are ticket machines that accept coins or notes. The minimum ticket price is ¥170, but it goes up to ¥310 in proportion to the distance traveled. Summary tables show the prices for each station. When these are only written in Japanese, as is quite often the case, pay the minimum and then pay an additional amount if the ticket is refused at the exit. **Fare adjustment machines** are provided for this purpose. Insert the ticket and the machine will calculate the amount owing and print a new ticket once the additional amount has been paid. Attendants on duty can also provide assistance.

☺ *Strangely for such a large, bustling city, the subway closes at around 12:30am.*

BY JR – The **Yamanote Line**, which makes a loop around the center of Tokyo, has an elevated track which provides an opportunity to see the city. *(Tickets from ¥140.)* The same fare adjustment system is applied as in the subway. A JR ticket is not valid for the subway, so if you haven't got an IC card watch out for journeys that combine both. The JR also uses the **Chuo Line** (Chuo-sen) that runs from Tokyo Station to Shinjuku and then out to the suburbs as far as Mount Takao. **The Sobu Line** (Sobu-sen, from Chiba in the east to Mitaka in the west) serves the same stations as the Chuo Line, crossing the downtown area. The one-day **Tokunai Pass** covers all JR trains in central Tokyo *(¥750, children ¥370).*

☺ The **Tokyo Free Kippu** pass *(¥1590, children ¥800)* is valid for 1 day on the subway, on the buses, and the JR inside Tokyo. However, if you plan to use the subway and metropolitan JR lines often over a period of several days, it's much better to buy a **PASMO** or **Suica** rechargeable IC card, which is valid throughout the Tokyo subway and JR trains, and even in some shops *(pasmo. co.jp/visitors/en; jreast.co.jp/e/pass/suica. html).* There's no prospect of savings here, as the card is debited by at least ¥170 per journey. However, it does save the need to buy tickets until the credit runs out. It can also be used in other Japanese cities.

BY BUS – Unlike the subway, buses, with few exceptions, display their destination in kanji. Polyglots and the adventurous pay *¥210 per ticket (¥110 for children)* for any distance, in the 23 districts of Tokyo. Day passes are *¥500 (¥250 for children).*

BY TAXI – *The first 1.2mi/2km costs around ¥730 and each additional 0.6mi/1km around ¥360. Fares increase by 20 percent between 10pm and 5am.* Taxis can prove practical for short distances and are essential after 12.30am, when the subway closes. Tokyo has a taxi fleet of 50,000 cars. Don't be surprised when the rear doors open automatically to let you in and close automatically, too.

☺ In view of the difficulties that some taxi drivers have in finding the correct destination, it's a good idea to ask someone at your hotel to write out the name and address in *kanji*, or to be able to point it out on a map. Without a map, it's a good idea to name an easily identifiable place (subway, department store, etc.) near your final stop and finish the journey on foot, to save you time.

BY BICYCLE – The citizens of Tokyo are keen cyclists. They prefer to ride on the pavement, weaving in and out of pedestrians, umbrella held aloft when it rains. A ring of the bell indicates to other cyclists and pedestrians that they are about to overtake. Some districts such as Ueno, Yanaka, and Asakusa are particularly suitable for cycling, while many hotels **rent bikes** out by the day for a modest sum *(around ¥300 per day).*

Cycle Rental – **Sumida Park Bicycle Parking**, near the Sumida Park water bus kiosk, Asakusa. Subway G19 (Map IV, C2). Open 6am–8pm. *¥200 for 4hr (return by 4.20pm), ¥300 per day (return by 8.30pm).*

Community Cycle, docks throughout the city. Register and pay by card online (docomo-cycle.jp/chiyoda/en), or pay in cash for a one-day pass atone of the counters *(¥2000).* Otherwise, *¥150 for first 30min, ¥100 for every 30min after.*

BY BOAT – The boats of the **Tokyo Cruise Ship Company** *(www.suijobus. co.jp/en)* sail between Asakusa (Azuma Bridge) and Odaiba along the Sumida River. There are different trips to choose from. One departs from Asakusa and stops at Hamarikyu-teien *(40min, ¥1040, includes entry to the garden).* In spite of the sprawling concrete buildings that frequently line the banks, boat trips have the advantage of providing another vantage point from which to see the city. From Hinode Pier, 5min walk from Hamarikyu, boats go on to Odaiba.

ADDRESSES

TOKYO

FOOD & DRINK

In a city with every culinary temptation imaginable, some come at a very high price. But even expensive restaurants often offer fixed price lunch menus for ¥3500 or under. It is also possible to eat for very little outlay in the cheap restaurant chains *(Matsuya, Yoshinoya, Sukiya, etc.)*. These offer a bowl of rice with meat and a choice of miso soup, fish, salad, etc. *(¥200–600)*, or generous portions of noodles. **Conbini** – Japanese convenience stores such as 7-Eleven and Lawson – have sandwiches and *onigiri* (rice balls) for around *¥130*, and *bento* (boxed lunches) for roughly *¥500*. Every *conbini* has a microwave.

Most **department stores** have vast basement food halls, with *bento* at a reasonable prices. Since all hotel rooms are equipped with a kettle, to save on breakfast prices, just buy some tea or coffee *(kohi)* along with a light breakfast from the *conbini* on the corner.

NIGHTLIFE

Metropolis *(metropolis.co.jp)*, a weekly English language publication, is useful for finding out what's on. Free copies are distributed in cafes, restaurants, and hotels. Another useful source of information is *realtokyo.co.jp/en* for cultural events in the capital, while *residentadvisor.net/guide/jp/tokyo* is the best source of information on club nights, music festivals and similar events.

Cinemas – There are numerous movie theaters. For programs and times, look in Metropolis *(see above). Average price per seat: ¥1800.*

National Theater of Japan 国立劇場 – *4-1 Hayabusa-cho, Chiyoda-ku (next to the supreme court). Subway Z05 or Y16 (Map II, A2). www.ntj.jac.go.jp/english.html.* Traditional performances including Kabuki, Noh, *bunraku*, and *kyogen*. *Tickets ¥3000–5000; audioguides usually available.*

Security – Tokyo is certainly one of the safest capitals in the world and you can walk about at any hour. Exceptions are the night spots of Roppongi, Kabukicho, and Ikebukuro, where there are hostess bars with conmen ready to slip a drug into your glass in order to steal your cards. Common-sense rules apply: don't leave your drink unattended.

SPORT AND LEISURE

Helicopter Flight – Excel Air Service エクセル航空ヘリコプタークルージング – *14 Chidori, Urayasu-shi, Chiba. Subway JE07, JR Keiyo Line, Maihama Station; then taxi (5min) or shuttle (from 4pm). Reservations online or on ✆047-380-5555 (11am–5pm). excel-air.com/english.* Tokyo Sky Cruise: 4pm (3:30pm winter) to 30min after dusk – 15min flight. *¥20,400 per person, ¥14,200 (children); Sat–Sun & public holidays ¥23,700, ¥16,600.* Tokyo Night Cruise: 30min after dusk to 8:45pm (8:15pm winter) – 15min flight. *¥23,700 per person, ¥16,600 (children); Sat–Sun & public holidays ¥26,800, ¥18,800.*

Tea Ceremony – Imperial Hotel 帝国ホテル – *1-1-1 Uchisaiwai-cho, Chiyoda-ku (Map III, A1). Open Mon–Sat 10am–4pm. Reservations online or✆03-3504-1111. imperialhotel.co.jp/e/tokyo.* Lesson lasts 20min, *¥2000.*

Sado Kaikan 茶道会館 – *3-39-17 Takadanobaba, Shinjuku-ku. Subway JY15, SS02 or T03, JR Yamanote, Seibu Shinjuku or Tozai lines, Takadanobaba Station (Map 1, A1). Mon–Thu 10am–3pm and 6pm–9pm. Reservations ✆03-3361-2446 or kitami@sadoukaikan.com. sadoukaikan.com.* Lesson lasts 1hr *(3 people minimum, ¥5000 per person).*

Ikebana – Ohara School いけばな小原流 – *Ohara Kaikan Bldg, 5-7-17 Minami-Aoyama, Minato-ku. Subway G02, C04 or Z02, Ginza, Chiyoda or Hanzomon lines, Omotesando Station, exit B3. (Map VII, B2). ohararyu.or.jp/english/lesson.html. Reserve in advance.* Class in English *Thu 10.30am–4pm, Sun 10.30am–2pm; ¥4000–6000.* Taster lesson in English (2hr) *Thu 10:30am–noon or 1–3pm, Sun 10am–noon or 12.30–2pm; ¥4000.* Observation only *¥1000.*

USEFUL INFORMATION
ASAKUSA

Asakusa Culture and Tourism center Center 浅草文化観光センター–
2-18-9 Kaminari-mon, Taito-ku. Subway A18, G19, TS01 or TX03, Asakusa Station (Map IV, C2). Open daily 9am–8pm. ✆03-3842-5566. Bureau de change on the 1F and cafe on 8F with a panoramic view.

UENO

Tokyo Tourist Information Center – *Ueno Station, opposite Keisei Line ticket gates in station (Map IV, A2). Open daily 8am–6.30pm.* ✆03-3836-3472.

TRANSPORTATION
ASAKUSA

BY BOAT – **Tokyo Cruise Ship Company**, *by Azuma Bridge. Subway A18, exit 4 (Map IV, C2). Open daily 10am–5pm. Departs every 20–30 min. www.suijobus.co.jp/en.* **Tokyo Mizube Line** – *embark by Senso-ji Nitenmonmae. Subway G19, exit 5 (Map IV, C2). Open Tues–Sun 9am–5pm. www.tokyo-park.or.jp/waterbus/index.html.* These two companies offer trips across Tokyo Bay, stopping notably at Hamarikyu-teien (♨garden, see p157). **Rickshaw** – *Map IV, C2.* If you fancy visiting Asakusa 19C-style, try a rickshaw. Drivers in traditional costume wait for customers in front of Kaminari-mon. *(Not so cheap at ¥2000 for 10min).*

ADDRESSES

ASAKUSA AND UENO

🍴STAY

ASAKUSA

🛏**Khaosan Tokyo Kabuki** カオサン東京歌舞伎 – *1-17-2 Asakusa, Taito-ku (Map IV, C2).* ✆03-5830-3673. *www.khaosan-tokyo.com/en. 11 rooms. Dorm ¥3600 per person.* Behind its kabuki theater-style façade, this branch the backpacker hostel chain is by far the most comfortable. Ideally situated close to the start of Nakamise shopping street, the dorms are good. The double rooms are good, equipped with private shower, as are the dormitories, which sleep up to four people in bunk beds.

🛏**K's House Tokyo Oasis** ケイズハウス東京オアシス – *2-14-10 Asakusa, Taito-ku (Map IV,C2).* ✆ 03-3844-4447. *www.kshouse.jp/tokyo-oasis-e/index.html. 12 rooms & 17 beds in dormitories. Dorm ¥2950 per person.* A well-kept hostel with very international clientele, basic dorms and decent private rooms.

🛏**Taito Ryokan** 台東旅館 – *2-1-4 Nishi-Asakusa, Taito-ku (Map IV, C2).* ✆03-3843-2822. *www.libertyhouse.gr.jp. 9 rooms. ¥6400.* 🍴. A small inn housed in a traditional building, charming if a little tired, and both low-budget and unpretentious. The friendly manager, who speaks English, has a relaxed approach. Shared showers. Two bikes are available to rent *(free, but ¥5000 security deposit)*.

🛏**Toyoko Inn Asakusa Kuramae Kaminarimon** 東横イン浅草蔵前雷門 – *1-3-13 Komagata, Taito-ku (Map IV; C2, off map).* ✆03-3841-1045. *www.toyoko-inn.com/hotel_list. 105 rooms. ¥9500.* 🍴. As with all the hotels in the chain, the rooms are small and characterless, but well-kept and functional. *Free shuttle bus available from JR Ueno Station.*

🛏🛏**Ryokan Asakusa Shigetsu** 旅館浅草指月 – *1-31-11 Asakusa, Taito-ku (Map IV, C2).* ✆03-3843-2345. *www.shigetsu.com/e/index.html. 21 rooms. ¥16,800. ¥1100–1300* 🍴. Hidden away in a narrow street near the temple of Senso-ji and the busy Nakamise-dori, this *ryokan* is a peaceful haven. The hearty and varied breakfast is a real treat. The top-floor *o-furo* has a view of the temple.

🛏🛏**Hotel Sunroute Asakusa** ホテルサンルート浅草 – *1-8-5 Kaminarimon, Taito-ku (Map IV, C2).* ✆03-3847-1511. *www.sunroute-asakusa.co.jp/en. 174 rooms. ¥21,600. ¥2530* 🍴. This business hotel with no special charm is still well placed to explore Asakusa. Small, well-equipped, soundproof rooms.

🛏🛏🛏**Kaminarimon Ryokan** 雷門旅館 – *1-18-2 Asakusa, Taito-ku (Map IV, C2).* ✆03-3844-1873. *www.kaminarimon.co.jp/en. 22 rooms. ¥28,300. Breakfast available.* Completely redone in 2019, this modern *ryokan* has beautifully kept Japanese- and Western-style rooms, with private or communal bathroom. English spoken. Some rooms have a view of Senso-ji.

🛏🛏🛏**Sukeroku-no-Yado Sadachiyo** 助六の宿 貞千代 – *2-20-1 Asakusa, Taitō-ku (Map IV, C2).* ✆03-3842-6431. *sadachiyo.co.jp/en. 20 rooms. ¥21,600. ¥1500* 🍴. JThis traditional *ryokan* is a welcoming break from the bustle of Asakusa. Rooms are

Japanese style, with futons and *tatami* mats, there are relaxing *o-furo*, and you can enjoy sumptuous Japanese cuisine *(dinner course from ¥5500)*. Front desk staff usually speak English.

UENO

🛏🛏 **Hotel Coco Grand** ホテルココグラン上野不忍 – *2-12-14 Ueno, Taito-ku (Map IV, A2).* 📞*03-5812-1155. www.cocogrand. co.jp/uenoshinobazu. 58 rooms. ¥16,800.* 🚇. An agreeable hotel opposite Ueno Park and Shinobazu Pond. Comfortable rooms with elegant decoration, some with a view of the park. *The Zen suites (¥1000 extra) are particularly nice. Spa on 2nd floor. A good price/quality ratio.*

🛏🛏 **Homeikan Honkan** 鳳明館本館 – *5-10-5 Hongo, Bunkyo-ku (Map IV; A2, off map).* 📞*03-3811-1181. www.homeikan. com/en-5. 31 rooms. ¥14,000. ¥1100* 🚇. Built in 1950, this establishment has real character – it's even been designated an Important Cultural Property. The floors in the lobby and corridors are made of black pebbles *(nachi ishi)* that shine as though they've been polished. Every bedroom is decorated differently, making use of wood, except for the "economy" bedrooms where the floors are lino. There are three private family bathroom. Also has two other properties nearby, the Morikawa and Daimachi annexes, in the same style.

🛏🛏 **Ryokan Katsutaro Annex** 旅館勝太郎 – *3-8-4 Yanaka, Taito-ku. 15min walk from Ryokan Katsutaro (Map IV; A1, off map).* 📞*03-3828-2500. www.katsutaro. com/indexf.html. 17 rooms. ¥14,800. ¥870* 🚇. Established in 2001 near a very busy pedestrian shopping street and the Yanaka Cemetery, this *ryokan* still feels fairly new. Its elegant façade of small gray bricks is indicative of its whole image: smart, serious, modern, and comfortable. If you plan to arrive back late at night, ask for the access code. Bicycle rental available *(¥300 per day)*.

🛏 **Sawanoya Ryokan** 澤の屋旅館 – *2-3-11 Yanaka, Taito-ku (Map IV; A1, off map).* 📞*03-3822-2251. www.sawanoya. com. 12 rooms. ¥11,000. ¥435* 🚇. An entire family greets you when you arrive at this 70-year-old *ryokan*: the grandmother and grandfather their two grandchildren, and the mother and father running back and forth between kitchen and bedrooms. About 30 percent of their (mostly international) visitors in the past 25 years have returned – the sign of a good place.

Ask for the key if you plan to come back after 11pm. All rooms are Japanese-style, and two have private bathrooms. Bicycle rental available *(¥300 per day)*.

🛏🛏 **Suigetsu Hotel Ogaisou** 水月ホテル鴎外荘 – *3-3-21 Ikenohata, Taito-ku (Map IV, A2).* 📞*03-3822-4611, www.ohgai. co.jp. 124 rooms. ¥16,000. From ¥2000* 🚇. Just behind the zoo, this hotel is composed of three buildings set around the house and garden of the novelist Mori Ogai, whose name alone seems to attract Japanese clients. The ambience aims to be traditional (Japanese bedrooms, but some slightly staid Western-style ones too), and the staff wear becoming kimonos. Two *o-furo* and one room for the teaceremony.

🍴 EAT

🍽 If you can't find a certain address, ask at the Asakusa Tourism and Culture Center, or at one of the district's police boxes *(koban)*.

ASAKUSA

🍜 **Sometaro** 染太郎 – *2-2-2, Nishiasakusa, Taito-ku (Map IV, C2).* 📞*03-3844-9502. Open Wed–Mon noon–10.30pm. From ¥550; lunch usually around ¥1200.* 🚇. Located near the Drum Museum, on a street that carries on from Kaminarimon avenue toward Hongan-ji Temple. You'll recognize this restaurant by its blue curtain with white *kanji* script; it opened in 1937, and the decor seems to have changed little since then. It's ususally crowded with locals and tourists, all here for its famous *okonomiyaki*. Seating is on *tatami* mats.

🍜 **Tanuki-dori** たぬき通り – *(Map IV, C2).* tanuki-dori.com/en. This pedestrian street decorated with statues of *tanuki* (raccoons) is well known for its restaurants (most 🚇) offering *okonomiyaki* at reasonable prices, recognizable by their hot plates.

🍜 **Asakusa Mizuguchi** 浅草 水口 – *2-4-9 Asakusa, Taito-ku (Map IV, C2).* 📞*030-3844-2725. asakusa-mizuguch.main.jp/ english. Open Thu–Tue 10am–9.30pm (Sat & Sun from 9am), last orders 9pm. Menu in English. Set meals from under ¥1000.* This pleasant, unpretentious *shokudo* (canteen) has been nourishing the people of Asakusa since 1950. You'll be seated with the locals, who watch TV with a glass of cold beer in one hand.

DISCOVERING TOKYO AND SURROUNDINGS

Namiki Yabu Soba 並木藪蕎麦 – 2-11-9 Kaminarimon, Taito-ku (Map IV, C2). 📞03-3841-1340. Open Fri–Wed 11am–7.30pm. Around ¥1000. In a small house squeezed between two large, modern buildings, this restaurant has been serving noodles since 1913. They pride themselves on their *juwari* (100 percent buckwheat) soba noodles; gluten-free diners can eat these, but not the strong, salty soy dipping sauce.

Kazunoya Oiwake 和の家追分 – 5-37-7 Asakusa, Taito-ku (Map IV, C1). 📞030-3874-0722. www.kazunoya-oiwake. com. Open Tue–Sun 5.30pm–midnight. Menu in English. ¥2000 table charge (includes snacks). One of Tokyo's few remaining *min'yo izakaya*, a kind of bar with food where the staff play traditional Japanese music. The main attraction here is the lively Tsugaru *shamisen* performances at 7pm and 9pm.

Asakusa Imahan 浅草今半 – 3-1-12 Nishi-Asakusa, Taito-ku (Map IV, C2). 📞03-3841-1114. www.asakusaimahan. co.jp/english. Open daily 11.30am–9.30pm, last orders 8.30pm. Menu in English. Lunch sets from ¥1600; dinner sets from ¥8000. Located on one corner of Kokusai Street, the restaurant sets out its stall with a stylized motif of an ox head on the exterior of the building. Their main claim to fame is to offer high-quality meat, served as *shabu-shabu* (a type of savory hotpot or stew) or *sukiyaki*.

RYOGOKU

Shinjuku Saboten 新宿さぼてん – 6F Solomachi, Tokyo Skytree Town, 1-1-2 Oshiage, Sumida-ku (Map IV; C2, off map). 📞03-6658-5300. Open 11am–11pm (last orders 10pm). Menu in English. Bento from ¥600; set meals from ¥1300. In Skytree Town, this branch of the large chain makes consistently good, crispy *tonkatsu* (deep-fried, breaded pork cutlets). You can help yourself to as much grated cabbage, miso soup and rice as you like.

UENO

Tonkatsu Musashino とんかつ武蔵野 – 2F 2-8-1 Ueno, Taito-ku (Map IV, A2). 📞03-3831-1672. tonkatsu-musashino. tokyo. Open daily 11.30–8.30pm. Lunch from ¥1000. A high-quality, traditional *tonkatsu* restaurant that has been in operation since 1948.

Korean Cafe Chung Hak Tong コリアン カフェ チョン・ハク・トン – 2-11-20 Ueno, Taito-ku (Map IV, A2). 📞03-5807-7399. Open 11am–midnight (Sun 10pm). Lunch from ¥600, dinner from ¥1300. A pleasant Korean restaurant situated opposite Ueno Park. The spicy soups and stews are perfect on a cold day.

Izuei Honten 伊豆榮本店 – 2-12-22 Ueno, Taito-ku (Map IV, A2). 📞03-3831-0954. www.izuei.co.jp/en. Open Mon–Fri 11am–3pm & 5–10pm, Sat & Sun 11am–10pm (last orders 30min before closing). From ¥3200. This elegant restaurant is well known to anyone who likes *unagi*. For those who've never had the flavourful grilled eel dish before, this is the perfect place to try it, served with a slightly spicy house sauce made from a secret recipe.

Hantei はん亭 – 2-12-15 Nezu, Bunkyo-ku (Map IV, A1). 📞03-3828-1440. www.hantei.co.jp. Open Tue–Sun, 11.30am–3pm & 5–11pm (last orders 2.15pm, 10pm). Lunch around ¥3200, dinner around ¥5000. This restaurant, in a beautiful historic house, is renowned for it *kushiage*: skewers of meat, fish, and vegetables coated with breadcrumbs and fried. The menu covers the classics, but also some truly original options: scallops, lotus roots, potato tofu, etc., all served with rice, soup, and tea.

TAKING A BREAK

ASAKUSA

Kamiya Bar 神谷バー – 1-1-1 Asakusa, Taito-ku (Map IV, A2). 📞03-3841-5400. www.kamiya-bar.com. Open Wed–Mon 11.30am–10pm. The first Western bar to open (in 1880) in Tokyo attracts a loyal local clientele. Try the *denki bran*, a turbo-charged brandy cocktail (the name means "electric brandy"). There are restaurants on the second and third floors of the building.

Kappabashi Coffee & Bar – 3-25-11 Nishiasakusa, Taito-ku (Map IV, A2). 📞03-5828-0308. www.facebook.com/kappabashi.coffeebar. Cafe open daily 8am–8pm, bar open Mon–Sat 6pm–1am. A stylish cafe serving fresh parfaits and delicious patisserie, generally popular with a younger crowd. Turns into a laidback bar in the evening.

From Afar Warehouse 01 From Afar 倉庫01 – 1-1-9 Hogashikomagata, Sumida-ku (Map IV;C2, off map). www.fromafar-tokyo.com/fromafarsoko01. Open daily noon–7pm, last orders 6.30pm. Just over the river from Asakusa Station is this arty coffee shop in a converted warehouse. The drinks and cakes are excellent, and the space also serves as a gallery, florist and craft store.

RYOGOKU

Beer Club Popeye 麦酒倶楽部POPEYE – 2-18-7 Ryogoku, Sumida-ku. (Map IV; C2, off map). www.lares.dti.ne.jp/~ppy. Open Mon–Thu 5–11.30pm, Fri 3.30–11.30pm, Sat 3–11.30pm. Tokyo's temple of beer! There are s70 on tap and the expert staff will provide advice. Enjoy Japanese, Belgian, and American craft beers to wash down good-value food. Happy hour is 5–8pm (Sat 3–8pm).

UENO

Books & Cafe Bousingot ブックス＆カフェ・ブーサンゴ – 2-33-2 Sendagi, Bunkyo-ku (Map IV; A1, off map). ℘03-3823-5501. www.bousingot.com. Open Wed–Mon afternoon–11pm (irregular opening hours). A cafe and bookstore where you can sip, among other things, mint diabolo, cappuccino, Corona, and French table wines. The decor is 1960s–70s, the atmosphere jazzy.

Nezu no Taiyaki 根津のたいやき – 1-23-9 Nezu, Bunkyo-ku (Map IV; A1, off map). ℘03-3823-6277. Open Wed–Thu & Sat–Mon 10.30am–12.30/2pm (irregular opening hours). Hayashi Shozo has been preparing taiyaki (small cakes shaped like a fish and stuffed with anko, red bean paste), which are the delight of the neighborhood, for some time. He has enjoyed international recognition since 1996, when the US Ambassador wrote to congratulate him, declaring that here he had found the true heart of Japan. The long queue marks out the place.

SHOPPING

ASAKUSA

Arai Bunsendo Nakamise-ten 荒井文扇堂仲見世店 – 1-30-1 Asakusa, Taito-ku. ℘03-3841-0088. Open daily 10.30am–6pm. Closed one Mon per month. Shop on Nakamise-dori which specializes in traditional fans. Great for souvenirs, but also does a roaring trade on muggy summer days.

Portrait of Sumo wrestler, Ryogoku station

© Eurasia Press/Photononstop

Kurodaya 黒田屋 – 1-2-5 Asakusa. Taito-ku. ℘03-3844-7511. Open Tue–Sun 11am–7pm. This store, which has been in business since the mid-19C, is particularly well known for its Japanese paper (washi) and small objects made of paper.

Miyamoto Unosuke Shouten 宮本卯之助商店 – 2-1-1 Nishi Asakusa, Taito-ku. ℘03-3844-2141. www.miyamoto-unosuke.co.jp/english. Open daily 9am–6pm. The taiko specialist, essential for all percussion enthusiasts. A museum (℘see p140) on the fourth floor contains some 900 percussion instruments.

Sukeroku 助六 – 2-3-1 Asakusa, Taito-ku. ℘03-3844-0577. Open daily 10am–6pm. A small store on Nakamise-dori specializing in handmade miniature dolls, and stages on which to display them. Good quality.

Marugoto Nippon まるごとにっぽん – 2-6-7 Asakusa, Taito-ku. ℘03-3845-0510. marugotonippon.com. Open daily: 1F & 2F 10am–8pm; 3F 10am–9pm; 4F 11am–11pm. This shopping mall has outlets selling a vast range of products manufactured in the different regions of Japan, including foodstuffs and high-quality craft items. Restaurants on the top floor.

KANDA-JINBOCHO

Given that this area is also known as "book town", it's no surprise that it has a number of excellent used-book stores and publishing houses, as well as stores selling antiques and curios.

Isseido Shoten 一誠堂書店 – *1-7 Kanda-Jinbocho, Chiyoda-ku.* ☏*03-3292-0071. www.isseido-books.co.jp/index_en.html. Open Mon–Sat 10am–6.30pm (public holidays 10.30am–6pm).* Without doubt Tokyo's most prestigious bookshop for ancient and rare books, both Japanese and foreign (arts, archeology, literature, religion, etc). Also sells a good variety of prints, historical maps, etc.

Ohya Shobo 大屋書房 – *1-1 Kanda-Jinbocho, Chiyoda-ku.* ☏*03-3291-0062 & 03-3295-3456. www.ohya-shobo.com/english.php. Open Mon–Sat 10am–6pm.* Bookshop and gallery crammed to the rafters with Japanese books from the Edo and early Meiji eras, plus ancient Japanese maps, and *ukiyo-e* prints from the Edo and Meiji eras.

Hara Shobo 原書房 – *2-3 Kanda-Jinbocho, Chiyoda-ku.* ☏*03-5212-7801, www.harashobo.com/english. Open Tue–Sat 10am–6pm.* Shop and gallery selling Japanese *ukiyo-e* prints, from 17C to 20C. Also has some modern illustrated titles, and reference books about *ukiyo-e* and Japan's historic print culture.

Yamada Shoten 山田書店 – *2F Yamada Bldg, 1-8 Kanda-Jinbocho, Chiyoda-ku.* ☏*03-3295-0252. www.yamada-shoten.com/english. Open Mon–Sat 10am–6.30pm.* Shop and gallery of *ukiyo-e* prints from the Edo, Meiji, and Taisho eras. Also sells modern engravings and prints.

SPORT AND LEISURE
RYOGOKU
Ryogoku Kokugikan 両国国技館 – *1-3-28 Yokoami, Sumida-ku (Map I, D2).* ☏*03-3623-5111. www.sumo.or.jp. Open Mon–Fri 10am–4.30pm; no charge, except for tournament days, when entry is by paid ticket only.* This stadium hosts 3 sumo tournaments a year (*2 weeks in Jan, May, & Sept*), but 6 tournaments are held in total in Japan per year. Tickets go on sale a month before the start of the competition. On the day, cheaper seats at the back of the terraces are put on sale (*¥2200*) from 8am at Kokugikan. The bouts begin at 10am, but the best *rikishi* (wrestlers) only enter the ring from 4pm.

USEFUL INFORMATION
IMPERIAL PALACE
Post Office/Withdrawals – *Tokyo Central Post Office (☏ see p179).*
JR East Travel Service Center – *Tokyo Station, Marunouchi North Entrance. Open daily 7.30am–8.30pm.* In Tokyo Station, information office (bureau de change, JR Pass, other passes and tickets, etc.).

ADDRESSES

IMPERIAL PALACE
🏨STAY
Capitol Hotel Tokyu キャピトルホテル東急 – *2-10-3 Nagatacho, Chiyoda-ku (Map II; A3, off map).* ☏*03-3503-0109. tokyuhotelsjapan.com/global/capitol-h. 251 rooms. ¥60,000. From ¥1300 (buffet ¥4700)* ☲. The Capitol offers a great location, comprehensive facilities and attentive service. Japanese design elements are seamlessly incorporated into the Western-style rooms. Breakfast is indulgent (dietary requirements fine with notice). There's an amazing view towards the Imperial Palace from the pool area, but access is quite restricted—no bikinis (full swimsuits only), and no tattoos.

Hoshinoya Tokyo 星のや東京 – *1-9-1 Otemachi, Chiyoda-ku (Map II, B2).* ☏*05-7007-3066. hoshinoya.com/tokyo/en. 84 rooms. ¥90,600. ¥4000* ☲. A perfect blend of modern, luxury hotel and traditional *ryokan*, a few minutes' walk from the Imperial Palace. The building has 17 floors, but as each one is reserved for guests staying on it, it feels quiet and private. The dramatic rooftop bath is filled with natural spring water pumped up from 1500m below Tokyo.

🍴 EAT
Tokyo Ramen Street 東京ラーメンストリート – *B1F First Avenue, Tokyo Station, near Yaesu South Exit (Map II, C3). Varies by shop, but open daily around 11am–10pm. From ¥800.* You'll find some of the best outlets dedicated to ramen here, each with their own specialty, some with English menus. All offer generous portions and good value for money. *Soranoiro* has vegan options.

⊜⊜🅑 **Mango Tree Tokyo** マンゴツ
リー東京 – *35F Marunouchi Bldg, 2-4-1
Marunouchi, Chiyoda-ku (Map II,B3).* 🕿*03-
5224-5489. mangotree.jp/shop/mangotree/
tokyo. Open 11am–3.30pm & 5–11pm (last
orders 2.30pm & 10pm). Lunch ¥2900,
dinner course ¥7000.* Delicious Thai lunch
buffet with a view. A la carte and course
menu options in the evening.

⊜⊜🅑 **Sens et Saveurs**
サンス・エ・サヴール – *35F Marunouchi
Bldg, 32-4-1 Marunouchi, Chiyoda-ku (Map
II, B3).* 🕿*03-5220-2701. pourcel.jp/eng/
sensetsaveurs. Open Mon–Fri 11am–1.30pm
& 5.30–9pm (Sat–Sun & public hols to
2pm & 8.30pm). Menu in English. From
¥4500 lunch, ¥10,200 dinner.* Tokyo on the
Mediterranean. A superb location on the
35th floor with a view of the Imperial
Palace. Vegan set menus available.

⊜⊜⊜🅑 **Tapas Molecular Bar** タパ
スモラキュラーバー – *38F Mandarin
Oriental Hotel, 2-1-1 Nihonbashi Muromachi,
Chuo-ku (Map II, C2).* 🕿*03-3270-8188.
www.mandarinoriental.com/tokyo/fine-
dining/tapas-molecular-bar. Open daily
for two seatings, 6–8pm & 8.30–10.30pm.
Reservation essential. ¥24,000.* Seats just 8
people around a bar, behind which a chef
prepares 20 or so dishes with scientific
precision and artistic flair. An intimate and
memorable dining experience.

SHOPPING

Character Street – *B1F First Avenue, Tokyo
Station, near Yaesu Central Exit. Open daily
10am–8.30pm.* Twenty or so shops selling
licensed cartoon character products
(Doraemon, Hello Kitty, Pokemon...). A
special mention for Donguri Republic,
where you'll find irresistible Studio Ghibli
items (Totoro, Kiki, Chihiro, etc.).

SPORT AND LEISURE

Sky Bus Tokyo スカイバス東京*Desk on
ground floor of Mitsubishi Bldg, opposite
Tokyo Station, Marunouchi South Exit (Map
II, B3).* 🕿*03-3215-0008. www. skybus.jp.*
Hourly departures *(around 10am–5pm)* for
a 50min–1hr 20min tour on a double-
decker bus *(¥1500–1800),* following 3
routes. There's one *(2hr)* in the evening,
departing 6pm or 8.30pm depending
on the season *(¥2100).* The hop on/hop
off Sky Hop Bus follows 3 routes *(around
9.30am–5pm);* tickets valid 24hr *(¥3500).*

ADDRESSES

GINGZA

🛏 STAY

⊜⊜ **Ginza Grand Hotel** 銀座グラン
ドホテル – *8-6-15 Ginza, Chuo-ku (Map
III; C2, off map).* 🕿*03-3572-4131. www.
ginzagrand.com/english. 257 rooms.
¥13,650. ¥2300* 🍽*.* Close to Shinbashi
subway, this hotel has well-equipped
rooms in various decorative styles, suiting
both business guests and tourists. Two
restaurants, plus a *conbini* on 1F

⊜⊜ **Hotel Gracery Ginza** ホテルグレイ
スリー銀座 – *7-10-1 Ginza, Chuo-ku (Map
III, C2).* 🕿*03-6686-1000. www.gracery.com/
english/ginza. 270 rooms. ¥16,100. ¥2160*
🍽*.* Comfortable, tastefully decorated
rooms in the heart of the district, chic
but quiet. Good value for money.

⊜⊜ **MUJI Hotel Ginza** MUJI ホテル銀
座 – *3-3-5 Ginza, Chuo-ku (Map III, B1).*
🕿*03-3538-6101. hotel.muji.com/ginza/en.
79 rooms. ¥19,000. ¥1800* 🍽*.* Taking up
the sixth to tenth floors of MUJI's flagship
store, the sleek lines, warm oak wood and
low lighting are a design-lover's dream.
Everything in the hotel is for sale on the
floors below, from the aroma diffusers to
the very comfortable bedding, and the 6F
Salon bar even has a "design chair menu".

🍴 EAT

🕭The area around the rail line between
Shinbashi and Yurakucho stations is full of
cheap restaurants, many serving yakitori
(grilled chicken skewers).

⊜ **Sakura Suisan Ginza Sanchome-ten**
さくら水産・銀座三丁目店 – *2F Ginza
Sunny Bldg, 3-4-16 Ginza, Chuo-ku (Map
III, B1).* 🕿*03-3561-3671. Open Mon–Fri
11am–2pm & 4pm–midnight; Sat–Sun
& public hols 4pm–midnight (last orders
11.15pm). English menu. Dishes from ¥300.*
"Always the same lowest price" is the
izakaya's slogan, displayed next to a
leaping fish. Order sashimi, tempura,
salads, and snacks by touch screen.
Popular, good quality and well priced.

⊜⊜ **Gonpachi G-Zone** 権八 G-Zone –
1-2-3 Ginza, Chuo-ku (Map III, 1). 🕿*03-5524-
3641. gonpachi.jp/ginza. Open 11.30am–
midnight (lunch menu till 3pm, last orders
dinner and drinks 11.30pm). Set lunch from
¥1000, dinner from around ¥2000.* The

interior of Gonpachi's Ginza *izakaya* is spacious and atmospheric, with prompt service of soba (buckwheat noodles), tempura and drinks.

😋🍴 **Sushizanmai Yurakucho-ten** すしざんまい・有楽町店 – *2-1-3 Yurakucho, Chiyoda-ku (Map III, B1). ☎03-3500-2201. www.kiyomura.co.jp. Open daily 24hr. Around ¥2000.* High-quality, no-frills sushi spot under the railway line. At 1am the chefs are still busy behind the counter, orders coming in thick and fast.

😋🍴🍴 **Shiseido Parlour Ginza Honten** 資生堂パーラー銀座本店 – *4–5F Shiseido Bldg, 8-8-3 Ginza, Chuo-ku (Map III, B2). ☎03-5537-6241. parlour.shiseido. co.jp. Open Tue–Sun 11.30am–9.30pm (last orders 8.30pm). Around ¥5000 for lunch, ¥7000 for dinner.* On the fourth and fifth floors of the Shiseido building (📍 *see p157*), this discreet luxury restaurant offers Japanese–European cuisine (*yoshoku*) elegantly served as in the Meiji era. Try the meat croquette or hayashi rice.

😋🍴🍴🍴 **Restaurant Dazzle** レストランダズル – *8–9F Mikimoto Ginza 2 Bldg, 2-4-12 Ginza, Chuo-ku (Map III, B1). ☎03-5159-0991. huge.co.jp/en/restaurant/dazzle. Open 11.30am–3pm & 5.30–11.30pm (last orders 2pm & 10pm). Dress code: smart. English menu. Lunch from ¥2200, dinner ¥6800.* Located at the top of the magnificent Mikimoto Building (📍 *see p156*), this opulent restaurant really lives up to its name. The wine store, sitting inside a glass tower that dominates the room, is an impressive sight, as are the modern Italian dishes.

😋🍴🍴🍴 **Fish Bank Tokyo** フィッシュバンク トウキョウ – *41F Shiodome City Center, 1-5-2 Higashi-Shinbashi, Minato-ku (Map III, B2). ☎03-3569-7171. fish-bank-tokyo.jp/en. Open daily 11.30am–3pm & 5.30–10.30pm (last orders 1.30pm & 9.30pm). Lunch menu from ¥3000, dinner from ¥9500.* In an elegant space with a spectacular view of Rainbow Bridge. The menu feautures subtle fish and seafood dishes prepared according to traditional French recipes adapted to local tastes.

TAKING A BREAK

Salon de Café サロン・ド・カフェ – *3F Shiseido Bldg, 8-8-3 Ginza, Chuo-ku (Map III, B2). ☎03-5537-6231. parlour.shiseido.co.jp. Open Tue–Sat 11.30am–9pm (last orders 8.30pm), Sun & public hols 11.30am–8pm (last orders 7.30pm).* On the third floor of the Shiseido Building, this elegant cafe offers a choice of pastries to nibble with your coffee in plush surroundings.

Uogashi-Meicha うおがし銘茶 – *5-5-6 Ginza, Chuo-ku (Map III, B1). ☎03-3571-1211. www.uogashi- meicha.co.jp/en. Open daily 11am–6pm.* Near Ginza Crossing, this modern cafe above a branch of the specialist teashop chain is the ideal place to try excellent green tea, an espresso or a *kakigori* (Japanese shaved ice dessert).

SHOPPING

Ginza Antique Mall アンティークモール銀座 – *1-13-1 Ginza, Chuo-ku (Map III, C1). ☎03-3535-2115. www.antiques-jp.com. Open daily 11am–7pm.* On three floors, Japanese and Western antiques, both good and bad. Prices tend to be quite high, but feel free to haggle.

Itoya 伊東屋 – *2-7-15 Ginza, Chuo-ku (Map III, C1). ☎03-3561-8311. www.ito-ya. co.jp/en. Open daily 10am–9pm (Sun & public hols 7pm).* On several floors, a good choice of Japanese paper and drawing materials, plus an art gallery and cafe.

Uniqlo Ginza ユニクロ銀座店 – *6-9-5 Ginza, Chuo-ku (Map III, B1). ☎03-6252-5181. uniqlo.com/jp/shop/ginza/?lang=en. Open daily 11am–9pm.* There's a Uniqlo in practically every city in Japan, but this store in Ginza is the biggest of all, with 12 floors of their signature wearable basics.

USEFUL INFORMATION
ROPPONGI

Bank/Foreign Exchange – World Currency Shop, *Roppongi Hills, 6F West Walk (Map I, B4). ☎03-5413-9722. Open Mon–Fri 11am–7pm, Sat–Sun and public holidays noon–5pm.*

ADDRESSES

ROPPONGI

🏨 STAY

😋🍴 **Hotel Asia Center of Japan** ホテルアジア会館 – *8-10-32 Akasaka, Minato-ku (Map I, B3). ☎03-3402-6111. www. asiacenter.or.jp/en. 175 rooms. ¥12,000. 🚇.* Not far from the Roppongi district, this recently-built hotel at the top of a hill offers simple accommodation in a calm and comfortable environment, and at a very reasonable price. A buffet breakfast is included for foreign guests.

🍴🍴🍴 **International House of Japan** 国際文化会館 – *5-11-16 Roppongi, Minato-ku (Map I, B4). ✆03-3470-4611. www.i-house.or.jp/eng/facilities/accommodations. 44 rooms. ¥26,300. ☕.* 10min walk from the Mori Tower. A magnificent traditional Japanese garden surrounds the Le Corbusier-inspired 1950s building. Hi-tech furniture, serious and sophisticated atmosphere. You must be proposed by a member to stay here.

🍴🍴🍴 **ANA Intercontinental Tokyo** ANA インターコンチネンタル東京 – *1-12-33 Akasaka, Minato-ku (Map I, B3). ✆03-3505-1111. anaintercontinental-tokyo.jp/en. 844 rooms. ¥28,000. ¥4200 ☕.* Attractive hotel occupying floors 1–36 of a 37-floor tower. The comfortable rooms are elegant and smart—some have beautiful views of the Imperial Palace, Tokyo Tower, and Roppongi Hills. Excellent restaurants.

🍴 EAT

🍴🍴 **Pintokona** ぴんとこな – *Roppongi Hills, B2F Metro Hat, Hollywood Plaza, Minato-ku (Map I, B4). ✆03-5771-1133. kiwa-group.co.jp/pintokona. Open daily 11am–11pm (last orders 10pm). English menu.* The decor at this classic *kaiten-zushi* (conveyor-belt sushi) place is Kabuki-theater inspired. Order what you want, or just reach out and help yourself; plates colors indicate price *(from ¥150)*.

🍴🍴 **Sankyu** 燦紅 – *1F Roppongi Shinsei Bldg, 3-1-18 Nishi-Azabu, Minato-ku (Map I, B3). ✆03-5771-6201. http://www.39jap.com/39tokyo. Open daily 6pm–4am (Sun to 11pm). English menu. From ¥1000.* Leave your shoes outside before entering this rustic-style restaurant. Australian or Japanese beef *(wagyu)* takes pride of place, the latter significantly more expensive (from ¥4400 for 100g).

🍴🍴🍴 **L'Atelier du Joël Robuchon** ラトリエ ドゥ ジョエル・ロブション – *2F Roppongi Hills Hillside, 6-10-1 Roppongi, Minato-ku (Map I, B4). ✆03-5772-7500. www.robuchon.jp/en/shop-list/latelier. Open daily noon–4pm, & 6–11pm (last orders 2.30pm & 9.30pm). English menu. Lunch from ¥3200, dinner ¥5200.* Clean

lines in a softly-lit red and black interior. Sophisticated yet relaxing, serving refined French cuisine.

🍴🍴🍴 **Hishinuma** 菱沼 (ひしぬ ま) – *B1F Axis Bldg, 5-17-1 Roppongi, Minato-ku (Map I, B3/4). ✆03-3568-6588. restaurant-hishinuma.jp. Open Mon–Sat 11.30am–2pm & 6–11pm (last orders 1.30pm & 8.30pm). Lunch menus from ¥3700, dinner from ¥13,200.* "Serving society through good eating" is the motto of chef Hishinuma Takayuki, who is as devoted to his customers as he is to his culinary creations. The menu is decided based on what's good at market that day, and might include vegetarian *kaiseki* dishes, grilled meats, or fresh sashimi.

🍴🍴🍴 **Tofuya Ukai Shiba** とうふ屋 うかい – *4-4-13 Shiba-Koen, Minato-ku (Map I, B4). ✆03-3436-1028. ukai.co.jp/english/shiba. Open Mon–Fri 11.45am–3pm & 5–10pm, Sat–Sun 11am–10pm (last orders 7.30pm). Closed two Mon per month. Lunch menu from ¥6000, dinner from ¥11,000.* At the bottom of Tokyo Tower is this charming *ryotei* surrounded by a 71,040sq ft/6600sq m Edo-era garden. You will enjoy unforgettable tofu and inventive seasonal dishes here.

NIGHTLIFE

Toho Cinemas TOHOシネマズ – *Roppongi Hills, Keyakizaka Complex, Minato-ku (Map I, B4). ✆050-6868-5024. www.roppongihills.com/en/cinema.* The biggest movie theater complex in Tokyo. All-night screenings some weekends.

Agave アガヴェ – *B1F Clover Bldg, 7-15-10 Roppongi, Minato-ku (Map I, B3) ✆03-3497-0229. agave.jp. Open Mon–Thu 6.30pm–2am (last orders 1.30am), Fri–Sat 6.30pm–4am (last orders 3.30am).* One of the biggest tequila bars in the world, with over 500 kinds of tequila and mezcal. Also serves Mexican food, and sells cigars which you can smoke in the bar.

Gen Yamamoto ゲンヤマモト – *1F Anniversay Bldg, 1-6-4 Azabu-Juban, Minato-ku (Map I, B4) ✆03-6434-0652. genyamamoto.jp. Open Tue–Sat 3–11pm (last entry 9.30pm). Cover charge ¥1000; tasting menus ¥4800–7800.* Undoubtedly one of Tokyo's best bars. With only 8 seats and no music in the chic, minimalist space, customers focus on Yamamoto's craftsmanship, as he creates 4 to 7 unique cocktails for each person.

Clubs – Shibuya may have more of a thriving club scene than Roppongi now, but it doesn't change the fact that there are still more clubs here, and foreigners come in large numbers.

USEFUL INFORMATION
SHINJUKU

Tourist Office – *Tokyo Tourist Information Center, 1F Metropolitan Government Bldg no. 1, 2-8-1 Nishi-Shinjuku, Shinjuku-ku (Map V, A2). ℘03-5321-3077. gotokyo.org/en/plan/tourist-info-center. Open daily 9.30am–6.30pm.* In addition to tourist information, guided tours in several languages, including English.

ADDRESSES

SHINJUKU

🛏 STAY

⊖⊟ **City Hotel Lonestar** シティホテルロンスター – *2-12-12 Shinjuku, Shinjuku-ku (Map V , C2). ℘03-3356-6511. www.thehotel.co.jp/en/lonestar. 50 rooms. ¥13,500.* 🖵. This small, pleasantly decorated hotel is well equipped and situated right next to a street full of cheap restaurants. Reductions available online.

⊖⊟ **Toyoko Inn Shinjuku Kabuki-cho** 東横イン新宿歌舞伎町 – *2-20-15, Kabuki-cho, Shinjuku-ku. (Map V; C1, off map). ℘03-5155-1045. www.toyoko-inn. com/hotel_list. 351 rooms. ¥10,000.* 🖵. This chain business hotel has small, well-kept rooms and is right in the heart of Shinjuku's nightlife district. Online discounts available.

🍴 EAT

⊖⊟⊟ **Mo-mo Paradise Kabuki-cho Honten** モーモーパラダイス歌舞伎町本店 – *8F Humax Pavilion, 1-20-1 Kabuki-cho, Shinjuku-ku (Map V, C1). ℘03-3208-0135. mo-mo-paradise.com/shopinfo_kabukicho.html. Open Mon–Fri 5–11pm, Sat–Sun & public holidays 11.30am–11pm (last orders 10.30pm). English menu. From ¥3000.* The specialties here are *shabu-shabu* and *sukiyaki*, both hot-pot dishes made with light broth, fresh vegetables and thinly sliced fatty meat. Served as an "all you can eat" deal within 1hr 40min.

⊖⊟⊟ **Shinjuku Tsunahachi** 新宿つな八 – *3-31-8 Shinjuku, Shinjuku-ku (Map V, C2). ℘03-3352-1012. www.tunahachi.co.jp/en/shop/shopinfo01.html#label01. Open daily 11am–10.30pm (last orders 10pm). Lunch from ¥1500, dinner ¥2500.* The main branch of a chain long famed for its light, crispy tempura. Even the smaller sets are filling, but it's hard to resist ordering more when it's this good.

⊖⊟⊟ **Le Mange-Tout** ル・マンジュ・トゥ – *22 Nandomachi, Shinjuku-ku (Map V; C1, off map). ℘03-3268-5911. le-mange-tout.com/en. Open Mon–Sat 6.30–9pm. ¥17,820. Dress fairly smartly.* A rigorous chef who studied in Alsace, Tani Noboru's French-Japanese fusion food is inventive and tasty. Arrive hungry.

Kabuki-cho at night

NIGHTLIFE

North of Shinjuku park is **Shinjuku Nichome** 新宿二丁目 *(map V, C2)*, the LGBTQ quarter of the capital, where there's a profusion of bars and clubs in a small area.

A-Un 阿吽 – *3F Taraku Bldg, 2-14-16 Shinjuku, Shinjuku-ku. ☎070-6612-9014. a-un.bz. Open daily 8pm–3am (Fri–Sat & public hols 5am).* Small, lesbian-friendly bar/club with an excellent sound system. The drinks are cheap, and there are often events with international DJs, but owner DJ Juri's sets are reason enough to visit.

New York Bar ニューヨーク バー – *52F Park Hyatt Hotel. 3-7-1-2 Nishi-Shinjuku, Shinjuku-ku. ☎03-5323-3458. restaurants. tokyo.park.hyatt.co.jp/en/nyb.html. Open 5pm–midnight (Thu–Sat 1am). Cover charge ¥2500 from 8pm (Sun 7pm).* If you can't stay in the Park Hyatt, like the characters in the film *Lost in Translation*, you can at least have a drink there, listening to jazz (daily from 8pm, Sun 7pm) while enjoying the stunning view of the city lights.

SHOPPING

Kinokuniya Shinjuku Honten 紀伊国屋書店 新宿本店 – *3-17-7 Shinjuku, Shinjuku-ku. ☎03-3354-0131. www.kinokuniya. co.jp/c/store/Shinjuku-Main-Store/ shopinfo_en.html. Open daily 10am–9pm.* One of the biggest bookstores in Tokyo (B1F–8F), with a good selection of English-language books and magazines available. Also has a cafe, Kino Chaya.

Hanazono-jinja Flea Market 花園神社青空骨董市 – *5-17-3 Shinjuku, Shinjuku-ku. ☎090-2542-0291. kottou-ichi.jp. Open Sun 6.30am–sunset.* A much-loved weekly flea market. Not held when there is a ceremony at the shrine.

USEFUL INFORMATION
SHIBUYA

Shibuya Tourist Information Center – *4F Mark City, the building directly adjacent to Shibuya Station (Keio Inokashira Line). Open daily 10am–7pm (Sat–Sun and public hols 6pm).* Information in English.

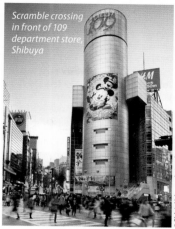

Scramble crossing in front of 109 department store, Shibuya

© Oleksiy Maksymenko/age fotostock

ADDRESSES

SHIBUYA

🛏 STAY

😊😊 **The B Sangenjaya** ザ・ビー 三軒茶屋 – *2-17-9 Taishido, Setagaya-ku (Map VI; A2, off map). ☎03-3795-0505. ishinhotels.com/en/theb/sangenjaya. 118 rooms. ¥15,000. ¥1100 🍽.* Near Shibuya, this modern hotel has ten floors and is situated in a lively district. Its small rooms are impeccably equipped. Guests have use of a coffee machine in the hall and a laundry on the tenth floor.

😊😊 **Hotel Unizo Shibuya** ホテルユニゾ渋谷 – *4-3 Udagawa-cho, Shibuya-ku (Map VI, A1–B1). ☎03-5457-7557. unizo-hotel.co.jp/ en/shibuya. 186 rooms. ¥18,900. ¥1240 🍽.* Reliable business hotel chain. Rooms are small and quiet, with safety deposit boxes and attractive bathrooms. The entrance is on a small street at the side of the hotel.

😊😊😊 **Shibuya Hotel EN** 渋谷ホテルえん – *1-1 Maruyama-cho, Shibuya-ku (Map VI, A2). ☎03-5489-1010. shibuyahotel.jp/ en. 55 rooms. ¥19,000. 🍽.* Opposite the entrance to the Bunkamura, this well-located hotel has nine floors of simple, comfortable rooms, though it's a little lackluster. A small breakfast of baked goods and coffee or tea is included.

😊😊😊 **Shibuya Tobu Hotel** 渋谷東武ホテル – *3-1 Udagawa-cho, Shibuya ku (Map VI, B1). ☎03-3476-0111. www. shibuyatobuhotel.com/en-us. 205 rooms.*

¥21,700. ¥1100 🚃*.* Near Shibuya Station, only about 500m from the Hachiko statue. Light and welcoming rooms with simple, comfortable furninshings. Several good restaurants and bars on site.

😋🍴🍴🍴🍴 **Shibuya Stream Excel Hotel Tokyu** 渋谷ストリームエクセルホテル東急 – *3-21-3 Shibuya, Shibuya-ku (Map VI, B2).* 🖉*03-3406-1090. tokyuhotelsjapan.com/global/stream-e. 177 rooms. ¥39,000. ¥2450* 🚃*.* The perfect central Shibuya location, perfect for exploring the area's nightlife, though the many good restaurants and bars housed in the same building also make a night in appealing. The hotel has a sleek, modern style enlivened with touches of mid-century design. Excellent views of the city lights.

🍴EAT

😋 **Curry House CoCo Ichibanya Udagawa-cho** 壱番屋渋谷区宇田川町店 – *1F Yokota Building, 24-10 Udagawa-cho, Shibuya-ku (Map VI, B2).* 🖉*03-5459-0460. tenpo.ichibanya.co.jp/map/2098. Open daily 24hr. English menu. ¥505–around ¥1300.* This popular chain restaurant (there are over 1200 branches in the country) is a great introduction to Japan's version of curry, *kare raisu*. It's usually based on pork stock, but this branch has vegetarian and halal options, too. Choose your spice level carefully, as it rises surprisingly fast.

😋 **Ramen Nagi Tonkotsu Shibuya** ラーメン凪豚骨渋谷店 – *1F Kaminato, 1-3-1 Higashi, Shibuya-ku (Map VI, C2).* 🖉*03-3499-0390. n-nagi.com/english. Open Mon–Sat 11am–3pm, Sun & public holidays 11am–9pm (last orders 2.30pm & 8.30pm). English menu. From ¥850.* 🚃*.* A great choice for high-quality, well-priced ramen, with a mouthwatering selection of toppings. Try the classic *tonkotsu* (pork), or go for one of the more international creations, like Black King, with a squid-ink and black garlic broth.

TAKING A BREAK

Chatei Hatou 茶亭羽當 – *1-15-9 Shibuya, Shibuya-ku (Map VI, B2).* 🖉*03-3400-9088. Open daily 11am–11.30pm.* 🚃*.* The archetypal Japanese *kissaten*, a type of coffee shop which feels like a slice of mid-20C life. The atmosphere is homely, with patterned crockery, dark wood and a beautiful ikebana arrangement. They

serve good pour-over coffee, teas and comforting snacks like buttered toast and chiffon cake. Note that smoking is allowed, as in most *kissaten*.

NIGHTLIFE

😋 Some of Tokyo's best bars and clubs are not in Roppongi, but Shibuya.

Mary Jane 渋谷メアリージェーン– *2F Fuji Shoji Bldg, 2-3 Sakuragaoka-cho, Shibuya-ku (Map VI, B2).* 🖉*03-3461-3381. maryjane.cocolog-nifty.com. Open Tue–Sun noon–11pm (Fri midnight).* A classic jazz cafe/bar, open since 1972. Sip a Japanese whisky or a cup of tea, and listen to the owner's superb jazz collection. A few snacks are available, including an excellent cheesecake.

Club Asia クラブエイジア – *1-8 Maruyama-cho, Shibuya-ku (Map VI, A2).* 🖉*03-5458-2551. clubasia.co.jp. Irregular opening hours, depending on events (see internet site).* Long-standing club which tends to play techno, hip-hop, and trance music. Often used as a live music venue.

Womb ウーム – *2-16 Maruyama-cho, Shibuya-ku (Map VI, A2).* 🖉*03-5459-0039. womb.co.jp/en. Open daily; check schedule online.* The most prestigious DJs and crowds flock to Womb, one of Tokyo's most famous clubs. Mainly techno and house music. ID required; door price usually around *¥3500* (cash only).

ADDRESSES

HARAJUKU

🍴EAT

😋😋 **Gut's Soul Yoyogi-ten** ガッツ・ソウル・代々木店 – *3F Oshiro Building, 1-32-1 Yoyogi, Shibuya-ku (Map I, A3).* 🖉*03-3320-1452. guts.gr.jp/shop/yoyogi.php. Open Mon–Fri 11.30am–3pm & 5–11.30pm (last orders 2.30pm & 11pm), Sat–Sun & public holidays noon–11.30pm. From ¥1100. Yakiniku* (barbecued meat) restaurant with generous all-you-can-eat offers (45min or 1hr 30min) starting at 5pm.

😋😋 **Lotus** ロータス – *4-6-8 Jingumae, Shibuya-ku (Map VII, B2).* 🖉*03-5772-6077. www.heads-west.com/shop/lotus.html. Open daily 11am–2am (last orders 1.30am). English menus. Lunch from ¥1000, dinner from ¥1500.* Raw concrete forms a pleasant contrast to the pink and purple touches, colors chosen to evoke the lotus flower. On the menu: pasta, risotto, pizza, meat dishes, and lots of tempting desserts.

BREIZH Café Crêperie ブレッツ カフェクレープリー表参道店 – 3-5-4 Jingumae, Shibuya-ku (Map VII, B2). ℘03-3478-7855. le-bretagne.com/e. Open daily 11.30am–10.30pm (Sun & public holidays 10pm). From ¥1050. BREIZH will transport you to France with its authentic and delicious buckwheat galettes, crêpes, cider, Calvados, etc.

Galali Aoyama Galali青山 – 3-6-5 Jingumae, Shibuya-ku (Map VII, B1/2). ℘03-3408-2818. galaliaoyama.com. Open Mon–Fri 11.30am–2pm & 6–11.30pm (last orders 1.30pm & 10.30pm), Sat 5–11pm (last orders 10pm). Lunch from ¥1080, dinner ¥4000. This izakaya mixes traditional Japanese food and style with modern elements. On the counter, made out of two solid beams, 12 sorts of salt are lined up ready to be taken with sake, tequila-style.

Benoit ブノワ – 10F La Porte Aoyama, 5-51-8 Jingumae, Shibuya-ku (Map VII; C2, off map). ℘03-6419-4181. benoit-tokyo.com/en. Open daily 11.30am–3.30pm & 5.30–11.30pm (last orders 2pm & 9.15pm). English menu. Prix fixe lunch from ¥4200, dinner from ¥6700. The Tokyo Benoit, like the one in Paris, is under the leadership of Alain Ducasse. Chic Mediterranean cuisine.

Shigeyoshi 重よし – 1F Co-op Olympia, 6-35-3 Jingumae, Shibuya-ku (Map VII, A2). ℘03-3400-4044. Open Mon–Sat noon–1.30pm & 5.30–10pm. Lunch around ¥8000, dinner ¥25,000. Reservation required. This restaurant serves kappo cuisine, multi-course meals similar to kaiseki. The chef uses the best seasonal produce, so the menu changes daily. Diners sit at a counter to watch him work.

TAKING A BREAK

Nalu 76 Cafe ナルーカフェ – MM Bldg, 4-9-2 Jingumae, Shibuya-ku (Map VII, B2). ℘03-5786-1781. number76.com. Open Tue–Fri 10.30am–8pm (Thu to 6pm), Sat & Sun 10am–7pm. An enduring trend in Tokyo is the cafe/hair stylist, and Nalu 76 Cafe is a great example. The cafe on 1F serves classic dishes like karaage (fried chicken), while on 2F you can get a excellent haircut by an English-speaking stylist.

On Sundays オン・サンデーズ カフェ – 3-7-6 Jingumae, Shibuya-ku (Map VII, B1). ℘03-3470-1424. watarium.co.jp/onsundays/html. Open Tue–Sun 11am–8pm (Wed 9pm). A stylish cafe and bookshop in the basement of the contemporary art gallery Watari-um. There's also a shop on 1F, which sells an excellent range of art goods and stationery.

Tourindou 桃林堂 – 3-6-12 Kita-Aoyama, Minato-ku (Map VII, B2). ℘03-3400-8703. tourindou100.jp/shop/list.html. Open daily 10am–7pm (Mon 5pm). Traditional Japanese sweets, preserved fruits, and vegetables. Many are seasonal specialties. All delightful to look at, and all delicious, but their taiyaki are especially famous.

Design Festa Cafe & Bar – 3-20-18, Jingumae, Shibuya-ku. ℘03-3479-0839. df-cafe.com/en/index.html. Open daily 11am–11pm. A bar, cafe, and design space all in one. Serves American-style comfort foods like hot dogs and milkshakes, and a good range of cocktails. The cafe is part of Design Festa, the innovative gallery just next door, which also runs nearby okonomiyaki restaurant Sakuratei.

USEFUL INFORMATION
ODAIBA
TRANSPORTATION
ON THE YURIKAMOME – See p172.

BY FERRY 水上バス – suijobus.co.jp. Less futuristic than the Yurikamome Line, it's still a spectacular way to approach Odaiba. Departures vary by season.
Asakusa–Odaiba (Daiba or Odaiba-kaihinkoen stations): departures 10am, 10.10am, 1.15pm, 1.25pm, 3.15pm, 3.25pm; return 12.20pm, 2.20pm and 2.25pm; return 12.20pm, 2.20pm, 2.25pm; 50min–1hr 10min trip; ¥1380 or ¥1720 one way.

Asakusa–Toyosu (Shijo-mae Station): departures 10am, 10.10am, 1.15pm, 1.25p

Hinode Pier–Odaiba (Daiba or Odaiba-kaihinkoen stations): regular departures 1.20pm, 3.10pm; 1hr 10min trip; return 12.45pm, 2.45pm, sometimes 4.40pm; ¥2220 one way.

Hinode Pier–Odaiba (Aomi or Tokyo Big Sight stations): regular departures 10.35am–5.35pm; return 10.30am–5.30pm; 25–35min; ¥460 one way.

ADDRESSES

ODAIBA

NIGHTLIFE

ageHa アゲハ – *Studio Coast, 2-2-10 Shin-Kiba, Koto-ku (Map I; D4, off map).* 📞*03-5534-2525. ageha-en.com. Open daily; check schedule online.* Tokyo's superclub, out in the Shin-Kiba area near Odaiba, regularly attracts major international DJs. Shuttle buses run from Shibuya.

ADDRESSES

KAGURAZAKA

🛏 STAY

🍴 **Tokyo Central Youth Hostel** 東京国際ホステル – *18F Central Plaza, 1-1 Kaguragashi, Shinjuku-ku (Map I, B2).* 📞*03-3235-1107. jyh.gr.jp/tcyh/e/top.html. 170 dormitory beds. ¥4050 per person. ¥700 🍴.* The hostel occupies the 18th and 19th floors of a high-rise building so there are fine views. Has 2 tatami rooms (sleep up to 6 people) as well as the 3- to 10-person dorms.

🍴🍴 **Tokyo Dome Hotel** 東京ドームホテル – *1-3-61 Koraku, Bunkyo-ku (Map I, C1).* 📞*03-5805-2111. www.tokyodome-hotels.co.jp/e. 1006 rooms. ¥15,400. ¥500–¥3000 🍴.* Designed by Tange Kenzo, this huge glass-walled hotel looms over Tokyo Dome. Rooms are spacious and elegant, many with great views. The hotel gets very full (and prices go up) when there's a baseball match in the Dome.

🍴 EAT

🍴🍴🍴 **Kagurazaka Shun Honke** 神楽坂SHUN本家 – *1F LV Annex, 3-2-36 Kagurazaka, Shinjuku-ku (Map I, B2).* 📞*03-3266-0560. www.kagurazaka-shun.jp. Open Mon–Fri 11.30am–2pm & 5.30–11pm, Sat–Sun & public holidays 11.30am–2.30pm & 5.30–10pm (Sat to 11pm). English menu. Lunch around ¥2000, dinner ¥5000. Book ahead.* Clean lines and soft lighting give this *izakaya* a soothing feel. The seasonal menu offers *kappo* multi-course dining or à la carte dishes.

🍴🍴🍴 **Ichimonji** 懐石・一文字 – *3-6 Kagurazaka, Shinjuku-ku.* 📞*03-5206-8223. Open daily noon–2pm & 6pm–9pm. Lunch from ¥10,000, dinner from ¥15,000. Reservations required.* A simple, sophisticated space in which to enjoy the very best of *kaiseki*, created by a master of the tea ceremony.

🍴🍴🍴 **Yamasaki** 山さき – *2F Fukuya Bldg, 4-2 Kagurazaka, Shinjuku-ku (Map I, B2).* 📞*03-3267-2310. Open Tue–Sat 6–10pm (last orders 8pm). From ¥10,000. Reservations required.* Only four modest tables here for Mika Yamasaki, a chef well-versed in the technique of preparing *nabe* (one-pot dishes). Try the warming *negima nabe* with tuna.

NIGHTLIFE

Iseto 伊勢藤 *4-2 Kagurazaka, Shinjuku-ku (Map I, B2).* 📞*03-3260-6363. Open Mon–Fri 5–9.30pm.* A bar that feels like it belongs in a different era, from the reed screens over the windows in summer to the lack of air conditioning or central heating. The wood-paneled interior has low tables and *tatami* flooring, and a reverent atmosphere for serving the sake (no other drinks are sold). Also serves delicious *otoshi* (small dishes served with your drink order) and snacks which pair well with sake.

ADDRESSES

MOUNT TAKAO

🍴 EAT

🍴🍴🍴 **Ukai Toriyama** うかい鳥山 – *3426 Minamiasakawa-cho, Hachioji (Map I; A3, off map).* 📞*042-661-0739. ukai.co.jp/english/toriyama. Open Wed–Mon 11.30am–10pm (Sat from 11am; last orders 3pm & 7.30pm), Sun & public hols 11am–9pm (last orders 7pm). Lunch from ¥5350, dinner from ¥5950. Free shuttle bus from Takaosanguchi Station.* This restaurant is housed in several traditional thatched houses nestled among the vegetation in a lush valley. Specializes in chicken and beef, cooked on an *irori* hearth and elegantly presented. The ideal finishing touch to a walk on Mount Takao.

South of Tokyo ★★

Although the cities of Yokohama and Kamakura are relatively close geographically, situated 15.5mi/25km and 31mi/50km south of Tokyo respectively, they are surprisingly different to each other. The Kamakura era gave birth to Japan's first military government in 1185, while in the 1850s, in the crucible of its early interactions with Westerners, Yokohama forged the largest industrial port in the country. Each has thus drawn from its changing fortunes a powerful history with which to confront the modern visitor. Kamakura's blend of warrior culture and Buddhism led to a new relationship with the divine, while Yokohama's openness to the world now extols a completely unabashed modernity: two realities which are still shaping modern Japanese society today.

YOKOHAMA★ 横浜
⌖ Map p200.

A Bit of History – Yokohama really started to flourish after the Treaty of Kanagawa was signed with the USA in 1854. Five years later, the port was opened and its seafront area divided, one section being reserved for foreigners, while the second, the Japanese area of Yokohama-cho, was split into

▸ **Population:** Yokohama: 3,733,000
Kamakura: 174,300

⌖ **Michelin Map:** Regions of Japan Map 1, Tokyo & Surroundings p131.

▸ **Location:** 15.5mi/25km south of Tokyo, Yokohama is the principal city in Kanagawa prefecture. Kamakura is 15.5mi/25km farther south, 31mi/50km from Tokyo.

▲ **Kids:** The view from the Landmark Tower and a visit to *Nippon Maru*, the beaches of the Miura Peninsula.

⌚ **Timing:** Allow a full day, leaving Tokyo early in the morning and finishing with dinner in the Chinese quarter.

☺ **Don't miss:** In Yokohama, the Yamate district and the garden of Sankei-en; Chinatown and its temple in the early evening. In Kamakura, the temples and shrines in Kita-Kamakura early in the morning.

five districts. Over a century and a half later (it celebrated its 150th anniversary in 2009), Yokohama is one of the largest ports in the country, and the

Japanese silk aids France

In the middle of the 19C the Second French Empire's economy was based on a textile industry that was a world leader in silkworm-breeding and the silk trade. However, between 1855 and 1860, two infections (nosema disease and flacherie) threatened to ruin France's silk industry. The French representative in Edo confirmed that the Japanese silkworm industry was able to compensate for the shortages in France. The archipelago became a much sought-after partner, and continued to be so until the early 20C. From 1860 onward, Duchesne de Bellecourt helped to establish the first merchants from Lyon in Nagasaki and Yokohama. Louis Bourret set up a spinning operation in the international concession of Yokohama. Raw silk from Japan, which was of better quality than silk from China, enabled the silk manufacturers of Lyon to maintain their premier position in the world silk trade.

Minato Mirai 21, Landmark Tower on the left

© SeanPavonePhoto/iStock

second largest city, with a population of 3.7 million. Located close to the capital, it's now part of the Tokyo conurbation. The *salarymen* who commute from Yokohama each day are too numerous to count and the Chinese community here is the largest in Japan. Yokohama has lost nothing of its original global and forward-looking character.

Although the city is constantly changing, the museums are a reminder of its history. Given the city's maritime nature, the presence of a Port Museum is not unusual, but the Silk Museum may seem surprising until you realize that silk is the commodity on which it built its fortune. Yokohama was quick to learn from Western models of modernity. A walk across town will reveal how its physical character changes, from the picturesque late-19C houses nestling on Yamate hill, to Minato Mirai 21, with its modern, futuristic architecture.

The town could be divided into four districts: the heights of **Yamate** ("The Bluff"), where foreigners have historically congregated; the central, administrative district of **Kannai**; the extensive **Chinatown**; and **Minato Mirai 21**.

YAMATE AND MOTOMACHI DISTRICT ★★ 山手・元町

&*Map; B2, off map. 2min walk from Ishikawa-cho Station, south exit.*
Motomachi, an elegant shopping street that developed when Westerners set-

tled in this residential district, leads to Yamate hill, on the southeast side of the downtown area. At the northeast end of the street a wooded promontory marks the beginning of the Yamate district. From there, paths wind up the hillside to **Harbor View Park**, which offers an excellent view over the port and bay.

You'll find the Yokohama British House in the park, and the **Yokohama Foreign General Cemetery** (&*open Tue–Sun 10am–5pm*) nearby, where around 5000 people representing some 40 different nationalities are buried. Some of the tombs show a touch of humor or *post mortem* professional loyalty—a former railway engineer, Edmond Morel, for example, has a headstone shaped like a train ticket. As you stroll along the road running beside the cemetery *(Yamate-Hon-dori)*, you'll see a dozen or so houses, some of them resembling small English country-manor residences, that occupy pride of place amid charming gardens. Most of these late-19C buildings were rebuilt after the 1923 earthquake, and seven of them now house temporary exhibitions and small museums full of atmosphere. The **Tin Toy Museum** (&*open Mon–Fri 9am–6pm, Sat & Sun 9.30am–7pm;* ⊜ *¥200*) has more than 3000 small-scale models dating from 1890 to 1960. The **Yamate Museum** (&*open Tue–Sun 11am–4pm;* ⊜ *¥200*), built in 1909, is the only house that remained intact after the earthquake.

USEFUL INFORMATION
YOKOHAMA

Tourist Offices – Sakuragicho Station *(Map, A2; ℘045-211-0111, open daily 9am–6pm)*, **Yokohama Station** *(Map, A1; ℘045-441-7300, open daily 9am–7pm)*, and **Shin-Yokohama Station** *(Map A1, off map; ℘045-473-2895, open daily 9am–9pm)*. English spoken at all three.

Bank/Foreign Exchange – **Prestia/ SMBC Trust Bank**, *Yokohama Station (Map, A1; open Mon–Fri 9am–3pm)*. Currency exchange, travelers' checks, etc. ATM daily, usually 24hr.

Post Office/Withdrawals – *1-1 Sakuragi-cho (Map, A2; open Mon–Fri 9am–6pm)*. ATM at entrance *(Mon–Fri 8am–9pm, 9am–7pm)*, post office services on 3F.

The Bluff Medical and Dental Clinic – *82 Yamate-cho, Naka-ku (Map B2, off map). ℘045-641-6961. bluffclinic.com. Open Mon–Fri 9am–12.30pm & 1.30–5pm, Sat 9am–1pm (dental clinic shut Wed)*. English-speaking doctors.

TRANSPORTATION

BY TRAIN – Yokohama Station *(Map, A1)* – Two lines link the Tokyo airports to Yokohama: the **Narita Express Line** departs from Narita *(1hr 30min journey, ¥4300)* and the **Keikyu Line** departs from Haneda *(25min, ¥450)*. The JR **Tokaido** *(27min, ¥470)*, **Yokosuka** *(30min, ¥470)*, and **Keihin-Tohoku** *(40min, ¥470)* lines all depart from Tokyo Station. Take the subway to Sakuragicho Station or Minato Mirai Station for easy access to most sights.

BY BUS – **Limousine Bus Company** departs from Narita International Airport *(www.limousinebus.co.jp/en; 1hr 50min, ¥3700)* and Haneda Airport *(hnd-bus.com; 30min, ¥590)*.

GETTING AROUND

ON FOOT – Follow the **Kaiko Promenade** *(a harborside route indicated by circular plaques set in the ground)* linking the main downtown sites.

BY SUBWAY – There are two subway lines running north–south. Allow ¥210–550 depending on distance.

BY TRAIN – Local trains *(Tokyu-Toyoko and JR Negishi)* are quicker and cheaper than the subway.

BY BUS – **Akai-Kutsu** tourist buses are recognizable by their retro red-and-yellow design. Regular departures from Sakuragicho Station for main tourist sites *(¥100)*. Stations are announced in English.

BY BICYCLE – **Rental**

Cycle Travelation *(cycletravelation. com/english/rental)*, near Yokohama Station. Open Tue–Sun 9am–6pm; from ¥2000 per day.

Bay Bike *(docomo-cycle.jp/yokohama/ en)*, cycle docks throughout Yokohama. Daily 24hr; from ¥150 per 30min.

USEFUL INFORMATION
KAMAKURA

Tourist Information – *Kakamura Station, east exit (Map, B2; ℘0467-22-3350, open daily 9am–5pm)*. English spoken.

TRANSPORTATION

BY TRAIN – Kamakura Station *(Map, B2)* – From Tokyo Station, the **JR Yokosuka Line** *(1hr journey, ¥920)*.

From Shinjuku, the **JR Shonan-Shinjuku Line** *(1hr, ¥920)*, or the **Odakyu Line** to Fujisawa *(55min, ¥590)* then the **Enoden Line** *(35min, ¥300)*; **Enoshima Kamakura Free Pass** *(¥1470)* covers a round trip.

From Shibuya, the **JR Shonan-Shinjuku Line** *(55min, ¥920)*, or the **Tokyu Toyoko Line** to Yokohama *(25min, ¥270)* then the **JR Yokosuka Line** *(25min, ¥340)*.

Enoshima – From Shinjuku, take the **Odakyu Line** to Fujisawa then the **Enoden Line** *(10min, ¥220)* to Enoshima. Covered by the Enoshima Kamakura Free Pass.

GETTING AROUND

BY TRAIN – From Kamakura, the **Enoden Line** to Hase *(5min, ¥190)* and **JR Yokosuka Line** to Kita-Kamakura *(3min, ¥140)*.

A **Kamakura Enoshima Pass** *(¥700)* allows you to travel freely on the Enoden Line, Shonan monorail and JR Yokosuka lines from Kamakura Fujisawa.

BY BUS – Numerous buses for the main temples depart from Kamakura station.

BY BICYCLE – Hase and Kita-Kamakura are a 15–20min cycle from Kamakura. *Kamakura Station (Map, B2). Daily 8.30am–5pm; from ¥600 per hour, ¥1600 per day.*

YOKOHAMA

0 — 250 — 500 m
0 — 250 — 500 yds

N

RAMEN MUSEUM, SHIN-YOKOHAMA STATION

WHERE TO STAY

Navios Yokohama...................................❶
PROSTYLE Ryokan Yokohama
  Bashamichi...❷
Richmond Hotel
  Yokohama Bashamichi.....................❸
Royal Park Hotel..................................❹
Yokohama Hostel Village...................❺

WHERE TO EAT

Bistrot El Ella.......................................❶
Kisoji...❷
Seiko-En Honkan................................❸

Yokohama Sta.
Shin-Takashima Sta.
Takashima-cho Sta.
CENTRAL WHOLESALE MARKET
RINKO PARK
Minatomirai Line
Yokohama Museum of Art
Minatomirai Sta.
Minato Mirai 21
SHINKO PARK
Mitsubishi Minatomirai Industrial Museum
Queen's Square Yokohama
Landmark Tower
Cup Noodles Museum
SHINKO ISLAND
BICYCLE RENTAL
Yokohama Port Museum
AKA RENGA PARK
Yokohama International Passenger Terminal
Sakuragi-cho Sta.
Bashamichi-dori
Bashamichi Sta.
KANAGAWA PREF. GOVERNMENT OFFICE
Yokohama Archive History
SAKURAGI-CHO
KANNAI DISTRICT
Keihin Kyuko Line
NOGEYAMA ZOOLOGICAL GARDEN
NOGE-CHO
Kannai Sta.
Nihon-odori Sta.
YAMASHITA PARK
Silk Museum
Hinodecho Sta.
NOGEYAMA PARK
JR Negishi Line
MINATO P.O.
Isezaki Mall
YOKOHAMA CITY OFFICE
YOKOHAMA STADIUM
Osanbashi-dori
CHINATOWN
Fujidana Isezaki
Kannai Sta.
ISEZAKI-CHO
Isezakichojamachi Sta.
Kentei-byo Temple
Kaganecho Sta.
NAKA P.O.
Ishikawacho Sta.
MOTOMACHI
Motomachi-dori St.
Bandobashi Sta.
Kariba Line
YAMATE DISTRICT SANKEI-EN
MOTOMACHI
SOJI-JI

The Treaty of Kanagawa

Commodore Perry's fleet moored in Edo Bay in July 1853. The US naval officer was carrying a letter from the American President, insisting that the shogun open up diplomatic and commercial relations between the two countries. On March 31, 1854, the Japanese signed the Treaty of Kanagawa with the United States. It brought an end to the political isolationism observed by Japan since the 1630s. Not only was the treaty to have a profound impact on Japanese society, it was also to discredit the shogun government in the eyes of its vassals, who were divided on which path to follow. The modernization sought by the Meiji state was under way. It proved fatal to shogun authority.

Sankei-en

© mahroch/iStock

Also worth seeing in the nearby Italian Garden is the **Diplomat's House** (🕐 *open daily 9.30am–5pm;* 🎟 *no charge)* and **Bluff 18 Ban-Kan** (🕐 *open daily 9.30am–5pm;* 🎟 *no charge)*. The first tennis court in Japan was installed in **Yamate Park** in 1876, hence the **Yokohama Yamate Museum of Tennis** (🕐 *open daily 10am–5pm;* 🎟 *no charge)*.

▶ From here it's an easy walk to Chinatown, over the Nakamura River.

Sankei-en ★★ 三渓園

♿ *Map; B2, off map. 58-1 Honmoku Sannotani, Naka-ku. From JR Negishi Station, bus 58, 99, 101, Honmaku stop, then 7min walk. sankeien.or.jp.* 🕐 *Open daily 9am–5pm.* 🎟 *¥700.*

Until 1906 the "third valley" (or "Sankei-en") was the property of silk merchant Hara Tomitaro. The traditional Japanese garden *(43.2 acre/17.5ha)* is divided into two areas: the external garden, which includes a three-tier pagoda, brought Kyoto's Tomyo-ji (1475), and a traditional house from the Hida region (the famous *gassho-zukuri*, with roofs "like hands joined in prayer," ♿ *see p275)*; and the internal garden, with a beautiful pavilion dating to the beginning of the Edo era (the *Rinshunkaku)*.

However, it's not the buildings but the garden itself, shaped into a variety of evocative, sweet-smelling landscapes, that attracts some 500,000 visitors a year. Go early in the morning, if possible.

KANNAI DISTRICT 関内
♿ *Map, B2.*

Kannai literally means "inside the barrier," as there used to be a barrier separating the houses occupied by foreigners from the municipal administrative buildings occupied by the Japanese.

Yokohama Archives of History ★ 横浜開港資料館

♿ *Map, B2. 3 Nihon-Odori, Naka-ku.* 🕐 *Open Tue–Sun 9.30am–5pm.* 🎟 *¥200. kaikou.city.yokohama.jp/en/index.html.* This museum, a must for anyone interested in the moment when not just Yokohama but the whole of Japan opened up to the outside world, is housed in the building where the Treaty of Kanagawa was signed. With over 200,000 pieces dating from the Edo era through to the early Showa era, it provides a fascinating look back in time with the aid of maps, models (ships, buildings, etc.), newspapers of the day, prints, photographs, postcards, and miscellaneous objects.

Since most of the official archives disappeared in the 1923 earthquake or the 1945 bombing raids, the fact that this collection has been assembled is remarkable. In the reading room you can see copies of early Japanese newspapers.

The tree in the inner courtyard is said to be a descendant of the *tabunoki* incense tree that features in most contemporary depictions of the arrival of Commodore Perry and his men.

Chinatown

Silk Museum シルク博物館

Map, B2. 2F Silk Center, 1 Yamashita-cho, Naka-ku. Subway Kannai or Nihon Odori. ⓞOpen Tue–Sun 9.30am–5pm. ✆¥500 (excluding special exhibitions). silkcenter-kbkk.jp/museum/en.

Despite its rather outdated presentation, this museum provides a good overview of the history of silk and how it is made, from silkworm to the creation of a kimono. It takes between 3000 and 9,000 silkworm cocoons to make a kimono, depending on size, complexity of design, the fullness of the sleeves, and accessories (*obi* sash, etc.); each cocoon provides around 4265ft/1300m of raw silk. You will also find out how the port of Yokohama became so important for the silk trade. Finally, temporary exhibitions compare the different silk production of other countries, like Laos or Uzbekistan.

CHINATOWN ★★ 中華街

♿Map, B2. To reach Chinatown from the Silk Museum, walk down Osanbashi-dori (10min walk). Subway Motomachi-Chugakai. chinatown.or.jp.

Like many of the world's ports, Yokohama has a Chinese community, and its Chinatown is today the biggest in Japan. The city was one of the first Japanese ports to open up commercially, and this, together with the subsequent dynamism of its commercial activities, was attractive to those who were forced to flee political upheavals in China.

Another factor was that, not used dealing with Japanese people, Western merchants used *compradore* as intermediaries, Shanghai natives who had aided Western traders in China following the Treaty of Nanking in 1842. This activity developed over the years as Yokohama's influence spread, and today it is supported by China's increasingly important role in international relations.

Chinatown is now a small, prosperous district that attracts impressive numbers of people to its 200 or so restaurants every weekend. In the middle of its narrow, bustling streets, the **Kantei-byo** Chinese temple (*ⓞopen daily 9am–7pm; ✆no charge*), richly decorated under its three baroque and rococo-style roofs, shimmers and gleams like a finely-cut ruby with thousands of golden lights shining beneath a bestiary of dragons and octopuses. It's dedicated to Guan Yu, a military hero and former Han general, recognizable by his red face. Deified as the god of war, he now guarantees his popularity with the people by also protecting the temple's riches.

MINATO MIRAI 21 ★★ みなとみらい21

♿Map, B1. Sakuragicho Station.

The solid but futuristic-looking 👥 **Landmark Tower ★★** (*Map, A1*) defines Yokohama's gleamingly modern seafront, known as Minato Mirai 21. Measuring some 972ft/296m, the

The Kamakura Period

Minamoto no Yoritomo (1147–1199) chose Kamakura for his capital in 1192, propelling the city into history in one of the turning points that have since defined the story of Japan. Though the Kamakura period itself didn't last even 150 years, ending in 1333, it established the mode of military government, the **shogunate**, that was to dominate until the mid-19C. Upon Yoritomo's death, his direct successors (his son Yoriie was assassinated) were ousted one after the next by a noble family of Taira ancestry, the Hojo clan, who took the reins and governed under the title of regent (*shikken*). Nine Hojo *shikken* in succession ruled for more than a century, pulling the strings of a power that was notionally exercised by shoguns they picked first from the Fujiwara family line, and then from among the imperial princes. During this period, Japan narrowly avoided occupation by the Mongols on two occasions (1274 and 1281), with the invasions being repelled at great cost by a warrior class that felt it had been poorly rewarded for its efforts. This discontent drove the emperor Go-Daigo (1288–1339) to take command of a coalition of forces with a view to restoring imperial power. The puppet emperor (Kogen) installed by the regency was driven from Kyoto with the aid of Ashikaga Takauji (1305–1358), the descendant of a faithful vassal of Minamoto no Yoritomo. Lord Nitta Yoshisada (1301–1338), Go-Daigo's most charismatic ally, conquered Kamakura and the city was laid waste in 1333, bring the Kamakura period to an end.

tower houses one of the highest observation decks (the Sky Garden) in Japan *(896ft/273m)* and probably one of the fastest elevators; it shoots skyward at a speed of 2,461ft/750m per minute, so that you reach the Sky Garden in just 40 seconds! (🕐*Open daily 10am–9pm, Sat 10pm;* 🎫*¥1000, children ¥500; yokohama-landmark.jp/skygarden).* Close by is the inevitable shopping mall, the **Landmark Plaza**.

Mitsubishi Minatomirai Industrial Museum
三菱みなとみらい技術館
Map, A1. 3-1 Minatomirai 3-chome, Nishi-ku; behind Landmark Tower. 🕐*Open Wed–Mon 10am–5pm.* 🎫*¥500. mhi.com/expertise/museum/minatomirai.* "To help young people launch themselves into the future more successfully" are the words chosen by Mitsubishi to explain the opening of this museum in

The first of the shoguns

In 1159, Yoshimoto, **Minamoto no Yoritomo**'s father, was crushed by his great rival Taira no Kiyomori. Yoritomo was condemned to exile and the Taira clan imposed their authority on the Imperial Court. However, this authority was gradually undermined by the intrigues of the Emperor, the intractability of the great lords, and the marriage of Yoritomo and Masako, daughter of Hojo Tokimasa (who became the first *shikken*). Yoritomo initiated a revolt and in 1185, the Taira troops were defeated once and for all on the beach of Danno Ura, near Shimonoseki. Yoritomo then assumed the title of *sei i taishogun* ("generalissimo who subdues the barbarians") ,and the village where he had established his base became the seat of his first military government *(bakufu).* Thus, in 1192, Kamakura became the capital city of the first Japanese shogun, a commander-in-chief in whom all power and authority resided; the Emperor retained only his position as religious leader, a role to which he was entitled because of his divine origins. The shoguns only finally died out with the Meiji Restoration in the latter half of the 19C.

1994 on its former industrial site. Its's broadly split into four areas *(Space, Sky, Sea, and Land)*, which take the visitor into a 3D virtual world. The simulated helicopter flight is one of the most popular attractions.

Cup Noodles Museum
カップヌードルミュージアム 横浜
Map, B1. 2-3-4 Shinko, Naka-ku. Subway Minato Mirai. Open Wed–Mon 10am–6pm. ¥500. cupnoodles-museum.jp/en.
Interactive museum where you can learn about the history of instant noodles, which were invented in Japan. One of the most fun parts is the My Cupnoodles Factory, where you can make your own bespoke instant ramen *(¥300)*. Also has a modern art section and the Noodles Bazaar, serving global noodle dishes

Yokohama Museum of Art
横浜美術館
Map, A1. 3-4-1 Minatomirai, Nishi-ku, opposite Mitsubishi Museum. Subway Minato Mirai. Open Fri–Wed 10am–6pm. ¥500 (excluding special exhibitions). yokohama.art.museum/eng.
This impressive museum of modern art and photography, designed by architect Tange Kenzo *(see p172)*, hosts top-quality temporary exhibitions, with a few recurring themes such as the beautiful sculptures of Isamu Noguchi (1904–88), who worked in the studios of Brancusi.

Yokohama Port Museum ★
横浜みなと博物館
Map, A2–B2. Opposite the Landmark Tower. Open Tue–Sun 10am–5pm. ¥600, children ¥300 including Nippon Maru. nippon-maru.or.jp/foreign.
The recently remodeled Port Museum covers the history of the Japanese Merchant Navy and include a fine collection of models. The visit continues on board the **Nippon Maru ★**, a retired sailing ship moored just outside, which makes for a truly beautiful sight when her sails are hoisted. She served as a training ship for 50 years, but has formed part of the museum since 1984. The whole ship is open to be explored.

AROUND YOKOHAMA
Soji-ji ★ 總持寺
Map; B2, off map. 2-1-1 Tsurumi, Tsurumi ward. Tsurumi Station, JR Keihin Tohoku Line, then 7min walk from west exit. Open Tue–Sun 10am–4.30pm. 1hr tour ¥400 (small booklet in English). English Zazen classes ¥500 (check schedule online). sojiji.jp/english.
The headquarters of the Soto sect and one of the principal Zen schools in Japan *(see box p209)*, this temple has 40 or so buildings, mostly constructed in the early 20C. Built in 1966, the spectacular Daisodo, the Great Hall of the founders, has a floor covered in 1000 *tatami* mats. Two hundred monks live here, a vibrant community where the youngest are tasked with cleaning the floor of the corridor *(Ichimonji Roka)* twice a day, while practicing *zokin-gake*. This involves running nonstop to the end of the corridor, a distance of 1969ft/600m, while polishing the floor with a cloth wrapped around the arms; breath control in difficult postures is an integral part of Zen discipline. Try not to miss the Room of the Purple Clouds *(Shi-untai)*, a reception room with panels painted by the best artists of the Taisho era (1912–26), reserved for important visitors.

Ramen Museum
新横浜ラーメンミュージアム
Map; A1, off map. 2-14-21. Shin-Yokohama, Kohoku. Subway Shin-Yokohama. Open daily 11am–10pm (Sun 10.30am). ¥310. raumen.co.jp/english.
In a replica Tokyo street from the 1960s learn about the history of ramen (wheat noodles originally from China). You can sample different regional varieties (some vegetarian choices available).

KAMAKURA ★★★ 鎌倉
Map, p205.
Surrounded by mountains on three sides, the only escape route from this town is across a steel-blue sea fringed with dark sand. Was it the limited horizon that compelled the population of this ancient village of storehouses

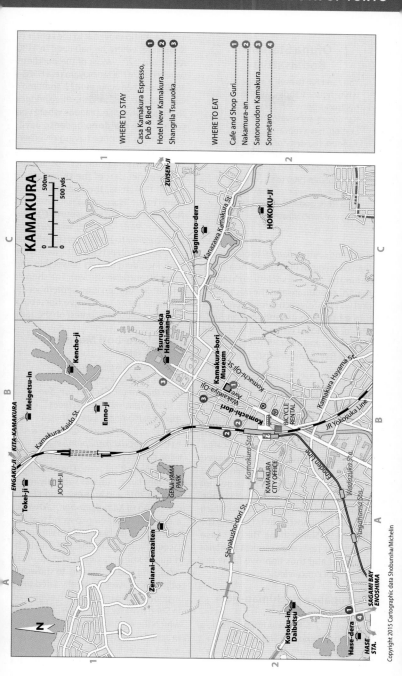

KAMAKURA

0 — 500m
0 — 500 yds

WHERE TO STAY

Casa Kamakura Espresso,
Pub & Bed............................ ❶
Hotel New Kamakura............ ❷
Shangrila Tsuruoka.............. ❸

WHERE TO EAT

Cafe and Shop Guri............... ❶
Nakamura-an........................ ❷
Satonoudon Kamakura......... ❸
Sometaro.............................. ❹

Copyright 2015 Cartographic data Shobunsha/Michelin

205

Ofuna Station Bodhisattva

You can't fail to notice a gigantic white figure standing by the rail tracks between Tokyo and Kamakura, surveying Ofuna Station. It is a representation of Kannon, the deity of compassion. Built in 1960, the statue, which is 82ft/25m tall and weighs 1,723,650lb/1900 tons, contains several stones takes from ground zero (the center of impact) at Nagasaki and Hiroshima.

(kura) and scythes (kama) to build more than 60 religious buildings? The answer lies in the military society created by the 12C shogunate and the bushi (warrior) way of life, which turned Kamakura into a breeding ground for Zen Buddhism. The town is one hour's journey from Tokyo and a paradise for surfers in Sagami Bay. Allow at least 2 days.

CENTRAL DISTRICT

As you leave Kamakura Station (east exit), you will see the start of two main roads to your left. The first, Komachi-dori, is a narrow, pedestrianized street given over to commerce: restaurants, cafes, stores, ice-creams and wasabi -flavored beans (wasabi-mame at a store called Kamakura Mameya). Three large torii (gates) mark out the attractive **avenue of cherry trees ★** (Wakamiya-oji), which extends for almost 4930ft/1500m to the Tsurugaoka Shinto shrine. The trees were planted at Yoritomo's request to honor the kami and thus improve his wife's chances of conceiving.

Tsurugaoka Hachiman-gu ★
鶴岡八幡宮

Map, B1. 2-1-31 Yukinoshita; 10min walk from Kamakura Station, east exit. Open daily 6am–8.30pm (5am Apr–Sept). No charge. tsurugaoka-hachimangu.jp.
The shrine was founded in 1063 by Yoriyoshi (grandfather of the Minamoto clan) in tribute to Emperor Ojin Himeg-

ami. Yoritomo moved it to the center of Kamakura, where he had lived in 1180 (see box p203). Most of the buildings were rebuilt in the Momoyama era (1568–1600), and then again in 1823. Yoritomo's wife, Masako, designed the three bridges that lead to a vast esplanade where you will find the **maidono** or dance pavilion, famous for once having reverberated under the feet of Shizuka, mistress of Yorimoto's half-brother, Yoshitsune. In the upper part of the shrine at the top of the steps, the kamino miya is home to the Tsurugaoka Hachiman-gu **National Treasure Museum** (open Tue–Sun 9am–4.30pm; tariff varies according to exhibition). It contains almost 5000 objects from the Kamakura area, including objects of worship and mikoshi (portable shrines). The shrine's annual celebration is on September 15, followed by an impressive horseback archery (yabusame) contest on the 16th.

Kamakura-bori Museum ★★
鎌倉彫資料館

Map, B2. 3F Kamakura-bori Kaikan, 2-15-13 Komachi; 5min walk from the station. Open Tue–Sun 9.30am–5pm. ¥300 (excludes special exhibitions). Cafe & shop on 1F; studios and craft workshops on 2F & 4F. kamakuraborikaikan.jp/museum.
If you can only visit one museum in Kamakura, make it this one. The building is not very large but was superbly renovated in 2016 and houses a magnificent collection of Kamakura-bori, artworks made of Judas or gingko wood that has been carved and varnished (using urushi lacquer) with remarkable skill. This technique is known as mokucho-saishitsu (sculpting and lacquering, to showcase objects that were generally fated to sit in poor lighting in temples). It originated in Song dynasty (960–1279) China, after which the techniques were developed in Japans. A very good and informative video explains the history of the craft. If your interest is picqued, try to book a place on a workshop (around ¥3200). At the excellent cafe (see Addresses p213), you can enjoy vegetarian shojin-ryori cuisine served on lacquerware.

Hokoku-ji★★★ 報国寺

Map, C2. 2-7-4 Jomyo-ji. Bus 23, 24, 36 from Kamakura station, Jomyo-ji bus stop. Open daily 9am–4pm. ¥300. houkokuji.or.jp.

This Zen temple belongs to Kencho-ji , a temple of the Rinzai sect. It was founded in 1334 by Tengan Eko (1273–1335) to honor the memory of Ashikaga Ietoki, grandfather of shogun Ashikaga Takauji. Apart from some beautiful **sculptures of the Buddha ★★** (14C) by sculptor Takuma Hogen and others *(in the central building and annex),* the temple's attraction lies mainly in its **bamboo forest ★★**, which includes some 2000 moso bamboos, the largest species of this woody plant. You can enjoy the view over a cup of *matcha* (powdered green tea) in the adjoining pavilion *(¥600).*

Bamboo forest, Hokoku-ji

© ranmaru_/iStock

Sugimoto-dera ★★ 杉本寺

Map, C2. 903 Nikaido; 10min walk from Hokoku-ji, on Kanazawa Kamakura St. Open daily 8am–4.30pm. ¥200. sugimotodera.com.

One of the oldest temples in Kamakura (734) is accessed via a magnificent flight of worn, moss-covered steps flanked by white flags bearing the names of donors. The two **guardian statues ★** flanking the entrance may have been sculpted by Unkei. Attributed to the priest Gyoki, this atmospheric temple houses three **statues of the eleven-headed Kannon ★★**, two from the Kamakura era. The temple was rebuilt in the 17C.

Zuisen-ji★ 瑞泉寺

Map; C1, off map. 710 Nikaido; 20min walk from Sugimoto-dera (signposted with arrows). Open daily 9am–5pm. ¥200. kamakura-zuisenji.or.jp/en.

Built at the end of the Kamakura era by Do-un Nikaido (1267–1334), a high-ranking general, this temple is visited mainly for its garden. This is the last remaining Kamakura-era garden, its most arresting feature the natural cave incorporated into the design. It was designed by a Zen priest of the Rinzai school, Muso Soseki (1275–1351), who was also known for designing the famous Moss Garden in Kyoto (see p 344).

Also called the Kamakura Temple of Flowers, there is a rich variety of endemic flora such as the *mitsumata*, a plant with white flowers used in the manufacture of *washi* (Japanese paper). It is also popular for the narcissi and plum trees that cover the Kimpei-san hill. From the top, the **Ichiran-tei** pavilion offers a **panorama** of Hakone and Mount Fuji.

HASE DISTRICT 長谷

Hase-dera ★★ 長谷寺

Map, A2. 3-11-2 Hase; 5min walk from Hase Station. Open daily: Mar–Sept 8am–5.30pm; Oct–Feb 8am–4.30pm. ¥400. www.hasedera.jp/en.

According to the story of this temple's foundation, in 721 the monk Tokudo Shonin found an enormous camphor tree in the forests of Nara, near the vilage of Hase. Realizing the tree was large enough to provide wood for two statues, he had two images of Kannon carved from it. The first was enshrined in a temple near Nara; the second was thrown into the sea in the hope that it would one day reappear to save the people. Fifteen years later it did so, on Nagai beach near Kamakura, and this temple was constructed in honor of the deity. The sculpture is now in the main **Kannon-do** pavilion, which dominates the inner part of the temple (with a magnificent **view** from the observation terrace). When you see how tall it is *(just over 30ft/9m),* you realize just how huge

Statue of the Buddha, Kotoku-in
© bhidethescene/iStock

the original camphor tree must have been, although the statue on show is a later reproduction. Kannon, the deity of mercy, is represented here with a staff in her right hand and a lotus flower in the left, symbols, perhaps, of the pilgrimages prompted by her reappearance. On the right, the **Amida-do** houses the seated statue of Yakuyoke, who guards against evil spirits. The golden statue, almost 10ft/3m high, was paid for by Yoritomo. On your way back, don't miss the **jizo-do** where Fukuju Jizo (the *jizo, or* boddhisatva, of happiness) is enshrined. The temple is surrounded by thousands of small stone *jizo*. A little farther down, **Benten-Kutsu** cave is dedicated to the goddess of the sea.

Kotoku-in and the Kamakura Daibutsu ★ 高徳院・鎌倉大仏
🕭*Map, A2. 4-2-28 Hase; 5min walk north of Hase-dera.* ⏰*Open daily: Apr–Sept 8am–5.30pm; Oct–Mar 8am–5pm (Buddha statue to 4.30pm).* 🌐*¥300; statue interior* 🌐*¥20. kotoku-in.jp/en.*
When Yoritomo's wife ordered the construction of a large statue of the **Buddha ★★** *(Daibutsu)* at this temple, she modeled it on the great, gilt bronze statue of the Vairocana Buddha of Todai-ji in Nara. Five years later, the wooden statue was destroyed by a typhoon. In 1252, it was replaced by this 125-ton bronze statue,

37ft/11.3m high, which was originally covered in gold leaf. The *jobon-josho mudra* (hands with upturned palms) indicates that the highest level of enlightenment has been achieved, which is evident when you gaze into the Buddha's half-closed eyes, which are almost 3ft/1m across.

Zeniarai-Benzaiten ★★
銭洗弁財天
🕭*Map, A1. Follow the arrows from Kotoku-in (20min walk).* ⏰*Open daily 8am–4.30pm.* 🌐*No charge.*
An unusual and atmospheric place, with just the *torii* (gates) set into a rocky wall to betray its existence to the outside world. Passing through the gates leading into a tunnel, you emerge in a large, open space carved out of the rock containing a beautiful shrine. At the back of a hidden cave there's a lovely freshwater spring, which, according to legend, was revealed to Minamoto Yoritomo on the day of the serpent, in the month of the serpent, in the year of the serpent. As such, it was dedicated to Benzaiten, goddess of snakes. She's also the deity of all things which flow, including water and money; if you wash your coins (and even your notes, drying them carefully in the curling fumes of incense) in the water at one of the shrine's many small altars, it's said that your money will be doubled.

KITA-KAMAKURA 北鎌倉

▶ The temples are located either side of the railway tracks. We suggest you start at the more pleasant eastern exit.

Engaku-ji ★★ 円覚寺

Map; B1, off map. 409 Yamanouchi; 5min walk from Kita-Kamakura Station, east exit. ○*Open daily: Mar–Nov 8am–4.30pm; Dec–Feb 8am–4pm.* ⌐¥300. engakuji.or.jp.
Kamikaze, which literally means "divine wind," was the name given to the typhoons that destroyed the Mongolian fleet on its way to invade Japan. Later, the name was adopted by Japanese pilots, who carried out suicide attacks near the end of World War II. This Zen temple was built by Hojo Tokimune (1251–84), eighth regent of Kamakura, to pay tribute to both the Japanese and Mongolians who perished during the two invasion attempts (1274 and 1281). It contains good examples of *kato mado* (bell-shaped windows) and *sankarado* (wooden latticework), two characteristic features of Zen temples. Though badly damaged in the 1923 earthquake, most of it was later rebuilt. The main attraction is the **Reliquary** *(Shari-den)*, which is reputed to contain a tooth of the Buddha. Karate enthusiasts may like to pay a visit to the tomb of Funakoshi Gichin (1868–1957), the founder of this martial art (*see p120*).

Meigetsu-in ★★ 明月院

Map, B1. 189 Yamanouchi; 10min from Kita-Kamakura Station. ○*Open daily 9am–4pm (Jun 8.30am–5pm).* ⌐¥500 (additional fee in June & late Nov).
Meigetsu-in, the "Bright Moon Hermitage," was founded in 1160 by Yamanouchi Tsunetoshi as a place of rest for the soul of his father, Toshimichi, who died in the Battle of Heiji (1159). The site was taken over by Hojo Tokiyori (1227–63), fifth regent of Kamakura, who turned it into a Buddhist temple when he retired. A **dry landscape garden** and beds of irises can be seen through the round doorway of the main building. The tombs are hollowed out of the rock walls, thus leaving space outside for meditation. The temple is also known as Ajisai-dera, or "**hydrangea temple**," for its profusion of blue blooms every June. It's almost as enchanting during the fall leaf-viewing (*momijigari*) season of late November.

Kencho-ji ★★ 建長寺

Map, B1. 8 Yamanouchi; 10min walk from Meigetsu-in via Kamakura-kaido St. ○*Open daily 8.30am–4.30pm.* ⌐¥500. kenchoji.com.
Founded by the regent Hojo Tokiyori, this temple bears the name of the period (Kencho, 1249–55) in which it was completed. The first and biggest Zen temple in Kamakura, it was built by the priest Rankei Doryu, a Chinese master who came to Japan to teach Zen.

Simplicity and Subversion

Zen, the Japanese form of *Chan* (the Chinese school opposed to all religious creeds and indoctrination, instead concentrating on direct experience and what comes from within), was brought to Japan by two monks of the **Tendai** Buddhist school. The first monk, **Eisai** (1141–1215), founder of the **Rinzai** branch, advocated an experimental approach to meditation, blending humor, paradox, and physical and mental challenges in the form of beatings and riddles *(koan)*. The second monk, **Dogen** (1200–53), author of the *Fukanzazengi (General Recommendations Concerning the Practice of the Way)*, established the **Soto** school, which teaches the *zazen* seated method of meditation. The aim of both is to lead the pupil to the *satori*, the awakening. These simple practices were encouraged by the shogun authorities because they were contrary to the way the Emperor exercised religious authority. Although of divine origin, the Emperor relied on complex rituals to raise him above the uneducated masses.

San-mon, Kencho-ji

© tupungato/iStock

The complex used to have almost 50 secondary temples, but only a dozen or so remain. Of particular interest is the *bonsho* **temple bell**, cast in 1255 and now classified as a National Treasure. On the other side of the San-mon (gate) are **juniper trees** over 700 years old. The *Butsuden* (Buddha hall) contains an unusual image of the **Jizo Bosatsu**. The garden outside the main hall was designed by Muso Soseki; the pond is in the shape of the ideogram for "spirit."

Enno-ji ★ 円応寺
Map, B1. 1543 Yamanouchi; opposite Kencho-ji. Open daily: Mar–Nov 9am–4pm; Dec–Feb 9am–3pm. ¥200.
The main feature of this small temple is the statue of Enma (Hindu god of death and hell), more than 750 years old, with a fierce expression. There is also a fine selection of bodhisattvas made of clay.

Tokei-ji ★★ 東慶寺
Map, B1. 1367 Yamanouchi; 275yd/250m from Kita-Kamakura Station (west exit) or 5min walk from Engaku-ji, down Kamakura-kaido St. Open daily Apr–Nov 8.30am–4.30pm; Oct–Mar 8.30am–4pm. ¥200. tokeiji.com/english/about.
Following the death of her husband, Hojo Tokimune, Kakusan-ni withdrew from the world as tradition demanded of a widow. This withdrawal was, however, into the temple that she founded after her husband's death. Thus it was that in 1285, one of the first Japanese nunneries appeared. Although women had few rights, the Tokei-ji managed to obtain extraterritorial status with legal privileges from the shogun government, in particular the right for a woman to divorce her husband provided she had lived in the temple for three years. As a result it became known as the "**Divorce Temple**." The privilege lasted until the Meiji reforms of 1873, when women were granted the right to divorce.

Walking in the **garden** is a real delight. The cherry, apricot, and peach trees, peonies, and irises form a wonderful picture at different times of year. The **Treasure House★** (*Matsugaoka Hozo; open Tue–Sun 10am–3pm*) contains a fine wooden statue of **Sho Kannon Bosatsu Ryuzo**. Its clay halo (*do-mon*) was made using a mold engraved with floral designs, a technique that was unique to Kamakura.

There are also some fine **Darumas** (round, hollow dolls with no arms or legs, representations of Bodhidharma, the founder of Zen) by the priest Hakuin (1685–1768), as well as the famous **Mikudari-han**, which literally means "three and a half lines": divorce letters given to wives by husbands signifying

A Dragon for Enoshima

According to an 11th-century account written by a monk named Kokei, a terrible, five-headed dragon that lived in a lake near Kamakura was laying waste to the surrounding area. In 552, the goddess Benzaiten appeared during an earthquake; she made the island of Enoshima rise up from the waves and then made it her home. The dragon proposed marriage to the goddess, but she refused to accept unless he chose to embrace goodness. The dragon consented, eventually turning into a mountain upon his death, and the island became a place of peace.In the 12C, the shogun Minato no Yoritomo visited to supplicate for the goddess' protection. Worship was reserved for the emperor and samurai until the 18C, but was opened up to all after that and the site subsequently become a very popular place of pilgrimage. Taking only 5 days from the penitent's departure from Tokyo, it had the advantages of being shorter than the Mount Fuji pilgrimage and not requiring a travel permit.

Today this devotional journey is most often undertaken with a group of people from the same district or company. Pilgrims head first to Mount Oyama *(see p238)* and then on to Enoshima, before finishing at Kamakura The island has often been chosen as a subject by woodcut artists, notably Hiroshige.

their agreement to the divorce. A copy was also registered in the temple.

Enoshima 江の島

Map; A2, off map. 5mi/8km east of Kamakura. Take the Enoden Line from Hase or Kamakura stations to Enoshima Station (25min, ¥260). Direct connection from Shinjuku in Tokyo by Odakyu railways. Fujisawa City Tourist Center – 1-14-8 Katase-kaigan, 5min walk from Odakyu Katase-Enoshima Station. Open daily 8.30am–5pm. Information available in English.

This little island in Sagami Bay, an hour by train from Tokyo, has been famed for centuries, not only for the beautiful views of Mount Fuji but also—and especially—as a sacred Buddhist site. Nowadays, tourists and Tokyoites alike flock here in great numbers to spend the day or the weekend.

Cross the bridge and you will find the great bronze *torii* that marks the entrance to the main road leading to the three shrines, which together make up **Enoshima Shrine** *(open daily 8.30am–5pm; no charge)*. The street is lined with *omiyage* (souvenir) stores and specialty snack stalls emitting mouth-watering aromas—a tempting place for a stroll or a little food-tasting!

A red *torii* indicates you have arrived at **Hetsunomiya**, the first temple *(you can take an escalator up; ¥200 to Hetsunomiya, ¥360 to top of island)*, whose origins date back to 1204. It is dedicated to Benzaiten, goddess of all things which flow (including music, love and prosperity), and who, according to the legend of the dragon of Enoshima (*see box above*), was also present at the creation of the island. Two statues of the goddess, one dating back to the Kamakura period (13C), are to be found in Hoanden Pavilion *(¥200)*.

The second temple, **Nakatsunomiya**, which is a little further up the hill (escalator access available) was originally constructed in the 9C and has been rebuilt countless times since. It is traditionally visited by Kabuki actors.

Before continuing, you might well be tempted to take a break in the **Samuel Cocking Garden** *(open daily 9am–8pm; ¥200, or ¥500 with observation tower)*, which was built by a British merchant in 1882. The **Enoshima Lighthouse Observation Tower** is a 390ft-/119m-high structure offering a 360° panorama of the bay and—during good weather—a view of Mount Fuji. **Okutsunomiya**, the third temple, houses an astonishing painting of a tortoise from the Edo period. You can extend your stroll by walking to the two **Iwaya grottos** (🕐open daily: Mar–Sept 9am–6pm; Oct–Feb 9am–4pm; 👛¥500), which are 500ft (152m) and 185ft (56m) long respectively; these were probably the first cult sites for spirit worship on the island.

ADDRESSES

🛏 STAY

YOKOHAMA

🚇 **Yokohama Hostel Village** ヨコハマ ホステルヴィレッジ– 1F Sanwa Bldg, 3-11-2 Matsukage-cho, Naka-ku (Map, B2). 📞045-663-3696. yokohama.hostelvillage. com/en. 37 rooms. ¥5000. 🍴. In the former workers' district of Kotobuki, this old day laborers' residence has been transformed into a hostel. Rooms are small but clean; mix of singles, Japanese-style twins, 2-person dorms, and a family room. Kitchen and coin laundry area, and roof terrace. Down-to-earth, friendly feel.

🍽 **Navios Yokohama** ナビオス横浜 – 2-1-1 Shinko, Naka-ku (Map, B2). 📞045-633-6000. www.navios-yokohama.com. 135 rooms. ¥16,600. ¥1200 🍽. A standard hotel with all modern conveniences. Ideally located, near to Minato Mirai 21.

🍽🍽 **PROSTYLE Ryokan Yokohama Bashamichi** PROSTYLE旅館横濱馬 車道 – 5-64 Tokiwa-cho, Naka-ku (Map, B2). 📞045-662-2222. prostyleryokan. com/yokohamabashamichi/en. 94 rooms. ¥19,000. ¥1600 🍽. Opened in 2018, this sleek and well-located hotel fuses Japanese and Western style, with *tatami* flooring and *jinbei*-style pyjamas, but also leather sofas and black marble shower rooms. *Shabu-shabu* restaurant on site.

🍽🍽 **Richmond Hotel Yokohama Bashamichi** リッチモンドホテル 横浜馬 車道 – 5-59 Sumiyoshi-cho, Naka-ku (Map, B2). 📞045-228-6655. richmondhotel.jp/en/ yokohama. 201 rooms. ¥10,100. ¥1100 🍽. A very practical location in the Kannai district, halfway between Chinatown and Minato Mirai and not far from JR lines and the subway. Good-sized rooms.

🍽🍽🍽 **Royal Park Hotel** 横浜ロイヤルパークホテル – 2-2-1-3 Minatomirai, Nishi-ku (Map, A1). 📞045-221-1111. www2.yrph.com/en. 603 rooms, 20

suites. ¥20,000. Discounts often available online. From ¥1900 🍽. Between the 52nd and 67th floors of the Landmark Tower, the rooms of the Royal Park Hotel all have a breathtaking view—including from the nautical-style portholes in the shower rooms. Several restaurants, some with vegan, gluten-free or Halal options. Try the sushi at Shikitei (68F), and a tea ceremony with a view (65F; ¥1500). Magic!

KAMAKURA

🍽 **Hotel New Kamakura** ホテルニュー 鎌倉 – 13-2 Onarimachi (Map, B2). West exit from the station, then the tunnel to the left beneath the rail line. 📞046-722-2230. newkamakura.com/index_en.asp. 24 rooms. ¥8000. Extra fee 🍽. 🍴. Just behind the station in a quiet square. Small, but very pleasant rooms, many Japanese-style. The new wing is more comfortable (and has wi-fi) but is also more expensive.

🍽🍽 **Casa Kamakura Espresso, Pub & Bed** カーサ 鎌倉 エスプレッソ パ ブ＆ベッド – 1-15-5 Hase (Map, A2). 📞046-755-9077. 2 rooms (1 twin, 1 bunk). ¥10,800. 🍽. Guesthouse located near the Daibutsu, opened in 2016 by a young, English-speaking architect couple. Rooms are simple, stylish and comfortable, the American breakfast is excellent, and the welcoming cafe-bar downstairs (open daily 10am–6pm) is always lively.

🍽🍽 **Shangrila Tsuruoka** シャングリラ 鶴岡 – 1-9-29 Yukinoshita (Map, B2). East exit from the station, then 5min walk to the left along Wakamiya-oji. 📞046-725-6363. 10 rooms. ¥11,000. 🍽. It has seen better days, but is ideally situated by Tsurugaoka Hachiman-gu. No breakfast but there is a cafe upstairs. The owner speaks English.

🍽🍽 **Iwamotoro** 岩本楼 – 2-2-7 Enoshima, Fujisawa (Map; A2, off map). 📞046-626-4121. iwamotoro.co.jp/english. 28 rooms. ¥25,000. 🍽. This historic *ryokan* on Enoshima has been attracting guests for generations. Fresh seafood cuisine, two unusual hot springs (a tiled Roman-style one and a Benzaiten cave one), and stunning views over the sea toward Mount Fuji. Incredible value for money.

🍽🍽 **Kamakura Park Hotel** 鎌倉パークホテル – 33-6 Sakanoshita, Hase (Map A2; off map). 📞046-725-5121. kamakuraparkhotel.co.jp/en. 46 rooms, 2 suites. ¥27,000. ¥2700 🍽. A little way from the town center, the Park Hotel offers comfortable rooms and a *rotenburo* (open-air bath), all with a view over the ocean. Very attentive staff.

⚑/EAT

YOKOHAMA

🍴🍴 **Bistrot El Ella** ビストロ・エルエラ – 1F Joy Motomachi, 3-132 Motomachi, Naka-ku (Map, B2). ℘045-212-3581. minatomirai21.com/shop/1781. Open daily 11am–9pm (last orders), dinner from ¥3000. Good French food, with an emphasis on meat dishes. Lunch *bento* are available to take out (¥500), and the nearby park is a great picnic spot

🍴🍴 **Seiko-Enn Honkan** 生香園本館 – 5-80 Aioi-cho, Naka-ku (Map, B2). ℘045-651-5152. shu-tomiteru.jp. Open daily 11.30am–9.30pm (Sun & public hols 9pm). Set menus from ¥4200. Cantonese food in a traditional setting. The seafood yakisoba is great, and well-priced.

☯Yokohama's **Chinatown** has a huge choice of restaurants, all on any Tourist Office map. For Cantonese cooking, **Heichinrou** 聘珍樓 (the oldest Chinese restaurant in Japan) and **Manchinro** 萬珍樓 are essential. Try Shanghai specialties like *dazha xie* and tasty crabs at **Jo Gen Ro** 状元楼; and Beijing food at **Torin** 東林 and **Kaseiro** 華正楼.

🍴🍴🍴 **Kisoji Bashamichi-ten** 木曽路・馬車道店 – B1F Yokohama Bashamichi Bldg, 4-55 Otamachi, Naka-ku (Map, B2). ℘045-664-2961. kisoji.co.jp/kisoji/english. Open daily 11.30am–3pm & 5–10pm (last orders 2.30pm & 9.30pm, or 9pm on Sun). Set menus from ¥4900. Kisoji's set menus are generous and good value for money. Try the *shabu-shabu* (beef hotpot) with *gomadare* (sesame sauce) with *kishimen* (noodles from Nagoya) on the side.

🍴🍴🍴 **Rinkaen** 隣花苑 – 52-1 Sannotani Honmoku, Naka-ku, behind Sankei-en garden (Map; B2, off map). ℘045-621-0318. Open Thu–Tue noon–8pm. Lunch from ¥3500, dinner 10,000. Reservations recommended. The 14C residence of a Shinto priest attached to a shrine in Izu, the house was moved here, and gives a rare insight into Izu architecture of the time. They serve first-class *sankei soba*, the recipe of which has been passed down from generation to generation. An unforgettable culinary experience.

KAMAKURA

🍴 **Nakamura-an** 中村庵 – 1-7-6 Komachi-dori (Map, B2). ℘046-725-3500. nakamura-an.com. Open 11.15am–5pm (closed one day a week, day may vary). From ¥800. 🍴 Soba noodles are the specialty here, prepared on the spot by a skillful cook. Very popular.

🍴 **Cafe & Shop Guri** CAFE&SHOP 俱利 – 1F Kamakura-bori Kaikan, 2-15-13 Komachi (Map, B2). ℘0467-33-5751. kamakuraborikaikan.jp/cafe. Open Tue–Sun 11am–5pm (lunch last orders 2.30pm). Lunch sets from ¥1500. Cafe in the Kamakura-bori Museum (◉see p140). Delicious Japanese cuisine, including vegetarian *shojin-ryori* and light snacks, served on beautiful lacquerware which you can buy in the shop.

🍴 **Satonoudon Kamakura** 里のうどん鎌倉店 – 5-18-2 Yukinoshita (Map, B1). ℘046-724-7631. Open daily 11am–8pm (Sat & Sun 8.30pm). Menu in English. Around ¥1000. A simple, welcoming restaurant a stone's throw from Tsurugaoka. The menu is extensive, with a focus on udon noodles. The *shirasu-don* (rice topped with fresh whitebait, a Kamakura specialty, ¥970) is also delicious.

🍴 **Shonan burger** 湘南バーガー – 2-1-6 Enoshima, Fujisawa (Map; A2, off map). ℘046-629-0688. Open daily 10am–7pm. Menu in English. From ¥500. Right by the entrance to Enoshima Island Spa is this burger restaurant with a focus on fish rather than meat. Go for the *satsuma-age* and *shirasu* burger, a deep-fried fish cake topped with fresh whitebait.

🍴 **Sometaro** 染太郎 – 3-12-11 Hase (Map, A2). ℘046-722-8694. okonomi-sometaro. com. Open Thu–Tue 11.30am–9pm (last orders). From ¥900. 🍴 A relaxed spot where you can personalize and cook your own *okonomiyaki* (Japanese pancakes) at the hot plate on the table.

🍴🍴🍴 **Hachinoki** 鉢の木 – 350 Yamanouchi, Kita-Kamakura (Map; B1, off map). ℘046-723-3723. hachinoki. yamato-ip.net/en/lp/hachinoki. Open daily 11.30am–2.30pm (Sat–Sun & public hols 3pm) & 5–7pm. Menu in English. Lunch from ¥2600, dinner ¥7000. The two elegant branches of Hachinoki are ideal places to try Zen cuisine. The Kitakamakuraten building serves *shojin-ryori*, while Shinkan serves *kaiseki*; both offer a masterclass in Japanese service and cuisine.

TAKING A BREAK

Shoyu Cafe しょうゆきゃふぇ– *1-77-4 Motomachi, Naka-ku, Yokohama (Map; B2, off map).* ℘*045-211-1101. elysee-hikaru. com/cafe/new_cafe.html. Open daily 9.30am–5pm (Sat–Sun 5.30pm). Closed 2nd Wed of the month.* In one of the most beautiful houses in Yamate district, the Ehrismann Residence, this tearoom is a haven of peace. the desserts and snacks all feature soy sauce; try the raw pudding, and the satisfyingly crusty bread.

NIGHTLIFE

Yokohama's **Chinatown** is one of the liveliest areas in the evening. Try the atmospheric *izakaya* in **Noge-cho** 野毛町 *(Map, A2; generally open 6pm–1am),* or **Motomachi-dori** 元町通り *(Map, B2)* for a more trendy area, popular with tourists.

SHOPPING

YOKOHAMA

Bashamichi-dori 馬車道通り – *(Map, B2)* Go window shopping and find *izakaya* in this street *(michi)* of horse-drawn carriages *(basha)*, a reference to the time when foreigners still rode down it in horse-drawn vehicles.

Motomachi-dori 元町 – *(Map, B2)* A popular shopping street with tourists.

Aka Renga Park 横浜赤レンガ倉庫 – *Minato Mirai 21 (Map, B2). www.yokohama-akarenga.jp/en.* An old silk warehouse which has been converted into a mall and cultural center.

The Miura Peninsula ★★

Just 1hr by train from Tokyo and 30min from Yokohama, the Miura Peninsula (*Miura hanto*) is a great alternative day trip or weekend excursion, with swimming, walking, and cycling on offer, plus plenty of art and history to explore. A popular holiday destination for the citizens of Tokyo, the Miura Peninsula boasts several lighthouses due to its location at the mouth of Tokyo Bay. Visit in the fall and winter, to see Mount Fuji from the western side of the peninsula.

- **Michelin Map:** Tokyo & Surroundings p131
- **Location:** South of Yokohama
- **Info:** Yokosuka Tourist Information Suka-navi i, 1-5 Wakamatsu-cho, Yokosuka. ℘046-822-8301. tic.jnto. go.jp. Open 10am–6pm. Information in English.

YOKOSUKA 横須賀

In the northeast of the peninsula. Keikyu Main Line from Shinagawa Station to Shioiri Station (50min, ¥640), or JR Yokosuka Line from Tokyo Station to Yokosuka (1hr 15min, ¥1080).

A major turning point in Japan's history took place at Yokosuka 150 years ago: Kurihama (southeast of the current naval base) is where Commodore Perry disembarked in 1853 to apply to the shogun to open up Japan up to trade with Western nations. Several years later, Léonce Verny, a French engineer sent by the shogun's government, supervised

TRANSPORTATION

Keikyu railway runs a bus and train service for the peninsula (see local signs for details). Passes available: Miura Hanto 1-day ticket *(¥1970 per person from Shinagawa)* or 2-day ticket *(¥2080 per person from Shinagawa).*

the construction of a dockyard in this sheltered harbor (&*see box opposite*). Modern-day Yokosuka (population 407,000) is now home to a large US-Japanese naval base and major ship-building and car-manufacturing facilities.

Yokosuka Military Port 横須賀軍港

Tour leaves from Shopper's Plaza Daiei. ⏲*Daily 10am–3pm; 45min.* ☞*¥1400. tryangle-web.com/en/index.html.*

The naval base can only be explored on a tour. You'll have a chance to look over different kinds of Japanese and US military vessels (including the only nuclear aircraft carrier stationed outside the USA) and the two docks built at the end of the 19C by Verny, which are still in use.

Verny Park ヴェルニー公園

Opposite JR Yokosuka Station; or 5min from Shiori Station. Museum: ○*open Tue–Sun 9am–5pm.* ○*No charge.*
Inside this small park by the naval base you will find busts of Léonce Verny and Oguri Kozukenosuke, plus the **Verny Commemorative Museum**, housing a collection of historical documents relating to the construction of the dockyard, including the steam press that Verny ordered in 1866 from the Netherlands.

Memorial Ship Mikasa 記念艦三笠

7min walk from Keikyu Yokosuka Chuo Station; or bus from Yokosuka Station to Saikaya Mae, then 7min walk. ○*Open daily: Mar & Oct 9am–5.30pm; Apr–Sept 9am–5.30pm; Nov–Feb 9am–4.30pm.* ○*¥600. kinenkan-mikasa.or.jp/en.*
Admiral **Togo** was aboard this battleship when he led the Japanese navy to victory over the Russian Baltic fleet on May 27, 1905, at the **Battle of Tsushima**. Japan's defeat of Russia at the end of a two-year conflict (1904–1905) was to have serious repercussions throughout the world; for the first time ever, an Asian country had carried the day against a Western power. Exploring the boat (whose equipment has been largely restored) will give you a detailed insight into the context and course of the battle and introduce its principal protagonists.

Kannonzaki ★ 観音崎

Shioiri Station to Maborikaigan Station (Keikyu Line, 12min, ¥160), then bus nos. 24 or 28 for Kannonzaki (10min, ¥250); get off at Yokosuka Bijutsukan-mae. ○*Open daily 10am–6pm. Closed 1st Mon of each month.* ○*¥310. Museum: www.yokosuka-moa.jp.*
This area of Yokosuka is clearly more seaside oriented, with a charming promenade along the shore from which you can watch the cargo ships crossing Tokyo Bay. Look out for the first Western-style lighthouse, built by Verny during his stay here, enjoy the beach, and visit the **Yokosuka Museum of Art**. The clean lines of this uncluttered building house a collection of modern and contemporary Japanese art; one pavilion is dedicated to Taniuchi Rokuro, a renowned illustrator from the 1950s.

A Fruitful Collaboration

After Japan had been opened up, **Oguri Kozukenosuke Tadamasa**, a senior samurai functionary at the Ministry of Finance, convinced the shogun's government of the necessity of ship building on Japanese soil. They contacted representatives of France, who deputed François Léonce Verny (1837–1908), a young polytechnic student who had already shown his mettle in Brest and Ningbo (China). Verny drew up plans for the future dockyards and then visited the site in 1866, turning up with 45 French engineers and foremen (with families in tow) in what at the time was only a fishing village. Over 3000 Japanese laborers were recruited to work on a construction site that took ten years to complete. Everything had to be built from scratch, starting with a foundry, but the dockyard eventually became a showcase for Western technology at the outset of Japan's industrialization. In 1870, Verny founded the first training school for Japanese technicians and engineers and French influence was also felt in areas of daily life such as cooking, fashion, and the institution of Sunday as a day of rest. Links with France are maintained to this day, as Yokosuka has been twinned with the city of Brest since 1971.

Mount Fuji viewed from Jogashima at sunset

© Torsakarin/iStock

Miura Beach ★ 三浦海岸
Southeast of Yokosuka. Take the Keikyu Line from Shioiri Station to Miurakaigan Station (24min, ¥240), then 3min walk.
👥 This sandy beach over half a mile (1km) long gets very busy and is popular with swimmers and windsurfers alike.

Arasaki Park 荒崎公園
Southwest of Yokosuka. Keikyu Line from Shioiri Station to Misakiguchi Station (25min, ¥280) then bus nos. 12, 22, 51 or 52 (25min, ¥320).
A path and picnic areas have been built along this rocky, jagged section of coast, which has many grottos to explore.

Hayama Marina and surrounding area ★ 葉山マリーナ
West of Yokosuka. Keikyu Line from Tokyo/Shinagawa to Shinzushi Station (55min, ¥640), then bus nos. 11 or 12 to Hayama Marina (5min, ¥200).
During the Meiji period, this area was very popular with foreigners living in Japan, who had their summer residences built here. While these are no longer to be seen, the "seaside resort" feel of the place is still a little different. From the marina, there is a beautiful view of Mount Fuji (fall and winter). You can hire a motorboat here and take a cruise round the bay *(45min, ¥2850 per person).*

Jogashima ★★ 城ヶ島
Southwest of Yokosuka, at the end of the peninsula. Keikyu Line from Shioiri Station to Misakiguchi Station (25min, ¥280) then bus no. 9 to Hakushushi-mae (28min, ¥400) and 10min walk.
🐚 The southern part of Jogashima Island, which is linked to the rest of the peninsula by a bridge, has been partly spared urbanization and has retained its unspoiled feel. Paths lead along the low cliffs, with views across the open water and, at the furthest southwestern tip of the island, of Mount Fuji.

ADDRESSES

🛏 STAY

YOKOSUKA

🍽🍽 **Mercure Hotel Yokosuka** メルキュールホテル横須賀 – 3-27 Honcho. ✆046-821-1111. mercureyokosuka.jp. 160 rooms. ¥12,000. ¥700 🖥. This contemporary hotel has an ideal setting near the naval base and stations. Rooms are fairly small, but comfortable. Superb views over the bay from the upper floors.

🍽🍽🍽🍽 **Kannonzaki Keikyu Hotel** 観音崎京急ホテル – 2-1157-2 Hashirimizu. ✆046-841-2200. kannon-kqh.co.jp/eng. ¥40,000. Offers sometimes available online. 🖥. This establishment boasts beautiful rooms with bay views in a seaside setting, just round the corner from the Yokosuka Museum of Art. Next door, you'll find the "Spasso" *onsen*, for which there is no charge for hotel guests.

🍴 EAT/ TAKING A BREAK

HAYAMA MARINA

🍽️🍽️ **La Marée** ラ・マーレ – 20-1 *Horiuchi, Hayama-machi. ℘046-875-6683. lamaree.chaya. co.jp. Open Tue–Sun*

11.30am–9pm (last order).Menu in English. Lunch from ¥1800, dinner from ¥2600. An extremely charming brasserie-style cafe with cosy, European-style décor, right next to the marina.

North of Tokyo

The mountainous region of Nikko is so enchanting that as long ago as the 8C it attracted the attention of influential priests. Protected by imposing Mount Nantei, Nikko is dotted with the shrines and temples that arose out of the many forms of worship here practiced in the "light of the sun" (as Nikko's name means). As Nikko was regarded as a holy place rich in *kami*, the first of the shoguns decided to build his mausoleoum here, to which his grandson added elaborate decoration. The result is the most dazzling mausoleum in Japan *(Tosho-gu)*. In 1999 UNESCO designated the shrines and temples of Nikko a World Heritage Site.

- ▶ **Population:** Nikko: 84,000;
- ⏱️ **Michelin Map:** Regions of Japan Map 1, Tokyo & Surroundings p131.
- ▶ **Location:** Tochigi prefecture, 87mi/140km from Tokyo.
- 👫 **Kids:** The avenue of *jizo* statues. If possible, visit May 17 and 18 for the **Yabusame Ceremony** (⏱️*see p222*).
- 🕐 **Timing:** Ideally allow 3 days for Nikko and at least 1 day for an excursion to Saitama or Gunma
- 🚫 **Don't miss:** Taiyu-in and Tosho-gu; an evening at the Takai-ya restaurant.

NIKKO ★★★ 日光

⏱️*Map, p219.*
The main road to the shrines of Nikko takes you over Shin-kyo, the vermilion-colored delicately arching bridge that crosses over the Daya River.

Shin-kyo Bridge ★ 神橋

⏱️*Map, B1.* 🕐*Open daily: Apr–Oct 8am–5pm; Nov–Mar 9am–4pm.* 🎫*¥300.*
In 767, the Buddhist priest **Shodo Shonin** (735–817) and his disciples were intent on exploring Mount Nantai, but were held back by the tumultuous waters of the Daiya River. In answer to their prayers the god Jinja Daio appeared with two snakes, one red and one blue, which entwined above the river to form a bridge *(span*

of 89ft/28m). Beside the bridge is the **Gejo Ishi**, a stone instructing everyone who intends to cross the bridge to dismount their horses *(gejo means "to set foot on")*.

The bridge took its current form when it was rebuilt in 1636 during the reign of the third Tokugawa shogun. In 1907, it was rebuilt again (in the same design) after being washed away by a flood, and strengthened with a *torii* (gate).

Kosugi Hoan Museum of Art
小杉放庵記念日光美術館

⏱️*Map, B1.* 🕐*Open Tue–Sun 9.30am–5pm (last admission 4.30pm).* 🎫*¥720. khmoan.jp/english.html.*
Works by the talented painter Kosugi Hoan (1881–1964) are displayed here. Kosugi is known particularly for the logo-style tiger roundel (Tora no Maki,

USEFUL INFORMATION
NIKKO

Tourist Offices – *(Map, C2)* ☎*0288-53-1525. nikko-travel.jp/english. In Tobu-Nikko station, open daily 8.30am–5pm, or JR Nikko Station, open daily 9am–5pm. English spoken.*

Post Office/Withdrawals – *896-1 Nakahatsuishi-cho. ATM Mon–Fri 8.45am–7pm, Sat–Sun 9am–5pm.*

TRANSPORTATION
BY TRAIN – **JR** and **Tobu Nikko Stations** – *South of downtown (2min walk apart from each other; map, C2).* From **Tokyo** *(Asakusa Station),* several direct trains per day on the **Tobu Line** *(2hr, ¥2800; may be with compulsory reservation depending on the train/time).* If you want to use a **JR Pass** you must take the **JR Utsunomiya Line** *(Yamabiko, Tsubasa or Nasuno trains)* from **Tokyo Station** to **Utsunomiya** *(50min),* then the **JR Nikko Line** *(45min; ¥5580; may be with compulsory reservation).* From **Shinjuku Station** in Tokyo, regular trains to **Utsunomiya** *(1hr 30min)* on **JR Shonan-Shinjuku Line**, then to Nikko *(45min; ¥2590).* If you want to get to **Niigata**, point of departure for Sado, you will have to go back through **Tokyo** *(Omiya).*

GETTING AROUND
ON FOOT – The Nikko temples can be visited on foot. 20min walk from the bridge Shin-kyo, itself 20/30min walk from Tobu Nikko Station.

BY BUS – There are regular services from Tobu Nikko station to the temples and the hotels lining the main road. Your best bet is to buy a single bus ticket *(¥310; ¥500 for a day pass)* to get there as soon as possible and then return on foot as far as Shin-kyo; you will be walking along National Route 119, which is interspersed with stores and restaurants.

Passes – the **Nikko All Area Pass** *(¥4520 Apr–Nov, ¥4150 Dec–Apr; 4 days)* includes the return journey between Asakusa and Nikko (Ltd. Express ticket not included), use of the Tobu Bus (World Heritage Loop) in Nikko, Chuzen-ji Onsen, Yumoto Onsen, and Kotoku Onsen. The **Nikko World Heritage Pass** *(¥2000; 2 days)* includes the return journey from Asakusa-Nikko (Ltd. Express ticket not included) and use of the World Heritage Loop and Tobu Buses in Nikko.

USEFUL INFORMATION
GUNMA PREFECTURE
MINAKAMI

Minakami Tourism Association – At entrance to the station *(Map, C2).* ☎*0278-62-0401. enjoy-minakami.com/en. Open daily 8.30am–5.30pm.*

Minakami Town Office, Tourism and Commerce division – *2min from the station.* ☎*0278-62-2111. www.town. minakami.gunma.jp. Open Mon–Fri 8.30am–5.15pm.*

the "Shotokan tiger") that he designed for the cover of the first book to be written about karate by Funakoshi Gichin, known as the "father of modern karate" (⌚*see p120).*

THE TEMPLES
Rinno-ji, Tosho-gu, Futarasan, and Taiyu-in are all on the same site, north of Shin-kyo Bridge.

Rinno-ji★★ 輪王寺
⌚*Map, B1. On the left after Shin-kyo at the top of the road, this is the first temple at the entrance to the site.* ○*Open daily: Apr–Oct 8am–5pm; Nov–Mar 8am–4pm.* ☜*¥400. rinnoji.or.jp.*

Shodo Shonin felt the mountainous region of Nikko was so pure that it was a fitting place for the god Kannon. The same year in which he crossed the Daiya River, he founded the first place of worship in Nikko: the Shironryu-ji (the temple's original name), which was built a short distance from the sacred bridge. After the monk Tenkai (1536–1643), patriarch of the Tendai-shu Buddhist sect, set about revitalizing the temples in the vicinity, the temple was renamed Rinno-ji and became a model for around 15 other Buddhist temples with the same name in the region.

Once past the large copper sculpture of Shodo, you enter the largest temple

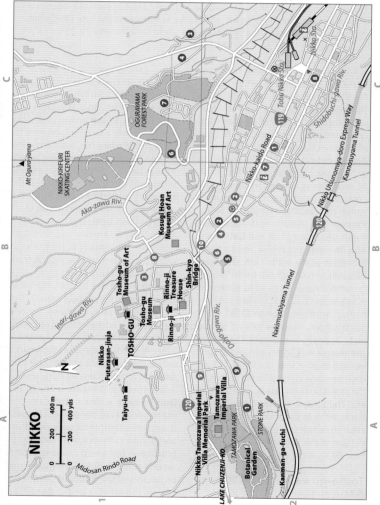

NIKKO

Mt Ogura-yama

NIKKO-KIRIFURI SKATING CENTER

OGURAYAMA FOREST PARK

Aka-zawa Riv.

Inari-gawa Riv.

Kosugi Hoan Museum of Art

Tosho-gu Museum of Art

Rinno-ji Treasure House

Shin-kyo Bridge

Tosho-gu Museum

Rinno-ji

TOSHO-GU

Nikko Futarasan-jinja

Taiyu-in

Daiya-gawa Riv.

Nikko-kaido Road

Tobu Nikko Sta.

Nikko Sta.

Shidobuchi-gawa Riv.

Nikko Utsunomiya-doro Express Way

Kannosuyama Tunnel

Nakimushiyama Tunnel

Midosan Rindo Road

Nikko Tamozawa Imperial Villa Memorial Park

Tamozawa Imperial Villa

TAMOZAWA PARK

STONE PARK

Botanical Garden

Kanman-ga-fuchi

LAKE CHUZENJI-KO

N

0   200   400 m
0   200   400 yds

Tokugawa Ieyasu, protector of the north

Before he died, the shogun Ieyasu (1542–1616) left specific instructions for his burial: "Bury me at Mount Kuno (Shizuoka prefecture) for the first five years after my death. Then build a small shrine at Nikko, in which you will place me as a god. I will then become the protector of Japan." The Emperor Go-Mizuno-o deified the first shogun of Edo as Tosho Daigongen, "The great spirit that lights up the East." Ieyasu chose the Nikko site for its position, north of Edo (now Tokyo), a direction in which all evil spirits were thought to gather, and so considered unlucky. It was Ieyasu's intention to defend the north like a *tenno*, a celestial guardian of altars. This proved a successful strategy and the Tokugawa shogunate of 1603 brought a stability to Japan that was to last until 1868, when the last shogun Tokugawa Yoshinobu was forced to step down.

in Nikko, listed in the architectural canons of the Tendai sect (a rarity in itself). The **Sanbutsu-do ★**, or "Room with the Three Buddhas" *(undergoing renovation until Mar 2021; usually ☜¥400, or ¥900 combined ticket with Taiyu-in)*, houses an enormous statue, 85ft/26m high, of **Amida-nyorai**, the Buddha Amitabha or "Buddha of infinite Light" *(can still be seen during the renovation work)*. Popular for his compassionate countenance, this Buddha is flanked by **Senju Kannon** (the goddess with a thousand hands; *☜see box p139*) and **Bato Kannon** (the goddess with a horse's head, protector of the animal kingdom and banisher of bad humor), two of the 33 forms that Kannon is said to assume. It is also in this hall that the annual rice-eating ceremony, **Gohan Shiki**, takes place in April, intended to ward off bad luck. Opposite the temple, the **Treasure House ★** (*☉open daily 9am–5pm; ☜¥300)* displays selections from its Buddhist heritage in rotation: 6000 objects, the oldest of which date back to the Nara era. The **Shoyo-en stroll garden ★★** *(included in Treasure House admission)*, created in the Edo era, is a miniature version of the landscape of Lake Biwa near Kyoto. Most enjoyable.

Tosho-gu ★★★ 日光東照宮

☉Map, B1. Behind Rinno-ji. ☉*Open daily: Apr–Oct 8am–5pm; Nov–Mar 8am–4pm. ☜¥1300. Audioguides ¥500 (English available). toshogu.jp/english.* Access to the largest Shinto shrine in Nikko is via the Sennin Ishidan, "the stone staircase of the 1000 men." At the top is an impressive *torii ★* (gate), made of granite from Kyushu (1618). This is the most imposing of the gates built in the Edo era. Its *shimenawa* (rice-straw rope indicating a sacred place, used for ritual purification) has been removed because of safety concerns as the weight of the rope *(661lb/300kg)* posed a threat to the *torii*. To the left of the *torii* is the **five-story pagoda ★**. Built in 1650, it was destroyed in 1815 and rebuilt three years later. Its central pillar, which is 24in/60cm in diameter and 98ft/30m high *(the whole tower is 118ft/36m in height)*, is suspended by chains from beams on the fourth level.

Floating free at the bottom, the pillar helps maintain the pagoda's equilibrium in the event of an earthquake. The animals depicted on the first level represent the 12 signs of the zodiac. The symbol of "three hollyhocks" *(not really hollyhocks, but wild ginger)* inside a black circle *(Mitsuba aoi)* is the Tokugawa clan crest. Another stone staircase leads to the **Omote-mon ★**, the entrance to the main precincts of the shrine. This gate is a good example of how Buddhist and Shinto architectures have sometimes been combined in one structure: on one side are the **ni-oh** guardians, protectors of the Buddhist pantheon, and on the other, a pair of **Karajishi**, the Chinese stone lions that mark the transfer from the secular to the sacred interior of a Shinto shrine. The lions are accompanied by 82 sculptures, including two feline creatures with different

© JTB Photo/UIG/age fotostock

Kara-mon, Tosho-gu

coats, one with stripes and one with spots—in the Edo era, it was believed that the leopard was the female of the tiger. Once through the door you enter a preliminary courtyard. On the right are three sacred storehouses (**Sanjinko**) containing everything required for the annual *matsuri* (festival) of the 1000 warriors who accompany the *yabusame* procession (🎧*see box p222*).

On the **Kamijinko** (the uppermost of the three storehouses), the elephant sculptures (after the drawings of Kano Tanyu) demonstrate the ability of an artist to represent animals he had never seen—hence their being depicted with claws. On the left, in the **Shinyo-sha** (sacred stables) a white horse, a gift from New Zealand, is traditionally kept. The stables are decorated with an illustration of the maxim "see no evil, hear no evil, speak no evil" by the sculptor **Hidari Jingoro** (1594–1634). In eight carved panels the **sansaru ★** ("three monkeys") explain that if we behave like the three wise monkeys Mizaru *(see no evil)*, Kikazaru *(hear no evil)*, and Iwazaru *(speak no evil)*, we too will be spared evil – three principles that are important in the Tendai Buddhist tenet and play on *zaru* (not) and *saru* (monkey).

At the end of the courtyard, after the **Rinzo** (the sacred library containing just over 6000 sutras), you reach the

Yakushi-do. This Buddhist temple was formerly part of Rinno-ji, but was allowed to remain in this Shinto part of the complex despite the separation of the two religions imposed by the Meiji reforms. Destroyed by fire, it was rebuilt in the 1960s, preserving the acoustics that seem to make the **Nakiryu** dragon painted on the ceiling roar when you clap your hands. The original dragon, the work

An ostentatious silence

Although Tokugawa Ieyasu wanted a modest shrine, in 1634 his grandson Tokugawa Iemitsu started to build the biggest mausoleum in Japan, wishing to give Ieyasu a setting befitting his immortality. No expense was spared therefore in the construction of this Momoyama-style building with Baroque highlights—140,000 trees were felled and 5173 sculptures created. Fifteen thousand craftsmen were employed from start to finish over a period of 17 months. The cost in today's money is estimated to be $330 million dollars. Today, the whole complex is UNESCO listed, and contains 8 national treasures.

of Kano Eishin Yasunobu (1616–85), was restored by Katayama Nanpu.

At the top of yet another flight of stairs is one of the Tosho-gu's finest features, **Yomei-mon ★★★**, "the Gate of Sunlight." Also called *Higurashino-mon*, "the gate that can be observed until dusk," because of its many carved works of art: there are 508 sculptures arranged in layers along its 36ft/11m height (thousands of craftsmen were involved). The point was not so much to entertain but to impress the lower-ranking samurai who had no other choice but to wait in front of the gate (through which they were not allowed to pass). This fantastic menagerie includes Chinese unicorns, dragon-horses, *iki* (Japanese dragons with tusks instead of whiskers), juxtaposed with scenes of children making a snowman. The gate is supported by twelve columns painted white using a pigment made from powdered shellfish and carved with scroll motifs known as *guri-mon*. Interestingly, on the left-hand column in the front of the gate, the curves are inverted—a deliberate act by the artists, to show the gods that they did not have the skills to be their rivals. With perfection being perceived as the beginning of decline, it was even common practice among several Buddhist schools to leave three tiles missing when building a roof. Also admire the images of **wooden tigers ★** in a medal-lion on one of the central columns, the fibres and grain of the wood forming the striped pattern of their coats. Just beneath the gate, two **dragons ★** stride across the platform, one drawn facing up and surveying the eight directions of the sky, and the other looking toward the earth and its four compass points. Both were created by **Kano Tanyu** (1602–74), the favourite artist of the Tokugawa shogunate (&see box p325).

Once past the Yomei-mon, you will enter another courtyard containing the sacred storage hall. The **Shinyosha** is used to store the three **mikoshi ★★**, portable shrines dedicated to Tokugawa Ieyasu, Toyotomi Hideyoshi, and Minamoto no Yoritomo. In 1636, their weight had to be reduced from 2470lb/1120kg to 1764lb/800kg to help the 55 bearers who carried the shrines in ceremonies. Inside, on the ceiling, are three depictions of **bodhisattvas ★**, some of the most beautiful in Japan.

At the north end of the courtyard, the beautiful **Kara-mon ★** Chinese gate dating from 1617 *(three of the seven divinities of good luck are carved on its west face)* leads to the main shrine, the **Honsha**. This is made up of the **Haiden** *(hall of worship)*, the **Honden**, and the **Ishi-noma** (the chamber of stones, whose main function is to link the world of humans in the Haiden to that of the gods in the Honden). The Honden *(undergo-*

Yabusame

Twice a year (May & Oct) during the Nikko Tosho-gu Festival, a *yabusame* ceremony is held at the lower end of the shrine. The participants have to shoot three targets placed along a track with a bow and arrow, while galloping by on horseback. *Yabusame* is neither a sport nor a martial art but a religious ritual, the aim of which is to delight the gods with a display of skill and power of concentration.

ing renovation until 2024) is the shrine's most sacred building as one of its three small rooms houses the *Nainaijin*, the *kami* of Ieyasu, Toyotomi, and Yoritomo *(rooms closed to the public)*.
If you don't visit the Honden, head past the Haiden to the corridor leading to Tokugawa Ieyasu's mausoleum. On the way you'll pass the **Treasure House** *(¥500)*, where precious objects belonging to Tosho-gu are displayed. The entrance to the corridor is famous for the **Nemuri neko** ★, carved beneath the lintel—*The Sleeping Cat*, attributed to the sculptor Hidari Jingoro (1594–1634), with a small sparrow to one side. This unlikely pairing symbolizes the desire for peace that Tokugawa Ieyasu expressed for his country before his death. After climbing around 200 steps, you will find his tomb at the end of a stone footpath and surrounded by magnificent Japanese cedars.

Tosho-gu Museum of Art ★ 日光東照宮美術館

Map, B1. Behind Tosho-gu. Open daily: Apr–Oct 8am–5pm; Nov–Mar 8am–4pm. ¥800.
In 1928, the high priest in charge of the Choyokaku, Tosho-gu's administrative offices, assembled talented artists such as Nakamura Gakuryo, Katayama Nanpu, and Arai Kanpo, working under the direction of Yokoyama Taikan (1868–1958), to complete the decoration of the offices. Now housing a museum, among the 150 works displayed are the **Old Pine Tree**, a drawing by Arai, and the **Camelia** by Katayama.

Tosho-gu Museum ★ 日光東照宮宝物館

Map, B1. South of Tosho-gu. Open daily: Apr–Oct 8am–5pm; Nov–Mar 8am–4pm. ¥1000; ¥2100 combined with Tosho-gu.
Just outside the paid area of the shrine is the modern Nikko Toshogu Museum, well worth a visit for its excellent collection of items relating to Tokugawa Ieyasu. It was opened to mark the 400th anniversary of his death

Agyo and Ungyo

The first sound we make in life, with the mouth wide open, is "ahhhh." The last sound, with the lips closed, is "ummmm." Sanskrit tradition put these two sounds together to form the sacred sound "Om or Aum," which Buddhism adopted. The two **ni-oh** statues that are found at the entrance to Buddhist temples in Japan are guardians and protectors; Agyo, is always represented with an open mouth, making the first sound *(Ah)* and his partner, with closed lips, the last one *(Um)*. The two divinities thus symbolize the beginning and the end of all things; a thought to guide our steps as we enter a sacred place.

Futarasan-jinja★ 二荒山神社

Map, A1. West of Tosho-gu. Open daily: Apr–Oct 8am–5pm; Nov–Mar 8am–4pm. ¥200; garden ¥200 extra.
Founded by priest Shodo Shonin in 782, this shrine, rebuilt in 1610, has a fine **Honden** ★ (main hall) in the Momoyama style. It was constructed in 1619 by shogun Tokugawa Hidetada (1579–1632), and is dedicated to Okuninushi no Mikoto, one of the mythical founders of Shintoism, and the divine spirits of the surrounding mountains.
The three portable shrines built in 1617 and kept in the **Shinyosha** ★ (sacred storage hall) are dedicated to the *kami* of Mount Nantai *(8156ft/2486m)*, Mount Nyotai *(8146ft/2,483m)*, and Mount Taro *(7769ft/2368m)*, symbolizing father, mother, and child respectively. Three ancient **black pines** *(kouyamaki)*, which according to legend were planted by the monk Kukai, capture many visitors' imagination, along with the old bronze lantern called the **ghost lantern**. It bears sword marks, caused according to legend by warriors who duelled with ghosts attracted by the light. Historians, however, suggest the cuts were dealt by guards to chase away the flying squirrels attracted by the oil of the lamps.

The **Yayoi Matsuri** (a parade of flower-covered floats from the different districts of Nikko) takes place each year (April 13–17) within the shrine complex.

Taiyu-in ★★ 家光廟大猷院

🚶 Map, A1. Opposite Futarasan-jinja.
🕐 Open daily: Apr–Oct 8am–5pm; Nov–Mar 8am–4pm. 💳 ¥550.

Tokugawa Iemitsu (1604–51), who was deeply respectful of his grandfather, the first of the Tokugawa shoguns, declared: "I shall serve Ieyasu even after my death." With a similar regard for *his* ancestor, Iemitsu's successor, Tokugawa Ietsuna, decided to build Iemitsu's mausoleum looking not southwest, as tradition required, but to the north so that he could face his grandfather in Tosho-gu. Today, Iemitsu's mausoleum is part of the Rinno-ji complex.

The **Nioh-mon** (gate), the first stage on the path to the mausoleum, is guarded by the famous *ni-oh* (🚶 see box p223). The second gate, or **Niten-mon ★**, is the most impressive in Nikko. The Gate of the Two Gods (Niten), it is dedicated to **Jikokuten** and **Koumokuten**. The former, Guardian of the East, carries a sword. The Guardian of the West carries a paintbrush and an unrolled scroll. The back of the gate is flanked by the divinities **Raijin**, god of lightning, with a drum and drumsticks, and **Fujin**, god of the wind, which he carries in a bolster-shaped bag on his shoulder.

Once through the gate you arrive at two towers, one with a bell in it (*shoro*), and the other a drum (*koro*), a musical yin and yang that sound in turn above the 33 lanterns lining the path. This leads first to **Yasha-mon ★**, a magnificent ornamental gate with a dominant motif of peonies (a symbol of prosperity), and then to **Kara-mon**, a Chinese-style gate. The mausoleum is a short distance from here, but first you reach the **Haiden ★** (hall of worship). Inside, **140 dragons** decorate a ceiling the size of 64 *tatami*-mats; on the wall near the entrance is a painting of a **Chinese lion**, the work of the brothers Kano Tanyu and Eishin. The main hall, the **Honden**, is dazzling. Amid the splendor, flying dragons roar, one up toward the sky (*shoryu*) and the other down toward the earth (*koryu*), under the impassive eye of a phoenix painted on the latticework ceiling.

After the Honden is the amazing white and gold gate **Koka-mon ★**. The gate is closed as it leads to **Oku-noin** (🔒 closed to the public), the sacred place where Iemitsu lies. He died in Ueno (north Tokyo) and was brought here to his final resting place.

WEST OF THE TOWN
Kanman-ga-fuchi Walk ★★
憾満ヶ淵
🚶 Map, A2. This lovely walk begins at Stone Park behind the Hotori-an Hotel.

This stretch of the Daiya River runs through a dramatic gorge, a geological phenomenon caused by lava from Mount Nantai, known as Kanman-ga-fuchi Abyss. There is a magnificent row of 👥 **Jizo statues ★★** below the attractive cemetery. Continue walking to the Dainichi Bridge, which takes you to the other side of the river.

Tamozawa Imperial Villa ★
日光田母沢御用邸
🚶 Map, A2. 8-27 Hon-cho. 🕐 Open Wed–Mon: Apr–Oct 9am–5pm; Nov–Mar 9am–4.30pm. 💳 ¥510.

This summer residence of the Imperial family was built around the first residence of the Tokugawa Kishu clan, transported from Edo in 1872. A great technical feat, its 106 rooms, linked by corridors, are all on one level. Created originally for Prince Yoshihito (the future Emperor Taisho), the villa had been used by three emperors up to 1947. Good English-language signage.

The splendid **garden ★**, which originally encompassed a botanical garden, is also open to the public.

EXCURSION
Chuzenji-ko ★ 中禅寺湖
🚶 Map; A2, off map. 19mi/30km northwest of Nikko. From JR and Tobu Nikko stations, bus no. 2, 1 or 11 (50min) to Chuzenji-ko. Add 30min for Yumoto. 💳 ¥1150 (one way) to Chuzenji-ko, ¥1700

Chuzenji-ko and Mount Nantai

(one way) to Yumoto, unless you have a Tobu Pass.

Once you have passed the famous "hill with 48 bends" on this stunning mountain road, make a stop at the Akechi-daira cable car *(¥710 round trip)* for a **view** over Lake Chuzenji and the **Kegon Falls ★**, an impressive 318ft/97m high. The lake shores are lined with beautiful **villas**, built soon after 1899, when the Imperial authorities granted permission for foreigners to travel freely in Japan. Particularly worth visiting is the one owned by the Italian Embassy, designed by architect Antonin Raymond, who came to Japan to assist Frank Lloyd Wright on the Imperial Hotel.

Once past the lake you can opt to cross the Senjogahara plateau to **Yumoto** ("the source of hot water") and its small lake Yunoko. This *onsen*, with nine hot springs, is one of the most highly regarded in the region.

ASHIKAGA 足利

♿*Map p131, B2. 50mi/80km northeast of Tokyo. Ryomo express train on Isesaki Line from Tobu Asakusa Station to Ashikaga-shi Station (1h 15min, ¥2000).*
Ashikaga is set in beautiful natural surroundings and has some important cultural sites. To the north it is overlooked by Mount Ashio, while to the south are expanses of fertile fields.

Ashikaga Gakko 足利学校跡

10min walk from Ashikaga-shi Station.
🕐*Open daily: Apr–Sept 9am–4.30pm; Oct–Mar 9am–4pm.* ✆*¥420.*
Japan's oldest academic institution is now a National Historic Site, and played an important role in Japan's educational history. The date of its founding is uncertain, but textbooks *(now National Treasures)* were provided by Uesugi Norizane in the Muromachi era (1336–1573). In 1550, over 3000 students studied Confucianism, divination, and Chinese medicine here. It closed in 1873.

Banna-ji ★ 鑁阿寺

Near Ashikaga Gakko. 🕐*Open Mon–Sat, hours vary. Temple precincts* ✆*no charge; main hall & Issai Kyodo tour* ✆*¥6000 for groups up to 15 people, ¥400 per extra person. ashikaga-bannaji.org.*
A National Treasure, this Buddhist temple of the Shingon sect consists of seven historic buildings. It was founded in 1196 by lord Ashikaga Yoshikane, and contains a large image of the god Dainichi (inherited from the Minamoto clan), and a 600-year-old gingko tree. Toward the end of his life Ashikaga Yoshiyasu, cousin of Minamoto no Yoritomo, withdrew to Mount Koya *(♿see p377)* to become a monk, subsequently returning to Ashikaga. Acknowledged as one of the three founders of the Shingon sect, Ashikaga Yoshiyasu is still revered by Shingon monks.

Ashikaga Orihime Shrine
足利織姫神社
15min taxi or 30min walk from Ashikaga Station. ⏰Open daily 10am–4pm. 🚇No charge. orihimejinjya.com.
Ashikaga was long famous for its textile industry. In tribute to textile workers of the past, volunteers from the town built this Shinto shrine in 1937, located on a hill with splendid **views** over the Kanto plain. This scenic spot is also popular with couples, as it enshrines the god of marriage. In 2004, it was classified as an Important Cultural Property.

Kurita Museum 栗田美術館
15min by taxi or 30min walk from Ashikaga Station. ⏰Open Tue–Sun 9.30am–5pm. 🚇¥1250. kurita.or.jp/english/index.htm.
This gallery contains the world's largest collection of **Imari and Nabeshima porcelain and ceramics**, made during the Edo era (1603–1867) by the Hizen Nabeshima clan. The first porcelain to be produced in Japan, Imari was exported to the West and throughout Asia by the Dutch East India Company. The gallery is set in a garden full of flowers and foliage, with some Japanese-style houses.

Ashikaga Flower Park
あしかがフラワーパーク
Opposite the Kurita Museum. ⏰Open daily: Mar–mid-Nov 9am–6pm; late Nov–Feb 10am–5pm; late openings for some events. 🚇¥300–1800, depending on season and events. www.ashikaga.co.jp/english.
A park covering an area of 430,555sq ft/ 40,000sq m, with a wide variety of flowers blooming in every season. Famous for its magnificent wisteria arbors, one of which is 2625ft/800m long, and which are lit up during the evening in their peak season of March and April (to 9pm). The park also has some beautiful azaleas, hydrangeas, and water lilies.

SAITAMA AND GUNMA PREFECTURES 埼玉県と群馬県
Tokyo & Surroundings Map p131.

One or two days in these two prefectures north of the capital provides a radical change in setting: unspoiled natural landscapes, mountains close to 6500ft/2000m high, wild flora and fauna, and plenty of hot springs (onsen) to relax body and spirit.
Escapees from the capital are numerous here on weekends, especially in the fall, but the typically Japanese atmosphere is appealing in every season.

Nagatoro 長瀞
🚃*Map, A1. The Seibu Chichibu line runs from Ikebukuro Station to Kaminagatoro (2hr–2hr 40min journey, 🚇¥1360–3000).*
With the Arakawa River running through it, Nagatoro is a perfect place to experience Saitama's beauty. You can rent bikes (ask at the tourist information office, opposite Minakami Station) to cross the city and, for experienced cyclists, continue to the top of Mount Hodo (20min, or 45 min on foot).
On your way back down, stop at **Hodosan-jinja ★**. Recently repainted, the brilliantly-colored sculptures decorating the walls of this shrine are worth seeing. Continue down the street, turn left at the large torii and take the second street on the right. After the bridge, turn left and you will see **Hozenji** on your right. This little country temple is home to a wall sculpture of dragons which still have their original (slightly faded) colors. Heading back to Tokyo, don't forget to keep an eye out for the old steam locomotive in the train station.

Saitama Museum of Natural History ★ 埼玉県立自然の博物館
200m/650ft on left from Kaminagatoro Station. ⏰Open Jul–Aug Tue–Sun 9am–5pm; Sept–Jun daily 9am–4.30pm. 🚇¥200. shizen.spec.ed.jp.
This museum has a unique way of presenting Saitama's past and present natural bounty. You'll encounter stuffed animals to be "touched gently," mountain scenes featuring local species, fossils and reconstructions of ancient creatures, and a model of a giant shark. There's a pleasant **walk** along the river from the museum.

River cruise, Nagatoro

© JTB/Photoshot

Minakami 水上

Map; B1, off map. 102mi/165km from Tokyo by shinkansen or local train to Takasaki, then the JR Joetsu Line to Minakami (approx 2hr journey ✆¥5490–¥6010 by shinkansen; or 3hr ✆¥3020 by local train).

Skiing, trekking, rock-climbing, rafting, canoeing, and *onsen* (hot springs): Minakami offers numerous invigorating activites in a natural setting, a three-hour drive from the capital. The town extends over a vast stretch of land along the Tonegawa River, on which four dams were built to supply water to Saitama and Tokyo prefectures' 30 million inhabitants.

The impressive mountain relief of Tanigawa-dake rises to the northwest. No fewer than 18 **hot springs** surge to the surface here, hence the many *ryokan* and *minshuku* (family-run lodgings).

Tanigawa-dake ★ 谷川岳

By route 291, or 55min by bus from Joma-Kogen Station.

Mount Tanigawa (6486ft/1977m) is beautiful in every season, but especially when the valleys turn gold in fall and when the deep snow of winter arrive. The Tanigawa Ropeway (daily: Apr–Nov 7/8am–5pm, Dec–Mar 8.30am–4.30pm; ✆¥2060 round trip) takes visitors to 4265ft/1300m; experienced hikers can then make for the peak (*5hr round trip*)

or return by foot to the valley. Several ski trails are open in the winter season.

Takumi no sato たくみの里

West of JR Joma-Kogen Station on route 17 (20min by Kan-etsu bus JS14; ✆¥730). takuminosato.jp. English map available at the Tourist Office.

The main reason to visit this sleepy village is for its profusion of craft workshops, at many of which you can see artisans working or even have a go yourself. It's also pleasant just to walk among the shops, restaurants, and farms, and visit Tainei-ji, a Kamakura-era temple. The village layout partly dates from the Edo era: Shukuba Avenue was then on the Mikuni road, via which gold from Sado Island (*see p304*) was taken to Tokyo.

Kusatsu Onsen 草津温泉

Map, A1. About 140km/87mi from Tokyo; 3hr 45min from Shinjuku by direct JR Express Bus. visitgunma.jp/en.

Kusatsu is one of Japan's most popular *onsen*, due to the quality and abundance of its waters (*7039gal /32,000l*). It has a long history, being mentioned in the tales of Yamato Takeru no Mikoto (legendary 2C hero) and Gyoki (8C Buddhist priest). Minamoto no Yoritomo, the first shogun, often visited to relax in the waters. Soldiers came here to bathe their wounds in the Civil Wars of the 16C, but when trouble broke out, Shingen

Tomioka Silk Mill

© JTB Photo/UIG/age fotostock

Takeda (one of the most powerful *daimyo* of the time) closed the baths. It was the German academic Erwin von Bälz (1849–1913), invited by the Meiji government to teach in the Faculty of Medicine in Tokyo, who saw the medicinal benefits of the waters in Kusatsu and promoted them outside Japan. In winter the spa also has a ski slope.

Today, you can take your pick of several onsen here, and watch the unusual and energetic Yumomi (traditional water-cooling performance). The three main public baths are all tattoo-friendly

Tomioka Silk Mill ★ 富岡製糸場

83mi/135km from Tokyo by shinkansen or local train to Takasaki, then Joshin line to Joshu-Tomioka (approx 2hr journey ¥5200–¥5520 by shinkansen; or 3hr ¥2730 by local train), then walk 15min. ⏰*Open daily 9am–5pm.* ¥1000. ☎*0274-67-0075. tomioka-silk.jp.*

This extraordinary site bears witness to Japan's entrance into the industrial revolution. It become the world's leading producer and exporter of raw silk, remaining so until 1914. The silk mill was designated a UNESCO World Heritage Sites and classified as a National Treasure of Japan in 2014.

In 1870, the new Meiji government decided to launch a national development project for industry, and built the world's largest silk mill in Tomioka, in a region with a strong silk-making tradition. Using equipment sourced in France and training from French spinners,

production started in this **large brick building** in October 1872. The mill was privatized and sold to the Mitsui Finance Group in 1893, and then passed first to the Sankei Hara raw silk exporters in 1902 and then the Katakura company in 1938. The last owners ceased production in 1987 but ensured all the workers' accommodation and factory buildings were preserved in perfect condition. The English audioguide gives valuable context to the beautiful buildings *(¥200, or download onto your smartphone for free).*

ADDRESSES

🛏 STAY

NIKKO

🏠 **Johsyu-ya Ryokan** 上州屋旅館 – *911 Nakahatsuishi-machi (Map, B2).* ☎*0288-54-0155. www.johsyu-ya.co.jp/ en/index.html. 8 rooms. ¥9090. ¥1000* 🍴. 🍽. This *ryokan* offers both Japanese and Western-style rooms. A central location, hot-spring bath, warm welcome, and plenty of charm at a modest price.

🏠 **Minshuku Rindo-no-ie** 民宿りんどう の家 – *1462 Tokorono (Map, C1).* ☎*0288-53-0131. 4 rooms. ¥7700.* 🍴. Charming, well-sized rooms in a family house. A bit out of the way in the east of Nikko, but has a free shuttle bus from Tobu Nikko Station.

🏠 **Nikko Park Lodge** 日光パークロッジ – *2828-5 Tokorono (Map, C1).* ☎*0288-53-1201. nikkoparklodge.com. 12 rooms, 1 dormitory. ¥5200; dorm ¥2400 per person.* 🍴. Lots of charm and good ideas—*o-furo,* decent wi-fi, yoga classes, vegetarian dinners—at this country house by the mountains. Away from the center, it's true, but Ken, the dynamic owner, will act as chauffeur for arrivals and departures. Also has a branch near Tobu Nikko Station.

Nikko Station Hotel Classic 日光ステーションホテル クラシック 3-1 (Map, C2). ℰ0288-53-1000. nikko-stationhotel.jp. 71 rooms. ¥16,000. ¥1000 ☕. This hotel opposite the station is a perfect choice in its category, with nicely furnished and immaculately kept room. The restaurant is welcoming and well-lit, and the terrace cafe pleasantly laidback. A very good *onsen* and *rotenburo* (tattoos are fine).

Nikko Koryu Sokushin Center Kaze-no-hibiki 日光市交流促進センター風のひびきー – 2854 Tokorono (Map, C1). ℰ0288-54-1013. www.nikko-kazenohibiki.com/en/index.shtml. 12 rooms. ¥16,000. ¥10,500 ☕. A modern hotel 20min walk from the station, reminiscent of a summer vacation camp. Both Japanese- and Western-style rooms.

Turtle Inn Nikko タートル・イン・日光 – 2-16 Takumi-cho (Map, A2). ℰ0288-53-3168. turtle-nikko.com/turtle. 10 rooms. ¥10,000. ¥1000 ☕. For almost 40 years the Turtle and its energetic owners have pulled out all the stops for a cosmopolitan, backpacking clientele. Slightly faded but comfortable rooms. Good Japanese dinner (¥2000).

Annex Turtle Hotori-an アネックスタートル・ほとり庵 – 8-28 Takumi-cho (Map, A2). ℰ0288-53-3663. turtle-nikko. com/hotori-an. 11 rooms. ¥13,400. ¥1000 ☕. A cozier version of the Turtle Inn. A *ryokan* with some rooms looking over the peaceful river bank, a wonderful *onsen*, and a pleasant lounge area.

Logette Saint Bois ロヂテ・サンボア – 1560 Tokorono (Map, C1). ℰ0288-53-0082. www.sunfield.ne.jp/~l-sanboa/eng.html. 8 rooms. ¥16,800. ☕. A 15min walk from the station and 30min from the temples. This small chalet off the beaten track has plenty of charm, and wildlife on the doorstep. Large o-furo. Arrival and departure transfers provided (¥150).

Nikko Kanaya Hotel 日光金谷ホテル – 1300 Kamihatsuishi (Map, B2). ℰ0288-54-0001. www.kanayahotel.co.jp/eng/nkh. 71 rooms. ¥20,000. ¥2600 ☕. One of Japan's oldest hotels, with everything

designed to appeal to the discerning eye. Coffered, decorative ceilings with moulding, an outdoor pool and a classic dining room. A choice of French cuisine in the dining room, sushi in the Japanese restaurant, or curry in the Craft Lounge. Free shuttle bus to Nikko Station.

ASHIKAGA

Hotel Wakasa ホテルわかさ – 2374-2 Daimondori. ℰ0284-44-5353. wakasa-h.co.jp. 41 rooms. ¥9240. ☕. A very well-kept business hotel at reasonable prices and ideally situated near Ashikaga Gakko, the oldest school in Japan.

New Miyako Hotel Ashikaga Honkan ニューミヤコホテル足利本館 – 4254-1 Minami-cho. ℰ0284-71-3333. newmiyakohotel.co.jp/en. 80 rooms. ¥9420. ¥1100 ☕. A clean, convenient business hotel just by Tobu Ashikaga Station. From the restaurant on the 9th floor there is a view over the Watarase River.

🍴 EAT

NIKKO

Hippari-Dako ひっぱりだこ – 1011 Kamihatsuishi-machi (Map, B2). ℰ0288-53-2933. Open Mon–Sat noon–5pm & 6.30–9pm. Menu in English. Around ¥1000. 🍴. A small room with tables and walls covered with businesss cards. Tasty, unpretentious dishes at modest prices: *yakitori* (grilled chicken skewers), *yakisoba* (fried noodles), udon noodles in curry sauce, etc.

Shokudou Suzuki 食堂すゞき – 581-2 Gokomachi (Map, B2). ℰ0288-54-0662. Open Thu–Tue 11.30am–2.30pm & 5.30–9pm. From ¥1000. 🍴. Italian cuisne, Chinese, Korean, Japanese... The varied, daily changing menu here is ideal if you can't make up their mind. The *yuba* course (¥2800) is excellent, and they've been selling *kakigori* (shaved ice with syrup, summer only; ¥880) for 50 years.

Eat Asai イートあさい – 894 Naka-Hatsuishimachi (Map, B2). ℰ0288-54-0110 . Open Wed–Mon 11.30am–2pm & 5–8.30pm. Menu in English. Lunch around ¥800, dinner ¥1300. A fusion of Chinese and Japanese dishes, with simple and tasty cooking based on local produce. Try the *yuba ramen* (¥870), noodles served with the tofu skin which forms on soy milk when it is heated. Long prized by Nikko's Buddhist monks, *yuba* is now just as popular with secular vegetarians for its

nutritional qualities. This tiny restaurant has a very congenial owner who speaks English and is happy to share tips about the city.

🍽 **Suzuya** 鈴屋 – *2315-1 Sannai (Map, B1).* 📞*0288-53-6117. Open daily 11am–3pm. Around ¥1200.* 🚭. Specializes in handmade soba, udon, and *yuba*, often seasoned with *sansho*, a peppery local plant used to spice up the dishes.

🍽🍽 **Beer Restaurant Nikko Enya** えんや – *443 Ichiyamachi (Map, C2).* 📞*0288-53-5605. www.nikko-enya.com. Open Wed–Mon 11am–2.30pm & 5–10.30pm (last orders 2pm & 9.30pm). Lunch from ¥850, dinner ¥2500.* Steaks, skewers, and *shabu-shabu*. A welcoming restaurant that also serves some excellent beers.

🍽🍽 **Koryori Shinmatsu** 小料理新松 – *934-1 Naka-Hatsuishimachi (Map, B2).* 📞*0288-54-0041. Open Thu–Tue 11am–3pm & 5.30–11pm. Lunch around ¥1500, dinner ¥2500.* 🚭. Three low tables alongside the counter and an efficient owner busy preparing vegetable tempura, sea bream sashimi, etc. *Yuba* is their specialty, served in set meals featuring several small, beautifully presented dishes.

🍽🍽🍽 **Unagi Sawamoto** うなぎ澤本 – *1037-1 Kami-Hatsuishimachi (Map, B2).* 📞*0288-54-0163. Open daily 11.30am–1.45pm & 5–6.30pm. From ¥3000.* 🚭. Eel has the place of honor in this family-owned restaurant near Shin-kyo bridge. A variety of carefully prepared set meals.

🍽🍽🍽 **Gyoshintei** 堯心亭 – *2339-1 Sannai (Map, B1), a few min east of Tosho-gu.* 📞*0288-53-3751. meiji-yakata.com/en/gyoshin. Open Fri–Wed 11am–7pm (last order; from 11.30am in winter). Menu in English. Lunch around ¥3000, dinner ¥4000–6000.* 🚭. A unique chance to experience highly renowned vegetarian Buddhist cuisine *(shojin ryori)* in the enchanting and historical Fudouen site. Served in the most traditional style, the *kaiseki zen* (set meal) may include a dozen dishes, including tofu, *yuba*, bamboo shoots, and Nikko *yokan* (a firm jelly made from sweetened bean paste). Simpler lunch sets available, such as barley rice with fresh *yuba* *(¥2000)*.

🍽🍽🍽 **Mihashi Steakhouse** みはしステーキハウス – *1115 Ichicho, Uehachi (Map, B2).* 📞*0288-54-3429. meiji-yakata.com/en/mihashi. Open Fri–Wed 11.30am–8pm (last orders; winter to 7.30pm). Menu in English. À la carte from ¥1700, set menu ¥4500.* The best steak in Nikko! Full menu or meat by weight *(from ¥2200/150g rump steak)*; serves *Tochigi wagyu*, a fatty, marbed cut of meat.

🍽🍽🍽🍽 **Takai-ya** 高井家 – *4-9 Honmachi (Map, A1–A2).* 📞*0288-53-0043. nikko-takaiya.jp/link2.html. Lunch ¥5500–6600, dinner from ¥6600. Reservation required.* This *kaiseki* restaurant has been run by the Takai family since 1805, and each year a descendant of the Tokugawa clan comes to dine here on the eve of Nikko Festival. The chef has a talent for blending flavors, like smoked trout marinated for three days in salted water, or rolls of *yuba* with wasabi. The space is intimate and peaceful— in order to look after their guests well, the Takais serve only a few people at once. Relax in the pauses between the whispering of the *shoji* (screens), listen to the croaking of frogs in the garden, and enjoy this extravagant and memorable meal.

TAKING A BREAK

NIKKO

Yuzawaya 湯沢屋 – *946 Shimo-Hatsuishimachi (Map, B2).* 📞*0288-54-0038. yuzawaya.jp. Open 10am–4pm.* Enjoy your cup of *matcha* with a *manju* (filled sweet dumpling), or perhaps a *yokan* (sweet red bean paste jelly) sundae at this teahouse. You can buy boxes of traditional Japanese sweets at the attached shop.

SHOPPING

Utakata うたかた – *9218 Nakahatsuishi (Map, B2).* 📞*0288-53-6465. luxe-nikko.com. Open daily 10am–5.30pm.* This store sells and rents kimonos, and superb fabrics.

SAITAMA & GUNMA PREFECTURES

🏠 STAY

MINAKAMI

🛏🛏🛏🛏 **Ryokan Tanigawa** 旅館たにがわ – *524-1 Tanigawa, Minakami-machi; next to Tanigawa onsen.* 📞*0278-72-2468. ryokan-tanigawa.com/en. 29 rooms. From ¥37,000 half board.* 🚇. A beautiful, recently built *ryokan* in traditional style. Western or Japanese rooms, and a good *onsen* featuring a *rotenburo*. Some rooms have a private hot-spring bath (*costs extra*), useful for guests with tattoos, who will not be allowed to use the main bath. Free shuttle to Minakami Station.

🍴 EAT

NAGATORO

🍱🍱🍱 **Irori-an Hanamizuki** 囲炉里庵 花水木 – *499 Nagatoro.* ☎0494-26-5058. *choseikan.com/dininginfo/*

irorianhanamizuki. Open 11am–2.30pm & 5.30–7.30pm (last orders). Lunch sets from ¥3500, dinner ¥5000. Reservations recommended. This charming restaurant with its river view serves delicious *udon* (*zuriage udon*) and grilled fish. You eat in a private room, around a square hearth cut in the ground (*iri*), where the food is cooked. You can also eat in the other, less expensive wing of the restaurant: **Iwazakura** (*岩ざくら; from ¥2000*).

East of Tokyo

Foreign tourists rarely linger east of Tokyo, contenting themselves merely with transiting through the vast airport at Narita. There are nonetheless some interesting things to do and see, all of which are easy to reach. The pleasant city of Narita is home to one of the most impressive temples in the country, while the streets flanking the canal at Sawara seem to be frozen in time in the Edo period.

NARITA 成田

⚓*Regional Map, B2. Access: JR and Keisei line trains every 30min to Ueno and Tokyo (40min–1hr 30min) and the airport (7–15min). Leave the JR station and follow scenic Omotesando, which is lined with the usual (but attractive) stores, to the city's main attraction:*

Naritasan Shinsho-ji ★★
成田山新勝寺
15min walk from JR and Keisei stations.
🕐*Open daily 24hr; free guided walks daily 10am & 3pm.* 🎟*No charge. naritasan.or.jp/english.*
Built in the 10C, this Shingon Buddhist temple is dedicated to Fudo Myo-o, the god of fire. Its impressive expansion began in the 17C when the capital was moved to Edo and a famous Kabuki actor made the figure of Fudo Myo-o extremely popular, having prayed to the god for a child and being granted his request. Since then, pilgrims have flocked to Narita and it now welcomes

▶ **Population:** Narita 131,000; Sawara 47,200.
⚓ **Michelin Map:** Tokyo & Surroundings Map p131.
🈁 **Tourist Info:** Omotesando, near the temple. ☎0476-24-3232. www.nrtk.jp. Tue–Sun 9am–5pm.
▶ **Location:** 37mi/60km from Tokyo, in Chiba prefecture.
🕐 **Timing:** Allow a day. You could also take in Narita and Sawara during a long stopover at Narita Airport.

Naritasan Shinsho-ji
© olsword/iStock

10 million visitors a year. Take a stroll among the different buildings (arranged in order of antiquity), looking out for the highly colorful ornamentation on

the pagoda next to the main hall, and enjoy the vastness of the surrounding grounds. The temple gets especially busy during extremely popular festivals such as New Year and Setsubun (Feb 3).

SAWARA 佐原

Map, B2. 17 km northeast of Narita Airport. Train JR Narita Line (30min, ☞¥500). This small city is renowned for its beautiful **canal district from the Edo period** (15min walk from the station), made up of the waterside houses of merchants who got rich on the river's rice trade, and traditional, photogenic inns.

Among all these remarkable buildings, look out in particular for the "jah-jah" (sound of dropping water) bridge and the house of cartographer Ino Tadataka (1745–1818), which is now a museum (open Tue–Sun 9am–4.30pm, ☞¥500) with good English signage.

Sawara is equally well-known for its charming biannual (July/Oct) **street festival**, during which giant representations of mythological heroes are borne shoulder-high by the crowds. You can see a few of these during the rest of the year at Dashi Kaikan (3368 Sawara-i, open Tue–Sun 9am–4.30pm, ☞¥400). Located 3mi/5km north of the city (20min by bus from the station), the unusual Sawara Aquatic Botanical Gardens (open Tue–Sun 8am–6pm, extended hours in summer; ☞¥500, or ¥700 during the iris festival) are famed for their 1.5 million irises that are in bloom between May and June, best viewed from a boat.

Mount Fuji★★★
富士山

"A wise man climbs Mount Fuji once. A madman climbs it twice." If this saying holds true today, the reason is less the difficulty of the walk up the mountain than the number of climbers with whom you share the privilege of reaching the highest summit in Japan … in single file! For many, such is the myth of the mountain, a potent symbol of Japan, that climbing it is as inevitable as it is unforgettable. Many Japanese people still view Mount Fuji as a sacred mountain, revered for at least 12 centuries and visited every year by 17 million people. As close to perfection in shape as it is possible to get, its snowcapped peak has graced millions of images across the world.

- ▸ **Population:** Hakone 11,786.
- **Michelin Map:** Regions of Japan Map 1, Tokyo & Surroundings p131, Mt. Fuji p236.
- **Location:** Hakone, Kanagawa, 62mi/100km from Tokyo; Mount Fuji, Yamanashi, 56mi/90km from Tokyo.
- **Kids:** Tenzan Onsen; Museum of the Little Prince; the Hakone Checkpoint.
- **Timing:** Allow two days for Hakone, and two for Mt. Fuji. Buses link both via Gotemba, but a car is more practical.
- **Don't miss:** Pola Museum of Art; Hakone Open-Air Museum; Itchiku Kubota Art Museum; Mishima Yukio Museum.

THE HAKONE REGION★
箱根

Tokyo & Surroundings Map p131.
Part of the **Fuji-Hakone-Izu National Park**, this region embodies all Japan's most characteristic geographic traits: volcanoes, lakes, thermal springs, and, where lava has not made the soil too impermeable, verdant forests. As a result, Hakone's onsen (hot springs), are among the finest in Japan—and just over an hour from Tokyo.

Lake Ashi and Mount Fuji in winter

THE HAKONE LOOP

The Hakone–Tozan rail line (9mi/15km long) connects Odawara and Hakone-Yumoto (12min journey); Hakone-Yumoto to Gora takes 40min. The "Loop" is a popular tourist route that takes in the major sites.

Tenzan Onsen (Tenzan Tohji-Kyo) ★ 天山湯治郷

Hakone-Yumoto, 550yd/500m past the Okada Hotel. Bus from Hakone-Yumoto Bus Station ¥100. Open daily 9am–10pm. ¥1300 (children ¥650). Bathing essentials not supplied.

One of the largest thermal bath complexes in Japan, with indoor and outdoor baths (including one in a cave) at different temperatures. Saunas and massages for head-to-toe relaxation. Refreshingly for such a traditional complex, guests with tattoos are welcome.

Hakone Open-Air Museum ★★ 彫刻の森美術館

1121 Ninotaira. Electric train from Hakone-Yumoto to Chokoku-no-Mori Station. Open daily 9am–5pm. ¥1600; online discounts available. hakone-oam.or.jp/en.

This open-air museum—Japan's first, which celebrated its 50th anniversary in 2019—is a pleasant surprise. Stroll through the grounds and discover the sculptures that stand out superbly against the natural backdrop. The exhibition centers around 120 contemporary sculptures (Henry Moore, Niki de Saint Phalle, etc.) and one pavilion, renovated in 2019, dedicated to Picasso.

Gora 強羅

At Gora, the Hakone–Tozan Line terminus, you'll find shops and accommodation. Further north, the beautiful countryside serves as the perfect setting for some excellent museums.

Pola Museum of Art ★★ ポーラ美術館

1285 Kozukayama, Sengokuhara. Bus (13min, ¥300) or taxi from Gora Station. Open daily 9am–5pm. ¥1800. English audioguide available, ¥400. polamuseum.or.jp/english.

This private museum is housed in a superb contemporary building surrounded by forest. It has an exceptional collection of 19–20C French painting (Monet, Renoir, Degas, Picasso, Matisse, Cézanne) amassed by Suzuki Tsuneshi, who was CEO of the Pola cosmetics group. There are collections of other artworks, cosmetics equipment, and sculpture to round off your visit.

Museum of the Little Prince ★ 星の王子さまミュージアム

909 Sengokuhara. Shisetsu-Meguri bus from Gora Station. Open daily 9am–6pm (last entry 5pm). ¥1600 (children ¥700). www.tbs.co.jp/l-prince/en.

Readers of the much-loved children's book *The Little Prince* by aviator Antoine de Saint-Exupéry (written in the Bevin House on Long Island, New York) will love this cute, quirky museum. The models and reconstructions of characters from the book are a little Disney-esque in style.

© motive56/iStock

USEFUL INFORMATION
HAKONE

Tourist Office – *Hakone-Yumoto Station.*
0460-85-5700. Open daily 9am–5.45pm.
Excellent information in English.

Post Offices/Withdrawals – Odawara
Post Office *(ATM Mon–Fri 8am–9pm, Sat &
Sun 9am–7pm)*, Yumoto Post Office *(ATM
Mon–Fri 8.45am–6pm, Sat &Sun 9am–
5pm)*, and Hakone-Gora Post Office *(ATM
Mon–Fri 9am–5.30pm, Sat 9am–12.30pm)*.

TRANSPORTATION

The **Hakone Free Pass** *(odakyu.
jp/english)* covers almost all journeys
departing from **Shinjuku**, plus local
transport and discounted entry for some
sites. *¥5700 (2 days)* or *¥6100 (3 days)*.
BY TRAIN – From Shinjuku Station
(Tokyo), regular departures on the
Odakyu Line's Romance Car *(about 1hr
25min, ¥2280)* or local trains *(2hr, ¥1190)*.
From **Tokyo Station**, regular departures
of the **shinkansen** *(35min, around ¥3500)*
and local trains on the JR Tokaido Line *(1hr
20min, ¥1500)* to Odawara.
On arrival at **Odawara Station**, allow
20min by bus *(¥370)* for Hakone-Yumoto,
40min for Moto-Hakone *(about ¥1180)*.
Or take the Hakone Tozan Tetsudo Line
(15min, ¥310) or Odakyu Line Ltd. Express
Hakone *(15min, ¥510)* for Hakone-Yumoto.
For Oyama, get off at **Isehara**.
By Bus – **Odakyu Hakone Highway
Bus** – around 18 buses per day
(depending on the season) leaving
Shinjuku Station for Sengoku *(around
2hr journey, ¥2000)*.

GETTING AROUND

If you're not coming from Shinjuku but
will travel around Hakone a lot, you could
get the cheaper **Hakone Free Pass**, which
only applies from Odawara onwards *(2
days ¥4600, 3 days ¥5000)*.

BY BUS – **Hakone Tozan Bus** and **Izu-
Hakone Bus** have regular connections to
main sites.

BY ELECTRIC FUNICULAR – The Hakone
Tozan Cable Car is picturesque, but also
practical for sites between Hakone-
Yumoto and Gora *(40min; ¥400)*.

USEFUL INFORMATION
MOUNT FUJI AND LAKE KAWAGUCHI

Fujiyoshida Tourist Office – *Fujiyoshida
Station (Map, B1). Open daily 9am–5pm.*
0555-22-7000. Maps and detailed
explanations. English spoken.

Fujisan World Heritage Center – *6663-1
Funatsu (Map, B1). 0555-72-0259.
Open daily: Mar–Jun, Oct & Nov 9am–5pm;
Jul–Sept 8.30am–6pm; Dec–Feb 9am–4pm.*
Information and exhibitions on the area.

Fujikawaguchiko Tourist Office
– *Kawaguchiko Station (Map, B1).
0555-72-6700. Open daily 9am–5pm
(longer in peak season).* Maps and detailed
explanations. English spoken.

Hakone Tozan Tetsudo Line

TRANSPORTATION

BY TRAIN – From Tokyo (Shinjuku Station), the **Chuo Line** goes to Otsuki (*8 direct trains per day, 1hr 30min journey, ¥1320; or 65min, ¥2770 by Ltd. Express*). Alternatively, take the **Keio Line**, changing at Takao (*1hr 30min, ¥1320*). At Otsuki, continue by the **Fuji–Kyuko Line** to Kawaguchiko (♿*Map, B1; 55min, ¥1340*).

BY BUS – Simpler and more practical than taking the train. From Shinjuku Station, regular departures for **Fuji-san Station** (*2hr, ¥1750*) and Kawaguchiko Station (*1hr 45min, ¥1750*). From Tokyo Station regular departures to Kawaguchiko Station (*around 3hr, ¥1800*). If you arrive from Mishima, take the **Express** **Fuji Bus** from Mishima to Kawaguchiko (*1hr 45min, ¥2260*). You may have to change at Gotenba.

GETTING AROUND

BY TRAIN OR BUS – Around 4 buses per hour run between Fujisan and Kawaguchiko stations, but the train is better (*5min, ¥220*). From Kawaguchiko Station, the yellow 1930s-style **Retrobus** tours the major sites (*¥1300 for 2 days*).

BY BICYCLE – Available at some hotels, as well as bicycle rental shops. Practical for getting to/from Kawaguchiko if you don't have luggage. There's a rental shop and baggage storage place 1min from Kawakuchiko Station (*fuji-bb.jp/welcome; ¥1500 per day, or e-bike ¥2600;* ⬚).

Lalique Museum Hakone ★
箱根ラリック美術館

186-1 Sengokuhara. From the bus station by Hakone train station, take the T Line bus (platform 3) to Sengoku Annaijo-Mae (25min). 🕐*Open daily 9am–5pm.* ✆*¥1500. lalique-museum.com.*

Nestled in an ornate garden, this museum houses an exceptional collection of works by the French glass-maker René Lalique (1860–1945). Among the 1500 or so items that make up the collection, the 230 works on display exemplify this genius of decorative art's talent and creative inspiration, which owed so much to his fascination with nature— an interest he shared with Japanese art. There is a wealth of delicate glass flasks on the ground floor and some very fine flower vases upstairs; the section devoted to jewelry—sadly small—is dazzling and a vibrant tribute to Lalique's original artistic vision which was so much a feature of the Art Nouveau and Art Deco periods. Round off your visit with a trip to the tearoom, looking out over a perfect lawn.

Owaku-dani Valley ★★ 大涌谷
From Gora Station, take the funicular to Souzan (9min), then the ropeway to Owaku-dani Station. ✆ *No charge* with the Hakone Free Pass (♿*see p234*), otherwise ¥820. If the cable car is closed due to volcanic activity (gas emissions), there may be a substitute bus service – information and prices at www.hakoneropeway.co.jp.*

It takes just eight minutes to rise from 2431ft/741m to 3425ft/1044m, from where you can look down over the "valley of hell," Owaku-dani. The valley appeared around 3000 years ago following a volcanic eruption that shook Kami-

Yoshida no Himatsuri

Attracting more than 200,000 people, one of Japan's most popular *matsuri* (festivals) takes place every year on August 26 and 27. It marks the end of the official Mount Fuji climbing season. Torches over 10ft/3m tall light 1.2mi/2km of the main trail from the town of Fujiyoshida. On the first day (*Chinkasai*), the gods leave the shrine and are carried in *mikoshi* (portable shrines) and *mikage* (a shrine in the shape of Mount Fuji) to the house of rest of the gods (*Otabisho*). On the second day (*Susuki*), they are returned to the shrine.

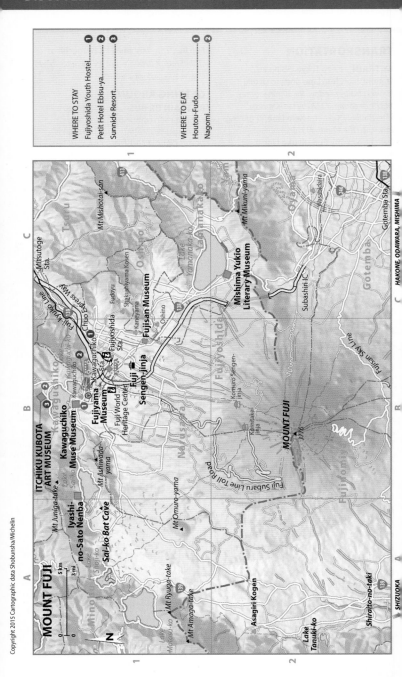

Copyright 2015 Cartographic data Shobunsha/Michelin

MOUNT FUJI

WHERE TO STAY

Fujiyoshida Youth Hostel...... ❶
Petit Hotel Ebisu-ya........... ❷
Sunnide Resort.................. ❸

WHERE TO EAT

Houtou-Fudo................ ❶
Nagomi.................... ❷

yama *(4718ft/1438m)*. The legacy of the eruption is a brown, ravaged volcanic landscape with active sulfur vents and tendrils of steam from the hot springs. Incidentally, the smell of sulfur was classified by the Environment Ministry as one of the 100 most common smells in Japan. Try local specialty *kuro tamago*, eggs that have turned black after being immersed in one of the boiling springs *(6 eggs around ¥500)*.

Owaku-dani Valley

Lake Ashi 芦ノ湖
Cable car from Owaku-dani to Togen-dai, then walk down to the pier to join a sightseeing cruise. hakone-kankosen. co.jp. ◐*Cruises daily: Mar 20–Nov 30 9.30am–5pm; Dec–Mar 19 9.30am–4.40pm.* ◉*¥1000 one-way, ¥1840 round trip (covered by Hakone Free Pass).*
Cruise boats designed to look like pirate ships leave Togendai and cross the waters of this large lake *(11mi/18km long)* to Hakone-Machi and Motohakone. It's an uneventful crossing, but the **views** of Mount Fuji are splendid.

Narukawa Art Museum
成川美術館
Very close to Hakone-Machi pier. ◐*Open daily 9am–5pm.* ◉*¥1300; discounts online. narukawamuseum.co.jp/en.*
A permanent exhibition of contemporary Japanese artists, but the museum also holds temporary exhibitions. A small collection of Noh masks and rare Chinese jade and ivory are also on display. There's a magnificent **view** to be enjoyed from the cafe, and the Panorama Lounge.

Hakone Checkpoint ★ 箱根関所
Walk north around Lake Ashi (about 15min). ◐*Open daily: Mar–Nov 9am–5pm; Dec–Feb 9am–4.30pm.* ◉*¥500 (children ¥250). hakonesekisyo.jp/ english/main/main.html.*
👥 A reconstruction of one of the checkpoints put in place by the Tokugawa shoguns during the Edo era. The checkpoint at Hakone was set up in 1619 and was the first of 53 control points on the Tokaido road (the route linking Edo to Kyoto). As well as checking the credentials of the

men who passed through with their weapons, and taxing goods, checkpoints were used to prevent women from leaving Edo. This meant that the *daimyo* had to leave their families behind in their residences near the capital, thus enabling the shogun to exert pressure on them. This system requiring alternate attendance in the lords' domain and at Edo *(sankin kotai, ◐see p134)* helped the shogun to suppress the power and wealth of his vassals. This careful reconstruction was six years in the making and gives a detailed picture of daily life at a checkpoint.

Old Tokaido road ★★ 旧東海道
Opposite the checkpoint, an avenue of cedars leads to the old Tokaido road.
The cedar trees planted along the Tokaido road were no doubt intended to provide shelter for travelers of high rank, particularly the shoguns. Those who had been newly promoted also took this road to the Imperial capital, Kyoto, in order to receive their honor from the Emperor. The protocol changed with the reign of Tokugawa Iemitsu when it became the Emperor's responsibility to send an emissary bearing the Imperial mandate to Edo. A stretch of around 1.2mi/2km of this beautiful **cedar-lined avenue ★★** still exists. Along the way, stop for *amazake* (a sweet, mild drink)

237

The Tokaido road as seen by Hiroshige

For an impression of the beauty of the land- and seascapes crossed or skirted by the Tokaido road, study one of the famous series of prints by the great artist Ando Hiroshige (1797–1858): *The Fifty-Three Stations of the Tokaido Road*, executed between 1832 and 1834. The series received such critical and commercial acclaim that in the following years, the artist produced other series devoted to the country's most beautiful landscapes, in particular *Thirty-Six Views of Mount Fuji* (1852 and 1858) and *One Hundred Famous Views of Edo* (1856–8).

and a sticky *mochi* (rice cake) at atmospheric **Amazake-chaya** (⟨*see p245*).

Hakone Shrine ★ 箱根神社
Moto-Hakone, back along the lake heading northwest. ⊚*No charge.*
The shrine's beautiful bright red *torii* (gates) set in the waters at the edge of Lake Ashi stand out from across the lake, contrasting with the background of greenery. Standing at the end of a magnificent **avenue of cypress trees ★★**, this shrine, built in 757, is one of the oldest in Kanto.

EXCURSIONS

Oyama ★ 大山
Northeast of Hakone. Odakyu Line from Shinjuku (1hr, ⊚¥590) or Odawara (32min, ⊚¥370) to Isehara Station. Leave by the northern exit, then take bus no. 4 (30min, ⊚¥310) to Oyama Cable. Then a 15min walk to the cable car.
This is a nice stop to slot in on your way to or from Hakone, ideally in spring or fall so you can admire the trees in all their glory.
Mount Oyama (*4108ft/1252m*), literally the "great mountain," is a pilgrimage site that has attracted visitors for centuries, especially during the Edo period. Having paid their respects at the shrines nestling along the side of the mountain, pilgrims then made their way to Enoshima (⟨*see p210*) and Kamakura, some 19 miles (30km) to the southwest. Even today, nigh on half a million people visit the site every year.
You can do the entire trip on foot or take the cable car for one or two sections (⊚¥630 to Afuri-jinja). **Koma-sando**, the path leading to the sanctuaries, is very picturesque, with its succession of souvenir stores (selling wooden tops in particular), *ryokan*, and restaurants, where you can try some tofu-based local specialties and sweet *manju* dumplings, awaiting you as you climb the hill.
Oyama-dera – *At the first cable car stop.*
The first temple was built in the 8C by a monk named Roben (689–773) from

Koshu, a purely Japanese wine

Although famous for its fruits (persimmons, apples, grapes), Yamanashi prefecture was the birthplace of the country's wine industry and is becoming increasingly recognized for its Koshu (the old name for Yamanashi) vines. Although grown in Japan since the 8C BC (probably introduced from the Caucasus via the Silk Road), the vines only started to be cultivated on any scale in 1877 after the establishment of the region's first viticultural society. Grapes are grown in the Katsunuma Valley in southeast Yamanashi and today provide 25 percent of Japanese wine. An unstructured dry white, slightly acidic with the aroma of lemons, is now exported to Europe. Grace Wine (*grace-wine.com*), set up in 1923 and one of Japan's largest winemakers (*there are now more than 60 in Yamanashi prefecture*), produces 250,000 bottles per year and its Grace Koshu has been acclaimed by critics. Lumiere Winery (*lumiere.jp/en*) produces sparkling and orange wines, and offers English-language tours. ⟨*Japanese amateur wine association: jp-wine.com/en.*

Todai-ji temple in Nara. The main building houses a national treasure: an iron statue of the Buddhist divinity Fudo Myo-o, dating back to the Kamakura period (12C), that can be viewed only on the 8, 18 and 28 of the month and at New Year (Dec 29–3 Jan).

Afuri-jinja – *At the highest cable car stop.* Lying at an altitude of 2300ft/700m, this sanctuary is dedicated to the mountain spirits "that make the rain come" and so is particularly venerated by farmers, fisherfolk and, during the Kamakura period, samurai, who traditionally offered a saber in exchange for divine protection—a very valuable and personal gift. From the esplanade, there is a superb **view ★★** in good weather of Sagami Bay, the Izu and Miura peninsulas, the Tanzawa Mountains, and Mount Fuji. The most indefatigable walkers can continue to the summit *(1hr 30min climb)*, where there is a small shrine.

Odakyu Railways' **Tanzawa-Oyama Freepass** may be worth considering if you want to stay overnight in the area. The cheapest type which includes the cable car *(2 days, ¥1750; odakyu.jp/english/passes/tanzawa_oyama)* also covers a stretch of the Odakyu Line, local buses and discounts at souvenir shops, restaurants and lodgings.

Odawara Castle 小田原城
9mi/14km northeast of Hakone-Yumoto. Hakone–Tozan Line train (17min, ¥310) to Odawara Station then 10min walk from east exit. Or Tokaido shinkansen from Tokyo Station (35min, ¥3540). Open daily 9am–5pm. Closed 2nd Wed in Dec & Dec 31– Jan 1. ¥500.
This is the nearest castle to Tokyo. Originally constructed in the mid-15C, as it occupies a strategic location it passed through the hands of various clans, most of whom redesigned it. It was famously besieged and occupied by the armies of Toyotomi Hideyoshi in 1590. After being destroyed in 1870, it was partially reconstructed in 1960 to plans dating back to the Edo period. You can now visit

the keep, with its four floors and three gates. Within the keep there is a well-illustrated museum trail detailing the history of the site. There is a beautiful view of Sagami Bay and the city from the observation platform on the top floor.

Yugawara ★ 湯河原
About 30km/17mi south of Hakone. JR Odoriko Express from Tokyo Station (1hr 15min, around ¥3000).
Yugawara benefits from a magnificent view over the bay of Sagami and a mild climate. It is known for its thermal spas, referred to in 7C literature. Visitors can appreciate the quality of the Doppu no Yu and Kogome no Yu public baths, or those in numerous *ryokan* in the town. Though near popular Hakone, Yugawara has preserved a peaceful authenticity. Heading up the Fujiki River you come to Oku-Yugawara, a forest with a sprinkling of traditional *ryokan*, where many Japanese writers drew inspiration: Shimazaki Toson, Natsume Soseki, and Akutagawa Ryunosuke, among others.

Manazuru Peninsula ★ 真鶴
3mi/5km from Yugawara. Tokaido line shinkansen from Tokyo Station (1hr 10min, ¥3390), or from Yugawara Station by bus or JR train (3min, ¥190).
There are nice walks to be had along the peninsula's coast or in its protected ancient forest (Uotsuki Forest Reserve) and its bathing resort; the ruins of an ancient castle, the little port, and even the beach at Kotogahama all combine to ensure a pleasant stay. From the headland (**Mitsuishi Seacoast**), there is a lovely view of Sagami Bay on one side and the Izu Peninsula on the other, as well as of the two "married" rocks. Don't miss sunrise, which attracts crowds on the first day of the new year.

If traveling by car, you can combine the three sites (Yugawara, Manazuru, and Odawara) before continuing on toward Kamakura *(located 26mi/42km east of Odawara; see p204)*, following the Shonan coast.

MOUNT FUJI ★★ 富士山
Map, p236. Allow 2 days.

The sight of the perfect peak of "Fuji-san" set against a vivid blue sky never fails to enthrall, wherever it is viewed, and it seems to be visible from just about everywhere in Yamanashi *(the north face)* and Shizuoka *(the south face)* prefectures. The summit of the volcano is permanently covered in snow and at an altitude of 12,389ft/3776m, it is the highest peak in Japan. Due to their destructive nature (the last eruption was in 1707), the *kami* (spirits) of Mount Fuji are treated with the utmost respect by the Japanese. However, for the visitor, the closer you get to this legendary mountain, the more your disenchantment may grow. The towns nearby are not of a great deal of interest and the mountain itself gets crowded with those intent on making the ascent, usually overnight in order to see the sunrise. Yet, there are some pleasant surprises, too, like the kannon with the head of a horse.

Mount Fuji, together with the shrines, springs and inns associated with the sacred climb to its summit, have been inscribed on UNESCO's World Heritage list since 2013. The five lakes (Fujigoko) surrounding it are one of the country's most popular tourist areas.

FUJIYOSHIDA 富士吉田
Map, B2.

A pilgrimage town, or more accurately, a town through which pilgrims pass on their way to the top of Mount Fuji, Fujiyoshida retains two fine buildings as reminders of its prosperous past.

Each town would send a group of pilgrims *(fujiko)* to Mount Fuji under the protection of the *oshi*, the priest responsible for the spiritual and material guidance of the pilgrims on the sacred heights of the mountain. Depending on its financial situation, a town would either shoulder the entire cost of constructing an *oshi* lodging house, or share the burden with other towns. By the end of the Edo era, Fujiyoshida had as many as 82 inns of this kind.

The point of departure for all the pilgrims, and the second point of interest in town, is **Fuji Sengen-jinja ★★** *(open daily 9am–5pm, no charge)*, reached via a beautiful avenue lined with moss-covered lanterns. Behind the *torii* (gates) the shrine complex, an area of almost 25 acres/10ha, has put down its roots alongside some glorious ancient cedar trees. The main building, the Honden, built in the Momoyama style and dating from the 17C, is dedicated to several *kami*, including Kono-hana Sakuya-hime, the goddess of flowering trees (her name is derived from the Japanese for "flowering cherry tree"). The highly fertile goddess was required to prove her worth by showing that she could give birth during a raging fire. This unprecedented act gave her additional powers from that time on: she became the protector from fire and the facilitator of child birth. One of the routes up the mountain, the **Yoshida Trail**, begins at the shrine; the trail's opening is celebrated each year on June 30.

Fujisan Museum ★
ふじさんミュージアム
2288-1 Kamiyoshida. Take a bus from Gotemba, Odakyu Line, and get off at Fujisan Paku. fy-museum.jp. Open Wed–Sun 9.30am–5pm.

Ashinoko Skyline

If you are traveling by car, don't miss this panoramic road ★★ which follows the high ground looking down over the western shore of Lake Ashi. Espeially if you travel from south to north (Yugawara, Odawara or Izu Peninsula), you will be playing hide-and-seek with Mount Fuji as it appears and disappears at the whim of the cloud cover. There are a number of viewing points along the route, particularly on Mount Mikuni (3615ft/1102m).

Fuji Sengen-jinja, Fujiyoshida

© PicturePartners/iStock

¥400; includes same-day admission to the Togawa Oshi House and English audioguide.

Fujisan Museum, which was renovated in 2015, traces the history of the religious worship associated with the most sacred mountain in Japan, from the first mystics, steeped in Shintoist and Buddhist ideas from the Heian period (794–1185), to the popularization of religious pilgrimage during the Edo period (1603–1868). The numerous display items, photographs and videos give a pretty comprehensive overview; the story ranges from the initial fear inspired by Fuji-san's violent eruptions to the fascination exerted by the beauty of its perfect cone. While an effort has been made to supply some information in English, the detailed descriptions of the objects on show are all in Japanese.

Oshi (Former Togawa Family House) 御師旧外川家住宅

3-14-8 Kamiyoshida. 5min from Fujisan Station or Hokuryo Koko bus stop. ⏰Open Wed–Sun 9.30am–5pm. ¥100, or ¥400 with same-day admission to Fujisan Museum.

The former residence of the Togawa family (18C) is a beautiful and historic house, long used as an *oshi* (lodging for pilgrims to Mount Fuji).

Fujiyama Museum
フジヤマ ミュージアム

Highland Resort Hotel & Spa, 5-6-1 Shinnishihara, Fujiyoshida. Free shuttles from Fujisan and Fujikyu Highland stations. ⏰Open Mon–Fri 10am–5.30pm, Sat 10am–8.30pm, Sun 9am–8.30pm. ⏰Irregular closures. ¥1000. fujiyama-museum.com/en.

Sleek, modern museum focused on the many and varied works of art inspired by mount Fuji, by artists ranging from Kusama Yayoi to Yasuda Yukihiko.

KAWAGUCHIKO ★ 河口湖
🗺Map, B1.

Lake Kawaguchi, by the town of the same name and not far from Fujiyoshida (1.9mi/3km), has excellent Mount Fuji **views**. In spring its cherry trees are a photographer's delight. Two museums also make the detour worthwhile.

Itchiku Kubota Art Museum
★★★ 久保田一竹美術館

🗺Map, B1. 2255 Kawaguchi, Fuji Kawaguchiko-machi. 25min by Omni Bus Red Line from Kawaguchiko Station. ⏰Open Wed–Mon: Apr–Nov 9.30am–5.30pm; Dec–Mar 10am–4.30pm. ¥1300. itchiku-museum.com.

This unique and original museum is dedicated to the great textile artist Kubota Itchiku (1917–2003). The central building, a pyramid-shaped structure

Itchiku Kubota Art Museum

framed by 16 ancient cypress trees, contains displays of large-scale contemporary kimonos. These "things to wear" (the meaning of "kimono") which each take an average of two years to make, weigh three or four times more than a regular kimono. Each thread has been produced with a dyeing technique *(tsujigahana)* used between the 14C and 17C, which Kubota revived. Part of his unfinished masterwork, "Symphony of Light," whic is made up of 80 kimonos inspired by the theme of the four seasons, is always on display.

The New Wing, inspired by Spanish architect Gaudi, houses a collection of Tombodama glass pearls from Mesopotamia dating back 3500 years. You will find a waterfall and a varied selection of sculptures in the garden, and a tearoom towards the back of the museum.

Kawaguchiko Muse Museum

★★ 河口湖ミューズ館（与 勇輝館）

&*Map, B1. Yagisaki Park, Fuji Kawaguchiko-machi. 12min Omni Bus Red or Green Line from Kawaguchiko Station.* ○*Open daily 9am–5pm.* ○*Closed Dec–Mar Thu & New Year public hols.* ▭*¥600. fkchannel.jp/muse/en.*

This small museum displays dolls made by Atae Yuki (born 1937), who has revived the craft of doll making in Japan. Made out of cotton fabric, many of his creations are modeled on Japanese children and are hauntingly beau-

tiful; he is particularly skilled in creating their individual expressions. Atae Yuki's dolls have been exhibited worldwide. There's also a good cafe, where you can enjoy cake sets, parfaits and traditional Japanese confections.

AROUND LAKE SAIKO 西湖

&*Map, A1–B1.*

The eruptions of Mount Fuji over thousands of years have considerably altered the landscape. Of the 80 caves in the area, the **Saiko Bat Cave** (○*open daily 9am–5pm;* ▭*¥300)* is the largest, reaching a depth of 1247ft/380m.

▷ From Saiko cave, take the Retrobus to the north of Lake Sai *(10min)*.

Iyashi-no-Sato Nenba

いやしの里根場

&*Map, B1. 2710 Saiko-Nenba, Fuji Kawaguchiko. Omni Bus Green Line from Kawaguchiko Station.* ○*Open Mar–Nov daily 9am–5pm; Dec–Feb Thu–Tue 9.30am–4.30pm.* ▭*¥350. fujisan.ne.jp/iyashi.*

Destroyed by a typhoon in 1963, this **traditional village** with a population of 235 was rebuilt as an open-air museum in 2003, to revive specialist skills that were in danger of being lost. Of the 40 houses that make up the village, just under 20 have been rebuilt with thatched roofs in the shape of a warrior's helmet *(kabuto-zukuri),* a skill which very few craftspeople still practice. Traditional crafts on display in some of the houses include pottery, weaving, doll making, and incense making (using powdered charcoal mixed with plum syrup to produce a characteristic scent).

AROUND LAKE YAMANAKA
山中湖
♿ *Map, C1/2.*

Situated at an altitude of 3215ft/980m, the largest *(8.4mi/13.5km long)* and highest lake in the region is very popular in summer, particularly with the citizens of Tokyo, who use it for watersports. Adjacent to the lake, in a wooded area (part of Bungaku no Mori park), are museums dedicated to the famous writer Mishima Yukio and influential author and journalist Tokutomi Soho. Work by the poet Tomiyasu Fusei is also displayed.

Mishima Yukio Literary Museum ★★ 三島由紀夫文学館
♿ *Map C2. 506-296 Hirano, Yamanakako; 5min from Bungaku no Mori Koen Mae bus stop.* ◷*Open Tue–Sun 10am–4.30pm.* ⊛*¥500. mishimayukio.jp.*

This museum is bursting with original documents and memorabilia of the great Japanese writer Mishima Yukio, including the desk at which he used to work. Mishima's major works, such as *Confessions of a Mask*, are on display.

ASCENT OF MOUNT FUJI★★
富士登山
♿ *Map, B2. fujisan-climb.jp. Climbing is authorized only between Jul 1 and mid-Sept. Take suitable clothing as the temperature is only 41°F/5°C at the top.*

Mount Fuji (12,389ft/3776m) is divided into 10 *gome*, or stations: the first, *Ichi-gome*, is at 4610ft/1405m; the second, *Ni-gome*, at 5236ft/1596m. Most climbers go straight to the fifth station, *Go-gome* (7562ft/2305m), by bus on one of the many services departing from Kawaguchiko, Fujinomiya and Gotenba stations. The 18.6mi/30km bus journey takes 50min–1hr.

🚶 There are several routes to *Go-gome* from the bottom of the mountain; the traditional one (the **Yoshida Trail**) starts at Fuji Sengen-jinja. *Allow around 5hr to reach the fifth station.* Alternatively, on the north face, the Lake Kawaguchi side, you can take the Sengen or Funatsu Trails; on the south face, the Shizuoka side, the Fujinomiya Gotenba Trail (quite challenging), or the Subashiri Trail.

From the fifth station there are just two trails, one each via the north and south faces. At the eighth station, the north-and south-face trails meet. (*Allow a 5–6hr walk from the fifth station, around another 4600ft/1400m of uneven terrain.*) Japanese climbers generally set off at around 11pm *(or before 8pm from the first station)* to reach the summit by dawn *(5am in summer).* At the top it takes about 1hr to walk around the crater *(2625ft/800m).* Allow at least 3hr to descend to the fifth station again.

ADDRESSES

🛏 STAY

HAKONE

🛏 **Hakone Tent**箱根テント – *1320-257 Gora.* ✆*0460-83-8021. hakonetent.com/en. 10 rooms. ¥10,300; dorm ¥3800 per person. ¥500* ⬛*.* ⬛*.* Excellent modern guesthouse just 2min from Gora station. Quiet rooms with blackout curtains for a good night's sleep, but also lots of events in the attractive common area. Dorms are *tatami* rooms with futons. Kitchen, good wifi and two relaxing *onsen*.

🛏 **Moto-Hakone Guest House** 元箱根ゲストハウス – *103 Moto-Hakone.* ✆*0460-83-7880. motohakone.com. 5 rooms. ¥9000.* ⬛ *(cards fine for room charge; cash only for tax).* 10min from Lake Ashi, a mini version of Fuji Hakone Guest House with the same people in charge, but guests are welcomed by their (English-speaking) friend. Pleasant and convenient, it makes a good base for the Lake Ashi area.

🛏🛏 **Choraku-so Nakaji Ryokan** 長楽荘中路旅館 – *525-58 Kowakidani.* ✆*0460-82-2192. 4 rooms. ¥11,400.* ⬛*.* A charming *ryokan* with good-sized rooms near the Open-Air Museum. The charming owner, whose energy is impressive given that she's over 90, decorates the rooms with her calligraphy. Tattoos are allowed in the *onsen*.

Fuji Hakone Guest House 富士箱根ゲストハウス – *912 Sengokuhara. ℘0460-84-6577. fujihakone.com/en. 14 rooms. ¥12,000. ¥810* . This welcoming guesthouse has four hot-spring baths, including a *rotenburo,* plus fast wifi, a kitchen, and a lounge. Best of all, it's run by the delightfully friendly, English-speaking Takahashi-san and family.

Hakone Suimeisou 箱根水明荘 – *702 Yumoto- Hakone. ℘0460-85-5381. suimeisou.com/english. 28 rooms. ¥29,000 half-board.* This modern *ryokan* situated near Hakone-Yumoto station features immaculate and spacious Japanese rooms, all with a view of the Haya River and several with a private bath *(costs extra)* on the terrace. There is also a resplendent top-floor *onsen* which has large picture windows.

Kiritani Hakone-so 桐谷箱根荘 – *1320-598 Gora. ℘0460-82-2246. kiritani-hakoneso.com. 24 rooms. ¥28,300 half-board.* . On the heights of Gora, a superb villa with an annex at the side, transformed into a *ryokan*. A splendid view of the mountain. *Onsen* and *tatami*-floored dining rooms lend it a traditional air. A very attractive place.

Fujiya Hotel 富士屋ホテル – *359 Miyanoshita. ℘0460-82-2211. fujiyahotel.jp/en. 146 rooms. ¥20,000.* Flower Palace, Kikka-so, Forest Lodge, Restful Cottage... the various buildings of this 19C hotel make up a veritable museum, blending architectural eclecticism with a colorful history. A 1hr guided tour will enable you to learn more, and follow in the footsteps of Einstein, Charlie Chaplin, and several members of Japan's Imperial Family, all of whom have stayed here.

Takumi-no-yado Yoshimatsu 匠の宿・桂松 – *521 Hakone-Machi. ℘0460-83-6661. takuminoyado.com. 19 rooms. ¥66,000 half-board.* A superb, elegantly designed *ryokan* enhanced by an internal garden and a magnificent *onsen* (you can see Mount Fuji from the *rotenburo*). Some rooms also have a Fuji view or private hot-spring bath *(costs extra).* Serves traditional Kyoto-style *kaiseki* cuisine.

OYAMA

Ryokan Asada 旅館あさだ – *594 Oyama Isehara-shi. ℘0463-95-2035. www5c. biglobe.ne.jp/~asada. 8 rooms. ¥29,800 half-board.* On Koma-sando, the street that leads to the shrines of Mount Oyama, you'll find this *ryokan* tucked away in a small garden. The meals are excellent, featuring delicious dishes based on tofu, the town's specialty.

YUGAWARA

Ryokan Fukiya ふきや旅館 – *398 Miyakami Yugawara-machi Ashigarasimo-gun. ℘0465-62-1000. yugawarafukiya.com/en/index.html. 20 rooms. ¥58,600 half-board.* A *ryokan* with refined architecture and decor. Seven types of thermal baths in various settings. Serves exceptional Japanese food.

MANAZURU

Shotokumaru しょうとく丸 – *1162-1 Manazuru-machi. ℘0465-68-1611. shoutokumaru.co.jp. ¥19,600 half-board.* Breathtaking sunrise and sunset views from the rooms. Meals feature fish and shellfish caught that morning.

AROUND MOUNT FUJI

FUJIYOSHIDA

Fujiyoshida Youth Hostel 富士吉田ユースホステル – *2-339 Shimo-Yoshida Honmachi (Map, B1). ℘0555-22-0533. www.jyh.or.jp/e/i.php?jyhno=2803. Closed Jan–Feb. ¥6800. . No meals.* A small Japanese-style guesthouse, run by an attentive and welcoming family.

KAWAGUCHIKO

Petit Hotel Ebisu-ya プチホテルエビスヤ – *3647 Funatsu (Map, B1). ℘0555-72-0165. park20.wakwak.com/~ebisuya. 8 rooms. From ¥10,500. ¥1575* . An imposing white building with red roof tiles near the exit to Kawaguchiko station. Japanese-and Western-style rooms, most with a view of Mount Fuji.

Sunnide Resortサニーデ・リゾート – *2549-1 Oishi (Map, B1). ℘0555-76-6004. www.sunnide.com/english.html. 29 rooms, 25 cottages. ¥28,000. ¥1000* .This old villa, once the property of a famous Kyushu nobleman, has views of Mount Fuji and Lake Kawaguchi. It was bought by the father of Mr Ide (hence Sunn-ide!), who opened first a restaurant and then a hotel. Today, the complex includes a *ryokan*, a renowned restaurant, and hillside cottages.

🍴 EAT

HAKONE

🔔 Few restaurants open in the evening, as most *ryokans* serve an evening meal.

🔔 **Gyoza Center** 餃子センター – 1300-537 Gora. ✆0460-82-3457. *Open Fri–Wed 11.30am–3pm & 5–8pm. Menu in English. Set menus around ¥1400.* 🍴. This simple, friendly spot is heaven for fans of *gyoza* dumplings. As well as the standard varieties, they have gingko and garlic (highly recommended), scallops, and several others, served with miso soup. The family-run store suffered a fire in 2018, but should be up and running again in sleek new premises by the time this guide goes to print.

🔔 **Hatsuhana Soba Honten** はつ花そば本店 – 635 Hakone-Yumoto. ✆0460-85-8287. *hatsuhana.co.jp. Open Thu–Tue 10am–7pm. From ¥900.* A famous heroine of last century, Hatsuhana, saved her sick husband by serving him *soba* noodles with yam paste. It happened in Hakone, in this very house, which has been full ever since. Most popular dish: *teijo soba* with yam paste, of course.

🔔🍽🍺 **Akatsuki-tei** 暁亭 – 182-4 Yumotochaya. ✆0460-85-7330. *Open Sat–Sun and public holidays 11.30am–2pm (last orders). Around ¥3300.* 🍴. *Book ahead.* A magnificent wooden building surrounded by a traditional Japanese garden. Dining rooms with clean lines and sophisticated set meals, specializing in tofu and *yuba*.

YUGAWARA

🔔🍺 **Shirako** しらこ – 1-5-15 Dohi Yugawara-machi. ✆0465-63-6363. *Open Tue–Sun 11.30am–2.30pm & 6–10pm. (last orders 1.45pm & 9pm). Lunch around ¥2000, dinner ¥5000.* A small Japanese restaurant close to the station, offering delicious, fresh fish and seafood meals.

🔔🍽🍺 **Herlequin Bis** エルルカンビス – 744-49 Miyakami-Yugawara-machi - Ashigarasimo-gun. ✆0465-62-3633. *herlequin.com. Open Thu–Tue 11.30am–1.30pm (last orders) & 6–8.30pm (last orders). Lunch menus from ¥4200, dinner ¥6500.* A charming setting amid rustling bamboo. French cuisine with a Japanese twist.

AROUND MOUNT FUJI

🔔 Around Mount Fuji the evening meal is usually eaten in the hotel or *ryokan*.

KAWAGUCHIKO

🔔 **Houtou-Fudo, Kawaguchiko-Minami-ten** ほうとう不動河口湖南店 – 1672-2 Funatsu (Map, B1). ✆0555-72-5011. *houtou-fudou.jp/english.html. Open daily 11am–7pm. From ¥1050.* A large, rustic place with *tatami* mats and low tables, where local specialty *houtou* (hot pot of udon noodles with vegetables and mushrooms) is served. You can also try *basashi* (raw horse meat) here. There are two other branches in town, all excellent.

🔔🍺 **Nagomi** 和 （なごみ） 2719-1114 Kawaguchi (Map, B1). ✆0555-76-6390. *navi-city.com/iine/nagomi. html. Open 11.30am–2.30pm & 5.30–10pm. Lunch from ¥1200.* 🍴. *Reservation required for dinner.* A small room with *tatami* mats and a view of Fuji, where you can try well-chosen, interesting dishes, such as pickled herring with soy beans, or seafood salad.

TAKING A BREAK

KAWAGUCHIKO

Tenka-chaya 天下茶屋 – 2739 Kawaguchi, Fujikawaguchikocho (Map, B1). ✆0555-76-6659. *tenkachaya.jp. Open daily 10am–5pm.* 🍴. This characterful tearoom, which is a little worn around the edges, is well known for having as one of its customers Dazai Osamu, the famous writer (◉*see p108*). Also serves hearty local dishes like *houtou*.

HAKONE

Amazake-chaya 甘酒茶屋 – 395-1 Futagoyama, Hatajuku, Ashigarashimo-gun. ✆0460-83-6418. *amasake-chaya. jp. Open daily 7am–5.30pm.* This rustic teahouse has been open for 400 years, and still offers the same menu that tempted samurai to stop by on their journeys between Kyoto and Edo. Try the *amazake* (a sweet rice drink) and delicious *chikara mochi* ("power mochi", sweet or savory sticky rice cakes).

SHOPPING

Rokuro-Kobo-Katase ろくろ工房かたせ – 103 Oshiba, Moto-Hakone. 0460-83-6405. *Open daily 10am–5pm.* For 60 years Mr Katase has been making beautiful *kokeshi* dolls (◉*see box p508*). Some are classical in style, others surprisingly contemporary, so there are dolls to suit all taste. They're also good value for hand-made items.

The Izu Peninsula ★★

伊豆半島

The Izu Peninsula is featured in Yasunari Kawabata's short story *The Izu Dancer* (1925) about a girl on a walking tour of the peninsula, which brings to life the beauty of the area. While it is true that in the 1920s the peninsula was accessible only along a network of winding tracks, as trains did not yet service the whole area, the region was nonetheless already attracting visitors, particularly from nearby Tokyo, who would come to recharge their batteries beside the glittering lakes carved directly out of the volcanic landscape. The area has been developed since then and Highway 414 winds its way across the peninsula and the famous Loop ("spiral") Bridge. Nonetheless, Izu has managed to avoid large concrete developments and has kept its old-style, traditional Japanese hotels.

SHIMODA ★★ 下田

Shimoda is an ancient site dating back to prehistoric times. Indeed, a great many remains from the Joman period

▶ **Population:** Shimoda: 21,400; Izu (Shuzenji): 30,600.

◔ **Michelin Map:** Regions of Japan Map 1, Tokyo & Surroundings p131.

▤ **Info:** See opposite.

◖ **Location:** Shizuoka prefecture, about 62mi/100km from Tokyo.

▲▲ **Kids:** The Wakano-ura and Chikurin no Komichi walks.

◔ **Timing:** Allow three days to enjoy the *onsen*.

◉ **Don't miss:** The view of Shimoda Bay; walking beside the Katsura River; treating yourself to a night in Arai Ryokan in Shuzenji (◔*see p251*).

have been found within the city limits. The town's history, however, revolves around the fact that under the terms of the **Shimoda Treaty,** signed on May 25, 1854, by Hayashi Daigaku (the plenipotentiary ambassador of the shogun government) and Commodore Matthew C. Perry of the American Navy, its port became accessible to Western powers. Despite its interesting history, it is Shimoda's physical beauty that puts it on the

Shirahama Beach, Shimoda

© Clover/Photoshot

USEFUL INFORMATION

SHIMODA – Tourist information, *1-4-28 Shimoda-shi, near the station. tic.jnto.go.jp/detail.php?id=1176. Open daily 9am–5pm.*

Shimoda International Club – A voluntary guide association *(tours around ¥200 per person)*. Email reservation required via: sicshimoda@yahoo.co.jp.

SHUZENJI – Tourist information, *Izu City Tourist Information, 341-7 Kashiwakubo. izushi.info/english/index.html.*

TRANSPORTATION

SHIMODA – BY TRAIN – From Tokyo Station, Odoriko or Superview Odoriko *(2hr 30–2hr 45min, around ¥6000)*. From Shinjuku, Superview Odoriko *(1 per day, 2hr 50min, ¥6640)*. Or shinkansen to Atami, then change for the Shimoda train.

👁 *Sit on the left on the train from Tokyo to enjoy views of the sea and the Izu coast.*

👁 *The JR Pass does not cover the Izukyu Rail-owned lines south of Ito, but some regional passes do, such as the JR Tokyo Wide Pass and most JR East passes.*

BY BICYCLE Rental – Noguchi Rent-A-Cycle, *1-3-14 Shimoda. 3min walk from the station. Open 9.30am–6pm (winter 4pm). ¥500 per hour, or ¥2000 per day.*

SHUZENJI – BY TRAIN – From Tokyo, direct Odoriko trains *(2hr 10min, ¥4500)* or change at Mishima for Shuzenji Station. For Nagoya, Izuhakone Sunzu Line to Mishima, then the Hikari shinkansen *(2hr 15min, ¥8570)*.

BY BUS – Train from Shimoda to Kawazu, then bus from Kawazu to Shuzenji *(13 per day, 1hr 30min, ¥1700)*.

---

tourist map. Situated at the southern end of the peninsula, which until recently was only accessible by boat, Shimoda's trump card is a magnificent bay, with almost tropical vegetation whose tangled roots cling to rugged contours. Nearby volcanic Mount Fuji has been on occasion a particularly noisy neighbor.

EAST OF SHIMODA

Nesugata-yama ★ 寝姿山

Take the cable car opposite Izukyu Shimoda Station (1min). 🕐*Open daily 9am–5pm.* 🎫*¥1030 round trip.*
Start by tackling Mount Nesugata (656ft/200m). The name means "sleeping posture", as apparently its shape is reminiscent of a reclining woman. From the top, you can enjoy a beautiful **view** over the town and bay.

Kaikoku Shimoda Minato
開国下田みなと

Walk 15min from the station toward the port area, crossing the Inouzawa River. This concrete building overlooking the bay hosts a Harbor Museum, covering the history of the Izu Peninsula and the town of Shimoda (🕐*open daily 9am–5pm;* 🎫*¥500)*. Below there is a color-

ful **fish market** each Sunday morning (🕐*open 8am–11am)*, and several cheap lunch spots serving delicious fish (🕐*generally 9am–1.30pm;* 🎫*¥1500)*.

Gyokusen-ji ★★ 玉泉寺

40min walk east of the station along the bay (or bus no. 10, ¥160). 🕐*Open daily 8am–5pm.* 🎫*No charge; museum ¥400.* This Zen temple housed the first American embassy for three years, before it was relocated to Tokyo. A small museum displays a collection of personal objects (china, glasses) belonging to Consul Harris, plus a model of him and Saito Okichi. Also noteworthy are a few daguerreotypes left behind by a Russian sailor and photographer, one of the first to use this photographic process invented in 1837. Above the temple, two small cemeteries face each other: one American and one Russian. They contain the tombs of sailors who were killed when a typhoon struck the *Diana*, the vessel of Russia's Admiral Putyatin, who was on a diplomatic mission to Japan. More unusual is the **milk monument**, commemorating the first official drinking of cow's milk in Japan; in the early 19C it was unknown as a drink to the vast majority of Japanese people.

FROM MAI MAI-DORI TO THE PORT

Hofuku-ji ★ 宝福寺

Mai Mai-dori, 10min from the station.
Open daily 8am–5pm. No charge;
museum ¥400.

Visitors to this temple come mainly because of its small museum and one of the tombs it contains. Both invoke the memory of **Saito Okichi** (1841–90).

At the age of 16, after two years of training to become a geisha, Okichi was forced by the shogun to become a *rashamen* ("sheep," the name given to Japanese women who took Westerners as lovers). It was thought that her great beauty would be an additional asset in the negotiations being undertaken with the US Consul General to Japan, Townsend Harris (1804–78), who was attempting to open up Japan to foreign trade.

After the treaty was signed and Harris had been assigned to other missions, Tojin Okichi, "Okichi the foreigner" as she was now called, was ostracized and began a life of wandering and alcoholism that finally ended when she drowned in the Inouzawa River. As no one claimed the body, a priest at Hofuku-ji gave her a burial, and in so doing unwittingly ensured the temple's popularity (he was in fact banished for this action). Kenji Mizoguchi, one of the first filmmakers to be interested in Okichi, made *Tojin Okichi (Mistress of a Foreigner)* in 1930. Since then, endless tributes have been paid to the woman who was so marked and ultimately destroyed by her association with a foreigner in the service of her country.

Namako Kabe ★ なまこ壁

10min walk east of the temple toward the Inouzawa River.

The walls (*kabe*) of the 13 traditional houses that remain in this part of Shimoda are clad with flat tiles, the joins sealed with rounded seams of white plaster said to resemble sea slugs (*namako* in Japanese). The advantage of arranging the tiles in this attractive, diamond-shaped cross-hatched pattern is that it doesn't allow water to collect (causing mold and damp). The plaster also helps with resistance to fire.

Shimoda History Museum ★★

下田開国博物館
Continue south down Mai Mai-dori.
Open daily 8.30am–5.30pm.
¥1200. shimoda-museum.jp.

This fascinating museum (with *namako kabe*-style walls) traces the development of the town after its encounter with Commodore Perry. A diorama shows how the port had to be adapted to meet the new steam ships' requirements for water and coal, as this type of ship had previously been almost unknown to the Japanese. It also shows how a typhoon that destroyed the Russian vessel commanded by Admiral Putyatin enabled the Russians and the Japanese to cooperate, providing each with an opportunity to learn and develop naval construction methods.

Ryosen-ji ★★ 了仙寺

At the junction of Mai Mai-dori and Perry Road, 5min from the History Museum and 15min from the station (bus no. 6, ¥160). Open daily 8.30am–5pm. ¥500; visit with English commentary (5 people or more) ¥1000. www.izu.co.jp/~ryosenji/eigo.html.

It was in this temple on May 25, 1854 that the shogun's ambassador Hayashi Daigaku and Commodore Perry signed the Treaty of Peace and Amity that was to lead to the opening of the port of Shimoda. The adjoining Museum of Treasures, run by the ebullient monk Daiei Matsui, contains more than 3000 original documents relating to this period. It's also interesting to see how Japanese artists represented the "foreign devils" who invaded their shores in the 19C. Today the temple is known as the "Hall of Opening the Nation." The temple is delightfully scented every May, when the Jasmine Flower Festival is held.

Choraku-ji ★ 長楽寺

Perry Road, 10min from Ryosen-ji.
Open 8.30am–5pm. No charge;
Treasure Museum ¥500.

The Peace Treaty between Russia and Japan was signed in this temple on October 15, 1854. Today, it's a charming, flower-filled place with a small museum

Shuzen-ji

© JTB/Photoshot

displaying a few historical souvenirs and cultural objects.

From the temple, stroll along **Perry Road** and the narrow canal lined with picturesque houses to discover the bust of Perry and the **Anchokuro**, the restaurant once run by Okichi Saito after Townsend Harris returned to America. A few traces of the original restaurant still remain inside. You can then continue on to the port.

Port and Wakano-Ura Walk★★ 下田港・和歌の浦

This pleasant walk goes round the port and then follows the shore as far as the aquarium. The path loops round a hill, where Shimoda Park is located.

SHUZENJI ★★ 修善寺

This small town was established during the Heian era. The monk Kukai (774–835), later known by the name of **Kobo Daishi**, founded the temple of Shuzen-ji after he discovered the Tokko no yu hot spring. The town of Shuzenji developed around the temple, which took on a new historical significance with the exile of **Minamoto no Yoritomo** to the Izu Peninsula in the 12C.

It was here that the man who would become the first shogun of Japan met his wife, Masako, daughter of his enemy Hojo Tokimasa. After Minamoto no Yoritomo's death, it was here that his son Yoriie was assassinated, too, with the complicity of Masako, by the man who became regent, Hojo.

The death mask

In 1203, **Minamoto no Yoriie**, 21-year-old son of the first shogun, was forced to seek refuge in the temple of Shuzen-ji; he had plotted against his maternal grandfather, the regent Hojo Tokimasa, who had removed him from power. One year later, Yoriie was assassinated. He was supposedly poisoned as he unwittingly immersed himself in a bath filled with lacquer. His contorted features are said to have been carved into his death mask that was sent to his mother (and which is now supposedly held at Shuzen-ji). Okamoto Kido (1872–1939), a talented exponent of the *torimonocho* or detective novel, turned the legend into the play *Shuzenji Monogatari* (1908) popularizing this tragic story: It was staged both at the Kabuki-za of Tokyo in 1911, and in Paris in 1927.

Chikurin no Komichi Walk with Katsura Bridge

Overcome with remorse, Masako had the temple of Shuzen-ji dedicated to her son. From then on the town became associated with this dramatic story worthy of a Shakespearean tragedy, as well as for its excellent hot springs.

The range of fine hotels frequented by top writers, especially during the Meiji Period of 1868–1912, adds to the overall appeal of the town and has put it firmly on the tourist map.

Chikurin no Komichi Walk ★★
竹林の小径
From Kaede Bridge to Katsura Bridge along the Katsura River (around 219yd/200m).

👥 Beside the Katsura River just past the bridge is a small pavilion that shelters the famous *onsen* of **Tokko no yu**, which, according to legend, appeared when Kobo Daishi struck a rock here with his *tokko* (ritual Tantric staff). The monk is said to have been touched by the sight of a child washing his father's diseased back with cold water. Since then the temperature has been a soothing 105.8°F/41°C.

Shuzen-ji ★★ 修禅寺
Opposite Tokko no yu. ⏱Open daily 8.30am–4pm. No charge; museum ¥300. shuzenji-temple.com.

The Buddhist temple around which the story of Shuzen-ji, from Kobo Dai-shi to the Hojo family, has evolved has experienced many ups and downs (the main hall has burned down on several occasions). When Hojo Soun (1432–1529) financed its reconstruction in the 15C, he placed the shrine under the protection of his cousin, the priest Ryukei Hanjoi, who belonged to the Soto Zen sect. So the temple, maintained first by the Shingon sect founded by Kukai in 807, then by the Rinzai sect from 1275, finally came under the jurisdiction of the Soto sect from 1489. It was destroyed in 1863 and rebuilt under the profoundly pro-Shinto and anti-Buddhist Meiji era.

Dating from the first period is the sculpture of the **Dainichi Nyorai** ★★ (the cosmic Buddha to whom the temple is dedicated), in Sanskrit Vairocana: "He who spreads light all around." The cosmic Buddha is the central figure of Shingon, the "True Word" in Japanese. Sculpted by Jikkei, it was commissioned by Masako for her son's seventh birthday. There are also beautiful Buddhist paintings on display, a saddle in mother-of-pearl, and of course the famous **death mask** with distorted features (ⓒ see box p249), said to be Minamoto no Yoriie's, in the adjoining **museum ★**.

Shigetsu-den ★★ 指月殿

Opposite Shuzen-ji. Cross the Katsura River and follow the signs.

In this small temple constructed entirely of wood, the oldest temple on the Izu Peninsula (13C), Minamoto no Yoritomo's wife Masako created a library of sutras (Buddhist texts) to appease her son's soul and to protect her own, since her complicity in his murder was undeniable. Next to the temple, in Genji Park at the bottom of Shikayama hill, is the grave of **Minamoto no Yoriie** (1182–1204), restored in 1703 to commemorate the 500th anniversary of his death.

ADDRESSES

🛏 STAY

SHIMODA

🛏 **Yamane Ryokan** やまね旅館 – *1-19-15 Shimoda.* ℘*0558-22-0482. www.shimoda-city.com/#we-page- home. 9 rooms. Around ¥10,000.* �　. *Reservations through the Tourist Office.* In the town center, a simple, well-kept *ryokan* run by an endearing, elderly couple who don't speak much English.

🛏🛏🛏 **Shimoda Bay Kuroshio** 下田ベイクロシオ – *4-1 Kakisaki.* ℘*0558-27-2111. baykuro.co.jp. 42 rooms. ¥20,000.* Although the exterior isn't up to much, there's a magnificent view from this *ryokan*, which has all modern conveniences. Rooms are an interesting mix of styles, with exposed concrete walls alongside *tatami* mats and bright bedspreads. Meals available.

🛏🛏🛏 **Kanaya Ryokan** 金谷旅館 – *114-2 Kochi.* ℘*0558-22-0325. 11 rooms. ¥16,000.* One of the finest *ryokan* in Japan, established in 1866, is 10min by taxi from Shimoda. Nobel Prize winner Yasunari Kawabata referers to it in his books, and the superb staircase was immortalized in the film of *The Izu Dancer*. Some rooms are surprisingly cheap, and they're attractive and well-kept, but for the full experience (including meals) you'll pay more. The *onsen* is excellent.

SHUZENJI

🛏🛏🛏🛏 **Yagyu-no-Sho** 柳生の庄 – *1116-6 Shuzenji.* ℘*0558-72-4126. yagyu-no-sho.com. 15 rooms. ¥90,500 half-board.* The Yagyu, a samurai family famous for being martial arts instructors to the Tokugawa shoguns, have created a perfect temple. No detail is left to chance, flowers are arranged by a great Ikebana professional in an *onsen* surrounded by roses. All suites have a private hot-spring bath. Adjoining *kendo dojo* (training school for fighting with bamboo swords). A truly once-in-a-lifetime stay.

🛏🛏🛏🛏 **Arai Ryokan** 新井旅館 – *970 Shuzenji.* ℘*0558-72-2007. arairyokan. net/english.* (℘*092-687-5312.) 24 rooms. ¥47,000 half-board.* If you can only stay in one *ryokan*, this should be a strong contender. Built in 1872, the hotel is a model of refinement and architectural subtlety, much of it listed. The 7C baths are outstanding. There are even organized visits for nonresidents, and a museum whih displays some of the *ryokan*'s 700 pieces in rotation.

🍴 EAT

SHIMODA

🍽 **Ra-maru** ラーマル – *Kaikoku Shimoda Minato, 1-1 Shimoda.* ℘*0558-27-2510. Open daily 10am–5pm. Around ¥1000.* This excellent American-style diner by the bay is famous for one thing: the Shimoda burger. Made with a huge piece of deep-fried *kin-medai* ("fish with golden eyes"), a chunk of brie, and a salty soy-based sauce. Delicious.

🍽🍽🍽 **Uo-Suke** 魚助 – *1-6-8 Shimoda.* ℘*0558-27-3330. Open Wed–Mon 11.30am–3pm & 5–10pm. Lunch around ¥2500, dinner ¥4000.* Bar or stylish dining room upstairs, serving a well-prepared selection of *izakaya* classics. Try the Shimoda specialty of *kin-medai.*

SHUZENJI

🍽🍽 **Bokunenjin** 朴念仁 – *3451-40 Shuzenji.* ℘*0558-73-0073. ginza-sasuga.jp/bokunenjin/index.html. Open Thu–Tue 11am–3pm. Closed 3rd Tue of every month. ¥2000.* �　. Just 7 tables in a *tatami* room, with splendid views of a river and bamboo forest. Try the soba noodles, and the deep-fried sakura shrimp.

🍽🍽 **Matsuba-chaya** 松葉茶屋 – *4281-66 Shuzenji.* ℘*0558-72-0576. Open Wed–Mon 10.30am–3pm & 5–6.30pm (last orders). Around ¥2000.* �　. The specialty here is *kamameshi*, a warming rice dish with vegetables, served in an attractive cast-iron pot.

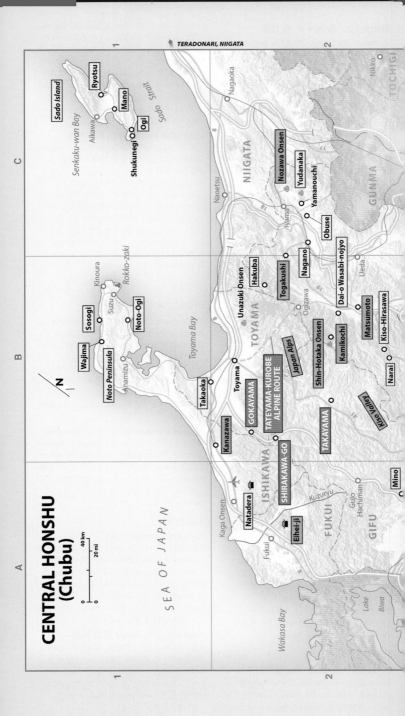

CENTRAL HONSHU (Chubu)

TERADONARI, NIIGATA

SEA OF JAPAN

N

0 ───── 40 km
0 ───── 20 ml

Wakasa Bay

Lake Biwa

FUKUI

Fukui

Eihei-ji

Natadera

Kaga Onsen

Kuzuryu

Gujo Hachiman

GIFU

Mino

ISHIKAWA

Kanazawa

SHIRAKAWA-GO

GOKAYAMA

TAKAYAMA

Kiso Valley

Narai

Kiso-Hirasawa

Matsumoto

Kamikochi

Dai-o Wasabi-noyjo

Shin-Hotaka Onsen

Japan Alps

TATEYAMA-KUROBE ALPINE ROUTE

Toyama

Takaoka

TOYAMA

Unazuki Onsen

Ogizawa

Togakushi

Nagano

Hakuba

Obuse

Yamanouchi

Yudanaka

Nozawa Onsen

NIIGATA

Iiyama

Naoetsu

Naetsu

Nagaoka

Ueda

GUNMA

Nikko

TOCHIGI

Noto Peninsula

Wajima

Sosogi

Noto-Ogi

Suzu

Kinoura

Rokko-zaki

Minamizu

Toyama Bay

Senkaku-wan Bay

Aikawa

Sado Island

Ryotsu

Mano

Ogi

Shukunegi

Sado Strait

C   **B**   **A**

1   2

252

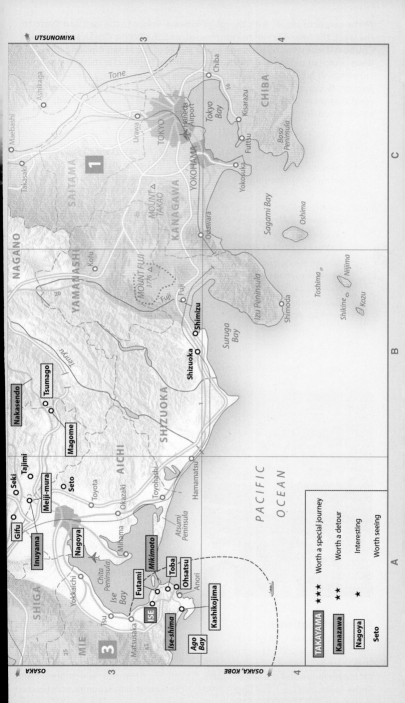

UTSUMOMIYA

PACIFIC OCEAN

TAKAYAMA ★★★ Worth a special journey
Kanazawa ★★ Worth a detour
Nagoya ★ Interesting
Seto Worth seeing

At the center of Japan, with the mega-cities of Tokyo to the east and Kyoto to the west, the Sea of Japan sea northward, and the Pacific Ocean southward, Chubu is dominated by the spectacular peaks of the Japan Alps and offers a wide choice of terrain and tourism possibilities. Popular for its ski trails, hot springs, and hiking trails, the region is a mix of great urban centers *(Nagoya, Niigata, Nagano)*, cities of history and art *(Takayama, Kanazawa)* and quaint rural villages nestling in narrow valleys. The ancient Nakasendo Road, constructed during the Edo era, still crosses the region today.

Highlights

1 The deeply spiritual atmosphere of **Ise-jingu** (p265)

2 Distinctive thatched houses of **Gokayama Valley** (p276)

3 **Zenko-ji**, home of a legendary 6C image of Buddha (p278)

4 **Matsumoto Castle**, guarding the gateway to the Japan Alps for centuries (p283)

5 The aesthetic perfection of **Kenroku-en** gardens (p296)

▶ **Population:** 23 million – Aichi, Fukui, Gifu, Ishikawa, Nagano, Niigata, Shizuoka, Toyama, and Yamanashi Prefectures.

◔ **Michelin Map:** Regional Map pp252–253, Regions of Japan Map 2.

◑ **Location:** Chubu occupies the central part of the island of Honshu: an area of 25,020sq mi/72,572sq km. The Japan Alps cut across the middle of the region, separating the northeast coast *(*Hokuriku*)* from the Pacific side (Tokai). Nagoya, with Centrair international airport, is the gateway to the region.

☺ **Don't miss:** The traditional districts of Takayama and Kanazawa; the Kiso valley; skiing at Hakuba; Nozawa Onsen; Ise shrine; Zenko-ji; Matsumoto Castle; the thatched houses of Shirakawa-go.

👪 **Kids:** The "snow monkeys" of Jigokudani Yaen-koen.

🕐 **Timing:** Allow a week for Nagoya and its region and another for a tour from Nagano to Kanazawa.

Nagoya with its castle

© peeterv/iStock

A land of contrasts

Considered Japan's "rice basket", the northern region, called Hokuriku, is a strip of land squeezed between a steep mountain range and the Sea of Japan. Snow-laden in winter, hot and humid in summer, this region is an industrial fiefdom and a place where traditional craftsmanship and sites have been preserved.

The peaks of the Japan Alps in the center of Honshu, which are among the highest in the country, often exceed 9843ft/3000m. The region's urban

Magome, Kiso Valley

© sasimotophoto/age fotostock

centers also have distinct identities: Nagoya, the fourth largest city in Japan, gave birth to Toyota Industries, whereas Nagano hosted the 1998 Winter Olympic Games. Cities like Kanazawa, once peopled with samurai and geisha, Matsumoto with its castle, Takayama, the city of carpenters with its traditional houses at the water's edge, or even the village of Gokayama, with its steeply thatched houses, their roofs reaching the ground, all leave the visitor with unforgettable memories of the history and culture of this region.

Uji Bridge, Naiku, Ise-jingu

© Sean Pavone/iStock

The Nakasendo Road

In 1603 the Tokugawa government settled at Edo (modern-day Tokyo). While in appearances granting the *daimyo* (feudal lords) autonomy, in reality they were controlled. The Tokugawa instituted a system of *sankin-kotai*, or alternating residency, so they could not grow too rich: the *daimyo* had to live every other year at Edo, and leave their wives and children there as hostages. This rule forced them to maintain a residence in the capital, a heavy financial responsibility. It was for this reason that the Nakasendo Road, connecting Kyoto and Edo and crossing the Kiso Valley in Chubu, was constantly busy with long processions of travelers.

The Tokaido Road

This ancient way also connected Kyoto and Edo, taking the coastal route to the south of the mountains, and was the most important of the Five Routes of the Edo period. There were 53 government-sanctioned stations, or *shukuba*, along the Tokaido, where travelers stopped for food and rest. This was in reference to the 53 Buddhist teachers the youth Sudhana visited in his quest for enlightenment, so that the Tokaido Road was a metaphor for his spiritual journey. These *shukuba* were later immortalized by the great *ukiyo-e* master Hiroshige in his series *The Fifty-Three Stations of the Tokaido*.

Nagoya★
名古屋

The prosperous city of Nagoya, the fourth largest in Japan, and the stronghold of the Toyota empire, has established itself as one of the most powerful engines of Japanese economic growth. From weaving looms to automobiles, by way of porcelain and *pachinko* (the pinball game was invented here), the city was the cradle of Japanese industrial capitalism at the beginning of the 20C.

A hundred years later, it is well on its way to becoming the country's second industrial hub. Badly damaged by air raids during WW II, Nagoya was recast in the Toyota company mold, a grid pattern of wide boulevards designed for cars straddled by walkways for pedestrians. Although hardly a magnet for tourists, this gray, sprawling metropolis is not lacking in leisure activities or places to visit, including an interesting castle, and an important shrine. Of the towns in the surrounding area, possible destinations for excursions are the castle town of Inuyama and various small towns specializing in traditional crafts.

SIGHTS

Around JR Nagoya Station

Virtually a city within a city, the central station of Nagoya, also known as Meieki, is used by more than a million passengers a day. Built in 1999, it is one of the largest stations in the world in surface area *(16sq mi/41sq km)*, and is teeming with shops, restaurants, and hotels. Above it are the two white **JR Towers** *(804ft/245m high)*, while below are nearly 3.5mi/6km of underground shopping arcades. Proudly ignoring the economic downturn, the surrounding area saw an explosion of new building in the early 21C: **Midland Square** *(810ft/247m)* in 2006, in front of the central exit from the station, was joined in

▸ **Population:** 2,283,000 (metropolitan region: 10.1 million) – Aichi Prefecture.

Michelin Map: Regions of Japan Map 2, Regional Map pp252–253 A3.

Location: Nagoya is on the Pacific coast, 224mi/360km west of Tokyo and 116mi/186km east of Osaka. Most of the city stretches east from its vast central station, where the JR lines (Shinkansen and others), Meitetsu and Kintetsu private lines, buses, and subways converge. The Sakura-dori subway line leads 2mi/3.5km to the east, to Hisaya-odori Park and Nagoya TV Tower. The downtown area is here, in particular Sakae, the city's nightlife center. The castle is farther north, the harbor and Atsuta-jingu to the south.

Kids: The port area; Karakuri-kan puppet museum; Meiji-mura open-air museum.

Timing: Allow one day for the city and two days for its surrounding area.

Don't miss: Tokugawa Art Museum and Port of Nagoya Public Aquarium; Inuyama Castle; Gifu crafts like Mino's paper and Seki's swords.

2007 by the **Lucent Tower** *(591ft/180m)* to the north, with its slightly curved outline; then in 2008, on the south side, by the startlingly innovative **Spiral Tower** *(558ft/170m)*. All these skyscrapers have **panoramic** bars and restaurants at the top, which are best at night.

USEFUL INFORMATION

Tourist Offices – In **Nagoya Station** *(open daily 8.30am–7pm, 052-541-4301, nagoya-info.jp/en), and in the Oasis 2 complex, basement level (open daily 10am–8pm, 052-963-5252).*
Nagoya International Center – *1-47-1 Nagono, Nakamura-ku, 3F Kokusai Center Bldg, on Sakura-dori. 7min walk from Nagoya Station. Open Tue–Sun 9am–7pm. 052-581-0100. nic-nagoya.or.jp/en.* Information in English (newspapers, TV), library, wifi.

TRANSPORTATION

BY PLANE – **Centrair** *(www.centrair.jp)* – **Nagoya International Airport** is on an artificial island in Ise Bay, 28mi/45km to the south, linking Chubu with other Japanese regions and international destinatons. The Meitetsu train line connects the airport to Nagoya Station *(30min, ¥890–1250).*
BY TRAIN – **Nagoya Station** – Numerous Nozomi or Hikari shinkansen to Kyoto *(35min, ¥5170),* Osaka *(50min, ¥5940),* and Tokyo *(1hr 50min, ¥10,560).* Limited Express trains to and from Nagano *(3hr, ¥6930),* Matsumoto *(2hr, ¥5610),* Takayama *(2hr 30min, ¥5610),* and Kanazawa *(3hr, ¥6930).*
BY BUS – **From Tokyo** – roughly hourly buses with the companies **Keio, Meitetsu,** and **Willer** *(5–6hr journey time, ¥2500–6000).* There are also buses to Kyoto and Osaka, and destinations in Chubu.

GETTING AROUND

BY SUBWAY – Very practical, with 6 lines serving the city. Tickets ¥210–330. There is a day pass *(¥600),* which also includes the bus. Signs in English.
BY BUS – The **Me-guru** tourist bus leaves once or twice every hour *(weekends every 20–30min, no service Mon)* from the bus terminal opposite Nagoya Station *(stop no. 8)* and serves the city's main tourist attractions, including the **Castle** and **Tokugawa Art Museum,** but not the harbor. *¥210 per journey or ¥500 for a 1-day pass.*

Noritake Garden ノリタケの森
Subway Kamejima. 10min walk north of the station. Museum and craft center open Tue–Sun 10am–5pm. Museum no charge, craft center ¥500. www.noritake.cojp/mori.

A center of ceramic production for centuries, the Nagoya region is today responsible for almost 90 percent of the exports of Japanese porcelain, of which the Noritake company, founded in 1904, is the country's biggest manufacturer. The site of the company's first factory is now a museum displaying some fine old pieces in Art Deco style, and also houses a studio where you can see and even try (from ¥1800) the techniques of painting on porcelain, which are still used today. There is, of course, a shop on the way out.

Toyota Commemorative Museum of Industry and Technology

トヨタ産業技術記念館
545yd/500m north of Noritake Garden. Subway Kamejima. Open Tue–Sun 9.30am–5pm (last admission 4.30pm);

Pachinko fever

Lined up in serried ranks, like bees in a hive, the solitary *pachinko* players are glued to their machines amid the flashing lights and incredible din of the pachinko parlors. Invented in Nagoya in the 1930s, *pachinko* is now ranked third in the Japanese leisure economy, after restaurants and tourism, with well over 10,000 *pachinko* parlors in the country. Nearly a quarter of all Japanese people—students, white collar workers, housewives, retired people—are said to play regularly, many of them addicts who spend whole days frittering away their wages. Being only just within the law (with a few exceptions, gambling is forbidden in Japan), *pachinko* is often accused of benefiting organized crime and even the North Korean regime, which is said to control much of the industry.

free English tours 2pm & 3.15pm. ≋¥500. www.tcmit.org/english.
The largest company in Japan and the world leader in automobile manufacture, the car giant Toyota owes its growth to an original and highly successful system of production based on the avoidance of the three forms **waste** *(muda, mura, muri)* that was perfected by its founder Toyoda Sakichi in the 1920s. He began by making the first sewing machines in Japan before investing in the burgeoning automobile industry. The museum, which occupies the former Toyota factory, traces the history of the business, from its beginnings to the present day.

Nagoya Castle★ 名古屋城

Subway Shiyakusho. ◑*Open 9am–4.30pm (dungeon 4pm); free English tour daily 1pm.* ≋¥500. www.nagoyajo.city.nagoya.jp.
Originally a fortified town on the Tokaido road linking Edo and Kyoto, Nagoya grew up around its castle, built in 1612 on the orders of the shogun Tokugawa Ieyasu for his ninth son Yoshinao. The citadel included a five-story keep, its roof proudly adorned with two gold dolphins *(kinshachi)*. The residence of the Owari branch of the Tokugawa until 1868, it was one of the best-preserved castles in Japan, but was unfortunately destroyed by bombs in 1945. The 151ft/46m-high **keep** was rebuilt in 1959 in a faithful replica of the original, although it is now made of reinforced concrete and an elevator takes you to the top, from where you can enjoy a fine **view** of the city.
The old wooden buildings of **Honmaru Palace**, which once stood beneath the keep, has been carefully reconstructed using authentic tools and techniques. This palace once houses, among other things, the magnificent Kano School painted screens and *fusuma*. To the east, the former castle grounds are home to the beautiful **Ninomaru Garden**, which is particularly attractive when the cherry trees are in blossom. You can see a Tea Ceremony in the pavilion.

Tokugawa Art Museum★★ 徳川美術館

Subway Ozone, exit 3, 10min walk. ◑*Open Tue–Sun 10am–5pm (last admission 4.30pm).* ◑*Closed Dec 15–Jan 3.* ≋¥1400, or ¥1550 with garden. tokugawa-art-museum.jp/en.
Located in a former private residence from the 1930s, this museum houses the family treasures of the Owari branch of the Tokugawa shoguns, especially those bequeathed by Tokugawa Ieyasu and his son Yoshinao. The collections, displayed in rotation, comprise more than 10,000 pieces, some 60 of which are classified as either National Treasures or Important Cultural Properties.
Among them are many samurai helmets, swords and pieces of armor, lacquerware, pottery, and other instruments connected with the Tea Ceremony, calligraphic scrolls and precious screens, and costumes and masks from the Noh theater. The museums greatest treasures are the 12C **painted scrolls★★★** *(emaki)* illustrating the *Tale of Genji*, the masterpiece of Japanese literature (◑ *see p348*). These fragile works are only on public show for one week a year, in November. For the rest of the year, they are replaced by facsimiles and video images. It's also worth spending some time in the museum's small, attractive garden, **Tokugawa-en**.

Atsuta-jingu★ 熱田神宮

3mi/5km south of the downtown area. Subway Jingu-Nishi, then 5min walk east. ◑*Daily 24hr; Treasure Hall daily 9am–4.30pm.* ◑*Last Wed & Thur every month. Shrine* ≋*no charge, Treasure Hall* ≋¥500. atsutajingu.or.jp/en.
Dedicated to the sun goddess Amaterasu (here called Atsuta-no-Okami), Atsuta-jingu is, after Ise and Izumo, the **third most venerated shrine in Japan,** visited by 9 million worshippers every year. Quite close in its architecture to Ise Shrine, it was rebuilt in 1955 after having burned down during the war.
According to the old chronicles, Atsuta-jingu was founded in the year 86 to house the sword of Amaterasu's brother, the *kami* (Shinto deity residing in trees,

rocks and other natural phenomena) Susano-o. It was thanks to this magic sword—known as *Kusanagi-no-tsurugi* (Grass-Cutting Sword), and as legendary in Japan as Excalibur in Britain—that Prince Yamato-takeru, the son of the 12th Emperor, was able to defeat his enemies. It is one of the Three Sacred Treasures symbolizing the legitimacy of the imperial throne, along with the jewel in the Imperial Palace in Tokyo and the mirror in Ise Shrine (♿ *see p265*). Hidden away in the main temple, it cannot be seen by mere mortals, who have to make do with the **Treasure Hall**'s displays of paintings, *bugaku* (dance) masks, pottery, and blades. At the entrance to the **wooded grounds**—a pleasant oasis of greenery—stands a magnificent, giant camphor tree dating from the 11C.

👥 Nagoya Port★ 名古屋港

Subway Nagoyako, exit 3, then 7min walk. Founded a century ago, this is one of the country's largest industrial ports. It stretches to the south of the city over a vast area partly reclaimed from the sea. Part of the port has been developed for tourists, and the area in and around here includes a number of **attractions**. Of most interest is the **"Fuji" Antarctic Museum** (◉*Open Tue–Sun 9.30am–5pm.* ✆¥300). Now at anchor in a dock in the port, this vessel was involved in a number of Antarctic expeditions between 1965 and 1983—328ft/100m long, and weighing 5200 tons, it could break up to 31.5in/80cm of ice. Life on board is realistically reconstructed, with costumed mannequins in the machine rooms, canteen, officers' mess, infirmary, and dormitories, and a moving floor as if at sea. A small museum traces the history of Japanese exploration in the South Pole. The **Maritime Museum**, meanwhile, gives more context about Nagoya's importance as a port.

Port of Nagoya Public Aquarium★★ –

◉*Open Dec–Mar Tue–Sun 9.30am–5pm; Jul 21–Aug 31 & Golden Week (end Apr–beg May) 9.30am–8pm, rest of the year 9.30am–5.30pm.* ✆¥2,030; ¥1,010 under 15; ¥500 under 4. www.nagoyaaqua.com/

english. . Opened in 1992 and enlarged in 2001, this is one of the largest aquariums in Japan, and probably the best. Its high-tech wizardry is extremely impressive, as well as admirably educational. The concept is that of an ocean voyage from the Sea of Japan to the Antarctic, by way of the Great Barrier Reef in Australia. Among the high points of the visit are: a hologram showing how land mammals evolved into cetaceans 50 million years ago; an artificial beach where sea turtles lay their eggs; a pool of 140 penguins, with snow falling as if on an ice floe; the enchanting underwater ballet of a shoal of 20,000 sardines; an Imax theater.

SC Maglev and Railway Park ★★
リニア鉄道館

Kinjofuto Station. ◉*Open Mon & Wed–Sun 10am–5.30pm (daily in Golden Week & mid-July–Aug).* ✆¥1000; driving simulators ¥100–500. museum. jr-central.co.jp/en.

Right at the south of Nagoya's dockland area, the SC Maglev and Railway Park is full of fascinating insights into Japan's famous railways. As well as examples of several different types of train (including the very impressive Maglev models), there are detailed dioramas with tiny trains shooting through, plus simulators for driving conventional trains or shinkansen. These are so popular they're by lottery only; drop your entry ticket in as soon as possible.

A helpful English audioguide is ¥500, or you can download a free smartphone app with English descriptions.

EXCURSIONS
♿*Regional Map.*

Seto 瀬戸

♿*Map, A3. 12.5mi/20km northeast of Nagoya. From Sakae-machi Station (in front of Sakae subway station), take the Meitetsu-Seto Line to Owari-Seto Station (35min, ¥460).*

In the 12C, Seto was the great center of Japanese **ceramics**. Its potters adapted Chinese forms to Japanese tastes, thus creating a specifically national style and establishing such a strong association between the town and the production of ceramics that the word *setomono* (objects from Seto) came to be used as the generic term for all ceramics, pottery, porcelain, and earthenware. Today, the town is trying to give a new impetus to an industry that has been in decline but still employs a third of its population. As techniques have evolved, new applications have been found to take advantage of ceramics' insulating properties—it is now used in the components for cell phones, computers, and semiconductors.

The town has several museums, as well as many workshops, where visitors can try their hand at pottery.

Seto Gura Museum – ○*Open daily 9am–6pm (last admission 5.30pm).* ⌾¥520. This large complex near the station *(on the other side of the river)* was built for Expo 2005. On three floors, it presents a large-scale reconstruction of Seto before the war, when the porcelain industry was still working at full stretch. There are old coal-fired ovens, trams, and period houses. The museum traces the history of Seto ceramics over the past 13 centuries. In the tearoom, you can choose a cup for your tea from a collection of valuable pieces.

Inuyama★★ 犬山
⌾*Map, A3. 15.5mi/25km north of Nagoya. From Nagoya Station, take the Meitetsu Line to Inuyama (35min, ⌾¥570). Tourist Office in the station (○open daily 9am–5pm; ℘0568-61-6000; inuyama.gr.jp). For the castle, get off at the next station (Inuyama-yuen), farther north, near the Kiso River.*

This sleepy little town on the banks of the Kiso River, in the northwest of Aichi prefecture, has the oldest castle in Japan. Its picturesque alleyways, temples, and shrines, and the nearby Meiji-mura are well worth a day's excursion. From June to mid-October, demonstrations of **cormorant fishing** take place on the Kiso River, around 1pm every day and from 7pm every evening.

Visitors can watch while dining on board flat-bottomed boats *(2hr30min, depar-*

tures around 11am and 5pm, reservation recommended, ℘*0568-61-2727;* ○*see box on p262).*

Inuyama Castle★★ 犬山城 – *10min walk west of Inuyama-yuen station.* ○*Open daily 9am–5pm.* ⌾¥550. *inuyama-castle.jp.* Designated a National Treasure, Inuyama Castle stands on a small hill, commanding a magnificent **view** of the Kiso River, Mount Ena, and Nobi Plain. It was built in 1537 by Oda Yojiro Nobuyasu, the uncle of Oda Nobunaga, who united the whole of Japan.

Its white keep, in the squat, sober Momoyama style *(four floors, 62ft/19m),* surrounded by a balcony and topped by an elegant roof with curved, turned-up edges, has miraculously survived civil wars, fires, and earthquakes. This makes it Japan's oldest surviving castle, though parts have of course been extensively renovated over the years. Inside, a rough-hewn central pillar, shiny with the patina of centuries, supports the whole structure. Belonging to the Naruse clan until the Meiji era, the castle was once surrounded by pavilions and turrets, which have not survived.

At the foot of the castle hill stretches the elegant Japanese garden of **Urakuen★** (○*open Mar–Nov 9am–5pm (Jul 15–Aug 9am–6pm), Dec–Feb 9am–4pm,* ⌾¥1000, tea ¥500) planted with maples, camellias, and bamboo. There are several tea houses including the **Jo-an★**, designated a National Treasure. This tiny pavilion, made of adobe and rice paper, is no bigger than three *tatami* mats—its sober simplicity is true to the spirit of austerity associated with the world of tea. It was Oda Nobunaga's younger brother, the warlord Oda Uraku (1547–1621), who, on retiring to devote himself to his passion for tea, built this small pavilion in the precincts of the Kennin-ji in Kyoto, in 1618. It was moved here in 1972.

♟♟ Karakuri-kan museum からくり展示館 – *On Honmachi, the street south of the castle.* ○*Open daily 9am–5pm.* ⌾¥100. *inuyama-castle.jp.* This small museum, which displays wooden puppets from the Edo period, is a real

delight. On Fridays and Saturdays, the last puppetmaker in the town comes here to give demonstrations.

👤👥 Meiji-mura★ 博物館明治村
4.5mi/7km east of Inuyama. Bus (every 30min, journey time 20min, ¥430) from Inuyama Station. ℘0568)-67- 0314.
🕐*Open daily: Mar–July, Sept & Oct 9.30am–5pm; Aug 10am–5pm; Nov 9.30am–4pm; Dec–Feb 10am–4pm.*
🕐*Irregular closures; check website.*
🎫*¥1700, children ¥600. meijimura.com.*
This open-air museum, located in a 247-acre/100ha park, contains 67 public and private buildings dating from the Meiji era (1868–1912), scattered around a lake. The brick, stone, or painted wood buildings come from Nagasaki and Kobe, and include offices, a Kabuki theater, banks, gothic churches, and villas with Victorian turrets. There are also some steam locomotives and old trams ferrying visitors across the grounds (not covered by entry fee). Not to be missed are the façade and lobby of Tokyo's **Imperial Hotel**, designed by Frank Lloyd Wright in 1923. He also designed the furniture used in the cafe.

Tajimi 多治見
🕐*Map, A3. 23.5mi/38km northeast of Nagoya (Gifu-ken). Access: JR Chuo Honsen Line (20–40min, 🎫¥680–1970).*
Like Seto, this town *(population 110,000)* specializes in **ceramics**, and a number of workshops are open to visitors. The best known is the **Kobei Kiln★★** *(10min by bus from the station, Minami Ichinokura stop;* 🕐*open daily 9 or 10am–5pm;* 🎫*¥300; koubei-gama.co.jp)*. Housed in a magnificent Edo period residence, it showcases the works of the Kato family, potters for seven generations, particularly those of **Kato Takuo**, father of the current master, whose output, influenced by ancient Persian art, earned him the title of Living National Treasure. The unusual **Ichinokura Sakazuki Art Museum** *(*🕐*open Wed–Mon 10am–5pm;* 🎫*¥400, sakazuki.or.jp)* is devoted to sake cups. During the Meiji era, Tajimi produced almost 80 percent of the sake cups in Japan, and over 1500 are on dis-

play here. The upper floor has cups for the tea ceremony made by the principal Living National Treasures of Japanese pottery. The museum also offers pottery experiences *(mosaic tiles from* 🎫*¥880, 2hr course with Kato Kohei* 🎫*¥3300)*.
Also worth a look is the **Tajimi Mosaic Tile Museum★** *(*🕐*open Tue–Sun 9am–5pm;* 🎫*¥300, mosaictile-museum. jp)*, with displays on this local industry and a workshop where you can make your own tiles. The biggest draw is the building, a huge clay structure which looks like it emerged from the ground, designed by Fujimori Terunobu.

Gujo Hachiman★★ 郡上八幡
🕐*Map, A2. 47mi/75km north of Nagoya. 1hr 40min by bus from Nagoya Station (2 daily; ¥2260).*
Gujo Hachiman is famous for its pure waters, which underpin its renowned sake and *ai-zome* (indigo dyeing) industries. In modern times, the town has also become Japan's leading producer of the food models you see in restaurant windows around the country. Try your hand at *ai-zome* at **Watanabe Dyehouse★** *(*🕐*open daily 10am–5pm; 2hr experience* 🎫*¥15,000; gujozome.jp)*, and making food models at many shops around town, such as **Sample Kobo** *(*🕐*open daily 9 or 9.30am–5pm; experiences from* 🎫*¥990; samplekobo.com)*.
Visit in summer if possible, for the lively **Gujo Odori★★**. Every night from mid-July to September, locals take to the streets to dance and sing in full costume. You can learn more (and practice the steps) at the **Hakurankan museum** *(*🕐*open daily 9am–5pm;* 🎫*¥520; gujo-hachiman.com/e_gujohaku)*.

Mino★ 美濃
🕐*Map, A2. 25mi/40km north of Nagoya. 1hr 30min by bus from Nagoya Station (hourly; ¥1260).*
Famous since the 8C for the production of traditional Japanese *washi* **paper**, this small town (population 21,000) retains a historic center dating from the early Edo period (17C). Its two parallel main streets are lined with superb merchant houses; to demonstrate their wealth, merchants

Fishing, Gifu-style

Though cormorant fishing (ukai) goes back 1300 years in Gifu, only six families now practice it. Fathers hand down to sons the privilege granted by the Imperial Household Agency, the fish caught at the season's start being served at the Emperor's table.

The long, wooden fishing boats set off at nightfall, the light of burning braziers hanging from the front attracting the fish. Two assistants navigate while the usho, the master fisherman, stands handling his team of 10 to 12 cormorants; traditionally he wears a black linen cloth and a hat, a navy blue kimono, and a skirt of braided rice straw. The trained birds, held on lashes, dive and capture in their beaks small, shiny fish similar to trout, called ayu. Metal rings on the cormorants' necks prevent them from swallowing their prey. The birds are pulled out of the water and their necks squeezed until they regurgitate the ayu; unsurprisingly, there is much debate surrounding this historic practice from the point of view of animal welfare

The season lasts from May 11-October 15 and takes place daily from 7.30pm (except during heavy rain or when the moon is full) in the clear waters of the Nagara River, 1.25 miles (2km) north of Gifu Station, near Nagarabashi Bridge. *From the station, take bus no. 11 to the quay where boats take out tourists. Buy Tickets at kiosks on the quay and in the hotels nearby, or reserve in advance from the Cormorant Fishing Boat Office (✆058-262-0104, www.gifucvb.or.jp/en/01_sightseeing/01_01.html). ¥3,400 for ~2hr30min, ¥6,000 with dinner on board.*

added lavish *udatsu* (earthenware roof struts), like those on the **Imai family residence** (🕐open daily 9am–4.30pm; 🎟¥300), a former *washi* paper wholesaler (now a museum).

The Akari festical, celebrating *washi* by lighting up historic streets with paper lanterns, is held each year on the second weekend in October. You can see some of the artistic creations year-round at the **Mino-washi Akari Art Gallery**(🕐open Wed–Mon 9am–4 or 4.30pm; 🎟¥200).

Seki 関

🚶Map, A3. 31mi/50km north of Nagoya. 1hr 20min by bus from Nagoya Station (hourly; ¥1060).

The capital of Japanese **sword** (katana) manufacturing, this little town has been producing the country's finest blades for eight centuries. In the Muromachi era (1338–1573), Seki had nearly 300 master swordsmiths, providing weapons for the greatest samurai in Japan. Today, there are still 18 of them, licensed to make 24 swords a year each, but the town mainly produces kitchen knives, razors, and scissors. To visit Marusho Kogyo forge, a reservation is required, direct from the forge (✆0575-22-0259, marusho-kogyo.jp/en).

The **Seki Traditional Swordsmith Museum** (5min walk from Hamono-kaikan-mae station; 🕐open Wed–Mon 9am–4.30pm; 🎟¥300) focuses on the history and techniques of sword making in Seki and development of the cutlery industry, with a monthly demonstration (first Sun, except Jan & Oct; 🎟¥300).

The **Seki Hamono Museum★** (10min walk from Akatsuchisaka bus stop; 🕐open daily 8.30am–5pm; 🎟no charge; hamonoyasan.com) has displays on how Seki's blades are created, and a small clear-walled demonstration forge. There are various experiences available, too (🎟¥6810 for 2hr; bit.ly/hamonoya).

Gifu★ 岐阜

🚶Map, A3. 22mi/35km north of Nagoya. 18min by train on the JR Tokaido Line (¥470) or 30min on the Meitetsu Line (¥550). Tourist Office (🕐open daily 9am–8pm) on Level 2 of the JR station. Formerly a staging post on the Nakasendo road, Gifu grew up beside its castle, south of the Nagara River. An earthquake in 1891 and the air raids of 1945 destroyed much of the town's heritage, but it still produces quality handicrafts and attracts crowds of tourists each summer for the cormorant fishing.

Gifu Castle – *Bus from the station to Gifu-koen-mae. A cable car (☎¥1080 round trip, or ¥900 for summer night viewings) goes to the top.* ⏰*Open daily: mid-Mar–mid-May 9.30am–5.30pm; mid-May–mid-Oct 8.30am–5.30pm (extended hours in summer for night viewing); mid-Oct–mid-Mar 9.30am–4.30pm.* ☎¥200. Gifu-jo was built as a fort in 1203 at the top of Mount Kinka *(formerly Mount Inaba; 1079ft/329m)*, but fell into the hands of Oda Nobunaga's clan in the 16C, and was finally destroyed in the early 17C. This modern reconstruction of the castle is worth a visit for the lovely **view** over Nobi Plain—on a clear day, you can see all the way to Nagoya.

Ozeki Lantern Factory – *6mi/1km south of Gifu-koen.* ⏰*Open Mon–Fri 9am–5pm.* ☎*No charge. ozeki-lantern.com.* Gifu's specialties are oil-paper umbrellas *(wagasa)* and *washi* or silk paper lanterns *(chochin)*, hand mounted on a slender framework of bamboo. For more than a century, this workshop has been producing the best lanterns in the town; it has more than 600 examples on display, some painted with landscapes or traditional patterns, others with more contemporary designs by Isamu Noguchi.

ADDRESSES

🏠 STAY

NAGOYA

😐😐 **Hotel Palace Nagoya** ホテルパレス名古屋 – *3-10-6 Taiko, Nakamura-ku.* ☎*052-452-7000. palace-nagoya.jp. 100 rooms. ¥10,450. ¥1100* 🍴. This business hotel is good value for money. A shuttle bus from Nagoya Station is available.

😐😐 **Nagoya Flower Hotel Part II** 名古屋フラワーホテルPART II – *5-6 Takehashi, Nakamura-ku.* ☎*052-451-2200. www.flowerhotel.co.jp/menu.html. 78 rooms. ¥9800. ¥400* 🍴. Well-maintained business hotel just 6min the station on foot. Only single and semi-double room types, though.

INUYAMA

😐 **Inuyama International Youth Hostel** 犬山国際ユースホステル – *162-1 Himuro, Tsugao, 1.2mi/2km from the castle.* ☎*0568-61-1111. jyh.gr.jp/inuyama. 27 rooms. ¥7800.*

¥750 🍴*, dinner from ¥1500.* 🍴. Modern hostel, with private rooms instead of dorms, in Japanese and Western style.

GUJO HACHIMAN

😐😐 **Nakashimaya** 中嶋屋 – *940 Shinmachi.* ☎*057-565-2191. nakashimaya.net. 8 rooms. ¥16,500. ¥1650* 🍴. Venerable ryokan in the heart of town, with a couple of lovely hot spring baths. The traditional breakfast is served in your room.

🍴 EAT

NAGOYA

😐😐 **Yabaton Honten** 矢場とん本店 – *3-6-18 Osu, Naka-ku.* ☎*052-252-8810. english.yabaton.com. Open daily 11am–9pm. Menu in English. Set meals from ¥1800.* 🍴. Pork is the specialty of the house, especially *miso-katsu* (pork topped with miso sauce).

😐😐😐 **Atsuta Houraiken** あつた蓬莱軒 – *503 Godo-cho, Atsuta-ku.* ☎*052-671-8686. houraiken.com. Open Thu–Tue 11.30am–2pm & 4.30pm–8.30pm. Closed 2nd & 4th Thu in month. Menu in English. Set meals from ¥3900.* Near the entrance to Atsuta shrine, this restaurant has been serving the legendary *hitsumabushi*, a delicious local eel dish, since the 1870s.

😐😐😐 **Torigin Honten** 鳥銀本店 – *3-14-22 Nishiki.* ☎*052-973-3000. torigin.co.jp. Open daily 5pm–midnight. Set meals from ¥4800.* 🍴. Restaurant specializing in Nagoya *cochin* chicken, served in every way possible: from the spurs to the comb, grilled or raw.

INUYAMA

😐😐😐 **Okumuratei** 奥村邸 – *395 Higashi-koken.* ☎*056-865-2447. f-narita.com. Open Wed–Mon 11am–3pm & 5.30–9pm. Set lunches from ¥2500, dinners from ¥4500. Reservation required for evening.* This splendid Edo-period house (1842) once belonged to a kimono merchant. Chef Kazuo Narita trained in French cuisine, hence the Franco-Japanese menu, featuring Marseilles-style bouillabaisse side by side with filet mignon à-la-Narita.

TAJIMI

😐 **Pizza Moon** ピッツァ・ムーン – *6-30-1 Ichinokura.* ☎*057-221-3353. moon-t-f.com. Open Mon–Fri 11am–5pm, Sat–Sun 11am–9pm. Lunch sets from ¥1350, dinners from ¥3500.* This friendly Italian taverna serves delicious wood-fired pizzas, as well as pasta and other options.

Ise-shima★★
伊勢・志摩

The Ise-Shima National Park covers most of the Shima Peninsula. It's best known for Ise Shrine, the most sacred building in Shintoism, which is dedicated to the sun goddess Amaterasu, mythical ancestor of the Imperial dynasty. An unusual feature of this shrine is that it is torn down and rebuilt every 20 years. A UNESCO World Heritage Site since 2004, it attracts more than 6 million visitors a year. The peninsula is home to other historic sites such as the two "wedded rocks," the Meoto-iwa. The town of Toba is famous for its female free-divers, the *ama*, and its cultured pearls. Farther south, along the magnificent jagged coastline of Ago Bay, is a multitude of islands, inlets, and promontories.

BACKGROUND

A mythical origin – Ise Shrine, and more particularly the Naiku, is believed to house the sacred mirror of the sun goddess Amaterasu, which is, with the sword and the jewel, one of the Three Sacred Treasures of the Imperial throne. A symbol of Amaterasu, the mirror is a reminder of the time when the gods lured her from the cave into which she had shut herself (in protest at her brother's actions), by arousing her curiosity with dancing and laughter. Amaterasu gave the mirror to her grandson Ninigi when he descended to rule the earth. It then passed to Jinmu, the first Japanese Emperor, the goddess's great-great-grandson.

According to the old chronicles, worship of Amaterasu was originally celebrated in the Imperial Palace, but was then transferred to Ise by Yamatohime, daughter of the 11th Emperor Suinin, in the year 4. But the actual date of Ise's foundation is more likely to have been later, somewhere around 478.

Imperial links – Ise Shrine has always been closely associated with the Imperial dynasty. An Imperial princess

▶ **Population:** Ise town: Population 127,800 – Mie Prefecture.

Michelin Map: Regions of Japan Map 2. Regional Map p252–3 A3.

▶ **Location:** The town of Ise is 62mi/100km south of Nagoya ; its main station is Ise-shi (Kintetsu and JR lines). Ise-jingu is divided into two large shrine compounds: Geku (10 minutes' walk from the station), and Naiku, (3.5mi/6km farther on) which can be reached by bus. The Kintetsu Line continues to Toba and then Kashikojima on Ago Bay.

🕐 **Timing:** Ideally allow two or three days, including a night in Toba.

Don't miss: The Naiku section of Ise-jingu; the *ama* divers near Toba.

has held the office of high priestess of Ise (*Saio*) since ancient times. The present holder is Emperor Naruhito's sister, Kuroda Sayako.

Although today Shintoism and the State are officially separated, Ise remains a place where religion, national sentiment, and politics are inextricably linked. The Emperor has a strong connection with Ise-jingu. For example, on his official travels, he is careful never to sit with his back turned to the shrine. In his palace in Tokyo, he symbolically grows rice and sends an envoy to Ise once a year to present the harvest to the goddess Amaterasu.

Despite these strong links to the Imperial Family, the popularity of Ise originates less in veneration of the Emperor than it does in the tradition of great pilgrimages, which developed in particular from the 16C. During the Edo period (1603–1867), Ise-jingu attracted millions of the faithful.

USEFUL INFORMATION

Tourist Offices – In **Ujiyamada Station** (Kintetsu Line), 5min from **Ise-shi** Station (open daily 9am–5.30pm; ℘0596-23-9655). Additional office at the entrance to the **Geku** (open daily 8.30am–5pm; ℘0596-23-3323).

TRANSPORTATION

BY TRAIN – Two lines link **Nagoya** with **Ise-shi**: Kintetsu (1hr 20min–1hr 40min, ¥1470–2810) and JR (1hr 30min, ¥2040). The same lines go on to Toba, but only the Kintetsu continues to Kagoshima and **Ago Bay**. From **Ise-shi**, Kintetsu also connects with **Kyoto** (2hr) and **Osaka-Nanba** (1hr 45min).
BY BUS – The **CAN Bus**, which leaves from Ise-shi station, loops between the Ise sites (**Geku, Naiku**), **Futami** and **Toba** (1-day pass ¥1000).

ISE 伊勢

ISE-JINGU★★★ 伊勢神宮

The Grand Shrine of Ise comprises two large compounds containing an inner shrine, the Naiku, and an outer shrine, the Geku. In addition, there are more than 100 small shrines scattered throughout the town and the surrounding area. A tour of the shrines normally starts with the Geku, but the Naiku is the more interesting of the two.

Naiku★★★ 内宮

From Ise-shi Stationor Ujiyamada Station, take bus nos. 51 or 55 to Naiku (15min, ¥440). ⏱*Open daily: Jan–Apr & Sept 5am–6pm; May–Aug 5am–7pm; Oct–Dec 5am–5pm.* ⬤*No charge. isejingu.or.jp.*

The inner shrine (also called Kotai-jingu, and dedicated to Amaterasu) lies in a forest of giant cedars, camphor trees, and cypresses that covers 13,591 acres/5500ha. Visitors enter via the 330ft/100m-long **Uji Bridge** over the clear waters of the Isuzu River. This bridge is also rebuilt every 20 years. The path turns right and leads across a landscape garden to the **Temizusha**, a

pool where the faithful wash their hands and mouth, a symbol of the purification of both body and mind. Others perform their ablutions on the river bank.

The members of the Imperial household and the clergy have special halls, the **Saikan** (purification hall) and the **Anzaisho** (hall for visitors from the Imperial household), between the great gates (*torii*) that mark the entrance to the sacred precinct. A wide stone staircase then leads to the edge of the inner sanctum, which only the Emperor, the Empress, and religious dignitaries are allowed to enter.

The crowd has to be content with looking on from behind a fence at the the white silk curtain concealing the entrance. It is a simple rectangular wooden building, raised on piles, with a thatched roof and two crossed beams at either end known as *chigi*. Beside the building is an empty space marked out by white pebbles indicating where the old shrine was (and where the next one will be built in 2033, for the 63rd time). As many as 10,000 trees more than 200 years old are needed to rebuild the Naiku and the Geku.

Ancient and modern

Every 20 years since the 7C, the two shrines of Ise have been demolished and rebuilt in their original form. A number of explanations have been put forward as to the origin of this costly ritual known as *Shikinen Sengu*, including the Shinto emphasis on rituals of purification and regeneration. Perhaps the fact that 20 years is about the time that their thatched roofs would normally last plays a part, or it may be that it is a way of ensure building techniques are passed on from one generation to the next. Whatever the answer, eternally renewed and yet always the same, Ise Shrine embodies both the ephemeral and the eternal. The next rebuilding ceremony will take place in 2033.

Oharai-machi★ – During the Edo period, the pilgrimage to Ise was so popular that it gave rise to a number of pleasure districts in the surrounding areas, where dances and purification rituals also took place. "There is so much business going on here that the noise is tremendous," a Japanese author wrote as early as the 17C. "Money flows like water, without a moment's pause." The area of bustling streets on the approach to the Naiku is called Oharai-machi. They are lined with traditional businesses, tea houses, restaurants, and shops selling local handicrafts.

Geku★★ 外宮

5min walk from Ise-shi station, on the CAN Bus Geku-Naiku loop.

Officially known as Toyouke Dai-jingu, the outer shrine is dedicated to Toyouke-no-omikami, goddess of agriculture and industry, protector of harvests and the home. Symbolically, it is she whose task it is to offer Amaterasu and the other *kami* the sacred food that the priests of Ise leave twice a day, morning and evening, in the Mike-den (a pavilion behind the Gosho-den, the principal shrine). This is also closed to the public, who have to remain behind a fence. Like the Naiku, the Geku is rebuilt every 20 years in identical style, give or take a few details, exhibiting the same bare, austere style regarded in Shintoism as the height of beauty and purity.

Kogakkan University, Faculty of Shinto Studies

The status of *bushi* (samurai) may be passed down generally from father to son, but a great deal of study at university or in the temple awaits aspiring priests. Kogakkan University in Ise is one of the best known for Shinto studies. Students study Japanese culture and history as well as the origins and practices of Shinto, and leave, after four years, clutching a license to be a Shinto priest.

EXCURSIONS
FUTAMI★ 二見

Regional Map. 4.5mi/7km east of Ise. 10min by JR train to Futaminoura station.

This small seaside resort, which grew up in the 1920s near Ise Shrine, is famous for its "wedded rocks"

Meoto-iwa★ 夫婦岩

15min walk east of the station.

These two much-photographed rocks lie just offshore. They are associated with Izanagi and Izanami—according to Japanese mythology, the creators of the Japanese archipelago and parents of Amaterasu. The larger "male" rock is 30ft/9m in height and has a small *torii* (gate) on the top. It is connected to the "female" rock (height 13ft/4m), by a *shimenawa*, a rope of braided rice straw used to mark out a sacred space in the Shinto religion.

The rope is 98ft/30m long and is replaced by priests three times a year (*May 5, Sept 5, & Dec 25*), in a ceremony accompanied by singing and drumming. From May to July, and notably during the Summer Solstice, you can see the sun rise between the two rocks and even glimpse the silhouette of Mount Fuji in the distance.

Hinjitsukan – On the seafront, 220yd/200m before the rocks. ◯Open Wed–Mon 9am–5pm (last entry 4.30pm). ⬡¥300. This majestic wooden building, dating from 1887, was where the Imperial Family and important state dignitaries would stay when they visited Ise Shrine. They would relax here and sometimes bathe in the sea. Now a museum, the building is notable for its large (120-*tatami*) hall and a beautiful, traditional garden.

TOBA★ 鳥羽

5mi/8km southeast of Futami. From Futaminoura, JR Line (10min, ¥210). From Ise, Kintetsu Line (15min, ¥330) or JR Line (15min, ¥240). Tourist Office at the station exit (◯open 9am–5.30pm).

A small, very tourist-oriented port town (*population 20,000*), Toba is the world center for cultured pearls, most of them produced by the Mikimoto company.

The mermaids of Toba

Gathering seaweed, sea urchins, abalones, lobsters, and oysters from the seabed, the *ama* are "daughters of the sea." Up until the 1950s, they would generally dive wearning only a *fundoshi* (loincloth), with ropes on their ankles connected to tubs bobbing on surface, acting both as floats and containers for the catch. But the tradition, handed down from mother to daughter, is in decline. Today it is mostly older women wearing special one-piece white bathing suits (or sometimes wetsuits) who carry it on; the average age is around 65. The strongest can go down as far as 82ft/25m, holding their breath for minutes at a time. As soon as they surface, they give a curious whistle to decompress the air in their lungs. A native of Osatsu, Nakamura Yasuko, now in her sixties, has been diving since the age of 15. "The white tunics we wear ward off sharks and make it possible for us to be seen in case of accident. It's a profitable profession, but it means spending hours in cold water. Our daughters are not as tough as we were, they all dream of a different life."

The region's rocky coastline, with its many small coves and rocky inlets, is also famous for its female divers, the *ama*, who for centuries have plunged into the sea here without the aid of breathing apparatus to collect seaweed, shellfish, and crustaceans.

Mikimoto Pearl Island★★
ミキモト真珠島
5min walk from the station. ○*Open daily: Jan–Nov 8.30am–5.30pm; Dec 9am–4.30pm (last entry 1hr before closing).* ○*Closed 2nd Tue, Wed & Thu of Dec.* ◐*¥1500. mikimoto-pearl-museum.co.jp.*

It was on this small island facing Toba harbor that Mikimoto Kokichi (1858–1954), known as "the pearl king," became the first person in the world to produce cultured pearls. The technique involves introducing a parasite into the shells of young oysters. Harvested after around four years, 1 percent of them will have produced perfect pearls.
There is a **museum** on the island that explains the process and displays jewelry and works of art made out of pearls, and, from April to November, tourists can see demonstrations of pearl fishing by *ama* divers.

🏊🏻 Toba Aquarium★   鳥羽水族館
In the harbor, just opposite the island. www.aquarium.co.jp. ○*Open 9am–5pm (Jul 20–Aug 30, 8.30am–5.30pm), last admission 1hr before closing.* ◐*¥2,500;*

¥2,100 over 65; ¥1,250 under 15; ¥630 under 6. www.aquarium.co.jp/en. Among the 850 varieties of marine and freshwater creatures in this aquarium is a group of seals and sea lions that give regular shows, much to the delight of children. The aquarium also contains flat-nosed dolphins from Ise Bay, manatees, sturgeons, dugongs, Amazonian pirarucu, and other unusual sea creatures.

Toba Sea-Folk Museum
海の博物館
5.5mi/9km south of Toba. Kamone Bus from Toba Station to Umi no hakubutsu-kan stop (35min, ¥500). umihaku.com. ○*Open daily: Mar–Nov 9am–5pm; Dec–Feb 9am–4.30pm (last admission 30min before closing).* ○*Closed late June & late Dec.* ◐*¥800.*

This museum contains around 40 traditional fishing boats from the villages on the peninsula and explains the fishing methods, traditions, and beliefs of the local seagoing people, especially the *ama* divers of Ise, whose practices go back over 1000 years.

Osatsu Kamado★
相差かまど
9.5mi/15km south of Toba. Kamone Bus from Toba Station (40min, ¥600). Lunch from ¥3500; tea and snack ¥2000. Reservation required. osatsu.org/en.
A small harbor in a rocky inlet, this is home to one of the main communities of *ama* on the Shima Peninsula. A wooden

hut near the shore, where the divers go to rest and warm themselves after they come out of the water, has been converted so that the tourists can meet them and chat while getting a taste of the day's catch.

Ago Bay★ 英虞湾

15.5mi/25km south of Toba. Take the Kintetsu Line to the terminus at Kashikojima (30–40min, ¥480–1000). This magnificent bay is the center for Japanese pearl cultivation. Just offshore lies a picturesque string of small, wooded islands.

Bay Cruises – *Opposite Kashikojima Station. 6–8 daily, 50min round trip. ¥1600. ℘0599-43-1023, shima-marineleisure. com/cruise/espana/info.* From **Kashiko-jima★** harbor, a Spanish-themed tourist boat cruises the bay, allowing visitors a close-up view of the oyster beds in the pearl farms.

Yokoyama Observatory★ – *2.5mi/4km north of Kashikojima. Kintetsu Line to Shima-Yokoyama station, then 30min walk. ℘0599-44-0567.* Perched at an altitude of 492ft/150m, the observatory provides a **panoramic view** of Ago Bay. There is a small information center for visitors (Ⓞ*open daily 9am–4.30pm*), and walks in the nearby woods. On the 10th and 20th of each month, there's a free English guided walk (*10am–noon, departing from the visitor center*).

ADDRESSES

🏨 STAY

ISE

🛏🛏 **Hoshidekan** 星出館 – *2-15-2 Kawasaki, near Ise-shi Station. ℘0596-28-2377. www.hoshidekan.jp. 10 rooms. ¥11,500. ¥1000 ☕.* On the edge of the Kawasaki Kaiwai district, once called "the kitchens of Ise," this splendid *ryokan* also has a lovely garden.

FUTAMI

🛏🛏 **Nisshokan** 日章館 – *537-1 Chaya, Futami-cho. 10min walk from Futaminoura Station. ℘0596-43-5000. 6 rooms. ¥13,200.*

¥1100 ☕. A friendly place by the sea, not far from the Meoto-iwa. Japanese rooms and *o-furo*. Free shuttttle from the station.

TOBA

🛏 **Road Inn Toba** ロードイン鳥羽 – *1-63-11 Toba. ℘0599-26-5678. 52 rooms. ¥7400. ¥700 ☕.* A classic business hotel with Western- and Japanese-style rooms. Wifi only in public areas, not in the rooms.

AGO BAY

🛏🛏🛏 **Shima Kanko Hotel The Classic** 志摩観光ホテル クラッシック – *731 Shinmei, Ago-cho, Shima-shi, near Kashikojima Station. ℘0599-43-1211. www.miyakohotels.ne.jp/shima/english. 114 rooms. ¥26,000. Around ¥4000 ☕.* A big hotel overlooking the bay, with a free shuttle to the station. Hosted the G7 Ise-Shima Summit in 2016, and has an excellent French restaurant.

🍴 EAT

ISE

🍴 **Daiki** 大喜 – *2-1-48 Iwabuchi. ℘0596-28-0281. ise.ne.jp/daiki. Open daily 11am–9pm. Menu in English. Bento lunches from ¥1100, set meals from ¥1600.* A highly regarded restaurant, with reasonable prices. Try the *tekone-zushi*, a traditional fish dish (steamed rice topped with flaked *bonito*). For those on more generous budgets, there are set *kaiseki* menus.

🍴 **Nakamura** 中むら – *12-14 Honmachi. ℘0596-28-4472. iseudon- nakamura.jp/ index.html. Open Mon–Fri 11am–4pm. Closed 2nd & 4th Mon each month. From ¥600.* 🍜 Since the Edo period, this inexpensive spot has been serving warming bowls of Ise udon, thick white wheat noodles cooked in a dried bonito stock, to pilgrims visting the shrine.

MATSUSAKA

🍴🍴🍴 **Wadakin** 和田金 – *1878 Nakamachi. 8min walk from Matsutaka Station. ℘0598-21-1188. e-wadakin.co.jp/ en. Open Mon–Fri 11.30am–8pm, Sat–Sun & public hols 11am–8pm. Closed 4th Tue each month. Bento lunches from ¥2000, set meals from ¥12,900.* 🍜 Located 6mi/10km north of Ise, the town of Matsusaka produces some of Japan's best beef, very much equal to the more famous Kobe beef. An institution dating from the Meiji era, this restaurant has its own ranch. Try the *sukiyaki* menu, a real treat.

Takayama★★★
高山

Surrounded by mountains that rise to over 9845ft/3000m, this "mini alpine Kyoto" seems frozen in time. Thanks to its historic districts dating from the Edo period, with their wooden houses, sake breweries, antiques shops, temples, and shaded shrines, this small city has plenty of character and atmosphere. As the former capital of Hida province, Takayama (often called Hida-Takayama) was famous for its carpenters, who built the opulent merchant houses in the town and also helped to build the temples of Kyoto. However crowded it gets, especially at weekends, Takayama is well worth a visit. In the surrounding area, the villages of Shirakawa-go and Gokayama have both been designated World Heritage Sites because of their *gassho-zukuri*, old thatched houses with sloping roofs where several generations live together.

BACKGROUND

The city of carpenters – Poor in agricultural resources but rich in wood for building, Takayama was renowned for its skilled carpenters, considered the best in Japan. Unable to pay the taxes in rice and cloth imposed by the Emperor, the villagers would instead leave for several months a year to work in the capital, Heian *(now Kyoto)*, where they built temples and palaces. On their return, they would put the knowledge they had acquired to good use, building houses and temples in their own city. These skills have been handed down to the present day. Not only was Takayama enriched by frequent contact with Kyoto, but after 1692 (when it was placed under the direct control of the shogunate, which appointed its governor), it also maintained close ties with Edo.

A place of harmony – A former fortified town, Takayama's castle was destroyed by the Tokugawa in 1695. The grid-style layout, inspired by Kyoto, was divided

- ▶ **Population:** 88,500 – Gifu Prefecture.
- ⚙ **Michelin Map:** Regions of Japan Map 2, Regional Map p252–3 B2, Takayama Map p270.
- ◖ **Location:** In the north of Gifu prefecture, 112mi/180km from Kanazawa, 103mi/165km from Nagoya, and 106mi/170km from Nagano, Takayama is on a plateau at an altitude of 1900ft/580m, surrounded by peaks more than 9845ft/3000m high. The old quarter of Sanmachi is a 15min walk to the east of the railway station, on the right bank of the Miya River. Most attractions are within walking distance and well signposted in English.
- ◷ **Timing:** Allow two days in Takayama, and two more for Shirakawa-go and Gokayama. If you plan to stay in the valleys, make reservations in advance.
- 👁 **Don't miss:** A leisurely stroll in the Sanmachi district, looking at the craft shops and lingering in the morning markets; staying in a farmhouse in Shirakawa-go or Gokayama.

between the samurai quarter near the Enako River, the temple quarter on the slopes of Higashiyama, and the merchants' quarter on the banks of the Miya River. It is this last area, known as Sanmachi, with its 17C wooden buildings, that attracts visitors today.

Neatly aligned one after the other, the merchant houses run the length of the narrow streets. One or two stories high, they have gently sloping roofs ending in wide canopies, and façades with dark wooden doors and complex latticework.

TAKAYAMA

WHERE TO STAY

Minshuku Kuwataniya	**1**
Minshuku Sosuke	**3**
Oyado Koto-no-Yume	**5**
Rickshaw Inn	**9**
Ryokan Kaminaka	**11**

WHERE TO EAT

EvilTex	**1**
Kakusho	**2**
Kitchen Hida	**3**
Koma	**4**
Kyoya	**5**
Susaki	**6**

The whole effect is one of harmony and coherence. Close by are canals that were used for washing clothes and as a source of water for quenching fires, and into which winter snow could be cleared.

Geography has kept the area somewhat isolated, allowing Takayama to develop something of its own culture over the past 300 years.

USEFUL INFORMATION

Tourist Office – Opposite Takayama Station entrance *(Map, B2)*. Open daily Apr–Nov 8.30am–7pm, Dec–Mar 8.30am–5.30pm. ☎0577-32-5328. www.hida.jp.

TRANSPORTATION

BY TRAIN – From Tokyo, Kyoto, or Osaka, the simplest route is via Nagoya, from where the Limited Express Hida leaves every hour *(2hr 30min, ¥5610)*.

BY BUS – The bus station, mostly served by Nohi Bus, is on the left as you exit the JR station *(Map, B2)*. ☎0577-32-1688, www.nouhibus.co.jp. Book tickets in advance.

To Kanazawa: 4 buses per day *(2hr 15min journey, ¥3600)*.
To Matsumoto: 4 buses per day *(2hr 20min, ¥3250)*.
To Gifu: 6 buses per day *(2hr, ¥2700)*.
To Nagoya: 12 buses per day *(2hr 40min, ¥3100)*.

GETTING AROUND

BY CAR – Taking the car is much more practical than going by bus for exploring Shirakawa-go and Gokayama. There are several car rental companies near the station, including **Toyota Rent-A-Car** ☎0577-36-6110. You can return the car in Kanazawa.

SIGHTS
👣Map opposite.

Kokubun-ji 飛騨国分寺
👣*Map, B2. 5min walk from the station.* 🕐*Open daily 9am–4pm.* 👝*¥300.*
Easily recognizable by its three-story pagoda, this is the oldest temple in the town. It was founded in 746 by Emperor Shomu and burned down several times. The main building dates from the 16C. In the courtyard is a 1200-year-old gingko tree with a gnarled trunk.

Morning markets 朝市
👣*Map, B1 & 2. Along the Miya River to Sanmachi & opposite Takayama Jin'ya.* 🕐*Open daily from 6 or 7am.*
Farmers from the surrounding area have been coming to these two markets at to sell vegetables, fresh fruit, flowers, and condiments for over 200 years.

Sanmachi District★★ さんまち
👣*Map, B1/2. 10min walk from the station.*
The best-preserved part of the city centers on three streets running parallel to the Miya River: Ichinomachi, Ninomachi, and Sannomachi ("streets 1, 2, and 3"). Most of the former merchant houses have been turned into museums or shops selling antiques, lacquerware, and pottery, recognizable by their blue curtains *(noren)*. There are also a number of sake breweries, which can be identified by the balls of cedar needles *(sugidama)* hanging in the entrances. Visitors are always welcome for a tasting.

Kusakabe Heritage House★ – Shimo-
Ninomachi. 🕐*Open Mar–Nov daily 9am–4.30pm; Dec–Feb Wed–Mon 9am–4pm.* 👝*¥500.* The former residence of a pawnbroker and silk merchant, rebuilt after a fire in 1879, this sturdy house is a fine example of traditional cypress-wood architecture. Its spacious interior, designed to let in maximum air and light, comprises an earth floor and a raised central space around the sunken hearth, the *irori*. The house has a garden, and a display of old objects and equipment used in handicrafts.

Yoshijima Heritage House★ – Next to
Kusakabe House. 🕐*Open Mar–Nov daily 9am–5pm; Dec–Feb Wed–Mon 9am–4.30pm.* 👝*¥500.* More sophisticated than the Kusakabe house, this sake merchant's residence dates from 1908. The wooden beams and pillars have a beautiful, glossy patina. The stairwell is built around a central column and bathed in the natural light from the skylight above. The part of the house facing the street was used for business, while the back rooms, opening onto a simple patio, were for family use. The building at the rear was used to store sake.

The floatmakers

The carpenters of Takayama show their mettle during the city festival, which takes place twice a year: Sanno Matsuri in spring (Apr 14–15) and Hachiman Matsuri in the fall (Oct 9–10). The ancestors of the woodworkers who now bring such fame to the craftsmen of Hida were involved in constructing the 25 floats for the very first Takayama festival; they were employed to do so by rich merchants looking for an opportunity to flaunt their wealth. In spring, a ceremony is held at the shrine at Hie to attract the goodwill of the gods, and the 12 floats then make their way through the city. In the fall, a procession of 11 floats (departing on this occasion from Sakurayama Hachiman-gu) gives thanks to the gods for their benevolence. Puppet shows dedicated to the gods are performed on the floats in both festivals, during the procession on the first day and when the floats take up positions across the city on the second. On both occasions, the crowds in the street can admire the many metal ornaments, wood-carvings, and swags of cloth that decorate every inch of these magnificent, lumbering floats as they cross Takayama. As night falls, the gold and lacquer adorning the floats are lit up by the hundreds of lanterns with which they are bedecked, and the water reflects their colors and lights as the procession crosses the city's crimson bridge.

Hirata Folk Art Museum★ – 39 Kami-Ninomachi. ⏰Open daily 9am–5pm. ⬥¥300. Set in a large, plain house built in 1897, which belonged to a merchant family that sold candles and ointments, this museum conveys an idea of daily life in a middle-class home of the Edo period, with its display of household utensils, mirrors, lacquerware, toiletries, toys, etc.

Takayama Museum of History and Art★ – 75 Kami-Ichinomachi. ⏰Open daily 9am–7pm. ⬥No charge. This small museum, housed in a restored 19C sake brewery, traces the history of Takayama through a collection of documents, handicrafts, and objects of archeological, ethnographic, or religious interest.

Sakurayama Hachiman-gu
桜山八幡宮
⏰Map, B1. 78 Sakuramachi. ⏰Open daily 24hr. ⬥No charge.
The doors of this elegant shrine, made from hinoki wood (Japanese cypress), bear emblems in the form of stylized cherry blossoms. The shrine is dedicated to Emperor Ojin, Takayama's guardian deity, and was founded in the 4C. The shrine precincts are surrounded by cedar trees; in Shintoism, it's said that

these trees' impressive height helps the gods to come down to earth.

Takayama Yatai Kaikan★★
高山屋台会館
⏰Map, B1. 78 Sakura-machi. ⏰Open daily: Mar–Nov 9am–5.30pm; Dec–Feb 9am–4.30pm. ⬥¥900.
This hall is used to display in rotation four of the 23 large, colorful floats (yatai) used in the city's festivals. The others are stored in warehouses in the downtown area. Dating from the 17C and 18C, the floats are richly decorated with gleaming lacquer, gilt, and mother-of-pearl inlays. Lanterns, drapes, and mechanized figures sitting on top of the floats complete the elaborate effect. In the adjoining exhibition hall is a large-scale model (1:10) of Nikko's Tosho-gu shrine.

Karakuri Museum★ 獅子会館
⏰Map, B1. 53 Sakuramachi, near the Yatai Kaikan. ⏰Open daily 9.05am–4.25pm. ⬥¥600.
More than 800 lion masks used in the traditional festival dances are exhibited in this small museum. The purpose of the dances is to purify the path of the procession before the altars bearing deities pass along it. More interesting are the short but amusing shows of karakuri

© Glen_Pearson/iStock
Sanmachi District

puppets, wooden automata dating from the Edo period. They sit atop the floats while their operators, concealed below, make them perform acrobatics to the sound of drums and flutes.

Higashiyama District 東山
Map, B1. 10min East of Sanmachi. Allow 1hr to explore it.
The atmosphere in this district, home to the bulk of Takayama's temples and shrines, is calm and soothing. You can follow a verdant 2mi/3.5km-long trail that takes in the main buildings. Some of the temples contain fine statues.

Takayama Jin'ya★★ 高山陣屋
Map, B2. 1-5 Hachikenmachi, in the south of Sanmachi. Open daily: Mar–Jul & Sept–Oct 8.45am–5pm; Aug 8.45am–6pm; Nov–Feb 8.45am–4.30pm. ¥440. Ask at the entrance for a free 40min tour in English.
Originally the residence of the Kanamori clan, this building served as the regional government office for Hida when the province was directly controlled by the Tokugawa shoguns, from 1692 to 1868. The only surviving building of its kind in Japan, it was used as a courthouse and as a tax collection center. The great courtroom is reached through an imposing door and a narrow vestibule. Ordinary people had to kneel behind a barrier and make their appeals to the authorities in the dark. One of the rooms close by was used for torture. The rest of the building lodged the *daikan* (local governor), his distinguished guests, and

the staff. To the south were the great storehouses for rice, wood, and other produce collected in tax, which was a heavy burden on the peasants in this poor, mountainous province, giving rise to frequent revolts.

Hida Takayama Museum of Art★★★ 飛驒高山美術館
Map, A2. 1mi/1.7km southwest of town, on the Hida-no-Sato road. "Sarubobo" bus from the station (¥210). Open daily 9am–5pm. ¥1300. htm-museum.co.jp/english.php.
Created by a wealthy and enthusiastic collector, Tetsuya Mukai, this museum houses a collection of beautiful **European Art Nouveau** glassware, furniture, and glass pieces by Tiffany, Lalique, Daum, and Gallé. Several rooms are devoted to the great masters of European decorative art in the pre-World War I period, such as Louis Majorelle, Charles Rennie Mackintosh, the Vienna Secessionists. The highlight has to be one of Lalique's **glass fountains** (1932) that once adorned the traffic circle on the Champs-Élysées in Paris.

Hida-no-Sato★★ 飛驒の里
Map, A2. 1.6mi/2.5km southwest of town. "Sarubobo" bus from the station (¥210). Open daily 8.30am–5pm. ¥700. hidanosato-tpo.jp.
In a small wooded valley beside a lake, this open-air museum contains a folk village of some 30 farmhouses, mostly dating from the 18C and 19C. They are large traditional rural houses or *minka*,

*Gassho-zukuri houses,
Shirakawa-go*

© JTB/Photoshot

with wide roofs of thatch, bark, or shingle and well-preserved interiors. In the center of the main room is an *irori*, a hearth hollowed out of the beaten-earth floor, around which the family would gather. The rooms and storehouses display farming tools and everyday objects that give a glimpse of life in the mountain villages. In some of the houses, people can be seen working at traditional crafts like ceramics, dyeing, weaving, and cabinetmaking. For those who don't have time to visit Shirakawa-go and Gokayama, this museum is a good way of discovering the famous *gassho-zukuri* style of building (☙*see opposite*).

EXCURSIONS
☙*Regional Map, B2.*

SHIRAKAWA-GO★★ 白川郷
50mi/80km northwest of Takayama. From Takayama Bus Station, hourly buses leave for Ogimachi, the main village in the valley (50min, ¥2470), 2 of which continue on to link Ogimachi and Kanazawa (1hr 15min, ¥1850). www.nouhibus.co.jp.

Tucked away in the heart of the mountains, the villages of Shirakawa-go are scattered about amid forests and paddy fields on the banks of the Sho River, which also flows through the adjoining valley of Gokayama. For centuries, Shirakawa-go and Gokayama were "lost valleys," cut off from the world by snow during the winter.

Due to their isolation, they developed a particular way of life based on a system of mutual cooperation between neighboring families. In 1995, both valleys were designated UNESCO World Heritage Sites, thanks to their traditional *gassho-zukuri* three- or four-story wooden houses. Their triangular thatched roofs slope at an angle of 60 degrees to withstand the heavy snow in winter. These giant farmhouses could accommodate up to 30 people from several generations of the same family; most are still lived in. Up until the 1970s, the attics were used for breeding silkworms and storing mulberry leaves, whose fibers were used to produce *washi* paper. Until the 19C, the region also manufactured gunpowder. Today, its main industry is tourism. The crowds who flood in during the day, especially at weekends, tend to somewhat spoil the magic of the place, which is best appreciated by spending a night here.

Ogimachi★★ 荻町
Map available at the Tourist Office where the buses park (🕐open daily 9am–5pm; shirakawa-go.gr.jp).

This well-preserved village on the east bank of the Sho River has 60 *gassho-zukuri* houses, most dating from the 19C and nearly half still inhabited. Each *gassho-zukuri* is surrounded by a plot of land, generally containing paddy fields and kitchen gardens.

The thatched roofs are completely replaced roughly every 30 years, but thanks to all the villagers pitching in and helping, this only takes a single day. On the last Sunday in October, the whole village is hosed down in a spectacular fire prevention exercise.

Start your visit by climbing to the **Shiroyama Tenbodai** viewpoint *(15min walk on a path to the northeast)*, which offers an overall **view★★** of the village. You will see how the houses are neatly arranged parallel to the river, aligned north to south to limit their exposure to bad weather.

Wada House★ – *In the north of the village.* ⏱*Open daily 9am–5pm.* ✆*¥300.* This house dates from the 18C and is the largest *gassho-zukuri* in Ogimachi. It belonged to the wealthy family that once ran the village and still live in it. Note the soot-blackened roof structure above the central hearth. The upper floors, which were used for breeding silkworms, have exhibits of period equipment. The beams and pillars are ingeniously held together, not with nails or screws but with ropes, which allow the structure to yield and sway slightly under the pressure of the snow and wind without breaking.

Myozen-ji★ – *At the foot of the mountain to the east.* ⏱*Open daily: Apr–Nov 8.30am–5pm; Dec–Mar 9am–4pm.* ✆*¥300.* In this Buddhist temple of the Jodo Shinshu sect, the temple bell is sheltered beneath a fine thatched roof. The vast *gassho*-style lodging adjoining the temple contains a display of everyday rural objects.

Gassho-zukuri Minka-en★★ – *In the south of the village, on the west bank of the river.* ⏱*Open Mar Fri–Wed 8.40am–5pm; Apr–Nov daily 8.40am–5pm; Dec–Feb Fri–Wed 9am–4pm.* ✆*¥600. shirakawago-minkaen.jp.* Twenty-five *gassho-zukuri* farmhouses from a nearby village, threatened with being swallowed up by the building of a dam in 1967, were moved into this open-air folk museum, which gives a good idea of traditional life in the area. Craft demonstrations

An explosive recipe

With little land available for rice cultivation, the villagers of Shirakawa-go and Gokayama made maximum use of the meager resources available to them. Having to spend the long winters in their farmhouses, they bred silkworms, feeding them on mulberry leaves. They made use of everything they could: the fibers of the mulberry tree were used to produce paper; the silkworms' excrement was stored in the ground, along with that of humans, to ferment until nitrate was obtained, and the nitrate was then mixed with charcoal and sulfur to make gunpowder. The products they made—silk, paper, and gunpowder—were then carried on the villagers' backs across the mountains to trade in Takayama and Kanazawa.

are given in some of the houses and it is possible to take part in dyeing or weaving workshops, or to try making soba (buckwheat noodles).

GOKAYAMA★★★ 五箇山
North of Shirakawa-go, on Route 156. From Ogimachi, a bus leaves 6 times daily for the villages of Suganuma (30min journey, ¥860) and Ainokura (45min journey, ¥1300), then continuing to Takaoka (1hr–1hr 20min journey, ¥1000–1200), from where a JR train can take you back to Kanazawa (30min). gokayama-info.jp/en.

This enchanting valley, adjacent to Shirakawa-go, has several hamlets scattered along the Sho River, each with its splendid *gassho-zukuri*. Less accessible than Shirakawa-go, Gokayama gets around half as many visitors. A rustic calm pervades the thatched houses, which double as inns, where you eat your dinner around the hearth. At night, the only sound is the croaking of frogs.

Suganuma★★ 菅沼

Route 156, 12.5mi/20km from Ogimachi.
Situated on a terrace above a bend in the river, Suganuma *(population 40)* proudly guards its nine surviving *gassho-zukuri.* Two of them house the **Folk Museum** (🕐*open daily 9am–4.30pm;* 🎟️*¥300),* which showcases the valley's past activities, including the making of gunpowder in secret for the Kaga clan.

Iwase House★★ – *Nishiakao, 2mi/3km upriver of Suganuma.* 🕐*Open daily 8am–5pm.* 🎟️*¥300. iwaseke.jp.* The Iwase family will show you around their magnificent *gassho*-style house, the largest of its kind in Japan *(five floors, 85ft/26m long, 43ft/13m wide, and 49ft/15m high),* which dates from the 18C.

Murakami House★★ – *Kamigachi, 3mi/5km downriver from Suganuma.* 🕐*Open Thu–Tue: Apr–Nov 8.30am–5pm; Dec–Mar 9am–4pm.* 🎟️*¥300. murakamike.jp.* This *gassho-zukuri* was built around 350 years ago, making it the oldest surviving example in Japan. The family living here will make you tea and sing you a folksong by the fire.

Ainokura★★ 相倉

6mi/10km from Suganuma. Buses stop 550yd/500m below the village. Map available at the information office in the car park, which is higher up (🕐*open daily 8am–5pm, g-ainokura.com).*
The main village in Gokayama, situated on a plateau overhanging the Sho River, contains 20 *gassho-zukuri.* It is almost identical in appearance to Ogimachi, but the atmosphere is more tranquil. Several of the farmhouses have been turned into *minshuku* and, if you want to relax after a hike in the forest, you can take advantage of a number of *onsen* nearby.

Ainokura Folk Museum – 🕐*Open daily 8.30am–5pm.* 🎟️*¥300 per building, or ¥500 for both.* This museum, housed in two *gassho-zukuri,* showcases the history and traditions of the valley, including the period in the 12C when it was used as a refuge by the surviving samurai of the Taira clan. Folk costumes and instruments, handicrafts and *washi* (traditional paper) from the region are also on display.

Washi Paper Workshop – 🕐*Open Mon–Sat 8.15am–5pm.* 🎟️*¥700 per sheet. www1.tst.ne.jp/gokawasi.* Small workshop where you can try making the fine *washi* for which the area is known.

ADDRESSES

🛏️ STAY

TAKAYAMA

🛏️ **Minshuku Kuwataniya** 民宿桑谷屋 – *1-50-30 Sowamachi (Map, B2).* 📞*0577-32-5021. kuwataniya.com. 9 rooms. ¥9100. ¥880* 🍽️*, dinner ¥2500.* A good, very friendly *minshuku,* with free bicycle rental.

🛏️ **Rickshaw Inn** 力車イン – *54 Suehiro-cho (Map, B2).* 📞*0577-32-2890. rickshawinn.com. 11 rooms. ¥8800. ¥550* 🍽️*.* A lovely place. The owner, the English-speaking Eiko, is a mine of information.

🛏️🛏️ **Minshuku Sosuke** 民宿惣助 – *1-64 Okamoto-cho (Map, A2).* 📞*0577-32-0818. irori-sosuke.com. 13 rooms. ¥11,000. ¥880* 🍽️. 🚭. A fine building with a traditional *irori* hearth, just 10min west of the station.

🛏️🛏️ **Ryokan Kaminaka** 旅館かみなか – *1-5 Hanaoka-cho (Map, B2).* 📞*0577-32-0451. ryokankaminaka.com. 10 rooms. ¥16,500. ¥550* 🍽️. 🚭. A welcoming family guesthouse surrounded by a lovely garden, with English-speaking staff. *Kaiseki* dinners available (request when booking).

🛏️🛏️🛏️ **Oyado Koto-no-Yume** おやど・古都の夢 – *6-11 Hanasato-cho (Map, B2).* 📞*0577-32-0427. kotoyume.com. 23 rooms. ¥22,300. ¥2000* 🍽️. 🚭. An oasis of refinement 55yd/50m from the station. Very good prices for such a superb *ryokan,* with indoor and outdoor hot-spring baths

SHIRAKAWA-GO

🛏️🛏️🛏️ **Gassho-no-yado Yokichi** 合掌の宿・よきち – *351 Ogimachi.* 📞*0576-96-1417. shirakawa-go.gr.jp/en/stay/3060. 5 rooms. From ¥22,000.* 🍽️*, dinner also included.* 🚭. Beautiful *gassho-zukuri* house, which serves generous portions of tasty regional dishes. *O-furo* for private use.

🍲🍱🛏 **Magoemon** 合掌乃宿・孫ェ門
– 360 Ogimachi, on the river bank, near the bridge. ☎0576-96-1167. shirakawa-go.gr.jp/en/stay/3081. 6 rooms. From ¥25,000. 🍽, dinner also included. 🚭. Lovely, traditional thatched building. Big meals (breakfast and dinner included in rate) are served around the *irori*, where a storyteller relates local legends each evening.

🍲🍱🛏🛁 **Tousuke-no-yu Fujiya** 藤助の湯ふじや – 325-1 Hirase, Shirakawa-mura. ☎05769-5-2611. tousuke-fujiya.com/en. 11 rooms. From ¥35,200. 🍽, dinner also included. 🚭. Refurbished riverside house, now an elegant, luxurious *ryokan*. Each attractive room has with its own *irori*, and the 4 baths can be booked for private use.

GOKAYAMA

🍲🛏 **Yomoshiro** 民宿・与茂四郎 – 395 Ainokura, in the center of the village. ☎0763-66-2377. 4 rooms. From ¥21,000. 🍽, dinner also included. 🚭. A rustic, family-run inn housed in a *gassho-zukuri*. All rooms have shared bathrooms. Meals are served convivially around the central heart; there may be folk music after dinner, played on the *sasara*, a traditional instrument.

🍴 EAT

TAKAYAMA

🍲 **Koma** 独楽 – 1-6 Hanaoka-cho (Map, B2). ☎0577-34-6488. koma.kaminaka.info. Open Wed–Mon 11am–9pm. Menu in English. From ¥600. 🚭. No-frills *teppanyaki* restaurant with friendly, mischievous owners. Great *okonomiyaki* and *yakisoba*.

🍲🍱 **EvilTex** イーブルテックス – 6-19 Hanasato-machi (Map, B2). ☎0577-57-5888. eviltex13.com. Open Mon & Wed–Sat 11.30am–10pm, Sun 11am–9pm. Menu in English. Around ¥1300. Hearty TexMex food, mouthwatering burgers and world beers in a bustling, friendly restaurant. Great for vegetarian and gluten-free meals, too.

🍲🍱🛏 **Kitchen Hida** キッチン飛騨 – 1-66 Honmachi (Map, B2). ☎0577-36-2911. kitchenhida.com. Open Thu–Tue 11.30am–3.30pm & 5–8.30pm (last orders 2.45pm & 7.45pm). Menu in English. Steaks from ¥5200. Hida's famous beef is served here in a variety of ways.

🍲🍱🛏 **Kyoya** 京や – 1-77 Ojin (Map, B1). ☎0577-34-7660. www.kyoya-hida.jp. Open Wed–Mon 11am–9pm (last orders 8.30pm). Set menu from ¥3800. 🚭. Kyoya has been specialising in *houda miso* (Hida beef with miso cooked on magnolia leaves) since 1979. This former farm building is now

one of the most beautiful restaurants in town, decorated in the rural style.

🍲🍱🛏 **Susaki** 料亭州さき – 4-14 Shinmei-cho (Map, B2). ☎0577-32-0023. ryoutei-susaki.com. Open daily 11.30am–2pm & 5pm–late (last seating 7pm). Set lunches from ¥6600; Sowaryu set ¥13,310. Reservation required. Seasonal foods, ceremoniously presented at a restaurant over 200 years old. Splash out on the indulgent Sowaryu Honzen Kuzushi set meal, with over a dozen dishes, if you can.

🍲🍱🛏 **Kakusho** 角正 – 2-98 Baba-cho (Map, B2). ☎0577-32-0174. kakusyo.com. Open daily 11.30am–2.30pm & 5.30–8pm (last orders 1.30pm & 7pm). Price varies; expect around ¥16,000. Six pavilions dotted around a magnificent garden, serving sumptuous *kaiseki* and *shojin-ryori* meals. Vegan options available; ask in advance.

TAKING A BREAK

TAKAYAMA

Fujiya Hanaikada – 46 Hanakawa-cho (Map, B2). ☎0577-36-0339. enakawakamiya.co.jp/shop. Open Fri–Wed 9am–5pm. Enjoy some creative and delicious Japanese patisseries in the surroundings of a one-hundred-year-old building decorated in a refined, modern style. Lovely!

Warajiya – 170 Hachimangu Keidai (Map, B1). ☎0577-33-6789. Open Sat–Thu 9.30am–5pm. Closed Dec–Mar. 🚭. After 30 years of selling pottery and ceramics here, the very friendly owners decided to turn their shop into a tearoom. Good coffee, too, though the fine ceramics are the star.

SHOPPING

TAKAYAMA

Kawakami Chokoku – 2-158 Ojinmachi (Map, B1). ☎0577-34- 9616. Open daily 9am–5pm. This shop near Hachiman-gu showcases the skill of Takayama's woodcarvers, with superb figures of deities, monks, animals, and so on.

SPORT AND LEISURE

TAKAYAMA

Satoyama Experience – satoyama-experience.com. Discover more about Takayama and the lifestyle of the people of Hida through activities such as guided cycle rides, stays in traditional houses, and tours based on the town's culinary specialties.

The Japan Alps★★
日本アルプス

Along with steep gorges and deep forests, the Japan Alps, in the center of Honshu, contain the highest peaks in the country after Mount Fuji, many of them more than 9845ft/3000m. The area's many excellent ski resorts have the advantage of also possessing hot springs, where visitors can relax after a day on the slopes. Nagano, made famous by the 1998 Winter Olympics, grew up around its ancient temple, Zenko-ji, which attracts more than 6 million visitors a year. In a lofty mountain setting at 1942ft/592m above sea level, the city of Matsumoto has one of the finest castles in Japan. Hiking enthusiasts will enjoy the nearby alpine trails of Kamikochi or, farther south, the lovely Kiso Valley. It was through this valley that the Nakasendo ("the road through the central mountains") passed, linking Edo (now Tokyo) and Kyoto inland, just as the Tokaido road connected them along the coast.

NAGANO★ 長野

Regional Map.

This modern city in the north of the prefecture *(1hr 40min from Tokyo by Shinkansen)* is surrounded by numerous ski resorts, all about an hour away by bus. Occupying the basin of the Shinano River, Nagano grew up in the 13C, around the vast Zenko-ji.

Zenko-ji★★★ 善光寺

1.2mi/2km north of Nagano Station. 30min walk along Chuo-dori or 15min by Gururin-go bus (¥150).
Open daily, roughly 5.30am–4pm (summer) or 7am–4pm (winter). Precinct ⌖no charge; San-mon, Museum, Naijin & O-kaidan ⌖¥1000.
A place that most people in Japan aim to visit at least once in their life, Zenko-ji is

▶ **Population:** Nagano: 378,000; Matsumoto: 243,000.
⌖ **Michelin Map:** Regions of Japan Map 2, Nagano Prefecture, Regional Map pp252–3 B2.
▶ **Location:** Nagano is 145mi/230km from Tokyo and 115mi/185km from Niigata. Matsumoto is 45mi/70km from Nagano, 60mi/95km from Takayama, and 120mi/190km from Nagoya. JR Shinano trains cross the region from north to south, from Nagano to Nagoya via Matsumoto and the Kiso Valley. The ski resorts and mountain villages are served by buses, but some roads are closed during winter.
▲ **Kids:** Seeing the snow monkeys at Jigokudani Yaen-koen; Nozawa Onsen; the Ninja Village at Togakushi Folk Museum.
⌖ **Timing:** Allow two/three days to visit the sights of Nagano and Matsumoto and their surroundings.
⌖ **Don't Miss:** Zenko-ji in Nagano; Nozawa Onsen; Matsumoto Castle; hiking at Kamikochi or between Tsumago and Magome.

the largest temple in Japan after Nara's Todai-ji (⌖see p362). Surrounded by a bustling religious district, it is also very lively—there is almost a fairground atmosphere on Nakamise-dori, the great avenue leading to the temple, lined with lodgings for pilgrims, abbey residences, and shops, which spill over onto the adjoining streets. Buses regularly disgorge streams of tourists eager to see the temple.

A mythical beginning – Legend relates that the temple was founded in order to house a statue of Amida (the Buddha of

USEFUL INFORMATION

Nagano Tourist Office – In the JR station. *Open daily 9am–6 or 7pm. ℘026-226-5626. go-nagano.net.*
Matsumoto Tourist Office – At the station. *℘0263-32-2814. Open daily 9am–5.45pm. visitmatsumoto.com.*

TRANSPORTATION

BY TRAIN – For Nagano, the Shinkansen leaves Tokyo every 30min *(1hr 30min, ¥7810)*, continuing on to Kanazawa *(1hr 20min, ¥8590)*. Matsumoto is on the JR Shinonoi Line between Nagano *(50min–1hr 15min, ¥1170–2370)* and Nagoya *(2hr, ¥5610)*.
BY BUS – *The terminal is opposite Nagano Station (west exit), in the West Plaza.* From Tokyo, highway buses leave from the Shinjuku Expressway Bus Terminal *(3hr 40min, ¥2900–4800)*.

the Western Paradise), a gift to Emperor Kinmei from Korea in 552, when Buddhism was introduced into Japan. The statue was thrown into a canal after an epidemic, but later retrieved by a poor man named Honda Yoshimitsu, who took it back to his village and built an oratory for it in 602. By 670, this had become a temple, which grew in size and popularity in the Kamakura era, a time when the cult of Amida was spreading through Japan. The temple has burned down on several occasions; the current structure, built between 1707 and 1726, is the 11th reconstruction.

A temple of tolerance – A vast complex, with many subsidiary temples, Zenko-ji has a number of unusual aspects. Firstly, it welcomes both the Jodo and Tendai sects, which take it in turns to hold services. Secondly, unlike most Japanese temples, it has always been open to women. Indeed, an abbess is in charge of the Jodo branch. Finally, the layout is unique: the temple runs from north to south, with Mount Omine, symbol of the Western Paradise, behind it. Many believers have built mausoleums at the foot of the mountain in the hope of future rebirth.

Visit – A long, paved ramp climbs gently upward, past the 30 or so temple lodgings where visitors can stay. It leads through the gate of **Nio-mon** (rebuilt in 1918), guarded by two impressive deities, past a row of *jizo (bodhisattvas)*, to the monumental, two-story **San-mon★** (1750), which offers glorious views and has a small attached museum. The avenue finally comes out onto a broad esplanade, where the **Hondo★★**, the two-story main hall, is located.

This huge building, designated a National Treasure, is made from 60,000 lengths of wood, with a roof of cypress bark. At the entrance to the vast, *tatami*-floored hall is a wooden statue

Hondo, Zenko-ji

© fazon1/iStock

of **Binzuru★★**, a disciple of Buddha said to be able to cure physical ailements—so many worshipers have touched it for help over the years that the features of the face have been worn away. At the far end, on the west side, a richly decorated altar contains the statue around which the temple grew up: the **Ikko Sanzon**, a golden triad depicting Amida flanked by the two *bosatsu*, Kannon and Seishi. The statue is kept hidden in a reliquary—not even the priests are allowed to see it—but a replica is shown at the Gokaicho Festival, every seventh year (2021, 2027, etc). The best view is from the open area in front of the altar, the **Naijin**.

To the right of the altar, a staircase leads to a dark underground corridor, the **O-kaidan**, where worshippers try to find a metal key mounted in the right-hand wall directly beneath the sacred statue. This is supposed to open the gates of paradise to them.

M-Wave Nagano Olympic Memorial Arena エムウェーブ

3mi/5km to the northeast. From the station, take bus no. 8 for Yashima; get off at the M-Wave-mae stop (20min, ¥360). ✆026-222-3300. nagano-mwave.co.jp. Check website for opening times. ☞¥2180 including hire of skates. A colossal covered arena *(787ft/240m long and 394ft/120m wide)*, with a speed-skating track built for the 1998 Olympic Games. There is a small **museum** about the Olympics *(○open Sat–Sun & public hols 10am–5pm)*, and a rink suitable for skaters of non-Olympic ability.

EXCURSIONS
⌖*Regional Map.*

Obuse★ 小布施

⌖*Map, C2. 10mi/16km northeast of Nagano. On the Nagano Dentetsu Line (35min, ¥680). Map and bicycle rental at the Tourist Office on the way into the center of town (○open daily 9am–5pm, obusekanko.jp).*
The main claim to fame of this small town *(population 11,000)* is that it was the place where the artist **Katsushika Hokusai** (1760–1849), the master Japa-

nese printmaker, chose to settle during the last years of his life. He bequeathed many works to the town. Obuse also has a number of small **museums** on various themes: bonsai, lamps, antique pottery, etc. There are some fine vineyards and chestnut groves in the area surrounding the town—chestnut-flavored ice cream and confectionery are its specialty.

Hokusai-kan★★ – *10min walk southeast of the station. ○Open daily: July–Aug 9am–6pm; Sept–June 9am–5pm. ☞¥1000. hokusai-kan.com.* Apart from 30 or so prints, the main attractions of this museum devoted to Hokusai (and his followers) are the his original works, which include ink drawings and *kakejiku* (wall scrolls). His genius lay in being able to capture the essence of a movement or the beauty of a kimono-clad courtesan in just a few strokes. The museum's exhibits also include ceiling panels and two festival floats decorated by the artist.

Takai Kozan Museum – *55yd/50m from the Hokusai-kan, at the end of the street. ○Open daily: July–Aug 9am–6pm; Sept–June 9am–5pm. ☞¥300.* Takai Kozan (1806–83), a wealthy Obuse merchant, was not only Hokusai's patron and friend, but also one of his pupils. His darkly ironic works depict demons and ghosts, ugly-looking fantasy creatures inspired by the traditional representation of the Buddhist hells.

Gansho-in – *30min walk east of the station. ○Open daily: Apr–Oct 9am–5pm; Nov 9am–4.30pm; Dec–Mar 9.30am–4pm. ☞¥300.* This Soto Buddhist temple, founded in 1472, bears on its ceiling a stunning phoenix painted by Hokusai.

Yudanaka★ 湯田中

⌖*Map, C2. 22mi/35km northeast of Nagano. Nagano Dentetsu Line (45min–1hr 10min, ¥1190–1290).*
An *onsen* resort in the district of Yamanouchi, Yudanaka nestles in a gorge of the Yokoyu River, below the ski resort of Shiga Koken. Most visitors come here to see the **wild monkeys** bathing in the mountain's hot springs.

Dawn ceremony

To see a small part of the ritual life of a Japanese temple, attend a morning service at Zenko-ji *(check on times the day before)*. It is celebrated by the high priest or priestess, who blesses the heads of the kneeling worshipper as they pass. Shaven-headed monks in scarlet silk robes makes their way in procession to the altar and kneel before it. Clouds of incense drift about the room while readings of sacred texts alternate with hypnotic chanting. When the gong sounds, a curtain in front of the altar is lifted to reveal a golden phoenix on a bright-red background. The second curtain reveals the reliquary containing the sacred statue. The priest pretends to open the chest, without in fact doing so. In accordance with tradition, the Buddha has to remain hidden.

Jigokudani Yaen-koen★ – *From Yudanaka Station, bus to Kanbayashi Onsen or Snow Monkey Park stops (hourly, 15min, ¥210), then 30min walk along the path. jigokudani-yaenkoen.co.jp.* ○*Open daily: Apr–Oct 8.30am–5pm; Nov–Mar 9am–4pm.* ☞*¥800.* A popular subject for amateur photographers, the colony of 200 or so macaques living near this pool in the monkey park visit regularly for an invigorating dip in the hot water as relief from winter temperatures. Their presence here is not entirely natural; local innkeepers took pity on the monkeys when they started venturing out of their forest to scavenge for food as a result of habitat destruction in the 1960s. Today it's the park keepers who put food out for them. The surroundings are not so natural either, spoiled by concrete and electric cables, but this is still a unique opportunity to see the mischievous monkeys playing and running about, oblivious to the presence of humans.

Nozawa Onsen★★ 野沢温泉
○*Map, C2. 28mi/45km northeast of Nagano. JR Iiyama Line to Togari-Nozawa-Onsen (1hr, ¥710), then bus (9 per day, 20min, ¥310). From the east exit of Nagano Station, there are also buses that go direct to the resort, but only Dec–Apr (bus no. 24, 2 daily, 1hr 15min, ¥1600). There's a Tourist Information Office in the middle of the village (*○ *open daily 8.30am–5.30pm;* ✆*0269-85-3155, nozawakanko.jp).*
Although at a relatively low altitude (5413ft/1650m), Nozawa Onsen's skiing area is excellent, thanks to the quality of its snow. Catering for both ski enthusiasts and families, the resort has retained the feel of an old-fashioned mountain village, its cobbled lanes echoing with the clack of wooden *geta* as holidaymakers walk to the baths. There are 13 public baths *(no charge)* in the village—a good way to relax after an energetic day

Skiing area – *nozawaski.com.* ○*Open Dec–early May daily 8.30am–5pm (8pm in season).* ☞*¥5200 for a 1-day pass.* Compact and easily reached, Nozawa Onsen has 31mi/50km of ski slopes, two cable cars, and 22 chairlifts. If you ski from top to bottom you will be descending 3560ft/1085m, and the longest slope is 6mi/10km. Downhill skiing, cross-country skiing, ski jumping, snowboarding... the resort can cater for all ski forms and levels, and there is also a children's club.

Public Baths – ○*Open daily: Apr–Nov 5am–11pm; Dec–Mar 6am–11pm.* ☞*No charge (bring your own towel).* The most popular of the baths is **O-yu★★**, housed in a fine wooden building which looks rather like a temple, in the middle of the village. Not far away is the hot spring **Ogama**, where the water is 176°F/80°C—so hot the villagers can boil their food in it and the craftsmen use it to soften the vine shoots with which they make toys. Last, but not least, there is **Sparena** *(north of the village;* ○*open Thu–Tue: Apr–Jun & Sept–Nov noon–8.30pm; mid Jul–Aug 9am–8.30pm; Dec–Mar 6.30am–8.30pm;* ☞*¥700),* a large, covered swimming pool with whirlpools, waterslides, a spa, and a sauna.

Cedar tree trail to Togakushi Okusha

© Christine Minato/iStock

Japan Museum of Skiing★ – *At the foot of the slopes. ◐Open Fri–Wed 9am–4pm (last admission 3.30pm). ☞¥300.* Housed in a building shaped like a church, this museum covers the history of skiing in Japan and the 1998 Winter Olympics at Nagano, several events of which were hosted by Nozawa Onsen. Portraits of the resort's stars are also on display—despite the village's small population of just 4200, it has produced no fewer than 15 Olympic champions over the years.

Togakushi★★ 戸隠

◐Map, B/C2. 12.5mi/20km northwest of Nagano. From Nagano Station (stop 7, outside the Zenko-ji exit) bus no. 70 takes the Togakushi Birdline Highway to the Chusha-Miyamae stop (12 per day, 1hr journey, ¥1250).A discounted round trip ticket (also covers buses in Togakushi) can be bought from the Alpico Kotsu agency, by Nagano Station. Nestling in the midst of a magnificent cedar forest, at an altitude of 3937ft/1200m, this alpine village *(population 5000)* welcomes skiers in winter, and hikers from the end of April. The three shrines, all within a relatively short distance, are popular hiking destinations: the **Hokosha★** *(lower shrine)*, **Chusha★** *(middle shrine)*, and **Okusha★** *(upper shrine)*. In the Middle Ages, Togakushi was a major center for Shugendo, an ascetic cult whose practitioners were warrior monks *(yamabushi)* who lived like hermits in the mountains. They are also said to have been skilled

in the *ninja* arts of espionage, illusion, and assassination. The village is also known for its bamboo handicrafts and its soba, noodles made from buckwheat harvested in the mountain pastures, and eaten hot or cold in the many restaurants along the village's main street.

Togakushi Folk Museum – *15min walk uphill from Chusha-Miyamae bus stop, opposite the Okusha gate. ◐Open late Apr–mid Nov daily 9am–5pm. ☞¥600. togakushi-ninja.com.* The museum tells the story of the *ninja* through displays featuring weapons, clothes, and photographs, and explains their techniques. The **Ninja Trick Mansion** next door is a maze-like building filled with traps, hidden doors, and secret staircases *(◐open Fri–Wed, 9am–5pm).*

Okusha-jinja – *45min walk from Chusha-Miyamae bus stop. ◐Open daily 9.30am–5pm. togakushi-jinja.jp.* A mountain **trail★★** leads through a forest of ancient cedars to this shrine hidden on the side of Mount Togakushi. According to legend, this mountain was formed from the rock which sealed the cave into which Amaterasu had withdrawn after being offended by her brother. When the chance arose, the *kami* Ame-no-tajikarao tossed the rock aside, and it landed here.

Hakuba★ 白馬

◐Map, B2. 37mi/60km to the west. From Nagano Station (stop 6, east exit), buses for Hakuba every hour (1hr 45min,

¥2200). Hakuba is also connected by train to Matsumoto (1hr 40min, ¥1170) and to Tokyo Shinjuku by bus (Apr–Dec, 5hr, around ¥5000. The Tourist Office is at the station (🕐open daily 8am–6pm; 📞0261-72-3000, hakubavalley.com).

Winter and summer alike, the resort of Hakuba (population 10,000) is a paradise for outdoor sports enthusiasts. At the heart of the Japan Alps, surrounded by towering peaks, it hosted the downhill, super-giant slalom, Nordic skiing, and ski jumping events in the Nagano Winter Olympics. Popular with young people for its après-ski options, it offers some of the best skiing in Japan, as well as some pleasant *onsen*. In the summer season, activities switch to hiking, climbing, camping, mountain biking, rafting, canoeing, canyoning, golf, and fishing.

Skiing area – 🕐*Open late Nov–early May.* 🎫*¥5500 for a 1-day pass to Happo-One.* There are seven resorts linked by bus, including the central resorts of Happo-One, Hakuba 47, and Goyu-Toomi. **Happo-One★** is at the foot of the mountains, just five minutes by bus from the station. The slopes cater for all levels of skier and snowboarder, and rise to a height of 6007ft/1831m. There are 13 slopes *(including a superb 2mi/3km slalom slope)* and 31 ski lifts.

Hakuba Ski Jumping Stadium – *At Happo-One.* 🕐*Open daily: Dec–Mar 9am–3.30pm; Apr–Nov 8.30am–4.30pm.* 🎫*¥460.* Built in 1992, there are two ski jumps, one normal (length 295ft/90m) and one large (394ft/120m). Take an elevator to the top of the slope to get an impressive "ski-jumper's eye view."

MATSUMOTO★★ 松本
🕐*Regional Map, B2.*

Spread out across a valley framed by the snowy peaks of the Japan Alps, Matsumoto is a major crossroads at the heart of Chubu. It is an attractive city, with a great deal of charm and a relaxed atmosphere. Originally called Fukashi, it developed in the 16C as a fortified town around the castle that still stands proudly at its center.

TRANSPORTATION
BY TRAIN – **Matsumoto Station** – Matsumoto is on the JR Shinonoi Line between Nagano *(50min–1hr 15min, ¥1170–2370)* and Nagoya *(2hr, ¥5610).*
BY BUS – **Matsuden Bus Terminal,** *opposite the rail station, below the ESPA store.* 6 buses per day to Takayama *(2hr 25min, ¥3250),* plus hourly trains from Shinjuku *(3hr, ¥3800).*

Designated a National Treasure, the castle has the oldest wooden keep in Japan. Farther south, the old merchant quarter of Nakamachi is full of fine storehouses from the Edo period, in stark contrast to the modern architecture of the **Matsumoto City Museum of Art** and the **Japan Ukiyo-e Museum.**

Matsumoto Castle★★★ 松本城
15min walk northeast of the station. 🕐*Open daily 8.30am–5pm.* 🎫*¥610 (including Matsumoto City Museum). matsumoto-castle.jp. Guided tour in English available, no charge.*

Many Japanese castles are merely restorations or reconstructions based on an original. Not so Matsumoto, which is a fascinating example of a fortified "flatland" castle *(hira-jiro),* one of the best-preserved in the country, still imbued with the smoke and clamor of past battles. Set in the heart of the city, it is surrounded by three deep moats filled with still water, where carp and swans swim lazily. Because of its black color, it is known as "Crow Castle", in contrast to the white Heron Castle in Himeji (🕐*see p417).* The history of the site begins in 1504, when the region was dominated by a small fortress built by the Ogasawara clan. In 1582, Toyotomi Hideyoshi (1536–98) gained control, and installed his loyal supporter, Ishikawa Kazumasa, who remodeled the building and added the great keep (1593).
Built in a period of unrest, Matsumoto Castle was designed for defense. Many of its features are familiar from medieval castles in Europe: moats, huge walls, walkways, narrow staircases, projecting

Matsumoto Castle and the Japan Alps peaks

© JTB Photo/UIG/age fotostock

galleries, and arrow slits, all designed to make it impregnable. The biggest difference is that the building is of wood and not stone. The sober elegance of the dark-wood keep may be aesthetically appealing, but from a military point of view it presented an easy target for the flaming arrows of attackers. However, potential assailants would still have to get past the three successive enclosures that sheltered the lord's palace and the living quarters of his 1200 samurai.

Visit – The keep stands on an artificial rise in the middle of a wide moat. The smooth convex walls of its stone base fall almost sheer to the water. Access is by a delightful vermillion bridge. Seen from outside, the 98ft/30m-high main tower appears to have five floors with flat roofs enlivened by triangular pediments, more rounded and ornate on the south side. In fact, as you can see inside, there are six floors; samurai would assemble in the dark, low-ceilinged secret third floor in case of siege. The keep is flanked by two secondary towers, to the southeast and northeast, linked by an elevated corridor. Visitors to the upper floors can see the forest of thick, rough-hewn wooden pillars that bear the weight of the structure. The display cases contain a collection of old swords and firearms. From the top floor, reached by a very steep, narrow staircase, there is a **panorama** of the mountains. In the ceiling is a small shrine dedicated to a goddess who prevents fires. The tour ends with the *tsukimi-*

yagura turret, added in 1636, and used as a moon-viewing pavilion.

Matsumoto City Museum – ⏲*Open daily 8.30am–5pm.* 🎫*Entry included in castle ticket.* On the way out of the castle, this small museum contains a model of the fortified town at the time of the Tokugawa shoguns (17C and 18C), plus swords and armor. The city's folk traditions are also represented in a collection of dolls, a specialty of Matsumoto.

Nakamachi District★ 中町

10min walk south of the castle. Walk down the big, tree-lined avenue called Daimyo-dori as far as the Metoba River. On either side of the river are the two attractive streets of Nawate-dori and Nakamachi-dori, lined with former storehouses *(kura)* from the Edo period. Their tiled roofs and thick walls decorated with black and white latticework were designed to protect the merchandise. Today, most have been turned into cafes, soba restaurants, art galleries, and trendy boutiques.

On Nakamachi-dori, **Nakamachi Kurassic-kan** (⏲*open daily 9am–5pm,* 🎫*no charge*) displays local crafts. Nearby, in the small **Geiyukan** theater *(performances Sun & public hols 1.30pm & 3pm; ¥1000),* you can listen to old songs accompanied by the *shamisen* (three-stringed instrument) while enjoying a green tea.

Matsumoto City Museum of Art 松本市美術館

5min walk southeast of Nakamachi, on Ekimae-dori. ◷*Open Tue–Sun 9am–5pm.* ✎*¥410. matsumoto-artmuse.jp.*
Opened in 2002, this museum shows the work of local artists, including the calligraphy of Kamijo Shinzan, the landscapes of Tamura Kazuo, and the colorful, avant-garde creations of Kusama Yayoi, one of the most famous living artists in Japan, who was born here.

Japan Ukiyo-e Museum★★
日本浮世絵博物館

2mi/3km west of the station. Town Sneaker bus Western Route to Ukiyo-e Hakubutsukan stop (¥200), or Dentetsu Kamikochi Line train to Oniwa station (¥180) then 15min walk. ◷*Open Tue–Sun 10am–5pm.* ✎*¥1100. japan-ukiyoe-museum.com.*
Although not easy to reach, this museum housed in an ultra-modern building is definitely worth a visit, as it contains the vast collection of the Sakai family. Among Matsumoto's richest merchants and patrons during the Edo period, over five generations the Sakai family collected more than 100,000 prints, paintings, screens, and old books, making it the largest private collection of its kind in the world, though only a fraction can be displayed at a time.
The *ukiyo-e* ("images of the floating world") woodblock prints are displayed in three-monthly rotation, in subdued lighting because of their fragility. The collection includes many masterpieces by Utamaro, Hiroshige, Hokusai, and Sharaku. *An English-lanugage brochure is available.*

EXCURSIONS
◷*Regional Map, B2.*

Daio-Wasabi Farm★
大王わさび農場

At Azumino, 9mi/15km northwest of Matsumoto. JR Oito Line train to Hotaka (25min, ¥340), then 15min by bicycle (rental outside the station, ¥200 per hour). ◷*Open daily: Apr–Oct 9am–5.30pm; Nov–Mar 9am–4.30pm.*

✎*No charge. daiowasabi.co.jp.*
This is the largest *wasabi* plantation in Japan, 37 acres/15ha of fields irrigated by spring water from the mountains. There are stands selling an endless variety of products made with the spicy, strongly flavored radish, including biscuits, tea, chocolate, ice cream, and even milkshakes.

Kamikochi★★   上高地

31mi/50km west of Matsumoto. Matsumoto Dentetsu Line to Shin-Shimashima (30min, ¥710), then hourly connecting bus (1hr journey, ¥2200). Kamikochi can also be reached by bus from Takayama (hourly, changing at Hirayu Onsen, 1hr 25min journey, ¥2650) or Matsumoto (1hr 50min journey, ¥2500). Cars must park at Nakanoyu, 5mi/8km from Kamikochi and linked to it by shuttle bus. The Information Center (◷*open late Apr–mid-Nov daily 8am–5pm, kamikochi.org) at the bus station has a free English hiking map.*
Situated on the banks of the Azusa River in a deep valley at 4921ft/1500m above sea level, this mountain resort set amid stunning scenery is one of the great centers for hiking and climbing in Chubu-Sangaku National Park. On any day in high season, hundreds of hikers set off to tackle its tallest peaks: **Hotaka-dake** *(10,466ft/3190m)* and **Yariga-dake** *(10,433ft/3180m).* Kamikochi itself consists of a mere handful of hotels and shops, and entry

An alpine missionary

The development of Kamikochi as a tourist center owes a great deal to the Reverend Walter Weston (1861–1940), an English missionary and amateur mountaineer, who climbed the peaks of the region and popularized mountaineering as a sport in Japan. Although he didn't coin the term "Japan Alps," Weston was responsible for putting the area on the mountaineering map in 1896, publishing *Climbing and Exploring in the Japanese Alps.*

Azusa River and Hotaka-dake, Kamikochi
© ChanwitOhm/iStock

by car is prohibited. It is possible to make a day excursion to Kamikochi, but if you spend the night here, then you can set off on a hike early the next morning before the crowds arrive.

🚶 **Azusa-gawa Valley★** – Two easy, well-signposed circuits (2hr round trip) follow the Azusa River in a loop, starting from the Kappa-bashi suspension bridge, near the bus station. The first, which goes south, leads to **Taisho-**

ike, a lake formed in 1915 when the Yake-dake volcano erupted and partly blocked the Azusa River. On the way back, cross Tashiro-bashi and see the statue of Walter Weston (📖 see box p285) on the left bank. The other loop, going north, runs along the right bank as far as Myojin-bashi. Cross the bridge for a view of the picturesque **Myojin-ike★** and the ring of snowy peaks reflected in its clear waters.

Shin-Hotaka Onsen★★
新穂高温泉
♿ *Regional Map, B2. 43.5mi/70km west of Matsumoto. Regular buses from Takayama (1hr 20min, ¥2200) and Matsumoto (2hr, ¥2930).*
This spa area, with its many hot springs, is famous for having Japan's first double-decker **cable car** (🚠 *¥2900 round trip*), taking visitors up to 7074ft/2156m on the 9544ft/2909m-high Mount Nishi-Hotaka. From there the **panoramic view★★** over the Japan Alps is simply breathtaking. From the point where the cable car drops you off on the mountain, it's a three-hour hike to Kamikochi.

KISO VALLEY★★ 木曽谷
♿ *Regional Map, B2/3.*
In the south of Nagano prefecture lies this heavily wooded valley, which forms a natural route across the Japan Alps. The Kiso River runs through the valley for around 43.5mi/70km. When the Tokugawa were in power (1603–1867), two main roads linked the shogun's capital Edo (present-day Tokyo) with the Imperial capital, Kyoto. The first, the Tokaido road, ran along the Pacific coast. The second, the **Nakasendo**, crossed the mountains between Matsumoto and Nagoya, following the Kiso Valley. Eleven of the road's 69 stations (*juku*, or post towns) grew up along the valley, places where the *daimyo* (feudal lords), forced to visit Edo regularly to pay tribute to the shogun, could stop off on their journey. At that time, it took three days to travel through the valley compared with a few hours by car or train today. Part of the 17C paved road is still visible in places.

The secret of lacquerware

Lacquer (*urushi*) is a resin extracted from the sumac shrub. It is applied in thin layers, which are sanded down and polished between each coat. The number of layers determines the ultimate quality of the object—Kiso lacquerware can have anything up to 18 layers. The color is obtained by incorporating natural (charcoal, cochineal) or chemical (iron oxide, mercury sulfate) pigments. Kiso lacquerware is of several types: *roiro* (shiny black, like the surface of a mirror), *shunkei* (wood coated a light red, so the grain is visible), and *tsuishu* (a mixture of colors, with mother-of-pearl inlays, giving a multicolored, marbled effect).

Kiso-Hirasawa★ 木曽平沢

&Map, B2. 22mi/35km south of Matsumoto. Access by JR Chuo Line (1hr 10min, ¥590).

During the Edo period, this town, set among vineyards, acquired a reputation throughout Japan for the quality and beauty of its lacquerware (&see box opposite), prompting many travelers on the Nakasendo to stop here. Today, the tradition continues, and the village and its surrounding area contains around 200 workshops employing 900 people, including around 60 master lacquerers. The main street is lined with shops selling china, boxes, containers, tables, furniture, screens, and panels of lacquered wood.

Kiso Center for Arts and Crafts – 15min walk north of the station. ○Open daily Apr–Nov 9am–5pm; Dec–Mar Wed–Mon 9am–5pm. ◎No charge. ☏0264-34-3888 (reservation required). Both shop and museum, this large gallery displays the work of some 50 lacquerers. You can even try your hand at the craft (◎from ¥700).

Narai★ 奈良井

&Map, B2. 3mi/5km south of Kiso-Hirasawa. Next station on the JR Chuo Line. Tourist Office in the village (○open daily 9am–5pm. ☏0264-34-3048, www.kankou-kiso.com/en).

Consisting of a single street 0.6mi/1km long, this former post town still has some fine old wooden houses with wide canopies and openwork façades. Now a protected site, the village (population 800) is almost identical to Tsumago and Magome, but far less crowded. Spend the night in one of its small inns and feel as if you are stepping back in time a century or two. It also specializes in making small lacquered combs.

Nakamura House – 10min walk south of the station. ○Open Apr–Nov daily 9am–5pm; Dec–Mar Tue–Sun 9am–4pm. ◎¥300. A superb example of an Edo-period house, with a central hearth (irori) and garden at the rear. It once belonged to a rich merchant who dealt in combs—the shop occupied the part of the ground floor facing the street.

Tsumago★ 妻籠

&Map, B3. 56mi/90km south of Matsumoto. JR Chuo Line to Nagiso (2hr journey, ¥1520), then a bus (10min, ¥300). There are 5 buses per day between Magome and Tsumago (25min, ¥600). The Tourist Office is in the village center (○open daily 8.30am–5pm; ☏0264-57-3123, tumago.jp/english).

Hemmed in by mountains, this former post town on the Nakasendo was abandoned after the opening of the Chuo railway and the main road in 1911. After decades of neglect, having miraculously escaped the sweeping modernization of the 1960s and 1970s, it was deemed the ideal candidate for a makeover as a tourist destination. The locals worked together to restore their town, with great success.

As in Narai and Magome, electricity cables, TV aerials, and telephone lines were buried or hidden, and the **wooden houses of the Edo period** restored and turned into museums, restaurants, inns, and shops. A long, paved street (pedestrian only) cuts through town. At one end is an old wooden noticeboard on which the shogun's edicts used to be displayed.

During the Edo period, the cypress forests of the Kiso Valley were closely guarded since they provided the wood used to build castles, temples, and national shrines. The town's inhabitants were forbidden, on pain of death, to cut down even the smallest tree.

Tsumagojuku Honjin – ○Open daily 9am–5pm. ◎¥300 (¥700 with Wakihonjin Okuya). This meticulously restored inn was an official stopping place for daimyo (feudal lords) on their way to Edo. The building is divided into two areas: a fine, spacious dwelling for the feudal lords and their men, and a smaller, plainer space for the Shimazaki family, who ran the village.

Wakihonjin Okuya – ○Open daily 9am–5pm. ◎¥600 (includes Rekishi Hakubutsukan; ¥700 with the Tsumagojuku Honjin). An imposing, two-story cypress wood building, with a delightful moss garden; it also served as a halt for passing samurai. It was rebuilt in 1877 and welcomed the Emperor Meiji on a brief stay in the region.

Rekishi Hakubutsukan – ○*Open daily 9am–5pm.* ❧*¥600 (includes Wakihonjin Okuya).* This local history museum next to the Okuya displays lacquerware, as well as models and photographs of Tsumago before and after its restoration.

🚶**Tsumago–Magome trail**★ *5mi/8km (2hr 30min walk). Baggage forwarding service available (mid-Mar–Nov only). Leave baggage before 11.30am at the Tourist Office in Magome or Tsumago, and it will be delivered by 5pm.* ❧*¥1000 per item.* A rural trail that makes its way beneath cypresses, past small waterfalls and hamlets bright with flowers in the summer months. The steepest section of the trail is between Magome village and Magome Pass, at 2625ft/800m, from where there is a magnificent view of the surrounding mountains. The route is usually tackled from the south, start-ing in Magome, but the route is well signposted from both ends.

Magome★ 馬籠
🧭*Map, B3. 56mi/90km from Nagoya. From Nagoya, take the Shinano Wideview train to Nakatsugawa (1hr 15min–2hr 30min, ¥1980–3840), then a bus (hourly, 25min, ¥560). There are 5 buses per day between Magome and Tsumago (25min, ¥600). The Tourist Office is in the village center (○open daily 8.30am–5pmr; ℘0573-69-2336, kiso-magome.com).*
Situated on a hillside facing west, the village stretches along a steep but lovely stone-paved street lined with souve-nir shops, restaurants, and *minshuku*. The restored buildings recreate the atmosphere of a post town in the Edo period. There is a small **Folk Museum** halfway along the street (○open daily 9am–5pm; ❧¥200), showcasing village traditions and crafts. In the lower part of the village is a beautiful **mill wheel**, for grinding buckwheat and hulling rice.

Kur Resort Yubunesawa – *2mi/3km south of Magome; free hourly shuttle bus from Nakatsugawa Station daily 9.55–11.55am & 1.55pm–4.55pm.* ○*Open daily 10am–10pm.* ❧*¥1000.* ℘*0573-69-5000, nakatsugawaonsen.com.* Fed by the hot springs of Mount Ena, this vast aqua spa complex has both indoor and outdoor baths, pools with water massage, two swimming pools with waterslides, etc. An ideal place to soothe tired muscles after a hike.

ADDRESSES

🛏 STAY
NAGANO
🛏 **Fuchino-bo** 淵之坊 – *462 Motoyoshi-cho.* ℘*026-232-3669. www.fuchinobo. or.jp. 8 rooms.* Magnificent *shukubo* (temple lodging) from the Edo period. Spacious Japanese rooms and divine vegetarian cuisine.

🛏🛏 **Nagano Tokyu REI Hotel** 長野東急REIホテル – *1-28-3 Minami-Chitose.* ℘*026-223-1090. www.tokyuhotelsjapan. com/global/nagano-r. 143 rooms. ¥10,100. ¥1400* 🍽. A well-maintained business hotel right opposite the JR station, fully renovated in 2016. Excellent value for money.

🛏🛏 **Shimizuya Ryokan Chuokan** 清水屋旅館中央館 – *49 Daimon-cho.* ℘*026-232-2580. chuoukan-shimizuya.com. 18 rooms. ¥12,000. ¥1000* 🍽*, dinner ¥3000.* A friendly, family-run *ryokan* in a superb 130-year-old house.

🛏🛏 **The Saihokukan Hotel** 犀北館 – *528-1 Agatamachi.* ℘*026-235-3333. saihokukan.com. 88 rooms. ¥11,000. ¥1800* 🍽*, dinner ¥3600.* An old hotel, opened in 1890, and somewhat extravagantly refurbished with marble columns. The Japanese restaurant is immaculate.

YUDANAKA
🛏🛏 **Uotoshi Ryokan** 魚敏旅館 – *2563 Sano, Yamanouchi.* ℘*0269-33-1215. www. avis.ne.jp/~miyasaka. 8 rooms. ¥9100 (Nov–mid-Apr ¥1100 supplement). ¥1100* 🍽*, dinner ¥3300.* A simple, family-run guesthouse with a magnificent cypress-wood *onsen*. English spoken.

NOZAWA ONSEN
🛏🛏 **Pension Schnee** ペンション・シュネ – *8276 Toyosato.* ℘*0269-85-2012.*

pensionschnee.com. 12 rooms. ¥18,200. Around ¥1000 🍴, dinner available. A pretty chalet below the ski slopes, run by a lovely family of former Olympic champions. The copious breakfast comes with homemade jams. Wifi only on restaurant floor; Western-style rooms.

🛏🛏🛏🛏 **Ryokan Sakaya** 旅館さかや – 9329 Nozawa-onsen-mura. ☎0269-85-3118. ryokan-sakaya.com. 29 rooms. ¥35,200. 🍴, dinner around ¥4000. This elegant *ryokan* has a wonderful *onsen* with indoor and outdoor baths. Delicious *shabu-shabu* dinners available. An unforgettable stay.

TOGAKUSHI

🛏🛏🛏 **Gokui Lodge** 宿坊・極意 – 3354 Togakushi. ☎026-254-2044. www.egokui. com. 8 rooms. ¥21,000. 🍴, dinner also included. Superbly located in a 400-year-old former *shukubo* (temple lodging) adjoining the Chusha temple. Friendly service and exquisite food.

HAKUBA

🛏🛏 **Yamano Hotel** 山のホテル – 3477 Hokujo. ☎0261-72-8311. hakuba-yamanohotel.com. 21 rooms. ¥15,000. 🍴, dinner ¥3500. Looking rather like a Swiss chalet, this hotel is close to the ski slopes and has comfortable, modern Japanese and Western rooms and hot-spring baths. English spoken.

MATSUMOTO

🛏 **Super Hotel Matsumoto Ekimae** スーパーホテル松本駅前 – 1-1-7 Chuo. ☎0263-37-9000. www.superhoteljapan. com/en/s-hotels/matumoto. 73 rooms. ¥8900. 🍴. A business hotel 220yd/200m from the station. Nothing out of the ordinary, but good value.

🛏 **Tabi-shiro** タビシロ – 1-3-6 Josei. ☎026-388-3453. tabi-shiro.com/en. 5 private rooms, 2 dorms. Dorms ¥3900 per person, rooms ¥9800. ¥400 🍴. 🍴. Welcoming, well-designed hostel near to the castle, with *tatami* rooms, a good kitchen, and a bar (open Fri & Sat only). Staff are very friendly and helpful.

🛏🛏🛏 **Hotel Kagetsu Matsumoto** 松本ホテル花月 – 4-8-9 Ote. ☎0263-32-0114. hotel-kagetsu.jp. 89 rooms. ¥11,100. ¥2400 🍴. A 5min walk from the castle, this old samurai house was converted some 130 years ago into a hotel of character. It offers spacious, attractive Western- and Japanese-style rooms. There's an *onsen* and the breakfast is generous.

🛏🛏 **Marumo Ryokan** まるも旅館 – 3-3-10 Chuo. ☎0263-32-0115. www.avis. ne.jp/~marumo/index.html. 8 rooms. ¥11,000. ¥1000 🍴. Friendly family *ryokan* with a garden. There's an *o-furo* for private use, and an excellent coffee shop (open to the public; daily 8am–6pm).

KAMIKOCHI

🛏🛏 **Nishi-Itoya Sanso** 西糸屋山荘 – 4469-1 Azumi. ☎0263-95-2206. www. nishiitoya.com/en.40 rooms, 10 dorms. Dorms ¥9000 per person, private roms ¥11,500. 🍴, dinner included. Open Nov–Apr only. Kamikochi's best budget accommodation. Note that the dorms are shared *tatami* rooms, rather than bunks.

SHIN-HOTAKA ONSEN

🛏🛏🛏🛏 **Hotakaso Sangetsu** 穂高荘山月 – Shin-Hotaka Onsen. ☎0578-89-2036. okuhida-sangetsu.jp/en. 49 rooms. ¥35,500. 🍴, dinner also available. 🍴. This large hotel may have an uninspiring exterior, but the glorious lobby with *irori* hearth, and splendid open-air *onsen* baths (with mountain views) more than make up for it. Shuttle buses to the hotel group's other properties mean access to more *onsen*.

KISO VALLEY

NARAI

🛏🛏 **Iseya** 民宿伊勢屋 – 388 Narai, Shiojiri-shi. ☎0264-34-3051. oyado-iseya.jp. 9 rooms. ¥19,600. 🍴, dinner also included. 🍴. This friendly *minshuku* occupies a fine Edo-period house on the main street, with an ornamental garden.

TSUMAGO

🛏🛏 **Koushinzuka** 民宿こおしんづか – 1775 Azuma. ☎0264-57-3029. kiso. ne.jp/~koosinzuka.nt. 3 rooms. ¥11,000. ¥1000 🍴, dinner ¥1000. 🍴. Old-style *minshuku* with calm, rustic atmosphere. Dinners around central *irori* hearth.

🛏🛏🛏 **Fujioto** 旅館藤乙 – Nagiso-cho. ☎0264-57-3009. tsumago-fujioto. jp. 7 rooms. ¥24,000. 🍴, dinner also included. A lovely *ryokan*, one of the most comfortable in the village, with a splendid garden and good meals. The owners speak English.

MAGOME

🛏🛏 **Tajimaya** 但馬屋 – 4266 Magome. ☎0573-69-2048. kiso-tajimaya.com. 10 rooms. From ¥18,400. 🍴, dinner also included. A *minshuku* in a traditional house. Rustic, but pleasant, with communal bathrooms. The copious meals are served at the *irori* hearth.

⚑ EAT

NAGANO

There are several places to eat, drink and relax at **Patio Daimon** (51 Daimon-cho; patio-daimon.com/english), a complex of restored kura storehouses near Zenko-ji.

⊜ **Motoya** そば処元屋 – 587-3 Daimon-cho. ☎026-232-8707. Open Wed–Mon 11am–3pm (last orders 2.30pm). Lunch around ¥1000, dinner ¥1500. ⊟. A popular—and always packed—restaurant specializing in the soba for which Nagano is famous. Also does good tempura, with noodles or on rice.

⊜ **Yayoiza** 弥生座 – 503 Daimon-cho. ☎026-232-2311. yayoiza.jp. Open Wed–Mon 11.30am–8.30pm (closed 2nd Wed in the month). From ¥1100. ⊟. Opened in 1847 and something of a local institution. Regional dishes like shabu-shabu, based around the famous Nagano beef.

⊜⊜⊜ **Bikura** 欅屋びくら – West Plaza Bldg, 1355-5 Suechiro-cho. ☎026-264-7717. bikura.com. Open Sun–Thu 4.30–11pm (last orders 10.15pm), Fri–Sat 4.30pm–midnight (last orders 11pm). Around ¥4500. Eclectic Japanese and Western cuisine in a 10th-floor restaurant opposite the station.

TOGAKUSHI

⊜ **Uzuraya** うずら家 – By Chusha shrine. ☎026-254-2219. Open Thu–Tue 10.30am–4pm. From ¥800. ⊟. The best place to sample Togakushi's famous soba noodles, served, for example, cold with a plate of tempura (tenzaru soba). The simple, attractive dining room upstairs has a view of a giant 800-year-old cedar.

MATSUMOTO

There are several 100-year-old restaurants on **Nawate-dori** serving soba (try **Benten Honten**; open Fri–Wed 11am–6.30pm), and pastries (such as **Sweet**; open Thu–Tue 9am–6pm; sweet-bakery.com).

⊜ **Shiduka** しづか – 4-10-8 Ote. ☎0263-32-0547. www.shiduka.co.jp . Open Mon–Sat noon–10pm (last orders 9.30pm). Lunch sets from ¥990, dinner from ¥1500. A few minutes from the castle, this elegant izakaya has a rustic appeal. The à la carte menu features the famous (but dear) beef from Nagano, served as a steak or on a skewer. There is also a good list of local nihonshu (sake).

⊜⊜⊜ **Kura** 蔵 – 1-10-22 Chuo. ☎0263-33-6444. Open Thu–Tue 11.45am–2.30pm & 5.30–9.30pm. Around ¥5000. ⊟. Located in a former fish canning factory, this restaurant serves kappo cuisine. The menu features unusual items like basashi (horsemeat sashimi) and hachinoko (bee larvae), as well as less challenging dishes.

KISO VALLEY

NARAI

⊜⊜ **Tokkuriya** 徳利屋 – 516 Narai. ☎0264-34-2189. Open daily 11am–5pm. English menu available. Around ¥1500. ⊟. Meals served around the hearth in one of village's oldest houses. The soba is the focus, but try the local gohei-mochi too.

SPORT AND LEISURE

HAKUBA

Evergreen Outdoor Center エヴァーグリーン・アウトドアセンター – 4377 Hokujo, Hakuba, Hakuba- mura. ☎0261-72-5150/0261-72-3200. evergreen-hakuba.com. Run by a cheerful Canadian, the center offers a full range of sporting activities, both in summer and winter: cross-country or off-piste skiing, kayaking, rafting, mountain biking, climbing, and more.

EVENTS AND FESTIVALS

NOZAWA ONSEN

Dosojin Fire Festival (Jan 15) – This popular matsuri includes one of Japan's three best firework displays.

MATSUMOTO

Yozakura Kai Festival (Apr) – Literally the "night of observing the cherry trees." Tea ceremonies take place and medieval music is played as night falls, and the cherry trees are artfully illuminated in the grounds of Matsumoto Castle.

FURUKAWA

Furukawa Matsuri (Apr 19–20) – This picturesque small town near Takayama holds a raucous festival each spring, with elaborate floats, taiko drumming, and loincloth-wearing men competing to place small drums on a stage.

SHOPPING

MATSUMOTO

Belle Amie ベラミみむら人形店 – 3-7-23 Chuo. Open Mon–Tue & Thu–Sat 9am–7pm, Sun 10am–6pm. ☎0263-33-1314. This shop-workshop-museum has been producing all kinds of good-quality dolls in regional styles for over 50 years.

Kanazawa★★
金沢

In the 17C, Kanazawa was one of the most powerful feudal cities in Japan. In terms of wealth, artistic influence, and size of population, it could more than hold its own with the great capitals of Europe at the time. Like Kyoto, it escaped the bombing of World War II, so, although it also has its fair share of modern architecture, the samurai and geisha quarters, with their winding alleys and little wooden houses topped with glazed tiles, are preserved intact. Famous for Kenroku-en, one of the three most beautiful gardens in Japan, as well as its fine cuisine, richly varied handicrafts, Noh theater, and museums, Kanazawa is definitely *iki*—tasteful, refined, and distinguished. For a pleasant excursion outside the city, the Noto Peninsula, with its jagged coastline, will plunge you into a rural Japan of wild beauty and sleepy fishing villages, where the pace of life is far gentler. Fukui Prefecture's Eihei-ji, meanwhile, provides a Zen retreat in the mountains.

A BIT OF HISTORY

Kanazawa, which literally means "golden marsh," is said to derive its name from a stream where the region's peasants once found deposits of gold. In the 16C, the city was ruled as an autonomous fiefdom by a Buddhist sect until it was seized by Maeda Toshiie, a vassal of the shogun Toyotomi Hideyoshi, in 1583. A castle was built and the small town was transformed into a powerful feudal city over which the Maeda clan would rule for three centuries.

The vast, fertile, wooded region of Kaga (*now Ishikawa prefecture*), which they controlled, made them so prosperous that they became the country's second most powerful family and, rather like the Medici in Italy, became patrons of the arts. Porcelain and pottery, silk dyeing, gold leaf, lacquerware, and Noh theater

▶ **Population:** 466,000 – Ishikawa Prefecture.

Michelin Map: Regions of Japan Map 2, Regional Map pp252–3 B2, Kanazawa Map p292.

▶ **Location:** Kanazawa is on the northern coast of Honshu, 93mi/150km from Takayama and 155mi/250km from Nagoya, on a narrow plain between the Sea of Japan and the Japan Alps, at the gateway to the Noto Peninsula. This sprawling city stretches between the Asano and Sai rivers. Its center is located around the Kenroku-en and the castle grounds, which can be reached by bus from the station. Farther south, the shopping area of Katamachi, near the Korinbo department store, is the liveliest part of the city. In the west is the old samurai quarter of Nagamachi and, to the south of the Sai-gawa, the Teramachi temple quarter. In the northeast of the city, across the Asano-gawa, is the geisha quarter of Higashi Chayamachi.

Timing: Allow two days to see the city.

Don't miss: Kenroku-en; the 21st Century Museum of Contemporary Art; the Nagamachi and Higashi Chayamachi districts.

all flourished under their patronage, and remain local specialties today.

SIGHTS

Map opposite.

From the JR station, the Kanazawa Loop Bus (*every 15min, ¥200 per journey, 1-day pass ¥500*) tours the city's main tourist sights.

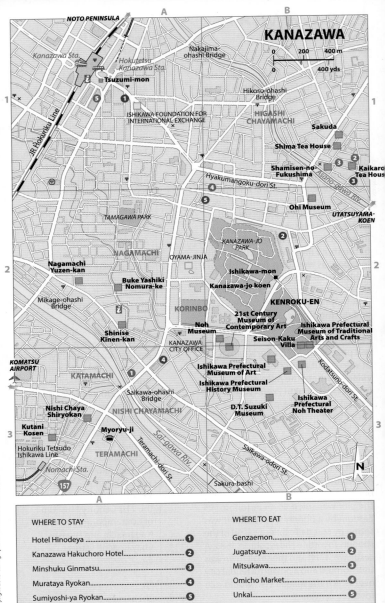

KANAZAWA

NOTO PENINSULA

Kanazawa Sta.

Hokutetsu
Kanazawa Sta.

JR Hokuriku Line

Tsuzumi-mon

Nakajima-
ohashi Bridge

Hikoso-ohashi
Bridge

ISHIKAWA FOUNDATION FOR
INTERNATIONAL EXCHANGE

HIGASHI
CHAYAMACHI

Sakuda

Shima Tea House

Shamisen-no-
Fukushima

Kaikaro
Tea House

Hyakumangoku-dori St.

Asano-gawa Riv.

Ohi Museum

UTATSUYAMA-
KOEN

TAMAGAWA PARK

KANAZAWA-JO
PARK

NAGAMACHI

OYAMA-JINJA

Ishikawa-mon

Kanazawa-jo koen

Nagamachi
Yuzen-kan

Buke Yashiki
Nomura-ke

Mikage-ohashi
Bridge

KORINBO

KENROKU-EN

21st Century
Museum of
Contemporary Art

Noh
Museum

Ishikawa Prefectural
Museum of Traditional
Arts and Crafts

Shinise
Kinen-kan

KANAZAWA
CITY OFFICE

Seison-Kaku
Villa

KOMATSU
AIRPORT

KATAMACHI

Ishikawa Prefectural
Museum of Art

Kodatsuno-dori St.

Saikawa-ohashi
Bridge

Ishikawa Prefectural
History Museum

Ishikawa
Prefectural
Noh Theater

Nishi Chaya
Shiryokan

NISHI CHAYAMACHI

D.T. Suzuki
Museum

Kutani
Kosen

Myoryu-ji

Sai-gawa Riv.

Hokuriku Tetsudo
Ishikawa Line

TERAMACHI

Teramachi-dori St.

Saikawa-odori St.

Nomachi Sta.

157

Sakura-bashi

N

Copyright 2015 Cartographic data Shobunsha/Michelin

0   200   400 m
0   400 yds

WHERE TO STAY	
Hotel Hinodeya	❶
Kanazawa Hakuchoro Hotel	❷
Minshuku Ginmatsu	❸
Murataya Ryokan	❹
Sumiyoshi-ya Ryokan	❺

WHERE TO EAT	
Genzaemon	❶
Jugatsuya	❷
Mitsukawa	❸
Omicho Market	❹
Unkai	❺

AROUND THE STATION
Tsuzumi-mon 鼓門
Map, A1. Leaving the JR station, take the tree-lined avenue, at the end of which is a fountain.

Kanazawa is more than a little proud of this magnificent contemporary structure designed by architect Shirae Ryuzo and built from pinewood. The gate's completion in 2005 marked the

Higashi Chayamachi District

end of an important renovation plan for the station. While its shape recalls that of the *torii* – the vermilion gates found at the entrance to Shinto shrines – its twisted pillars are reminiscent of the *tsuzumi* drums used in Noh theater performances. Not only is the gate a superb sight, it supports the glass dome atop the station, collecting rainwater which is then sluiced away through the two pillars, within which you can see metal piping among the beams. The apparent fragility of the dome is in stark contrast to the brute strength projected by the gate. Take a step or two back, and the whole thing looks a little like a samurai helmet.

Omicho Market★　近江町市場

Map, B1. 10min walk from the station. Musashigatsuji bus stop (no. 18).
Open daily 9am–6pm.
There are hundreds of stands selling fruits and vegetables, fish and other foodstuffs in this covered market that is nearly 300 years old. A feast for the senses, the maze-like market also houses a number of food stands and restaurants serving seafood and sushi (see Addresses p303).

Higashi Chayamachi District★
ひがし茶屋街

Map, B1. 1.2mi/2km east of the station. Ashiba-cho bus stop (no. 6).
The grace and refinement of the pleasure district of Higashi Chayamachi,

founded in 1820 and located in the east of the city, near the Asano River, remains unchanged. Glimpsed through the dark wooden latticework of its geisha houses, it is a closed, secretive universe, like the Gion district of Kyoto. In fact, Kanazawa is the only place outside Kyoto where old-style geisha training still occurs.

Some 50 geisha, or *geigi* in the local dialect, still practice their profession here, entertaining clients with poetry recitals, tea ceremonies, elegant conversation, and song and dance accompanied by the *shamisen*. Two geisha houses on Higashi Chaya-gai can be visited:

Ochaya Shima★ – *Open daily 9am–6pm. ¥500. ochaya-shima.com.* The luxurious interior of this well-preserved tea house on two floors has *shamisen*, combs, games, and kitchen utensils on display, as well as superb pieces of lacquered wooden furniture.

Kaikaro★ – *Open daily 10am–5pm. ¥750. kaikaro.jp/eng.* On the other side of the street is the largest tea house in the city, whose pure lines are nearly 200 years old, though some chich modern touches have also been added. Inside are gold-fringed *tatami* and a gleaming lacquered staircase. There is also a Japanese garden.

Sakuda gold & silver leaf shop – *1-3-27 Higashiyama. Open daily 9am–6pm. No charge. goldleaf-sakuda.jp.* Gold

USEFUL INFORMATION

KANAZAWA

Kanazawa Tourist Information Center – *By the east entrance to the JR station (Map, A1). Open daily 8.30am–8pm.* ✆*076-232-6200. visitkanazawa.jp.*

Goodwill Guides – *Open daily 9am–5pm.* ✆*076-232-3933. kggn.jp.* An English-speaking guide service. Reserve at least 2 weeks in advance.

Ishikawa Foundation for International Exchange – *Rifare Bldg, 1-5-3 Honmachi (Map, A1). 5min walk from the station. Mon–Fri 9am–6pm, Sat 9am–5pm).* ✆*076-262-5931. ifie.or.jp.* International exchange foundation with a bookshop on the second floor, with foreign newspapers and internet access

THE NOTO PENINSULA

Wajima Tourist Office – In the bus station. ✆*0768-22-1503. Open daily 8am–6pm.* Only scant information in English.

TRANSPORTATION

GETTING TO AND FROM KANAZAWA

BY PLANE – **Komatsu Airport**, *located 19mi/30km southwest of Kanazawa (Map; A3, off map). komatsuairport.jp.* 10 flights per day from Tokyo Haneda; 1 flight per day from Tokyo Narita; 1 flight per day from Sapporo; 2 flights per day from Sendai; 4 flights per day from Fukuoka; 1 flight per day from Okinawa (Naha). A Limousine Bus *(50min, ¥1150)* connects the airport with the city center.

BY TRAIN – **JR Station** *(Map, A1)* – Kanazawa is on the Hokuriku Shinkansen line, which should have been extendedto Kagaonsen, Fukui and Tsuruga by 2022. To and from Nagoya, 8 trains per day by Ltd Express Shirasagi *(3hr, ¥6810)*. From Takayama, Ltd Express Hida to Toyama *(1hr 30min, ¥2890)* then 21 Shinkansen per day *(25min, ¥2810)*.

To and from Tokyo by Shinkansen, 21 trains per day *(2hr 50min, ¥13,600)*. To/from Osaka by Ltd Express Thunderbird *(2hr 40min, ¥7130)*.

BY BUS – *Bus terminal by the east exit from the train station (Map, A1).* 11 buses per day to Wajima *(2hr, ¥2300)*, 8 buses per day from Tokyo *(7hr 30min, ¥4100)*, 10 buses per day from Nagoya *(4hr, ¥4500)*.

GETTING AROUND KANAZAWA

BY BUS – The easiest way for tourists to get around is to take the Kanazawa Loop Bus *(every 15min 8.30am–6pm, 1-day pass ¥500)*, which makes a circuit of the city's tourist attractions. Buses leave from the east exit of the JR station, platform 7. Alternatively, take the Kenrokueen Shuttle *(departures from platform 6, ¥200 Mon–Fri, ¥100 Sat–Sun & public hols)* or see the city by night with the Light-up Bus *(Sat only, 7–9.10pm, ¥300)*.

BY BICYCLE – **Machinori** – Rent a bike from one of the 21 Machinori cycle ports around the city, including in Kanazawa Station *(machi-nori.jp/en; ¥200 per day, plus additional fee for rides over 30min)*.

GETTING TO AND FROM THE NOTO PENINSULA

BY PLANE – **Noto Airport**, located 62mi/100km northeast of Kanazawa. 2 flights per day from Tokyo aneda *(1hr, ¥24,000)*.

BY TRAIN – From Kanazawa, JR Nanao Line to Nanao *(1hr 30min, ¥1230)* or Ltd Express Thunderbird to Nanao *(50min, ¥2090)* or Wakura Onsen *(1hr, ¥2230)*.

BY BUS – From Kanazawa: 11 buses per day for Wajima *(5.55am–7.10pm, 2hr, ¥2300)*, some via Anamizu. From Wajima, 10 buses per day for Sosogi *(40min, ¥760)*. From Sosogi, take the bus along the lovely coast road, passing through Sosogi-Kinoura, Kinoura, Rokugo-zaki, the thermal baths at Yoshigaura, Suzu, and finally, Ogi.

leaf is one of the great craft specialties of Kanazawa, which supplies around 98 percent of the Japanese market (including for Kyoto's famous Kinkaku-ji). It is used to decorate the altars of shrines and temples, fans, and other objects. Gold powder is used as a decoration on lacquerware in a technique called *maki-e*.

The workshop here gives visitors an opportunity to watch the *kinpaku* gold leaf technique, which consists of hammering an ingot down to a microscopic thinness (1/10,000th of a mm). Gilded screens are displayed on the upper floor and there is a shop selling various gilded objects (lacquerware, pottery, chopsticks, lotions containing specks of gold, etc). 1hr workshop on gold-leaf gilding possible (from ¥600).

Fukushima Sangenten – ⏱*Open Mon–Sat 10am–64m.* ⏱*Closed 2nd & 4th Sat every month.* ✆*¥500.* In this 100-year-old shop, the Fukushima family makes superb *shamisen*, the three-stringed, long-necked lutes used by the geisha. The sound box is traditionally made of ebony, sandalwood, or oak, and covered in snake- or catskin. Here you can learn more about the instrument, and maybe try plucking one, and enjoy a cup of green tea.

AROUND THE CASTLE

Ohi Museum★ 大樋美術館

📍*Map, B2. 2-17 Hashiba-cho. 8min from Higashi Chayamachi, Hashiba-cho bus stop (no. 7).* ⏱*Open daily 9am–5pm.* ✆*¥700. ohimuseum.com.* Ohi pottery *(named after a village in the suburbs of Kanazawa)* is quite similar in style to the raku pottery of Kyoto, on which it is based (📍*see p 324).* It was introduced into Kanazawa in 1666 by the Chozaemon family, who arrived as part of the entourage of a master of the tea ceremony invited by Maeda Tsunanori. The same family has continued the tradition ever since—the current master is **Ohi Chozaemon Toshio**, the eleventh generation and a highly regarded artist. Shaped by hand, without a potter's wheel, Ohi ware is characterized by its black or amber glaze, obtained by slow firing, and is intended specifically for the tea ceremony. With its pure forms, rough surfaces, and monochrome colors, it embodies the essence of *wabi-sabi*: simple, imperfect beauty.

If you buy a café ticket (¥1000), you can enjoy tea from whichever of the beautiful, handmade bowls you select.

Kanazawa-jo-koen 金沢城公園

📍*Map, B2. Kenrokuen-shita bus stop (no. 9).* ⏱*Open daily: Mar–mid-Oct 7am–6pm; mid-Oct–Feb 8am–5pm.* ✆*No charge; entry to historic buildings (all open 9am–4pm)* ✆*¥320. bit.ly/kanazawa-jo.*

The castle park sheltered the residence of the powerful Maeda lords for 14 generations, from 1583 to 1869. Kanazawa Castle was ravaged by fire in 1759, and again in 1881; all that remains of the original building is the monumental gateway, the **Ishikawa-mon★**, built in 1788, in the southeast of the grounds. Its fine wrought-iron work is a reminder of this historic feudal city's former greatness. The first part of a long-term reconstruction of the site was completed in 2001: the former arsenal, the Gojikken Nagaya, flanked by two turrets, the Hishi Yagura and Tsuzuki Yagura. Great care was taken to ensure only traditional methods of construction were used, with no nails or screws. Raised on a stone base, the walls are made of bamboo latticework filled in with adobe and covered in several layers of plaster.

Kenroku-en★★★ 兼六園

📍*Map, B2. Kenrokuen-shita bus stop (no. 9).* ⏱*Open daily: Mar–mid-Oct 7am–6pm; mid-Oct–Feb 8am–5pm.* ✆*¥320. bit.ly/kenroku-en.*

Considered one of the three most beautiful gardens in Japan, alongside those of Mito and Okayama, Kenroku-en (28.2 acres/11.4ha) attracts more than 2 million visitors a year. Created in 1676, and enlarged and improved by successive generations of Maeda lords, it once formed the outer grounds of Kanazawa Castle. Its name, meaning "garden

© Joaquin Ossorio-Castillo/iStock

of six combined elements," refers to the six attributes it is said to possess: spaciousness, seclusion, artifice, antiquity, water, and panoramas—although, to escape the crowds and fully appreciate these qualities, it is best to go early or at the end of the day. Ponds, streams, waterfalls, artificial hills, groves, rocks, paths—everything in the Kenroku-en has been carefully designed to create aesthetic perfection. In addition, unlike many other gardens in Japan, the **views** are not spoilt by ugly buildings in the background.

Like all great landscape gardens, its atmosphere and colors change with the seasons and flowering times: plum trees in the spring, cherry trees in April, azaleas in May, and irises in the summer mists. Chrysanthemums and red maples mark the advent of the fall, while in winter, branches of pines are supported by ropes tied to pillars to stop them from breaking beneath the weight of the snow.

Visit – At the edge of Kasumi Pond is the famous **Kotoji-toro**, a stone lantern supported on two long legs that resemble the bridge of a *koto* (the Japanese zither). In the southeast, beside Hisago Pond, stands the **Yugao-tei Tea House**, built by Kobori Enshu in the 17C. Look out for the oldest fountain in Japan, powered by an ingenious system based on the differing water levels of two ponds. Last but not least, you can try a cup of *matcha* and elegant

confectionery *(daily 9am–4.30pm, ¥720)* in the Shigure-tei Tea House.

Seison-kaku Villa★ – *5min southeast of Kenroku-en.* ⏲*Open Thu–Tue 9am–5pm.* ¥700. *seisonkaku.com.* This magnificent residence adjoining the garden was built in 1863 by Maeda Nariyasu for his mother. Beneath a curved roof of cypress shingles, the house is an elegant succession of *tatami* rooms with finely decorated sliding doors inlaid with rare Dutch colored glass.

Ishikawa Prefectural Museums
石川県立美術館

♿*Map, B3. 5min walk southeast of Kenroku-en, near Seison-kaku Villa.*
These small museums are not exceptional, but they are certainly worth a visit if you have the time.

Ishikawa Prefectural Museum of Traditional Arts and Crafts – ⏲*Open 9am–5pm: Apr – Nov daily; Dec–Mar Fri–Wed (last admission 4.30pm).* ⏲*Closed 3rd Thu in month Apr–Nov.* ¥210. *ishikawa-densankan.jp.* Examples of the crafts for which the region is famous (Kutani ceramics, Kaga Yuzen dyed silk, lacquerware, gold leaf), along with the tools and techniques used to produce them. There are regular demonstrations.

Ishikawa Prefectural History Museum – ⏲*Open daily 9am–5pm (last admission 4.30pm).* ¥300. *ishikawa-*

rekihaku.jp. The collections and displays in this museum, housed in three brick buildings of a former military arsenal, date from the beginning of the 20C and recount the story of the Ishikawa region from the Jomon period to the present day.

Ishikawa Prefectural Museum of Art – *Open daily 9.30am–6pm (last admission 5.30pm). ¥370 (excludes special exhibitions). ishibi.pref.ishikawa. jp.* Among the finest pieces in this museum's collection, all dating from the period of the Maeda lords, are precious scrolls, lacquerware, Kutani porcelain, and old kimonos. There are also a number of contemporary works by artists living in the Ishikawa region, often the subject of special exhibitions.

Ishikawa Prefectural Noh Theater – *Open Tue–Sun 9am–10pm (tours until 5pm). No charge.* This theater has continued the traditions of the Kaga Hosho school of Noh since the Edo period. Performances are given at 1pm on the first Sunday of every month except August, and the second Sunday in April and September. On other weekends you may come across a rehearsal.

21st Century Museum of Contemporary Art★★
金沢２１世紀美術館

Map, B2/3. Hirosaka (no. 10) or Korinbo (no. 15) bus stops. Open daily 9am–10pm (public spaces), Tue–Thur & Sun 10am–6pm & Fri–Sat 10am–8pm (museum). Varies by exhibition. kanazawa21.jp/en.

Opened in 2004, Kanazawa's Museum of Contemporary Art is a major player in its field, showing the work of Japanese and foreign artists of international caliber. This vast, circular glass building created by architects Sejima Kazuyo and Nishizawa Ryue, places the emphasis on light and movement. Split into a series of zones *(gallery, theater, children's workshops, media laboratory, library)*, the museum is intended to be accessible to everyone and inspires a sense of playful discovery. Among the works on permanent display are installations by the American James Turrell, Frenchman Patrick Blanc, Britons Anish Kapoor, Damien Hirst, and Tony Cragg, the Italian

The Swimming Pool *(2004) by Leandro Erlich, 21st Century Museum of Contemporary Art*

Photo by Atsushi NAKAMICHI/NACÁSA & PARTNERS, Courtesy of 21st Century Museum of Contemporary Art, Kanazawa

Francesco Clemente, and Argentinian Leandro Erlich.

The museum often has artists in residence. Its collections, which include not only art but also handicrafts, design, fashion, and films, make a conscious attempt to keep abreast of new forms of expression emerging around the world.

Noh Museum 金沢能楽美術館

♿Map, B2. Next to the previous museum, near Kanazawa City Hall. ⏱Open Tue–Sun 10am–6pm. ⊜¥310. kanazawa-noh-museum.gr.jp.

Noh flourished in Kanazawa under the patronage of the Maeda clan during the Edo period. The local Kaga Hosho school popularized this classical Japanese opera well beyond the samurai class for which it was traditionally reserved. Since Noh was so deeply rooted in the hearts of the city's inhabitants, it was able to survive the abolition of feudalism and the warrior clans. This small museum explains the structure of Noh performances and displays a precious collection of **kimono** and **masks** worn by the actors. You can even try on one of the elaborate costumes yourself (Tue–Sun 10am–4pm, ⊜no charge).

D.T. Suzuki Museum 鈴木大拙館

♿Map, B3. 820yd/750m south of the Noh Museum. 3-4-20 Honda-machi. ⏱Open Tue–Sun 9.30am–5pm (last admission 4.30pm). ⊜¥300. kanazawa-museum.jp/daisetz.

This impressive, modern museum offers a stroll in the footsteps of Zen Buddhist philosopher Daisetz Suzuki (1870–1966), with low lighting, plants and a calm central pool prompting reflection.

Teramachi District 寺町

♿Map, A3. 20min walk south of Kenroku-en. Jusangen-machi or Hirokoji bus stops (no. 13).

On the opposite bank of the Sai River, the tranquil quarter of Teramachi contains no fewer than 70 temples, a reminder of the 15C when the city was a Buddhist principality. To counter the monks' influence, the temples were moved away from the castle into this area, which marked the city limits at the time.

Myoryu-ji★ ⏱Open daily for tours (1–2 per hour, 40min): Mar–Nov Mon–Fri 9am–4pm, Sat–Sun 9am–4.30pm; Dec–Feb 9am–4pm. ⊜¥1000. Tour is in Japanese, but an English brochure is provided. ☎076-241-0888. Maeda Toshitsune used this temple as a secret hiding place in the 17C. Also known as the Temple of the Ninja, it is a dizzying labyrinth crammed full of ingenious traps, secret passages, and concealed rooms designed to catch possible attackers unaware. There are no fewer than 29 staircases connecting its 23 rooms and corridors. From the outside, this temple-fortress seems to have only two floors. Once inside, it can be seen that there are in fact four, plus three intermediate levels. According to one legend, there is also a tunnel underneath the well, linking it to Kanazawa Castle. You can visit the precincts for free, but it's worth taking a tour to get a look inside the fascinating building.

Nishi Chayamachi District にし茶屋街

♿Map, A3. 5min walk west of Teramachi, on the other side of Minami-odori.

After Higashi Chayamachi, this was Kanazawa's second pleasure district. Although smaller in size, it is still home to five pretty tea houses (ochaya) with openwork sliding doors, presided over by some 20 geisha.

Nishi Chaya Shiryokan – ⏱Open daily 9.30am–5pm. ⊜No charge. The interior of this tea house has been reconstructed, including the room where the geisha would entertain customers to the sound of the shamisen.

Kutani Kosen★ – 15min walk to the southeast, following the rail line. ⏱Open daily 9am–5pm. ⊜No charge. kutanikosen.com/en. A pottery kiln with displays of traditional Kutani porcelain, characterized by its bright colors and floral patterns. Visitors can also try their hand at painting on pottery (daily 9am–3.30pm, ⊜from ¥1300).

© Kana Design Image/iStock
Nagamachi District

▶ Back in the city center, walk through the Katamachi district, the focus for the city's shopping and nightlife, then, after the Korinbo department store, turn west toward Nagamachi.

Nagamachi District　長町
&Map, A2. 5min walk from Korinbo bus stop (no. 15).
The former samurai quarter of Nagamachi, with its beautiful cobbled alleys that wind between low walls of ocher cob, old canals, and sumptuous residences, has been preserved. It plunges the visitor into the atmosphere of Kanazawa in feudal times.

Buke-yashiki Nomura-ke★★ – *1-3-32 Nagamachi.* ◷*Open daily: Apr–Sept 8.30am–5.30pm; Oct–Mar 8.30am–4.30pm.* ☞*¥550. nomurake.com.* This luxurious samurai residence, built entirely of dark brown wood, belonged to Nomura Denbei Nobusada, one of Maeda Toshiie's closest associates in the 16C. Twelve generations of the Nomura family lived here, until the Meiji era, enriching the house with a delightful ornamental garden, complete with miniature waterfall. The *Jodan no ma* or art room, a later addition, has magnificent latticework and carved caissons of mahogany, ebony, and cypress.

Shinise Kinen-kan★ – ◷*Open 9.30am –5pm (last admission 4.30pm).* ☞*¥100. kanazawa-museum.jp/shinise.* Originally in the south of the city, this former Chinese herbalist's shop, founded in 1779, was moved to the entrance of the Nagamachi district and turned into a museum. The shop, with its impressive pharmacy cabinets, is on the ground floor, on the side facing the street (the rear part comprises private quarters and a garden).

Nagamachi Yuzen-kan – *In a modern building near Chuo-dori, in the western part of the district.* ◷*Open Mar–Nov Thu–Mon 9.30am–5pm.* ☞*¥350. kagayuzen-club.co.jp/en/yuzenkan.* This workshop showcases the techniques for making traditional Kaga Yuzen dyed silk. Visitors can try wearing a kimono (*¥1300*) or painting on silk (*¥4000*).

EXCURSIONS
&*Regional Map.*

SOUTH OF KANAZAWA
&*Map, A2.*
The region south of Kanazawa and around **Fukui** (*53mi/85km from Kanazawa*) includes several places of interest for excursions. Aside from the famous cliffs at Tojinbo and the four hot spring towns which make up **Kaga Onsen**, two Buddhist monasteries in particular are worth a detour.

☺ You might like to extend your visit to the area by staying in Fukui (numerous hotels in all price categories), one of the Kaga Onsen hot spring towns, or Eihei-ji.

© MasaoTaira/iStock

Kaga Onsen★ 加賀温泉

*26mi/42km southwest of Kanazawa.
JR Hokuriku Line train to Kagaonsen
(25min–1hr, ¥770–1530; Shinkansen
from 2022), then CAN Bus (1-day pass
¥1000). The Tourist Office is in the
station.* ⏰*Open daily 8.45am–5.30pm.*
☎*0761-72-6678. visitkaga.com.*

This attractive cluster of traditional hot
spring towns, on the Sea of Japan coast
between Kanazawa and Fukui, is well
worth a couple days' visit. **Katayamazu**
sits by Shibayamagata Lagoon, and
has an impressive lakeside public bath
(⏰*open daily 6am–10pm, ☞¥440, sou-
yu.net)*; **Yamashiro** is a historic town
with a glorious Meiji-style bath house in
the main square *(Ko-soyu;* ⏰*open daily
6am–10pm, ☞¥500)* and links with artist
Kitaoji Rosanjin; **Yamanaka** boasts an
impressive mountain setting and variety
of cultural attractions, from theaters to
sake breweries; and at **Awazu** you can
stay in the oldest *ryokan* in the country,
possibly the oldest hotel in the world still
operating, Hoshi Ryokan (⏰*see p302).*

Natadera★ 那谷寺

*5mi/8km east of Kagaonsen Station. CAN
Bus (25min) from Kaga Onsen.* ⏰*Open
daily: Mar–Nov 8.30am–4.45pm; Dec–
Feb 8.45am–4.30pm. ☞¥600.* ☎*076-65-
2111. natadera.com.*

This Shingon Buddhist monastery was
founded by a monk named **Taicho** in
717 as part of his quest for harmony
between man and nature. Set within
extensive, undulating grounds, the
many buildings lie among camellias,

cedar trees, and bizarre rock formations.
They were mostly reconstructed in 1640
by Kaga lord Toshitsune, who had both
an incense pavilion and a three-storey
pagoda built beside the central pavilion. As you walk from one to the other,
down flights of steps cut into the rock,
between enormous tree trunks and
past a tunnel, you will discover hidden
jizo statues, altars, serene gardens, and
a charming viewpoint. Crowds gather
in the main temple, which has been
partially converted into a grotto and
decorated with animal sculptures, to
stand before a renowned and venerated
wooden statue of Kannon.

In the fall, the forest explodes in a riot
of red, yellow, and orange, attracting
many walkers who come to follow in
the footsteps of the poet **Basho** (17C),
who was so inspired by the place that he
commemorated it in a *haiku.*

Eihei-ji★★ 永平寺

*20mi/32km east of Fukui. Trains every
20min from Kanazawa to Fukui (45min,
¥1340); Hokuriku Shinkansen service
from 2022. From Fukui there is a direct
bus service (35min, ¥780). Or, take the
local train to Eiheiji-guchi (25min, ¥460)
and then a bus (15min, ¥410).* ⏰*Open
daily 8am–5pm. ☞¥500.* ☎*0776-63-
3012. Tourist Information Office at Fukui
Station.* ⏰*Open daily 8.30am–7pm.*
☎*0776-20-5348. fuku-e.com.*

Founded by **Dogen** in 1244, the "temple
of eternal peace" is made up of dozens of
buildings nestling in a majestic forest of
cedars and cypresses spread across the

side of a mountain and surrounded by babbling streams. This bastion of Buddhist spirituality is the seat of the **Soto school of Zen** and dedicated to *zazen*, or meditation in a seated position.

On a stroll around the buildings, you'll see the priests' hall (Sodo), where training in *zazen* is undertaken; the Sanmon gate, the oldest structure in the complex (1749); the Hatto, where various ceremonies take place; the Daikuin (kitchens); and the Joyoden, Dogen's mausoleum. Eiheiji offers *shukubo*, or temple lodging, to those interested in Zen *(¥9000–10,000, reservation required)*, which bring you into closer contact with the community of 200 shaven-headed monks who are making their way toward Enlightenment in this idyllic setting, through meditation and carrying out daily chores (housework, gardening, cooking, washing). If you're interested but feel nervous about the pre-dawn wake-up times, staying at the new Zen Village at the base of the mountain is a good option (♨see p302).

NOTO PENINSULA★ 能登半島
♨*Map, B1.*

North of Kanazawa, the Noto Peninsula is regarded by many Japanese people as a place where the frenetic pace of modern life has still not taken hold quite yet. Its secluded nature is one of its attractions, along with its coastal scenery. One of the peninsula's fishing villages was the setting for director Imamura Shohei's film *Warm Water Under a Red Bridge*, in which a disillusioned Tokyo dweller, having divorced his wife and lost his job, rediscovers enjoyment of life. In fact, the eastern coast is highly urbanized, and only the western part of the peninsula has remained rural and traditional, with its wild natural beauty and rugged coastline.

Wajima★ 輪島
81mi/130km northeast of Kanazawa.

A small fishing port *(population 31,000)* on the northwest coast of the peninsula, Wajima is one of the area's principal attractions. Its main claims to fame are its highly regarded lacquerware *(Wajima-nuri)* and lively **morning**

market★ (♨*open daily 8am–noon;* ♨*closed 2nd & 4th Wed of the month)*. Tourists and villagers flock to the 100-odd stands, which sell dried fish, seafood and a vast array of lacquerware. The fish vendors hail customers in loud, cheeky voices. Continuing north along the main street *(Asaichi-dori),* you will reach the **harbor**, where fishermen calmly mend their nets oblivious to the big black crows circling overhead.

Wajima Lacquerware Center★ – *15min walk southwest of the market, next to Shin-bashi bridge.* ♨*Open daily 8.30am–5pm.* ✆*¥200.* Over 5000 pieces made by the 170 members of the Wajima Association of Lacquerers are on display at this museum, alongside some much older items (some over 400 years old). Lacquerware is also on sale; depending on the process used, it may take up to 120 applications over six months to produce a bowl, hence the prices *(for a soup bowl, ¥8000–¥50,000)*. You may be able to watch artisans at work.

Kiriko Kaikan★★ – *20min walk east of the station or 5min by bus, Kiriko Kaikan stop.* ♨*Open daily 8am–5pm.* ✆*¥620.* This exhibition hall has a collection of some fine *kiriko*—giant, colored paper lanterns—that are paraded during Wajima's festivals to attract the attention of the gods, many around 33ft/10m high. A video of the festivals is also shown.

Soji-ji★ – *Monzen village, 16mi/25km southwest of Wajima on Route 249 (45min by bus).* ♨*Open daily 8am–5pm.* ✆*¥400. sojiji.jp.* Founded in 1321, this magnificent temple was one of the main bases of the Soto school of Zen Buddhism until it was destroyed by fire in 1898. Subsequently restored and relocated, it still has some superb buildings containing interesting Buddhist statues. The temple has a room where visitors can take part in a *zazen* morning meditation session *(Sept–Jun daily, ¥500; book ahead)*, and tours by monks are available in English *(¥400; book ahead)*.

Sosogi★ 曽々木

10.5mi/17km east of Wajima.
Noto's magnificent **coast road★** runs past the scenic terraced paddy fields of Senmaida and the jagged inlets of the coastline to the small village of Sosogi, which has two interesting buildings. These thatched houses once belonged to the Tokikuni family, descended from Taira Tokitada, one of the survivors of the Taira clan, who took refuge here. **Shimo Tokikuni-ke**, or "low house" *(10min walk from Sosogi bus stop;* Open *Apr–Nov Sat–Sun 10am–4pm,* ¥500, *tokikunike.com)*, was built in 1590, and has a fine garden. The larger **Kami Tokikuni-ke**, or "high house" (Open *daily: Jul–Sept 8.30am–5.30pm; Oct–Jun 8.30am–5pm,* ¥520, *tokikunike.jp)*, was built at the beginning of the 19C for another branch of the same family.

Cape Rokko-zaki

16mi/25km to northeast.
Once beyond Sosogi, the road leads past a succession of undulating hills and sheer cliffs until it reaches Rokko-zaki, the farthest point on the peninsula.

There are several hiking trails near Rokko-zaki lighthouse, which are particularly pleasant in summer.

Noto-Ogi★ 能登小木

16mi/25km south of Sosogi.
Protected by a deep fjord, Noto-Ogi is mainly worth a visit for its magnificent **bay**, filled with deep-sea fishing boats, with rows of lamps suspended above their decks. Squid fishing by lamplight is in fact quite common in Japan—not surprising when you consider that the Japanese consume more squid than any other nation in the world.

ADDRESSES

🛏 STAY

KANAZAWA

🛏 **Minshuku Ginmatsu** 民宿銀松 – 1-17-18 Higashiyama (Map, B1). ℘076-252-3577. 5 rooms. ¥7600. ¥1000 ⌷. 🖶. This simple, clean *minshuku* is located in

attractive Higashi Chayamachi. Guests get free use of a local *sento* (public bath).

🛏 **Hotel Hinodeya** ホテルひので屋 – 2-17-25 Honmachi (Map, A1). ℘076-231-5224. hotelhinodeya.com. 20 rooms. ¥6600. ¥500–700 ⌷. A well-maintained, comfortable business hotel, just a few minutes from the JR station (east exit).

🛏 **Murataya Ryokan** 村田屋旅館 – 1-5-2 Katamachi (Map, A3). ℘076-263-0455. murataya-ryokan.com. 11 rooms. ¥10,400. ¥550–850 ⌷. This friendly *ryokan* is ideally situated for an evening out. The lady of the house speaks English and will shower you with information.

🛏🛏 **Sumiyoshi-ya Ryokan** 旅館すみよし屋 – 54 Jukken-machi (Map, B2). ℘076-221-0157. sumiyoshi-ya.com. 8 rooms. ¥13,000. ¥1200 ⌷, dinner also available. A lovely *ryokan* in a spectacular building, serving beautiful Japanese meals.

🛏🛏🛏 **Kanazawa Hakuchoro Hotel Sanraku** 金沢白鳥路ホテル山楽 – 6-3 Marunouchi (Map, B2). ℘076-222-1212. sanraku.premierhotel-group.com/kanazawa. 85 rooms. ¥28,600. ⌷. A beautiful hotel dating from the beginning of the 20C, close to Kenroku-en. Rooms are larger than average, and there's a magnificent *onsen* and lovely Japanese garden.

KAGA ONSEN

🛏🛏 **Hoshi Ryokan** 法師 – Wa-46 Amazu-machi. ℘0761-65-1111. ho-shi.co.jp. 70 rooms. ¥13,300. ¥2200 ⌷, dinner around ¥5000. Apparently the world's oldest hotel, founded over 1300 years ago by Garyo Hoshi, the son of a traveling companion of the monk Taicho. This beautiful *ryokan* satisfies any craving for "traditional Japan": enjoy natural hot springs, elegant *kaiseki* cuisine and the tea ceremony. Wifi available, but only in the lobby.

EIHEI-JI

🛏🛏 **Hakujukan** 柏樹関 – 6-1 Shihi, Eiheiji-cho. ℘0776-63-1188. hakujukan-eiheiji.jp. 18 rooms. ¥32,000. ⌷, dinner also included. Built in 2019 at the base of the holy mountain where Eihei-ji sits, in collaboration with the temple, Hakujukan offers hotel comforts with temple-stay activities. You can enjoy *shojin-ryori* meals, practice *zazen*, and try sutra copying.

NOTO PENINSULA

🛏 **Minshuku Yokoiwa-ya** 温泉民宿・横岩屋 – Ku-2 Machino-machi, Sosogi.

🎣 0768-32-0603. wajima.gr.jp/yokoiwaya.
7 rooms. ¥9450. ¥840 🍴, dinner around
¥1400. Friendly inn ideally located by the
sea, with an *o-furo*. Pick-up from Sosogi-
guchi bus stop available.

🍲 **Noto-Isaribi Youth Hostel** 能登漁
火ユースホステル – *Yo 51-6, Noto-Ogi.*
🎣 0768-74-0150. bit.ly/notohostel. 5
dorms. ¥3900 per person. ¥600 🍴, dinner
¥1200. 🍴. A lovely hostel with *tatami*
dorms, owned by a friendly fisherman.
Unsurprisingly, the meals feature
delicious, fresh seafood.

🍲🍲 **Hotel Koushuen** ホテル高州園 –
2-31-6 Tsukada-machi, Wajima. 🎣 0768-22-
8888. koushuen.co.jp. 132 rooms. ¥16,800.
¥1650 🍴, dinner available. This large hotel
complex overlooking the coast offers a
vast range of services. Bar and karaoke
available after nightfall. Japanese and
Western rooms.

🍲🍲🍲 **Hyakuraku-so** 能登九十九
湾百楽荘 – *11-34 Otsusaka, Noto-Ogi.*
🎣 0768-74-1115. 100raku-noto.com. 27
rooms. ¥35,500. ¥1100 🍴, dinner ¥3300.
This unusual *ryokan* overlooks the
superb Tsukumo Bay. A tunnel takes you
98ft/30m down to sea level, where there
is a wonderful *onsen* in a cave.

🍴 EAT

KANAZAWA

🐟 Fish and seafood reign supreme in
Kanazawa. The city makes something of a
specialty of *kaiten-zushi*, those restaurants
where plates of sushi revolve on a
conveyor belt.

🍲 **Omicho Market** 近江町市場 –
50 Kami-omicho (Map, B1/2). 🎣 076-231-
1462. ohmicho-ichiba.com. Market open
daily 9am–5pm (approx). Of the many
stands and restaurants at this market,
the *kaiten-zushi* restaurant **Okura** (open
10.30am–6.30/7pm) and more upmarket
Ichinokura (open 11am–10pm), are
among the best. Freshness is guaranteed.

🍲🍲🍲 **Genzaemon** 源左エ門 – *5-3
Kigura-machi (Map, A3).* 🎣 076-232-7110.
Open daily 5pm–midnight. Around ¥5500. A
50-year-old *izakaya*-style restaurant well
known for the freshness of its fish. The
friendly, twinkly-eyed owner, Hayashi,
fillets fish at the speed of light!

🍲🍲🍲 **Jugatsuya** 十月亭 – *1-26-16
Higashi Chayamachi.* 🎣 076-253-3321.
Open Thu–Tue 11.30am–10pm. Lunch
from ¥3000, dinner from ¥9000. Book well
ahead for dinner. In a lovely traditional

building, close to the Shima teahouse
in the Higashi Chayamichi district. You
can sample traditional Kanazawa cuisine
here.

🍲🍲 **Unkai** 雲海 – *16-3
Showamachi (Map, A1).* 🎣 076-224-9805.
anacrowneplaza-kanazawa.jp/rest/unkai/
index.html. Open daily 11.30am–2.30pm
& 5–9.30pm. Lunch from ¥2700, dinner
¥7000. Next to a Japanese garden on the
fifth floor of the ANA Crowne Plaza Hotel,
this restaurant offers refined cuisine in an
elegant setting.

🍲🍲🍲🍲 **Mitsukawa** みつ川 – *1-16-2
Higashiyama.* 🎣 076-253-5005. sushi-
mitsukawa.jp. Open Thu–Tue noon–2pm
& 5.30–10pm. Lunch from ¥6600, dinner
from ¥11,000. Book well ahead. In Higashi
Chayamichi, not far from Kaikaro tea
house. The sushi is exceptional, prepared
in front of you.

TAKING A BREAK

KANAZAWA

Kaburaki – *1-3-6 Nagamachi (Map, A2).*
🎣 076-221-6666. kaburaki.jp. Open Tues–
Sat 9am–10pm, Sun–Mon 9am–6pm. The
city's oldest shop specializing in Kutani
porcelain, in the heart of the samurai
district. *Matcha* is served in beautiful
cups, and there's a small, free museum.

Café Kotomi – *1-2-27 Hirosaka (Map, B2).*
🎣 076-222-5103. kotomikanazawa.jp/
cafe. Open Tue–Sun 11am–6pm. A haven
of peace above a pastry shop, this cafe
has picture windows, soft music, retro
furniture, and serves Japanese treats.

SHOPPING

KANAZAWA

Hakuza Hikarigura – *1-13-18 Higashiyama
(Map, B1).* 🎣 0176-251-8930. hakuza.co.jp.
Open daily 9.30am–6pm (5.30pm winter).
Gold leaf adorns many items in this shop,
from decorative objects and jewelry to
white wine and cakes. Look out for the
sumptuous, gilded *kura* (storage room).

Kanazawa Crafts Hirosaka – *1-2-25
Hirosaka (Map, B2).* 🎣 076-265-3320. crafts-
hirosaka.jp. Open Tue–Sun 10am–6pm.
Two floors of items made by Kanazawa
craftspeople, from papier mâché animals
and Mizuhiki brooches to colorful
Temari balls and ceramics. Temporary
exhibitions highlight the work of young
designers.

Sado Island★★
佐渡島

Sado is popular among the Japanese holidaymakers as a place where both nature and traditions have been preserved. During the Middle Ages, it was the island to which aristocrats and samurai defeated in power struggles would be sent into exile. But Sado turned a curse into an asset. Given those sent into exile were often highly cultured, they stimulated the island's artistic life, which has flourished ever since. Among the most notable were Emperor Juntoku (1197–1242), the monk Nichiren (1222–82), and Zeami (1363–1443), one of the creators of Noh, a form of theater still widely practiced here, with no fewer than 34 stages scattered throughout the island. Sado is also famous for its *bunya ningyo* puppets, and for the Kodo drummers, who have superstar status in Japan. In the 17C, the island experienced a gold rush, and artists and noblemen were replaced by thousands of convicts sent to work in the mines, a backbreaking activity that went on for more than three centuries. Today, Sado mainly attracts city dwellers in search of a little of old Japan, as well as hikers who like to camp in summer in its flower-strewn fields or near the rocky capes used as a refuge by migrating birds.

▶ **Population:** 55,500 – Niigata Prefecture.

Michelin Map: Regional Map pp252–3 C1.

Location: 22mi/35km off Niigata, in the Sea of Japan, Sado Island covers an area of 330sq mi/855sq km, which makes it the sixth largest island in the country. It consists of two mountain ranges with a broad rice-growing plain in the middle, hence the characteristic "S" shape. The island's capital, Ryotsu, is connected to Niigata by ferry and hydrofoil. The other notable town is Mano, on the west coast. Ogi, in the south of the island, is where ferries from Naoetsu land. Buses (passes 1–3 days, ¥1500–3000) serve the main points on the island, but with a reduced service Nov–Mar. Bike rental is a good option for shorter trips.

Kids: A *bunya ningyo* puppet show; a tub boat ride; Kodo drumming.

Timing: Allow at least two days to tour the island. Renting a car (several services in Ryotsu) will make getting about a lot easier.

Don't miss: The Earth Celebration, in August; the gold mine at Sado Kinzan.

SIGHTS

RYOTSU★ 両津
The main harbor town of Sado, Ryotsu is, logistically, the most convenient point of entry to the island, but it is not the most attractive of its towns.

Futatsu-game and Ono-game★★ 二つ亀・大野亀
From Ryotsu, Uchikaifu Line bus to Washizaki (about 1hr journey time).
These two superb rocky sites, linked by a footpath, are in the northeast tip of the island. The name of the first means "two turtles," because of its natural shape. There is also a popular **black-sand beach** here. Given the size of the second rock *(550ft/167m)*, the locals believe that, like all unusual natural sites, it houses a deity. On the path between the two, you pass **Sai no kawara**, a natural cave containing hundreds of small *jizo* statues, symbolizing the children who it's believed make their last stop here on their way to heaven.

Paddy fields by Lake Kamo, Ryotsu

© helovi/iStock

Sado Kinzan★ 佐渡金山

1305 Shimo-Aikawa. Nanaura-kaigan Line buses from Ryotsu to Aikawa (around 1hr journey), then Sado Kinzan bus (10min journey), or a pleasant walk (parallel to the main road rather than long it). In summer, buses go directly to the site. ◷Open daily: April–Oct 8am–5.30pm; Nov–March 8.30am–5pm. ◷¥900 for each tunnel, or ¥1400 for both. sado-kinzan.com.

This **gold mine** dates back to 1601 and remained in use until 1989. During its 380-odd years as a working mine, 80 tons of gold were extracted from its 250mi/400km of galleries. More than half of this went to the coffers of the Tokugawa Shogunate. In the **Sodayu Tunnel**, animatronic miners are used to explain the various extraction processes. The system for pumping spring water to supply the upper galleries is particularly ingenious. The **Doyu Tunnel** is less interesting in itself, but emerges to a stunning and unusual view.

MANO★ 真野

16mi/26km west of Ryotsu on Route 350 (45min by Minamisen Line bus).

The town of Mano, near the bay of the same name, the most sheltered on the island, is surrounded by sites of historical and religious interest, and also has a good **beach**.

Konpon-ji★ 根本寺

Konponjimae bus stop on Minamisen Line. ◷Open daily: Apr–Oct 8am–4.30pm; Nov–Mar 8am–3.30pm. ◷¥300. www.sado-konponji.com.

This temple is one of the 44 principal centers of the Buddhist sect founded by the monk Nichiren. Its fine buildings, with their impressive thatched roofs, are arranged around a pleasant garden.

Kokubun-ji 国分寺

2.5mi/4km walk from the previous temple along the footpath. ◷Open daily dawn–dusk. ◷No charge.

The oldest temple on Sado. The present building dates from 1679, but excavations (visible in a large field, west of the current temple complex) have revealed foundations apparently laid in the 8C by Emperor Shomu.

Sado Rekishi-Densetsukan Museum 佐渡歴史伝説館

2mi/3km walk from Kokubun-ji, on the same path. ◷Open daily: Apr–Nov 8.30am–5pm; Dec–Mar 9am–4.30pm. ◷¥800. sado-rekishi.jp.

This museum has a hi-tech approach, using hologrms and robots to illustrate the island's history and tell its folk stories. The shop has a lot of local craft items, and there's a good, simple restaurant on site too.

USEFUL INFORMATION

TOURIST OFFICES

Ryotsu – *On the ground floor of the Kisen Ferry Terminal. Open daily 7am–6pm. ☏0259-27-5000. visitsado.com/en.* **Ogi** – *On the ground floor of the Marine Plaza Bldg. Open Mon–Sat 8.30am–5.30pm. ☏0259-86-3200.*

TRANSPORTATION

If you have a JR East Pass, it's worth buying a **Sado-Niigata Pass** (*¥4000, sado-niigata.com/pass*), which covers the return ferry trip, a 3-day bus pass on Sado, and e-bike rental.

RYOTSU

BY TRAIN – From **Tokyo to Niigata**, Shinkansen Max Toki *(2hr, ¥10,230).* **BY BOAT** – From **Niigata**, boats roughly hourly for Ryotsu *(ferry 2hr 30min, ¥2420 each way; jetfoil 1hr, ¥6510 each way).*

OGI

BY TRAIN – Shinkansen Hakutaka then Ltd Express Shirayuki from **Kanazawa to Naoetsu** *(1hr 30min, ¥6180).* Shinkansen Hakutaka and Myoko Haneuma Line from **Nagano to Naoetsu** *(1hr, ¥3110).* Both via Joetsumyoko. **BY BOAT** – From **Naoetsu**, 3–5 boats per day Mar–Oct for Ogi *(1hr 40min, ¥3840 each way).*

GETTING AROUND THE ISLAND

BY BUS – The island has 15 bus lines: *www.visitsado.com/en/tosado/insado.* **Bus pass:** *1/2/3 days, ¥1500/2500/3000.* **By Car** – Several rental companies at Ryotsu ferry terminal exit. *From around ¥6500 per day.* **BY BIKE** – Bike rental is available at Ryotsu, Osi and Aikawa Tourist Offices. *Around ¥1500 per day, ¥2000 for e-bikes.*

Myosen-ji 妙宣寺

20min walk west of the museum. 🕑*Open daily dawn–dusk.* ☞*No charge.* The first disciple of the Buddhist monk Nichiren, Nittoku Abutsubo, is believed to have founded the shrine in 1221. Two generations of carpenters are said to have worked on its impressive five-story pagoda *(79ft/24m in height),* which was finally completed in 1825.

OGI★ 小木

11mi/17km southwest of Mano (50min by Ogi Line bus). The gateway to the southwestern part of the island, with its maritime links to Naoetsu, Ogi *(population 3000)* was the port through which gold products were exported to Edo between the 17C and the 19C. A rather sleepy place today, the town comes to life every year for the great **Earth Celebration** *(Aug 18–20, kodo.or.jp),* featuring the Kodo *taiko* drums. Another big draw for tourists are the **tarai-bune**, large round tubs used by the villagers as boats to collect seaweed and abalone. For a modest sum, wearing their traditional costume, women will take you out in their boats for a trip around the harbor *(¥500 for 10min, Mar–Nov daily approx. 9am–4.30pm, bit.ly/ogi-boats).*

Sadokoku Ogi Folk Museum★

佐渡国小木民俗博物館

West of Ogi on Route 45 (Shukunegi Line bus, Ogi Minzoku Hakubutsukan-mae stop; 11min journey). 🕑*Open 8.30am–5pm: Apr–Oct daily; Nov–Mar Tue–Sun.* ☞*¥500. bit.ly/sadokoku.* This museum displays various relics from the island's past, including a fine reconstruction of an Edo-period ship. A former school from the 1920s adjoining the museum houses thousands of everyday objects used by the islanders.

Sado Island Taiko Center★★

佐渡太鼓体験交流館

West of Ogi on Route 45 (Shukunegi Line bus, Taiko-taiken-koryukan stop; 10min journey). 🕑*Open Tue–Sun 9am–5pm; drumming lessons Sat–Sun 10am, 1.30pm & 3pm, weekdays with reservation.* ☞*¥2000 for 1hr drumming lesson. sadotaiken.jp.*

This attractive timber building contains a large hall where the Kodo drummers teach visitors how to play the traditional *taiko* drums. A lot of fun (andgood exercise) for both adults and children.

Shukunegi 宿根木

1mi/1.5km from the previous museum.
In a village known for its shipyards, it is not surprising to find in its narrow streets some fine old houses built of planks taken from disused boats. Three of them are open to the public, including the **Seikuro house** (🕐open Sept–Jun 9am–4pm, Jul–Aug 8.30am–5pm, 👓 ¥400). On a nearby street corner is a house shaped like a boat.

Shukunegi is also a good place for *tarai-bune* rides, and while the Ogi tub boats are generally made from fiberglass, here they're still wooden (*¥800–2000 for 15–35min, Mar–Nov daily 9am–6pm*).

ADDRESSES

🏯 STAY

RYOTSU

🛏 **Green Village Patio House** グリーンヴィレッジ・ユースホステル – *750-4 Niibo Uryuya, 9km outh of Ryotsu.* 📞*0259-22-2719. bit.ly/sado-greenvillage. 6 rooms. Dorms/twins ¥3850 per person, singles ¥4180. ¥770 ☕.* Former youth hostel with 2 single rooms and 4 others with bunk beds (can be booked as private twin rooms). Simple, light decor and functional comfort.

MANO

🛏🍽 **Itoya** 伊藤屋 – *278 Mano-Shinmachi, in the heart of Mano, on the main road.* 📞*0259-55-2019. itoyaryokan.com. 15 rooms. ¥12,200. ¥1000 ☕, dinner ¥5000.* This gorgeous *ryokan* is just 220yd/200m from the beach, and offers good-quality service and facilities. All rooms are Japanese style.

OGI

🛏🍽**Hana-no-Ki** 花の木 – *78-1 Shukunegi.* 📞*0259-86-2331. sado-hananoki.com. 7 rooms. ¥13,260. ¥550 ☕, dinner ¥4950.* This exquisite *ryokan* is an elegantly decorated with stone, wood, and traditional Japanese screens. Dinners are sumptuous; specialties include *zuwai-*

gani (crab, except in Jan, Feb & Sept), but food can be vegetarian on request. Pottery classes available. You can arrange to be picked up from the jetty.

🛏🍽 **Kamome-so** かもめ荘 – *11-7 Ogi.* 📞*0259-86-2064. sado-kamomesou.com. 11 rooms.¥12,400. ¥1100 ☕* The *onsen* at this well-maintained, modern *ryokan* are superb and also open to non-residents (*open daily 10am–9pm; ¥450*).

🍽 EAT

RYOTSU

🍽 **Tenkuni** 天國 – *206 Ryotsu-Minato.* 📞*0259-23-2714. Open 11am–3pm & 6–10pm. Around ¥1100.* 🍴. Simple, copious Japanese food. Especially good for sashimi or tempura *donburi* style (on rice).

MANO

🍽🍽 **Toki** 登貴 – *743-2 Mano-Shinmachi.* 📞*0259-55-2137. Open Tue–Sat 5–9pm. Set meals around ¥1200.* 🍴. This friendly *izakaya* serves all kinds of fish and seafood, depending on the catch of the day, usually charcoal grilled.

OGI

🍽 **Cafe Nano** カフェなの – *426 Shukunegi.* 📞*0704-314-7862. Usually open Fri–Mon 11am–4.30pm. Lunch around ¥1000.* 🍴. In an old wooden building in sleepy Shukunegi, this welcoming cafe serves waffles and home-made ice cream, plus heartier meals and good coffee.

KYOTO AND KANSAI

Kansai is one of the most popular of Japan's regions, and for several reasons, not least its exceptional geographical location. Covering 12,740sq mi/33,000sq km *(11 percent of Japan)*, it lies at the center of the Japanese archipelago open to three bodies of water: the Sea of Japan to the north, the Pacific Ocean to the south, and the Inland Sea facing the island of Shikoku; despite the region's mountainous relief, these three seas are interconnected by convenient land "corridors" made up of plains *(Osaka, Wakayama)* and basins *(Kyoto, Nara, Shiga)*. Kansai is also viewed as the cradle of Japanese civilization.

Highlights

Japan: past, present, and future

In the 8C, first Nara and then Kyoto were adopted as the Imperial capital, Kyoto remaining so for a thousand years. Their golden age is well represented in their cultural heritage, both cities having mercifully been spared serious damage from earthquakes and war. Containing as it does the cities of Kobe, Kyoto, and Osaka, Kansai is also the country's second most important economic region.

Home to one-fifth of Japan's population and well-positioned geographically, the region makes the most of its commercial and port facilities. It's also a major IT, manufacturing, and science center, with the Kansai Science City, straddling the prefectures of Kyoto, Osaka, and Nara, playing a vital role. Thus the region is not only a big draw for tourists, but also attracts increasing numbers of professionals from Japan and overseas to service its dynamic economy. That said, it's seen even greater growth in tourism than most of the rest of the country in recent years, with over 17 million visitors staying overnight in the region in 2017.

▶ **Population:** 23 million.

Michelin Map: Regions of Japan Map 3, Regional Map opposite .

Location: Kansai *(or Kinki)* means "province of the west", Kanto "province of the east," as they're the regions west and east of the famous Tokaido road between Kyoto and Tokyo. Kansai, in southern Honshu, covers 12,740sq mi/33,000sq km divided into five *ken* (prefectures): Mie, Shiga, Hyogo, Nara, and Wakayama; and two *fu* (urban prefectures): Kyoto and Osaka.

Kids: The International Manga Museum in Kyoto; a boat trip on the Hozu River in Arashiyama; Shirahama Onsen; the Nachi waterfall with overnight stay in a *shukubo* (temple lodging).

Timing: A week and a half: 3 days in Kyoto, 2 in Nara, 1 in Ise, 1 day on Mount Koya, 2 nights in Osaka to sample the food and nightlife, and the last day in Kobe for Himeji Castle *(itinerary of about 168mi/270km, starting from Kyoto; mostly covered by JR Kansai Wide Area Pass)*. An extra 2 days? Relax at Kinosaki Onsen, or enjoy Ine's coastal charm.

Don't miss: Kyoto, Himeji Castle, Nara, Osaka nightlife, Mount Koya, and Kumano Sanzan shrines.

KYOTO AND KANSAI

```
0                    40 km
0        20 mi
```

TOTTORI

Tottori

4

Kinosaki Onsen

Toyooka

Izushi

Tango Peninsula

Ine

OKAYAMA

Wadayama

Amano Hashidate

Miyazu

SEA OF JAPAN

Wakasa Bay

HYOGO

Takeda Castle Ruins

Maizuru

Ikuno Silver Mine

Tsuruga

FUKUI

Aioi

Japanese Toy Museum

KYOTO

Imazu

Harie

Lake Biwa

HIMEJI

Kakogawa

Takarazuka

KYOTO

Ohara

Nagahama

Mii-dera

Mount Hiei-zan

Hikone

Akashi

Kobe

Itami Airport

Otsu

Uji

MIHO MUSEUM

Honpuku-ji

Osaka Bay

Osaka

Ishiyama-dera

Yodo

SHIGA

Awaji-shima

Kansai International Airport

Sakai

Shigaraki

Kibukawa

Sumoto

Kishiwada

NARA

Yokkaichi

Kii Channel

OSAKA

Hahimoto

HORYU-JI

Kashihara

Suzuka

MIE

Wakayama

Sakurai

Tsu

Ise Bay

WAKAYAMA

KOYA-SAN

Yoshino-yama

Matsusaka

NARA

Ise

KUMANO HONGU TAISHA

KUMANO KODO

Ago

Kii-Tanabe

Tamaki-jinja

Ago Bay

Toba

Shirahama Onsen

Yunomine Onsen

Kumano

Mt Nachi

Kumano Hayatama Taisha

NACHI NO TAKI

Shingu

Kumano Nachi Taisha

Nachi

Kushimoto

Kii-Katsuura

PACIFIC OCEAN

N

KYOTO	★★★	Worth a special journey
Osaka	★★	Worth a detour
Kobe	★	Interesting
Kashihara		Worth seeing

Kyoto★★★
京都

There are 1600 Buddhist temples, 400 Shinto shrines and 200 listed gardens in Kyoto … a substantial 20 percent of Japan's National Treasures, and several UNESCO World Heritage Sites. If to this we add 37 universities which have produced Nobel Prize winners, it becomes abundantly clear why this ancient city is still thought of as the cultural heart of Japan. So much for the overview of the city, only part of which has retained its original green setting. Though it served as Japan's capital for 11 centuries and has been spared many scourges, such as earthquakes and World War II bombing, the city has sadly not escaped urbanization. Development has transformed (for those who don't take the time to get acquainted with it) the city into a series of beautiful but isolated enclaves, leaving visitors often scurrying across stretches of concrete jungle in order to reach the next exquisite temple or peaceful garden. It nevertheless remains an exceptional city, and even within the less picturesque areas there's much to be enjoyed.

A BIT OF HISTORY
Kyoto, the "capital of peace and tranquility"

The Yamashiro basin, enclosed by mountains to the north, and fed by the waters of the Kamo-gawa to the east and the Katsura-gawa to the west, was an ideal place in which to lay out a city according to the then current principles of Chinese geomancy. Kyoto was founded in 794 by Emperor Kanmu (reigned 781–806), who wanted to free his capital (Nara) from the excessive influence of Buddhist monks. The new city was named **Heian-kyo**, the "capital of peace and tranquility." To counter the power of the Nara monks, the emperor went so far as to encourage the founda-

▶ **Population:** 1,475,000

⏚ **Michelin Map:**
Regions of Japan Map 3, Regional Map p309 B2, Kyoto maps p312, p314, p318.

▶ **Location:** Both municipality and urban prefecture *(fu)*, Kyoto consists of 11 districts *(ku)* covering roughly 232sq mi/600sq km. Built to a grid plan, the city is easy to find your way around.

👥 **Kids:** Kyoto International Manga Museum; the Gion district; an *odori* show; a boat trip on the Hozu River at Arashiyama; Toei Studio Park.

🕐 **Timing:** You need several days for Kyoto, or ideally a week. Alternate walks around different districts with visits to temples, going to the most popular early in the day. Tickets for some (e.g. Saiho-ji), need to be reserved well in advance *(possible online for some sights)*.

😊 **Don't miss:** The **temples** of Sanjusangen-do, Kiyomizu-dera, Ginkaku-ji, Daitoku-ji, Kinkaku-ji, Ryoan-ji; the **districts** of Pontocho and Gion; the Philosopher's Path. Kyoto Station; Katsura Imperial Villa; Saiho-ji; Byodo-in (Uji); the Miho Museum; Lake Biwa.

tion of new Buddhist sects, with doctrines introduced by two monks who have since become legendary: Saicho (767–822) and Kukai (774–835), founders of the Tendai-shu and Shingon-shu sects respectively. The new city was laid out *(like Nara)* on a **square grid plan** modeled on the Chinese Tang dynasty capital of Chang'an *(now Xian)*.

Higashiyama district with Yasaka pagoda, Hokan-ji

Once the Imperial Palace had been erected (facing the inauspicious north), temples and shrines were built to protect the different entrances to the city: **To-ji** and **Sai-ji** to the south, **Kamigamo-jinja** in the northwest, and **Enryaku-ji** (founded by Saicho on Mount Hiei in 788) to the northeast.

An aristocratic crossroads of art and religion

The new Japanese capital enjoyed its heyday during the Heian period (794–1185), and began to develop its own national style after the fall of the Tang dynasty (907). Heian-kyo then became a great aristocratic crossroads of the arts and religion under the aegis of the **Fujiwara** family. By introducing a regency system, with the role of regent being passed from father to son, the Fujiwara were able to retain power until the end of the 12C (❂ *see box, below*). This continuity of power fostered Kyoto's cultural development, as can be seen from Byodo-in, erected in the south of the city. As a result, the Chinese style of painting was superseded by the Yamato style, better suited to the movable features of Japanese buildings (sliding panels, screens, etc.). As the worship of Amida gained ground, a suitable way of representing the Buddha had to be found, one worthy of "this Buddha of infinite light," and so the technique of *kirikane* (gold leaf decoration) came to dominate sacred iconography. The Fujiwara family prospered but toward the end of the 12C, they could not prevent the growing influence of the Taira clan over Emperor Go-Shirakawa (1127–92). There was increasing rivalry in the corridors of power and open warfare eventually broke out between the Taira and Minamoto clans. This led to the first decentralized shogunate at Kamakura.

Sessho and sekkan – the Fujiwara regents

The Heian era (794–1185), also known as the Fujiwara period, reflects the dominance of the Fujiwara family, which became powerful through its influence, alliances, and marriages with members of the Imperial Family, a process that culminated in the creation of the new role of regent. **Fujiwara no Yoshifusa** (804–72) became *sessho*, "regent for an emperor while still a minor," to Seiwa (850–80), who was just eight years old when he became Emperor in 858. Yoshifusa's son, **Fujiwara no Mototsune** (836–91), strengthened the family's power, and in 884 introduced the position of *kanpaku*, or regent for emperors who had already attained their majority, including Yozei, Koko, and Uda. This new hereditary office, which gave the Fujiwaras full powers, was referred to as *sekkan*, a contraction of *sessho* and *kanpaku*.

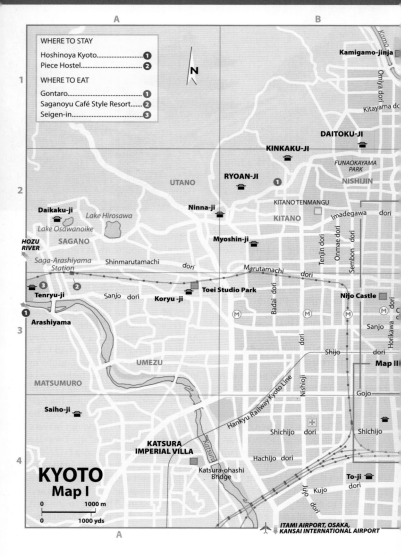

WHERE TO STAY

Hoshinoya Kyoto.....................❶
Piece Hostel............................❷

WHERE TO EAT

Gontaro...................................❶
Saganoyu Café Style Resort.......❷
Seigen-in................................❸

KYOTO
Map I

0   1000 m
0   1000 yds

Higashiyama—The culture of the "Eastern Mountains"

During the Kamakura period (1185–1333) Kyoto became less important. It was not until the Ashikaga shoguns, descendants of the Minamotos, came to power that Imperial rulers returned to the city. During the Ashikaga era (1333–1573), also known as the Muromachi era *(named after the district of Kyoto where the shoguns lived),* the arts once again flourished in Kyoto. The **Golden Pavilion** *(Kinkaku-ji)* was built during the rule of the third shogun **Ashikaga Yoshimitsu** *(1358–1408).*

But this period, though innovative, was followed by years of violence and chaos during which rivalries between feudal lords led to the terrible Onin War (1467–77), which escalated nationwide. The war reduced Kyoto to ashes, but eventually a new artistic and philosophical movement began to gain strength, inspired by the eighth shogun

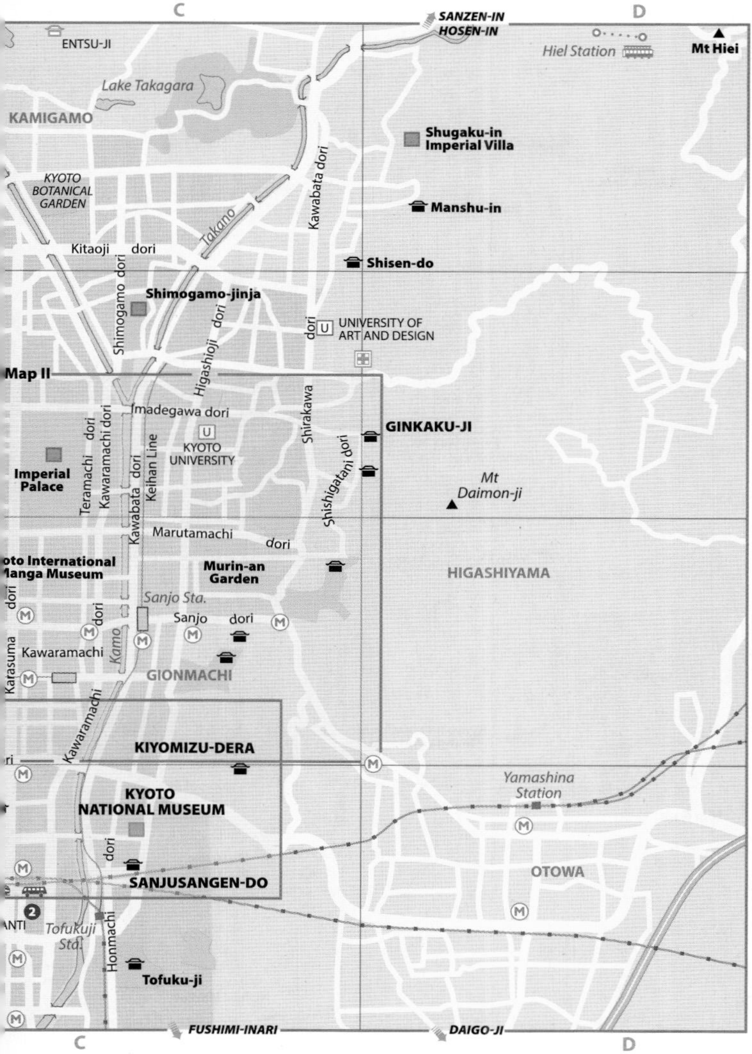

Map labels

ENTSU-JI

SANZEN-IN HOSEN-IN

Hiel Station ▲ **Mt Hiei**

Lake Takagara

KAMIGAMO

■ **Shugaku-in Imperial Villa**

Kawabata dori

KYOTO BOTANICAL GARDEN

Takano

🏠 **Manshu-in**

Kitaoji dori

🏠 **Shisen-do**

Shimogamo dori

Shimogamo-jinja

Higashioji dori

🔲 **UNIVERSITY OF ART AND DESIGN**

Map II

Imadegawa dori

Shirakawa

GINKAKU-JI

Teramachi dori
Kawaramachi dori
Kawabata dori
Keihan Line

🔲 KYOTO UNIVERSITY

Shishigatani dori

Imperial Palace

Mt Daimon-ji ▲

Marutamachi dori

Murin-an Garden

HIGASHIYAMA

Kyoto International Manga Museum

Sanjo Sta.

Sanjo dori Ⓜ

Karasuma
Kawaramachi
Kamo

Ⓜ Kawaramachi

GIONMACHI

KIYOMIZU-DERA

KYOTO NATIONAL MUSEUM

Yamashina Station

OTOWA

dori

SANJUSANGEN-DO

② ANTI *Tofukuji Sta.*

Honmachi

Tofuku-ji

FUSHIMI-INARI *DAIGO-JI*

Body text

of the Muromachi *bakufu*: **Ashikaga Yoshimasa** (riegned 1449–73).

Retiring to the Eastern Mountains (*Higashiyama*), Yoshimasa focused on the study of Zen Buddhism and the accompanying pared-back aesthetics. The **Silver Pavilion** (Ginkaku-ji, modeled on the Golden Pavilion, Kinkaku-ji), became the style's prototypical structure (👆 *see p337*), and courtly and samurai arts were combined and elevated even further.

The aristocracy was won over to a more ascetic lifestyle, at once in harmony but also in conflict with the turmoil of the period, which was softened or sublimated by cultural pursuits such as the formal tea ceremony (*cha-no-yu*), the art of creating dry landscape gardens (in which the spirit is nourished rather than the physical senses), or the pleasures of flower arranging (*ikebana*). When Yoshimasa died, Kyoto lapsed into a state of anarchy.

Nishijin
Textile Center

Raku Museum

Imadegawa Sta.

Imperial
Palace

OMIYA GOSHO

SENTO GOSHO

KYOTO GYOEN

Kamo-gawa River

Kawaramachi-dori Ave.

KYOTO PREF.
GOVERNMENT OFFICE

Marutamachi-dori Ave.

Marutamachi Sta.

Nijo Castle

Horikawa-dori St.

Karasuma-dori Ave.

Nijo-dori St.   ❶

Kyoto
Shiyakusho-
mae Sta.

Kyoto International
Manga Museum

❼

23

10

❼

KYOTO CITY
OFFICE

Oike-dori Ave.

26

❾

Nijojo-
mae Sta.

Karasuma-
Oike Sta.

Nijo jinya

Sanjo-dori

21

NAKA P.O.🏣

Museum
of Kyoto

13

❶

8

16

❸

5

Pontocho
Kaburenjo
Theater

Teramachi Shopping Arcade

15

19

12

6

koji St.

11

Pontocho-
dori

11

25

Nishiki
Nishiki Market

20

ℹ

Omiya Sta.

Hankyu Kyoto Line
Shijo-Omiya Sta.

Karasuma Sta.

Shijo-dori Ave.

❾

Kawaramachi
Sta.

Shijo Sta.

Seishu Netsuke
Art Museum

14

❸

❺

❷

22

12

❶

367

❹

❿

Gojo Sta.

Copyright 2015 Cartographic data Shobunsha/Michelin

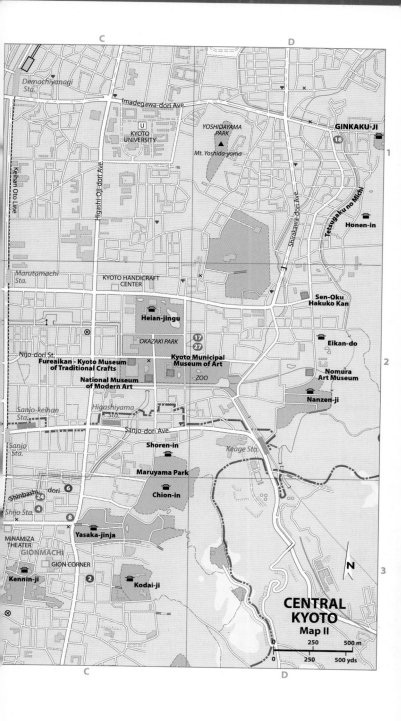

Demachiyanagi Sta.

Imadegawa-dori Ave.

YOSHIDAYAMA PARK

KYOTO UNIVERSITY

Mt. Yoshida-yama

GINKAKU-JI

18

Tetsugaku no Michi

Honen-in

Shirakawa-dori Ave.

Higashi-Oji-dori Ave.

Keihan Oto Line

Marutamachi Sta.

KYOTO HANDICRAFT CENTER

Sen-Oku Hakuko Kan

Heian-jingu

OKAZAKI PARK

17
27

Eikan-do

Nijo-dori St.

Fureaikan - Kyoto Museum of Traditional Crafts

Kyoto Municipal Museum of Art

Nomura Art Museum

National Museum of Modern Art

ZOO

Nanzen-ji

Sanjo-keihan Sta.

Higashiyama Sta.

Sanjo-dori Ave.

Sanjo Sta.

Shoren-in

Keage Sta.

Maruyama Park

Chion-in

Shinbashi-dori

6

24

Shijo Sta.

4

8

MINAMIZA THEATER

Yasaka-jinja

GIONMACHI

GION CORNER

Kennin-ji

2

Kodai-ji

N

CENTRAL KYOTO
Map II

0   250   500 m

0   250   500 yds

CENTRAL KYOTO
Map II

WHERE TO STAY

Hirota Guesthouse.............**1** B2
Hotel in Gion Maifukan.............**2** B3
Inn Kawashima.............**3** B3
Itoya.............**4** B3
Khaosan Kyoto Guest House.............**5** B3
Mume Boutique Hotel.............**6** C3
Nishiyama Ryokan.............**7** B2
Royal Park Hotel Kyoto Sanjo.............**8** B2
Ryokan Kinmata.............**9** B2
Ryokan Sawai.............**10** B3
Super Hotel.............**11** B3
9 Hours.............**12** B3

WHERE TO EAT

Bio-Tei.............**1** B2
Bussarakan.............**2** B3
Ganko Sanjo Honten.............**3** B2
Gonbe.............**4** C3
Grilldorebun.............**5** B2
Hale.............**6** B3
Honke Owariya.............**7** B2
Izuju.............**8** C3
Kerala.............**9** B2
Kushikura.............**10** B2
Kyomachi.............**11** B3
Kyoto Gogyo.............**12** B3
Misoka-an Kawamichiya.............**13** B2
Miyakoyasai Kamo.............**14** B3

Mukadeya.............**15** A3
Musashi.............**16** B2
Okakita.............**17** C2
Omen Ginkakuji Honten.............**18** D1
Ootoya.............**19** B3
Tomi Zushi.............**20** B3
Ukiya.............**21** B2
Waka.............**22** B3
Watanabeya.............**23** B2
Yagenbori Sueyoshicho-ten.............**24** C3
Yamatomi.............**25** B3
Yoshikawa Inn.............**26** B2
Yamamotomenzo.............**27** C2

KYOTO STATION
Map III

WHERE TO STAY

Aranvert Hotel.............**1** A1
Dormy Inn Premium Kyoto Ekimae.............**2** B2
Gion Guesthouse IKKUU.............**3** B2
Hanakiya Inn.............**4** D1
Hotel Iida.............**5** B2
Kikokuso Inn.............**6** B2
K's House.............**7** B2
Ryokan Shimizu.............**7** A2

WHERE TO EAT

Kyosuishin.............**1** B2
Okutan.............**2** D1
Ramen Alley.............**3** B2

For the military leader **Oda Nobunaga,** who established his headquarters in the neighboring region of Gifu, it was necessary to re-establish authority over Kyoto. In 1573, during the Sengoku of "Warring States" period, he finally drove the last shogun of the Ashikaga dynasty from the Imperial capital.

Once established in his power base, Nobunaga began to build the castle of Nijo, but he was betrayed soon after (1582) and committed *seppuku*, leaving his lieutenants, **Toyotomi Hideyoshi** and **Tokugawa Ieyasu**, the task of completing it and transforming it into an aristocratic residence *(shoin-zukuri)*.

Saved by a miracle

In fact, the new shogun, Ieyasu, already had a castle and therefore preferred, in 1603, to move his headquarters to Edo *(Tokyo)*. Though Kyoto continued to be the Imperial capital, power was henceforth exercised from elsewhere. For more than 250 years, the Tokugawa reigned unopposed until 1869, when Emperor Meiji transferred his capital to Tokyo, already the seat of administrative power, thus restoring Imperial authority. Kyoto was left to its golden slumbers. Luck was with Kyoto during World War II, when it became the only large Japanese city to escape the destruction unleashed by the conflict. It was even spared the atomic bomb, despite being on the list of potential targets, when an advisor with a soft spot for Japanese culture (there's disagreement over exactly who) told President Truman that the country would never recover from the loss of Kyoto's historical and cultural riches. Kyoto was spared, and in its place Nagasaki was targeted.

Japan's seventh most populous city, Kyoto is now a magnet for tourists and a center of highly sophisticated traditional craftsmanship. Since the signing of the Kyoto Protocol (December 1997), the city has also become synonymous with the world's efforts to combat the threat of climate change and global warming.

SIGHTS

AROUND THE STATION
Allow 2 days.

Kyoto Station★ 京都駅
🕭*Map III, B2.* 🅸*Kyoto's main tourist office is on the 2nd floor. kyotostation.com.*
Opened in 1997 to mark the 1200th anniversary of the foundation of Heian-kyo, Kyoto's station is strikingly modern. However, according to architect Hara Hiroshi (born 1936), the layout of the vast complex reflects the history of the city, as well as its geographical location, combining plain and mountains under a wide expanse of sky. Thus, the station's immense atrium *(89ft/27m wide by 197ft/60m high by 1542ft/470m long)*, modeled on the traditional grid pattern of Chinese towns, combines a flat, low area *(the entrance to the station, representing the plain)* and upper levels *(the mountains)* at the top of which is a roof garden, from where there is a fine **panoramic view★** out over Kyoto.

The 250,000-odd travelers who pass through this monumental steel-and-glass construction each day are implicitly walking in the footsteps of their ancestors, except that here, the "mountain," consisting of 16 floors *(three of them below ground level)*, is scaled by an immense escalator that cuts across the atrium like a *kamishide* (one of the white-paper zigzag shapes often hung at the entrance to a shrine).

While the architect Hara may have wished to convey the sacred associations of high places, he did not neglect the many more usual functions offered by Japanese stations. A luxury hotel and entertainment venue *(900 seats)* form its east wing, while the Isetan department store, with its array of shopping arcades and restaurants, always full to capacity, occupies the west side.

Kyoto Tower 京都タワー
🕭*Map III, B2.*
It's hard to miss the giant silhouette of Kyoto Tower as you exit the station. It's a far cry from the dreams of pagodas and teahouses that recently disembarked tourists might have been harboring, and it certainly attracted criticism from the more conservative Kyotoite circles when unveiled. Built by Tanahashi Makoto in 1964 for the Tokyo Olympics, it is 430ft/131m high and features a UFO-like bulge near the top, a peculiarity that sets it apart from Eiffel Tower wannabes like its cousins in Nagoya, Sapporo, and Tokyo. Although no longer quite at the cutting edge of fashion, it is still the only tower in Kyoto and the local skyline is impossible to imagine without it. You can take an elevator to its **panoramic viewing platform** (🕔*open daily 9am–9.20pm, ¥800*), although the view is ultimately no more impressive than from the roof of the station.

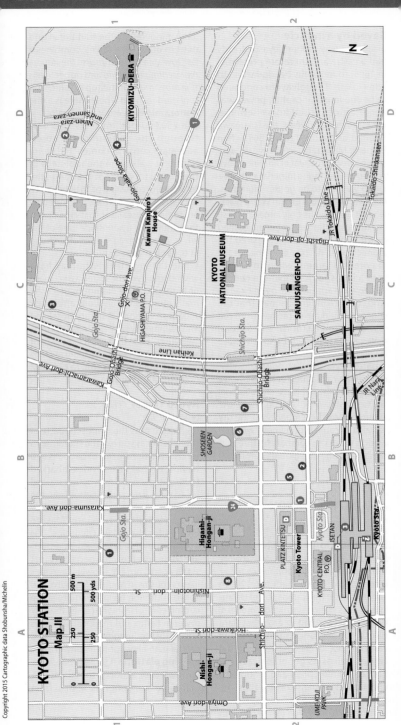

KYOTO STATION
Map III

Copyright 2015 Cartographic data Shobunsha/Michelin

KIYOMIZU-DERA

Ninen-zara and Sannen-zara

Gojo-zaka Slope

Kawai Kanjiro's House

Gojo-dori Ave

HIGASHIYAMA P.O.

Gojo Sta.

KYOTO NATIONAL MUSEUM

SANJUSANGEN-DO

Higashi-oji-dori Ave

JR Tokaido Line

Tokaido Shinkansen

Keihan Line

Shichijo Sta.

Kawaramachi-dori Ave

Gojo-Obashi Bridge

Shichijo-Obashi Bridge

JR Nara Line

SHOSEEN GARDEN

Karasuma-dori Ave

Gojo Sta.

Higashi-Hongan-ji

PLATZ KINTETSU

Kyoto Tower

KYOTO CENTRAL P.O.

Kyoto Sta.

ISETAN

Kyoto Sta.

Nishinotoin-dori St.

Shichijo-dori Ave

Horikawa-dori St.

Nishi-Hongan-ji

Omiya-dori Ave

UME-KOJI PARK

500 m
500 yds
0   250   500

To-ji★★ 東寺

Map I, B4. 10min walk southwest of the JR station, or 5min from Toji Station (Kintetsu Line), or buses no. 202, 207 & 208. Open daily: mid-Apr– mid-Sept 8.30am–5pm; mid-Sept–mid-Apr 8.30am–4pm. ¥500–1300. Prices and entry fees vary, so check the website before your visit. toji.or.jp/en.

When the capital was relocated to Heian-kyo in 794, the "Temple of the East" was quickly erected to protect this key point of the new town. The work was entrusted to the monk Kukai, who, at the beginning of the 9C, introduced from China the teachings of the Buddhist Shingon-shu ("True Word") sect. Placed under the jurisdiction of Kukai in 823, To-ji naturally became (with Kongobu-ji on Mount Koya, *see p377*) the main center for the dissemination of this esoteric form of Buddhism. The most noticeable structure is the five-story **pagoda★★**, the highest in Japan at 187ft/57m. It was rebuilt in the 17C, as were most of the buildings in the temple precincts. To the south, the main hall, or **kondo★** houses the triad of **Yakushi Nyorai★★** (*see box p320*). In the **kodo★**, the lecture hall, there is a large sculpted **mandala★★** consisting of the tutelary figure of the solar Great Buddha, **Dainichi Nyorai**, surrounded by 21 satellite statues arranged in groups: Buddhas *(Nyorai)*, bodhisattvas *(Bosatsu)*, and, third in the hierarchy of Buddhist divinities, the five *Myo-o*, or "kings of magic knowledge." In the center stands **Fudo Myo-o★**, "the immutable one"—the defender of Buddhist law is always depicted with a straight sword *(tsurugi)* and a cord.

On the 21st of each month, a lovely flea market (antiques, secondhand items, old kimonos) is held at To-ji.

Nishi Hongan-ji★ 西本願寺

Map III, A1/2. 10min walk northwest of the JR station. On several bus routes. Open daily 5.30am–5pm. No charge. hongwanji.or.jp/english.

A modest temple was first built in the mountains to the east of Kyoto around the mausoleum of Shinran Shonin (1173–1262), founder of the Jodo Shin-shu sect (*see box p322*). In 1591, after various changes of fortune, the mausoleum was transferred to its present location when land was given to the sect by Toyotomi Hideyoshi. The **San-mon★** *(main gate, 1645)* of Nishi Hongan-ji, or "Western Temple of the Original Vow," leads straight into the **Hon-do** *(main hall, 1760)*. It houses statues of Amida, Prince Shotoku, and the monk Honen. The prayer hall has sliding panels decorated with phoenixes and peacocks painted by Kano-school artists. Farther south, the **Daishi-do** *(founder's hall, 1637)*, houses a seated statue of Shinran Shonin.

Higashi Hongan-ji★ 東本願寺

Map III, B1/2. 5min walk east from Nishi Hongan-ji or north from Kyoto station; entrance on Karasuma-dori. On several bus routes. Open daily Mar–Oct 5.50am–5.30pm; Nov–Feb 6.20am–4.30pm. No charge. higashihonganji.or.jp/english.

A counterpart to Nishi Hongan-ji, Higashi Hongan-ji, or "Eastern Temple of the Original Vow," was built as a result of a handover of power complicated by sibling political rivalry. On the death of the chief abbot Kosa (1543–92), responsibility for the Nishi Hongan-ji, which generally devolved on the eldest son, passed to his third son, as Kosa and Toyotomi Hideyoshi had decided. Ten years later, Japan's new strongman, Tokugawa Ieyasu, in turn donated a plot of land, but this time to the eldest son, who had not yet received anything. As a result, in 1602 Higashi Hongan-ji was erected to the east of Nishi Hongan-ji. With the backing of the shogun, this temple became the new headquarters of the Jodo Shin-shu sect and the mausoleum of Shinran Shonin was transferred here. More imposing than its rival the Western Temple (the founder's hall, **Goei-do★**, is one of the largest all-wooden buildings in the world), the Eastern Temple is also rather more austere in appearance, having burned down on numerous occasions in the past. The present structure is as recent as 1895.

Some of the 1001 statues of Kannon, Sanjusangen-do

© Christophe Boisvieux/age fotostock

Strolling along the corridor connecting the Goei-do with Amida Hall, you will see a glass case displaying one of the ropes used to raise the huge beams of the Goei-do. Known as a **kezuna**, it is made from hair donated by the faithful. The largest rope *(16in/40cm in diameter)* is 33ft/10m long and weighs a ton.

▶ Walk through the little Shosei-en garden *(daily: Mar–Oct 9am–5pm, Nov–Feb 9am–4pm; ¥500)* and cross the Kamon River, heading southeast.

Sanjusangen-do★★★
三十三間堂

Map III, C2. 15min walk east of Kyoto station, or Shichijo Station (Keihan Line), or buses no. 100, 206 & 208. Open daily: Apr–Oct 8am–5pm; Nov–Mar 9am–4pm. ¥600. sanjusangendo.jp. Founded in 1164 by the charismatic warlord Taira no Kiyomori, this temple dates from 1266, its predecessor hav-

ing been burned down in 1249. The first surprise is its sheer size: the main hall is 394ft/120m long. This partly explains the temple's name, which translates as "Hall with Thirty-three Spaces Between Columns," since the hall is divided into 33 *(san-ju-san)* bays. Nor is this a random number, since the goddess of mercy, Kannon *bosatsu*, to whom the temple is dedicated, changed form 33 times in order to rescue mankind.

The second surprise is the veritable forest of statues, shimmering like a magnificent brass orchestra as you walk past them in the semi-darkness. Under the gaze of the visitor, the **1001 statues of Kannon★★★** seem to stare back in return, each with a slightly different expression on its gilded face. With the exception of the 124 dating from the original foundation of the temple, they were carved by the best artists of the Kamakura period, such as **Unkei** and his son **Tankei**. Head of the renowned

The Buddha of Healing

Yakushi Nyorai can be recognized by the small pot of medicine he carries in his left hand. He is in fact the only Buddha depicted holding an object. The pot he holds normally has 12 facets, representing the 12 redemptive tasks Yakushi undertook to fulfill in order to become a Buddha. His right hand sketches out the *mudra* (gesture) of "the dispelling of fear." The skilled Buddha of Healing is always accompanied by an even number of servants, such as the divinities Nikko ("Sunlight") and Gakko ("Moonlight"). His is an important role since his task is to cure, day and night, the deadliest of diseases: ignorance, the source of all our desires and the cause of humanity's suffering.

Kei-ha Buddhist school, Tankei also masterminded the immense statue of **Kannon with 11 heads ★★★** *(10ft/3m high)* presiding over the center of the building. While this group of 1001 statues is an amazing sight *(80 artists are said to have worked on them over more than a century)*, the sculptural quality of each of the **28 divinities★★★** arrayed at their feet *(Kamakura period)* is no less impressive. These deities are of Hindu origin. Guardians of the goddess of mercy, they wear intimidating expressions. The realism and vivacity of their features, and the intensity of their inlaid crystal eyes, is truly striking.

Look out for Naraen-Kengo *(Nayarana in Sanskrit)*, Karura *(Garuda)*, Mawara-nyo *(Maha-bala)*, Missha-kong *(Vajra-pani)*, and the elderly Basu-sennin *(Vasu)*.

😊 *An archery contest involving more than 600 competitors is held annually on the nearest Sunday to January 15, on the veranda of Sanjusangen-do.*

Kyoto National Museum★★★
京都国立博物館

🖐 *Map III, C2. Opposite Sanjusangen-do. Temporary exhibitions:* 🕐 *Open Tue–Sun 9.30am–4.30pm.* 💴 *¥530 (supplement for special exhibitions). www.kyohaku.go.jp.* 💬.

The reforms introduced by Emperor Meiji (1868) were the inspiration for the monumental **Meiji Kotokan**, the red-brick building on your right as you enter the museum grounds. Architecturally, this hall in the Kyoto National Museum reflects the foreign influences welcomed by Katayama Tokuma, the emperor's official architect. Pediments, terraces, and rooflines suggest the Baroque.

The irony is that the museum was inaugurated in 1897 with the intention of protecting Kyoto's cultural and architectural heritage, which were threatened by the emperor's modernization program. A similar concern lay behind the foundation of the national museums in Tokyo and Nara. Since 2014, this symbolic building has no longer held the museum's permanent collection, instead hosting temporary exhibitions

---

The Development of Carved Wooden Statues

The "joined-block" construction for wooden statues, *yosegi-zukuri*, as seen at Sanjusangen-do, is still rudimentary: only the upper limbs are sculpted separately before being affixed to the main statue, carved from a solid block of wood. It was not until the sculptor **Jocho** *(whose oldest works date from 1022)* that sculptors in wood began to create statues by assembling a number of carved wooden blocks using mortise and tenon joints. Jocho's best-known work is the Amida Buddha at Byodo-in in Uji.

---

that change several times a year (keep a lookout for them as they are normally worth seeing).

The permanent collection is now presented in the **Heisei Chishinkan**, a brand new annex designed by Taniguchi Yoshio, who was notably also responsible for the redesign of MoMA in New York. The building combines concrete, glass, water, and a linear design that is reminiscent of traditional Japanese houses. Inside the vast open spaces, subdued lighting and transparent cubes throw the focus on the remarkable pieces being exhibited on three levels. The upper level is devoted to ceramics and archeological discoveries. The intermediate level presents Japanese and Chinese painting. On the lower level immense sculptural works and items of calligraphy, textiles, metal and lacquerware are displayed.

The 12,500 items, which cover prehistory up to the start of the Meiji era, are exhibited in rotation, but some masterpieces are always on show. In room 4, you can admire a magnificent Chinese funerary statue: **Lady of the Palace Holding a Pekinese★★** *(Tang dynasty, 8C)*. Gallery 5 is dominated by four gigantic kings guarding each of the cardinal points. The most important, **Tamon-ten Vaisravana★★★** *(late Heian period, 11C)*, has the task of defending the northern gate, the one most

Pure Land and True Land Buddhism

Amida, the Japanese pronunciation of the Sanskrit Amitabha, "infinite light," and of Amitayus, "eternal life," was the name adopted by the monk Dharmakara after he had refused enlightenment for himself, unless he could bring nirvana to anyone who appealed to his name. This bodhisattva, who became a Buddha under the name of **Amitabha**, is one of the most popular in Great Vehicle, or *Mahayana*, Buddhism (one of the two main schools). The paradise offered by his branch of Pure Land Buddhism is easily accessible: the worshipper simply needs to recite the Nembutsu: "Namu Amida butsu" ("In the name of Amida Buddha"). From the dozen or so sects spawned by Amida, two main streams emerged: the Jodo-shu or "Pure Land" school, founded by Honen Shonin (1133–1212), also known by his posthumous name of Enko Daishi; and the "True Pure Land" school or **Jodo Shin-shu**, established by Shinran Shonin (1173–1262). Their differences are less to do with doctrine and more about power struggles, to which not even the Pure Land sect proved immune.

exposed to malevolent spirits according to Chinese geomancy. He therefore holds himself upright, impassable and menacing, while the other guardians are more relaxed and dressed in flowing garments. His attributes include a *stupa* (votive tower symbolizing Buddhism) in his left hand and a *halberd* (two-handed pole weapon) grasped in his right. This room also houses some fine wooden sculptures of **Jizo Bosatsu**★★ *(Heian period, 9C)*, a popular divinity devoted to helping the suffering.

Among the collections of **paintings**★★ *(galleries 8 to 12)*, which span the Heian and Edo periods, are works by Sotatsu, an exponent of the more narrative and typically Japanese *Yamato-e* style of illustration, which emerged during the Heian period. Two of the museum's masterpieces are portraits on **kakemono**★★★ (hung scrolls, literally "the thing which hangs") by Fujiwara Takanobu (1142–1205), depicting the leaders of the rival clans during the Kamakura period: **Minamoto no Yoritomo** (1147–99) and **Taira no Shigemori** (1138–79). With its stark geometrical composition, the latter exhibits the dark asceticism of a *raku*. Painted on a roll of paper, the **Gaki-zoshi**★★★ *(Heian period, 12C)* depicts hungry ghosts *(gaki)*, a rare subject in Japanese painting, treated here with ethereal vivacity. Eight panels depicting the world of **birds and flowers in each**

of the four seasons★★, originally from Daisen-in temple, are one of the major works of Kano Motonobu (1476–1559). Descending from the heavens on a peacock encircled in clouds, the **Mayura Vidyaraja**★★ is a silk painting of Chinese provenance *(Song dynasty, 11C)*, from Ninna-ji temple. Look out also for some magnificent **kosode**★★, forerunners of the modern kimono, with narrow openings for the hands at the ends of the sleeves.

Kawai Kanjiro's House★
河井寛次郎記念館
♿Map III, C1. 10min walk north from the National Museum, or Kiyomizu Gojo Station (Keihan Line), or several bus routes. ⏱Open Tue–Sun 10am–5pm. ⏱Closed Aug 11–20 & Dec 24–Jan 7. 💰¥900. kanjiro.jp.

A visit to the workshop of Kawai Kanjiro (1890–1966), one of the world's greatest potters, includes a tour of the *machiya* (♿*see box p324*) where he lived. The interior is beautifully furnished, and there's a lovely, simple garden.

THE CENTER
♿Maps I and II. Allow a day, to go from the Imperial Palace in the morning to the Pontocho district by early evening. With its all-too clearly delineated grid of wide streets that meet at right angles, Kyoto's city center can seem boring. You might even be put off walking from

one sight to the next, to avoid being confronted with the concrete face of modern Kyoto and having your whole fantasy of the ancient city (geishas walking through falling cherry blossoms from temple to temple, etc.) undermined. This, of course, would be a mistake.

It's undeniable that a good few of the long and tedious boulevards really don't lend themselves to a stroll, but you need only walk a little farther, perhaps on a smaller parallel side street, to find you are suddenly sharing the asphalt with several cyclists on the wrong side of the road, some noisy cats, narrow, improvised gardens that are slowly encroaching onto public spaces, and perhaps shopkeepers hosing down the ground in front of their shops in the morning. There are a few treasures here and there: a whiff of lacquer, the smell of wood, something frying. A workshop, a store from a bygone age rubbing shoulders with a young designer's boutique. You may get so carried away by the serene atmosphere of your surroundings that you reach the temple or museum you are aiming for without even noticing.

The city center also has its hotspots, busting with businesses of all kinds: Shijo-dori and Kawaramachi-dori are lined with big stores, while the Teramachi arcade and the surrounding area are a magnet for young, stylish locals. The area just north of here, near the town hall (Shiyakusho), has been the preserve of antiques dealers for decades, while only the most strong-disciplined of visitors will be able to leave Nishiki Market, just off Teramachi, without plenty of delicious foodie souvenirs.

Imperial Palace★ 京都御所
Map II, B1/2. Imadegawa or Marutamachi stations (Karasuma Line). Several bus routes. Kyoto Gyoen: Open daily 24hr. Kyoto Gosho and Sento Gosho visits by guided tour only; book ahead for Sento Gosho at the IHA (see box p323). Kyoto Gosho: Tue–Sun 10am & 2pm (English). Sento Gosho: Tue–Sun 9.30am, 11am, 1.30pm, 2.30pm & 3.30pm (Japanese, with English audioguide). No charge.

The Imperial Household Agency

You'll need to apply at the **Imperial Household agency (IHA)** for access to some sights: Kyoto Gosho, Sento Gosho, Katsura Imperial Villa, and Shugaku-in Imperial Villa. Apply in person (the office is in the Imperial Park, north of the main entrance on Karasuma-dori; Mon–Fri 8.45am–noon & 1–4pm; 075 211 1215) or online (sankan. kunaicho.go.jp/multilingual/lang/en/information.html) as far in advance as possible. You'll need to **bring your passport** both for applications at the office, and when actually visiting the sights.

sankan.kunaicho.go.jp/english/guide/kyoto.html.

At the heart of the Imperial Park—or **Kyoto Gyoen** (210-acre/85ha), a popular green space in the heart of the city—lies **Kyoto Gosho**, the Imperial Palace, its sheer size evident from the surrounding wall. The various buildings of the Palace, past which a terse guide urges you at the double, are set in grounds of 25 acres/10ha. Originally erected in 794 1.2mi/2km west of its present site, the palace suffered 16 fires between 960 and 1227. Time and again it rose phoenix-like from its ashes, but finally in 1788 it was decided to transfer it to this location, an area thought (wrongly, as it turned out) to be much safer.

The present version dates from the late 19C, reproducing the palace as it was in the golden age of Japanese civilization during the **Heian period**. Of the various buildings before which the guide calls a halt, the **Shodaibunoma★**, or courtesans' salon, is one of the more interesting. It consists of a hall divided into three rooms arranged hierarchically, their status reflected in the paintings that adorn the doors and sliding panels (fusuma) of each. Thus, the **Tiger**, **Stork**, and **Cherry Tree** rooms were occupied by courtesans of progressively lower rank. In the Palace's main pavilion, the **Shishin-den**, is

Machiya

Referred to by the locals as *unagi-no-nedoko*, or "eel beds," these town *(machi)* houses *(ya)* are typical of old Kyoto. The front generally serves as a shop, behind which the rest of the building extends. This long, narrow layout is due to the fact that tax used to be calculated not on floor area but on the length of street frontage. A string of several workshops may therefore share a single shop window. A courtyard garden lets in light and the buildings are often raised on supports so that air can circulate beneath. Very few have survived.

the room where the Taisho and Showa emperors were crowned. Of special interest is the next pavilion, the **Seiryo-den**, once the emperor's residence. At the end of your visit, the peaceful **Oike no niwa★** garden provides a moment of calm.
In the southeast of the palace grounds, the **Sento Gosho★★** is a serene garden designed by Kobori Enshu (1579–1647). It's especially beautiful in May, when the wisteria is in full, glorious bloom.

▶ Walk west along Naka-dachiuri from Karasuma-dori, keeping to the west side of the Imperial Palace.

Raku Museum★★   楽美術館
Map II, A1. 10min walk from the Imperial Palace or Imadegawa Station (Karasuma Line). ◯*Open Tue–Sun 10am–4.30pm.* ⊚*Entry charge varies according to exhibition (usually around ¥1000). raku-yaki.or.jp.*
This small museum stands next door to the home of the Raku family. It was opened in 1978 by the 14th generation of this family of ceramic artists. Austere as the tea bowls on display, the building houses some magnificent pieces ranging from the earliest *raku* made by Chojiro *(born 16C)* to those of Raku Kichizaemon *(born 1949, 15th generation).*
The method of production *(rapid firing followed by accelerated cooling)* was first used at the beginning of the Momoyama

period. The simplicity and austerity of these thick-walled, rustic-looking bowls immediately appealed to those who, like Ashikaga Yoshimasa *(◖see p90),* wished to transform the tea ceremony into an occasion for meditation.

▶ From the Raku Museum, walk up Horikawa-dori to the southwest corner of the Horikawa-dori and Imadegawa-dori intersection (roughly 15min).

Nishijin Textile Center
西陣織会館
Map II, A1. Subway Imadegawa Station, then 10min walk. Several bus routes. ◯*Open daily: Mar–Nov 10am–6pm; Dec–Feb 10am–5pm.* ⊚*No charge. nishijin.or.jp.*
A branch of the powerful Hata clan arrived in this district 1500 years ago, bringing new agricultural techniques and a knowledge of silkworm breeding, a lucrative industry and one of the reasons why Emperor Kanmu moved his capital to Kyoto. Nowadays, this former workshop and exhibition center, located in the weavers' district of Nishijin, explains various weaving techniques. Fashion shows are also held to display the finished products *(9.30am–3.30pm).* You can buy or hire all kinds of kimono, or have yourself photographed in a kimono of your choice *(¥4000–13,000).*

Nijo Castle★★   二条城
Map II, A2. 10min walk southwest of the Imperial Palace. Nijojo-mae Station (Tozai Line). Bus nos. 9, 12, 50, 101 & 111. ◯*Open daily: Jul–Aug 8am–6pm; Sept 8am–5pm; Oct–Jun 8.45am–5pm (last admission 1hr before closing).* ◯*Closed Dec 26–Jan 4, and Tue in Jan, Jul, Aug & Dec.* ⊚*Castle and palace ¥1030, castle only ¥620, gallery ¥200; audioguide ¥500. nijo-jocastle.city.kyoto.lg.jp.*
Erected by Ieyasu, who in 1603 became the first Tokugawa shogun, this castle was the symbol of **Tokugawa** power for some 15 generations until 1867, when the last shogun abdicated. It was then taken over by the Imperial government, (which made it its headquarters). It now belongs to the municipality of Kyoto.

The beginning of the 17C saw the end of the Momoyama period, and with it, the ostentatious splendor in which Toyotomi Hideyoshi (1536–98) had so delighted. His Tokugawa successor also wished to display his power over the newly unified country, but had to find a more discreet way. Though constructed in the style of a *shoin-zukuri*, or aristocratic residence, usually unsuited to siege warfare, this castle was by no means defenseless.

Once through the richly sculpted and gilded **Kara-mon★** *(Chinese gate)*, you reach **Ninomaru Palace★★**, designated a National Treasure. The 30 or so rooms cover 32,300sq ft/3000sq m, and feature some outstanding decoration: majestic *tokonoma* (alcoves), *chigai-dana* (staggered shelves) of extreme delicacy, coffered ceilings embossed with brightly colored motifs, and *fusuma* (sliding panels) painted by artists of the Kano School (*see box below*). Behind these gilt partitions, however, are concealed countless alcoves, once occupied by guards ready to spring forth. The beautiful **garden★** with its lake and rocks is attributed to the great landscape designer Kobori Enshu.

Ninomaru Palace will be closed 2022–25, after work on the Honmaru-Goten Palace is completed in 2021, as part of a large-scale **restoration project**.

Nijo jinya★ 二条陣屋

Map II, A2. 5min walk south of the castle on Omiya-dori. Visit by 1hr Japanese-language guided tour only; book by phone at least 24hr ahead. Arrange an interpreter in advance (see list on website; free, but you'll need to pay their entry fee). ¥1000. 075-841-0972, nijyojinya.net/English.html.

This inn was built in the 17C to accommodate visiting *daimyo* (feudal lords). As they demanded the highest levels of security, the building had to be proofed against threats of all kinds. Behind its reinforced, fireproof walls, a maze of corridors serves 24 cunningly constructed rooms. Secret passages, trapdoors, hidden stairways, false ceilings, and "nightingale floors" make this historic inn a fascinating place to visit. The volunteer interpreters' level of English varies widely, so it's best to read up on the property before you arrive, so you know what to look out for.

Walk east for 15min, toward Karasuma-dori via Oike-dori.

Kyoto International Manga Museum★

京都国際マンガミュージアム
Map II, B2. Karasuma-Oike Station, exit 2. Open Thu–Tue 10am–6pm. ¥800 (children ¥300). kyotomm.jp/en.

This museum, established in 2006 in a former primary school dating from the late-19C, comes as a wonderful surprise. It is as playful as its subject: manga, a word invented in the 19C by master printmaker Hokusai (1760–1849), which translates as "derisory image" (*see Understanding Japan p96*).

Around 50,000 volumes of manga fill a whole wall of shelving 460ft/140m long. As well as these comics (all browsable inside or on the deck and lawn outside, including the English-language section)

The Kano School

This school of painters was in existence for eight generations, replacing the monks who, until that time, had carried out the shoguns' commissions. The founder, **Kano Masanobu** (1434–1530), excelled in a monochrome decorative style based on black ink. In the Momoyama period, gold leaf was introduced by Kano Eitoku (1543–90), which greatly appealed to Toyotomi Hideyoshi. Eitoku's grandson, Kano Tanyu (1602–74), became official painter to Tokugawa Ieyasu *(decorating, for example, Nijo Castle)*. His realistic style, featuring herons and peacocks against a background of gold leaf, snow, or *sakura*, celebrated nature.

the museum houses an archive of 15,000 items covering the history of manga to the present day. Upstairs there are permanent exhibitions featuring stories and drawings *(174 plates depicting maiko, apprentice geisha, are on display)* as well as temporary exhibitions. In one small classroom, you can listen to a storyteller *(3 performances per day; no English-language shows)* demonstrate *kamishibai*, a traditional form of usually comical storytelling with illustrations. The storytellers used to go from one village to the next to perform, their illustrations in the paniers of their bicycles. There were once 50,000 of them in Japan, but they gradually disappeared with the advent of television.

○ Walk down Karasuma-dori for 5min, then turn left onto Sanjo-dori.

Museum of Kyoto
京都文化博物館
Map II, B2. 5min walk from Karasuma-Oike subway or 8min Karasuma Station (Hankyu Line). *Open Tue–Sun, 10am–7.30pm (special exhibitions usually 10am–6pm).* *¥500. bunpaku.or.jp/en.*

With its fine red-brick façade facing Sanjo-dori, this municipal museum *(not to be confused with the Kyoto National Museum, see p321)* is proof of how important the **Sanjo-dori** road was at the beginning of the Edo period. It was originally the only way of reaching Sanjo Bridge across the Kamo River, and then the Tokaido road.

The old bank building is now an annex, with most exhibitons held in the modern building attached. In the permanent exhibition *(2nd floor)*, the city's history is illustrated by fine models. A lack of information in English makes things difficult, but the museum does have volunteer English-speaking guides.

There's also a small **cinema** *(3rd floor)*, screening classic Japanese films every month, and regular special exhibitions. On the first floor *(ground floor)* is a reconstructed street of Edo-era shops, "Roji Tempo," where you can have a meal or snack and buy traditional craft items.

Around the museum are plenty of cafés, boutiques, and restaurants, creating a pleasant, lively atmosphere. Lovers of 20th-century architecture will note some interesting façades. Apart from the museum itself, look for the **Sacra** building (corner of Tominokoji-dori) erected in 1916 with decoration inspired by the Viennese Secessionst style. The **1928** building (corner of Gokomachi-dori), influenced by Art Deco, may also catch your eye. The *Mainichi Shinbun* daily newspaper used to have offices here; today it is a cultural complex, with a lovely period theater.

PONTOCHO AND SURROUNDINGS★ 先斗町
Map II, B/C2. Allow the latter part of an afternoon, and spend the evening at one of Pontocho-dori's restaurants.

Nishiki Market★ 錦市場
Map II, B3
The first store opened here in 1310, giving rise to a market focused on seafood; over time it diversified, becoming the "kitchen of Kyoto." This pedestrianized, covered street is packed with stands selling many of the ingredients of traditional Kyoto cuisine: wild vegetables, spices, dried fish, and Uji tea. It is popular with gourmets and fans of traditional crafts. Good-quality cutlery and crockery is also on sale *(see Addresses p356)*. It runs into Teramachi Arcade.

The market is at its liveliest around lunch, but if you come early in the morning you'll see the stands being set up and can savor the smells of frying and pickling, and perhaps chat with the storeholders before things get really busy.

Teramachi Arcade 寺町通
Map II, B2.
What may seem at first like just another run-of-the-mill shopping arcade, extending from one side of Shijo-dori to the other, Teramachi is actually full of specialist stores and dotted with tiny temples *(its name means "temple town")*. Many stores specialize in fashion for the young, but there are also some more tra-

Pontocho-dori

© greir/iStock

ditional shops *(books, stationerery)* and restaurants. Send some time browsing in the print store Nishiharu, where you will be welcomed by one of Japan's great experts in the field of *ukiyo-e* (woodblock prints). The quality of the goods on sale is matched only by the courtesy of the owner (☝*see Addresses p360*).

▶ Return to Shijo-dori and head east toward the river. On the sidewalk to the right are the entrances to two of Kyoto's largest stores: **Takashimaya** and **Hankyu**. Pontocho-dori is the narrow street on your left, just before Shijo-bashi, the bridge over the Kamo.

Pontocho-dori★ 先斗町通
☝*Map II, B/C2.*
Running parallel with the Kamo River, this lane lined with small wooden houses is barely 6.6ft/2m wide and gets very crowded at night. Popular since the early 18C on account of its many *ochaya* (geisha tea houses), today it is the bars, restaurants, and *izakaya* (bars serving food and drink) that attract visitors. In the height of summer, many or the riverside restaurants construct terraces called *yuka* over the water. The level of service in the restaurants and bars varies, and some are members-only, so it's best to pick a destination in advance (☝*see Addresses p 361*).
At the end of Pontocho-dori, you will see the facade of **Pontocho Kaburenjo Theater** (☝*Map II, B2*). Every year since

its opening in 1895, the theater has presented the **Kamogawa Odori** or "Dance of the Kamo River" (☝*see Addresses p361*), one of Kyoto's most successful geisha festivals. *To extend your visit, follow the Takasegawa Canal, where the bars are much more free and easy.*

Seishu Netsuke Art Museum★
清宗根付館
☝*Map II, A3. 7min walk from Omiya (Hankyu Line) or Shijo-Omiya (Randen tram) stations.* ◷*Open Tue–Sun 10am–5pm.* ⟳¥1000. *netsukekan.jp.*
This delightful museum, housed in a former samurai residence on a quiet, residential street, is the only one in the country dedicated to *netsuke*. These small decorative toggles first appeared in the 17C and were used to attach small containers such as pouches to traditional clothing. The craftsmen who made them in bone, ivory, wood, metal, or porcelain were drew inspiration from animals, flowers, mythical creatures, etc.

EAST OF THE CENTER: AROUND HEIAN-JINGU
Allow a morning or afternoon.

Heian-jingu★ 平安神宮
☝*Map II, C2. Sanjo Station (Keihan Line). Several bus routes. Shrine:* ◷*Open daily: mid-Feb–mid-Mar & Oct 6am–5.30pm; mid-Mar–Sept 6am–6pm; Nov–mid-Feb 6am–5pm. Gardens:* ◷*Open daily: Mar–Sept*

8.30am–5.30pm; Oct 8.30am–5pm; Nov–Feb 8.30am–4.30pm. ⊷Shrine no charge; garden ¥600. heianjingu.or.jp.
This Shinto shrine was erected in 1895 to mark the 1100th anniversary of the city. Standing in the north part of Okazaki Park, it is a 5:8 scale replica of the Gosho, the former Imperial Palace built in the 8C. It is dedicated to the Emperor Kanmu, founder of Kyoto, and Komei, the last sovereign to reside there. The height of the ridge of the impressive *torii* (entrance gate) is the same as the water level of Lake Biwa. Behind the shrine, the **gardens★** are known for their cherry trees, irises, and maples.

National Museum of Modern Art★
京都国立近代美術館
Map II, C2. 10min walk from Higashiyama Station (Tozai Line). Bus nos. 5, 46 & 100. Open Tue–Thur & Sun 9.30am–5pm, Fri–Sat 9.30am–8pm. ⊷¥430 (¥220 in the evenings); special exhibitions around ¥1300. www.momak.go.jp.
The permanent collections of this important museum consist of paintings in the **Nihonga style** by artists such as Nishiyama Suisho (1879–1958) and Hirota Tatsu (1904–90). There are also works in the **Yoga style** (the Western painting style first practiced in the Meiji period) by such artists as Kuroda Jutaro (1887–1970), Suda Kunitaro (1891–1961), Kishida Ryusei (1891–1929), and of course **Léonard Foujita** (1886–1968), including a wonderful **Reclining Nude★★★** dating from 1937. Ceramic works by Kitaoji Rosanjin (1883–1959) are exhibited alongside some of the 420 items created by the prolific Kawai Kanjiro (1890–1966, *see p322*). These are complemented by works from Western artists including Piet Mondrian (*see Katsura Imperial Villa p339*), Max Ernst, Matisse, and Odilon Redon, who is represented with a magnificent *Youthful Buddha* (1905). The museum also has a fine **photographic collection** (Ansel Adams, Alfred Stieglitz).

Kyoto City KYOCERA Museum of Art 京都市京セラ美術館
Map II, C2. Opposite the National Museum of Modern Art. Open Tue–Sun 10am–6pm. ⊷¥730 (excluding special exhibitions). kyotocity-kyocera. museum.
This museum, thoroughly renovated between 2017 and 2020, primarily exhibits works from the Meiji era or later, and includes both local and international artists. A selection of pieces is shown in the purpose-built collection room, with the display changed according to the season. There are also temporary exhibitions, varying in focus from Sugimoto Hiroshi to Van Gogh.

Fureaikan (Kyoto Museum of Traditional Crafts)
京都伝統産業ふれあい館
Map II, C2. 5min walk from the preceding museums, in the basement of the Miyako Messe, opposite Heian-jingu. Open daily 9am–5pm. ⊷No charge. kmtc.jp/en.
This museum is devoted to traditional craftsmanship, with the emphasis on the history of technology. Workshops and classes are occasionally held.

THE NORTHEAST
Allow a full morning or afternoon.

Shimogamo-jinja★ 下鴨神社
Map I, C2. Demachiyanagi Station (Keihan or Eizan lines). Buses no. 4 & 205, Shimogamo-mae stop. Open daily 6.30am–5pm. ⊷No charge. www. shimogamo-jinja.or.jp.
Founded in the 6C by Emperor Kinmei *(and rebuilt in the 19C)*, Shimogamo is one of Kyoto's oldest shrines and has a twin, Kamigamo, in the northwest of the city (*see box p335*). Shimogamo-jinja is dedicated to the mountain god and his wife, the river goddess, who are lavishly honored here in the heart of a large park fed with water from the Kamo-gawa. A magnificent tree-lined avenue provides the setting for the spectacular *yabusame* (mounted archery contest) that accompanies the **Aoi Matsuri** each year in mid-May (*see box p329*).

© EvergreenPlanet/iStock

Aoi Matsuri

Initially a purification rite to guard against bad harvests, the **Hollyhock Festival** *(May 15, from 10.30am)* is now more a commemoration of the Heian era. The slow, rather formal procession departs from the Imperial Palace and heads for the first shrine built in Kyoto, Kamigamo-jinja. At the halfway point, a halt is called at its twin shrine of Shimogamo. The hollyhock not only has protective properties, but was also the emblem of the Tokugawas.

Shisen-do 詩仙堂
Map I, C1. Ichijoji Station (Eizan Line), then 10min walk. Buses no. 5 & Kita-8, Ichijoji Sagarimatsu-cho stop, then 5min walk. *Open daily 9am–5pm.* *Closed May 23.* *¥500. kyoto-shisendo.com/Ja.html.*

Now a Zen temple belonging to the Soto sect, this thatched villa was founded in 1631 by the poet Ishikawa Jozan (1583–1672), who had been expelled by Shogun Tokugawa. It contains 36 beautiful ink portraits of Chinese poets, but the main draw is the remarkable **garden★**. Defying the convention of the time, it combines dry landscape, tea garden, and stroll garden features (*see p114*).

Manshu-in★ 曼殊院
Map I, D1. 30min walk from Shisen-do. Shugaku-in Station (Eizan Line), or bus no.5, Ichijoji Shimizu-cho stop, then 15min walk. *Open daily 9am–5pm.* *¥600. manshuinmonzeki.jp.*

Originally sited on the northern slope of Mount Hiei, this temple was relocated during the Edo period and rebuilt with a number of different *shoin* (pavilions). Its rooms feature some very fine *fusuma* (sliding panels), painted by Kano Eitoku (1543–90) for the Tiger Room, and by Kano Tanyu (1602–74) for the main pavilion. Of later date, the Bamboo and Peacock Rooms were decorated by Ganku Kishiku (1756–1839). In the **dry landscape garden★** outside, a magnificent five-needle pine rises from a bed of painstakingly raked white sand. It has stood on its tiny green island for more than 400 years.

Shugaku-in Imperial Villa★★ 修学院離宮
Map I, D1. 20min walk north of Manshu-in. Shugaku-in Station (Eizan Line), then 20min walk, or bus no. 5, Shugakuin Rikyu-michi stop, then 10 min walk. *Visits by guided tour only; book ahead at the IHA (*see box p323*).* *Tue–Sun 9am, 10am, 11am, 1.30pm & 3pm (Japanese, with English audioguide).* *No charge. sankan.kunaicho.go.jp/english/guide/shugakuin.html.*

Lying at the foot of the Higashiyama mountain chain, this villa derives its name from the old Shugaku temple, which it replaced in the 16C. Three villas were built here by order of the shogun as a vacation residence for the retired Emperor Go-Mizuno'o (1596–1680). It consists of a number of pavilions, laid out on different levels in a fine 69-acre/28ha **park★**. Following the tour route, the lower villa *(Shimo no chaya)* is reached first, followed by the middle villa *(Naka no chaya)*, where one of the pavilions, the **Kyaku-den**, has a magnificent **kasumidana★★** (shelves arranged to represent mist or clouds against a background of painted panels), and some cedar doors decorated with chariots *(hoko)* and carp. The tour proceeds next to the upper villa *(Kami no chaya)*, by far the most interesting. The first of its two pavilions, the **Rinuntei**, "the pavilion near to a cloud," has a clear **view★** over the Yokuryuchi pool, in the middle of which rises a majestic tea pavilion, the **Kyusui-tei**.

THE EAST: THE PHILOSOPHER'S PATH AND SURROUNDINGS
Allow a full day.

The **Tetsugaku no Michi**, or **Philosopher's Path★★** *(Map II, D1)*, was apparently named for the philosopher Nishida Kitaro (1870–1945), who always walked this route deep in thought while on his way to work at Kyoto University. The path follows a small canal shaded by weeping willows and cherry trees.

Ginkaku-ji★★★ 銀閣寺
&Map II, D1. Several bus routes.
⏲Open daily: Mar–Nov 8.30am–5pm; Dec–Feb 9am–4.30pm. ✺¥500.
shokoku-ji.jp.

The **Silver Pavilion** is of course reminiscent of the Golden Pavilion (&see p312). Built a little later, what it lacks in ostentation—despite its name, it isn't coated in silver as Kinkaku-ji is coated in gold—it gains in modesty. Ashikaga Yoshimasa (1435–90), eighth shogun and grandson of Yoshimitsu (&see p337), built his own retirement villa on a much smaller scale than that of his ancestor. He had just introduced the Higashiyama culture, the "culture of the Eastern Mountains," rooted in a form of Zen philosophy closely tied to the easthetic princple of *wabi-sabi* (refinement in simplicity, or the beauty of imperfection). The tea ceremony *(cha-no-yu)* is perhaps the fullest expression of this idea, and Yoshimasa is said to have played a key role in its development from an everyday activity into a formal ritual.

The first such ceremony is believed to have been held in a small room just a few feet square *(chashitsu)* in the middle of this garden. The room is said to have been designed by Zen'ami (1386–1482), a gardener belonging to the *eta* (outcast) class, who were regarded with distaste by the Zen masters. Redesigned on many occasions, the **garden★★** consists of two parts. The first combines *Kogetsu-*

Philosopher's Path

© SeanPavonePhoto/iStock

330

Ginkaku-ji

© coward_lion/iStock

dai, cones of sand designed to reflect the moon's rays, and *Ginsadan*, long strips of alternately rough and smooth sand. The second, hugging the hillside *(with pine trees, a small lake, and rocks)*, draws its inspiration from the Moss Garden (&see p340) that a century before had influenced the garden of the Golden Pavilion.

Honen-in 法然院

&*Map II, D1. 10min walk south of Ginkaku-ji, on the left of the canal. Grounds:* ○*open daily 6am–4pm. Main hall:* ○*open Apr 1–7 & Nov 1–7 9am–4pm.* ∞*Usually no charge; ¥500 early Apr, ¥800 early Nov. honen-in.jp.*

This quietly lovely temple is approached via a magnificent avenue of maples, cedars, weeping cherries, camellias, and clematis. To your right, on the hillside, a small cemetery shelters the tomb—marked by a tree planted between two stones—of **Tanizaki Jun'ichiro**, author of the seminal essay on Japanese aesthetics *In Praise of Shadows*.

The temple has a small, dry landscape garden. It is dedicated to the founder of the Buddhist Jodo-shu sect, the monk **Shonin Honen** (&*see box p322*). The main hall, which houses a beautiful black Amida Buddha statue, is only open in early April (when the camellias are blooming) and November (for fall leaf-viewing). A small *kura* (traditional storehouse) holds temporary special exhibitions, usually well worth seeing, of works by local artists.

Sen-Oku Hakuko-kan★

泉屋博古館

&*Map II, D2. 20min walk back down the Philosopher's Path; cross the canal after Otoyo shrine. Several bus routes.* ○*Usually open Tue–Sun 10am–5pm (varies by exhibition).* ∞*¥800. sen-oku. or.jp/kyoto/english.html.*

This collection of 3000 items acquired by the Sumitomo family is exhibited in rotation in a minimalist setting. The highlights are some **Chinese bronzes★★** from the Shang and Zhou dynasties (17C BC–AD 453). The museum also possesses some fine mirrors dating from the Han (202 BC–AD 220) and Tang (618–907) periods, some Ming (1368–1644) and Qing (1644–1911) dynasty paintings, plus a few works by the painter Shi Tao (1642–1707). The visit ends with a collection of **Noh masks★★** and costumes (16C and 18C), and a pleasant **garden**.

Eikan-do★ 永観堂

&*Map II, D2. Roughly 5min walk south of Sen-Oku Hakuko-kan. Bus no. 5 to Nanzenji Eikando-michi.* ○*Open daily 9am–5pm (last admission 4pm). Fall leaf viewing & illuminations:* ○*Open daily Nov 8.30am–9pm.* ∞*¥600 (¥1000 in Nov before 5pm). eikando.or.jp.*

This Buddhist temple, first of Shingon then of Jodo allegiance (&*see box p322*), bears the name of the monk Eikan (1033–1111, real name Yokan). He devoted his life to the poor and infirm and built a hospital in the temple precincts.

Nanzen-ji

Eikan found his vocation after meeting Amida, an event depicted in the sculpture **Mikaeri Amida Nyorai★**, *Amida Looking Over His Shoulder.* The Buddha *(Nyorai)* is said to have revealed himself to Eikan while he was saying his prayers. The figures in the sculpture are shown in a pose that was very innovative for the time. There is also a fine silk painting: **Yamagoshi Amida★**, *Amida Appearing Behind the Mountains.* This vertical scroll *(a National Treasure)* depicts Amida receiving a dying man and guiding him toward the Pure Land Western Paradise, a major theme in Buddhist iconography. The temple complex is popular in the Fall on account of its **gardens**, when the leaves of the maples turn red and gold; try to avoid weekends, when the crowds are overwhelming. To the rear of the gardens is a pagoda, from which there is a fine **view** of the city.

Nomura Art Museum
野村美術館
♿*Map II, D2. 2min walk south of Eikan-do, or 10min from Keage Station (Tozai Line).* ◷*Open early Mar–early Jun & early Sept–early Dec Tue–Sun 10am–4.30pm. nomura-museum.or.jp.*
This recently refurbished museum is devoted to the tea ceremony and all its trappings, and also has some interesting objects relating to Noh theater. It was founded by wealthy businessman

Nomura Tokushichi (1878–1945), who made his fortune in stockbroking, banking, and insurance.

Nanzen-ji★★ 南禅寺
♿*Map II, D2. 5min walk south of Eikan-do. Keage Station (Tozai Line).* ◷*Open daily: Mar–Nov 8.40am–5pm; Dec–Feb 8.40am–4.30pm (Tenju-an later in fall).* ☞*Temple complex no charge; Hojo (with garden) ¥500, San-mon ¥500, Nanzen-in ¥300, Tenju-an ¥500, Konchi-in ¥400. nanzenji.com.*
This temple was originally a villa built for Emperor Kameyama (1249–1305). Toward the end of his life the emperor became the disciple of a great Buddhist teacher, and in 1291 the villa was converted into a temple. The Zen Temple of the South *(Nanzen-ji)* became the headquarters of the Rinzai sect, whose teachings were introduced to Japan in 1191 by the Chinese monk Eisai (♿*see box p209).*
Destroyed during the terrible Onin War (15C), it was largely reconstructed in the 17C, along with the triple gate **San-mon★** with its ceiling painted by artists of the Kano School. Just past the San-mon, the **Hojo seiryo-den★★★** is the most important pavilion. Its two rooms *(Dai-hojo and Ko-hojo)* have been designated a National Treasure for their sliding panel *(fusuma)* paintings. The *24 Paragons of Filial Piety* and the celebrated

Mizunomi no Tora★★, *Tiger Drinking Water*, were painted by Kano Eitoku (1543–90) and Kano Tanyu (1602–74) (⏺*see box p325*). The **Leaping Tiger Garden★** attached to the *hojo* is a fine example of a *kare-sansui* (dry landscape garden), laid out by Kobori Enshu. An imposing massif of rocks and plants, supposed to recall the tiger painted by Tanyu, stands out boldly between the gravel and a white wall.

There are several secondary temples set in Nanzen-ji's 27-acre/11ha wooded park. **Nanzen-in★**, comprised of Emperor Kameyama's mausoleum and a fine 14C landscaped garden, is hidden away behind a magnificent Meiji period **aqueduct** (1890).

South of the San-mon, **Tenju-an★** is flanked by a fine dry landscape garden, and another garden around a pond which is particularly lovely in the fall, when the leaves are illuminated in the evening (*¥600*).

Konchi-in★, southeast of the gate and just outside the temple enclosure, boasts another fine garden by Kobori Enshu. A stork and tortoise are symbolized by two facing groups of rocks.

THE EAST: FROM KIYOMIZU TO MARUYAMA PARK
Allow a full day, starting early in the morning for a quiet stroll around Kiyomizu-dera.

Kiyomizu-dera★★★ 清水寺
⏺*Map III, D1. Bus nos.100, 202, 206, 207, Kiyomizu-michi or Gojozaka stop, then 10min walk.* ⏺*Open daily 6am–6pm (sometimes to 9pm).* ⬡*¥400. kiyomizudera.or.jp/en. Several pavilions are/will be undergoing restoration.*

Consisting of seven pavilions, including a bell tower (*shoro*) and a **pagoda** (*sanjunoto*) built at different levels on the slopes of Higashiyama, this temple is notable for its main hall and waterfall. Founded in 798 by the monk Enchin (*last rebuilt in the 17C under the patronage of Tokugawa Iemitsu*), the "Temple of Clear Water" (*Kiyomizu-dera*) rises from a tall wooden platform built on piles (*roughly 66ft/20m high*). Providing a

breathtaking **view** over Kyoto, this **immense terrace★** has also seen its share of tragedy: in the Edo period, it was popularly believed that those who jumped and survived would see their dreams come true. The temple treasury houses an 11-headed statue of Kannon (⏺*see p321*) that is put on display every 33 years (*the number of her reincarnations; next will be 2033*). Lower down the mountainside, the **Otowa-no-taki** is famed for its sacred waters, celebrated regularly with processions.

▶ Go back down from the temple, then take the stairway on the right.

Ninenzaka and Sannenzaka
二年坂・三年坂
⏺*Map III, D1.*

Sannenzaka ("Three-year Slope") is the favored route of pilgrims who have been staying at Kiyomizu-dera. A cobbled street lined with old wooden town houses, it is a reminder of the Higashiyama culture (⏺*see Silver Pavilion p330*). There are shops selling the famous local Kyo-yaki (or Kiyomizu-yaki) pottery used for the tea ceremony, alongside antique dealers, souvenir shops, and restaurants, all overlooked by the remains of an ancient Buddhist temple complex: the four-story **Yasaka★** pagoda. This is to your left, in a street at right angles to **Ninenzaka** ("Two-year Slope"), which takes over from Sannenzaka and runs alongside the **Ryozen Kannon** memorial. This immense concrete statue (*79ft/24m high*) is a monument to the Japanese people who lost their lives in World War II. Ninenzaka then becomes Nene Street (*Nene-no-michi*), deriving from the nickname of the female founder of Kodai-ji, to which it leads.

Kodai-ji★★ 高台寺
⏺*Map II, C3. 15min walk from Kiyomizu-dera or 10min from Gion (Yasaka-jinja). Buses no. 86, 202, 206, 207, Higashiyama-yasui stop.* ⏺*Open daily 9am–5.30pm (sometimes to 10pm for illuminations).* ⬡*¥600 (temple and small museum below). kodaiji.com.*

My name is Fumihana, maiko, trainee geisha

"I come from Chiiba, my name is now Fumihana." Just 13 when she decided to become a *maiko*, Fumihana (written with the kanji 'wealth, beauty, intelligence') became one of the 100 apprentice geisha active in the city (there are also around 100 geisha). "When I finished junior high school, I left for Kyoto. I was just 15." Her deportment, devotion to tradition, fierce determination to learn the *shamisen*, *koto*, singing and dance, and the consent of her parents soon convinced an *okaasan*, head of one of Kyoto's geisha houses in Miyagawa-cho, to take her on and train her. "I immediately learned the Kyoto dialect," a prerequisite for continuing her training. "It took me two years, but the apprenticeship to become a *geisha* may last up to five, all paid for by my *okaasan*. At the end of this first stage, I shall be allowed to paint my bottom lip red. It is not until I become a full *geiko* [the Kyoto dialect word for geisha] that I will also be able to paint my upper lip. Then I shall be ready to show my *okaasan*'s clients all she has taught me."

Kita no Mandokoro (Nene to her friends) founded this temple after the death of her husband, Toyotomi Hideyoshi, with the intention of retiring and becoming a Buddhist nun, a practice common among high-ranking noblewomen. A subtemple of the Kennin-ji, Kodai-ji was famed for its beauty. Having been burned down a number of times, it has unfortunately lost much of its former glory. The few pavilions that remain intact nevertheless are reminders of the original splendor, in particular **Kaisan-do**, the founder's hall, which was decorated by artists of the Kano and Tosa schools.

The mortuary chapel, **Otama-ya★**, dedicated to the *daimyo* Toyotomi Hideyoshi, has some fine Momoyama period *maki-e* (lacquerwork items inlaid with precious materials, in this case gold). The **garden★★**, created by Kobori Enshu (1579–1647), is another of the site's attractions.

On leaving Kodai-ji, make a slight detour by taking one of the streets that climb up the hillside to reach the entrance to **Kyoto's cemetery**. From the top there is an interesting **view★**, with the shapes of the tombs and buildings merging to create an unusual harmony.

▶ Now return to Nene-no-michi; bordered by flowering cherry trees in spring and fiery maples in the fall, it runs alongside Maruyama Park.

Maruyama Park and Yasaka-jinja★ 円山公園・八坂神社

♿ *Map II, C3. Both* ⏰ *open daily 24hr.* 🎫 *No charge. yasaka-jinja.or.jp*

This is east Kyoto's green lung. Covering some 25 acres/10ha, its fragrant lawns are dotted with rare tree species, including a wonderful **flowering weeping cherry★** (*shidare-zakura*). Stands selling postcards and all kinds of wares line the main path leading due west to **Yasaka-jinja★**. The shrine funds the important annual festival, **Gion Matsuri**, which is held in July. The entrance to the shrine's enclosure is marked by an immense scarlet stone *torii* (gate), facing Shijo-dori.

▶ 550yd/500m northeast of the park, you arrive at Chion-in.

Gion Matsuri

This spectacular festival, which goes on throughout July, culminates in a great parade on the 17th, which has its origins in a procession to ward off the plague of 869. Thirty or so floats, decorated with flowers and brightly colored fabrics, process through the streets of Gion from the Yasaka-jinja, to the sound of drums and flutes. The evening before, the streets are lit with lanterns and filled with crowds.

Chion-in★ 知恩院

Map II, C3. Shijo or Sanjo stations (Keihan Line). Several bus routes.

Open daily 9am–4.30pm (sometimes later). ¥500. chion-in.or.jp.

This temple was built in the 13C next to the mausoleum of Honen, founder of the Jodo school (*see box p322*), to which Chion-in belongs. Once through its colossal gate, the **San-mon★**, you reach the **Miei-do★** on the north side of the courtyard. The most important of the temple buildings, this hall is dedicated to Honen, as can be seen from the central statue, thought to be a self-portrait. A walkway to the east connects the pavilion to the **Amida-do**, the hall of Amida Buddha, venerated by the Jodo sect. A second walkway to the north leads to the monks' assembly hall, with access to the guest rooms to the east: one large (**Ohojo**) and one small (**Kohojo**). Rebuilt in the 17C, like most of the pavilions on this site, they are decorated with fine **paintings★** by artists of the Kano School. The **garden** was designed by Kobori Enshu. Honen's mausoleum stands on the hillside, east of the Miei-do. To the rear of the complex is **Daisho-ro**, at 67 tonnes the biggest bell in Japan.

Shoren-in★ 青蓮院

Map II, C2. 5min walk north of Chion-in. Higashiyama Station (Tozai Line). Buses no. 70 (Sat–Sun only), Jingu-michi stop. Open daily 9am–5pm. ¥500. shorenin.com.

Though burned down in a serious fire in the 19C, Shoren-in still has some fine features: a 700-year-old **camphor tree**, some **paintings** of the celebrated Kano and Tosa Schools, and in particular, the magnificent **gardens★** laid out by Soami and Kobori Enshu.

5min walk from Maruyama Park, heading southeast.

GION DISTRICT★★
祇園周辺

Map II, C3. Gion-Shijo Station (Keihan Line). Buses no. 12, 46, 86, 100, 106, 110, 201, 202, 203, 206 & 207.

Kyoto's most famous *hanamachi* (literally "flower town") or geisha district, Gion was, during its golden age in the early 19C, home to more than 3000 geisha in some 700 *ochaya* (tea houses), a time portrayed with realism in Mizoguchi's 1936 film *Sisters of the Gion*. Though somewhat spoiled by mass tourism these days, it is still a fascinating area. North of Shijo-dori, the **Shinbashi** district is a warren of romantic cobbled streets bordering the canal. The willow-shaded **Shirakawa-dori★** has some venerable *ochaya* and *okiya* (geisha houses), where *maiko* come and go in their *okobo* (high-soled clogs).

South of Shijo-dori, turn into **Hanami-koji★**, which runs at right angles to it. On the corner is Gion's most famous *ochaya*: **Ichiriki**, recognizable by its red panels. This beautiful area has suffered particularly from mass tourism; from 2019, signs were put up visitors that they'd be fined ¥10,000 if they took photos on private property, part of an effort to make tourists behave with a bit more thought for the locals.

If you want to meet a geisha, you usually need an introduction and

Shinto shrines: two styles, one purpose

The style of **Kamigamo-jinja**, with its gently curving lines emphasised by the roof projecting beyond the wall, marks a radical break with the straight lines of the Nara period. It is characteristic of 80 percent of the 80,000 surviving Shinto shrines, the remainder being more similar to **Ise Shrine**, whose double roof is secured by a ridge beam weighted down with 10 ridge billets, with extended barge boards ending in crossed finials at either end. Though constructed differently, both shrines are dismantled and reconstructed every 20 years (Ise) and every 21 years (Kamigamo); 15.5 tons of cyprus bark are needed just to reconstruct the roof of Kamigano-jinja.

Dry landscape garden of Daisen-in, Daitoku-ji

several hundred thousand yen to spare. On Hanami-koji, the **Gion Kobu Kaburenjo Theater** *(Gion Corner)* offers a brief glimpse of the traditional arts of the geisha. More *ryokan* are starting to offer dinner shows, too, so you can see geisha performing and, in some cases, even briefly meet them.

Kennin-ji★ 建仁寺

♿Map II, C3. 2min walk south of Gion Kobu Kaburenjo. ◷Open daily: Mar–Oct 10am–5pm; Nov–Feb 10am–4.30pm. ✆¥500. kenninji.jp.
This is one of Japan's oldest **Zen temples**, and Kyoto's oldest, founded by the monk Eisai (1141–1215) in 1202. The Gate of the Imperial Messenger *(Chokusimon)* and the adjacent small **Zen garden** are well worth a visit. There's also an interesting modern painting of a dragon on the Hatto hall's ceiling.

THE NORTHWEST
Allow at least a day. Keifuku Line trains enable you to combine a visit to this district with Arashiyama in one day, helpful if you are pressed for time.

Kamigamo-jinja★ 上賀茂神社

♿Map I, B1. Buses no. 4, 9 & 46, Kamigamo-jinja-mae stop. ◷Open daily 5.30am–5pm. ✆No charge. kamigamojinja.jp.

A UNESCO World Heritage Site, Kyoto's oldest shrine is in a splendid location. Covering 163 acres/66ha, its precincts are overlooked by the sacred mountain of Ko-yama. The complex consists of more than 30 buildings, the main one surrounded by two waterways. Dedicated to the god of thunder, who regularly hurls lightning bolts at Ko-yama, it was founded in the 7C. The shrine became the main center of worship in Heian-kyo (now Kyoto) when Emperor Kanmu made the city his new capital. It was therefore vital in the spiritual genesis of Kyoto, as can be seen from the annual **Aoi Matsuri** (♿see box p329). Passing through the first *torii* (gate), you reach the shrine via a long avenue *(sando)* shaded by cedar trees. Behind the second *torii*, two cones of sand with purifying properties ward off evil spirits. On the top of each are set two pine needles, commemorating the thunderbolt which split a pine tree in two on the day the shrine was consecrated. After crossing the Neigibashi (a second stage of purification), pilgrims arrive at the main building *(honden)*.
Reconstructed for the seventh time in 1863, the **honden** is still modeled on the original structure built in the Heian period, a golden age for the arts, and has been a model for shrine architecture ever since (♿see box p335).

Daitoku-ji★★★ 大徳寺

🚶*Map I, B1. Several bus routes.* 🕐*Open daily: temple precincts 24hr; sub-temples approx. 9am–4.30pm.* 🎫*Temple precincts no charge; Ryogen-in ¥350, Zuiho-in ¥400, Daisen-in ¥400, Koto-in ¥400. zen.rinnou.net. Allow half a day.*

This immense enclosure is as quiet as a graveyard. The complex was built by monk Daito Kokushi of the Rinzai sect at the request of Emperor Go-Daigo (1288–1339). Only four of the 22 buildings are open to the public.

If you enter by the south gate of the monastery *(Kitaoji-dori)*, the first building you reach is **Ryogen-in★** (established 1502), with a *hojo* (abbot's living quarters) flanked by five wonderful **gardens**. The oldest of them, the **Ryogin-tei★**, was designed by Soami. Adjacent to it is the **Totekiko**, Japan's smallest dry landscape garden.

A hundred yards farther on, on your left, **Zuiho-in★** has fine gardens designed by Shigemori Mirei (1896–1975), his avant-garde concepts beautifully attuned to the enigmatic abstraction of Zen gardens. The **Garden of the Cross**, however, bears witness to the conversion to Christianity of its former owner, the *daimyo* Otomo Sorin.

Farther north, **Daisen-in★★** *(the most visited of the temples)* is strikingly beautiful but less peaceful. It was built in 1509 by Kogaku Shoko, who was also an excellent gardener. The **fusuma★★** (sliding panel) paintings by Soami, Kano Motonobu, and Kano Yukinobu (15C and 16C) are beautiful. The pavilion is surrounded by three **dry landscape gardens★★★**, reproducing in three dimensions the characteristic black-and-white style of *sumi-e* paintings (ink and wash), framed here by black-fringed walls. The northeastern garden (created by Soami or Kogaku) is divided by a partition wall and opens onto a cascade of white gravel, leading in turn to a sand pathway. The flow of the path is a metaphor for life: as it negotiates the obstacles it encounters, it is transformed into a powerful river. In the same way, once our problems have been overcome, we can look to the horizon *(symbolized here by a boat)* and lose ourselves in the sea of eternity.

Returning southwestward *(turn off when you get to the bell of the tower on your right, then take the first alley on your left just after the Zuiho-in)*, at the end of a magnificent, tree-lined pathway you will discover **Koto-in★**. Founded in 1601 on the orders of Hosokawa Tadaoki (1563–1645), a great warrior who fought under Toyotomi Hideyoshi, this temple is a haven of peace.

Kinkaku-ji★★★ 金閣寺

🚶*Map I, B2. Several bus routes.* 🕐*Open daily 9am–5pm.* 🎫*¥400. shokoku-ji.jp.*

Set among luxuriant greenery reflected in the waters of a lake *(the Mirror Pond)*, at first glance the **Golden Pavilion** looks like a mirage. But the crowds approaching in serried ranks, cameras at the ready, soon remind us that this is a World Heritage Site, with all its attendant disadvantages. Yoshimitsu (1358–1408), third shogun of the Ashikaga dynasty, relinquished power in 1397 to become a monk under the name of Rokuon, and went on to build the Golden Pavilion, its name derived from the fact that the two upper stories are clad in gold leaf. This retreat stands in the vast Rokuon-ji temple enclosure, modeled on the stroll garden of the Moss Temple.

As **Ashikaga Yoshimitsu** was a great devotee of Zen philosophy, it is not surprising that his pavilion was converted into a temple after his death. For several centuries, the pavilion (though not all the buildings of the Rokuon-ji) miraculously escaped the ravages of Kyoto's civil wars, in particular the devastating fire of the Onin War (1467–77) caused by Ashikaga Yoshimasa's successor (founder of the Silver Pavilion). It did, however, go up in flames in 1950, when a mentally disturbed monk set fire to it, an event which, six years later, inspired Mishima Yukio to write *The Temple of the Golden Pavilion*. The pavilion was subsequently rebuilt.

Its **first level** is in the style of an aristocratic dwelling of the Heian period *(shinden-zukuri)*, and is reserved for

Kinkaku-ji

meditation; the **second**, which houses Buddhist relics, is in the style of a samurai residence, with the roof curving slightly upward like a saber; the **third** and **last** is in the *karayo* style of Zen temples. The roof is dominated by a Chinese phoenix, an appropriate symbol as the bird is believed to rise from its own ashes.

Ryoan-ji★★★ 龍安寺

Map I, B2. 15min walk southwest of Kinkaku-ji, or bus no. 59, Ryoanji-mae stop. Open daily Mar–Nov 8am–5pm; Dec–Feb 8.30am–4.30pm. ¥500. www.ryoanji.jp.

Almost everything that can be said about this Zen garden has been said, to the point where the Buddhist temple for which it was created, the **Temple of the Peaceful Dragon**, is almost forgotten. It was founded in 1473 by one of the most powerful feudal lords of the time, Hosokawa Katsumoto, vassal of the Shogun **Ashikaga Yoshimasa**, the founder of the Silver Pavilion. Knowing he had not long to live, he decided to build it and retire there with the monks. He did indeed die in the year the temple was built, too soon to meditate overlooking the Zen garden.

The **garden★★★** is said to have been designed by the painter/gardener Soami (1472–1525) at the end of the 15C. Rectangular in shape, 80ft/25m from east to west and 33ft/10m from south to north, it is enclosed on three sides by clay walls. On a finely raked surface of white sand, 15 rocks *(divided into five groups)* are carefully arranged on a bed of moss, posing a perpetual *koan*, or riddle, for the Zen Rinzai School. What did the artist have in mind? Does the sand suggest the sea? Why can you only see 14 rocks at any one time? Unfortunately, your reflection is often interrupted by the crowds who now throng to the garden; visit early or late in the day if possible.

Ninna-ji★ 仁和寺

Map I, A–B2. 10min walk southwest of Ryoan-ji. Omuro-Ninnaji Station (Keifuku Kitano Line), or buses no. 10, 26 & 59, Omuro Ninnaji stop. Open daily: Mar–Nov 9am–5pm; Dec–Feb 9am–4.30pm. Grounds no charge (¥500 in cherry blossom season); palace & gardens ¥500. ninnaji.jp/en.

This temple was originally the Omuro Gosho palace, the Imperial Palace of the Omuro district. Begun by Emperor Koko, it was completed by his son, Emperor Tenno (867–931), who became a monk and retired here. The palace was then converted into a temple for the Buddhist Shingon sect, with monks chosen exclusively from the ranks of the Imperial Family until the time of the Meiji Restoration. The present buildings date from the 17C. One of its emblems is the **Niomon** (the gate of Ni-oh Ungyo and Agyo). Commissioned by Tokugawa Iemitsu, it is one of the three great gates of Kyoto. Among the temple's notable sights are the **kondo** (a National Treasure), the **five-story pagoda★** (108ft/33m high), and two magnificent **gardens★**: a kare-sansui (dry landscape) garden and a second, featuring a pond and a bridge (chisenkaiyushiki), by the **goten** building. The grounds are also famous for their **Omuro cherry blossoms**, the latest blooming sakura trees in Kyoto.

Myoshin-ji★ 妙心寺

Map I, B2. 15min walk southeast of Ninna-ji. Keifuku Kitano Line, Myoshinji Station. Bus nos. 10, 26, 91, 93, Myoshin-ji-mae stop. Open daily 9am–5pm. Temple precincts no charge; Taizo-in ¥600; Keishun-in ¥400; Daishin-in ¥300. myoshinji.or.jp.

This 776-acre/310ha complex is the headquarters of the Myoshin-ji school of the Buddhist Rinzai sect, which has more than 3000 temples throughout Japan. Founded in 1338 by Kanzan Egen with the support of Emperor Hanazono, it comprises a central temple and 46 secondary temples. From the first, you can view the **Yokushitsu★**, an ingenious wooden structure (1656) used by the monks for bathing, with an area that could be transformed into a steam room. The **Hojo**, the Abbot's quarters, and the **Hatto**, the Dharma hall, house some magnificent sumi-e (ink and wash paintings) by Kano Tanyu (1602–74). From a height of 66ft/20m, the intense black eyes of the **dragon★★** painted on the ceiling of the Hatto seem to follow you around (the dragon plays a protective role).

Of the secondary temples open to the public, the **Keishun-in, Daishin-in,** and **Taizo-in★★**, the last is the most interesting. It houses a masterpiece known as **Hyonenzu★★**, Catching a Catfish with a Gourd, painted by Josetsu. This Japanese painter of Chinese origin (1405–96) is regarded as the founder of the Zen art of sumi-e ("the way of black ink"), a monochrome technique used to promote Zen philosophy. The temple has a magnificent **garden★★** (often not too busy) dating from the Muromachi period (1336–1573). It was designed by the great master Kano Motonobu (1476–1559) at the very end of his life. If you have not yet found the answer to Josetsu's riddle about catching a catfish with a gourd, take a close look at the shape of the pond: rather gourd-like, perhaps?

Leave this complex by the north gate and return to Ryoan-ji, a pleasant walk of about 20min.

Koryu-ji★★ 広隆寺

Map I, A3. Uzumasa (JR Sagano Lines) or Uzumasa-Koryuji (Keifuku Arashiyama Line) stations, or buses no. 11, 72, 73, 75, 76 & 77. Open daily: Mar–Nov 9am–5pm; Dec–Feb 9am–4.30pm. ¥700.

Dating from 1165, the **kodo★** (lecture hall) of this temple is one of Kyoto's oldest buildings, and houses a 9C statue of Amida Buddha (see box p332). At the back of the kodo, the **taishido**, dedicated to **Shotoku Taishi** (574–622), displays a statue of this celebrated prince who drew up the Jushichijo no Kenpo, or "Constitution in 17 Articles." This charter promised social harmony through the new religion of Buddhism, which the Prince was instrumental in spreading throughout Japan.

Shotoku Taishi is said to have given the founder of Koryu-ji the magnificent statue that has been displayed ever since in the **Reiho-kan** (treasure hall). It depicts the **Miroku Bosatsu★★★** (Maitreya in Sanskrit), the Buddha who is to arise several million years after his master, Amida Buddha, and lead human beings to final enlightenment. Dating from the first half of the 7C and finely carved in red pine, the statue's enigmatic smile under half-closed eyes radiates sweetness and serenity.

Toei Studio Park 東映太秦映画村

Map I, A3. Short walk from Koryu-ji. Uzumasa-Koryuji Station (Keifuku Arashiyama Line). Open daily Mar–Nov 9am–5pm; Dec–Feb 9.30am–4.30pm . ⌖¥2400 (children ¥1400). toei-eigamura.com.

Children (and adults) will enjoy wandering around the costume drama film sets of this famous Japanese studio—Kurosawa Akira himself filmed here. You can be a ninja, find out about sound effects and film posters, and do some animation... It's just a pity that the more interesting attractions are only available on paying a supplement.

THE SOUTHWEST
Allow half a day for each site.

Katsura Imperial Villa★★★
桂離宮

⌖Map I, A4. 20min walk from Katsura Station (Hankyu Line), or bus no. 33, Katsura Rikyu-mae stop, then 8min walk. ⌖Visit by guided tour only (1hr, in English); reserve in advance at the IHA (⌖see box p323). ⌖Tue–Sun 9.20am, 11.20am, 1.20pm, 3.20pm & 4.20pm. ⌖¥1000. sankan.kunaicho.go.jp/english/guide/katsura.html.

The garden and Imperial villa of Katsura were commissioned by Prince Toshihito (1579–1629) and his son Prince Toshitada (1619–62). A number of graceful *shoin* (pavilions), completed in 1664, are arranged around the lake, along with a platform from which to watch the moon rise. Raised on delicate wooden piles,

they are slightly staggered to form a "flying geese" configuration. Their minimalist façades combine dark-wood with the white paper of sliding doors and windows, forming geometrical shapes. The stroll garden (⌖see p115), and some of the pavilions, are attributed to architect and gardener Kobori Enshu.

Saiho-ji (Moss Temple)★★★
西芳寺 (苔寺)

⌖Map I, A4. 3km northwest of Katsura Imperial Villa. Buses no. 28, 63 & 73, Matsuo Taisha-mae stop, then 15min walk. ⌖Daily, hours vary; visit (2hr) by appointment only. ⌖¥3000. Book 1–2 months in advance (check website for details). saihoji-kokedera.com.

The **Moss Temple** is truly enchanting, especially after the rains of May and June. Designed in 1339 by Buddhist monk Muso Soseki (1275–1351) on the site of a monastery dedicated to Amida Buddha (which had itself replaced an older villa belonging to Prince Shotoku), the Moss Temple—officially Saiho-ji, but better known as **Koke-dera**—is laid out on two levels. The **lower garden**, showing Heian influence, is arranged around a lake; the **upper garden**, clinging to the hillside, mimics the bed of a rocky cascade.

This was the first Zen garden and has since influenced many others, such as the gardens of the Golden and Silver

Katsura Imperial Villa

USEFUL INFORMATION

Tourist Offices – Kyoto Tourist Information Center, *Kyoto Station Bldg, 2F, next to the Isetan department store (Map III, B2).* ✆*075-343-0548, kyototourism.org. Open daily 8.30am–7pm.* Information in English on the city and prefecture.

Kawaramachi Sanjo Tourist Information Center, *Kawaramachi-dori, between Shijo and Sanjo (Map II, B3).* ✆*075-213-1717. Open daily 10am–6pm.* Information in English, in the city center.

Randen Arashiyama Station Center, *In the Keifuku station, Arashiyama. Open daily 9am–6pm (8pm Apr–Nov).* Has free maps of the area.

Tour Guides – Kyoto SGG Club, *Kyoto Station, Shinkansen Hachijo exit. kyotosgg.sakura.ne.jp. Open daily 10am–4pm.* Information and guiding services in English, free of charge *(apart from transport costs and meals, which you are expected to cover).* Book online 2 weeks in advance.

WaRaiDo Guide Networks, *waraido. com/walking.* Guided walking tours, in English, Mar–Nov every Mon, Wed & Fri, starting at 10am from Kyoto Station *(duration 5hr, ¥2000 per person; no reservations).* The program includes temples, shrines, gardens, and the old artisans' districts.

Bank/Foreign Exchange – ATMs accepting foreign cards are available at **post offices**, usully with hours lsightly longer than the post office itself. At the Central PO (⏱*see below*), the ATM is accessible 24hr. **Prestia/ SMBC Trust Bank** also has 24hr International ATMs, as do most **7-Eleven** *combini.*

Post Offices – Central Post Office, *main exit from Kyoto Station, west side (Map III, B2). Open Mon–Fri 9am–9pm, Sat–Sun & public hols 9am–7pm.* In the south wing of the building, a post office counter is open 24hr.

Nakagyo Post Office, *corner of Sanjo-dori and Higashi-Notoin (Map II, B2). Open Mon–Fri 9am–7pm, Sat–Sun & public hols 3pm.* Has a window open 24hr for express mail and stamps.

Health – Japan Baptist Hospital, *47 Yamamoto-cho, Kita-Shirakawa, Sakyo-ku.* ✆*075-781-5191. www.jbh. or.jp.* English-speaking doctors on site.

Sakabe International Clinic, *435 Yamamoto-cho, Gokomachi Nijo-sagaru, Sakyo-ku.* ✆*075-231-1624, sakabeclinic.com/english. Open Mon–Sat (except thur & Sat afternoon).* Clinic run by English-speaking staff.

TRANSPORTATION

BY PLANE – Kansai International Airport (KIX), Osaka *(Map I, B4; off map).* ✆*072-455-2500. kansai-airport. or.jp/en.* The airport, on an island in Osaka Bay, has a rail link to Kyoto Station on the JR Haruka Line *(every 30min, journey time about 1hr 15min, ¥2900 without reservation, ¥3430 with reservation).* The airport is also served by bus: terminal 1, stop 8; terminal 2, stop 2 *(every 20–30min, journey time 1hr 45min, ¥2600).* The stop in Kyoto is in front of the Avanti department store, by Kyoto Station's south (Hachijo) exit. Alternatively, minibuses run by **Yasaka** *(*✆*075-803-4800, yasaka.jp/english/shuttle)* and **MK Taxis** *(*✆*075-778-5489, mktaxi-japan. com)* provide a door-to-door service between Kansai International Airport and Kyoto city center *(around ¥4000 per person, sometimes with supplement for luggage).* Both companies have desks in the arrivals hall. Book your seat before departure at least 2 days in advance.

Itami International Airport (ITM), Osaka *(Map I, B4; off map).* ✆*06-6856-6781, www.osaka-airport. co.jp.* The domestic (despite its name) airport has a bus link with Kyoto Station *(every 25min, journey time around 55min, ¥1340).* The stop in Kyoto is in front of the Avanti department store by Kyoto Station's south (Hachijo) exit. Minibuses run by MK Taxis also provide a door-to-door service between Itami Airport and Kyoto city center *(¥3000 per person, plus luggage supplement).*

BY TRAIN – **Kyoto Station** *(Map I, C4)*. The station is served by JR and Shinkansen trains, and is the terminus for the Kintetsu Line. **Kawaramachi Station** *(Map I, C3)* serves the Hankyu Line. The Keihan Line operates out of **Sanjo Station** *(Map I, C3)*. The Shinkansen Nozomi departs for Tokyo *(every 10min, 2hr 20min journey, ¥13,320)*, Nagoya *(every 10min, 40min journey, ¥5170)*, Hiroshima *(every 20min, 1hr 40min journey, ¥10,770)*, and Fukuoka *(Hakata Station, every 30min, 2hr 50min journey, ¥15,400)*. There are also slower, cheaper trains along this route. For Nara, take the JR Line *(every 15min, journey 45min, ¥720)* or Kintetsu Line *(Ltd Express, hourly, journey 35min, ¥1160)*. For Kobe, JR Line *(every 10min, journey 55min, ¥1100)* or Hankyu Line *(Kobe-Sannomiya Station, Ltd Express, every 10min, journey 1hr 10min, ¥630)*, changing at Juso in Osaka. For Osaka, JR Line *(every 10min, journey 30min, ¥570)*, Hankyu Line *(Umeda Station, Ltd Express, every 10min, journey 45min, ¥400)* or Keihan Line *(Yodoyabashi Station, Ltd Express, every 10min, 50min journey, ¥420)*. For Himeji, JR Line *(every 15min, journey 1hr 30min, ¥2310)*. For Ise, Kintetsu Line *(Ise-shi Station, Ltd Express, every 30min, 2hr 25min journey, ¥3690)*, changing at Yamatoyagi.
BY BUS – Though slower than trains, buses can be much cheaper, and night buses will also save you night's accommodation if you can sleep on them. Prices will vary a lot by time of year, comfort of seat, etc. **Willer Express** *(stop on south side of Kyoto Station)* runs services to Fukuoka, Hiroshima, Matsuyama, Niigata, Takayama and Tokyo. **JR Highway Buses** *(stop on north side of Kyoto Station)* serve Hiroshima, Kanazawa, Nagano, Nagoya and Tokyo. **Keihan Buses** *(stop on south side of Kyoto Station, by Hotel Keihan)* go to Fukuoka, Kanazawa, Tottori and Tokyo.

GETTING AROUND KYOTO
BY SUBWAY – The network consists of two lines: the **Karasuma Line** (north–south) and **Tozai Line** (east–west), which intersect at Karasuma-Oike Station. *(Map II, B2)*. Convenient for moving quickly around the city center, but not very useful for visiting the more out-of-the-way temples. Trains run 5.29am–11.49pm, depending on the line. *Tickets ¥210–¥350, depending on distance; 1-day pass ¥600, available from subway stations, tourist information centers, and many hotels.*
BY TRAIN – Several lines serve Kyoto. The **Hankyu Line** runs southwest from Kawaramachi Station to Katsura Villa, and northwest into the Arashiyama district. Arashiyama is also served by the **Randen-Keifuku Line**, from Shijo-Omiya Station, and by the **JR Sagano Line**, from Kyoto Station. The northeast of Kyoto is served by the **Eizan Line**. The **Keihan Line** from Sanjo-Keihan Station heads south to Osaka.
☺ *To find your way around the labyrinth of Kyoto Station, check online or ask at the tourist office for a floor guide.*
BY BUS – A dense network of bus routes enables you to get to almost all the temples and places of interest, most services run by **Kyoto City Bus** (the green buses) but a few by **Kyoto Bus** (cream and red colored). *Buses run 6am–10pm, and some until 11pm. The same fare (¥230; 1-day pass ¥600, buy on the bus or at tourist information centers, the Bus Information Center, or many hotels)* applies for any destination within the central zone, which covers almost the whole of Kyoto. The **Raku Bus** (operated by Kyoto City Bus; usually brightly colored) serves the main tourist sites: buses no. 100 (east of the city), 101 (center and northwest), and 102 (connects east–west). A **bus route map**, with explanatory notes, can be obtained from Kyoto Tourist Information and from the information office at the main bus terminal, opposite the main entrance to Kyoto Station.
☺ Buses do not arrive at regular

intervals and are sometimes stuck in traffic. Make long trips by subway or train, then take a bus for the final leg of the journey.

PASSES – A **Kyoto Subway & Bus One-day Pass** *(¥900/1700; onedaypass.kyoto)* allows you unlimited busand subway travel for 1 or 2 days, and can be purchased at any station or the Bus Information Center by Kyoto Station. A **Kansai Thru Pass** allows you unlimited travel on all subway lines, trains *(apart from the JR network)*, and regional buses (Kyoto, Osaka, Kobe, Himeji, Nara, and Koya-san) for 2 days *(¥4400)* or 3 days *(¥5500)*, as well as discounts at many places of interest. It can be purchased at Kyoto Station's Bus Information Center, Kansai International Airport, large tourist information centers, or online ahead of your trip *(surutto.com/tickets/kansai_thru_english.html)*. The JR network has a wide range of travel passes in the region. Among the most useful is the **JR Kansai Area Pass** *(1 day ¥2300, 2 days ¥4600, 3 days ¥5600, 4 days ¥6600, half-price for children 6–11 years, under 6 years no charge)*, which can be used on the JR Kansai network (covers Kansai International Airport, Kobe, Osaka, Nara, Himeji, and Kyoto). The **JR Kansai Wide Area Pass** *(5 days ¥9200, half-price for children 6–11 years, under 6 years no charge)* covers a larger area, including the Sea of Japan Coast and down onto the Kii Peninsula. The **JR San'yo-San'in Area Pass** *(¥19,400, half-price for children 6–11 years, under 6 years no charge)* covers a broader area still, including Hiroshima and Fukuoka, and is valid for 7 consecutive days of travel. JR passes can be bought online in advance, or in Japan at JR stations *(supplement applies)* on presentation of a passport.

BY TAXI – Taxis will carry up to 4 people and there are usually plenty of them. The fare is around ¥640 for the first 1.2mi/2km, then around ¥80 every 0.2mi/300m. If you plan to spend all day visiting temples, involving a lot of walking, they are handy for the short distances between the temple complexes. There are **"Foreigner Friendly" taxi stands** *(daily 9am–5pm)* on either side of Kyoto Station, with drivers who speak either English of Chinese. Otherwise, it's useful to have the name and address of your destination written down in Japanese to show your driver.

BY BICYCLE – The most practical way to get around the city. Apart from the steep hills to the east, the terrain is flat, sloping slightly from north to south, and you can ride on the wide pavements of the city's avenues. Also make the most of the fine cycle path that runs north–south along the Kamo River. Be careful to park in official areass, though; it's annoying and expensive *(¥2300)* to retrieve impounded bicycles. *English information on Kyoto cycling rules, official parking areas, rental, routes, etc. on kyoto-bicycle.com/foreigners.*

Bicycle Rental – **Kyoto Cycling Tour Project**, *just west of the Central Post Officeg.* ☏*075-354-3636. kctp.net. Open daily 9am–6pm.* Rents bikes *(from ¥1000/day).* and e-bikes *(from ¥2300/day)* and organizes guided bicycle tours *(from ¥6500/person for 3hr).*

Fuune Rental Biycles, *163 Komeya-cho, Shimogyo-ku, opposite Nishi Hongan-ji.* ☏*075-354-7070, fuune.jp. Open daily 9am–6pm.* Bike *(from ¥1000/day)* and e-bike *(from ¥1800/day)* rental. Helpfully, a day's rental allows you to return it by 10am the next day. Also has tandems *(from ¥2500/day).*

Kyoto Eco Trip, *58 Higashikujo, Minami-ku, south of Kyoto Station.* ☏*075-692-0794, kyoto-option.com. Open daily 9am–6pm.* Near the station, you can hire town bikes *(from ¥900/day)* and e-bikes *(from ¥2000/day).* A convenient shop if you're planning to cycle to Fushimi.

Pavilions. Interestingly, the 120 varieties of moss for which it is now famous did not grow here until the Meiji period, when the garden fell into neglect.
All visits begin with a short Zen service and sutra copying, after which you're free to explore the lushly beautiful grounds for the remainder of the time.

THE SOUTHEAST
Allow at least a full day.

Tofuku-ji★★ 東福寺
Map I, C4. Tofukuji Station (Keihan & JR Nara lines), or buses no. 202, 207 & 208, Tofukuji stop, then 10min walk southeast. Open daily: Apr–Oct 9am–4.30pm; Nov–late Dec 8.30am–4.30pm; late Dec–Mar 9am–4pm. Garden ¥400, bridge & Kaisan-do ¥400. tofukuji.jp.
Headquarters of the Rinzai school of Zen Buddhism, this temple was built in 1236 by the monk Enni under the guidance of Kujo Michiie (1193–1252), *sessho* (regent) for Emperor Chukyo (reigned 1221). This great statesman of the Kamakura period wanted to build a vast edifice modeled on Todai-ji and Kofuku-ji in Nara—Tofuku-ji is a combination of the two names. Although destroyed by fire on numerous occasions—in the Meiji period, it even lost its Buddha hall *(butsu-den)*—this temple has many interesting features: the **Tsuten-kyo★★**, a bridge set in a magnificent forest of maples; the **San-mon★★**, a gate with a majestic half-hip roof, decorated with sculptures of the Buddha and 16 *arhats* (sages) carved by Teicho on the first floor. Listed as a National Treasure, this is the oldest-surviving Zen gate in Japan (13C). Within the enclosure, the meditation room *(zendo)*, toilets *(tosu)*, and bathroom *(yokushitsu)* all date from the Muromachi period (14C). The **Hojo★** (abbot's quarters) is nevertheless the highlight, not on account of its age *(it was reconstructed in 1890)*, but because of the way it is laid out: unusually, it opens on every side onto a magnificent **garden★★**, creating some interesting juxtapositions. The western garden, for instance, consists of splendid mosses

and is counter-balanced on the south side by a dry landscape garden with seven cylindrical stones representing the constellation of the Great Bear. Blending the Zen simplicity of the Kamakura period with the geometrical abstraction of modern art, it was designed in 1945 by **Shigemori Mirei** (1896–1975), a leading exponent of the movement to revitalize the art of the Japanese garden.

Fushimi-Inari Taisha★★ 伏見稲荷大社
Map I, C4, off map. Fushimi Inari (Keihan Line) or Inari (JR Nara Line) stations, then 5min walk east. Open daily 24hr. No charge. inari.jp. Be sure to wear good shoes.
The central shrine is one of over 30,000 Inari shrines in Japan, and one of the most unusual places of worship in the whole of the country. A path wends its way for approximately 2mi/4km up the hillside to the shrine, passing through hundreds of vermilion **torii★★** (gates). Ukanomitama no Mikoto (better known as Inari) is the tutelary goddess of rice, Japan's staple cereal. It is therefore easy to understand why, ever since the 8C, the faithful have been seeking Inari's favor by erecting *torii* branded with their names. Since rice attracts rodents, it is also logical that at intervals along the tunnel created by the gates, there are small stone statues of foxes, predators of the rodents, including one with the key to a rice granary in its jaws, a metaphor for its protective role.
Nowadays, farmers imploring the goddess for bumper crops have been superseded by those seeking greater wealth.

Daigo-ji★★ 醍醐寺
Map I, D4, off map. Daigo Station (Tozai Line), exit 2, then 15min walk east. Buses no. 22, 22A & 301, Daigoji stop. Shimo Daigo: Open daily: Mar–Nov 9am–5pm; Dec–Feb 9am–4pm. ¥800 (¥1500 mid-Mar–mid-May & mid-Oct–mid-Dec). Kami Daigo: Open daily: Mar–Nov 9am–4pm; Dec–Feb 9am–3pm (must be back at the base

of the mountain before 5pm). ¥600. daigoji.or.jp.

This famous temple of the Shingon school is now a UNESCO World Heritage Site. At the top of Mount Kasatori, the Buddhist monk Shobo, better known by his posthumous name of Rigen Daishi (832–909), discovered a spring with life-giving powers. In 874 he built a monastery dedicated to the Kannon, which expanded over several levels until the 13C. Seriously damaged in the civil wars, the complex was rebuilt in the late 16C on the orders of Toyotomi Hideyoshi.

Access to the lower temple, or **Shimo Daigo**, is via the Kamakura period (13–14C) **Nio-mon★**. Within the enclose are the main hall *(kondo)*, the lecture hall *(kodo)*, and the treasure hall, but it is the **five-story pagoda★** that really catches the eye. Intended for Emperor Daigo (897–930), but not completed until 951, it is one of the oldest in Japan. Inside *(generally closed to the public),* its precious mandalas *(designs of concentric circles)* painted on wood are indicative of the earliest art forms of tantric Buddhism.

It is a 45-minute walk from the Nio-mon along the path to the upper temple, or **Kami Daigo**, an architectural masterpiece from the Momoyama period, rebuilt in 1606. It's up here that you can drink the famous "life-giving" waters. On the way back to the lower temple, you will see *(opposite the Nio-mon)* the former residence of the principal of Daigo-ji: the **Sanpo-in★**, which literally means "House of Three Treasures" (Buddha, Dharma, Sangha). It opens onto a magnificent **tea garden★★** in the style of the lavish Momoyama era. It combines a tea pavilion, a *kare-sansui* (dry landscape) garden, and *sakazukushi (moss on a background of white sand)* garden. It was designed by master gardener Takeda Baishoken, again on the orders of Toyotomi Hideyoshi, who visited to admire the cherry trees and decided to settle there. In the spring of 1598, he even organized a cherry-blossom viewing party *(hanami)* for more than 900 guests. He died later that same year, and the event is now commemorated in the annual Hideyoshi Hanami Parade on the second Sunday in April *(information from the Tourist Office).*

GETTING AROUND

The small trains with violet carriages on the Randen-Keifuku Line serve Arashiyama from Shijo-Omiya *(20min journey; Map II, A3).* The Keifuku-Kitano Line links the town with the northwest sites from Katabira no Tsuji Station. It's a practical option for visiting both Arashiyama and the northwest in one day *(¥220 per journey, children ¥110 see randen. keifuku.co.jp/en).*

ARASHIYAMA★ 嵐山

Map I, A2/3. Allow a day. JR Sagano, Keifuku, or Hankyu lines to Arashiyama or Saga-Arashiyama stations. Buses no.11, 28, 91 & 93. Tourist Offices in Arashiyama (Keifuku Line) and Saga-Arashiyama (JR) stations.

Popular with tourists, the suburb of Arashiyama is in a beautiful natural setting, although spoilt in parts by the inevitable souvenir shops, but you can soon get away from them. **Togetsu-kyo**, literally "the bridge that spans the moon," now has to make do with the Katsura River and is where tourists tend to congregate. Bicycles, rickshaws, and boats are all options to hand for exploring its busy surroundings. There's a lovely view over the river which flows between steep, wooded banks, colorful in fall.

Arashiyama is a great place to cycle. You can hire bikes at Saga-Arashiyama and Arashiyama stations (prettily decorated with a kimono "forest") and cycle the paths in the extreme west of the town *(open 9am–5pm; ¥1000/day).*

Tenryu-ji★ 天竜寺

Map I, A3. 330yd/300m north of Togetsu Bridge. Open daily: late Mar–late Oct 8.30am–5.30pm; late Oct–late Mar 8.30am–5pm. ¥500 (garden only), ¥800 (with temple). tenryuji.com.

Dating from the 14C, the "Temple of the Celestial Dragon," belonging to the Rinzai sect of Zen Buddhism, was almost entirely rebuilt in the Meiji period. The **garden★**, one of the oldest in Japan, was designed by Muso Soseki (1275–1351).

Detour via Sagano

At the end of the Tenryu-ji garden, you can walk through a beautiful **bamboo grove★★** (open daily 24hr, no charge, hanatouro.jp/arashiyama). This stand of giant bamboo swaying in the wind has appeared in a number of films, and is now so popular the crowds may spoil it for you; there's a separate, quieter path for bikes and rickshaws, though, a much more rewarding experience. The route leads to **Okochi Sanso** (open daily 9am–5pm, ¥1000, including green tea), the private villa of Okochi Denjiro, star of many 1930s samurai films, which has a beautiful **view★** over the Kyoto Valley. It's a great place to escape the crowds, on foot or by bike, along small lanes that zigzag between temples, gardens, fields, and peaceful residential areas. You'll soon reach **Saga-Torimoto** (a road at an incline), with some well-preserved machiya (townhouses) from the Meiji era. Today these old houses are occupied by restaurants and boutiques.

A little farther on, in the temple of **Otagi Nenbutsu-ji** (open daily 8am–5pm, ¥300), 1200 stone statues are lined up, all slightly different and many with funny or cheeky expressions. See if you can find the two friends sharing a drink.

Daikaku-ji★ 大覚寺

 Map I, A2. Around 0.5mi/1km north of Arashiyama Station (JR). From Tenryu-ji, bus no. 28; from Shijo-dori, bus no. 91. Open 9am–4.30pm. ¥500. daikakuji.or.jp.
Originally the country retreat of the Emperor Saga, this building was converted into a temple of the Shingon school in 876. The emperor was a great friend of the monk Kukai, known posthumously as Kobo Daishi, who had introduced from China the "True Word" school of Buddhism, Shingon-shu. The

main hall (shinden) has some wonderful fusuma (sliding panel) **paintings★** by the Kano School.

👥 Boat Trip on the River Hozu★ 保津川下り

 Map I; A2, off map.
There are two options for this very popular trip, especially in spring and fall.

JR Line + boat – Allow 1hr 20min. JR Sagano Line to Kameoka Station (1–3 stops after Arashiyama, depending on the train). On leaving the station, turn left and head toward Hozugawa-kudari (10min walk to Kameoka pier). The boats arrive near Togetsu Bridge and depart roughly every hour; open daily: Mar 10–Nov 9am–3.30pm; early Dec 9am–2.30pm; mid-Dec–Mar 9 10am–2.30pm. ¥4100. hozugawakudari.jp/en. This trip runs the rapids of the Hozu River in a flat-bottomed boat: spectacular, and quite safe in the hands of skilled oarsmen. The trip finishes by Togetsu-kyo, in the center of Arashiyama.

Sagano Scenic Railway + boat – From Torokko-Saga or Torokko-Arashiyama stations, take the scenic railway, also known as the Sagano Romantic Train to the terminus Torokko-Kameoka (open Mar–Dec 9am–5pm, one train an hour, 25min journey, ¥620, sagano-kanko. co.jp/en). From there, a bus (15min, ¥310) takes you to Kameoka pier where you can catch a boat (as described above). This option is probably less efficient, but the scenic train journey is gorgeous, gliding above the Hoze River along a former JR San'in Line, in carriages with panoramic windows. It gets very busy with groups, though, and is definitely a touristy operation.

EXCURSIONS

UJI★ 宇治

 Regional Map, B2. Allow half a day to a day, as a trip from Kyoto. 2.5mi/4km south of Kyoto. JR Nara Line (15–30min, ¥240). Tourist offices in the JR station, near the south exit, and by the river near Byodo-in (both open daily 9am–5pm, kyoto-uji-kankou.or.jp).

Phoenix Hall, Byodo-in

Famous for its **green tea**, and for featuring in *The Tale of Genji*, this pleasant, rural area near Kyoto also boasts the magnificent Byodo-in, which features on all ¥10 coins.

Byodo-in★★ 平等院

A 10min, well signposted walk from the station. Garden: ⏰*open daily 8.30am–5.30pm. Hoshokan Museum:* ⏰*open daily 9am–5pm.* 👟*¥600.* 👣*Phoenix Hall visits are by guided tour only,* ⏰*every 20min 9.30am–4.10pm.* 👟*¥300. byodoin.or.jp.*

Exemplifying the splendor of the Heian period, this former country residence was built by the regent (*sessho*) Fujiwara no Michinaga (966–1028), who retired here just before the year 1000 to practice meditation. On his death, his son Yorimichi converted it into a temple dedicated to the Amida Buddha (1052). The central pavilion, with its two open wings, represents a bird in flight. In 1994, the remarkable temple was added to the UNESCO list of World Heritage Sites.

The central **Phoenix Hall★★** houses a National Treasure: a great statue of the **Amida Buddha★★★** dating from the 11C and attributed to the monk **Jocho** (👀 *see box p321*). On the walls are nine color paintings of the Amida Buddha descending from the Pure Land *(Western Paradise)* over which he presided, as he had undertaken to receive all the dying who wished to enter his Pure Land, a key concept during the Heian period (794–1185). The fact that there are nine paintings is an allusion to the number of levels of salvation in the Pure Land. Created in 2000 by Akira Kuryu, the **museum★** houses a fine collection of works of art, including the oldest examples of the *yamato-e* painting style in the world.

Taiho-an★ 市営茶室・対鳳庵

On leaving Byodo-in, turn right and follow the river for 330yd/300m. ⏰*Open daily 10am–4pm.* ⏰*Closed 2 weeks end Dec/beg Jan.* 👟*¥500. Tickets can be purchased at the Tourist Information Center.*

This charming wooden pavilion is an authentic tea house, and was built to teach people the elaborate code of rules governing the tea ceremony. The main room is called the *Honseki*; other rooms are the *hiroma-chaseki* and *ritsurei-seki*.

EXCURSIONS AROUND LAKE BIWA 琵琶湖

Allow around four days for all the sights, with two nights at Otsu and one at Makino (between Hikone and Harie).

There's a selection of sites around Lake Biwa, the largest lake in Japan, which is more like a small sea (260sq miles/ 670sq km): Ostu and the area around it; the Miho Museum; Hikone to the east; and Harie to the west. They can be treated as single destinations, reached by train or car, or you can see several in one trip. It's also worth stopping off at one or more of the beaches along the lake.

The Tale of Genji

The power of the Fujiwaras reached its peak under **Fujiwara no Michinaga** (966–1028). He managed to marry his three daughters to three successive Emperors: the eldest, Shoshi, to Emperor Ichijo (980–1011), 66th Emperor of Japan; the second to Emperor Sanjo (976–1017), Ichijo's cousin; and the third to Go-Ichijo (1008–36), the son her elder sister Shoshi had borne to Ichijo. Fujiwara no Michinaga is believed to have partially inspired the main character in *Genji Monogatari (The Tale of Genji)*, the world's first novel, written by empress-consort Shoshi's governess **Murasaki Shikibu** (973–1014) around 1008.

On the opposite bank of the Ujigawa River, 10min walk from Byodo-in, the small but well presented **Tale of Genji Museum** is dedicated to this important literary work *(45-26 Higashiuchi; Open Tue–Sun 9am–5pm, ¥600, English audioguides no charge; 0774-39-9300, bit.ly/genjimuseum)*.

OTSU AND SURROUNDINGS 大津
Regional Map, B2. 10mi/16km from Kyoto. Allow two or three days.
Some of the sites on the southwest side of the lake, around the town of Otsu, are included in UNESCO's Historic Monuments of Ancient Kyoto list.

Hiei-zan and Sakamoto★ 比叡山・坂本
From Sanjo Keihan, buses no. 16 & 17; from Kyoto Station, buses no. 18 &19 (around 1hr journey, ¥770).
Dispatched to China for a year by Emperor Kanmu to seek out new doctrines, the monk Saicho (767–822), returned in 805 with the teachings of the Tendai school. The monastic complex that he founded at **Enryaku-ji** on Mount Hiei to the northeast of Kyoto became the headquarters of the Tendai sect.

Sanzen-in★ 三千院
From Ohara Station, walk east up the path lined with stands selling pickles (the local specialty) following the river (10min walk). Open daily: Mar–Oct 8.30am–5pm; Dec–Feb 9am–4.30pm. ¥700. sanzenin.or.jp/en.
The main attraction in the small country town of Ohara, apart from its local specialty of "Ice Kyuri," Japanese cucumbers delicately marinated in "kelp water," is **Sanzen-in**, founded by the monk, Saicho. The main hall of the temple houses a valuable statue of Amida Buddha meditating.

Behind it is a lovely **garden★** planted with maples and cedars, and full of small *jizo* (bodhisattva) statues. Jizo Bosatsu, who vowed to help alleviate the suffering of all creatures in hell is, much-loved throughout Japan.

Hosen-in★ 宝泉院
On leaving Sanzen-in, turn right. Hosen-in temple is just after Shorin-in. Open daily 9am–5pm. ¥800, including green tea. hosenin.net.
A wonderful 700-year-old **pine tree★** graces the garden of this little-visited temple. Inside, the ceiling still bears traces of the blood shed by the 370 samurai who committed *seppuku* (ritual suicide) after the Battle of Sekigahara (1600), in which General Tokugawa Ieyasu defeated Hideyoshi's son (*see p132*). The ceiling is made from the floor of the mighty castle Toyotomi Hideyoshi (1536–98) had built on Fushimi Hill, where the grisly act took place. The castle was destroyed in 1622 and the hill transformed into a peach orchard.

Enryaku-ji★ 延暦寺
There are two cable cars up to Enryaku-ji, Sakamoto and Eizan. Sakamoto is more convenient, dropping you almost 1km closer to the To-do, and has glorious views over Biwa-ko (every 30min, journey time 10min; ¥860 single/¥1620 return). Open daily 9am–4pm. ¥700, English audioguide ¥500. hieizan.or.jp.

Little now remains of the large monastic complex built on Mount Hiei by **Saicho** (767–822), one of the patriarchs of the Buddhist Tendai school. Enryaku-ji was the base from which Saicho taught the doctrine of the Tendai school.

Having become increasingly powerful over the centuries at the expense of its rivals, the complex was finally destroyed in the 16C by General Oda Nobunaga (1534–82), who captured Kyoto and brought the dominance of the Ashikaga clan to an end.

Of the former complex of more than 3000 pavilions and temples, just three principal groups of buildings now remain: **To-do** to the east, **Sai-to** to the west, and **Yokawa** to the north (of lesser interest). In the first group, don't miss the statues in the **Kokuho-den★** and the great hall of **Konponchu-do★**, the main building, which conmtains flames apparently burning continuously now for 1200 years. In the second group, it is worth seeing the **Shaka-do★**, rebuilt by Hideyoshi, and the **Hokke-do**, for its praying monks.

Hiyoshi-taisha★ 日吉大社

Near Hieizan-Sakamoto Station (JR Kosei Line from Kyoto). ◷*Open daily 9am–4.30pm.* ◉*¥300. hiyoshitaisha.jp.*
The divinity of **Mount Hiei**, at the base of which you'll find the shrine of is the **Hiyoshi-taisha**, is tasked with protecting the ancient city of Kyoto from evil spirits. Go past the imposing **Omiya stone bridge** and you will see the **sanno torii** marking the entrance to the shrine precincts, which unusually features a triangle at its apex that opens out to form the kanji for "mountain."
A little farther on, the roof of the **Nishi-hongu romon** gate, which opens onto **Nishihongu honden,** the main hall, is supported by **two monkeys**, the messengers of the god of the shrine. At 5am on the first day of each year, a 10minute **Noh play,** to which admission is free, is put on in the temple's Noh arena, performed by actors who have come from Kyoto.

Former Chikurin-in 旧竹林院

Leave Hiyoshi-taisha and continue straight on for a couple of minutes, then take the first turning on the left. ◷*Open Tue–Sun 9am–4.30pm, last admission 4.30pm.* ◉*¥320.*
This picturesque traditional building set in lush green gardens used to be a *satobo*, or retirement villa for monks. Visitors today can appreciate the quiet, meditative atmosphere over a cup of green tea (there are two tea houses).

▶ Leave the former Chikurin-in and follow the road down past the buildings constructed on the terraced walls on both sides, turn left and continue straight on for another 440yd/400m, then take a right. Sakamoto Station is a little farther on.

Mii-dera★ 三井寺

Take the Keihan Railway from Sakamoto Station to Mii-dera Station. ◷*Open daily 8am–5pm.* ◉ *¥600. shiga-miidera.or.jp.*
The sprawling monastic complex of **Onjo-ji** temple is made up of 40 buildings. Its nickname, **Mii-dera** (literally, "three wheels"), comes from the three emperors who were first bathed in **Akaiya**, the sacred spring, which is now to be found in the grounds of the **Kondo**, or **main hall.**
Founded in the 7C, this temple of warrior monks has been involved in numerous wars and was burnt down dozens of times in the past. Fortunately, each of the **little statues** of the Buddha was entrusted to a monk whose job it was to save it from the flames. These statues—some of which date back to before the Kamakura period—are exhibited in the Kodo, the fabric of which dates from 1599.
Less conveniently, you will not be able to admire the seven metal Buddha statues contained in the **zushi,** a chamber in the main hall that was sealed up upon the death of the last Buddha; it will not be opened until the coming of the next Buddha, in 7670 million years…

Entrance Hall, Miho Museum designed by I. M. Pei

OTSU 大津

JR train from Kyoto to Otsu (15–20min).
Located at the far southern end of
Lake Biwa, Otsu enjoyed a brief spell
as capital in the 7th century and grew
rapidly as an important staging-post
on the Tokaido road. It is now a densely
populated city of 300,000 inhabitants,
the capital of the Shiga Prefecture, and
a major tourist destination. Its mostly
Japanese visitors come here to enjoy a
walk beside the lake, a boat tour, one of
its many festivals, or even the immense
water fountain displays (amongst the
most powerful in the world) known as
Biwa-ko Hana-funsui. The city can
also be used as a base for exploring the
temples described in the next chapter.

Ishiyama-dera 石山寺

*Take the Keihan Railway from Mii-dera
(or Otsu) Station to Ishiyama-dera
Station. If coming from Kyoto, take Jr
Biwa-ko Line to Ishiyama, then the
Keihan Line to Ishiyama-dera Station.*
○*Open daily 10am–4.30pm.* ☜*¥600
(special exhibitions around ¥500).
ishiyamadera.or.jp.*
This "Temple of the Stony Mountain" is
where **Murasaki Shikibu** was inspired
to write the **Tale of Genji.** To commemorate this fact, a room in the temple has
been reserved for a life-size figure of the
author that can be viewed from outside.
There is even a little Murasaki automa-

ton exhibited in a glass case! There is
also a museum with exhibits relating by
turns to both the temple and the *Tale of
Genji* (⌖*see box p348).* The **gardens★**on
the mountainside surrounding the temple are always in flower, whatever the
season, but are particularly beautiful in
April, when the cherry trees are in blossom and the temple is lit up.

MIHO MUSEUM★★
ミホミュージアム

⌖*Regional Map, B2. Allow a morning or
afternoon, including journey time. About
12.5mi/20km southeast of Kyoto. JR
Biwako Line to Ishiyama Station (15min,
¥250), then Teisan bus to the terminus
(5–7 per day, 9.10am–1.10/2.10pm
out, 11am–5pm return, 50min, ¥840;
teisan-konan-kotsu.co.jp).* ○*Open Tue–
Sun 10am–5pm (last admission 4pm).*
○*Closed for much of the year; check
website for details.* ☜*¥1100.* ℘*0748-
82-3411, miho.jp/en.* ☕.
In complete harmony with the mountainous landscape south of Lake Biwa,
this museum by architect I. M. Pei
(designer of the Louvre Pyramid in Paris),
takes the visitor by surprise in more ways
than one.
On arrival, a small electric vehicle takes
you through a tunnel to re-emerge after
a few hundred yards in front of a building
set into the mountainside (you can also
walk, about 10min). Inside, the exhibits

The Children's Kabuki Festival of Nagahama

For close to 250 years, every year in mid-April magnificently decorated floats parade in Nagahama's streets with a miniature Kabuki troupe, its actors aged 5 to 12. Two and a half centuries ago Kabuki existed for children here, but they had no stage, hence the idea of floats. Supported by rich families rivaling each other in the pomp and wealth they could display in this manner, the **Nagahama Hikiyama Festival** is today one of **Japan's three greatest float parades**, as well as one of the only Kabuki performances given by children.

The boys undergo two relentless months of training in this traditional art to strive to meet the expectations of both families and instructors. Then, in the festival held on **April 13–16**, clothed in magnificent costumes and wearing heavy wigs, the boys ceaselessly perform their play over and over on their "traveling art musuem", before an audience of thousands.

From Kyoto take the Shinkansen Hikari to Maibara, then Hokuriku Line to Nagahama (40min, ¥2330). From Hikone take the Hokuriku Line to Nagahama (20min, ¥240). Outside of the festival, the floats are housed in the Nagahama City Hikiyama Museum (🕐 open daily 9am–5pm, 🎫¥600, nagahama-hikiyama.or.jp).

(from the ancient civilizations of Japan, China, the Middle East, and the Greco-Roman world) are displayed with an elegant simplicity. They include a **Buddhist statue from the Gandhara★★★** *(modern-day northern Pakistan and eastern Afghanistan)* carved shortly after the reign of King Kanishka I (2C), and a **mosaic of Dionysus★★** discovering Ariadne on Naxos *(stone tesserae, of 3C or 4C Romano-Syrian origin)*.

The **north wing** features Japanese arts and hosts special exhibitions. It also houses the collection of Koyama Mihoko, who in 1970 founded the Shinji Shumeikai sect, one of Japan's "new religions," which believes that the contemplation of art and living in harmony with nature gives meaning and enjoyment to life. The sect now has 300,000 devotees worldwide, and the museum is staff who live and work here are all members.

HIKONE CASTLE★ 彦根城
🚗*Regional Map, B2. Allow a morning or afternoon, including the journey. About 25mi/40km northeast of Kyoto. JR Biwa-ko Line (every 30min, 50min journey time, ¥1170). 10min walk up the main street from Hikone Station. 🕐Open daily 8.30am–5pm. 🎫¥600 (castle & Genkyu-en) or ¥1000 (castle, Genkyu-en & museum). visit.hikoneshi.com/en/castle*

& hikone-castle-museum.jp/en.
Dominating the east bank of **Lake Biwa** and built between 1603 and 1622 by the warlord Ii Naosuke, Hikone Castle is one of Japan's oldest remaining Edo-period castles. Its keep, moat, and ramparts are well-preserved.

From the terrace of the **Tenshu★**, which caps the three stories of the keep, there is an uninterrupted **view** over the lake. On the northeast side of the castle, follow the path that is marked out to the **Genkyu-en★**, a beautiful landscaped garden of Chinese inspiration where you can drink Uji green tea. The castle also houses a small **museum** *(collections of armor and Noh theater costumes)*.

HARIE 針江
🚗*Regional Map, B2. About 37mi/60km northwest of Kyoto. From Hikone, JR Biwa-ko Line to Shin-Asahi Station via Omi-Shiotsu (1hr 15 min, 🎫¥1170). From Hieizan-Sakamoto Station, Kosei Line to Shin-Asahi Station (40min, 🎫¥680). From Shin-Asahi Station, 15 min walk.*
Not caring for modern water systems, this little village has developed a unique lifestyle: each home has its own spring sheltered in its own shed, or *kabata*, used as both well and kitchen. For ¥1000, you get a pass to wander around the village and enter the homes indicated by signs to take a look at the *kabata*.

Amanohashidate
© MasaoTaira/iStock

Don't miss the little Shinto shrine in the middle of the village, of course devoted to a water divinity.

THE TANGO PENINSULA
丹後半島
⟟*Regional Map, B1.*
Tango-hanto, a peninsula located in the northernmost reaches of Kyoto prefecture on the Sea of Japan, features an extremely jagged coastline in which rocky headlands alternate with little coves and deeper bays, and the fairly unspoilt countryside still exudes an atmosphere of authenticity. The main tourist sites can be reached by rail and bus, but the easiest way to explore the region is by car.

Amanohashidate★★ 天橋立
From Kyoto, take a Ltd Express on the JR San'in Line to Fukuchiyama, then take the privately owned Kita-kinki Tango Tetsudo Line to Amanohashidate Station (2hr 50min, ¥3310). Infrequent trains go directly from Kyoto 2hr 10min, ¥4010). ⓘ*Tourist Information Office in the station (*⏰*open daily 9am–6pm, amanohashidate.jp).*

Considered one of the three most beautiful views in Japan (along with Miyajima, ⟟*see p443, and Matsushima, *⟟*see p474),* the scenery formed by this narrow sandbar stretching out across Miyazu Bay is certainly an astonishing sight.

Its name—literally, the "bridge linking earth and heaven"—is a reference to Shinto mythology: it was said that the god Izanagi would use this "bridge" to pass from heaven to earth and back again, but one day the "bridge" collapsed. Nonetheless, it seems not to have affected the relationship between the gods and man, and it's certainly helped the tourist industry over the centuries.

➤ The "bridge", which is 2.3mi/3.6km long and planted with 8000 pine trees, can be crossed on foot or by bicycle, and you can stop off at one of the beaches (only one beach with summer lifeguard surveillance, at the far south on the Amanoshidate Station side). If you wish to admire the unique scenery properly, you are better off taking to the hills and ascending Mount Nariai as far as **Kazamatsu Park** (*cable car* ⏰ *open daily 8am–5.30pm, every 15min,* ⛟ *¥680 round trip, tankai.jp/amanohashidate_cablecar_chairlift).* It's traditional to take in the view from the observation platform by placing your head between your knees: the "bridge" then seems to be hovering between earth and the heavens.

On one of the legs of the journey, be sure to stop off at the **Motoise Konojinja**. Founded more than 2000 years ago, this shrine predates even the one at at Ise (⟟*see p265) and throughout its long existence has always been closely associated with the Imperial family.

A 20min walk up the mountain from Kasamatsu Park is rustic, atmospheric Nariai-ji, founded in 704 and dedicated to Kannon (◐*open daily 8am–4.30pm,* ◉*¥500, nariaiji.jp)*

Ine 伊根

Tankai bus from Amanoshidate Station (55min, ◉¥400) or national highway 178. 🔲*Tourist Information Office in Fuya-no-Sato Park (◐open daily 9am–5pm, ine-kankou.jp). You can rent e-bikes here (◉¥2000/day), and ask about the free bicycle rental scheme around the village.* The charming fishing village of **Ine**, which has been completely preserved (a rarity in Japan), is magnificent. Sheltered by an island, there is a little circular bay and, nestling at the base of cliffs covered in vegetation, a straggling line of wooden houses, seemingly built onto the water. Known locally as **funaya**★★, these houses are unique examples of their kind: the lowest floor, at sea level, is used as a boathouse and storeroom, while the upper floor is living space. This type of building dates back to the Edo period, and there are still 230 remaining in the village (a couple even from the Edo period). It's best experienced by staying overnight in one of the funaya, but if you can only come for the day, head to Fuya-no-Sato for the best views, or out on a sightseeing boat (◐*daily 9am–4pm, 25min tour* ◉*¥800, inewan.com/#kankousen; or ask about sea taxi rides, usually* ◉*¥1000/30min for min. two people).*

Maizuru 舞鶴

From Kyoto JR San'in line to Higashi-Maizuru (1hr 40min, ◉¥3400).
The largest city on the Tango Peninsula *(pop. 84,000)*, Maizuru has boasted a major port since the Middle Ages, with the *kitamaebune* (🕯*see p432)*, ships traveling from northern Japan, making a stop here. Because of the docks' strategic location on the Sea of Japan, the Meiji government decided in 1898 to turn the harbor into a military port that was to play an essential role during the Russo-Japanese War (1904–1905). It is now the third-largest Japanese naval base, and also houses several large civilian shipyards.

On the eastern side of the city there is a nice selection of Meiji-era brick buildings, collectively known as the **Maizuru Brick Park**. Here you'll find the **World Brick Museum**, which looks back over the global history of bricks, in a former torpedo hangar that was built in 1903 *(15min walk from Higashi-Maizuru Station, ◐open daily 9am–5pm, ◉¥300, akarenga-park.com)*. The **Maizuru City Commemoration Hall** *(exhibitions, concerts, café, ◐open daily 9am–5pm, ◉no charge)*, which is just next door, and the **Maizuru Wisdom Warehouse** *(◐open daily 9am–5pm, ◉no charge)* are also worth a look.

To continue your Sea of Japan coastal trip westward, see Kinosaki Onsen (🕯*see p400)* and the San'in Coast (🕯*see p450)*.

ADDRESSES

🛏 STAY

🛏 Many hotels and *ryokan* adjust their prices according to demand, so good reductions can be obtained during the week on the spot or via the internet. High season prices *(Apr–May, mid-Aug, Nov and New Year)* in this region can be around 10–30 percent higher than at other times.

AROUND KYOTO STATION

🛏 **K's House** ケイズハウス京都 – 418 Naya-cho, Shichijo-agaru, Dotemachi-dori, Shimogyo-ku (Map III, B2). ☎075-342-2444. *kshouse.jp/kyoto-e*. 65 rooms. Dorms ¥2500 per person, doubles ¥6600. Occupying a neat yellow house, this hostel with English-speaking staff is a model of cleanliness and friendliness. Pleasant lounge, well-equipped kitchen, patio, lockers, and bicycle rental *(¥700 per day)*.

🛏 **Piece Hostel Kyoto** ピースホステル京都 – 21-1 Higashi Kujo Higashisannocho. (Map I, C4). ☎075-693-7077. *piecehostel.com/kyoto/en*. 50 rooms. Dorms ¥2900 per person, doubles from ¥7600. 🚻. A particularly pleasant youth hostel. The communal areas are welcoming and encourage mixing among guests: library, lounge, kitchen open 24hr, terrace. The rooms, from 18-bed dorms to private doubles, are comfortable and well equipped (wifi, soft mattresses).

🛏🛏 **Hotel Iida** ホテル飯田 – 717 Higashi shiokoji-cho, Akezu-no-mon-dori, Shimogyo-ku (Map III, B2). ☎075-341-3256. www.hotel-iida.co.jp. 27 rooms. ¥17,600. ¥1650 🍴, dinner from ¥4400. This small hotel-ryokan is in a quiet road, with 23 of the simple but pleasant rooms Japanese-style. Staff speak both English and Spanish. Separate baths for men and women on the lower ground floor.

🛏🛏 **Ryokan Shimizu** 京の宿しみず – 644 Kagiya-cho, Shichijo-dori, Wakamiya-agaru (Map III, A2). ☎075-371-5538. kyoto-shimizu.net. 9 rooms. ¥15,400. 🚭. A modern, well-maintained ryokan in a quiet street. The owners are attentive to your needs and speak English. Cedarwood o-furo (reserve a time), internet, bicycle rental (¥770 per day).

🛏🛏 **Aranvert Hotel** アランヴェール ホテル京都 – 179 Higashi, Kazariya-cho, Gojo-dori, Shimogyo-ku. (Map III, A1). ☎075-365-5111. aranvert.co.jp. 183 rooms. ¥25,400. ¥1500 🍴. Near the subway and several bus stops, this hotel manages to combine modernity and tradition. On the top floor there's a lovely view of the surrounding mountains from the baths. If you don't fancy the hotel breakfast, head to Cafe Open a few doors east (daily 8.30am–8pm) for a good-value "morning set."

🛏🛏🛏 **Dormy Inn Premium Kyoto Ekimae** ドーミーインPREMIUM京都駅前 – 558 Higashi Shiokoji-cho, Shichijo-Kudaru, Higashinotoin-dori, Shimogyo-ku. (Map III, B2). ☎075-371-5489. dormy-inn-premium-kyoto-ekimae.hotel-ds.com/en. 200 rooms. ¥26,000. ¥2000 🍴. Modern business hotel, well situated near Kyoto Tower, just a 3min walk from Kyoto Station. Small rooms, but well soundproofed and comfortable. Onsen on the top floor.

🛏🛏🛏 **Kikokuso Inn** 枳殻荘 – Kawara-machi, Shichijo-agaru, Hitosujime nishiiru, Shimogyo-ku. (Map III, B2). ☎075-371-7781. www.oak.dti.ne.jp/~kikokuso. 4 rooms. ¥20,000. ¥2200 🍴. A lovely, intimate old-style ryokan, in a house more than a century old. The rooms (only one with an en-suite bathroom) are laid out along a wooden veranda overlooking a delightful courtyard garden. There is a picturesque o-furo in a rock garden setting. Has wifi.

KYOTO CITY CENTER

🛏 **9 Hours** ナインアワーズ – 588 Teianmaeno-cho, Teramachi-dori, Shijo-sagaru (Map II, B3). ☎075-371-353-7337. ninehours.co.jp. ¥7900. Everything in this stylish capsule hotel is an immaculate white, with the ultra-modern sleeping pods worthy of a science fiction film. Slippers, yukata, and toiletries provided. Bring earplugs, in case whoever's in the next capsule snores. Prices vary widely by day, and are discounted if you book online well in advance.

🛏 **Khaosan Kyoto Guest House** カオサン京都ゲストハウス – 568 Nakano-cho, Bukkoji-agaru, Teramachi-dori, Shimogyo-ku. (Map II, B3). ☎075-201-4063. kyoto.khaosan-tokyo.com. 46 rooms. Dorms ¥3500 per person, doubles ¥8400. 🚭. Pleasant, backpacker-oriented hostel on a quiet road. The small rooms are well-kept, with bunk beds.

🛏🛏 **Super Hotel** スーパーホテル京都・四条河原町 – 538-1, Shin-Kyougoku-dori, Sijyo-agaru, Nakano-cho Nakagyo-ku. (Map II, B3). ☎075-255-9000. www.superhoteljapan.com/en. 177 rooms. ¥13,500. 🚭. A pleasant, modern hotel, with pared-back service (reception is only open until 3pm) to keep prices low. The rooms, all en suite, are well appointed and you can select your preferred pillow type. Weekday discounts available online.

🛏🛏 **Hirota Guesthouse** 広田ゲストハウス – 665 Seimei-cho, Nijo-tominokoji-nishiiru, Nakagyo-ku. (Map II, B2). ☎075-221-2474. 5 rooms. From ¥17,500 for 2 people. Meals extra charge 🍴. From the exterior, you wouldn't guess at the oasis of calm that lies behind. At the bottom of the garden, the "cottage" comprises 2 Japanese-style rooms, a bathroom, and kitchen, ideal for a group. The house has 5 bedrooms (tatami floors), which share a bathroom. The owner is a retired guide and interpreter; she speaks perfect English. Bicycles available to rent (free).

🛏 **Inn Kawashima** 川嶋旅館 – 207-2 Ayanokoji-dori, Yanaginobanba-nishiiru, Shimogyo-ku. (Map II, B3). ☎075-351-2089. 5 rooms. 🛏¥18,000. ¥1300 🍴. Located in a machiya (wooden house) typical of old Kyoto, and in a quiet street, this charming ryokan has rooms arranged around a well-maintained courtyard garden. The owner speaks English and a little French. The only drawback is that everyone shares just 1 bathroom. Reduction on prices out of season.

🛏🛏 **Royal Park Hotel Kyoto Sanjo** ロイヤルパークホテル京都三条 – Kawaramachi Higashi-iru, Sanjo-dori, Nakagyo-ku. (Map II, B2). ☎075-241-1111. the-royalpark.jp/en. 172 rooms. ¥17,000.

¥2200 🛏. A stone's throw from Pontocho and the Kamo River, a modern hotel that is very comfortable with tasteful rooms. A good restaurant in the basement, relaxing cocktail bar, and excellent service.

🛏🍽🛌 **Itoya 糸屋** – 712 Yakushimae-cho, Karasuma-dori, Matsubara -agaru. (Map II, B3). ☎075-365-1221. itoyahotel.com. 64 rooms. ¥21,000. ¥1320 🛏. In a small, modern and elegant building, this hotel was opened in 2013 and is comfortable and well situated. The decor is sober but tasteful. Bike rental available (¥1500/day).

🛏🍽🛌 **Nishiyama Ryokan 西山旅館** – 433 Yamamotocho, Goko-machi, Nijyo-sagaru, Nakagyo-ku. (Map II, B2). ☎075-222-1166. ryokan-kyoto.com. 30 rooms. ¥28,000. ¥3000 🛏, dinner ¥10,000. Behind the facade of this contemporary ryokan you will find a beautiful interior garden with a small waterfall. There is also a very relaxing o-furo in the basement. The rooms are large, attractive, and well laid out, if a little faded, and the bathrooms are very small.

🛏🍽🛌 **Ryokan Kinmata 宿・近又** – 407 Gokomachi-dori, Shijo-agaru. (Map II, B3). ☎075-221-1039. kinmata.com/english/index.html. 7 rooms. ¥99,400. 🛏, dinner also included. Built in 1801, this distinguished ryokan, which has been in the same family for seven generations, still has its superb, original wooden decor and antique furniture. The owners provide sophisticated, delicious kaiseki cuisine (also available without accommodation; from ¥6600 for lunch). The bedrooms overlook two perfectly tended courtyard gardens. As is usual in traditional inns, they're not en suite, but hot baths can be enjoyed in theluxurious cedarwood o-furo. A truly special, memorable experience of old-style Kyoto hospitality.

GION AND KIYOMIZU-DERA

🛏🛌 **Hanakiya Inn 花喜屋** – 583-101 Higashi-Rokucho-me, Gojobashi, Higashiyama-ku. (Map III, D1). ☎075-551-1397. hanakiya.jp.net. 6 rooms. ¥8500 (min. stay 2 nights). Hidden away in a lane near Kiyomizu-dera, this small, family-run B&B has simple Japanese-style rooms opening onto a little courtyard. Guests share a bathroom. There's a cosy lounge with book and coffee, and free wifi throughout.

🛏🛌 **Gion Guestouse IKKUU 祇園ゲストハウス一空** – 400-6 Nishigomon-chō Matsubara-sagaru. (Map III, C1). ☎075-741-6544. guesthouse-ikkuu.com. 4 rooms.

¥8700. 🚿. This small, friendly guesthouse is tucked away down a lamplit pedestrian road in Gion. Rooms are small and simple, but full of traditional character, and it's a steal in Gion. Free wifi throughout.

🛏🛌 **Hotel in Gion Maifukan 祇園の宿・舞風館** – Gion Yasaka-jinja Minami-momae, Higashiyama-ku. (Map II,C3). ☎075-525-5514. maifukan.com/en. ¥18,900. Japanese or Western rooms (including family rooms), all very well kept and comfortable, close to Gion and the temples in the east of the city. The staff are friendly and efficient, and speak English. Breakfast is taken in a cafe close by. Cycle hire available.

🛏🛌 **Mume Boutique Hotel ホテル・ムメ** – 261 Shinmonzen-dori, Umemoto-cho, Higashiyama-ku. (Map II, C3). ☎075-525-8787. hotelmume.jp. 7 rooms. ¥25,000. 🛏. In a street full of antiques shops, the façade of this charming hotel is discreet and sober, apart from its bright red door. Tradition and modernity have been blended successfully and very comfortably in the rooms decorated in one of four themes (flowers, wind, moon, butterfly). Comlimentary coffees and cocktails.

🛏🛌 **Ryokan Sawai 澤食** – 4-320 Miyagawasuji, Higashiyama-ku. (Map II, B3). ☎075-561-2179. kyoto-sawai.jp. 5 rooms. ¥20,200. 🚿. In the southern part of Gion, this sensitively restored ryokan is run by a retired university professor of great charm and occupies one of the oldest ochaya in the district. A simple, family guesthouse with oddly shaped rooms, creaking floors, and dividing walls affording little privacy. One shared bathroom.

OTSU

🛏🛌 **Biwako Hotel 琵琶湖ホテル** – 2-40 Hama-machi, Otsu-shi. ☎077-524-7111. keihanhotels-resorts.co.jp/biwakohotel. ¥20,900. Around ¥2450 🛏, dinner also available. This well-designed hotel on the shores of Lake Biwa has an onsen on the fourth floor, and another on the terrace with a beautiful view of the lake, especially at night. The restaurant's immense bay windows mean you can enjoy a meal overlooking the water.

ARASHIYAMA

🛏🛌 **Hoshinoya Kyoto 星のや京都** – 11-2 Genryokuzan-cho. (Map I, A3, off map). ☎050-3786-1144. hoshinoyakyoto.jp. ¥133,900. 🛏, dinner also included. For a completely indulgent stay in elegant

Arashiyama, look no further. You arrive by the hotel's private boat from Togetsu-kyo, and stay in your own villa overlooking a quiet stretch of the Hozu-gawa. The food and service are, of course, exceptional, and there are plenty of seasonal activities on offer, focused on Kyoto's crafts and the natural setting.

⁎/EAT

AROUND THE STATION

☕ **Ramen Alley** 拉麺小路 –*Isetan department store, Kyoto Station, 10F. (Map III, B2). kyoto-ramen-koji.com. Open daily 10am–10pm. From ¥700.* If you like ramen, this is the place to go. The types of ramen are so varied that you can effectiveky take a tour of the regions of Japan in this one small corner of Kyoto Station.

☕☕ **Kyosuishin** 京すいしん – *SK Bldg 1F, 719 Higashishiokoji-cho, Karasuma-dori-agaru, Shimogyo-ku. (Map III, B2). ℘075-365-8888. suishin.co.jp/shop/kyosuishin. Open daily 11.30am–3pm & 5–11.30pm. Menu in English. Lunch from ¥1850, dinner ¥4000.* Sushi, sashimi and tempura are all on the menu of this vast restaurant decorated in traditional style. Eat sitting on *tatami* mats or chairs.

KYOTO CITY CENTER

☕ **Bio-Tei** びお亭 – *2F M&I Bldg, 28 Umetadacho, corner of Sanjo-dori and Higashinotoin. (Map II, B2). ℘075-255-0086. Open Tue–Wed & Fri 11.30am–2pm & 5–8.30pm, Thur 11.30am–2pm, Sat 5–8.30pm. Menu in English. Set meals around ¥900 (lunch), ¥1300 (dinner).*🍴. Friendly, family bistro consisting of a counter and a few wooden tables. Serves tasty and inexpensive organic dishes: tofu and vegetable salads, chicken curry, soy croquettes, and sashimi, as well as yogurts, ice creams, and homemade cakes. Some vegan options available.

☕ **Ganko Sanjo Honten** がんこ京都 三条本店 – *101 Nakajima-cho, Sanjo-dori, Kawaramachi-higashiiru. (Map II, B2). ℘075-255-1128. www.gankofood. co.jp/en. Open daily 11am–11pm. Menu in English. From ¥800.* You can try most local specialties at more than reasonable prices in this large, very lively restaurant.

☕ **Hale** 晴 – *198-1 Higashi-Uomachi, Nishiki-koji. (Map II, B3). ℘075-231-2516. kyoto-nishiki.or.jp/stores/hale/index. html. Open Tue–Sun 11.30am–4pm & 6–9pm. Lunch around ¥1100, dinner sets ¥2200.* Nishiki Market is a good place for lunch on the hoof: fried food, omelets,

takoyaki... Head for this vegan restaurant, sitting discreetly among the boutiques, for a delicious, unpretentious sit-down meal with local specialties like *yuba*.

☕ **Honke Owariya** 本家尾張屋 – *Nishiki-koji Fuyacho Nishi-iru. (Map II, B2). ℘075-231-2516. honke-owariya.co.jp. Open daily 11am–7pm. Menu in English. Seiro soba ¥990, nishin soba ¥1430.* Kyoto's oldest noodle restaurant, dating back to 1465; official purveyor to the Imperial Family. Specialties include *hourai soba* (noodles with mushrooms, eggs, shrimp, and white radishes) and *nishin soba* (soba in broth with herring).

☕ **Kerala** ケララ – *KUS Bldg 2F, Kawaramachi-dori, Sanjo-agaru, Nakagyo-ku (Map II, B2). ℘075-251-0141. Open daily 11.30am–3pm & 5–10pm (last orders 2pm & 9pm). Lunch set from ¥900, dinner ¥2600.* Excellent Indian food, especially dishes typical of the southern state for which the restaurant is named: shrimp curry, chicken, and vegetables, *masala dosa* (spiced potato in Indian pancakes), and plenty more.

☕ **Kyoto Gogyo** 京都五行 – *452 Jumonji-cho, Takoyakusi- agaru, Yanaginobamba-dori. (Map II, B3). ℘075-254-5567. ramendining-gogyo.com. Open Mon–Fri 11.30am–3pm (Sat–Sun & public hols to 4pm) & 5–11pm. From ¥980.* A well-maintained place with wood details, this welcoming restaurant pleases right from the start. Excellent ramen on the menu, but also tasty salads and various accompaniments that are hard to resist.

☕ **Miyakoyasai Kamo** 都野菜・賀茂 – *276 Ogisakaya- cho, Ayanokoji- sagaru, Higashitoin-dori. (Map II, B3). ℘075-351-2732. nasukamo.net. Open daily 7–10am, 11am–4pm & 5–11pm. Lunch from ¥980, dinner ¥1500 (slightly more Sat–Sun & public hols).*🍴. South of Shijo-dori, this restaurant attracts many clients thanks to its rich and colorful buffet, with raw and cooked vegetables picked from the owner's own kitchen garden. Although most of the diners are vegetarians, meat and fish lovers are not forgotten, particularly in the evening.

☕ **Musashi** 寿司のむさし – *440 Kawaramachi-dori, Sanjo-agaru. (Map II, B2). ℘075-222-0634, sushinomusashi. com. Open daily 11am–9.45pm. Around ¥1500.* Reliable *kaiten-zushi* place near Teramachi, very often packed with tourists as well as locals.

☁ **Okakita** おかきた – *34 Okazaki-minami Gosho-cho, Sakyo-ku. (Map II, C2). ✆075-771-4831. kyoto-okakita.com. Open Wed–Mon 11am–8pm. Closed early Jan and 1st & 3rd Wed in month. From ¥940.* 🍴 Near Heian-jingu, Okakita is a must for fans of udon and soba, and has been keeping them happy for the past 70-odd years.

☁ **Ootoya** 大戸屋京都錦小路店 – *98 Nishiuya-cho, Sanjo-dori, Kawaramachi-higashi-iru (Map II, B3). ✆075-744-0853. ootoya.com. Open daily 11am–10pm. From ¥890.* Next to the west entrance to Nishiki Market, this is a branch of a well-established chain offering Japanese food at budget-friendly prices. Try complete sets based on meat or fish, seasonal dishes (such as oysters), salads, and desserts, using the photo menu as a guide.

☁ **Ukiya** 有喜屋 – *Museum of Kyoto 1F, 623-1 Higashikatamachi, Takakura, Sanjyo-agaru (Map II, B2). ✆075-255-2078. www.ukiya.co.jp/shop. Open Tue–Sun 11.30am–3pm & 5–8pm. Around ¥1100.* On the first (ground) floor of the museum, on the Edo-style shopping street, delicious fresh soba made by hand, and a good choice of tempura.

☁ **Waka** 和香 – *397-9 Shinkai-cho, by Bukko-ji (Map II, B3). ✆090-9707-6191. oterahouse.com/cafe. Open Wed–Sat 11.30am–3pm. Around ¥1000.* 🍴 Accessible, well-priced *shojin-ryori* (Buddhist vegetarian) set meals, in a lovely traditional house which also holds exhibitions in the gallery upstairs.

☁ **Yamamotomenzo** 山元麺蔵 – *34 Okazaki-minami Gosho-cho, Sakyo-ku. (Map II, C2). ✆075-751-0677. yamamotomenzou.com. Open Fri–Tue 11am–6pm, Wed 11am–2.30pm (earlier if sold out). Closed early Jan, 4th Wed in month. From ¥880.* 🍴 Right next to Okakita, near Heian-jingu, this restaurant is equally renowned for its excellent udon dishes.

☁☁ **Grilldorebun** ぐりる・ど・れぶん – *126 Ishiya-cho, Sanjo-kudaru Higashi-iru, Nakagyo-ku. (Map II, B2). ✆075-221-8756. Open Wed–Mon 11.30am–3pm & 5pm–3am. Closed 2nd & 3rd Wed each month, plus dinner 2nd & 3rd Tue each month. Lunch around ¥1500, dinner ¥4000.* A stone's throw from Sanjo Bridge, a small friendly restaurant that is very reminiscent of the 1960s and the films of Ozu Yasujiro. Mr Kudo serves delicious *yoshoku* (Western-influence) cuisine. Try a vegetable, beef or tofu hotpot.

☁☁ **Kushikura** 串くら – *584 Hiiragi-cho, Takakura-dori, Oike-agaru. (Map II, B2). ✆075-213-2211. kushikura.jp. Open daily 11.30am–2.30pm & 5–10.30pm (last orders 9.45pm). Set menus from ¥2000.* Housed in a fine old *machiya* with a pleasant courtyard garden, this restaurant specializes in succulent *yakitori* and other grilled skewers, cooked on a charcoal grill.

☁☁ **Misoka-an Kawamichiya** 晦庵・河道屋本店 – *Shimohakusan-cho, Fuyacho-dori, Sanjo-agaru, Nakagyo-ku. (Map II, B2). ✆075-221-2525. kawamichiya.co.jp/english.html. Open Fri–Wed 11am–8pm. Menu in English. Lunch around ¥15000, dinner ¥3000.* A charming 300-year-old soba (buckwheat noodle) restaurant. Their specialty is *hokoro* (for two people), a hotpot of noodles, pieces of chicken, tofu, mushrooms, and vegetables. Also try the delicious *oyako-nanban*; hot noodles with chicken, egg, and onions.

☁☁ **Watanabeya** わたなべや – *124 Sakyo-cho, Oshikoji-dori, Higashitoin-Higashiiru, Nakagyo-ku. (Map II, B2). ✆075-203-0651. Open daily 5.30pm–12.30am. Around ¥4000.* A good local restaurant specializing in seafood. You can dine at a collective table, or one floor up on *tatami* mats. The fish is ultra fresh and served as sashimi, tempura, grilled, and in salads, all at reasonable prices.

☁☁ **Yamatomi** 山とみ – *26 Nabeya-cho, Pontocho-dori, Shijo-agaru, Nakagyo-ku. (Map II, B3). ✆075-221-3268. kyoto-yamatomi.com. Open Mon & Wed–Fri 11.30am–2pm & 4–11pm, Sat–Sun & public hols 11.30am–11pm. Lunch from ¥1500, dinner ¥3000.* 🍴 Halfway along Pontocho, on the river side, this welcoming *izakaya* benefits from a pleasant waterside terrace. The best strategy is to order a number of small dishes such as *age-yuba* (deep-fried soy-milk skin), slices of roast duck, fried tofu, *teppan-age* (assorted kebabs), grilled chicken wings, etc.

☁☁☁ **Bussarakan** 佛沙羅館 – *173-1 Minoya-cho, Kiyamachi-dori, Matsubara-agaru. (Map II,B3). ✆075-361-4535. Open Jul–Aug daily; rest of the year Thu–Tue 11.30am–3pm & 5–10pm. Lunch around ¥2000, dinner ¥4500.* On fine summer days, it's a pleasure to eat on the terrace of this Thai restaurant raised up on stilts beside the Kamo River. Sophisticated cuisine and subtle flavors, such as fried chicken served in a banana leaf, or beef curry with coconut milk.

😑🍶🍴 **Kyomachi** 京町 – 156 Umenoki-cho, Pontocho-dori, Shijo-agaru, Nakagyo-ku. (Map II, B3). 𝒫075-223-2448. Open Mon–Sat 5.30–10.30pm. Around ¥7000. A venue ideally located in the middle of Pontocho, serving delicious local cuisine, such as traditional *hamo* (a kind of eel). Enjoy your meal on the summer terrace or indoors, in a *tatami* room. Reservations are advised.

😑🍶🍴 **Mukadeya** 百足屋 – 381 Mukadeya-cho, Shinmachi-cho, Shinmachi Nishiki-agaru, Nakagyo-ku. (Map II, A3). 𝒫075-256-7039. Open Thu–Tue 11am–2.30pm & 5–9.30pm. Menu in English. Set lunch from ¥3300, dinner from ¥5400. This magnificent *machiya* houses a sophisticated restaurant serving succulent vegetarian dishes of Zen inspiration, plus other *obanzai* (traditional cuisine; not all vegetarian) specialties.

😑🍶🍴 **Tomi Zushi** とみ寿司 – 578-5 Nakano-cho, Shinkyogoku-dori, Shijo-agaru. (Map II, B3). 𝒫075-231-3628. Open Fri–Wed 5pm–midnight. Around ¥3500. A little lost among the alleyways of boutiques in the commercial district, this small restaurant is an accessible spot to try some excellent sushi, made right in front of you as you perch at the counter.

😑🍶🍶🍴 **Yoshikawa Inn** 料理旅館・天ぷら吉川 – Tominokoji-dori, Oike-agaru, Nakagyo-ku. (Map II, B2). 𝒫075-221-5544. kyoto-yoshikawa.co.jp/en. Open Mon–Sat 11am–1.30pm (last orders), 5pm–8pm (last orders). Counter lunch from ¥3300, dinner ¥9200; kaiseki lunch from ¥11,500, dinner ¥13,800. 🥢. A renowned *kaiseki* restaurant in a historic setting, specializing in tempura. You can eat at the counter or in *tatami* rooms beside the garden. Vegetarian menu available; check in advance.

GION AND KIYOMIZU-DERA

😑 **Gonbe** 権兵衛祇園店 – 254 Kitagawa, Gion-cho, Higashiyama-ku. (Map II, C3). 𝒫075-561-3350. Open Fri–Wed 11.30am–8pm (last orders). Around ¥1500. 🥢. Near Gion, this popular Japanese restaurant prepares succulent dishes of soba, udon, and *donburi* (bowl of rice with a topping) with loving care. Its *tori nanban*, a bowl of noodles with duck, or *tamago toji*, the same with half a boiled egg, are filling and cheap.

😑🍶 **Izuju** 祇園いづ重 – 292-1 Gion-machi, Kitagawa, Higashiyama-ku. (Map II, C3). 𝒫075-561-0019. gion-izuju.com. Open

Thu–Tue, 10.30am–7pm. Saba zushi ¥2300. Behind its unassuming street frontage, this sushi restaurant (established in 1892) conceals a delightful old-style dining room decorated with Imari porcelain. It specializes in *saba zushi* (square-shaped pickled mackerel sushi), among other varieties local to Kyoto, and is particularly known for its *inari zushi* (sushi rice in fried tofu pockets).

😑🍶🍴 **Okutan** 奥丹 – 3-340 Kiyomizu Higashiyama-ku. (Map III, D1). 𝒫075-525-2051. tofuokutan.info. Open Fri–Wed 11am–4pm. Yudofu set menus from ¥3300. 🥢. One of Kyoto's best tofu restaurants, tucked away in a lovely peaceful Japanese garden. Its specialty is *yudofu*, a light yet filling tofu hotpot served with yam soup, rice, and vegetable tempura.

😑🍶🍴 **Yagenbori Sueyoshicho-ten** やげんぼり末吉町店 – Gion Sueyoshi-cho, Kiritoshi-kado, Higashiyama-ku. (Map II, C3). 𝒫075-551-3331. yagenbori.co.jp. Open daily noon–2pm & 5–11pm (last orders 10.15pm). Kaiseki lunch from ¥4000, dinner ¥8700. A place beside the romantic Shirakawa Canal to enjoy typical local dishes: tempura, *hoba-misoyaki* (miso, mushrooms, chicken, and grilled onions in magnolia leaves), and *shabu-shabu*. The excellent *kaiseki* menus here are more affordable than in the large *ryotei*.

PHILOSOPHER'S PATH

😑🍶 **Omen Ginkakuji Honten** おめん銀閣寺本店 – Ginkaku-ji. (Map II, D1). 𝒫075-771-8994. omen.co.jp. Open Fri–Wed 11am–3.30pm & 5–9pm. Noodles from ¥1150. Near the Silver Pavilion, this branch of the very popular local noodle chain (3 branches) serves udon in a satisfyingly hearty vegetable and sesame broth.

ARASHIYAMA AND NORTHWEST KYOTO

😑🍶 **Gontaro** 権太呂 – 26 Hirano Miyaziki-cho, Kita-ku. (Map I, B2). 𝒫075-463-1039. gontaro.co.jp. Open Thu–Tue 11am–9.30pm. From ¥880, nabe from ¥4400. Not far from the Golden Pavilion, this restaurant enjoys an excellent reputation for its soba, udon and *donburi* dishes, and its generous, steaming *nabe* (hotpots).

😑🍶 **Seigen-in** 西源院 – 13 Goryonoshita-cho, Ryoan-ji, Ukyo-ku. (Map I, A3). 𝒫075-462-4742. Open daily 10am–5pm. From ¥1500. 🥢. In Ryoan-ji temple, this restaurant looks out on an enchanting garden and is renowned for its *yufodu*, tofu hotpot with vegetables and herbs.

🍜 **Saganoyu Café Style Resort** 嵯峨の湯 カフェスタイルリゾート – *Imahori-cho, Saga Tenryu-ji. (Map I, A3). ☎075-882- 8985. sagano-yu.com. Open daily noon–7pm. Lunch around ¥1300.* Between the two stations at Sagano, a stone's throw from Arashiyama, this places is a bit out of the ordinary: a former *sento* (public bath) of the district transformed into a very pleasant café. The decor is light and airy, with white ceramics, mirrors, parquet flooring and large bay windows. The lunch menu is a bit limited but well made: sandwiches, salads, pasta, curry. A good choice of drinks and desserts.

OHARA

🍜 **Seryo Jaya** 芹生茶屋 – *Sanzen-in, Ohara, Sakyo-ku. (Map I, D1, off map). ☎075-744-2301. seryo.co.jp/cyamise. Open daily 9am–5pm. Menu in English. Noodles from ¥800, set meals from ¥1050.* 🍴. On the left of the entrance to Sanzen-in, this fine traditional restaurant has table and *tatami* seating, plus shaded benches outside in the lovely garden. Excellent soba and traditional set lunches, plus country dishes such as trout with seasonal vegetables.

OTSU

🍜 **Honke Tsuruki soba** 本家鶴喜そば – *4-11-40 Sakamoto, Otsushi, Shiga-ken. ☎077-578-0002. tsurukisoba.com. Open daily 10am–5.30pm. Closed 3rd Fri of month. From ¥1100.* This welcoming restaurant with magnificent wooden frontage offers all kinds of hot and cold soba dishes and generous set menus.

TAKING A BREAK

KYOTO

Café 363 カフェ363 – *363-1 Funaya-cho, Nakagyo-ku. (Map II, B2). 080-2454-8902. cafe363.com. Open 10am–6pm (last orders 5pm). Closed 1st Wed in month.* In a chic and arty area, this nice café and pancake house offers a warm welcome, plus delicious crepes and galettes.

Café Bibliotic Hello! – *650 Seimei-cho, Sanjo-Yanaginobaba, Higashi-iru. (Map II, B2). ☎075-231-8625. cafe-hello.jp. Open Tue–Sun 11.30am–midnight (last orders 11pm).* An intriguing name and unusual look behind giant banana trees. Somewhere you might like to linger if it's not too crowded (which it often is). A

pleasant setting, gallery, bookshop, bakery. Good coffee, cakes and tasty snacks.

Kanoshoju-an 叶匠壽庵 – *2-1 Nyaku-oji, Sakyo-ku. (Map II, D2). ☎075-751-1077. kanou.com/shop/chashitsu. Open Thur–Tue 10am–5pm.* Hidden away behind a bamboo hedge, an authentic, traditional tea house, well away from the tourist cafés on either side of the walk.

NIGHTLIFE

🎵 Kyoto's bar and nightclub district is on Kiyamachi-dori *(Map II, C2/3)*, the street parallel to Pontocho, between Shijo-dori and Sanjo-dori. *Drinks usually cost around ¥600. You may have to pay a cover charge, especially for live-music evenings.*

BARS

Yoramu よらむ – *35-1 Matsuya-cho Nijo-dori, Higashinotoin Higashi-iru. (Map II, B2). 075-213-1512. sakebar-yoramu.com. Open Wed–Sat 6pm–midnight.* Fabulous sake bar run by an Israeli man with an in-depth knowledge of Japan. The drinks list includes some intriguing aged sakes with lemon, rosé wine, plum, and coffee flavors. A tasting flight (3 glasses) is *¥1600.*

Rag ライブスポットラグ – *5F Empire Bldg, Kiyamachi-dori, Sanjo-agaru. (Map II, C2). ☎075-241-0446. origin.ragnet.co.jp/livespot. Hours vary; usually open 6pm–1am.* Bar featuring live music, with regular jazz, rock, blues, funk, and "world music" gigs. There's even a recording studio on site, so it's a real hub for the local music scene

CLUBS

Metro メトロ – *Marutamachi Station, exit 2. (Map II, C2). ☎075-752-4765. metro.ne.jp. Hours vary.* Popular local club held underground in a section of a subway station. Live music, from punk to reggae, and international DJs. *Entry usually ¥1000–3000.*

West Harlem ウエストハーレム – *Reiho Bldg B1F, 366 Kamiya-cho Nishikiyamachi-dori, Shijo-agaru, Nakagyo-ku. (Map II, B3). ☎050-1016-0099. westharlemkyoto.com. Hours vary; usually open 7pm–2am (Sat–Sun 5am).* For lovers of latin jazz, salsa, *bachata*, etc. Dancefloor with DJ in attendance, or bands at the weekend.

SHOPPING

🛍 For any Kyoto shopping expedition, **Teramachi** and the streets around it are a good place to start *(Map II, B2/3)*. Apart from Loft, Muji, Uniqlo, and other chains, you will find plenty of independent stores selling craft items, souvenirs, clothes and accessories inspired as much by traditional Japan as by modern trends. Also worth wandering around are the roads around the **Museum of Kyoto**, where you'll find a number of small boutiques. There are also innumerable boutiques and workshops in **Gion** and **Higashiyama** keeping the rich tradition of Kyoto crafts alive, and where young designers and craftspeople are having an impact today.

TEA

Ippodo 一保堂 – *52 Tokiwagi-cho, Teramachi-dori, Nijo-agaru. (Map II, B2). 075-211-3421. ippodo-tea.co.jp. Open daily 9am–6pm.* A fine old tea store (*matcha, sencha, ujishimizu*, etc.) with a small seating area for tasting. There's a comprehensive menu in English.

CRAFT ITEMS

Asahi-do 朝日堂 – *1-280 Kiyomizu. (Map III, D1). 075-531-2181. asahido.co.jp. Open daily 9am–6pm.* The most famous store in the temple district, known for its *Kiyomizu-yaki* pottery.

Kintake-do 金竹堂 – *263 Gion-machi Kitagawa. (Map I, C3). 075-561-7868. Open Fri–Wed 10am–8pm.* Workshop specializing in combs and brooches for geisha, traditionally made of mother-of-pearl, wood, or horn.

Miyawaki-baisen-an 宮脇賣扇庵 – *80-30 Daikoku-cho, Rokkaku-dori, Tomino-koji Higashi-iru. (Map II, B2). 075-221-0181. baisenan.co.jp/en. Open daily 9am–6pm (summer 9am–7pm).* Since 1823, Miyawaki has been making superb fans from silk, paper, wood, mother-of-pearl, and laquerware, in folding and non-folding versions.

Kyukyo-do 鳩居堂 – *520 Shimo-Honnojimae-cho, Aneyakoji-agaru. (Map II, B2). 075-231-0510. kyukyodo.co.jp. Open Mon–Sat 10am–6pm.* A firm specializing in fragrant incenses, incense burners, calligraphic inks, and brushes. Also has a fine selection of Japanese paper.

Miura Shomei 三浦照明 – *284 Gion-machi-Kitagawa. (Map II, C3). 075-561-2816. miurashomei.co.jp. Open Mon–Sat 10am–7pm. Closed public hols.* A store selling elegant traditional and modern *washi* paper lanterns, and bamboo, bronze, or stone lamps.

PAPER

Suzuki Shofudo 鈴木松風堂 – *Izutsuya-cho, Yanaginobanba, Rokkaku-sagaru. (Map II, B2/3). 075-231-5003. shofudo-shop.jp. Open daily 10am–7pm.* This store specializes in the strong yet delicate Japanese *washi* style of paper.

LACQUERWARE

Zohiko 象彦 – *719-1 Yohojimae-cho, Teramachi-dori, Nijoagaru, Nishigawa, Nakagyo-ku. (Map II, C2). 075-229-6625. zohiko.co.jp/en/shop. Open daily 10am–6pm.* A supplier to the Imperial court, Zohiko is an example of Japanese excellence in lacquerware. A beautiful selection of objects (bowls, trays, boxes, etc.), at a wide range of price points.

ANTIQUES/PRINTS

Explore the streets around **Shinmonzen-dori** 新門前通 (Map II, C3), in Kyoto's Shinbashi district. Good quality, and usually high prices. more affordable, if more touristy, is the **Kyoto Antiques Center** 京都アンティークセンタ, a complex of 20 or so boutiques. *Teramachi-dori, north of Nijo-dori. (Map II, B2/3). 075-222-0793. Open Wed–Mon 10.30am–7pm. Closed 3rd Mon in month.*

Kyoto's main **flea market** is held on the 21st of each month at the To-ji temple (Map III, A2/3), in the south of Kyoto.

Nishiharu 西春 – *1 Ishibashi-cho, Sanjo-diri, Teramachi-Higashi-iru. (Map II, B2/3). 075-211-2849. nishiharu-kyoto.com. Open daily 11am–7pm.* Mr Tohru Sekigawa, the respected owner, receives his customers in a tiny *tatami* room, where he displays Edo and Meiji period *ukiyo-e* (wood block prints), all with a certificate of authenticity.

CLOTHING AND FABRICS

Aizenkobo 愛染工房 – *Nakasuji Omiya-nishi, Yoko-omiya-cho, Kamigyo-ku. 075-441-0355. www.aizenkobo.jp. Open Mon–Fri 10am–5.30pm, Sat & public hols 10am–4pm.* The Utsuki family has made fabrics for 17 generations. In their boutique you'll find bedspreads, pillowcases, scarves, chemises, and kimono worked in batik (*shibori*).

BSC Gallery BSCギャラリー – *420 Sakurano-cho, Teramachi. (Map II, B2/3). 075-351-0033. r.goope.jp/bsckyoto. Open daily 11am–9pm.* Shop selling *sukajan*, embroidered silk bomber jackets. The best-quality items are upstairs.

Kikuya キクヤ – *567 Katada-cho, Shimigyo-ku. (Map II, B2). 075-212-3717. Open Mon–Sat 9am–6pm. Closed public hols.* A store specializing in antique and secondhand kimonos.

Mimuro みむろ – *Matsubara-nishi-iru-kitagawa, Karasuma-dori, Shimogyo-ku. (Map II, B3).* 🖉*012-036-6529. mimuro.net. Open daily 10am–6.30pm.* Five floors with more than 50,000 different kimono.

COSMETICS

Kamiya 加美屋 – *270 Gion-machi Kitagawa. (Map II, C3).* 🖉*075-561-8878. kami-ya.jp/open.htm. Open Mon–Sat 11am–7pm.* Branch of a popular local chain selling cosmetics and skincare goods inspired by geisha. Also has a few stationery items.

ENTERTAINMENT

DANCE

In spring and fall, the geisha and *maiko* (apprentice geishas) from Kyoto's five entertainment districts put on **dance performances** *(odori)*. They perform several times in the afternoon in their colorful traditional dress with immaculate hair and makeup *(tickets ¥2000–8500.)* Detailed information can be obtained from your hotel or a Tourist Office.

The season opens with the **Kitano Odori**, held late Mar–early Apr at the Kamishichiken Kaburen-jo Theater. *Imadegawa-dori, east of the shrine Kitano Tenmangu, (Map I, B2);* 🖉*075-461-0148, maiko3.com/index.html.*

The oldest of the *odori*, established in 1872, is the **Miyako Odori**, held Apr 1–30, at the Gion Kobu Kaburen-jo Theater. *Hanamikoji-dori (Map I, C3);* 🖉*075-541-3391, miyako-odori.jp.*

The **Kyo Odori** usually takes place 1st Sat–3rd Sun in April at the Miyagawa-cho Kaburenjo Theater. *Miyagawasuji;* 🖉*075-561-1151, miyagawacho.jp.*

The **Kamogawa Odori** takes place May 1–24 at the Ponton-cho Kaburenjo Theater. *Pontocho-dori, Map II, C2;* 🖉*075-221-2025, kamogawa-odori.com.*

In early Oct, the **Onshukai** is held at Gion Kaburenjo Theater. *Hanamikoji-dori (Map I, C3);* 🖉*075 541 3391, miyako-odori.jp/onsyukai.*

The **Kotobukikai** takes place around Oct 8–12, at the Kamishichiken Kaburen-jo Theater. *Imadegawa-dori, east of the shrine Kitano Tenmangu, (Map I, B2);* 🖉*075-461-0148, maiko3.com/kotobuki-kai.html.*

In mid-Oct is the **Mizuekai**, which takes place in Miyagawa-cho's Kaburenjo Theater. *Miyagawasuji;* 🖉*075-561-1151, miyagawacho.jp/mizuekai.html.*

The season ends with the **Gion Odori**, Nov 1–10, at the Gion Kaikan Theater. *Near the shrine Yasaka-jinja, Map II, C3;* 🖉*075-561-0224, gionkaikan.jp.*

You can also attend performances all year round at **Gion Corner** ギオンコーナー (*Yasaka Hall, 570-2 Gion-machi-minamigawa, Map II, C3;* 🖉*075-561-119, kyoto-gioncorner.com).* As well as dances performed by *maiko*, these sessions *(6pm & 7pm, 50min duration, ¥3150)* include demonstrations of *ikebana* (flower arranging), *gagaku* (court music), *bunraku* (puppetry), and *kyogen* (comic theater). Geared toward passing tourists, these performances give just a surface idea of the arts involved.

NOH THEATER

Kanze Kaikan 京都観世会館 – *44 Okazaki Enshoji-cho, Sakyo-ku. (Map II,C3).* 🖉*075-771-6114. kyoto-kanze.jp.* Several performances at the weekend *(from ¥3000).*

Takigi-Noh 京都薪能 *Heian-jingu. (Map II, C2).* 🖉*075-771-6114. Jun 1–2, from 5.30pm.* This atmospheric performance of Noh theater takes place at Kyoto's Heian shrine by torchlight.

KABUKI THEATER

Minami-za Theater 南座 *Shijo-Ohashi Higashi-zume. (Map II, C3).* 🖉*075-561-1155. kabukiweb.net/theatres/minamiza.* Kyoto's main Kabuki theater. In december, major actors perform short sections from their most famous roles in the *kaomise*, or "face showing."

MEDITATION

Kennin-ji 建仁寺 – *Komatsu-cho, Yamatooji-dori, Shijo-sagaru. (Map II, C3).* 🖉*075-561-6363. kenninji.jp/experience.* The venerable temple organizes zazen meditation sessions, 2nd Sun in month, 7.30am *(no charge).*

Nanzen-ji 南禅寺 – *Nanzen-ji Fukuchi-cho. (Map I, D4; off map).* 🖉*075-771-0365. nanzen.net.* Meditation sessions held 6am, 2nd & 4th Sun in month *(no charge).*

Ryosen-an 龍泉庵 – *107 Murasakino-daitokuji-cho. (Map I, B1).* 🖉*075-491-0543. Reservations required.* Meditation sessions Wed–Sun 7am (1st, 15th, 22nd of month & Aug; *no charge).*

Nara★★★
奈良

Nara, even more thant its neighbor Kyoto, has made an alliance with nature, and has planted its pagodas and monasteries among its lush vegetation. At the heart of the city is a beautiful 1480-acre/600ha park, a wide, verdant space with views of the wooded mountains surrounding the city. Around 1200 deer are allowed to roam freely in the park, venerated as messengers of the gods. Heijo-kyo (as Nara was formerly known) was established at the end of the Silk Road. It was Japan's first permanent capital, a position it occupied from 710 to 784. This marked the beginning of a strong, centralized state, a catalyst for the growth of a national identity. Buddhism, an import from China and Korea, took root here, flourishing under the patronage of successive sovereigns, including four empresses. Walking through the calm streets of Nara today is like skimming the pages of a history book. A cradle of Japanese tradition and literature, this city has never lost its human scale and possesses some of the finest artistic treasures and some of the oldest buildings in the country, including several UNESCO World Heritage Sites.

A BIT OF HISTORY

The Nara period – Nara has played a crucial role in Japanese history, having been founded in 710 as the first true capital of the country, under the name Heijo-kyo ("city of peace"). It remained so until the capital was transferred elsewhere in 784. Until 710, the capital had changed with each succeeding monarch because of Shinto traditions concerning death; whenever a monarch died, his palaces were considered impure and had to be destoyed and rebuilt elsewhere. This entailed a costly and destabilizing move with each new

▶ **Population:** 360,000 – Nara prefecture.

Michelin Map: Regions of Japan Map 3, Regional Map p309, Nara Map p369.

Location: Nara, capital of Nara prefecture, is in the north of the prefecture on its only plain, the Yamato. Both Kyoto *(28mi/45km)* and Osaka *(19mi/30km)*, are easily accessible by train. Nara's relatively small size and grid layout make it easily manageable on foot, apart from the western suburbs. The principal sights are around Nara Park and not far from the Kintetsu and JR stations. The main shopping areas are the Sanjo-dori thoroughfare, and the pedestrian arcades to the south of the Kintetsu-line station.

Kids: Children will love feeding special crackers to the deer in the park, available everywhere from street vendors.

Timing: A day should be enough to see Nara's key sights. Limit yourself to the park area (Todai-ji, Nara National Museum, Kofuku-ji, Kasuga Taisha), finishing up with Horyu-ji. For a longer visit, spend one night in the city. Avoid weekends, especially in April and May, because of the crowds.

Don't miss: Horyu-ji, the oldest Buddhist temple in Japan; the charming Naramachi district; Todai-ji, one of the largest wooden buildings in the world; a stroll in the forest around Kasuga Taisha.

USEFUL INFORMATION

Tourist Offices – Nara City Tourist Center, Sanjo-dori (Map, B2). ✆0742-22-3900. narashikanko.or.jp/en. Open 9am–6pm.

JR Station Tourist Office (Map, B2). ✆0742-27-2223. Open daily 9am–9pm.

Kintetsu Station Tourist Office (Map, B1). ✆0742-24-4858. Open daily 9am–9pm.

Nara Visitor Center & Inn, 3 Ikeno-cho, south of Sarusawa Pond (Map, B2). ✆0742-81-7461. sarusawa.nara.jp. Open daily 9am–9pm.

All four branches provide maps, brochures, and information in English, and the Sarusawa branch also offers free (short-term) luggage storage.

Guided Tours – Nara SGG Club ✆0742-22-5595, narasggclub.web.fc2. com; **Nara Student Guide** ✆0742-26-4753, narastudentguide.org; **EGG Nara (YMCA)** ✆0742-45-5920, egg-nara.org. All three services offer English-speaking tours. Tours are free, but you may need to cover transport, lunch and/or entry fees for your guide. Reserve in advance.

Bank/Foreign Exchange – Most banks are on **Sanjo-dori** (Map, B2). **Post Office ATMs** (e.g. 30 Noborioji-cho, open Mon–Fri 9am–5.30pm) accept foreign cards, as do ATMs at some combini, such as **7-Eleven**.

Post Offices – 1 Ogawa-cho, next to JR Nara Station (Map, A2). Open Mon–Fri 9am–7pm, Sat 9am–5pm.
24 Higashimuki Kita-machi, 220yd/200m northeast of Kintetsu Station (Map, B1). Open Mon–Fri 9am–7pm, Sat–Sun & public hols 9am–pm.

GETTING THERE

BY TRAIN – **Kintetsu Nara Station** (Map, B1) is the more central of the two stations. Trains to Kyoto (Ltd Express trains: every 30min, journey time 35min, ¥1160), Osaka-Namba (every 10min, journey time 40min, ¥570), and Kansai International Airport via the Nankai Line to Namba (every 20min, journey time 1hr 40min, ¥1500).

JR Nara Station (Map, A2) is in the southwest, 10min walk from the center: trains to Kyoto (Ltd Express trains: 8 daily, journey time 45min, ¥720), Osaka (Tenno-ji, every 15min, journey time 35min, ¥470), and Kansai International Airport via Tenno-ji (every 30min, 1hr 30min, ¥1740).

BY BUS – **Terminus at Kintetsu Nara** (Map, B1) and **JR Nara** (Map, A2) stations. Buses to Kansai International Airport (every hour, journey time 1hr 30min, ¥2100), Itami Airport (about every hour, journey time 1hr, ¥1510), and Tokyo by the Nara Kotsu night bus (1 daily, journey time 8hr, ¥8880–12,300).

GETTING AROUND

BY BUS – There are many bus routes crisscrossing the city, and most buses stop at the JR and Kintetsu stations. **Bus route no. 2** does a complete circuit of the city and the park in a clockwise direction; **no.1** goes counterclockwise. **Bus nos. 70 and 97** serve the temples of the southwest. ¥ Standard fare ¥220.

BY BUS – Available at both stations: 1-day Nara Bus Pass (¥500); 1-day Nara Bus wide Pass (also covers Horyu-ji; ¥1000); 2-day Nara Bus Wide Pass (¥1500); Kintetsu Rail Pass (1–5 days ¥1500–3900; also covers buses).

BY BICYCLE – Practical for getting around the park and Naramachi.
Nara Rent-A-Cycle (Kintetsu Nara Station, exit 7; open daily: Mar–Nov 8.30am–5pm, Dec–Feb 9am–3pm; from ¥500 per day). Some hotels also offer bike hire for guests.

---

monarch and was hardly conducive to the establishment of a well-run state.
To overcome this, and perhaps also because the growing influence of Buddhism had swept away some of these taboos, Empress Genmei issued an edict soon after her accession to the throne in 707, ordering the establishment of a permanent capital and thus putting an end to the Court's wanderings.

Hungry deer

The sacred deer of Nara are in fact Sika deer *(Cervus nippon)*. Their hazelnut-brown coat with white spots turns a dark gray in winter. The mating season is in the fall, and in the spring the hind gives birth to a single fawn, which stays with its mother for six months. Once believed to be messengers of the gods (until 1637, killing one was punishable by death), these deer have now been designated National Treasures. The deer have become so accustomed to being fed by visitors to the park that they follow them constantly, trying to eat whatever comes within their reach, to the extent that plastic wrappers have become the main cause of death among the herd.

Built on the model of Chang'an, the capital of the Chinese Han (206BC–220AD) and Tang (618–907) dynasties, Nara's design, later to be adopted in Kyoto, followed a geometrical grid intended to proclaim the glory of a dynasty whose descent from the gods was traced in the *Kojiki*, a book compiled in 712 describing the creation of the *kami* and the Earth.

The great temples of previous reigns, such as Kofuku-ji and Yakushi-ji, were moved to Nara; others, such as Todai-ji, were created anew.

The new city comprised palaces, shrines, public buildings, houses, and well-laid roads, covering a square-shaped area of about 6200 acres/2500ha, with a population estimated at about 100,000. Thanks to the support of successive emperors, Buddhism flourished here, initiating a period of unprecedented artistic and intellectual richness exemplified by the creation of the great bronze Buddha *(Daibutsu)* of Todai-ji between 747 and 752.

Thirteen centuries of history – Over time, the great temples of Nara came to hold ever-greater sway over political life, so the Court decided to counter this by relocating the capital, first to Nagaokakyo in 784, and then to Kyoto (Heian) in 794. Nara lost some of its importance and saw its religious preeminence challenged by the monks of Enryaku-ji on Mount Hiei, who also launched attacks against it. The city was sacked and burned a number of times during the Civil Wars, notably in 1180 and again in 1567, with disastrous consequences for the temples. Nonetheless, they managed to recover from these depredations, being rebuilt and refurbished, first during the Kamakura period and then during the Edo era. The year 2010 marked the 1300th anniversary of Nara's foundation, with the occasion

Herds of deer, Nara Park

© Nathanphoto/Dreamstime.com

marked by the former Imperial Palace, in the northwest of the city (see p323), being rebuilt.

NARA
 Map, p369.
Starting from the JR station, **Sanjo-dori** is the principal throughfare across the city center. Lined with shops and restaurants, it crosses the commercial arcades of **Machidono** (which connect it with the Kintetsu Station) toward Kofuku-ji, the ususal first stop in Nara Park.

SIGHTS

AROUND NARA PARK★★
奈良公園
Created in 1880, the vast lawns of Nara Park (Nara-koen), interspersed with ponds, wooded groves, and avenues, lie at the foot of the gently sloping Mount Wakakusa. Herds of **deer**, venerated since ancient times as messengers of the kami (the Shinto gods), are allowed to roam freely. Visitors can enjoy feeding them little crackers called shika-senbei.

Kofuku-ji★★ 興福寺
 Map, B1/2. Grounds: Open daily 24hr. No charge. Buildings: Open daily 9am–5pm. Tokon-do ¥300, Kokuhokan ¥700 (combined ticket ¥900), Chukon-do ¥500. kohfukuji.com.
Built in 669 in Uji, south of Kyoto, then transferred to Nara in 710 by the powerful Fujiwara family, to whom it belonged, this **temple** expanded as its owners grew in influence. In its glory days, from the 8C to the 12C, it covered an area of 130,000sq ft/12,000sqm and comprised some 175 buildings. Despite subsequent damage and reconstruction, it is one of the few Buddhist structures to have kept its original architectural style, known as the wayo style (a purely Japanese aesthetic approach, not influenced by Chinese models). As the center of the **Hosso School**, one of the many Japanese Buddhist sects, it has a large number of masterpieces in its collections.
Before entering the precinct from the south side, pause to enjoy the **view**

of the **five-story pagoda**★ reflected in Sarusawa Pond (Sarusawa-no-ike). The pagoda looks light and airy, as if it is about to fly away across the temple compound. Built in 730, it burned down several times (in 1017, 1060, 1180, 1356, and 1411), but was always reconstructed, the last reconstruction dating back to 1426, during the Muromachi period. At 164ft/50m it is the second-highest pagoda in Japan after that of To-ji in Kyoto, and is one of the great landmarks of Nara.
After many years of reconstruction, in 2018 the **Chukon-do**★ (Central golden Hall) reopened. The building is huge and elaborate, with vermilion pillars and gold details, and houses a figure of the historical Buddha as its principal icon.
Tokon-do★★, the Eastern Golden Hall, was built in honor of Empress Gensho in 726. Destroyed five times by fire, it was last rebuilt in 1415. With its broad, straight roof, seven bays, terrace and dark interior, it is typical of the 8C. The monks held their ceremonies outside the hall. Yakushi Nyorai, the Buddha of Healing (see box p320), was worshipped here, and his large bronze statue (1415) dominates the middle of the hall, flanked by the bosatsu Gakko (symbol of the moon) on the right and Nikko (symbol of the sun), left, both dating from the end of the 7C. Figures of celestial guardians and fierce-lookng generals stand at the four corners, defending the faith.
The **Kokuhokan**★★, the former refectory of the monks, is now used as the Treasure House. It contains a number of old statues, including a bronze **Buddha's head**★★ from 685, depicting Yakushi Nyorai, all that remains of a statue that once stood in the Tokon-do. Its eyes show a Chinese influence. There is also a **Senju Kannon**★★ here, a thousand-armed deity from the Kamakura period (12C) in lacquered and gilt wood, its beauty matched only by an extraordinary 8C three-headed **Ashura**★★★ (guardian of the Law) in lacquered hemp, with six arms as long and thin as tentacles.

Daibutsu-den behind Naka-mon, Todai-ji

© SeanPavonePhoto/iStock

Nara National Museum★★
奈良国立博物館

Map, C1. 15min walk from Kintetsu Station, 25min from JR station. Open Tue–Thur & Sun 9.30am–5pm, Fri–Sat 9.30am–8pm. Most of the museum is closed late Oct–early Nov for Shoso-in Treasures exhibition. ¥520, special exhibitions ¥1100. www.narahaku.go.jp. Volunteers at reception offer free guided tours (30min).

Opened in 1895, Nara National Museum houses a major collection of Buddhist art presented chronologially, spread over two buildings connected by an underground passageway.

Old Building – The main works on display here are Japanese Buddhist sculptures (galleries 1, 2, 3, and 8 for the bronzes) from the Asuka to the Kamakura periods, most of which have been left here in trust by the great monasteries of Nara and the surrounding area.

The works are shown in rotation, with displays changing each season. Strikingly realistic statues of monks alternate with grandly meditative Buddhas (Yakushi, Amida, Shaka), graceful *bosatsu* (Kannon, Nikko, Gakko), and fierce-faced protectors. The building also houses Buddhist statues from Gandhara, China, and Korea (galleries 4 and 6), Chinese bronze vases (galleries 14 and 15), and *gigaku* masks (gallery 7).

Modern Building – This new building is mostly used for special exhibitions. At the end of October and beginning of November, the museum displays the magnificent **treasures of Shoso-in★★** (objects brought from the continent via the Silk Road) usually kept at Todai-ji (*see opposite*), the origins of which go back to the Nara period.

Isui-en ★ 依水園

Map, C1. Open Wed–Mon (daily in Apr, May, Oct & Nov) 9.30am–4.30pm. ¥900. isuien.or.jp/en.

Somewhat off the tourist circuit, this traditional garden provides a relaxing interlude from sightseeing. It comprises two gardens dating from the Meiji era: the one on the west side *(turn right after the entrance)* is a stroll garden (*see p115*) laid out around a small pond; its counterpart on the east side uses the "borrowed landscape" (*shakkei—see p113*) of Wakakusa Hill in the background to create an appealing effect of depth.

Todai-ji★★★ 東大寺

Map, C1. 25min walk from Kintetsu Station. Daibutsu-den: open daily: Apr–Oct 7.30am–5.30pm; Nov–Mar 8am–5pm. ¥600 (¥800 with museum); English audioguides ¥500. Museum: open 9.30am–5/5.30pm. ¥500 (¥800 with Daibutsu-den). Nigatsu-do: open daily 24hr. No charge. Hokke-do: open daily: Apr–Oct 7.30am–5.30pm; Nov–Mar 8am–5pm. ¥600. Kaidan-in: open daily: Apr–Oct 7.30am–5.30pm; Nov–Mar 8am–5pm. ¥600. todaiji.or.jp.

In 743, Emperor Shomu commissioned an ambitious project: a building to house what was to be the most colossal bronze statue in the world, the **Great Buddha of Nara**, which was eventually consecrated in 752. Because of the major role it played in the country's religious history, Todai-ji always enjoyed the emperors' favor, even after the capital was moved to Kyoto. The original plan included two seven-story pagodas, now no longer in existence, one on each side of the central building. Twice burned down (1180 and 1567), Todai-ji was last rebuilt in 1708 on an area two-thirds of its original size. At the rear of the hall is a 1:50 scale model of the original temple, and some of its later iterations.

At the entrance, visitors pass through the **Nandai-mon★**, the Great South Gate with its five bays and two roofs. Its pillars tower over two impressive wooden statues: the **Ni-oh guardians★★** (1203), made by the sculptors Unkei and Kaikei. One guardian has his mouth open, the other's mouth is closed, symbolizing the beginning and end of life (ⓘ see p223).

The **Todai-ji Museum★** is to the left of the main avenue. The large collection of the temple's religious artifacts is exhibited on rotation, with the superb statues of Buddha of particular note.

At the end of the avenue is the Great Buddha Hall, the **Daibutsu-den★★**. Even though the most recent reconstruction has reduced its size and changed its proportions, it remains one of the largest wooden buildings in the world (*159ft/48.5m high and 187ft/57m wide*). A fine, eight-sided bronze lantern from 752, decorated with musical *bosatsu*, stands in front of it. Traditionally, the building's central skylight is opened twice a year (*Aug 15 & Dec 21–Jan 1*) to show the people the face of the deity.

The interior reveals the great, gilt bronze statue of **Daibutsu Vairocana★★**, the cosmic Buddha, sitting on a lotus flower in a state of enlightenment. Its enormous height (*50ft/15m*) and weight (*250 tons*) make it the largest bronze Buddha in the world. Created in 751 by the Korean Kimimaro—supposedly aided by 370,000 workers—the work has been

The Shuni-e ceremony

The monks of Todai-ji have performed the same ceremony every year for the past 1200 years: *Shuni-e*, a ritual of repentance in which they confess their sins to the Kannon in the Nigatsu-do. They must purge themselves of the "three poisons" greed, anger, and stupidity, which contaminate their souls and prevent them from seeing the truth. The rituals continue for two weeks at the beginning of March. At nightfall, the monks run along the balcony of the **Nigatsu-do**, waving huge torches and chanting. Finally, they offer sacred water to both the deity and the watching crowd.

restored many times. Only the pedestal is original: the head dates from the 17C. To the left of Daibutsu is Nyoirin Kannon, who grants wishes, and to his right, Kokuzo Kannon, symbol of wisdom.

You may also notice a hole in one of the building's pillars, the same size as the Buddha's nostril: it is said that those who manage to slip through it will go to paradise, and a significant number of the three million people who visit Todai-ji annually try their luck at it, a fun sight even if you don't attempt it yourself.

▶ Turn left on the way out and follow the path going east for about 440yd/400m, until near the belfry and the vermilion torii.

Rebuilt in 1667, **Nigatsu-do★** is a temple supported on piles, resembling a smaller version of Kiyomizu-dera in Kyoto (ⓘ see p332). There is a fine **view** of Nara from its terrace.

Farther south, **Hokke-do★★**, also known as Sangatsu-do, is the oldest building in Todai-ji (*erected in 746, but partially rebuilt in the Kamakura era*). It houses 16 remarkable statues from the Nara period, of which 12 are designated National Treasures. In the middle is a dry-lacquer statue of **Fukukensaku**

Lanterns, Kasuga Taisha

© Alberto Sánchez cerrato/iStock

Kannon★★, its hands joined in prayer, flanked by two beautiful bodhisattvas and a host of celestial guardians with terrifying faces.

About 330yd/300m to the west, on a small hillock on the other side of Daibutsu-den, stands **Kaidan-in★**, in which four precious statues of the celestial kings dating from the Nara period are preserved. Finally, head north, leaving a pond to your left, and you reach **Shoso-in★**, a curious storehouse made of logs and mounted on piles (⊶*closed to public*). It is used to store the ritual utensils for the ceremonies at the Todai-ji, as well as the treasures bequeathed to the temple by Emperor Shomu: thousands of objects (screens, ceramics, masks, fabrics, etc.) brought along the Silk Road from China, India, Persia, and Byzantium. Every year in the fall, some of these are put on display in the Nara National Museum.

From the vast Todai-ji site, marked paths lead to the south of the park (toward Kasuga Taisha). The main trail passes below the bare hill of **Wakakusayama** (1122ft/342m). From late March to mid-December you can climb it (⊶¥150) for a fine view of the town and its temples, among the spring cherry blossoms or colorful fall leaves.

Kasuga Taisha★★ 春日大社

🕐Map, C2. 15min walk from Todai-ji. Shrine: 🕐open daily dawn–dusk. ⊶No charge; inner shrine ¥500. Homotsu-den: 🕐open daily 9am–5pm.⊶¥500. Gardens: 🕐open daily: Mar–Nov 9am–

5pm; Dec–Feb 9am–4.30pm. ⊶¥500. *kasugataisha.or.jp.*

Located in the eastern part of Nara Park, Kasuga Taisha (Kasuga Grand Shrine) lies at the foot of two sacred mountains, Kasuga-yama and Mikasa-yama, once venerated as places chosen by the *kami* to come to earth. Shaded by Japanese cedars, the shrine buildings lie on the edge of a picturesque and well-preserved **primeval forest★**. Founded in 768 (or 710, according to some sources), the shrine's significance in Japanese history is that it housed the guardian deities of the Fujiwara clan. In about the 10C, during the Heian era, it was affiliated to Kofuku-ji, an association that would last until 1868, when Shintoism was separated from Buddhism by the Meiji Restoration.

Kasuga Taisha is famous for its **3000 lanterns**, donated by the faithful over the centuries. Moss-covered stone lanterns line the main avenue from the great *torii* to the entrance; others, in bronze, hang in the corridors of the buildings. All are lit twice a year during the **Mantoro festivals** (Aug 14–15 & Feb 3). The shrine is also notable for its **architecture★**, even though most of the buildings are 19C reconstructions. The long and narrow main building has a large thatched and gabled roof. It integrates well into its surroundings, large red pillars contrasting effectively with the green of the trees and the mauve of the wisteria, a flower with which the shrine is closely associated:

WHERE TO STAY

GH Sakuraya........................ ❶
Hotel Fujita Nara................. ❷
Kasuga Hotel....................... ❸
Nara Hotel.......................... ❹
Nara Ugaya Guesthouse....... ❺
Ryokan Matsumae................ ❻
Ryokan Seikanso.................. ❼
Super Hotel Lohas............... ❽
Toyoko Inn Nara Kintetsu..... ❾

WHERE TO EAT

Kura.................................... ❶
Mangyoku........................... ❷
Miyoshino........................... ❸
Mizuho............................... ❹
Okaru................................. ❺
Shunsai Hiyori..................... ❻
Yamatoan............................ ❼
Yamazakiya......................... ❽

NARA

SITE OF HEIJO PALACE

YAKUSHI-JI TOSHODAI-JI

HORYU-JI, CHUGU-JI

JR Yamatoji Line

Kintetsu Nara Line

Saho-gawa River

Shin-Omiya Sta.

CHUO P.O.

Sanjo-dori

Yasuragi-no-michi St.

Kintetsu Nara Sta.

NARA WOMEN'S UNIVERSITY

Nobori-oji Ave.

Konishi Arcade

Nara Sta.

Nara-Okuyama Driveway Toll Road

Shoso-in

TODAI-JI

Daibutsu-den

Nigatsu-do

Hokke-do

Kaidan-in

Todai-ji Museum

Isui-en

Kagami-ike Pond

Nandai-mon

Nara Park

Nara National Museum

Kofuku-ji

Sarusawa Pond

Ara-ike Pond

Sagi-ike Pond

Mt.Yuga-san

Naramachi Shiryokan Museum

Gango-ji

NARAMACHI

Naramachi Koshi-no-ie

Kasuga Taisha

Shin-Yakushi-ji

Irie Taikichi Memorial Museum of Photography

500 m
250
0

500 yds
250
0

N

Copyright 2015 Cartographic data Shobunsha/Michelin

the shrine's priestesses even wear clusters of wisteria in their hair.

To the west of the shrine, the **Homotsu-den** (Treasure Hall) displays *bugaku* masks, Noh costumes (⬤*see p109*), and old weapons and armor, several of them National Treasures.

Close by, the **gardens** (Kasuga Taisha Shin-en) are enchanting, especially when the wisteria blooms (May). It also contains all the plants and herbs cited in the *Man'yoshu* (the "Collection of Ten Thousand Leaves," the oldest known collection of Japanese poetry, 4–8C).

⬤ When you leave the shrine, follow the path on the left, which leads south through the woods. Leaving the forest after about another 875yd/800m, take the road on the right and then, 110yd/100m farther on, the street on the left, which leads to Shin-Yakushi-ji, as indicated by a sign.

Shin-Yakushi-ji★ 新薬師寺
⬤*Map, C2. 10min walk from Kasuga Taisha.* ◷*Open daily 9am–5pm.* ⬤*¥600. shinyakushiji.or.jp.*

At the edge of the town, near paddy fields, built in 747 at the request of Empress Komyo to thank the gods for restoring her husband, Emperor Shomu, to health, this temple was once one of the largest in Nara. The main hall, the only original building, houses a fine 8C **statue★** depicting Yakushi Nyorai (the Buddha of Healing, ⬤*see box p 320*) accompanied by 12 celestial guardians, each brandishing a different weapon. The temple is set in a peaceful residential district, where you'll also find the **Irie Taikichi Memorial Museum of Photography** (600-1 Takabatake-cho ✆0742-22-9811, ◷*open Tue–Sun, 9.30am–5pm,*⬤*¥500*). It is housed in a beautiful modern building, and celebrates the work of Irie Taikichi, who immortalised Nara over decades.

NARAMACHI★ 奈良町
⬤*Map, B2.*

This former merchant quarter, stretching south of Sarusawa Pond around the quiet temple of **Gango-ji** (◷*open daily*

9am–5pm, ⬤*¥500, gangoji-tera.or.jp*), is a maze of tranquil, picturesque little streets lined with wooden *machiya* houses used as shops, workshops, and private dwellings by the same families for generations. Some are now handicraft shops or cafes. The atmosphere is traditionally Japanese. ⬤ In between the numerous shop fronts you might see the door to the well-known **Harushika sake brewery** (⬤*see Shopping p376*).

Naramachi Koshi-no-ie
ならまち格子の家
⬤*Map, B2. 44 Gangoji-cho.* ◷*Open Tue–Sun 9am–5pm.* ⬤*No charge.*

This restored *machiya* typifies the layout of a traditional Nara house: a low façade, a tiled roof, windows protected by wooden latticework, and a long, narrow interior opening at the rear onto a small garden and storehouse.

Naramachi Shiryokan
奈良町資料館
⬤*Map, B2. 14 Nishonoshinya-cho.* ◷*Open daily 10am–5pm.* ⬤*No charge. naramachi.co.jp.*

This Edo period *machiya* is a museum housing a varied assortment of objects: porcelain, signs, old coins, and prints. Note the small red-and-white stuffed monkeys hanging from the canopy, which are "substitute monkeys," belonging to the Chinese cult of *koshin*. Each little monkey represents a member of the family, whom it is supposed to protect from misfortune and suffering by taking on these problems itself.

THE WEST OF THE CITY★
Nara Palace Site Historical Park 平城宮跡歴史公園
⬤*Map, A1, off map. Allow a half day minimum to fully explore the site. From Kintetsu Nara Station, take the Kintetsu Line one stop to Yamato Saidaiji, leave by the south exit and walk 20min east. Hours vary by building, but generally:* ◷*open Tue–Sun 9am–4.30pm.* ⬤*No charge. heijo-park.go.jp/en.*

Situated in the northwest of modern-day Nara, the former Heijo Palace (710–84) covered an area of 320 acres/130ha and was surrounded by a 16ft/5m-high clay rampart with 12 entrances. This Imperial complex included buildings where political and religious ceremonies were held, including the **Daigoku-den** (audience hall), **Chodo-in** (ceremonial hall), and **Dairi** (Imperial residence), as well as offices, shops, workshops, etc. Each building had its own base, tiled roof, and vermilion laquered pillars.

These wooden buildings may have disappeared but the site, which has been occupied by paddy fields ever since, still conceals archeological finds. Excavations have revealed, for example, a garden of Chodo-in to the east.

In 2010, in celebration of Nara's 1300th anniversary, an ambitious program of reconstruction was launched. Using traditional methods, the reconstruction of the **Suzaku-mon** (Great South Gate) took six years, while **Daigoku-den** (Imperial Audience Hall) took nine years. The project is ongoing, with the Minami-mon (South Gate) still being worked on at the time of research.

The sites museums give an overview of the program, and explain more of the history of Heijo Palace. To the south is the Guidance Center in **Suzaku-mon Square**, where you can see an impressive modl of the city as it was 1300 years ago. The **Nara Palace Site Museum**, by the west entrance, exhibits photographs of the excavation process, plus information on the traditional construction techniques used. To the east is the **Excavation Site Exhibition Hall**, with ceramics, tiles and tablets found during the work.

Toshodai-ji★ 唐招提寺

♿️*Map, A2, off map. Kintetsu Line to Nishinokyo Station, then 10min walk, or buses no. 72, 78 & 98 to Toshodai-ji or Toshodai-ji-higashiguchi stops (20min journey, ☏¥270). Temple complex:* 🕐*open daily 8.30am–5pm. ☏¥600. Mieido:* 🕐*Open Jun 6 only. ☏¥500. toshodaiji.jp.*

Although it has undergone much restoration over the centuries, Toshodai-ji nevertheless remains a harmonious example of Nara-period architecture. A temple belonging to the Ritsu sect, it is the work of Ganjin (688–763), a Chinese monk invited by Emperor Shomu to teach Buddhism in 759. Ganjin had an unusually hard time crossing the Sea of Japan, suffering shipwreck five times, and by the time he reached Japan, he had gone blind.

The **Mieido**, the hall at the far end of the garden, contains a **statue★** of Ganjin, the oldest lacquered effigy in Japan. The **Kondo★★**, the temple's principal pavilion and a designated National Treasure, has a colonnade of eight pillars at the front. The interior contains three large, dry-lacquer statues of the Buddhas Yakushi and Rushana, and the *bosatsu* Senju Kannon. Behind it is the lecture hall, the **Kodo★**, with a curved roof, which was originally part of Heijo Palace and contains several valuable statues, including a large 8C **Miroku Bosatsu★**.

Yakushi-ji★ 薬師寺

♿️*Map, A2, off map. 5min walk south of Toshodai-ji, partly closed for restoration until 2020.* 🕐*Open daily 8.30am–5pm: temple complex year round; Genjō-sanzōin Garan Mar–Jun & mid-Sept–mid-Jan. ☏¥1100 (Mar–Jun & mid-Sept–mid-Jan), or ¥800 (mid-Jan–Feb & Jul–mid-Sept). nara-yakushiji.com.*

Founded by Emperor Tenmu in 680 and moved to Nara in 718, this temple, the center of the Hosso sect, is one of the oldest and most sacred in the city. Seriously damaged by fire in 973 and again in 1528, it has been entirely rebuilt, with work on the beautiful **To-to★★**, East Pagoda only completed in 2020, after almost a decade. Three storys and 111ft/34m high, it appears to have six levels because of the canopies between the floors. The principal hall, the **Kon-do** (1635), houses a large bronze triad of the **Buddha Yakushi★★** dating from 697 and strongly influenced by the naturalist style of the Chinese Tang dynasty, while the showpiece of the **Toin-do**, or East Hall (1285), is a 7C **Sho Kannon★** showing Indian influence.

Kondo, Horyu-ji

© Joshua Hawley/Shutterstock

EXCURSIONS

HORYU-JI★★★ 法隆寺

Regional Map, p309, B2. From JR Nara Station, Yamatoji Line to Horyu-ji Station (15min, ☜¥230), then 20min walk to the north (map available at the station), or bus no. 72 (5min, ☜¥200). Alternatively, from JR Nara or Kintetsu Nara stations, bus no. 98 to Horyu-ji-mae stop (1hr, ☜¥770). Temple: ⊘open daily: mid-Feb–early Nov 8am–5pm; early Nov–mid-Feb 8am–4.30pm. ☜¥1500. Yumedono: ⊘open mid-Apr–mid-May & end Oct–end Nov, check online for details. horyuji.or.jp/em.

Located in the town of Ikaruga, 7.5mi/12km southwest of Nara, Horyu-ji, the "Temple of the Flourishing Law," features the oldest wooden buildings in the world. These masterpieces of the Asuka period were built in 607 on the orders of Empress Suiko and Prince Regent Shotoku. Some of the buildings may have been destroyed by a fire in 670 and rebuilt in the 8C. Horyu-ji was the first place in Japan to be designated a UNESCO World Heritage Site.

Sai-in (Western Precinct)★★★ – An avenue lined with pine trees leads to **Nandai-mon**, the Great South Gate, which dates from the Muromachi period (14C). Farther on is a much older gate (late 7C), **Chu-mon★**, with bulbous pillars, flanked by two **guardians★** (Kongorikishi), one of clay (711), the other of wood (12C).

In the middle of the central courtyard is the oldest and most sacred of the buildings, the **Kondo★★★** or Golden Hall. It contains a triad of **Shaka Nyorai★★** (Sakyamuni, the historical Buddha) from 623, by the sculptor Tori. The almond-shaped eyes, elongated face, the draping of the clothing, and the direct attitude of the sculpture are strongly influenced by the stone statues of the Chinese Northern Wei dynasty (386–534). The wall paintings depict the Buddhist paradise in the style of the Indian frescoes of Ajanta. Most are replicas, the originals lost in a fire in 1949.

Beside the Kondo is the **Gojuno-to★★★**, a five-story pagoda probably built in about 700, making it the oldest pagoda in Japan. Each level symbolizes one of the five tantric elements: earth, water, wood, air, and space. The base has clay statues illustrating the life of the Sakyamuni Buddha; the one facing north depicts his ascent to nirvana.

At the far end of the precinct, on the right, is the **Daihozo-in** (Treasure Hall), which displays several pieces from the Asuka period (7C), including a camphor-wood **Kudara Kannon★★★**, a masterpiece of grace and refinement, and the **Tamamushi no zushi★★★**, the altar of Empress Suiko, which is covered in 9000 iridescent beetle wings.

To-in (Eastern Precinct)★ – The main focus here is the **Yumedono★★**, or Pavilion of Dreams (739), where Prince Shotoku received answers to his political and philosophical questions in his dreams. Mounted on a stone podium, this eight-sided building houses a perfectly-preserved 7C gilt wooden statue of **Kuze Kannon★★**.

Chugu-ji★ 中宮寺

Map, A2, off map. *Open daily: mid-Mar–Sept 9am–4.30pm; Oct–mid-Mar 9am–4pm .* *¥600. chuguji.jp.*
A passageway at the far end of Horyu-ji's Eastern Precinct leads to this small temple, founded by Prince Shotoku in honor of his mother in 621. It is worth visiting for its black camphorwood statue of **Miroku Bosatsu★★★** (Buddha of the Future), seated in a meditation position, a masterpiece of Japanese statuary.

KASHIHARA 橿原

Regional Map, p309, A-B2. About 12mi/20km south of Nara. From Kintetsu Nara Station, take the Kintetsu Line to Yagi-nishiguchi Station via Yamato Saidaiji (45min, ¥440). On leaving the station, turn right, then right again, go straight and turn left after the traditional bridge. After 1300ft/400m you come to Hanairaka, the Imai-cho cultural exchange center.

Hanairaka 華甍

Open daily 9am–5pm. No charge.
This great wooden edifice dates from the Meiji period (1903) and is today a tourist center and museum; *you can ask for a plan and brochures on the Imai district and its history.* A model also presents it as it was during the Edo period.

Imai-cho★ 今井町

This district, with its rows of 17C houses, brings the day-to-day of the Edo period to life with several dwellings open to the public. Founded by a monk, the trade town of Imai belonged to a Buddhist temple which waged battle against Oda Nobunaga's army in 1570 before surrendering; in exchange, it received the status of autonomous city. It was therefore built based on the plan for a fortified town: the streets are not entirely straight, so that arrows can't reach their targets; and every house's façade has at least one iron ring to tie horses to.
The **Imanishi Residence** (*open Tue–Sun 10am–5pm; reservation required, call ✆0744-25-3388 10am–4pm; ¥400*) dates from 1650 and exhibits the interior of a rich merchant's home.

▶ From Yaga-nishiguchi Station, take the Kintetsu Line to Kashihara Jingumae Station (5min, ¥210).

Kashihara-jingu 橿原神宮

Daily 6.30am–5pm. No charge, Treasure Hall ¥300.
According to Shinto mythology, this temple was where the **first emperor of Japan**, Jinmu, was enthroned. Behind the temple, a little pebbled path takes

Imai-cho
© Travel and Still life photography/iStock

Yoshino-yama in spring

© davidevison/iStock

you to the summit of Unebi Mountain. The shrine's small **Treasure Hall** contains some interesting artefacts, from calligraphy to swords.

Yoshino-yama★ 吉野山

♿*Regional Map, p309, A2. About 26mi/42km south of Nara. Take the Kintetsu Line from Kashihara Jingumae Station (55min, ⊛¥470; from Nara, 1hr 30min, ⊛¥860) to Yoshino Station. From there, walk 10min to Senbonguchi Station for the cable car up Yoshino-yama (one way ⊛¥450, round trip ⊛¥800). www.yoshinoyama-sakura.jp.*

Perched at 3280ft/1000m on Yoshino Mountain, Yoshino village is famous for its **30,000 cherry trees** that bloom for an entire month, which thousands of Japanese people come to admire. Four areas at different altitudes explain this long season: **Shimonosenbon** (at the base of the mountain), **Nakasenbon** (about halfway up), **Kaminosenbon** (at the top), and **Okunosenbon** (behind the Kamisenbon).

Founded by the priest Gyoki in the 8C, then rebuilt in the 15C, **Kinpusen-ji★** (⏱*open daily 8.30am–4.30pm, main hall ⊛¥500, kinpusen.or.jp)* is said to be the second-largest wooden building in Japan after Todai-ji; it stands about 111ft/34m high. The last great religious waystation before climbing **Mount Omine**, this Buddhist temple also traditionally welcomes women on pilgrimage in the Kii Mountains (♿*see Kumano Kodo, p383)*, but who could not enter the sacred circle of the peak, where mountain ascetics trained and women were not allowed.

Along the main road coming down from Kinpusen-ji, shops and restaurants jostle with smaller temples, shrines, and tourist sites. **Yoshimizu Shrine** (⏱*open daily 9am–5pm, ⊛¥400, yoshimizu-shrine.com)* is worth a stop for its beautiful **painted screens**. A little farther on is **Gunpoen★** (⏱*open daily 8am–sunset, ⊛¥300)*, a garden in the precincts of a magnificent temple (now a *ryokan*) with a beautiful weeping cherry tree.

At the **Hanayagura viewpoint** *(20min by foot)* there is a beautiful **panorama** of the mountain. Nearby, the seven water divinities of the **Mikumari Shrine★** (⏱*open daily 8am–4pm, ⊛no charge)* live side by side in the sanctuary's right wing, in altars flanked on each side by two protective demons turning their backs on those of the altar.

ADDRESSES

🛏 STAY

NARA

🏠 **Nara Ugaya Guesthouse** 奈良ウガヤ ゲストハウス – 4-1 Okukomori-cho (Map, B2). ☏0742-95-7739. ugaya.net. 5 rooms. Dorms ¥2500 per person, doubles ¥6000. 🛏. Friendly guesthouse near the stations, with a cozy book-lined common area and organic coffee shop. Mixed and women-only dorms, plus private rooms (all with shared bathrooms).

🏠 **Ryokan Seikanso** 旅館静観荘 – 29 Higashi-Kitsuji-cho (Map, B2). ☏0742-22-2670. nara-ryokanseikanso.com. 9 rooms. ¥8800. ¥495/770 🛏. A delightful *ryokan*, built in 1916 around a magnificent inner garden. The friendly owner speaks a little English. The rooms, though slightly faded, are pleasant and well-lit. Try to book one of the six rooms that looks onto the garden. O-furo, wifi, and bicycle rental.

GH Sakuraya ゲストハウス桜舎 – *1 Narukawa-cho (Map, B2). ☏0742-24-1490. www.guesthouse-sakuraya.com. 3 rooms. ¥10,400.* ☐. A perfect address in the heart of the charming Naramachi district. The rooms in this renovated traditional building are Japanese style, and there are cultural activities on offer, plus a pretty interior garden, a friendly, obliging owner, and French- and English-speaking staff.

Hotel Fujita Nara ホテルフジタ奈良 – *47-1 Shimosanjo-cho (Map, B2). ☏0742-23-8111. en.fujita-nara.com. 117 rooms.* ☐. *¥16,000. ¥3040* ☐. Conveniently located, with friendly, English-speaking staff, bright, soundproofed rooms, two restaurants, and an attractive bar with a garden view. This hotel is a good mid-range choice.

Ryokan Matsumae 旅館 松前 – *28-1 Higashiterabayashi-cho (Map, B2). ☏0742-22-3686. matsumae.co.jp. 15 rooms. From ¥11,000. ¥990* ☐. A tranquil *ryokan* located in a little street not far from Sarusawa Pond. The owner speaks good English. Small, clean rooms with and without en-suite bathrooms.

Super Hotel Lohas スーパーホテルLohas・JR 奈良駅 – *1-2 Sanjo-honmachi (Map, A2). ☏0742-27-9000. superhoteljapan.com/en.* ☐. *233 rooms. ¥10,400.* ☐. Modern, welcoming and well-kept, this business hotel has compact rooms and is right next to JR Nara Station. There's also a pleasant *onsen*.

Toyoko Inn Nara Kintetsu 東横イン奈良近鉄 – *16-1 Nishi-Mikado-cho. (Map, B1). ☏0742-85-1045. toyoko-inn.com/e_hotel/00249/index.html. ¥10,500.* ☐. Near Kintetsu Station, this simple but comfortable business hotel suits guests who want to drop off their luggage and explore the city immediately.

Nara Hotel 奈良ホテル – *Nara-koennai (Map, B2). ☏0742-26-3300. narahotel.co.jp.* ☐. *129 rooms. ¥24,000. ¥3500* ☐. This hilltop hotel near the park, built in 1909, is Western in style apart from the cypresswood façade inspired by the Momoyama period (16C). Many celebrities have stayed here, from Einstein to the Dalai Lama. Room in the older part of the hotel are more atmospheric, with high ceilings, old wall-lights, and fireplaces.

Kasuga Hotel 春日ホテル – *40 Noborioji-cho (Map, B1). ☏0742-22-4031. kasuga-hotel.co.jp. 30 rooms.* ☐. *¥34,100. ¥2000* ☐. The exterior of this hotel reproduces the architectural style of the wooden buildings of the Tenpyo period (late-8C). The interior has spacious, well-equipped, light-filled Japanese- and Western-style rooms with high-tech equipment. Excellent *kaiseki* cuisine and a superb o-furo, complete with a waterfall, surrounded by rocks and greenery.

YOSHINO-YAMA

Chikurin-in-Gunpoen 竹林院群芳園 – *21-41 Yoshinoyama. ☏746-32-8081. chikurin.co.jp/e/home.htm. 41 rooms.* ☐. *¥30,000.* ☐, *dinner also included.* In the heart of a Japanese garden, this former Buddhist temple turned into a *ryokan* offers you stunning traditional rooms in an idyllic setting. Very beautiful *rotenburo*. Shuttle from Yoshino's Kintetsu Station *(except Apr)* from 2.30pm, by reservation.

⛴ EAT

NARA

Kura 蔵 – *16 Komyoin-cho (Map, B2). ☏0742-22-8771. Open daily 5–9.30pm. From ¥300 (per dish).* At the edge of Naramachi, this *izakaya* serves good-value, well-made Japanese dishes. Notable on the menu is a fragrant, hearty *oden* (a traditional stew).

Miyoshino 三好野 – *27 Hashimoto-cho (Map, B2). ☏0742-22-5239. bikkuriudon.com. Open Thu–Tue 11am–8.30pm. Lunch menus from ¥870.* ☐. This small, family-run cafe on Sanjo-dori specializes in udon dishes, many of which (with eggs, beef, tempura, etc.) are pictured on the wall.

Mizuho 瑞穂 – *12 Michiidono-cho (Map, B2). ☏0742-93-5071. tempura-bowl-restaurants-12.business.site. Open Mon–Wed & Fri–Sun 10.30am–9pm. Lunch from ¥800.* In Naramachi's pedestrianized arcades, near Sarusawa Pond, this tiny restaurant with jovial staff is a real find. The tempura is crisp and light, the set meals are extremely generous, and the range of beer and sake is impressive. Try the fried sweet-potato ice cream *(¥680)*.

Okaru おかる – *13 Higashimuki-minami-machi (Map, B2). ☏0742-24-3686. Open Thur–Tue 11am–9.30pm. From ¥1100.* ☐. The best *okonomiyaki* in Nara: savory pancakes stuffed with octopus, squid, pork, leek, or shrimp. The decor is fairly simple, and diners eat either at tables or on *tatami* mats.

☺ **Yamatoan** やまと庵本店 – *495-1 Sanjō-cho (Map, A2).* ☏*0742-26-3585. Open daily 11.30am–3pm & 5pm–midnight. From ¥700 (per dish).* At the start of Sanjo-dori coming from the JR station, look for the pretty façade. Serves alluring dishes mostly based on local chicken, pork and beef; try them in tempura or stews.

☺☺ **Yamazakiya** 山崎屋 – *5 Higashimuki-minamimachi (Map, B2).* ☏*0742-27-3715. ajiyama.com. Open Tue–Sun 11am–9pm. Menu in English. Lunch from ¥900, kaiseki from ¥4000.* Restaurant behind a famous store selling pickled vegetables. The menus feature the same with appetizing preparations that suit all tastes and budgets, from sushi or grilled meat to tempura or *kaiseki*.

☺☺☺ **Mangyoku** まんぎょく – *9 Ganrinin-cho (Map, B2).* ☏*0742-22-2265. Open Tue–Sun 6–11pm. Around ¥3000.* ☑. Located in a small street near Sarusawa Pond, this is a typical old Nara house with lanterns and a hurdle fence. Inside, old furniture, prints, a polished parquet floor, and wooden beams make for a pleasant setting. Good home-style dishes like *nikujaga* (beef stew), steamed chicken, grilled salmon, and other seasonal food.

☺☺☺ **Shunsai Hiyori** 旬菜・ひより – *26 Nakanoshinya-cho (Map, B2).* ☏*0742-24-1470. naramachi-hiyori.jp. Open Wed–Mon 11.30am–2.30pm & 5–10pm. Lunch from ¥1760, dinner from ¥3960.* At the edge of Naramachi, a lovely room of light wood with red walls. The enthusiastic chef makes multi-dish meals featuring vegetables from his own garden.

HORYU-JI

☺ Along the tree-lined avenue leading to the temple, a succession of restaurants is designed to lure the flood of visitors. **Sabo Shokodo**(茶房松鼓堂 – *open daily 9am–5pm)* is a popular spot with substantial portions of soba or udon *(from ¥880).* Near the information center is **Hirasou** (平宗 – *0745-75-1110, open daily 9am–5pm, hiraso.jp),* a shop and restaurant serving mackerel sushi *(ayu zushi)* and excellent ice cream.

KASHIHARA

☺☺☺ **Suian** 粋庵 – *1-4-35 Imai-cho.* ☏*0744-29-3807. Open Tue–Sun 11.30am–1.30pm & 5–10pm. Lunch around ¥1500, dinner ¥4500.* At the heart of the Imai-cho district, this traditional restaurant with its wooden frontage serves good soba set menus.

TAKING A BREAK

Gluten Free is the New Black – *11-43 Shibatsuji-cho (Map, A1).* ☏*080-6189-7925, glutenfreeisthenewblack.info. Open Tue–Wed 10am–5pm, Fri–Sun 10am–6pm.* Not only is everything in this welcoming cafe gluten free, but much of it is also vegan. Try the filling avocado toast, or perhaps by a cake or brownie to take away.

Mellow Cafe メローカフェ – *1-8 Konishi-cho (Map, B2).* ☏*0742-27-9099, mellowcafe. jp. Open daily 11am–11.30pm.* This trendy cafe with attractive terracotta decor makes a relaxing place for a drink in the afternoon or early evening. Also serves Italian meals; try the Narazuku (local pickles) and sake lees pizza *(¥1100)*.

Nonhana Ohka 野の花・黄花 – *13 Nakashinyamachi (Map, B2).* ☏*0742-22-1139. Open Tue–Sun 11am–5pm.* In a pretty Naramachi street, a pleasant cafe with an attractive room and terrace. Salads, desserts, and various teas and coffees.

SHOPPING

Handicrafts – **Nara Craft Museum** なら工藝館 – *1-1 Azemame-cho (Map, B2).* ☏*0742-27-0033. Open Tue–Sun 10am–6pm.* This lovely museum in the Naramachi district both displays and sells traditional handicrafts from Nara: wooden dolls, ceramics, laquerware, etc.

Souvenirs – **Yu Nakagawa** 遊 中川 – *31-1 Ganriin-cho (Map, B2).* ☏*0742-22-1322. Open daily 10am–6.30pm.* Tasteful souvenirs, notably those made of material (handkerchiefs, silk scarfs, bags, etc), wiith the Nara deer taking center stage.

Ink – **Kobaien** 古梅園 – *433-1 Zoshi-cho.* ☏*0742-22-6337. kajisyouten.com Open daily: Apr–Oct 9am–5pm; Nov–Mar 9am–4.30pm.* Shop linked to one of the oldest *sumi* ink factories in the country. The workshops can be visited and the shop sells sticks of colored ink.

Paper – **Akemitori** 朱鳥 – *1 Hashimoto-cho (Map, B2).* ☏*0742-22-1991. akemitori. jp. Open daily 10am–7pm.* A shop in the pedestrian arcades of Sanjo-dori specializing in *tenugui*, printed cotton clothes used as decoration or accessories.

Sake – **Harushika** 春鹿 – *24-1 Fukuchi-in-cho (Map, B2).* ☏*0742-23-2255. harushika. com. Open daily 9am–5pm.* Shop attached to a famous brewery that has been operating since 1884. You can try five different drinks for *¥500*, and can even take the cup home.

Koya-san★★★
高野山

Koya-san, the largest grouping of monasteries in Japan, stands at the summit of a densely forested mountain (Koya-san is also the name of the mountain). Almost a thousand Buddhist monks pray and meditate here, high up in the clear skies. For 12 centuries, Koya-san has been to Japan what the Santiago de Compostela is to Europe: a famous center for devotion that attracts around a million pilgrims a year. In times gone by, only the bravest would climb the arduous trails up to the lofty retreat. In spite of its isolation, Koya-san was a powerful religious center in the Middle Ages, housing approximately 1500 monasteries, of which around a hundred survive today, including 30 temple lodgings (shukubo), offering food and accommodation to travelers. Designated a UNESCO World Heritage Site, along with the other sacred sites and trails on Kii Peninsula, this town—shrouded in mist and incense—gives visitors the opportunity to enter a mysterious, esoteric Japan.

▶ **Population:** 3,300 – Wakayama Prefecture.

Michelin Map: Regions of Japan Map 3, Regional Map p309, Koya-san Map p379.

Location: Koya-san occupies a mountainous plateau at 2953ft/900m on the Kii Peninsula, 53mi/85km south of Osaka and 41mi/66km east of Wakayama. From the plain, a cable car will take you up to the station, located 2mi/3km north of the town. The main street becomes Rte 371 to Okuno-in, continuing south to connect with Kii-Katsuura and Kumano Sanzan.

Kids: A shukubo (temple stayy) up in the mountains is a great family activity.

Timing: One day should be enough for a visit, but if you really want to savor the mystical atmosphere, stay overnight. If you wish to visit the Kii Peninsula too, it's advisable to rent a car.

Don't miss: A night in a temple and the dawn ceremony.

AN OVERVIEW

A legendary founder – The history of Mount Koya goes back to 816, when the monk Kukai, known as **Kobo Daishi**, who had studied Buddhism in China, obtained permission from the Emperor to create a hermitage on the mountain. Legend relates that he was led to this isolated site by the Shinto deities of the peninsula. In 832, he founded the first monastery here—Kongobu-ji—in order to preach his new doctrine, Shingon. From that point, Koya-san continued to grow in influence. At its height, in the 15C, over 90,000 monks lived here, enjoying the protection of powerful lords.

These monks were also soldiers who were always ready to interrupt their prayers and descend from their entrenched position in the mountains to launch armed raids on the rival monasteries of Kyoto, especially those of Mount Hiei. In retaliation, Koya-san was attacked and burned down on several occasions. To put an end to these constant conflicts, the Tokugawa shoguns decided, in the 17C, to cut off the monasteries' means of subsistence by confiscating their vast estates. This was the beginning of a slow decline.

Koya-san today – The life of this tranquil town, a UNESCO World Heritage Site since 2004, is entirely centered on the monasteries, where nearly 1000 monks devote themselves to prayer and meditation. As elsewhere in Japan, their principal function, for which they are paid, is to perform funeral rites and honor the memory of ancestors. But in

Kukai, a sacred figure

Kobo Daishi, whose real name was Kukai, was born in 774 on the island of Shikoku, which today is dotted with temples dedicated to his memory (*see p563*). An aristocrat, he studied classical Chinese letters, but left university to become a wandering ascetic. From 804 to 806 he was in China, where he was able to study the Tantric doctrine of Chenyang, which he brought back to Japan, renaming it Shingon.

Honored by the Emperor on his return, he became a spiritual guide to the Court and in 823 was put in charge of To-ji in Kyoto. Nevertheless, he spent most of his life at Koya-san. After his death in 835, many legends spread about his miracles and other exploits. Venerated by the common people as if he were a god, Kukai was also a great humanist, poet, calligrapher, and philosopher, one of the fathers of classical Japanese culture. He is often credited, for example, with the invention of the *hiragana* syllabary.

Koya-san, this activity takes on a different dimension, thanks to the fervent cult surrounding Kobo Daishi since his death. His disciples claim that he is still alive, in a state of meditation (*samadhi*), waiting for Miroku, the Buddha of the Future. Twice a day, the monks go in procession to his mausoleum in Okuno-in cemetery and take him a meal. The legendary powers of the holy man have also attracted thousands of the faithful to be buried beside him, hoping in this way to be reborn in paradise. Spread throughout the town, the *shukubo* (temple lodgings), maintained by monks, provide accommodation for pilgrims and tourists.

The Shingon school – Claiming 12 million followers and 12,000 affiliated monasteries around the world, Shingon

USEFUL INFORMATION

Tourist Office – Koya-san Shukubo **Association**, by the Senjuin-bashi bus stop *(Map, B2). Open Jan–Feb 9am–5pm; Mar–Dec 8.30am–5pm.* ℹ*0736-56-2616. shukubo.net.* Rents audioguides to Koya-san's main sights *(¥500)*.
Bank/Foreign Exchange – Kiyo Bank, 55yd/50m to the left of the post office (*see below).Open Mon–Fri 9am–3pm.*
Post Office/Withdrawals – Opposite the Tourist Office. *Open Mon–Fri 9am–5pm.* **ATM** *Open Mon–Fri 8.45am–6pm, Sat 9am–5pm, Sun 9am–3pm.*

TRANSPORTATION
BY TRAIN – From Namba Station in Osaka, take the Nankai Koya Line to Gokurakubashi. Four Limited Express trains per day *(1hr 20min, ¥1680)* or Express trains via Hashimoto *(1hr 40min, ¥890).*

From Gokurakubashi, cable car *(5min, ¥390)* to Koya-san Station, 2mi/3km north of the town. Buses go from the station to Senjuin-bashi stop *(10min, ¥290).*

GETTING AROUND KOYA-SAN
The most central bus stop, **Senjuin-bashi**, is at the intersection on the main street *(Map, B2).* The town stretches from **Dai-mon** gate in the west to **Okuno-in** cemetery in the east. A bus *(every 15–30min)* serves the whole route, but it's an easy walk.

☃ If you're only staying one night, get the **Koya-san World Heritage Ticket** at Namba Station, a 2-day pass *(¥2900),* which includes the Osaka–Koya-san round trip and reduced prices in the town itself. The **Kansai Thru Pass** *(from ¥4300)* is also an option. Check online for points of sale.

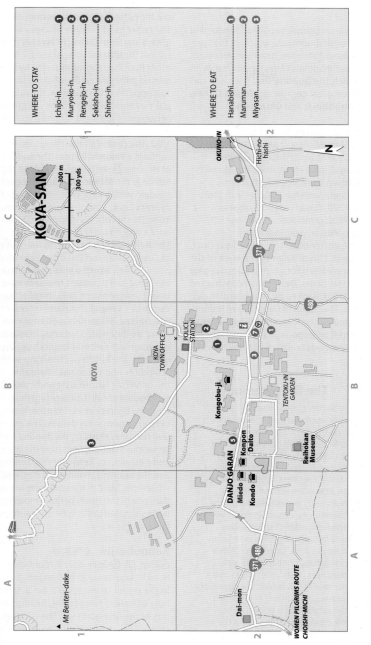

KOYA-SAN

300 m
300 yds

WHERE TO STAY

Ichijo-in............. 1
Muryoko-in.......... 2
Rengejo-in.......... 3
Sekisho-in........... 4
Shinno-in............ 5

WHERE TO EAT

Hanabishi........... 1
Maruman............ 2
Miyasan............. 3

Buddhism, the True Word sect, is an esoteric doctrine that states everyone on earth can achieve enlightenment and become a Buddha through the repetition of mantras (incantations) and the use of *mandalas* (symbolic images) as an aid to meditation.

SIGHTS

Koya-san occupies a plateau surrounded by eight mountains, which, in the symbolism of Shingon Buddhism, represent the eight petals of the lotus blossom on which the Buddha sits. Koya-san has three great complexes: **Danjo Garan**, **Kongobu-ji**, and **Okuno-in**.

Danjo Garan★ 壇上伽藍

Map, B2. Temple precincts open daily 24hr; Daito & Kondo open daily 8.30am–5pm; Reihokan Museum open daily: May–Oct 8.30am–5.30pm, Nov–Apr 8.30am–5pm. Daito ¥200; Kondo ¥200; Reihokan ¥600; combination ticket ¥1500. reihokan.or.jp/en/index.html

The entrance to this sacred precinct, about 330yd/300m to the west of the complex, is through an impressive gate on two floors, **Dai-mon** (reconstructed in 1705), flanked by two guardian deities. The center of Danjo Garan is dominated by the **Konpon Daito★**, a large, vermilion pagoda 165ft/50m high. The original was built by Kobo Daishi in 816,

but the present version dates from 1947. The rather gaudy interior houses a large gilded statue of **Dainichi Nyorai** (the cosmic Buddha) accompanied by four other Buddhas and surrounded by lacquered pillars painted with *bosatsu*.

Just opposite is the **Kondo★**, the principal pavilion, where major religious ceremonies are held. Erected in 819, it was rebuilt for the seventh time in 1932. The central altar in the gilded hall contains a **Yakushi Nyorai** (the Buddha of Healing; *see box p320*). Behind the Kondo is the **Miedo** (1848), an elegant pavilion with a vast, protecting roof of cypress bark, containing portraits of Kobo Daishi with his disciples (*open once a year on Mar 21*).

The **Reihokan Museum★**, to the south of Danjo Garan, on the other side of a pond, is well worth a visit as it is here that Koya-san's greatest treasures have been preserved since 1939. Its collection comprises several thousand works, of which about 200 are displayed in rotation. Many are designated National Treasures or Important Cultural Properties. The galleries are full to overflowing with sculptures and mandalas (diagrams of the universe), whose style and esoteric symbolism recall Tibetan tantric art: terrifying figures leaping from the flames, benign or grimacing deities. The great wall hangings extolling the Buddha and his various manifestations have the grace and freshness of Renaissance painting and the teeming vividness of medieval altarpieces. Most of the sculptures are in the style of the Heian period: imposing bodies, detailed clothing, fierce or austere faces, and so on.

Kongobu-ji★ 金剛峯寺

Map, B2. Open daily 8.30am–5pm. ¥500. koyasan.or.jp/en/kongobuji.

In the center of the town is Koya-san's holy of holies, Kongobu-ji, headquarters of the Shingon sect. The complex comprises administrative buildings, a religious university, and a temple open to visitors. Built in 1593 by Toyotomi Hideyoshi, it has been destroyed and rebuilt several times (*the last time in 1863*). The main hall, **Ohiroma★**, con-

---

The fire ceremony

At 5a, the gong sounds to announce that the service is about to start. The fire ceremony (*goma*) is held in all the temple dwellings at dawn and guests are cordially invited. In the half-light of the shrine, the priest sits down before an altar laden with offerings, bells, and candlesticks, and burns bundles of sticks in a bronze bowl. The fire crackles, burning away illusions and liberating men from their passions. Lined up on either side, sitting on their heels with their eyes closed, the monks chant mantras in low voices. The clouds of incense, the tinkling of little bells, the candlelight reflected on the silk robes: everything about the ceremony is eerie and spellbinding. When the ritual is over, the monks turn back into hosts, washing floors, cleaning rooms, and preparing breakfast.

Unusual monks

The main function of the monks of Koya-san may be to pamper the souls of the dead, but they also like the good things in life. Far from being hermits, they in fact lead comfortable lives, open to the outside world. They do not take vows of abstinence (most are married), and they are not averse, when the opportunity arises, to eating meat, drinking sake, or singing karaoke. All this is a long way from the austerity originally preached by the Buddha. But here it is believed that Buddhism can be a skill, adaptable to the pleasures of modern life without hypocrisy. "For us," says one of the monks, "Buddhism isn't about suffering and renunciation, but about trying to find happiness through spiritual elevation."

tains beautiful *fusuma* (sliding panels) by Kano Motonobu, founder of the Kano School during the Muromachi period (16C). The Willow Room, decorated by one of his pupils, was where Hideyoshi's nephew Toyotomi Hidetsugu committed ritual suicide in 1595. At the far end of Kongobu-ji is the largest rock garden in Japan, **Banryu-tei★**, whose rocks evoke mountains (some say two dragons) emerging from a sea of clouds. The visit ends with the monastery's huge **kitchen,** where meals (mainly rice) were cooked for about 2000 monks.

Okuno-in★★ 奥の院

&*Map, C2; off map. 30min walk east of village.* ○*Open daily 24hr; Toro-do 6am–5.30pm.* ⊂*No charge.*

Okuno-in, the **cemetery,** is unquestionably the most fascinating place in Koyasan. Here, in the bluish shade of age-old Japanese cedars with giant trunks, nearly **200,000 graves** are scattered. Famous names, shoguns, samurai, high priests, and artists lie side by side with ordinary people. Flashy modern gravestones alternate with older examples, moving in their simplicity. Some are distinctly comical, such as the cup and the giant rocket, erected by a coffee company and an aeronautics firm respectively, or the monument built by an insecticide manufacturer to beg forgiveness of the ants he exterminated. For all that, many Japanese still regard the possibility of placing their parents' urn under the protection of Kobo Daishi as a huge privilege and an assurance that they will one day be reborn in paradise. Such is the demand for the limited number of plots that prices have become astronomical.

From the first sacred bridge *(Ichi-no-hashi;* you should bow here to show respect to Kobo Daishi) at the entrance, a **flagstoned path★★** of 1.2mi/2km, lined with moss-covered stone lanterns, leads through this strange, melancholy undergrowth, amid lichen-eroded gravestones rising in tiers up the slopes. Silence reigns over this city of the dead, occasionally interrupted by the clicking of *geta* (wooden shoes worn by the monks) or the tinkling of bells carried by the white-clad pilgrims. Near the third bridge *(Mimyo-no-hashi)* is a picturesque row of bronze statues, popular deities in scarlet bibs, which visitors sprinkle with water to purify the karma of the dead. Soon after the bridge, at the top of a flight of 30-odd steps, you will come to **Toro-do★**, the Lantern Hall, the lights of which glitter on the ceiling like stars in the night sky. Donated by the faithful, some have been burning for hundreds of years. Behind this building is **Gobyo★**, the mausoleum of Kobo Daishi, who is

Flagstoned path, Okuno-in
© coward_lion/iStock

believed to have been in a state of meditation for nearly 1200 years. Twice a day, monks come here in procession to offer him not only food, but also fans in summer, heating in winter, new clothes once a year, and so on. To acquire merits and beg favors of the holy man, entire families pray fervently at the mausoleum. Most leave generous offerings.

✦ WALKS

🚶 **Women Pilgrims Route** – *Map, A2; off map.* Until 1872, Koya-san, rather like Mount Athos in Greece, was forbidden to women. They were, however, allowed to take the forest trail skirting the eight peaks that surround the basin where the holy site lies. Now well-signposted, the complete circuit takes about 5hr 30min, but you can do just part of it and stop to contemplate the many beautiful **views**.

🚶 **Choishi-michi** – *Map, A2, off map.* Before the cable car was installed at the beginning of the 20C, this 14mi/22km trail *(7hr walk)* was the only way to get to Koya-san. It is still much used by pilgrims, especially those who have previously gone around the 88 temples on the island of Shikoku (*see p563*). Granite slabs stand every 354ft/108m to mark the path. The trail starts in the plain, at the temple of Jison-in in the village of Kudoyama, one train stop before the terminus at Koya-san. Because of the marked difference in height from bottom to top *(2297ft/700m)*, this walk is only recommended to trail-hardened hikers.

ADDRESSES

🛏 STAY
KOYA-SAN

There are no hotels in Koya-san, only **shukubo** *(temple lodgings)*, all providing Japanese-style accommodation. The comfort level may be rudimentary at times, but there's no denying the charm. Vegetarian meals, included in the price and usually served in the rooms, are the default. Reservations required. All examples below are on 🔗 **eng.shukubo. net/temple-lodging.html**; check the site

for further information, and price and booking enquiries. All half board & 🗪.

🔗🔗 **Shinno-in** 親王院 – *144 Koya-san (Map, B2).* ☎0736-56-2227. *7 rooms.* A small temple, which means you won't run into large groups in high season. A well-preserved old setting, a pleasant *o-furo*, and rooms decorated with attractive *fusuma.*

🔗🔗 **Muryoko-in** 無量光院 – *611 Koya-san (Map, B2).* ☎0736-56-2104. muryokoin. org. *25 rooms.* A friendly temple, with fairly spartan rooms. One of the monks is a French-speaking Swiss man, who will hold forth passionately about Koya-san.

🔗🔗 **Sekisho-in** 赤松院 – *571 Koya-san (Map, C2).* ☎0736-56-2734. sekishoin.jp/ koyasanguide.html. *60 rooms.* A temple much-appreciated by tourists, with lovely rooms in the old part. Those in the modern annex have private bathrooms, but less character.

🔗🔗 **Rengejo-in** 蓮華定院 – *700 Koya-san (Map, B1).* ☎0736-56-2233. *48 rooms.* The rooms of this temple have gorgeous sliding panels. The best rooms have a view of the garden, and all guests can enjoy refined cuisine. Fluent English spoken.

🔗🔗 **Ichijo-in** 一乗院 – *606 Koya-san (Map, B2).* ☎0736-56-2214. itijyoin.or.jp. *22 rooms.* This temple, gleaming with gold, serves excellent, copious meals. Rooms are comfortable and attractive. The newest—and most expensive—have bathrooms, air conditioning, and wifi.

🍴 EAT
KOYA-SAN

🍽 The **shukubo** all serve vegetarian food *(shojin ryori)*. The number of dishes varies according to the price of the room, but Koya-san also has a few restaurants.

🍴 **Miyasan** 宮さん – *401 Koya-san (Map, B2).* ☎0736-56-2827. *Open Mon–Sat 4.30–10pm. Menu in English.* 🗪. Students, monks, town employees: the whole of Koya-san rubs shoulders in this tiny, friendly *izakaya.* Great for vegetarian food, but the fried chicken is the local favorite.

🍴🍴 **Maruman** 丸万 – *778 Koya-san (Map, B2).* ☎0736-56-2049. *Open daily 9am–6pm.* 🗪. A good variety of standard Japanese dishes (sushi, *tonkatsu*, udon, curries, etc.), with quick service.

🍴🍴🍴 **Hanabishi** 花菱 – *769 Koya-san (Map, B2).* ☎0736-56-2236. hanabishi-web.jp. *Open daily 11am–6pm.* Koya-san's chicest restaurant. Refined *kaiseki* cuisine at reasonable prices, including sushi and, in winter, *yosenabe* (one-pot cooking).

Kumano Kodo ★★★
熊野古道

The Kumano Kodo is a network of pilgrimage routes that covers the whole Kii Peninsula. After Buddhism was introduced into Japan in the 6C, the Kumano region gradually absorbed the new religion—especially its ascetic practices—giving rise to an extraordinary fusion of Shintoism and Buddhism (the local deities are considered manifestations of Buddhist deities). All these beliefs juxtaposed gave birth to a universal spirituality, open to all pilgrims. The geography of the area is interpreted as a representation of the sacred cosmos, and Kumano Kodo as where the divinities reside. But more than that, it is in the sacred mountains that spirits meet. For some years, Wakayama prefecture has been actively encouraging the revival of these routes, which have been twinned with the Camino de Santiago de Compostela since 1988 and a UNESCO World Heritage Site since 2004.

- **Michelin Map,:** Regions of Japan Map 3, Regional Map p309.
- **Info:** For details on the pilgrimage routes: tb-kumano.jp/en. To reserve accommodation & for other services: www.kumano-travel.com (office next to Tanabe Station).
- **Location:** Kumano Hongu Taisha is 250mi/400km south of Kyoto. The JR Kisei line from Wakayama connects Kumano with Shirahama, Kii-Katsuura, Nachi and Shingu.
- **Kids:** Walking the pilgramage routes; Nachi waterfall; Yunomine Onsen; Shirahama Onsen.
- **Timing:** Allow a day for Shirahama and Kii-Katsuura, from where you'll leave the next morning after visiting the fish market; a day at Kumano Hongu Taisha and Yunomine Onsen; a day for the pilgrimage route and shrines of Kumano Sanzan.
- **Don't miss:** Kumano Hongu Taisha, Hayatama Taisha, Nachi Taisha and Tsubo-yu.

SIGHTS

Shirahama Onsen 白浜温泉
Regional Map, p309, A3. 15min by bus from JR Shirahama Station. Bicycle rental at the station (open daily 9am–6pm, from ¥500/day).
This well-known thermal spa, one of the three oldest in Japan *(the others being Arima Onsen and Dogo Onsen)*, is more than 1300 years old. Among its other attractions is a splendid white sandy **beach**, one of the cleanest and most pleasant in the whole of Japan. Bathing is possible from the beginning of June to the end of September.

Sakino-yu – *Open Thu–Tue: Apr–Jun & Sept 8am–6pm; Jul–Aug 7am–7pm; Oct–Mar 8am–5pm. ¥500.* This public bath 0.6mi/1km south of the beach has a delightful open-air pool at the edge of a rocky shore. Tattoos allowed.

From Shirahama Station, take the JR Kisei Line to Kii-Katsuura Station *(2hr 10min journey, ¥1520; or 1hr 20min, ¥2840).*

Kii-Katsuura 紀伊勝浦
Regional Map, p309, A3. 50mi/80km from Shirahama.
Nestling in a magnificent but unfortunately somewhat built-up bay, Kii-Katsuura is one of the principal tuna fishing ports in Japan. The **tuna market** held here every morning at dawn can hold its own against Tokyo's fish market. The

Kumano Mandalas

Painted on paper with inexpensive ink, and about 40in/100cm high and 60in/150cm wide so easy to transport, mandalas are religious visualizationtools for teaching. The Kumano Bikuni, itinerant nuns, promoted the Kumano pilgrimage with these paintings, where each object and character has a story. Historically, only the Nachi shrine possesses mandalas, dating from the 16C and 17C, but in 2007, renowned Japanese painter Tanaka Shigezo prepared mandalas for the Hongu and Hayatama shrines.

Hotel Urashima, on the island opposite the harbor, has a lovely *rotenburo* (outdoor hot-spring pool) open to visitors (*see Addresses p387*).

▶ From Kii Katsuura, take the JR Kisei Line to Nachi Station *(5min, ¥140)* or the bus from Kii-Katsuura Station to the Daimon-zaka Chushajo-mae stop *(20 min, on the hour 6am–6pm, ¥420)*.

Kumano Sanzan★★★ 熊野三山
The Shinto worship of nature is well represented by Kumano Sanzan, the three sacred shrines of **Kumano Hongu**, **Kumano Hayatama**, and **Kumano Nachi**, at the tip of the peninsula.

During the Middle Ages this region was identified with the Buddhist paradise of the Pure Land. Pilgrims flocked here along old, paved trails *(kumano kodo)* that cut through the steep mountainsides and dense forests.

Several routes converge on the shrine **Kumano Nachi Taisha**. The Nakahechi route (*see p387*), the most popular, was used by pilgrims from Kyoto, who took 30 to 40 days to complete the 497-mile (800km) round trip. The Kohechi route, linking Koya-san with Kumano Sanzan, was one of the quickest but also most difficult due to the three passes that had to be crossed at heights of 2280ft (1000m). All along the trails a concentrated network of secondary shrines, the 99 *oji*, enabled pilgrims to make offerings and perform rituals, and provided a chance to rest. Another peculiarity of the Kumano, the mounds of sutra along the way, are evidence of the devotion of those who bury these sacred texts to preserve the teachings of the Buddha for the future, to enhance their spiritual worth, or to simply help the repose of the souls of the dead.

Kumano Nachi Taisha★★
熊野那智大社
Follow the pilgrimage route, or Kumano Kotsu bus from Kii-Katsuura (30min, ¥620) or Nachi Station (20min, ¥480). Useful stops are Daimonzaka. Nachi-san

Kumano Kodo

© ziggy_mars/iStock

Nachi no Taki and the pagoda of Seiganto-ji

© CSP_sepavo/age fotostock

TRANSPORTATION

To/from Shirahama – JR Kisei Line, Ltd Express Kuroshio for Shin-Osaka *(2hr 30min journey, ¥5170)*. Transfer at Hineno from Kuroshio Ltd Express to JR semi-express Kankukaisoku for Kansai International Airport *(2hr 10min, ¥4280)*.

To/from Shingu – JR Ltd Express Wide View Nanki for Nagoya *(3hr 30min journey, ¥7000)*.

GETTING AROUND

The area is known for its hiking, but also has buses and cable cars; see information in the site descriptions.

(for the shrine) and Taki-mae *(for the waterfall)*. *Shrine ⏱ open daily 24hr, ∞no charge; treasure house ⏱open daily 8am–4pm, ∞¥300; waterfall viewing platform ⏱ open daily 7am–4.30pm, ∞¥300. kumanonachitaisha.or.jp.*

🐾●**Daimon-zaka★★★** is an old ,moss-covered paved path which winds its way uphill beneath a canopy of cedar trees, to Nachi Taisha. A detour from the path takes you to a perfect example of the natural forces that characterize the Shinto religion, the majestic waterfall **Nachi no Taki★★★**. Venerated since ancient times, it attracts ascetics who come to be purified in its icy waters. It stands out, 436ft/133m high, like a long, white veil against the dark green vegetation. From here you can head to Kumano Nachi sanctuary.

Continuing along Daimon-zaka, you'll reach **Nachi Taisha★★**. This shrine has its roots in cult worship dedicated to Hiryu Gongen, the *kami* (god) of Nachi no Taki. **Seiganto-ji**, a Buddhist pagoda lying adjacent to the shrine and its small **treasure house**, bears witness to the site's religious syncretism.

The Fire Festival

The Nachi Fire Festival, intended to purify the portable shrines that play host to the *kami* of Nachi no Taki, is held on July 14. Once night has fallen, 12 shrines, carried at top speed to the top of the waterfall, catch fire on contact with the sparks leaping from 12 torches symbolizing the 12 divinities of the shrine. An impressive fiery spectacle.

▷ Return to JR Nachi Station and take the JR Kisei line to Shingu *(20min, ¥240)*.

Kumano Hayatama Taisha★★
熊野速玉大社

15min walk from Shingu Station. ⏱Open daily 8am–5pm. ∞No charge. Shinpokan (Treasure House) ⏱open daily 9am–4pm. ∞¥500. kumanohayatama.jp.

Resplendent in vermilion, the shrine is dedicated to **Hayatama**, the Shinto god of the life force, later associated with

Yakushi Nyorai, the Buddha of Healing (see box p320). Rebuilt in 1894, it houses a large number of votive objects. To the south, a sloping flight of steps leads down to a sacred rock, **Gotobiki-iwa**, where the deities of Kumano are said to have "landed."

Kumano Hongu Heritage Center★ 世界遺産熊野本宮館
Kumano Kotsu, Nara Kotsu, and Meiko buses go to Hongu from Shingu Station (14 buses daily, 1hr 20min) and from Kii-Tanabe (10 buses daily, 2hr). Open daily 9am–5pm. No charge. www.city.tan-abe.lg.jp/hongukan/en.
Facing Kumano Hongu ·Taisha, the Kumano Hongu Heritage Center has exhibitions on the UNESCO World Heritage listed Sacred Sites and Pilgrim-age Routes in the Kii Mountains. The Wakayama World Heritage Center permanent exhibition presents Kumano mandalas—absolutely not to be missed.

Kumano Hongu Taisha★★★ 熊野本宮大社
Facing the Kumano Hongu Heritage Center. Open daily 6am–7pm. No charge. Treasure Hall open daily 10am–4pm. ¥300. hongu.jp/en.
At the top of the long staircase in the shade of cryptomeria trees can be seen the Hongu Shrine to the divinity Ketsu-miko, later equated with the Buddha Amida. In 1889, the building was carried off by a flood; hence it was moved here, west of its original location on a bank of the Kumano River, where giant *torii* stand. At the entrance to the site, are

Cedar Compasses
The giant cedars of the Kumano forest, some of which are 700 years old, are known as Ipposugi, which can be succinctly translated as "cedars whose branches all point the same way." In this case, it is south, the sacred direction of paradise and consecrated to the Buddhist god Kannon.

banners with its emblem: a crow *(yata-garasu)* whose three feet symbolize the heavens, the earth, and humanity. This shrine is over 800 years old, one of the oldest in Japan. The use of natural, unfinished materials creates harmony with the surrounding forest. Instead of nails and bolts, complex joinery fits pieces of wood together, reinforcing the impression of coherency. The beautiful arched roof is covered with cypress bark and decorated with bronzes, as well as rounded wooden blocks and crossed beams pointing skyward. Peering between chinks in the fencing reveals the sacred corridor under the pavilion's verandas, specific to the Kumano style: it was here that monks went to devote themselves to meditation, prayer, and sutras, and to commune with the divine.

Oyu no Hara 大斎原 – *10min walk from Kumano Hongu Heritage Center.* In the Oyu no Hara clearing, the original site of the Kumano Hongu Shrine, you pass through the **O-Torii★★**, an immense steel arch, at 111ft/34m high the world's tallest *torii*. Legend says the Kumano divinities came down to earth as moons in a great oak in the clearing, rendered sacred. At first only a purified space for rituals and offerings, with Buddhist influence the clearing gradually became a shrine with several pavilions. It was only after the great 1889 flood that the sacred clearing, a place of nature worship for over 2000 years, returned to its natural state. During festivals, the *torii* is lit at night, creating a magic atmosphere to bring man closer to the divinities.

A pleasant trail through woods and paddy fields *(1hr walk)* leads to the small, hot-spring village of **Yunomine Onsen**, where you can spend the night.

Yunomine Onsen 湯の峰温泉
Walk from Hongu, or bus from Kumano Hongu Taisha (15min, ¥300).
Lying in a valley, the village of Yunomine has one of Japan's most ancient hot springs, discovered 1800 years ago and linked closely to the Kumano pilgrimage. The inhabitants boil vegetables and eggs (which can be purchased in local shops) in

hot springs dedicated to cooking, known as **Yuzutsu**. A little farther on you can also bathe in UNESCO-listed **Tsubo-yu★★**, a small stone-lined pool enclosed in a small wooden structure (⏰*open daily 6am–9.30pm; 30min session, 2 people max*, 💰*¥770, reservation required*). The curative waters give pilgrims a brief moment to soothe both body and soul. There are two other public baths at Yunomine; all three accept tattoos.

Hosshinmon-oji★ 発心門王子

Ryujin bus from Yunomine Onsen (35min). ⏰*Open daily 24hr.* 💰*No charge.*
To reach the sacred space of Kumano Hongu Taisha, pilgrims must achieve various levels of spiritual awakening along the pilgrimage route. Hosshinmon-oji is one of the five principal *oji* (secondary shrine of Kumano), and the first of the physical stations marking these ritual steps in mortal reincarnation ("Hosshin" means "spiritual awakening").
🚶 From Hosshinmon-oji, a section of the **Nakahechi pilgrimage★★** route takes in panoramic mountain views and quaint village roads, vistas of terraced tea plantations and restful forest paths. After the **Fushiogami-oji** viewpoint, from which **Oyunohara Island** can be seen surrounded by mountains, the road takes you to Kumano Hongu Taisha. It's a walk not to miss, but do take a companion, and maps from the hotel or a Tourist Information Center.

EXCURSION
Mount Tamaki 玉置山

🧭*Regional Map, p309, A3. From Totsukawa Onsen, about 30min by taxi or hotel bus to the Tamaki-jinja parking lot, from where the path starts.*
☝*A guide is necessary in the mountains: ask at your hotel.*
🚶 At dawn from the top of the sacred mountain of Tamaki *(3530ft/1076m)*, clouds can be seen enveloping the **Kumano Mountains**. It is a sight worth getting up early to see at sunrise, reached by a 20min walk on paths shaded by giant cedars. Near the summit, **Tamaki-jinja★** (⏰*open daily 8am–5pm*, 💰*no charge*)

rises among thousand-year-old trees and sacred sites; a deified tree, 3000 years old, protects the shrine. Rooms are available for pilgrims wishing to spend the night near the summit.

ADDRESSES

🛏 STAY
KII-KATSUURA

🛏🍴 **Hotel Urashima** ホテル浦島 *1165-2 Katsuura.* ☎*0735-52-1011. hotelurashima.co.jp/en. ¥26,400.* 🍽*, dinner also included.* Served by shuttle, this concrete colossus has some great assets: 2 swimming pools and 6 *onsen*, including a fantastic one in a sea cave.

🛏🍴 **Hotel Nakanoshima** ホテル中の島 *1179-9 Oaza Katsuura* ☎*0735-52-1111. kb-nakanoshima.jp/en. 139 rooms. ¥50,600.* 🍽*, dinner also included.* This large, recently renovated complex occupies the entire island. Beautiful traditional rooms with balcony and view of the sea, and very good cuisine, plus Olympic pool, and superb outdoor and indoor *onsen* overlooking the sea. Can reserve *onsen* for private use.

YUNOMINE ONSEN

🛏🍴 **Ryokan Azumaya** 旅館あづまや *122 Yunomine, Hongu-cho- Tanabe.* ☎*0735-42-0012. adumaya.co.jp. From ¥32,750.* 🍽*, dinner also included.* In the heart of the Kumano forest, this *ryokan* offers traditional rooms, simple and welcoming, and excellent cuisine steamed in the *onsen*. Relax in the indoor wooden bath, or outside in a stone *onsen* among trees. The charming owner offers *bento* for eating on the pilgrimage routes.

MOUNT TAMAKI

🛏🍴 **Hotel Subaru** ホテル昴 *909-4 Hiratani, Totsukawa.* ☎*0746-64-1111. hotel-subaru.jp. ¥27,500.* 🍽*, dinner also included.* This superb hotel at the foot of the mountains has 7 indoor and outdoor *onsen*, as well as a pools fed by the same spring. An old hand-run cable car carries visitors a little way up the mountain. Refreshingly enough, the whole place is tattoo-friendly.

Osaka★★ 大阪

When greeting each other, Osakans don't say *"Konnichiwa"* but *"Mokari makka?"* (literally, "Making any money?"). Osaka has always been a city of merchants. With its harbor, and its many canals ideal for transporting goods, it was even, in the 16C, the principal trading center in Japan, and was known as "the kitchen of the nation"—hence its tradition of hospitality, zesty dialect (Osaka-ben), and wonderful food. Osakans are known for being extrovert, enterprising, and hedonistic, and generally love eating well and going out. Osaka's *mizu shobai* nighttime entertainment industry is a teeming maelstrom of neon lights, pachinko halls, karaoke joints, Ferris wheels, bars, hostess clubs, and "maids cafes"—all places to unwind from the stresses of living in Japan's second megalopolis, an urban monster full of underground shopping malls and futuristic skyscrapers. Where Kyoto and Nara are windows onto an age-old Japan, Osaka is a vibrant showcase of the latest contemporary trends.

A BIT OF HISTORY

A city of water – Osaka was founded in the 3C. The city, then called Naniwa, grew up around its port. Emperor Kotoku even made it his capital from 645 until his death in 654. Naniwa established commercial and diplomatic ties with Korea and China, and was instrumental in the spread of Buddhism in Japan, through the temple of Shitenno-ji, built in 593. The inhabitants built many canals and bridges to facilitate the transportation of goods and strengthen the city's vocation as a commercial center.

"The pantry of Japan" – Things really took off toward the end of the 16C, when the shogun Toyotomi Hideyoshi—the man who unified Japan—built his castle here. The city grew in prosperity in the 17C, when it was the hub of Japanese agricultural output, supplying rice to the new capital Edo and becoming known as

▶ **Population:** 2,709,167 (Osaka/Kobe/Kyoto: 19.3 million).

Michelin Map: Regions of Japan Map 3, Regional Map p309, Osaka maps p391, p392.

▷ **Location:** Osaka, on a bay on the Inland Sea, 25mi/40km from Kyoto and 20.5mi/33km from Kobe, is served by Kansai International Airport, located on an artificial island to the south. Te north of the city, Kita-Umeda, spreads around JR Osaka Station, the commercial heart of Osaka and an area of skyscrapers and big stores. The south, Minami, stretches from Namba Station via the Dotonbori Canal to the Shinsaibashi district, and is Osaka's nightlife district, full of restaurants and bars. Farther east is the castle area; to the southeast, the area around Tenno-ji; and finally, to the west, Osaka Bay. Note the shinkansen arrive at Shin-Osaka Station, 5min by subway north of JR Osaka Station.

Kids: Osaka Bay: the aquarium, the Ferris wheel, and Universal Studios Japan. Spa world. Homeland for White Stork.

Timing: Two days should be enough to see the main sights. Make sure you have a good map of the city, and use the subway and trams for moving around.

Don't miss: Dotonbori by night; the view from Umeda Sky Building and Abeno Harukas 300; a *bunraku* puppet show (*see p387*); Kinosaki Onsen.

Dotonbori at night

"the granary of the nation." The wealthy merchants of Osaka became patrons of literature and theater, especially Kabuki and *bunraku* (ⓒ *see p110*), the latter having been created in Osaka. In the 19C, the city specialized in textiles, the electrical industry, and manufactured products. Until the 1920s, Hanshin—the great coastal industrial area in which Osaka played the pivotal role—remained the economic engine of the country.

Tokyo's rival – A prime target for American bombs, Osaka was almost razed to the ground during World War II, then rebuilt to a modern blueprint. In 1970, it was the site of the first Universal Exposition to be held in Asia. Already the third largest commercial port in the country, Osaka's ambition to become a major player in pan-Asian trade came a step closer to fruition with the opening in 1994 of Kansai International Airport.

SIGHTS
THE NORTH (KITA-UMEDA)

The main terminus for bus, subway, and public and private train lines, this bustling urban conglomeration surrounds a vast station (ⓒ *Map I*) topped with an impressive sloping roof suspended over the tracks and platforms. The area is crammed with big stores (Daimaru, Hanshin, Hankyu, Bic Camera, Herbis Plaza), underground shopping malls (Whity Umeda, Diamor Osaka), and an endless labyrinth of footbridges and pathways. It doesn't take long for

> ### Japanese Innovation
>
> The economic capital of Kansai, a region with a Gross Domestic Product greater than that of most countries, Osaka is a place where many inventions first saw the light of day: instant noodles, prefabricated houses, automated ticket machines, moving walkways, vacuum-packed meals, Walkmans, utility knives, calculators, and many more. Several multinationals also started out in Osaka, such as Matsushita (Panasonic), Suntory, Sharp, Sanyo, and Glico. And among the celebrities born in Osaka are the two biggest stars of contemporary Japanese architecture, Tange Kenzo and Ando Tadao.

the newcomer to get lost in this huge concrete jungle, where the skyscrapers vie for space. Huddling in the shadow of these giants of glass and steel are narrow streets packed with *izakaya*, bars where you can have a quick meal at the counter. By day, Kita is the ideal place for shopping and having fun at the same time: a good example is the trendy shopping complex **Hep Five** (ⓒ *open daily 11am–9pm;* ⓒ *Map I, B1*), which has a giant whale in its atrium and an impressive 348ft/106m-high Ferris wheel on the roof.

Umeda Sky Building★ ♿Map I, A1; off map. Observatory ⏰open daily 10am–10.30pm. 🎫¥1500. www. skybldg. co.jp/en.

To the west of Hankyu Umeda station, an underground passageway leads to this futuristic building built in 1993 by the architect Hara Hiroshi. This "city in the sky" consists of twin towers joined, at a height of 568ft/173m, by a circular terrace, the **Floating Garden Observatory**, which offers a stunning 360-degree **view★★**.

The sight is especially bewitching at night, when the city is all lit up. But beware: the glass elevator that takes you up to the top is not recommended for anyone who suffers from vertigo.

Nakano-shima 中之島
♿Map 1, A2; off map.

The island of Nakano-shima, sandwiched between the Dojima and Tosabori Rivers, is home to the towers of government buildings and elegant historic constructions from the early 20C (Bank of Japan, Central Public Hall), plus several interesting museums.

Museum of Oriental Ceramics★ 東洋陶磁美術館
5min north of both Yodoyabashi and Kitahama subway stations. ⏰Open Tue–Sun 9.30am–5pm. 🎫¥500 (excluding special exhibitions). www.moco.or.jp/en. 🚻.

This museum, founded in 1982, has one of the largest collections of ceramics in the world: some 2700 rare items displayed in rotation. The highlight of the Chinese collection is the wonderful **celadon★** (pottery) from the Song dynasty (960–1279), which shimmers in the natural lighting. There are also ceramics from Korea, and, to a lesser extent, Japan.

National Museum of Art, Osaka 国立国際美術館
15min walk west of the Ceramics Museum. ⏰Open Tue–Thur & Sun 10am–5pm, Fri–Sat 10am–8pm. 🎫¥430 (excludes special exhibitions); 🎫¥250 Fri–Sat after 5pm. www.nmao.go.jp.

It is difficult not to be moved by this impressive metallic structure that, according to the Argentinian-American architect César Pelli, represents the swaying of reeds in the wind. The legacy of a gallery created during Expo '70, this underground museum exhibits a constantly renewed selection from its rich collection of 6000 Japanese and international works (engravings, sculptures, paintings, and photographs), by the likes of Picasso, Cézanne, and Foujita, and a number of postwar artists. Pieces on loan from other national art museums are included to lend the finishing touches to temporary exhibitions of great quality.

Osaka Museum of Housing 大阪くらしの今昔館
♿Map1; B1, off map. Subway Tenjinbashisuji 6-chome (exit 3). ⏰Open Wed–Mon, 10am–5pm. 🎫¥600 (excluding special exhibitions). konjyakukan.com.

Located right at the end of the interminable Tenjinbashisuji shopping arcade, on the 8th floor of a modern high-rise building, you will unexpectedly chance upon a reconstruction of a **district from the Edo period**, with private dwellings, bungalows, workshops, and bathhouses. Another room houses superb dioramas showing the evolution of housing in Osaka from the 19C to the present day (traditional merchants' areas, industrialization, post-war collective housing).

Robots and "replicants"

In a few years' time, Osaka could well look like a set from a Ridley Scott movie, filled with robots and "replicants." Increasingly involved in cutting-edge technology, the city aims to become the world robotics capital, and is investing heavily in this emerging sector. Since 2004, Robot Laboratory, which brings together a number of different companies operating in this field, has been supportive of some 20 experimental projects. Japan is a forerunner in the robotics market and Osaka has no intention of being left out.

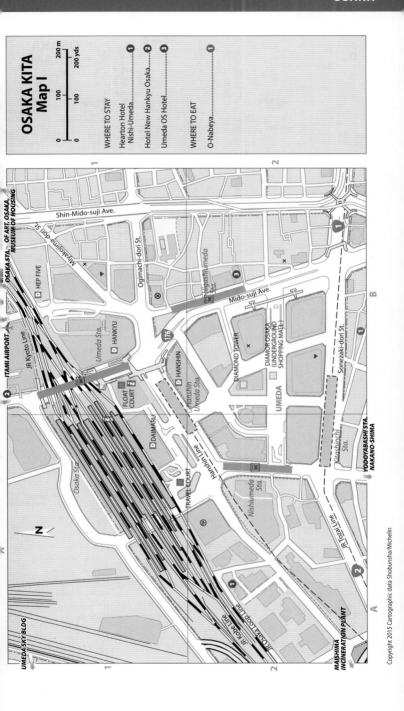

OSAKA KITA
Map I

0	100	200 m	
0	100	200 yds	

WHERE TO STAY

Hearton Hotel
Nishi-Umeda.................... ❶

Hotel New Hankyu Osaka.... ❷

Umeda OS Hotel................ ❸

WHERE TO EAT

O-Nabeya....................... ❶

Copyright 2015 Cartographic data Shobunsha/Michelin

Map labels:

UMEDA SKY BLDG.

OSAKA STA., OF ART OSAKA, MUSEUM OF HOUSING

ITAMI AIRPORT

JR Kyoto Line

Shin-Mido-suji Ave.

Miyakojima-dori St.

HEP FIVE

Ogimachi-dori St.

HANKYU

Umeda Sta.

Higashiumeda Sta.

Mido-suji Ave.

Osaka Sta.

FLOAT COURT

DAIMARU

HANSHIN

Hanshin Umeda Sta.

DIAMOND TOWER

UMEDA

DIAMOR OSAKA (UNDERGROUND SHOPPING MALL)

TRAVEL COURT

Hanshin Line

Nishiumeda Sta.

JR Tozai Line

Kitashinchi Sta.

Sonezaki-dori St.

YODOYABASHI STA., NAKANO-SHIMA

JR Kobe Line

JR Osaka Loop Line

MAISHIMA INCINERATION PLANT

N

391

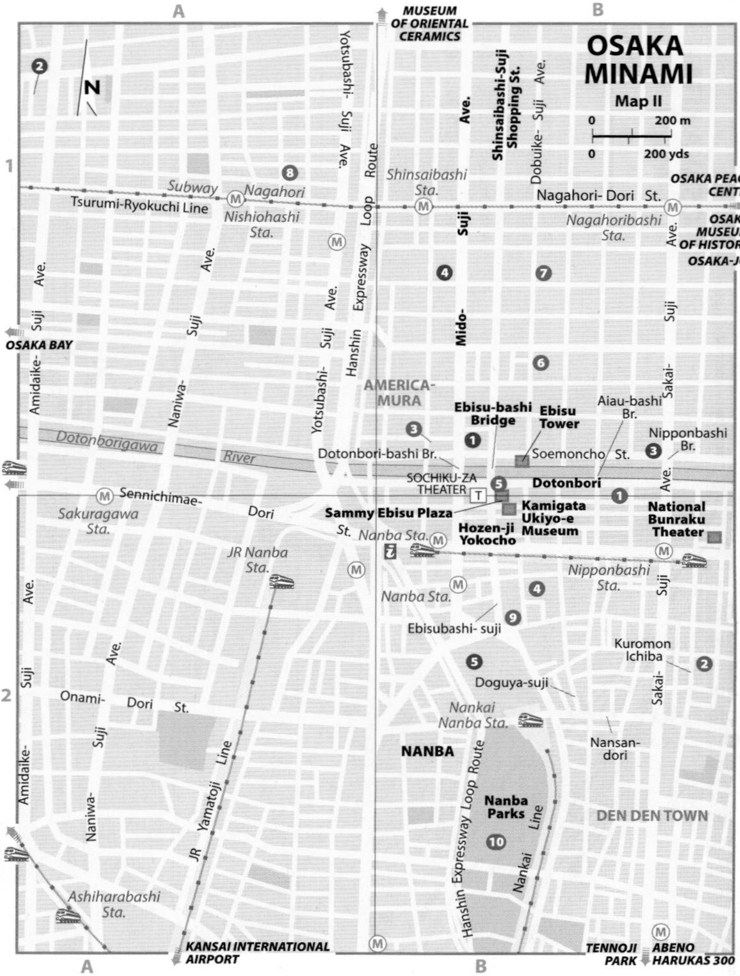

OSAKA MINAMI

Map II

0   200 m
0   200 yds

MUSEUM OF ORIENTAL CERAMICS

Yotsubashi- Suji Ave.

Shinsaibashi-Suji Shopping St.

Dobuike- Suji Ave.

② N

Subway
Tsurumi-Ryokuchi Line
Nagahori
⑧
Nishiohashi Sta.

Shinsaibashi Sta. Ⓜ

Nagahori- Dori St.

OSAKA PEACE CENTE

Nagahoribashi Sta. Ⓜ

OSAKA MUSEUM OF HISTOR

OSAKA-JO

Suji

④   ⑦

Mido-

⑥

Ave.

Suji

Yotsubashi- Suji Ave.

Hanshin Expressway Loop Route

OSAKA BAY

Amidaike- Suji Ave.

Naniwa- Ave.

Dotonborigawa   River

AMERICA-MURA

Ebisu-bashi Bridge
③
Ebisu Tower

Aiau-bashi Br.

Nipponbashi Br.

Dotonbori-bashi Br.

Soemoncho St.
③

Sakai-

Sennichimae- Ⓜ

Dori

SOCHIKU-ZA THEATER
T

Dotonbori
①

Sakuragawa Sta. Ⓜ

Sammy Ebisu Plaza

Kamigata Ukiyo-e Museum

National Bunraku Theater

St. Nanba Sta. Ⓜ

Hozen-ji Yokocho
i

JR Nanba Sta.

Ⓜ

Nanba Sta.

Nipponbashi Sta. Ⓜ

④

Ebisubashi- suji

⑨

Kuromon Ichiba

②

Onami-
Suji

Dori

St.

Amidaike- Suji

Naniwa-
Ave.

JR Yamatoji Line

⑤

Doguya-suji

Nankai Nanba Sta.

NANBA

Nankai Line

Nansan-dori

Sakai-

Ashiharabashi Sta.

Nanba Parks
⑩

Hanshin Expressway Loop Route

Nankai Line

DEN DEN TOWN

Ⓜ

KANSAI INTERNATIONAL AIRPORT

TENNOJI PARK

ABENO
HARUKAS 300

Ⓜ

Copyright 2015 Cartographic data Shobunsha/Michelin

WHERE TO STAY

Cross Hotel.. ❶
FON-SU Bed & Breakfast............................. ❷
Kaneyoshi Ryokan .... ❸
Nikko Osaka.. ❹
Swissôtel Nankai Osaka.............................. ❺

WHERE TO EAT

Chibo... ❶
Daikichi... ❷

Ganso Ajiho.. ❸
Jiyuken .... ❹
Kani Doraku... ❺
Ma-Nabeya .... ❻
Nishiya.. ❼
Vrai de Vrai/Chez Hijo................................ ❽
Watami Namba-ekimae-ten........................ ❾
Yasaiya Mei and
    Gumbo & Oyster Bar............................... ❿

Osaka skyline with the castle and its remaining structures

AROUND OSAKA CASTLE

Osaka Castle★ 大坂城

Map II; B1, off map. 15min west of Tanimachi 4-chome. Castle tower: open daily 9am–5pm, ¥600. Nishinomaru Garden: open Tue–Sun, Mar–Oct 9am–5pm, Nov–Feb 9am–4.30pm (until 9pm in cherry blossom season), ¥200–350. osakacastle.net.

Surrounded by attractive grounds planted with plum and cherry trees, the canopied roofs of Osaka Castle rise against a background of towering skyscrapers. It's a striking contrast, but somewhat deceptive, as the keep is actually a skillful concrete reconstruction from the 1930s. All that remains of the powerful fortress built by the shogun Toyotomi Hideyoshi in 1583 is the base of massive, irregular stones.

In 1997, the castle was completely renovated and an elevator installed inside. Although it may not have the appeal of Japan's oldest castles, it does—at least from the outside—give a good idea of a military structure from the feudal age, with its double ring of moats reinforced by thick granite walls. The original keep, completed in 1585, must have cut a fine figure, with its gilded beams. First destroyed in the attack led by Tokugawa Ieyasu in 1615, it was rebuilt by his heir Tokugawa Hidetada in 1620, then again destroyed by a fire in 1665, before achieving its present form in 1931.

Swords, armor, and documents relating to the life of Toyotomi Hideyoshi are on display inside. On the third floor is a replica of the gleaming Golden Tearoom, where the shogun performed the tea ceremony. The **observation post** on the eighth floor has a view all the way to Osaka Bay and the mountains.

A particularly attractive section of the grounds, **Nishinomaru Garden**, is especially popular in cherry blossom season, as it has no fewer than 600 *sakura* trees dotted around it.

Osaka Museum of History ★ 大阪歴史博物館

Map II; B1, off map. 3min north of Tanimachi 4-chome subway station. Open Wed–Thur & Sat–Mon 9.30am–5pm, Fri 9.30am– 8pm. ¥600, special exhibitions around ¥1000. www.mus-his.city.osaka.jp/eng.

Southwest of the castle grounds, in the NHK Building, this museum traces on four floors the history of the city chronologically from the 4C to the present day. The presentation is vivid (screens, reconstructions) and there are explanations in English. Maps and models help to explain the city's development amid its geographical constraints, the use of rivers, industrialisation, and so on. In the basement are the excavated foundations, some 1400 years old, of the Imperial Palace of Naniwa.

Osaka International Peace Center 大阪国際平和センター

🔊 *Map II; B1, off map. 5min west of Morinomiya subway station.* 🕐*Open Tue–Sun 9.30am–5pm.* 🎫*¥250. peace-osaka.or.jp.*

In the southeast of the castle grounds, 10 minutes' walk from the Museum of History, Osaka International Peace Center commemorates the victims of the aerial bombardment of the city during World War II, and of the atom bombs dropped on Hiroshima and Nagasaki. With its detailed displays of the horrors inflicted during the conflict, the center aims to instill in future generations a genuine desire for peace.

Expo '70 Commemorative Park 万博記念公園

🔊 *Map II, off map. Monorail to Banpaku Kinenkoen stop.* 🕐*Open daily 9.30am–5pm.* 🎫*¥260. expo70-park.jp.* About half an hour from central Osaka, this vast public park hosted the 1970 World Expo. The arresting **Tower of the Sun**, by artist Taro Okamoto, still presides over the area today. Visitors can even go inside it, and find out more in the attached museum (🎫*¥720, book in advance).* Elsewhere in the park are more museums, a Ferris wheel, the Expocity shopping mall, and several thousand cherry trees, which make it a popular *hanami* (blossom-viewing) spot in spring.

MINAMI: DOTONBORI AND NAMBA★

An entertainment district if ever there was one, Minami is a kind of Japanese Las Vegas: picturesque, noisy, and fascinating, a vast leisure and pleasure zone stretching from Namba Station in the south to the Honmachi district (north), packed with restaurants, bars, theaters, fairground attractions, and amusement arcades beneath an incredible array of neon lights, gaudy signs, and giant screens on the sides of buildings.

Around Dotonbori★★ 道頓堀

The epicenter of this visual anarchy is the pedestrian thoroughfare of **Dotonbori★★** (🔊*Map II, B1)* and its adjoining canal, where all the lights in Osaka seem to be concentrated. The area has to be seen at night, lit up by its signs: giant crabs with moving pincers, inflatable *fugu* fish, kitsch red dragons, and Glico's iconic running man. Glico, a company producing candy and cookies, has had that same sign above the bridge, **Ebisubashi** (🔊*Map II, B1),* since 1919, and it has since become one of the most famous visual landmarks in the city. Around the bridge there's a constant parade of students showing off their style, their bags and phones often covered in badges, soft toys, and other *kawaii* (cute) accessories. Here and there, you'll see *yatai* (food stands) selling an Osakan specialty: *takoyaki,* small octopus dumplings with a delectable, sweet-and-savory sauce.

Hozen-ji Yokocho★ 🔊*Map II, B2 –* South of Dotonbori, this narrow paved street, with plenty of faded charm, leads to the little temple of Hozen-ji, lit by attractive paper lanterns. It is dedicated to the goddess Mizukake ("water splashing") Fudo, whose moss-covered statue is sprinkled with water by passers-by hoping for good luck.

Kamigata Ukiyo-e Museum 🔊*Map II, B2.* 🕐*Open Tue–Sun 11am–6pm.* 🎫*¥500. kamigata.jp/kmgt/english.* This small print museum is located in a yellow house on the west side of Hozen-ji. The production of prints, linked to the Kabuki Theater, flourished in Osaka during the Edo period *(17C and 18C).* Some 30 original works are on display, and you can even try making your own *(from ¥500 for 30min).*

National Bunraku Theater★ 🔊*Map II, B2.* Traditional puppet shows, presented by Master Yoshida Minosuke III, a Living National Treasure, and his company (🔊*see Addresses/Nightlife p404).*

USEFUL INFORMATION

**Tourist Offices – Osaka Visitors'
Information Centers,** *at the airport
and stations. osaka-info.jp.*
Shin-Osaka, *3F (Map I, B1; off map).*
*℘06- 6305-3311. Open daily 8am–
10pm.*
Osaka Umeda, *north central exit
(Map I, B1). ℘06-6345-2189. Open daily
8am–5pm.*
Nankai-Namba Station, *Nankai bldg,
1F (Map II, B2). ℘06-6131-4550.Open
daily 9am–8pm.*
Osaka Station, *central concourse 1F
(Map I, A1). ℘06-6131-4550, open daily
7am–11pm.*
Kansai International Airport, ♿*see
p341. ℘072-456- 6025.*

**Guided Tours – Osaka SGG
Club,** *osakasgg.org/eng/index.html.*
English-speaking volunteer guides.
Transportation and meals extra. Apply
at least 2 weeks in advance.

Bank/Foreign Exchange – ATMs in
all post offices, including the central
post office *(see below).*
Prestia/SMBC Trust Bank, *Midosuji
Diamond Bldg, 2-1-2 Nishi-Shinsaibashi
(Map II B1). ATM 24hr.*
Sumitomo Mitsui, *Hankyu-Umeda
Station, lower ground floor (Map I B1).
Open Mon–Fri 9am–9pm, Sat–Sun
10am–5pm.* This bank exchanges most
currencies and has an international
ATM *(open daily 7am–11pm).*

Post Office/Withdrawals – **Central
Post Office,** *Osaka-Ekimae no. 1 bldg,
1-3-1 Umeda, south exit from the JR
station (Map I, A2). 24hr.* Exchange
service *(open daily 9am–6pm)* and ATM
*(open Mon–Sat 24hr, Sun midnight–
8pm).*

TRANSPORTATION

**BY PLANE – Kansai International
Airport (KIX) –** *kansai-airport.or.jp.*
Japan's second-biggest airport is
on an artificial island, 25mi/40km
southwest of Osaka. Connections to
50 cities in some 20 countries. Tourist

Information Center (TIC), exchange
bureau, and international ATM in
arrivals hall.
From Airport to Center – By train
(station on level 2F): trains to Namba
Station with Nankai Airport Line
*(Express every 15min, 45min journey,
¥930; Ltd. Express Rapid every 30min,
40min journey, ¥1450),* Tennoji with
JR Kansai Airport Line *(Express every
15min, 50min journey, ¥1060; Ltd.
Express Haruka hourly, 35min journey,
¥1740),* Osaka Station with the JR
Kansai Airport Line *(Express every
15min, 1hr 10min journey, ¥1210),* and
Shin-Osaka by JR Ltd. Express Haruka
(every 30min, 50min journey, ¥2380).
By bus: buses to Namba OCAT *(every
30min, 50min journey, ¥1100)* and Osaka
Station *(every 20min, 1hr journey, ¥1600).*
There is also a direct bus to Nara
from the airport, a train and bus link
to Kyoto, and a bus and fast boat
to Kobe. See information on these
destinations in the guide.
Itami Airport (ITM) – *www.osaka-
airport.co.jp.* Located 6mi/10km north
of Osaka, the city's second airport is
connected to some 30 Japanese cities.
**From the Airport to the Center – By
monorail and train:** Osaka Monorail
to Hotarugaike *(5min, ¥200),* then
transfer to the Hankyu Hotarugaike
Line for Umeda *(15min, ¥230).*
By bus: buses to Namba Station *(every
15min, journey time 30–40min, ¥650)*
and Shin-Osaka Station *(every 15min,
journey time 25–30min, ¥510).*
BY TRAIN – Shin-Osaka Station *(Map
I, B1; off map)* – Shinkansen to Tokyo
(2hr 30min journey, ¥13,870), Hiroshima
(1hr 25min, ¥9890), and JR Hakata in
Fukuoka *(2hr 30min, ¥14,750).*
Osaka Station *(Map I, A1)* – Trains to
Kobe *(every 10min, journey time 30min,
¥410),* Kyoto *(every 10min, journey time
30min, ¥570)* and Nara with JR lines
(every 30min, journey time 50min, ¥810).
Umeda Station *(Map I, B1)* – Trains to
Kobe-Sannomiya with the Hankyu
Line *(Ltd. Express, every 15min, journey
time 30min, ¥320),* or the Hanshin
Main Line *(Ltd. Express every 10min,*

journey time 30min, ¥320); trains to Kawaramachi in Kyoto with the Hankyu Line (every 5min, journey time 45min, ¥400).

Yodoyabashi Station (Map I, A2; off map) – Trains to Sanjo in Kyoto with the Keihan Line (Ltd.Express every 5min, journey time 50min, ¥420).

Osaka-Namba Station (Map II, A–B2) – Trains to Kintetsu-Nara with the Kintetsu Line (every 5min, journey time 40min, ¥570).

BY BUS – Umeda Terminus (Map I, B1), Abenobashi (Tenno-ji) and Namba OCAT at JR Namba (Map II, A2) – www.kousokubus.net/JpnBus/en andwillerexpress.com/en. Buses to Tokyo (8hr 30min, ¥4000/8000), Hiroshima (5hr, about ¥4000), Nagasaki (10hr 45min, about ¥8000), and many other cities.

BY BOAT – Nanko Ferry Terminal – www.osaka-ferry.net. Boats to Shikoku: Matsuyama (8hr, around ¥6000); to Kyushu: Shinmoji (12hr, around ¥7000), Beppu (12hr, around ¥12,000), Kagoshima (15hr, around ¥13,000); and to Okinawa (38hr, around ¥20,000). Cosmosquare subway; 30min journey to Umeda, ¥280, change at Honmachi.

GETTING AROUND OSAKA

BY SUBWAY – Osaka Municipal Transportation Bureau, ℰ06-6582-1400, open daily 5am–midnight approx., tickets ¥180–400 (depending on distance). Subway is best way to get around Osaka. The network has 8 lines, plus the circular JR Osaka Loop Line.

☺ **Passes** – It's worth using a prepaid card like Icoca if you're staying for a few days. The **Kansai One Pass** works the same way, but also gived foreign visitors discounts at some attractions.

Osaka Enjoy One-Day Eco Card – ¥800, Sat–Sun & public hols ¥600. Gives unlimited travel on buthe subway (but not JR trains) and buses for 1 day.

Osaka Amazing Pass – 1 day (¥2700) or 2 days (¥3600). Valid for travel on the subway, and free entry or at a reduced price to most of the city's museums and attractions. Available in Tourist Offices and subway stations.

JR Kansai Passes, Kansai Thru Pass, and **Kansai Wide Area Pass** – ☺see p37.

BY TAXI – Average trip ¥2000. ☺ Use **MK Taxi** for the lowest fares. ℰ06-6452-4441. mktaxi-japan.com.

Shinsaibashi 心斎橋

The long avenue called **Mido-suji** has wide sidewalks planted with ginkgo trees. Many of the big luxury brand names have stores here. The beautiful brick facade of the store Daimaru (look at the interior, too) draws the eye, as does the Hips building, flanked by a climbing wall. Running parallel with it to the east, the **Shinsaibashi-suji** shopping arcade (☺Map II, B1) houses a host of shops, and, in the basement, what's reputed to be the largest underground mall in western Japan: **Crysta Nagahori**.

North of this area, architecture enthusiasts should look up to see the ochre facade of the **Organic Building** (1993; two blocks west of exit 3 from Shinsaibashi subway), designed by Italian architect Gaetano Pesce. It is characterized by its pocket balconies (inspired by bamboo) where dozens of kinds of plants grow.

Amerikamura アメリカ村

☺Map II, B1.

This bohemian village full of boutiques selling new and second-hand clothes has developed over the last few decades into the district for young Osakans. Spreading out from around the triangular "square" of Mitsu park, where people congregate by the small replica Statue of Liberty, it attracts fashionistas, musicians, and designers who browse the vintage wear and unusual boutiques (Alice on Wednesday, for example) for inspiration, and relax in the restaurants, cafés, and clubs.

Shinsekai with Tsutenkaku Tower

© ferrantraite/iStock

Namba District 難波

&Map II, B2.

Thousands of commuters and customers pass through Namba's vast station and enormous Takashimaya store every day. To the south, the immense and amazing **Namba Parks** shopping center (nambaparks.com, ⏰open daily: gardens 10am–midnight; shops 11am–9pm; restaurants 11am–11pm) snakes along a canyon (whose curves and colors are reminiscent of the Siq at Petra) topped with gardens arranged in terraces. A nice example of optimal use of limited space! East of Namba Station, the covered mall **Doguya-suji** specializes in kitchen utensils and china. Knives, saucepans, tableware: there's a bit of everything here, even those wax models of dishes displayed in Japanese restaurant windows. A short distance away is **Kuromon Ichiba** (kuromon.com; &Map II, B2), the largest market in Osaka, which has been in existence for around 100 years.

There are around 660yd/600m of stands selling fruit, vegetables, fish, and other foodstuffs. To the south, the **Den Den Town** district (&Map II, B2) has a string of stores selling electronics at bargain prices, as well as shops selling colorful ornaments and figurines, and *maid cafés*, which attract the *otaku* of the city,

TENNO-JI

Built around the temple Shitenno-ji, this district has become one of the main transport hubs of this giant city.

Tennoji Park 天王寺公園

&Map II, B2; off map.

This park near Tennoji station includes a zoo, a botanical garden, and the Municipal Museum of Art. Other attractions are located nearby.

Osaka City Museum of Fine Arts 大阪市立美術館 – ⏰Open Tue–Sun 9.30am–5pm (last admission 4.30pm). ☞¥300 (excluding special exhibitions). osaka-art-museum.jp. This 1930s building houses a large collection of Japanese and Chinese artworks ranging from the 12C to the 19C, including some fine *maki-e* (gilded lacquerware). There are also temporary exhibitions.

Shitenno-ji 四天王寺 – ⏰Open Apr–Sept 8.30am–4.30pm; Oct–Mar 8.30am–4pm. ☞¥300, Treasure Hall ¥500, Garden ¥300. shitennoji.or.jp. To the northeast of the park, this temple was built in 593 by Prince Shotoku and would be the oldest in Japan if it hadn't been flattened by bombs in 1945. The reconstruction, although faithful to the original, is unfortunately made of concrete, not wood. Gokuraku-jodo Garden, dotted with teahouses and waterfalls, is designed to call to mind the Western Paradise of Amida Buddha, while the Treasure Hall holds exhibitions from its impressive collection of sacred, historic and artistic objects. Good flea market on 21 and 22 of each month.

Shinsekai 新世界 – *shinsekai.net*. The "modern world" is slightly less cutting-edge now, with some of the narrow streets and covered shoipping arcades looking distinctly old-fashioned, but they still attract tourists for their atmosphere. They surround the 338ft/103m-high **Tsutenkaku Tower** (*upper platform* ○*open daily 8.30am–9.30pm, outer deck 10am–6/8pm;* ◎*¥800, plus ¥500 for outdoor deck; tsutenkaku.co.jp;* ⌕). Built in 1956 and modeled on the Eiffel Tower, it was the symbol of the postwar reconstruction of Osaka. See also the narrow alleyway **Jan Jan Nokocho**, lined with popular eateries and clubs.

♨♨Spa-World★ スパワールド – *Subway Dobutsuen-mae.* ○*Open 10am–8.45am (following day).* ◎*¥1300, plus ¥1450 midnight–5am (children ¥1000), plus extra for certain pools and areas. spaworld. co.jp,* ⌕. Spread over six floors, this vast bathing complex attracts thousands of visitors a day. Each bath has a different theme: Roman baths, Turkish baths, Finnish saunas, Balinese spas, etc. You will also find a swimming pool with water slides, open-air baths, a gym, water sports, massage parlors, etc. Note that all tattoos are prohibited, and the rule is strictly enforced.

Abeno Harukas 300★ ハルカス300 – *abenoharukas-300.jp/en.* Opened in 2014, this slender tower now dominates the Osaka skyline. It contains a hotel, an immense shopping mall, and a number of restaurants (14th–15th floors). Two elevator journeys will take you to the 58th and 60th floors and an altitude of 985ft/300m, where there is a vast terrace (○*open daily 9am–10pm,* ◎*¥1500*) with a breathtaking **panoramic view★★★**

across the sprawling megalopolis, taking in railroad tracks and freeways, low and high-rise districts, the industrialized bay and Mount Rokko. If the weather is (very) good, you can even see Kyoto! You can stop off on the 16th floor (where you change elevators for the viewing platform) for a free view from the gardens, and for the **Art Museum** (○*open Tue–Fri 10am–8pm, Sat–Sun 10am–6pm,* ◎*varies by exhibition*) which hosts some interesting temporary exhibitions.

♨♨Osaka Bay★ 大阪湾
🔗*Map II, A1, off map.*
The ultra-modern harbor district (*Tenpozan*) has many attractions.

Tenpozan Ferris Wheel 天保山大観覧車 – ○*Open 10am–10pm.* ◎*¥800 (children 3 years and under no charge).* At a height of 368ft/112m, this is one of the largest Ferris wheels in the world. It affords a magnificent view over Osaka Bay and the coast as far as Kobe.

Universal Studios Japan ユニバーサル・スタジオ・ジャパン – *From JR Osaka Station, Yumesaki Line to Universal City Station (10min). Or, boat from Tenpozan Pier (¥600).* ○*Open daily 9am–10pm (times vary according to day and season).* Day passes from ◎*¥7600 (children 4–11 years ¥5200). usj.co.jp/e.* Modeled on its American counterpart and much-loved by Japanese families, this theme park features 17 attractions inspired by famous Hollywood blockbusters such as *Spiderman, Jaws, E.T., Jurassic Park,* and *Terminator,* as well as a plentiful supply of cafes and restaurants.

Maishima incineration plant – *Tours (in Japanese) Mon–Sat 10am, 1pm & 3pm, reservation required. osaka-env-paa.jp.* Located on the neighboring island of Maishima, this astonishing construction was designed by the Austrian architect F. Hundertwasser, and the Viennese artist's style, inspired by Klimt and Gaudí, is difficult to miss, with its colorful mosaics and gilded onion domes.

Otani River, Kinosaki Onsen
© CMYK/Shutterstock

Osaka Aquarium Kaiyukan★★

海遊館 – *Subway Osakako. www.kai-yukan.com/language/eng/.* ○ *Daily 10am-8pm and 8:30am-8:30pm some days in May, July, Aug, and Sept. See web.*◎¥2,300; ¥2,000 (over 60); ¥1,200 (under 15); ¥600 (under 6); under 3 free. An army of uniformed hostesses greets you at the entrance to this aquarium devoted to the marine life of the Pacific Ocean. In an unusual building with walls covered in "marine" mosaics, the Kaiyukan is one of the biggest and most beautiful aquariums in the world. The collection comprises some 580 marine species. The main tank measures 190,699 cubic ft /5,400 cubic m, and contains 11,000 tons of water.

The star of the show is a huge whale shark, but you will also see an incredibly large sunfish, king penguins, rays, dolphins, seals, turtles, and tropical fish. You won't forget the jellyfish or the enormous army of crabs, motionless on a sandy floor, the playful sea otters, or the ballet performed by shoals of shimmering sardines and anchovies.

EXCURSIONS

♣♣ Tezuka Osamu Manga Museum★ 手塚治虫記念館

JR (25min, ◎¥330) or Hankyu (35min, ◎¥280) lines from Osaka. ○ *Open Thur–Tue 9.30am–5pm.* ◎¥700, children ¥100–300. *tezukaosamu.net/en.* This museum

in **Takarazuka★** provides a complete overview of the works of the renowned *manga-ka* Tezuka Osamu (◔*see p97).* It also includes a library and an animation workshop that kids will love.

Kinosaki Onsen★★ 城崎温泉

⊙*Regional Map, A1. 120mi/190km northwest of Osaka. 2hr 50min journey from Osaka on JR Ltd. Express Konotori or Hamakaze (◎¥5170). Or JAL flight from Itami to Tajima airport (35min, from ¥8500) then Zentan bus (30min, ¥500).Or take a Zentan bus from Hankyu Sanban-Gai terminal (Hankyu Umeda Station Terminal Bldg North, 1st F; 5 daily, 3hr 20min, ◎¥3800).* ⓘ*Tourist Information Center "Sozoro" near the station,* ○*open daily 8.45am–6pm. visitkinosaki.com.*

To escape hectic Osaka, there's nothing better than planning a stay in this charming spa town where you can get a taste of a Japanese way of life. No less than **seven public baths** (◎*No charge for those with an overnight reservation at one of the city's ryokans; otherwise,* ◎¥600–800 *depending on the bath; map and opening times available in the Tourist Office).* All have differing architecture and atmosphere and are spread across the city center and along the Otani River, shaded by weeping willows and cherry trees. Tattoos are allowed in all seven. Entirely rebuilt after an earthquake in 1925, the city went to some trouble to

© MasaoTaira/iStock

Izushi town

preserve the traditional style that lends it considerable charm. The delights of the *onsen* are augmented with those of the table, as Kinosaki is located close to the Sea of Japan and is particularly well-known for the quality of its crabs, the *matsuba kani* (November to March).

Ropeway and Onsen-ji – *20min walk from the JR station. Cable car: ◐open daily except 2nd & 4th Thu in month, 9.10am–5.10pm. ◉¥900 round trip, or ¥560 to Onsen-ji. It is also possible to walk*

up *(approx. 40min)*. The platform at the top of Daishi-yama looks out over the city, the vast estuary of the Maruyama River, and the sea, a **view★** that is particularly beautiful in the colors of the fall. Halfway up you will find **Onsen-ji** (*◐open daily except 2nd & 4th Thu in month, 9am–4.30pm)*, a temple founded 1300 years ago by the *bonze* Douchi-Shonin who, after 1000 days of prayer, had caused water to spring forth from the rocks (on the site of the modern-day Mandara-yu), thus creating the spa

A Symbolic Bird

The Oriental stork (*Ciconia boyciana*, *kounotori* in Japanese), which originates in Siberia, is larger than its European cousin (approx. 4.5ft/1.4m long with a weight up to 11lb/5kg) and it has a black beak. The stork forms part of the identity of the Toyooka region, and for this reason their decline in numbers since the 1960s has provoked a bout of conscience-searching about the destruction of the environment. A reintroduction program has been in place since 1965 but the first birds raised could not be released into the wild until 2005. At the same time, campaigns involving the entire community were set in motion to reduce the use of pesticides in the paddy fields, re-establish wetlands, plant pine trees, etc, and to provide the storks with more favorable living conditions. Nowadays, there are around 40 of the birds living in the region and the Toyooka experiment is proving an inspiration for other cities in Japan, as well as Korea and China.

👥 To see the storks, head for the **Hyogo Park of the Oriental White Stork**: ◐*open Tue–Sun 9am–5pm, ◉no charge. By train: take the JR San'in line from Kinosaki Onsen to Toyooka (15min, ◉¥200) then a Zentan bus (Danti line,15min, ◉¥250), getting off at Kounotori no Sato park. stork.u-hyogo.ac.jp/en.*

resort. The temple boasts a number of remarkable objects, including a large statue of Kannon, 7ft/2.1m high, that is safely enclosed in a reliquary and exposed to public gaze only every 33 years, for a duration of three years (the latest being 2018–21). Fans of Buddhist statuary can round off their visit at the neighboring **Kinosaki Art Museum** (🕐open daily except 2nd & 4th Thu in month, 9am–4.30pm, ⊚¥400).

♣♂ Beaches – *For Kehi: several buses daily from the station for Mihara or Kehi, get off at Minato Chugakko (10min, ⊚¥210),or taxi around ¥1700. For Takeno: rail access via the JR San'in Line (10min, ⊚¥200), get off at Takeno Station then 15–20min walk or cycle ride from the station.* The Sea of Japan coast, which is just around the corner, is worth a detour for the beauty of the unspoilt scenery that has been incorporated into the San'in Kaigan National Park (🚶*see also Tottori p450*). There are two very pleasant beaches: **Kehi**, to the east, on the other side of the Marayama River, and **Takeno** to the west, the largest and most beautiful. The fine sand and translucent water may tempt you to a swim, but note that swimming is not advised after Aug 15 because of the jellyfish.

Izushi 出石
Take the JR San'in line from Kinosaki Onsen to Toyooka Station (15min, ⊚¥200), then a Zentan bus (30min, ⊚¥570). izushi.co.jp/en.
This "town beneath the castle" is very well-known for its *sara soba* (buckwheat noodles served cold on little porcelain plates) and has several well-preserved buildings that will allow you dive back into the atmosphere of 19C Japan.
Shinkoro – Built in 1871, this tower contains a *taiko* (drum) used for raising the alarm; it has become a symbol of the town.

Eirakukan – 🕐*Open Fri–Wed 9.30am–5pm. Tours:*⊚*¥30, Japanese but with brochure in English.* This Kabuki theater, the oldest in the region, was built in 1901 in an Edo period style and you will get to see the auditorium, the curtains, and the astonishing stage machinery in the basement, should you drop in. Performances are only held in November.

Karo-yashiki – 🕐*Open daily 9.30am–5pm.* ⊚*¥100.* The only house from the Edo era to survive the great fire that ravaged the town in 1876. Exhibition of costumes and spears used during Oshiro Matsuri on November 3.

Sakagura – Within these high adobe walls (with windows few and far between) you will find some sake breweries that are still in operation to this day.

ADDRESSES

🍴 STAY

KITA (UMEDA) AND THE CASTLE

⊜ **Shin-Osaka Youth Hostel** 新大阪ユースホステル – *Koko Plaza 10F, 1-13-13 Higashinakajima (Map I, B1; off map). Direction JR Shin-Osaka.* ✆*06-6370-5427. osaka-yha. or.jp/shin-osaka-eng. Dorms ¥3500, doubles ¥9400. ¥520⊡.* A practical choice just 5min walk from the shinkansen station, this hostel is well equipped and welcoming.

⊜ **Umeda OS Hotel** 梅田ＯＳホテル – *2-11-5 Sonezaki, Kita-ku (Map I, B2). ✆06-6362-6610. www.hankyu-hotel.com/hotel/ch/umeda. 283 rooms. ¥8860. ¥1100⊡. MasterCard not accepted.* A luxurious hotel for the price, in a big concrete tower in the south of Umeda. Comfortable, soundproofed rooms (some of them non-smoking) with good facilities.

⊜⊜ **Hearton Hotel Nishi-Umeda** ハートンホテル西梅田 – *3-3-55 Umeda, Kita-ku (Map I, A2). ✆06-6342-1111. hearton. co.jp/hotel/nishi-umeda. 471 rooms. ¥11,550. ¥1320⊡.* This large building near JR Osaka Station houses a clean, modern hotel with efficient service. The soundproofed rooms are cozy, and most overlook the rail tracks.

⊜⊜ **Hotel New Hankyu Osaka** 新阪急ホテル – *1-1-35 Shibata, Kita-ku (Map I, B1). ✆06-6372-5101. hankyu-hotel.com/ hotel/hh/osakashh. 961 rooms. ¥16,500. ¥1980 ⊡.* This huge, top-class hotel, directly connected with Osaka-Umeda station, has spacious, quiet rooms with all modern conveniences, as well as shops, bars, and restaurants. Airport shuttle from the main entrance.

🛏🍴 **Nine Hours Shin-Osaka** ナインアワーズ新大阪 – *1-19-9 Higashinakajima (Map I, B1; off map). Direction JR Shin-Osaka. ☎06-6195-9509. ninehours.co.jp/shin-osaka-station. ¥4900 per person. ¥500☕.* An excellent, design-led capsule hotel right opposite the shinkansen station. Staff are very friendly, pods are comfortable (though bring ear plugs just in case), and the communal areas are modern and attractive. Good discounts through the website if you book well ahead

MINAMI (NAMBA, DOTONBORI)

🛏 **FON-SU Bed & Breakfast** フォンス―ベド&ブレックファスト – *3-11-20 Shinmachi (Map II, A1). ☎06-6556-6586. fonsubedbreakfast.business.site. Dorms ¥3900, doubles ¥9000. ¥600☕.* A charming hostel, with a good variety of rooms (both Japanese and Western private rooms) and well-kept communal areas (retro 1950s/60s design). The excellent dorms are so spacious they're more like small, semi-private rooms.

🛏🍴 **Carpe Diem** カルペ・ディエム – *3-2-14 Nakahama, Joto-ku (Map II, B1 off map). ☎06-6961-0444. carpediem-osaka.jp. 4 rooms. ¥21,000 (price reduces from 2nd night).* 🍴. Located east of the castle, this lovely residence has three pavilions in a magnificent garden. The first has a loft room with traditional Japanese bath. The second can be booked as 2 en-suite rooms, separated by paper sliding doors, or 1 large room. The last *(the "tea ceremony room")* has 1 bedroom and a living room. Also offers cultural events such as soba making and calligraphy.

🛏🍴 **Cross Hotel** クロスホテル大阪 – *2-5-15, Shinsaibashi (Map II, B1). ☎06-6213-8281. crosshotel.com/osaka. 229 rooms. ¥25,500. ¥2970☕.* Situated between Dotonbori, Namba, and Amerikamura, the Cross is in the heart of the action. Decorated in browns and reds with little design touches, efficient bilingual staff, and large Western rooms and Japanese bathrooms, this is an excellent hotel.

🛏🍴 **Hotel Nikko Osaka** ホテル日航大阪 – *1-3-3 Nishi-Shinsaibashi (Map II, B1). ☎06-6244-1111. hno.co.jp/english. 635 rooms. ¥23,500. ¥1200☕.* Reliably good in the downtown area, located in an imposing 32-story tower near Shinsaibashi subway station. A vast, elegant lobby,

English-speaking staff who will attend to your every need, and immaculately clean rooms with contemporary decor in warm colors. Swimming pool, sauna, bars, restaurants, and airport shuttle.

🛏🍴 **Kaneyoshi Ryokan** かねよし旅館 – *3-12 Soemon-cho (Map II, B1). ☎06-6211-6337. kaneyosi.jp. 15 rooms. ¥20,900. ¥1650☕.* This friendly, modern *ryokan*, ideally located beside Dotonbori Canal, has clean, bright, spacious rooms.

🛏🍴 **Swissôtel Nankai Osaka** スイスホテル南海大阪 – *5-1-60 Namba, Chuo-ku. ☎06-6646-1111. swissotel.com/hotels/nankai-osaka. 546 rooms. ¥35,000. ¥3650☕.* In the heart of the Namba district, this luxurious hotel offers rooms with an impressive view of the city, and use of a superb Olympic pool.

TENNO-JI/NAGAI

🛏🍴 **Marriott Miyako Hotel** 大阪マリオット都ホテル – *1-1-43 Abeno-suji (Map II, B2 off map). ☎06-6628-6111. marriott.com/hotels/travel/osamc-osaka-marriott-miyako-hotel. 360 rooms. ¥40,850. ¥3600☕.* A reasonably new hotel, the Marriot occupies the upper floors of the Abeno Harukas Tower. Very comfortable, with impeccable service, and a stunning view over Osaka from your bed!

KINOSAKI ONSEN

ℹ️ The town has an efficient information and reservation system available in English, via *kinosaki-web.com/en*, or in person in the office opposite the station *(open daily 9am–5pm, ☎0796-29-4188)*. Free shuttles offer transfer to ryokan and hotels from the station. Cycle rental is available *(around ¥400/2hr, ¥800/day)*. During the crab season *(Nov–Mar)* tariffs tend to be higher.

🛏🍴 **Yamamotoya** 山本屋 – *643 Yushima, Toyooka. ☎0796-32-2114. yamamotoya.kinosaki.com. 20 rooms. ¥20,500. ¥2160☕.* A well-maintained *ryokan* in a good location on the main street, not far from the Ichi no yu baths.

🛏🍴 **Nishimuraya Honkan** 西村屋本館 – *469 Yushima. ☎0796-32-2211. nishimuraya.ne.jp/honkan. 34 rooms. ¥200,500. ☕, dinner also included.* This famously luxurious *ryokan* has been welcoming guests for 150 years. Very elegant decoration, exceptional service, private garden, *onsen*, and fine cuisine.

☕️/EAT

Osaka is a food lover's paradise. The choice is incredibly varied and almost never disappointing. The city's (informal) motto: eat 'til you drop!

KITA (UMEDA) AND THE CASTLE

🍽 **O-Nabeya** 大鍋や – *1-9-24 Sonezaki-shinchi, Kita-ku (Map I, B2). ☎06-4796-3225. o-nabeya.com. Open Mon–Fri 5pm–5am, Sat 5pm–midnight, public hols 5–11pm (last orders 1hr before closing).* A friendly restaurant specializing in *oden* (eggs, vegetables, and fishcakes in broth) and *kushikatsu* (meat coated in breadcrumbs and deep-fried on skewers).

🍽 **Kiji** きじ – *Umeda Sky Bldg B1F, 1-1-90 Oyodonaka (Map I, A1; off map). ☎06-6440-5970. osietesite.com/gourmet/ osaka/osakawasyoku/kiji. Open Fri–Wed 11.30am–9.30pm. From ¥730.* Some of Osaka's best *okonomiyaki* is served in this small restaurant in the Sky Building's Showa-style "entertainment district." Look for the green walls outside, and business cards on every surface inside; the long line is also a clue. The owner is a dab hand at calligraphy, and often gives customers a handwritten memento of their visit.

🍽🍽🍽 **Umeda To-ka** 梅田燈火 – *2-5-28 Sonezaki-shinchi, Kita-ku (Map I, A2). ☎06-6345-8118. opefac.com/store/umeda_toka. Mon–Sun noon–3.30pm & 5–11.30pm, Sun & public hols noon–3.30pm & 5–10.30pm. Lunch around ¥3500, dinner ¥5500.* A restaurant with contemporary decor and creative Japanese cuisine. Dishes such as sea bream with sake or lotus root, shrimp with taro, langoustine croquettes, etc.

MINAMI (NAMBA, DOTONBORI)

🍽 **Kuromon Market** 黒門市場 – *(Map II, B1).* A few minutes' walk from Namba Station, ideal for a lunch on the hoof. The stalls selling tempura or sashimi will soon give you an appetite. The food at **Daikichi** (大吉, *☎06-6643-2678, kuromon. com/jp/daikichi, Mon–Sat 8.30am–4pm)* is based on *dashi* broth, with soba, udon, and duck. A limited choice, but tasty dishes, and not expensive.

🍽 **Ganso Ajiho** 元祖・味穂 – *2-8-33 Nishi-shinsaibashi (Map II, B1). ☎06-6213-8806. Open Tue–Sun 6pm–2am. Lunch around ¥500, dinner ¥1000.* At the corner of a street in Amerikamura, this fried food spot is very popular with the young people who fill the boutiques. Warming classics like *takoyaki, okonomiyaki, shabu shabu, oden,* and *yakisoba,*.

🍽 **Jiyuken** 自由軒 – *3-3-134 Namba. (Map II, B2). ☎06-6631-5564. jiyuken. co.jp. Open Tue–Sun 11.30am–9pm. From ¥770.* 🖐 This restaurant in the Namba Center shopping mall south of Dotonbori is famous for its curried rice. Try the *meibutsu curry,* a dish of saffron-flavored rice with beef and onions.

🍽🍽 The commercial center of Namba Park has several interesting restaurants on the 6th floor, such as **Yasaiya Mei** *(Map II, B2, ☎06-6636-2240. eat-walk.com/nanba. Open daily 11am–11pm. ¥1500/4500),* where, in a modern setting, you can taste some excellent cuisine based on fresh and seasonal vegetables. The staff are amiable and efficient. Opposite is **Gumbo & Oyster Bar** – *(Map II, B2, ☎06-6644-3627. oysterbar.co.jp. Open daily 11am–11pm. ¥1500/4500),* with a wide range of dishes based on oysters: natural, in soup, in croquettes, salads, grilled, etc.

🍽🍽 **Chibo** 千房道頓堀店 – *1-5-5 Dotonbori (Map II, B1/2). ☎06-6212-2211. chibo.com. Open Mon–Sat 11am–1am, Sun & public hols 11am–midnight. Menu in English. ¥1,500/3,900.* The specialty of this five-story restaurant is one of Osaka's most popular: *okonomiyaki.* On the top floor is "President Chibo," a slightly more upmarket steakhouse.

🍽🍽 **Nishiya** にし屋 – *1-18-18 Higashi-Shinsaibashi (Map II, B1). ☎06-6241-9221. nishiya-shinsaibashi.com. Open Mon–Sat 11am–11pm, Sun & public hols 11am–10pm. ¥1500/6000.* Built of wood, like the old *sukiya*-style tea houses, this restaurant specializes in udon. Try the *kitsune udon,* noodles served in a light broth, with slightly sweet fried tofu on top.

🍽🍽🍽 **Ma-Nabeya** ＭＡ～なべや – *Fuku Bldg Shinsaibashi 4F, 2-8-26 Higashi-Shinsaibashi (Map II, B1). ☎06-6212-4130. ksnetwork.com/chain/nabeya/osaka. Open daily 5pm–midnight. Tabehodai from ¥3390.* A stylish restaurant with good *tabehodai* (all-you-can-eat, for a fixed price) deals: eat as much as you like for 1hr 30min. Feast on beef *shabu-shabu* or *sukiyaki.*

🍽🍽🍽 **Kani Doraku** かに道楽本店 – *1-6-18 Dotonbori (Map II, B1). ☎06-6211-8975. douraku.co.jp/kansai/honten. Open daily 11am–11pm (last entry 10pm). Set lunch from ¥2970, dinner 5500.* This restaurant in the pedestrian section of Dotonbori is easily identified by the giant crab on the front. Crab is the house specialty, caught in the cold waters of

Tenjin Matsuri

© HunterKitty/iStock

Hokkaido, and cooked in sushi, *nabe*, tempura, and various inventive ways.

🍴🍴🍴 **Vrai de Vrai/Chez Hiro** ヴレ・ド・ヴレ／シェ・ヒロ – *1-24-8 Shinmachi, Nishi-ku (Map II, A1).* ☎*06-6535-7807. Open Tue–Sun 11.30am–3pm & 6–11pm. Around ¥3500/¥8500.* French cuisine by Japanese chef Hiro. Excellent beef stew. Eat inside, in an intimate setting, or on the little terrace lined with olive trees.

TENNO-JI

🍴🍴 **Sora** 空 – *1-10 Shimo Ajihara-cho, Tennoji-ku (Map II, B1, off map).* ☎*06-6773-1300. yakinikusora.jp. Open Mon & Wed–Fri 5–11pm, Sat–Sun & public hols 4–11pm). ¥1500/4000.* One of the best Korean restaurants in Osaka, in the heart of Tsuruhashi's maze of little streets. Good choice of grills, with *kimchi* (spicy pickled cabbage).

🍴🍴 **Zuboraya** づぼらや新世界本店 – *2-5-5 Ebisu-higashi, Naniwa-ku (Map II, B2; off map).* ☎*06-6633-5529. zuboraya. co.jp/shop01.html. Open daily 11am–11pm (last orders 10.30pm). Menu in English. Set menus ¥2000/4000.* On corner of the street by Tsutenkaku Tower; look for the giant *fugu*-shaped lanterns outside. *Fugu*, a white fish that can release a deadly poison if prepared incorrectly, is the house specialty, served as sushi, sashimi, fritters, croquettes, and so on.

IZUSHI

🍴 **Jinbe** 甚兵衛 *14-16 Kobito, Izushi-cho, Toyooka.* ☎*0796-52-2185. www.jinbe.com/ en. Open Thu–Tue 11am–6pm. ¥165 per plate, sides ¥200.* Taste the town specialty seated on *tatami* mats: cold, refreshing *izushi sara soba*, with dipping sauce and sides. Traditionally the noodles are served on five small porcelain plates, but you can have as many or few as you'd like; if you manage 17 you'll even get a small prize.

NIGHTLIFE

Minami is the epicenter of Osaka's nightlife, with hundreds of bars and clubs on Dotonbori, and in Shinsaibashi and Amerikamura. The buzz is incredible

Bars – Billboard Live ビルボードライブ – *Herbis Plaza Ent B2F, 2-2-22 Umeda (Map I, A2).* ☎*06-6342-7722. billboard-live. com. Open daily; hours vary deending on performance.* An institution in Osaka, with the greatest names in jazz, soul, funk, and world music.

Bears ベアーズ – *Shin-Nihon Namba Bldg B1F, 3-14-5 Namba-naka (Map II, B2).* ☎*06-6649-5564. namba-bears.main.jp. Open daily around 6.30–10pm.* One of the top local spots for live music, especially rock.

Theater– National Bunraku Theater 国立文楽劇場 – *1-12-10 Nipponbashi (Map II, B2).* ☎*06-6212-2531. www.ntj.jac. go.jp. Open Jan, Apr, end Jul–beg Aug & Nov; shows daily 11am & 4pm. Bunraku,* or Japanese puppet theater, was created in Osaka at the end of the 17C. This theater, built in 1984, presents shows for 3-week periods four times a year. English audioguide available (from ¥500).

EVENTS

Tenjin Matsuri 天神祭 *(Jul 24–25)*: Osaka's most spectacular festival, including a procession to Tenman-gu shrine, a night parade of boats on the Okawa River, and a closing fireworks display.

Kobe★
神戸

From the Chinese quarter, little Nankin, the aromas of Peking duck and *dim sum* fill the air. Old-fashioned street lamps and a large Bavarian-style house with a weathervane on top rub shoulders with a synagogue, a mosque, and a Jain temple in the European district. With its fine houses perched on hills overlooking the sea, Kobe—like Yokohama and Nagasaki—is a port with a strongly international, cosmopolitan feel. The city had links with China a thousand years ago, and was one of the first to open up to the West at the beginning of the Meiji era. American and European merchants and sailors imported their own culture and customs: fashion, jazz, movies, steaks (the famous Kobe beef), and pastries. Hit by a terrible earthquake in 1995, Kobe has risen from the ashes, a modern city gradually reclaiming land from the sea. Heavily built-up as it is, it's still a pleasant city to walk around in, and at night, when its lights are reflected in the bay, the view is picture-postcard romantic. Last, but by no means least, a visit to Kobe is highly recommended thanks to the proximity of the finest castle in Japan: Himeji Castle.

BACKGROUND

A cosmopolitan flavor – The name Kobe is said to derive from Kamibe, "guardians of the gods," after the Ikuta-jinja shrine, founded in the year 201. As early as the Nara period, the city had links with China. Thanks to its trading connections, the port grew, adopting the name Hyogo in the 13C. In 1868, at the beginning of the Meiji era, Kobe was one of the first five ports authorized to trade with the outside world, bringing Japan's two centuries of isolation to an end. Many Westerners settled in Kobe, first near the harbor, then in the Kitano district, where they built sumptuous

▶ **Population:** 1,525,000 (Metropolitan Area: 2,420,000) – Hyogo Prefecture.

Michelin Map: Regions of Japan Map 3, Regional map p309, Kobe Map p408.

▷ **Location:** Kobe extends along a narrow coastal strip, 20.5mi/33km from Osaka and 46.5mi/75km from Kyoto, between the peaks of Maya and Rokko. A large thoroughfare, Flower Road, crosses the city from Shin-Kobe station (where the shinkansen arrives), to the harbor in the north. The liveliest area is around Sannomiya, the main station, where local JR trains arrive. Pedestrian malls lead to the Chinese quarter of Nankin-machi and the business area around the Old Foreign Settlement. North of the railway is the European quarter of Kitano. It's easy to get around Kobe on foot, and there are plenty of street signs in Roman letters.

Kids: Maritime Museum; Tetsujin 28 robot; Suma Beach.

Timing: Allow a day in Kobe, then a half day visit to Himeji. The Kobe City Loop Bus is very practical.

Don't miss: the view from Kitano, or Mount Rokko and Mount Maya. A walk on Akashi Bridge.

residences. It was this period that gave Kobe its cosmopolitan flavor, and its reputation as an economic powerhouse—the reason why it was heavily bombed at the end of World War II.

A city reborn – Devastated by the Kobe earthquake of January 17, 1995

Kobe port with Port Tower

© Sean Pavone/iStock

(🔊 *see box p407*), the city was fairly quickly rebuilt and recovered much of its economic dynamism. The fourth-largest merchant port in Japan, it has a major industrial park built on land reclaimed from the bay *(more than 2470 acres/1000ha)*, as well as a large foreign population, numbering around 42,000. In addition, many foreign multinationals, such as Nestlé and Procter & Gamble, have their Japanese headquarters in Kobe. Expatriates enjoy the city for its relaxed pace, nightlife (including jazz clubs), hot springs (Arima Onsen), and twice-yearly fashion shows (the Kobe Collection).

SIGHTS

THE CENTER AND THE BAY
The area around Sannomiya Station *(Map, B1)* and Motomachi station *(Map, B2)* is where the big stores and shopping arcades can be found. As you descend toward the harbor, you come to the **Old Foreign Settlement** (Kyu Kyoryuchi; *Map, B2*), between Flower Road and Meriken Road ("street of Americans"). This is where foreigners lived before they settled on the Kitano hills farther

---

Foreigners in Kobe

Approximately 42,000 foreigners live in Kobe, from over 100 different countries. The five largest communities are Koreans (around 22,200), Chinese (13,200), Vietnamese (6000), Taiwanese (1300) and Americans (1300).

---

north. The district is dotted with Western-style buildings from the end of the 19C and the beginning of the 20C, such as the former American consulate (1880), now a cafe. The pavements are wide and tree-lined, and the street lamps may remind you of North American cities.

Kobe City Museum★★
神戸市立美術館
🔊 *Map, B2.* 🕐 *Open Tue–Fri & Sun 10am–5pm, Sat 10am–9pm.* 💴 *¥300 (excluding special exhibitions), 1F only ◎no charge. kobecitymuseum.jp.* 💻.
Housed in a former bank (1935) in neo-Classical style with Doric columns, and extensively renovated in 2019, the City Museum showcases cultural exchanges between Asia and the West. It also evokes the small changes in daily life that occurred with the arrival of things like street lighting, European furniture, and even new hairstyles at the end of the 19C.
One of the highlights of its collections is the rare series of **Nanban paintings★★** from the 16C and 17C. These works, on screens and scrolls, are inspired by the European Renaissance art introduced by the missionaries. Some vividly depict the arrival of Portuguese ships (the word *nanban* means "southern barbarians"). Unfortunately, they are so fragile that they can only be displayed for 40 days a year *(end Jul–early Sept)*. For the rest of the time, visitors have to be content with facsimiles, and the other rooms showcasing the archeology and history of Kobe (an interesting model of the Old Foreign Settlement). Models and town

plans help to evaluate the urban boom that the port city has undergone.

Cosmic Elements Waterfall & Earthquake Memorial
慰霊と復興のモニュメント

In Higashi Yuenchi Park behind City Hall. Set in a landscaped area of red brick and green trees, the water tumbles down a black granite construction. Beneath the waterfall is an underground section, the walls of which are inscribed in gold with the names of the 6434 victims of the 1995 earthquake.

Nankin-machi (Chinatown)
南京町

 Map, A–B2.

On the other side of Meriken Road, a big gate adorned with dragons marks the entrance to Kobe's Chinatown. It's difficult to miss the roads saturated with red and golden dragons. More modest in size than the Chinatowns of Yokohama or Nagasaki, it is a small but teeming enclave of a few streets. A host of restaurants vie for your attention, with brightly colored signs, the shouting of touts, and the enticing smells of cooking. This is a pleasant area to stroll in at night, when the shops are all lit up.

Soraku-en 相楽園

 Map, A1. Nakayamade-dori . 078-351-5155. Open Fri–Wed 9am–5pm. ¥300. sorakuen.com.

Now owned by the city of Kobe, this Japanese garden has been established since 1885. Stand in this calm oasis, ringed by tall buildings, and wonder at the immense trunk of a camphor tree, several centuries old, and feel the spines on the leaves of a forest of sago palms. The paths are flooded with color in April and May, when the azaleas bloom across the garden.

Around the port

 Map, A–B2.

The seafront of central Kobe is a nice walk, taking you from museum quays to giant shopping malls. Leisure pursuits, shopping, and culture are on the agenda, to be enjoyed from beautiful

panoramic vantage points, looking out across the city.

Meriken Park – Map, B2. kobe-meriken.or.jp. Meriken Road leads to the wharf, where foreign ships once unloaded their cargo. On the east side of the park, part of the wharf hit by the 1995 earthquake has been deliberately left in a damaged state: the only trace of the earthquake still visible today.

 Kobe Maritime Museum – Map, B2. Open Tue–Sun 10am–5pm. ¥600 (or ¥1000 with the Port Tower). kobe-maritime-museum.com. The roof of this modern building, made of steel tubes, is designed to resemble the slender prow of a ship. The museum's collections follow the maritime history of Kobe. They include some interesting model ships, among them a 29.5ft/9m replica of *HMS Rodney*, the flagship that led the first Western flotilla into Kobe harbor in

The Kobe Earthquake

On January 17, 1995, at 5.46am, an earthquake of magnitude 7.2 shook the Kobe region. The hypocenter in fact lay near the harbor, along a fault line that crosses the strait between Awaji Island and Kobe.

The shocks, which were remarkable for involving an exceptional degree of vertical movement *(up to 3.3ft/1m in places)*, brought buildings down like houses of cards. A mere 20 seconds were enough to leave over 6000 people dead, tens of thousands wounded, and 100 billion dollars' worth of damage. The much-criticized late arrival of the Emergency Services forced the panic-stricken inhabitants to mount the rescue operation themselves with whatever was to hand. This disaster was a trauma for the whole nation, shattering the myth of Japan's preparedness for earthquakes, and led to changes which had a huge impact on readiness for and response time to future disasters.

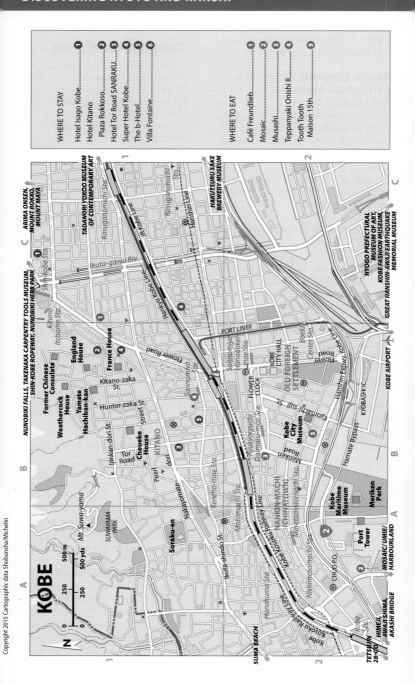

WHERE TO STAY

Hotel Isago Kobe........ ①
Hotel Kitano............... ②
Plaza Rokkoso............ ③
Hotel Tor Road SANRAKU... ④
Super Hotel Kobe........ ⑤
The b-Hotel................ ⑥
Villa Fontaine.............

WHERE TO EAT

Café Freundlieb......... ①
Mosaic........................ ②
Musashi...................... ③
Teppanyaki Onishi II... ④
Tooth Tooth
Maison 15th............... ⑤

KOBE

Copyright 2015 Cartographic data Shobunsha/Michelin

Weathercock House and the view over the city of Kobe

© LeeYiuTung/iStock

1868, and a scale model, adorned with precious stones, of the *Oshoro Maru*, one of the first Japanese sailing ships.

The museum also houses **Kawasaki Good Times World**, a high-tech interactive space run by the Kawasaki company, manufacturer of motorcycles, ships, trains, and aircraft, which started in Kobe. Among many other attractions is the flight simulator, giving visitors the experience of piloting a helicopter.

Port Tower – *Map, A2. Open daily: Mar–Nov 9am–9pm; Dec–Feb 9am–7pm. ¥700 (¥1000 with Maritime Museum).* An amazing structure in latticed steel, the Port Tower is a dramatic sight when lit up at night. Built in 1963, it soon became the symbol of the town. From the top (354ft/108m), there is a 360-degree panoramic view of the bay, with Mount Rokko in the background.

Mosaic/Umie – *Map, A2; off map.* Anchored like an immense ship and sign-posted with a giant wheel, this complex of stores and restaurants (*see Addresses p416*) draws the crowds at the weekend and is the best seat in the house to watch the sun go down, lighting up the buildings along the bay. **Harbourland**, just round the corner, is flanked by even more shopping malls, past which you can walk all the way to Kobe station.

KITANO AND THE HEIGHTS

KITANO DISTRICT★ 北野
Map, B1/2. Kitano-cho Plaza, open daily Mar–Oct 9am–6pm; Nov–Feb 9am–5pm.

From 1887, foreigners began to abandon the concession near Kobe harbor and settle in this hilly neighborhood,

Legendary beef

The pampered Kobe cattle are regularly massaged, listen to Mozart, and (rumour has it) even have beer added to their water. The result is an exceptional marbled beef, soft as butter, which melts in the mouth. The meat contains a higher than normal percentage of unsaturated fat, which is distributed in, rather than around, the muscle, creating the marbling. However, the prices are astronomical. In theory, the label "Kobe beef" is exclusive to a single breed of cattle *(wagyu)* raised locally. In reality, the cows are often raised elsewhere (Kyushu, California, or Australia, for example) before being sent to Kobe for slaughter. Only Matsusaka beef comes anywhere close to matching the quality of Kobe.

somewhat reminiscent of San Francisco. Kitano is a microcosm of Kobe's cosmopolitan heritage; there are some 30 *ijinkan* (houses of European merchants), a dozen of which are open to visitors, Catholic and Protestant churches, European cafés, a mosque, a synagogue, and even a Jain temple. All this foreign flavor brings in crowds of domestic tourists, and young married couples in search of a romantic spot to immortalize their union.

🕭A number of the *ijinkan* can be visited with the Ijinkan Group Ticket *(from ☜¥1400; kobe-ijinkan.net/en)*.

#Weathercock House – 🕭*Map, B1.* 🕙*Open* daily *9am–6pm.* ☜*¥500 (¥650 with Moegi House, next door). kobe-kaza-midori.com.* Built by a wealthy German merchant in 1909, this brick residence is best-known for the weathervane on its roof. It must be said that the interior is only moderately interesting, a patchwork of Biedermeier furniture and Art Nouveau decoration with a few mock-Gothic touches.

Yamate Hachiban-kan★ – 🕭*Map, B1.* 🕙*Open daily: Apr–Sept 9.30am–6pm; Oct–Mar 9.30am–5pm.* ☜*¥550.* A curious cross between a Tudor mansion and a Japanese pagoda, this residence houses several bronzes by Rodin, Bourdelle, and Renoir, and a few fine Buddhas from Thailand and Gandhara.

France House★ – 🕭*Map, B1.* 🕙*Open daily: Apr–Sept 9.30am–6pm; Oct–Mar 9.30am–5pm.* ☜*¥550.* Built in 1904, this elaborately decorated house originally contained apartments for foreigners. You can see some beautiful examples of Lalique glassware, and a set of handsome Louis Vuitton steamer trunks.

If you're in the mood, you can also visit English, Danish, Dutch, and Austrian houses, the former Chinese and Panamanian consulates (the latter now a trick art museum), and so on.

Nunobiki Herb Park
布引ハーブ園

🕭*Map, C1; off map. Access by the Shin-Kobe Ropeway, from just behind the Shin-Kobe Oriental City building.*

🕙*Open mid-Mar–mid-Jul Mon–Fri 10am–5pm, mid-July–Aug daily 10am–8.30pm, Sept–Nov Sat–Sun & public hols 10am–8.30pm, Dec–mid-Mar daily 10am–5pm.* ☜*¥1500 with ropeway (round trip), or ¥900 after 5pm. kobeherb.com/en.*

This herb garden on Mount Rokko *(altitude 131ft/400m),* to the north of Kitano, is mainly of interest for the **view★**. It's especially stunning at night, when the whole vast Kobe-Osaka conurbation is spread out below like a carpet of light.

Nunobiki Falls ★ 布引の滝

🕭*Map, C1; off map. Access road behind Shin-Kobe JR shinkansen station.*

These beautiful 140ft/43m falls are made up of four cascades and have provided inspiration for poets and writers for many years, as commemorated by the stone pillars marking out the path. Climb the steps that have been cut into the rock for around 45min to be rewarded with a spectacular view across the sea and the city of Kobe.

Takenaka Carpentry Tools Museum ★★ 竹中大工道具館

🕭*Map, CI; off map. 7-5-1 Kumochi-cho Chuo-ku. JR Shin-Kobe Station (shinkansen and subway), central exit, then 2min walk. Or City Loop Bus to 12 Shin-Kobe Station stop, or Kobe City Bus (lines no. 2 & 18) to Kumochi 6-chome stop, then 3min walk.* 🕙*Open Tue–Sun 9.30am–4.30pm.* ☜*¥500. dougukan.jp.*

This arts and traditional woodcraft museum is housed in a pleasant contemporary building made of wood and glass that blends well with the greenery surrounding it. The displays are based on three topics: the history of woodworking, the invention of woodworking techniques, and the teaching of carpentry skills. Discover everything there is to know about carpentry, from joinery tools to prehistoric Jomon stone axes and modern Western tools, as well as traditional carpentry techniques, the skills of master artisans, and the different timbers used in construction.

USEFUL INFORMATION

Tourist Office – At the main (east) exit of Sannomiya station *(Map, B1). Open daily 9am–7pm. ℘078-322-0220. feel-kobe.jp.* Additional offices at Shin-Kobe and Kitano stations.

Bank/Foreign Exchange – In post offices *(ATM 24hr)* and 7-Elevens. For foreign exchange, Sumitomo Exchange Corner, 2F Sannomiya Station. *Open Mon–Fri 11am–7pm, Sat–Sun 9am–5pm.*

TRANSPORTATION

BY TRAIN – **Sannomiya Station** *(Map, B1)* – The more central of the two stations, served by JR, Hankyu, and Hanshin lines. **Kobe Station** *(Map, A2)* farther out, a 5min journey to west, near Harbourland.

To Osaka-Umeda: JR Line *(around 25min, ¥410)* or Hanshin and Hankyu lines *(30min, ¥320).*

To Kyoto: JR Line *(55min, ¥1100)* or Hankyu Line to Kawaramachi via Osaka-Juso *(1hr 10min, ¥630).*

To Nara: JR Line to Osaka, then Yamato JR Line *(1hr 15min, ¥1270).*

To Himeji: JR Rapid *(40min, ¥990).*

Shin-Kobe Station *(Map, C1),* farther north, has frequent Nozomi shinkansen for Kyoto *(30min journey, around ¥2860),* Hiroshima *(1hr 10min, around ¥9670),* Fukuoka (Hakata) on the Island of Kyushu *(2hr 15min, around ¥ 14,420),* and Tokyo *(2hr 50min, around ¥14,420).*

BY PLANE – Kobe Airport - ℘078-304-7777. kairport.co.jp. Linking the city with the rest of the country (Sapporo, Tokyo Haneda, Naha, Kagoshima, etc.), the airport is on an artificial island (Port Island) served by the Port Liner Monorail from Sannomiya Station *(20min, ¥340).* You can also connect with **Kansai International Airport** by rapid boat shuttle *(kobe-access.jp, 30min, ¥1880).*

BY BOAT – Various ferry companies serve Kobe, generally leaving from one of three ferry terminals: Rokko Island (to Oita with Hankyu Ferry, Shin-moji with Ferry Sunflower, Niihama with Orenji Ferry; Naha with A Line); Kobe Sannomiya (to Shodo-shima and Takamatsu with Jumbo Ferry, and Miyazaki with Miyazaki Car Ferry); and Kobe Port Terminal (for China). For information on services and companies see: *bit.ly/kobeferry.*

GETTING AROUND KOBE

Kitano, the city center, and the port are fine for walking around, but take the subway or train to sites farther afield.
Pass for the bus and subway – *¥1040 for one day.*

Kobe City Loop – Very practical, this bus line loops around Sannomiya, the port, Kitano, and Shin-Kobe, stopping at the main tourist sites. *Every 15/20min, Mon–Fri 9am–5.30pm, Sat–Sun & public hols 9am–7pm), ¥260, day pass ¥680.*

WEST OF THE CITY

👤👥 **Tetsujin 28-go** 鉄人28号 モニュメント

🕐 *Map, A2; off map. JR train (10min journey, 🚇 ¥180) or subway (10min journey, 🚇¥240) from Sannomiya to Shin-Nagata. kobe-tetsujin.com.* In 2009, this typical Japanese suburban residential area (station, tower blocks, shopping arcade) decided to attract tourists by installing a giant steel statue in one of its pedestrianized areas: Tetsujin 28, **a giant robot** 60ft/18m high and weighing 50 tons, symbolizes the city rising up after the disaster of 1995. It was plucked from the frames of a manga and *anime* by Yokoyama Mitsuteru (born in Kobe; 1934–2004), the first in a long line of the *mecha* genre published in the 1950s and 1960s.

THE EAST OF THE CITY

Hyogo Prefectural Museum of Art★ 兵庫県立美術館

Map, C2; off map. From Sannomiya Station, Hanshin Line to Iwaya Station, then 8min walk south. Open Tue–Sun 10am–6pm (Fri–Sat to 8pm during special exhibitions). ¥500 (excluding special exhibitions). www.artm.pref. hyogo.jp.

Designed in 2004 by the architect Ando Tadao, this impressive concrete building on the seafront has a fine collection of works by 20C Japanese and international artists. These include sculptures by Henry Moore, Giacometti, Arp, and Brancusi, and Western-style canvases by two well-known Japanese painters, **Koiso Ryohei** and **Kanayama Heizo**. There are also temporary exhibitions, which will enable you to discover some interesting contemporary Japanese artists.

Great Hanshin-Awaji Earthquake Memorial Museum★ 人と防災未来センター

Map, C2; off map. 328yd/300m from the preceding museum, following the main road west. Open Mon–Thur & Sun 9.30am–5.30pm (Jul–Sep to 6pm), Fri–Sat 9.30am–7pm; last admission 1hr before closing. ¥600. www.dri.ne.jp/ en.

A highly instructive museum devoted to the terrible earthquake of 1995. A film on a giant screen simulating the quake and a life-size reconstruction of devastated streets give visitors the feeling that they are watching the event live. The presentation is so realistic it's hard not to come out feeling shaken. The museum also covers what happens in the days after an earthquake, and the latest disaster prention measures.

Hakutsuru Sake Brewery Museum 白鶴酒造資料館

Map, C1; off map. From Sannomiya Station, Hanshin Line to Sumiyoshi Station, then 5min walk south. Open daily 9.30am–4.30pm. Closed summer hols. No charge. hakutsuru. co.jp/english/culture/museum.html.

The **Nada district**, near the coast, is famous for its many sake breweries. In fact, it is the leading center for sake production in Japan: more than a quarter of the bottles sold in the country originate here, and sake has been made in the area for nearly 700 years. Some of the breweries may be visited, including this one—accommodated in a former storehouse with a nice smell of straw and old wood. The museum uses life-size models to explain the various stages of the production process. Video and brochures are available in English. *A free tasting concludes the visit.*

Kobe Fashion Museum
神戸ファッション美術館

Map, C2; off map. Hanshin Line to Uozaki Station (or JR Sumiyoshi Station), then Rokko Line monorail to Island Center Station, then 2min walk from the southeast exit. Open Tue–Sun 10am–6pm. Varies by exhibition. fashionmuseum.or.jp.

This museum is the only really interesting attraction on Rokko Island. The collections in this futuristic building (which resembles a spaceship) include dazzling kimono, rare fabrics, and precious brocades, along with classic dresses by Dior, Cardin, and Yves Saint-Laurent. A rich fashion library and temporary exhibitions complete the visit. It's a pity that the museum tends to overlook the great Japanese couturiers working today.

Tadanori Yokoo Museum of Contemporary Art ★
横尾忠則現代美術館

Map, C1; off map. 3-8-30 Harada-dori, Nada-ku. Hankyu Line to Oji-koen Station, then 5min walk; or JR Line to Nada Station, then 10min walk; or Hanshin Line to Iwaya Station, then 15min walk. Open Tue–Thur & Sun 10am–6pm, Fri–Sat 10am–8pm. Varies by exhibition. www.ytmoca.jp/ english/en_guidance.html.

This museum devoted to **Yokoo Tadanori** (born 1936), the Japanese "Andy Warhol," is spread out over two floors and contains several separate collections. On the first floor, an exhibition of works addresses the topic of war, a favourite of the artist, while the second floor deals with pop culture, with displays that are original and often challenging, including posters, collages, illustrations, videos, and paintings by this unique graphic designer and visual artist, all shouting for attention with their bright colors, exuberant shapes, and sometimes audacious content.

MOUNT ROKKO & MOUNT MAYA

The Mount Rokko chain looking out over Kobe runs for nearly 31mi/50km, and features several summits with excellent views over the city and the bay.

Mount Rokko 六甲山

🚠 *Map, C1; off map. City Bus nos. 6 or 106 leave from Mikage Station (Hanshin Line) and Rokkomichi Station (JR Line), or Rokko (Hankyu Line, around 15–30min journey), for the Rokko Cable-shita stop. Then, take the Rokko Cable Car: 10min journey, ⏰ open daily 7.10am–9.10pm, 3 departures per hour, ☞¥1100 round trip. rokkosan.com/en.*

The temperature at the summit of Mount Rokko (3054ft/931m) is on average nearly 50°F/10°C lower than at sea level, which goes some way toward explaining the popularity of the site with tourists – winter or summer – since the turn of the 20C. The old **funicular railway** has now been renovated and takes visitors up to the Art Deco Rokko Sanjo Station. From **Tenran Observatory** there is an unobstructed view over the immense Kobe-Osaka conurbation.

Rokko Alpine Botanical Garden★

– ⏰ *Open mid-Mar–mid-Nov Thur–Tue, 10am–5pm.* ⏰ *Closed early Sept.* ☞¥620. ☕. Built in 1933 at an altitude of 2830ft/865m, and with an average annual temperature of 48°F/9°C, this garden contains more than 1500 species of Japanese Alpine plants, including several that are endemic and indigenous to Mount Rokko and other mountainous regions of the world (rhododendrons from the Himalayas, Komakusa roses, Edelweiss, etc). These beautiful plants and flowers extend over more than

124 acres/50ha, criss-crossed by small paths that hug the slopes and terraces constructed by the designers, linking forest zones, rock gardens, and a pond.

▶ Take the Rokkosanjo bus and get off at the Rokko Garden Terrace stop, or continue on foot.

You will find restaurants, cafés, and stores at **Rokko Garden Terrace** (a replica of a European village).

Rokko Shidare Observatory★ – *12min by cable car to Rokko Arima Ropeway departure point. ☞¥1900 round trip. Also accessible from Arima Onsen.* ⏰*Open daily: Apr–Nov 10am–8.30pm; Dec–Mar 10am–6pm. ☞¥310.* A truly amazing structure that lights up at night. In addition to the very pretty view over Kobe and Osaka Bay from the viewing platform, the observatory (designed by Sanbuichi Hiroshi) manages to combine sustainable development with architecture; thanks to an ingenious system that collects rainfall, snow, and frost, the building is naturally air-conditioned.

Arima Onsen ★ 有馬温泉

🚠*Map, C1; off map. Bus from Sannomiya Station (1–2 per hour) or subway to Tanigami Station, then change to Kobe Dentetsu Line for Arima Onsen (35min journey). Alternatively (though it takes longer), take the cable car to Mount Rokko, which links to the Arima cable car.*

Located on one side of Mount Rokko, Arima is one of the three oldest hot springs in Japan, documented as early as 631 in the *Nihon shoki*. After years of being flooded with tourists, the resort is gradually recovering its former charm thanks to judicious redevelopments in the heart of the old city center, including craft workshops, a toy museum, and the construction of traditional housing.

Mount Maya 摩耶山
Kikuseidai observation platform
★★ – *From Sannomiya Station (JR/Hankyu/Hanshin Lines and subway) to Kobe, take the City Bus no. 18 to Maya*

Cable-shita Station (25min journey), then the Maya View Line to the Hoshi no Eki stop (15min). Ropeway: ⏱*Open Mon–Fri 10am–5.20pm, Sat–Sun in winter 10am–7.40pm, Sat–Sun in summer 10am–8.40pm.* ⬤*¥1560 round trip. www.koberope.jp/en.*

Lying at an altitude of 2290ft/698m, Kikuseidai ("the hill where you can scoop up a handful of stars") has probably the best view of Kobe, Osaka, Akashi Kaikyo Bridge, and Awaji Island. Unlike the excesses of urban design at Mount Rokko, the viewing platform here blends in with the natural surroundings. You can camp here overnight to appreciate the twinkling of the stars as they mingle with the lights of Osaka Bay *(tent hire from* ⬤*¥1000 at Café Monte 702, right beside the viewing platform).*

Tenjo-ji★ 摩耶山天上寺

10min walk from the Hoshi no Eki stop. ⏱*Open daily 9am–5pm.* ⬤*No charge. www.mayasan-tenjoji.jp.*

This temple was founded at the behest of Emperor Kotoku in 646 by the hermit Hodo Sennin, who brought with him from China a golden statue of Maya, the mother of the Buddha, who became the temple's guardian. A fire destroyed the ancient wooden temple in 1975, but it was immediately reconstructed a little to the north of the original site, near the summit of Mount Maya. In good weather, there is a fabulous view from the terrace (with its Japanese rock garden) over the Inland Sea and Awaji Island, with Akashi Kaikyo Bridge in the distance.

AWAJI-SHIMA 淡路島

Around 18mi/30km southwest of Kobe.

Akashi Bridge & Maiko Marine Promenade★★ 明石海峡大橋・舞子海上プロムナード

Take the JR Line to Maiko Station (45min journey), then 5min walk south. ⏱*Open daily: Apr–Jun & Sept 9am–6pm, Jul–Aug 9am–7pm. Maiko Marine Promenade:* ⬤*¥250 Mon–Fri, ¥300 Sat–Sun. To visit the bridge and the top of one of the pillars:* ⬤*¥3000 (reservation required, check online). hyogo-maiko-park.jp/en.*

This bridge between the islands of Honshu and Awaji is the longest suspension bridge in the world (4km/2.5mi long, 2km/1.2mi wide and with central pillars 300m/984ft high). This technological feat can withstand the harshest of weather, the strong currents of the Inland Sea, and even substantial seismic tremors. **Maiko Marine Promenade** is an observation walkway, 300m/984ft out from the shore and 50m/164ft above the sea, from where you can view the bridge through large windows. If you book, you can take the elevator to the top of one of the bridge's pillars.

Awaji (Awaji-shima) is the largest island of the Inland Sea. The birthplace of **Ningyo Joruri**, puppet theater, it is also the main producer of **Japanese incense** and continues to supply 70 percent of the market. This sweet-smelling wood is said to have been discovered in the 6C by fishermen sifting through driftwood after a storm. The island is home to two major works by architect Ando Tadao: Awaji Yumebutai Hotel and Honpuku-ji temple.

Awaji Yumebutai 淡路夢舞台

2 Yumebutai, Awaji-shi. ☎*0799-74-1111.* This huge complex by Ando Tadao includes a conference center, a hotel, and a memorial to the victims of the 1995 earthquake. The **tea pavilion** hidden within a cylindrical maze of running water and stones, the **amphitheater** with its interplay of water and lights, and the **chapel** are all works of art in themselves, structures that you can enter for contemplation. Viewed from above, **Hyakudan Garden** is made up of a hundred small stone squares planted with shrubs and flowers, descending the hillside in terraces

Honpuku-ji★★ 本福寺

20min walk from Higashiura Bus Terminal. ⏱*Open daily 9am–5pm.* ⬤*¥400.* Concealed behind two concrete walls, just the roof of the temple is visible, which on closer inspection turns out to support a pond. A staircase splits it

Awaji Ningyo-za Puppet Theater

in two and disappears as it descends between multicolored lilies (open in the mornings).

At ground level the rounded walls and the predominance of the color red give the place an enclosed and secret feel, at its most profound when the rays of the sun light up the statue of Buddha *(around 4pm in summer and 3pm in winter)*. Climbing back up the staircase, the sky fills your field of vision like a final homage to the pure lines of architect Ando Tadao's transcendent design, completed in 1991.

Nojima Fault Preservation Museum & Hokudan Earthquake Memorial Park ★

野島断層保存 北淡震災記念公園

JR Line to Maiko Station (45min), then the express bus from Kosoku Maiko bus terminal over the Akashi Bridge to Hokudan Earthquake Memorial Park stop. Or boat from Akashi Port to Iwaya Port, then bus to Hokudan Earthquake Memorial Park stop. ⏱*Open daily 9am–5pm.* ⏱*Closed late Dec.* ∞*¥730. nojima-danso.co.jp/nojima.html.*

This memorial museum devoted to the terrible earthquake of 1995 was erected on the site of the epicenter and the Nojima fault created by the quake. Educational displays and a preserved section of the fracture line make it pos-

sible to grasp the scope and violence of the disaster. Memorial House is one of the few buildings to have miraculously survived. The living room simulates what the earthquake felt like over a 40 second period, thanks to a mechanism in the floor. Documentary films with powerful images are also shown.

Awaji Ningyo-za Puppet Theater ★★ 淡路人形座

JR Line to Maiko Station (45min journey), then the express bus from Kosoku Maiko bus terminal over the Akashi Bridge to Fukura stop (1hr 10min), then a short walk. ⏱*Open Thu–Tue 9am– 5pm. Shows (45min) at 10am, 11.10am, 1.30pm & 3pm.* ∞*¥1500. English-language audioguide on website. awajiningyoza.com*

Opened in 2012, this theater is keeping alive a puppetry tradition that goes back 500 years on Awaji Island. The artform combines operating the marionnettes (each puppet is worked by three black-clad stagehands), music played on a *shamisen* (a three-stringed instrument) and narration provided by the *taiyu*. The troupe give explanations in English before each performance. The beauty of the costumes, the precision of the puppets' movements, and the musical atmosphere evoke great emotion in the audience.

◗ You can continue south toward the Island of Shikoku (☉see p546).

ADDRESSES

🏠 STAY

KOBE

◖◗ **The b-Hotel** ザ・ビー神戸 – *2-11-5 Shimoyamate-dori. (Map, B1).* ✆*078-333-4880. ishinhotels.com/en/theb/kobe. 168 rooms. ¥20,000. ¥1100⛶.* In the heart of the lively Sannomiya area, an ochre-colored building with practical but pleasant rooms.

◖◗ **Hotel Isago Kobe** ホテルいさご神戸 – *4-3-7 Kumochi-cho (Map, C1).* ✆*078-241-0135. isago.co.jp. 27 rooms. ¥14,300. ¥1650⛶.* An excellent little hotel, combining Japanese tradition and modernity. Cozy but elegant Japanese and Western rooms, attentive but unobtrusive service, and top-quality food.

◖◗ **Hotel Kitano Plaza Rokkoso** ホテル北野プラザ六甲荘 – *1-1-4 Kitano-cho (Map, B1).* ✆*078-241-2451. kourituyasuragi.jp/kobe. 49 rooms. ¥12,800. ¥1650⛶.* A lovely hotel, renovated in light beige tones. Clean, quiet rooms, most with an attractive view.

◖◗ **Hotel Tor Road** ホテルトアロード – *3-1-19 Nakayamate-dori (Map, B1).* ✆*078-391-6691. sanraku.premierhotel-group.com/kobe. 77 rooms. ¥10,400. ¥1900⛶.* A very cozy establishment. The rooms on the 9th and 10th floors are decorated in typically English style. Other rooms are more standard, but equally well maintained.

◖◗ **Super Hotel Kobe** スーパーホテル神戸 – *2-1-11 Kano-cho (Map, B1).* ✆*078-261-9000. www.superhoteljapan.com/en/s-hotels/kobe. 87 rooms. ¥10,200. ⛶.* A simple, reasonably priced business hotel. The rooms are small, but clean and well equipped.

◖◗ **Villa Fontaine** ヴィラフォンテーヌ神戸三宮 – *4-1-4 Asahi-dori. (Map, C1).* ✆*078-224-5500. www.hvf.jp/eng /location/sannomiya.php. 185 rooms. ¥13,200. ¥1700⛶.* Just 5min from Sannomiya Station. Its rooms are modern (though a bit small), welcoming, and well designed. Little touches and smart communal areas raise it a step above its competitors.

🍴 EAT

KOBE

◖◗ **Cafe Freundlieb** カフェ・フロインドリーブ – *4-6-15 Ikuta-cho (Map, C1).* ✆*078-231-6051. freundlieb.jp .Open Thu–Tue 10am–7pm.* Lodged beneath the nave of a former Lutheran church, this German tearoom serves good salads, sandwiches, and pastries.

◖◗ **Musashi** とんかつ・武蔵 – *Moritani shoten Bldg 2 F, 1-7-2 Motomachi-dori (Map, B2).* ✆*078-321-0634. Open Mon–Tue & Thu–Fri 11am–8pm, Sat–Sun & public hols 11am–8.30pm.* Established in 1939, this restaurant specializes in *tonkatsu*: breaded pork cutlets, fillets, and shrimp.

◖◗ In the **Mosaic** complex *(Map, A2)*, on the sea front *(☉see p409)*, there's a great choice of restaurants to suit all tastes and budgets, including **Brasiliano** ブラジリアーノ *(3F, ✆078-360-2996, umie.jp/shop/detail/202 ; open Mon–Fri 11am–3pm & 5–10pm, Sat–Sun & public hols 11am–1pm)*, with its popular buffet-grill inspired by Brazilian cuisine. At **Oyster Bar** ザ オイスターバー神戸 *(2F, ✆078-371-7300, theoysterbarkobe.owst.jp; open daily 11am–10pm; menu in English)* you can sample oysters served in several different ways *(¥1300–2800)*, while **Frantz** 神戸フランツ *(3F, ✆078-360-0007, www.frantz.jp; open daily 10am–9pm)* serves irresistible little pots of creamy pudding (around ¥400).

◖◗ **Tooth Tooth Maison 15th** トゥーストゥース・メゾン15 – *15 Naniwa-machi (Map, B2).* ✆*078-332-1515. toothtooth.com/restaurant/maison-15th. Open daily 11am–11pm. menu in English.* Behind the Kobe City Museum, an elegant historic building where you can snack on coffee and a patisserie, or enjoy a salad for lunch. European feel and welcoming.

◖◗◗ **Teppanyaki Onishi II** 鉄板焼大西II – *3F Kitano Phoenix Bldg, 1-17-6 Nakayamate-dori (Map, B1).* ✆*078-332-4029. Open Tue–Sat 6pm–2am, Sun & public hols 5pm–9.30pm. Set menus from ¥8600 for 2 people. ⛶.* This is an excellent *teppan-yaki* restaurant (food cooked on a hot plate): the famous Kobe beef ihere, flavored with brandy, is just about as tender and juicy as anyone could ever wish for. This, together with the friendly atmosphere, makes for a great experience.

NIGHTLIFE

For bars, restaurants, and bright lights, the **Sannomiya** area north of the station is the place to go. Kobe is also known for its **jazz clubs**, with shows generally taking place around 6.30–10pm. Try **Sone** ソネ 1-24-10 Nakayamate-dori, west of Kitano-zaka (Map, B1). 078-221-2055. kobe-sone.com/index.html. Open daily 5pm–midnight.

SPORT AND LEISURE

Boat Rides – Naka Pier Cruise Terminal 中突堤ターミナル (Map, A2). 078-322-5670. Trips usually around 50min, ¥1200. Several companies offer cruises along the bay; try the trip at night.

Beaches – In summer, Kobe's residents flock to the lovely **Suma Beach** 須磨海岸 (Map, A2; off map), 20min by train to the east of Kobe (Suma Station). Nearby is **Akashi Kaikyo Bridge** 明石海峡大橋, the longest suspension bridge in the world (12,830ft/3910m), linking the Kobe region with Awaji Island.

Nada sake factories – Free visits and 10-minute explanatory film in English, with a tasting.

Kiku-Masamune Sake Brewery Museum 菊正宗酒造記念館 – 1-9-1 Uozaki-Nishimachi, Higashinada-ku. 078-854-1029, kikumasamune.com. Open daily 9.30am–4.30pm.

Kobe Shu-Shin-Kan Brewery 神戸酒心館 – 1-8-17 Mikagetsukamachi, Higashinada-ku. 078-841-1121, enjoyfukuju.com/en/visitus. Open daily 10am–6pm; and its restaurant **Sakabayashi** さかばやし (open daily 11.30am–2.30pm & 5.30–10pm; menu in English).

AWAJI-SHIMA

Matsuho no Sato Onsen 松帆の郷温泉 – 77 Iwaya, Awaji-shi, Hyogo-ken. 079-973-2333. matsuho.com/hotspring. Open daily 11am–10pm (last admission 9pm). ¥700. There are a great many baths to be enjoyed in this onsen complex, which has a beautiful view of Akashi Kaikyo bridge.

Himeji★★

The amazing Himeji feudal castle, designated a National Treasure and on the UNESCO World Heritage List, is without doubt one of the most iconic of Japanese monuments and is known globally. Exploring this 17C masterpiece of architecture has to be one of the highpoints of any visit to Japan. The town of Himeji is also very pleasant, and the presence of several sites of interest in the vicinity make it worthwhile prolonging your stay.

HIMEJI CASTLE★★★ 姫路城

Map, B1. A 15min walk from Himeji JR Station (north exit), or take one of the frequent shuttle buses. Open late Apr–Aug 9am–6pm; Sept–late Apr 9am–5pm; last admission 1hr before closing. ¥1000 (¥1050 with combined Koko-en garden ticket). himejicastle.jp/en. English tours: daily 10am & 1pm; 45min. ¥1000.

- ▶ **Population:** 530,500 – Hyogo Prefecture.
- ◖ **Location:** 31mi/50 km west of Kobe (40min by train). A shuttle leaves Kansai airport (2hr 10min). Himeji can be visited easily on foot.
- **Kids:** The castle, the Japanese Toy Museum.
- ◔ **Timing:** Allow a day.
- **Don't miss:** A walk in the gardens of Koko-en and Enkyo-ji.

One of the great masterpieces of Japanese architecture, Himeji Castle is known as the **White Heron Castle** (Shirasagi-jo). Its graceful outlines (a central five-story keep surrounded by three smaller bastions) and white plaster walls resemble a bird taking flight. Built on a hill in the middle of a vast plain, this impregnable fortress is a model of the art of defense: a labyrinth of moats, ditches,

Himeji Castle

© Sean Pavone/iStock

and traps, fan-shaped ramparts, loop-holes (*sama*), projecting parapets, and passages leading nowhere, all designed to keep attackers at bay. But Himeji was also, and above all, a symbol of the shogun's prestige, hence the beautiful swooping curves of its roofs, like waves on the ocean. Because it is in an excellent state of preservation, the castle has featured in a number of period films, including Kurosawa Akira's *Ran* (1985).

History – In spite of all its defenses, the castle has never been fought over in its over four centuries of existence. It stands on the site of an older fort, built in 1346 by Akamatsu Sadanori. Toyotomi Hideyoshi seized it in 1577 and enlarged it to make a strategic fortress, around which a town began to grow. This is where he executed his famous U-turn to avenge the death of Nobunaga. After the Battle of Sekigahara (1600), Tokugawa Ieyasu entrusted the castle to his son-in-law Ikeda Terumasa, who expanded it to its present form between 1601 and 1609. Control of the complex subsequently passed to a number of clans, who added various buildings and turrets. Slightly damaged by air raids in 1945, its wooden structure was entirely refurbished and strengthened between 1956 and 1964, and a vast program of restoration work was completed in 2015.

Visit – The route, marked with arrows (*about 2hr*), leads through a maze of doors, staircases, and corridors to a

USEFUL INFORMATION

Himeji Tourist Office – entrance west of the station. ☏ *079-287-0003, himeji-kanko.jp. Open daily 9am–7pm.* English-speaking staff can supply maps and explain where to withdraw cash. *Free bicycle hire daily 9am–4pm.* The **"Castle View" observation platform** is an ideal place from where to take a photo of the castle, and is just above the Tourist Office.

TRANSPORTATION

BY TRAIN – **Himeji Station** *(Map, A3)* – The simplest way to get to Himeji is to take the JR Special Rapid from Kobe *(40min journey, ¥990)*, from Osaka *(1hr, ¥1520)*, or from Kyoto *(1hr 30min, ¥2310)*. Alternatively, from Kyoto, if you have a JR Pass it's better to take the shinkansen *(45min, ¥4840)*.

GETTING AROUND HIMEJI

The castle is 15min from the station: keep walking straight ahead. You can also get there by bus (**Loop Bus**, *every 15/30min, ¥100 per journey, one-day pass ¥300*), or ask at the tourist information center about renting a free bicycle for the day.

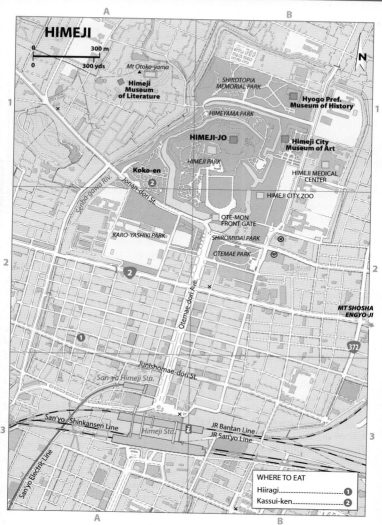

HIMEJI

0   300 m
0   300 yds

Mt Otoko-yama ▲

Himeji Museum of Literature

SHIROTOPIA MEMORIAL PARK

中央 ...

Hyogo Pref. Museum of History

HIMEYAMA PARK

HIMEJI-JO

Himeji City Museum of Art

HIMEJI PARK

Koko-en ❷

Jonan-dori St.

HIMEJI MEDICAL CENTER

Sentō-gawa Riv.

HIMEJI CITY ZOO

OTE-MON FRONT GATE

KARO-YASHIKI PARK

SHIROMIDAI PARK ⊗

OTEMAE PARK 🚻

❷

MT SHOSHA ENGYO-JI

Otemae-dori Ave.

372

❶

Junishomae-dori St.

San'yo Himeji Sta.

San'yo Shinkansen Line

Himeji Sta.

JR Bantan Line
JR San'yo Line

San'yo Electric Line

WHERE TO EAT	
Hiiragi	❶
Kassui-ken	❷

Copyright 2015 Cartographic data Shobunsha/Michelin

vast courtyard planted with cherry trees and pines *(nishi-no-maru)*, where the lord, his family, and his vassals had their quarters. Next follows the main enclosure *(honmaru), where the* **central keep** *(tenshukaku)* is to be found. The 151ft/46m-high tower, designed both as a watchtower and a final bastion in case of attack, has five floors plus a base of irregular stones held together by lime-based cement. The roof combines triangular peaks *(chidori-hafu)* and curved gables *(kara-hafu)*. At the very top are two *shachihoko* (a mythical animal with the head of a tiger and the body of a fish), 6.6ft/2m high. Inside, a series of dark, narrow staircases leads to the top, from where there is a clear **view** of the town. Note the massive cypresswood pillars, the bases of which are 3ft/95cm across. The oldest is 780 years old. Collections of armor, swords, and rifles are on display on the different floors.

What remains of the western citadel **Nishi-no-maru**, where the *daimyo* lived, is now a succession of 17C tow-

Takeda Castle Ruins

© Yoshitsugu Nishigaki/Alto/age fotostock

ers linked by a very long, split-level corridor. Some were used as apartments by employees of Princess Sen (Sen-hime, 1597–1666, a frequent character in historical fims and tales), who made herself beautiful in what was known as the "cosmetic" tower. Nowadays, you can walk the length of the complex and, in a number of rooms, explore small exhibitions about both the castle's defensive system, and everyday life within its walls.

Around the Castle
Koko-en★ 好古園
🕐Map, A1. 🕐Open late Apr–Aug 9am–6pm; Sept–late Apr 9am–5pm. 🎫¥300 (🎫¥1050 with combined Himeji Castle ticket). himeji-machishin.jp/ryokka/kokoen/en.
These nine delightful gardens, modeled on the gardens of the samurai residences of the Edo period, date from 1992. One of them, **Cha-no-niwa**, has a teahouse, Souju-an (🕐Open daily10am–4pm; matcha and traditional sweet 🎫¥500).

Himeji City Museum of Art★ 姫路市立美術館
🕐Map, B1. 🕐Open Tue–Sun 10am–5pm. 🎫¥210 (excluding special exhibitions). bit.ly/himejiart.
This small brick building houses a fine collection of Impressionist and modern paintings, including works by Corot, Courbet, Monet, Matisse, Derain, and Delvaux. The annex displays works by Japanese artists from the 19C through the present day.

Hyogo Prefectural Museum of History 兵庫県立歴史博物館
🕐Map, B1. 🕐Open Tue–Sun 10am–5pm. 🎫 ¥200 (excluding special exhibitions); 1F 🎫no charge. bit.ly/hyogohistorymuseum. 🔲.
Designed by the architect **Tange Kenzo**, this museum showcases the history of Japanese castles, with scale models of 12 castles in Japan that have kept their original structure. There are also a few antiquities, including some Buddhas.

Himeji Museum of Literature 姫路文学館
🕐Map, A1. 550yd/500m west of the Museum of History. 🕐Open Tue–Sun 10am–5pm. 🎫¥300 (excludes special exhibitions). himejibungakukan.jp/en.
The museum buiding was designed by **Ando Tadao**. While there's not much English description of the displays, it's all nicely enough put together that lovers of Japanese literature will find some interest in it.

Engyo-ji★ 圓教寺
🕐Map, B2; off map. From the stop outside the station, bus no. 6 or 8 to Mount Shosha Ropeway stop (25min journey, 🎫¥280). After the cable car ride (5min, 🎫¥1000 round trip), 30min walk or bus (20min, 🎫¥500 round trip). 🕐Open daily 8.30am–6pm (varies slightly by season). 🎫¥500. shosha.or.jp/_en.
This temple complex (Tendai sect) on **Mount Shosha** (to the north of Himeji) romantically combines Buddhist art with nature. Lined with maples, cherry trees, and statues of the thousand-armed deity Kannon, the trail leads to Daiko-

do, a pavilion where some scenes from the movie *The Last Samurai* were shot.
The **Shoshazan Ropeway Combination Ticket** covers buses between Himeji Station and the ropeway, and the cable car round trip (*¥1420; available at the bus terminal by Himeji Station*). The ropeway closes for a week in February.

EXCURSIONS

Japanese Toy Museum★
日本玩具博物館
Around 6.2mi/10km north of Himeji. By train: JR Bantan Line to Koro Station, then 15min walk. By car: Chugoku Expressway to Fukusaki interchange, then 4mi/7km south. Open Thu–Tue 10am–5pm. *¥600 (children ¥200–400). japan-toy-museum.org.*
This museum is spread over six separate buildings, linked by short tree-lined paths. Since 1974, **Inoue Shigeyoshi** has accumulated a priceless collection of over 80,000 toys from 145 countries. Beautifully displayed, popular Japanese toys (*hina* dolls, puppets, kites, *temari*, soft toys made of silk) rub shoulders with dolls' houses and Christmas toys from all over the world. In one room, you can play with old wooden toys, most of which are unique.

Ikuno Silver Mine ★   生野銀山
JR Bantan Line to Ikuno Station, then bus to Ikunoginzan-guchi stop (10min journey) and 10min walk. Open Mar & Nov daily 9am–5pm; Apr–Oct daily 9am–5.30pm; Dec–Feb Wed–Mon 9.30am–4.30pm. Wear good shoes and a sweater (average temp. 5°F/13°C). *¥900. ikuno-ginzan.co.jp.*
This silver mine was operational from 807 to 1973. When it was mined, huge quantities of silver and over 70 types of ore (gold, lead, copper, etc.) were extracted from 350km/217mi of tunnels. An underground museum (good English signage) charts the different techniques used to mine the rock in chronological order, from pickaxes to explosives in the 19C. The mine has been designated an Important Cultural Property.

Takeda Castle Ruins★★
竹田城跡
JR Bantan Line to Takeda Station, then bus to Takeda-jo Seki stop and 20min walk along the trail; or on foot from the station via one of three steep trails (1hr). Open daily: mid-Mar–May 8am–6pm; June–Aug 6am–6pm; Sept–Nov 4am–5pm; Dec 1–mid Dec 10am–2pm. *¥500. www.city.asago.hyogo.jp/takeda.*
Takeda Castle, often likened to Machu Picchu, is among the country's most beautiful historic sites. At an altitude of 353m/1158ft, the remains (mainly foundations) emerge out of a sea of cloud, hence its poetic nickname, "**castle in the sky**" (best seen Oct & Nov at sunrise). From the top of this must-see site, you will be rewarded with a breathtaking view over the surrounding green valleys. The feudal lord Sozen Yamana had this fort built in 1431 to protect Tajima from attacks from neighboring regions.

ADDRESSES

EAT
Kassui-ken 活水軒 – *68 Honmachi (Map, A1). 079-289-4131. himeji-machishin.jp/ryokka/kokoen/en/kassuiken. Open daily: May–Aug 9.30am–4.30pm; Sept–Apr 9.30am–5.30pm. Menu in English.* Nestled in the gardens of Koko-en, this restaurant has a heavenly view of a small pond and a waterfall. It serves Himeji's specialty, *anago* (grilled conger eel), as well as noodle and rice dishes. Arrive early to avoid the lunch crowds, or just drop in for an afternoon drink.

Hiiragi 柊 – *88 Junicho-mae (Map, A2). 079-284-1239. www.anago-hiiragi.com. Open Mon–Tue & Thur–Sat 11am–2pm & 5–11pm, Sun 5–10pm. From ¥1900.* A welcoming spot to try *anago*, served as part of a set meal or as *donburi* (on rice).

SPORT AND LEISURE
Sake Brewery Nadagiku 灘菊酒造 – *1-121 Tegara. 079-285-3111. nadagiku.co.jp/en. Open daily 10am–6pm.* A well-known brewery established in 1910 by the Kawaishi family. Visits in English available; reserve in advance.

WESTERN HONSHU (CHUGOKU)

Chugoku occupies the southwestern tip of the island of Honshu. Its name, literally meaning "middle country," harks back to the time when Japan was divided into the near country (Kingoku), the middle country (Chugoku), and the far country (Ongoku)—relating to their distance from the capital, which was first Nara, then Kyoto. Mountainous and heavily forested, the Chugoku mountain chain running across the center splits the region into two quite distinct areas: San'in, in the north, and San'yo, in the south.

Highlights

1 The gardens of **Koraku-en**, beautiful in any season (p425)

2 Pausing for remembrance and reflection at **Hiroshima's A-Bomb Dome** (p439)

3 Sacred island **Miyajima** (p423)

4 An early-morning visit to the **Tottori** sand dunes (p451)

5 Shopping for pottery in the workshops of **Hagi** (p458)

▶ **Population:** 7.6 million – Okayama, Hiroshima, Yamaguchi, Shimane, and Tottori Prefectures.

Michelin Map: Regions of Japan Map 4, Regional Map opposite.

Location: At the western tip of the island of Honshu, Chugoku covers an area of approximately 12,239.4sq mi/31,700sq km. The three principal cities in the region are Hiroshima, Okayama, and Tottori. A Shinkansen line runs along the San'yo coast, from Kobe to Kyushu, while the JR San'in line runs along the north coast.

Timing: Allow four days for San'yo and an equal amount of time for San'in. If possible, do a circular tour that takes in both.

Don't miss: The shrines of Miyajima and Izumo; Peace Memorial Park in Hiroshima; Koraku-en in Okayama; Adachi Museum in Matsue; the Ohara Museum in Kurashiki; the dunes of Tottori; Iwami Ginzan Silver Mine.

The Region Today

San'in ("the shady side of the mountain") faces the Sea of Japan, looking toward Korea and Russia. The terrain is somewhat inhospitable, with only a few narrow, lowland areas into which rivers flow. Nature reigns supreme and the climate is harsh with snowy winters and rainy summers. From the sand dunes of Tottori to the samurai quarters of Hagi, life in Chugoku moves at a slow pace. The old traditions are respected in all aspects and walks of life, whether praying in the shrines that cling to mountainsides, bathing in the sleepy seaside *onsen*

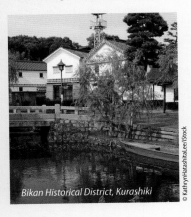

Bikan Historical District, Kurashiki

© KathrynHatashitaLee/iStock

resorts, or working in the kilns, where pottery has been fired for over 300 years, or in the sake breweries handed down through the generations. Foreign travelers, still a rare sight here, are always treated with great hospitality.

San'yo ("the sunny side of the mountain") has a milder climate and is more urban and industrial, especially along the stretch of coast encompassing Okayama,

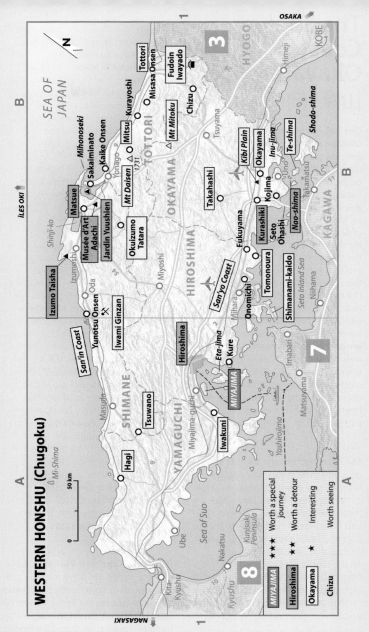

WESTERN HONSHU (Chugoku)

SEA OF JAPAN

ILES OKI

OSAKA

KOBE

HYOGO

Himeji

Tottori
Misasa Onsen
Fudoin Iwayado
Chizu

Mihonoseki
Sakaiminato
Kaike Onsen
Mitsu-Kurayoshi
Mt Mitoku

Matsue
Musée d'Art Adachi
Jardin Yuushien
Okuizumo Tatara
Shinji-ko
Yonago
Mt Daisen
1731

Izumo Taisha
Izumoshi
Oda

TOTTORI

OKAYAMA

Tsuyama

Kibi Plain
Okayama
Inu-jima
Te-shima
Shodo-shima

Takahashi
Uno
Kojima
Seto
Ohashi
Kurashiki
Nao-shima

Takamatsu

KAGAWA

San'in Coast
Yunotsu Onsen
Iwami Ginzan

Miyoshi

HIROSHIMA

Fukuyama
San'yo Coast
Onomichi
Tomonoura
Shimanami-kaido
Mihara
Niihama
Seto Inland Sea

Masuda

SHIMANE

Hiroshima
Eta-jima
Kure
MIYAJIMA

YAMAGUCHI

Tsuwano

Hagi

Mi-Shima

Miyajima-guchi
Yashirojima

Imabari

Matsuyama

Iwakuni

Sea of Suo

Kunisaki Peninsula

Ube
Nakatsu

Kyushu
Kita

NAGASAKI

MIYAJIMA ★★★	Worth a special journey
Hiroshima ★★	Worth a detour
Okayama ★	Interesting
Chizu	Worth seeing

0   50 km

Hiroshima and Yamaguchi, home to major steelworks. The dynamic city of Okayama has built its prosperity on agriculture, wood, textiles, and trade. Hiroshima, rebuilt after the terrible atomic bomb attack of 1945, is today a thriving metropolis. However, the region is also an area of great natural beauty, with an indented coastline of channels, inlets, and bays looking out over an endless string of islands floating on the great blue expanse of the Inland Sea (Seto Naikai).

423

The San'yo Coast★: Okayama★

山陽：岡山

One hour by shinkansen from Osaka, Okayama is the gateway to Chugoku and, via the Great Seto Bridge (8mi/13km) over the Inland Sea, also to the island of Shikoku. Wedged between the sea and the mountains, this commercial hub lies at heart of an historic region (the old kingdom of Kibi) with a mild, sunny climate ideal for fruit farming. Although the city itself is not especially attractive, it is well worth a visit for the wonderful Koraku-en, one of the most beautiful stroll gardens in Japan. It is also a useful base for exploring the surrounding area: Kurashiki, a picturesque merchant enclave from the Edo era with its well-preserved old houses; and the town of Takahashi, with its elevated castle. And if you want to sample the charms of the countryside, nothing beats a bicycle ride around the paddy fields on the Kibi Plain.

SIGHTS

The center of the city, with its streets on a grid plan, is easy to negotiate on foot. All the usual supsects in terms of the Japanese urban landscape are there: the main avenue, covered malls and commercial centers, a district of bars and restaurants near the station, and cultural infrastructure.

All the tourist sites are a stone's throw from JR Okayama Station, at the end of Momotaro-dori, but the bus and tram systems are useful if you're not keen on a walk.

Yumeji Art Museum★

夢二郷土美術館

⚭Map, C1. By the main (north) entrance of Koraku-en. ◷Open Tue–Sun 9am–5pm. ◉¥700. yumeji-art-museum.com. ▱.

▶ **Population:** 720,000 – Okayama Prefecture.

⚭ **Michelin Map:** Regions of Japan Map 4, Regional Map p423, B1. Okayama Map p426.

▷ **Location:** Okayama is a medium-sized city on the shores of the Inland Sea, 100mi/161km from Hiroshima, 112mi/180km from Osaka, and 45mi/72km from Takamatsu. The downtown area lies between the station to the west and the Asahi River to the east. This is also where the museums are concentrated, around Koraku-en and the castle. The commercial district is close to the river, while the area around the station is much livelier at night.

👥 **Kids:** Don't miss the unusual Japan Rural Toy Museum in Kurashiki.

◷ **Timing:** Allow a day or two for Okayama and Kurashiki, or alternatively Takahashi, the Kibi Plain, and the ports of Tomonoura and Onomichi. This is also the easiest jumping off point for the Art Islands of the Inland Sea (⚭see p554).

☺ **Don't miss:** A stroll through Koraku-en; Ohara Museum in Kurashiki.

The artist **Takehisa Yumeji** (1884–1934), a native of Okayama, was one of the leading lights of the Romantic movement during the Taisho era (1912–26). Sometimes called the Japanese Toulouse-Lautrec, he shared the French artist's desire to make his art more accessible by producing posters and prints. But whereas Toulouse-Lautrec gave an unflinching picture of the Bohemian life of Montmartre, which included prostitutes, Yumeji preferred

Irises by Ryu-ten pavilion, Koraku-en

© mura/iStock

to depict slender young women with delicate features—*bijin-ga* (elegant beauties)—in traditional kimono, embodying a certain ideal of purity. His work, employing a number of different media (ink, pastels, charcoal, watercolors, etc.) reveals a self-taught artist with a fresh style, who combined strong lines with muted colors, and tried to achieve a blend of some elements of Japanese tradition with the modern Western trends that were inescapable in Japan at the beginning of the 20C.

Koraku-en★★★ 後楽園

Map, C1. Main (north) entrance by Tsurumi Bridge; south gate opposite the castle. 25min walk from station, or tram no.1 to Shiroshita (¥100) then 15min walk, or bus no. 1 (12min). okayama-korakuen.jp. Open late Mar–Sept 7.30am–6pm; Oct–late Mar 8am–5pm. ¥410 (¥580 with castle, ¥980 also with Hiyashibara Museum of Art).
Stalls in Koraku-en sell oniwa-sodachi bento, takeout meals that match the garden's seasonal colors (¥1100), to eat in the open air, weather permitting.

Situated on an island in the middle of the Asahi River, once only accessible by boat (there are now three bridges), this exceptional garden was created in 1700 by the *daimyo* of Okayama, Ikeda Tsunamasa. Anxious to have a place near his castle where he could relax,

receive guests, and practice riding and archery, he spent no less than 14 years perfecting the garden. Today, Koraku-en is considered one of the three finest gardens in Japan, the others being Kairaku-en in Mito and Kenroku-en in Kanazawa.

It is not exceptionally large *(32 acres/13ha)*, but it is beautiful, varied, and in flower throughout the year, changing color with the seasons. A *kaiyu* (stroll garden, see p115), it is filled with wide lawns, hills, ponds, and tea houses, with paths winding in between, as well as a 2100ft/640m-long stream of pure water, making the garden pleasantly cool in summer. Although since the Meiji era the former fields and rice paddies have been replaced by lawn, there is still a working tea plantation. The plums *(ume)* gathered in the garden are used to make a sweet liqueur called *umeshu*. Every January 1 and 3, to celebrate the New Year, the Japanese cranes that are raised here are released to fly over the garden—with a wingspan of nearly 10ft/3m, they are a spectacular sight.

Visit: *From the main, north, entrance, turn right and walk counterclockwise.*

The first building is **Enyo-tei**, the main pavilion, from where the lord enjoyed the view of the garden and its "borrowed landscape" (*shakkei*— see p113) of Mount Misao in the background. Behind the pavilion is a small **Noh theater**, reconstructed after the

OKAYAMA

300 m
300 yds

WHERE TO STAY

Excel Okayama.................... 1
Hotel Granvia...................... 2
Hotel Via Inn...................... 3
Okayama Plaza Hotel......... 4

WHERE TO EAT

Toritetsu........................... 1
Toriyoshi........................... 2
Yamato.............................. 3

TAKAHASHI

OKAYAMA AIRPORT

OKAYAMA INTERNATIONAL CENTER

JR San-yo Shinkansen

Okayama Sta.
Okayamaeki-mae

Eki-mae

KURASHIKI, HIROSHIMA

Shiyakusho-suji St.

Nishi-kawa Riv.

Momotaro-odori St.

Nishikawa

Yanagawa

Yanagawa-suji St.

Korakuen-dori St.

Joka-suji St.

Okayama Orient Museum

Shiroshita

OKAYAMA SYMPHONY HALL

Yubinkyoku-mae

OKAYAMA CHUO P.O.

Teramachi

Tamachi

Kencho-dori

BANK OF JAPAN

Okayama Electric Tramway
Higashiyama Line

Okayama Electric Tramway
Saidaibashi Line

OKAYAMA PREF. GOVERNMENT OFFICE

Hayashibara Museum of Art

Okayama-jo

Tsukimi-bashi Bridge

Asahi-gawa Riv.

Aoi-bashi Bridge

KORAKU-EN

BOTANICAL GARDEN

Sawa-no-ike Pond

Kasayo-no-ike Pond

Kayou-ike Pond

Horai-bashi Bridge

Tsurumi-bashi Bridge

Shin-Tsurumi-bashi Bridge

Yumeji Art Museum

N

426

USEFUL INFORMATION

TOURIST OFFICES – All have English-speaking staff, and English maps.

Okayama City Tourist Office – By the shinkansen exit, Okayama Station. ℘086-222-2912. okayama-kanko.net/sightseeing/en. Open daily 9am–6pm.

Okayama Momotaro Tourist Information Center – Ichibangai Ekimotomachi, by the station. ℘086-222-2912. okayama-japan.jp/en. Open daily 9am–8pm.

Okayama International Exchange Center – 2-2-1 Hokan-cho. ℘086-256-2914. www.opief.or.jp. Open Mon–Sat 9am–5pm. Information on the prefecture and city of Okayama.

Kurashikikan Tourist Center – Kurashiki-kan, 1-4-8 Chuo. ℘086-422-0542. kurashiki-tabi.jp. Open daily 10am–6pm.

Kurashiki Station Tourist Center – By the south gate, Kurashiki Station. ℘086-424-1220. Open daily: Apr–Sept 9am–6pm; Oct–Mar 9am–7pm.

TRANSPORTATION

BY PLANE – Okayama Airport (okayama-airport.org/en; Map A1, off map) – 10 flights daily to Tokyo Haneda (1hr 15min, ¥36,000), 1 to Sapporo (1hr 50min, ¥50,000), 1 to Naha, Okinawa (2hr 5min, ¥40,000). Buses run between the airport and Okayama Station (30min, ¥760).

BY TRAIN – Okayama Station (Map, A1/2) – The city is on the San'yo Line shinkansen. Trains every 15min to Tokyo (3hr 20min, ¥16,600), Kyoto (1hr, ¥7140), and Hiroshima (35min, ¥5610). For Shikoku, JR Seto-Ohashi Line to Takamatsu (55min, ¥1550).

war. Farther down, a superb weeping cherry tree droops over **Kayo Pond** (Kayo-no-ike), which is fed by a waterfall. In summer, a myriad of big white lotuses bloom here. In the middle of the water sits a huge granite rock (25ft/7.5m high and with a circumference of 66ft/20m). It was moved here three centuries ago, having been cut into 90 pieces to make it easier to transport. As you continue, you pass the remains of the **jetty** where the daimyo moored his boat when coming from the castle, now covered by a thicket of bamboo. Just after the south gate is the little **Renchi-ken** tea house, where you can enjoy some tea while contemplating the view. Climb **Yuishin Hill** for a magnificent **view★★** of the garden, particularly impressive in May, when the azaleas are in bloom.

At **Sawa Pond** (Sawa-no-ike), the largest in the garden, look for carp swimming between the small islands covered in green pines and white sand. Farther south is the **Ryu-ten** pavilion, and nearby a stream running over a bed of colored pebbles that leads to fields of irises, in bloom in June. In the eastern part of the garden, near **Kako Pond** (Kako-no-ike) and its waterfall,

are groves of plum and cherry trees. After pausing in front of a patch of land planted with rice and lotuses, look north to see row upon row of **tea plants**.

▶ Leave by the south gate of the garden, then cross the footbridge to get to the castle.

Okayama Castle★ 岡山城

⌚Map, C2. Tram no.1 from Okayama Station to Shiroshita (⊝¥100), then 10min walk. ⌚Open daily 9am–5.30pm. okayama-kanko.net/ujo/english. ⊝¥320, excluding special exhibitions (¥580 with Koraku-en, ¥980 also with Hiyashibara Museum of Art). Built by the daimyo Ukita Hideie in 1597, Okayama Castle is also known as U-jo, "Crow Castle," because of its black wooden walls. Black was synonymous with strength and sobriety, white with wealth and splendor. The one exception here is the gilded shachi (mythical fish protecting the building from fire) at the corners of the roofs. A flatland castle (built on a plain), it is protected on the east side by the Asahi River. On one of the first levels is a **keep** in the shape of a pentagon, decorated with curved canopies. The whole building occupies six floors. Unfortunately, the castle die not withstand the bombing of World War II, and in 1966 it was rebuilt in reinforced concrete. The engineers even installed an elevator. Apart from the stone base, the only part of the castle that is now original is the **Tsukimi turret** in the northwest corner of the enclosure.

Still, it's an attractive building, and hosts some fun activities: you can try on a very regal kimono *(5 times daily, 5 people per session;* ⌚ *no charge)* or try making *bizen-yaki (Bizen ceramics; 5 times daily;* ⌚*¥1250)*. The interior also houses objects *(armor, swords, lacquerware)* that belonged to the Ukita and Ikeda clans.

Hayashibara Museum of Art★
林原美術館
⌚ *Map, C2. 5min walk from the castle. hayashibara-museumofart.jp.*
⌚*Open Tue–Sun 10am–5pm.* ⌚*¥500, excluding special exhibitions (¥980 with Koraku-en and Okayama Castle).*

Formerly located within the castle grounds, this building belonged to the Ikeda clan before being bought by Hayashibara Ichiro, a wealthy industrialist, who in 1964 turned it into one of the first private museums in Japan. It houses an extensive collection, displayed in rotation, of more than 10,000 items from ancient Japan, including **kimono★** from the Noh theater of the late Muromachi era, a **screen★★** decorated with a view of Kyoto in the 18C, as well as armor, swords, lacquerware, and paintings in ink inherited from the Ikeda family.

Okayama Orient Museum★
オリエント美術館
⌚*Map, B1/2. 15min walk from the station, or tram no.1 to Shiroshita (*⌚*¥100). www.orientmuseum.jp.*
⌚*Open Tue–Sun 9am–5pm.* ⌚*¥300, excluding special exhibitions.*

Housed in a big, concrete building, this museum of Middle Eastern art and archeology was created in 1947, thanks to a donation from a wealthy Okayama businessman. It contains some 5000 items, mostly from the **ancient Persian empires**. Its two floors are arranged around a large, central patio containing a marble fountain reminiscent of the courtyard of an early caravanserai. The works are displayed in chronological order: prehistoric hunter-gatherers, the rise of cities, and ancient empires, Persia and Greece, Islamic civilization. Among the finest pieces is a bas-relief from the Assyrian royal palace of Nimrod (Iraq, 9C BC), a funerary bas-relief from Palmyra (3C BC), fragments of Roman mosaics from Syria (5C), and glazed pottery from Iran (13C and 14C).

EXCURSIONS
KIBI PLAIN★ 吉備平野
This cycle route begins 9mi/15km west of Okayama. Take the JR Kibi Line to Bizen Ichinomiya Station (12min journey, ⌚*¥210), where bikes can be rented (open daily 9am–6pm, around* ⌚*¥400/2hr,* ⌚*¥1000/day). They can be dropped off on arrival at Soja Station. From there, you can get a train back to Okayama (30–40min,* ⌚*¥420–510), or on to Kurashiki (10min,* ⌚*¥240) or Bitchu-Takahashi (25min,* ⌚*¥420). Allow around 4hr if cycling, ideally between May and Sept when the paddy fields are green, or a day on foot.*

The 10.5mi/17km-long Kibi Plain Bicycle Route is a specially designed trail across the Okayama countryside. If the weather is fine it is a real pleasure to cycle the small roads that wind between the paddy fields, hamlets, meadows, and wooded hills, scattered with remains dating back to the old kingdom of Kibi *(4–5C)*. Places of interest along the way include the **Kibitsu-jinja**, a shrine built in 1425 and dedicated to Prince Kibitsuhiko, the inspiration for the legend of Momotaro *(*⌚*see box opposite);* **Tsukuriyama-kofun**, an imposing 5C burial mound; and **Bitchu Kokubun-ji** and its five-story pagoda, near Soja.

TAKAHASHI★ 高梁
31mi/50 km northwest of Okayama. Bitchu-Takahashi Station, on the JR Hakubi Line to Okayama (55min, ⌚*¥860) or Kurashiki (35min,* ⌚*¥590).*

A small town hemmed in by mountains and surrounded by paddy fields, Takahashi has a well-preserved historic quarter 0.6mi/1km north of the station, centered on the area known as Ishibiya-cho, which is lined with merchant and samurai houses from the Edo period. Some are open to visitors, such as **Buke Yashiki-kan** (🕐*open daily 9am–5pm;* ⊜*¥400),* two houses (the former Orii and Haibara residences) which have several traditional rooms you can explore, including kitchens, plus gardens, and a storehouse where armor is displayed. On the same street, the Rinzai Zen temple **Raikyu-ji** (🕐*open daily 9am–5pm;* ⊜*¥300)* has a gorgeous **dry landscape garden★** designed in 1604 by the famous architect, gardener, and tea master Kobori Enshu (1579–1647). Its borders of raked sand combining rocks and azalea groves stand out gracefully against the borrowed landscape *(shakkei)* of Mount Atago. But, although not easy to reach, Takahashi's main point of interest remains its castle.

Bitchu-Matsuyama Castle★
備中松山城

3mi/5km north of the station. Access by taxi (around ⊜*¥1400 from the station), or on foot (approx. 1hr 20min).* 🕐*Open daily: Apr–Sept 9am–5.30pm; Oct–Mar 9am–4.30pm.* ⊜*¥300.*

Perched high on Mount Gagyu, at an altitude of 1410ft/430m, this fortress is the highest in Japan. The original structure, built in 1240, was enlarged at the beginning of the 16C at the time of the Sengoku wars. After the Meiji Restoration, the castle was forgotten until the town undertook to restore it in the 1950s. The small (two-story) **keep** was rebuilt in wood. From the castle terrace, there is a lovely **view** of the river below and the surrounding mountains.

KURASHIKI★★ 倉敷

15.5mi/25km west of Okayama. JR San'yo Line from Okayama (15min, ⊜*¥330). The shinkansen stops at Shin-Kurashiki Station, a 10min local train ride (*⊜*¥1200) from the more central Kurashiki Station.*

Momotaro the hero

According to a legend from the Edo period, still a story taught to every Japanese child in shool, the little boy Momotaro was found floating down a river in a giant peach by an elderly couple. He set off to fight the ogres of the island of Onigashima, in the Inland Sea. On the way, he befriended a dog, a monkey, and a pheasant, who all helped him to defeat the ogres.

An obligatory stop on the San'yo road between the Inland Sea and the northern regions, this merchant town prospered, thanks to the rice and textile trades. Enjoying the status of a free port, linked to the sea by canals, it became so rich that it was placed under the direct supervision of the shogunate during the Edo period. Today, Kurashiki (population 477,000) is the largest center for the production of jeans in Japan.

Located 875yd/800m to the south of the station *(10min walk),* the **historical district of Bikan★★**, with its storehouses and romantic canals lined with weeping willows, has retained its old character. Today, its many art museums, restaurants, *ryokan,* and handicraft shops make it a lively tourist center.

🚤*Boat rides on the canals (Tue–Sun 9.30am–5pm, 30min,* ⊜*¥500) are available Mar–Nov.*

Ohashi House 大橋家住宅

3-21-31 Aichi, at the entrance to the Bikan district, behind the Dormy Inn Hotel. ohashi-ke.com. 🕐*Open Dec–Feb Sat–Thur 9am–5pm; Apr–Oct Sat 9am–6pm, Sun–Fri 9am–5pm; Mar & Nov daily 9am–5pm.* ⊜*¥550.*

The Ohashi family built its fortune in the 18C on salt and rice. Because of the influence they exerted, they were given permission by the shogunate to build this residence in 1796. The wide front door leads to an open space separating the house from the street: a style theoretically reserved for the samurai class. The original house had more than

A family of art patrons

Ohara Ken-Ichiro, director—and grandson of the founder—of the Ohara Museum of Art, traces the history of the collection: "My grandfather Magosaburo was a cotton baron but also a philanthropist, who among other things founded the hospital in Kurashiki. When it came to art, his first interest was Eastern art of the past, but then his friend, the artist Kojima Torajiro, introduced him to Western painting. Between 1912 and 1923, Kojima made several trips to Paris, Belgium, Germany, and Switzerland to buy modern paintings for Magosaburo, visiting Monet's studio at Giverny and Matisse's studio in Paris. At the time, very few Western works could be seen in Japan. Magosaburo's one wish was to enlighten the Japanese public by showing his collection. The works acquired during that period form the kernel of the museum's holdings. My father Soichiro added artists belonging to the Mingei movement, and modern European, American, and Japanese art. I myself continue to buy a great deal of contemporary art."

25 rooms, and about 30 people lived here, including servants. The interior is typical of the houses of rich Kurashiki merchants, with *tatami* rooms at the front for business and for entertaining guests, and private rooms at the rear. On the upper floor, an attic was used for storing the family's possessions (kimono, ceramics, scrolls). At the far end of the garden is a storehouse that has been turned into an exhibition hall.

▶ Cross the avenue called Chuo-dori to get to the main canal of Bikan, where the principal museums can be found.

Ohara Museum of Art★★
大原美術館

1-1-15 Chuo. ◐*Open Tue–Sun 9am–5pm.* ◉*¥1300 (with Kojima Torajiro Memorial Hall), audioguide ¥500. ohara.or.jp/en.*
In 1930, **Ohara Magosaburo**, who had made his fortune in textiles, created a museum to display his **collection of Western art**, one of the finest in Japan. Located on the right (west) bank of the canal, the building has a colonnaded façade like a Greek temple, a copy of the entrance to the Royal Museum in Ghent, Belgium.
The **Main Gallery** showcases Western sculptures and paintings, including a comprehensive survey of the various early-20C French and European movements: Barbizon school, school of Paris, Impressionists and post-Impressionists,

Nabis, Fauvists, Symbolists, and academic painters. Highlights include a vibrant Monet *Waterlilies* (1906), a Gauguin from the Tahitian period (1892), and an *Annunciation* by El Greco (late 16C), as well as works by Renoir, Toulouse-Lautrec, Pissarro, Puvis de Chavannes, Modigliani, Matisse, and Foujita.
Among the postwar artists represented are Fautrier, Soulages, Pollock, Warhol, and De Kooning. Sculptures by Rodin, Bourdelle, and Henry Moore are on display in the garden. At the far end, the museum's **annex**, built in the style of a traditional Kurashiki storehouse, is devoted to modern and contemporary Japanese artists such as Fujishima Takeji, Koide Narashige, Aoki Shigeru, Kumagai Morikazu, Kishida Ryusei, and Yasui Sotaro. The **Craft Art Gallery** displays the work of some of the leading artists of the Folk Art or *Mingei* movement (◐*see p115*). Finally, in the adjoining **Asiatic Art Gallery**, housed in some restored traditional warehouses, is the work of some of the leading lights of the Mingei movement: Hamada Shoji, Kawai Kanjiro, Munakata Shiko, and Yanagi Soetsu. The Chinese Room, just before the exit, has a beautiful stone Buddha of the Northern Wei Dynasty (386–534).

▶ Before carrying along the river bank, south, stop to look at two lovely houses. The **Ohara House** on the left is a superb example of a rich merchant's home, and beside it is the **Villa Yurinso**, both thinked to the family which founded the art museum.

Kurashiki Museum of Folkcraft★ 倉敷民芸館

1-4-11 Chuo. ◯*Open Tue–Sun (daily in Aug): Mar–Nov 9am–5pm; Dec–Feb 9am–4.15pm.* ◉*¥700. kurashiki-mingeikan.com.*

Opened in 1948, this museum is housed in a former rice *kura* (storehouse) typical of Kurashiki, with whitewashed cob walls with black tiles. It is the largest museum of popular **Japanese handicrafts** after the one in Tokyo. The collection comprises about 15,000 items *(displayed in rotation)*, most of them ordinary objects made by anonymous artisans. The prime objective is to demonstrate the beauty in everyday objects, but the museum also serves tosupport local craft traditions. Apart from the pottery, furniture, fabrics, and glassware of Kurashiki, you can see examples of weaving and basketwork from Africa, Southeast Asia, and South America.

👥 Japan Rural Toy Museum★ 日本郷土玩具館

1-4-16 Chuo, not far from the folkcraft museum. ◯*Open daily: Mar–Nov 9am–5pm; Dec–Feb 10am–5pm.* ◉*¥400 (children ¥200). gangukan.jp.* ▱.

No fewer than 5000 toys on display and 40,000 in storage. Children of all ages will love this colorful museum with its dolls, automata, lucky charms, wooden or papier mâché *(hariko)* animals, and figures, kites, miniatures, and games from across Japan. You stroll about beneath the gaze of some favourite Japanese animals (owls, foxes). There are some rare items from the Edo period in display cases on the ground floor and the attic. The museum has a little **shop** selling the ubiquitous *maneki-neko* (cats with raised paws) and Daruma dolls (lucky figurines of Buddhist origin). You can also see traditional crafts in the attached **Plus One Gallery**, a chic, modern space, and buy locally made tableware at the **Side Terrace** shop.

▶ Walk back along the canal and cross the little bridge opposite the Tourist Office. Carry straight on, then turn right onto Honmachi-dori.

Honmachi-dori 本町通り

This narrow lane is lined with picturesque traditional houses, with roofs of silver-gray tiles and whitewashed walls adorned with wooden latticework, attractive old shops, sake breweries, cafes, and galleries. To the south of the street is **Ivy Square**, formerly the site of a textile mill. Today it accommodates more restaurants, shops, and cafes, as well as the **Kojima Torajiro Memorial Hall** (◯*open Tue–Sun 9am–5pm;* ◉*¥1300 combined ticket with the Ohara Museum of Art)*, an Impressionist painter who helped Ohara Magosaburo to build his collection *(✦see box opposite)*.

KOJIMA 児島 AND THE SETO OHASHI★ 瀬戸大橋

From Okayama, rail access via the Seto Ohashi Line to Kojima Station (Ltd Express, 25min journey, ◉*¥510); from Kurashiki, bus to Kojima Station.*

This small coastal town 12mi/20km south of Kurashiki and 16mi/25km from Okayama is renowned as the **Japanese jeans capital**, with everything from stores and workshops to buses decorated like denim. More than anything, however, it is known for being the town closest to the famous **Seto Ohashi** (Great Seto Bridge). Opened in 1988 after several decades of construction work, it is in fact six bridges (road, freeway, rail) in a line, linking Honshu and Shikoku from island to island across 8mi/13km. To fully admire this remarkable structure, which makes use of a number of construction techniques (suspension bridges, cantilevered bridges, etc.), climb the little hill near the town center; the view is amazing at sundown. Alternatively, you could take a little boat trip from the quay opposite Kojima Station *(daily 9am–3pm, Sat–Sun only in winter, 45min,* ◉*¥1600)*. There are plenty of attractions associated with the bridge to try in the area, including a museum, viewing points, and a bus tour.

Fishing port, Tomonoura

© sanoaku/iStock

TOMONOURA★ 鞆の浦

48mi/78km southwest of Okayama.
To Fukuyama: 15min from Okayama
(✍¥2760) or 10min from Shin-Kurashiki
(✍¥1460) by JR San'yo Line shinkansen
to Fukuyama Station, or local JR train
(1hr from Okayama, ✍¥990; 45min from
Kurashiki, ✍¥770). Then Tomotetsu
bus to Tomonoura (30min, ✍¥520) or
Tomoku (35min, ✍¥550), from platform
no. 5, outside Fukuyama Station. 🄸The
Tourist Office is by Tomonoura bus
stop (🕐open daily 9am–4.30pm;
audioguide ✍¥500; maps, brochures
and smartphone app alternative to
audioguide ✍no charge; tomonoura.jp).
If you wish to enjoy the countryside and
atmosphere of the Inland Sea, or learn
a little more about its history, Tomonoura (and Onomichi, *see p433*) makes
an interesting stop on the journey to
Hiroshima or a day-trip from Okayama.

You will have to pass through the city of
Fukuyama *(🄸Tourist Office in the JR sta-*
tion, 🕐open daily 9am–5pm, fukuyama-
kanko.com).
Situated in a little bay surrounded and
sheltered by islands, this fishing port
dates back to ancient times and inspired
some of the poems incorporated into the
Man'yoshu ("Collection of 10,000 Leaves,"
7–8C). The town center is easy to explore
on foot and has retained much of its Edo-
period beauty, leaving a picturesque
environment that inspired the director
Miyazaki Hayao to make his film Ponyo
(2009). Anyone who has seen it will inevitably be reminded as they watch the little
delivery trucks picking their way through
the narrow streets down by the sea, or
stroll round the fishing port in the early
morning, or just sit and watch the sun go
down over the islands of the Inland Sea.

An Important Trade Route

During the time Japan was cut off from the rest of the world (17C to mid-19C),
international commercial exchanges were limited and circumscribed (*see p78*).
Domestic interaction developed considerably, however, and one of the most
important of these trade routes was the sea route used by the *kitamaebune*
(literally "the ships coming from the north"), linking the island of Hokkaido with
Osaka via the Sea of Japan coast, the Kanmon Straits, and the Inland Sea. By the
end of the Edo period, approaching 400 commercial ships, large-sailed junks
capable of transporting 150 tons of cargo, were plying this route. The many ports
along the way in which they stopped off—such as Tomonoura, Onomichi, and
Sakata (*see p496*)— grew rich from trading: wood, coal, rice, salt, potatoes,
seaweed, herrings, and more were transported first to Osaka and then to Edo.
Such exchanges also encouraged intense cultural and social interaction.

The village and the temples

Taichoro – ⏱*Open daily 8am–5pm.* 🎫*¥200.* This house (very late 17C) located in the grounds of **Fukuzen-ji** was intended as a place to host Korean ambassadors visiting the shogun's court during the Edo period. Since this time, it has become famed for the panoramic views it allows of the surrounding islands (spoilt a little nowadays by modern construction work). The temple has an unusual object, too: the **Maria Kannon**, a statue of the Virgin Mary disguised as Kannon, when Chrstianity was suppressed in Japan during the Edo period. A dozen other temples are spread across the base of the hill and can be explored as you stroll through the pretty lanes of the village.

Around the port

Irohamaru Museum – ⏱*Open daily 10am–6pm.* 🎫*¥200.* This museum tells the story of the shipwreck of the Irohamaru, which happened off the coast of Tomonoura in 1867. The event is well-known in Japan as the famous samurai **Sakamoto Ryoma** (1836–67) was on board (👣*see p573*); he survived the wreck, but was assassinated later that same year. There is still a stone lantern and quays (*gangi*) built during the Edo period to admire in the old port.

Ota residence – ⏱*Open Wed–Mon, 10am–5pm.* 🎫*¥400.* This vast complex, made up of nine buildings dating back to the 18C, belonged to a rich family of brewers. It was used to make *homeishu*, a popular local plant-based liqueur.

Sensui-jima – 🚢 A stone's thrown from the village and accessible via ferry (*daily 7am–9.30pm, 5min crossing, ¥240 round trip*), this little island is just the place for walkers to enjoy a number of pretty beaches, and views of the islands and shipping traffic from a number of vantage points. There's also a hotel, with beautiful outdoor baths open to non-staying guests (*open daily 10am–9pm, ¥550;* 👣*see p435*).

ONOMICHI 尾道

Located 56mi/90km west of Okayama. 30min by JR San'yo Line shinkansen from Okayama to Shin-Onomichi (🎫¥3100), or 1hr 20min by local JR train to Onomichi (¥1340). 🚉*Tourist Offices in both stations (JR Shin-Onomichi Station:* ⏱*open daily 9am–6pm; Onomichi Station:* ⏱*open daily 9am–6pm; English brochures and maps). See city. onomichi.hiroshima.jp & ononavi.com.*

This large port (population: 138,600) is located along the shores of a narrow sound. Six little islands, linked by bridges, separate it from the island of Shikoku, 43mi/70km distant (👣*see p546*). This strategic positioning allowed the port to play a key role in the commercial traffic that grew up in the Inland Sea from the Middle Ages, bringing it wealth and prosperity.

Stretched out along gentle hills, the city is extremely agreeable for strolling around and there is always something of interest in the sound: shipping traffic (little ferries on their way to Mukaishima across the water, large cargo ships), giant cranes, and the distant sounds of the docks and the naval yard. You can take a shuttle from the ferry port (beneath the Green Hill Hotel) to the surrounding islands as easily as you would a bus.

There is no shortage of restaurants offering seafood and ramen (for which Onomichi is one of Japan's leading cities), and you can stroll along the peaceful lanes running up and down the hills with only cats for company. The lanes lead from temple to temple with a myriad of beautiful views of the city.

Senko-ji Park – *Bus from JR Onomichi Station to Nagaeguchi, then walk or cable car.* ⏱*Open daily 9am–5pm. Cable car:* 🎫*¥320 one way, ¥500 round trip.* Perched on a hill, this park boasts a **panoramic view★** of its surroundings: the island of Mukaishima, located on the other side of the sound; the unceasing ballet of the little ferries shuttling between the two banks; the string of islands; and the bridges connecting them all the way to Shikoku. From the temple, there is a pleasant walk that will take you down

Shimanami Kaido over Innoshima Bridge

© JTB Photo/age fotostock

to the sea through a maze of pretty cobbled lanes.

You might stop off en route at the nearby **Onomichi City Museum of Art** *(17-19 Nishi Tsushido-cho, ☏0848-23-2281, 🕐open only during temporary exhibitions, Tue–Sun 9am–5pm, ✆varies by exhibition).* Located 5 minutes' walk from the viewing point and not far from a romantic orchard garden (a lovers' place, as the sign there points out), this museum, expanded by Ando Tadao, puts on some interesting exhibitions of local and international art and design.

Jodo-ji – *Take a bus from JR Onomichi Station to Jodoji-shita.* This Buddhist temple, founded by prince Shotoku at the beginning of the 7C, and thus one of the oldest in the country, is home to a great number of national treasures, notable a statue of Kannon dating from the Heian period (which is exhibited once every 33 years) and a screen (15–16C) decorated with scenes from the *Tale of Genji*. The last scene of Ozu Yasujiro's film *Tokyo Story* was shot on the esplanade beside the sea here. This is the easternmost stop on Onomichi's **Historical Temple Path**; follow it to explore the other temples scattered across the hills, 25 of which now remain out of the 80 that have been built over

the centuries with donations given by rich merchants from the city. Route map in English available from the tourist information offices.

Shimanami Kaido★★ – A **maintained cycling route** *(blue markings on the ground)* from Onomichi to Imabari on the island of Shikoku, which has the unusual feature of crossing six islands and seven bridges. It is an ideal way to enjoy the scenery and different light conditions of the Inland Sea. You can cover either its whole length *(44mi/70km)* or just a part, taking time to explore the islands and take in the beaches.

🛈*There are good English-language cycling maps from the Tourist Offices. The U2 building (onomichi-u2.com/en) is also a helpful place to visit; you can hire bikes here, get repairs, and pick up any information you might need about the route. The same services are available at the other end of the Shimanami Kaido, in Imabari (🕐 see p446).*

You can hire a bike (cross bike, tandem or e-bike) at either end of the route (shimanami-cycle.or.jp/rental/english), dropping it off at any of 14 bike hire points along the route (except e-bikes, which must be returned to the same place) and continuing/returning by bus. ✆¥1100–1600/day, plus a deposit of ✆¥1100 (refundable if you return the bike to the same place). Giant bike rental is also possible (bicyclerental.jp/en; store in the U2 building, ⏰ open daily 9am–7pm), but you can't drop the bike off along the route. ⛟¥4400–14,300/day, plus ⛟¥3000 surcharge to drop the bike off at the other end of the route.

Nao-shima ★★ *see Islands of the Inland Sea, (⏰ see p554).*

ADDRESSES

🏠 STAY

OKAYAMA

🛏🛏 **Excel Okayama** エクセル岡山 – *5-1 Ishizeki-cho, Kita-ku (Map, B2). ☎086-224-0505. excel-okayama.com. 89 rooms. ¥10,200. ¥850 🍴.* A business hotel ideally located near the castle and the museums. Small but functional rooms.

🛏🛏 **Hotel Via Inn** ヴィアイン岡山 – *1-25 Ekimoto-cho, Kita-ku. (Map, A1–2). ☎086-251-5489. viainn.com/en/okayama. 251 rooms. ¥13,600. 🍴.* A reasonably new tower block near the railway. Standard business hotel rooms, practical and with a good view over the town from the upper floors. The sound of trains will either rock you to sleep or keep you awake.

🛏🛏 **Okayama Plaza Hotel** 岡山プラザホテル – *2-3-12 Hama, Naka-ku (Map, B2). ☎086-272-1201. oplaza-h.co.jp. 80 rooms. ¥11,600. ¥800 🍴.* A chain hotel with all modern conveniences, close to Koraku-en. All rooms are non-smoking.

🛏🛏🛏 **Hotel Granvia** ホテルグランヴィア岡山 – *1-15 Ekimoto-cho, Kita-ku (Map, A2). ☎086-234-7000. granvia-oka. co.jp. 329 rooms. ¥23,760. ¥1980 🍴.* Rooms are well-maintained and beautifully decorated. There are 11 banqueting rooms and restaurants. Pool, sauna and jacuzzi on site.

KURASHIKI

Apart from the business hotels near the station (🛏🛏 *Alpha-One, Tokyo Inn, and the pleasant Dormy Inn*), there are several pretty *ryokan*.

🛏🛏 **Kurashiki Ivy Square** 倉敷アイビースクエア– *7-2 Honmachi. ☎086-422-0011. ivysquare.co.jp. 149 rooms. ¥13,320. ¥1980 🍴.* This red-brick building from the end of the 19C, a former courthouse converted into a cotton mill in 1899, is now a charming hotel.

🛏🛏🛏 **Ryori Ryokan Tsurugata** 料理旅館鶴形 – *1-3-15 Chuo, ☎086-424-1635. turugata.jp. 11 rooms. ¥47,400. 🍴, dinner also included.* Attractive traditional rooms around the garden of a former residence. The restaurant is highly recommended, with its elegant but unpretentious Japanese cuisine.

TOMONOURA

🛏🛏 **Kokuminshukusha Sensui-jima** 国民宿舎仙酔島 – *3373-2 Tomo-cho, Fukuyama-shi. ☎084-970-5050. tomonoura. co.jp/sen/02shukusha.html. 13 rooms. ¥19,360. 🍴, dinner also included.* On the island of Sensui-jima (⏰ see p433), this hotel is close to nature (beach, coastal paths) and is great for rest and relaxation. Japanese or Western rooms and nice baths, plus a good restaurant.

ONOMICHI

🛏 **Green Hill Hotel Onomichi** グリーンヒルホテル尾道 – *9-1 Higashi-Gosho-cho. ☎0848-24-0100. shimanami-gho.co.jp. 92 rooms. ¥9510. ¥1650 🍴.* Functional but pleasant hotel between the port and the JR station. Great view of the small ferries that serve the Island of Mukaishima.

🛏🛏 **Hotel Alpha-1 Onomichi** ホテル・アルファーワン尾道 – *1-1 Nishi-Gocho-cho. ☎0848-25-5600. alpha-1.co.jp/onomichi. 196 rooms. ¥10,700. ¥900 🍴.* A good-value option with small, standard business hotel rooms. No surprises, but well situated.

🛏🛏🛏 **Hotel Cycle** ホテルサイクル – *5-11 Nishi-Gosho-cho. ☎0848-21-0550. onomichi-u2.com/en. 28 rooms. ¥22,000. ¥1620 🍴.* An unusual concept for a hotel, in a former U2 warehouse by the sea. The modern, comfortable rooms are artfully decorated in a blend of industrial and traditional style. A good base for those tackling the Shimanami Kaido; there's even a space specifically for storing your bike in your room.

🛏🛏🛏🛏 **Bella Vista Spa & Marina Onomichi** ベラヴィスタスパ＆マリーナ尾道 – *1344-2 Oobiraki, Urasaki-cho. ☎084-987-1122. bella-vista.jp. 45 rooms. ¥44,000. ¥4950 🍴.* Several miles from Onomichi and Fukuyama, this hotel on a hill benefits from a magnificent view over the inland sea. Elegant, spacious Japanese- and Western-style rooms. *Onsen* and multiple restaurants.

🍴 EAT

OKAYAMA

🍜 **Toritetsu** とり鉄岡山錦町店 – 3-101 Nisiki-cho. (Map, A2). 📞086-235-3681. tori-tetsu.com/shop/304p. Open daily 11.30am–3pm & 5pm–midnight (Fri–Sat to 1am). A small *yakitori* restaurant with a young, trendy vibe.

🍜 **Yamato** やまと – 1-9-7 Omote-cho. (Map, B2). 📞086-232-3944. shokudou-yamato.com. Open Wed–Mon 11am–7pm. 🍱. Unpretentious and very popular. You can replenish your energy reserves with classic Japanese curry, ramen, *katsudon*, etc., without breaking the bank.

🍜🍜 **Toriyoshi** 鳥好駅前本店 – 5-8 Honmachi, Okayama Station. (Map, A2). 📞086-233-1969. Open daily 4pm–midnight. Menu in English. This popular place is a tavern, where the waitresses bustle about between huge wooden tables. Oysters in vinegar, sashimi, tempura, etc.

KURASHIKI

🍜 **Miyake Shouten** 三宅商店 – 3-11 Honmachi. 📞086-426-4600. Open Mon–Fri 11.30am–5.30pm, Sat 11am–7.30pm, Sun 8.30am–5.30pm (varies by season). Lunch from ¥900. 🍱. A restaurant in an old store, with tables of bare wood, simple, well-made dishes at lunchtime and excellent cakes and hot drinks.

🍜🍜 **Taishoutei** 大正亭 – 2-14 Honmachi. 📞086-422-8100. kurashiki.co.jp/taisyotei. Open daily noon–2pm & 5.30–9pm. 🍱. The specialty is the *mamakari-zushi* (a member of the herring family).

🍜🍜 **Mingeijaya Shinsui** 民芸茶屋新粋 – 11-35 Honmachi. 📞086-422-5171. k-suiraitei.com/shinsui. Open Mon–Sat, 5–10pm. A vast wooden counter surrounds the cooks, occupied with cutting up fish when they are not making *oden* (the local hot pot).

🍜🍜🍜 **Terrace Kurashiki Ryokan** 旅館くらしき –4-1 Honmachi. 📞086-422-0730. ryokan-kurashiki.jp/en. Open Tue–Sun 11am–5pm. Menu in English. Lunch around ¥1850; kaiseki lunch from ¥6250, dinner ¥10,000. The café belonging to Kurashiki *ryokan* offers excellent seasonal menus in an agreeable setting. Try the *sanpo-michi* lunch box with 12 dishes. Only *kaiseki* courses in the evening.

TOMONOURA

🍜 **Café @** – 844-3 Kojimachi, Fukuyama-shi. 📞084-982-0131. tomonoura-a-cafe. jp. Open Thur–Tue 10am–6pm. Lunch from ¥990. A smiling welcome awaits you at this laidback cafe in a rustic, traditional building. Sandwiches, pasta, fresh juices.

🍜 **Chitose** 千とせ – 552-7 Tomo-cho-tomo. 📞084-982-3165. Open Wed–Mon 11.30am–3pm & 6–9pm. Lunch around ¥900, dinner ¥2000. 🍱. Hearty meals in this restaurant on a quiet village street. An excellent place to try the region's fish and seafood.

ONOMICHI

🍜🍜 **Yamaneko Mill** ヤマネコ ミル – 5-2 Higashi-Gosho-cho. 📞848-36-5331. ittoku-go.com. Open Tue–Sun 10am–8pm. Menu in English. Set menus around ¥3000, a la carte cheaper. A good bet for a quick bite near the station, with an Italian-influenced menu. Try the Onomichi pudding, beautifully presented in small glass bottles.

🍜🍜 **Onomichi U2** オノミチ ユーツー – 5-11 Nishi-gosho-cho. 📞0848-21-0550. onomichi-u2.com. Yard Cafe & Butti Bakery: open Mon–Fri 9am–6pm, Sat–Sun 8am–7pm. The Restaurant: open Mon–Fri 7–10am & 11.30am–4.30pm, Sat–Sun also 5.30–9.30pm. Kog Bar: open daily 5.30–9.30pm. Menu in English. Restaurant lunch around ¥2000, dinner ¥3500. Situated on the promenade, past the Green Hill Hotel, this former warehouse has been totally renovated to house a lovely bar-restaurant-hotel complex. A bright interior respects the building's industrial past, and with attentive staff and a varied range of menus, it's a great success. There are excellent Viennese cakes and patisserie at Butti Bakery, while the Yard Cafe is ideal for coffee and a snack. The seafood is excellent at the international/Japanese The Restaurant, and you can round off the night at the chic Kog Bar.

SHOPPING

Each town on the coast is proud of its specialties and local produce (fish, fruit...), used in everything from cakes to the Kit-Kat that you can eat on the spot or offer as a present. White peaches and *mamakari* (herring-like fish) from Okayama, figs, citrus, and ramen from Onomichi, strawberries from Te-shima.

SPORT AND LEISURE

Cycling – Cyclists should not miss the two superb cycle ways around Okayama: the Kibi plain (👟see p428) and the Shimanami Kaido (👟see p434).

The San'yo Coast★: Hiroshima★★

山陽：広島

Some people visit the city out of a sense of duty, while others prefer to avoid the experience for fear of finding it too upsetting, but nobody can be indifferent to Hiroshima, a charming city which has the sad distinction of tbeing the first city to be struck by an atomic bomb, in August 1945. Within just a few seconds, the explosion had turned the center of the city into a wasteland. Today, only the charred framework of the A-Bomb Dome remains to bear witness to the nuclear inferno. The destruction of Hiroshima was a turning point in world history, and the city has worked tirelessly to deliver a warning to future generations, seen by most visitors through its Peace Memorial Park.

But like a phoenix reborn from its own ashes, Hiroshima has also looked to the future and today it is a dynamic city (the largest in Chugoku) and active port, with sports and cultural activities, and a vibrant nightlife. A couple of miles away, the island of Miyajima has one of the most famous views in Japan: the *torii* (gate) of Itsukushima Shrine, which appears to float in the water just offshore. The little town of Iwakuni, once a samurai stronghold, has a well-preserved and picturesque wooden bridge.

BACKGROUND

A strategic base – Hiroshima was founded in 1589 by the feudal lord Mori Terumoto, who built his castle on the largest of the islands formed by the branches of the Ota River—hence the name of the city (*Hiro* means "large" and *shima* "island"). It expanded during the Edo period, and became industrialized soon after the Meiji Restoration. During

▶ **Population:** 2 million – Hiroshima Prefecture

⌚ **Michelin Map:** Regions of Japan Map 4, Regional Map p423, Hiroshima Map p438.

▷ **Location:** Situated on the Inland Sea, 99mi/160km from Okayama and 175mi/280km from Fukuoka, Hiroshima occupies the delta of the Ota River, which divides the city into several islands. It is easily covered on foot or by tram. The JR station is to the east of the downtown area, the Peace Memorial Park to the west.

👥 **Kids:** Some of the images and eyewitness accounts presented in the Peace Memorial Museum may be disturbing for younger children, but the Peace Park should be fine; Miyajima, with its deer and walking trails, will appeal to the whole family.

🕐 **Timing:** You can visit Hiroshima and Miyajima in one day, but it's more sensible to allow two days. Reckon on spending one night in Hiroshima and the other on Miyajima.

☺ **Don't miss:** Peace Memorial Park; the island of Miyajima.

the First Sino–Japanese War (1894–95), the Imperial High Command was based here, and in the 1930s, the armaments industry became established. Hiroshima Bay, including the Kure naval center, became the principal military base in the west of Japan. During World War II, Hiroshima was a strategic base maintaining southern Japan's land defenses. **August 6, 1945** – Under the code name "Manhattan Project," the Americans had been secretly working on an atomic bomb since 1942. In September 1944,

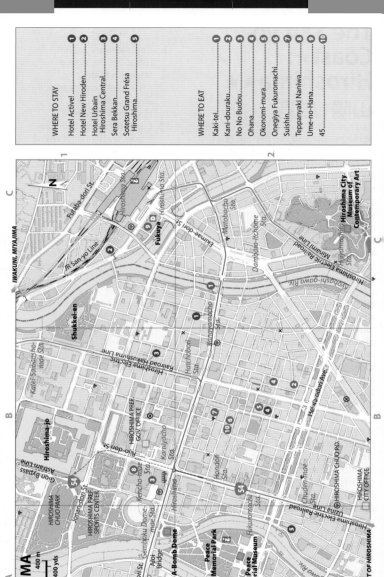

HIROSHIMA

Copyright 2015 Cartographic data Shobunsha/Michelin

N

IWAKUNI, MIYAJIMA

0   400 m
0   400 yds

WHERE TO STAY

Hotel Active! 1
Hotel New Hiroden 2
Hotel Urbain
  Hiroshima Central 3
Sera Bekkan 4
Sotetsu Grand Frésa
  Hiroshima 5

WHERE TO EAT

Kaki-tei 1
Kani-douraku 2
No No Budou 3
Ohana 4
Okonomi-mura 5
Onegiya Fukuromachi 6
Suishin 7
Teppanyaki Naniwa 8
Ume-no-Hana 9
45 10

Shukkei-en

Hiroshima-jo

HIROSHIMA PREF.
GOV. OFFICE

HIROSHIMA
CHUO PARK

HIROSHIMA PREF.
SPORTS CENTER

Fukuya

Hiroshima City Museum
of Contemporary Art

A-Bomb Dome

Peace
Memorial Park

Peace
Memorial Museum

HIROSHIMA CHUO P.O.

HIROSHIMA
CITY OFFICE

PORT OF HIROSHIMA

HIROSHIMA AIRPORT

438

the decision was taken to use it against Japan. A first test took place on July 16, 1945, in the desert of New Mexico. Four days later, the American high command finalized their list of potential targets: Hiroshima, Kokura, Niigata, and Nagasaki. In the early hours of the morning of August 6, 1945, the B-29 bomber *Enola Gay* took off carrying a 4-ton uranium-235 bomb nicknamed *Little Boy*. By dawn, the skies were clear over Hiroshima, and the city was chosen as the target. The bomb, dropped at 8.15am, exploded 1900ft/580m above the ground, directly over Shima Hospital in the heart of the city. Immediately, the sky was split by a flash of light and a terrifying explosion. A mushroom-shaped cloud rose over the horizon and the sky turned black. The explosion, equivalent to 15,000 tons of TNT, instantly razed the city to the ground. Of the 350,000 inhabitants and military personnel present at the time of the attack, including thousands of Korean slave laborers, 80,000 people were immediately killed.

In the following weeks, another 60,000 died, and 92 percent of the city's buildings were completely destroyed. Eyewitness accounts by survivors describe nightmarish visions: wounded people with disfigured faces and mutilated bodies staggering through the rubble like sleepwalkers, their clothes in tatters; others, horribly burned, screaming with thirst as they lay dying. Little known at the time and long suppressed by the American authorities, the secondary effects of radiation were equally terrifying: loss of hair, anemia, internal bleeding, fever, and infections. Subsequently, many of those exposed to radiation died of cancer, leukemia, and other diseases. Still today, we have every right, when confronted with these horrors, to wonder about the military purpose and moral validity of unleashing such a weapon on a civilian population.

Capital of peace – There were many who believed that the city would never come back to life and that it would be at least 75 years before any plants could be grown there again. Nevertheless, the population managed to rebuild it

> ### *Hibakusha*, the open wounds of the A-bomb
>
> Known as *Hibakusha* in Japanese, the living survivors of the atomic bomb in 2019 numbered, officially, 145,844. One of them, Mito Kosei, is a volunteer guide in Hiroshima. He was still in his mother's womb when exposed to radiation:
>
> "Since 1957, *Hibakusha* like me have been entitled to free medical treatment, but many are ashamed of their condition and prefer not to identify themselves."
>
> In addition to their physical suffering, the *Hibakusha* were for a long time covertly discriminated against. The US occupying authorities suppressed any reporting on the effects of the bomb in Japan for years, adding to the fear, shame and confusion endured by the survivors.

quite quickly, and in 1949, Hiroshima was proclaimed a City of Peace by the Japanese parliament. Reconstructed on a grid plan, the new city regained its pre-eminence in the region and its economic dynamism. Hiroshima may now look like any other Japanese city, but it has not forgotten its past, and continues to honor the memory of its dead through museums, annual ceremonies, and many initiatives for peace.

SIGHTS

A-Bomb Dome★ 原爆ドーム

🕐*Map, A1. 35min walk from Hiroshima Station, or 15min by tram (lines 2, 6, 1, subway M10, Genbaku Dome-mae).*
Facing Aioi Bridge and the Motoyasu River, the A-Bomb or Peace Memorial Dome (*Genbaku Domu*) is one of the few structures left standing after the atomic blast. Designed by the Czech architect Jan Letzel in the European style and erected in 1915, it was the Industrial Promotion Hall. All that remains now—left as a reminder of the catastrophic event—is the blackened metal structure, some twisted girders,

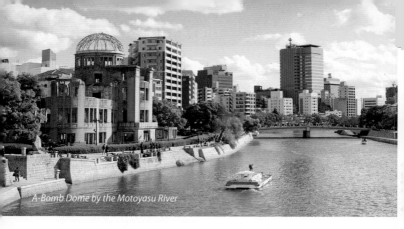
A-Bomb Dome by the Motoyasu River

and ruined walls. The surrounding buildings were destroyed, but because the bomb exploded almost vertically above it, the dome was partially spared. In December 1996, it was designated a UNESCO World Heritage Site. To prevent it from collapsing, it has had to be strengthened on several occasions, notably in 2002.

◐ Cross the river to the park opposite.

Peace Memorial Park★★
平和記念公園
🕭*Map, A2.*

Created in the 1960s by Tange Kenzo and planted with camphor trees and oleanders (the first flowers to start blooming again after the bombing), the park covers 30 acres/12ha. It lies at the northern tip of the island between the Ota and Motoyasu Rivers, in a part of the city that was completely destroyed by the bomb. It includes a number of monuments (fountains, towers, and columns) to the memory of the 140,000 victims who died, including the Peace Memorial Museum and the Memorial Cenotaph. Every year, on August 6, a ceremony of commemoration is held in the park.

Children's Peace Monument★
原爆の子の像

This statue, on a granite pedestal, was erected in memory of a girl named Sasaki Sadako, who was born on January 7, 1943, and died on October 25, 1955, at the age of 12 of leukemia caused by radiation. Sadako was two years old at the time the explosion took place, and was 1.2mi/2km from the epicenter. Most of her neighbors were killed, but she emerged unscathed, only to be diagnosed with leukemia in 1954.

Hoping to recover, Sadako set about folding 1000 origami cranes. According to Japanese tradition, anyone who accomplishes this task will see their wish granted. She had time to make 644 of these cranes before she died. Her classmates were so moved by her story that they continued folding cranes, and collected money to erect a monument to her (1958). Ever since then, every year, children around the world have been folding cranes and sending them to Hiroshima, where they are placed around the statue. Some come to place them personally on school trips. Thanks to Sadako, the origami crane has become an international symbol of peace.

Black Rain: the ordeal of the *Hibakusha*

A film by Shohei Imamura, 1988. Hiroshima, August 6, 1945. Yasuko is going to her uncle's house on board a boat when the bomb explodes; it is followed by a black rain that falls on the passengers. Unaware she has been irradiated, it is only some years later, when she is living peacefully in the country, that death begins to stalk her. Through the story of this young woman, the film tells of the ordeal lived by many **Hibakusha**: to their physical suffering was added the deep pain of being shunned by society and being labeled "contagious."

Memorial Cenotaph
原爆死没者慰霊碑
Designed by Tange Kenzo, the Cenotaph is in the form of an arch. Beneath it lies a tomb containing the names of all the victims of the bomb, inscribed with the epitaph: "May all the souls here rest in peace, for we shall not repeat the evil." Beside it burns the **Peace Flame**, which will only be put out when every last nuclear weapon on earth has been destroyed.

National Peace Memorial Hall★
国立広島原爆死没者追悼平和祈念館
🕐*Open daily: Mar–Jul & Sept–Nov 8.30am–6pm; Aug 8.30am–7/8pm; Dec–Feb 8.30am–5pm.* ✍*No charge. www.hiro-tsuitokinenkan.go.jp.*
To the right of the cenotaph, this gray marble-and-glass building built in 2002, again the work of Tange Kenzo, honors the memory of the victims of the bomb by presenting the full horror of the event. In the circular central hall, a fountain marks ground zero, its water having the symbolic function of soothing the souls of those who died thirsty. A 360-degree image shows the devastated city after the catastrophe. In the basement, computers show video testimonies and films shot at the time. The archives contain about 100,000 eye-witness accounts, all of them very moving. A wall screen displays the names and photographs of the dead.

Peace Memorial Museum★★★
広島平和記念資料館
🅖*Map, A2.* 🕐*Open daily: Mar–Jul & Sept–Nov 8.30am–6pm; Aug 8.30am–7/8pm; Dec–Feb 8.30am–5pm.* ✍*¥200, English audioguide ¥400. hpmmuseum.jp. Guided tours available 10.30am–2.30pm, 1hr–1hr 30min; ask at the Informatin Counter. Sometimes holds talks by hibakusha (🕐see p439).*
Also designed by Tange Kenzo, this harrowing museum shows the consequences of the atomic explosion through a large collection of photographs and objects that belonged to the victims. One of the two buildings displays a very realistic reconstruction

Historic Tramways
Among the trams in service today in Hiroshima, two (nos. 651 and 652) were circulating on the morning of August 6, 1945, and survived the effects of the atomic bomb. The Hiroshima Electric Railway Co. Ltd. (Hiroden for short) was founded three years later. The company's fleet of trams is unique as they date from different eras—the oldest dating back to 1925—and come from different cities—Kobe, Osaka, Kyoto, Fukuoka, and even Hannover and Dortmund)—which is why it has been dubbed "the Museum of Wheeled Transport."

of the ruins after the cataclysm, with terrible waxwork figures and genuine remnants of the tragedy: tattered clothes, melted bottles, vitrified tiles, twisted girders, and clocks with their hands frozen at 8.15am. The mechanism of the A-bomb and the damage caused by it are meticulously described, as well as the suffering endured by the population. There is also an informative overview of Hiroshima before and during the war, tracing the course of events leading up to the bombing, and attempting to explain why the city was chosen as a target by the US army.

Japanese militarism and its own many atrocities do not go unmentioned, nor does the fact that, among the victims, there were many Koreans and Chinese who had been working in the city as forced laborers. The American viewpoint, depicting Hiroshima as a "necessary sacrifice" to hasten the end of the war, is also called into question: could it be that the United States was also trying to beat its rivals, the USSR, to domination of the region?

The last section of the museum uses charts and scale models to show the current state of the world's nuclear arsenal, emphasizing the threat that the arms race poses to the future of mankind, and Hiroshima's commitment to peace.

USEFUL INFORMATION

Tourist Offices – All with English-speaking staff. hiroshima-navi.or.jp/en & visithiroshima.net.

Hiroshima Tourist Information – *South exit of Hiroshima Station. (Map, C1). Open daily 6am–midnight.* ☎082-263-5120.

Hiroshima City Tourist Information Centers – *Peace Memorial Park. (Map, A2). Open daily from 8.30am: Mar–Jul & Sept–Nov to 6pm; Aug to 7/8pm; Dec–Feb to 5pm.* ☎082-247-6738.

Shareo Kaimya-cho Underground Shopping Center. (Map, B2/3). Open daily 11am–5pm. ☎082-243-5716.

TRANSPORTATION

BY PLANE – **Hiroshima Airport** – *25mi/40km east of the center (A2 off map). www.hij.airport.jp.* Flights to Tokyo *(15 daily, 1hr 20min, ¥35,000)*, and the main Japanese cities.
Limousine Bus *(1hr, ¥1340)* to the city
BY TRAIN – **Hiroshima Station** – Hiroshima is on the Tokyo–Osaka–Hakata shinkansen Line. Links to Fukuoka *(Hakata; 1hr 5min, ¥8570)*, Shin-Osaka *(1hr 20min, ¥9890)* and Tokyo *(4hr, ¥18,380)*.

BY BOAT – setonaikaikisen.co.jp.
To the islands and Shikoku – The ferry terminal is at the end of tram lines 1, 3, and 5 from downtown, and 5 from the station. Allow 30min to get there. Regular links to the neighboring islands (Etajima, Ninoshima) and

Matsuyama (Shikoku), often stopping at Kure. Ferry *(10 per day, 2hr 40min to Matsuyama, ¥3670)* or speed boat *(12 per day, 1hr 10–20min, ¥7230)*.
To Miyajima – ♿*see Miyajima opposite.*

GETTING AROUND HIROSHIMA

BY TRAM – The 9 lines of the Hiroshima Electric Railway Co. Ltd *(hiroden.co.jp/en;* ♿*see box p441)* enable you to move about town easily. *Open daily approx. 5.30am–11pm, depending on the line. ¥190 per ticket in the city center. 1 Day Streetcar Pass ¥600 (¥840 with ferry for Miyajima). The Visit Hiroshima Small Area pass (2 days ¥1500) covers trams, buses and ferry to Miyajima; the Middle and Wide Area passes cover destinations further afield. Passes can be bought at Tourist Information Centers, on board the tramway, or at the Train Information Desk at the station (opposite the tramway departure platforms).*
Astram Line – This under/overground line leaves the city center (Hondori Station on Rijo-dori) and serves the northern and western suburbs for 12mi/18km *(¥490 to the end of the line).*
BY BOAT – **Gangi Taxi** – These are small boats (6 passengers max.) that go up and down the city's rivers. There are many boarding/disembarking points on the quays *(gangi)*: you can hail a boat or reserve one in advance *(☎082-230-5537, from ¥500 per person for 10min).*

Shukkei-en★ 縮景園
♿*Map, B–C1. Kaminobori-cho. 20min walk northeast of Peace Memorial Park.* ○*Open daily: Apr–Sept 9am–6pm; Oct–Mar 9am–5pm.* ✺*¥260. shukkeien.jp.*
This small garden *(10 acres/4ha)* was designed in 1620 by the local *daimyo* Asano Nagaakira. It is situated close to the Kyobashi River, from which it draws the water for its pretty central pond. The pond itself was modeled after the West Lake in Hangzhou, China, former capital of the Southern Song dynasty

(1127–1279). Wiped out by the A-bomb, Shukkei-en was rebuilt in 1951 from the original plans. Since then, the trees have had time to reach their adult height, shielding the park from its urban surroundings. The garden contains miniaturized versions of some of the country's most famous landscapes—the main hill, for example, symbolizes Mount Fuji, and the pond, with its many small islands, evokes the Inland Sea. Around the lake, several tea pavilions with thatched roofs add to the air of calm.

Hiroshima City Museum of Contemporary Art
広島市現代美術館

&Map, C2. 1-1 Hijiyama-koen. Tram Line 5, Hijiyama-shita stop. Open Tue–Sun 10am–5pm. ¥300 (excludes special exhibitions). hiroshima-moca.jp. Erected in 1989, this circular building set around a central open space is situated in Hiyajima Park on top of a hill planted with cherry trees. It was designed by the architect Kurokawa Kisho, who is associated with the Metabolist movement (see p101) and also designed the National Art Center in Tokyo. In addition to temporary exhibitions, there is a permanent collection of works by postwar Japanese and foreign artists, including a number from China and Korea.

EXCURSIONS
&Regional Map, A1.

Miyajima★★★ 宮島

Information booth at the ferry terminal (open daily 9am–6pm, &0829-44-2011). Also miyajima.or.jp & visit-miyajima-japan.com/en.

Access by train/tramway + ferry – From Hiroshima Station, JR San'yo Line to Miyajima-guchi (every 10min, journey time 25min, ¥420), or tramway line 2. Ferries, JR (jr-miyajimaferry.co.jp) or Miyajima Kisen (miyajima-matsudai.co.jp), depart from the pier in front of the station (10min crossing, ¥360 round trip); last returning boat 22.14pm.

Access by boat – From Hiroshima port to Miyajima (6/8 sailings a day, 30min crossing, ¥1900 one way, setonaikai-kisen.co.jp). From the Peace Park to Miyajima by fast boat (3–12 sailings a day, 45min crossing, ¥2200 one way, aqua-net-h.co.jp/en).

If you have the time, it's worth spending a few days in Miyajima. Firstly to see the village and its temples before/after the hoards of tourists, but also to explore its forests and landscape (Momiji Park, near the village, gives you a good idea of this) and surrounding beaches. Miyajima has been a sacred Shinto site since ancient times. With a surface area of 12sq mi/30sq km, it is forbidden either to be born or to die here, so there is no maternity hospital or cemetery on the island. The unusual feature of its main attraction, the beautiful **Itsuku-shima Shrine**, is that it is partly built in the sea. At high tide, the shrine appears to be floating on the water. The **view** of its great red *torii*, set in the water a short distance offshore, is one of the most famous in Japan.

Miyajima's mountains, forests, beaches, hiking trails, and freely roaming deer make it a favorite with families. The island was designated a UNESCO World Heritage Site in 1996.

Itsukushima Shrine★★★
厳島神社

15min walk from the ferry terminal. Open daily: Jan–Feb & mid-Oct–Nov 6.30am–5.30pm; Mar–mid-Oct 6.30am–6pm; Dec 6.30am–5pm. Treasure Hall: open daily 8am–5pm. ¥300, Treasure Hall ¥300, combined ticket ¥500. en.itsukushimajinja.jp.

Built on piles within a rugged bay, the shrine of Itsukushima is a superb example of how a man-made structure can complement its natural surroundings. Rated one of the three most beautiful **views** in the whole country (with Matsushima, see p474, and Amanohashidate), thousands of visitors come here every year to admire this classically beautiful building. According to tradition, the shrine dates from 593.

However, most of the buildings were not erected until the Heian period (in the *shinden* style used for aristocratic residences) by Taira no Kiyomori (1118–81), head of the Taira clan and governor of the region, who made Itsukushima his palace. Restored and enlarged several times, notably in 1556, the shrine is dedicated to the three daughters of the god Susano-o, of whom the eldest, Itsukushima, is the goddess of the sea.

The famous "**floating**" **torii★★★** about 656ft/200m offshore was rebuilt in 1875. Made of vermilion-lacquered camphorwood, it is 52.5ft/16m high. The fact that it stands offshore is thought to

© jon chica parada/iStock

relate to the sacred nature of the island: ordinary people were not allowed to set foot on it and had to approach by sea, through this gate, in order to get to the temple. The "floating" effect is strongest at high tide, but at low tide, when the sea floor is exposed and strewn with fragments of shell, it's possible to walk to the *torii* and get a better sense of how huge it is. The *torii* blazes with color in the evening sunset like a vast Japanese ideogram, and is attractively illuminated at night—artificially until 11pm, and then more subtly by the moon.

The shrine itself comprises several buildings linked by pontoons and verandas, including the hall of worship (**haiden**), the pavilion of offerings (**heiden**), and the main hall (**honden**). On the jetty facing the bay is the oldest **Noh theater stage** in Japan (16C).

The **Treasure Hall**, in a pavilion a little apart from the other buildings, includes a number of objects (sacred scrolls, weapons, musical instruments, masks, fans), offerings from the Taira, and others over the centuries. At the rear of the building is the **Tahoto**, a two-story pagoda.

Miyajima Public Aquarium
宮島水族館

10-3 Miyajami-cho (5min walk south from Itsukushima Shrine). ℰ0829-44-2010. www.miyajima-aqua.jp/english/ 🚻 ⏱*Open 9am–5pm (last admission 4pm).* 🎫*¥1,420; ¥710 under 15; ¥400 under 6; under 4 free).*

👥This aquarium presents the flora and fauna of the Inland Sea as well as of

other parts of the world, with a total of 350 different species. There's an interesting reconstruction of a local oyster farm.

Daisho-in★★ 大聖院
5min walk along the path that climbs up to the south of the shrine. ⏱*Open daily 8am–5pm.* 🎫*No charge. daisho-in.com.*

This colorful temple at the foot of Mount Misen has all the ususal sights of a Buddhist temple, from sutra-engraved prayer wheels to a pond with koi carp. More unusual, though, is the huge collection of statues, lining stairways, peeking out of the undergrowth, and filling a lantern-lit cave. From the terrace, there is a fine **view** of Miyajima.

Senjokaku 千畳閣（豊国神社）
On the hill to the north of the shrine. ⏱*Open daily 8.30am–4pm.* 🎫*¥100.*

Built by Toyotomi Hideyoshi at the end of the 16C, but never completed, this huge camphorwood temple is the largest building on the island, with a surface area of 857 *tatami* (Senjokaku means "hall of one thousand mats"). It is dominated by an elegant five-story **pagoda**, **Gojuno-to★**, actually older than the hall itself, which dates from 1407.

Miyajima History and Folklore Museum★
宮島歴史民俗資料館
Just west of the shrine. ⏱*Open Tue–Sun 9am–5pm.* 🎫*¥300.*

Housed in a fine 19C merchant house with a garden, half of which has been

Generations of bridge building

Ebizaki Kumetsugu is the head carpenter of Kintai Bridge, like his father before him, and so on all the way back to 1673. He and his team have the task of maintaining the bridge, which is made of Japanese cypress wood *(hinoki)*. "Everything is done by hand. We rely on our own experience and don't calculate anything by computer. The hardest thing is to anticipate how the wood will react over time,

© Tanawin Tananankul/iStock

how it will withstand bad weather. The most recent rebuilding work was in 2004. With the quantity of wood that we used, we could have built 50 houses."

preserved to show how the original owners lived. The other half is given over to exhibits tof everyday objects from the Edo period, notably a giant rice spoon, reproductions of which can be found in most shops on the island.

Mount Misen Observatory★
弥山展望台

10min walk to the cable car in Momijidani Park from the shrine (or free bus to the start at Itsukushima), then 20min in two stretches by cable car (⊙open daily 9am–5pm; ☞¥1000 one way, ☞¥1800 round trip) to Shishi-iwa, then 30min walk to the top.

🚶 With an altitude of 1739ft/530m, this is the highest point on the island. From the terminus of the cable car, a path lined with several Bhuddist pavilions leads to the summit.

From the terrace of the observatory, a beautiful structure of wood and glass opened in 2013, there is a spectacular **view★★** of the shrine and the islands of the Inland Sea. The mountain, which has preserved its luxuriant primeval forest where monkeys and deer roam freely, has some pleasant hiking trails. There are three well-trodden paths heading back down towards the village: Momijidani, Daisho-in and Omoto-koen hiking trails *(1–2hrs).*

IWAKUNI★ 岩国
25mi/40km soutwest of Hiroshima. Trains every 15min on the San'yo Line (50min, ☞¥770). From Iwakuni Station, there is a shuttle bus service (stop no. 2) to Kintai Bridge (20min, ☞¥300).

Don't be put off by the industrial complexes and huge military base which "welcome" you at Iwakuni when you arrive by train. Situated at the mouth of the Nishiki River, in Yamaguchi prefecture, this town *(population 137,000)* has much to recommend it, including a fine five-arched wooden bridge.

Kintai Bridge★★ 錦帯橋
⊙*Open daily 24hr. ☞¥300 (combined ticket with cable car & castle ☞¥940). kintaikyo.iwakuni-city.net/en*

In 1673, Kikkawa Hiroyoshi, *daimyo* of Iwakuni, tired of seeing the bridges over the Nishiki River washed away every rainy season, ordered a Chinese-style bridge to be built, with humpback arches resting on solid stone pillars able to withstand floods. Thanks to the skill of the local carpenters, the elegant Kintai Bridge stood proudly for almost three centuries until it was brought down by a typhoon in 1950: it was reconstructed in identical form three years later. Until the Meiji Restoration, the use of the bridge was reserved for noblemen and samurai, the common people having to cross the river by boat. Known as the "Brocade Sash Bridge" because of the curtain effect produced by its five arches, it is 16.5ft/5m wide and 633ft/193m long. It is a fine example of the effectiveness of traditional building techniques, in which not a single nail was used. Its arches rise to a height of 36ft/11m above the river.

▶ On the other side of the bridge, head for the cable-car station.

Iwakuni Art Museum★
岩国美術館

℘0827-41-0506. ○*Open daily: Mar–Nov 9am–5pm; Dec–Feb 9am–4pm.* ✆*¥800. iwakuni-art-museum.org.*
Located in the town's historic samurai quarter, this museum has a fascinating collection of weapons, helmets, and armor. The upper floors also display *maki-e* (gilded lacquerware), ceramics, paintings in the classic *yamato-e* style, and some particularly lovely screens from the Edo period.
Opposite the museum, in a small **vivarium** (○*open daily 9am–5pm; ✆¥200*), you can see the **white snake of Iwakuni**, a rare variety of red-eyed albino snake. The town has the only captive specimens in the world of this fast-disappearing species. Outside the museum, there's a pleasant park in which to walk, admiring the cherry trees beside the river in spring, and the colors of the maple leaves in fall.

Iwakuni Castle 岩国城

Access by cable car (every 20min, daily 9am–5pm, ✆¥550) 5min walk from Kintai Bridge. ○*Open daily 9am–4.45pm. ✆¥260 (combined ticket with cable car & Kintai Bridge ✆¥940).*
Standing at the top of Shiroyama, the castle is a concrete reconstruction dating from 1962. The original was built in 1608 by the local lord, Kikkawa Hiroie, and was destroyed just seven years later on the orders of shogun Tokugawa Iemitsu. The ruins of the old castle can still be seen some 164ft/50m away, those responsible for the reconstruction

having evidently preferred to move it to the edge of the hill.
The interior is of no great interest, but the position offers a good **view** of the town below and, on a clear day, the islands of the Inland Sea.

EXPLORING HIROSHIMA BAY
Kure 呉

Located 15mi/24km south of Hiroshima. By train: JR Kure Line from Hiroshima Station (30–50min, ✆¥500). By ferry (which continues to Matsuyama; setonaikaikisen.co.jp & ishizakikisen.co.jp): super-jet 25min, ✆¥2130 per crossing, or 45min, ✆¥940 per crossing. 🛈 *Kure Tourism Information Plaza, follow the passage on the 2nd floor of JR Kure Station.* ○*Open daily 9am–7pm. kuremachidiary.jp/en.*
This large port city *(population 228,000)* on Hiroshima Bay has played a significant role in the history of modern Japan. This sheltered location was chosen as the site for a military port and ordnance store in 1889 and a military base and enormous naval dockyards are to be found here to this day.

Yamato Museum★ – *5min walk from Kure Station.* ○*Open Wed–Mon 9am–6pm. ✆¥500. yamato-museum.com/en.*
The *Yamato*, the largest battleship ever built at the time, left the Kure slipway in December 1941. Presented as a symbol of Japanese military might just as the war in the Pacific began, the ship never fulfilled the hopes that were placed in it; when ordered to Okinawa on a suicide mission in April 1945, it was sunk by the Americans off the coast of Kyushu.
The museum recounts this story in a very instructive manner (there is an impressive 1/10 scale model). But above all, is at pains to show the wider perspective of how cutting-edge technology developed during the ship's construction benefited post-war Japanese industry, for example in the development of the shinkansen, in automobile manufacturing, and in naval construction. The 3rd floor reviews current naval construction techniques.

The famous ship has inspired a number of films, including *Yamato* (2005) and *Space Battleship Yamato* (2010), the latter based on an *anime* by Leiji Matsumoto which (considerably) reworked history of the *Yamato* in science-fiction style, and enjoyed resounding success at the end of the 1970s.

Iron Whale Museum – *Close to Yamato Museum.* ⏱*Open Wed–Mon 9am–5pm.* ⁂*No charge. jmsdf-kure-museum.go.jp/ en.* 🚻. The Japanese Navy's home defense forces set out their wares (minesweepers and submarines) in this museum. The main attraction is a **submarine tour** of the *Akishio*, decommissioned in 2004 and "moored" alongside the museum.

Etajima 江田島

Located 16mi/27km south of Hiroshima. Ferries run from Hiroshima to the various ports on the island, of which the most useful are Kirikushi (10min, ⁂¥930), Nakamachi (30min, ⁂¥960), and Koyo (25min, ⁂¥1060). There are also connections departing from Kure (to Koyo: 10–20min, ⁂¥390–550).

This vast island with its many bays is known mostly for its oyster farming and its *mikan* plantations (a kind of mandarin), but there is also a very wide variety of very charming scenery to explore by bike. The nicest excursion (2–3hr) is without doubt the ride along the coast, from the port of Kirikushi (*docks 3 & 4 from Hiroshima*) in the northeast to Nakamachi.

You can hire a bike in Kirikushi, from the Etajima City Tourism Association (⏱Tue–Sun 9am–5pm). The maximum rental period is 2 days, and you can drop the bicycle off at several points on the island. Bikes ⁂¥1000/day, e-bikes ⁂¥1500/day, plus a deposit of ⁂¥1000 (refundable if you return the bike to the same place).

Former Naval Academy – *Ferry to Koyo port, then a bus from Dock 1 for Ogaki, getting off at Jukka-gakko (5min, ⁂¥160). Only accessible by guided tour (1hr 30min) in Japanese (brochure in English):* ⏱*Open Mon–Fri 10.30am, 1pm & 3pm, Sat–Sun &*

public hols 10am, 11am, 1pm & 3pm. ⁂*No charge. mod.go.jp/msdf/onemss/english/ information.html.* The Imperial Naval Academy was relocated in 1888 from Tsukiji in Tokyo to this facility on the island of Etajima, close to the military port of Kure. The school was occupied by the American army from 1945 to 1956, since which times it has housed the 1st Technical School and the officer cadet school for the naval homeland defense forces. Today, it's the island's flagship attraction.

On site is the **Museum of Naval History** (*closed 2nd & 4th Mon each month*), which has nearly 14,000 objects on display, notably moving wills and personal effects left behind by kamikaze pilots during World War II.

👣Other places of interest to see in the area include Tomonoura and Onomichi (👣*see p433*). Connections from Hiroshima to Onomichi (*53mi/85km to the east*): 40min by Shinkansen on the JR Sanyo Line to Shin-Onomichi (⁂*¥3130*) or 1hr27min by JR Local train to Onomichi (⁂*¥1450*).

ADDRESSES

🏨 STAY

🛏 **Grand Prince Hotel** グランドプリンスホテル広島 – *23-1 Motoujina-machi, Minami-ku. (Map, A2; off map).* 📞*082-256-1111. www.princehotels.com/hiroshima. 510 rooms. ¥9380. ¥2500* 🚻. High-quality hotel near the port with an exceptional view over Hiroshima Bay and the islands. Direct boat connection with Miyajima from the pier at the bottom of the hotel.

🛏 **Hotel Active!** ホテルアクティブ広島 – *15-3 Noboricho, Naka-ku. (Map, C2).* 📞*082-212-0001. hotel-active.com/hiroshima. 157 rooms. ¥9600.* 🚻. Modern, functional, welcoming, well situated, and good value for money. This business hotel is a step above most others, and worth trying. The breakfast is healthy and varied.

🛏 **Hotel Urbain Hiroshima Central** アーバンイン広島セントラル – *5-20 Teppo-cho, Naka-ku. (Map, B1).* 📞*082-511-5211. urbainhiroshimacentral.com. 170 rooms. ¥6460.* 🚻. A large green star announces this classic business hotel. Well designed, it enables you to stay in the center without breaking the bank. Another hotel in the same chain (more luxurious) is just north of the station (**Hotel Urbain Hiroshima Executive**; *6-13 Wakakusa-cho, Higashi-ku; Map C1, off map); ℘082-567-6600, urbain-hotels.com/hex; ¥8080,* 🛏*).*

🍽 **World Friendship Center** ワールド フレンドシップセンター – *8-10 Higashi Kan-on (Map, A2; off map). ℘082-503-3191. wfchiroshima.com. 6 rooms. ¥4200.* Small guesthouse run by an American pacifist association founded in 1965. The rooms are bright and pretty. Sometimes holds events where you can meet A-bomb survivors, and listen to their experiences.

🍽🛏 **Sotetsu Grand Fresa Hiroshima** 相 鉄グランドフレサ広島 – *3-3-1 Otemachi, Naka-ku. (Map, A2). ℘082-249-3600. fresa-inn.jp/hiroshima. 283 rooms. ¥10,450. ¥1675* 🛏*.* The main advantage of this chain hotel is—beyond its practicality—its situation, a stone's throw from the Peace Park. Some rooms have a lovely view over the park.

🍽🛏 **Hotel New Hiroden** ホテルニュ ーヒロデン – *14-9 Osuga-cho. (Map, C1). ℘082-263-3456. newhiroden.co.jp. 256 rooms. ¥10,400. ¥1320*🛏*.* Usefully situated 3min from the JR station and close to the Kyobashi River. Functional rooms, restaurant, and bar.

🍽🛏🛏 **Sera Bekkan** 世羅別館 – *4-20 Mikawa-cho (Map, B2). ℘082-248-2251. serabekkan.jp. 35 rooms. ¥22,550.* 🛏*.* One of the few traditional *ryokan* in the heart of Hiroshima. *O-furo* on the top floor.

MIYAJIMA

🍽🛏 **Kikugawa** 菊がわ – *796 Miyajima-cho, Hatsukaichi. ℘0829-44-0039. kikugawa.ne.jp/en. 7 rooms. ¥15,400. ¥1430*🛏*.* In the heart of the village, this pretty guesthouse is good value for money. Japanese or Western rooms. The *kaiseki* dinner is recommended.

🍽🛏🛏🛏 **Iwaso Ryokan** 岩惣 – *Momiji-dani, Hatsukaichi. ℘0829-44-2233. iwaso. com/english. 38 rooms. ¥57,500.* 🛏*, dinner also included.* The most famous roykan in Miyajima, by the Mitarai River. Traditional, luxurious rooms and lavish meals.

🍴/EAT

HIROSHIMA

Oysters are the city speciality, along with *okonomiyaki* (pancakes stuffed with shredded cabbage, noodles and eggs, plus often pork or shrimp, topped with a flavorful brown sauce).

🍴 **Okonomi-mura** お好み村 – *5-13 Shin-tenchi. (Map, B2). okonomimura.jp/foreign/english.html. Hours vary by store; generally open daily 11am–11pm.* 🍴*.* Several floors of stalls selling the famous local *okonomiyaki*. Some have English menus, but all serve variations on the same theme anyway. A clasic Hiroshima experience.

🍴 **Ohana** お花 – *2-1 Nagaregawa-cho, Naka-ku. (Map, B2). ℘082-205-7317. Open Mon–Thur 6pm–2am, Fri–Sat 6pm–3am.* A lively *izakaya*, ideal for a drink and a skewer of *yakitori* while sitting at the counter.

🍴🍴 **45** キャラントサンク – *1-18 Fukuromachi, Naka-ku. (Map, B2). ℘082-545-1225. commercial-art.net/shop/45_hiroshima. Open 11.30am–2pm (Sat–Sun to 3pm) & 5–11pm. Menu in English. Lunch around ¥1200, dinner ¥1800.* A bar open to the road, in a large room of concrete and wood. The menu is inspired by European cuisine but based on local products. Long list of wines and alcohol, and quality service. At lunch, the bread and patisserie are a bargain, while in the evening there's a choice of more substantial dishes. The name is pronounced as in French.

🍴🍴 **No No Budou** 野の葡萄 – *Pacela Credo Building 7F, 6-78 Motomachi, Naka-ku. (Map, B1). ℘082-502-3340. nonobudou-hiroshima-pacela.owst.jp. Open daily 11am–4pm & 5.30–10pm. Lunch around ¥1800, dinner ¥2200.* Very popular with shoppers after a long day of retail therapy, this large buffet places the emphasis on fresh, organic food (large salads, cooked vegetables, some meat and fish, desserts, various drinks). Great view of the castle park from the terrace.

🍴🍴 **Kaki-tei** 牡蠣亭 – *11-11 Hashimoto-cho, Naka-ku. (Map, C2). ℘082-221-8990. kakitei.jp. Open Wed–Mon, 11.30am–2.30pm & 5–10pm. Lunch around ¥1300, dinner from ¥3000.* This tiny restaurant-kiosk (an extension of a terrace) by the Kyobashi River is ideal for tasting one of the region's specialties, oysters, prepared here in multiple ways.

🍴🍴🍴 **Kani-douraku** かに道楽広島店 – *7-4 Nagarekawa-cho, Naka-ku. (Map, B2). ℘082-244-3315. douraku.co.jp/west/hiroshima. Open 11am–11pm (last orders 10pm).* Dishes that are a paean to the crab *(kani)* in every form possible, from the very simplest to the most refined of preparations.

🍴🍴🍴 **Onegiya Fukuromachi** おねぎ や袋町店 – *1-13 Fukuromachi. (Map, B2). ℘082-243-6351. Open daily 5pm–12.30am.*

Menu in English. As its name and sign indicate, this place specialises in leeks and the whole onion family. A very elegant Japanese interior, with courteous service and tasty, often surprising dishes, such as braised leeks with bacon.

🍜🍶🍱 **Suishin** 釜飯酔心本店 – *6-7 Tatemachi, Naka-ku. (Map, B2).* 📞082-247-4411. suishin.or.jp/honten. Open daily 11.30am–10pm (last orders 9pm). A centrally located restaurant specializing in *kamameshi,* grilled fish, and *donburi* (fish, meat or vegetables served on rice).

🍜🍶🍱 **Teppanyaki Naniwa** 鉄板焼なにわ – *Rhiga Royal Hotel 6F, 6-78 Motomachi, Naka-ku. (Map, B1).* 📞082-228-6762. www.rihga.com/hiroshima/restaurant. Open daily 11.30am–2.30pm & 5.30–9.30pm. Lunch around ¥3000, dinner ¥9600. An ideal spot for the evening, serving Hiroshima's best and most inventive *teppan-yaki.*

🍜🍶🍱 **Ume no Hana** 梅の花 – *Fukuya Station Square Bldg 11F, 9-1 Matsubara-cho, Minami-ku. (Map, C1).* 📞082-506-2066. umenohana.co.jp/n_english. Open daily 11am–4pm & 5–10pm. Meaning "plum blossom," this restaurant specializes in soy, with everything from simple simmered *yuba* dishes to a tofu terrine served in an earthenware pot with soy lollipops.

MIYAJIMA

Fresh oysters, grilled or in fritters, grilled conger eel *(anago)* and *momiji manju* (cakes made with rice and buckwheat flour, in the shape of maple leaves) are the specialties of the island. The former are sold on roadside stands in the village center; the latter are sometimes still made in 19C factories using cast-iron molds.

🍜 **Sarasvati** サラスヴァティ – *407 Miyajima-cho Hatsukaichi.* 📞0829-44-2266. itsuki-miyajima.com/shop/sarasvati. Open Thur–Tue 8.30am–8pm. Lunch around ¥1400. 🗓. The delicious smell of coffee will guide you to this charming place at the foot of the steps to Senjokaku. There are also excellent cakes and, at lunchtime, a simple but tasty menu (pasta, warm oysters, toasted sandwiches, etc.).

🍜🍶 **Fujitaya** ふじたや – *125-2 Miyajima-cho-Hatsukaichi .* 📞0829-44-0151. Open daily 11am–5pm. Menu in English. Lunch around ¥2400. 🗓. Away from the busy village center, on a small road that climbs to Daisho-in, this eatery attracts fans of *anago-meshi* from all over the world. Slices of meltingly delicate, fragrant grilled fish on a bowl of rice, with *tsukemono* on the side: simple and perfectly done. Get ready to stand in line at the weekend.

SHOPPING

Sake – the city of **Saijo** 西条, 30min by train from Hiroshima *(JR Sanyo Line for Fukuyama),* is famed for the quality of its sake. There are eight breweries side-by-side in the city center, immediately recognisable by their tall brick chimneys and white latticed facades. Most offer a tour, free tasting and shop. Information and brochures are available from the Tourist Office *(opposite the station, open Tue–Sun,10am–4pm; saijosake.com).*

NIGHTLIFE

Cafés, bars, and clubs are legion around the Hondori shopping mall in Hiroshima, particularly to the east of the arcade – try 45, also a good restaurant (🕯see opposite).

EXCURSIONS

Kagura Monzen Toji-mura 神楽門前湯治村– *Akitakata.* 📞0826-54-0888. toujimura.com. 1hr drive north of Hiroshima. You can see performances of *kagura,* masked dancing originating in the Shinto tradition, put on by amateur groups in the Kagura Monzen Toji Village, in Akitakata City. Round off the trip with a meal at a restaurant, some shopping, or a visit to an *onsen. Performances: Fri, Sat–Sun & public holidays Apr–Jul & Sept–Nov 12.30pm & 2.30pm; Aug–Sept 12.30pm, 2.30pm, 8pm & 8.45 pm.* 🎫¥500.

ACTIVITIES

Bus – "Sightseeing Buses" follow two circular routes of sights and museums across the city center, departing from the station. *chugoku-jrbus.co.jp. One trip ¥200, day pass ¥400.*

Sightseeing boats – With an enormous port, nearby islands which nonetheless feel a world away, beaches, oyster farms, and sunsets, Hiroshima Bay is not short of interesting things to do and see. You can explore them under your own steam by taking one of the regular ferries to the islands (Miyajima, Etajima, etc.) or take an organized cruise. Have a look at the various types online, or ask at the tourist office. Alternatively, join the regular city river cruises *(Thur–Tue 10am–4.20pm, every 40min; 25min; departs from near the Peace Memorial; ¥1200; hiroshima-water-taxi.com).*

The San'in Coast
山陰

A tour of the San'in coast in the north of Chugoku, on the shores of the Sea of Japan, is a journey into *Ura-Nihon*, the hidden Japan. Well away from the main tourist routes, it is a wild, thinly populated region, where age-old traditions are still respected. It is full of stunning landscapes, fascinating cultural sites, delightful *onsen*, and old feudal towns steeped in history, and there are plenty of open-air activities to enjoy too.

TOTTORI★ 鳥取

Regional Map, B1.
Famous for its vast sand dunes, part of the **San'inkaigan National Park**, this large port city at the mouth of the Sendai River is fairly unremarkable in itself, but its mountainous hinterland, especially Daisen-Oki National Park, to the west, is full of fine temples, pleasant *onsen*, and opportunities for hiking.

Tottori Folkcraft Museum
鳥取民芸美術館

651 Sakae-machi. 5min walk northeast of Tottori Station. Open Thu−Tue 10am–5pm. ¥500. mingei.exblog.jp.
In a small, wooden merchant house from the Edo period, this museum is affiliated to the Mingei movement, which aims to promote traditional crafts. Its collection comprises nearly 5000 objects illustrating the Japanese concept of *wabi-sabi* (finding beauty in simple, used, imperfect things), among them some lovely Japanese and Korean pottery, old furniture, kimono, bamboo utensils, etc.

Kannon-in Garden 観音院庭園

162 Uemachi. 10min east of Tottori Station by bus (¥100). Open daily 9am–5pm. ¥550, including matcha tasting. kannonin33.jimdo.com.
Commissioned in the 17C by the feudal lord Ikeda Mitsunaka, this temple garden is thought to have been designed by a pupil of the famous tea master

- **Population:** Tottori: 193,000, Matsue: 205,400. Hagi: 50,000.
- **Michelin Map:** Regions of Japan Map 4, B3, Regional Map p423.
- **Location:** By the Sea of Japan, the San'in Coast comprises Tottori and Shimane prefectures, and northern Yamaguchi prefecture. Tottori is 88mi/142km from Okayama, Matsue 76mi/122km from Tottori, and Hagi 137mi/220km from Tottori.
- **Kids:** Tottori Sand Dunes; Matsue Vogel Park; a boat trip on the moats at Matsue Castle; the steam train at Tsuwano; Yonago Waterbird Sanctuary.
- **Timing:** Allow at least four days, stopping over at Tottori, Matsue *(two nights)*, and Hagi. If you have a car, stop at Misasa Onsen, Kaike Onsen, or Yunotsu Onsen. Most towns and places of interest can be reached with the JR San'in Line, which runs along the coast, or failing that, local buses. Always check when the buses are running, as some only run at weekends or during the summer.
- **Don't miss:** Tottori sand dunes; Adachi Museum of Art near Matsue; the shrine of Izumo Taisha; Iwami Ginzan Silver Mine; the old streets of Tsuwano; the pottery kilns and Uragami Museum in Hagi.

Kobori Enshu, and modeled on the tea gardens of Kyoto. It includes a small, rock-strewn hill and a fine pond in the center of which are two small islands representing the turtle and the crane

Tottori Sand Dunes

© winhorse/iStock

(symbols of longevity). It also benefits from a superb "borrowed landscape" in the background, completely free of urban development.

Jinpukaku Mansion 仁風閣
2-121 Higashi-machi. 10min northeast of Tottori Station by minibus (🚌¥100). ⏰*Open Tue–Sun 9am–5pm.* 🚌¥150. *www.tbz.or.jp/jinpuukaku.*
Located at the foot of Mount Kyusho, where Tottori Castle once stood, this immaculate, white European-style residence was built in 1907. The first building in the town to have electricity and a telephone, it played host to Prince Yoshihito (the future Emperor Taisho) whenever he stayed in the area. The interior houses a few items of imported European furniture. At the rear, there is a pleasant Japanese garden and a large lawn.

👥 Tottori Sand Dunes★★ 鳥取砂丘
3mi/5km north of the city. From Tottori Station, bus every 20min to Tottori Sakyu stop (20–30min journey, 🚌¥300–370). Camel rides and cart rides are available throughout the year. From Apr to Nov, there are opportunities for sandsurfing, parascending, and hang gliding. ℹ️*Details on all these activities from the Sand Pal Tottori Information Center at the Sakyu Kitaguchi stop, just before the dunes,* 📞*0857-20-2231.*

These yellow and brown sand dunes are unique in Japan and stretch along the coast for 10mi/16km, reaching a width of 1.2mi/2km in places. Some of the dunes reach a height of 295ft/90m. They were created tens of thousands of years ago by sediment carried out to sea by the Sendai River, then pushed back to shore by the marine currents. Their changing shapes, and the interplay of light and dark as they shift in the wind, recall the most beautiful Saharan landscapes. In winter, covered with a thin white blanket of snow, the effect is quite surreal.

The dunes are home to a major center for research into agriculture in dry environments. Set back from the coast are vast plantations of shallots, the largest in Japan.

😊The best time to visit the dunes is early in the morning, when the amazing shapes created by the wind during the night are revealed. It is dangerous to swim near the dunes; a safer alternative is **Uradome Beach** *(3mi/5km to the east).* Also from Uradome, you can take a **boat trip** *(Mar–Nov daily 9.10am–4.10pm, 40min,* 🚌*¥1300; small boats Apr–Oct 9am–4pm,* 🚌*¥2100)* along the jagged coastline with its magnificent caves and pine-covered islands.

To the west of Tottori, 7.5mi/12km away, is **Hakuto Beach**, popular with surfers and windsurfers.

EXCURSIONS
Regional Map, B1.

Chizu 智頭

18.5mi/30km south of Tottori. Access by the JR Imbi Line (30min journey, ¥1350). Perched at an altitude of 984ft/300m, near the source of the Sendai River, this delightful little town *(population 7000)* was a large forestry center during the Edo period. Five minutes' walk from the station is **Ishitani House** (*open Apr–Nov Thu–Tue 10am–5pm, ¥500, ifs.or.jp,*), an impressive 40-room residence that once belonged to a wealthy Chizu merchant. Lord Ikeda of Tottori would stop here whenever he made his biennial journey to Edo to pledge allegiance to the shogun.

The massive roof is supported by imposing cedarwood pillars, and there is a delightful garden at the rear. Another place worth a visit, also on the main street is the **Suwa sake brewery** (suwai-zumi.jp) dating from 1859, where you will be able to taste a wonderfully light and fragrant *daiginjo-shu* (sake made with polished rice milled to at least 50 percent).

Mount Mitoku★★ 三徳山

25mi/40km west of Tottori. JR San'in Line to Kurayoshi Station, then bus (every hour, 40min journey) to Mitoku-san. The last bus coming back leaves at 3pm. Open daily 8am–3pm. ¥410. The difficult upper part of the trail is only suitable for adults in good physical condition, and is impassable in rainy or snowy weather.

The 2953ft/900m-high Mount Mitoku (*"Mountain of the Three Virtues"*) is a former shrine of the Buddhist Tendai sect used during the Heian era (794–1185) as a school and retreat for monks. A series of stone staircases leads first to **Sanbutsu-ji**, the main temple, surrounded by 1000-year-old cedars. The **Treasure Hall** is open to visitors (*open daily 8am–5pm, ¥400, 0858-43-2666*). Behind it, a steep path takes you through the luxuriant vegetation to **Monjudo**, perched on a precipice from where there is a splendid **view** of the valley.

The climb continues, with the help of creepers and chains as handrails, until you reach a rocky ridge and at last see **Nageiredo★★**, a 12C temple built into a rift in the cliff and designated a National Treasure. How this building was erected on such a vertiginous site remains a mystery.

Misasa Onsen 三朝温泉 – This town on the road between Kurayashi and Mount Mitoku has been known for almost 1000 years for its hot springs, believed to have rejuvenating powers because of their high radium content. There are a dozen *ryokan* dotted along the river, as well as a free public *rotenburo* (outdoor hot-spring pool).

Mount Daisen★ 大山

From Tottori, JR San'in Line to Yonago Station (1hr, ¥2890), then bus (hourly, 50min, ¥720) to Daisen-ji.

Reaching a height of 5673ft/1729m, this massive extinct volcano rises directly from sea level. From a distance, it resembles Mount Fuji. In winter, its snowy slopes attract skiers and snowboarders, replaced by hikers when spring arrives. Getting to the top (or 20m below it; the peak is inaccessible for 66ft/20 years due to unstable rocks), from the temple of Daisen-ji, takes about five hours each way. The whole region is part of **Daisen-Oki National Park**. It's particularly stunning in the fall, when the forest vegetation turns flame-red.

Daisen-ji 大山寺 – *Open daily 9am–4pm. ¥300. daisenji.jp.* From the bus stop in the village, in front of the Tourist Information Center, cross the river to reach the lovely cedar-lined avenue that leads to the temple. Founded in 718, it was an active center of the Tendai sect until the 16C, and at its height boasted nearly 3000 monks. Unfortunately, most of the buildings were destroyed in successive fires, leaving only a small part of the original complex. To the left of the temple, a path leads to **Ogamiyama Shrine**, an integral part of the temple before the separation of Buddhism and Shintoism in the Meiji era.

USEFUL INFORMATION
TOURIST OFFICES

Tottori – In the station. *Open daily 8.30am–5.30pm.* ℰ*0857-22-7935. tottori-tour.jp/en*

Matsue – Outside the JR station. *Open daily Jun–Oct 7am–7pm; Nov–May 9am–6pm.* ℰ*0852-21-4034. visit-matsue.com.*

Hagi – Next to Higashi-Hagi Station. *Open daily: Mar–Nov 9am–5.45pm; Dec–Feb 9am–5pm.* ℰ*0838-25-3145. hagishi. com/en.* There is another office at Hagi station in the south *(same hours.* ℰ*0838-25-1750).*

TRANSPORTATION

BY TRAIN – **Okayama and Tottori**, JR Ltd. Express Super Inaba, Imbi Line *(6 per day, 1hr 50min journey, ¥4470).*
Tottori and Matsue, JR Ltd. Express Super Matsukaze and Super Oki *(5 per day, 1hr 30min, ¥3630).*
Matsue and Okayama, JR Ltd. Express Yakumo *(several per day, 2hr 40min, ¥5610).*
Matsue and Hagi, JR San'in Line & JR Ltd. Express Super Oki via Masuda *(3 per day, 3hr 30min, ¥5390).*
Hagi and Hiroshima, via Nagatoshi and Asa *(7 per day, 3hr–3hr 30min journey, ¥6910).*
Hagi and Fukuoka (Hakata), via Naga-toshi and Asa *(7 per day, 4hr, ¥5830).*

BY BUS – **Matsue and Hiroshima**, Ichibata Bus and Hiroshima Electric Railway *(3hr 30min, ¥3900).*
Hagi Bus Center, located downtown. Regular buses to Shin-Yamaguchi *(Bocho bus, 1hr 15min, ¥2060)* and Hiroshima *(4hr, ¥3700).*

Kaike Onsen 皆生温泉 – *3mi/5km north of Yonago Station, access by shuttle bus (20min journey, ⮑¥280).* This hot-spring resort, full of big seaside hotels, is famous for its waters, rich in mineral salts and calcium, bubbling up directly from beneath the sand.

👥 Yonago Waterbird Sanctuary
米子水鳥公園 – *20min by bus from Yonago Station.* 🕐*Open Wed–Mon: Apr–Oct 9am–5.30pm; Nov–Mar 8.30am–5.30pm, Sat–Sun and public hols 7am–5.30pm).* ⮑ *¥200, children* ⮑ *no charge. yonago-mizutori.com.* This lagoon attracts the largest concentration of migrating birds in Japan during the winter. More than 75,000 varieties winter here, including whistling swans from the Siberian tundra.

MATSUE★★ 松江
🕐*Regional Map, B1.*
Known as the "water city" because of its many canals, Matsue stands by the sea, where Nakaumi lagoon and Lake Shinji meet. A former feudal stronghold, capital of Izumo province (now Shimane prefecture), this pleasant city is a mine of cultural and historical treasures, such as its castle, one of the best-preserved in the country.

Matsue also prides itself on having been the adopted home of the writer **Lafcadio Hearn** (1850–1904), the author of many books on Japan, who became a Japanese national under the name Koizumi Yakumo (🕐*see box p455).*

✍️*On presentation of a passport, foreign tourists get reductions of 30–50 percent on admission prices to museums and tourist attractions in Matsue and its surroundings. To get around, rent a bicycle at the station (generally ⮑¥300–500/day) or use the Lakeline Bus (every 20min, ⮑¥200/ journey, ⮑¥500/day), which does a circuit of the principal sights.*

Matsue Castle★ 松江城
1.2mi/2km north of Matsue Station. 🕐*Open daily: Apr–Sept 7am–7.30pm; Oct–Mar, 8.30am–5pm (dungeon Apr–Sept 8.30am–6.30pm; Oct–Mar, 8.30am–5pm).* ⮑*¥670 (children ¥290). matsue-castle.jp.*
The dark silhouette of the keep of Matsue Castle rises in the center of a

Matsue Castle moat

© MasaoTaira/iStock

hill surrounded by moats. Built in 1611 by the *daimyo* Yoshiharu Horio, it is a fine example of military architecture—although it never came under attack—and one of the best-preserved in Japan. Six storys high *(98ft/30m)*, it has a wooden framework adorned with gables and roofs that turn up at the ends. Inside, documents, scale models, weapons, and armor trace the history of the city. When you get to the top, don't miss the 360-degree **view** over Matsue and its surroundings, Lake Shinji, and Mount Daisen.

👥 Horikawa Sightseeing Boat 堀川遊覧船

Pick up and drop off at the castle entrance. ⏱*Open daily: spring and fall 9am–5pm; summer 9am–6pm; winter 9am–4pm. Trip: 30min.* 🎫*¥1000 (children ¥500). www.matsue-hori-kawameguri.jp.*

The castle moats, known as *Horikawa*, are linked to a network of canals that were once used for transporting goods. This pleasant tour in a flat-bottomed boat, steered by an often-talkative boat-man, will take you beneath bridges and past banks fringed with cherry trees and willows. It's a good way to soak up the relaxed atmosphere of the city.

Buke Yashiki 武家屋敷

10min walk north of the castle. ⏱*Open daily: Apr–Sept, 8.30am–6.30pm; Oct–Mar 8.30am–5pm.* 🎫*¥310. www.matsue-bukeyashiki.jp/en.*

Situated midway along Shiominawate-dori, a beautiful street lined with Edo-period houses, this samurai residence dating from 1730—the largest in Mat-sue—once belonged to the Shiomi, a medium-ranking military family in the service of the Matsudaira lords. The grand appearance of the front gate contrasts with the Spartan sobriety of the interior, which still contains furniture and domestic objects.

Meimei-an 明々庵

In a little street to the north. ⏱*Open daily: Apr–Sept 8.30am–6.30pm; Oct–Mar 8.30am–5pm.* 🎫*¥410.*

This superb tea house, with its curved thatched roof, was built in 1779 in the garden of the residence of one of his vas-sals by the feudal lord Matsudaira Fumai, the seventh of that name, a respected master of the tea ceremony. Restored and moved here in 1966, it regularly attracts experts in the art of tea.

Lafcadio Hearn Memorial Museum and Old Residence
小泉八雲記念館・旧居

On Shiominawate-dori. ⏰*Open daily: Apr–Sept 8.30am–6.30pm; Oct–Mar 8.30am–5pm. Museum:* 🎫*¥410. www. hearn-museum-matsue.jp. House:* 🎫*¥310. www.matsue-castle.jp/kyukyo.*
Although the writer Lafcadio Hearn spent barely 15 months in Matsue, where he taught English in the city's high school, it was this city that sparked his love of Japan—he recorded his impressions of it in *Glimpses of Unfamiliar Japan.*
The museum has a large collection of his letters and manuscripts, as well as objects recalling his life in Japan. Next door is the house where he lived, barely changed since his departure, and with a pretty garden. The writer's great-grandson still lives in Matsue, where he teaches literature at the university.

Tanabe Art Museum 田部美術館
Next to Lafcadio Hearn Memorial Museum. ⏰*Open Tue–Sun 9am–5pm.* 🎫*¥700. www.tanabe-museum.or.jp.*
This museum devoted to the Tanabe clan displays objects amassed by the family over 25 generations. Most are related to the tea ceremony, especially ceramics, but the collection also includes calligraphy, paintings, prints, and other antiques.

Shimane Prefectural Art Museum★ 島根県立美術館
On the lake shore, 15min walk from Matsue Station. ⏰*Open Wed–Mon: Mar–Sept 10am–30min after sunset; Oct–Feb 10am–6.30pm (last admission 30min before closing) Collection:.* 🎫*¥300. Special exhibition:* 🎫*¥1000. Combined ticket:* 🎫*¥1150. www. shimane-art-museum.jp/en.*
This futuristic, light-filled building has a permanent collection of modern and contemporary Japanese and Western artworks, and also holds (usually excellent) temporary exhibitions. There are works on the theme of water, sculptures on wood, photographs, and many prints, including Hokusai's famous *Views*

Japanophile Lafcadio Hearn

Born in 1850 to an Irish father and a Greek mother, the writer and journalist **Lafcadio Hearn** was a tireless globetrotter (London, New York, Canada, Martinique). But it was in Japan, where he arrived in 1890, that he found his spiritual home. In Matsue, he met and married a samurai's daughter, converted to Buddhism, and took Japanese citizenship under the name Koizumi Yakumo. Appointed Professor of English Literature at the University of Tokyo, he taught there until his death in 1904, and published several books on Japanese culture, myths, and folklore, becoming a true link between Japan and the West.

of Mount Fuji, and Hiroshige's series on the Tokaido road. Visit toward evening, as this is an ideal place to see the romantic **sunset★** over Lake Shinji.

EXCURSIONS

👥 Matsue Vogel Park
松江フォーゲルパーク

7.5mi/12km west of Matsue. Take the Ichibata tram line from Matsue Shinjiko Onsen Station to Vogel Park Station (15min journey). ⏰*Open daily: Apr–Sept 9am–5.30pm; Oct–Mar 9am–5pm (last admission 45min before closing).* 🎫*¥1500 (children* 🎫*¥700). www. ichibata.co.jp/vogelpark.* ♨.
Created in 2001 on the shores of Lake Shinji, midway between Matsue and Izumo, this theme park has four huge **tropical greenhouses** containing a richly colored abundance of irises, fuchsias, orchids, and begonias. The park also houses some 80 varieties of exotic bird. Children love feeding the toucans, watching demonstrations of falcons in flight, and seeing penguins from the Cape. Beside a duck pond is a small restaurant serving *soba* (buckwheat noodles).

Izumo Taisha Shrine

Adachi Museum of Art★★
足立美術館

12.5mi/20km south of Matsue. JR San'in Line to Yasugi Station (15min journey), from where a free shuttle bus serves the museum (15min). ◔*Open daily: Apr–Sept 9am–5.30pm; Oct–Mar 9am–5pm.* ◎*¥2300, English audioguide ¥500. www.adachi-museum.or.jp/en.*

In 1970, Adachi Zenko (1899–1990), a business tycoon who made his fortune in Osaka, built this museum to display his collection of modern Japanese art in his native region. He also set about creating, with a team of gardeners, a remarkable **Japanese garden★★★**, which the American magazine *Journal of Japanese Gardening* has rated the most beautiful in Japan (ahead of the garden of the Katsura Imperial Villa in Kyoto). The garden covers an area of 41 acres/16.5ha and has four different sections: a dry landscape garden, a moss garden, a pond garden, and a white gravel and pine garden, with the wooded ridge of the mist-shrouded mountains in the background. Visitors are not admitted to the garden, but have to look at it through the windows of the museum, which nevertheless effectively frame the **views**. Works by various Japanese artists are on display, notably **Yokoyama Taikan** (1868–1958), and are changed with the season.

Izumo Taisha★★ 出雲大社

◔*Regional Map, B1. 22mi/35km west of Matsue. Take the Ichibata tram line from Matsue Shinjiko Onsen Station to Izumo-Taisha-mae Station (1hr,* ◎*¥81).* ◔*Open daily 24hr; Treasure Hall daily 8.30am–4.30pm.* ◎*No charge. Treasure Hall:* ◎*¥300. izumooyashiro.or.jp.*

The great shrine of **Izumo Taisha**, also called Izumo Oyashiro, is the **second most important Shinto shrine** in Japan after Ise (◔*see p 265*) and where all the gods in Japan gathered once a year. It is dedicated to the *kami* Okuninushi, god of the earth and the harmony of nature, agriculture, and medicine, who is said to bring happiness and harmony to human relationships, especially marriage, which is why the shrine attracts a lot of people hoping to get married. To begin a prayer here, clap your hands not twice, as is usual, but four times to draw the deity's attention not only to you, but also to your loved one.

Izumo Taisha is said to be the oldest shrine in Japan and is known to have existed since at least the 7C. The area where it stands was once an island, separated from the coast by a sound that has since been filled in by alluvial deposits. Most of the existing buildings, however, date from 1874, and the main building from 1744 (apparently its 25th reconstruction). The main shrine is surrounded by a rectangular double fence. It is accessed via an avenue of pines twisted by the wind, then through the **o-torii**, the largest shrine gate in Japan, adorned with a huge sacred rope of rice straw (shimenawa) 21ft/6.5m long and weighing 1 ton. The **Honden** (main hall), 79ft/24m high, is on a raised platform. This is typical of the architectural style known as taisha-zukuri, the oldest style used for shrines, characterized by a roof of cypress bark with a double slope and curved canopies, and an imposing front staircase on piles. Its proportions are modest in comparison with the previous building dating from the Heian period (around 1200 years ago) which, with a towering height of 157.5ft/48m, was then the largest wooden building in Japan, ahead of Todai-ji in Nara.

The small **Treasure Hall** contains some interesting items, including paintings and highly ornamented sacred objects, but unfortunately there's little in the way of English signage.

Ideally, visit the shrine early in the morning (around 6.30am– 8.30am) for the beautiful, clean air and lack of crowds.

Shimane Museum of Ancient Izumo
– To the right of the shrine. ○Open daily: Mar–Oct 9am–6pm; Nov–Feb 9am–5pm. ○Closed 3rd Tue of the month. ⊜¥310 (excluding special exhibitions). www. izm.ed.jp/english. Opened in 2007, this museum traces the history of the region of Izumo. Relics unearthed by archeological excavations (bronze bells and swords, pottery, funerary objects) are on display. A 1:10 scale model gives an idea of how the shrine looked 1000 years ago, when it stood on high piles and was reached by a huge 358ft/109m-long staircase.

Hinomisaki – 6mi/10km along the coast road. There are regular buses (35min journey). This magnificent cape to the northwest of Izumo, watched over by a lighthouse dating from 1903, attracts many walkers. Visitors can climb to the top of the **lighthouse** (○open daily 9am–4.30pm; ⊜¥210), which is the oldest in Japan, to see the **view**. On the left, a trail runs along the coast, which leads, after 0.6mi/1km, to a small harbor, where the 400-year-old **Hinomisaki Shrine** lies hidden.

Iwami Ginzan Silver Mine★
石見銀山

♿Regional Map, B1. 48mi/77km west of Matsue. JR San'in Line to Oda-shi Station (1hr 10min journey, ⊜¥1170). From there, there are regular buses to Omori Daikansho stop (30min, ⊜¥630), at the entrance to the site. ○Open daily: Mar–Nov 8.30am–6pm; Dec–Feb 8.30am–5.30pm. ○Closed last Tue of month. ⊜¥300. ginzan.city.ohda.lg.jp.

A UNESCO World Heritage Site since 2007, the former Iwami Ginzan Silver Mine was at its production peak in the 16C and 17C. It is estimated that at that time 38 tons of pure silver were being extracted each year—one-third of all the silver produced in the world. Much of the ore was transported to the coast to be turned into small oval bars, which were used as currency in trade, first with Korea and China, then with Europe.

The mining region of Iwami Ginzan played a major role in the economic expansion of Japan—several hundred shafts were sunk here—with mining villages, a network of roads, and commercial ports. The whole area was under the direct control of the Edo shogunate. Today, it is possible to visit the **Ryugenji Mabu★** deposit, situated at an altitude of 1970ft/600m, where you can explore part of a long underground tunnel shored up by wooden planks. The working conditions in the dark, damp tunnels were harsh and the life expectancy of the miners barely exceeded 30. The site is 35 minutes' walk from the pretty village of **Omori**, where you can visit the small **Iwami Ginzan Museum** (○open daily 9am–5pm, ☜¥500). The nearby 18C stone temple **Rakan-ji** (🕐open daily 9am–5pm, ☜¥500) contains statues of the 500 *rakan* (disciples of the Buddha), each with a different expression, who watch over the souls of dead miners.

🚶 **Yunotsu Onsen** – 6mi/10km from Iwami Ginzan along a descending trail (3hr hike, or bus to Nima or Oda-shi, then JR San'in train to Yunotsu). Nestling in a deep valley, this little port, which once used to export the silver ore, is linked to the mining area by a flagstoned path that winds through the woods. Its old-fashioned atmosphere, two public baths, *ryokan,* and tranquil cafes are all good reasons to stop here.

▶ From Yunotsu, take the JR San'in Line to either Matsue or Hagi.

HAGI★ 萩
🕐*Regional Map, A1.*
A former feudal town hemmed in between the hills and the sea, Hagi has preserved its old samurai quarter intact. The modern world seems to have bypassed this sleepy little town with an Edo-period atmosphere. In spring, the scent of orange flowers rises from the orchards. The town is also famous for its kilns, making *hagi-yaki* ceramics, with their milky, pink-beige coloring. It played a vital role in the revolutionary

movement of the Meiji era, which, in 1867, brought down the shogunate, restored the Emperor, and opened the country to the West.

😊*Don't get off at JR Hagi Station, but at Higashi-Hagi farther east, which is the more central of the two. Bikes are a practical and pleasant way to explore Hagi,and there are several bicycle rental shops on the way out of the station (around ☜¥1000/day). Alternatively, buses (every 30min, ☜¥100) do a circuit of the town.*

Teramachi, Jokamachi, and Horiuchi Districts★
寺町・萩城城下町・堀内
The town center of Hagi lies to the west of Higashi-Hagi Station, on the island formed by the delta of the Abu-gawa. Farther west still is the site of the former Hagi Castle. It is reached through the **Teramachi district**, famous for its many small temples. To the north is **Kikugahama Beach**, with its exceptionally clear waters.

Shizuki-koen – 🕐Open daily: Apr–Oct 8am–6.30pm; Nov–Feb 8.30am–4.30pm; Mar 8.30am–6pm. ☜¥210. This park lies on the former site of Hagi Castle, of which only the outer walls and inner moats remain today. Built by the Mori clan (the local lords) in 1604, it was demolished in 1874 during the Meiji

The Miwa, a great dynasty of potters

The potteries of Hagi owe their reputation to the quality of their *chawan*, the bowls used in the tea ceremony. According to the saying, "*Ichi* Raku, *ni* Hagi, *san* Karatsu," the *raku*-style is the ideal pottery to use for the tea ceremony, followed by the pottery from Hagi, and finally that from Karatsu. What makes Hagi ceramics special is their porous glaze, which allows the tannin from the tea to seep through its cracked surface, so that the pastel tones—pink or ivory—of the stoneware take on a slightly beige hue as the bowls age. The process was introduced by Korean artisans around 1600.

Today, Hagi has many kilns and pottery workshops, some of them open to visitors. **Miwa Jusetsu** (1910–2012) was the eleventh generation of a family of potters and one of the most famous in Hagi, designated a Living National Treasure. He worked hard to revive the art of ceramics, and his tea bowls routinely fetch several million yen. His son, **Miwa Kazuhiko,** has taken a more avant-garde approach, veering away from the utilitarian context.

Jokamachi, Hagi

Restoration. From the castle ruins, a 20-minute walk will take you to the top of Shizuki Hill *(469ft/143m)*.

Horiuchi – The district at the foot of the castle was where high-ranking samurai, such as the Kuchiba, the Suu, the Masuda, and the Fukuhara, had their residences. Protected by long, rough walls of whitewashed cob, the houses of the aristocrats still retain their Edo-period wooden entrances.
The **Hagi Museum**, built in 2004 in the style of the neighboring old buildings (⏰*open daily 9am–5pm,* 🎫*¥510),* traces the history of the city.

Jokamachi – Farther east is this quarter that housed samurai of lower rank and wealthy merchants. The best preserved residences are on two streets that run parallel: **Edoya** and **Kikuya**.
Among these is **Kikuya House** (⏰*open 8.30am–5.30pm,* 🎫*¥600),* built by a powerful merchant family in 1604, which has a lovely garden. Around it are arranged the living quarters, the kitchens, and the storehouses, where period objects and utensils are on display.
Farther north, the **Kumaya Museum of Art** (⏰ *open Tue, Thur & Sat–Sun 9am–4pm,* 🎫*¥700)* displays objects that once belonged to the wealthy Kumaya family, including a large number of ink paintings and objects relating to the tea ceremony.

Hagi Uragami Museum★★
山口県立萩美術館浦上記念館
South of Jokamachi, on the other side of the canal. ⏰*Open Tue–Sun 9am–5pm.* 🎫*¥300 (excluding special exhibitions).*
In a spacious modern building dating designed by Tange Kenzo, this museum has an excellent collection of nearly 5000 *ukiyo-e* prints, among them Hokusai's famous *Thirty-six Views of Mount Fuji* (including *The Great Wave off Kanagawa*) and portraits of Kabuki actors by Sharaku and courtesans by Utamaro. It also houses a large collection of Korean and Chinese ceramics and porcelain.

Shoin-jinja 松陰神社
10min walk south of Higashi-Hagi Station. ⏰*Open daily 24hr.* 🎫*No charge. shoin-jinja.jp/en.*
This shrine is dedicated to the memory of **Shoin Yoshida** (1830–59), one of the leaders of the Meiji Restoration. A low-ranking samurai, he led a brief, tragic life, and was beheaded at the age of 30 for rebelling against the authority of the shogun. While under house arrest toward the end of his life, he founded a school, **Shoka-sonjuku** (⏰*open daily 8am–5pm,* 🎫*no charge).* The shrine preserves this just as it was: a small building open to the elements, with modest *tatami* rooms and paper windows, where the master preached the spirit of resistance and the idea of nationhood to his pupils. Several future prime ministers were once pupils at the school.

Toko-ji – ⏱*Open daily 8.30am–5pm.* ✎*¥300.* Five minutes' walk along the river east of the shrine, at the foot of a wooded hill, is this late-17C temple, in the style of a Chinese pagoda. Behind it, an atmospheric avenue lined with 500 stone lanterns leads to a mausoleum housing five of the Mori clan lords' tombs.

EXCURSIONS
⏱*Regional Map, A1.*

Tsuwano★ 津和野
40mi/65km northeast of Hagi. Direct bus (Bocho Bus, 1hr 45min, ✎¥2130) or train via Masuda (2hr 35min, ✎¥1620). 🛈*Tourist Information Center by the station (*⏱*open daily 9am–5pm).*
A former fortress town huddling deep in a valley, Tsuwano can still boast charming old streets, lined with well-preserved samurai houses and picturesque sake breweries. A canal full of colorful carp and fringed with irises runs alongside the main street, Tonomachi-dori.

Maria Seido Chapel – *20min walk from the station.* ⏱*Open daily 24hr.* ✎*No charge.* Small chapel in a wooded grove in the foothills. Built in 1931 in tribute to Jesuit missionary the 36 Japanese Christians martyred here for refusing to renounce their faith in 1868.

Taikodani Inari Shrine – *15min walk from the station to the first torii. Shrine office:* ⏱*open daily 9am–4pm.* ✎*No charge. taikodani.jp.* Perched on the side of a hill, this shrine is one of the sacred sites of Inari, the Shinto deity of harvests and trade, whose messenger is a fox (kitsune). It was built in 1773 and modeled on Fushimi-Inari in Kyoto. Access to the shrine is through a long tunnel of 1045 vermilion *torii* (gates).

Tsuwano Castle Ruins – *1hr 10min hike from the station, or 30min walk then 5min chairlift (*⏱*open daily 9am–4.30pm,* ⏱*closed Dec–Feb;* ✎*¥450 round trip) and 15min hike.* The remains of this 1325 fortress are perched on the top of the hill overlooking Tsuwano. From here, there is a magnificent **view★** of the valley.

👥 **Steam train** – The *SL Yamaguchi-go (Mar–Nov Sat–Sun, or daily in Golden Week & Jul–Aug; 2hr trip;* ✎*¥1700),* makes a round trip between Shin-Yamaguchi and Tsuwano. From Shin-Yamaguchi, you can connect to the shinkansen line for Hiroshima on the San'yo coast (⏱*see p437)* or Fukuoka (⏱*see p 577)* on the island of Kyushu *(about 40min).*

ADDRESSES

🛏 STAY

TOTTORI
🍴🛏 **Hotel New Otani Tottori** ホテルニューオータニ鳥取 – *153 Ima-machi.* ☎*0857-23-1111. newotani-tottori.jp. 136 rooms. ¥14,300. ¥1500🍴.* A comfortable, well-maintained, Western-style business hotel opposite the station.

🍴🛏 **Shiitake Kaikan Taisuikaku** しいたけ会館・対翠閣 – *1-84 Tomiya.* ☎*0857-24-8471. taisuikaku.com. 31 rooms. ¥13,000. Around ¥1000🍴, lunch and dinner also available.* Simple, excellent *ryokan,* 5min walk south of the station. Four Western rooms with en suite, and a lovely communal *o-furo* for the Japanese rooms.

🍴🍴🛏 **Kansui-tei Kozeniya** 観翠庭こぜにや – *651 Eiraku Onsen-cho.* ☎*0857-23-3311. kozeniya.com. 25 rooms. ¥20,100. ¥1210🍴.* Elegant modern *ryokan,* 10min walk northeast of the station; Japanese and Western rooms, with and without bathroom, around ornamental pond. Indoor and outdoor *onsen.*

AROUND TOTTORI: MISASA ONSEN
🍴🛏 **Izanro Iwasaki** 依山楼岩崎 – *365-1 Misasa.* ☎*0858-43-0111. izanro.co.jp/en. 87 rooms. ¥17,600. ¥2200🍴.* Behind a large building, this *ryokan* is magnificently situated amid gardens and waterfalls. Has 12 different baths, all wonderful.

MATSUE
🍴🛏 **Matsue Excel Hotel Tokyu** 松江エクセルホテル東急 – *590 Asahimachi.* ☎*0852-27-0109. tokyuhotelsjapan.com/global/matsue-e/. 163 rooms. ¥18,000. ¥2200🍴.* A basic, practical business hotel opposite the station. Buffet breakfast.

🍴🍴🛏 **Naniwa Issui** なにわ一水 – *63 Chidori-cho.* ☎*0852-21-4132. naniwa-i.com. 25 rooms. ¥26,150. ¥2750🍴.* An elegant *ryokan* in the Shinjiko Onsen district, in east Matsue, with romantic view of the lake. Well-equipped rooms, some with Western-style beds. Magnificent *onsen*.

🛁🛁🛁 **Ohashikan** 大橋館 – *40 Suetsugu Honmachi. ✆0852-21-5168. ohashikan.jp/english.html. 20 rooms. ¥26,600. ¥1080 🍽.* This *ryokan* with an American owner is near the main bridge. Spacious rooms and a pleasant *onsen*. Good local cuisine.

IWAMI GINZAN

🛁🛁🛁 **Nogawaya Ryokan** 旅館のがわや – *Ro-30 Yunotsu, Yunotsu-cho. ✆0855-65-2811. www.nogawaya.com. 10 rooms. ¥24,500. 🍽, dinner also included.* A warm and friendly *ryokan* with an *onsen*, in the picturesque hot spring resort town of Yunotsu Onsen. Delicious *kaiseki* cuisine.

HAGI

🛁🛁 **Senshunraku** 萩焼の宿千春楽 – *467-2 Kikugahama, Horiuchi. ✆0838-22-0326. senshunraku.jp. 100 rooms. ¥17,900. ¥1100 🍽.* This *ryokan* in the center of town, facing Kikugahama Beach, has a pleasant garden and a number of baths, some covered, some open-air. Japanese and Western rooms. Meals are excellent, focusing on fresh seafood.

🛁🛁🛁🛁 **Hagi Honjin** 萩本陣 – *385-8 Chinto. ✆0838-22-5252. hagihonjin.co.jp/english. 85 rooms. ¥38,400. 🍽, dinner also included.* Situated east of Higashi-Hagi Station, this large *ryokan* is one of the finest in the city, with Japanese and Western rooms. A superb *onsen* and a *rotenburo* on the top of a hill, reached by private monorail.

🍴 EAT

TOTTORI

🍜 **Izakaya Tottori Daizen** 居酒屋鳥取大善 – *715 Sakae-machi. ✆0857-27-6574. tottori-daizen.com/english. Open Mon–Sat 11am–midnight, Sun 11am–11pm. Menu in English.* The menu in the casual *izakaya* includes sushi, *katsudon* (bowl of rice with pork), assorted tempura, and *yakiniku* (grilled meat). Good choice of local sakes. The owner speaks English.

🍜🍜 **Takumi Kappo** たくみ割烹店 – *652 Sakae-machi. ✆0857-26-6355. Open 11am–2.30pm, 5pm–10pm (last orders 2pm & 9pm). Closed 3rd Mon of month (except in Aug & Dec). Menu in English.* A lovely wood-paneled room in the Tottori Folkcraft Museum. Try the beef *shabu-shabu*, crab sushi, and other local specialties.

CHIZU

🍜 **Mitaki-en** みたき園 – *707 Ashizu, Chizu-cho. ✆0858-75-3665. ashidumitakien.jp/en. Open daily 10am–4pm (food 11.30am–2pm). Closed Dec–Mar. ¥2750–6050. Booking required.* Truly special restaurant, hidden away in a forested garden. The roof is in cedar bark and the *tatami* rooms are heated by *irori* (sunken hearths); in summer you can eat at the riverside. Serves fresh *sansai-ryori* (mountain vegetable cuisine).

MATSUE

🍜 **Yakumo-an** 八雲庵 – *308 Kitahori-cho. ✆0852-22-2400. yakumoan.jp. Open daily 10am–3pm (last orders 2pm). Menu in English.* 🍽. This lovely soba and udon restaurant in an 18C former samurai residence, near Buke Yashiki, has a tranquil garden with a carp pond; if you ask when booking, they may seat you in the private *tatami* room overlooking the garden.

🍜🍜 **Garden Restaurant Minami** 庭園茶寮みな美 – *14 Suetsugu Honmachi. ✆0852-21-5131. minami-g.co.jp/minamikan/18_english.php. Open 11.30am–3pm & 5.30–10pm. Lunch from ¥1600 (kaiseki much more).* This elegant restaurant in a lakeside *ryokan* near Matsue Ohashi serves sea bass in parcels (*suzuki-yaki*) and steamed rice with bream (*tai-meshi*). You can also book a private *tatami* room for a more elaborate *kaiseki* meal.

IWAMI GINZAN

🍜 **Shinyu Café Kuranojo** 震湯カフェ内蔵丞 – *7-1 Yunotsu , Yunotsu-cho. ✆0855-65-4126. yunotsu.com/cafe. Open Fri–Wed 11am–5pm.* An ideal place for a coffee or a light meal, in an old house full of period character. The owner speaks English and arranges guided tours.

HAGI

🍜🍜 **Nakamura** なかむられすとらん – *394 Hijiwara. ✆0838-22-6619. Open Thur–Mon, 11am–2pm & 5–8pm. Around ¥1800.* This restaurant in the center of Teramachi, though slightly old-fashioned, is rightly popular for its seafood specialties.

🍜🍜 **Ajiro** 懐石料理あじろ – *67 Minami-katakawa-cho. ✆0838-22-0010. hagi-ajiro.com. Open Thur–Tue 11.30am–2pm & 5–9pm. Lunch from ¥2300, dinner ¥2800.* 🍽. The seasonal ingredients are always fresh, the sashimi and tempura delicious, and the presentation very elegant, with Hagi ceramics.

NORTHERN HONSHU (TOHOKU)

Tohoku, the northeastern part of Honshu, is the largest region in Japan after the island of Hokkaido to the north. Apart from having been the homeland of the Ainu people and, for centuries, also the Emishi people, the privilege (or handicap) Tohoku shares with Hokkaido is of being considered the "end of the world" in Japanese culture. The chilly northern end of Honshu, Japan's central island, lies far from Kansai and Kanto, the imperial anchor points of Japanese civilization for more than a millennium. For a long time, Kyotoites visited Tohoku—a place they considered hostile, with backward customs—only cautiously, almost unwillingly, and this view of the region as wild and untamed, perhaps even a little uncivilized, lingers on.

Highlights

1 Sailing amid the stunning scenery of **Matsushima Bay** (p476)

2 **Zuigan-ji**, founded more than 1000 years ago (p474)

3 The opulent golden hall of **Konjiki-do** at Chuson-ji (p487)

4 The "Living Buddha" mummified monk of **Churen-ji** (p495)

5 Rich and unique biodiversity in the forests of **Shirakami-sanchi** (p510)

▶ **Population:** 8,682,000.

Michelin Map: Regions of Japan Map 5, Regional Map opposite.

Location: Tohoku is 25,870sq mi/67,000sq km in 6 prefectures: **Fukushima** *(5322sq mi/13,784sq km, pop. 1.8 mil)*; **Miyagi** *(2812sq mi/7282sq km, pop. 2.3 mil)*; **Yamagata** *(360sq mi/9325sq km, pop 1 mil)*; **Iwate** *(5898sq mi/15,275sq km, pop. 1.2 mil)*; **Akita** *(4493sq mi/11,638sq km, pop. 970,000)*; and **Aomori** *(3724sq mi/9646sq km, pop. 1.2 mil)*.

Kids: Date Masamune's armor at Sendai City Museum; Shiogama fish market; a boat trip around Matsushima Bay; the monk mummy at Churen-ji, Tsuruoka; a stroll in Shirakami-sanchi forest.

Timing: 1–2 days, Sendai; 1 day, Matsushima; half day, Shiogama; 3 days, Tsuruoka; 3–4 days for Hirosaki area.

Don't miss: Matsushima Bay; Mount Haguro & a night in a *shukubo*; Kakunodate samurai district; Nyuto Onsen; the Sanriku Fukko (Reconstruction) National Park; the Oirase Valley trail; the Shirakami-sanchi mountains.

The region known as Michinoku, "the land beyond roads," was so far removed from these loci of power that it could only be inhabited by marginal figures, outcasts *(eta)* or the asocial, such as the *yamabushi*, "the people who sleep in the mountains," peripatetic hermits who lived ascetic lives in the wilderness. **Power and poetry** – Despite being overlooked or disdained for so long, this vast area of course produced several people of note, chief among them the *daimyo* Date Masamune (1567–1636), a native of Yamagata nicknamed "the One-Eyed Dragon." He had lost an eye to a childhood illness, but it presented no barrier to his military domination of the region. In fact, it became part of the mystique that grew up around him—that even with one eye he was the fiercest warrior in the land.

With powerful nature and even more powerful warlords to contend with, few people chose to venture past the Shirakawa barrier (which ran along the frontier between the central provinces and Tohoku). One of these curious souls

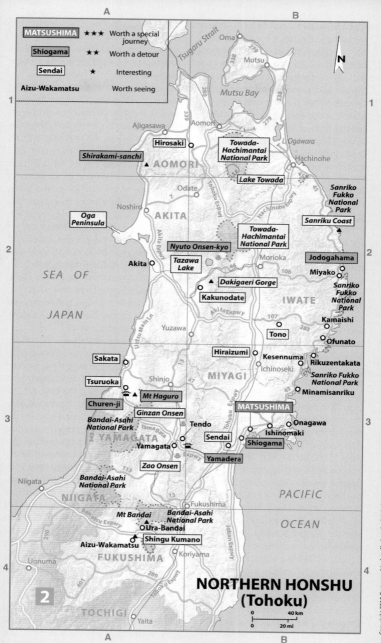

NORTHERN HONSHU (Tohoku)

Map legend:

MATSUSHIMA	★★★	Worth a special journey
Shiogama	★★	Worth a detour
Sendai	★	Interesting
Aizu-Wakamatsu		Worth seeing

Tsugaru Strait

Oma

Mutsu

Mutsu Bay

Ogawara

Hachinohe

Ajigasawa

Aomori

Hirosaki

Towada-Hachimantai National Park

Shirakami-sanchi ▲ AOMORI

Lake Towada

Sanriko Fukko National Park

Odate

Noshiro

AKITA

Towada-Hachimantai National Park

Sanriku Coast ▲

Oga Peninsula

Nyuto Onsen-kyo

Morioka

Jodogahama

Akita

Tazawa Lake

Miyako

Dakigaeri Gorge ▲

Sanriko Fukko National Park

Kakunodate

IWATE

Kamaishi

Yuzawa

Tono

Ofunato

SEA OF JAPAN

Hiraizumi

Kesennuma

Rikuzentakata

Sakata

Ichinoseki

MIYAGI

Sanriko Fukko National Park

Tsuruoka

Minamisanriku

Churen-ji

▲ Mt Haguro

Ginzan Onsen

MATSUSHIMA

Bandai-Asahi National Park

Tendo

Onagawa

YAMAGATA

Sendai

Ishinomaki

Yamagata ○

Shiogama

Zao Onsen

Yamadera

Bandai-Asahi National Park

Niigata

PACIFIC

NIIGATA

Fukushima

OCEAN

Mt Bandai ▲

Bandai-Asahi National Park

Uonuma

Ura-Bandai

Aizu-Wakamatsu ▲ Shingu Kumano

FUKUSHIMA

Koriyama

TOCHIGI

Yaita

0   40 km
0   20 mi

N

Copyright 2015 Cartographic data Shobunsha/Michelin

---

was Japan's most famous poet, Basho (1644–1694). In the opening of his *Narrow Road to the Deep North*, he felt possessed by the spirits of wanderlust, saying wistfully, "I can think of nothing but the moon at Matsushima." He spent months wandering through Tohoku, composing many beautiful works along the way.

Nature meets nuclear – While Matsushima Bay has, since Basho's time, been recognized as one of the three most beautiful landscapes in Japan, Tohoku is also known for its scenic mountainous terrain and sometimes inhospitable climate. When the first nuclear power plants were established along the coastal zone of Fukushima Prefecture in the 1970s, atomic power promised thousands of jobs for a region whose economy principally relied on tough fishing and agriculture work, and many viewed the Fukushima Nuclear Power Plant as a godsend for the area.

But on March 11, 2011—40 minutes after a magnitude-9 earthquake that had occurred 80mi/130km off the coast of the city of Sendai—a tsunami of incredible strength crashed into the eastern seaboard, with waves 77ft/23.6m high in the city of Ofunato. It ravaged 372mi/600km of coast between the prefectures of Aomori to the north and Iwate, Miyagi and Fukushima to the south.

Part of the destruction wrought was a meltdown at the Daiichi Fukushima nuclear power plant, resulting in severe radioactive fallout in the worst nuclear accident since Chernobyl. It later became clear that the damage could have been prevented, had proper safety standards been applied at Fukushima Daiichi.

As a result of the earthquake and tsunami, 15,900 people died, with over 2,500 missing and 6,200 injured.

Repair work – Though the majority of the necessary infrastructure was repaired impressively fast, there's still much left to do, even around a decade after the disaster. Seawalls are being built everywhere, structures are being raised up out of danger, terraces are being built, and an ambitious plan to convert abandoned areas into a renewable (projected completion date around 2025). Locals are gradually returning to the coast, which looks out over one of the richest fishing areas in the world.

Much is still absent, however (public services and accommodation), and 50,000 evacuees remain displaced. An exclusion zone is likely to remain in place around Fukushima Daiichi for a long time, and around half of the people evacuated from areas adjacent to the long-term exclusion zone say they have no plans to return, even if the radiation levels are declared safe.

Decontamination work at and around the ruined power plant is far from finished, and it remains a complex problem; decommissioning it fully will likely take another 40 years. All that said, visitors need go nowhere near the plant, and certainly should not be put off from traveling in Tohoku on its account. As the name of the nuclear power plant included "Fukushima," many tourists became fearful of the whole area which bears this name. However, most of the prefecture was not evacuated and saw little change in radiation levels. Fukushima City, for instance, which is a full 50mi/80km from the Daiichi Plant, now has radiation levels comparable to cities such as Hong Kong, and presents no risk to the people living there, let alone visiting for a few days.

Recovery and tourism – "Ganbaro Tohoku," as the locals say—"Hang on in there, Tohoku!" The region has worked hard to rebuild and safeguard against future disasters, but shaking off the stigma is proving harder. Tourism, already a vital part of the region's economy before 2011, is now more important than ever. There's much to see in this vast area, and no barriers in terms of safety or infrastructure to accessing most of it. In recognition of Tohoku's great cultural and natural importance, the monuments and sites of Hiraizumi (🅒 see p484) were inscribed on the UNESCO World Heritage list in June 2011, followed by the Shirakami-sanchi mountains (🅒 see p510) a few years later. On the eastern coast, existing national parks were combined into the Sanriku Fukko (Recovery) National Park, a glorious stretch of coastline dotted with fishing villages and rice paddies, criss-crossed by walking routes (including the 1000km-long Michinoku Coastal Trail; tohoku.env.go.jp/mct/english), and full of opportunities to learn more about the communities affected by the disaster, and to help in the recovery efforts.

Aizu-Wakamatsu and surroundings
会津若松

One of the main cities in Fukushima Prefecture has retained, or rather reconstructed, numerous parts of its past despite the fire that ravaged the city in September 1868 during the famous Boshin War, in which the emperor took on troops from the Tokugawa Shogunate. The Aizu clan, one of the most loyal supporters of the shogun, were finally defeated by imperial forces after a month of bloody resistance; they fought passionately, as evidenced by the famous Byakkotai or "White Tiger Force," a reserve unit of which some twenty young members commited *seppuku* on thinking they saw their castle in flames. This act contributed without a doubt to the notoriety of the city, which was best known to merchants because of its role as a trading crossroads between Niigata and Western Japan. This strategic position made it possible for the merchants to rebuild the city, as is demonstrated to this day in the famous Nanokamachi Road.

▶ **Population:** 120,700.

Map: Regions of Japan Map 5, Regional map p463, B3, Sendai Map p469.

Location: Aizu-Wakamatsu is located 180mi/290km north of Tokyo, in Fukushima Prefecture.

Timing: Allow a day for Aizu-Wakamatsu and a night at Higashiyama.

Don't miss: Nanokamachi Road and the Shiroki lacquer store; a night at the Mukaitaki ryokan to experience the *onsen* at Higashiyama.

USEFUL INFORMATION

Tourist Office – Inside Aizu-Wakamatsu station. ℘024-232-0688. *samurai-city.jp/en. Open daily 9am–5.30pm.*

TRANSPORTATION

BY TRAIN – From Tokyo Station, take the Shinkansen Yamabiko to Koriyama *(1hr 15min, ¥7810)*, then the JR Ban'etsu West Line *(1hr 10min, ¥1170)*.
BY BUS – From Tokyo, take the JR Shinjuku highway bus *(several daily, 4hr 50min–7hr, ¥4800)* to Aizu-Wakamatsu Station.

SIGHTS
Nanokamachi-dori
15min walk from JR Aizu-Wakamatsu Station, or direct from Nanukamachi Station.
This is the nerve center of the city of Aizu-Wakamatsu, through which the main roads of the Edo period ran. The most interesting part is from Osakaya Hotel to the old Nanukamachi (also written Nanokamachi) Station with its retro cafe.

Sazaedo Pagoda ★ さざえ堂
30min walk from JR Aizu-Wakamatsu Station, or 15min by Akabe bus to Iimoriyama-shita stop (☞¥210) then 5min walk. ⏲*Open daily: Jan–Mar 9am–4pm; Apr–Nov, 8.15am–sunset.* ☞*¥400. sazaedo.jp.*

Built in 1796 on the hillside at Iimoriyama, this beautiful Buddhist temple is a three-storey pagoda (54ft/16.5m high) incorporating an extremely rare structure in Japan: a double helix ramp that allows visitors to go up and down without passing one another. The walls and ceilings within are covered with inscriptions recording the importance of this pilgrimage site during the Edo era, with each visitor adding their name to show they had been there. The original statues are no longer visible, however, as they are too fragile.

Tsuruga Castle 鶴ヶ城

40min walk from JR Aizu-Wakamatsu Station or 15min by Haikara-san bus to Tsurugajo-iriguchi stop (¥210), then 5min walk. ◐*Open daily 8.30am–5pm. ¥410, or ¥510 with tea. tsurugajo.com.*
The graceful outline of this white castle with a tiled roof is particularly photogenic when the cherry trees are in bloom. Destroyed by imperial troops in 1874, the current building was reconstructed in the 1960s, although its origins are far older as the first castle was built here in the 14C. Pay a visit to the interesting historical museum and enjoy the view over the town from the 5th floor. The castle **grounds** are home to the **Rinkaku**, a tea pavilion built by the son of tea master Sen no Rikyu (16C).

Oyakuen Garden 御薬園

45min walk from JR Aizu-Wakamatsu Station, or 25min by Haikara-san bus to Oyakuen stop (¥210), then 1min walk. ◐*Open 8.30am–5pm (last admission 30min before closing). ¥330, or ¥810 with tea. tsurugajo.com/oyakuen*
Created for the feudal lord of the town some 600 years ago and remodeled several times over the centuries, Oyakuen is now a peaceful landscaped garden. A tea pavilion from the Edo period stands on the center of the island surrounded by a pond. The **house** on the banks of the pond dates from the same period, as does the **medicinal garden** of over 400 plants. The two-story building **(Chouyoukaku)** in the herb garden was named by Princess Setsuko, grand-daughter of the last feudal lord of Aizu.

EXCURSIONS
◐*Regional Map.*

Higashiyama Onsen

3.5mi/6 km southeast of Aizu-Wakamatsu Station. Bus from Akabe to Spa Higashima stop (20min, ¥210), or allow around ¥2200 by taxi. aizu-higashiyama.com.
This historic village founded some 1300 years ago contains a few excellent hotspring baths and beautiful old buildings. Stay overnight if you can, at one of the magnificent *ryokan* (◐*See Addresses).*

Shingu Kumano Shrine ★ 新宮熊野神社

◐*Map, A4. 10.5mi/17km north of Aizu-Wakamatsu. JR Ban'etsu-West Line to Kitakata (15min, ¥320), then 15min by bus to Shingu-mae stop, or a "Buraringo" bus (Apr–Nov 8am–5pm).* ◐*Open Apr–Nov daily 8am–5pm; Dec–Mar Sat–Sun & public hols 9am–4pm. ¥300.*
This major Shinto shrine was founded in the 11C by Minamoto no Yoriyoshi. The **Nagatoko**, a remarkable building and unique in Japan, is a huge prayer hall open to the elements and supported by 44 pillars beneath a thatched roof. The three small shrines a little farther up the mountain are home to statues of divinities (not visible). The **treasure house** features several Important Cultural Properties, including a copper basin (1341) and a statue of Buddha seated on a lion, dating from the Heian period (794–1185). Come in fall if you can, to see the shrine blanketed in bright yellow leaves from the 800-year-old gingko tree.

Ura-Bandai 裏磐梯

◐*Map, A4. 12mi/20km north of Aizu-Wakamatsu.* 🏠*Ura-Bandai Visitor Center: Goshikinuma Iriguchi.* ✆*0241-32-2850.* ◐*Open Thur–Tue: April–Nov 9am–5pm; Dec–Mar 9am–4pm. urabandai-inf.com.*
At the center of the vast **Bandai-Asahi National Park** stands Mount Bandai, a huge volcano that has split into three summits (the highest 5950ft/1816m above sea level). The surrounding landscape is impressive and wild, to the south around **Lake Inawashiro** and to the north on the Bandai Plateau **(Ura-bandai)**. The area is known for its superb walks, notably around Goshikinuma, the "five-colored pools."
Goshiki-numa★ – *JR Ban'etsu-West Line to Inawashiro Station (35min), then a Bandai Toto Bus to Goshikinuma Iriguchi stop or Urabandai Kogen Eki (around 30min).*
🐾In the heart of the national park, at an altitude of 800m/2624ft, the 3.5km/2.2mi-long path beside these brightly colored pools unveils an exceptional natural landscape. The ponds were formed from the eruption of **Mount Bandai** in 1888, which also caused the

bright hues: the acidic, volcanic water turns amazing colors, from green to red to blue.

Planted after the eruption, a magnificent forest is home to a rich diversity of wildlife and plants. A must-see in autumn.

⚓ *Much farther north, Bandai-Asahi National Park also includes the sacred mountains of **Dewa Sanzan** (⚓ see p494), a place of pilgrimage for centuries, and still home to many yamabushi.*

ADDRESSES

🛏 STAY

AIZU-WAKAMATSU

🛏 **Hotel Alpha-1** ホテル・アルファーワン会津若松 – 5-8 Ekimae-machi. ☎0242-32-6868. alpha-1.co.jp/aizuwakamatsu. 81 rooms. ¥9600. ¥700/800🍴. A classic business hotel 5min from the station, practical and well-kept but a bit soulless.

🛏 **Ekimae Fuji Grand Hotel** 駅前フジグランドホテル – 5-25 Ekimae-machi. ☎0242-24-1111. fujigrandhotel.co.jp. 151 rooms. ¥9000. 🍴. Next to Hotel Alpha-1, with similar facilities and friendly staff in a less impersonal, if slightly faded, setting. Western or Japanese breakfast, wifi, and free guest access to adjoining onsen.

HIGASHIYAMA ONSEN

🛏🛏 **Kutsurogijuku Chiyotaki** くつろぎ宿千代滝 – 43 Yumoto Terayashiki. ☎0242-26-0001. kutsurogijuku.jp. 64 rooms. ¥13,600. ¥1000🍴. Large, charming and well-priced ryokan. The onsen are elegant and the food excellent. Wifi available.

🛏🛏🛏🛏 **Ryokan Mukaitaki** 会津東山温泉向瀧 – 200 Yumoto Kawamukai. 6min walk from the bus terminal. ☎0242-27-7501. mukaitaki.jp. 24 rooms. ¥39,900. 🍴, dinner also included. 🚭. A lovely ryokan that has only improved with age, simple and in harmony with the gardens over which the rooms look out. With a relaxing onsen and rotenburo, and sumptuous meals, everything oozes tradition. Wifi available.

URA-BANDAI

🛏 **Bandai Lakeside Guesthouse** バンダイレークサイドゲストハウス – 1096-444 Soharayama Hibara. ☎0241-23-8757. bandai.ski. 5 rooms. Dorm ¥4320, doubles ¥13,770. 🍴, dinner ¥1500. Welcoming guesthouse on the shores of a picturesque lake. Japanese-style rooms, good meals, and a laidback bar area. The friendly, English-speaking staff can help with activities and equipment rental.

🍴 EAT

AIZU-WAKAMATSU

🍴🛏 **Shibukawa Donya** 渋川問屋 – 3-28 Nanokamachi-dori. ☎0242-28-4000. shibukawadonya.com. Open daily 11am–9pm. Ramen or katsudon ¥500–1000; wagyu ¥2200 per 30z/80g. These former seafood warehouses are now home to a restaurant that has gained popularity for its setting and it culinary specialities, such as wagyu beef. There's an option to dine with a geisha show (reserve 3 days in advance; ¥11,000), and the adjoining hotel hasfour very comfortable rooms (from ¥26,500 for 2 people).

HIGASHIYAMA ONSEN

🍴 **Yoshinoya Shokudo** よしのや食堂 – 113 Idaira Oaza Yumoto. ☎0242-27-2341. Open daily 11am–2.30pm & 5.30pm–8.30pm. Ramen or katsudon ¥500–1000. It may not look terribly promising, but this restaurant offers a warm welcome to everyone from students to spa-goers who choose not to dine in their ryokan. A slice of local life. As you leave, have a look at the Shatekiba just opposite (open daily 4–9pm), a rifle-shooting stand that is a long-standing local curiosity.

KITAKATA

🍴 **Makoto Shokudo** まこと食堂 – 7116 Odazuki-michishita. ☎0241-22-0232. Open Tue–Sun 7.30am–3pm. Lunch under ¥1000. A great place to stop on your way to/from Shingu Kumano. Tatami rooms, delicious local ramen, and good prices.

SHOPPING

AIZU-WAKAMATSU

Shirokiya – 1-2-10 Omachi, Nanokamachi-dori. ☎0242-22-0203. shirokiyashikkiten.com/english. Open 9am–5pm: Dec–Jun Thur–Tue; Jul–Nov daily. This store specializing in lacquerware opened during the Kyoho period (1716–1736) and it is now like visiting a three-story museum. Prices to suit every pocket.

HIGASHIYAMA ONSEN

Ishimotoya – 115 Idaira Oaza Yumoto. ☎0242-27-2024. This wine merchant's has been open for business since 1900 and is renowned for its fine selection of sake from Aizu and elsewhere.

Sendai★ and surroundings★★★
仙台

Like many provincial cities, Sendai owed its influence to a strong overlord. While the all-powerful Tokugawa shogunate united the country by eliminating their rivals, the *daimyo*, General Date Masamune (1567–1636), managed to impose his authority over the Miyagi region, later extending it throughout Tohoku and building a castle at Sendai, from which to rule his territories. Sendai has prospered ever since, rebuilding after its almost total destruction in WW II, and again after the tsunami in 2011, which left almost a thousand people dead in its suburbs. Sendai is a tough, forward-looking city: it recovers quickly, but without ever forgetting. It's also known as "the city of universities and schools," and as "Mori no Miyako," the city of trees; for many inhabitants, the zelkova species (elms imported from the Caucasus) has become an important anchor point to cling on to since the catastrophe that ravaged Tohoku.

▶ **Population:** 1,089,000.

Michelin Map: Regions of Japan Map 5, Regional Map p463, B3, Sendai Map opposite.

Location: Sendai is 232mi/373km north of Tokyo. It is the regional capital of the prefecture of Miyagi (population 2.3 million), bounded by the Pacific Ocean to the east, Fukushima Prefecture to the south, Yamagata to the west, Akita to the northwest, and Iwate to the north.

Kids: A boat ride from Shiogama to Matsushima.

Timing: Allow a day for Sendai, a morning for Shiogama, and a day for Matsushima.

Don't miss: Matsushima Bay; the auction at Shiogama fish market; Sendai's restaurants and bars; Entsu-in temple (Matsushima); Arahama Elementary School.

SIGHTS
Map, opposite.

The city developed alongside the Hirose River, overlooked by Sendai Castle, before extending east of this natural frontier. The eastern districts are divided by main arteries, the largest being Aoba-dori, intersected by the scovered shopping arcades of Ichiban-cho. **Jozenji-dori★** (*Map, B1*) is famous for its September Jazz Festival (*2nd weekend*), December lights and **Mediatheque★** (*open daily 9am–10pm, closed 4th Thu in month; Map, B1*), whose innovative architecture by Ito Toyo is daringly built around a still tubular lattice structure that glows artificially from within. The more historic western districts, by contrast, are home to parks, museums, and university buildings.

WEST OF THE CITY CENTER
Zuiho-den★★ 瑞鳳殿
Map, B2. 23-2 Otamayashita, Aoba-ku. 25min walk from Sendai Station, or 15min by Loople Bus. Open daily: Feb–Nov 9am–4.30pm; Dec–Jan 9am–4pm. ¥550. zuihoden.com.

This mausoleum was built for Date Masamune in the year after his death (*see box p470*). It was inspired by Nikko's famous Tosho-gu shrine, built-between 1634 and 1636, which became the model for all *daimyo* in search of postmortem splendor (*see p145*). Destroyed during the 1945 bombings, it was rebuilt almost identically during the 1970s, with concrete replacing the original wood. A short distance from the temple a path leads to tombs of Date's descendants and followers.

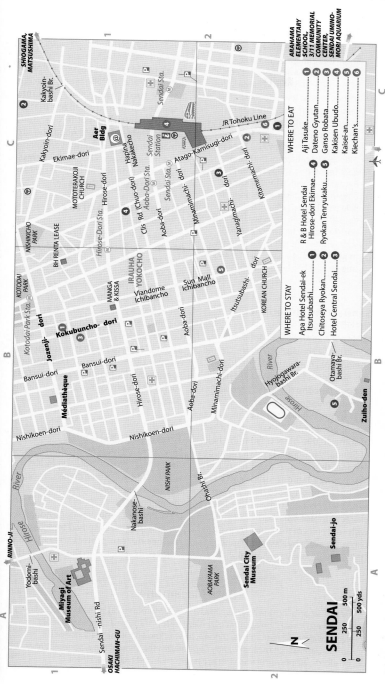

WHERE TO EAT

Aji Tasuke........... 6		Dateno Gyutan....... 4
R & B Hotel Sendai		Ganso Robata........ 5
Hirose-dori Ekimae. 1		Kakisen Ubudo...... 2
Ryokan Tennyukaku... 2		Kaisei-an...........
Hotel Central Sendai. 3		Kiechan's...........

WHERE TO STAY

Apa Hotel Sendai-ek	
Itsutsubashi......... 1	
Chitoseya Ryokan.... 2	
Hotel Central Sendai. 3	

SENDAI

N

| 0 | 250 | 500 m |
| 0 | 250 | 500 yds |

Copyright 2015 Cartographic data Shobunsha/Michelin

469

Daruma at Matsushima

This rather tubby papier mâché figure is Daruma, better known as Bodhidharma, founder of Zen. Before he founded this Buddhist school, he meditated for nine years. Unsurprisingly, after going so long without using them, Daruma awoke to find his legs and arms had shriveled away—hence the roly-poly shape of the Daruma dolls found throughout Japan. Because he lived in the temple of Zuigan-ji, he's particularly popular in Matsushima. Traditionally, dolls are sold with the eyes left unpainted, the better to "define" your wishes. The left eye is painted in when making a wish, the right one when it has been fulfilled.

Sendai City Museum★★
仙台市博物館

Map, A2. 26 Kawauchi, Aoba-ku. 10min by the Loople Bus (catch at Sendai Station) from the mausoleum. Open Tue–Sun 9am–4.45pm. ¥460. English audioguide: no charge. city.sendai.jp/ museum/museum/index.html.

This impressive historical museum was opened in 1961, thanks to the gift of some 10,000 objects from the heirs of Sendai's founder, Date Masamune. Among the unique exhibits is Date Masamune's famous armor, including the helmet thought to have served as a model for the costume of the darkest character in *Star Wars*, Darth Vader, along with souvenirs of the journeys to Christian lands made by Hasekura Tsunenaga (1571–1622), *daimyo* of Sendai.

Sendai Castle   仙台城跡

Map, A2. 1 Kawauchi, Aoba-ku. Museum: open daily 9am–5pm. ¥700. honmarukaikan.com.

Date's castle was destroyed by bombing in 1945 and nothing remains except a stone turret and a few remnants dispersed around the terrace that so splendidly overhangs the city. Built on the heights of Mount Aoba, the site remains a strategic point overlooking the gorge and river. The small, interesting museum on site includes a simulation of the inside of the castle.

Miyagi Museum of Art
宮城県美術館

Map, A1. 34-1 Kawauchi-Moto-hasekura, Aoba-ku. 15min walk from the castle. Open Tue–Sun 9am–5pm. ¥300 (excluding special exhibitions). www.pref.miyagi.jp/site/museum-en.

Opened in 1981, the museum's core collection features Japanese art from the Meiji era to modern times. In addition to work by Japanese artists such as Sato Churyo, Takahashi Yuichi, and Matsumoto Shunsuke, it also displays some work by major overseas artists such as Kandinsky, Klee, and sculptor Barry Flanagan.

NORTH OF THE CITY CENTER

Rinno-ji★   輪王寺

Map, A1; off map. Mount Kitayama. 25min from JR Sendai Station by bus nos. 13, 14, 24. Open daily 8am–5pm. Temple: no charge; garden: ¥300. rinno-ji.or.jp.

As a simple castle was not enough to defend Sendai, Date had temples and shrines built to protect the city from evil spirits. Erected in the north of the

Date Masamune

One of Japan's most revered warlords, Date Masamune was nicknamed "the One-Eyed Dragon" on account of the eye he lost through a childhood illness. Perhaps even more than this, though, he was known for the elegance of his armor. Date, which means "Dandy," epitomizes the style of the Japanese feudal overlords, all-powerful and with great presence and charisma. He fought alongside Toyotomi Hideyoshi and then Tokugawa Ieyasu, before retiring finally to the Tohoku region.

USEFUL INFORMATION
TOURIST OFFICES
SENDAI – Sendai Station, 2F. *Open daily 8.30am–7pm.* ☎022-222-4069. *sendai-travel.jp.* Information in English on Sendai and Miyagi prefecture.

MATSUSHIMA – By JR Matsushima-Kaigan Station. *Open daily: Apr-Nov 8.30am–5pm, Dec–Mar 8.30am–4.30pm.* ☎022-354-2618. *matsushima-kanko.com.*

Post Office/Withdrawals – Sendai Eki-nai Central Post Office, 1F, Sendai Station. *ATM open Mon–Fri 7am–11pm, Sat 9am–9pm, Sun 9am–7pm.*

TRANSPORTATION
GETTING TO AND FROM SENDAI
BY PLANE – The airport is southeast of the city. *sendai-airport.co.jp/en.* Trains every 30min to Sendai Station *(25min journey, ¥650).*

BY TRAIN – From **Tokyo**, Yamabiko, Hayabusa, Komachi , and Hayate Shinkansen depart every 30min (JR Tohoku Shinkansen Line). The Komachi and Hayabusa are the fastest and most expensive *(1hr 30min; ¥11,210).* From Sendai, the JR Tohoku Line serves **Shiogama** *(15min, ¥240),* the Senseki Line **Matsushima** *(25min, ¥420)* and **Hon-Shiogama** *(30min, ¥330).*

BY BUS – Bus Center – *1-6-31 Chuo, Aoba-ku.* ☎022-261-533. Long-distance buses for Aomori, Tokyo, Nagoya, etc. Buses are around half the cost of the train, but take much longer.

From Sendai to Tsuruoka – Shonai Kotsu *(shonaikotsu.jp/english),* buses every hour from 7.05am to 8.35pm *(2hr 30min, ☞¥3200 one-way).*

Sendai Marugoto Pass – Unlimited transport on JR trains, bus, subway, Abukuma Express, Sendai Airport Access Line for two days between Sendai, Matsushima, Shiroishi, and Yamadera *(¥2720, children ¥1350, sendaitravelpass.jp).* There's a similar one-day pass *(¥ 1320, children ¥660).*

GETTING TO AND FROM SHIOGAMA
BY TRAIN – The train station is in the city center. *See connections with Sendai.*

GETTING TO AND FROM MATSUSHIMA
BY TRAIN – Matsushima-kaigan Station is more convenient for the main sights than Matsushima Station. *See connections with Sendai.*

GETTING AROUND SENDAI
The main buses leave from Sendai Station. The **Loople Bus** *(west exit from the station, stop no. 16; loople-sendai.jp/en)* covers the main tourist sites *(every 15–30min; ¥260 per journey, one-day pass ¥630; 1-day pass for bus & subway ¥920).* The **subway** serves the city from north to south and west to east. The first 3 stations cost ¥200, the next three ¥250, and on to the terminus ¥300 *(one-day pass ¥840; www.kotsu.city.sendai.jp/subway).*

GETTING AROUND SHIOGAMA AND MATSUSHIMA
BY BOAT – Between Shiogama's **Marine Gate Building** and **Matsushima** (next to the Tourist Office), and in a loop from each, boats every hour, approx. 9am–4pm *(50min, ¥1500; marubun-kisen.com/english/matsushima).*

city, the Buddhist temple of Rinno-ji was intended to guard what was considered to be the most inauspicious compass point. The beautiful **garden★**, complete with a koi-filled pond and a pagoda, is the highlight of the visit.

Osaki Hachiman-gu★★
大崎八幡宮
🕐*Map, A1; off map. Hachimangu-mae. 15min from the JR Sendai Station by bus nos. 10 or 15.*

Construction of this shrine was ordered by Date Masamune, who wanted to establish the guardian deities of his castle here. Built in 1607 on the top of a hill, it is a fine example of the architecture of the Momoyama era (1573–1603). Its flamboyant **porch**★★ and also the **coffered ceiling**★★ decorated with 55 brightly colored hand-painted flowers relieve the handsome austerity of gold and black lacquer. Every year on January 14, during the **Dontosai Matsuri**, a long procession of men files past on the way to burn their New Year decorations in front of the Hachiman shrine.

EAST OF THE CITY CENTER

The Tozai subway line crosses Sendai from west to east: from Tagima Zoo in the west to Arai rail station *(7.5mi/12km from the central station)*. Many of the buildings in this neighborhood are new, built to house tsunami victims, in particular former residents of the Miyagino and Wakabayashi districts; these areas had been integrated into Sendai's municipal authority in 1989 as part of its ongoing urban expansion towards the sea, but were completely wiped out in 2011. Temporary accommodation is being phased out in favor of new housing developments, a great improvement for the people who lost their homes in the disaster. The developments are somewhat homogeneous, though, as they had to be mass-produced quickly to get people out of their emergency shelters (140,000 buildings were completely destroyed in Sendai), while also dealing with a fresh influx of migrants from the coast.

Sendai 3/11 Memorial Community Center – Ġ*Map, C2; off map. 15min subway ride from Sendai Station,* ✆*¥300.* ⏰*Open Tue–Sun 10am–5pm,* ✆*no charge, brochure in English.* Constructed at the heart of Arai Station, with the intention of preserving the memory of the catastrophe for later generations, this community center also serves to bring together the neighborhood's new inhabitants. The multi-level building features various exhibitions to help visitors better "think of the future, face up to the past, share and talk together,"

as the exhibitors put it. For many inhabitants, the trauma will remain always, and just a look at the first diorama, a side-by-side comparison of two photographs of the same place, before and after the tsunami, makes it easy to see why—the difference is quite staggering.

Arahama Elementary School
仙台市立荒浜小学校
Ġ*Map, C2; off map. From Arai Station, take bus no. 2 (every hour, 10am–4.30pm, 15min journey,* ✆*¥240).* ⏰*Open daily 10am–4pm.* ⏰*Closed 2nd & 4th Thur of the month.* ✆*No charge.*
This "ghost building" has been preserved, and open to visitors since 2017. It is the former elementary school for the district of Arahama (a suburb of Wakabayashi), an area totally wiped out by the tsunami of March 11. It was on the top floor of this structure, built in 1873, that 320 people—among them students, school staff and locals—took refuge immediately after the earthquake. An army helicopter eventually winched the survivors to safety from the torrent that had been unleashed beneath them. Along with some very evident reminders of the tsunami—doors blown out, ironwork twisted, and balconies torn off—there is a display of photos and videos that demonstrate the violent force of the catastrophe which claimed the lives of 930 people in the city of Sendai alone. Only the classrooms in the uppermost floors remained untouched, and there are several unfinished lessons still to be seen on blackboards. Looking out from the roof, it is hard to imagine that 2200 people once lived in the immediate area in more than 800 houses. If you look towards the coast (half a mile/around 800m away), you will see the immense, newly constructed seawall, the large banks of earth rising more than 20ft/6m above the new highway.

Sendai Umino-Mori Aquarium★ 仙台うみの杜水族館
Ġ*Map, C2, off map. 4-6 Nakano, Miyagino-ku.* ✆*022-355-2222. www.uminomori.jp/umino/en/index.*

html. ⏰*Open summer 9am–7.30pm, winter 9am–5.30pm, rest of the year 9am–6.30pm (last admission 30min before closing). ⮞¥2,200; ¥1,600 under 18/over 65; ¥990 under 12; ¥600 over 4; under 4 free. From Arai Station, take the free shuttle in summer and on public holidays. From Sendai Station take the Tohoku Line to Nakanosakae Station (18min journey, ⮞¥200) then a shuttle (every 30min, 8.45am–4pm, no charge), or a 15min walk.*

This new aquarium blends two entirely disparate approaches, the first being informative and educational. The eastern shores of Tohoku and the coastal region of Sanriku, the easternmost area jutting out into the sea, look out onto an ocean that is rich in fishing resources. This deep body of water (93% of its expanse is more than 650ft/200m deep) is also known as the "the sea of fertility" and lies at the confluence of a warm *(oya-kurio)* and a cold current *(oya-shio)*. The result is a body of water full of rich micronutrients.

The area's marine riches and fishing resources are investigated from a variety of angles and presented in numerous vast tanks that house more than 200 species. As you make your way through room after room, you cannot escape the feeling that everything possible is being done to gradually reconcile coast-dwellers with the sea and its deep waters once more—mistrusted ever since the trauma of 2011, despite the visceral connection that ties the people of the area with this stretch of sea. The rare and spectacular species you can see here include the singular mola mola or ocean sunfish, a bony fish with no tailfin that can weigh more than a ton!

The second part of the visit is considerably more playful: the pool outside contains dolphins, sealions, and penguins that perform tricks and eat quantities of food, amusing the youngest visitors but at the cost of respect for the animals on show.

EXCURSIONS
⚑*Regional Map, B3.*

Shiogama★★ 塩竈
Located around 18.5mi/30km northeast of Sendai, Shiogama is best known for its large tuna market, which supplies some of Tokyo's best restaurants. The town is also the ideal starting point for reaching Matsushima by boat.

Fish market★★ 塩釜水産物仲卸市場
15min walk from Higashi-Shiogama Station. The tuna auction is held 5min from the market. ⏰Open Mon–Tue & Thur–Fri 3am–1pm, Sat 3am–2pm, Sun 6am–2pm. ⮞No charge. nakaoroshi. or.jp/lang/en.

This lively market, which employs nearly 400 people, has four sections (deep-sea fish, small fish, salted fish, and other seafood products such as dried seaweed). There are a few restaurants where you can sample most of the produce sold on the stands. Miyagi specialties include *hoya* (sea pineapples), *shako-ebi* (with the texture and taste of shrimp), the famous Matsushima *kaki* (oysters), and tuna, sold at the special tuna market where auctions take place daily between 7am and 8am.

Shiogama-jinja★★ 鹽竈神社
Ichimori-yama, above the city. ⏰Open daily 5am–8pm. shiogamajinja.jp.
Rebuilt in the 17C, this shrine with asymmetric roofs in the *Nagare-zukuri* style is actually made up of three buildings (Ugu, Sagu, Betsugu), each dedicated to one of the three local deities responsible for Tohoku's well-being. Of these, **Shiotsuchi-Oji no kami**, housed in the Betsugu, is by far the most important. As protector of fishermen and all who live by the sea, the *kami* taught the locals how to extract salt from seawater, a technique integral to the process of **preserving food in brine**, which became widespread in Japan. It also protects pregnant women, which raises the question of a link between salt and pregnancy—*shio* means salt, but it also

Kuri, Zuigan-ji

© mfaira/Shutterstock

signifies the tide. There is also a Japanese saying that births occur during an incoming tide when the moon is high in the heavens, its roundness perhaps evoking the fullness of pregnancy.

There is a small **museum** with various exhibits linked to salt production and inshore fishing methods (🕐*open daily: Apr–Sept 8.30am–5pm; Feb–Mar & Oct–Nov 8.30am–4.30pm; Dec–Jan 8.30am–4pm; ☞¥200).*

MATSUSHIMA★★★ 松島

Located 25mi/40km northeast of Sendai, Matsushima Bay, the "island of pines", contains more than 260 islands. "Matsushima ah! A-ah, Matsushima, ah! Matsushima ah!" according to the well-known *haiku*, expressing the feeling of being at a loss for words when faced with the bay's beauty, at one time thought to have been penned by poet Matsuo Basho. It has since been classified as one of the three most beautiful landscapes in Japan. In addition to the beauty of their landscape, these many islands, covered with pine trees *(matsu)* came to the rescue in the face of the tsunami in 2011, damping the violence of the swell and reducing the waves to a height of 4ft/1.3m at the seafront, limiting the destruction at the edges of the residential areas.

While the temple Zuigan-ji has been restored, the magnificent tree-lined boulevard leading to the central building is no more; the century-old pines were almost all uprooted in the disaster. Other trees have been planted along a straight corridor, and in years to come may be just as magnificent.

Zuigan-ji★★★ 瑞巌寺

91 Chonai, Matsushima. 🕐*Open daily: Apr–Sept 8am–5pm; Mar & Oct 8am–4.30pm; Feb & Nov 8am–4pm; Dec–Jan 8am–3.30pm.* ☞*¥700 (including museum). zuiganji.or.jp/en.*

Built by the monk Ennin (794–864) in 828, during the Heian period, Zuigan-ji was one of the first sites of worship from which the great Buddhist patriarch of the Tendai school spread Buddhism throughout northern Japan. During the Kamakura period (1185–1333, 🚶 *see p77)*, Zuigan-ji became one of the principal temples of the Rinzai branch of the Zen Buddhist sect (which emphasizes achieving enlightenment through meditation), breathing new life into a Buddhism that was fashionable during those chaotic times. Having fallen into neglect from the 15C, the temple owes its renaissance to Date Masamune. In 1604, the powerful *daimyo* needed an aristocratic residence not far from Sendai. Like Nijo Castle (Kyoto), completed by Tokugawa Ieyasu at the beginning of the 17C (🚶*see p325)*, although Zuigan-ji was remodeled in elegant fashion, it was not left defenseless.

Kano School gilding and painting decorate the *fusuma* (sliding panels), while the corridors are laid with "nightingale floors" *(uguisubari)*—planks that squeak like birds to betray the steps of intruders. Date transported the best carpenters and sculptors from Kyoto and

Wakayama to work on the cedars *(sugi)* brought directly from Mount Kumano. Of the rooms in the Hondo, the **Shitchu** or **Kujaku no ma★★★**, the central space reserved for religious use, is of particular interest. Its pictures, painted on **fusuma** by Sakuma Shuri in 1622, depict on one side **pines** (trees that do not shed their leaves in winter and thus symbolize the strength and perseverance required by man), and on the other, **peacocks** (an iconographic motif much loved by Buddhists, who saw in the iridescent dark blue "eyes" adorning its outspread tail a proof of origins shared with the Buddha: heaven on earth).

The **Bunno no ma★★★** room was painted by Hasegawa Toin in 1622. The **Jodan no ma**, a room reserved exclusively for the lord, is resplendent with its black-striped lacquered alcove *(tokonoma)* of "offset" chigai-dana shelves. To the right of the Hondo is the **Kairo★**, a corridor with Chinese-style doors *(karato)* and a magnificent carved lintel *(ranma)* whose "nightingale floor" leads to the **Kuri★**, a Zen kitchen notable for its lofty, powerful wooden frame.

The visit may be continued with the **Zuiganji Art Museum★★**, whose numerous exhibits include a bell *(upan)* made in 1326 to announce mealtimes; a wooden statue of Date Masamune (1593), and various family portraits of the Date clan; not to mention a great number of pieces of calligraphy and **paintings on fusuma★★★**. Having been transferred from the Hondo to one of the rooms in the museum, they are rarely exhibited, for conservation reasons (you're mostly looking at masterful reproductions within the Hondo itself). These paintings by Hasegawa Toin are accompanied by a **wooden Godai-Myo★★★** statue (10–11C)

Entsu-in★★ 円通院

67 Chonai, Matsushima. ◷Open daily: Apr–late Oct 8.30am–5pm; late Oct–Nov 8.30am–4.30pm; Dec–Mar 9am–4pm; ☜¥300. entuuin.or.jp.
If you are fortunate, you may be able to visit this temple with Amano Haruka, a Zen monk, who is the daughter of the

senior monk. Haruka is one of only two women to have been admitted to the rank of monk in the Tohoku region. She also runs rosary-making workshops at the temple *(20min, ☜¥1000 including entry fee)*.

Entry is by the garden of "great sorrow," through a moss garden and then a dry landscape garden. Representing the bay of Matsushima, it is composed of rough, streaked, and smooth stones, respectively referring to birth, apprenticeship, and accomplishment—the three stages of life. The path is bordered by maples, azaleas, and camellias, and leads to the **Sankei-den★★**, the mausoleum of Mitsumune, the grandson of Date Masamune, who died aged 19 in Edo Castle in 1645, probably by poisoning.

Suspicion fell on the Tokugawa family, since, with a gift for military strategy, at some point he would have posed a threat for the shogunate, already barely able to hang onto its political power. In this small, magnificently decorated shrine can be seen the hopes the Date clan had cherished for this promising grandson. A statue of Mitsumune riding a white horse stands out against walls skillfully overlaid in sparkling gold. He is accompanied by his seven faithful retainers, all of whom committed *seppuku* when he died.

Above the right- and left-hand doors are painted a rose and a narcissus with white petals respectively. Symbolizing Rome and Florence, and testifying to the visit made by Tsunenaga to the Pope on Date's orders, these two flowers so detestable to the Tokugawa (all allegiance to Christianity being severely punished by the shogunate) were not rediscovered until 1945, nearly 300 years after the tomb was built in 1646. These flowers are exhoed in the Western-style rose garden in the grounds, which is very unusual for a Buddhist temple.

▷ Return to the bay (220yd/200m).

Matsushima Bay★

On a crescent of land overlooking the bay you will find the **Kanran-tei★** tea house *(a short distance from the pier*

Matsushima Bay

© JTB Photo/Universal Images Group/Getty Images

at 56 Chonai; ☎022-353-3355; ⏰ *open daily: Apr–Oct 8.30am–5pm, Nov–Mar 8.30am–4.30pm;* ✍*¥200, tea* ✍*¥500).* This "place to view the ripples on the water" offers a splendid **view** of the bay. Its doors in the *shoin-zukuri* style are embellished with beautiful paintings by Kano Sanraku (1559–1635). Left of Kanran-tei, the islet of **Godaido★** has a small temple hall *(open to the public every 33 years, next opening in 2039)* in Momoyama style, rebuilt in 1609 by Masamune. The prefix "Go" ("five" in Japanese) refers to the statues of the five Buddhist guardians kept in the temple; they represent the *Mikkyo*, the "secret teachings" of Shingon Buddhism. A **red footbridge** *(Fukuura-bashi)* connects the islet of **Fukuura★** to the shore. It is a botanical reserve, where some 250 plant species have been recorded *(⏰ open daily 8am–5pm;* ✍*¥200).*

Facing Fukuura, the **Date Masamune Wax Museum** *(Matsushima Kaigan, on the seafront walkway opposite;* ⏰*open daily: mid-Mar–late Dec 8.30am–5pm, late Dec–mid-Mar 9am–4.30pm;* ✍*¥500)* exhibits 25 dioramas detailing his life, plus a gallery of famous Tohoku personalities.

The Most Beautiful Views over the Bay★★★
Shintomi-yama, a small hill behind the Wax Museum, is an ideal place from which to view the sunset. The park of **Saigyo Modoshi no matsu★★**, literally, "the pine tree that compelled Saigyo to

depart from Matsushima," commands one of the finest viewpoints over the bay, while **Ogitani★★** *(on the N45 coming from Sokanzan)* and **Sokanzan★** "the hill with two views" *(from where you can see Shiogama and Matsushima Bay in one panoramic view),* are two popular observation points.

EXCURSIONS
Ishinomaki
5.5mi/25km east of Matsushima. JR Senseki Line from Matsushima-kaigan Station, 45min, ✍*¥510.* 🚩*Ishinomaki Community & Information Center, on the main road west of the river (also serves as the place to learn about the ongoing reconstruction work);* ⏰ *open Mon & Wed–Sun 9.30am–6pm.*

This small city is filled with manga—everything from signs to street furniture—having been the favorite town of the famous illustrator **Ishinomori Shotaro** (1938–1998). A native of Tome, as a boy he would cycle two or even three hours to the **Okada Theater** in Ishinomaki to watch the films that were to prove such a stimulus to his imagination. Having achieved worldwide renown for his *shonen manga* (for young adults) in 1964, he published Cyborg 009, the first Japanese series to feature multiple heroes in costumes with special powers. **Ishinomori Manga Museum★** – *15/20min walk from the station on a little island in the Kyu Kitami River (map from Tourist Office); mangattan.jp/manga;* ⏰ *open Mar–Nov daily 9am–6pm,*

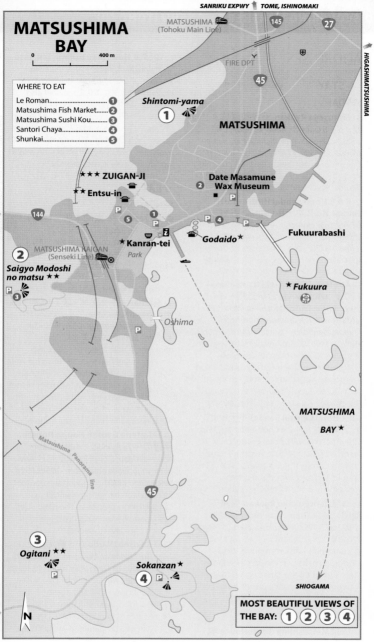

MATSUSHIMA BAY

0 — 400 m

WHERE TO EAT

Le Roman............................. ①
Matsushima Fish Market....... ②
Matsushima Sushi Kou.......... ③
Santori Chaya...................... ④
Shunkai............................... ⑤

MATSUSHIMA ⬛
(Tohoku Main Line)

145

27

FIRE DPT

45

HIGASHIMATSUSHIMA

Shintomi-yama
①

MATSUSHIMA

144

★★★ **ZUIGAN-JI**

★★ **Entsu-in**

**Date Masamune
Wax Museum** ②

P

①
⑤
P
P
④
P

ℹ️

★ **Kanran-tei**
Park

Godaido ★

Fukuurabashi

MATSUSHIMA KAIGAN
(Senseki Line)

②

**Saigyo Modoshi
no matsu** ★★
P
③

★ **Fukuura**

Oshima

Matsushima Panorama line

**MATSUSHIMA
BAY** ★

45

③
Ogitani ★★
P

Sokanzan ★
④ P

SHIOGAMA

N

**MOST BEAUTIFUL VIEWS OF
THE BAY:** ① ② ③ ④

*closed 3rd Tues of each month; Dec–Feb
Wed–Mon 9am–5pm* ⊜ *¥800, children
¥200–500).* Built just round the corner
from Nakaze Park, the museum was
designed by Ishinomori in the form of a
spaceship, an unmissable stop for manga
lovers. Unfortunately, the 160-year-old

Okada Theater, which used to stand next
door, was swept away by the tsunami
just five days after a total restoration had
been completed.

⤷*See Sanriku Coast p481 if you would like
to stay for longer farther north.*

ADDRESSES

🛏 STAY

SENDAI

🛏 **Chitoseya Ryokan** 千登勢屋旅館 – *6-3-8 Odawar, Aoba-ku (Map, C1).* ✆*022-222-6329. ryokanchitoseya.co.jp/en. 13 rooms. ¥6300. ¥770🍴.* A little away from the center in northern Sendai. A charming inn with a small garden and shrine. Wifi, *o-furo*, bicycle rental.

🛏 **R & B Hotel Sendai Hirose-dori Ekimae** R&B ホテル仙台広瀬通駅前 – *2-6-37 Hon-cho, Aoba-ku (Map, C1).* ✆*022-726-1919. randb.jp/sendai. 202 rooms. ¥9720.* 🍴. In the center of town, specializing in "singles." Functional but rather souless business hotel rooms.

🛏 **Apa Hotel Sendai-eki Itsutsubashi** ア パヴィラホテル〈仙台駅五橋 – *3-1-1 Itsutsubashi, Wakabayashi-ku (Map, C2).* ✆*0570-023-111. apahotel.com/hotel/ touhoku/sendaieki-itsutsubashi. 610 rooms. ¥9000. ¥1400🍴.* 8min walk from Sendai Station and 2min from Itsutsubashi Station, this business hotel is good value for money. Very comfortable rooms and fairly quiet, even those that are above the railway. An *onsen* and a restaurant.

🛏🍴 **Hotel Central Sendai** ホテルセントラル仙台 – *4-2-6 Chuo, Aoba-ku (Map, C2).* ✆*022-711-4111. hotel-central.co.jp. 97 rooms. ¥17,820. ¥1485🍴.* A former *ryokan*, now a business hotel with practical double and single rooms. A warm welcome just 3min from the station.

🛏🍴🛁 **Tenryukaku Ryokan** 旅館天龍閣 – *22-20 Otamayashita (Map, B2).* ✆*022-222-9957. tenryukaku.com. 25 rooms. ¥20,200.* 🍴. A beautiful *ryokan* at foot of Zuiho-den, with a dining room of 105 *tatami* mats overlooking the Hirose River—ideal for the Tanabata Festival fireworks. An *onsen* and a type of sauna on a bed of stones (*ganban-yoku*).

MATSUSHIMA

🛏 **Uchi Matsushima Guest House** 宇智松島民宿 – *121-3 Chonai Matsushima.* ✆*022-765-1397. www.uchi-matsushima. com. 6 rooms. ¥7200.* 🍴. Opened in 2016 by Eiju Nakamura, this guesthouse is ideally placed, just minutes from the temples. A little basic but the rooms are well-kept. WC and shower on the landing. Free welcome drink on arrival, and simple breakfasts.

🛏🍴🛁 **Hotel Matsushima Taikanso** ホテル松島大観荘 – *10-6 Inuta Matsushima.* ✆*022-354-2161. taikanso.co.jp/ en. 256 rooms. ¥31,020.* 🍴, dinner also included. With its Japanese and Western rooms, *rotenburo*, *onsen*, pool, and seven restaurants with Japanese and French cuisine, this hotel offers something for everyone. Luxury accommodation and a wonderful view across the bay.

🍴 EAT

SENDAI

🛏 **Aji Tasuke** 味 太助本店 – *4-4-13 Ichiban-cho (Map, B1).* ✆*022-225-4641. aji-tasuke.co.jp. Open Wed–Mon 11.30am–10pm. From ¥600, set meals from ¥2000.* 🍴. Avid meat eaters shouldn't visit Sendai without trying the local specialty, *gyutan*; charcoal-grilled beef tongue.

🛏 **Kiechan's** キーチャンズ – *1-1-8 Chuo, Wakabayashi-ku. (Map, C2).* ✆*022-713-9277. www.kiechans.jp. Open Wed–Sat 4.30pm–1.30am, Sun–Tue 4.30pm–midnight.* A half dozen or so *izakaya* (including Kiechan's) jostle for space 7min from Tsutsubashi Station, in front of the Apa Hotel. Whichever of the many dishes you choose (skewers, sushi, omelets, etc.) wash it down with some sake and enjoy the friendly and relaxed atmosphere.

🛏🍴 **Dateno Gyutan Honpo Honten** 伊達の牛たん本店 – *4-10-11 Chuo, Aoba-ku (Map, C2).* ✆*022-722-2535. www. dategyu.jp. Open daily 11am–10pm. Fixed lunch menu ¥1800 .* Sitting at the counter you can watch meltingly tender ox tongue being prepared. The head chef, Yoshitsugu Sawabe, is a great friend of French chef Joël Robuchon.

🛏🍴 **Kakisen Ubudo** かき鮮海風土 – *1-1-1 Tsutsujigaoka, Miyagino-ku (Map, C1).* ✆*022-212-2340. Open daily 10am–10.30pm. Table charge ¥400.* One of the best sushi restaurants in Sendai. The quality of the seasonal food, including oysters (*kaki*), is excellent. Fans of oysters should try out their different preparations (winter only).

🛏🍴🛁 **Kaisei-an** 開盛庵 – *1-2-21 Ichiban-cho, Aoba-ku (Map, B2).* ✆*022-266-2520. en.kaiseian.jp. Open daily 11.30am–9pm.* A warm welcome to a restaurant that has been serving *unagi* (eel) for 126 years. Reservations required for the *tatami* rooms on the second and third floors, including one suberb room guarded by a vigilant *daruma*.

🍴🍶🍱 **Ganso Robata** 元祖・炉ばた – *2-10-28 Kokubun-cho (Map, B1).* 📞*022-266-0897. Open Mon–Sat 5–10pm. Closed public holidays.* 🍴. A celebration of Japanese style, opened in 1950. Seating is at a U-shaped bar around the central open hearth, where a rack with brass carafes dangles. You will be offered a glass of sake and various amuse-bouches to start with.

MATSUSHIMA

By midday the cheap eateries are busy offering their local specialties: oysters, *sasakamaboko* (a fishcake with *mirin*, sugar and potato flour, steamed or grilled), squid, shellfish, and *zunda mochi*, made with sticky rice and edamame purée.

🍴 **Matsushima Fish Market** 松島さかな市場 – *4-10 Fugendo.* 📞*022-353-2318. sakana-ichiba.co.jp. Market open daily 8am–5pm, sit-down eateries 8am–5pm.* 🍴. Lots of eateries offering superb fresh oysters (*yakigaki*) and grilled seafood.

🍴 **Santori Chaya** さんとり茶屋 – *24-4-1 Senzui.* 📞*022-353-2622. Open Thu–Tue 11.30am–3pm & 5–10pm.* The only restaurant offering fresh oysters all year round, Santori also specializes in *sokadon* and excellent fish, sushi, eels, and tuna. Fine view of the bay and the islands.

🍴🍶 **Shunkai** 旬海 – *51-2 Chonai.* 📞*022-353-4131. sensinan.co.jp/syunkai. Open Thur–Tue 11.30am–3pm & 5.30–10pm (Dec–Apr reservation required for dinner).* One of the few local restaurants open in the evening. Grilled fish, sashimi, and soba noodles. Rooms with *tatami* mats and a convivial bar favored by the locals.

🍴🍶🍱 **Matsushima Sushi Kou** 松島 寿司幸 – *88-1 Chonai.* 📞*022-355-0021. Open Thu–Tue 11am–9pm. Lunch around ¥2500, dinner ¥3000.* 🍴. Open in the evening, this restaurant (counter and tables) is one of the best *sushi-ya* in town. The menu is packed with local produce: abalone, scallops, and sea urchins. Deliciously fresh sashimi and sushi.

🍴🍶 **Le Roman** ロマン – *10-174 Inuta.* 📞*022-354-2778. Open Wed–Mon 11am–5pm. Reservations not accepted.* 🍴. Simple meals in the park of Saigyo Modoshi no Matsu, a stone's throw from one of the most amazing panoramic views over Matsushima (📖*see p418*). It's the ideal place for lunch, or to watch the sunset. The park has some 250 cherry trees, gorgeous in spring when in blossom.

SHIOGAMA

🍴 **My Kaisendon** 松島さかな市場 – *Shiogama Fish Market* (📖*see p471*). 📞*022-362-5518. nakaoroshi.or.jp/lang/en. Open Mon–Fri 6.30am–12.30pm, Sat–Sun 6.30am–1.30pm.* 🍴. Take your pick of the market's fresh seafood, to have here with rice and miso soup (*¥400*). A delicious *sashimi-don*, with only your favorite fish.

NIGHTLIFE

SENDAI

Kokubun-cho 国分町 is Sendai's nightlife quarter, its tangle of streets full of bars, restaurants, *pachinko*, and massage parlors. A European ambiance can be found at the excellent **Gulp Down Cafe** ガルプダウンカフェ *(3F Fox Bldg, 2-10-30 Kokubun-cho, Aoba-ku, facebook.com/GulpDownCafe)*, Middle Eastern ambience at **Sindbad** シンドバッド *(1F Ex Plaza, 2-2-22 Kokubun-cho, Aoba-ku; ¥450 table charge)*.

SHOPPING

SENDAI

Culinary Specialties – **Kanezaki Kamaboko** 鐘崎 – *3-5-16 Ichiban-cho, Aoba-ku.* 📞*022-231-5141. kanezaki.co.jp/shop/kanezaki. Open daily 10am–7pm.* Specializes in *sasakamaboko*. The flesh of the fish is ground and grilled, and presented in the shape of a bamboo leaf. They can be made with shrimp, ham, lotus, wasabi, etc. Prices from *¥120* each.

Ocha no Igeta お茶の井ケ田 – *3-8-11 Ichiban-cho, Aoba-ku.* 📞*022-261-1351. Open daily 10am–7.30pm. Matcha* green tea, plus elegant cakes and confectionery.

Crafts – **Tsutsumi-no-Ohinakkoya** つつみのおひなっこや – *2-10-10 Tsutsumi-cho.* 📞*022-233-6409. tsutsumi-n.net. Open daily 9am–6pm.* Sato is one of the last makers of *tsutsumi*, small painted terracotta dolls. Family museum, shop, and doll-making *(daruma)* workshop; *reservations required.*

EVENTS AND FESTIVALS

SENDAI

Tanabata Matsuri 仙台七夕まつり – In summer *(Aug 6–8)*, Sendai's streets fill with 1500 decorated bamboo poles; fireworks the evening before the festival.

Dontosai Matsuri どんと祭 – A large procession of men, clad only in white loincloths, a piece of white paper clenched between their teeth, gather to pray for a prosperous year *(Jan 14;* 📖*see p472)*.

The Sanriku Coast
三陸海岸

The titanic amount of repair work here gives an idea of the scale of the disaster, even so many years after the tsunami that hit on March 11, 2011, devastating more than 370mi/600km of coastline between the prefectures of Amori to the north and Iwate and Miyagi to the south. Many public works are still in progress, reconstructing, reinforcing, raising, building and remolding the landscape. Seawalls, housing, factories, ports—everything has to be reconsidered and planned to anticipate the unforeseeable, as the force of the tsunami confounded all expectations, including those of the marine research instutions. Some 8700mi/14,000km of a total of 21,750mi/35,000km of coastline were thought to have had adequate protection against tsunamis, but it proved to be quite the contrary after the destruction of the three famous seawalls at Kamaishi, whose foundations (more than 205ft/63m deep along a total length of over 6230ft/1900m) had made it into the record books. While a visit to this stretch of coastline will inevitably bring you face to face with the destructive power of the sea, you'll also be confronted by its beauty and its bounty. What's more, tourism is a vital part of the recovery process for the region, showing the inhabitants of the Sanriku Coast that they, and the beautiful stretch of coastline they call home, have not been forgotten.

RECOMMENDED ROUTE
♿Regional Map.
The railway line was destroyed and has been rebuilt as a road. An efficient BRT (bus) service therefore now runs where the trains once did, and even sounds a horn when entering the tunnels. If you're a fan of hiking or cycling, it's worth add-

- ♿ **Michelin Map:** Regional map p463, B3.
- ▶ **Location:** This part of the coastline lies between Matsushima and Kamaishi, around 175mi/280km on the Pacific coast of Tohoku.
- ◷ **Timing:** Allow three days and two nights.
- ☺ **Don't miss:** Minami-Sanriku Hotel Kanyo; Kesennuma fish market; Iwate Tsunami Memoria; the huge works at Kamaishi.

USEFUL INFORMATION
Sendai Tourist Office – (♿see p471). **Kamaishi Tourist Office** – Kamaishi Station. ☎0193-22-5835. *Open daily 9am–6pm.*

TRANSPORTATION
GETTING TO AND FROM SANRIKU COAST
Easy access points on the Tohoku Shinkansen route include Sendai, Ichinoseki and Hachinohe. The JR bus (BRT) runs on adapted rail lines.

ing a section of the spectacular, 620mi-/1000km-long Michinoku Coastal Trail *(tohoku.env.go.jp/mct/english)* onto your trip, which runs from Hachinohe down to northern Fukushima prefecture, taking in the **Sanriku Fukko (Reconstruction) National Park** *(www. env.go.jp/en/nature/nps/park/sanriku)* along the way.

Minamisanriku 南三陸町
♿*Map, B3. From Sendai or Matsushima, JR Tohoku Line to Kogota, then JR Ishinomaki Line to Maeyachi. Then take the JR bus (BRT) for Minamisanriku (Shizugawa Station). 2hr 40min journey from Sendai, ☞¥1570.* 🌐*m-kankou.jp.*
On March 11, 2011, 832 people were killed or went missing, and 3400 buildings were destroyed: 60% of the town, which had a population of 17,666 before the tsunami, was wiped out. Reconstruction work is still under way; the projects

11 March 2011 and After

The Minami-Sanriku Hotel Kanyo, an immense hotel looking out over the sea, is one of the few buildings in the town of Minamisanriku to escape being swept away by the tsunami. There were 350 people inside the building when the catastrophe struck and, as the only shelter in an area that had been completely devastated, it immediately became a temporary home for 250 refugees, who were joined by medical teams and volunteers in the weeks that followed. Through the commitment and resourcefulness of Mrs Abe Noriko and her staff (it took 8 weeks to reconnect the electricity and 4 months for the water), it was possible to feed and house up to 1000 people, and a library and a classroom were set up for the children. Dozens of events were organized in the two years that followed to support the refugees and maintain community cohesion.

are immense but economic activity is gradually picking up, organized around the **Sun Sun Shopping Village** (sansan-minamisanriku.com), originally a temporary structure but now permanently established on higher ground in attractive, chalet-style buildings. Time is pressing, as a large proportion of the locals are still waiting to be rehoused. The population has now fallen to around 14,000, with many having left to live elsewhere. What remains of the Crisis Management Center in the ravaged downtown area has become a symbol of the municipality, a place to welcome visitors, and the center of the **Memorial Park**.

Kesennuma 気仙沼

Map, B3. JR bus (BRT) from Minamisanriku (1hr 15min, ¥770), or JR trains from Ichinoseki (1hr 15min, ¥1170). kesennuma-kanko.jp.

This town of 75,000 people was seriously affected by the tsunami, which had reached a height of about 65ft/20m as it entered the bay; over 800 people lost their lives, and 1000 more declared missing, while 20,000 houses were destroyed or badly damaged, and more than 500 fishing boats were swept away. But Kesennuma is now gradually rebuilding itself, and is worth visiting if only to enjoy its location on a pretty bay that contains the forested island of Oshima, known as the "Green Pearl."

Fish Market★ – *At the port. Open Mon–Fri from 7am. No charge for access to the walkway (it is not permitted to enter the actual market area without a guide).*

A walkway has been set up upstairs so you can watch the bustling activity in this market which is a conduit for the fish caught from some of the largest ports on the northeastern coast of Japan. Look out for bonito, swordfish, and even shark, as well as shellfish (oysters and sea urchins), fresh off the boat and prepared and sold before your very eyes. A rare treat and a reminder that this part of the Pacific is one of the richest fishing areas in the world.

Just around the corner, on the first floor of the Uminoichi center, you will find a **Tourist Office** and the **Shark Museum** (*uminoichi.com; museum open daily 8am–5pm, ¥500*), with detailed information (in Japanese only) on this fascinating animal, illustrated with photos and models. One room in the museum is dedicated to eyewitness accounts and documents relating to the tsunami.

Sitting atop a hill looking out over Kesennuma (*2mi/3km from the port; taxi approx ¥2000*) is the **Rias Ark Museum of Art** (*rias-ark.sakura.ne.jp/2; open Wed–Sun 9.30am–5pm, ¥500*). Since opening in 1994, this art museum has focused increasingly on contemporary art, with one section strongly emphasizing ethnography and local history, including, of course, the tsunami. Being on high ground, the museum served as a refuge after the disaster. Museum staff collected everything they could to document the tragedy; there are now more than 30,000 photos and 250 items of debris, displayed in a new, dedicated permanent space.

Rikuzentakata 陸前高田

⚓*Map, B3. Take the JR bus (BRT) to Rikuzentakata: 35min from Kesennuma, ⊜¥510. Or Iwateken Kotsu buses from Ichinoseki: 1hr 50min, ⊜¥1630.*

This fishing port, which boasted 24,000 inhabitants before the 2011 catastrophe, also took the full force of the tsunami and lost more than 1700 people. The town center was completely destroyed but is due for reconstruction as soon as the work is finished to shore up the area nearest to the sea.

Iwate Tsunami Memorial★ いわて TSUNAMIメモリアル – *iwate-tsunami-memorial.jp,* 🕐*open daily 9am–5pm,* ⊜*no charge.* This excellent modern museum is part of the **Memorial Park** (opened in stages 2019–22). Its sobering displays of objects from the debris, details of disaster history and management in Japan, and good English signage make it a memorable and worthwhile stop. This stretch of coast was previously famed for its pine forest, which ran along 1.25mi/2km of the beach at Rikuzentakata. It was completely flattened by the tsunami: of 70,000 trees, some of them 350 years old, only one was left standing. Though the 90ft/27.5m **Miracle Pine** finally died in 2012, it was preserved as a symbol of the town's endurance and incorporated into the park.

Kamaishi 釜石

⚓*Map, B2. Take the JR bus (BRT)Ofunato Line to Sakari (45min from Rikuzentakata, ⊜¥420), then Sanriku Railway Rias Line to Kamaishi (50min, ⊜¥1100).*

There is an option to stop off en route at **Ofunato**, where you can spend the night and visit the port *(BRT, 45min Rikuzentakata to Shimofunato, ⊜¥240).* The reconstruction of the port will take your breath away, having been built at a point where tsunami waves more than 65ft/20m high swept away everything for more than 1.8mi/3km inland.

On top of the hills of **Kamaishi** is a gigantic statue of Kannon, **Kamaishi Dai-Kannon** (*kamaishi-daikannon.com,* 🕐*open daily Mar–Nov 9am–5pm, Dec–Feb 9am–4pm, ⊜¥500; 10min by taxi from Kamaishi Station, around ⊜¥1300*).

Rising to a height of 159ft/48.5m (you can climb up inside the monument and enjoy a spectacular view), the goddess has embodied compassion for 50 years in a city that was similarly devastated by the tsunami—despite its three sea walls of differing lengths (3248ft/990m, 2198ft/670m, and 1083ft/330m) and foundations more than 206ft/63m deep, which were intended to protect the city and the entrance to the bay. After three decades of studies and expenditure of nearly 2 billion dollars, the walls were finally inaugurated a few weeks before the tsunami hit. New structures, of even more titanesque dimensions, are still under construction.

The planners are likely looking to the small town of **Fudai**, 71mi/115km north of Kamaishi, the only place to escape the 66ft/20m-plus waves thanks to its sea defences —only one person in this village of 2600 was lost. The defences include a floodgate 51ft/15.5m high, condemned as a waste of public funds when constructed in the 1970s and '80s; after the disaster, many local residents visited the grave of the mayor who approved the project, to thank him.

Kamaishi's reconstruction has also included the building of a 16,000-capacity sports stadium: the town has long been obsessed with rugby, and hosted two matches in the 2019 Rugby World Cup, symbolizing the region's movement towards recovery, and its ongoing vitality, resilience and warm hospitality.

▷ From Kamaishi, return inland to the Tono, 18mi/45km to the west (*JR Kamaishi Line, 50min journey, ⊜¥860*).

ADDRESSES

🏨 STAY

MINAMISANRIKU

🌊🏨🏨 **Minami-Sanriku Hotel Kanyo** – 南三陸ホテル観洋 – *99-17 Kurosaki, Minamisanriku-cho. ☏022-646-2442. mkanyo.jp. 244 rooms. ¥24,900. ⫍, dinner also included.* This great ocean liner of a hotel overlooking Shizugawa Bay features huge Japanese rooms, *onsen (rotenburo)* with a magnificent view of the bay, and several restaurants. It also played a key role after the disaster (⊘ see p481) Free shuttle to Sendai *(reservation required)*.

KESENNUMA

🛏 **Guesthouse Kakehashi** ゲストハウス架け橋 – *55-3 Nagaisomae-bayashi. ☎022-625-7739. 2 dorm rooms. dorms ¥3900 per person. ¥500 🍴*. This welcoming guesthouse first opened to accommodate volunteers helping the recovery efforts. A warm welcome, and opportunities to get involved in the local community.

RIKUZENTAKATA

🛏🛏 **Hakoneyama Terrace** 箱根山テラス – *Otomocho, Myoga 1-232. ☎019-222-7088. hakoneyama-terrace.jp. 14 rooms. ¥11,000. ¥1500 🍴*. The trump card of this cypresswood eco-establishment in the Rikuzentakata Hills is its unbeatable bay view. Basic but extremely comfortable rooms, with a beautiful, serene terrace.

OFUNATO

🛏 **Ofunato Plaza Hotel** 大船渡プラザホテル – *7-8 Chayamae. ☎019-226-3131. ofunatoplaza.com. 34 rooms. ¥10,000. ¥1000 🍴*. This business hotel by the Ofunato BRT stop has well-appointed, comfortable rooms, and a very generous buffet breakfast. Restaurant and wifi.

KAMAISHI

🛏🛏 **Hotel Route-Inn Kamaishi** ホテルルートイン釜石 – *2-17-17 Omachi. ☎050-5847-7701. inn.co.jp/hotel_list/iwate/index_hotel_id_619/. 58 rooms. ¥11,950. 🍴*. This business hotel, which opened in 2014, is 15min walk from Kamaishi Station and is one of the best places to stay places in town. Well-appointed, comfortable rooms. Wifi and *onsen*.

Hiraizumi 平泉 and surroundings★

The glory of Hiraizumi is bound up with the fate of the Fujiwara family, who it into an absolute treasure-house from the 12C onwards as they mined the enormous gold reserves located at Mutsu, east of Oshu, now situated between the prefectures of Fukushima and Aomori. The riches and power of the Fujiwaras attracted envy and anger, condemning Hiraizumi to constant attack from Minamoto no Yoritomo, the first shogun. Having been razed to the ground, hardly a hint of Hiraizumi's former splendors now remains, with the exception of Chuson-ji, which has been listed as a UNESCO World Heritage Site since 2011.

SIGHTS

Hiraizumi 平泉
From the station, take the main road to the gate of Motsu-ji (0.5mi/700m), 15min walk or 5min by bus.

Motsu-ji 毛越寺
🕐 *Open daily: Nov–Apr 8.30am–4.30pm; May – Oct 8.30am–5pm. 🎫¥500. motsuji.or.jp. 🍴.*

⚓ **Michelin Map:** Regional map p463, B3.
▶ **Location:** The temple Chuson-ji is north of the town, while Motsu-ji is south, 1.25mi/2km apart. Tono is 5mi/93km to the northwest of Hiraizumi.
🕐 **Timing:** Allow a day and a night in Hiraizumi, and the same for Tono.
😊 **Don't miss:** The Konjiki-do at Chuson-ji; Yanagata House at Tono; the farms of Tono Furusato Mura.

Like Chuson-ji, Motsu-ji was built in the 9C by the priest Jikaku Daishi. In the 12C, this monastic complex included more than 50 pagodas and some 500 dwellings for priests and other temple associates, again testifying to the power of the Fujiwara family. Before it was reduced to ashes in a great fire in 1226, the richness of the central pavilion was unequaled in Japan. The original buildings have never

USEFUL INFORMATION

Hiraizumi Tourist Office – One inthe station, one just outside. *Open daily 9am–5pm. ℘0191-46-2110. hiraizumi. or.jp.* Both rent audioguides (*¥500*) with information on the main sights.
Tono Tourist Office – Opposite the station. *Open daily 8.30am–5.30pm. ℘0198-62-1333. tonojikan.jp.* Ask about the combination ticket (*¥1290*), which gives you access to 5 out of 7 nearby attractions.

GETTING TO AND FROM HIRAIZUMI

From Sendai – Shinkansen Hayabusa or Yamabiko for Ichinoseki, then JR Tohoku Line for Hiraizumi (*1hr, ¥3850*).

From Hiraizumi to Tono – JR Tohoku Line for Hanamaki, then JR Kamaishi Line to Tono (*1hr 50min, ¥1690*).

GETTING AROUND HIRAIZUMI AND TONO

The Hiraizumi Run-Run loop bus (*from the JR station*) takes in all the main tourist sites, with a ticket valid for multiple stop-offs (*¥150 per journey, 1-day pass ¥400 pass*). You can hire bicycles from Hiraizumi Rent-a-cycle, by the station (*bikes ¥1000/day, ebikes ¥1300/day*).
You can also hire bikes from the tourist office in Tono (*¥1020/day, ebikes ¥1320/day*). In Tono itself, all the sites can be seen on foot.

---

been rebuilt but their foundations are laid out in the **Jodo teien★**, a Heian-style garden, intended to represent the paradise of the Pure Land Buddha. On the fourth Sunday in May, the **Goku-sui-no-en** takes place on the banks of the Yarimizu stream that winds through the garden; it's a recreation of an elegant, aristocratic country outing such as took place during the Fujiwara era. The participants write *waka* (traditional poems), as cups of sake are floated to them on the stream.

▶ Retrace your steps and turn left onto a road that runs in front of Mairuru-ga-ike Pond (*0.5mi/800m*).

Hiraizumi Cultural Heritage Center 平泉文化遺産センター

7min by Run-Run loop bus from the JR station. ◯*Open daily 9am–5pm. Donations welcome.*
The six sites at Hiraizumi, which include the sacred mountain of Kinkeisan, the temples, gardens, and the archeological sites representing the Buddhist "Pure Land," were inscribed as UNESCO World Heritage Sites in 2011. The center has provided a range of different interactive panels to help visitors find out more

about the last remnants of this ancient kingdom, with interesting commentaries that can easily fill an hour (information in English).

When **Fujiwara no Kiyohira** (1056–1128) developed the great "Oku Daido" frontier way to cross **Michinoku**—"the land beyond roads," the old name for Tohoku, whose extent ran from its southern border, the Shirakawa barrier, to the Aomori town of Soto no hama at its northern limits—he had a very specific intention in mind: to build the temple of Chuson-ji at the very center of Michinoku. To make sure of this, he erected *sotoba* (wooden tablets bearing an image of Amida) at 358ft/109m intervals along the road (a reference to *mala*—prayer beads—which generally have 108 elements linked by a cord and a 109th on which is placed the knot that holds the whole thing together) and he had the temple built at the precise centerpoint between the two geographical frontiers, his mental template being the layout of the Buddha's Pure Earth, to which every Buddhist aspires after death.

▶ Continue to the north (*over 0.5mi/700m*).

Glory and Dreams at a World Heritage Site

At its height, Hiraizumi had risen to a population of 100,000 and become the administrative heart of Japan's western kingdom. To lend a spiritual dimension to the riches they had accumulated from the gold mines in their provinces, the powerful Fujiwara clan from Mutsu wished to create a "Buddhist paradise on Earth" with four gardens that would blend the Buddhist concepts of Pure Earth with entirely Japanese ideas; the Chuson-ji monastery, with all its inlaid stone, silver, pearls, and gemstones, was duly founded in 1105. The dream was to prove short-lived, however, and Hiraizumi was ravaged by incessant wars from the end of the 12C. While the majority of its monasteries had been razed to the ground before the close of the Middle Ages, Chuson-ji was to prove an exception, and it was in this waning city in 1186 that one of the most popular heroes in Japanese history, **Minamoto no Yoshitsune** (1159–1189), accompanied by his faithful companion, the monk Benkei, came to seek refuge from his half-brother and rival Yoritomo. Unfortunately, the great warrior was betrayed and found himself surrounded by the enemy; he was forced to commit suicide by *seppuku* while Benkei bravely fought on, eventually falling in battle, pierced with a thousand arrows. His tomb is to be found at the foot of Chuson-ji.

Chuson-ji★★ 中尊寺
About 1mi/1.6km north of Hiraizumi Station. 10min by Run-Run loop bus from the JR station. ○*Open daily: Mar–Oct 8.30am–5pm; Nov–Feb 8am–4.30pm.* ✎¥800 (including Konjiki-do, Kyozo and Sankozo). ▫.

The Tsukimizaka slope leading to the temple is lined with cryptomeria trees planted 350 years ago by the Date clan. The temple was founded in 850 by the priest Jikaku Daishi (794–864) under the aegis of Enryaku-ji temple at Mount Hiei (north of Kyoto, ⌚*see p349*). Having been destroyed and rebuilt several times, there is nothing left of the temple but the **Kyozo** (the Treasure Hall where the *sutra* were kept) and, in particular, the **Konjiki-do★★★**, which was encased in a modern building in 1963. The golden temple was completed in 1124 and partially gilded with gold leaf, shining like the Pure Earth (*jodo* in Japanese) promised to his devotees

Kyozo, Chuson-ji

© yspbqh14/Shutterstock

Boat trip on the Satetsu River, Geibikei

© CHENG FENG CHIANG/iStock

by **Amida Nyorai**, the Buddha of infinite light who has been worshipped since the Heian period. Unlike the Buddha Sakyamuni, Amida is not a historical figure but a creature of fable, promising and providing (to those who fervently believe in him) an earthly paradise that is perfect and shining in every way. In the turmoil that held sway during the period, it may have seemed wiser not to rely only on yourself (a proposition that was just too uncertain) but to have faith in the compassionate power of Amida. The craftsmanship – the work of artisans is also a prayer addressed to Amida – is of immense sophistication, the apotheosis of the Buddhist art of the period, combining all the symbolic attributes that make it possible to guarantee such a post mortem transformation and elevation: either side of Amida we find, to the right, Kannon, the divinity of Compassion, and to the left, Seishi, the Bodhisattva of wisdom. Six saviors from hell and two guardian kings round off this happy scene, along with carved peacocks on the lower binding of the altar, whose shimmering outstretched tails are similarly tokens offered to the faithful of the paradise to come (🖉 *see Zuigan-ji, p474*).

Unusually, four generations of the Fujiwara family are entombed beneath the various altars: the central altar houses the remains of Kiyohira; the one to the right is the resting place of the severed head of Yasuhira (1155–1189), where sev-

eral lotus flower seeds were discovered (the same lotuses that are to blossom on the Buddha's Pure Earth) and which science has brought to bloom again, nine centuries later.

The small **Sankozo★★** museum just around the corner houses some extremely pretty **sculptures★★**, including of Amida Nyorai (12C) who stands beside Yakushi Nyorai. There is also the **Kinginji Kosho Issaikyo★★★**, complete *sutras* written in alternating lines of gold and silver on blue paper, which were commissioned by Kiyohira.

The café Kanzantei (🕐 *open 9.30am–4.30pm*) is a good place to relax, and there is a terrace and magnificent view. Ideal for a coffee and snack.

AROUND HIRAIZUMI
Genbikei★ 厳美渓
From Hiraizumi, take the train to Ichinoseki, then a bus from the station's west exit to Genbikei (20min).

👥The tumultuous waters of the Iwaigawa cut through the gorge down through nearly 1.2mi/2km of waterfalls, hot-water springs, and gnarled outcroppings. Enjoy a walk alongthe river and over scenic bridges, stopping for a "flying *dango*" —an enterprising local restaurant set up a line over the river. Put ¥400 in the basket attached to it, hit the gong to alert the restaurat's staff, and they'll pull the basket over, take your payment, and send back some delicious *dango* (sweet dumplings) and green tea.

Geibikei★ 猊鼻渓

From Hiraizumi, take the JR Tohoku Line to Ichinoseki, then JR Ofunato Line to Geibikei Station (1hr, ⚏¥590). The gorge is a 5min walk from the station. Flat-bottomed boat trips (1hr 30min): ◷*open daily: Apr–Aug 8.30am–4.30pm; Sept–late Nov 8.30am–3.30pm; late Nov–Mar 9.30am–3pm.* ⚏*¥1800. geibikei.co.jp.*

👥👤The best way to enjoy the Satetsu River meandering between sheer cliffs is from a boat, steered along for 1.2mi/2km by storytelling, folk-singing guides. At the far end of the gorge, you can throw *undama* ("luck stones" with kanji for love, work, etc. on them) at a small opening in the rock. Get one in, and you'll be lucky in whichever area of life that kanji represents.

RECOMMENDED ROUTE

♿*Regional Map, B2.*

Tono★ 遠野

58mi/93 km northwest of Hiraizumi. Access by train (♿see Useful Information p485).

This charming small city is inseparably linked with the memory of **Yanagita Kunio** (1875–1962), who is considered the father of Japanese ethnology thanks to his "Tono Monogatari" (The Tales of Tono), published in 1910. It was the very first compilation of legends and regional stories, creating a folklore bestiary populated with *yokai*, supernatural creatures that have fired the imaginations of several generations of artists, from the renowned *mangaka* Mizuki Shigeru (1922–2015) to author Murakami Haruki and film-maker Miyazaki Hayao. As you stroll through the streets, you will find the *yokai* still stalk the city, notably the *kappa* (water sprites), who you'll see popping up everywhere in the form of signs, statues and posters. Tono has been tirelessly restoring its old farms, inviting storytellers and opening up paths so you can stroll along the old routes used by the *kappa*.

◯ Take the main road from the rail station, which will take you to Ote-bashi bridge *(10min walk).*

Yanagita Kunio and the *yokai* of Tono

Yanagita Kunio first visited Tono in 1909, and was captivated by the rich folk tales he heard there. Fearing that these traditions would be lost in Japan's ruh to modernization, he set about recording the local tales in what later became the Tono Monogatari. In this work, he demonstrated that subject matter that was essentially oral and ephemeral—deemed "fit only for children," as was thought at the time—actually amounted to a genuine source of ethnographic material worthy of study, that made it possible to "understand the paths that have been taken to get to where we are now."

This collection of work from the local inhabitants had already been initiated by **Kizen Sasaki** (1886–1933), a native of the Tono region and a noted Japanese folklorist.

Folktale and Storytelling Center とおの昔話村 – ◷*Open daily 9am–5pm, ⚏¥500.* Beside the river you will find this modern museum, with an old inn attached, Yanagita Kunio's preferred place to stay in town. The museum features learning trails for visitors (with unfortunately little information in English) describing the area's rich folk tales, with interactive exhibits and a small library. There are daily storytelling sessions in which the tales are dramatically performed, too.

Tono Municipal Museum 遠野市立博物館 – *tonoculture.com/tono-museum,* ◷*open Apr–Oct daily 9am–5pm; Nov–Mar Tues–Sun 9am–5pm, ⚏¥300 (English audioguides ⚏no charge).* On the other side of the bridge, next to the library, Tono's impressive municipal museum is a treasure trove of information on the local area and traditions.

Tono Furusato Mura★ 遠野ふるさと村 – *7.5mi/12km. From Tono Station. Regular buses from Tono via Densho-en (40min, ⚏¥830).* ◷*Open daily: Mar–Oct*

9am–5pm; Nov–Feb 9am–4pm; last entry 1hr before closing. 👓*¥540, workshops ¥600–1000. tono-furusato.jp.* 🛏.

The "home country village" is made up of five regional farms (which were dismantled and rebuilt here); the most historic is more than 200 years old. The particular feature of these structures, known as *magari-ya* (literally, "folded houses"), is that they are L-shaped. The inhabitants spent most of their time looking after their horses, with the stable in one of the wings of the house, adding the warmth of the animals to the home —particularly desirable in such a cold region.

This practice dates back to the Edo Era, when Tono acquired great renown for its horse-rearing, in particular for the Nambu breed (named after the clan that ruled Tono at the time). Through selective pairing and cross-breeding, this stocky breed (which probably originated in Korea; there is some archeological evidence from the 7C) also gave rise to larger, more robust horses that were as popular with the military as they were with merchants. All this took place before European-bred horses flooded into Japan from the 16C onwards.

As horses were of prime economic importance, it became the custom to carve images of them on wooden panels (*ema*) to be used for votive purposes, and these were hung up in temples to beseech the *kami* (gods) to spare their precious livestock from perils and plagues. These heartfelt wishes are still being expressed today, as *ema* are to be found everywhere in shrines.

Some of the houses feature workshops and craft demonstrations (pottery, cabinet-making, cooking with *soba*, etc.).

ADDRESSES

🛏 STAY

HIRAIZUMI

🛏🛏🛏**Hiraizumi Hotel Musashibo 平泉ホテル武蔵坊** – *15 Hiraizumi Osawa, Nishiiwai-gun, 12min from the station, or take the Run Run loop bus.* 📞*0191-46-2241. www.musasibou.com/en/. 48 rooms.*

¥22,000. 🛏*, dinner also included.* Ideally located between the two temples, this hotel lcould really do with some modernization, but nonetheless has much going for it: a lovely *onsen* with a view over Tabashine Mountain, a good restaurant, and a warm welcome. Instead of the small Western-style rooms, go for the Japanese ones

AROUND HIRAIZUMI

🛏🛏🛏**Genbikei Itsukushi-en 厳美渓いつくし園** – *15 Minamitakinoue, Genbi-cho, Ichinoseki-shi. 5min walk from Genbikei Station, or free shuttle bus.* 📞*0120-155-940. itsukushien.co.jp. 47 rooms. ¥23,100.* 🛏*, dinner also included.* A *ryokan* overlooking Genbikei Gorge, with *tatami* rooms, *onsen*, and Japanese cuisine. No wifi.

TONO

🛏🛏**Minshuku Tono 民宿とおの** – *10min walk behind the station, 2-17 Zaimoku-cho.* 📞*0198-62-4395. minshuku-tono.com. 11 rooms. ¥15,400.* 🛏*, dinner also included.* 🍴. This typically Japanese boarding house (shared *o-furo* and toilets) is an enjoyable immersion in Japanese culture. The room set aside for the Japanese breakfast is marvellous, with a traditional open hearth.

🛏🛏**Aeria Tono あえりあ遠野** – *1-10 Shinmachi.* 📞*0198-60-1700. aeria-tohno.com. 62 rooms. ¥14,200. ¥1300*🛏. Located a 15–20min walk from the station, opposite the library, this hotel is generally full of groups. Not the most exciting place, but with plus points: a restaurant, *onsen*, bar, and good Western-style rooms.

🍴 EAT

HIRAIZUMI

🍽**Izumi Sobaya 泉そばや** – *75 Izumiya. 3min from the station, at the main intersection on your right.* 📞*0191-46-2038. Open Wed–Mon 9am–5pm. Set menus from ¥570.* 🍴. Managed by an elderly couple, Izumi sobaya is famed for its fresh, flavorful home-made soba noodles.

TONO

🍽🍽🍽**Kuishinbo Chikara くいしんぼちから** – *10-4 Chuodori.* 📞*0198-62-1771. Open Mon–Sat 5.30pm–midnight.* Good, simple local *izakaya*; don't forget to try *dobekko* (alcohol made from fermented rice) at the end of the meal.

Yamagata and surroundings
山形

With its wide-open spaces punctuated by large trunk roads lined with with low-rise buildings, the city of Yamagata is both the capital of the eponymous prefecture and a good place to stroll around. While its places of interest are limited, the city—which is on the shinkansen network – makes a good base for day-trips to the numerous places of interest and ruins that surround it: mountain temples, world-class skiing, atmospheric *onsen*, unusual festivals, and much more besides.

SIGHTS

Kajyo Kouen park is 15min walk from Yamagata Station (head due north beside the railway). The city's green lung is also an extremely historic site as it contains the ruins (restored at great expense) of the castle built by Mogami Yoshiaki (1545–1614). The founder and planner of the town was a skilled warrior to boot, improving its fortunes to such an extent that he was dubbed the "founding father of Dewa (the former name of an area now shared between the prefectures of Yamagata and Akita) with a million *goku*." A *goku* or *koku* was the equivalent of 330lb/150kg of rice, the amount required to feed a person for an entire year.

There are a number of museums in the immediate vicinity of this historic area, and one of the most important exhibits in the small historical museum devoted to the town founder, the **Mogami Yoshiaki Historical Museum** (○open Tue–Sun 9am-4.30pm, ⊗no charge), is the beautiful **black lacquered helmet★★** weighing more than 6.6lb/3kg that still bears the mark of the bullet which struck it during the siege of Hasedo in 1600.

Less than 330ft/100m away, you will find **Yamagata Art Museum★** (✆023-622-3090; yamagata-art-museum.or.jp/en;

▶ **Population:** 249,700

⌀ **Michelin Map:** Regional map p463, B3

▷ **Location:** Yamagata is located 223mi/359km north of Tokyo and 40mi/65km west of Sendai. It is the capital of the eponymous prefecture (population 1.08 million) and is surrounded by the Sea of Japan to the west and the prefectures of Fukushima to the south, Miyagi to the east, and Akita to the northwest.

○ **Timing:** A couple of days at Zao Onsen; there is plenty going on there in both summer and winter; one or two nights in Ginzan Onsen; half a day at Yamadera.

⌗ **Don't miss:** Yamadera; the Dai Rotenburo at Zao Onsen; a night at Ginzan Onsen; the Tendo festival.

USEFUL INFORMATION
Yamagata Tourist Office – West exit from the station (1F Kajo Central Bldg). ✆023- 647-233. yamagatakanko.com. Open daily 9am–5.30pm.

TRANSPORTATION
From Tokyo (Ueno), take the Shinkansen Tsubasa (2hr 40min journey, ¥10,430). **From Sendai**, take the Senzan Line for Yamagata (1hr 15min, ¥1170).

○open Tue–Sun 10am–5pm, ⊗¥600), which features a very interesting permanent collection that has been assembled from two major donations: the Hasegawa collection (163 pieces) includes works by Matsuo Basho, Kumashiro Yuhi, and Yokoyama Kazan, among others; and the Western collection, an impressive donation by Yoshino Gypsum Co. The latter contains more than a hundred works, mainly Impressionist, featuring Monet, Renoir, Cézanne, Degas, Pissaro, and more.

On the city center side, the main road will take you to an old administrative building constructed in the Renaissance style at the turn of the 20C. The **Bun-shokan** (⊙ *open daily 9am–4.30pm*, ⊙ *closed 1st & 3rd Mon each month*, ⊶ *no charge*) appears in the distance like a mirage, an attractive but incongruous sight in a Japanese city.

EXCURSIONS

Yamadera★★ 山寺

2.5mi/4km northeast of Yamagata. 5min walk from the JR Yamadera Station (serves Sendai, 1hr 15min journey, and Yamagata, 20min journey, via the JR Senzan Line. ⊙ Open daily 6am–6pm. ⊶¥300. Konpon Chudo: ⊙ open daily 8am–5pm. ⊶¥200. Allow at least 1hr for the ascent.

This spectacular collection of Buddhist temples nestled on this mountain gradually heaves into view as you ascend (1015 steps), revealing its setting among ancient trees and strangely shaped rocks. Officially known as **Risshaku-ji**, the site was founded in 860 by the monk Ennin and was visited in the 17C by the poet **Basho**, who composed one of his most famous haikus there: "The silence broken/the cries of the cicadas/penetrate the rocks." The first temple (**Konpon Chudo**) is the oldest (14C) and houses cherished statues of the Buddha and a flame "that never goes out," which was brought here from Mount Hiei in Kyoto. Around the half-

way point, be sure to take the left fork before you ascend to the uppermost temple, so that you can take in the glorious view from the **Godaido** pavilion.

Zao Onsen★ 蔵王温泉

11.5mi/18.5km southeast of Yamagata. From Yamagata Station, buses every hour, 40min journey, ⊶¥1000. Direct express buses from Sendai in ski season, 1hr 40min journey, ⊶¥1600). 🛈Tourist Office in the station: ⊙ open daily 9am–6pm, ⊙ closed Mar & every Wed out of season. zao-spa.or.jp.

At the foot of Mount Zao (6040ft/1841m), the town is famed as a **ski resort and spa**. Its extensive slopes attract sports enthusiasts of every level who get to admire the *juhyo*, or "snow monsters" (frozen, snow-covered trees with impressive silhouettes), as they schuss downhill. You can also get a great view of these from **Juhyo Kogen**, accessible by ropeway (*zaoropeway.co.jp*). There are plenty of walks to enjoy in the area, and the numerous hotels, *ryokan*, and public bathhouses welcome guests all year round.

Zao Onsen Dai Rotenburo – *15min walk from the center. ⊙Open May–mid-Nov daily 6am–7pm (varies by season). ⊶¥550. jupeer-zao.com/roten.* The acidic hot springs at Zao Onsen, with their high sulfur content, are among the most popular in the country and have been prized for centuries for their therapeutic benefits, especially for skin conditions (they have been nicknamed the "source of beauty"). Enormous open-air baths

---

Ningen-Shogi: The Festival Of Live Pawns

Tendo is where 95% of shogi sets are manufactured. Shogi, literally the "generals' chess game," is played by more than 15 million Japanese people and is part of the wider family of chess-style games. Having first appeared in Japan some time around the 11C, and probably derived from China's Xiang-Qi, the rules were finalized around the 16C. Tendo's headline event since 1956 has been the **Ningen-shogi**, which sees the *shogi-ban*, a board of 81 squares, scaled up to human size (56ft/17m long and 46ft/14m wide), with shuffling human chess pieces dressed up as samurai. The Ningen-shogi is held every April during the cherry blossom festival. (✆023-653-1680. japan.travel/en/ spot/1794. Accessible by train on the JR Ou Line from Yamagata (20min, ⊶¥250).

have been set up at the foot of the mountain and have been blended perfectly into their natural surroundings. Once you have got used to the strong sulfurous smell and the milky color of the water, you can enjoy relaxing in the restorative hot-spring waters.

Zao Okama★ – *From Zao Onsen, take the Zao Ropeway (cable car) to Jizo San-cho Station (zaoropeway.co.jp, ◷open daily: Apr–mid-Dec 8.30am–5pm, mid-Dec–Mar 8.15am–4.45pm; ⇔¥1500 one way, ¥3000 round trip) then around 1hr walk. By bus, from JR Shiroishi Zao Station to Kattadake Peak (2 daily, 1hr journey, ⇔¥1500). By car, take the Zao Echo Line route to the parking lot below Zao Mountain Peak Restaurant (toll ⇔¥550; route closed mid-Nov–Apr), then 5min walk.*

👣The walk from Zao Onsen to this crater lake at an elevation of 5577ft/1700m on Mount Zao is unmissable for the athletically inclined. The name Okama, which means "pan for cooking rice," is a reference to its circular shape. It is also known as "the lake of five colors," because its acidic, limpid waters—frequently emerald green—can change hue several times a day, depending on the amounts of sunshine and the season. The lake was formed after an eruption of Mount Zao in the 18C.

Ginzan Onsen★★ 銀山温泉
37mi/56km north of Yamagata. From Yamagata Station, take the JR Yamagata Shinkansen to Oishida (30min, ⇔¥1440) then the bus (40min, ¥720 one way). 🔖ginzanonsen.jp.
The isolated location of this **spa town** (literally "the hot springs of the silver mountain") is not without its charms. Its main—and only—road is pedestrianized and runs along both sides of the river, passing about a dozen *ryokan* mostly dating back to the years between 1910 and 1920 (most have since been renovated), public bathhouses (all of which are indoor, with the exception of the *ashiyu* foot baths), and stores. It is even prettier at night, with its old-fashioned lighting (the electric cables

have been sunk underground), and in winter, when the snow picks out every architectural detail. It is only a few minutes' walk to the Shirogane waterfall (72ft/22m high).

👣 Allow about 40min (return trip) to visit the summit of the silver mountain. The very well-signposted path takes walkers through the galleries of the old silver mine (**Nobezawa-Ginkodo**); the precious metal was discovered more than five centuries ago and made the place's fortune.

▷ You can return to Tsuruoka or Sakata, on the Sea of Japan coast, from Ginzan Onsen or Yamagata *(take the JR Rikuu West Line from Oishida station).*

ADDRESSES

🏠 STAY

YAMAGATA
⊜⊜ **APA Hotel Yamagata Ekimae** アパ ホテル山形駅前大通 – *Tokamachi 4-1-8. ☎023-633-9111. apahotel.com/en/hotel/ touhoku/yamagata-ekimae/. 56 rooms. ¥10,450. ¥1100⊟.* Located a 7min walk from Yamagata Station, this hotel features all the modern conveniences you would expect from business hotels in the APA chain. Well-appointed, functional rooms.

ZAO ONSEN
⊜⊜ **Ohira Hotel** 大平ホテル – *825 Zao Onsen. ☎023-649-9422. oohira.co.jp. 24 rooms. From ¥7500 per person, including breakfast. ¥16,800. Breakfast and dinner available.* This *ryokan* located a 15min walk from the station looks more like a *minshuku* and is convenient for Zao Onsen Dai Rotenburo (above the station). The Ohira has its own very pleasant spa and *rotenburo*. Plain but nice rooms.

⊜⊜ **Zao Spa Hotel Kiraku** ホテル喜ら く – *825 Zao Onsen. ☎023-694-9422. www. zao-kiraku.co.jp/. 24 rooms. From ¥16,200. Breakfast and dinner available.* This *ryokan* is close to the resort, just before the small bridge that leads to the cable car (Sanroku Line). Well-kept and quite elegant, it has good, comfortable rooms and a lovely spa and *rotenburo*.

GINZAN ONSEN

🛏🍴🛁 **Kozan Kaku** 古山閣 – 423 Ginzanshinhata, Obanazawa. ✆023-728-2039. kozankaku.com. 12 rooms. ¥29,000. 🍴. 🛁. This magnificent *ryokan*, burnished by time and set in wooded splendor, has extremely beautiful rooms and plain but elegant baths.

🛏🍴🛁🛁 **Fujiya** 藤屋 – 443 Ginzanshinhata, Obanazawa. ✆023-728-2141. www.fujiya-ginzan.com. 8 rooms. ¥63,000. 🍴, dinner also included. The essence of tradition has been revisited by architect Kuma Kengo, the master of contemporary design, in this 350-year-old *ryokan* that has been completely reimagined. The result is a unique, neatly stripped-down space in which each building material (bamboo, paper, glass) comes into its own magnificently.

EVENTS

YAMAGATA

Imoni-Kai Festival – 3rd Sun in Sept. This annual event that takes place close to the source of the Mamigasaki River, which crosses the city of Yamagata, brings together 30,000 people around a giant cauldron, 20ft/6m in diameter, dangling from the arm of an earth excavator, in which *taro* (a vegetable) and beef are cooked.

Tsuruoka 鶴岡 and surroundings★

Situated at the foot of a volcanic, mountainous region bordering the Sea of Japan, Tsuruoka benefits from a favorable natural environment. This peaceful little provincial city is not without attractions and is the ideal starting point for a tour of the "Dewa Sanzan," the three sacred mountains most closely linked with the *yamabushi* hermits (🔎*see box p497*). Nearby Sakata, Yamagata prefecture's second city, has a number of museums with cutting-edge modern architecture.

SIGHTS

Situated 1.5mi/2.5km southwest of the station, Chido Museum lies in Tsuruoka Park, formerly overlooked by **Sakai Castle** (the seat of one of Yamagata's leading families).

Chido Museum★ 致道博物館

10-18 Kachushin-machi. 5min walk from Tsuruoka City Hall, 10min by bus or taxi from Tsuruoka Station. ⏱Open Mar–Nov daily 9am–5pm; Dec–Feb Thur–Tue 9am–4.30pm. ✎¥800. chido.jp.
This museum comprises various buildings that were transferred here and turned into mini museums on Tsuruoka's history and culture. Chido Museum was launched during the 1950s by the

- ▶ **Population:** Tsuruoka 129,600; Sakata 105,000.
- **Michelin Map:** Regions of Japan Map 5, Regional Map p463 A3.
- **Location:** In Yamagata Prefecture. **Tsuruoka** is bound by Mount Chokai to the north, the sacred Dewa mountains to the east, the Asahi mountain chain in the south, and the Sea of Japan to the west. **Sakata** is about 18.5mi/30km northwest of Tsuruoka.
- **Kids:** A trip to Mount Haguro and a night in its *shukubo*.
- **Timing:** Allow a full day for Tsuruoka and the environs, and another day for Sakata.
- **Don't miss:** Churen-ji and Mount Haguro in the Tsuruoka region; the Honma Museum of Art and the Domon Ken Museum of Photography at Sakata.

influential Sakai family, owners of the park. The collection includes two magnificent buildings from the Meiji era: the **first district administrative cen-**

USEFUL INFORMATION

TOURIST INFORMATION CENTERS

TSURUOKA – *In Tsuruoka Station. ℘0235-25-7678. www.tsuruokakanko. com. Open daily: Mar–Oct 9.30am– 5.30pm; Nov–Feb 10am–5pm.*

SAKATA – *In Sakata Station. ℘0234-24-2233. sakatacity. com. Open daily 10am–6pm.*

Sakata Tour Guide – *℘0234-24-2233. Allow ¥1000 for an hour.*

TRANSPORTATION

TSURUOKA

BY TRAIN – **JR Tsuruoka Station** – From **Tokyo**, take the Joetsu Shinkansen to Niigata *(1hr 30min)*, then the Uetsu Honsen Line for Tsuruoka *(1hr 50min)*. From **Sendai**, take the Senzans Line for Yamagata *(1hr 10min)*, then the Uetsu Honsen Line for Tsuruoka *(2hr 10min)*.

SAKATA

BY TRAIN – From **Tsuruoka** to **Sakata** *(17mi/ 28km),* around every 30min. JR Uetsu Line *(35min, ¥510)* or the Inaho Ltd. Express *(20min, ¥1750)*. From **Sakata** to **Hirosaki** *(157mi/253km)*, take the JR Uetsu Line to Akita, then the JR Ou Line *(5hr 30min, ¥5870)* or take the Inaho Ltd. Express to Akita, then the JR Ou Line *(4hr 15min, ¥5870)*.

TSURUOKA

BY BUS – **Tsuruoka Bus Terminal (Shoko Mall)** – *℘0235-24-7600.* From Tsuruoka to Sendai *(generally every 1hr 30min 2hr 35min/2hr 50min journey, from¥5600 round trip)*. From Tsuruoka to Sakata (JR station), *9 per day (Sat– Sun & public hols 4 per day), 1hr 10min journey, from ¥840.* From Tsuruoka to Dewa-Sanzan, *10 buses daily* (via Haguro-machi) to the top of Haguro-san. *shonaikotsu.jp.*

SAKATA

BY BUS – **Sakata Bus Terminal** – To Sendai, usually every hour *(3hr 30min journey, from ¥6000 round trip)*.

GETTING AROUND TSURUOKA

Taxi Companies – *Shoko Hire Co. ℘0235-22-0055, Hire Center Co. ℘0235-22-5155.*

GETTING AROUND SAKATA

Bicycles can be rented from the Tourist Information Center in Sakata Station *(open daily 9am–5pm; no charge)*. **Run-Run buses** serve the city's tourist sights for an all-in fare of ¥100.

ter★ *(former Nishitagawa District Office)*, dominated by a clock tower (1881), and the **first police station★** (1884), with an exhibition of historical documentation on the region. These buildings were originally commissioned by the prefec-

One prayer, three gods

Gas-san, Haguro-san, and Yudono-san, collectively known as **Dewa Sanzan**, are the three sacred mountains of Yamagata prefecture (formerly Dewa province), located in one of the sections of Bandai-Asahi National Park. Each has a precise significance. Haguro-san symbolizes prosperity in the present life, Gas-san the world of the dead, and Yudono-san that of reincarnation and rebirth. For nearly 1500 years, these three mountains have been venerated by pilgrims who would willingly climb them all, if not for the fact that heavy snows make the ascents of Gas-san *(6509ft/1984m)* and Yudono-san *(4934ft/1504m)* impossible. As such, Gosai-den temple on Haguro-san, which is lower *(1358ft/414m)* and therefore accessible all year round, has come to represent the spirits of all three mountains. Gas-san was featured in a novel by Mori Atsushi, who won the Akutagawa Prize in 1973.

😊 Tsuruoka 😊

Tsuruoka is celebrated in Japan for producing what are considered the country's most delicious—and costliest—soybeans. Legend has it, they are so good that a feudal lord of the Sakai clan had his retainers bring him some every day.

tural governor who, after the prefectures were created in 1871, took over regional responsibility for the Meiji government's policy of encouraging Western architectural styles. The **farm★** *(former Shibuya family home)*, with its curved, thatched roof in *kabuto-zukuri* style (shaped like a samurai helmet), is an example of a traditional rural dwelling.

The **Folklore House★** *(Mingu no kura)* is home to an interesting ethnographic museum devoted to fishing-related topics. Note the commemorative steles designed to appease the souls of caught salmon. The highlight of the visit is the Sakai family's **Japanese garden★★**, one of the finest in Tohoku. It is next to a rather special tea house, which has two openings (one is more usual, since darkness helps the meditation required for the tea ceremony). In fact, this tea house also served as a work room, specifically as a place for doing calligraphy.

EXCURSIONS
🕐*Regional Map, A3.*

Churen-ji★★   注連寺
Nakadai, Oami. Bus from Tsuruoka Station (40min, ¥1000 round trip). Get off at Oami bus stop, then 25min walk north. 🕐*Open daily 8am–5pm. ¥500.*
The big attraction in this temple, built in the time of Kobo Daishi, is the **mummy★★** of the monk Tetsu-monkai Shonin (1768–1829), who auto-embalmed himself during his lifetime through drastic fasting and practices of mortification (now illegal). To become a living mummy, a monk would eat only nuts and seeds for 1000 days, and for a further 1000 days, only bark and pine roots *(mokujiki)*. Following these two

stages, the monk would drink a tea made from the sap of the *urushi* tree. This toxic substance, generally used to make lacquer, would preserve the body while warding off flesh-eating maggots. Finally, the monk would retire to meditate in an underground chamber connected to the surface by a bamboo breathing tube until death intervened. If his body did not decompose after death, he would become a *sokushinbutsu* (there are around 20 in Japan), someone who achieved nirvana while still living.

The temple's **coffered ceilings★**, painted during the 1980s, are also interesting. Painted in the modern manga style, they are intended as charms designed to protect the roof from fire. Before leaving the temple, take a look at the magnificent **wooden bell★** hanging in the entrance. Made in the Meiji era, its name, *wani-guchi*, means "crocodile's mouth."

👥👤 Mount Haguro★★   羽黒山
🕐*Regional Map, A3. From Tsuruoka Station take the Shonai Kotsu bus toward Mount Haguro, terminating at the summit (around 50min, ¥850, dewasanzan.jp & hagurokanko.jp/access). Or get off at the foot of Mount Haguro and hike up (allow 1hr).*
Haguro-san, Gas-san, and Yudono-san (🕐*see box opposite)* are the sacred sites of Shugendo (🕐*see p497)*, an ancient belief system dating from the 7C, which combines Shinto and Buddhist beliefs. Along with Omine-san (in the Kii Peninsula), these mountains are the most sacred sites for the *shugenja*, the followers of Shugendo. The path up the mountain to its summit at 1358ft/414m includes 2446 stone steps that take an hour to climb. It follows a magnificent **trail★★★** lined with hundreds of cedars, many 350 to 500 years old, and takes you past a superb **five-story pagoda★★** boasting five symmetrical roofs, 98ft/30m in height. The pagoda is surrounded by more cedars, **Cryptomeria japonica**, including the 1000-year-old "grandfather of cedars," and is the oldest pagoda in Tohoku. It was constructed by Taira no Masakado during the Heian era

(937), although thought to have been rebuilt in 1400. Unusually, there are no other shrines in this sacred place as many were destroyed during the Meiji reforms that separated Shintoism and Buddhism. Just before the summit, you can visit—or even stay in—the **Saikan shukubo ★★** (temple lodgings, *see Addresses*). Reconstructed in 1697, it is the sole survivor of 30 monasteries destroyed during the Meiji era, although between times, this building was turned into a Shinto shrine. At the summit is the **Gosai-den★★**, a temple with an impressive thatched roof (6.9ft/2.1m). Its shared Buddhist and Shinto influences make it one of the rare examples of architectural syncretism to have escaped the Meiji fury. Perhaps it was protected by the Gosaiden, guardian of the spirits of the three mountains.

SAKATA★ 酒田
Regional Map, A3.

Sakata owes its prosperity to its geographical situation at the heart of the trading routes along the western coast of Japan. The city was a transit port for *kitamae bune* (large cargo vessels that plied the Sea of Japan from Osaka to Hokkaido) and during the Edo period (1603–1867) became Japan's second port after Sakai *(near Osaka)*.

Tucked into the mouth of the Mogami River that empties into the Sea of Japan, it is also the port from which the many commodities produced in the region were shipped out (notably to Kyoto).

They included rice and sake, and other commodities such as the lucrative virgin safflower oil, formerly used as a dye. It is not surprising, therefore, that the city still bears traces of its prosperous merchants, including the old, still influential **Honma** family, without whom Sakata would probably not be what it is today, one of the most visited cities in the Yamagata prefecture.

Apart from the two museums (of Art and Photography) 3mi/5km southwest of Sakata Station (around 20min by bus), the tourist highlights are all close to each other. A good way of getting around is by bike: bicycles are available on loan free of charge at Sakata Station (open 10am–5pm). The most logical route for a half-day tour is: Honma Museum of Art, the Somaro house (see Addresses), the Honma Residence, Sankyo Rice Warehouses, then return to Sakata Station.

Honma Museum of Art★
本間美術館

7–7 Onari-cho. 5min walk from Sakata Station. Opendaily: Apr–Oct 9am–5pm; Nov–Mar 9am–4.30pm. Closed Tue–Wed Dec–Feb. ¥1000. homma-museum.or.jp.

In 1947, the Honma family opened the first private Japanese museum. Originally focused on objects from the Sakai family, over time the collection was enlarged to reflect the region's culture. Variously themed temporary exhibitions (from early to contemporary art) are in a

Shugendo and Yamabushi

Practitioners of Shugendo, the sect whose goal is the search and attainment of the way *(do)* to divine spiritual powers *(gen)* through ascetic practices *(shu)*, are known as *shugenja* or *yamabushi* ("one who lies in the mountains"). Living an ascetic life in Japan's mountainous regions, many go to Mount Haguro to make solitary retreats, during which they subject themselves to feats of endurance such as *nanibushi*, when the *yamabushi* retires to a cave to inhale the irritant fumes of peppers, or meditating for several days under a waterfall. Most of the rites remain a secret, however. *Yamabushi* can be recognized by their costume, unchanged for more than 1000 years; it includes the *hangai*, a hat woven from cypress wood, and the *horagai*, "conch shell of the Law," used to signal to each other their presence in the mountains.

Five-story pagoda, Mount Haguro

recent building at the entrance to the garden, and in the **Seienkaku★** at the end of the garden, a handsome wooden building which was formerly the summer residence of the Sakai overlord. It was built in 1813, at the same time as the **Kakubu-en garden★★**.

Typical of stroll gardens (see p115) that flourished in the great cities of the time, Kabuki-en is a harmonious grouping of pools, islets, artificial hills, rocks, and lanterns.

Here is also **Mr Ikeda's studio**, an artist-potter making tea ceremony bowls, known as *Honmayaki*, after a technique developed by Honma Yusuke, a former museum director. Each weighs exactly 21.2oz/600g, for a perfectly weighted bowl in the hand. It's not usually possible to visit the studio, but *Honmayaki* is sold in the museum shop.

Honma Residence★★
本間旧本邸

0.7mi/1.2km from Sakata Station (20min walk). 7min by Run-Run bus from Sakata Station, Nakamachi stop. Open daily: *Mar–Oct 9.30am–4.30pm; Nov–Feb 9.30am–4pm.* ¥800. hommake. sakura.ne.jp.

Thanks to its wealth, reputed to have made the Honma a far more powerful clan than most *daimyo* in Tohoku, this merchant family's residence has a unique feature. Built in 1768 by the Honma family, it also provided a residence for the Sakai overlord during his regional inspection tours. As a result, it combines a Shoin-style exterior worthy of a samurai with an elegant interior appropriate to a merchant. This unusual division of a common space is reflected in every detail of the house. The quality of the wood, the decoration, and even the height of the floor change when you move from one part of the house to another. The house is proof of the social hierarchy prevailing under the Tokugawa.

Sankyo Rice Warehouses
山居倉庫

Sankyo-machi 1-1-20, 1mi/1.6km from Sakata Station (20min walk). Take the Run-Run bus from the JR station (8min) to Sankyo Higashi-cho stop. sakatacity.com/todo/ sankyo-soko-rice-storehouses.

Built in 1893 by a rice merchant, these 12 wooden warehouses along the bank of the Niida River are shaded by large zelkova trees, protecting them from summer sun and icy winter winds, keeping the rice at the ideal temperature. Still in use today, three of them now perform other functions.

The first building is now the **Shonai Rice Historical Museum** (open daily: *Mar–Nov 9am–5pm, Dec 9am–4.30pm;*

¥300). The 11th, **Hana no Yakata**, has been turned into a museum on the history and culture of Sakata (◑open daily: Jan–Nov 9am–5pm, Dec 9am–4pm; ¥300). Highlights include the works of Tsujimura Jusaburo, a famous maker of dolls and puppets. The 12th warehouse, **Sachi no Yakata**, currently serves as a Tourist Office and souvenir shop selling local products (◑open daily 8.30am–5.30pm). There's also a cafe with a zelkova-shaded terrace, as well as the Hokotei restaurant. Bicycle rental available.

▶ Cross the Mogami River and Kyoden. The two museums are about 109yd/100m from each other.

Ken Domon Museum of Photography★★
土門拳記念館
3mi/4.8km from Sakata Station. 20min by Run-Run bus from the Sakata Station (¥100), Domon Ken Kinen Kan stop. www.domonken-kinenkan.jp/english/. ◑*Open 9am–5pm: Apr–Nov daily; Dec–Mar Tue–Sun.* ¥440. *domonken-kinenkan.jp.*

A native of Sakata, Domon Ken (1909–90) was one of the great masters of photographic realism. This museum, the first of its kind in Japan, is devoted to his work. The building appears to float on a manmade lake. It was designed by Taniguchi Yoshio, the famous Japanese architect best known for his redesign of New York's Museum of Modern Art several years later.

Sakata City Museum of Art★
酒田市美術館
◑*Open Apr–Nov daily 9am–4.30pm; Dec–Mar Tue–Sun 9am–5pm.* ¥550. *sakata-art-museum.jp.*

This hillside museum opened in 1997. Ikehara Yoshiro's building is a triumph, merging with the surrounding garden, Mount Chokai area, Mogami River, and city of Sakata. the two main collections focus on the works of painter Morita Shigeru (1907–2009) and sculptor Taka-hashi Tsuyoshi (1921–91).

ADDRESSES

🛏 STAY
HAGURO-SAN
Mount Haguro Saikan 羽黒山斎館 – *0235-62-2357. dewasanzan.jp/publics/index/64. 120 beds. ¥17,300. ☕, dinner also included.* A unique experience, this is a 300-year-old *shukubo* (temple lodging). Fabulous views, and great vegetarian meals.

SAKATA
Hotel Inn Sakata Ekimae ホテルイン酒田駅前 – *5min walk from in front of the station, toward the left. 1-10-20 Saiwai-cho. 0234-26-8800. ekimae.hotelinn.jp. 93 rooms. ¥8400. ☕.* Impeccable service and nice staff, with well-kept and very functional rooms. Two restaurants on site (*French and Italian, daily11.30am–2pm & 5.30–9pm*) and fast wifi.

🍴 EAT
TSUROUKA
Al Checciano アル・ケッチァーノ – *83 Ichirizuka, Shimoyamazoe. 0235-78-7230. alchecciano.com. Open Tue–Sun 11.30am–2pm & 6–9pm.* Inventive Japanese and Italian fusion cuisine from chef Okuda Masayuki, using quality regional products.

SAKATA
Sakata Fish Market さかた海鮮市場 – *10min by bus from Sakata Station (¥150), Koto stop. 2-5-10 Funaba-cho. 0234-23-5522. kaisen-ichiba.net.* The market stands are on the ground floor (*open daily 8am–6pm*), the restaurants above; Tobishima is good value (*open daily 7am–7pm*).

Kitamae Yokochou 北前横丁 – *2-6-1 Nakamachi. kitamae-yokochou.com. Open daily 5pm–midnight.* In the heart of Sakata, at the commercial intersection of the Marine 5 Shimizuya Department Store. A dozen or so small bistros where you can dine, relax, and enjoy a beer.

Somaro 相馬楼 – *Maikozaka 1-2-20 Hiyoshi-cho. 0234-21-2310. somaro.net. Open Thu–Tue 10am–5pm. Lunch & performance from ¥5000.* The best known of Sakata's "Edo-era restaurants" serves classic cuisine accompanied by *maiko* singing and dancing. Two performances per day, at noon (*1hr, with food only*) and 2pm (*15min, around ¥1000*). Reservation required 2 days before (on 0234-21-8015).

Akita 秋田 and surroundings

It may not be very evident at first sight, but the regional capital of Akita has a number of attractions just a few steps from the train station. A park laid along its northern slope offers a first panoramic view of the city, and Akita has a treasure that alone is worth the trip: a masterpiece by the painter Foujita. The beautiful, wall-sized painting is a wonderful guide to the local traditions, such as the Neburi-nagashi, the spectacular festival of lanterns which attracts visitors from all over the world each August.

WALKING TOUR

Located 10min northwest of the train station (*take the main road, Hirokoji-dori, then, immediately on your right, Otemon-dori*), **Senshu Park** is the green lung of the city. At the entrance to the park, the **Satake Historical Museum** (*open daily 9am–4.30pm; ¥100*) introduces the figure who founded the city of Akita: the *daimyo* **Satake Yoshinobu** (1566–1633). Defeated by Tokugawa Ieyasu during the famous Battle of Sekigahara (October 20, 1600), was forced to retreat to much smaller landholdings, with an accordingly reduced income.

The Satake clan continued on the Kubota Domain, also known as the Akita Domain, until the Meiji Restoration, which abolished the samurai class for good. Different military artefacts (armor, helmets, standards, etc) in the museum bear witness to this period.

As for Kubota Castle, the final stronghold of the Satake family built by Yoshinobu in 1603 on Shinmei hill (now Senshu Park), all that remains is its layout and some archeological grids, which can be found by heading up the northwest slope of the park. One of the eight turrets that used to be on top of on the hill was rebuilt on its original spot in 1989. From the top floor of this guard post,

▸ **Population:** 306,700

Michelin Map: Regional map p463, A2.

Location: Akita, capital of the eponymous prefecture, is 159mi/256km northeast of Sendai and 67mi/108km north of Sakata. The town is served by the shinkansen.

Timing: A day in Akita, finishing at the Akita Museum of Art; one day and night at Kakunodate; the same for Lake Tazawa; one night in Nyuto Onsen or Oga Peninsula.

Don't miss: The Foujita painting and the Kanto festival (Neburi-nagashi) in Akita; the samurai houses and warehouses of Kakuno-date; a walk at Lake Tazawa.

Osumi-Yagura (*open daily 9am–4.30pm, ¥100*), you can enjoy a stunning **panoramic view★** of the city. Coming back down from the park (*southwest exit*), keep walking (*around 8min on foot*) towards the **Kanto Festival Center★** (*Neburi-Nagashi-kan, 1-3-30 Omachi, open daily 9.30am–4.30pm, ¥100, including Old Kaneko Family House*). This large hall displays numerous *kanto*: long bamboo poles, several meters high, spanned by crossbars holding paper lanterns shaped like rice bales. Videos and demonstrations (*held Apr–Oct: Sat–Sun & public hols*) show the incredible skill of the lantern-bearers, working under significant constraints. They have to carry the *kanto* without holding them in their hands but balancing them on their forehead, hips, palms, etc. This is a particularly daunting challenge when the largest of them, called *o-waka,* can reach 32ft/10m in height and weigh, fully loaded with 46 lanterns, up to 132lb/60kg.

Next to the Neburi-Nagashi building is the **Old Kaneko Family House** (*same ticket*). This family home is attached to the clothing warehouse it managed

USEFUL INFORMATION

Akita City Tourist Information Center – In Akita Station. *☎018-832-7941. akita-yulala.jp. Open daily: Apr–Oct 9am–7pm; Nov–Mar 9am–6pm.* Good, competent staff that speak English. Bicycle hire available (no charge, but only 10 available).

Kakunodate Tourist Information Center – In Kakunodate Station. *☎018-754-2700. kakunodate-kanko.jp. Open daily 9am–6pm.* Luggage storage for ¥500/day.

Tazawako Tourist Information Center – In JR Tazawako Station. *☎018-743-2111. Open daily 8.30am–5.15pm.*

Oga Tourist Information – In JR Oga Station. *☎018-524-4700. Open daily 9am–5pm.*

TRANSPORTATION
BY TRAIN

To Akita – From Tokyo, Shinkansen Komachi *(4hr, ¥17,780)*. From Sendai, Shinkansen Komachi *(1hr 20min ¥10,220)*. From Morioka, Shinkansen Komachi *(1hr 40min, ¥4500)*.

To Kakunodate and Lake Tazawa – From Akita, Shinkansen Komachi *(50min, ¥2870; 1hr 10min, ¥3220)*. Or, JR Yamagata Line to Omagari, then JR Tazawako Line to Kakunodate *(1hr 30min, ¥1340)* or Lake Tazawa *(2hr, ¥1690)*.

To Sakata – From Akita, JR Uetsu Line *(1hr 55min, ¥1980)*.

To Hirosaki – From Akita, JR Ou Line *(1hr 30min, ¥2640)*.

BY BUS

Ugo Kotsu bus – From Kakunodate to Lake Tazawa *(Mon–Fri 7.31am–4.11pm, Sat–Sun and public hols 8.16am–3pm, 45min, ¥600)*.
From Lake Tazawa (Tazawako station) to Nyuto Onsen *(daily 6.55am–6.20pm, 50min, ¥850)*.

---

from 1854 to 1975. Apart from the living quarters and their architectural divisions based on the social status of its occupants (masters and servants), you can see the traditional mud walls and the very impressive armored doors that protected the contents of the warehouse against the omnipresent scourge of the Edo period, with its wooden buildings: the threatening contagion of fire.

Further south *(5min walk, still on Omachi-dori)* the distinctive red brick façade of the **Akarenga Folk Museum** (◒*open daily 9.30am–4.30pm, ☜¥210*) stands out. Built at the end of the Meiji era, this building was formerly the central branch of the Akita Bank. Its lofty interiors, with their baroque shapes and materials, now house museum displays. On the ground floor you can see a stunning, gleaming cylindrical radiator imported from the United States. Among the many exhibits showcasing local crafts, it is worth spending a little time among the magnificent collection of **wood engravings★** by Akita native

Katsuhira Tokushi (1904–1971), whose works are in complete synergy with the local traditions.

By the time you return to the Asahi River night may be falling, which is when the very lively **Kawabata district** (◒*see box above*) comes into its own. The street running along the river contains innumerable pubs, bars and restaurants. Heading back in the direction of Senshu Park, cross the central district of Nakaichi, which is enclosed between two main thoroughfares, Chuo-dori to the south and Hirokoji-dori running along the park to the north. This is where Akita Museum of Art is located *(20min walk)*.

Akita Museum of Art★★
秋田県立美術館

1-4-2 Naka-dori (opposite Senshu Park). ☎018-853-8686. ◒Open daily 10am–6pm. ☜¥310. www.akita-museum-of-art.jp.

This museum, the work of architect Tadao Ando (2013) in his signature stripped-back style, is specially designed for viewing an unusually large painting (67ft/20.5m long and 12ft/3.65m wide) from two different levels (head and balcony height). This painting, produced in 1937 by painter **Fujita Tsuguharu** (1886–1968), better known by his French name Léonard Foujita, was commissioned by the Japanese collector Hirano Masakichi (1895–1989). The art lover, tired of the painter's boasting, set him a challenge: "If you are truly the greatest artist of the century, you should be able to paint the biggest picture in the world." Foujita immediately took the Akita native at his word. The challenge was a daunting one, however, both to find a subject strong enough to hold its own over a length of about twenty meters, and to work out the material conditions of its execution – finding for example an artisan able to join together several canvases into one and a space able to accommodate the gigantic project. The artist finally took over the collector's largest rice barn. After only 17 days, with 10 hours of work per day, the canvas was finally completed. Entitled **"The Events of Akita"**★★★, it presents the festivals of the four seasons. An artistic achievement of extraordinary vitality and documentary insight, it shows the signature customs, festivals and manners of the Akita region. The painting is made up of two parts on either side of a bridge. On the right side are the annual events and festivals (Kanto festival) connected with Tomachi, the merchant district of Kubota castle where the collector's family made its fortune. On the left side is the daily life of the people in the midst of Tomachi's winter cold. Hirano's collection includes many other high quality paintings by Foujita, such as *Sleeping Woman*, and other Western paintings, including ones from the École de Paris and his friends from Montparnasse.

EXCURSIONS
Regional Map, p463

Kakunodate ★ 角館
Map, B2. 42mi/68km east of Akita.

During the Edo period (1603–1868), Japanese society was organized according to the very rigid hierarchy of the *shinokosho* class system, which classified individuals according to their social background and occupation. At the top of the hierarchy was the warrior class (*bushi*), including the samurai who depended on the shogun and the *daimyo*. Then the peasant class (*nomin*), the artisans (*kogyo*), and then the class who live without creating, the merchants (*shonin*), the most despised group in this hierarchy, which is still reflected in the socio-urban division of Kakunodate. In the north, the direction from which evil spirits enter, is the samurai district, which has existed almost unchanged for nearly four centuries. In the south are the often opulent houses of the merchants, flanked by their impressive *kura*, old warehouses

The Beauties of Akita

Until the Second World War, there were still almost 200 geisha in Akita, whose distinct beauty and culture was said to be specific to Akita's damp climate. These "beauties of Akita" (*Akita bijin*)—maiko as well as geisha—flourished apart from the rise of Kyoto's Gion district (*see p335*), which was the model for the image of the geisha at that time in the Japanese archipelago. Geisha houses thrived in the lively district of Kawabata (literally "the opposite side of the river") which still glitters today with a thousand much more modern and noisy lights over the waters of the Asahikawa. New young women are seeking to revive this tradition in Akita, and these "servants of the codified art" can once again be seen and heard in some places. For all information: Sen Co. Ltd. 1-3 Senshu-koen. *018-827-3241, akitamaiko.com. Geisha shows held in the famous former restaurant Matsushita, a cultural center since 2016 (matsushita-akita.jp). Information available at the tourist office in Akita station (English: *018-832-7941).

The Great Parades Of Neburi-Nagashi

Literally meaning "washing away drowsiness", *Neburi-nagashi* was originally a custom where people submerged themselves in the waters of a river to dissolve harmful energies and cast off the evil spirits that were believed to cling to sleeping bodies. Awakened, purified, and in a state to pray to their ancestors' spirits for good harvests, practitioners hung multiple lanterns from the top of long poles (*kanto*) to welcome and guide the spirits, a custom that is reminiscent of the age-old tradition of honoring one's deceased family at Obon, one of the most popular Japanese festivals during the Edo period. Since 1881, the *Neburi-nagashi* has been known as Kanto. Thousands of lanterns come together in Akita's **Kanto Matsuri**, held every year from August 3 to 6. The swaying lights, depending on the skill of the bearer, should match the gentle undulation of the ears of wheat, rice, and millet, the cereal crops that once fed the community. The whole parade takes place to the rhythm of drums and flutes, urged on by chanting spectators.

later rebuilt in red brick, with armored doors like safes to protect their contents against the frequent fires of that time.

Samurai district of Kakunodate (Buke-Yashiki) ★★
武家屋敷

Around 20min walk from Kakunodate Station. Take the main road opposite the station and walk for 10min, then turn right; the district starts at Yoko-machi. Ishiguro Samurai House: ○*open daily 9am–5pm,* ✆*¥400. Aoyagi Samurai Manor Museum:* ○*open daily: Apr–Nov 9am–5pm, Dec–Mar 9am–4.30pm,* ✆*¥500; Iwahashi, Kawarada & Odano Samurai Houses:* ✆*no charge. samurai-world.com.*

This magnificently preserved district is home to samurai residences, each of which is set in a garden planted with weeping cherries and other ancient trees. Six of the houses are open to the public, of which the two most note-worthy are Ishiguro house, the oldest and still inhabited, and Aoyagi house, whose several buildings contain varied collections curated by the family over the centuries (weapons, crafts, photos). Iwahashi, Kawarada and Odano houses

Samurai district, Kakunodate

© JTB Photo/Universal Images Group/Getty Images

Lake Tazawa in autumn

© Pirih_Hant/iStock

are not quite as opulent, but also worth a visit, especially if you've a particular interest in the Edo period.

Kakunodate Denshokan Museum (Heritage Center)
角館樺細工樺伝承館

10-1 Omote-machi. 5min walk from Aoyagi Samurai Manor Museum.
○*Open daily: Apr–Nov 9am–4.30pm; Dec–Mar 9am–4pm.* ☜*¥300.*
Kabazaiku, which is the art of working with cherry bark, has been one of the craft specialities of Kakunodate for over 200 years. A visit to the museum will acquaint you with a collection of objects manufactured using this technique *(*tea chests, caskets, *inro)* and you will also be able to see demonstrations by master craftsmen. Also on display are a collection of samurai armor of the Satake clan (☾*see p499*), pottery, and objects and tools of daily life. There is a large shop on the ground floor.

Merchant district★ 外町
South of the Yoko-Machi intersection, there are several houses worth a visit. Some still sell the products that made them their fortune, such as the beautifully maintained **Ando House**, but most of them open up a few private areas as museum spaces during visiting times. Also worth visiting are **Tatesu House** with its lovely little back garden, and **Nishinomiya House**.

Petasites Japonicus

Petasites japonicus—a symbol and motif of the Prefecture of Akita that is reproduced on clothing and paper and represented many times in the prints of Hokusai—is an umbrella plant so enormous it can be used as a sunshade. The leaves of the largest species, roughly circular but with a wedge missing, can measure up to nearly 4ft/1.2m in diameter. Prepared properly to remove their toxicity, the spring buds of the plant are a mouthwatering delicacy for tempura lovers. Each year at the beginning of June, near the village of Niida (3.5mi/6km south of Akita station), people flock to see the harvesting of the butterbur (its English name) stalks, which are later found in the restaurants of Akita.

AROUND KAKUNODATE
🐾*Regional Map, B2.*

Dakigaeri Gorge★ 抱返り渓谷
6mi/9km east from Kakunodate.
Taxis available at JR Kakunodate and Tazawako stations; in the fall a free shuttle service operates from JR Kakunodate and a bus from JR Tazawako.

🐾 A path *(1hr 30min round trip)* with two suspended footbridges and several tunnels leads to Mikaeri falls (30m/98ft high). The incredibly dense primeval forest seems to tumble into the mountain stream. Depending on the season, the water flowing through the steep gorge is either turbulent or calm and changes from emerald green to dark blue. The site is extremely popular in spring and fall.

Lake Tazawa★ 田沢湖
12mi/20km northeast from Kakunodate. By train, Akita Shinkansen to Tazawako station, then bus (15min, ⊜¥360) to Tazawa-kohan stop, the main village on the eastern side. There is also a bus service around the lake (including the statue of Tatsuko). There are also boats across the lake from Tazawa-kohan to the statue of Tatsuko (🕐open Apr–early Nov daily, 40min trip, ⊜¥1300).

👥 In addition to stunning scenery, this crater lake (the deepest in Japan, 423m/1388ft) is the setting of a popular legend, according to which the maiden Tatsuko, who is said to have prayed to the gods to keep her beauty, was turned into a dragon. Her picture postcard bronze statue standing on the western shore of the lake is a popular holiday snapshot, as is the bright red *torii* (gate) of **Goza no Ishi** shrine on the northern shore. It is not possible to walk around the lake, but the road offers many viewing points; it is possible to cross the lake by boat.

🐾 Experienced walkers can hike on **Mount Akita Komagatake**, a series of three summits, the highest of which reaches 1637m/5370ft, overlooking the lake *(Jun–Oct: 7 buses from Tazawako station per day, 1hr, ⊜¥1100; get off at the 8th stop, where the trail to the summit starts; allow around 1hr 30min walk).*

Nyuto Onsen-kyo★★ 乳頭温泉郷
Akita Shinkansen to Tazawako station, then bus (55min) to Tazawa Kōgen Onsen stop.

This group of 7 onsen (hot springs and hotels), tucked away on the slopes of Mount Nyuto in the countryside, brings the guarantee of an authentic stay in Japan. For centuries, the sulfur-rich water has been renowned for its therapeutic virtues and most have mixed baths. The oldest, **Tsuru-no-yu,** still has baths in thatched-roof buildings dating

Tsuru-no-yu, Nyuto Onsen

© Narongsak Nagadhana/Shutterstock

from the Edo period. **Kuro-yu**, the farthest, is some 330 years old. This rustic riverside hamlet is steeped in charm, with several excellent accommodation options (🛏️see Addresses). The baths are open to non-guests during the day. *Tsuru-no-yu: 📞018-746-2139, 🕐baths open daily 10am–3pm, 💴¥600; Kuroyu: 📞018-746-2214, 🕐baths open mid Apr–mid-Nov daily 9am–4pm, 💴¥600.*

Oga Peninsula ★ 男鹿

(🛏️Map, A2. 29mi/46km northwest of Akita (1hr by JR Oga Line trains, 💴¥780). This peninsula, with its jagged coastline, encroaches into the Sea of Japan. At Cape Shiosezaki to the south, you can see some unusual volcanic rocks, including the famous Godzilla Rock. Cliffs, caves, and waterfalls alternate along the west coast and the area is a designated **geopark**. The region is also famous for its *onsen* and thriving folklore and traditions, such as the **Namahage Festival** (Dec 31). Renting a car is the best way to get around the peninsula, which is not easily accessible by public transport, and has a glorious coastal road, with numerous off-road parking areas from which to admire the view.

Namahage Museum and Oga Shinzan Folklore Museum★ なまはげ館

20min taxi from Hadachi station, JR Oga Line. Aza–Mizukuisawa, Shinzan, Kitaura, Oga. 🕐Open daily 8.30pm–5pm. Namahage Museum 💴¥550, combined ticket 💴¥880–1100. Namahage ritual reenactments every 30min (in Japanese; brochure in English). namahage.co.jp/namahagekan.
The Namahage Festival is alive and kicking in the region. On December 31, the men of every village, dressed in straw and wearing scary masks, visit all the houses to see whether the children have been good that year. As representatives of the mountain spirits, they bring good luck for the new year. The museum is full of information about this ritual and boasts a wonderful collection of masks. You may also have a chance to watch an artisan in the process of sculpting one.

The adjacent Folklore museum offers the chance to witness a re-enactment of a visit of the Namahage.

Shinzan shrine 真山神社

97 Aza-Mizukuisawa, Kitaura Shinzan.
This Shinto shrine, said to have been founded by the legendary 12th emperor (1C), is the most important of the Oga peninsula. It is made up of three pavilions: the main one is easily accessible, while the third is a 1hr walk up the mountain. The shrine is still associated with the Namahage. These spirits descended from the mountain gather together on January 3rd and the 2nd weekend of February (Sedo Festival) to take part in ceremonies with dancing and music.

ADDRESSES

🏠 STAY

AKITA

🛏️🛏️ **Comfort Hotel Akita** コンフォートホテル秋田 – *3-23 Senshukubota-machi. 📞018- 825-5611. choice-hotels.jp/hotel/akita. 159 rooms. ¥13,700. 🚃.* 5min from the station (west exit), the rooms in this business hotel are rather cramped but very well maintained and functional.

KAKUNODATE

🛏️🛏️ **Onsen Machiyado Nekonosuzu** 温泉 町宿 ねこの鈴 – *28 Shitachu-cho, around 10min walk from the station, a few min walk to the left of the central post office. 📞018-742-8105. oogiri.co.jp/nekonosuzu. 13 rooms. ¥13,500. ¥1400🚃.* Comfortable *ryokan*, popular with Japanese guests, with an *onsen* that's open to the public. Western and Japanese rooms. Japanese breakfast in the adjacent building.

NYUTO ONSEN-KYO

🛏️🛏️🛏️ **Kuroyu** 黒湯温泉 – *2-1 Tazawako Seiho-nai. 📞018-746-2214. kuroyu.com. Open mid Apr–mid Nov. ¥24,000. 🚃, dinner also included.* Deep in nature, this hot-spring hotel complex, over 300 years old, includes several buildings with Japanese-style rooms of differing sizes and standards. A charming welcome and fabulous baths. Can collect you from the bus stop if required.

🛏🍽 **Iori** いおり – *65 Maeda, Ogata.* ☎*018-755- 2262. 5 rooms. ¥12,200. ¥500 ☕, dinner also available.* 🚭. This rural inn *(minshuku)* has lovely Japanese rooms. It is worth a detour for its tasty food prepared with local produce. The charming owner doesn't speak English, but you can book via the Tourist Office.

🍽 EAT

AKITA

🍽 **Nakakoji Coffee and Wine** 仲小路コーヒー＆ワイン – *2-1-48 Nakadori .* ☎*018- 583-0730. nakakoji-coffee.com. Open Tue 11am–6pm, Wed–Sun 11am–10pm.* A friendly, laidback little spot near the Akita Museum of Art. Hot drinks, cakes and sandwiches in the day, wine and light meals in the evening.

🍽🍽 **Kamakura no Sato** かまくらの郷 – *4-13-1 Nakadori.* ☎*018-874-8313. akitasuisan.co.jp. Open From ¥1500.* With decor that gives a nod to the famous igloo snow houses *(kamakura)* carved out of the ice for the Yokote Festival (Feb 15–16), this restaurant is very popular with young Japanese people and serves a local cuisine based on raw or cooked fish, accompanied by the famous Akita rice, said to be one of the best in Japan.

🍽🍽 **Mikuriya Kourin** 御廚 光琳 – *Nakaichi, 1-4-3 Nakadori.* ☎*018-832-2002. kourin.net. Open daily 11am–3pm & 5–11pm.* Situated opposite Akita Museum of Art (on the 2nd floor of a department store), this restaurant is one of the best in the district. Menus start around ¥1500, including delicious grilled fish with rice and vegetables. Takeout lunches available.

KAKUNODATE

🍽 **Sakura no Sato** 桜の里 – *9 Higashi Katsuraku-cho.* ☎*018-754-2527. Open daily 9am–5pm. Menus from ¥900.* This small restaurant in an attractive samurai residence is packed at the weekends. Local specialities at good prices, including the famous *inaniwa udon*, which are stretched until they are thinner than normal udon noodles.

🍽 **Sakuramaru Coffee** 櫻丸珈琲 – *24-1 Machiokachi-machi.* ☎*018-749-7339. Open daily 10am–5pm.* Modern coffee shop near the samurai quarter. The veranda is especially lovely when the cherry trees are in bloom. Serves green tea, good coffee drinks, and sweet and savory snacks.

SHOPPING

AKITA

Akita Citizen's Market – *4-7-35 Nakadori.* ☎*018-833-1855. akitashiminichiba.com. Open Mon–Sat 5am–6pm.* With over 80 stalls and shops, this market is the perfect spot to pick up local products: dried fish, mountain vegetables, mushrooms, and not forgetting the famous giant butterbur plant (♿*see box p503*). It is also worth taking a look at the department store **Topico** *(train station 1F & 2F, open daily 7am–10pm)* for rural and local produce. Souvenirs on the 2nd floor.

KAKUNODATE

Ando Fermentation – *27 Shimoshinmachi.* ☎*018-753-2008. andojyozo.co.jp. Open daily 9am–5pm.* Ando Fermentation has been specialising in making miso and soy sauce since the beginning of the 18C, today housed in beautiful 19C buildings. Look out for the two brick storehouses *(kura)* where the reception and a cafe/book store are now located. Free tastings of the house products are available.

EVENTS

AKITA

Akita Kanto – *Aug 3–6.* This paper lantern festival *(see p453)* runs alongside a food festival. It is perfect for discovering local products such as *kiritanpo* (sticks of rice grilled over a flame), *gakko* (pickles) and the well-known sake products from dozens of local brewers.

YOKOTE

Kamakura Snow Festival – *Feb 15–16 (JR Yamagata Line from Akita, 1hr 20min, ¥1340).* Around 100 kamakura (snowhouses), with children inviting you in to try a waring cup of *amazake*, a sweet drink made with fermented rice. By the river, tiny *kamakura* with candles in them glitter as night falls.

KAKUNODATE

Cherry Blossom Festival – *Late Apr–early May.* Held in the samurai district, along a good mile of the bank of the River Hinokinai. A mass of beautiful flowering cherry trees.

Kakunodate Matsuri – *Sept 7–9.* This fall festival has been running for 350 years. A long procession of fantastic floats, culminating in a battle on the last day.

Hirosaki★
弘前

Spared the damage suffered by other cities during World War II, unlike Aomori which was razed to the ground, Hirosaki has many attractions, such as the thousands of ancient cherry trees surrounding the castle that are the pride of the city every spring. This rural region is Japan's leading apple producer and an important university center. Along with the other *daimyo*, the Tsugaru clan, who ruled the city from the 17C onward, lost their high office in the Meiji era. However, taking advantage of the drive toward modernization and higher education under the Meiji reforms, they sent family members to study in Tokyo, who greatly benefited the city upon their return.

- ▶ **Population:** 174,170.
- ⏱ **Michelin Map:** Regions of Japan Map 5. Regional Map p463 A–B2.
- ◐ **Location:** Hirosaki is in Aomori prefecture, 37mi/60km northwest of Lake Towada.
- 👫 **Kids:** Neputa-mura and the Oirase Gorge; a stroll in the beech forests of the Shirakami mountains.
- ◑ **Timing:** Allow a full day for Hirosaki, two days for the Lake Towada region, and another two days for the Shirakami-sanchi mountains.
- ◉ **Don't miss:** Cherry-blossom time in April; the Hirosaki Neputa Matsuri, August 1–7; towada Art Center; dinner at Anzu.

SIGHTS

Hirosaki grew up around its castle, protected by Shinto shrines to the north and Buddhist temples to the southwest. Bounded to the west by Mount Iwaki, the city sprawls over the flat land to the east, where the railway station is located.

Hirosaki Castle　弘前城

Shimoshirogane-cho. Bus to Hirosaki, Shiyakusyomae stop. ◐*Apr–late Nov daily 9am–5pm (longer during festivals).* ◉*¥320 (¥520 with botanical gardens & Fujita Kinen Teien). hirosakipark.jp/en.* Completed in 1611, the castle was occupied by generations of the Tsugaru clan until the Meiji era, but apart from moats and ramparts, little remains of

USEFUL INFORMATION

Hirosaki Tourist Office – At the station central exit. English spoken. *⌖0172-26-3600. hirosaki-kanko.or.jp. Open daily 8.45am–6pm.*

TRANSPORTATION

By Train – From Hirosaki to Towada: Take the Tsugaru Ltd. Express to Aomori, then the Aomori Tetsudou to Misawa *(70mi/112km, 2hr 10min journey, ¥2510)*. Then from Misawa, take the Towada Kankou Dentetsu bus to Towada-shi *(9mi/15km, 30min, ¥600)*. **From Hirosaki to Shirakami:** Take the JR Ou Line to Futatsui *(1hr 15min journey, ¥1340)*. From there, take the bus to Fujisato *(6mi/10km, every hour, 7.15am–6pm, around ¥500)* or a taxi *(about ¥4000)*. At Fujisato, get off at the **Shirakami-sanchi World Heritage Conservation Center** *(shirakami-fujisatokan.jp/en, open Jan–Mar Wed–Sun 10am–4pm, Apr–Dec Wed–Mon 9am–5pm)* to pick up information on visiting Shirakami-sanchi.

Floats, Hirosaki Neputa Matsuri

© JTB Photo/age fotostock

it today except five gates designated Important Cultural Assets.

The castle keep was rebuilt in 1810 and has now been turned into a small historical **museum** (🕐 *open 9am–5pm; ✍¥300)*, which dominates the 121-acre/ 49ha **public park★**, famous throughout Japan for the flowering of its 2,600 cherry trees. At the end of April, crowds of people descend to picnic beside the moats, an event often filmed by Japanese television. The **botanical gardens** are worth strolling through, to see the many styles of gardens laid out to bloom in different seasons.

Note that the castle is undergoing **restoration work until 2023**, so accessible areas and times throughout the castle park may change.

SOUTH OF THE CASTLE
Fujita Kinen Teien★
藤田記念庭園

8-1 Kamishirogane-cho, on the castle park's southern edge. 🕐*Open mid-Apr–Nov, Tue–Sun 9am–5pm.* ✍*¥320 (¥520 with castle & botanical gardens).* This elegant Japanese garden, which incorporates Mount Iwate using the "borrowed scenery" technique, was created in 1919 by Fujita Ken'ichi (1873–1946), one of the most suc-

cessful businessmen in Japan. In its 26,312sq yd/22,000sq m area, you will find a **Japanese house** with a floor made from *yakusugi* (ancient pines from Yakushima), an **archeological hall** (with exhibits dating back to the pre-Jomon era), a tea ceremony pavilion, and a somber Taisho-era dwelling with a magnificent **veranda★**.

Mysterious *kokeshi*

The earliest *kokeshi* (traditional wooden dolls with enlarged heads but no limbs) appeared in Tohoku at the end of the 19C. Their origin is unclear and open to various interpretations, especially since the word is spelled in *hiragana* (syllables) and not in the conventional *kanji* (characters). Explanations include: a doll with a head in the shape of a poppy seed; souvenirs sold by local artists to passing tourists on their way to an *onsen*, for whom the doll's cylindrical shape would be a reminder of the massage-tables; or votive dolls designed to appease the souls of dead babies.

The denizen of the forest

The woodpecker is famed for the staccato blows (about 15 per second) that it can deal a tree trunk with its beak, without suffering the slightest harm itself. Various biomechanical explanations have been suggested: its brain, located above the axis of its beak, limits the effects of the shock wave and cartilage at the base of the beak serves as a shock absorber, while the woodpecker's head is of a small size and is entirely filled by its brain. Other suggestions favor the bird's tongue; this incredibly prehensile muscle is made up of curved, bony material able to enclose the brain. Whatever the cause, you may well hear it echoing through the forests of northern Japan.

Zenrin-gai★ 禅林街

15min walk south from Fujita Kinen Teien. Thirty-three temples (recalling the number of reincarnations undergone by the goddess Kannon) flank this peaceful "Buddhist way" leading to the Tsugaru family temple of Chosho-ji.

At the start is an octagonal tower (the shape is unusual in Japan) called **Sazae-do★**, built in 1839 by a local merchant in memory of those who died in two terrible famines—the Tenmei (1783) and Tenpo (1833–39). Inside, the corridor is decorated with images of Kannon's reincarnations.

At the end of the avenue stands **Cho-sho-ji★** (©open Apr–Oct daily 9am–4pm; ◉¥310) with its majestic gate, the **San-mon★★**, 52.5ft/16m high, built in 1629 by Nobuhira, the second Tsugaru overlord. Chosho-ji contains 500 small statues of the disciples of Buddha.

NORTH OF THE CASTLE
Nakacho Historic Quarter★ 仲町

The people who served the *daimyo* lived in this district until the Meiji Reformation. Several houses are open to visitors: the **Iwata House★** (31 Wakado-cho; ©open Jul–Oct Tue–Wed & Fri–Sun, 10am–4pm; Nov–Mar Sat–Sun 10am–4pm; ◉no charge) shows how a samurai family would have lived at the time.

♁♁ Neputa-mura 津軽藩ねぷた村

61 Kamenokomachi, at the northeast corner of Hirosaki Castle's park. ©Open daily 9am–5pm. ◉¥550. neputamura.com.

A center containing workshops devoted to the many local crafts and customs of the Aomori region northeast of Hirosaki, such as dolls (kokeshi, ©see box p508), pottery, lacquer, *shamisen*, tea houses, etc. The highlight is undoubtedly the **Hirosaki Neputa-no-Yakata Museum★**, containing some of the the highly decorative festival floats with illuminated screens or giant fans used during the famous Hirosaki festival, the **Neputa Matsuri**. The word *neputa* derives from *nepute* or "drowsiness" in the local dialect, allegedly referring to the farmers' custom of placing giant lanterns along the river bank in order to keep them awake when they were returning late from a hard day's work.

EXCURSIONS
©*Regional Map.*

♁♁ Towada-Hachimantai National Park★
十和田八幡平国立公園
©*Map, B1–2.*

Towada Park and the **Hachimantai plateau** (205,100 acres/83,000ha) together constitute one of northern Japan's most beautiful National Parks, the lushly forested Towada-Hachimantai National Park. To reach it, take the train to Towada-Minami Station, then the bus in the direction of Lake Towada.

Get off at the Ishigido stop and continue on foot along the road beside the river that meanders through the stunning **Oirase Gorge★★** to Nenokuchi, on the edge of Lake Tow-

Oirase gorge

© magicflute002/iStock

ada *(around 3hr walk, 5mi/8km)*. There are spectacular **waterfalls** at **Kumoi** and **Choshi**.

A short distance from Nenokuchi's JR bus terminal, is **Lake Towada★**, where you can take a boat trip to Yasumiya *(toutetsu.co.jp/ship.html; mid-April to early Nov, every hour, 50min, ☎¥1430; fewer, shorter trips in winter, ☎¥1230)*. It runs back and forth between the two headlands of **Nakayama** and **Ogura** that project into the southern part of this ancient crater lake, one of the largest in Japan, perched at 1316ft/401m above sea level.

👪 Shirakami-sanchi★★
白神山地

Get off the bus at the Shirikami-sanchi Conservation Center (🕭 see p507), where you can find practical information about getting to Shirakami-sanchi, depending on the season and time. The site itself is 14mi/22km (45min) from here.

Shirakami-sanchi is a mountainous area covering 321,235 acres/130,000ha, straddling the border between the prefectures of Akita and Aomori. Their slopes covered in forest, the mountains here are 328–3937ft/100–1200m above sea level. The central area of around 42,000 acres/17,000ha has been designated a Natural Heritage

Site by UNESCO. Remote and inaccessible from urban centers, the site comprises a unique **beech forest** virtually untouched by man. Its Siebold beeches represent the last remaining large area of the great primary forests that once cloaked the slopes of Japan's northern mountains. The leaves of the trees trap rainwater, which then trickles down the trunks to the forest floor, forming pockets of water that sustain a whole ecosystem. The region is home to more than 500 plant species and a wide variety of animals, including around 15 species of large mammal, such as the Japanese **serow** (a type of goat-antelope) and the Japanese **black bear**.

Eighty-four species of bird have also been recorded, including **golden eagles** and green and black woodpeckers, as well as over 2000 different species of insects.

Shirakami-sanchi World Heritage Conservation Center
白神山地世界遺産センター藤里館
30min by bus from Futatsui Station to Akikita, Yunosawa Satoguri stop. Fujisato Ranger Office, Satokori 63. ☎0185-79-3001. ⏰Open Jan–Mar Wed–Sun 10am–4pm, Apr–Dec Wed–Mon 9am–5pm. ☎No charge. shirakami-fujisatokan.jp/en.

Shirakami-sanchi

© JTB Photo Communications, Inc./age fotostock

Four Unesco Natural Heritage Sites

Yakushima (Kagoshima prefecture), **Shirakami-sanchi** (Tohoku region), **Shiretoko** (Hokkaido prefecture,) and the **Ogasawara Islands** (Tokyo prefecture) are the four sites in Japan to be inscribed on the UNESCO World Heritage list under natural criteria, the first two in 1993, Shiretoko in 2005, and Ogasawara in 2011. Inscription is intended to safeguard natural beauty with an exceptional universal significance, and emphasizes that such heritage is to be preserved for generations to come. The many other Japanese sites listed are all cultural and historical assets.

The Center (960sq yd/800sq m in area) provides comprehensive information on the fauna and flora of this Natural Heritage Site, the first in Japan to obtain international listing. You'll learn how bonsai growers love the Japanese beech *(Fagus crenata)*, which is famous for its property of marcescence (leaves that dry during fall, but remain on the tree throughout winter, finally dropping when the new buds open in spring). An adjacent room displays the work of local artists, some of them well-known, such as the talented **Hirano Shoji.**

  As Shirakami is difficult to access, a visit is best accompanied by a ranger, who has a thorough knowledge of the wood's ecosystem and its wildlife. There are also some well-signposted pedestrian trails.

Towada City★ 十和田市
 Map, B1. Towada Kanko Dentetsu bus from Shichinohe-Towada or Hachinohe stations to Towada City (every 1–2hr;

40min–1hr). The JR Oirase-go service goes from Hachinohe station right to the Art Center (3 daily; 40min), then on to Lake Towada (1hr). towada.travel/en/learn/city-of-towada.

This small regional city *(population 62,800)* boasts one very unexpected attraction: one of the best contemporary art galleries in Japan. It was created as part of a project which has helped to revitalize the whole city, the Arts Towada Project, and makes the area well worth a detour from Hirosaki or Lake Towada.

●● Towada Art Center★★★
十和田市現代美術館
10-9 Nichiban-cho. Open Tue–Sun 9am–5pm. ¥510, special exhibitions ¥800, combination ticket ¥1200. towadaartcenter.com/en.

With a collection ranging from sculptures to videos to interactive installations, Towada Art Center focuses on showing contemporary works which are fun and thought-provoking for people of all ages. The gallery itself is light, airy and welcoming, but the works are not confined to the building: there are also several located across the road in an open area, where kids can play on Yayoi Kusama's vibrant scultures, and explore the puffy, marshmallow-like house by Erwin Wurm.

If you have enough time, head across town to the tiny, unassuming **Matsumoto Tea Stall** (17-5 Inao-cho; ○ open daily 9.30am–7pm), where you'll find a couple of extra works added by the artists providing pieces for the museum. The shopkeeper is a very knowledgeable about the Arts Towada Project, and delights in sharing the whimsical pieces with customers.

ADDRESSES

🏨 STAY

HIROSAKI
🛏 **Route Inn Hotel Hirosaki Ekimae** ホテルルートイン弘前駅前 – 5-1 Ekimae-cho, Hirosaki. ℘0172-31-0010. route-inn.co.jp/hotel_list/aomori/ index_hotel_id_258/. 212 rooms. ¥9600. ⬜. Opened in 2008, this hotel in the famous Route Inn chain is a short distance from the station, close to the post office. Modern, practical, and comfortable, it is popular with the region's salarymen.

🛏🛏🛏🛏 **KAI Tsugaru** 界 津軽 – 36-1 Aza-Kamibotan-mori, Owani, 17km from Hirosaki. ℘057-007-3011. kai-ryokan.jp/en/ tsugaru. ¥48,000. ⬜, dinner also included. A modern take on a *ryokan*, offering huge *tatami* rooms with Western-style beds, daily performances of Tsugaru *shamisen* (and the chance to try the instrument yourself), and excellent hot spring facilities (small tattoos accepted if covered; staff can provide patches). One of the best hotels in the area. Free shuttle bus (5min) to Owani Onsen Station, which has public footbaths to use while you wait for your train (JR Ou Line to Hirosaki, 10min).

TOWADA
🛏🛏 **Hotel Towada-so** ホテル十和田荘 – 340 Yasumiya, Towada-kohan. ℘0176-75-2221. towadaso.co.jp. 234 rooms. ¥10,400. ¥1000⬜. A huge hotel complex situated on the lakeside (facing the Nakayama promontory), offering many facilities with a wide range of prices.

🛏🛏🛏 **Oirase Keiryu Hotel** 奥入瀬 渓流ホテル – 231 Tochikubo, Okuse. ℘050-3786-1144. www.oirase-keiryuu. jp/en. ¥26,000. ⬜, dinner also available. Large resort hotel in the beautiful Oirase Gorge, with Japanese- and Western-style rooms with modern design touches, and two towering hearths in the lounge areas designed by Okamoto Taro. Lovely *onsen* baths, helpful staff and a perfect location.

FUJISATO (SHIRAKAMI-SANCHI)
🛏🛏 **Hotel Yutoria Fujisato** ホテルゆと りあ藤里 – 1-2 Kamiyunosawa, Fujikoto, Fujisatomachi, Yamamoto-gun, Akita. Bus or taxi from the station (about 5.5mi/9km). ℘0120-53-5362. hotel-yutoria.com. 21 rooms. ¥13,500. ¥1100⬜. This hotel has many facilities (swimming pool, *onsen*, boutiques, restaurant) and is an ideal location for visitors to Shirakami-sanchi. Just a few minutes from the upper reaches of the Shirakami-sanchi World Heritage Conservation Center. Western-style rooms.

🍽/EAT

Especially if staying in the Towada-Hachimantai National Park, it's best to book meals at your accommodation if possible, as options can be somewhat limited in the evenings.

HIROSAKI
🛏 **Anzu** 郷土料理店・杏 44-1 Oyakata-amchi. ℘0172-32-6684. anzu. tsugarushamisen.jp. Open daily 5–11pm. ¥3000–8000. This welcoming *izakaya* features experienced *shamisen* students, who play the instrument in the lively local style every evening. They are among the best in Japan. Simple, tasty cooking.

🛏🛏🛏 **Suimeiso** 翠明荘 – 69 Motodera-machi. ℘0172-32-8281. suimeiso.co.jp/en. Open Thur–Tue 11am–10pm (last orders 8.30pm). Lunch from ¥3400, dinner from ¥9000. Lunch in this 1895 *shoin-zukuri*-style house is a memorable experience. Elegant wood paneling and a well tended Japanese garden, plus exceptional traditional food.

"In the ideal geography of the Japanese, Hokkaido is a blank space. Most Japanese in their forties have never been there, will never go there, and would be hard pressed to express an opinion about it. For them, this land has no prestige because it has almost no history." That was written 45 years ago by Swiss writer Nicolas Bouvier in his *Japanese Chronicles*. The land does, however, have a history, a powerful one, much of it tied to the land's indigenous inhabitants—the Ainu. Toward the end of the 19C, the Meiji government decided to launch a full-scale colonization of Hokkaido ("road to the northern sea"). By 1922, 2 million Japanese immigrants had flocked to these vast landscapes, bringing with them their culture, agricultural methods, and cattle, and forcing the Ainu to adjust to the settlers' way of life. Only in the 21C were the Ainu officially recognized as an indigenous people of Japan.

Highlights

1   The festival atmosphere during **Yuki Matsuri** ice sculpture competition *(p514)*

2   **Shiretoko Goko** in the fall *(p529)*

3   **Goryokaku** fortress *(p531)*

4   View from **Mount Hakodate** *(p538)*

5   Walks in the densely forested wilderness of **Lake Akan** *(p543)*

Pristine National Parks

"It is Japan, but yet there is a difference somehow," wrote explorer Isabella Bird in the 19C. Indeed, the history of Hokkaido reaches farther back than the rest of Japan; the expressive terra-cotta figurines of the ancient Jomon era were found here. Over the centuries pioneers, farmers, disgraced samurai, and gold

▸ **Population:** 5,281,000.

◔ **Michelin Map:** Regions of Japan Map 6, Regional Map opposite, Sapporo Map p515.

▸ **Location:** The great northern island *(about 20 percent of the total landmass of Japan)*, 932mi/1500km from Tokyo, is surrounded by the Pacific Ocean, the Sea of Japan, and the Sea of Okhotsk.

▲▲ **Kids:** The Sapporo Snow Festival (Yuki Matsuri).

◔ **Timing:** At least aday each in Sapporo and Otaru, and two days for Noboribetsu and its surroundings. One day in Hakodate.

◉ **Don't miss:** The National Parks *(Daisetsu-zan, Shiretoko)*; Noboribetsu Onsen *(especially Dai-ichi Takimoto-kan)*; Shiretoko Peninsula; Hakodate; experiencing Ainu culture.

Asahi-dake, Daisetsu-zan National Park
© PY Lee/iStock

prospectors came to this remote land with its harsh climate, thick forest, and icebound coasts. Rice cultivation developed in the west, and cattle ranching in the north and east, carving new landscapes out of what are still vast areas of forest (70 percent of the island). In 1972, the Winter Olympics at Sapporo (the first held outside Europe or the United States) not only put Hokkaido on the map in terms of winter sports,

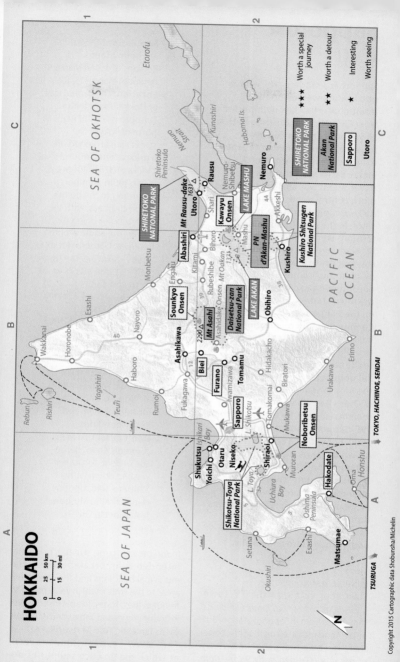

HOKKAIDO

0 25 50 km
0 15 30 mi

SEA OF JAPAN

SEA OF OKHOTSK

PACIFIC OCEAN

Etorofu

Kunashiri

Habomai Is.

Nemuro Strait

Shiretoko Peninsula

SHIRETOKO NATIONAL PARK

Mt Rausu-dake 1631

Rausu

Utoro

Shari

Abashiri

Kawayu Onsen

LAKE MASHU

Mashu

Nemuro

Nemuro-Shibetsu

Akkeshi

Kushiro

Kushiro Shitsugen National Park

PN d'Akan-Mashu

LAKE AKAN

Monbetsu

Engaru

Kitami

Rubeshibe

Bihoro

Sounkyo Onsen

Mt Odkan

Asahidake Onsen

Mt Asahi 2290

Daisetsu-zan National Park

Obihiro

Esashi

Nayoro

Asahikawa

Biei

Furano

Kamizawa

Tomamu

Hidakacho

Hidaka

Haboro

Fukagawa

Wakkanai

Horonobe

Rebun

Rishiri

Yagishiri

Teuri

Rumoi

Shukutsu

Yoichi

Otaru

Niseko

Ishikari Bay

L. Shikotsu

Shikotsu-Toya National Park

Sapporo

Shiraoi

Noboribetsu Onsen

Tomakomai

Mukawa

Biratori

Urakawa

Erimo

Muroran

L. Toya

Uchiura Bay

Hakodate

Oshima Peninsula

Oma

Esashi

Setana

Okushiri

Matsumae

Honshu

N

TOKYO, HACHINOE, SENDAI

TSURUGA

★★★ Worth a special journey
★★   Worth a detour
★   Interesting
        Worth seeing

SHIRETOKO NATIONAL PARK

Akan National Park

Sapporo

Utoro

Copyright © 2015 Cartographic data Shobunsha/Michelin

they also aroused a new interest in the island within Japan. Ever since, Japanese tourists have been coming to the archipelago's second-largest island in huge numbers (around 50 million every year), aware that its natural heritage (no fewer than six National Parks) is a great asset.

Sapporo★

札幌

Sapporo is a modern city, whose grid layout owes less to the traditional urban layout imported from China than to the pragmatism of colonizers influenced by the American farmers invited to Japan to introduce new agricultural methods. In 1868, the new Meiji government was anxious to gain as much control as possible over this Ainu-occupied territory, particularly since, in the sea off Hokkaido, tensions were growing with the Russians over the question of the sovereignty of Sakhalin and the neighboring islands. Hence instead of continuing to develop Hakodate, the town strategically situated on the Tsugaru Strait, where the Commission for Colonization was based, the government decided to build its regional capital farther to the east. It chose a place called Sat poro pet—"large dry river" in the Ainu language—to the south of Otaru Bay, a harbor that always remains ice-free. By the end of the 19C, Sapporo had a population of 2600, but within a century, it had grown to nearly 2 million. Today, although the fifth largest city in Japan is an aggressively modern metropolis, nature is everywhere in Sapporo, from the many gardens dotting the city to the winter snow that forces its inhabitants underground into huge malls.

▶ **Population:** 1,958,000.

Michelin Map: Regions of Japan Map 6, Regional Map p513, B2.

▶ **Location:** The capital city of Hokkaido prefecture, Sapporo is 655mi/1054km north of Tokyo. The streets are arranged on a grid pattern, around blocks of 328ft/100m by 328ft/100m, numbered according to the points of the compass, with the central point being the TV Tower. The address of the Botanical Gardens, for example—N3 W8—can be read as: three blocks to the north and eight blocks to the west of the TV Tower.

Kids: Yuki Matsuri (one week a year at the beginning of February); Dai-ichi Takimoto-kan at Noboribetsu.

Timing: If time is limited, allow a day and a night in Sapporo, and a day for Noboribetsu and its surroundings.

Don't miss: Yuki Matsuri; "Genghis Khan" barbecue or *bata-kon ramen* washed down with a Sapporo beer; Upopoy National Ainu Museum; Noboribetsu Onsen.

SIGHTS

Sapporo Map, opposite.
Start your visit with the **TV Tower** (295ft/90m; *tv-tower.co.jp/en*; *Map, B2*), 15min walk from JR Sapporo Station. Built in 1957 and modeled on the Eiffel Tower, there is a beautiful panoramic **view★** of the city (*open daily 9am–10pm; ¥720*) from the top.
To the west is **Odori Park** (*Map, A–B2*), a green artery through the city, 345ft/105m wide by 0.9mi/1.5km long

(*odori* means "large street"), originally intended a firebreak between the municipal buildings and the residential areas to the south, which were prone to frequent fires. Today, the park is crowded in both summer and winter, and is famous for its fantastic **Yuki Matsuri★★★**.
This Snow Festival (*snowfes.com*), at which gigantic ice sculptures are displayed, has been attracting hundreds of thousands of visitors every February since the 1950s. Some of the sculptures can weigh more than 700 tons.

SAPPORO

0 — 300 m
0 — 300 yds

WHERE TO STAY

Capsule Hotel Safro Spa.......... ❶
Hotel New Budget....................... ❷
Nakamuraya Ryokan.................. ❸
Richmond Hotel
Sapporo Odori............................. ❹
Sapporo Grand Hotel................ ❺
Toyoko Inn Sapporo
Eki Kita-guchi............................. ❻

WHERE TO EAT

Daruma... ❶
Ganso Ramen Yokocho............. ❷
Hiraku... ❸
Ramen Kyowakoku...................... ❹

MOERENUMA-KOEN

SAPPORO BEER MUSEUM

HOKKAIDO MUSEUM

HISTORICAL VILLAGE OF HOKKAIDO

NEW CHITOSE AIRPORT

OTARU

CHUO-ku

JR Hakodate Line

JR Tower

Sapporo Sta.

Sapporo Sta.

Kita-Sanjo-dori St.

Soseigawa-dori St.

Bus Center Mae Sta.

Chuo Bus Terminal

Tokei-dai

Tokeidai-dori St.

SAPPORO CITY OFFICE

Odori Sta.

TV Tower

Nijo Market

Botanical Garden of Hokkaido University

Ainu Museum

Natural History Museum

Old Hokkaido Government Building

Odori-koen

Kita1chijo-dori St.

SUSUKINO

Susukino Sta.

Susukino Sta.

Hosui

NAKAJIMA PARK

SAPPORO CONCERT HALL

Tanukikoji Shopping arcade

Tram

Tram

Tsukisamu-dori St.

Ishiyama-dori St.

Nishi 11 chome Sta.

Shiryokan

HOKKAIDO MUSEUM OF MODERN ART

JOZANKEI ONSEN, NISEKO

HOKKAIDO JINGU, OKURAYAMA JUMP STADIUM

MONT MOIWA

MAKOMANAI TAKINO

DO-O Expressway

Copyright 2015 Cartographic data Shobunsha/Michelin

515

Yuki Matsuri ice sculptures and TV Tower

© F. Fotonokum/Shutterstock

NORTH OF ODORI PARK
Near the corner of Tokei-dai-dori.

The clock tower **Tokei-dai** *(sapporoshi-tokeidai.jp;* ○*open daily 8.45am–5.10pm;* ∞*¥200;* ◖*Map, B1)* was erected in 1876 by Americans from Massachusetts as part of the drill hall of the former Sapporo Agricultural College. The first of its kind in Japan, run by three American teachers at the request of the Japanese government, the college was intended to educate the new migrants settling on Hokkaido. The clock still has its original chimes. Rewound every four days, it has been maintained by the Inoue family for two generations. The college hall now houses a small museum and a municipal library.

Built in 2003, the **JR Tower** *(◖Map, B1)* next to the station, offers excellent **views** of Sapporo. At 568ft/173m, the observation platform on the 38th floor is the place to be during the Yuki Matsuri *(jr-tower.com;* ○*open daily 10am–11pm, last admission 10.30pm;* ∞*¥740).*

To the east of the station *(10min by bus)* is the **Sapporo Beer Museum** *(◖Map, C1; off map),* a red-brick building dominated by a tall chimney bearing the pole-star symbol. The former Sapporo brewery, the first in Japan and now a **museum** *(sapporobeer.jp/brewery;* ○*open Tue–Sun 11.30am–8pm;* ∞*no charge, tour with beer tasting* ∞*¥500),* is a popular spot in the evenings, thanks to its large restaurant with a quasi-German atmosphere *(◖see Addresses).*

Opposite the station (two blocks to the west), about 330yd/300m away, is a fine red-brick building dating from 1888: the **Old Hokkaido Government Building** *(◖Map, B1),* former seat of the prefectural government of Hokkaido, whose interior displays period furniture and paintings, and houses the archives of the Commission for Colonization.

▷ Continue west for 550yd/500m.

Hokkaido University Botanical Gardens★ 北大植物園
◖Map, A1. N3 W8. ℘*011-221-0066.* ○*Open Tue–Sun: late Apr–Sept 9am–4.30pm; Oct 9am–4pm.* ∞*¥420. Greenhouses only:* ○*Open Nov–Apr Mon–Fri 10am–3.30pm, Sat 10am–12.30pm.* ∞*¥120. hokudai.ac.jp/fsc/bg/index_e.html.*

Completed in 1886, these Botanical Gardens cover 32 acres/13ha and were originally intended to help the migrant farmers understand their new homeland, with its harsh sub-Arctic temperatures. They include an **arboretum** *(elms, conifers, maples),* an **alpine garden**, a 13,993sq ft/1300sq m **greenhouse** *(mainly orchids),* and an **ethnobotanical section** listing 180 species of plant used by the Ainu for food, medicine, clothes, and transportation.

The **Ainu Museum★★**, located just inside the entrance to the garden, has exhibits of clothes made from elm bark,

USEFUL INFORMATION

Tourist Offices – Hokaido-Sapporo **Tourist Information Center**, *1F JR Sapporo Station west concourse (Map, B1). Open daily 8.30am–8pm.* 📞*011-213-5088. sapporo.travel.*

Sapporo International Communication Plaza, *3F MN Bldg, N1 W3, opposite the clock tower (Map, B1).* 📞*011-211-3678. Open Mon–Sat 9am–5.30pm.* Maps, brochures, and information in English.

Bank/Foreign Exchange – **Hokkaido Bank Honten**, *Odori W4-1 (Map, B2). Open Mon–Fri 9am–3pm; ATM open 7am–9pm. Closed public hols.* **Hokkaido Bank Minami Ichijo-ten**, *S1 W10-3. Open Mon–Fri 9am–3pm; ATM open 8am–7pm. Closed public hols.*

Post Office/Withdrawals – **Central Post Office**, *N6 E1-2-1 (Map, B1). Open Mon–Fri 9am–8pm, Sat 9am–7pm, Sun & public hols 9am–5pm; ATM open Mon–Fri 7am–11pm, Sat 9am–9pm, Sun & public hols 9am–7pm.* **Odori Post Office**, *Odori W2-9 (Map, B2). Open Mon–Fri 9am–7pm, closed public hols; ATM open Mon–Fri 8.45am–9pm, Sat–Sun & public hols 9am–5pm.*

TRANSPORTATION
GETTING TO AND FROM SAPPORO

BY PLANE – **New Chitose Airport** *(Map, C2; off map) – 23mi/37km southeast of Sapporo. new-chitose-airport.jp.* Flights to Tokyo, Haneda Airport *(every 30min, 1hr 30min journey, around ¥39,000)*, Osaka, Itami Airport *(10 flights per day, 1hr 55min, around ¥48,000)*, and other large cities in Japan. There are also flights to the main towns in Hokkaido *(about 1hr)*.

Airlines – JAL, *new-chitose-airport.jp/en/airport/airline/jal.html,* 📞*0570-025-071.* ANA, *new-chitose-airport.jp/en/airport/airline/ana.html,* 📞*0570-029-333.*

From the airport to the center – The quickest route is by JR trains to Sapporo Station. Trains every 20min *(40min, ¥1150)*. The station is below the arrivals lounge. Buses are slower,

but a good option for downtown hotels *(1hr–1hr 20min, ¥1100)*.

BY TRAIN – **Sapporo Station** *– 10min walk from the center (Map, B1).* From **Tokyo**, take the Shinkansen Hayabusa to Shin-Hokuto, then change to the Ltd. Express Hakucho *(around 8hr journey, ¥27,500)*. Many trains to towns on Hokkaido: 12 Hokuto Ltd. Express services per day from **Hakodate** *(3hr 50min, ¥8910)*; to and from **Noboribetsu**, several Ltd. Express Super Hokuto trains per day *(1hr 15min, ¥4250; station 5mi/8km south of the center, about ¥2500 for a taxi into the town)*; trains every 30min to and from **Otaru** *(30min, ¥750)*; trains every hour (every 30min in rush hour) to and from **Asahikawa** *(1hr 30min, ¥4690)*; 6 trains per day to and from **Kushiro** *(4hr, ¥9460)*; 2 direct trains per day to and from **Abashiri** *(5hr 30min, ¥10,010)*. 🚃 The **JR Hokkaido Rail Pass** *(www2.jrhokkaido.co.jp/global/english/railpass/rail.html)* covers trips on the JR Hokkaido network for 3 days *(¥17,400)*, any 4 days within a 10-day period *(¥23,500)*, 5 days *(¥23,500)*, or 7 days *(¥25,800)*. Buy online in advance, or at the station or the airport in Japan (slightly more expensive). If getting the train from Honshu, it's also worth looking at the **JR Tohoku-South Hokkaido Rail Pass** *(¥19,750 for 5 days in a 14-day period)* and the **JR East-South Hokkaido Rail Pass** *(¥26,900 for 6 days in a 14-day period; both passes jreasthokkaido.com/e)*.

BY BUS – **Sapporo Station Bus Terminal** *– On the left as you come out of Sapporo Station (Map, B1).* **Eki-mae Bus Terminal**, *Odori E1 (Map, B1)*. Buses are often the cheapest, fastest way of getting around Hokkaido. **Hakodate** *(5hr journey time, around ¥5000)*: Chuo Bus *teikan.chuo-bus.co.jp/en;* Hokuto Kotsu Bus *hokto.co.jp;* Hokkaido Bus *hokkaidoubus-newstar.jp.* **Toyako Onsen** *(4 buses per day, 2hr 40min journey, around ¥3000)*: Donan Bus 📞*0142-75-2351.* **Abashiri** *(6hr, around ¥6500)*: Chuo Bus; Kitami

Bus *h-kitamibus.co.jp*; Abashiri Bus *abashiribus.com*. **Noboribetsu Onsen** *(14 buses per day, 1hr 40min, around ¥2500)*: Donan Bus; Chuo Bus.

GETTING AROUND SAPPORO

ON FOOT – The downtown area is manageable on foot. If it's rainy use the Pole Town underground mall between Odori and Susukino.

BY SUBWAY – Three lines cover the city, the most useful being the Nanboku Line *(green)*, linking Sapporo Station with Susukino and Nakajima-koen. *Tickets from ¥210.* A 1-day pass costs ¥830 *(¥520 Sat–Sun & public hols)*.

BY BUS – From Sapporo Station, tourist buses make continuous circuits of the city, stopping at the principal sights *(Sapporo Walk,*

one journey ¥210; day pass ¥750). Departures every 20min, 7am–11pm, Chuo Bus, *☎011-231-0500, teikan. chuo-bus.co.jp/en.* The same company also runs day excursions to Niseko, Lake Shikotsu, Otaru, Furano, and Biei.

CAR RENTAL – **Nippon Rent-A-Car,** *N6 W4, north exit from the JR station, left near the North Gate Hotel (Map, B1). ☎011-746-0919. www.nipponrentacar. co.jp, open 7am–11pm.* **Nissan Rent-A-Car,** *Hokkaido kensetsukaikan Bldg, 1 F, N4 W3 (south exit, near the Tokyu department store (Map, B1). Open 8am–10pm. ☎011-233-4123. nissan-rentacar.com. Open 8am–10am.*

BICYCLE RENTAL – **Porocle,** bicycle sharing service throughout the city. *¥150 for first 30min, then ¥100/30min; one-day pass ¥1500. porocle.jp/en.*

women's sealskin dresses, and many ritual objects such as the skulls of bears and turtles. A rare 13-minute **ethno-graphic film** made in 1935 shows the ritual slaughter of a bear in a ceremony known as the *iyomante*—the bear's spirit returns to the land of the gods, so that the deities who had temporarily appeared disguised as bears to answer the needs of men could again manifest themselves in this form that provided meat and fur.

The poisoned arrows used to kill the bear during this ceremony are soaked in *torikabuto* (a kind of aconite of the *Ranunculaceae* family)—a poison itself considered a deity, whose role is to persuade the bear to accept the invitation of the god of fire. Young bears were always spared because the gods residing in them are not yet able to escape by their own means.

The **Natural History Museum**, about 110yd/100m inside the garden, contains displays of stuffed animals, including the unusual Japanese flying squirrel *(musasabi)*.

▶ Continue west for 550yd/500m.

Hokkaido Museum of Modern Art★
北海道立近代美術館

Map, A2I off map. N1 W17. Subway: Nishi-Juhachome (Tozai Line), exit 4, then 5min walk north. ☎011-644-6882. Open Tue–Sun 9.30am–5pm. ¥510 (tariffs vary according to exhibition).

The collection, numbering around 4300 items, is displayed in rotation and is divided into three categories: Hokkaido artists from the Meiji period onward; modern and contemporary Japanese artists; and artists from around the world. This last section concentrates on paintings from the School of Paris, along with Art Nouveau and Art Deco, and includes Pascin, Kisling, Soutine, Chagall, Rouault, Foujita, Tiffany, Lalique, and Gallé. The great Hokkaido artist **Kataoka Tamako**, who was born in Sapporo in 1905 and died in 2008 at the age of 103, is also represented. She was an exponent of the technique known as *nihon-ga* (literally, "Japanese-style painting").

SOUTH OF ODORI PARK

The nightlife district of **Susukino** (*Map, B2; Subway Susukino*) lies between blocks S3 and S7, and is full of the usual features of Japanese cities at

The Ainu, recognition at last

The Ainu settled in the northern parts of Japan *(Tohoku, Hokkaido)* before the Jomon era (10,000–300 BC), and also on Sakhalin and the Kuril Islands. The other main ethnic group in the area was the Emishi; there is still debate about how closely related the two groups were, if at all. After centuries of co-existence (with periods of both peace and conflict, but mostly mutually profitable trade), the Meiji government in 1869 made colonization of Hokkaido an official policy, following the lead of Western Imperialist powers. Discriminated against and stigmatized for their different cultural traditions, which for example utilized hunting and gathering more than large-scale agriculture, the Ainu were forced to assimilate in order to survive, losing their language, culture, and land in the process.Although their claims finally drove the Japanese Parliament to pass a law in 1997 for the promotion of Ainu culture, it was not until June 6, 2008 that the Japanese Parliament finally passed a resolution recognizing them as an indigenous group "with its own language, religion, and culture." In 2019, this became law, at last granting full legal recognition to the Ainu.

night: karaoke clubs, pachinko parlors, hostess bars, and so on. By day, you can enjoy some fresh air in **Nakajima Park** *(&Map, B2; off map; 15min walk farther south, or Nakajima-koen subway station, after Susukino).*

It has a number of facilities, including a sports center, an astronomical observatory, a pond, and Japanese garden, a **tea house** (dating from the 17C, commissioned by the tea master Kobori Enshu and brought here from Honshu), the **Hokeikan** guesthouse (where members of the Imperial Family have stayed), and the **Sapporo Concert Hall (Kitara)**. The hall's innocuous exterior conceals a magnificent 2000-seater, **arena-style auditorium★★**, much-admired for its acoustics, with a great organ built by French company Alfred Kern.

AROUND THE CITY
Historical Village of Hokkaido★ 開拓の村
&Map, C1; off map. 9.5mi/15km east of Sapporo center. Nopporo Forest Park. From Sapporo Station, train to Shin-Sapporo (20min), then bus (10min to Shinrin-Koen stop) or taxi (about ¥1100). ⏰*Open May–Sept daily 9am–5pm; Oct–Apr Tue–Sun, 9am–4.30pm.* ¥800, or ¥1200 with Hokkaido Museum. kaitaku.or.jp.
Visitors can gain an impression of what life was like in the early days of the

island's colonization in this open-air museum. It has around 60 meticulously reconstructed buildings representing the Meiji and Taisho eras, divided into four areas (town, farm, fishing village, and mountain village). In winter, you can get around the museum's site *(133acres/54ha)* on a sleigh (¥270).

Hokkaido Museum★
北海道開拓記念館
&Map, C1; off map. Nopporo Forest Park. 5min walk from the Historical Village. ☎*011-898-0466.* ⏰*Open Tue–Sun: May–Sept 9.30am–5pm; Oct–Apr 9.30am–4.30pm.* ¥600, or ¥1200 with Historical Vilage. English audioguide ¥280. www.hm.pref.hokkaido.lg.jp/en.
This huge museum is organized chronologically, covering everything from the morphogeographical beginnings of the island 2 million years ago to its Ainu ocieties, colonization and the most recent economic developments. We learn, for example, how in the 7C the Satsumon culture laid the foundations for what would become the Ainu culture, and how, from the end of the 12C, the first Japanese shogunate gradually began to encroach upon their daily lives.
At that time, the *wajin* (the name given to migrants from Honshu) were settling en masse in the southern part of Hokkaido *(*called **Ezochi** until 1869),

almost overwhelming the indigenous population, the Ezo, who rebelled for the first time in the middle of the 15C. The Meiji period when colonization really began to be pushed as the official Japanese policy, is brought to life with archive material and documents.

Moerenuma Park★★
モエレ沼公園

Map, C1; off map. About 6mi/10km northeast of Sapporo. Subway Kanjodori-higashi (Toho Line), then buses no. 69 or 79 to Moere-koen Higashiguchi, the east entrance to the park (25min). Open daily 7am–10pm (last admission 9pm). No charge. moerenumapark.jp.

Designed by Japanese-American sculptor **Isamu Noguchi** (1904–88), this 467-acre/189ha park is almost a sculpture in its own right. The early stages of construction commenced in 1982, but the park was not opened until 2005. Noguchi conceived of it as part of a vast project to surround the Sapporo with a green belt, and it was built on a site originally earmarked for an immense waste treatment plant. This ground, "plowed into a landscape of dreams," in the sculptor's own words, has seen the flowering of some often-spectacular geometric constructions, such as the Tetra Mound, the Play Mountain, and Mount Moere, which looks rather like a pre-Columbian monument redrawn by Mondrian. A beautiful and thought-provoking place to stroll around for an afternoon.

EXCURSIONS
See Regional Map.

OTARU 小樽

Map, A2. 25mi/40km northwest of Sapporo. By train see p517. Otaru International Information Center, Canal Plaza Tourist Information, at the end of Chuo-dori, near the canal. Open daily 9am–6pm. 0134-33-1661. www.city. otaru.lg.jp/kankou.

This city (population 115,300) also functions as Sapporo's port and has the advantage of being ice-free throughout the year. Otaru built its fortune on two different kinds of business: herrings and banking. During the Meiji era, to capitalize on the island's economic development, it was chosen by the Bank of Japan as the location for its Hokkaido branch. Its importance increased after Japan's adoption of the gold standard, when it was entrusted with buying the gold mined on Hokkaido.

The gold bolstered the central bank's reserves, thus ensuring the viability of the yen and guaranteeing its international credibility. Otaru thus became the Wall Street of northern Japan.

The town
On leaving the station, take the Chuo bus to Mount Tengu *(12min journey, ¥220)*, and the foot of the **Otaru Tenguyama Ropeway**. The cable car *(open mid-Apr–Jun 9.30am–9pm; Jul–Aug 9am–9pm; Sept–early Nov 9.30am–9pm; ¥1140 round trip)* rises to an altitude of 889ft/271m in a few minutes. The small museum devoted to skiing *(no charge)* is a reminder that Otaru is popular as a winter sports resort. The slopes of Mount Tengu were chosen to host some of the events in the Sapporo Winter Olympics in 1972. Another room has a display of around 700 masks of **Tengu**—a Japanese folk deity with a red face and very long nose.

From the **observatory★**, there is a magnificent **view** of the town and its harbor.

▶ From the station, walk down the main street (Chuo-dori), then turn right when you reach the Temiya Line railway track (10min walk).

Otaru City Art Museum *(open Tue–Sun 9.30am–5pm; ¥300, excluding special exhibitions)*. Works by many of the artists connected with the town, such as Nakamura Zensaku (1901–83), a native of Otaru, whose Hokkaido landscapes can also be seen in many of Japan's major museums. Nearby is the **Otaru City Museum of Literature** *(open Tue–Sun 9.30am–5pm; ¥300)*. Otaru's two most important literary figures are **Ito Sei** (1905–69), famous in Japan for translating *Lady Chatterley's Lover*, and **Kobayashi Takiji** (1903–33), who wrote about the working classes and whose most important book, *Kanikosen (The Factory Ship)*, is still relevant today. The story of sailors on a fishing boat who rebel against their working conditions actually became a bestseller among Japanese youth faced with increasingly uncertain employment prospects in 2008.

Walk back toward the central avenue until you come to **Unga Plaza,** where you will find a selection of local products—cookies, sake, etc.—in the oldest storehouse in Hokkaido (⊙*open daily 9am–6pm,* ⊛*no charge*), renovated in the Taisho style.

The nearby **Otaru Canal Building Museum** (⊙*open daily 9.30am–5pm;* ⊛*¥300*) showcases the history of the city, especially through its herring industry (50 years ago, it produced close to 1000 tons; today it's about a third of that). Then walk along the magnificent **Otaru Canal**, which is always very lively, but especially after nightfall. End your tour of Otaru with a visit to the glassblowers' district to the east of **Sakaimachi-dori**, where you'll find the **Kitaichi Glass Factory** and its **Museum of Venetian Art** (*venezia-museum.or.jp;* ⊙*open daily 8.45am–6pm;* ⊛*¥700*), which also has a good cafe. This local craft of glassware has its origins in the old practice of fishing by lamplight, which is how the Otaru fishermen used to catch anchovies.

▶ From Otaru, return to Sapporo, then take the JR Chitose Line *(25.5mi/41km, 40min,* ⊛*¥820).*

SHIKOTSU-TOYA NATIONAL PARK★
支笏洞爺国立公園
Regional Map, A–B2.
Founded in 1949, this park encompasses many important sites, including **Lake Shikotsu**, **Noboribetsu**, **Lake Toya**, and the seething **Usu volcano**.

Lake Shikotsu★ 支笏湖
From Chitose Station, take the south exit. From stop no. 3, bus every hour 8.50am–4.50pm (allow 45min, ⊛*¥920). You can also rent a bicycle (⊙open 9am–5pm,* ⊛*¥300/day) and reach the lake along the cycle trail (allow 2hr).* ⓘ*Tourist Office at Chitose Station, Chitose Station Plaza 2F.* ✆*0123-24-8818. 1000sai-chitose. or.jp/en.* ⊙*Open daily 10am–8pm.*

Shikotsu ("large pool" in Ainu) is a crater lake formed 40,000 years ago by the collapse of the upper part of the cone after a volcanic eruption. What makes it unusual is that the lake never freezes, even in winter, thanks to the fact that its waters reach a depth of 1191ft/363m in places, giving the lake a constant temperature of 38.5°F/3.6°C.

🚶 The **Visitor Center** (⊙*open daily: Apr–Nov 9am–5.30pm; Dec–Mar 9.30am–4.30pm*) provides maps and information on hiking trails around the lake. With so many mountains to climb, enthusiasts could easily stay for a week. **Mount Eniwa** *(4331ft/1320m),* for example, was used for downhill events at the Sapporo Winter Olympics in 1972. There are also many waterfalls and hot springs, and, at 1873ft/571m above sea level, the emerald-green **Lake Okotanpe**. Sticking to the simplest route, allow around two hours to hike around the lake, making sure you visit the famous moss cave mentioned in all the leaflets.

▶ From Chitose, take the Ltd. Express Suzuran to Noboribetsu Onsen *(43.5mi/70km, 45min, ¥2830).*

Noboribetsu Onsen★
登別温泉
5mi/8km north of JR Noboribetsu Station. About ⊛*¥1500 for a taxi.* ⓘ*Tourist Office, 60 Noboribetsu Onsen-cho,* ✆*0143-84-3311, noboribetsu-spa. jp,* ⊙*open daily 9am–5pm.*

Lying at the foot of Hiyoriyama, 656ft/200m above sea level, this hot-spring resort is one of the most famous on Hokkaido. Noboribetsu (from *Nupurupetsu*, "dark, cloudy river" in Ainu)justifies its name with the 10,000 tons of muddy, sulfurous water that well up every day from this *jigoku-dani* ("hell valley"), stoked by a seething volcano. The quality and great mineral variety of these thermal waters are what gives this resort its current reputation. First developed in the Taisho era (1912–26), it takes pride in now having the most impressive *onsen* in Japan.

The onsen – Most Japanese tourists paddle about in the hot-spring baths of their hotels, and many of these baths are also open to non-residents for a small fee. The Tourist Office, located midway along the main thoroughfare of this little resort, will give you a list. The most spectacular—and the most expensive— is **Dai-ichi Takimoto-kan★**, located at the far end of the resort (takimotokan. co.jp/en; ⏰open daily 9am–9pm, last admission 6pm). For ¥2000 (or ⬤¥2500 with lunch), you will gain entrance to a large *onsen* complex (53,820sq ft/5000sq m) divided into 30 pools composed, unusually, of seven waters with different mineral properties (sodium bicarbonate, naturally hydrated sodium sulfate, ferrous sulfate, etc.).

To fully appreciate the waters that well up from the ground here at temperatures ranging from 122°F/50°C to 194°F/90°C, follow one of the paths that lead to an observation platform. After a walk of less than 15 minutes from the Tourist Office you will be able to look down on the whole spectacular **Hell Valley**.

In another 20 minutes you will arrive at the hot-water lake **Oyu numa**. However, you would be advised to skip a visit to the bear park which you'll see signposted hereabouts; the conditions in which the bears are kept are upsetting, and go against the respect with which Ainu culture traditionally treats these animals.

▶ From Noboribetsu Station, take the JR Muroran Line to Shiraoi (12mi/19km, 20min, ¥370).

♨♠Upopoy National Ainu Museum and Park★★ ウポポイ
国立アイヌ民族博物館・共生公園

2-3-4 Wakasusa-cho, Shiraoi-gun. 15min walk from the station. ⏰Open Tue–Sun: Apr–Oct 9am–6/8pm; Nov–Mar 9am–5pm. ⬤¥1200. ainu-upopoy.jp/en. ▭.

On the shores of serene Lake Poroto, this new museum (opened 2020) is mainly focused on the Ainu people, both historically and in modern Japan. The name, **Upopoy**, comes from the Ainu for "singing in a large group", indicating the sense of community and connection which the project aims to create.

The modern museum building houses exhibits on everything from Ainu clothing to language and religion. In the park is an **open-air museum** section, where you can enter traditional Ainu homes, see performances and try making crafts and foods. Also in the park is the Irei Shisetsu (慰霊施設), a **memorial** and space for reflection and rituals.

▶ From Noboribetsu, take the JR Muroran Line to Toya Station, via Higashi Muroran (33mi/53km, 1hr 10min, ¥1060).

Lake Toya★ 洞爺湖

This crater-lake, covering a surface area of 27sq mi/70sq km, is at an altitude of 272ft/83m. The Usu volcano lies on its southern rim. It erupts not just from the top, but also through vents at its base, as it did in 2000. This unpredictability has resulted in a very uneven landscape with a constantly seething layer of magma not far below the surface.

The ♨♠**Volcano Science Museum★** (15min by bus from Toya Station) explains more about Usu, one of the most active volcanoes in Japan (toyako-vc.jp/en/volcano; ⏰open 9am–5pm; ⬤¥600, children ¥300). A number of excursions are available, depending on the volcano's mood. The most popular involves taking the **cable car** from Sanroku Station (15min from the bus terminal by Donan Bus; ⏰open daily: summer 8.15am–5.30pm, rest of the year 9am–4pm; ⬤¥1600 round trip) to Showa Shinzan.

ADDRESSES

🛏 STAY

SAPPORO

🛏 **Sapporo International Youth Hostel** 札幌国際ユースホステル – 6-5-35 Toyohira Rokujo (Map, C2; off map). ℘011-825-3120. youthhostel.or.jp/kokusai. 35 rooms. Dorms ¥3200, doubles ¥7000. ¥680⌷. 10min by subway from the downtown area; excellent for a limited budget. Ultra-clean dormitories (4 beds) and rooms. O-furo or private showers upstairs. Note that unmarried couples cannot share private rooms.

🛏 **Hotel New Budget** ホテルニューバジェット札幌 – S3 W6-7-1 (Map, B2). ℘011-261-4953. newbudget.com. 161 rooms. ¥9200. ⌷. 🚗. Unbeatable prices at this business hotel in Susukino. Service is cut to the minimum: almost everything can be bought from vending machines. Rather cramped rooms, but sufficient.

🛏 **Capsule Hotel Safro Spa** スパ・サフロ – S6 W5 (Map, B2). ℘011-531-2424 or 2233. safro.org. 104 capsules. ¥4100 per person. ¥630⌷. Capsule hotel in the heart of the nightlife district. Access to an excellent spa in the same building. Men and women sleep in separate sections.

🛏 **Toyoko Inn Sapporo Eki Kita-guchi** 東横イン札幌駅北口 – N6 W1-4-3 (Map, B1). ℘011-728-1045. www.toyoko-inn.com/eng/index.html. 357 rooms. ¥8500. ⌷. Large business hotel near the station (exit 16). Well-equipped rooms with wifi, safe, refrigerator, etc. Good breakfast.

🛏🛏 **Richmond Hotel Sapporo Odori** リッチモンドホテル札幌大通 – S2 W4-4-1 (Map, B2). ℘011-208-0055. richmondhotel.jp/sapporo-odori. 200 rooms. ¥11,200. ¥1200⌷. Comfortable Western rooms at reasonable prices.

🛏🛏 **Nakamuraya Ryokan** 中村屋旅館 – N3 W7-1 (Map, A1). ℘011-241-2111. nakamurayaryokan.com. 26 rooms. ¥12,600. ⌷. Comfort and an authentically Japanese atmosphere at this ryokan right opposite the Botanical Gardens.

🛏🛏 **Sapporo Grand Hotel** 札幌グランドホテル – N1 W4 (Map, B1). ℘011-261-3311. grand1934.com. 504 rooms. ¥13,400. ¥2600⌷. The oldest hotel in Hokkaido (1934) impresses with its size, many and varied restaurants, and spacious rooms.

NOBORIBETSU ONSEN

🛏🛏 **Kashoutei Hanaya** 花鐘亭はなや – 134 Noboribetsu-onsen-cho. ℘0143-84-2521. kashoutei-hanaya.co.jp. 21 rooms. ¥20,150. ¥1800⌷. Close to Noboribetsu Onsen (Byouin-mae bus stop), this ryokan is one of the town's most enchanting, with a fine rotenburo.

🍴 EAT

SAPPORO

🍴 Apart from seafood, beer, and bata-kon ramen (noodles with butter and corn), Sapporo is famous for its "Genghis Khan," a mutton and vegetable barbecue named for the plate on which it's grilled, which looks a little like the warlord's helmet. Surprisingly few restaurants are open in the evenings, as most visitors dine in their hotels.

🍴 **Ramen Kyowakoku** 札幌ラーメン共和国 – 10F Esta Bldg, N5 W2 (Map, B1). ℘011-209-5031. sapporo-esta.jp/ramen. Open daily 11am–10pm. 🚗. On the top floor of the shopping mall, eight stands serving noodles from Hokkaido's different regions. Friendly, retro ambience, with red lanterns and old posters.

🍴 **Ganso Ramen Yokocho** 元祖ラーメン横丁 – S5 W3 (Map, B2). ganso-yokocho. com. Hours vary; generally 11am–2pm. Most 🚗. A tiny but famous street in Susukino, lined with noodle houses.

🍴🍴 **Daruma** だるま本店 – S5 W4 (Map, B2) ℘011-552-6013. best.miru-kuru. com/daruma. Open daily 5pm–3am. Unpretentious barbecue restaurant on a narrow street, run by three lively ladies. It's a little hard to find: look for the sign showing a bald, bearded Genghis Khan.

🍴🍴🍴 **Sapporo Beer Garden** サッポロビール園 – N7 E9 (C1, off map) ℘0120-150-550. www.sapporo-bier-garten.jp. Open daily 11.30am–10pm. Restaurant in the former Sapporo brewery. A giant beer vat sets the tone; visitors come here to feast on "Genghis Khan" barbecue and beer, plus sushi and crab menus.

🍴🍴 **Hiraku** 開（ひらく）– 2F President Matsui Bldg, S1 W5 (Map, B2) ℘011-241-6166. Open Mon–Sat 5–11pm. Menu in English. Restaurant specializing in oysters (cooked or raw), soba, sushi, and seasonal dishes. Try the oyster stew.

OTARU

🍵🍶🍴 **Masazushi** 政寿司本店 – *1-1-1 Hanazono, Sushiya-dori.* *☎0134-23-0011. masazushi.co.jp. Open Thu–Tue, 11am–3pm & 5–9.30pm Menu in English.* Otaru's great sushi restaurant. People come from Sapporo just to try its famous snow crab.

NIGHTLIFE

Clubs – **Booty** ブーティー*S7 W4 (Map, B2).* *☎011-521-2336. booty-disco.com.html. Open Mon–Sat, ususally 9pm–4am. No table charge. Drinks about ¥500.* Funk, hip-hop, R & B, rap, and reggae. Relax in the lounge bar on the first floor. This French-owned club is Sapporo's trendiest.

Bars – **Hallstairs** ホールステアーズ – *Seibido Bldg. B1F, S3 W3.* *☎011-242-2252.*

miyakoshiya-coffee.co.jp/jp/shopinfo/ hseb_gig. Open Mon–Thur & Sat 2pm–2am, Fri 2pm–3am, Sun 2pm–midnight. Rock, soul, jazz and a relaxing atmosphere in this coffee shop/performance space.

Bar Habana バー ハバナ – *6 Tanuki-koji.* *☎011-219-8870. Open Tue–Sun, usually 6pm–2am.* A colorful bar with Cuban-style music, and sometimes salsa classes.

Jersey Bar ジャージー バー – *W6-10-4.* *☎011-242-4335. Open Tue–Sun, usually 6pm–1/2am.* Irish pub much-loved by both expatriates and locals.

Rad Brothers ラッド ブラザーズ – *LC Nibankan Bldg, S7 W3.* *☎011-561-3601. radbrothers.owst.jp/en. Open daily 6pm–6am.* A very lively, young crowd, standard bar food, and good music.

Daisetsu-zan National Park★★
大雪山国立公園

In the heart of Hokkaido, Daisetsu-zan is Japan's largest National Park by some margin. Its 888sq mi/2300sq km encompass a number of volcanic peaks, including Mount Tomuraushi, Mount Tokachi, and Mount Asahi, which rises to 7513ft/2290m. The "Roof of Hokkaido" is known as Kamui Mintara ("playing field of the gods") by the Ainu. Gorges, cliffs, waterfalls, lakes, and hot springs wreathed in steam draw the crowds, both in summer and winter, to these luxuriant foothills in one of the most impressive mountain ranges in Japan.

> ▶ **Population:** Asahikawa 352,100.
> ⏱ **Michelin Map:** Regions of Japan Map 6, Regional Map p513.
> ▷ **Location:** Asahikawa is 87mi/140km east of Sapporo.
> 👪 **Kids:** A walk on Mount Asahi; the cable car to Kuro-dake; a night at the youth hostel to take advantage of its magnificent *rotenburo*.
> 🕐 **Timing:** At least one day to take advantage of the hiking opportunities around Sounkyo and Mount Kuro. Spend the night in the park itself so that you can soak lazily in an *onsen* as evening falls.
> 🔍 **Don't miss:** Sounkyo Gorge; a walk on Mount Asahi.

SIGHTS
ASAHIKAWA 旭川

⏱*Regional Map, B2.* 🚉*The well-stocked Tourist Information Center is in the station, by the exit.* *☎0166-26-6665. asahikawa-tourism.com.* 🕐*Open daily: Jun–Sept 8.30am–7pm; Oct–May 9am–7pm. English spoken.*
The second-largest city on Hokkaido lies at the confluence of the rivers flowing

down from the Daisetsu-zan massif. Visitors to the National Park can rent their winter sports equipment here. Asahikawa's claim to fame is as the home town of writer Inoue Yasushi (1907–91), whose novel *The Hunting Gun* has been translated into many languages. A small museum stands on the site of his birthplace, the **Inoue Yasushi Memorial**

TRANSPORTATION

BY TRAIN – From Sapporo – Take the Ltd. Express Super Kamui or Rairakku to **Asahikawa** (87mi/140km, every 30min–1hr, 1hr 30min, ¥4690).

Hall (5-7 Shunko; inoue.abs-tomonokai.jp; ⊙open Tue–Sun 9am–5pm; ⊕¥200). It is to the northeast of the station, on the opposite side of the Ishikari River, which can be reached on foot along the town's main thoroughfare, Heiwa-dori. On the west side of the river, near the Asahi Bridge, is the **Kawamura Kaneto Ainu Memorial Hall** (11 Hokumon-cho; ⊙open daily 9am–5pm, to 6pm Jul–Aug 6pm; ⊕¥500), devoted to Ainu culture.

▶ For Sounkyo, take bus no. 3 outside the station (1hr 50min journey, ⊕¥2000) or a JR Sekihoku Line train to Kamikawa Station (31mi/50km, 1hr 10min, ⊕¥1100). From Kamikawa, Dohoku Bus (3min walk from the station) to Sounkyo terminal (30min, ⊕¥1000).

SOUNKYO★ 層雲峡

🛈Tourist Information Center ✆01658-5-3350. sounkyo.net. ⊙Open Nov–Apr Thu–Tue 11.30am–5pm.
The northern gateway to Daisetsu-zan National Park, this small hot-spring resort lies at the foot of Kuro-dake, near beautiful waterfalls. Relax in one of the many onsen or in the **Kuro-dake no yu** public bath (sounkyo.com/kurodakenoyu.html; ⊙open 10am–7pm: Nov–Apr Thu–Tue, May–Oct daily; ⊕¥600) in the village. The bus terminal and post office are close to the Tourist Information Center, on the other side of the river.

Kuro-dake★ 黒岳

Allow half a day. Take good shoes and warm clothes.
🚶 Take the cable car (rinyu.co.jp/kurodake; ⊙open daily: summer 6am–6pm, winter 8am–4.30pm, with variations by month; ⊕¥2400 round trip) to Kuro-dake Station (4265ft/1300m), which has an observation point on its roof (⊕no charge). Food and equip-

ment for winter hiking are available. A chairlift 220yd/200m from the cable car exit takes 15 minutes (schedule varies by season; ⊕¥800 round trip) to reach the seventh station of Mount Kuro (altitude 4987ft/1520m). From here, you can follow the steep trail that leads to the summit (6509ft/1984m; about 1hr 30min). There is a beautiful **panoramic view★★** from the top—you can see the peaks of Keigetsu-dake (6358ft/1938m), Ryoun-dake (6972ft/2125m), and Hokuchin-dake (7362ft/2244m).

Sounkyo Gorge★★ 層雲峡

15.5mi/25km downhill from central Sounkyo. Allow 40min walk/15min cycle to the most spectacular waterfalls. Bicycle rental at Northern Lodge Hotel (⊕¥1100/day). 🛈Sounkyo Visitor Center has helpful information on the National Park in English (sounkyovc.net; ⊙open Jun–Oct daily 8am–5.30pm, Nov–May Tue–Sun 9am–5pm).
Winding for nearly 15mi/24km along the magnificent Daisetsu-zan mountain range, the Soun gorge (kyo) is a spectacular sight, especially the **Ryusei and Ginga waterfalls★★** (295ft/90m and 394ft/120m high respectively), which hurtle down the rocky cliffs
🚶 For a view of both falls, take a trail from the rear of the car park through the forest to emerge after 15 minutes at a wonderful **panorama★**.

▶ From Asahikawa Station, take bus no. 66 to Asahidake Onsen (4 daily; 1hr 20min journey; around ⊕¥1500).

Asahi-dake★★ 旭岳

A young volcano, Asahi-dake is the highest peak in the Daisetsu mountain range, which stretches for over 31mi/50km, and includes a number of peaks above 6562ft/2000m. The rocky faces of Mount Asahi, often wreathed in cloud, are steep, but the lovely Sugatami plateau nearby (altitude 5249ft/1600m) is more accessible. Toward the end of the day, head for the small resort of **Asahidake Onsen**. Some of its many hot springs are in the open air, in an enchanting alpine setting.

Sugatami Region★★ 姿見

The easiest way to reach the plateau is by Asahidake Ropeway (asahidake.hok-kaido.jp/en; ⏰ *open daily; hours vary by season, ranging from 6am–6pm to 9am–4pm;* 🎫 *¥2200 round trip late Oct–May, ¥2300 Jun–late Oct). Or a fairly steep and challenging hike (2hr).*

🚶 Various walks are possible from the point where the cable car drops you off, with a guide (English-speaking guides available) or without. There are a number of observation points along the walking trails where you can see plants (*chinguruma*, rhododendron) and animals (brown bear, red squirrel, rabbit, pika), and bubbling pools—a reminder, like the wisps of smoke rising up from the ground, that the volcano is still very much an active one.

The peak can be reached in about 2hr, depending on the weather.

ADDRESSES

🛏 STAY

ASAHIKAWA

🛏 **OMO7 Asahikawa** OMO7旭川 – ☎*0166-29-2666. omo-hotels.com/ asahikawa/en. 237 rooms. ¥8500. ¥2000☕.* Well-designed resort-style hotel, with friendly English-speaking staff, several restaurants and an *onsen* and sauna area *(¥1000)*, perfect after a day hiking or skiing; tattoos accepted if they're small enough to be covered with four seals (available free at the hotel). Shuttle buses to Asahidake *(reservations required, no charge).*

ASAHIDAKE ONSEN

🛏🍴 **Daisetsuzan Shirakaba-so** 大雪山 白樺荘 – ☎*0166-97-2246. shirakabasou-asahidake.com. 4 dorms, 14 private rooms. Dorms ¥7890 per person, doubles ¥17,880. ☕, dinner also included.* A great *rotenburo* makes this simple guesthouse a top place to stay. English spoken.

Shiretoko National Park ★★★
知床国立公園

The Shiretoko National Park (*shiretoko* means "the end of the earth" in the Ainu language) covers the northern half of this 40mi/65km-long peninsula shaped like a finger pointing toward the Sea of Okhotsk. Founded in 1964, the park has a surface area of 149sq mi/386sq km. Still virtually unspoilt, at its center is a volcanic ridge culminating in Mount Rausu (5449ft/1661m), with, to the north, the slightly lower peaks of Mount Lo (5128ft/1563m) and Mount Shiretoko (4114ft/1254m). Covered in coniferous forests, their slopes end in sheer cliffs dropping down to the sea, which is sometimes covered with ice. Brown bears wander in the park, which has been attracting increasing numbers of

▶ **Population:** Abashiri: 35,200.

🕐 **Michelin Map:** Regions of Japan Map 6, Regional Map p513.

▶ **Location:** The peninsula lies in the northeast of Hokkaido. Sapporo to Abashiri: 220mi/355km; Abashiri to Utoro: 48mi/77km; Utoro to Rausu: 18mi/30km.

👨‍👧 **Kids:** A boat trip beside the cliffs.

🕐 **Timing:** Allow at least three days.

😍 **Don't miss:** The five lakes trail (Shiretoko Goko); Kamuiwakka Falls.

tourists, mostly Japanese, especially since Shiretoko was designated a UNESCO World Heritage Site in 2005, because of the interaction between its marine and terrestial ecosystems.

USEFUL INFORMATION

Tourist Office – **Abashiri Tourist Information**, in the JR station. *Open Mon–Fri noon–5pm Sat–Sun 9am–5pm. Closed most of Jan & early Apr–start of golden Week. abakanko.jp/en.*
Shiretoko Nature Center and Rausu Visitor Center – *see p529.*

TRANSPORTATION

BY PLANE – **Memanbetsu Airport** – *0152-74-3115, mmb-airport.co.jp.* Planes from Sapporo *(6 flights per day, 45min, around ¥25,000)*, Tokyo *(6 flights per day, 1hr 50min, around ¥47,000)*, and Nagoya *(1 flight per day, 2hr10min, around ¥50,000)*. The Abashiri bus connects the airport with Abashiri *(35min, ¥910)* and Utoro *(Abashiri Bus 0152-43-4101, abashiribus.com; and Shari Bus 0152-23-2451, sharibus. co.jp; 3 buses per day mid-Jun–mid-Oct & end Jan–mid-Mar, 2hr 20min, ¥3300).*
BY TRAIN – **From Sapporo** – 2 Ltd. Express Okhotsk trains per day to Abashiri *(5hr 30min, ¥10,010)*, then 7 trains per day on to Shiretoko-Shari *(45min, ¥970)*, the station closest to Shiretoko National Park *(25mi/40km).*

BY BUS – **From Sapporo** – 9 buses per day to Abashiri *(6hr, around ¥7000)*. From there, you can get buses to Utoro *(Airport-Liner: Abashiri Bus and Shari Bus for Utoro; 3 buses per day mid-Jun–mid-Oct & end Jan–mid-Mar; 1hr 40min journey, ¥2600)*, but buses are more frequent from Shari, with Shari bus *(7 per day in summer, 4 per day in winter; 1hr, ¥1650).*
From Utoro – Buses *(6 per day in summer)*, serve Shiretoko Nature Center, Iwaobetsu, and the five lakes (Shiretoko Goko; *3 buses per day in winter to Shiretoko Nature Center)*. From mid-Jun to mid-Oct, 4 buses per day link Utoro with Rausu via the Shiretoko Pass *(50min, around ¥1500)*. In Aug, the shuttle bus linking Shiretoko Nature Center with Kamuiwakka Falls leaves every 20/40min *(50min, around ¥1400).*
BY CAR – **Car Rental** – **At the airport or outside Abashiri station:** Nippon Rent-A-Car *0152-74-4177*, Nissan Rent-A-Car *0152-74-3785*. There is another branch of Nippon Rent-A-Car at Abashiri Station *0152-44-0919.*

SIGHTS

Regional Map.

ABASHIRI 網走

Map, B1. Allow half a day.
Situated 230mi/371km to the east of Sapporo, the climate of this port town is harsh and its landscape inhospitable. As the fresh water of the Abashiri River flows into the Sea of Okhotsk, the north-ernmost of Japan's seas, diluting its salinity, ice forms more easily. As a con-sequence, the sea is blocked by ice from January to April. It perhaps comes as no surprise to learn that there is a prison here, where political prisoners were sent during the Meiji era. Most tourists stop in Abashiri just long enough to explore the lagoon, before rushing on to Shire-toko National Park, but there are a few good museums worth visiting.

Ice spectacular

The spectacle of thousands of blocks of ice bristling from the sea, creating an immense but mobile white landscape is a striking one, and a great number of Japanese tourists make the journey to see it. This natural phenomenon is unique in Japan, but is now under threat as the climate warms. It can be observed both at Abashiri and along the coast toward Utoro.

Abashiri Prison Museum★
博物館網走監獄

7min south of the station by bus no 2. Open daily: May–Sept 8.30am–6pm; Oct–Apr 9am–5pm (last admission 1hr before closing). ¥1100. kangoku.jp/ multilingual_english.

The Japanese Alcatraz was for criminals, but political prisoners who opposed or rejected the reforms imposed by the Meiji Emperor were also sent here. What made conditions for the prisoners all the more unbearable was that the jail was unheated. The museum is housed in the old prison buildings, where the suffering of their daily lives is illustrated with waxwork figures. The prison was moved to a new, more humane location and building in 1984.

Okhotsk Ryuhyo Museum★
オホーツク流氷館
30min walk from Abashiri Prison Museum, or 5min by bus. ⏰*Open May–Oct 8.30am–6pm; Nov–Apr 9am–4.30pm.* ☞*¥825. ryuhyokan.com.*
To get an idea of what the conditions are like in winter in this part of Japan, the visitor puts on a woollen coat similar to those worn by the Ainu, and enters a room where the temperature does not exceed -15C/5F. The experience continues with a look at what are known here as "sea angels" or *Clione limacina*. These small, translucent, orange mollusks are one of the first links in the food chain.

Hokkaido Museum of Northern Peoples★
北海道立北方民族博物館
5min walk from Okhotsk Ryuhyo Museum. ⏰*Open Jul–Sept daily 9am–5pm; Oct–Jun Tue–Sun 9.30am–4.30pm.* ☞*¥550. hoppohm.org.*

This museum demonstrates how the northern peoples classified as "Arctic," whether hailing from Siberia, northern Europe, or North America, were able to develop ways of life adapted to extreme conditions (a harsh climate, sparse vegetation, the Polar night, etc.). Among these, of course, are the Ainu. The striking thing that emerges from this fine ethnographic collection is how much the cultures of such very different people have in common.

SHIRETOKO NATIONAL PARK★★★ 知床国立公園
♿*Regional Map, C1/2. Allow at least 2 days.* 👁*This park is probably the wildest on Hokkaido so comes with a few warnings. Brown bears can be dangerous, particularly if surprised and especially females with their young. Be particularly cautious in the fall when they are more active, and always make your presence known, such as by wearing a small bell around your neck. You are advised not to enter the park in the early morning, at dusk, or alone. It is advisable to hire a Japanese guide, especially if you are planning a long excursion, such as to Cape Shiretoko. Picchio (shiretoko-picchio.com) is a good choice for nature and wildlife tours, with experienced, English-speaking guides, offering activities such as whale watching, bear spotting, hiking and snowshoeing. On your right (4mi/7km before Utoro), you will see the spectacular 263ft/80m-high*

Hokkaido Museum of Northern Peoples

Shiretoko Goko, Shiretoko National Park

Oshinkoshin no taki★, a waterfall considered one of the hundred most beautiful in Japan. From the little port of Utoro, huddled at the foot of this enormous rock, a coast road follows the western side of the park until a left fork leads to Shiretoko Nature Center, Shiretoko Goko (the five lakes), and Kamuiwakka Falls.

Shiretoko Nature Center

知床自然センター

3mi/5km from Utoro. 🕐*Open daily: late Apr–late Oct 8am–5.30pm; late Oct–late Apr 9am–4pm.* 🐾*No charge. center. shiretoko.or.jp/en.*

You can get more information on the local flora and fauna in this center, and follow the circular trail which start behind the centers to **Furepe no taki★**, a **waterfall** that gushes down the cliff and plunges into the Sea of Okhotsk. **Rausu Visitor Center** (🕐*open daily: Mar–Oct 9am–5pm; Nov–Apr 10am–4pm*), on the other side of the park, also has interesting information and exhibits, but little English signage.

Shiretoko Goko★★ 知床五湖

9.3mi/15km from Utoro. Information at Field House: 🕐*Open daily: hours vary by season, ranging from 7.30am–6.30pm to 8.30am–4pm. goko.go.jp.*

🚶 A 2mi/3km hiking trail *(about 1hr walk)* will take you around the five lakes, along fragrant paths and buttressed footbridges over swamps. The trail is especially enchanting in fall, when the maples turn a blazing red.

Kamuiwakka-no-taki★★
カムイワッカ湯の滝

6.2mi/10km from Shiretoko Goko along a dirt track. Barred to cars mid-Jul–mid-Sept. Take the shuttle bus (🕐see Transportation, p527). From the bus stop, about 30min walk.

This hot-spring area is dominated by a mass of hot water cascading from pool to pool, a dramatic and inviting spectacle. Don't forget a swimming costume and non-slip shoes, necessary to make your way up the cascades.

Unfortunately, at the time of research only the lower section of the falls was open to the public, for safety reasons. Check in advance of your visit how much is accessible.

East of Utoro ウトロ

After the fork, Route 334 crosses the mountainous ridge of the peninsula and then descends to Rausu, a small port on the west coast.

🖐 *Note there is no access to Shiretoko Pass (2493ft/760m) in winter, and sometimes even up until mid-June, because of the snow.*

🚶 Climbing imposing **Rausu-dake** *(5449.5ft/ 1661m)* is only for experienced hikers. For a less testing climb, take the trail from Utoro instead. It is not signposted, but is quite easy to spot, and begins behind Chinohate Hotel in Iwaobetsu (🕐*open Jun–Oct only, about 8hr round trip*).

Walking back down to Rausu is not advisable *(5hr walk)* because of snow patches and the risk of getting lost; it's better to take the bus back to JR Shiretoko Shari Station.

ADDRESSES

🛏 STAY

ABASHIRI

🍴 **Business Ryokan Miyuki** ビジネス旅館みゆき – S4 W4. ℘0152-43-4425. www5b.biglobe.ne.jp/~myk4425. 8 rooms. ¥7000. ¥500🍴. On the main street, 10min walk from the station, is this small family-run ryokan. Basic, but clean and friendly, and has an o-furo.

🍴🍴 **Abashiri Central Hotel** 網走セントラルホテル – S7 W2. ℘0152-44-5151. abashirich.com. 96 rooms. ¥12,000. ¥1400🍴. A stylish and very comfortable hotel right in the middle of town.

UTORO

🍴 **National Shiretoko Camp** 国設知床野営場 – Kagawa. ℘0152-24-2722. shiretoko.asia/hotel/camp_utoro.html. Closed Oct–May. 7 cabins (2–4 people), plus pitches. Pitches ¥400 per person, cabins ¥3200. 🍴. For properly equipped campers, this well-kept site amid the trees, with toilets and sinks, is ideal. No showers, but you can wash in the adjoining onsen (open daily 2–8pm, ¥500), which makes life difficult for guests with tattoos. Stunning views over the sea at sunset.

🍴 **Iwaobetsu Youth Hostel** 知床岩尾別ユースホステル – Iwaobetsu, Shari-cho. ℘0152-24-2311. shiretoko-guide.com/stay. 11 dormitories. Around ¥4000 per person (tariff varies by month). 🍴. Hostel in the middle of the countryside; a useful base for hikers who want to climb Rausu-dake. It also organizes sea-kayaking excursions. Spartan dormitories, but clean. Dinner available (around ¥2500).

🍴🍴 **Minshuku Lantan** 民宿ランタン – 85 Utoro-nishi, Shari-cho ℘0152-24-2654. lantan.jp. 12 rooms. ¥19,000. 🍴, dinner also included. 🍴. Easy to spot because of the surfboards at the entrance. Friendly wooden guesthouse with pleasant Japanese rooms and a light-filled dining room. O-furo.

🍴🍴 **Iruka Hotel** いるかホテル – 5 Utoro-nishi, Shari-cho. ℘0152-24-2888. iruka-hotel.com. 13 rooms. ¥11,200. Cozy hotel with pretty blue decor and clean, small rooms (both Japanese and Western), a rotenburo, and a pleasant terrace facing the sea. The owner arranges excursions to see bears and dolphins, as well as ice diving. Self-catering facilities; no meals.

🍴🍴🍴 **Hotel Kifu Club** ホテル季風クラブ知床 – 318 Utoro-higashi, Shari-cho. ℘0152-24-3541. kifuu.com. 14 rooms & 2 chalets. ¥28,400. 🍴, dinner also included. Lovely wooden house with large picture windows and a chimney. Spacious rooms with views of the sea, fine cuisine, a vast o-furo, and two rotenburo. The owner can arrange bear- and deer-watching walks.

🍴🍴🍴 **Kitakobushi Shiretoko Hotel & Resort** 北こぶし知床ホテル＆リゾート – 172 Utoro-higashi. ℘0152-24-2021. shiretoko.co.jp/en. 181 rooms. ¥20,600. 🍴. In the center of Utoro, this excellent luxury hotel (recently refurbished) has both Western and Japanese-style rooms. An onsen on the roof, with a view of the sea, restaurants, and boutique.

🍴 EAT

ABASHIRI

🍴🍴 **Sushi Kappou Hananoren** 鮨かっぽう花のれん – S5 E2. ℘0152-44-7576. Open daily 11am–2.30pm & 5–9pm. Delicious sushi prepared in front of you. You can also try hot dishes in different small rooms. Good value for money.

🍴🍴🍴 **Kiyomasa** 鮨 – S3 W3. ℘0152-61-0003. seiwa-dining.com. Open Mon–Sat 5pm–midnight. Simple but good sushi restaurant Food can be made to order by the chef or chosen from the conveyor belt (kaiten).

UTORO

🍴 **Cafe Fox** カフェ・フォックス – 96-5 Utoro-higashi, Shari-cho. ℘0152-24-2656. cafefox.jp. Open Apr–Oct daily 8am–6pm. 🍴. Unpretentious eatery, practical for take-out picnics. The fish burger is particularly good.

🍴 **Coffee Albireo** コーヒー・アルビレオ – 14 Utoro-higashi. ℘0152-26-8101. Open Fri–Mon 11am–5pm. 🍴. Simple, laidback cafe serving tea, coffee and snacks, plus warming set meals like ochazuke (green tea over rice) with grilled salmon.

Hakodate and around ★

函館

Wide avenues following the lines of the coast, an old merchant quarter with an East-meets-West atmosphere, churches and temples of all stripes, a rocky headland reaching toward the island of Honshu and overlooking the city, offering Japan's most beautiful panoramic views to be seen by night—with all this, Hakodate lives and breathes the sea. An appealing, pleasant city, it is proud of its beautiful monuments, including a citadel that could have been designed by French military architect Vauban, and is today a superb park. Hokkaido's leading port, its fish market is busy in the early hours as the first boatloads arrive. You can enjoy a treat in

▶ **Population:** 264,800.

♿ **Michelin Map:** Regions of Japan Map 6, Regional Map p513, Hakodate Map p534.

▶ **Location:** Hakodate is about 198mi/320km from Sappororo and 422mi/680km north of Tokyo.

👪 **Kids:** See beautiful Ainu clothing at the Museum of Northern Peoples.

🕐 **Timing:** Give yourself two days to get a sense of the city, which is bigger than it first appears, and to walk up Mount Hakodate.

😊 **Don't miss:** The slopes of Motomachi; the panoramic view from Mount Hakodate, especially by night; an early morning breakfast of sushi at Asal-chi fish market.

From the Treaty Of Kanagawa to the Last Samurai

Under the terms of the Treaty of Kanagawa in 1854, the Japanese were to allow American trading vessels to enter the domestic ports of Hakodate and Shimoda. This treaty, signed by the shogun and Admiral Matthew C. Perry, opened the way for other accords and there was soon a Western presence in several ports across Japan, including Tokyo, Yokohama, Nagasaki, Niigata, Kobe, and Hakodate. Jules Brunet, a Frenchman hoping to take advantage of such agreements, left for Japan in 1867 and this artillery instructor was to be one of the inspirations, many years later, for the film *The Last Samurai*. He was a member of a military mission sent by France to modernize the army at the request of the shogun Tokugawa Yoshinobu, but later refused to abandon those he had trained, and supported them when the shogun was defeated by the emperor in 1868. They thus retreated to Hakodate, accompanied by Admiral Takeaki Enomoto and a handful of foreigners (mostly French). It was here that Enomoto founded the shortlived **Independent Republic of Ezo**, of which he was elected leader.

The state was to last barely six months but was recognized by foreign powers for a short period. On May 11, 1869, a force of 8000 imperial troops disembarked at Hakodate and attacked the fortress at Goryokaku. Overwhelmed by the bombardment, the 800 defenders surrendered. Jules Brunet managed to flee with the last French survivors, taking to a boat anchored off Hakodate Port. Enomoto was apprehended but went on to to pursue a successful diplomatic career during the Meiji period; Toshizo Hijakata, another fervent supporter of the short-lived republic, met his end in June 1869 but is now celebrated as a genuine local hero; you will see a statue of him as you tour the fort.

USEFUL INFORMATION

Tourist Offices – In Hakodate JR Station, *12–13 Wakamatsu-cho, Hakodate. ℘0138-23-5440. hakodate-kankou.com/en.* Most information is available in English (and Russian). *Open daily: Apr–Oct 9am–7pm; Nov–Mar 9am–5pm.*

Motomachi Tourist Office – *12-18, Motomachi, Hakodate, ℘0138-27-3333. Open Apr–Oct 9am–7pm, Nov–Mar 9am–5pm. Closed Dec 31–Jan 1.*

Post Office/Withdrawals – Ekimae **Post Office** – *7-18 Wakamatsu-cho. ℘0138-22-9909. Open 9am–5pm. ATM open Mon–Fri 9am–7pm, Sat–Sun & public hols 9am–5pm.*

Bank/Foreign Exchange – Hokuyo **Bank** – *15-7-11 Wakamatsu-cho. ℘0138-23-8511. Open 9am–3pm. ATM open Mon–Fri 8am–7pm, Sat–Sun & public hols 9am–7pm.*

Hokkaido Ekimae-ten Bank – *20-1 Wakamastu-cho. ℘0138-22-8161. Open 9am–3pm. ATM open Mon–Fri 8.45am–7pm, Sat–Sun & public hols 9am–5pm.* ATMs in 7-Eleven/late-night *conbini.*

Health – Check *hakodate.travel/en/information/emergency.html* for emergency information.

Hakodate Goryokaku Hospital – *38-3 Goryokaku-cho. ℘0138-51-2295.* Some staff speak English.

Tsuruha Drug Hakodate Matsukaze – *12-6 Matsuykaze-cho. tsuruha.co.jp/en. Open daily 9am–10pm.*

TRANSPORTATION

BY PLANE – **Hakodate Airport** is 4.5mi/7km from the center, in the east of the town. *airport.ne.jp.*
Flights to **Tokyo Haneda**, around 1hr 20min (JAL, AIR DO, and ANA); **Narita** (Vanilla Air); **Osaka Itami Airport**, in 1hr 35min; **Sapporo** in 45min.

From the airport to the center – A bus leaves every 20min for the JR station *(20min journey, ¥420).* Teisan bus *℘0138-55-1111. By taxi allow around ¥3000.*

BY TRAIN – The **JR station** is in the center of town, near the port *(Map, C1).* From Tokyo, the **Shinkansen (Hayabusa)** for Shin-Hakodate-Hokuto, then the Hakodate Liner, connecting with Hakodate Station in 20min *(5hr total journey, ¥23,760).* Connections to towns in Hokkaido via Sapporo *(3hr 40min, ¥8910),* and New Chitose Airport *(3hr 25min, ¥8050).* You can also use on of the **JR Hokkaido Rail Passes** (*see p517).*

BY BUS – From Hakodate Station to Sapporo *(approx. 5hr):* Chuo Bus, *teikan.chuo- bus.co.jp/en;* Donan Bus; Hokuto Kotsu, *hokto.co.jp;* Hokkaido bus *hokkaidoubus-newstar.jp (all approx. ¥5000).*

GETTING AROUND HAKODATE

ON FOOT – The town is not that big, only the old town and hillside are worth seeing on foot but take the tramway for Goryokaku.

BY TRAM – Practical with a slightly retro feel and 26 stations. Fares from *¥210.* 1-day tram pass *¥600 (children ¥300).* 1-day bus & tram pass *¥1000 (children ¥500).* Buy on the tram or from the kiosk in front of the station. Show passes on exiting the tram or bus.

BY BUS – A good network, including to sites farther out (Trappestines Con.)

CAR RENTAL – There are plenty of options at Hakodate Airport.

the restaurants surrounding the recently refurbished docks. The area around Hakodate offers numerous opportunities for excursions, from old towns and villages to beautiful natural sites.

SIGHTS
Hakodate Map.

Goryokaku★★ 五稜郭跡
Map, C1; off map. 43-9 Goryokaku-cho. Tramway stop Goryokaku Koen Maie, then 15min walk. ℘0138-51-4785.

© kanuman/iStock

Goryokaku

Tower ⏱ *open daily: late Apr–late Oct 8am–7pm; late Oct–late Apr 9am–6pm.* 💴 *¥900 (children ¥450–680). goryokaku-tower.co.jp. Park* 💴 *no charge.*

The fortress of Goryokaku was built in the late Edo period, to protect the port opened to Westerners in 1854. Designed by architect Ayasaburo Takeda, its five-branched star design takes inspiration from European "Vauban" forts and was the first Western-style fort in Japan. This not only limited the number of blind spots where cannon could not fire, but also created many more gun emplacements than on a traditional Japanese fortress.

Its bastions, turned into gardens, are especially pleasant in springtime when the **cherry trees** are in blossom or in the autumn when the leaves turn brilliant colors. The moats, dry or filled with water, create beautiful perspectives against the hand-hewn stonewalls. In 2010, a re-creation of the Ezo Governor's Palace gave additional cachet to the site. During a visit, the **observation tower**, that more than anything recalls an airport control tower, may seem slightly out of place. Nevertheless, the museum presentation of the historic events is interesting and the **view★★** to be had at the top, at 351ft/107m, is quite simply spectacular. Moreover, the majesty of the citadel is heightened by the rocky headland of Hakodate overlooking the straits.

Open-air plays about the town's history are held every July and August, with 500 enthusiastic amateur performers.

Hakodate Museum of Art
道立函館美術館

37-6 Goryokaku. Open Tue–Sun 9.30am–5pm. 💴 *¥260 (excluding special exhibitions).* 📞 *0138-56-6311. dokyoi. pref.hokkaido.lg.jp/hk/hbj.* 💻.

This modern building is home to 19C and 20C Japanese art collections. Rodin's statue of Balzac is here, as well as, works by Bourdelle and Renoir. Interesting temporary exhibitions are also organized, often highlighting artists from Japan.

The Port Area★

Hakodate's busy port is a place of both local everyday life and vestiges of the past. Early birds can enjoy octopus sushi at the "Asai-chi" fish market (📍*Map, C1*) close to the station (⏱*open from 5am*). Its some 300 shops are a cheery, colorful show. Just behind the station, the **Mashu Maru**, the last ferry linking Hakodate and Aomori before the Seikan tunnel opened, has been turned into a museum.

Head along Tomoe Ohashi street towards Mount Hakodate, and you'll

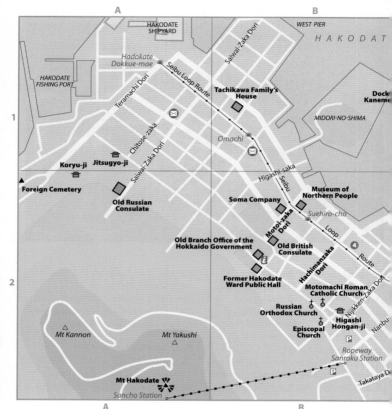

The map shows labels including:
HAKODATE SHIPYARD
WEST PIER
HAKODAT
HAKODATE FISHING PORT
Hadokate Dokkue-mae
Seibu Loop Route
Teramachi Dori
Saiwai-Zaka Dori
Tachikawa Family's House
Dock Kaneme
MIDORI-NO-SHIMA
Chitose-zaka
Omachi
Koryu-ji Jitsugyo-ji
Saiwai-Zaka Dori
Higashi-saka
Seibu
Museum of Northern People
Foreign Cemetery
Old Russian Consulate
Soma Company
Motoi-zaka Dori
Suehiro-cho
Loop
Old Branch Office of the Hokkaido Government
Old British Consulate
Route
Former Hakodate Ward Public Hall
Hachimanzaka Dori
Motomachi Roman Catholic Church
Russian Orthodox Church
Nijikken-Zaka Dori
Nanbu
Mt Kannon
Mt Yakushi
Higashi Hongan-ji
Episcopal Church
Ropeway Sanroku Station
Mt Hakodate
Sancho Station
Takataya D

A B
1
2

soon come to the wholesale fish market; it's difficult to enter the market, but it's worth peeking in if you can. Adjacent are the old docks. All along the sea are the red-brick façades of the old warehouses with their pretty Meiji pediments. They have been converted to contain a multitude of souvenir shops within an entire panoply of products that Japanese tourists adore. The numerous restaurants as well as the Jiyu fish market (⏱open all day) make the docks the liveliest place in town.

Behind the docks, city side, the former post office built in 1911 is also home to a great many restaurants and shops. A visit to the **Kahei Takadaya Museum** (*13-22 Suehiro;* ⏱*Map, C2;* ⏱*open Fri–Wed 9am–5pm;* ✆*0138-27-5226;* ➽*¥300)* is a chance to see the inside of a **strong-box-house**★ with its thick shutters. You

will come across these houses several times when visiting the Motomachi district. Hakodate owes much to this great merchant, Kahei Takadaya, born at the end of the 18C; he is often credited with the significant development and thriving of both the city and its port. The house holds many interesting objects recalling the life of this great benefactor.

Motomachi★★ 元町坂

▷ Take the tramway to its terminus, Hakodate Dokku-Mae Station; then head up Uomi-Zaka street to the Foreign Cemetery.

Foreign Cemetery★ 外人墓地
⏱*Map, A2.*
Overlooking the sea in a calm, serene setting, one reaches the cemetery

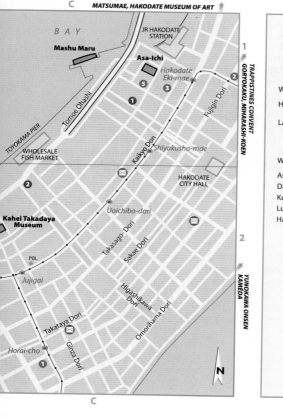

HAKODATE

0		200 m
0		200 yds

WHERE TO STAY

Hakodate Danshaku
  Club Hotel and Resort.......❶
La Vista Hakodate Bay..........❷

WHERE TO EAT

Asari Honten............................❶
Daimon Yokocho....................❷
Kurobe.......................................❸
Lucky Pierrot...........................❹
Hakodate Market....................❺

---

where foreigners have been laid to rest
by taking little streets running between
historic residences. Different sections are
set aside for the Chinese, Orthodox Russian, Christian, Protestant, and Catholic
people. The surprising nature of the place
recalls that the city of Hakodate has been
open to the rest of the world since 1854.

◗ Retrace your steps until you come
to the temple of Koryu-ji.

Koryu-ji★ 高龍寺
21-11 Funami-cho. ◷*Open daily 9am–
4pm.* ◌*No charge.* ☏*0138-23-0631.*
This temple is unquestionably the most
beautiful in Hakodate. Unpainted, built
of wood, one can feel a certain spirituality. Although settled in this location in the early 18C, it was founded in
the early 17C. Destroyed by a fire dur-

ing an attack on the city (1868) by the
Imperial forces, it was rebuilt between
1900 and 1911. The **imposing gates,**
abundantly carved with lions, dragons,
and phoenix, give onto the courtyard,
where the main building stands. To the
right, behind the curious gallery fitting
into the terrain, there is a charming
garden planted with pines and azaleas.
Among the interesting artworks belonging to the temple, there is a representation of Buddha on his deathbed, painted
by Hakyo Kazizaki in 1811.

◗ Take the next first street on
your right after the temple. On the
hillside's flank, on the slopes of Mount
Hakodate, it will take you to the
district surrounding the town hall and
containing the churches.

Jomon art

The Hakodate figurine *(dogu)* has become the symbol for Jomon culture, which first came into being on the island of Hokkaido. Magnificently well-preserved, it is one of the world's most beautiful vestiges of the prehistoric era. A copy can be seen in the Hakodate City Hall lobby. The many Jomon objects found bear witness to a mastery of the arts, with real finesse in their execution. With numerous sites throughout northern Tokoku and Hokkaido, there is more and more interest in the ancient Jomon civilization among Japanese people today. In 2009 Japan requested classification on the UNESCO World Heritage list for all these sites; the procedure is not yet concluded. But regardless of whether they're registered, the sites are remarkable, and well deserve the increasing attention they're receiving.

Jitsugyo-ji 実行寺
Map, A1. Open daily dawn–dusk. No charge.
Located in a pleasant garden, this temple is surrounded by an immense **cemetery** containing a bilingual French-Japanese commemorative monument. It relates the disembarkation of the French in 1855, recorded by the monk Matsuo Nichiryu, whose statue overlooks the setting.

Take Saiwai Zaka, heading up and right, to pass in front of the former Russian Consulate (1908), a vast edifice of wood and brick; its advanced state of deterioration unfortunately makes it impossible to visit. Then head downward to the left of Tokiwa Zaka to the bottom.

Tachikawa Family's House 太刀川家
Map, B1. Cafe: open Tue–Sun 10am–6pm. 0138-22-0340.
Notice the pretty, slightly curved green façade of this old home belonging to a rich Meiji era family. Today it contains a rather nice cafe, a good chance to see inside one of these historic buildings.

Now take the boulevard until you come to Yayoi Zaka. Notice on the corner the impressive 1930s façade of the old Nishi police station.

Museum of Northern Peoples★ 北方民族資料館
Map, B2. 21-7 Suehiro-cho. Open daily: Apr–Oct 9am–7pm;Nov–Mar 9am–5pm. ¥300 (children ¥150). Combined ticket with the Old British Consulate, Hakodate City Museum of Literature, Former Hakodate Ward Public Hall, ¥840 (three museums ¥720, two museums ¥500). 0138-22-4128. www.zaidan-hakodate.com/hoppominzoku.
This interesting museum, housed in a lovely 1920s building, explores the culture of the Ainu, and other northern peoples. Among the exhibits are beautiful items of clothing, jewelry, and paintings. There are occasionally events and workshops held here.

Motoi Zaka★ 基坂
Map, B2.
There is a majestic **view** of the Hakadate City Hall from this sloping road. Notice at the corner and imposing green building bearing the name of the **Soma Company★**, built in 1913.

Old British Consulate 旧イギリス領事館
Map, B2. 33-14 Motomachi. 0138-27-8159. Open daily: Apr–Oct 9am–7pm; Nov–Mar 9am–5pm. ¥300 (children ¥150). Combined tickets available (see above). hakodate-kankou.com/british/en.
Built in the 1930s in a style more Portuguese than English, this residence stands in the middle of a very pleasant garden.

It is home to a small **museum** and (naturally, for the British consulate) **tearoom**.

▶ Now cross Motomachi Park.

Old Branch Office of the Hokkaido Government
旧北海道庁函館支庁庁舎

🚶 *Map, B2*. 12-18 Motomachi. 📞0138-27-3333. 🕐*Open daily: Apr–Oct 9am–7pm; Nov–Mar 9am–5pm.* 🎫*No charge.*
This harmonious building, built in 1909, stands out owing to a peristyle, where four tall, slender columns surmounted with Corinthian capitals are embellished with a carved pediment. Inside, a fascinating **museum** traces the history of **photography** and exhibits a few old cameras. It also houses a Tourist Office.

Former Hakodate Ward Public Hall★★ 旧函館区公会堂

🚶 *Map, B2*. 11-13 Motomachi. 🕐*Open daily: Apr–Oct 9am–7pm; Nov–Mar 9am–5pm.* 🎫*¥300 (children ¥150). Combined tickets available (🚶see opposite). www.zaidan-hakodate.com/koukaido.* 📞0138-22-1001.
At the gardens' high point, the former City Hall is a beautiful wooden edifice built in 1910 after the great 1907 fire that ravaged the city and destroyed 12,000 homes. In yellow and blue, its balconies, columns, and small windows overlook the bay.
The first floor of this long building is surmounted with a sloping roof ending in two imposing triangular pediments. The façade is broken up into three porches on the ground floor; there is a charming loggia on the first floor.
The inside consists of a series of salons furnished in the style of the early 20C. There is a **superb view★★** of the bay and city from the balcony.
Note that the building was undergoing a **major restoration** at the time of research; check the progress of the works before visiting.

▶ Turn right on leaving, and take the cobbled street heading to the religious buildings district. You will come to Hachiman Zaka first.

Hachiman Zaka★ 八幡坂
🚶*Map, B2*.
With its cobblestones, streetlamps, and trees, this very photogenic avenue offers a birds' eye **view** of the bay and the old *Mashu Maru* ferry.

Religious Buildings★ 大三坂周辺の教会
🚶*Map, B2*.
The bell towers and domes of three churches can be found emerging somewhat incongruously from among the small houses and cobbled streets.
Russian Orthodox Church★ – Built in 1916, this is in the middle of a beautiful flowery garden. Its octagonal belltower, roofs, and green onion domes surmounted with crosses comprise a successful and typically Byzantine grouping. Inside, you can admire the beautiful icons and wooden altarpiece decorated with paintings, most of which are attributed to **Rin Yamashita**. She drew inspiration from the Italian Renaissance, and studied the art of icon painting in St. Petersburg (📷*photographs are not authorized inside*).
Motomachi Roman Catholic Church – Preceded by a small forecourt and dominated by a square belltower ending in a tower with an octagonal spire, the Catholic Church also dates from the early 20C. The **interior★** is in the Neo-Gothic style, abundantly decorated, its rib-vaulted ceiling painted blue, and sprinkled with little golden stars.
Episcopal Church – The strange white cruciform building of this modern church, its arched roof rising from the center, stands out over the trees.

▶ Take the street that heads out opposite the Catholic Church and that runs along the buildings of the Hongan-ji temple. Then turn left and head down Nijukken-Zaka.

Higashi Hongan-ji ★ 東本願寺函館別院
🚶*Map, B2*. 16-15 Motomachi. 🕐*Open daily 7am–5pm.* 🎫*No charge.*
Of imposing proportions, Higashi Hongan-ji was built in the early 20C. It

© mantaphoto/iStock

is the first reinforced concrete temple to be built in Japan; hence the impressive size of its tiled roof. The interior remains rather traditional, with an especially beautiful coffered ceiling.

Nearby, you can see a German-style half-timbered house; it is home to a butcher's shop making delicious Carl Raymon sausages. They recall once again the Western presence in Hakodate.

MOUNT HAKODATE★ 函館山

Map, A2. 19-7 Motomachi. Cable car: open daily: late Apr–late Oct 10am–10pm; late Oct–late Apr 10am–9pm. One way ¥1000 (children ¥500), round trip ¥1500 (children ¥700). 334.co.jp/eng. 0138-23-3105.

Symbol of the city, Mount Hakodate culminates at an altitude of about 1000ft/334m, advancing majestically into the Tsugaru strait. Originally volcanic, the sea has beaten its black rock to form tall cliffs shrouded in rich vegetation. Numerous walking paths crisscross it, offering beautiful **views**. The Senjojiki plateau is best to enjoy these wild seascapes. The cable car takes you quickly to the mountaintop, from where there is an extraordinary **panoramic view★★★** of Hakodate, lovely by day or night. Though it can get crowded, in 2009 it was rated as the favorite tourist destination among Japanese travelers, ranking before even Kyoto.

Yunokawa Onsen 湯の川温泉

Map, C2; off map. Tramway, Yunokawa Onsen stop. hakodate-yunokawa.jp.

A spa district is developing to the west of the city, with numerous hotels and Japanese baths. There is a good **view** of Mount Hakodate from the beach. At night in the open sea, the lights of fishing boats track down squid drifting through the water.

Miharashi-koen★ 見晴公園

Map, C1; off map. Miharashi Koen-dori. 0138-57-7210.

This park on the heights was created by the Iwafune family at the end of the Meiji era. The only large park of its type on the whole island of Hokkaido, it is magnificent, especially in spring and in fall, a favorite with amateur photographers. The former summer pavilion is a beautiful wooden construction, set in a little Japanese garden.

Trappistine Convent トラピスチヌ修道院

Map, C1; off map. 346 Kamiyunokawa-cho. Bus from the station or Yunokawa tramway terminus, Trappistine Iriguchi stop, then 10min walk. Access to park and museum only. Open Thu–Tue: late Apr–Oct 8am–5pm; Nov–late Apr 8am–4.30pm. No charge. 0138-57-3331. ocso-tenshien.jp.

Founded by eight French Trappists in 1898, this convent is now home to about 60 nuns. The brick buildings are not especially interesting, but the statue of Archangel St. Michael and the re-created Lourdes cave, in the park, are quite pretty, and interesting to see in a Japanese context. There is also a lovely **view** of the city and its surroundings, and a small museum about the Cistercian Order.

EXCURSIONS
Kameda Peninsula 亀田半島

Map, C2; off map.

Kameda Peninsula offers superb landscapes. Route 278 runs along the ocean and leads to **Mount Esan**, a volcano still active; its base is covered with azaleas in springtime. **Cape Esan**, turned into a park, overlooks the sea. The road then heads through the verdure toward Mina-mikayabe, then Ofune, both important sites in Jomon civilization. In Ofune, the **archaeological museum** exhibits many objects unearthed at archaeological digs (open late Apr–mid-Nov daily 9am–5pm; ¥300). From Shikabe, you reach **Lake Onuma★**.

The grim mass of the Komagatake vol-cano dominates the beautiful landscape. The area around the lake has plenty of **sports activities**, from skiing to hiking to golf, while the lake itself is dotted with 126 lislands. Farther south, **Nanae** is a ski area with a marvelous view of Hakodate.

Matsumae 松前

 Map, C1; off map. Bus directly from Hakodate Station.

This pretty little town was the first in Hokkaido to welcome a clan from Hon-shu, the Matsumae feudal lords who bestowed their name on the place in 1604. It has numerous parks, their paths edged with over 10,000 **cherry trees**. The **castle** (open mid-Apr–mid-Dec daily 9am–5pm; ¥360)stands out, with its two-story keep. Rebuilt in 1854, it was again rebuilt in 1949, following a fire. It is home to an interesting **his-tory museum**. You can also visit **Mat-sumaehan Yashiki** (open Apr–Oct daily 9am–5pm; ¥360), a re-created Edo-period village, as well as the **tem-ple district**, which contains 55 graves of members of the Matsumae clan.

ADDRESSES

🛏 STAY

 Hakodate Danshaku Club Hotel & Resort Hakodate 男爵倶楽部ホテル&リゾーツ – 22-10 Otemachi (Map, C1) 0138-21-1111. danshaku-club.com. 52 rooms. ¥15,500. ¥1650 .Next to the fish market; high-tech, design-led rooms.

 La Vista Hakodate Bay ラビスタ函館ベイ – 12-6 Toyokawa (Map, C2). 0138-23-6111. hotespa.net/hotels/lahakodate/. 350 rooms. ¥22,000. .Right

in the center of town. Beautiful modern rooms and a lovely view.

 Wakamatsu 割烹旅館 若松 – 1-2-27 Yunokawa (C2, off map). 0138-59-2171. wakamatsuryokan.com/hakodate. 24 rooms. ¥30,000. ¥3800 . A very beautiful hotel in traditional *ryokan* style. A nice view of the sea and Mount Hakodate.

🍴 EAT

Hakodate is known for its seafood and fish. The squid *(ika)* is prepared in many different ways, including in thin slices as sushi. Ramen is another specialty. You'll find a great many restaurants in the lively old docks district, and around the station. The Motomachi district, on the other hand, is pretty quiet.

 Fish Market 函館朝市 – (Map, C1). . You can enjoy fish specialties here from 5am that are easy on the wallet, if you feel so inclined. Try especially the *kaisen-don*, a bowl of rice topped with fish.

 Lucky Pierrot ラッキーピエロ – 23-18 Suehiro-cho (Map, B2). 0138-26-2099. luckypierrot.jp/en. Open Mon–Fri & Sun 10am–12.30am, Sat 10am–1.30am. Menu in English. . Japanese fast food chain. Varied, generous hamburgers at unbeatable prices, albeit in slightly alarming clown-themed surroundings.

 Daimon Yokocho 大門横丁 – 7 Matsukaze-cho (Map, C1). hakodate-yatai.com. Hours vary; usually open 5pm–midnight, some restaurants at lunchtime in season. 0138-24-0033. hakodate-yatai.com. . This small district has built up around two narrow pedestrian streets, with about 30 restaurants with outside seating. You can have your pick of sushi, *yakitori*, ramen, tempura, etc.

 Kurobe くろ兵衛 – 8-23 Wakamatsu-cho (Map, C1). 0138-22-7147. Open Mon–Fri 5pm–1am. Grilled chicken, in every possible form, in a lively and friendly setting.

 Asari Honten 阿さ利本店 – 10-11 Hourai-cho (Map, C2). 0138-23-0421. Open Thur–Tue 11am–9.30pm. Menu in English. In an old house near the religious buildings quarter and the departure point for the cable car *(about 650yd/600m)*. You will be welcomed in small rooms, where you will be served *sukiyaki*, a delicious dish of thin slices of beef dipped in egg yolk, served with vegetables.

Akan-Mashu National Park ★★
阿寒摩周国立公園

With its volcanoes, mountain lakes with clear waters and hot springs, Akan-Mashu National Park offers tourists magnificent excursions. With the wide, open skies and immense horizons, no matter the time of year, the beauty of the landscapes is always impressive. Nature here is completely unspoilt: night skies sparkle with a thousand stars, cranes skim across the heavens and bears are never far away, as is indicated by the numerous forest signs warning walkers out for a stroll!

SIGHTS

Akan Park extends over 222,395 acres/90,000ha. It can be divided into two sections – the east, around the lakes of Kussharo and Mashu, and the west, around Lake Akan. Established in 1934, it has a remarkable ecosystem, with numerous deer and foxes, and all kinds of conifers, while the icy waters of the lakes are full of fish. Along with areas of forest and grassland, there are wild flowers and azaleas whose perfume is pronounced in spring.

Lake Kussharo★★ 屈斜路湖
35mi/57km in circumference, the largest lake on the island of Hokkaido is also the second-largest in Japan; it lies in a former gigantic crater. Its maximum depth reaches 387ft/118m; the center is occupied by the immense island of Nakajima, (about 7.5mi/12km in circumference), the den of a local monster called Kusshi. His silhouette, which strangely enough recalls that of the Scottish "Nessie", can be seen on the beach at Sunayu to the delight of both children and adults.

Kawayu Onsen★ 川湯温泉
This major spa resort, a bit off the beaten track, is a good base for exploring the lakeshore. There are numerous paths accessible from the Tourist Office or from the **museum** devoted to

- **Michelin Map:** Regions of Japan Map 6, Regional Map p513, National Park Map 542.
- **Location:** Akan is located southwest of Hokkaido and about 248mi/400km from Sapporo.
- **Kids:** A fishing trip at Lake Akan; or to the Akan International Crane Center to see hundreds of these beautiful Japanese birds in flight.
- **Timing:** Give yourself about three days.
- **Don't miss:** Akan Lake and the climb up the volcanoes; the Akankohan and Kawayu Onsen; the panoramic views of Lake Mashu.

sumo wrestler **Taiho Koki** that weave between the wisps of steam in a pretty, wooded environment. There are a good many *ashiyu* (hot foot baths) found regularly along the way.

Sunayu 砂湯
This popular beach has one interesting characteristic: if you dig into the sand, hot water springs forth! There is also a beautiful **view★** of the lake from the old wooden jetty here.

Wakoto Peninsula★★ 和琴半島
Accessible by foot, bike or car, it's worth going out of your way to visit the *onsen* here: a basin simply dug and set into the shore of the lake. It's especially magical in winter, when you can contemplate the frozen lake among wisps of steam rising around you. The water in the basin is very hot, but a bit nearer to the lake the water is closer to warm as it mixes. To warm up or just to relax, you can then take the footpath running 1.5mi/2.5km along the point.

USEFUL INFORMATION

Akan Tourist Office – 2-6-20 Akan-ko Onsen. ℘0154-67-3200. en.kushiro-lakeakan.com. Open daily 9am–6pm. Information in English, maps for hiking, activity programs, etc., and on hiring bikes, canoes, etc.

Akan Nature Center organizes excursions all year round to the volcanoes and lakes *(frozen in winter)*. Reservation required. 5-3-3, Akan-ko Onsen. ℘0154-67-2801. akan.co.jp. *Open daily Jan–Mar & May–Oct daily 8am–8pm.*

Kawayu Onsen Tourist Office, 2-3-40, *Kawayu Onsen.* ℘0154-83-2670. Open Tue–Sun 9am–9pm.

TRANSPORTATION

BY PLANE – The quickest way to Akan-Mashu National Park is to fly to **Kushiro Airport** *(kushiro-airport.co.jp)*, which is the closest to Akan-kohan. Regular flights from Sapporo *(45min)* and Tokyo *(1hr35min)*. **Memanbetsu Airport** is also a possibility *(see Transportation, Shiretoko National Park p527)*.

GETTING AROUND AKAN

BY BUS, THEN TRAIN – From Memanbetsu Airport, take the bus to Abashiri center, just over 0.5mi/1km from the JR train station. Trains leave from there for Kushiro toward the south, via Shiretoko Shari *(45min)* and serve Kawayu Onsen *(45min)*, Biruwa and Mashu *(around 20min)*.

BY BUS – From Kushiro (station and airport), the Akan travel company offers day trips by bus to the Akan lakes, Mashan and Kussharo (several trips possible, depending on the season) as well as regular buses. *(Kushiro Station to Lake Akan 2hr, ¥2750 one way; uu-hokkaido.com/corporate/akanbus.shtml#rosen)*.

CAR RENTAL – www.nipponrentacar.co.jp and nissan-rentacar.com.

An alternative *onsen*, also right on the lake and slightly less touristed, is just east around the lake at **Kotan Onsen** (*kotan* means village in Ainu, as this is an Ainu settlement).

Mount Iou★ 硫黄山

The road between Kawayu Onsen and the train station crosses vast extents of moors spotted here and there with azaleas; it runs alongside the mountain continually shrouded in the mist. It then comes to Mount Iou, a fair-sized volcano *(1883ft/574m)*, which they say sleepswith one eye open. The Ainu call it Atosanu-puri, the "naked mountain". Beyond the parking lot, the earth is white, encrusted with yellow and blue sediments amid the roiling clouds of vapor and small geysers of boiling water. The strong odor of sulfur smells like nothing so much as rotten eggs. It's fascinating to see the effects on the landscape: normal plant growth stops abruptly where the sulfurous steam rolls over the ground.

 Access is regulated and you should not to go beyond the safety barriers.

 Now continue on Route 52, which gradually zigzags its way up to Lake Mashu.

Lake Mashu★★★ 摩周湖

This lake, overlooked by Mount Mashu, occupies the crater of a volcano. Of a circumference of 12mi/20km and a total depth over 656ft/200m, it makes a strong impression with its stark slopes dropping almost straight down to the clear waters. The lake's color is so particular that you'll find products all over attempting to replicate "Mashu blue."
It is not possible to go all the way around the rim of te lake, in order to protect its delicate ecosystem, but there are three observation towers from which you can admire its beauty.

The first, **observation tower no. 3★★**, offers a **view** made even more beautiful by the fact that it is possible to see

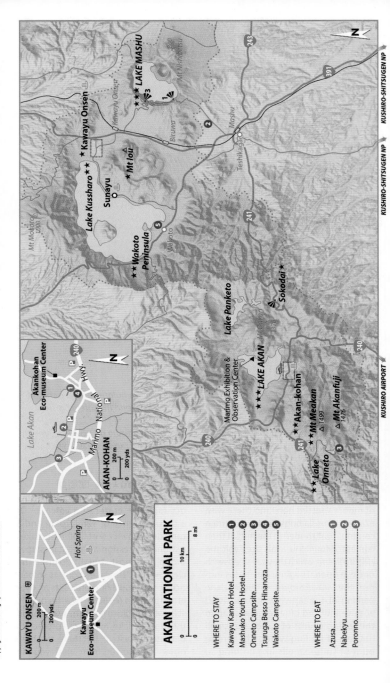

Copyright 2015 Cartographic data Shobunsha/Michelin

542

KAWAYU ONSEN
Kawayu Eco-museum Center
Hot Spring
N
0   200 m
0   200 yds

AKAN-KOHAN
Lake Akan
Akankohan Eco-museum Center
Marimo National
N
0   200 m
0   200 yds

AKAN NATIONAL PARK
0   10 km
0   8 ml
N

LAKE MASHU ★★★
★ Kawayu Onsen
Kawayu Onsen
Mt Nishibetsu
Mashu
243
391
Mt Iou ★
Lake Kussharo ★★
Sunayu
Wakoto Peninsula ★★
Mt Motokoi 1000
Teshikaga
Bihoro
240
241
Lake Panketo
Sokodai ★
Marimo Exhibition & Observation Center
LAKE AKAN ★★★
Akan-kohan ★★
Mt Meakan ★★
△ 1499
△ Mt Akanfuji 1476
Lake Onneto ★★
240
241
240

KUSHIRO-SHITSUGEN NP
KUSHIRO-SHITSUGEN NP
KUSHIRO-SHITSUGEN NP
KUSHIRO AIRPORT

WHERE TO STAY
Kawayu Kanko Hotel..............❶
Mashuko Youth Hostel............❷
Onneto Campsite.....................❸
Tsuruga Besso Hinanoza.........❹
Wakoto Campsite....................❺

WHERE TO EAT
Azusa.......................................❶
Nabekyu...................................❷
Poronno....................................❸

Lake Mashu in summer

the sea in the distance. Next best is **observation tower no. 1★★**, where the birds'-eye **view** onto the lake is impressive. It is only regrettable that the place is so popular, and packed with souvenir shops and restaurants.

▶ Head back down to Mashu Onsen and take Route 241 to Akan, which gradually rises through the forest.

At **Sokodai★** *(parking lot with toilets, to the left of the road by taking a path that heads upward)* there is a wonderful **view** of Lake Panketo. As you drive along the weaving roads you will catch sight of the imposing mass of **Mount Akan**, and in the distance, **Mount Meakan**.

Lake Akan★★★ 阿寒湖
Dominated by the haughty mass of the volcano, you'll find here magnificent flora and fauna, and experience absolutely unforgettable walks. To make it a little easier to get across the lake's 16mi/26km circumference, numerous boats leave from Akan Onsen so that you can discover the treasures the area has to offer. Serious nature lovers can go fly-fishing along the banks, the waters of the lake not being too deep.

Akan-kohan★★ 阿寒湖畔 – The pleasant spa resort of **Akanko Onsen** (阿寒湖温泉) is home to many hotels and auberges, some of them with rather

high standing, and all in the wooded setting of the lakeside. Visitors will either be attracted or aggravated by the extremely tourist-oriented nature of the place, although it must be admitted it brings a certain liveliness. Once again, there are a great many **footpaths** along the streets of the small town.

🐾 **The lakeside★** – There is a track that takes you around the lake, making for a very pleasant walk at sunrise. Beyond the landing stage, you can take the park's natural paths to discover numerous hot springs. You will also see a great many animals such as squirrels and birds in their natural habitat.

Eco-museum★ – 1-1 Akanko Onsen. 🕐 *Open Wed–Mon 9am–5pm.* 🎫 *No charge.* 📞*0154-67-4100. business4.plala. or.jp/akan-eco.* The floor of this museum reproduces an aerial view of the region. The modern and educational presentation shows the various interesting animal species living in Akan.

Maeda Ippoen Foundation – Near the museum, a lovely chalet-like stone house with a 1950s design is home to the Maeda Ippoen Foundation. This important dignitary of the Meiji era, who loved Akan deeply, passed that love of the forest onto his family. His daughter-in-law, Mitsuko, established the foundation in 1983. She manages close to 16sq mi/4000ha of the forest, especially the west bank of the lake, with a view to restoring the forests the way they were three centuries ago. A great deal of planting has been done, especially to reestablish the balance between conifers and leafy trees. Mitsuko also aims to protect the trees from the deer fond of nibbling on the bark.

Akanko Ainu Kotan★ – ⏱*Open daily 10am–9pm;* ✏*¥500, or ¥1100 with performance; akanainu.jp/en.* This Ainu village lies at the end of a large street of shops with about 36 homes, containing about 200 people. It has the look of a large sloped square surrounded by souvenir shops and restaurants. Tall totems stand at the center. At the high end of the village, the large communal house, *onne-chisse*, offers **performances**. In the back, it also has an arena for night performances to close the Ainu market.

Boating excursion on the lake★★ – Generally ⏱*open mid-Apr–Nov, daily 6am–5pm in season; around* ✏*¥2000/1hr 15min boat trip; akankisen.com/_eng.* Pleasant cruises make it possible to visit the island of Churu; there is a small aquarium there with algae shaped like balls, called *marimo*.

Climb up Mount Akan – The boat can also make a stop at the landing stage, the departure point for a strenuous climb *(count on about 5hr 30min to head up and a good 2hr to come back down).* From the summit (4495ft/1370m) there is a beautiful **panoramic view★★** of the lake and the mountains toward Mount Akan.

Lake Onneto★★ オンネトー湖 – Baptized the "lake of five colors", Onneto lies in a landscape of great beauty, edged with fir trees and overlooked by the smoking shape of Mount Meakan. A signposted path runs along its eastern edge. After about 50min you will come to the **Yunotakia Falls★** *(164ft/ 50m high),* the waters are at a temperature of about 110°F. A basin has been dug and arranged so as to make it possible to bathe there.

Mount Meakan★★ 雌阿寒岳 – ⟋🐾 This young volcano, only about 20,000 years old, produces gas eruptions, the last one being in 1959. Around 2000 years ago a second crater, Mount Akanfuji, grafted itself onto the southern side of the mountain. There are two paths leading to the summit. The first one, which you will encounter coming from Akan, after Nonaka Onsen, is easier; it takes about 2hr. The other path, at the far end of the lake, can take up to 3hr. At an altitude of 4918ft/1499m, the **view** from the top is splendid. The volcano still being active, it would be foolhardy to go into the crater. You can then retrace your steps or head back down to Akan-kohan, which takes about 3hr.

KUSHIRO AREA
Tsurui Ito Tancho Sanctuary
⏱*Open Oct–Mar Thur–Mon 9am–4pm.* ✏*No charge. wbsj.org/en/tsurui.*
Heading in the direction of Kushiro and its airport, Route 240 gradually heads downward into a large cultivated valley. This area is part of **Kushiro Shitsugen National Park**, a wetland preserved in part for conservation of the **Red-crowned cranes (tancho)**, found in the area. A special center has been created here to help Japanese cranes find food in the winter. The show the birds put on in the snow *(Nov–Mar),* battling sometimes with eagles to save their food, is quite spectacular. Many amateur photographers come here to see the performance.

Akan International Crane Center 阿寒国際ツルセンター
23-40 Kamiakan, Kushiro. ⏱*Open daily 9am–5pm; observation center Nov–Mar.* ✏*¥470. aiccgrus.wixsite.com/aiccgru.*
You can find out everything you ever wanted to know about Japanese cranes in this information facility, with an attached breeding center and winter feeding ground.

Kushiro 釧路
The town of Kushiro has a pleasant, modern port with many facilities. In the surrounding national park is an immense marshland sheltering some 2000 spe-

cies of plants and animals. There are a number of lookouts and observatories; the closest to Kushiro is Hosooka *(20min by train from Kushiro on the JR Semmo Line to Kushiro Shitsugen, then a 10min walk).*

ADDRESSES

🏨 STAY

AKAN

🛏 **Onneto Campsite** オンネトー国設野営場 – *Moashoro, Ashoro-cho.* ☎0156-25-2141. *Open Jun–end Oct. 10 pitches. ¥400 per person.* 🚻. Although the standard is fairly basic, this is a good, peaceful site, somewhere you can immerse yourself in nature and maybe see some wild animals. Ask at the Toust Office about booking. *Onsen* on site (**admission charge**). Out of season, bears may visit, so take usual precautions about food storage etc.

🛏🛏🛏🛏 **Tsuruga Besso Hinanoza** 鶴雅別荘鄙の座 – *2-8-1 Akanko Onsen, Akan-cho.* ☎0514-67-5500. www.hinanoza.com/en. *25 rooms. ¥80,000.* 🍽, *dinner also included.* This magnificent *ryokan*-like hotel is a unique experience. There's a wonderful view of lake from the rooms, the restaurant is superb, and the bar is very welcoming. Some suites have a Japanese bath outside but there is also an open-air *onsen* on the top floor. A unique and unforgettable experience.

KUSSHARO

🛏 **Wakoto Campsite** 和琴半島湖畔キャンプ場 – *Wakoto-hanto, Kussharo-ko.* ☎015-484-2835 (in season), 015-483-2567 (out of season). en.bes.or.jp/branches/kawayu. *Open late Apr–mid Oct. From ¥1000 per person.* 🚻. On the shores of Lake Kussharo, facing Mount Wakoto, an ideally located campsite with interior and exterior *onsen* (no charge).

🛏 **Mashuko Youth Hostel** 摩周湖ユースホステル – *883 Teshikaga-genya, Teshikaga- cho.* ☎0154-82-3098. youthhostel.or.jp/mashu. *¥4500 per person.* 🚻. A very pleasant youth hostel near Mashuko and the lake.

🛏🛏 **Kawayu Kanko Hotel** 川湯観光ホテル –*1-2-30 Kawayu Onsen, Teshikaga-cho.* ☎015-483-2121. iionsen.com/en/. *67 rooms. ¥10,600.* 🍽. A lovely traditional hotel, with a very Japanese ambiance, in the heart of Kawayu Onsen.

🍴 EAT

AKAN-KOHAN

🍽🍽 **Pan de Pan** パンデパン *1-6-6, Akanko Onsen.* ☎0154-67-4188. tsurugasp.com/akan-pandepan. *Open daily 8.30am–6pm; closed 1st & 3rd Wed each month.* European-inspired snacks, pastries and hot chocolate in this tearoom in a lively, colorful setting.

🍽🍽 **Nabekyu** 奈辺久 – *4-4-1 Akanko Onsen.* ☎0154-67-2607. *Open daily 11am–3pm & 6–8pm. Menu in English.* Restaurant offering good fish specialties, excellent tempura served on rice (ten-don), and generous servings.

🍽🍽 **Azusa** あずさ – *1-6-8 Akanko Onsen.* ☎0154-67-2474. *Open daily 11.30am–9pm. Menu in English.* For a quick and economical dinner; mostly meat dishes, though the menu also features the unusual "Marimo" ramen, topped with a type of sea plant.

🍽🍽 **Poronno** ポロンノ – *4-7-8 Akan-kohan Onsen.* ☎0154-67-2159. poronno.com. *Open daily: May–Oct noon–3pm & 6.30–9.30pm; Nov–Apr 12.30–8.30pm. Menu in English. Reservations required in winter.* Discover Ainu specialties, such as delicious, spicy *yukku* curry, served with plenty of vegetables.

ACTIVITIES/FESTIVALS

Boat trips – **Akan Sightseeing Cruise Company** 阿寒観光汽船 *1-5-20 Akanko Onsen.* ☎0154-67-2511. akankisen.com/_eng/index.html. Tour of the lake with a stop on the island to visit the *marimo* observation center. Ferries (1hr 25min, ¥2000, children ¥1040). Motorboat rentals, small hovercraft *(price varies by course).*

Procession – **Torch procession** イオマンテの火祭り nightly with **Ainu songs and dances**. Depart 8.20pm from Marimukan parking lot to Ainu village. Performance in the open-air theater *(Sept 1–Nov 30; adults ¥1100; children no charge).*

Festival – 3 days in early October, the Ainu hold the colorful **Marimo Matsuri** まりも祭り celebrating the spherical green algae clusters found in the lakes, a symbol of Hokkaido that you will find in all the souvenir shops.

SHIKOKU

Smallest and least populated of the four main Japanese islands, Shikoku was divided into four provinces—hence its name: *shi* (four) and *koku* (lands)—which became Ehime (Matsuyama), Kagawa (Takamatsu), Tokushima, and Kochi prefectures. For centuries, difficult accessibility kept it off the great trade routes of the Inland Sea reaching out to China and Korea, though its rich nature and important pilgrimage route attracted travelers to its forested mountains, rugged coastline and bubbling hot springs.

Highlights

1 Lounging on a secluded beach on sleepy **Hon-jima** (p558)
2 A dip at **Dogo Onsen**, one of the oldest in Japan (p561)
3 Exploring **Nao-shima**, and its art galleries and installations (p554)
4 Kayaking down the **Oboke Gorge** in the Iya Valley (p566)
5 Browsing for fresh produce and local crafts at **Kochi Market** (p574)

Shikoku Today

Shikoku is linked to the main island of Honshu by a system of three long bridges mostly used by those taking buses along the old Shikoku Temple Pilgrimage route, in the footsteps of Buddhist sage Kobo Daishi (774–835). Somewhat neglected, this still relatively unspoilt island hides quaint temples and villages, beautiful verdant mountains, and rice paddies.

▶ **Population:** 3,721,200 – Ehime, Kagawa, Tokushima, and Kochi Prefectures.

◔ **Michelin Map:** Regions of Japan Map 7, Regional Map & Inland Sea opposite.

◗ **Location:** South of Honshu and east of Kyushu, Shikoku covers 7,258.7sq mi/18,800sq km. The island's highest peak is Mount Ishizuchi *(6503ft/1982m)* in Ehime prefecture. The rail network has three main lines: the JR Yosan Line (leaving Okayama to run west along the coast from Takamatsu to Matsuyama), the JR Dosan Line (transversing the island from Takamatsu to Kochi via Oboke), and the JR Kotoku Line (along the eastern coastline from Takamatsu to Tokushima).

👫 **Kids:** Head for the Pacific coast, with Katsurahama Beach and Kochi whale-watching cruises.

🕐 **Timing:** About 3 days in Matsuyama and Takamatsu; a week for the complete Takamatsu–Kotohira–Iya Valley–Kochi–Cape Ashizuri–Uchiko–Matsuyama tour.

🅰 **Don't miss:** Dogo Onsen in Matsuyama; Ritsurin-koen garden at Takamatsu; the Iya Valley countryside; the Cape Ashizuri cliffs; the art islands of the Inland Sea.

Iya Kazura-bashi, Iya Valley, Tokushima

© okimo/iStock

HIROSHIMA · ONOMICHI

SHIKOKU

4

0   40 km
0   20 mi

Inland Sea

Shimanami-kaido · Takamatsu · Hon-jima

Sadamisaki Peninsula

Imabari

Matsuyama · Dogo Onsen

Marugame · Noguchi Garden Museum

Tadotsu · Shodo-shima

Yawatahama · Ozu

Niihama

Uchiko

Kotohira · Shikoku-mura

Mt Ishizuchi 1982 △

KAGAWA

Uwajima

EHIME

Oboke

Awa Ikeda

Naruto

Niyodo

Iya Valley · Tokushima

Shimanto-gawa

Kochi

Yoshino

Iya

KOCHI

TOKUSHIMA

Naka

Nakamura

Tosa Bay

Katsurahama

Hiwasa

Sukumo

Monet-Marmottan Garden

Tosa-Shimizu

Ashizuri-misaki

Muroto-misaki ▲ · Muroto

N

PACIFIC OCEAN

NARUTO WHIRLPOOLS, NAO-SHIMA, KOBE, OSAKA

Matsuyama	★★	Worth a detour
Takamatsu	★	Interesting
Hon-jima		Worth seeing

OKAYAMA

Kurashiki

Shinokayama

Hoden

INLAND SEA

4

Inu-jima

0   10 km
0   6 mi

HONSHU

Shodo-shima

N

OKAYAMA

Te-shima

Tonosho

Kankakei Gorge
777 △

HIROSHIMA, FUKUYAMA

Kojima

Uno

Miyanoura

Ieura · Karato

Ikeda · Kusakabe

Honmura

KOBE, OSAKA

Nao-shima

Seto Ohashi

Hon-jima

SHIKOKU

KAGAWA

7

Takamatsu

MARUGAME

A

B

Nao-shima	★★	Worth a detour
Te-shima	★	Interesting
Shodo-shima		Worth seeing

It also offers many leisure pursuits: hiking, rafting, bathing, ocean boating trips, etc. The steep mountains inland are among western Japan's highest, stretching east to west to separate Shikoku in two. A narrow coastline northward edged by the Inland Sea (*Seto Naikai*) has long been the most populated, developed part of the island; its main towns are Takamatsu eastward and Matsuyama to the west.

The Inland Sea's peaceful, sunny shores and mild climate are ideal for growing olives, peaches, and citrus fruits right across the scattering of small islands here, which nowadays are better known for their modern art exhibitions.

Rain is much more prevalent in the south, where the Pacific's waters are warm and fish abundant. While the coast is often struck by typhoons, vegetation is lushly subtropical with bamboo, banyans, camellias, and palm trees. There are only a few isolated fishing villages, meaning the natural environment has been preserved along the coast, where promontories carve out delightful bays.

Takamatsu★
高松

The main access port to the island of Shikoku, Takamatsu is situated on the coast of the Inland Sea. Severely damaged by bombing during World War II, which destroyed the castle dating from the end of the 16C, this modern, industrialized town nevertheless managed to salvage its principal attraction, Ritsurin-koen, a magnificent stroll garden dating from the Edo era. An hour's train journey to the southwest, Kotohira Shrine is one of the most sacred in Japan.

SIGHTS

You can rent bicycles at the station to get around the town. Otherwise, take the local JR line trains or those of the Kotoden Line.

Ritsurin-koen★★★ 栗林公園

Map, A3. 1.6mi/2.5km south of JR Takamatsu Station (30min walk). Train to JR Ritsuin-koen-kitaguchi Station or Kotoden Risturin-koen Station. Bus nos. 9 or 10. Open daily: hours vary by season, between 5.30am–7pm (Jun–Aug) and 7am–5pm (Dec–Jan). ¥410. my-kagawa.jp/en/ritsurin.

Backing onto Mount Shiun-zan to the west, whose wooded peak forms a natural backdrop to the vista, this stroll garden *(kaiyu)* extends over an area of 39.5 acres/16ha *(185.3 acres/75ha, including the mountain)*. Designed in 1625 by Ikoma Takatoshi, the feudal lord of the province, it was enlarged and embellished over a period of 100 years until 1745, by five generations of the Matsudaira, who inherited the fiefdom.
Sandy paths wind their way among a string of ponds full of colored carp; small valleys alternate with low hills in an undulating landscape. Lakes are dotted with islands studded with strangely shaped rocks and artistically distorted black pines, whose twisted branches suggest dragons, or cranes in flight. The park contains some 160 types

- ▶ **Population:** 419,000 – Kagawa Prefecture.
- **Michelin Map:** Regions of Japan Map 7, Regional Map p547, Takamatsu Map p550.
- **Location:** Northeast of Shikoku in Kagawa Prefecture, 120mi/195km from Matsuyama and 100mi/160km from Kochi, Takamatsu is linked to Okayama by the Great Seto Bridge. The railway station is in the north, close to the port, and from there a busy thoroughfare, Chuo-dori, leads to the south as far as Ritsurin-koen. From the port, boats serve the islands of Nao-shima and Shoda-shima.
- **Timing:** One day is enough for a visit to Takamatsu. An extra day would allow you to explore the surrounding countryside and Kotohira or the islands.
- **Don't miss:** Ritsurin-koen; Konpira-san; the local specialty, *sanuki udon*.

of trees and flowers that change with the seasons: camellias, plum trees, and magnolias in winter; cherry trees, wisteria, and rhododendrons in spring; iris, lilies, and lotus in summer; desmodiums and maple trees in the Fall. This harmonious blend of panoramas, landscapes, and buildings is a masterpiece of the art of the Japanese garden.
Visit – Round trip *(1hr) leaving from the East Gate. Another possibility is to start from inside the North Gate.*
Just beyond the East Gate, to the right, the **Sanuki Folkcraft Museum** (*open Wed–Sun 8.30am–5pm; no charge*) contains displays of regional furniture and traditional craft items, including colored kites. Sanuki is the name of the ancient province that became Kagawa Prefecture. Next, take a left in front of

Engetsu-kyo, Ritsurin-koen

the Commerce and Industry Promotion Hall, toward the **South Garden** *(Nantei)*, which is the best preserved. Following the bank of the North Pond, you reach the **black pine path★★** *(Hako-matsu)*, a row of brooding trees with twisted branches like candlabras. Beyond a bridge *(to the right)*, is the **Higurashi-tei**, or "Pavilion of the Setting Sun," a thatched tea house dating from 1898. Farther along is the **Kikugetsu-tei★★**, the "Holding the Moon" tea house dating from 1640, where the lords of Matsudaira came to perform the Tea Ceremony and compose *haikus*. You can drink green tea here, served with a piece of candy. A tour of

Did you know?

The town of Takamatsu is one of the main centers for the cultivation of **bonsai trees** in Japan, particularly pines—it supplies 80 percent of Japan's pine bonsai. The main nurseries are at Kinashi, 3.7mi/6km south of the town center.

the South Lake enables you to admire the **Engetsu-kyo★**—an elegant, crescent-moon-shaped wooden bridge—reflected in the water. Finally, the **Hiraiho★** offers the best **view** over the park. The less

USEFUL INFORMATION

Tourist Office – At JR Takamatsu Station exit *(Map, A2)*. Open daily 9am–8pm. ☎087-826-0170. my-kagawa.jp/en.

TRANSPORTATION

BY AIR – Takamatsu Airport *takamatsu-airport.com/en*. 10.5mi/17km south of the JR station *(A3, off map)*. Flights for Tokyo *(Haneda Airport, 1hr 10min, about ¥34,500.*

BY BUS – Buses to JR station *(frequency depends on flights, 45min journey, ¥780)*.

BY TRAIN – **JR Takamatsu Station** *(Map, A2)* – To Okayama, JR Marine Liner *(55min, ¥1550)*; from Okayama, Shinkansen Nozomi to Shin-Osaka *(45min, ¥5610)*. For Matsuyama, Ltd. Express Ishizuchi *(2hr 30min, ¥5760)*. To Tokushima, Uzushio Ltd. Express, JR Kotoku Line *(1hr, ¥2670)*. 🚆 The **All Shikoku Rail Pass** is practical *(3–7 days, ¥9000 – 13,500)*.

BY BOAT – From Kansai, ferry links between Kobe and Wakayama and Tokushima. Various ferries serve the islands of the Inland Sea. For Naoshima *(🔖see p554)* and Shodo-shima *(🔖see p558)* from **Sunport Ferry** *(Map, A1)*, a 5min walk from JR Takamatsu Station, and link to Kobe in Kansai *(4hr, around ¥2000)*.

Copyright 2015 Cartographic data Shobunsha/Michelin

stylized **North Garden** (Hokutei) is set around two lakes: the **Fuyosho**, where lotus grows in profusion, and **Guno-chi** Pond where the lord used to hunt ducks.

Shikoku-mura★ 四国村

↻Map, C2. 3mi/5km east of the center of Takamatsu. 10min walk from JR Yashima Station (Shido Line) or 5min walk from Yashima-Kotoden Station. ◷Open Apr–Oct 8.30am–6pm; Nov–Mar 8.30am–5.30pm. ⊛¥1000. shikokumura.or.jp.

The volcanic plateau of **Yashima**, which rises to an altitude of 961ft/293m, was the site of a bloody battle that took place in 1185 between the Minamoto (or Genji) clan and the Taira (or Heike), ending in defeat for the latter. On a clear day there is a fine **view** of the islands of the Inland Sea from the plateau. The **open-air museum of Shikoku-mura** lies at its foot, where 33 village houses and ancient buildings have been reassembled from all over the island, including a delightful Kabuki theater

A Myriad of Islands

Many of the Inland Sea's islands are uninhabited, while others are well-known and rich with legend; **Megi-jima**, for example, the "island of ogres" off the Takamatsu coast, is supposedly where the little hero Momotaro slayed a demon. The landscape of **Shodo-shima** is reminiscent of the Mediterranean, with its olive groves and mock Greek temples. **Awaji-shima**, the largest island, on the Naruto Strait, between Shikoku and Kansai, is also of interest. *Ningyo joruri* puppet theater has been performed here for over 500 years and the island is also the main producer of incense, supplying 70 percent of the Japanese market. It is said this fragrant material was discovered accidentally in the 16C by Awaji fishermen. Having found pieces of dark wood in debris a storm washed ashore, they were amazed at the enchanting scent it gave off when burned. They proclaimed it a miracle, and took it to the emperor, thereby bringing about creation of the Japanese incense craft known today.

built by the peasants of Shodo-shima during the Edo era, various thatched huts where they squeezed the juice from sugar cane and broke down the bark of mulberry trees with steam to make paper *(washi)*, a mill, and houses occupied by lighthouse keepers. The museum also includes an exhibition room with a small indoor garden designed by the architect **Ando Tadao**.

Isamu Noguchi Garden Museum★
イサム・ノグチ庭園美術館
Map, C2. 5mi/8km east of the center of Takamatsu. 3519 Mure, Mure-cho. 10min by taxi from the JR station or Yashima-Kotoden Station. ℘087-870-1500. Access by guided tour (1hr) only; reserve at least 2 weeks ahead. Open Tue, Thur & Sat at 10am, 1pm, & 3pm. ¥2200. isamunoguchi.or.jp.
Talented American-Japanese sculptor and designer **Isamu Noguchi** (1904–88) divided his time between two studio-residences: one in New York and one situated here, at Mure, an area once inhabited by stone-cutters and now absorbed by the galloping urbanization of Takamatsu. The studio, formerly a sake brewery during the Edo era, contains various bronzes and stone sculptures. Other examples of his work, some of them unfinished, are scattered about the garden. Influenced by Brancusi as much as by the Zen spirit of the Japanese gardens, Noguchi carved

thick granite monoliths, contrasting rough and polished surfaces, and sharp angles with feminine curves. On a grassy incline, stones form a sacred circle around the sculptor's tomb, symbolized by a sculpture in the form of an egg.

EXCURSIONS
Regional Map, B1.

Kotohira★★ 琴平
18.5mi/30km southwest of Takamatsu. Access by train (1hr) on the JR Dosan (¥840) or Kotoden (¥620) lines, then 15min walk. town.kotohira.kagawa.jp.
The main attraction of this small town is the Kotohira-gu Shrine, more usually called **Konpira-san★★**, built at the top of the steep-sided Mount Zozu at a height of 1709ft/521m. It is dedicated to *kami* Omono-nushi, protector of sailors and fishermen. A famous place of worship since the 11C, it receives four million pilgrims every year. The entire complex was originally dedicated to Konpira Daigongen, a Shinto-Buddhist deity likened to Kunbhira, the crocodile god of the sacred waters of the Ganges. Following the separation of religions during the Meiji Restoration, in 1878 the shrine was rededicated solely to the Shinto divinity.
To reach the main temple, you must climb 785 stone steps. Shaded by cherry and other trees, the way is lined with stands selling candy, stone lanterns, and votive tablets. Just before the

top, be sure not to miss the **Shoin★★** (🕐 *open daily 8.30am–5pm;* 🎫 *¥800)*, the old reception hall, built in 1660, which houses a collection of fine *fusuma* painted by Maruyama Okyo (1733–95): tigers, herons, flowers, and birds, and Chinese sages in mountain landscapes. Climb a few steps higher to see the Shrine of the Rising Sun, **Asahi no Yashiro** (1837), dedicated to the goddess Amaterasu, which has finely sculpted roof timbers. More steps lead to the **Hongu**, the main hall, and to the **Ema-do★**, where there is an exhibition of marine objects, models of boats, and votive plaques. From there, the remaining 583 steps lead to the Okusha, the inner sanctuary.

Kanamaru-za★ – *At the foot of the hill.* 🕐 *Open daily 9am–5pm.* 🎫 *¥500.* During the Edo era, there were many theaters, markets, lotteries, and sumo contests to entertain the pilgrims. Built in 1835, the **Kabuki theater** is the oldest in Japan. Inside, go backstage to see the ingenious wooden mechanism used to rotate the scenery. Occasional performances are held during the season *(Apr–mid-May).*

Marugame   丸亀

18.5mi/30km west of Takamatsu. Access by train (25min) on the JR Yosan Line (🎫 *¥560)*. 🛈 *www.city.marugame.lg.jp.* This port *(population 110,000)* lies at the foot of one of the stretches of the Great Seto Bridge. South of the railway station, a 15min walk away, the **Marugame-jo** (🕐 *open 9am–4.30pm;* 🎫 *¥200)*, its castle built at the end of the 16C, is one of the rare examples to have retained its original wooden keep. This fan-shaped building sits on top of an artificial, 164ft/50m-high mound.
At the port, a 10min walk north of the station, the small **Uchiwa no Minato Museum** (🕐 *open Tue–Sun 9.30am–5pm;* 🎫 *no charge)* is dedicated to the traditional paper fans *(uchiwa)* that are manufactured in Marugame—the town produces 90 percent of the national production.

The Naruto Whirlpools
鳴門の渦潮

41mi/66 km southeast of Takamatsu in Tokushima prefecture. By train on the JR Kotoku or JR Naruto line (1hr 30min), then a bus for Narutokoen (25min).
This natural phenomenon occurring in the straits of Naruto between the islands of Shikoku and Awaji-shima is caused by the difference in level between the waters of the Inland Sea and the Pacific Ocean. Whirlpools form at every tide and can reach a diameter of 22 yards/20 m in spring and fall. There are several options if you would like to see them: you can either go to the glass viewing platform on Onaruto Bridge or leap aboard a boat *(20–30min round trip).*
Access via bridge (Uzu-no-michi promenade): 772-0053 Naruto Park, Naruto-cho. uzunomichi.jp/lang_en. 🕐 *Open daily 9am–6pm (Oct–Feb 5pm).* 🎫 *¥510. Boat trips (there are two companies operating from Tokushima port): Uzushio Kankosen (uzusio.com/en), departures every 35min, daily 9am–4.20pm; from* 🎫 *¥1800/person. Uzushio Kisen (uzushio-kisen.com/ en), departures every 30min, daily 8am– 4.30pm;* 🎫 *¥1600/person.*

Tokushima★★ 徳島
44mi/70 km southeast of Takamatsu. JR Kotoku line trains (1hr, 🎫 *¥2670) or a Kotoku express bus (1hr 30min, around* 🎫 *¥1750).* 🛈 *Tourist information office on the JR station, 6F;* 📞 *088-656-3303;city. tokushima.tokushima.jp;* 🕐 *open daily 10am–6pm.*
This large city *(population 270,000)* on the northeastern coast of the island is the capital of the eponymous prefecture. At the foot of Mount Bizan on the Yoshino River estuary, it is one of the principal entry ports for visitors to Shikoku, thanks to the Onaruto Bridge that links it to the main island of Honshu. It is famed for its great summer festival of Awa Odori and for being the departure point for an ancient pilgrimage route to 88 temples.

Awa Odori Kaikan – *15min walk from the JR station. 2-20 Shinmachibashi, on the 3F.* 🕐*Open daily 9am–5pm; for evening performance 8–9pm. Museum* 🎫*¥300 (day performances ¥800, evening ¥1000).* The exhibits include documents and objects recounting the history of the Awa Odori festival; the most interesting part is the performance at the end of the tour *(30min, only in Japanese)*. A cable car will whisk you from the same building to the summit of Mount Bizan (920ft/280m), from where you can admire the view over the city and along the coast *(🕐open daily: Apr–Oct 9am–9pm; Nov–Mar 9am–5.30pm;* 🎫*¥1020 round trip).*

Awa Jurobe Yashiki puppet theater – *184 Miyajima Motoura, Kawauchicho, Tokushima-shi. 20min by bus no. 7 from JR Tokushima Station, Jurobe Yashiki stop.* 🕐*Open daily: Sept–Jun 9.30am–5pm; Jul–Aug 9.30am–6pm. Performances in Japanese daily 11am & 2pm.* 🎫*¥410. joruri.info/jurobe/english.* Awa Ningyo Joruri is a style of theater originating from the area around the Inland Sea in the 17C. Each large puppet is operated by three people accompanied by a narrator and several musicians. The little museum describes the creation of the wooden puppets as well as the art of bringing them to life. These performances are very popular in the Tokushima region and were once a regular fixture in Shinto shrines.

Historic street, Mima City 美馬

Located 31 mi/50 km west of Tokushima, access via JR Tokushima Line, get off at Anabuki Station.
This 440-yd/400-m street in the Waki-machi district is lined with a beautifully preserved group of merchants' houses dating from the Edo and Meiji periods. An architectural oddity shared by all is the *udatsu* (firebreak) on the second floor. *Udatsu* gradually became symbols of wealth in a city that grew prospserous on the back of manufacturing and the indigo and silk trades. You can visit the residence of the Yoshida family, one of the richest in the city *(*🎫*¥500).*

ADDRESSES

🛏 STAY

🛏 **Takamatsu Hotel Sakika** 高松ホテルさきか – *6-9 Hyakken-cho (Map, A2).* ☎087-822-2111. www.netwave. or.jp/~nmimatsu/english/room.html. *21 rooms. ¥8400. ¥880*⊡.🚭. This simple, well-kept hotel offers the best value for money in town.

🛏 **Takamatsu Super Hotel Kin-en-kan** スーパーホテル高松禁煙館 – *1-4-12 Kanko-dori (Map, A2).* ☎087-833-9000. superhotel.co.jp/s_hotels/takamatsu. *68 rooms. ¥8640.*⊡. A typical business hotel, practical and comfortable, and entirely non-smoking. There's another Super Hotel in the shopping arcade *(1-1 Tamachi).*

🛏🛏 **Kiyomi Sanso Hanajukai** 喜代美山荘花樹海 – *3-5-10 Saiho Cho (A2, off map).* ☎087-861-5580. hanajyukai.jp/ akebono_en. *40 rooms. ¥17,300. ¥2420*⊡. A superb hotel built in a small wooded area. A panoramic guest lounge and great *onsen* provide unequaled views over Takamatsu Bay.

🛏🛏🛏 **Rihga Hotel Zest Takamatsu** リーガホテルゼスト高松 – *9-1 Furujin-machi (Map, A2).* ☎087-822-3501. *119 rooms.* rihga.com/kagawa. *¥23,300. ¥1750*⊡. A good central hotel, well kept and very comfortable, with 3 restaurants.

🍴 EAT

🍽 **Waraya Udon Restaurant** うどんのわら家 – *91 Yashima-nakamachi (Map, C2).* ☎087-843-3115. www.wara-ya.co.jp. *Open Mar–Nov daily 10am–7pm; Dec–Feb Mon–Fri 10am–7pm, Sat–Sun 10am–6.30pm.*🚭. A very popular and cheap country-style restaurant specializing in *sanuki udon*.

🍽🍽 **Tenkatsu Honten** 天勝本店 – *7-8 Hyogomachi (Map, A2).* ☎087-821-5380. tenkatsuhonten.jp. *Open Mon–Fri 11am–2pm & 4–10pm, Sat–Sun 11am–9pm. Menu in English.* This sushi and tempura restaurant has had an unrivaled reputation since 1866! The weekday lunche sets are great value.

🍽🍽🍽 **Alice in Takamatsu** アリスイン高松 – *2-1 Sunport (Map, A2).* ☎087-823-6088. aliceintakamatsu.com/restaurant. html. *Open 11.30am–3pm & 5.30–9.30pm. Menu in English.* In the tallest tower in Shikoku, this gastronomic restaurant with French-leaning cuisine "floats" above the beautiful blue of the Inland Sea.

The Inland Sea★★
瀬戸内海

Whether you think they resemble rocks strewn like confetti in the sea (Inu-jima) or a Japan in miniature (Shodo-shima), the thousand or so islands of the Inland Sea form a scattered sub-archipelago whose inhabitants make a living from fishing and farming in tiny villages. With a view to checking emigration from these hamlets, a 1980s philanthropist dreamt up a rejuvenation program for Nao-shima that would focus on art—and it worked! The project soon spread to the neighboring islands, which in turn filled up with works of art and museums with spectacular architecture. The islanders stayed, the green shoots of recovery reappeared in the paddy fields, and the tourists came in droves. Whether you visit on foot or by bike, you will encounter surprise after surprise as you observe and take part in island life.

SIGHTS
Inland Sea Map, p547.

NAO-SHIMA★★ 直島
The island has two ports, Miyanoura in the west (the main port) and Honmura in the east. From Takamatsu, ferries for Miyanoura (shikokukisen.com/en; 5–10 per day, 30–50min crossing, ✆¥520–1220 one way) and Honmura (1–2 per day, 30min, ✆¥1220). From Okayama, take the Seto Ohashi Line train to Chayamachi, then the Uno Line to Uno (50min, ✆¥600). The ferry terminal is opposite Uno Station. Ferries for Miyanoura (13 per day, 20min, ✆¥300) and Honmura (5 per day, 20min, ✆¥300). Nao-shima also has connections with Te-shima and Inu-jima.
This little island tucked away among a hundred others in the Inland Sea, half-way between Okayama and Takamatsu, Nao-shima *(3sq mi/8sq km, population 3100)* is a unique place. Today it blends

▶ **Location:** Regions of Japan Map 7, Inland Sea Map p547. The islands extend from Shikoku to Okayama. Access is mainly by boat (see each island description).

Kids: Enjoying the beaches; interacting with public art on Nao-shima.

🕓 **Timing:** This is a pleasant area to visit whatever the season, but be aware that boat links are less frequent in winter. You should try to spend at least a day on each island (a few hours for Inu-jima), but taking your time will allow you to appreciate island life. Avoid the often crowded weekends, when finding accommodation will be difficult.

☺ **Don't miss:** Crossing the islands by bike; the Art House Project and the museums designed by Ando Tadao on Nao-shima; Te-shima Art Museum; the rocks at Shodo-shima.

contemporary art with a well-conservenatural environment, combining the preservation of the past and avant-garde artistic enterprise.

Once a sleepy island of fishing villages, Nao-shima emerged from anonymity in 1992, when the Benesse Group chose it to establish a museum of contemporary art doubling as a hotel. The architect **Ando Tadao** was given the task of designing this highly original complex. Since then, the project has been enlarged, and the island has become very fashionable.

Your arrival at the little port of **Miyanoura** sets the tone, as you are welcomed by a large red Pumpkin sprung from the imagination of Yayoi Kusama before passing through the light and airy ferry terminal designed by SANAA. Once in

USEFUL INFORMATION
TOURIST OFFICES
Nao-shima Tourist Office – Miyanoura Port. *☎087-892-2299. naoshima.net/en. Open daily 8.30am–6pm.*

Te-shima Tourist Office – Ieura Port; left luggage facilities. *☎080-2850-7330. teshima-navi.jp/en. Open daily 8.30am–6pm.*

Shodo-shima Information Office – Tonosho port. *☎087-962-1666. www.town.shodoshima.lg.jp/en. Open daily 8am–6pm.* Information also available at Takamatsu Tourist Office (*see p549*).

TRANSPORTATION
The islands are accessible from Shikoku and the San'yo coast. See *benesse-artsite.jp/en/access* for updated information. Times and frequency vary by season.

GETTING AROUND THE ISLANDS
Cycling is good way to get around, also on foot, and by bus.

BY BICYCLE – **Nao-shima** – Allow 1–2hr to tour Nao-shima. There are several rental locations *(around ¥500/day; naoshima.net/en/access/rental)*.
Te-shima – Cycle rental at the piers of the two ports *(¥100 per hour; teshima-navi.jp/en/rental)*.
Shodo-shima – Bicycles and cars can be hired in Tonosho.
Hon-jima – Cycle rental at the pier.
BY BUS – **Nao-shima** – From the port, a regular bus tours the island, passing Honmura, the Benesse House, and the Chichu Art Museum *(¥100 per journey)*.
Te-shima – A regular bus service between the two ports *(¥200)*.
Inu-jima – No public transport, but the island is small and so is accessible on foot.
Shodo-shima – Buses serve the whole island, from the main port of Tonosho. 1-day pass *(¥1000)*, or 2-day pass *(¥1500)*.
TRIENNALE PASSPORT – This gives access to most of the sites for ¥4000–5000. Buy it from one of the information boothes/offices on each island or at Takamatsu and Uno ports.

---

the peaceful village, enter the **Naoshima Bath★** and take to the relaxing waters in fabulous surroundings (*open daily 1–9pm; ¥660; tattoos allowed*).

Benesse House★ ベネッセハウス
In the south of the island. Access by island shuttle bus, on foot, or by bicycle. Open 8am–9pm (last admission 8pm). ¥1050. benesse-artsite.jp.
The architect **Ando Tadao**, well known for his sober, minimalist concrete buildings has succeeded brilliantly in matching the museum's architecture with its natural environment. Nestling amid the vegetation, the various sections of the building hug the contours of the land, rising in stages, interspersed with greenery, to the top of a hill overlooking the sea. The works on display were all produced specially for these surroundings. They are not numerous, but all are shown in a way that enhances them, whether Bruce Nauman's neon lights blinking in the middle of a vast cylindrical space, Iannis Kounellis's wall of lead, Richard Long's stone and wood circles, or Yasuda Kan's monumental pebbles. What makes Benesse House so unique is that it is also a hotel, with rooms featuring contemporary works by artists such as Sol LeWitt, Thomas Ruff, Christo, and Keith Haring. A small monorail (for guests only) leads to the Oval, a structure in the center of which is an ornamental pond.

There are additional rooms in two annexes built in 2006, one of which has a restaurant and leads onto the beach. The grounds of the house are also dotted with installations. Notable among them is Kusama Yayoi's huge pumpkin, positioned on a jetty facing the sea like a child's toy forgotten by a giant.

Chichu Art Museum★
地中美術館

20min walk from Benesse House or by island shuttle bus. ◐Open Tue–Sun: Mar–Sept 10am–6pm; Oct–Feb 10am–5pm. ◉¥2100. ⌨. benesse-artsite.jp/en/art/chichu.html.

Buried beneath the slope of a hill overlooking the islands and former salt-marshes of the Inland Sea, the Chichu Museum, opened in 2004 and again the work of Ando Tadao, is an unsettling space. It houses only a small number of works, but they benefit from a very theatrical presentation, in which visitors are led on a journey that is sensory, intellectual, and emotional.

Along with the sequence of Monet Waterlilies are contemporary site-specific installations by James Turrell and Walter de Maria.

Lee Ufan Museum
李禹煥美術館

Access on foot from the Benesse House or by island shuttle bus. ◐Open Tue–Sun: Mar–Sept 10am–6pm; Oct–Feb 10am– 5pm. ◉¥1050. benesse-artsite.jp/en/art/lee-ufan.html

Ando Tadao has designed a stripped-down, bare concrete setting for Korean artist Lee Ufan's minimalist work (sculptures and paintings from the 1970s to the present day). A place of peace and meditation.

Art House Project★★
家プロジェクト

Honmura village. Access by bus, on foot, or by bicycle. ◐Open Tue–Sun 10am–4.30pm. ◉¥1050 for six installations, or ◉¥420 for one. Kinza site: ◐Open Thur–Sun 11am–1pm & 2–4pm. ◉¥520. Reservations required 2 days in advance for the Kinza site (𝄞087-892-3223). benesse-artsite.jp/en/art/arthouse.html.

A brochure in English, available in the village, lists the various sites to visit. Honmura, in the east of the island, had its time of glory in the 17C and 18C. Situated on the maritime trading route between the island of Shikoku and the ports on Honshu, the village became a pirate den, led by the Takahara family. There are still some fine traditional houses that can be seen from that time, in dark wood with heavy gray-tiled roofs. In 1998, in collaboration with the Benesse Foundation, the municipality began to renovate some of them to accommodate contemporary art installations. The temple **Minami-dera★**, for example, has been restored by James Turrell and provides an interesting visual experience for visitors, while **Kadoya**, more than 200 years old, accommodates the light installations of Miyajima Tatsuo.

Ando Museum – *Honmura village.*
Access by island shuttle bus, on foot or by bike. ◐Open Tue–Sun 10am–4.30pm. ◉¥520. benesse-artsite.jp/en/art/ando-museum.html. The museum, which has been incorporated into a traditional house built a century ago, is a harmonious combination of traditional materials and Ando Tadao's trademark concrete slabs. The exhibits on display examine the works of Ando Tadao and the history of Naoshima Island.

Te-shima★ 豊島

East of Nao-shima. Access via two ports: Ieura (the main port) and Karato.
Take a ferry to Ieura from Takamatsu, (shikokukisen.com/en; 4–5 ferries per day, 35min crossing, ◉¥1330). Access from Uno (see Nao-shima): the ferries to Shodo-shima (◐see p558) stop off at the two ports: Ieura (40min, ◉¥780) and Karato (1hr, ◉¥1050). Boat for passengers for Ieura only (25min, same fare). Also regular departures for passengers bound for Inujima and Nao-shima (Miyanoura 20min, ◉¥300, and, less frequently, Honmura).

This pretty island of hills, beaches, and forests is increasingly popular with those who have been charmed by Nao-shima and wish to extend their enjoyment. Ieura and Karato, the two main ports, and the road between them are all enlivened by a few artworks, some of them temporary. The best approach is to arrive at one port and leave from the other, linking the two by bus, on foot, or by bike (watch out for the hills).

Betting On Contemporary Art

Launched by the president of the Benesse correspondence and education publishing group, Nao-shima's revitalization through contemporary art project has been so successful that it's now extending to the other islands of the Inland Sea. In 2010 (Jul–Oct) the first **Setouchi International Art Festival** was held, and by now this **Setouchi Triennale** is a firm fixture. Its first year featured 75 international artists (including Christian Boltanski, Mariko Mori, and Olafur Eliasson), who were called upon to create projects on the seven islands (Nao-shima, Te-shima, Megi-jima, Ogi-jima, Shodo-shima, O-shima, Inu-jima, and Takamatsu Port). The project is evolving constantly, with each year (2019, 2022, erc.) bringing something new and surprising. The 2013 festival, for example, took place on twelve islands, making one of its key focuses the involvement of the local inhabitants, in order to highlight their cultural heritage. While some of the exhibits are temporary, many pieces have been left in situ, enriching the islands for years after their installation. *Further information at setouchi-artfest.jp.*

Teshima Yokoo House★ – *Ieura.* *Open Mar–Sept Wed–Mon 10am–5pm; Oct–Nov Wed–Mon 10am–4pm; Dec–Feb Fri–Mon 10am–4pm.* ¥520. *0879-68-3555. benesse-artsite.jp/en/ art/teshima-yokoohouse.html.* Another collaboration between an architect (Nagayama Yuko) and an artist (Yokoo Tadanori), providing a striking contrast to the Chicken Art Museum. The place is a riot of colors, with a transformed traditional house surrounding the sort of garden Gaudí might have designed. The pictures exhibited seek to elicit a reaction from visitors walking on soft *tatami* mats or looking out over carp that are as colorful as the works on display. And the silo beside the complex is dangerously close to inspiring vertigo.

Some 3mi/5km separate Ieura from Teshima Art Museum and you can stop off on the way at the little hill village of Karato Oka, where you can inspect several art installations and call in to the Shima Kitchen restaurant.

Teshima Art Museum★★ – *0.6mi/1 km beyond Karato Port.* *Open Mar–Oct Wed–Mon 10am–5pm; Nov Wed–Mon 10am-4pm; Dec–Feb Fri–Mon 10am–4pm.* ¥1570. *0879-68-3555. benesse-artsite.jp/en/art/teshima-artmuseum.html.* The fruits of a collaboration between the architect Nishizawa Ryue and the artist Naito Rei, this museum/artwork is reminiscent of a bubble, a UFO, or a shell placed on a hillside between the sea and the terraces of paddy fields. Having removed your shoes, you walk in, curious, unsettled, all your senses alert; two immense apertures allow wind and shifting light to enter, along with a leaf, or a butterfly. The ground and the walls are blank and soft; from the former there spring silent drops of water that pool, separate, intertwine, become stationary, accelerate... An experience to enjoy "as alone as possible", ignoring your watch. The neighboring "bubble" houses a pretty café, and don't forget to climb the hill to contemplate the beautiful tableau of the museum, paddy fields, and sea.

Les Archives du Coeur – *Located in Karato.* *Open Mar–Oct Wed–Mon 10am–5pm; Nov Wed–Mon 10am-4pm; Dec–Feb Fri–Mon 10am–4pm.* ¥520. *0879-69-3555. benesse-artsite.jp/en/ art/boltanski.html.* This space, imagined by the French artist Christian Boltanski, archives and plays recordings of the heartbeats of those who wish to use it to bear witness to their visit and their own existence. You can record your own, accompanied with a message, to join the movement.

Inu-jima 犬島

7.5mi/12km north of Nao-shima. Shuttle (shikokukisen.com/en; 45min) from Nao-shima (Miyanoura ¥1880 one way) and Te-shima (Ieura, 25min, ☞¥1250) or ferry (10min) from Hoden Port (☞¥300 one way). Museum: ⏱Open 9.30am–4.30pm: Mar–Nov Wed–Mon; Dec–Feb Fri–Mon. ☞¥2100. ✆086-947-1112. benesse-artsite.jp/en/art/seirensho.html.

Like many islands in the Inland Sea, Inujima *(0.2sq mi/0.5sq km, population 50)*, housed a copper refinery *(seirensho)*, no longer in use. Once again thanks to the Benesse Foundation, this vast brick shell has now been transformed into an unusual museum, **Inujima Seirensho Art Museum**, with a cafe and a bookshop. A work by the artist Yanagi Yukinori is currently on display, while other buildings on the island have been converted into galleries. As on Nao-shima, the Setouchi Triennale arts festival also takes place on Inu-jima.

Shodo-shima 小豆島

Approx. 19mi/30km northeast of Takamatsu. From Takamatsu Port there are services to the ports of Kusakabe (40min/1hr via Uchinomi Ferry Ltd.), Ikeda (1hr via International Ferry Ltd., and Tonosho (30min/1hr via Shikoku Ferry Ltd.). There are also services to Himeji, Okayama, Kobe, and Osaka.

The second-largest island in the Inland Sea *(60sq mi/153sq km, population 14,400)* has a touch of the Mediterranean about it, with orchards of olive trees and scenery that attracts a great number of Japanese tourists. The island is also famed for its *shoyu* (soy sauce) and *somen* (wheat noodles). You can do a smaller version of the 88-temple pilgrimage with the walk to the summit of Mount Kakankei.

Kankakei Gorge★

– *3mi/5km from Kusakabe Port, access by car. Cable car: ⏱open daily 8.30am–5pm (timetables vary seasonally), departures every 6 to 12min, 5min journey. ☞¥1760 round trip (¥980 one way). kankakei.co.jp.* These spectacular cliffs in the northern part of the island, towering to a height of 2600ft/800m, were sculpted by erosion more than a million years ago. A cable

car will take you to 2000ft/612m, from where there is a magnificent view of the coast and the Inland Sea. Paths have been laid to link various vantage points from which you can see the sometimes bizarre rock formations and the primeval forest that covers the mountainside. The most enthusiastic walkers may choose to climb or descend the mountain on foot.

Nakayama paddy field terraces – These terraced paddy fields near the village of Nakayama lend the countryside a serene feel. Follow the little paths among the cultivated fields; the oldest date back to medieval times. Nearby, there is a Shinto shrine and a small 17C Kabuki theater with a thatched roof (performances once a year in Oct).

Hon-jima 本島

6mi/10km off the coast of Marugame. 8 ferries per day serve the port (35min crossing, ☞¥1150 round-trip, last boat back at 7.30pm). There are also 4 ferries per day to Kojima (30min, ☞¥660 round trip). Tourist information available at the port, ✆0877-27-3578.

The main island of the seven Shiwaku islands, Hon-jima *(2.7sq mi/7sq km, population 650)* used to be a hideout for pirates *(wako)*, who scoured the Inland Sea. The pirates also traded with China, Korea, and Vietnam. Eventually recruited by the shoguns, from the end of the 16C to the Meiji era they served as customs officers, collecting a tax on maritime traffic heading for Osaka. The island's main village, **Kasashima**, still has the ancient customs house from the Edo era. With its many wooden houses from the Edo and Meiji eras, the island has a timeless feel.

ADDRESSES

🏠 STAY

🛏 A list of accommodation options is available at *naoshima.net/stay,* and help in making reservations can be found at Miyanoura Tourist Office. Reservations are strongly advised for weekends.

NAO-SHIMA

🛏 **Minshuku Okada** 民宿おかだ – *199-1 Tsumiura-cho.* 📞*087-892-3406. 4 rooms. ¥8400. ¥800* 🍴. Conveniently located between Benesse House and the village of Honmura, and run by a delightful, friendly couple.

🛏 **Naoshima Furusato Umi-no-ie Tsutsuji-so** 直島ふるさと海の家つつじ荘 – *352-1 Naoshima-cho.* 📞*087-892-2838. tsutsujiso.com/english. 10 yurts (40 beds), caravans, and 3 pavilions. Yurts ¥3850 per person, pavilions ¥4840 per person. ¥660* 🍴. 🍴. Very close to the beach. The yurts are basic but air-conditioned. Showers in adjacent mobile homes.

🛏🛏🛏🛏 **Benesse House Museum** ベネッセミュージアムハウス – *Gotan-ji.* 📞*087-892-3223. benesse-artsite.jp/en/stay. 65 rooms (4 buildings). ¥67,000.* 🍴. Rooms on the upper floor of the museum, with a view of the Inland Sea, and free admission to the museum.

SHODO-SHIMA

🛏🛏🛏🛏 **Shimayado Mari** 島宿 真理 – *Ko-2011 Noma.* 📞*0879-82-0086. mari. co.jp. 7 rooms. ¥61,300.* 🍴, *dinner also included.* A former factory renovated in a contemporary style. The best rooms have a private *onsen*. The restaurant (reservation required) serves local dishes.

🍴 EAT

NAO-SHIMA

🛏🛏🛏 **Cafe Salon Naka Oku** カフェ・サロン中奥 – *1167 Honmura Nakaoku.* 📞*0878-92-3887. cafesalon-naka-oku.jimdofree.com. Open Wed–Mon 11.30am–3pm & 5.30–9pm.* Shabby-chic cafe/restaurant in a beautiful old building. Curries, salads and traditional Japanese dishes, plus good coffee and cakes.

Matsuyama★★ 松山

The lively main town of Shikoku, Matsuyama, has grown up around a superb castle perched on the top of a hill. Situated at the center of the great Temple Pilgrimage route, the town itself boasts seven temples, including the eminent Ishite-ji. But the main local attraction has to be a visit to the delightful baths at Dogo Onsen, one of the oldest thermal spas in Japan, which, apart from steam, also exudes a delightful old-fashioned atmosphere.

SIGHTS

Matsuyama Castle★★ 松山城
10min walk east of the JR station. Take Tramway stop Kencho-mae or Ookaido, then the cable car or chairlift (🚠¥510 round trip). 🕐*Open daily: Feb–Nov 9am–5pm; Aug 9am–5.30pm; Dec–Jan 9am–4.30pm.* 🚠*¥510. Four footpaths also lead to the castle. matsuyamajo.jp.* The castle at Matsuyama is undoubtedly among the finest in Japan because of its impressive position on the slope of a hill at a height of 433ft/132m, with

▶ **Population:** 509,800 – Ehime Prefecture.

⚲ **Michelin Map:** Regions of Japan Map 7, Regional Map p547, A1.

▶ **Location:** The town is on a plain in the island's northwest, 121mi/195km from Takamatsu. The JR station is 550yd/500m to the west of the castle. Dogo Onsen, 1.2mi/2km to the east of the center, is served by trams, as is the whole of the town. The ferry port is 6mi/10km to the north, at Takahama.

👥 **Kids:** The *Botchan Ressha* steam train.

🕐 **Timing:** One day is all you need to see the places of interest, unless you stay at Dogo Onsen and/ or take the Shimanami Kaido cycle path.

😊 **Don't miss:** The castle; a bath at Dogo Onsen; the Shimanami Kaido.

Matsuyama castle

© Raga/Getty Images

spectacular **views★** overlooking the town and the Inland Sea. The warlord Kato Yoshiaki began construction of the castle in 1602. Twenty-six years later, a five-story fortress and other palatial buildings, enclosed by walls had been built halfway up the hill.

Below the castle lay the fortified town, surrounded by moats; the western part was inhabited by samurai and the eastern part by craftsmen and tradesmen; the temples were situated to the north. Since then, like many castles Matsuyama-jo has undergone various reconstructions.

The main keep, destroyed by lightning in 1784, was restored as a three-story building in 1854. Further work was also carried out in 1968 and 1986 in order to restore it to its original style, employing only techniques and materials used in its original construction (no nails or concrete).

Having passed through the **Tonashimon**, you emerge onto a wide plateau planted with cherry trees. Inside the keep is a large collection of sabers, armor, ancient documents, objets d'art, painted panels, and pieces of calligraphy that belonged to the feudal lords Kato, Gamo, and Matsudaira.

▷ Walk back down the hill by the path on the west side, behind the castle.

USEFUL INFORMATION

Tourist Offices – At JR Matsuyama Station *(open daily 8.30am–8.30pm; ☎089-931-3914, en.matsuyama-sightseeing.com)* and at the foot of the mechanical clock at Dogo Onsen *(open daily 9am–8pm; ☎089-921-3708)*. For English-speaking volunteers: Matsuyama International Center, 4-6-20 Samban-cho *(Tue–Sun 9am–5.30pm. ☎089-943-2025, mic.ehime.jp)*.

TRANSPORTATION

BY AIR – Matsuyama Airport – 3.5mi/6km west of the town *(bus every hour from the JR station, 15min)*. Flights for Tokyo *(1hr 30min, around ¥39,000)*, Osaka *(50min, ¥22,000)*, and also Nagoya, Fukuoka, and Okinawa.

BY TRAIN – To and from **Takamatsu** – JR Yosan Line *(2hr 30min, ¥5760)*. To and from **Okayama** – JR Yosan Line *(2hr 40min, ¥6420)*. **To and from Kochi** – via Tadotsu *(3hr50min, ¥9,230)*.

BY BOAT – There are connections to **Hiroshima** *(1hr 10min by speed boat, around ¥7200; 2hr 40min by ferry, ¥3700)*, and Kokura (Fukuoka). For the port (Matsuyama Kankoko), take the Sightseeing Port Limousine Bus from Dogo Onsen tram station *(40min, ¥630)* or from Matsuyama Station *(20min, ¥470)*.

GETTING AROUND THE TOWN

There are five tram lines *(¥160 per journey, 1-day pass ¥400)*. Line 5 serves the JR station at Dogo Onsen.

Ninomaru Shiseki Teien – ○*Open daily: Feb–Nov 9am–5pm; Aug 9am–5.30pm; Dec–Jan 9am–4.30pm.* ⊜*¥200.* At the bottom of the hill, this garden occupies the site of the old feudal palace, which burned down in 1872. The remains of the old palace walls now enclose a rock garden and pools into which a waterfall cascades.

Bansui-so – *3min walk from Ninomaru Shiseki Teien.* ○*Open Tue–Sun 10am–6pm.* ⊜*¥300. bansuisou.org/en.* To the south, at the foot of the castle hill, this impressive villa was built in the French neo-Classical style in 1922 by Count Hisamatsu Sadakoto, 15th lord of the Castle. Today it serves as an annex to the Ehime Prefectual Art Museum and displays Japanese 20C art.

Saka no ue no Kumo Museum – *3min walk from the garden.* ○*Open Tue–Sun, 9am–6.30pm.* ⊜*¥400 (audioguide in English ¥200). sakanouenokumomuseum.jp.* This museum was inspired by a best-selling novel by Shiba Ryotaro (1923–1996) that tells the story of the poet Masaoka Shiki (↻ *see box above*) and the brothers Akiyama, Saneyuki (1868–1918), and Yoshifuru (1859–1930), who both played a key role in the modernization of the Imperial army after the Meiji Restoration. From a wider perspective, the exhibits represent the entry of Japan into the modern world at the turn of the 20C. The building was designed by the great architect Ando Tadao.

Dogo Onsen★★ 道後温泉

1.2mi/2km east of Matsuyama. Tram Line 5 (⊜¥160) or Botchan Ressha. ○*Open daily 6am–11pm.*
The atmosphere in this small *onsen* town is relaxed; people using the spa wander around the hotels and souvenir shops in *yukata* (cotton kimonos). Dogo Onsen is one of the oldest in Japan. Its alkaline springs *(108°F/42°C)* are even mentioned in the *Nihon Shoki (Japanese Chronicles,* 720) and have been visited by many emperors and eminent historical figures. The baths also feature in writer Natsume Soseki's novel *Botchan* (1906), set in Matsuyama and read by nearly all Japanese schoolchildren. Virtually

Did you know?

Matsuyama is proud of being the capital of the **haiku** a short, yet meaningful poem consisting of 17 syllables. Born in the town, the poet Masaoka Shiki (1867–1902) revitalized and modernized this traditional form of poetry, of which Basho (1644–1694) is acknowledged as the great master.

everything at the *onsen* is still as it is described in this largely autobiographical work, beginning with the small steam train imported from Germany in 1887: the **Botchan Ressha** *(iyotetsu. co.jp/botchan/index.html;* ⊜*¥800).* It has only recently been put back into service and renamed in his honor.
Arriving at the square where the tram station is located—also now restored—visitors are greeted by a large clock, **Botchan Karakuri**, erected in 1994. Small mechanical figures enact scenes from the novel at each quarter hour, accompanied by music. Close by is a foot bath *(ashiyu),* where tired feet can be soothed in its thermal waters. A shop-lined arcade leads to the baths.

Dogo Onsen Honkan ★★★ – *Undergoing restoration work for several years from 2019; some sections may be closed or under scaffolding. dogo.jp/en.* Constructed in 1894, this large and rather surreal wooden building looks like a cross between a Japanese castle and a seaside villa, with its mix of pagoda-style roofs, colonnades, balconies, paper lanterns, glass windows, and paper partitions. At the top is a turret bearing the figure of a white heron, recalling the *onsen's* mythical origin. The building served as the bathhouse in the film *Spirited Away* by the Japanese director Miyazaki Hayao. At the reception desk you can obtain a leaflet in English listing the prices and how to use the *onsen.*
Decorated with beautiful mosaics, there are two baths (single sex) and four rates: the **Kami-no-yu** *("Bath of the Gods")* is the cheapest and most popular, with a

Dogo Onsen Honkan

© JTB Photo/UIG/age fotostock

communal changing room (⏰*open daily 6am–11pm;* ¥420). The **Tama-no-yu** ("Bath of the Spirits") is a little more intimate (⏰*open daily 6am–11pm;* ¥1250). The second floor of the building houses a display of objects linked to the baths or to the tea ceremony, and some ancient calligraphy. You could also take the tour of the **Yushinden** (⏰*open daily 6.30am–9pm;* ¥260), baths reserved for the Imperial Family that were still in use until 1950. On the third floor is a room dedicated to Natsume Soseki.

You can bathe in a replica of the Yushinden(⏰*open daily 6am–10pm; 1hr 30min private booking, with tea and sweets, from* ¥2040/group) in the attractive **Annex**, opened in 2017.

Finally, just a few minutes' wak away is the **Tsubaki-no-yu**, "the Camellia Bath," which is very popular with local retirees (⏰*open daily 6.30am–11pm;* ¥400). Refreshingly, tattoos are accepted in all of the baths at Dogo Onsen Honkan. Most of the *ryokan* in Dogo Onsen have their own baths, too; you'll need to check their policies individually.

Ishite-ji★ 石手寺

0.5mi/1km east of Dogo Onsen. 15min walk from the tram station, bus nos. 52 or 8 towards Oku-Dogo (¥160). ⏰*Open daily 24hr.* No charge.

Of the 88 temples of the Shikoku Temple Pilgrimage, Ishite-ji, the 51st, is the most impressive and the most famous. It is also the most-visited after Zentsuji, near to Kotohira, where Kobo Daishi grew up. Constructed during the Kamakura era, around 1330 (its origin goes back to the 9C), it contains some beautiful, Chinese-style architecture. Of particular note are the Ni-mon, a gate with a floor built above it, the belfry, and a three-story pagoda.

EXCURSIONS
🧭*Regional Map, p547.*

TOWARD THE INLAND SEA

Imabari 今治
31 mi/50 km northeast of Matsuyama. By train from JR Matsuyama Station (40min by the Ltd. Express Shiokaze towards Okayama ¥1500).

This coastal city of 170,000 inhabitants has the strange feature of having been Japan's principle manufacturer of towels since the end of the 19C.

Castle – *25min walk from the JR station or 10min by bus.* ⏰*Open daily 9am–5pm.* ¥520. Two things immediately strike you: its location on the coast, affording views of the traffic on the Inland Sea, and its defensive moats that are filled by the tide. An exhibition of armor, swords, and other historical items is to be found in the donjon tower (restored in 1980) and there is a superb view of the city and the Kurushima Straits from the 6th floor. Designed by Todo Takatora, the castle was considered an architectural touchstone for its time (early 17), so much so that the original keep was reproduced near Kyoto in 1610.

ڶڶ Imabari is the arrival (or departure) point for the **Shimanami Kaido★**, a superb cycle route crossing the Inland Sea to Onomichi on Honshu *(◐ see p434 for information)*. If you take a car, you can visit the sites described below and explore the countryside as you go where the bridges and islands take you.

Murakami Suigun Hakubutsukan – *Northeast of Oshima, 1285 Miyakubo, Miyakubo cho. ◐Open Tue–Sun 9am– 5pm. ✆¥320.* This museum is dedicated to the Murakami clan, on of the most powerful families in the Inland Sea from the mid-14C to the mid-16C. Settled on several of the islands stretching out

beween Imabari and Onomichi and pos- sessed of a large fleet, they monitored all the traffic in the area as *suigun* (a sort of coastguard); in return for a toll, they authorized boats to pass and assisted with navigation. This epic tale is illus- trated with maps, models, and objects from daily life *(brochure in English)*.

Toyo Ito Museum of Architecture, Imabari (TIMA) – *In the southwestern part of Omishima Island, 2418 Urado Omishima cho. ◐Open Tue–Sun 9am– 5pm. ✆¥840. tima-imabari.jp/en.* Situ- ated in a magnificent landscape of islands that stretch away to the hori- zon, this museum resembles the career

© JTB Photo/UIG/age fotostock

A Thousand-Year-Old Pilgrimage

For 1000 years, pilgrims *(henro-san)* traversed the island of Shikoku in a clockwise direction, in the search for enlightenment. Easily recognized by their white clothing (representing purity), conical straw hats, sticks, and little bells, today's pilgrims make the same journey as the one made by the famous monk **Kukai** in the 8C *(known posthumously as Kobo Daishi)*, founder of the Buddhist Shingon school. They carry a small booklet which is stamped as they stop at each of the island's 88 sacred temples, 88 being the number of sins that the Shingon doctrine proclaims a person must cleanse themselves of before they can achieve beatitude.

The route in fact includes 89 stops, because from temple 88 *(Okubo-ji)* pilgrims must complete the loop by revisiting temple 1 *(Ryozen-ji)*. This temple is at Tokushima in the northeast of the island, from where the route heads south to Cape Muroto. This where Kukai meditated in a cave by the ocean and had a mystical experience at the age of 19. On foot it takes two months to walk the 745mi/1200km route. People often offer the pilgrims small gifts *(osettai)* or even shelter for the night, although these days many of the 100,000 pilgrims that come here annually travel by car or in air-conditioned tourist buses.

of its creator, the celebrated architect Ito Toyo, in that it is astonishing and exciting. The first building, the "Steel Hut," a kind of origami structure in black steel facing out to sea, houses an exhibition about his work and some themed displays, while the second, the "Silver Hut" (originally the architect's Tokyo home), contains workshops for children and architecture students.

Tokoro Museum Omishima – *In the southwestern part of Omishima Island, 2362-3 Urado Omishima-cho.* ◷*Open Tue–Sun 9am–5pm.* ☞¥310. This unusual little museum just round the corner from TIMA was built at the behest of a businessman in order to accommodate his collection of contemporary sculpture. Work by Japanese and Western artists—Takashi Fukai, Norichika Hayashi, Noe Katz, Marisol and even Giacomo Manzu—combine to form an original and poetic ensemble. The terrace looking out over the countryside is an inviting place to sit and cogitate.

SOUTHWEST
Uchiko ★ 内子
25mi/40km south of Matsuyama. Access by JR Yosan Line trains (1hr; ☞¥780). ⓘInformation kiosk and bicycle rental at Uchiko Station exit, ◷*open Thu–Tue 9am–4pm.*

In the early years of the Meiji era, this little town of 20,000 inhabitants began specializing in the production of vegetable wax *(moku-ro)*. Derived from the berries of the sumac tree *(urushi)*, it is used to make candles, polish, cosmetics, pencils, and medical ointments, and also for waterproofing the traditional paper umbrellas. Uchiko is also the birthplace of Oe Kenzaburo, who won the Nobel Prize for Literature in 1994.

The center of the town is a 15min walk from the station. It's worth stopping by the splendid **Yokaichi Street★**, a charming, flower-filled main road lined with delightful houses from the Edo era, old candle makers still in business, a sake brewery, a tea house, and various souvenir and craft shops. The **Uchiko-**

za★ (◷*open daily 9am–4.30pm;* ☞¥400) the local Kabuki theater built in 1916 and faithfully restored, presents *bunraku* shows in August. You can visit the auditorium *(650 seats)*, the backstage areas, and the basement, with its complex machinery for changing the scenery, made entirely from wood.

Uchiko still has several wax merchants' residences from the Edo era, particularly **Kami-Haga-tei** (◷*open 9am–4.30pm;* ☞¥510), built in 1894 by the Hon-Haga family, where you can see a typical Japanese interior of the time, a collection of buildings connected with the manufacture of wax, and a small museum.

Ozu 大洲
About 8mi/13km from Uchiko by Route 56; 15min by the JR Yosan train line, Iyo Ozu stop. Bicycle rental by the station.

Like its neighbor Uchiko, Ozu grew in the late-Edo era around the manufacture and trade of wax extracted from plants. It is today still a good example of a town that developed at the foot of a castle. The street of Obanahan-dori bears witness to this period, with well-preserved former merchant homes on the left and former samurai homes to the right. There are also a few early residences in neighboring streets.

The late-19C **Garyu Sanso villa★** was built by the Jokos, a successful family of merchants; it alone makes a visit to Ozu worthwhile *(30min walk from station;* ◷*open daily 9am–5pm;* ☞¥550, *or ¥880 with castle; brochure in English).* The villa's sober interior – inspired by the Imperial villa of Katsura in Kyoto – shows extreme refinement in every detail. At the far end of the mossy garden there is a pavilion on piles, overlooking the Hiji River; every summer, traditional cormorant fishing takes place here.

The **castle** in the town was rebuilt in 2004, following an original 17C model, and with early techniques using no nails or concrete. The various phases of reconstruction are presented in the four-story dungeon. On the top floor there is a beautiful view over the town and river (◷*open daily 9am–5pm;* ☞¥550).

Uwajima 宇和島

17mi/28km from Ozu by Route 56.
45min by the Yosan JR train line taken to the terminus.

An elegant three-story **castle★** overlooks the town and its port. This is one of 12 castles in the country having preserved their original structures, designed in the late-16C by the famous architect **Todo Takatora** (1556–1630), who also built the castles in Ozu, Kyoto, and Edo. There is a stunning **panoramic view** of the town from the top floor (🕐*open daily: Mar–Oct 9am–5pm; Nov–Feb 9am–4pm; ≈¥200).*

The Date clan administrated the town for 250 years, Tokugawa Ieyasu having first entrusted the stronghold to Date Hidemune, Masamune's son, in 1614. The **Tensha-en** garden (🕐*open daily Apr–Jun 8.30am–5pm; Jul–Mar 8.30am–4.30pm; mid-Dec–Feb closed Mon; ≈¥300)* bears witness to the family's great wealth. Created in 1866 by Date Munetada, the clan's seventh *daimyo*, this decorative garden is especially beautiful in April, when wisteria and irises are in bloom. The central pond, with its ornamental stones, as well as **Harusame Tei** *(calligraphy pavilion)* and **Senen Kan** *(tea ceremony house)*, all make this a remarkable place.

ADDRESSES

🛏 STAY

MATSUYAMA

🛌 **Hotel MYSTAYS Matsuyama** ホテルMYSTAYS松山 – *1-10-10 Otemachi. ☎089-913-2580. mystays.com/en-us/hotel-mystays-matsuyama-ehime. 161 rooms. ¥8000. ¥1500☕.* A large business hotel that is well situated in the center, near the JR station. A range of different standard rooms, some with a view of the castle.

🛌 **Matsuyama Shinsen-en Youth Hostel** 松山神泉園ユースホステル – *Otsu 22-3 Dogo-Himezuka. ☎089-933-6366. www.matsuyama-yh.com. 47 beds. Dorms ¥2200, single rooms ¥3520. ¥550☕ + dinner.* All mod cons at this rather Alpine chalet-style inn. One of Japan's best

youth hostels, with discounts for foreign guests. *O-furo.* Breakfast and dinner available; oddly, it's cheaper to get both .

🛌🛌 **Hotel Patio Dogo**ホテルパティオ・ドウゴ – *20-12 Yuno-machi, Dogo Onsen. ☎089-941-4128. patio- dogo.co.jp. 101 rooms. ¥12,000. ¥800☕.* Chaming, well situated hotel looking out onto the Dogo baths building. Spacious rooms.

🛌🛌 **Dogo Kan** 道後館 – *7-26 Dogo Tako-cho, Dogo Onsen. In the commercial center behind Tsubaki-no-yu. ☎089-941-7777. dogokan.co.jp. 90 rooms. ¥21,200. ¥2600☕.*The resort's most luxurious hotel, with lovely Japanese and Art Deco rooms. A very good restaurant and a fabulous private *onsen* (indoor and open-air baths).

OZU

🛌🛌 **Obayu Hot Spring** 小薮温泉 – *1433-1 Uwagawa, Hijikawa-cho. ☎089-334-2007. oyabu-hotspring.com/shukuhaku.html. 7 rooms. ¥14,300. ¥600☕.* A centuries-old, *ryokan. Tatami* mats, *onsen* bath, and a charming welcome. Extra fresh produce from the river and mountains finds its way to the table.

🍴EAT

MATSUYAMA

🍽 **Goshiki** 五志喜本店 – *3-5-4 Sanban-cho. ☎050-3476-1491. s422500.gorp.jp. Open 11am–3pm & 5–11pm. English menu. Lunch around ¥1400.* Near the main post office, south of the chateau. Famous for its *goshiki somen*, thin noodles in five colors.

🍽🍽 **Dogo Bakushukan** 道後・麦酒館 – *20-13 Dogo-Yunomachi. ☎089-945-6866. dogobeer.jp/bakusyukan-restaurant. Open daily 11am–10pm. Menu in English.* Not far from Dogo Onsen Honkan, this *izakaya* is ideal for a cool beer and a dish of octopus with vinegar, *konnyaku* (from the *taro* family), grilled bonito, sashimi, etc.

ACTIVITIES

Shimanami Kaido cycle path しまなみ海道 – You can hire a bike or e-bike at either end of the route *(shimanami-cycle. or.jp/rental/english)*, dropping it off at any of 14 bike hire points along the route (except e-bikes, which you'll need to drop back at the same point). You can continue or return by bus or ferry. *≈¥1100–1600/day, plus a deposit of ≈¥1100 (refundable if you return the bike to the same place).*

The Iya Valley★
祖谷渓

Hidden among the high mountains at the center of the island of Shikoku, the Iya Valley is one of the most isolated regions of Japan. Dotted with cottages, its slopes covered with maple forests, steep-sided gorges, and ancient vine bridges spanning emerald-green torrents, the effect is very picturesque. Due to its inaccessibility, the valley provided a refuge for the survivors of the Taira clan after their defeat by the Minamoto at the Battle of Yashima in 1185. Swapping the sword for the hoe and scythe, the warriors became farmers and today, many villagers can claim to have ancestors who served at the Court during the Heian era. A rural paradise until the 1970s, the valley was disrupted by economic development, with the construction of buildings, roads, car parks, and water courses; a frenzied round of concrete-laying that affected agriculture and spoilt the beauty of the countryside. Despite that, Iya remains a haven of peace, where you can enjoy many outdoor activities, from rafting to hiking.

▸ **Population:** 5,000 (*Miyoshi District: Population 24,300*) Tokushima Prefecture.

Michelin Map: Regions of Japan Map 7, Regional Map p547.

▶ **Location:** The Iya Valley is at the center of Shikoku, 47mi/75km west of Tokushima, 37mi/60km south of Takamatsu, and 28mi/45km north of Kochi. The Iya, which has its source on Mount Tsurugi (*6414ft/1955m*), follows a course about 37mi/60km to the east of the Yoshino River, of which it is a tributary. The JR Dosan Line (Takamatsu–Kochi) serves Awa Ikeda and Oboke, at the entrance to the valley.

Kids: A boat trip through the Oboke Gorge.

Timing: Few buses run in the valley, so if short on time, you could rent a car or opt for a day's bus tour (*see opposite*). Otherwise, allow for a two-day stay.

Don't miss: Oboke Gorge; the bridge at Kazura-bashi.

SIGHTS
Regional Map, B1.

OBOKE 大歩危
From Awa Ikeda, Route 32 and the railway line follow the course of the Yoshino River right through a spectacular gorge, as far as Oboke, 15.5mi/25km farther south.

The name of this otherwise fairly insignificant small town literally means "Great Dangerous Step," because of the extraordinarily steep-sided aspect of the valley here.

Oboke Gorge★ 大歩危峡
Boats leave the pier below Mannaka restaurant, 20min walk north from Oboke Station. Boat trips: open daily 9am–5pm, 30min, ¥1200. mannaka.co.jp.

The result of natural erosion, the spectacular gorges of the Yoshino River run for about 2.5mi/4km between Oboke and Koboke in the hollows of steep chalk cliffs streaked with shale varying in color from gray, black, and red-brown. The dark-green waters of the river are particularly good for rafting and kayaking (*see Addresses*). Among the thick vegetation covering the banks you can see traces left by wild animals (woolly macaques, deer), as well as huge, evocatively shaped rock formations.

Lapis Oboke ラピス大歩危
Route 32, between the gorge and Oboke Station. Open 9am–5pm: Dec–Feb Wed–Mon; Mar–Nov daily. ¥500.

USEFUL INFORMATION

Tourist Offices – *miyoshi-tourism.jp/en.* On the right as you leave Awa Ikeda Station. *℘0883-76-0877, open daily 7am–6pm.* Another office at Road Side Station Oboke. *℘0883-84-1489, open daily 9am–5pm.*

TRANSPORTATION
GETTING TO AND FROM THE IYA VALLEY

BY TRAIN – The Awa Ikeda and Oboke stations are served by the JR Dosan Line. Awa Ikeda is also on the JR Tokushima Line.
Trains run to and from Takamatsu *(1hr 10min, ¥2000),* to and from Kochi *(1hr 10min, ¥2860),* and to and from Tokushima *(1hr 15min, ¥2860)* by Ltd. Express.

GETTING AROUND

BY BUS – From JR **Awa Ikeda Station**, round-trip several times daily to Nishi Iya *(Iya Onsen and Kazura-bashi).* From Oboke Station, regular buses Apr–Nov for Kazura-bashi and Higashi Iya. For Chiiori, Oboke bus to Oshima tunnel.
BY CAR – Rental companies at JR Awa Ikeda Station (JR Rent-a-Car, *℘0883-72-0022*) and at Mannaka Hotel (*℘0883-84-1216*). *Around ¥7200 per day; reserve in advance.*
BY TOUR BUS – **The Bonnet Bus**, a small old-fashioned bus, leaves JR Awa Ikeda Station at 10.40am, tours the places of interest (Oboke Gorge, Kazura-bashi, Iya Onsen), and returns at 4.40pm *(¥8500, with boat trip and lunch; reservations required; ℘0883-72-1231, yonkoh.co.jp/teikan).*

This *michi no eki* (roadside station) contains a museum on the geological history of Shikoku, with various examples of rocks and crystals from all over the world, including a meteorite from Mars.

Heike Yashiki 平家屋敷
Route 45, 2.5mi/4km east of Oboke Station. ⏱*Open daily: Mar–Oct 8am–6pm; Nov–Feb 8am–5pm.* ⌖*¥500.*
This thatched house was originally the residence of Emperor Antoku's doctor, who fled here after the defeat of the Heike in 1185 (the emperor commited suicide by throwing himself into the sea). The interior has retained its fine timber structure and displays a varied collection of agricultural and craft tools.

NISHI IYA★★ 西祖谷
Accessible from Oboke or Awa Ikeda, the western part of the Iya Valley *(Nishi Iya)* is the most tourist-oriented. Cut off from the world for a long period, it survived by growing buckwheat, barley, tobacco, and millet.
Despite a scattering of unattractive buildings, it has been reasonably successful in resisting the excessive tide of concrete, particularly along the **panoramic route★★** (the old Route 32) that

winds over 12.5mi/20km between the hamlets of Nishi Iya and Iya-guchi in the north, in the direction of Awa Ikeda. Along the way are several **spectacular viewpoints** of the gorges, whose slopes are covered with conifers and wild cherry trees. The statue of the **Manneken-pis** is a copy of the one in Brussels, built on a rock overlooking a 656ft/200m precipice. The nearby **Iya Onsen Hotel** has a wonderful, open-air *onsen* on the banks of the river, reached by cable car *(iyaonsen. co.jp/en/spa;* ⏱*open daily 7.30am–6pm;* ⌖*¥1700, including cable car).*

Kazura-bashi★ 祖谷のかずら橋
Route 32, 7mi/11km east of Oboke Station. ⏱*Open daily dawn–dusk.* ⌖*¥550.*
It is this river crossing built from vines, 148ft/45m long and 49ft/15m above the water, that makes this area famous. It dates from the 12C, when the Taira clan took refuge in the valley. If threatened by possible attackers, the warriors could easily cut the cords of the bridge to block their way. A score of identical bridges onced crossed the river, but only this one and two others farther up the valley have survived. The bridge is remade every three years using the traditional techniques for plaiting the

Awa Odori, Japan's biggest festival

The town of Tokushima is famous for its folk dance festival Awa Odori, the most impressive in the country. From August 12 to August 15, during *Bon*, the **Festival of the Dead**, more than 100,000 dancers, both men and women, dressed in brightly colored kimonos, parade through the streets to the sound of *shamisen* (three-stringed instrument plucked with a plectrum), drums, brass, and flutes. Kicking up their feet and keeping time with their arms, the dancers move forward maintaining a bewitching rhythm, something like a samba, and chanting *"Ah! Yatosa! Yatosa!"* It is known as the "dance of the lunatics" because the lyrics state: "You're a fool if you dance, you're a fool if you don't dance, so you might as well dance!"

lianas, but is now reinforced with carefully concealed steel cables. The logs that make up the walkway are spaced so that a foot can pass between them, which makes crossing the bridge a little nerve-wracking. There is a small **waterfall** 164ft/50m upstream.

Chiiori★ ちいおり

12.5mi/20km east of Oboke Station. After Kazura-bashi, continue for about 3mi/5km on Route 32 to the Oshima tunnel. From there, the road to the right climbs for 3mi/5km (1hr 30min walk) to the house. ⊙*Visit by appointment only.* ⊗¥500. ☎0883-88-5290. chiiori.org.
In the tiny hamlet of Chiiori, the "House of the Flute" is a thatched house dating from 1720, bought and restored by American writer Alex Kerr. Arriving in the valley in the early 1970s, he was the first to issue an environmental wake-up call. In his 1993 book *Lost Japan* Kerr recounts how, in the process of modernization, the country is gradually disfiguring the environment. Out 30,000 streams and rivers only three have escaped the ravages of concrete in some form. Most of

the thatched roofs have been replaced by corrugated iron or tiles. The author founded an association that fights for the valley's ecological preservation. Chiiori now proudly shows off its ancient architecture, and enjoys a **panoramic view** of the valley. Accommodation is available for visitors, who must help with the chores.

HIGASHI IYA★ 東祖谷

More difficult to access than Nishi Iya, the eastern part of the valley *(Higashi Iya)* sees far fewer visitors.

Ochiai-Shuraku 落合集落

Route 439, 11mi/18km east of Kazura-bashi.
The hamlet of Ochiai, with its terraces rising up the mountain slope, planted with rice and tobacco, is thought to have been founded in the Middle Ages by the former samurai-turned-farmers of the Heike clan. Most of the houses date from the Edo era; some of the old-style thatched roofs are under restoration.

Oku Iya Kazura-bashi★ 奥祖谷かずら橋

Route 439, 19mi/31km east of Kazura-bashi. ⊙*Open Apr–Nov daily dawn–dusk.* ⊙*Closed Dec–Mar.* ⊗¥550.
At the foot of Mount Tsurugi *(6414ft/1955m)*, the second highest summit on Shikoku, is this pair of vine bridges—the longest and highest nicknamed "the husband" *(Otto no hashi)*, and the smaller one "the wife" *(Tsuma no hashi)*. Reinforced with steel cables, they are rebuilt at intervals. As with the Kazura-bashi, though safe, the bridges can feel rickety when crossing. Farther upstream, you can cross in a gondola mounted on a cable and pulled by a rope.

ADDRESSES

🛏 STAY

🛏🛏🛏 **Oboke-kyo Mannaka** 大歩危峡まんなか – *1644-1 Yamashiro-cho-Nishiu.* ☎0883-84-1216. mannaka.co.jp. 23 rooms. ¥26,500. 🍴, dinner also included. The hotel overlooks the Oboke Gorge. Comfortable

Western and Japanese rooms, high-quality cuisine, and a spacious, relaxing *onsen*.

🍲🍲🍲 **Iyashi-no-Onsenkyo** いやしの温泉郷 – *28 Higashi Iya-Sugeoi. ☏0883-88-2975. iyashino-onsenkyo.com. Open Apr–Nov only. 8 rooms, 5 bungalows. ¥22,000. Around ¥1000🍴.* On Route 439, right at the end of Higashi Iya, is a welcoming collection of thatched cottages built of wood and stone, offering Japanese or Western rooms. There is a good restaurant serving soba made on the premises, and a pleasant *onsen*, with open-air bath.

🍲🍲🍲🍲 **Iya Onsen Hotel** ホテル祖谷温泉 – *367-28 Matsuo Matsumoto. ☏0883-75-2311. iyaonsen.co.jp/en. 20 rooms. ¥41,000. 🍴, dinner also included.* Japanese-style rooms and divine *kaiseki* cuisine. You can also add lunch without breaking the bank. The *onsen*, at the foot of the gorge, is a pure delight.

🍴 EAT

The hotels mentioned also have good restaurants. Near Kazura-bashi, cheap cafes serve *yakizakana*: fish grilled on charcoal.

SPORT AND LEISURE

Rafting – Two companies with English-speaking staff organize trips down the Oboke Gorge, as well as kayaking and canyoning. *Around ¥5500 for a half-day.*

Mont-Bell モンベル大歩危店 – *☏0883-76-8110, montbell.jp. Mon–Sat 10am–6pm. Closed public hols Nov–Feb.*

Happy Raft ハッピーラフト – *☏0887-75-0500, happyraft.com.*

Kochi and the Pacific Coast★
高知・太平洋側

Separated from the rest of Japan by mountains on one side and the Pacific on the other, the Kochi region has retained its own character and special features, notably its dialect, Tosa-ben, which was also the name of the province until the beginning of the 17C. Washed over by the warm, fish-laden waters of the Kuroshio Current—the Japanese equivalent of the Gulf Stream—the coast enjoys a warm, humid climate, with the country's highest annual rainfall after Okinawa. Kochi has a glorious castle and a fine botanical garden. The neighboring beach at Katsurahama is considered one of Japan's most beautiful. To the southwest, the coast is carved out of virgin tropical vegetation, as is the Shimanto, claimed to be Japan's last remaining free-flowing river. At the westernmost point of the coast, the waves of the Pacific beat against the spectacular promontories of Cape Ashizuri, while the spectacular rocks of Cape Muroto bear witness to the island's geological history.

▶ **Population:** Kochi: Population 337,875 – Kochi Prefecture.

Michelin Map: Regions of Japan Map 7, Regional Map p547.

Location: South of Shikoku, 87mi/140km from Matsuyama; 100mi/160km from Takamatsu, Kochi is on the Pacific. Cape Ashizuri is 93mi/150km farther southwest. A wide avenue and tramway run north from the JR station into town.

Kids: Makino Botanical Garden; Katsurahama beach; summer whale-watching cruise.

Timing: 3 days, including travel, for Kochi, the Shimanto River, Cape Ashizuri, Cape Muroto. Kochi on Sunday for the market.

Don't miss: The Kochi Castle; the Cape Ashizuri panorama; *katsuo no tataki*, a Kochi specialty.

The market town

The Sunday market is Kochi's largest and best known but it is not the only one: every day, except Monday, a market is held somewhere in the town, the largest being on Tuesdays and Fridays.

SIGHTS

Opposite the JR Kochi Station, a major road leads to the south and **Harimaya-bashi** *(about a 10min walk)*, the center of the town. There, tucked away amid some modern buildings, is Harimaya-bashi's small red bridge. Crossing an arm of the river that has now been filled in, it was the scene of a secret lovers' tryst between a Buddhist monk and a young servant-girl in the 19C.

Farther to the north, the **Sunday Market★** (Nichi-o-ichi) has taken place along a stretch of the Otesuji-dori (road) for nearly three centuries. Several hundred stands sell the products of the region's farmers, fishermen, and craftsmen—vegetables, fruit, flowers, fish and shellfish, coral artifacts, knives, pottery, etc.—laid out over 0.75mi/1.2km. The Otesuji-dori comes out at the entrance to the castle.

Kochi Castle★★ 高知城

15min walk west of Harimaya-bashi.
Open daily 9am–5pm. ¥420.
kochipark.jp/kochijyo.

Originally built as a prestigious pleasure palace and not simply an austere fortress, Kochi Castle is among the most classically elegant and well-preserved in the whole country. Built in 1603 by the feudal lord Yamanouchi Kazutoyo, it was rebuilt after a fire in 1748. Entry is through the impressive **Ote-mon★**, a gate enhanced by fine ironwork and flanked by thick stone walls.

High on the ramparts, trapdoors and slits in the walls allowed projectiles to be aimed at possible assailants. Just beyond the entrance you can see the statue of Itagaki Taisuke, a native of Kochi and founder of the Freedom and People's Rights Movement, which pushed for democracy during the Meiji era. A wide stone staircase leads to the top of the hill *(141ft/43m high)* on which were built the houses of residential lords (Ninomaru). These were destroyed during the Meiji Restoration in 1873 to make room for a park planted with cherry trees.

The only part to survive was the six-story **keep★★**, which stands in the center of the internal defensive compound (Honmaru). It is reached by a roundabout route, with a staircase that comes to a dead end in an attempt to fool the

Kochi castle

© MasaoTaira/iStock

USEFUL INFORMATION

Tourist Offices – visitkochijapan. com/en. On the right, leaving JR Kochi Station (south exit). ☏088-879-5489, open daily 8.30am–7.30pm. Another office around 3min walk from JR Nakamura Station, turn left on leaving the station. ☏0880-35-4171, open daily 8.30am–5.30pm.

TRANSPORTATION

BY PLANE – Kochi Airport 6mi/10km east of Kochi (kochiap.co.jp/en). Bus (1–3 every hour, 35 min, ¥740) for JR Kochi Station. Flights for Tokyo (1hr 20min, around ¥39,000), Nagoya, Osaka, and Fukuoka. **BY TRAIN** – Kochi is on the JR Dosan Line. Trains run to and from **Takamatsu** (2hr 30min, ¥4650) and from **Okayama** (2hr 30min, ¥5540). **BY BUS** – 10 buses daily for **Matsuyama** (2hr 35min, around ¥3700), other large towns, and Shikoku and Honshu. **BY FERRY** – Ferries to **Oita (Kyushu)** from Sukumo port (3 per day, 3hr 10min, around ¥2700) in southwest Kochi (2hr 15min by train from Kochi, then 10min by bus from JR Sukumo).

enemy. From the top there is a lovely **view** over the whole of the town.

👥 Makino Botanical Garden★

牧野植物園

On the hill at Godaisan, 3mi/5km to the east. Buses run from Kochi Station (every hour, 30min journey) to Makino-shokubutsuen-mae. ◷Open daily 9am–5pm. ☞¥720. makino.or.jp. Founded 50 years ago by Makino Tomi-taro (1862–1957), father of Japanese botany, this center for the research into and conservation of plant species includes a museum, a restaurant, and a 14.8-acre/6ha park, with flowerbeds and greenhouses full of orchids, hibiscus, lotus, and bonsai trees—in total there are almost 3000 varieties of plants.

Chikurin-ji★ 竹林寺

Opposite the Botanical Garden. ◷Open daily 8.30am–5pm. Grounds ☞no charge; treasure hall ☞¥400.

No. 31 of the 88 sacred temples on the Temple Pilgrimage route, the "Temple in the Bamboo Forest" was founded in 724 by Gyoki, a Buddhist monk. Its six-story pagoda was refurbished in 1970, but the temple contains a lovely **Zen garden** (designed in the 14C by Muso Soseki) and some fine statutes from the Heian and Kamakura eras (10–13C) in the **Treasure House★**.

Biodiversity in danger

Professor Koyama Tetsuo, the Director of the Makino botanical gardens, has a gloomy outlook for Japan's native flora: "Nature has been devastated over the last decades and many species have disappeared. Fortunately, the Kochi region has largely been spared. The people of Japan care little about ecology and their botanical education is lacking—most can't tell the the difference between uniform, artificial plantations of cedars or cypress trees and truly natural biodiversity. They see a bit of green and that seems to be enough for them."

EXCURSIONS

◷Regional Map, B1.

There are some beautiful excursions in the Kochi region around the Pacific coast, where you can explore charmingly unspoilt scenery such as the Shimanto River and Cape Ashizuri in the southwest and Cape Muroto in the southeast.

👥 Katsurahama★ 桂浜

7.5mi/12kmi south of Kochi. Bus (every hour, journey time 50min) from Harimaya-bashi.

Ashizuri-misaki

© pinboke-oyaji/iStock

Forming a promontory at the southern end of Urado Bay, the popular **beach★** at Katsurahaman is long, sandy, and lined with pine trees. Note that swimming s prohibited, though, due to strong currents. On the promenade bordering the beach is a statue of **Sakamoto Ryoma**, a celebrated local hero (see box opposite).

The Sakamoto Ryoma Memorial Museum – 830 Urado-shiroyama, above Katsurahama Beach. ⏰Open daily 9am–5pm. ☞¥490–700. ryoma-kinenkan.jp.
Reproductions of letters, photos, and objects tell the story of the life and times of Sakamoto Ryoma, a well-known historical figure, in this modern museum.

Shimanto River★ 四万十川
68mi/110km southwest of Kochi. Train to Nakamura (1hr 45min, ☞¥420). From the JR station, walk to the river, where there are boat trips (1hr, around ☞¥2000).
The Shimanto-gawa (122mi/196km) is claimed to be the **last large free-flowing river in Japan**, unspoiled by dams or concrete dikes. Its clear water is full of ayu trout, which the local people fish from the beginning of the summer. The bridges have no parapets, so that the floodwaters flow over them rather than washing them away. The sandy islands and banks are covered in dense vegetation, where herons and egrets

nest. **Dragonflies** and **fireflies** swoop and flutter everywhere. From Nakamura, a town located near the estuary, you can also rent kayaks in which to paddle upriver.

Ashizuri-misaki★★ 足摺岬
100mi/160km southwest of Kochi. Train to Nakamura (1hr45min, ☞¥4140), then bus to Ashizuri-misaki (1hr 45min).
At the southern tip of Shikoku, Cape Ashizuri forms a spectacular spur. The base of its steep cliffs, 263ft/80m below, is lashed by the foamy waves of the ocean. At the entrance to the site is a bronze statue of **John Manjiro** (1827–98), a prominent local figure and the first Japanese to visit the United States. A path follows the coastline beneath an archway formed by numerous camellias (in flower Jan–Mar).
From the lighthouse, built in 1914, there is a fine **view★★** over the ocean, where it is sometimes possible to catch glimpses of **turtles**. Near the lighthouse, the **Kongofuku-ji temple 38** on the pilgrimage route was founded in 822 by Kobo Daishi in honor of the thousand-armed divinity Kannon.
The buildings date from 1662. Near the town of **Tatsukushi** (9.5mi/15km to the west of the cape, as the tide goes out), **rock formations** emerge from the seabed looking like the felled trunks of fossilized trees. Close by is an underwater park, where you can climb

down an enclosed spiral staircase to the sea floor and watch fish from an observation room.

Monet Marmottan Garden in Kitagawa village

北川村 "モネの庭" マルモッタン

In Kitagawa, 33mi/54km southeast of Kochi. By train on the Gomen-Nahari Line (1hr) then 5min by bus from Nahari Station, get off at Monet no niwa stop. ⏱*Open daily 10am–5pm.* ⚬*¥700. kjmonet.jp/english.html.*

There is a nice story behind this splendid garden nestling at the foot of the mountains. In 1883, the painter Claude Monet was inspired by the Japaneses prints he had been collecting to create his garden at Giverny; 114 years later, the Claude Monet Foundation granted the village de Kitagawa the right to recreate the garden and, after several changes required by the climate had been effected, the gates were thrown open in 2000. Changing constantly with the seasons, its masterpiece is the water garden with its blue water lilies *(Jul–Oct).*

Muroto-misaki 室戸岬

50mi/80km southeast of Kochi on highway 55. Direct bus connection from Kochi (2hr 40min) or by train on the Gomen-Nahari Line (1hr 30min), then bus from Nahari Station (40min), get off at Muroto misaki or Kannoura

stop. ℹ*Muroto Geopark Information Center, at the base of the lighthouse:* ⏱*Open daily 9am–5pm,* ⚬*no charge. Brochures in English.*

Cape Muroto lies at the southeastern-most corner of Shikoku on the Pacific coast, and its unique and spectacular geology and scenery have justly earnt it classification as one of UNESCO's geoparks. You can see strata of solidified rock that once were ancient seabeds and have been lifted by a series of seismic shocks dating back around 14 million years. A 1.25mi/2km path has been laid to allow visitors to walk around the site and the subtropical vegetation is as extraordinary as the views, the *ficus superba* in particuliar.

ADDRESSES

🛏 STAY

KOCHI

🛏 **Seven Days Hotel** セブンデイズホテル – *2-13-17 Harimaya-cho.* ✆*088-884-7100. 7dayshotel.com. 80 rooms. ¥8000. ¥220*☕*. Very central, stylish business hotel. Rooms small, but well-maintained. The copious breakfast is recommended.*

🛏🛏🛏🛏 **Jyoseikan** 城西館 – *2-5-34 Kamimachi.* ✆*088-875-0111. jyoseikan. co.jp. 62 rooms. ¥26,400.* ☕*. Near the castle; an institution for over a century, and where the emperor stays when in Kochi. Luxurious Japanese-style rooms.*

Sakamoto Ryoma (1836–67)

The turbulent life of this native of Kochi was retold in a 2010 serial made by the public broadcasting chain NHK (Ryomaden) that was extremely popular with audiences. His journey is representative of the troubled period at the end of the shogunate (*bakumatsu*) and the Meiji Restoration.

Born into a family of samurais, he very soon became involved with the opposition movement to the shogun and so was obliged to flee Tosa, his home fiefdom. While still playing a key role in the anti-shogunate movement (and acting as a negotiator netween the clans of the southwest, the Satsuma, Choshu, and Tosa), he began a career in business and founded an import/export company in 1865; he was convinced of the necessity of modernizing Japan in order to offer greater resistance to pressure from the West. He was assassinated in Kyoto in 1867, possibly by supporters of the shogun, and his tomb now lies in the Ryozen Gokoku jinja shrine in Kyoto.

Hirome Ichiba

© winhorse/iStock

NAKAMURA

😴🍵🍴 **Shimanto no Yado** 四万十いや しの宿 – *3370 Shimoda.* ☏*0880-31-1600. shimantonoyado.co.jp. 30 rooms. ¥24,600. 🛏️. Overlooking Shimanto estuary, this eco-hotel makes much of space, light, and wood. The beautiful, Japanese-style rooms may have a futon or a bed; some have a terrace and private *rotenburo*. A pleasant *onsen*, including seawater and medicinal herb baths.

ASHIZURI-MISAKI

😴🍵 **Ashizuri Thermae** 足摺テルメ – *1433-3 Higashi Hata, Ashizuri-misaki.* ☏*0880-88-0301. terume.com/english. 41 rooms. ¥12,100. ¥1650*🛏️. In a wild setting facing the sea, and of interest for its extensive thermal spa facilities: swimming pool, sauna, indoor and outdoor *onsen*. The restaurant serves good French food.

🍴 EAT

In Kochi, be sure to try the local specialty of *katsuo no tataki*, bonito served lightly grilled, with an effect similar to rare steak.

🍵 **Hirome Ichiba** ひろめ市場 – *Hirome Market, 2-3-1 Obiyamachi.* ☏*088-822-5287. hirome.co.jp. Open Mon–Sat 9am–11pm, Sun 7am–11pm.* This popular covered market has sixty or so cheap eating places serving Chinese dishes and local specialties.

SPORT AND LEISURE

The Sunday market is the biggest and best-known in Kochi, but there are others. A market takes place somewhere in Kochi every day apart from Monday, including two large markets on Tuesday and Friday. Ask for information at the Tourist Office.

👥👤 **Whale Watching** – Whaling was carried out for nearly 500 years from the villages and towns along this part of the coastline. While Japanese whaling remains a contentious issue both domestically and internationally, in the waters around Kochi at least whales have come to be seen as a source of income in a different way: whale watching trips, and by extension, conservation of these majestic marine mammals.

Whale Watching Usa boats leave from Usa port at 8am, 9am and 12.30pm *(1hr by bus from the JR Kochi Station; ☏088-856 -1133, usaww.jp/pc; mid-Apr–Oct, reservation nececessary; ¥6000 per person; around 5hr).*

Also **Ogata Whale Watching** from Irino port (Nakamura side) at 8am, 10am & noon *(☏0880-43-1058, nitarikujira.com/ english; mid-Apr–Oct, reservation required; ¥6000 per person; minimum 4 people required for a trip).*

In the far southwestern corner of the Japanese archipelago is Kyushu, Japan's third-largest island, with a tropical feel in the southern part and a more temperate climate to the north. The island is mountainous, with two volcanic chains meeting in the center at Mount Aso *(5223ft/1592m)*, and its many National Parks contain luxuriant forests dominated by holm oaks, camphor trees, bamboos, cedars, and magnolias. A myriad of smaller islands, many uninhabited, are spread out across the East China Sea. The name Kyushu means "nine provinces," referring to the original provinces into which the island was divided before the seven present-day prefectures were created.

▶ **Population:** 13.1 million – Fukuoka, Kagoshima, Kumamoto, Miyazaki, Nagasaki, Oita, and Saga prefectures.

⌖ **Michelin Map:** Regions of Japan Map 8, Regional Map p576.

▶ **Location:** To the southwest of Honshu, the island of Kyushu covers an area of 14,202sq mi /36,782sq km, slightly less than that of Switzerland. There are airports at Fukuoka, Oita (Beppu), Nagasaki, Kagoshima, Kumamoto, and Miyazaki. JR express trains run between the main cities. A shinkansen service operates between Kagoshima in the south and Fukuoka-Hakata in the north.

▲▲ **Kids:** Dolphin-spotting on a boat trip from Tsuji-shima harbor.

🕑 **Timing:** Allow at least a week to see the island's main sights. Hiring a car will enable you to get around more quickly, particularly in the south.

☺ **Don't miss:** A bath in the hot sands at Ibusuki, a riverside *onsen* at Kurokawa; Nagasaki Bay; the Kyushu National Museum; trips to Yakushima, Mt. Aso and Mt. Unzen; the Christian villages of Amakusa.

Highlights

1 Futuristic **Fukuoka** urban renewal: **Canal City** and **Hawks Town** (p578 and p581)

2 Stopping for noodles in Chinatown, **Nagasaki** (p592)

3 Scaling **Mount Unzen** on the Shimabara Peninsula (p595)

4 Sunset at **Kunimigaoka** (p604)

5 An immersive black sand treatment at **Takegawara Onsen**, **Beppu** (p621)

A Land of Fire

Kyushu's vast moonlike caldera is one of the largest in the world. Also known as "the land of fire," Kyushu is an area of intense volcanic activity, as demonstrated by the steaming "hells" of Beppu and a multitude of other hot springs, such as Kurokawa Onsen, Ibusuki, and Yufuin. But the sea is never far away, and the jagged coastline forms a striking contrast with the mountains. Thanks to the deep waters of these sinuous bays, great ports such as Kagoshima and Nagasaki grew up here.

Kyushu is the cradle of the most ancient of the Japanese cultures *(Yayoi era, 300BC to 300AD)*. Its proximity to Korea and China made it the main point of contact between Japan and mainland Asia. It was also the point of entry for the first Westerners to visit Japan: the Portuguese who landed on the island in the 16C, followed by the Spanish, British, and Dutch. With the arrival of European missionaries, notably the Jesuit priest St. Francis Xavier, Christianity spread rapidly throughout the island, making many converts. Long persecuted by

the central government and forced to practice their faith in secret, today the island is dotted with their small mock-Gothic Christian churches. The Korean and Chinese influences gave birth to a rich and varied ceramic art, from the sober pottery of Karatsu to the multi-colored porcelain of Arita and Imari.

In the north, the port of Fukuoka, the main entry point by sea, is an energetic, modern city, bucking the national trend with its growing population. Farther west, Nagasaki has a more romantic feel,

with a mixture of European and Asian influences. Kagoshima, in the south, lies in the shadow of Sakurajima, a volcano as graceful as Mount Fuji in appearance—but when angry, still spewing clouds of ash into the air. Last, but not least, the island of Yakushima contains a magnificent forest of 1000-year-old cedars. Kyushu is also Japan's fourth economic zone, after the main metropolitan areas of Tokyo, Osaka, and Nagoya, accounting for approximately 10 percent of the country's GNP.

Fukuoka★
福岡

Throughout its entire 2000-year history, the largest city in Kyushu has been a gateway to Asia, and the place where the culture of the mainland has most impinged on the Japanese archipelago: Fukuoka is closer to both Seoul and Shanghai than it is to Tokyo. The present-day metropolitan area is the result of the merger in 1889 of the feudal city of Fukuoka and the commercial city of Hakata. As the capital of a rapidly developing region, it has become one of the most dynamic cities in Japan.

THE CITY TODAY

Its innovative architecture includes an overabundance of hair-raisingly futuristic buildings, the work of such world-famous architects as Reem Koolhaas, Michael Graves, Cesar Pelli, and Isozaki Arata. Pinning its hopes on cutting-edge technologies, the city has also created a research park by the sea, where dozens of high-tech companies are inventing tomorrow's world. But, side by side with this flashy modernity, Fukuoka has also preserved its historical heritage, and its *yatai*: old-fashioned food stands that are set up on the streets in the evening and dismantled the following morning. These serve simple dishes in a noisy, aroma-filled atmosphere recalling the great, teeming capitals of Asia.

▶ **Population:** 1,588,900 – Fukuoka Prefecture.

Michelin Map: Regions of Japan Map 8, Regional Map opposite.

Location: Facing Hakata Bay and the Sea of Genkai, the city is divided down the center by the Naka River (Naka-gawa). To the west, the old quarter of Fukuoka Castle is today the main commercial area, called Tenjin. To the east, near the JR station, are the district of Hakata and the Canal City complex. In the middle, the island of Nakasu is noted for its bars and nightlife. The JR station is called Hakata and the airport Fukuoka.

Kids: Robosquare in Momochi; activities at Canal City; the Hakata Machiya Folk Museum; the National Museum in Dazaifu.

Timing: Allow two or three days, including excursions outside the city.

Don't miss: Dinner in a *yatai*; the Kyushu National Museum.

USEFUL INFORMATION

Tourist Office – In Hakata Station. *Open 8am–9pm.* ℰ*092-431-3003, yokanavi.com/en.* Volunteers offers guided tours in English (ℰ*092-725-9100; acros.or.jp/english*).

TRANSPORTATION

BY PLANE – Fukuoka Airport – Two subway stops from JR Hakata Station *(5min, ¥270)* on the Fukuoka Airport Line. From Tokyo, departures almost every 20min, between 6.15am and 8pm *(2hr, around ¥32,000).*

BY TRAIN – Hakata Station – From Tokyo, the fastest train is the Shinkansen Nozomi *(5hr, ¥22,220)*, but it's not covered on the Japan Rail Pass. The JR Pass can be used on Hikari and Sakura trains, but you have to transfer once on the way *(6hr, ¥22,220)*. The **JR Kyushu Pass** covers the whole of the JR network in Kyushu for 3 or 5 days *(¥15,300/¥18,400)*. JR South Kyushu *(3 days, ¥7500)* and North Kyushu *(3/5 days, ¥8700/¥10,200)* passes also sold.

A BIT OF HISTORY

Mongolian hordes and the *kamikaze* – Rice cultivation and techniques for casting iron and bronze were introduced to the north of Kyushu from the Korean peninsula more than 2000 years ago. From there, they spread throughout Japan. By the 6C, Dazaifu, the regional capital (later moved to Fukuoka), was maintaining diplomatic relations with the Chinese Sui dynasty (581–618). In the Middle Ages, Nanotsu—the old port of Fukuoka—became one of the most prosperous in Japan. It aroused the envy of the Great Mongolian emperor, Kublai Khan, who made two attempts to invade, in 1274 and 1281, raising one of the largest armies in history, consisting of 150,000 soldiers and 4400 ships.

The Japanese were massively outnumbered, relying on their modest fortifications built along the shoreline to repel the invading hordes. Defeat seemed inevitable, until the area was providentially hit by a typhoon that destroyed the invaders' fleet and forced them to retreat. The Japanese called it *kamikaze*, the "divine wind" that saved Japan.

Yamagasa Matsuri

Every year for the past 700 years, from July 1 to 15, this colorful festival in Fukuoka culminates in a furious race between teams of 26 men, representing the different districts of the city. Each team has to carry a float weighing almost a ton over a 3mi/5km course in a specified time, while the spectators throw water over them as they pass. The contestants run dressed in a simple costume consisting of a *shimekomi* (or *fundoshi*), the loincloth worn by sumo wrestlers, a light cotton jacket bearing the insignia of their team, and sandals made of straw. The festival was inscribed on UNESCO's Intangible Cultural Heritage list in 2016.

SIGHTS

The Fukuoka Tourist City Pass (¥820, ¥1340 combined with Daizafu) gives access to public transport (train, subway, and bus) for a day. For a list of outlets selling the pass: yokanavi.com/en/tourist-city-pass.

HAKATA DISTRICT

Canal City Hakata
キャナルシティ博多
10min walk west of JR Hakata Station.
Almost a city within a city, this huge American-style shopping mall opened in 1996, covering a staggering 2,580,000 sq ft/240,000sq m near the Naka-gawa. Part of this river has been diverted to form an **artificial canal** that flows through the middle of a central atrium; huge jets of water erupt from the canal at regular intervals.
The mall also houses a **13-screen multiplex cinema,** hotels, a **variety theater,** and hundreds of **boutiques, restaurants,** and **gaming halls**. Street performances and concerts take place throughout the day.

Kushida-jinja   櫛田神社
10min walk from Gion subway station. *Open daily 4am–10pm; museum open Tue–Sun 10am–5pm.* ¥310.
A beautiful and very old *gingko biloba* tree marks the entrance to this shrine founded in 754 (the present buildings date from 1587), which is also the starting point every summer for the spectacular Yamagasa Matsuri (*see box left*). A small **museum** displays the huge, richly decorated floats that are carried during the festival.

Hakata Machiya Folk Museum★ 博多町屋ふるさと館
Opposite the shrine. *Open daily 10am–6pm.* *Closed 4th Mon every month.* ¥200. hakatamachiya.com.
The collections of this museum, devoted to the traditional culture and lifestyle of Hakata, are displayed in a number of restored merchants' houses from the Taisho era (1912–26). There are faithful reconstructions of shop interiors

from the beginning of the century, and regular demonstrations of local crafts: doll making, silk weaving, the making of spinning tops. There is also a 20min video about the Yamagasa Matsuri.

Shofuku-ji 聖福寺

15min walk north from JR Hakata Station, or 5min walk from Gion subway station. ○*Open daily 25hr.* ∞*No charge. shofukuji.or.jp.*

This is the oldest Zen temple in Japan, founded by the monk Eisai (who also introduced tea to Japan) on his return from China in 1195. The fine wooden building with its double roof (○—*closed to the public*) has, as is so often the case in Japan, been destroyed and rebuilt several times over the centuries. Only the garden is open to the public.

Tocho-ji 南岳山 東長密寺

A 5-min walk from Shofuku-ji. ○*Open daily 24hr.* ∞*No charge.*

Concealed within this Shingon sect temple, which was built in the 9C by the monk Kobo Daishi upon his return from China, you will find the largest seated wooden Buddha statue in all Japan. The figure is more than 33ft/10m tall and was completed in 1992 after four years of work. Lurking behind the statue there is a treasure room that is open to the public, while outside, you will find an 85ft/26m, five-story pagoda, painted bright vermillion, that was built in 2011 to commemorate the 1200th anniversary of the temple. The tombs of various members of the Kuroda family, the feudal lords of Fukuoka Prefecture, lie scattered among the trees.

Nakasu foodstalls

© masanv78/Shutterstock

Asian Art Museum★★
福岡アジア美術館

7F–8F Riverain Center Bldg. Subway Nakasu-Kawabata, exit 6. Museum: Open Thur–Tue & Thur 9.30am–7.30pm (Fri–Sat to 8pm). Asia Gallery: Open Thur–Tue 9.30am–6pm (Fri–Sat to 8pm). ¥200 (excluding special exhibitions). faam.city.fukuoka.lg.jp/en. .

Situated within a large, light-filled modern building, opened in 1999, this museum is the first in the world to be entirely devoted to modern and contemporary Asian art, bringing together some 2300 works by painters and sculptors from India, China, Myanmar, Malaysia, Thailand, the Philippines, Pakistan, and of course Japan. There are no statues of Buddha here—the museum displays original and unusual works, sometimes humorous or eccentric, sometimes based on folk and ethnic traditions, and always of high quality.

As well as the work of already-celebrated artists such as **Nam June Paik**, **Zhang Xiaogang**, and **Jamini Roy**, there are temporary exhibitions by young artists in residence, as well as a triennial exhibition of contemporary art.

NAKASU AND TENJIN
中州・天神

The island of Nakasu in the middle of the Naka-gawa comes to life after nightfall, when its neon lights cast colored reflections on the water, and thousands of *salarymen* (office workers) converge on the area, sitting shoulder to shoulder on the wooden benches of the *yatai* (mobile foodstalls), devouring bowls of noodles or *yakitori*, washed down with sake. Farther west, the **Tenjin** area is a shopper's paradise, full of fashionable boutiques and department stores. The **ACROS building**, designed by Emilio Ambasz, dates from 1995. On its south side is a spectacular terraced garden.

CHUO DISTRICT 中央

1.2mi/2km west of Tenjin district. Subway Kuko and Nanakuma lines, Ohorikoen-mae (2 stops west of Tenjin) or Ropponmatsu stops.

The central district isn't the focus of tourism in Fukuoka, but it has a couple of sights worth visiting The green space of Ohori Park makes an excellent place for a stroll, and is home to the city's **castle ruins** (open daily 24hr, no charge).

👥 Fukuoka City Science Museum★
– Ropponmatsu station, exit 3. Open Wed–Mon 9.30am–9.30pm. ¥400 (children ¥200), planetarium ¥600 (children ¥300). fukuokacity-kagakukan. jp. Opened in 2017, all six floors of the city science museum are packed with interactive exhibits and science demonstrations. Reservations advised for the very comfortable and atmospheric planetarium. On the 5th floor is Robosquare, where around 100 robots are on display.

MOMOCHI DISTRICT★
シーサイドももち

2mi/3km northwest of the center. Subway Nishijin (Kuko Line), then 15min walk to the north.

The ultramodern district of Momochi is built on land reclaimed from the sea.

Fukuoka Tower – *Open daily 9.30am–10pm. ¥800.* The tower is 768ft/234m high and covered in 8,000 sheets of mirror glass. At 404ft/123m, its observation deck has magnificent **views**★ over the city.

Fukuoka City Museum – *5min walk south. Open Tue–Sun 9.30am–5.30pm. ¥1400. museum.city.fukuoka.jp/en.* Among the recently renovated city museum's exhibits are a **gold seal**★ given to Fukuoka in the year 57 by a Chinese emperor of the Han dynasty (206BC–AD220).

EXCURSIONS
Regional Map.

DAZAIFU★★ 大宰府
Map, B2. 9.3mi/15km southeast of Fukuoka. From Nishitetsu Fukuoka Station in Tenjin, take the Nishitetsu Omuta private train line and change at Nishitetsu Futsukaichi (30min, ¥400). Tourist Office and bicycle rental outside the station.

Dazaifu Tenman-gu★
大宰府天満宮

5min walk north of the station. Open daily 24hr. No charge.

A beautiful arched bridge over a pond leads to this shrine, founded in 905. The present building, in Momoyama style (1586), is listed as a National Treasure. It was erected in memory of Sugawara-no-Michizane (845–903), a famous scholar, poet, and minister, who lived at the court of Kyoto before falling into disgrace and being exiled to Dazaifu. After his death, he was deified as a *kami* (god) of literature and calligraphy under the name **Tenman Tenjin** (or Tenman-gu). Shrines dedicated to him can be found all over Japan. The shrine's pleasant garden contains thousands of Japanese plum trees *(ume);* there is a festival every year on February 25 to celebrate their blossoming.

Kyushu National Museum★★★ 九州国立博物館
Adjoining the shrine. Open Tue–Thur & Sun 9.30am–5pm, Fri–Sat 9.30am–8pm. ¥430 (children ¥130). www.kyuhaku.jp/en.

Opened in 2005 and designed by Kikutake Kiyonori, the museum is an architectural curiosity in itself, with its gigantic blue titanium roof *(525ft/160m long by 263ft/80m wide)* that undulates like a wave, and its wide plate-glass windows reflecting the surrounding forest. The light-filled interior is vast. The newest of the national museums, after those in Tokyo, Kyoto, and Nara, it focuses on the history of Japan's cultural exchanges with the rest of Asia. The permanent collections, displayed in rotation, are arranged in chronological order, covering prehistoric times and the Jomon era (room 1); the Yayoi and Kofun eras *(room 2)*; the ancient eras of the Nara and Heian (room 3); the Middle Ages: the Kamakura and Muromachi eras (room 4); the modern age, from the Momoyama to the Edo era. The **Ajippa** interactive space on the ground floor allows children to discover Japan's different cultures.

ADDRESSES

STAY

Ryokan Kashima Honkan 旅館・鹿島本館 – *3-11 Reisen-machi, Hakata-ku. 092-291-0746. kashimahonkan.jp. 27 rooms. ¥7280.* An elegant *ryokan* built in the Taisho era (1912–26). Beautiful surroundings, Japanese rooms, and a very friendly welcome in English. *O-furo.*

Takakura Hotel Fukuoka タカクラホテル福岡 – *2-7-21 Watanabe-dori, Chuo-ku. 092-731-1661. takakura-hotel.co.jp. 107 rooms. ¥11,900. ¥2000.* Beautiful rooms, and impeccable service. Fixed (higher) prices in Golden Week (*see p11*).

Hotel Forza Hakata ホテルフォルツァ博多 – *4-16 Hakataeki Chuogai, Hakata-ku. Hakata Station. 092- 473-7111.*

hotelforza.jp/hakata. *170 rooms. ¥21,000.*
¥1500 ⊡. Contemporary, functional hotel
in an ideal Hakata location.

⊖⊜▦ **Royal Park Hotel Fukuoka**
ロイヤルパークホテル福岡 – *2-14-15*
Hakataekimae, Hakata-ku. 5min from
JR Hakata Station, West 13 Exit. ☏*092-*
414-1111. the-royalpark.jp/the/fukuoka.
172 rooms. ¥20,010. ¥1815 ⊡. A modern
building in a good location, next to the
station, but in a small quiet road. The
rooms and bathrooms are a good size.

♉ EAT

FUKUOKA

☺ There are many late-opening eateries
for hungry night-owls, plus the 100 or so
stands (*yatai*) along the Naka-gawa.

⊖ **Maruyoshi** まるよし – *5 Kokutai-dori,*
Chuo-ku. ☏*090-9071-1083. Open Mon–Sat*
7pm–3am. ⊡. This restaurant was opened
in the 1930s. Try the house specialty of
motsu-nabe.

⊖ **Canal City Hakata** キャナルシティ博
多 – *1-2-25 Sumiyoshi, Hataka-ku. canalcity.*
co.jp/english. Open daily 11am–11pm.
¥700–5000. Nine restaurants on the mall's
top floor, serving ramen from the four
corners of Japan.

⊖⊜ **Motsu Ryori Kawano Haruyoshi**
Honten もつ料理かわ乃・春吉本店 –
2-16-8 Haruyoshi, Chuo-ku. ☏*092-761-2926.*
motsunabeya.com/haruyoshi. Open daily
5pm–midnight. A fifties-style restaurant
serving traditional local dishes. The menu
varies, but tripe is always in season.

⊖⊜ **Shinshusoba Murata** 信州そば む
らた – *2-9-1 Reisenmachi, Hakata-ku. Gion*
subway station. ☏*092-291-0894. Open Tue–*
Sun 11.30am–9pm. Lunch menus around
¥3000, dinner menus ¥5000. A good choice
of soba dishes (buckwheat noodles),
served hot or cold.

⊖⊜▦ **Sushi Yamanaka** 寿司やま
中 – *2-8-8 Watanabe-dori, Chuo-ku.* ☏*092-*
731-7771. www.sushi-yamanaka.jp. Open
Mon–Sat 11.30am–9.30pm. Lunch menus
from ¥22200 , dinner from ¥8800. A sushi
bar with a gleaming interior design; best
fresh fish and seafood.

⊖⊜▦ **Yoshizuka Unagiya** 吉塚うなぎ
屋 – *2-8-27 Nakasu, Hakata-ku. 7min walk*
southwest from Gion subway. ☏*092-271-*
0700. yoshizukaunagi.com. Open Thu–Tue
11am–8.30pm. Closed mid-Aug & Dec–beg
Jan. Lunch menus around ¥3000, dinner
¥6000. ⊡. On the island of Nakasu. You
may need to wait for get a table at this
restaurant known for its eel dishes.

DAZAIFU

⊖⊜ **Ume-no-hana** 梅の花 – *4-4-*
41 Zaifu. ☏*0120-28-7787. umenohana.*
co.jp/n_english. Open daily 11am–9pm. A
superb traditional tofu restaurant, with
very reasonable prices. Good lunches
from ¥2700. Generous servings.

Saga 佐賀 and surroundings

Located north of Kyushu, between
the prefectures of Fukuoka and
Nagasaki, Saga has been famous
throughout Japan since the 17th
century for the quality of its
ceramics. Still very productive,
the historic centers of Karatsu,
Imari, and above all Arita are
the most important, because of
their essential contribution to
elevating this Korean-born craft
to an artform and making it world
famous. As elsewhere on Kyushu
Island, Saga is subject to the
intense volcanic activity of the
island and has several famous spas.

▸ **Population:** Population
236,300 – Saga Prefecture

⟳ **Michelin Map:** Regional
map p576, B1.

▸ **Location:** Saga 48mi/78km
southeast of Fukuoka.

⚐ **Kids:** Saga Castle;
Saga Prefectural Space
& Science Museum.

⟳ **Timing:** Allow one day
for the town and another
for the surrounding area.

⚑ **Don't miss:** Arita
village with its shops
and craft workshops;
Okawachiyama ;
Karatsu Kunchi Matsuri
(festival in fall).

The Origins of Japanese Porcelain

Following the Japanese invasions of Korea between 1592 and 1598, many talented potters and ceramists were brought back by force to northeast of Kyushu. Around 1615, at the site of Izumiyama near Arita, one of them, Yi Sam-pyeong, discovered a deposit of high-quality kaolin. This highly resistant material would allow the production of simple white porcelain, with blue enamel underglaze, and celadon porcelain, known as Ko-Imari.

The kilns of Okawachiyama, a small village that was guarded and kept secret by the Nabeshima clan, multiplied. Prized by the high society of Japan's cities and the European courts for their great quality, the ceramics of Imari-yaki, Arita-yaki, and Hizen-yaki were exported to Europe until 1757 via the port of Imari, on board the ships of the Dutch East India Company. Very beautiful pieces from this period can be seen today in European museums, such as the Ariana Museum in Geneva (Switzerland) or the Zwinger porcelain collection in Dresden (Germany).

SIGHTS

Saga 佐賀

Capital of the prefecture of the same name, Saga is located by the Ariake Sea. Prosperous throughout the Edo Period under the yoke of the Nabeshima clan, due in particular to the ceramic products of Karatsu, Imagi, and Arita, the town was officially founded in 1889 after the Meiji Restoration. Saga beef, tender and flavorsome, is famous throughout Japan.

Saga Castle History Museum
佐賀城本丸歴史館

10min by bus from JR Saga Station (exit 3), Sagajo-ato stop, or 25min on foot. ○*Open daily 9.30am–6pm.* ∞*No charge, but donations welcome. saga-museum.jp/sagajou.*

👥 The castle was built in the early 17C by the powerful Nabeshima clan in the Saga plain on the site of a fortified village. All that remains today of the initial construction is the massive stone Sachi Gate. In 2004, the main building was restored to its state of 1838. It remains the largest wooden castle reconstruction in Japan, representing a beautiful example of traditional architecture of the late Edo Period. Today it houses the City History Museum.

USEFUL INFORMATION

Saga Tourist Information Center – In JR Shin-Tosu station, JR Nagasaki Line. *Open daily 9am–6pm.* Information in English. Also **Saga Travel Call Center** – 24hr in English ℘*095-220-160; free app from saga-travelsupport.com/lp.*
Karatsu Tourist Office – In Karatsu station. ℘*095-572-4963. Open daily 9am–6pm.*
Imari Tourist Office – In Imari station. ℘*095-523-3479. Open daily 9am–6pm.*
Arita Tourist Office – Opposite Arita station. ℘*095-542-4052. Open daily 9am–5pm.*

TRANSPORTATION

From Hakata to Saga, Ltd Exp. Kamome *(40min journey time, ¥1970).*
From Saga to Nagasaki – Ltd Exp. Kamome *(1hr 15min, ¥3420).*
From Hakata to Arita – trains every hour, JR Midori Line *(1hr 15min, ¥2800).*
From Arita to Imari– Matsuura Railway *(3 per hour, 30min, ¥460).*
From Arita to Takeo Onsen *(15min, ¥280/590)* Ltd Exp. Midori or JR Sasebo Line.
From Arita to Nagasaki via Haiki – Ltd Exp. Midori, then JR SeaSide Liner *(2hr, ¥1990).*

© bee32/iStock

Yoshinogari Historical Park★★
吉野ヶ里歴史公園

JR Nagasaki Line, Kanzaki or Yoshinogari Koen stops, then 15min walk. yoshinogari.jp/en/. ⊙Open daily 9am–5pm (Jun–Aug 6pm). ☞¥420. Between the 3C BC and 3C AD, the inhabitants of northern Kyushu, in addition to migrants from Korea and China, settled near the rice paddies. In the wake of archaeological digs, elements of the **Yayoi** culture, such as moats, large watch-towers and half-buried thatched roof houses, have been reconstructed at the foot of the lush green hillsides of Yoshinogari. Clay artefacts and impressive burial jars are elegantly displayed.

Karatsu 唐津 and the Higashi Matsuura Peninsula★
東松浦半島

⟁Regional Map, A1. 31mi/50km northwest. From JR Saga station, JR Karatsu Line (approx. 1hr 10min, ¥1110). Tourist Office in the station. This harbor town is famous throughout Japan for its **pottery**. Fired at a high temperature, these Korean-influenced ceramics are covered in a thick, dark brown or black glaze, or a white glaze scratched with floral motifs. Very sought after by tea ceremony aficionados, they often fetch astronomical prices. In the city, many kiln-workshops allow visitors to watch the artisans at work.

Nakazato Taroemon Kiln★ – *5min on foot, southeast of the JR station. ⊙Open Thu–Tue 9am–5.30pm. ☞No charge. nakazato-tarouemon.com.* The famous three-chamber kiln of Nakazato Taroemon has been in operation for 14 generations, and is still used once a month for a couple of days. It also includes a gallery-museum.

Karatsu Castle – *20min on foot, north of the station. ⊙Open daily 9am–5pm. ☞¥500.* Perched on a mound overlooking the sea, Karatsu Castle was built in 1602 by the *daimyo* Terasawa Hirotaka, a vassal of Toyotomi Hideyoshi. Dismantled during the Meiji era, it was rebuilt in 1966.

Former Takatori Residence ★ – *10min walk from the castle or 20min from JR Karatsu Station. ⊙Open Tue–Sun 9.30am–5pm. ☞¥520. Reservation essential: ℘095-575-0289.* Takatori Koreyoshi (1850–1927), a coal baron, had this luxurious seaside residence built with an incredible sense of detail. Beautifully restored, it illustrates the lifestyle of the upper middle classes during the Meiji Period. The residence is divided into two parts, one for the family and the other for guests, and includes a Zen garden, tearoom, and Noh theatre. On the first floor, the view of the garden that blends so perfectly with the beach and the islands of Karatsu bay in the background is stunning.

Niji-no-Matsubara pine forest – *5min walk from Higashi-Karatsu (Karatsu Line) or 2min from Niji-no-Mastubara Station (Chikuhi Line).* In the foothills of Mount Kagami, bordering the long beach of Matsubara, the "rainbow pine forest" is a magnificent plantation of black

pines that dates from the 17C. Some 500m/1640ft wide and 5km/3mi long, it counters erosion by blocking the wind and strong tides in the bay.

Hikiyama Exhibition Hall★ – *10min walk from Karatsu Station, JR Karatsu and Chikuhi Lines.* 🕐*Open 9am–5pm.* 👓*¥310 (children ¥150). karatsu-bunka.or.jp/hikiy-ama.html.* This exhibition hall showcases the 14 floats that take part in the **Kunchi Festival** organized every autumn by the neighbouring Shinto shrine. These giant lacquered floats are made out of wood, clay, hemp, and paper and weigh between 2 and 5 tons. Since 1819, the floats in the shape of samurai helmets, lions, dragons, and fish are pulled through the streets of Karatsu by 14 teams corresponding to the 14 former merchant districts of the town.

Mount Kagami Observatory★ – *10min by taxi from JR Niji-no-Matsubara Station.* Covered in a thick carpet of azaleas and cherry trees in springtime, Mount Kagami is 284m/931ft high. An observation platform at the top commands a stunning view of Karatsu Bay.

😊 The easiest way to visit the sites on the Higashi-Matsuura Peninsula described below is by car.

Yobuko Fish Market – *40min by bus from Karatsu (Showa Bus, Yobuko direction), then a 5min walk along the pedestrianized road Sakana Ichiba.* 🕐*Open daily 5.30am–noon.* To make sure you miss nothing of this popular, picturesque and colorful market selling squid, octopus, and sea urchins, make sure you arrive early. After being dried on strange turnstiles along the wharves, the squid is sold in batches strung together by wire. Be warned, though, that many of the neighboring restaurants serve the squid alive, sliced into sashimi.

Saga Prefectural Nagoya Castle Museum★ – *40min by bus from Karatsu (Showa Bus, direction Hado Misaki, Nagoya-jo Hakubutsukan Iriguchi stop), then 5-min walk.* 🕐*Open Tue–Sun 9am–5pm.* 👓*No charge. saga-museum.jp/nagoya.* The castle was built in 1591 by order of General Toyotomi Hideyoshi to serve as a basecamp for the (failed) invasion of Korea and China; it was later abandoned and dismantled. All that remains of the huge original building are the foundations and outer walls. The on-site museum has a digital tablet with a virtual view of how the fortress used to look as you walk around. The main plateau commands a stunning view of the Genkai Sea.

Hamanoura terraced rice paddies★ – *20min by bus from Yobuko or 45min from Karatsu, Hamanoura/Genkai stop.* Thanks to their position in a hollow facing the Genkai Sea, the terraced rice paddies of Hamanoura are unique and quite beautiful. Visitors come here in spring to admire unforgettable sunsets reflected in the countless, curved, terraced pools; there's an excellent view from the observatory above.

CITIES OF CERAMICS

22mi/35 km south of Karatsu (50min by train, JR Chikuhi Line, 👓¥670).
The cities of **Imari★** (伊万里) and **Arita★** (有田) have been famous worldwide since the 17C for their skill in the field of ceramics, an art that is still alive today.

Okawachiyama★★ – *3.5mi/6km from JR Imari Station. 10min by bus or taxi, bus stop in front of the Imari-Arita Ware Traditional Crafts Center at the entrance to the village.* In the upper part of the town of Imari, nestling in a hollow of the wooded, steep mountainside, this village keeps alive the tradition of porcelain made from kaolin found in the surrounding region. After crossing the bridge adorned with white and cobalt blue ceramic, walk along the pedestrian lanes lined with old buildings, many of which are still home to active **kilns, workshops,** and **galleries.**
Since the 17C, the best of the work produced here has borne the Nabeshima Ware stamp. You will be able to admire the beauty of the pieces produced and the architectural variety of the merchant

houses whose history spans the Edo, Meiji, Taisho, and Showa periods. From the Tuzan shrine and the monument dedicated to Yi Sam-pyeong (☞see box p583), there is a superb panoramic view of the village in its deep valley.

Kyushu Ceramic Museum★ – *In Arita (25min by train from Imari, Matsuura Line, or 40min by train from Saga, JR Sasebo Line, then 10min walk).* ○*Open Tue–Sun 9am–5pm.* ☜*No charge (except special exhibitions). saga-museum.jp/ceramic.* An ideal starting point to find out more about the different styles of Kyushu pottery, this museum explains in detail the characteristics of each period. The display rooms are devoted to the history of local ceramics, the first examples of Imari-yaki pottery, pieces in the Kakiemon and Kanbara styles, masterpieces from Hizen Kokaratsu and Nabeshima Ware, and especially, 1000 Arita-yaki pieces from the Shibata collection dating from the Edo Period.

Kakiemon Kiln★ – *352 Nanzan. 10min by bus or taxi from JR Arita Station.* ○*Open 9am–5pm.* ☜*No charge. kakiemon.co.jp/en.* The artisans at this kiln have been using the techniques of their grand master, Kizaemon Sakaida (17C), for 15 generations, and in particular the ingenious Akae process of enamel decoration on porcelain. The white background color varies from bright to off-white depending on the colour of the clay used. There are two exhibition halls, one of which is a salesroom, and a lovely garden.

China on the Park★ – *10min from the JR Arita Station by Saihi Bus, Sasebo direction, Haraake stop, then 10min walk.* ○*Open daily 9am–5.30pm.* ☜*No charge. www.fukagawa-seiji.co.jp.* The prestigious Fukagawa-Seiji workshop produces, among other things, tea services for the Imperial family. Its gallery-museum, a large contemporary structure with a mezzanine tearoom, houses some superb pieces of transluscent white porcelain as well other more colorful and elaborate pieces, dating from the 19C. Visitors can paint their own piece of ceramic in the workshop next to the shop.

Gen-Emon Kiln★ – *2726 Maruo-hei, 10min by bus or taxi from the JR Arita Station.* ○*Open Mon–Sat 8am–5pm;* ○*closed some Sat.* ☜*No charge. gen-emon.co.jp/english.* Standing on a hillside, this famous kiln heated by red pine logs has been in operation for 250 years. Every step of the production of contemporary pottery is still carried out by hand, with each craftsman having their own specialty: shaping, painting, etc. The site offers the rare opportunity to see workshops from behind a window or what the interior of a kiln looks like. After the first firing, the black cobalt lines miraculously turn blue.

TAKEO ONSEN AND SURROUNDINGS

Takeo Onsen 武雄温泉
10mi/15km east of Arita (20min by train, JR Sasebo Line. ☜*¥280). Pubic baths around* ☜*¥500.*
At the foot of Mount Horai, the spa resort of Takeo has been attracting visitors for 1300 years thanks to its hot alkaline springs, reputed to leave the skin soft and supple. The spa buildings are located in the center of the historic town behind the huge red Romon tower gate, topped with a pagoda roof in 1914, designed by Tatsuno Kingo, architect of Tokyo railway station. Still open to the public, **Tonosama-yu**, the oldest bathing house in Japan decorated in marble, was reserved for the aristocracy back in the 18C.

Saga Prefectural Space & Science Museum ★
佐賀県立宇宙科学館
10min by bus from Takeo-Onsen Station, JR Sasebo Line. ○*Open Tue–Fri 9.15am–5.15pm, Sat–Sun 9.15am–6pm.* ☜*¥520 (children ¥100–310; planetarium only* ☜*¥520 (children ¥100–310); combined ticket* ☜*¥930 (children ¥180–550). yumeginga.jp.*
👤 The museum's daring architecture reproduces a rocket launch, although

the rocket is in fact a central elevator to 3 levels; the first is devoted to activities for children, the second to the Earth and universe, and the last to the region's different ecosystems.

The planetarium is one of the most modern in the world, complete with moving seats and 3D-vision. Notable attractions include an earthquake simulator, astronaut training gyroscope, and a weightlessness simulator.

Yutoku Inari-jinja★
祐徳稲荷神社

17mi/28km south of Takeo Onsen. 30min by train from Takeo-Onsen, JR Sasebo and Nagasaki Lines, change at Hizen-Yamaguchi (☺¥560) then 10min by bus from JR Hizen-Kashima Station, Yutoku Inari jinja-mae stop. ⏰Open daily. ☺No charge. yutokusan.jp/en.

Built against the flank of the hillside on stilts, Yutoku Inari-jinja is the third largest Shinto Inari shrine of Japan. Every year thousands of pilgrims come here in search of prosperity and good luck in business, particularly at the New Year. The oldest structure, devoted to the guardian spirit of the Nabeshima clan, dates from 1688. Iwasaki-Sya, the god of marriage who brings happiness and wealth, is worshipped in the enclosure of the main building.

ADDRESSES

🛏 STAY

KARATSU

☺☺ **Dai-ichi Riviere** 第一 リベール – *1-9 Higashimachi* ☏*095-575-2000 - kugimoto.co.jp/dai-ichi/en. 154 rooms. ¥8200 . ¥800☕.* Some of the rooms, and the *onsen,* in this modern hotel beside the Matsuura River have views of the castle and Niji-no-Matsubara pine forest.

TAKEO ONSEN

☺☺☺☺ **Ogiya** 扇屋 – *7399 Takeomachi.* ☏*095-422-3188 . ougiya.com. 8 rooms. ¥61,600 . ☕, dinner also included.* A magnificent *ryokan* where you will appreciate all the refinement of Japanese tradition. Japanese-style rooms, including some with private bath.

🍴 EAT

KARATSU AND THE HIGASHI MATSUURA PENINSULA

☺☺☺ **Yamashige** 山茂 – *1674 Konyamachi.* ☏*0955-573-0201. Open Mon–Sat 11.30am–2pm & 4.30–10pm. Lunch menus from ¥1800, dinner menus around ¥4000; seat charge ¥340/450.* Just a 2min walk from the JR station, this restaurant offers a wide range of seafood, plus the famous Saga beef.

ARITA

☺ **Kiln Café** – *972-31 Hommachi-hei.* ☏*090- 525-9389. Open daily 9am–5.30pm.* This friendly, laidback cafe housed in a shipping container serves warming lunch dishes such as curry and *ten-don* (tempura on rice), plus hot drinks and snacks. It also incorporates the town's ceramics tradition, so you might end up sipping coffee from an elegant, blue-and-white glazed glazed cup. The Arita tourist information center is in the same complex.

ACTIVITIES

Nanatsugama Sea Caves – *40min by Showa bus from Karatsu to Yoboku port, then 5min walk to the Marinepal jetty for sightseeing boats. Open Mar–Nov daily 9.30am–4.30pm, departures every hour, 40min. ¥1500, (children ¥750).* The seven Nanatsugama sea caves can only be seen by boat from Yobuko. The volcanic rock has been shaped here by the waves of the Genkai Sea over the centuries. In good weather, the dark basalt inside the caves contrasts with the bright light and the grass plateau above the cliff. At high tide with a calm sea, the boats can penetrate around 160ft/50m into one of the caves beneath 10ft/3m-high vault. Quite spectacular.

EVENTS

Arita Ceramic Faire – *end Apr–beg May.*

Saga International Balloon Fiesta – *late Oct–early Nov.* An international event with a hundred or so balloons from all over the world.

Karatsu Kunchi Festival – *Nov 2–4.* 14 floats parade through the town and across the beach (🕯*see p584*). A colorful folk festival.

Nagasaki★★
長崎

Nagasaki (the "long cape") winds along a long, narrow bay, overlooked by old colonial houses clinging in picturesque fashion to the surrounding hills. As early as the 16C, this natural deep-water harbor was attracting attention from foreign nations—Portuguese galleons and Chinese junks, Jesuit priests and merchant adventurers all made their way here. During Japan's two centuries of isolation (sakoku), from 1641 to 1853, Nagasaki was its only link with the outside word. Thanks to the city's history and its mixture of Eastern and Western influences, Nagasaki today has a discreetly cosmopolitan charm and a large Christian minority, much-persecuted over the centuries. As the victim of the second atomic bomb, after Hiroshima, Nagasaki has its own Peace Park as a poignant reminder of the tragedy. That terrible episode in its history has not stopped the place from being reborn as a lively, modern, port city, fueled by the dynamism of the great Mitsubishi dockyards.

- ▶ **Population:** 429,500 – Nagasaki Prefecture.
- ⚙ **Michelin Map:** Regions of Japan Map 8, Regional Map p576, Nagasaki Map p590.
- ▷ **Location:** Nagasaki stretches along the Urakami River and around a narrow harbor, 68mi/110km southwest of Fukuoka. Several tram lines cross the city from the station: 1.5mi/2.5km north of the station is the Urakami district and the Peace Park; 0.6mi/1km to the south lies the Shian-bashi district, noted for its nightlife, Chinatown, and the colonial villas of Glover Garden on the hills.
- ◷ **Timing:** Allow two days for the city and one for Shimabara. Ferries to Amakusa from the port.
- ☺ **Don't miss:** The Atomic Bomb Museum; the view from Mount Inasa; a bowl of chanpon noodles in Chinatown; Glover Garden. Shimabara Peninsula and Mt. Unzen.

A BIT OF HISTORY

The " Christian century" – The arrival of Portuguese and Chinese ships in 1571 marked the beginning of the transformation of Nagasaki from a small fishing village to a bustling trading port, and products from China and Europe came flooding in: tobacco, bread, clothes, firearms. Some products, now made in the city, have kept their original Portuguese names, like the famous Nagasaki honey cake, Castella (kasutera).

Following in the wake of Spanish missionary Francis Xavier, who preached in Japan from 1549 to 1552, the Jesuit fathers founded hundreds of churches in Nagasaki and in the south of Kyushu. With the aid of books, artistic exchanges, and a growing awareness of Western medicine, Christianity became influential for a brief period, but things soon turned sour. Worried by the widespread influence of the Jesuits, the shogun ordered their expulsion in 1597. It was accompanied by a wave of anti-Christian persecution, culminating in the great Shimabara Rebellion of 1637, when nearly 40,000 peasants, many of them Christian, rose up against the shogunate and were slaughtered. For the next 250 years Japanese Christians were forced to practice their religion in secret. Today, there are about 30,000 Christians in the city of Nagasaki.

Dejima, a door half-open – Less concerned with proselytizing than the Portuguese, the Dutch were able to continue discreetly doing business in Japan. In 1641, the artificial island of Dejima, in Nagasaki Bay, constructed on the orders of Tokugawa Iemitsu, was allocated as a

USEFUL INFORMATION

Tourist Offices – In the concourse of the JR station *(Map, A2)*. Open daily 8am–8pm; *095-823-3631, travel.at-nagasaki.jp/en.*

Unzen Tourist Association – Information center opposite the post office. *320 Unzen Obamacho. Open daily 9am–5pm.* *0957-73-3434.*

Shimabara City Office – Information office in row of houses, to the left on leaving Shimabara Station. *537 Kamimachi.* *095-763-1111. www.city.shimabara.lg.jp/kanko. Open daily 8.30am–5.15pm.*

Bank/Withdrawal – Juhachi Bank Honten, *1-11 Douzamachi (Map, B3).* Open Mon–Fri 9am–3pm.

Post Office – 1-1 Ebisumachi *(Map, A2).* Open Mon–Fri 9am–7pm, Sat 9am–5pm, Sun 9am–12.30pm.

TRANSPORTATION

BY PLANE – From Tokyo – 17 flights daily to Nagasaki *(1hr 40min, around ¥37,000).* Solaseed Air has a special offer for tourists at ¥10,500. Shuttles between the airport and Ken-ei Bus Nagasaki Terminal *(50min, ¥920).*

BY TRAIN – To and from Tokyo – You have to travel via Fukuoka-Hakata, *(5hr by shinkansen, about ¥25,060).* Link for **Fukuoka** by Ltd. Express Kamome *(2hr, ¥4270).* For Kumamoto, Ltd. Express Kamome, change at Shin-tosu for shinkansen Sakura *(2hr, ¥7080).*

BY BUS – Ken-ei Bus Nagasaki Terminal – *Opposite the JR station (Map, A2).* Buses are the cheapest and simplest way to get around the region. Regular departures for Kumamoto *(3hr 30min, arond ¥3800)* and Beppu *(4hr, around ¥4750).*

BY BOAT – For Amakusa, take bus no. 10 from Kenei terminal, opposite the JR station, to Mogi port *(30min, ¥280),* then a ferry to Tomioka, in the north of the island *(45min, ¥2100).*

GETTING AROUND NAGASAKI

BY TRAM – 6.20am–11pm, ¥130 per ticket, ¥500 1-day pass. The blue *(no. 1)* and red *(no. 3)* lines run between west *(Akasako terminus)* and east *(Hotarujaya terminus for Line 3, Shokakuji-shita terminus for Line 1)*; 30min between the two termini, 5mi/8km. The yellow *(no. 4)* and green *(no. 5)* lines run north–south across the east part of the city.

---

base for Dutch trading activities. Strictly confined to this island, they remained (along with China, and with the then-separate Ryukyus and Ezo, now Okinaa and Hokkaido) Japan's only point of contact with the outside world until 1855. When the ban on Dutch books was lifted in 1720, hundreds of students flocked to Nagasaki to study European art and science. With the Meiji Restoration, the

The "Hidden Christians"

After the decree of 1614 in which their religion was banned, the 400,000 Japanese Christians had to either renounce or conceal their faith. "The crackdown was brutal," says Father Renzo De Luca, who runs the museum at the 26 Martyrs Memorial. "For more than two centuries, hundreds of Christians who refused to recant were executed on this hill: crucified, burned alive, or hanged." Thousands of others continued to worship in secret, venerating Buddhist figures like the compassionate goddess Kannon, who reminded them of the Virgin Mary—the museum contains a number of statuettes of Maria Kannon, their backs marked with concealed crosses. The authorities offered rewards for anyone who would inform on the Christians. Suspects were forced to trample on biblical images in order to prove they were recanting their faith, in a ritual known as *fumie*.

NAGASAKI

Ohashi Sta.

Peace Statue ②

Urakami Cathedral

Peace Park

206

Matsuyama-machi Sta.

Atomic Bomb Museum

MT. KOMPIRA-SAN

0 — 500 m
0 — 500 yds

KITA P.O.

URAKAMI

Urakami-Ekimae Sta.

Urakami Sta.

NAGASAKI CITY HISTORY AND FOLKLORE MUSEUM

Urakami-gawa Riv.

JR Nagasaki Line

Mount Inasa

AERIAL TRAMWAY

TATEYAMA PARK

Nishiyama-gawa Riv.

Urakami-gawa Riv.

④

26 Martyrs Memorial St Philippe Church

Nagasaki Sta.

NAGASAKI PARK

Nagasaki Museum of History and Culture

Nagasaki Electric Tramway

Nagasaki-Ekimae Sta.

34

Nagasaki Electric Tramway Hotarujaya Line

Asahi-ohashi Bridge

Kokaidomae Sta.

Nishizashira Sta.

Kofuku-ji

KAZAGASHIRA PARK

Megane-bashi

KOTAI-JI

202

NAGASAKI PREF. GOVERNMENT OFFICE

Tsukimachi Sta.

CHINATOWN

MT. KAZAGASHIRA-YAMA

① Dejima Sta.

Nagasaki Dejima Museum of History

499

⑤ ③

Sofuku-ji

Nagasaki Prefectural Art Museum

④

② Shokakuji-Shita Sta.

HAMANI MACHI

Nagasaki Port

NOGUCHI YATARO MUSEUM OF ART

Oranda Zaka

③

Nagasaki Dejima Toll Road

324

③ ① Koshi-byo

Oura Catholic Church

Ishibashi Sta.

Glover Garden

Kyushu-shozen Ferry

WHERE TO STAY		WHERE TO EAT	
ANA Crowne Plaza Nagasaki Gloverhill	❶	Nagasaki-koh	❶
Nagasaki Catholic Center Youth Hostel	❷	Ryotei Kagetsu	❷
Nagasaki Washington Hotel	❸	Shikairou	❸
The Hotel Nagasaki BW Premier Collection	❹	Yossou	❹
Victoria Inn	❺		

city again became a rapidly expanding, cosmopolitan port.

The atomic bomb—During World War II, with its many factories producing arms, ships, and planes, Nagasaki was one of the linchpins of the Japanese military-industrial complex. It was not, however, the main target of the American B-29 bomber that took off from the US base on the island of Tinian in the Pacific on the night of August 9, 1945, three days after the bombing of Hiroshima. But, finding its original target, the industrial center of Kokura (now Kitakyushu), obscured by clouds, the bomber fell back on Nagasaki. Released blindly at 11.02am, the bomb exploded at an altitude of 1903ft/580m, not over the Mitsubishi steelworks which might have been an expected target, but, by a cruel twist of fate, over Urakami Cathedral, where people were at prayer, celebrating the Western faith for which their ancestors had given their lives. The bomb, *Fat Boy*, containing 15.4lb/7kg of plutonium, killed 70,000 instantly and a similar number subsequently died from the effects of radiation. It was 10 times more powerful than *Little Boy*, which had struck Hiroshima; the death toll would have been far higher had the hills around Nagasaki not contained the blast and helped shield the south.

SIGHTS
Map, opposite

URAKAMI DISTRICT★   浦上
Map, A1. Matsuyamamachi tram stop, Lines 1 and 3.
A long flight of steps leads up to the esplanade of **Peace Park** (*Map, A1*). Here, a huge statue points a finger skyward, the direction from which the nuclear cataclysm came on August 9, 1945. Below, a black marble column marks the hypocenter of the explosion. Beside it is what remains of the old **Urakami Cathedral** (*Map, A1*), which was destroyed by the blast. Built in 1895, it was Japan's largest Roman Catholic cathedral and the largest church in Asia. The present cathedral is a replica of the original red-brick building, with its two towers. It was rebuilt in 1959 on its original site, some 1640ft/500m northeast of the hypocenter. The statues in front of the cathedral still bear the scorch marks of radioactive fallout. To the north of the new cathedral is the **house of Dr Nagai Takashi** (*5min walk north of the Peace Park,* open daily 9am–5pm; ¥100), now a small museum commemorating the work of this radiologist (1908–51), who devoted his last years to caring for those affected by radiation sickness before himself dying of leukemia.

Atomic Bomb Museum★★
長崎原爆資料館
Map, A1. 3min north of Hamaguchi-machi tram station, or 3 min south of Matsuyama-machi tram station. Open daily: May–Aug 8.30am–6.30pm (Aug 7–9, 7.30pm); Sept–Apr 8.30am–5.30pm. ¥200. nabmuseum.jp/genbaku.
This moving and informative museum shows scenes of Nagasaki, both before and after the explosion, presenting a vivid picture of the devastation caused by the bomb and an appeal for world peace and nuclear disarmament. The photos and films taken in the aftermath of the catastrophe show the horribly disfigured bodies of the dead, the wounded, and the dying.

National Peace Memorial Hall★
国立長崎原爆死没者追悼祈念館
Open daily: 8.30am–5.30pm (May–Aug, 6.30pm; Aug 7–9, 8pm . No charge. www.peace-nagasaki.go.jp.
Next to the museum are the twin rectangular glass structures of the Peace Memorial Hall, set in a pool lit at night by 70,000 fiber-optic lights. Below ground, 12 pillars of light symbolize the hope for peace. This is a resource center, displaying both written and video testimonies by survivors. It also houses a cenotaph before which the inhabitants of Nagasaki pray for the departed.

AROUND THE STATION
26 Martyrs Memorial★
日本二十六聖人記念碑
Map, A2. 15min walk from Nagasaki Station. 26martyrs.com.
This monument was erected on Nishizaka hill in 1962 as a tribute to the 26 Christians—6 Europeans and 20 Japanese—forced to walk from Kyoto to Nagasaki, where they were crucified on February 5, 1597. The martyrs were canonized by the Catholic Church in 1862, by Pope Pius IX. Behind the monument is a small museum that traces the history of the "hidden Christians" of Nagasaki through sacred objects, relics, etc. There's a museum at the site (open daily 9am–5pm, ¥500).

Lantern Festival

In February, for the Chinese New Year, the streets of Chinatown are lit by some 15,000 colored lanterns. Thousands of people come to see the fireworks, acrobatic displays, demonstrations of martial arts, and the dragon dances.

Nagasaki Museum of History and Culture 長崎歴史文化博物館

♿ Map, B2. 5min walk north of Sakuramachi tram stop, Line 3. ⏰ Open daily: Apr–Nov 8.30am–7pm; Dec–Mar 8.30am–6pm. ⏰ Closed 3rd Mon of the month. 💰¥600. www.nmhc.jp.

Opened in 2005, this museum tells the story of Nagasaki and its dealings with the outside world through many objects brought to the city by Portuguese, Chinese, and Dutch mariners.

AROUND THE PORT

Nagasaki Dejima Museum of History★ 出島

♿ Map, A3. Dejima tram stop, Line 1. ⏰ Open daily 8.30am–9pm. 💰¥520. nagasakidejima.jp/en.

A small, artificial island in the shape of a fan, built in 1636 to house Nagasaki's European community and restrict the expansion of Christianity. For more than 200 years, Dejima was the only point of contact between Japan and the outside world. When the shogunate expelled the Portuguese, the Dutch were obliged to transfer their trading operations to Dejima. Once a year the Dutch merchants were authorized to leave the island and travel to Edo to pay tribute to the shogun. Just a dozen employees of the Dutch East India Company, all men, lived permanently on the island in one-story wooden houses, their existence enlivened only by occasional visits from prostitutes. While the Dutch traded in gold, silver, ivory, spices, silks, and porcelain, the Japanese were more interested in acquiring Western technological know-how by studying medical and scientific treatises translated from the Dutch.

When Japan opened up again in 1853, the island enclave lost its purpose and the surrounding land was gradually filled in. Today, swallowed up in the general urban sprawl, the site has become a museum. Over the past several years, 10 buildings including warehouses, houses, and a Protestant church, have been rebuilt and furnished in early 19C style. To complete the reconstruction of the original island, there is a proposal to dig a canal around the site.

Nagasaki Prefectural Art Museum★ 長崎県美術館

♿ Map, A3. 3min walk southwest of Dejima. ⏰ Open daily 10am–8pm. ⏰ Closed 2nd & 4th Mon in month. 💰 No charge, apart from exhibitions. www.nagasaki-museum.jp/english.

Opened in 2005, this museum is worth a visit, if only for its striking new building with slender lines and vast glass windows reflected in water. The roof terrace (reached by elevator) has a fine **view** of the harbor. The group of 500 Spanish paintings (the largest of its kind in Asia) bequeathed to the museum by Suma Yakichiro, a former diplomat who lived for many years in Spain, forms the core of the museum's collections.

Among the artists represented are **Picasso** (including a superb Still Life with Pigeon of 1941), Miró, Dalí, and Goya. The museum also displays paintings by local artists, and temporary exhibitions are often held here.

Chinatown 中華街

♿ Map, B3. Near the Tsukimachi tram stop, Lines 1 and 5.

Four gates decorated with multicolored dragons mark out Nagasaki's Chinatown. Although smaller than the Chinese districts in Yokohama and Kobe, it is the oldest Chinatown in Japan. It stretches for 218.7yd/200m along a busy street lined with shops and restaurants, which close early. In the 17C, approximately 10,000 of Nagasaki's 60,000 inhabitants were Chinese. Still an energetic and thriving community today, the Chinese have played an important role in shaping parts of the city, influencing

East meets West in More Ways Than One

During the Meiji era, it was quite common for expatriate European and American businessmen in Nagasaki to "marry" courtesans in order to ensure exclusive rights to their favors, in return for which the women would receive accommodation and money. This somewhat questionable arrangement gave rise to the romantic, fictional character of Madame Butterfly, whose passion for an American officer ends in tragedy when he abandons her. The more mercenary figure of "temporary wife" Madame Chrysanthème, in the story by French writer Pierre Loti, was based on a real person: the young Okane-san, who was Loti's "temporary wife" when he served as a naval officer in Nagasaki. The gentle and beautiful Otaki-san was the companion of German doctor and naturalist Philipp Franz von Siebold, who spent six years on Dejima in the 1820s. Siebold discovered a new species of hydrangea, which he named *Hydrangea otakusa* after Otaki-san. Their daughter, Kusumoto Ine, became Japan's first female doctor.

its art, architecture, and culinary traditions. Take a break here and try the local specialty, *chanpon*—a soup made with thick noodles and other ingredients (pork or seafood, cabbage, and vegetables).

HAMANO-MACHI DISTRICT
Sofuku-ji ★ 崇福寺
Map, B3. Shokakuji-shita tram stop, the terminus of Lines 1 and 3. Open daily 8am–5pm. ¥300.

At the end of the street of temples stands this flamboyant building, built by the Chinese community of Nagasaki in 1629 and associated with the Obaku Zen Buddhist sect. Chinese sailors worshipped their protecting deity, Masa, here and left behind a statue to him. The second of its three gates (*daiippo-mon*) and the Buddha Hall (*daiohoden*) have been designated National Treasures.

Kofuku-ji 興福寺
Map, B2/3. 5min walk from Kokaido-mae tram stop, Lines 3, 4, and 5. Open 8am–5pm. ¥300.

This Ming-style temple in the Teramachi district was founded by an Obaku Zen monk in 1620. Enjoy a cup of *matcha* while looking out over its peaceful garden.

Megane-bashi 眼鏡橋
Map, B3. Between Kofuku-ji and Nigiwaibashi tram stop, Lines 4 and 5.

This Chinese-style "spectacles bridge," so-called because of the way its two arches are reflected in the waters of

the Nakashima River, dates from 1634 and is the oldest stone bridge in Japan.

AROUND ORANDA ZAKA
オランダ坂
Map, A3. 5min walk from Shiminbyoin-mae tram stop, Line 5.

With the opening up of Japan to the outside world in 1859, foreigners were allowed to leave Dejima and many settled in this residential district. Its gently sloping cobbled streets earned it the name *Oranda Zaka*, or Dutch Slopes (at that time, all Europeans were still called "Dutch" by the inhabitants of Nagasaki). The banks and commercial buildings were all located at the bottom of the hill, while Western-style houses, schools, and consulates clung to the hillside itself. Several wooden houses in the district have been restored and contain small museums, including a **photography museum** (*4min from Ishibashi tram stop, open Tue–Sun, 9am–5pm; ¥100*), where you can see a collection of photographs of Nagasaki from the end of the 19C and the beginning of the 20C.

Glover Garden ★★ グラバー園
Map, A3. 5min walk from Ouratenshudo-shita tram stop, Line 5. Open daily 8am–6pm (Golden Week, Jul 19–Oct 9, and Dec 22–25: 8am–9.30pm). ¥610.

It was on this hill overlooking the harbor at the southern edge of the former

European concession that a small group of wealthy Westerners lived in the middle of the 19C. The area is now a park and open-air museum in which nine of the elegant, colonial-style mansions have been reconstructed.

The meticulously detailed presentation, interiors, antiques, and family photos evoke the 19C well, despite the crowds and slightly kitsch ambience.

▶ Start your visit from the top of the hill, reached by moving walkways.

Walker House – Born in England in 1851, Captain Robert N. Walker became involved in the Japanese shipping industry. In 1898, together with Thomas Glover, he went on to set up the first soft drinks factory in Japan (in Nagasaki), producing Banzai lemonade and cider, which later became the Kirin Brewery.

Ringer House – More opulent than Walker House and built of stone, this house dates from 1865. British businessman Frederick Ringer ran a number of companies, including a tea export business and a gas and electricity company.

Alt House – Another British tea merchant, William Alt, lived for three years in this impressive house built in 1864. It has a wide porch and fine veranda supported by Tuscan-style columns.

Glover House★ – Built in 1859, this is the most imposing of all the mansions. It belonged to Thomas Glover, a Scottish adventurer whose various enterprises included shipbuilding, brewing, and arms dealing. With its four wings forming a cross, it is the oldest European-style wooden residence in Japan. It is known as **"Madame Butterfly's House"** because Glover's wife, a former geisha, is said to have been the inspiration for the story on which Puccini's famous opera was based. Above the house is a statue of the Japanese singer Miura Tamaki (1884–1946), noted for her performance in the role. Toward the exit, in another building, you can see the fabulous dragons and floats used during the Kunchi Festival in the fall.

Koshi-byo 孔子廟

🜂 Map, A3. 3min walk from Ouratenshudo-shita tram stop, Line 5.
🕐 Open daily 8.30am–5pm. ∞ ¥600.
This **colorful shrine** at the foot of Higashi-yamate hill was built in 1893 by the Chinese of Nagasaki in honor of Confucius. The **statues** of the master's 72 disciples were a gift from China, which financed the complete restoration of the building in 1980. Beside it is a small historical **museum** displaying pieces on loan from the National Museum of China and the Palace Museum in Beijing.

Oura Catholic Church 大浦天主堂

🜂 Map, A3. Near Glover Garden.
🕐 Open daily 8am–5.30pm. ∞ ¥1000.
nagasaki-oura-church.jp.
A wooden mock-Gothic church with fine stained-glass windows, built in 1865 by

"Under the banner of God"

While it was Toyotomi Hideyoshi who decreed the expulsion of all Christian missionaries in 1587, persecution only became extreme and systematic under Tokugawa Iemitsu in the second decade of the 17C. All the missionaries were slain or forced out of the country and Japanese converts (at the end of the 16C are estimated at about 300,000) were obliged to recant or be martyred. As a result, about thirty Christians were thrown into the "hellfire" of Unzen in 1627. In 1637, thousands of farmers from Amakusa and Shimabara, mostly former Christians, rose up in insurrection against their local lords, who were loading them with taxes. Led by the very young **Amakusa Shiro Tokisada** (aged 16), they took refuge in Hara castle in the south of the peninsula. Despite resisting fiercely, they were overcome by an army dispatched by the shogun; 37,000 people died in the ensuing massacre and Japanese Christianity was officially wiped out for two centuries (🜂 see also p606).

Japanese carpenters under the direction of the French priest Father Petitjean, bishop of Nagasaki, who helped to restore the Catholic Church's links with the "hidden Christians." The church commemorates the 26 martyrs of 1597.

Mount Inasa★ 稲佐山

Map, A2. Access by cable car. Open 9am–10pm; ¥730 one-way, ¥1250 round trip. 5min walk west of the Takaramachi tram stop (Lines 1 & 3), or bus from the JR station (20min, ¥160). From the top of this 10935ft/333m high hill, the **view★★** of Nagasaki Bay is magical by day or night.

EXCURSIONS
Regional Map, A2.

SHIMABARA PENINSULA★
島原半島
About 37mi/60km southeast of Nagasaki. The landscapes and volcanic waters of **Unzen Amakusa National Park** *(Japan's leading National Park, created in 1934)* are a welcome contrast to the city.

Unzen★ 雲仙
Access by bus from Nagasaki (from the airport or the Nagasaki medical care center stop, 1hr 45min) or by Route 57. For over 300 years this spot at the foot of one of Mount Unzen's craters has been appreciated for the therapeutic virtues of its sulfured waters. They boil up naturally from the ground (248°F/120°C), releasing steam and gases that give a certain odor to the downtown area. As at Beppu (*see p621*) they are called "**hells★**" (*jigoku*). People come to relax in one of the many hotels or *ryokan* nearby, or to admire the seasonal changes against the backdrop of volcanic reliefs.Unzen, at an altitude of 2296ft/700m, also has temperate summers that from the late 19C to WWII many Westerners came to enjoy. Western-style hotels were built to welcome them, and though they have just about completely disappeared, with the exception of the Unzen Kanko Hotel (*see Addresses*), the city has kept several buildings from that period, inspired by Western architecture.

Oura Catholic Church

Unzen is quieter, escaping the mass tourism so apparent in resorts like Beppu.

Mount Unzen 雲仙岳
About 4mi/7km from Unzen. Take Route 57, then follow the "Nita Pass" signs. Mount Unzen is a volcanic grouping comprised of several cones, including mounts Myoken (*4373ft/1333m*), Fugen (*4458ft/1359m*), and Heisei Shinzan (*4875ft/1486m*); this last was formed during the most recent—and terrible —eruption, in 1991 (*see below*).
The cable car (*unzen-ropeway.com;* open daily: *Apr–Oct 8.30am–5.25pm, Nov–Mar 8.30am–5pm;* ¥1300 round-trip; *go in the morning before the mist forms*) leaving from Nita Pass at 3510ft/1070m takes you to the slopes of Mount Myoken, from where there is superb **panorama★★** of the peninsula from the observation platform, as well as of the Ariake Sea, Amakusa Archipelago, and Heisei Shinzan. Unzen Golf Course, Japan's first opened in 1913, is below. Azaleas cover Mount Myoken's slopes in spring.

Shimabara 島原
Mount Unzen Disaster Memorial Hall – *1-1 Heiseimachi, 10min from the ferry terminal.* Open daily 9am–6pm (last admission 5pm). ¥1000, audio guide in English available. This museum Japan's various volcano type and describes the violent 1991 eruption in detail; 43 peo-

ple died and several districts of the town were destroyed. Shimabara and the peninsula are part of UNESCO's global Geopark program.

Shimabara Castle – The original 17C castle was rebuilt in the 1960s. The museum evokes the Christian era, in the keep *(shimabarajou.com;* ⏱*open daily 9am–5.30pm;* 🎫*¥540).*

Bukeyashiki★ – About .5mi/700m from the castle, the samurai district remains authentic, especially Shitanocho Street, with its little water supply canal. Three Edo period residences can be visited.

ADDRESSES

🛏 STAY

NAGASAKI

🛏 **Nagasaki Catholic Center Youth Hostel** 長崎カトリックセンターユースホステル – *10-34 Uenomachi (Map, A1).* ℘*095-846-4246. e-yh.net/nccyh.* 🛏 *19 rooms. ¥2200.* 🍴 Part youth hostel, this is the Catholic center where Pope John Paul II stayed in 1981. Fairly spartan, but clean, quite comfortable and well kept.

🛏 **Victoria Inn** ビクトリア・イン長崎 *24 Doza-machi (Map, B3).* ℘*095-828-1234. www.victoria-inn.jp. 87 rooms. ¥8100. ¥1200*🍴. This Victorian-style hotel exudes shabby-chic charm and is well located with good transport links; it boasts comfortable and well-appointed rooms.

🛏 **Nagasaki Washington Hotel** 長崎ワシントンホテル – *9-1 Shinchimachi (Map, B3).* ℘*095-828-1211. washington-hotels.jp/ nagasaki. 300 rooms. ¥7280. ¥1430*🍴. A good hotel at the entrance to Chinatown.

🛏🛏 **ANA Crowne Plaza Nagasaki Gloverhill** ANAクラウンプラザホテル長崎グラバーヒル – *1-18 Minami-Yamatemachi (Map, A3).* ℘*095-818-6601. www.ihg.com. 216 rooms.* Near Minami-Yamate hill and Glover Garden, a very good hotel with three restaurants: Japanese, French, and Chinese.

🛏🛏🛏 **The Hotel Nagasaki BW Premier Collection** ザ・ホテル長崎BW プレミアコレクション – *2-26 Takaramachi (Map, A2).* ℘*095-818-6601. www.ihg.com/ crowneplaza/hotels/us/en/nagasaki/ngsgh/ hoteldetail. 216 rooms. ¥12,300. ¥2500*🍴. This hotel near the station stands out for its spaciousness and the beautiful views

across the city from the bay windows of its rooms and restaurant.

🍽 EAT

NAGASAKI

🍴 **Shikairou** 四海楼 – *4-5 Matsugae-machi (Map, A3).* ℘*095-822-1296. www.shikairou.com. Open daily 11.30am–3pm, 5pm–9pm (last orders 8pm).* A Chinese restaurant in the chic Glover Garden district that has been serving *chanpon* (a cheap noodle dish) for four generations.

🍴🍴 **Yossou** 吉宗 (よっそう) 本店 – *8-9 Hamamachi (Map, B3).* ℘*095-821-0001. yossou.co.jp. Open 11am–9pm (last orders 8pm). Closed 2nd Tue every month.* Enjoy the famous *mushi-zushi,* a cod and rice-based local specialty, seated on cushions on the *tatami*-covered floor.

🍴🍴 **Nagasaki-koh** 長崎港 – *1-F (Map, A3).* ℘*095-811-1877. nagasakikou.com. Open daily 11am–2pm & 5–10pm.* Serving fresh fish and seafood, this restaurant is located beside the marina on a terraced jetty looking out over the sea where you can watch the sun go down behind Mt. Inasa. An ideal place to forget about the hustle and bustle of the city.

🍴🍴🍴🍴 **Ryotei Kagetsu** 料亭花月 – *2-1 Maruyama-machi (Map, B3).* ℘*095-822-0191. ryoutei-kagetsu.co.jp. Open daily noon–3pm & 6–10pm (last orders 2pm & 8pm). Reservation required.* A high-class restaurant in an historic location with a magnificent garden. Famous revolutionary Sakamoto Ryoma numbers among past clientele.

TAKING A BREAK

Setre Café セトレ – *2-28 Minami Yamatemachi.* ℘*095-827-7777. Open Wed–Mon noon–5pm. hotelsetre.com/nagasaki/ restaurant.* Beside Glover Garden, this cafe belonging to the Setre Glover's House hotel has been entirely renovated and now has a smooth jazzy feel. Meals must be ordered in advance, but you can always stop in for a drink and a snack.

UNZEN

Unzen Kanko Hotel 雲仙観光ホテル – *320 Unzen, Obama machi.* ℘*095-773-3263. Open daily until 11pm. unzenkankohotel. com/dining_bar.* The only hotel left from the time when Unzen was a summer retreat for Westerners. English-style woodwork and fabric lend an old-fashioned charm when sipping a drink at the bar.

In The Land of the Volcano God

A Country Of Mountains And Flames

Volcanic activity is of Japan's very essence. Mount Fuji, a symbol of purity and eternity, is the perfect emblem for a country with an impressive tally of 110 active volcanoes, nearly 10 percent of all the volcanoes in the world. This concentration is the result of the collision of four tectonic plates (the Pacific, Eurasian, North American, and Philippine), a pile-up that caused Japan to appear above the waves in the first place. It is thus hardly surprising that the Land of the Rising Sun is also a country of mountains and flames. The Pacific ring of fire, which runs the entire length of Japan, first makes itself apparent at Kyushu, then at the Fossa Magna between Toyama and the Izu Peninsula, before reappearing in Tohoku and ultimately Hokkaido.

Volcanic Tourism

Volcanoes are inextricably bound up with the tourist industry in Japan: whether they come to see the fumaroles and clouds of steam at Sakurajima (Kyushu), to sniff the sulfur vents at Akan (Hokkaido), or to pass through the lunar landscape of toxic fumes at Mount Aso (Kyushu), crowds of Japanese flock along the paths leading to the country's craters. And that's not even counting the innumerable visitors from both Japan and further afield who stream to the foothills of Mount Fuji in July and August. The *onsen* (hot springs with medicinal qualities) and *ryokan* (historic inns with a traditional welcome for visitors) are also no strangers to the volcanoes' success with tourists—of which the "eight hells" of Beppu (Kyushu) or indeed the spa resort of Hakone (Kanto) are perfect illustrations. Volcanoes are a flourishing business!

Dangers and Monitoring

Japan's volcanoes remain a source of constant threat, however. One of the most sadly infamous is Mount Unzen (Kyushu), which disgorged a dome of lava in 1792, unleashing a mudslide onto the town of Shimabara and killing more than 14,500 people. Sakurajima (Kyushu) ejected more than 3 billion tons of lava in 1914 with the result that the straits separating the mountain from the peninsula were filled in, connecting it to the mainland. It is precisely because so many of them are still active and dangerous that Japanese volcanoes are amongst the most studied in the world, and this knowledge is spread and shared with the public in centers that also use fun to educate.

Mount Aso Volcano Museum (🕭 *see p602)*, **Mount Unzen Disaster Memorial Hall** (🕭 *see p596)*.

The Gods Of The Mountain

Under the influence of Shintoism, Japanese mountains and volcanoes have often been raised up to divine status. The most highly venerated of all is the goddess Sengen, to whom a temple is dedicated on the summit of Mount Fuji. Until 1872, women, who were considered impure, were even forbidden to set foot on the mountain. As you make your way up the slopes of a volcano, don't think twice about stopping off at one of the numerous temples or altars and making an offering to the local divinity—you will appease their wrath and spare yourself any nasty surprises of an eruptive nature.

Kumamoto★ and Mount Aso★★

熊本・阿蘇山

A prosperous city during the Tokugawa Shogunate (1603–1867), Kumamoto grew up around its castle facing Shimabara Bay. Perched on a hill and surrounded by high walls, the castle is one of the finest reconstructed examples in Japan. Kumamoto is also known for its beautiful garden, Suizen-ji, and in modern times for its bear mascot, Kumanon—probably the most successful in Japan. There are plenty of opportunities for excursions in the surrounding area. To the south is the Amakusa Archipelago and its spectacular mosaic of small islands, home to the descendants of Japan's "hidden Christians," where churches pop up in surprising fashion from deep inside little rocky creeks. To the northeast stands Mount Aso, the world's largest caldera covered with green meadows, lakes, forests, thermal springs, and smoking craters, their slopes a mass of different hiking trails.

▶ **Population:** 738,900 (Prefecture: 1.75 million) Kumamoto Prefecture.

⊙ **Michelin Map:** Regions of Japan Map 8, Regional Map p576, Mount Aso Map p600.

▷ **Location:** Kumamoto is located 68.4mi/110km south of Fukuoka, 105mi/170km north of Kagoshima and, going west, 31mi/50km from Aso and 93mi/150km from Beppu. A tram line links the JR station and the downtown area 1.6mi/2.5km to the northeast, where you will find the castle, the bus station (Kotsu Center), and the main shopping district.

👥 **Kids:** A boat trip to see the dolphins at Tsuji-shima; a horse or pony ride in the meadows of Mount Aso.

🕐 **Timing:** Allow two or three days. From Mount Aso, you can continue toward Yufuin and Beppu. From Amakusa, you can get to Nagasaki. Renting a car is a useful way to get around the region.

☺ **Don't miss:** Kumamoto Castle; the Mt. Aso caldera.

SIGHTS

Kumamoto Castle★ 熊本城

10min by tram from the JR Kumamoto Station, Kumamoto Castle-City Hall stop. The castle suffered serious damage in the the earthquake of April 2016, and had to be closed. however, as the restoration proceeds, different areas are slowly beinf reopened: in 2019, a walkway to see some of the outside of the keep; in 2020, walkways to cover some of the inner grounds as well; and in 2021, the inside of the main keep. Check the website ahead of your visit for the latest information. kumamoto-guide.jp/kumamoto-castle.

Situated on a hill surrounded by moats and strong stone fortifications, Kumamoto Castle was once deemed impregnable and is now the symbol of the city. Built between 1601 and 1607, under the guidance of the local lord Kato Kiyomasa, this citadel was a model of military engineering for its time. It included a number of defensive innovations in its design—smooth-surfaced, gently curving (*mushagaeshi*) ramparts to prevent attackers from climbing them, projecting parapets, loopholes—and no fewer than 49 towers and 29 gates. Despite these precautions, the castle was besieged and burnt down in 1877, during the Satsuma Rebellion. The keep was restored in 1960, in a similar style to the original, but with a concrete

USEFUL INFORMATION
Tourist Offices
Kumamoto Tourist Office–
In the concourse of the JR Kumamoto Station. ✆096-327-9500.kumamoto-guide.jp/en. Open daily 8am–7pm.
Amakusa Tourist Office –
Amakusa Treasure Islands Tourist Association. 15-7 Chuoshin-machi, Amakusa-shi (in a building near the Kotsu Center bus station). ✆096-922-2243. www.t-island. jp/en. Open daily 9am–6pm.

TRANSPORTATION
GETTING TO AND FROM KUMAMOTO
BY TRAIN – The JR Hohi Line which connects Kumamoto with Aso is partially shut following the April 2016 earthquake. For information see *www. jrkyushu.co.jp/english/train/oudan.html (1hr 10min, ¥1750, by Ltd. Express)* and Beppu *(3hr, ¥4650)*.
Trains run to and from Fukuoka-Hakata *(40min, ¥4700, by shinkansen)*. To and from Kagoshima-chuo *(1hr, ¥6540, by shinkansen)*. To and from Nagasaki *(via Shin-Tosu, 2hr 15min, ¥7080)*.

BY BUS – Kotsu Center bus station *(✆096-361-5233)* is located downtown, near the Kumamotojo-mae tram stop *(15min by tram from the JR station)*. Regular buses to Nagasaki *(3hr, around ¥3700)*, Aso *(1hr 30min)*, Beppu *(3hr 40min)*, Kagoshima *(3hr 30min)*, and Fukuoka *(2hr)*.
BY BOAT – Shin-ko ferry terminal can be reached by bus *(35min)* from the Kotsu Center. Ferries for Shimabara *(7 per day, 30min, ¥1100)*. Ferries also leave for Amakusa from Misumi-ko port *(3 per day 1hr, ¥2300)*, which can be reached from Kumamoto Station by JR Misumi Line *(50min)*.

GETTING AROUND KUMAMOTO
BY CAR – Renting a car for the day is an ideal way to explore Mount Aso and the Amakusa islands. Reserve in advance. At Aso Station: **Eki Rent-A-Car** *✆0967-34-1120*. In Hondo port (on Shimo-shima), **Toyota Rent-A-Car** *✆0969-23-0100*.

---

framework. Some of the other buildings have also been rebuilt, restoring at least some of the castle's former splendor. To reach the main courtyard, you must make your way round a maze of walls, but here you will find the **keep**, flanked by two smaller towers. It contains some interesting exhibits: samurai armor, models of the castle, manuscripts, and paintings. To the west of the keep is the **Uto-Yagura watchtower**, the only surviving section of the original castle.

▶ Walk west across the castle grounds (Ninomaru).

Kyu-Hosokawa Gyobu-tei★
旧細川刑部邸
Having been damaged in the earth-quake of April 2016, the building remains closed at the time of going to press.

This 300-year-old residence constructed in the *shoin-zukuri* style (a Chinese-inspired style typical of the houses of high-ranking samurai) was once the property of a member of the Hosokawa family, which controlled Kumamoto from 1632 until the Meiji era. With its large porch, it is representative of the aristocratic residences built in that period.

Kumamoto Prefectural Art Museum★
熊本県立美術館本館
In the grounds of the castle. ◷*Open Tue–Sun 9.30am–5.15pm. Exhibition room ⊚¥270, annex ⊚¥210, combined ticket ⊚¥420. www.museum.pref. kumamoto.jp.*
In a large brick building, this museum houses a collection of Japanese and Western works from various periods.

MOUNT ASO

WHERE TO STAY

Aso-no-yu **1**
Grandvrio Hotel
Aso Resort **2**
Yasuraginoyado
Shukubo Aso **3**

0   3 km

0   2 mi

KUROKAWA ONSEN

Kabutoiwa View Point

ASO

ASO CITY OFFICE

Aso-jinja

Aso Sta.

Namino Sta.

Miyaji Sta.

Koinomeni

Mt Takazuka

Mt Ojo-dake

Mt Aso-san

Mt Kishima-dake

Mt Naraomao-dake

Mt Neko-dake

Mt Taka-dake

Mt Naka-dake

AERIAL TRAMWAY

Naka-dake Crater

MINAMI-ASO

TAKACHIHO

Mt Korne-zuka

Mt Eboshi-dake

Aso Volcano Museum

YUNOTANI

YUNOTORI

HINOTORI

JIGOKU

TARUTAMA

TOCHINOKIHARA

TOCHI(NOKI)

CHOYO VILLAGE OFFICE

Minamiaso Tetsudo Line

AKAMIZU

Kurozu Sta.

Akamizu Sta.

Sugatani no Taki

57

212

57

265

265

225

N

Suizen-ji Garden

© T J/Shutterstock

Buddhist statues and examples of calligraphy can be seen alongside prints, engravings, and watercolors by Renoir, Gauguin, and Picasso.

A new gallery devoted to the **Hosokawa collection★** displays the works in rotation (calligraphy, paintings, pottery, armor) of the Eisei Bunko Museum, Tokyo, where the inheritance of the Hosokawa clan is preserved.

▶ Retrace your steps to the Shiyakusho-mae tram stop.

Suizen-ji Garden★★
水前寺公園

Near the Suizen-ji-koen-mae tram stop.
◷*Open Mar–Oct 7.30am–6pm; Nov–Feb, 8.30am–5pm.* ✎¥400.
Situated outside the center of the city, this garden was created in 1632 by Hosokawa Tadatoshi. It combines the simple, unadorned style of the tea gardens of the Momoyama era with the grander, more detailed layout of an Edo stroll garden (ℂ*see p115*).
Intended as a place of relaxation, its 158-acre/64ha area includes reproductions of the 53 famous natural sights of the Old Tokaido road (ℂ*see p238*), such as a hillock representing Mount Fuji, or a pond evoking Lake Biwa, its pure

water fed from an underground spring on Mount Aso.

The garden also contains a Shinto shrine, a Noh theater, and a delightful tea pavilion: a perfect place to enjoy a green tea. Although less famous than the gardens of Okayama, Mito, or Takamatsu, Suizen-ji is one of the most beautiful gardens in Japan and deserves to be better known. The one regret is that it is in the middle of a heavily built-up area, depriving the visitor of any natural views beyond the garden itself.

The Satsuma Rebellion

The Satsuma (Kagoshima) Rebellion, led by the warrior Saigo Takamori in 1877, was the last stand of the samurai who rejected the Meiji Restoration and the modernization that would cause the old feudal system to disappear and with it, the loss of their social status and privileges. The rebels laid siege to Kumamoto before being ruthlessly slain by an Imperial army that outnumbered them 10 to one. To avoid capture, Saigo committed *seppuku*.

Naka-dake Crater, Mount Aso

© KiraVolkov/iStock

EXCURSIONS
Regional Map.

MOUNT ASO★★ 阿蘇山
31mi/50km east of Kumamoto. Access by train on the JR Hohi Line (1hr 10min–1hr 30min journey). Tourist Office (*0967-34-0751,* open daily 9am–6pm). *Bicycle and car rental outside Aso Station. From there, regular bues go to the Volcano Museum and the cable car that goes up to Naka-dake crater (35min, ¥1200 round trip).* All access will be restricted when the volcano is particularly active, so check in advance.

In the center of Kyushu, halfway between Kumamoto and Beppu, Mount Aso National Park includes the gigantic **caldera** of Mount Aso, formed when the volcano collapsed some 80,000 years ago. With a circumference of 75mi/120km, it is among the largest in the world.

The town of Aso *(population 30,000)* lies to the north of this vast depression, which contains a dozen villages with a total population of about 100,000. The fertile slopes are covered with lush grazing pastures, terraced fields, lakes, forests, and hot springs used for *onsen*. Within the caldera are five volcanic cones: Naka-dake *(4941ft/1506m, the only active one of the five)*, Taka-dake *(5223ft/1592m, the highest)*, Neko-dake *(4619ft/1408m, recognizable by its craggy peak)*, Kishima-dake *(4167ft/1270m)*, and Eboshi-dake *(4386.5ft/1337m)*.

Classified as a "gray" volcano—one that sporadically sends up hot clouds of ash and scoria—Naka-dake has erupted almost 170 times. The oldest recorded eruption dates back to 553. Closer in time are the eruptions of 1884, when ash fell on Kumamoto, and those of 1933 and 1957, which were equally powerful. The most recent were in 2005 and 2007. This is still a dangerous place; visitors have been hurt, and even killed, by falling rocks and sulfurous emissions (not recommended for those with respiratory problems). *Check with the authorities if you plan any walks in the vicinity.*

Aso Volcano Museum
阿蘇火山博物館
Map, B2. 9mi/15km south of Aso along Route 111. Open daily 9am–5pm. ¥880. asomuse.jp.
This museum presents the geology of the volcano and the surrounding countryside with photos, models, and a short explanatory film. Cameras positioned inside the most active part of the volcano relay its activity live to the musem. *A map of the hiking trails around the volcano is available from the museum and there are volunteers who can act as guides. Ask at reception.*

Plain of Kusasenri★ – Beyond the museum stretches this lush, grassy plain. In the distance is Mount Eboshi, reflected in the clear waters of a lake. Children can enjoy pony rides here.

Komezuka★ – On the road from Aso, stop to climb *(10min)* this small, perfectly shaped volcanic cone, said to resemble an upturned bowl of rice.

Naka-dake Crater★★
阿蘇中岳東火口
♿*Map, B3.* 🕐*Closed in the event of eruptions, or emissions of toxic gases (and may also be closed following earth tremors).* ⚠*Not recommended for those in poor health.*

A smell of sulfur fills the air, and steam, smoke, and gas rise constantly from this active crater but the **view** is stunning. At the bottom of the crater, 1968.5ft/600m wide and 525ft/160m deep, is a dark green acid lake with a temperature close to 608°F/320°C. Around it, a panorama of black rocks stretches as far as the eye can see. Concrete bunkers are provided as shelter in case of emergency. Several signposted hiking trails start from the crater, the best leading to the top of Taka-dake *(5223ft/1592m)*. From there, you can see the whole of the caldera.

Aso-jinja 阿蘇神社
♿*Map, B1. Ichinomiya Village, 3mi/5km northeast of Aso. Access from JR Miyaji Station.*

This Shinto shrine, dating back nearly 2000 years, is dedicated to the 12 *kami* of Mount Aso, the most important of whom is Takeiwatatsu, grandson of the mythical Emperor Jinmu, traditional founder of Japan. It is one of the few shrines in the country to have retained its Buddhist gate with two roofs, which dates from 1850.

Kurokawa Onsen★★ 黒川温泉
♿*Map, C1, off map. 18.6mi/30km northeast of Aso. Buses running between Kumamoto and Beppu connect Aso Station and Kurokawa Onsen (1hr). From the information office at the car park (*📞*0967-44-0076,* 🕐*open daily 9am–6pm), you can obtain a map and a pass (*💶*¥1300) to three onsen of your choice. kurokawaonsen.or.jp/eng_new.*

Halfway between Kumamoto and Beppu, huddled in a narrow valley, this small village (population 400) hugs the Tanoharu River. Exceptionally well preserved, it is one of the most charming thermal sites in the country. Apart from the birdsong and the sound of the river, there is only the clip-clop of the *geta* (wooden sandals) worn by the *yukata*-clad bathers to disturb this tranquil place. There are almost 30 *onsen*, which double as inns, along the banks of the river. They all provide hot baths in the open air, set among the rocks of the river, or in small wooden clearings.

Yokagura, The Dance Of The Gods

Every year, from mid-November after the rice harvest to mid-February, the men of Takachiho dance the generations-old Yokagura, a cycle of 33 masked dances following episodes from Shinto mythology; the full performance lasts an entire night. The rest of the year, only four dances are performed. Over the last 20 years the Yokagura's renown has gone beyond Japan's borders, with performances abroad, particularly at European festivals. Yet it is primarily a community experience—450 men of all generations take turns to cover the performances—as well as, according to one of the oldest members of the troupe, the means for entering into contact with ancestors, thanking them for the harvest and asking for their protection for the future.

In 21C Japan, it's as if this recitation of "the slowly negotiated agreement between a benevolent Heaven and its earthly posterity, and the uninterrupted Imperial ascendancy that bears witness to it" (Nicolas Bouvier) has lost nothing of its power. *Performances mid-Feb–mid-Nov (1hr) daily at 8pm, Takachiho-jinja,* 💶*¥700; from mid-Nov–mid-Feb, about 20 complete performances; contact the Tourist Office* 📞*098-273-1213, takachiho-kanko.info/en.*

Manai cascade, Takachiho gorge

© tanukiphoto/iStock

TAKACHIHO 高千穂

About 50mi/80km from Kumamoto (2hr, 1hr from Mt. Aso), about 74mi/120km from Miyazaki by Route 218 (3hr). Takachiho–yama summit is at 5164ft/1574m. takachiho-kanko.info/en.
Part of Miyazaki Prefecture, Takachiho is nevertheless closer geographically to Kumamoto and Mount Aso.

Takachiho-jinja 高千穂神社
Next to Miyako bus station.
A large staircase, slightly off-center to the main building to avoid turning one's back to the altar when coming back down, leads to this Shinto shrine said to be founded 1800 years ago. The serene atmosphere is troubled only at night by spectators come to attend the Yokagura given during part of the year in a neighboring building (♨ *see p603*).

⚓ Takachiho Gorge, on the Gokase River 高千穂峡
About 0.6mi/1km west of the town center; by car, take Route 218. A trekking path (0.6mi/1km circuit, 30min, signs in English) looks down on the gorge. The gorge can also be reached by rowboat by river (30min, ☞¥2000, max. 3 people per boat; ⏰ open daily: Sept–Jun 8.30am–5pm; Jul–Aug 7.30am–6pm).

The Gokase River weaves between two high basalt flows hardened here 120,000 years ago when Mount Aso erupted. The path takes you first to a sacred pond and then to waterfalls, including the Manai cascade, the most impressive, as well as whirlpools, rocky masses, and at the narrowest point, three superposed bridges.

Kunimigaoka 国見ヶ丘
5min by car heading west of the town center, Route 218.
This site, literally called "sea of clouds", is especially imposing at sunset when the clouds cling to the rocky peaks surrounding the town. The **panoramic view★** is impressive; in clear weather it is possible to see as far as the craters of Mt. Aso. Three large statues recall one of the versions of Shinto mythology according to which Ninigi-no-mikoto, grandson of goddess Amaterasu O-mi kami, came down to earth at Takachiho.

⚓ Ama-no-Iwato jinja 天岩戸神社
About 5mi/8km east of the town center (20min by car or bus from Takachiho Bus Center).
The shrine was built overlooking the Gokase River, where, according to Shinto mythology, the sun goddess **Amaterasu O-mi kami**, ancestor of the Imperial Family, closed herself into a cave to punish her brother Suzano-no-mikoto, thereby causing continual night.
After having passed a tall, rough wood *torii* (gate), a beautiful avenue shaded by trees leads to the shrine. Behind the main building (accessible only with shrine priest), it is possible to make out Amaterasu's cave, in the cliffside on the other side of the river. The oldest building (left of the entrance) contains the mirror that is a symbol for the goddess. The path continues down to the river. After a few minutes it reaches the little Ama-no-Yasukawara shrine hidden in the depths of the cave. All around the shrine and at the river's edge is a multitude of piled flat pebbles, each one left by a visitor having made a wish.

MINAMATA

Regional Map.

The town is associated with a major ecological and public health disaster. Between 1930 and 1960, the Chisso chemical factory, in collusion with politicians and media entrusted with minimising the crisis, discharged vast quantities of methylmercury into the sea. The effect of eating contaminated fish resulted in deformities among the local population. The 15,000 victims were only recognised in 2004, when the state admitted liability. Reparations and decontamination operations have since been carried out and Minmata's goal is now to become a model environmental and eco-friendly city.

Minamata Eco Park

From JR Shin-Minamata Station take a Sankou Line bus and get off at the Roadside Minamata stop (15min journey), then a 5min walk to the park. www.minamata195651.jp.

This park was built to replace the 40ha/98acre-site that had been polluted. There are now many initiatives to repair the damage of the past. Thousands of tons of earth were brought here to build a trail by the water's edge, an orchard, a rose garden, and sporting facilities. Visitors can once again appreciate the panoramic view of the islands.

Minamata Disease & Archives Museum

From JR Shin-Minamata Station take a Sankou Line bus and get off at the Roadside Minamata stop (15min journey), then a 15min walk to the museum. Open Sun–Fri 9am–5pm. No charge. minamatadiseasemuseum.net.

This museum chronicles the region's environmental pollution. Scientific data, videos, and photographs relate the terrible effects of mercury poisoning, giving an insight into the scope of the disaster caused by Japan's hyper-expansionist post-war economic policy. Eyewitness accounts and testimonials encourage us not to repeat the mistakes of the past.

USEFUL INFORMATION

MINAMATA

GETTING THERE

BY TRAIN – from JR Hakata Station *(5min from Fukuoka Airport by subway)* to JR Shin-Minamata Station with the Kyushu Shinkansen Line *(1hr journey);* from JR Kumamoto Station to JR Shin-Minamata Station with the Kyushu Shinkansen Line *(30min);* from JR Kagoshima Chuou Station *(40min from Kagoshima Airport by shuttle bus)* to JR Shin-Minamata Station with the Kyushu Shinkansen Line *(30min).* EFrom Kagoshima Airport by shuttle bus to JR Shin-Minamata Station *(2hr). See www.city. minamata.lg.jp.*

Yunotsuru Onsen

5mi/8km southeast from the coast at Minamata. From JR Shin-Minamata Station take a local bus to Yunotsuru Onsen town center (35min journey, ¥150; 4/6 buses per day).

This spa resort has been nestling in a peaceful valley surrounded by trees for nigh on 700 years. Lined with tiny traditional houses, the river is spanned by delightful small bridges. The water supplying the *onsen* of the town's five *ryokan* originates from underground volcanic sources. It has traditionally been held that drinking it is good for diabetes and gout, while bathing in it is alleviates pain from arthritis or simply from muscle soreness after trekking all day in the neighboring mountains. *(Onsen open: Ryokan Hotarunoyu 10am–8.30pm, ¥200; Ryokan Kikuya 8am–10pm, ¥200; Ryokan Youraya Honten 10am–8pm, ¥200 (private bath ¥1000); Ryokan Tsurusuzu 11am–7pm, ¥500 (private bath ¥2000); Ryokan Asahisou 10am–8pm, ¥300.)*

The Tensho Embassy

At the invitation of an aristocratic convert, the Jesuits founded a great seminary (collegio) at Amakusa, in which they taught theology, science, and music. It was from the ranks of this institution that four young men were selected to be sent as a delegation to Pope Gregory XIII. In 1582, Martinão Hara, Julião Nakaura, Mancio Ito, and Miguel Chijiwa set off for a European odyssey of several years' duration that would take them from Lisbon to Rome. By their return, eight years later, however, the first decree expelling all the missionaries from Japan had been pronounced. All four nonetheless took holy orders. Several years later, with anti-Christian persecution having reached virulent heights, one of the four, Julião Nakaura, came to a tragic end, being arrested and martyred in Nagasaki in 1633. In 2008, he became one of 188 Christians beatified by Pope Jean-Paul II. The dramatic history of this diplomatic mission is recounted in a little museum, the Amakusa Collegio, with replica exhibits of objects brought back by the legation: a printing press, which notably enabled the missionaries to edit a Portuguese–Japanese dictionary, and some musical instruments (🕐 open daily 8.30am–5pm, 💰¥200, only in Japanese).

AMAKUSA ARCHIPELAGO★
天草諸島

46.6mi/75km southwest of Kumamoto. From the Kotsu Center, buses (2hr30min, ¥2240) serve Hondo, the main town of the island of Shimo-shima, which is also served by ferry from the Shin-ko ferry terminal in Kumamoto. 🚉*Tourist Office (🕐 open daily 9am–5pm) and car rental on arrival. There are few buses on the island itself.*

South of Shimabara Peninsula, between Nagasaki and Kumamoto, Amakusa-shoto comprises a string of around 100 islands, the main island being the mountainous Shimo-shima (220sq mi/570sq km), with a jagged coastline. Historically, Amakusa was one of the principal strongholds of **Christianity**, which was introduced to Japan by Portuguese Catholic missionaries. In 1589, the archipelago contained 30 churches, a Jesuit college with printing facilities and, out of a total population of 30,000, no less than 23,000 converts. After Christianity was banned at the beginning of the 17C, many renounced their faith, but thousands of others were executed. Some continued to worship in secret before small statues of the Virgin disguised as Kannon. They became known as the hidden Christians (👣*see p589*). From 1873,

with the reestablishment of religous freedom, many French missionaries established themselves in the islands, where they rebuilt churches to revive their faith. Today, nearly 10 percent of the island's inhabitants are Catholic (one percent in the rest of Japan).

Shimo-shima★ 下島

The capital, **Hondo**, a small town of 40,000 inhabitants, is on the northeast coast. It is linked to Kumamoto by a series of five spectacular bridges connecting several of the islands.

Sakitsu port – *In the southwest of the island, 11mi/18km from Hondo.* At the end of a narrow fjord, surrounded by low mountains, nestles this modest fishing village. There is a small mock Gothic **church** with a steeple and gray-tiled roof, built in 1928. The floor is covered with *tatami* mats, so you must take off your shoes to enter. Nearby, a statue of the Virgin looks out over a rocky cape at the exit to the bay. Fishermen setting out to sea beg her protection.

Oe Village★ – *3mi/5km north of Sakitsu along the coast.* A white **church** stands on a green hill overlooking the sea. Inside, the rib-vaulted ceiling is decorated with bright flowers. It was built and entirely financed in 1933 by Father Garnier, a kindly priest who is still affectionately remembered by the villagers. Below the church, near the cemetery, a statue of the Virgin of Lourdes stands hidden amid the bougainvillea. The nearby **Rosary Museum** (⏱*open daily 8.30am–5pm;* ☜*¥300)* displays objects related to the Marian cult of the "hidden Christians" and examples of the religious images they were forced to trample underfoot as a sign that they had renounced their faith. The museum also tells the story of the great Shimabara Rebellion of 1637, when 40,000 rebels—Christians and starving peasants—were mercilessly slaughtered by the shogun's troops.

ADDRESSES

🛏**STAY**

MOUNT ASO

😊😊 **Aso-no-yu** 阿蘇乃湯 – *6 Ozato (Map, B1).* ☎*0967-32-1521. asonoyu.com/ english.html. 11 rooms. ¥12,300. ¥1000*☐. 🍴. A rustic setting, Japanese rooms, and *o-furo*.

😊😊 **Grandvrio Hotel Aso Resort** 阿蘇リゾート・グランヴィリオホテル – *Komezuka-onsen (Map, A2).* ☎*0967-35- 2111. www.aso-hotelresort.com. 180 rooms. ¥15,100.* ☐. A large, beautiful hotel in the heart of the caldera.

😊😊 **Yasuragino-yado Shukubo Aso** やすらぎの宿・宿房あそ – *1076 Kurokawa, Aso-shi (Map, B1/2).* ☎*0967-34- 0194. aso.ne.jp/syukubou-aso. 12 rooms. ¥24,000.* ☐*, dinner also included.* A superb traditional *minshuku* run by delightful owners. *O-furo*.

AMAKUSA

😊😊 **Amakusa Prince Hotel** 天草プリンスホテル – *92 Higashi-machi, Hondo City. 10min walk from ferry pier* ☎*0969-22-5136. www.amakusa-prince hotel.jp. 28 rooms. ¥15,400.* ☐. A comfortable hotel near the port.

😊😊😊😊 **Gosoku no Kutsu** 石山離宮 五足のくつ *2237 Shimoda-Kita, Amakusa- machi, Amakusa-shi. Around 15mi/25km from Hondo and 7mi/12km from Oe.* ☎*0969-45-3633. rikyu5.jp. ¥59,400.* ☐*, dinner also included.* Clinging to a hillside in one of the most unspoilt parts of the west coast, this establishment is a real haven of peace. The rooms are in contemporary Japanese-style houses nestled in greenery. Vast, refined, with views of both sea and garden.

🍴 **EAT**

KUMAMOTO

😊😊 **Suzunoya** 鈴の屋 – *2 F Ryukyu-ya Bldg, Sannenzaka-dori.* ☎*096-324-5717. www.tofu-suzunoya.com. Open Tue–Sat 11am–10.30pm, Mon & Sun 11am–3pm.* A traditional ambience with a hint of modernity. Varied Japanese cuisine.

😊😊😊 **Ohako** おはこ – *13-2 Hanabata- cho.* ☎*096-324-4930. Open daily 5.30pm– midnight.* 🍴. Excellent, reasonably priced food. Specialties include *basashi* (horsemeat sashimi).

AMAKUSA

😊😊😊 **Yakko Sushi** 奴寿司 – *76-1 Higashi-machi.* ☎*0969-23-4055. Open Tue–Sun, noon–2.30pm, 5.30pm–9pm.* The highest quality fish, rice, *wasabi*, etc., are served in this sushi bar.

SHOPPING

Kumamoto Prefectural Traditional Crafts Center 熊本県伝統工芸館 – *3-35 Chibajo-machi.* ☎*096-324-4930. kumamoto-kougeikan.jp. Open Tue–Sun 9am–5pm.* A variety of wooden, ceramic, and bamboo artifacts from the region.

SPORT AND LEISURE

👥 **Boat Trips** – Iruka Club イルカClub, *Tsuji-shima port (Tsuji-shima Island) off the northern side of Amakusa (Shimo-jima island).* ☎*0969-33-0198.* Several trips a day to see the island's dolphins.

👥 **Horse Riding** – エルパティオ牧場 – *2305-1 Sanno, Ichinomiya-machi.* ☎*0967- 22-3861.* Short rides in the parkland of the caldera.

Kagoshima★
鹿児島

The southernmost city on Kyushu, charming, sun-drenched Kagoshima is often compared to Naples, with which it is twinned. Surrounded by purple mountains, it curls around a deep-set bay, in the threatening shadow of the ever-smoking Sakurajima volcano, the local Vesuvius, which regularly spews forth plumes of ash. A former samurai stronghold, for centuries it was controlled by the Shimazu clan, which at a long and therefore safe distance from Edo, could rule the province of Satsuma (now Kagoshima prefecture) and the Ryukyu Islands (Okinawa) more or less as it pleased. Chinese and Korean influences, brought here across the sea, have also left their mark on the local ceramics and on the city's culinary traditions, with its emphasis on pork (especially from black pigs) and sweet potato. *Shochu*, an alcoholic drink made from sweet potato is a local specialty—there are 120 distilleries in the city! Kagoshima was also Japan's first point of contact with Christianity, when Jesuit priest Francis Xavier arrived on the island in 1549. Another important figure in local history was Marshal Saigo Takamori (1827–77) who, after helping to restore the Meiji emperor, changed sides and led the Satsuma Rebellion. Kagoshima Bay is bordered on one side by the Satsuma Peninsula, where the *onsen* resort of Ibusuki, popular for its hot sand baths, nestles in an attractive setting.

SIGHTS

⊛ From the main station of Kagoshima-chuo, a tourist bus *(every 30min, ⊛¥190 per journey or ¥600 for a 1-day pass)* makes a circuit of the city's main sights.

▶ **Population:** 599,800 – Kagoshima Prefecture.
⊛ **Michelin Map:** Regions of Japan Map 8, Regional Map p576.
▣ **Location:** In the far south of Kyushu, 121mi/195km from Kumamoto and 196mi/315km from Fukuoka, Kagoshima is located on a bay. It has two train stations: Kagoshima, near the harbor, and the main station, Kagoshima-chuo, which is farther south. The downtown area is situated between the two stations, around the Tenmonkan-dori shopping mall, and is served by buses and two tram lines.
⊛ **Kids:** The sand baths at Ibusuki beach.
⊛ **Timing:** Allow one day for the city and another for Chiran and Ibusuki. From there, jetfoils go directly to Yakushima.
⊛ **Don't miss:** Sakurajima volcano; the sand baths at Ibusuki.

Kagoshima City Art Museum★
鹿児島市立美術館
15min by bus from Kagoshima-chuo Station. ⊕*Open Tue–Sun 9.30am–6pm (last admission 5.30pm).* ⊛¥300.
Built on the ruins of Tsurumaru Castle, at the foot of Shiroyama hill, this museum houses the city's modern art collections. Most of the works on display are by local Japanese artists from the end of the 19C and the beginning of the 20C, who were influenced by the great Western schools of the same period. The Paris-trained painter **Kuroda Seiki** (1856–1924) is well represented. Another room displays an assortment of **European works**, from the Impressionists to the 1950s: Monet, Renoir, Cézanne, Ernst, Matisse, Picasso, Mondrian, Kandinsky, Fautrier.

USEFUL INFORMATION

Tourist Offices – **Kagoshima Tourist Office** – *Central office Kagoshima-chuo Station concourse.* ℘099-253-2500. www.kagoshima-yokanavi.jp/english. Open daily 8am–7pm.
Kagoshima Prefectural Visitors Bureau – *Kagoshima-ken Sangyo Kaikan, 9-1 Meizan-cho.* ℘099-223-5771. www.kagoshima-kankou.com/for. Open Mon–Fri 8.30am–5.30pm. Visits in English can be organized by the office.

TRANSPORTATION

BY PLANE – **Kagoshima Airport**, 18.6mi/30km to the north, can be reached by bus from Kagoshima-chuo Station *(every 15min, journey time 40min, ¥1250)*. Daily flights to Tokyo *(1hr 40min, from ¥20,000 with Jet Star; Solaseed Air has a special offers for foreign vsitors)*. For Naha *(1hr 30min, around ¥40,000 with ANA, Solaseed Air ¥11,500)*. For Yakushima *(35min, around ¥28,000 round trip)*. Also flights to Osaka, Nagoya, Seoul, Shanghai Taipei, and Hong Kong.
BY TRAIN – A **Shinkansen** line links Kagoshima-chuo with Fukuoka-Hakata *(1hr30min, ¥10,450)*, Beppu *(via Kokkura, 3hr, around ¥16,000)*, Kumamoto *(50min, ¥7200)*, and Nagasaki *(via Shin-Tosu, 3hr, ¥14,000)*, and also connects with Osaka, in Kansai *(4hr, ¥22,500)*.
BY BUS – Long-distance buses leave from the Express Bus Center, outside Kagoshima-chuo Station. Regular services to Kumamoto *(3hr 30min)*, Oita *(5hr 40min)*, Fukuoka *(4hr)*, and Osaka *(11hr 40min)*.
BY BOAT – For Yakushima, jetfoils Toppy and Rocket serve the island from Kagoshima *(6 per day, 2hr–2hr 30min, around ¥8500)*.
The **Orita Kisen** ferry leaves Kogoshima at 8.30am *(4hr, about ¥5000*. The **Iwasaki Corporation** ferry leaves Kagoshima at 6pm and serves Tanegashima Island and goes on to Miyanoura port at 7am the following day *(13hr, ¥3700)*. Ferries for Okinawa *(Marix Line, 1 per day, 25hr, ¥21,000)* leave from Shin-ko port, farther south.
Ferry Sunflower *(℘099-473-8185)* leaves Shibushi port (east of the Osumi peninsula) for Osaka *(1 per day, 15hr crossing at night, ¥14,500)*.

A final section is devoted to the decorative arts of Satsuma, ceramics from the Momoyama era (end of the 16C), and crystalware from the end of the 19C.

Reimeikan (Prefectural Museum of Culture)★

黎明館（鹿児島県歴史資料センター）
218.7yd/200m walk from the previous museum. Open Tue–Sun 9am–6pm. ¥400.

Also located on the site of the former castle (the moats and some pieces of wall are all that remain), this museum is laid out on three floors and showcases the history of the region from prehistoric times to the Meiji Restoration.
The southern part of Kyushu, birthplace of the Jomon civilization some 10,000 years ago, was open to Chinese and Western influences from an early date. It was a powerful feudal fiefdom under the control of the Shimazu clan from the 12C to the 19C.

Sengan-en★ 仙巌園（磯庭園）

1.9mi/3km northeast of the center. 35min by bus from Kagoshima-chuo Station. Open daily 8.30am–5.30pm. ¥1000. www.senganen.jp/en.

Also known as Isotei-en, this garden was originally commissioned in 1658 by Shimazu Mitsuhisa, the nineteenth lord of the Shimazu clan, who had a villa constructed here. With its well-tended tropical plants, bamboos, and ornamental pond, it is a beautiful spot, with fine distant **views** of the bay

Sakurajima viewed from Kagoshima City

© José Fuste Raga/age fotostock

and the smoking cone of Sakurajima. Unfortunately, the immediate view is spoilt by the sight of the main road and the rail tracks in the foreground. Just outside the garden, the collections of the **Shoko Shusei-kan** are housed in what was once the first Western-style factory in Japan, founded in 1855, which produced glassware, ceramics, and weapons. Behind the museum building, you can visit the workshops and watch the glassblowers at work.

Dolphin Port

ドルフィンポート

20min by bus from Kagoshima-chuo Station or 10min walk from Kagoshima Station.

This shopping mall stretches along the boardwalk by the harbor. There are plenty of restaurants.

Kagoshima City Aquarium★ – *On the North Pier. 099-226-2233. http://ioworld.jp/english. . Open 9.30am–6pm (last admission 5pm). ¥1,500 (children ¥750, 4 years and under ¥350)*. One of the largest in Japan, this aquarium covers several floors, and provides an excellent introduction, both entertaining and educational, to the tropical marine life of Kagoshima and Okinawa. The visit ends with a dolphin show in a large pool.

Sakurajima★★ 桜島

From the terminal by the North Pier, ferries (every 10–15min, journey time 15min, ¥160) serve the peninsula. Tourist Office (open daily 9am–5pm) and bicycle rental beside the ferry terminal. A bus service (every 30min) makes a circuit of the peninsula.

The "house of fireflies"

This small cafe in the center of Chiran has been turned into a museum. Owned by Akihisa Torihama, it is called *Hotaru-kan*, the "house of fireflies". It was here that his grandmother, Tome-san, cooked a last meal for the young kamikaze pilots before they left on their missions. Out of affection for her, they all called her *Oka-san*, "mother." Many secretly entrusted her with letters for their girlfriends or families to escape the military censors. "Contrary to the legend, these young men weren't fanatical patriots who set off full of enthusiasm," explains her grandson. "They weren't even volunteers, but under pressure from society and the high command, they couldn't refuse. Knowing that the war was lost, they thought their sacrifice was pointless. Rather than fanaticism, their letters express their sadness at having to die so young and their sorrow at leaving their loved ones."

Hotaru-kan: *5min by bus from Chiran Peace Museum, to Nakagori stop; open daily 9am–5pm, ¥400.*

Sakurajima, to the north of Kagoshima Bay, is one of the most active volcanoes in Japan. It consists of three peaks, the highest reaching an altitude of 3665ft/1117m. Sakurajima is active more or less constantly, raining ash down on Kagoshima at regular intervals. In a major eruption in 1914, which claimed many lives, the volcano spewed out 3 billion tons of lava that engulfed the surrounding villages and filled in the 1312ft/400m-wide strait, thus joining what was then an island of 31sq mi/80sq km to Kyushu. Canals, barriers, and basins have been built on its slopes in order to channel the flow of lava and reinforced concrete shelters are intended to provide protection against falling volcanic debris.

Yunohira★ – 🚶 From the harbor, a road *(2hr walk there and back)* winds between the lava fields and the pine forests to this magnificent **observation point** over the volcano and the bay.

EXCURSIONS
🌀*Regional Map, A3*

Chiran 知覧
21mi/34km south of Kagoshima. Regular bus service from Kagoshima-chuo Station (1hr 20min; ¥840).
A quiet town surrounded by wooded hills and tea plantations, Chiran was one of the 113 fortresses built to protect the feudal lords of Satsuma, and also one of the principal bases from which kamikaze missions set off during World War II (🌀*see box opposite*).

Buke-yashiki★ 武家屋敷
Near the town center. ◷Open daily 9am–5pm. ⊜¥530. c hiran-bukeyashiki.com.
Seven samurai houses dating from the Edo period (mid-18C) stand side by side on a long street lined by a low stone wall. A stream filled with carp flows through a specially-cut channel. All the houses have delightful rock gardens that cleverly incorporate the "borrowed scenery" of the surrounding hills.

Peace Museum
知覧特攻平和会館
1.2mi/2km west of the town. The bus from Kagoshima also stops at the museum. ◷Open daily 9am–5pm (last admission 4.30pm). ⊜¥500. www.chiran-tokkou.jp/english.
During the Battle of Okinawa, toward the end of World War II, most Japanese kamikaze planes took off from Chiran. Almost all the pilots were young men between the ages of 17 and 28. The museum commemorates the 1036 kamikazes (or *tokkotai*, "special attack units") from Chiran, who committed suicide by flying their fighter planes crammed with explosives directly into American ships. The display cases show some of the letters they left for loved ones, and personal belongings.

▷ From Chiran, buses go to Ibusuki or to Kiire Station, where you can catch a train to Ibusuki.

IBUSUKI★ 指宿
31mi/50km south of Kagoshima. From Kagoshima-chuo Station, JR Ibusuki Line (1hr, ⊜¥1050).
👥 This *onsen* resort at the end of the Satsuma Peninsula has a glorious natural setting, surrounded by white sandy beaches and rocky inlets filled with tropical vegetation; the cone of the **Kaimon-dake** volcano can be seen in the background. Nearby, eels swim in the clear waters of the vast **Lake Ikeda** in the caldera of a former volcano.

Ibusuki Sunamushi Onsen★★
指宿砂むし温泉
Sunamushi Kaikan, near the beach. 20min walk from the station. ◷Open daily 8.30am–9pm. ⊜¥1080. sa-raku. sakura.ne.jp/en.
Ibusuki is famous for its volcanic sand baths, reputed to have a beneficial effect on neuralgia, rheumatism, and other aches and pains. Japanese travelers have been flocking here for three centuries, to be buried up to their necks by elderly ladies, who are dab hands with a shovel. The steam from the thermal waters beneath the beach heats the sand to a

Ibusuki Sunamushi Onsen

© Christophe Boisvieux/hemis.fr

temperature of 131°F/55°C. This steam is full of marine minerals, and the heat speeds up the circulation of the blood.

Satsuma Denshokan Museum★ 薩摩伝承館

Opposite the Ibusuki Hakusuikan Hotel. 5min by taxi from the JR station. ⏰*Open daily 8.30am–6pm (last admission 5.30pm).* ⌓¥1500. *www.satsuma-denshokan.com.*

Opened in February 2007, this superb building, surrounded by water, reproduces the architecture of the Heian era temples, in particular that of Byodo-in in Uji. Its collections of Satsuma porcelain—nearly 3000 pieces assembled by the family of the institution's founder—are unique, and trace the history of these intricately decorated ceramics, which became popular in Europe toward the end of the 19C. The ground-floor rooms display massive *kirande* vases ornamented with multicolored and gilded decorations. The first floor showcases Chinese ceramics, notably masterpieces from the Imperial porcelain of the Song dynasty (960–1279).

KIRISHIMA KINKOWAN NATIONAL PARK★ 霧島屋久国立公園

About 40mi/65km north of Kagoshima. From Kagoshima Station take the Nippon Main Line to Kirishima-jingu (50min, ⌓¥930*), then a first bus to Hotel Iwasaki (11 per day, 20min,* ⌓¥410*) to arrive at Takachiho-gawara, from where you can begin the trek up Mt. Takachiho.*

Nature-lovers will enjoy an escape to this natural park, its territory including the originally volcanic **Kirishima Mountains**. There is a superb landscape of about 20 mountain peaks, many of them over 3281ft/1000m in altitude; crater lakes and plateaus rival each other in beauty. Spring and fall are the best seasons for both the weather and for admiring the vegetation, especially the azaleas. There are several signposted trails of varying degrees of difficulty, crisscrossing the territory which was the first in Japan to be recognized as a National Park, in 1934 *(for information:* 🏢*Takachiho-gawara Visitor Center;* 📞*099-557-2505, www4.synapse.ne.jp/ visitor/index.html;* ⏰*open daily 9am–5pm).*

Mount Takachiho *(5,164ft/1,574m)* stands out among the peaks as having greater importance in Shinto mythology; it was here that Ninigi-no-mikoto, grandson of goddess Amaterasu and therefore ancestor of the current emperor, is said to have come down to earth to bring rice to Japan.

Kirishima jingu★ 霧島神宮

About 4.5mi/7km south of Mt. Takachiho. ⊙*Open daily 24hr.* 🐚*No charge.*

Mount Takachiho has long been viewed as a deeply sacred area, and has been home to important Shinto shrines. The first was built in the 6C; its founding is mentioned in the oldest official chronicles, the *Kojiki* and the *Nihon shoki* (8C). The current shrine dates from the Edo era and was financed by the 21st Lord of Satsuma. Throughout the year, numerous ceremonies are held in the main building (*honden*) in connection with rice, which recalls the myth; most of them the public is not allowed to attend. The annexed building (*kagura den*) is, however, open to the general public for various ceremonies.

ADDRESSES

🛏 STAY

KAGOSHIMA

🛏 **Little Asia Guest House** 鹿児島リトルアジア – *2-20-8 Nishida.* ☎*099-251-8166. www.kagoshimaguesthouse.com/kagoshima-English. Dorms ¥1650 per person, private rooms ¥4400.* 🛏. A family guesthouse for young travelers. Laundry, bike rental (*free for 1hr, ¥500/day*), a kitchen for residents. The owners speak English.

🛏🛏 **Hotel Nakahara Bessou** 温泉ホテル中原別荘 – *15-19 Terukunicho.* ☎*099-225-2800. nakahara-bessou.co.jp. 57 rooms. ¥13,500. ¥1650*🛏. A well-located, comfortable family hotel with Japanese and Western rooms with bathrooms and a lovely *onsen*.

🛏🛏🛏 **Castle Park Hotel** 城山観光ホテル – *41-1 Shinshoin-cho.* ☎*099-224-2211. shiroyama-g.co.jp. 365 rooms. ¥26,900. ¥2750*🛏. Kagoshima's finest hotel, at the top of Shiroyama hill, with four restaurants and a view of the volcano.

IBUSUKI

🛏🛏🛏🛏 **Ibusuki Hakusuikan Hotel** 指宿白水館 – *12126-12 Higashikata, Chirin-no-Sato.* ☎*0993-22-3131. hakusuikan.co.jp. 205 rooms. ¥44,000.* 🛏, *dinner also included.* Like a small village beside the sea with gardens, swimming pool, luxurious rooms (beds or futons), four restaurants, and huge baths modeled on those in the Edo era.

🍴 EAT

KAGOSHIMA

🍽🍽 **Kumasotei** 熊襲亭 – *6-10 Higasi-sengoku-cho.* ☎*099-222-6356. kumasotei.com. Open 11am–2.30pm & 5–10pm (last orders 2pm & 9.30pm).* Private rooms with *tatami* mats, menu in English, try the local cuisine: *kibinago*, pork *shabu-shabu*, etc.

🍽🍽 **Ajimori** あぢもり – *13-21 Sennichi-cho.* ☎*099-224-7634. adimori.com. Open Thur–Tue 11.30am–2.30pm, 5.30pm–9.30pm.* An old-style restaurant specializing in *kurobuta* and *tonkatsu*.

CHIRAN

🍽 **Taki-an** 高城庵 – *6329 Chiran-cho-koori.* ☎*0993-83-3186. takian.jp. Open daily 10.30am–4.30pm (last orders 4pm)*🛏. In a building over 250 years old. Try refreshing soba (noodles) while seated on *tatami* mats and admiring the garden.

SHOPPING

KAGOSHIMA

Sakamoto Kurozu Jouhoukan Tsubobatake 坂元のくろず 壷畑 情報館 – *3075 Fukuyama -Fukuyama-cho, Kirishima-shi.* ☎*099-554-7200. www.tsubobatake.jp. Open daily 9am–5pm.* Black vinegar (*kurozu*) has been produced in the Kagoshima region since the early 19C. Its three ingredients (rice, water, and yeast) are left to ferment outside in earthenware jars (with careful quality control) for between six months and five years, which produces this condiment that is sought-after among Japanese gastronomes. In the shop/museum you can see a film describing the different stages of production (in Japanese only), buy different products, and try recipes based on the vinegar in the **restaurant:** *fixed price menus for lunch from ¥1700, open daily 10am–5pm.*

Yakushima★★★
屋久島

Surrounded by coral reefs and often shrouded in mist, much of Yakushima is like a lush primeval forest. The island has a high level of biodiversity and is covered with a subtropical rainforest containing many *sugi*, Japanese cedars, some of the tallest of which are among the most ancient trees in the world. Designated a UNESCO World Heritage Site in 1993, the island is a place of extremes: on the coast the heat is positively tropical, with white sandy beaches, while in the mountains the cold is alpine, with snowcapped peaks in winter. Pentagonal in shape, the island bristles with some 50 mountains that are over 3280ft/1000m in height. The tallest, Mount Miyanoura *(6348ft/1935m)*, is the highest peak in southern Japan. The island's craggy contours and tropical latitude combine to give it record levels of rainfall: 157.4in/4m per year on the coast and more than 315in/8m in the mountainous interior. Locals say it rains 35 days in every month! But this drawback is fully compensated by the luxuriant plant life and the enchantment of the dense forest with its numerous trails, which make Yakushima a genuine paradise for hikers.

AN OVERVIEW

The "Alps of the ocean" – The result of a volcanic eruption 14 million years ago, Yakushima is distinguished by its highly mountainous terrain.

The island has several peaks that are more than 5905ft/1800m high, including Miyanoura-dake *(6348ft/1935m)*, Nagata-dake *(6188ft/1886m)*, and Okinadake *(6102ft/1860m)*, the highest peaks in the whole of Kyushu.

This rugged appearance is echoed on the coasts, especially in the southwest, where rocky cliffs plunge straight into the sea. To the north and east, the shoreline slopes more gently, lapped by the warm waters of the Kuroshio Current, which sustain a large variety of corals and tropical fish.

An abundance of vegetation – Forest covers 90 percent of the surface of the island. While the coast basks in a subtropical climate similar to that of Okinawa, the mountain peaks, snowcapped in winter, plunge to temperatures worthy of Hokkaido.

▶ **Population:** 13,180 – Kagoshima Prefecture.

Michelin Map: Regions of Japan Map 8, Regional Map p576.

Location: 37.3mi/60km to the south of Kagoshima, the island has a surface area of 193sq mi/500sq km and a circumference of 83.9mi/135km. The population is concentrated in two urban centers: Miyanoura, the principal town, in the north, and Anbo, in the east. The airport is located halfway between the two. Most boats land at Miyanoura. A road runs around the edge of the island, passing through the small town of Onoaida in the south.

Timing: Allow two or three days. Take a good pair of shoes, warm clothes, an umbrella, and a raincoat for hiking. Avoid Japanese public holidays, when the hotels are full and the trails get too crowded; also June—July (the rainiest season).

Don't miss: Mononoke forest; hiking in Yakusugi Land or, for the more adventurous, Jomon-sugi; the Oko no taki waterfall.

USEFUL INFORMATION

Tourist Offices – In **Miyanoura,** at the port terminal (*open daily 9am–5pm; ☎0997-42-1019, www.yakushima-marche.com/en*). In **Anbo,** in the center of the village, on the main road (*open daily 9am–5.30pm; ☎0997-46-2333*). There is another office on the left as you come out of the **airport** (*open when planes land, ☎0997-49-4010*).

TRANSPORTATION

☺ *There is no connection between Yakushima and Okinawa; you have to go via Kagoshima.*

BY PLANE – The JAC company, a subsidiary of JAL, connects Kagoshima and Yakushima (*5 flights per day, 35min, ¥15,600*). The airport is on the northeast coast, halfway between Miyanoura and Anbo, and can be reached by taxi or bus.

BY BOAT – ☺ *see page 609.*

GETTING AROUND YAKUSHIMA

BY BUS – A bus makes a circuit of the island every hour in both directions, between Miyanoura port and Oko no taki (*¥1,870*), via the airport, Anbo, Onoaida, and Yudomari. Another bus connects Miyanoura port and Shiratani Unsuikyo (*¥550*). A third goes from Miyanoura to Arakawa Tozanguchi via Anbo and Yakusugi Land.

BY TAXI – Several companies operate on the island, including **Yakushima Kotsu Taxi** (*☎0997-46-2321/ 0997-42-0611*).

BY CAR – Reckon on paying between ¥6,000 and ¥10,000 per day to rent a small car. The rental companies are at the airport. **Suzuki Rent-A-Lease,** ☎0120-80-1772. Matsubanda Rent-A-Car ☎0997-43-5000.

The vegetation reflects these differences: near the coast it is tropical (mangrove swamps, deeply shaded forests of bay trees, camphor trees, camellias, banyans, and fig trees), becoming more temperate (mixed forests of oaks, larches, maples, cypresses, and cedars), and finally subalpine (rhododendrons, mosses, and lichens) the higher you climb. As the island is a microcosm of all the ecosystems in Japan, the plant life is lush and extremely varied for the surface area: there are nearly 1,900 species and subspecies of plant and flower, many of them endemic to the island, especially in the mountains. The acidity of the soil and the high humidity favor the proliferation of ferns and epiphytes (lianas and mosses), which cover the trunks and branches of the trees.

Ancient cedars – Between 1,968.5ft/ 600m and 5,249.3ft/1,600m, the warm temperate forest is characterized by the abundance of *Cryptomeria japonica* or Japanese cedars (*sugi*), including many extremely old specimens. Cedars more than 1,000 years old are known as *yaku-sugi*, and younger trees *kosugi*. Since the soil is relatively poor in nutrients, the trees grow slowly, making their wood exceptionally dense and resilient. Venerated in ancient times, these trees were cut down in large numbers for logging by the Shimazu clan. During the Edo period (1603–1867), they were used to provide the shingles for temple roofs in Kyoto. In 1964, much of the forest was declared a National Park.

SIGHTS

☺ Buses are infrequent, so if you're in a hurry or simply prefer the comfort of a car, it's a good idea to rent one to get around the island (☺*see Addresses*).

Yakushima Environmental and Cultural Village Center
屋久島環境文化村センター

5min walk from Miyanoura port. ⏰*Open Tue–Sun 9am–5pm.* ✉¥530. www.yakushima.or.jp/en/village.html. This information center presents a broad outline of the geography, history, and culture of Yakushima. An IMAX film, projected on a giant screen, takes you on a dizzying flight over the mountains

Yaku-shika

© jaimax/iStock

Wildlife

Yakushima is of interest for its animal life, which is quite different to that in the rest of Japan. Hidden in the island's forests are large colonies of red-faced macaques (*yaku-zaru*, around 7000) and small wild deer (*yaku-shika*, around 18,000). Notable among the 150 species of bird are the Japanese robin (*komadori*) and the Japanese wood pigeon. Last, but not least, the island has 15 species of reptile (including a poisonous snake, the *mamushi*, and several hundred varieties of insect).

and ancient forests in the interior of the island. *There's a cafe-restaurant serving meals and Western-style breakfasts.*

Shiratani Unsuikyo★
白谷雲水峡
7.5mi/12km south of Miyanoura (30min by bus, ¥300).
🚶 At an altitude of 2,624.7ft/800m, this deep ravine conceals a magnificent rainforest of conifers, including many *yakusugi* cedars. Three easy, well-sign-posted hiking trails (*1hr, 1hr40min, and 3hr*) take you along the Shiratani River, passing some truly ancient trees on the way, including **Yayoi-sugi★**, a 1,200-year-old cedar. The three-hour trail is the most rewarding—it takes you across a hanging bridge and several clear, fast-flowing streams, before reaching the **Mononoke forest★★** (👝¥500), so-named in tribute to the filmmaker Miyazaki Hayao (👝*see p177*) who used it as the inspiration for his film *Princess Mononoke*.

Nagata Inakahama★
永田いなか浜
13mi/21km west of Miyanoura (35min by bus).
This long beach of white sand near the village of Nagata is ideal for bathing and is also one of the largest nesting sites in the world of the endangered **logger-**

Shiratani Unsuikyo

© Tsuyoshi_Kaneko/iStock

Nagata Inakahama

head turtles. Between May and August, as many as 500 turtles at a time come per night to lay their eggs on the beach where they were born, 10–20 years earlier. Each female makes two or three trips here per season, each time burying around 100 eggs. Of the young turtles that hatch, only a small number will escape predators. The small **Umigame-kan Museum** in Nagata (℘0997-49-6550, www.umigame-kan.org; ⓞ open Wed–Mon 9am–5pm; ☞¥300; ⓞ closed Oct14–Mar 9) has information about sea turtles and their life cycle.

The Southwest Coast★
南西海岸
26mi/42km (1hr by car) from Nagata to Yudomari. There are no buses along the forest road.
Seibu Rindoh forest road★★★ – Skirting sheer cliffs down which icy streams tumble, this spectacular narrow road crosses one of the wildest parts of the island. It is not uncommon to come across herds of small deer, or groups of monkeys busy delousing one another, or gleaning berries that have fallen onto the road. Don't feed them or go too close, you may get bitten or scratched.

Oko no taki waterfall★★ – *16.2mi/26km from Nagata, 21.7mi/35km (1hr by bus) from Anbo.* From the car park, a path leads along the riverbed to a large natural swimming pool, turquoise in color, fed by water cascading down from a height of 288.7ft/88m with a deafening roar. The waterfall is classified as one of the 100 most beautiful in Japan.

Hirauchi Kaichu Onsen – *40min by bus from Anbo.* ☞¥110. *Bring your own towel.* Accessible only at low tide, these pools have been carved out of the rocks by the sea. Bathing is mixed, so the more modest come here at night.

Yakusugi Museum 屋久杉自然館
1.9mi/3km from Anbo, on the road to Yakusugi Land. ⓞOpen 9am–5pm *(last admission 4.30pm).* ⓞ Closed 1st Tue of the month. ☞¥600. *www.yakusugi-museum.com.*
This museum traces the long history of logging on the island, especially during the Edo period. It shows how the trunks of trees that have been cut down or are left lying on the ground can regenerate and grow new shoots. A cross-section of a 1660-year-old tree is also on display. An annex to the museum has exhibits on the crafts that use wood from the cedar tree.

Yakusugi Land★★ ヤクスギランド
10mi/16km west of Anbo (40min by bus, ☞¥500).
🚶 A winding road leads to this **forest reserve** that rises in tiers between the altitudes of 3280ft/1000m and 4265ft/1300m. The forest here con-

tains age-old cedars with thick, gnarled trunks measuring between 16.4ft/5m and 29.5ft/9m in circumference. Forced to survive in difficult conditions, most have developed a complex network of roots in order to gain a foothold in cracks in the rocks. Some of the trees have become intertwined, while others have twisted branches and form a profusion of contorted shapes in the dim light of the undergrowth.

Four hiking trails (30min–2hr 30min) crisscross the valley. You may have to negotiate some wooden steps and well-secured hanging bridges along the way, but will pass by several superb *yakusugi* (trees), including the 3000-year-old **Kigen-sugi★★**.

Jomon-sugi Hiking Trail★★★
縄文杉ルート

1.9m/3km before Yakusugi Land, follow the right fork. The bus arrives at Arakawa Tozanguchi, the starting point of the trail, at 6.30am and returns at 5pm. About 10hr walk there and back.

Starting from the small car park, the trail straddles a precipice and then, for the first two hours, follows an old abandoned rail track. After about 50min, you will reach **Kosugi Dani**, a former camp where 500 or so woodcutters and their families lived between 1920 and 1970. The trail then plunges deep into the forest, passing the first ancient tree, **Sandai-sugi**, which is some 500 years old. The next part of the trail is a tough, steep climb, but you can pause for breath at **Wilson Kabu★**, named after the English plant collector Ernest Henry Wilson, who, in 1914, discovered the stump of this giant tree, which had been cut down in 1586. Its cavernous roots form a gaping hole large enough for several people to stand upright.

A little farther along the trail is the ancient 3,000-year-old **Daio-sugi★** and its companion **Meoto-sugi★**, intertwined like a couple of lovers locked in an eternal embrace. Finally, at an altitude of 4265ft/1300m, you reach **Jomon-sugi★★**, an immense giant of a tree that according to legend is 7200 years old, though in fact it is closer to 2600.

ADDRESSES

🛏 STAY

🛎 Always phone in advance for reservations. You will be collected on arrival.

MIYANOURA

🛏🌊 **Seaside Hotel Yakushima** シーサイドホテル屋久島 – *1208-9 Miyanoura.* ☎*0997-42-0175. ssh-yakushima.co.jp.* *80 rooms ¥21,400.* 🍽. A comfortable, practical hotel, spacious Western and Japanese rooms, some with a sea view. Outdoor swimming pool in summer.

🛏🌊 **Yaedake Sanso Lodge** ロッジ八重岳山荘 – *2191 Miyanoura. Sometimes closed in winter.* ☎*0997-42-1551. yaedake. jp. 8 cottages. ¥10,100. ¥700*🍽. Idyllic, in a forest next to a river for swimming and kayaking. The rooms have *tatami* floors and toilets, but no private baths. Meals with other guests in a separate room.

SOUTH OF THE ISLAND

🛏🌊🍽 **JR Hotel Yakushima** JRホテル屋久島 – *136-2 Onoaida, 9.3mi/15km south of Anbo.* ☎*0997-47-2011. jrk-hotels.co.jp/Yakushima/. 46 rooms. ¥26,700.* 🍽. The island's best hotel, facing the ocean. Elegant, luxurious Western-style rooms, some with fabulous views.

🍴 EAT

In the evenings, expect to be able to have dinner only where you are staying.

MIYANOURA

🌊 **Yakushima Kanko Center** 屋久島観光センター – *799 Miyanoura.* ☎*0997-42-0091. www.yksm.com. Open daily 8am–7pm (Dec–Feb 6pm).* Above a large store selling souvenirs and camping and hiking equipment. *A varied menu, try the delicious deer sashimi.*

🌊 **Shiosai** 潮騒 – *305-3 Miyanoura.* ☎*0997-442-2721. Open Fri–Wed, 11.30am–2pm & 5.30–9.30pm.* A modest bistrot with good traditional cuisine. *Saba -nabe* is a specialty (mackerel hot pot).

ANBO

🌊🍽 **Chaya Hirano** 茶屋ひらの – *2617-3 Anbo.* ☎*0997-46-2816. goyakushima.com. Open 11am–3pm & 6–9pm. Reservation required.* A lovely restaurant with cedar-wood decor. Fixed price menus with vegetables, fresh fish sashimi, etc.

Miyazaki

宮崎

With its palm-fringed avenues, peaches, and sub-tropical climate—it's the sunniest place in Japan— Miyazaki draws many Japanese and Korean holiday-makers who come to enjoy watersports and golf here. It is also known throughout Japan as the winter training base for professional sports teams, especially the prestigious Tokyo Yomiuri Giants baseball team.

▶ **Population:** 401,150 – Miyazaki Prefecture.
⚐ **Michelin Map:** Regions of Japan Map 8.
ℹ **Info:** Miyazaki Convention & Visitors Bureau, Kiten Bldg, 3F, 1-10 Nishiki-machi. ℘0985-26-6100. www.kanko-miyazaki.jp. Open 8h30am–5.45pm. Information booth also in the JR Miyazaki Station. ℘0985-22-6469. www.miyazaki-city.tourism.or.jp/en/. Open 9am–6pm.
▷ **Location:** On the southeast coast of Kyushu, 130km/80mi from Kagoshima and 175km/108mi from Kunamoto.
🕓 **Timing:** Allow a day.
👁 **Don't miss:** Shinto shrines along the Nichinan coast.

SIGHTS

The town and its surroundings are part of important episodes in Shinto mythology. The two great shrines on the Nichinan coast, standing in a remarkable and fairly unspoiled natural setting, alone make a trip here worthwhile. Despite the passing of centuries, they have undeniably managed to preserve a certain mysique.

Aoshima jinja★★ 青島神社

About 3mi/5km south of Miyazaki by Route 377. From Miyazaki Station take the bus to Aoshima stop (40min, ¥740) or the JR Nichinan to Aoshima Station (30min, ¥380). A bridge links the island to the coast.

The shrine is in a unique natural setting: an island about 1mi/1.5km across, shaped by erosion some 10- or 15,000 years ago, surrounded by astonishing rocky formations of basalt nicknamed "the giants' washboard" (*Oni-no-sentaku-ita*).

Set in a magnificent forest of palm and other centuries-old trees, the shrine is to the divinities Hikohohodemi-no-Mikoto and Toyotamahime.

There is a small **museum** recounting the main episodes of Shinto mythology, with mannequins and explanatory panels (in English). The last room is devoted to more contemporary "gods"—the Tokyo Yomiuri Giants baseball players, who come to the shrine to make their wishes during the winter training season in Miyazaki.

TRANSPORTATION

BY PLANE – **JAL** and **ANA** offer flights from Tokyo Haneda (*1hr 45min, about ¥49,000*) and Solaseed Air (*special offer for foreigners ¥11,500*). From Osaka Itami flights with Peach (*1hr, about ¥21,000*). JAL, ANA, and IBEX connect Miyazaki with Fukuoka (*45min, about ¥14,000*).
From the airport to Miyazaki: JR (*10min, ¥360*) or bus (*30min, ¥450*).
BY TRAIN – **To/from Kagoshima:** the JR Nippon-Honsen Line connects Kagoshima and Miyazaki stations (*2hr10min, ¥4200, by Ltd. Express Kirishima*).
To/from Beppu: the Ltd. Express Nichiri (*every hour, 3hr 30min, ¥5500*).

Udo jingu★ 鵜戸神宮

About 25mi/41km south of Miyazaki by Route 220. Take the bus from Miyazaki bus station to the Udo Jingu stop (1hr 15min, ¥1500). Climb the 700 stone steps from the parking lot to reach the shrine.

Udo jingu

© kanonsky/iStock

This Shinto shrine devoted to the Imperial cult (*jingu*) is on a cliffside at the edge of the sea. After having gone past two gates and two bridges, you come to the entrance to the cave in which the main building (*honden*) blazes with color and decoration.

According to Shinto mythology, it is here that the goddess Toyotamahime, daughter of the god of the sea and wife to Hikohohodemiho-no-Mikoto (grandson of Ninigi-no-Mikoto) came to give birth to her son. Although she had asked her spouse not to attend the birth, he could not refrain from entering the cave. He then discovered that Toyotamahime had assumed her original appearance, that of a water dragon *(wani)*. Unable to bear the discovery of her secret, she left immediately for the land of the sea, abandoning her son.

Behind the main building (*honden*), the protuberances in the rock are supposed to represent the breasts the goddess left behind to nourish her son, because water sweats from them at certain times of the year. This is why it is a special place of prayer for women who are pregnant, breast-feeding, or who wish to have a child.

Below the entrance to the cave, a large rock shaped somewhat like a tortoise is also part of the myth; he is said to have brought the goddess here for the birth and is thought to be still waiting for her return. Little earthenware amulets *(undama)* are sold in the shrine; men throw them with their left hand, and women with their right, to make wishes; if it reaches the part of the rock marked off with a rope, the wish is thought to come true.

Hikonagis-Takeugaya-Fukiaesu-no-Mikoto, the son of the goddess, is the father of Kamuyamato-Iwarebiko-no-Mikoto, better known under the name of Jinmu, the first emperor of Japan.

ADDRESSES

🏠 STAY

🛏 **Youth Hostel Sunflower Miyazaki** ユースホステル・サンフラワー宮崎 – *1-3-10 Asahi. ✆0985-24-5785. mfkaikan.jp/en. 1 dorm, 4 rooms. Dorm ¥3600 per person, private rooms ¥7200. ¥550⛉.* 15min walk from the railway station, this pleasant youth hostel has spacious *tatami*-mat or Western-style dormitories at reasonable rates. There's a 10pm curfew. Japanese breakfast available if you order the night before.

◎◎ **Hotel JAL City Miyazaki** ホテルJAL
シティ宮崎 – 4-2-30 Tachibanadori Nishi,
Miyazaki-shi. ✆0985-25-2580. miyazaki-
jalcity.co.jp. 210 rooms. ¥17,000. ¥1600⌷.
Dependable city-center business hotel
10min walk from the railway station and a
20min taxi ride from the airport.

◎◎ **Miyazaki Kanko Hotel** 宮崎観光
ホテル – 1-1-1 Matsuyama, Miyazaki-shi.
✆0985-27-1212. miyakan-h.com. 348 rooms.
¥18,000. ¥1700⌷. On the north bank of
the Oyodo river, this modern hotel has
everything you could need: *onsen* and
rotenburo facilities; five restaurants serving
a variety of international cuisine; a bar; a
tea lounge; several shops (florist, bakery,
souvenirs); and a spa.

◎◎◎◎ **Sheraton Grande Ocean
Resort** シェラトン・グランデ・オーシャ
ンリゾート – Hamayama, Yamasaki-cho.
✆0985-21-1133. www.marriott.com/hotels/
travel/kmisi-sheraton-grande-ocean-resort.
743 rooms. ¥30,600. ¥2500⌷. At the
center of the Phoenix Seagaia Resort, this
five-star skyscraper from Sheraton has all
the features you'd expect: Japanese and
Western rooms, suites, fitness center with
large pool and spa, shops, karakoke room,
restaurants, bars, non-smoking floor,
private *rotenburo* (¥500/hour). It's close to
the Phoenix Country Club, which has one
of Japan's top-three golf courses.

Beppu★
別府

Beppu is a strange sight from the
air, its plumes of steam making it
look like an industrial zone; yet it
is rather a "paradise of hells," the
near-boiling waters of the thermal
spas being highly regarded by the
Japanese. Several million people
visit every year to enjoy the town's
various *onsen*, over 3000 hot springs
pumping out 21 million gal/100
million l of water a day, with baths for
every taste: mud baths, sand baths,
open-air baths, baths containing iron
or clay. Nevertheless, few come here
just for the health benefits; with the
almost hedonistic atmosphere, this
is far more a place to relax and make
friends. Unfortunately, Beppu has
not escaped mass tourism, to the
degree that it is nicknamed the "Las
Vegas of *onsen*." If the rustic appeals,
opt for neighboring Yufuin.

SIGHTS

In Beppu, you can easily spend several
days going from one bath to another. With
the many free public baths, don't forget
to take a towel, a *yukata* (light kimono),
and soap, as these are not provided.

▶ **Population:** 122,600 –
Oita Prefecture.
◔ **Michelin Map:** Regions
of Japan Map 8,
Regional Map p576.
▷ **Location:** Northeast coast
of Kyushu, 6.2mi/10km to
the north of Oita (airport).
The main sights are in Beppu
and Kannawa, 3.7mi/6km
north of the station. Each of
Beppu's 8 districts has spas.
◔ **Timing:** Allow two days.
◉ **Don't miss:** Takegawara
and Hyotan Onsen. Yufuin.

Takegawara Onsen★★★
竹瓦温泉

10min walk southeast of the station.
◔*Open: hot sand bath 8am–10.30pm
(last entry 9.30pm),* ◎¥1050; normal
bath 6.30am–10.30pm (last admission
9.30pm),* ◎ ¥110. ◔Closed 3rd Wed of
month. city.beppu.oita.jp/sisetu/shieion-
sen/detail4.html.

The magnificent well-preserved wooden
architecture here immediately transports
you to the Meiji era, with its dimly lit, simple, and old-fashioned interior. Visitors
are buried up to the neck in one of the

USEFUL INFORMATION

Tourist Office – Beppu Station. *Main exit (east) of station. ☎092-687-6639. www.discover-oita.com. Open daily 8.30am–5.30pm.* Another office on corner Ekimae-dori/Ginza Arcade. *1-3-15 kitahama. Open daily 10am–4pm. ☎0977-23-1119.* Free wifi.

TRANSPORTATION

BY PLANE – **Oita Airport** connects with JR Beppu Station by bus *(50min, ¥1600).* Flights to Tokyo *(1hr 30min, about ¥14,000, with Jet Sat; Solaseed Air offer for tourists ¥11,500).*
BY TRAIN – To/from Fukuoka-Hakata, Ltd. **Express Sonic** *(2hr 10min, ¥5530).*

For Nagasaki, Ltd. Express Sonic to Fukuoka-Hakata, then Ltd. **Express Kamome** *(4hr, ¥10,200).* For Miyazaki, Ltd. **Express Nichirin** *(3hr 15min, ¥6000).* At the time of going to press, the JR Hohi Line that serves Beppu, Kumamoto, and Aso is partially closed following the 2016 earthquake. For more information: *www.jrkyushu.co.jp/ english/train/oudan.html.*
BY BOAT – To Osaka, **Sunflower Ferries** *(☎0120-56-3268, www. ferry-sunflower.co.jp)* have 1 ferry per day, a 12hr night crossing. To Kobe, Sunflower Ferries have 1 ferry per day, an 11hr 20min night crossing.

tubs of scorching hot black sand, before rinsing off and taking a quick dip in a hot bath of water, rich in iron.

Hyotan Onsen★★★ ひょうたん温泉
Kannawa district. From the station, bus no. 20 to Jigokubaru stop, or bus no. 24 to Sunabaru stop. 🕐*Open daily 9am–1am, ✒¥780; after 8pm ¥580. hyotan-onsen.com.*
Approximately 2300ft/700m east of the main bus station of Kannawa, this *onsen* in delightful green surroundings includes a sand bath, a *rotenburo* (open-air bath), a gourd-shaped indoor bath (*hyotan*), a sauna, and a waterfall bath for shoulder massage.

Kaihin Sunayu★★ 海浜砂湯
Beside the sea, near Beppu Daigaku Station. From the station, bus no. 20, 26, or 26A to Rutkosoen stop. 🕐*Open daily: Mar–Nov 8.30am–6pm; Dec–Feb 9am–5pm (last entry 1hr before closing). ✒¥1050. city.beppu.oita.jp/sisetu/ shieionsen/detail9.html.*
This sand bath by the beach is heated by water welling up from the ground. One of the most popular in Beppu, smiling old ladies shovel hot sand over visitors until they are buried up to the neck. The idea is to then remain motionless, and sweat it out for as long as possible.

Onsen Hoyo Land★
別府温泉保養ランド
Myoban district. From Beppu Station (west exit), bus no. 5, 9 or 41 to Konya Jigokumae (25min). 🕐*Open daily 9am–8pm. ✒¥1100. hoyoland.webcrow.jp.*
Despite its dilapidated appearance, this building contains several wonderful mud baths, including a large, mixed open-air pool.

Jigoku Meguri★ 別府地獄めぐり
Kannawa district. From Beppu Station (west exit), bus no. 2, 5, 7, 9 or 41 to the Kannawa bus terminal (20min). 🕐*Open daily 8am–5pm. Combined ticket for 8 jigoku ✒¥2000. beppu-jigoku.com.*
The most impressive of the town's sights are the pools spitting out water and mud, and belching gas, and some of these are now mini theme parks. Try **Umi jigoku** (Sea Hell), a beautiful pool surrounded by vegetation; silica and radium make it a deep cobalt blue. **Shiraike jigoku** (White Pool Hell) is milky-white, with sulfurous and slightly fetid vapors. Two other "hells" are worth visiting, 1.9mi/3 km to the north *(5min by bus no. 16 or 2)*: ferrous oxide makes **Chi-no-ike jigoku** (Blood Pool Hell) blood-red, while nearby **Tatsumaki jigoku** (Tornado Hell) spurts its geyser at every 25 minutes precisely.

Chi-no-ike jigoku, Jigoku Meguri

© Rita Ariyoshi/age fotostock

EXCURSION
🅖*Regional Map, B2.*

YUFUIN★★ 由布院
18.6mi/30km west of Beppu. From JR Beppu Station, take the JR Kyudai Line (1hr 15min) or a bus (1hr, 🚌¥910). Tourist Office (℘0977-85-4464, 🕐open daily 9am–7pm) and bicycle rental outside the station. www.yufuin.gr.jp.
This thermal spa lies at the foot of the majestic Mount Yufu-dake (5197ft/1584m). It is home to a good dozen *onsen* and a myriad of *ryokan*, each with its own hot baths, along with restaurants, cafes, museums, and art galleries. At dawn, the steam rising from **Lake Kinrin-ko** wreathes the town in a dreamlike mist.

Yufuin Station – Designed by Isozaki Arata, this train station is a small gem, traditional in style. It houses an art gallery *(🚌no charge)* and—at the other end of the platform, an *ashiyu*— a thermal foot bath. From the station, a **tsuji basha**, (a horse-drawn cart), is available to take families on a pleasant tour of the town *(operate Mar–early Jan, every 30min: Mar–Nov, 9am–4pm; Dec– early Jan, 9.30am–3pm; tour lasts 50min; 🚌¥1620 per person).*

ADDRESSES

🏨 STAY
BEPPU
🛏 **Happy Neko** ハッピーネコ – *1 Kumi kita-ju.* ℘097-775-8838. happyneko.com. *3 rooms. ¥5500.* A charming guesthouse with traditional rooms. Well situated, not far from the town *onsen*, compensating for the lack of bathrooms. The owner will meet you at the station for *¥600.* He also organizes a free evening walk to Beppu Castle, and a 2hr excursion to an *onsen* in the countryside *(¥100 per person)*, compensating for the hotel's lack of shower/bath.

🛏🛏 **Yamada Besso** 山田別荘 – *3-2-18 Kitahama.* ℘0977-24-2121. www. yamadabessou.jp. *10 rooms. ¥15,350. ¥1000🍽.* A beautiful family-run *ryokan*, Japanese rooms; a superb *rotenburo* in the garden.

🛏🛏 **Ryokan Sennari** 旅館千成 – *2-18 Noguchi-motomachi.* ℘0977-21-1550. www.beppu-sennari.com/en. *8 rooms. ¥16,600. 🍽🍴.* Less than 2min from the station. Excellent service and a beautiful, quiet garden.

YUFUIN
🛏🛏🛏🛏 **Saigakukan** 彩岳館 – *2378-1 Kawakami, Yufuin-cho.* ℘0977-44-5000. saigakukan.co.jp. *24 rooms. ¥39,600. 🍽, dinner also included.* A pleasant *ryokan* with a good view of Yufu-dake.

OKINAWA ARCHIPELAGO

Also known as the Ryukyu Islands, the 60-odd islands that form the Okinawa Archipelago are spread out in an arc over more than 620mi/1000km between the south of Kyushu and Taiwan. The largest, Okinawa-honto, is also the political and economic center of Okinawa Prefecture. Its capital, Naha, contains most of the cultural attractions, several large hotels, and theme parks.

Highlights

1 Exploring the sacred sites of **Sefa-utaki** (p630)
2 Watching **humpbacked whales** in season (p632)
3 Diving in **Manta Ray Scramble** (p634)
4 **Kayaking** up the Urauchi River (p635)

▶ **Population:** 1,451,900 – Okinawa Prefecture.

Michelin Map: Regions of Japan Map 9, Regional maps opposite.

Location: Around 1000mi/1600km southwest of Tokyo, the East China Sea lies to one side of the Okinawa Archipelago and the Pacific Ocean to the other. The main island, Okinawa-honto, contains Naha, the capital (international airport). 185mi/300km to the south are the Miyako islands, 95mi/150km farther southwest, the Yaeyama Islands, including Ishigaki-jima. The climate is subtropical, with an average temperature of 74°F/23°C.

Timing: The best time to visit is between October and April. Avoid the typhoon season between June and October, and the main public holidays. Three days is the minimum recommended. You could save time by flying to Okinawa rather than taking a boat.

Don't miss: Ishigaki, Taketomi, and Iriomote islands; for diving, Zamami, Ishigaki, and Iriomote islands.

Tropical paradise

More sparsely populated and better preserved are the Yaeyama Islands, which lie farther south: Ishigaki-jima with its splendid bays, the mangrove swamps and wild jungles of Iriomote-jima, and Taketomi-jima, with its stone houses and fields of sweet potato and sugarcane. These are tropical paradises with a real South Seas flavor. Beneath an azure sky, the ocean shimmers emerald and turquoise, while its depths teem with marine life, including colorful fish, manta rays, and whale sharks, and the beaches glitter with fine white sand against a backdrop of tropical vegetation bursting with flowers.

But this picture postcard view is not quite the whole story. For centuries, Okinawa was an independent kingdom with a strong sense of identity. It was also unfortunately the scene of one of the bloodiest battles of WWII, in which a third of the population perished and the local cultural heritage was almost completely destroyed. Even though the islands were ceded back to Japan in 1972 after a quarter of a century of occupation, American military bases remain, and still exert considerable influence on the local economy. The main island has also suffered from the uncontrolled spread of industry and tourism. Fortunately, the indigenous culture has not entirely given up the ghost. It still survives in old legends and ancestor worship, in the local language, food and crafts (textiles and pottery), and in drum dances and slow songs accompanied by *yup* guitars made from the skin of the *habu*, a poisonous snake found on the islands.

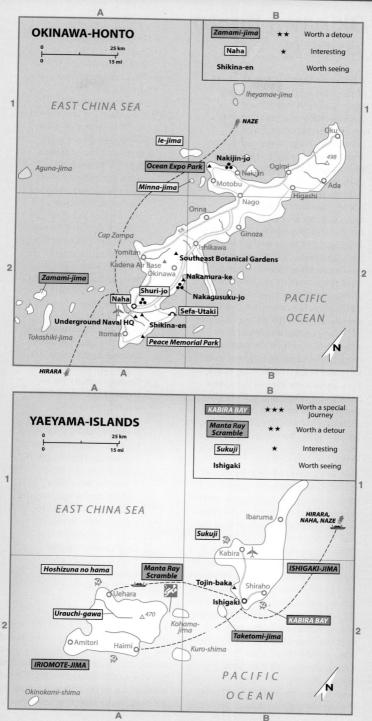

OKINAWA-HONTO

Zamami-jima	★★	Worth a detour
Naha	★	Interesting
Shikina-en		Worth seeing

0 ————— 25 km
0 ————— 15 mi

EAST CHINA SEA

Iheyamae-jima

NAZE

Oku

Ie-jima

Nakijin-jo

Ogimi

498

Ocean Expo Park

Nakijin

Ada

Minna-jima

Motobu

Higashi

Aguna-jima

Nago

Onna

Cap Zampa

Ginoza

58

Ishikawa

Yomitan

Southeast Botanical Gardens

Kadena Air Base

Okinawa

Nakamura-ke

Zamami-jima

Shuri-jo

Nakagusuku-jo

Naha

Sefa-Utaki

Underground Naval HQ

Shikina-en

Itoman

Tokashiki-jima

PACIFIC OCEAN

Peace Memorial Park

N

HIRARA

A   B

Copyright 2015 Cartographic data Shobunsha/Michelin

YAEYAMA-ISLANDS

KABIRA BAY	★★★	Worth a special journey
Manta Ray Scramble	★★	Worth a detour
Sukuji	★	Interesting
Ishigaki		Worth seeing

0 ————— 25 km
0 ————— 15 mi

EAST CHINA SEA

Ibaruma

HIRARA, NAHA, NAZE

Sukuji

Kabira

Hoshizuna no hama

Manta Ray Scramble

Tojin-baka

ISHIGAKI-JIMA

Uehara

Shiraho

Urauchi-gawa

470

Ishigaki

KABIRA BAY

Amitori

Kohama-jima

Haimi

Taketomi-jima

Kuro-shima

IRIOMOTE-JIMA

Okinokami-shima

PACIFIC OCEAN

N

A   B

Copyright 2015 Cartographic data Shobunsha/Michelin

Okinawa-honto
沖縄本島

The former center of the kingdom of the Ryukyu, the archipelago's main island, Okinawa-honto (also known simply as Okinawa) unfortunately lost much of its cultural heritage in the air raids of World War II. Today, it is the most Westernized of the islands owing to the omnipresence of American bases in the central part of the island. The surrounding urban areas provide rest and recreation for the 45,000-odd GIs, with plenty of drugstores, drive-ins, pizzerias, bars, and nightclubs. Naha, the ever-expanding capital, is almost a mini-Tokyo with its tall, ill-assorted buildings, bustling nightlife, and traffic jams. Hidden in the shadow of the skyscrapers, the potters' quarter of Tsuboya is like a survivor from a vanished world. In the south of the island, the ravages of war have left deep scars. The moving Peace Park gives some idea of the sheer horror of the fighting. In the north, the Motobu Peninsula has areas of untouched countryside, plus a sprinkling of charming islands.

A BIT OF HISTORY

The kingdom of the Ryukyus – Thanks to its geographical position, the Okinawa archipelago was, for several centuries, the center of an independent civilization, and played an important role in trade between Southeast Asia, China, Korea, and Japan. The Ryukyu culture evolved from the 7C onward, borne of the different cultural influences of Chinese, Korean, Malay, Japanese, and Micronesian migrants. Toward the 10C, Okinawa-honto was ruled by several warlords, who built a host of small forts that also served as places of worship. In 1429, these separate fiefdoms were united in one kingdom. Having come under the influence of the Chinese Empire, to which it paid tribute, the kingdom of Okinawa experienced

▶ **Population:** Island: Population 1,384,700, Naha: Population 317,400.

Michelin Map: Regions of Japan Map 9, Regional maps p625.

Location: The main island of Okinawa stretches for 84mi/135km from north to south; it varies in width from 3 to 12.5mi/5 to 20km. Planes land at Naha International Airport in the southwest, Naha being the principal city and transport hub. A monorail links the airport to the downtown area, which is centered on the main thoroughfare, Kokusai-dori. An expressway (Highway 330) crosses the island from Naha to Nago in the north via Okinawa City in the center.

Kids: The beach at Minnajima; whale-spotting at Zamami-jima.

Timing: If your time in Okinawa is limited, don't waste too much of it on Okinawa-honto: the smaller islands to the south are more interesting and peaceful. Three days should be enough to see the main points of interest on Okinawa-honto by car, but watch out for traffic jams in the south and center of the island.

Don't miss: In Naha, Tsuboya district and Kokusai-dori; in the south, Peace Park.

a golden age in the 15C and 16C before being subjugated in 1623 by the lord of the Shimazu clan from Satsuma (now Kagoshima) in the south of Kyushu. The island nevertheless continued to trade with China until 1879, when it was finally annexed by the Japanese government.

USEFUL INFORMATION

Tourist Offices – At Naha Airport *℘098-857-6884. Open daily 9am–9pm.* In Naha, on Kokusai-dori, Tenbusu Naha Bldg *℘098-868-4887. Open daily 9am–8pm. visitokinawa.jp.*

TRANSPORTATION

BY PLANE – **Naha Airport** – 2mi/3km to the southwest of the city. Access by monorail from Kencho-mae Station *(15min, ¥270)* or taxi *(about ¥800)*. Flights to Tokyo *(2hr 20min journey, about ¥50,000)*, Osaka *(2hr, about ¥42,000)*, Kagoshima *(1hr 30min, around ¥33,000)*, and most other large Japanese cities. Also flights to Seoul, Taipei, and Shanghai.

BY BOAT – **Naha-ko port** – Ferries connect with Kagoshima *(1 per day, 25hr 30min crossing, around ¥15,000)*. Access: 15min walk north of Asahibashi Bus Station.

Naha-shin-ko port – Ferries to Osaka and Kobe *(around 4 per month, 43hr, about ¥20,000)*. Access: bus no. 101 *(25min)* from Asahibashi Bus Station.

Tomari-ko port – Ferries to the small islands of Kume and Kerama. Access: buses nos. 99 and 26 *(¥240)* from Naha Airport, buses nos. 23, 27 and 28 from Asahibashi bus station *(Tomari Takahashi stop)*.

GETTING AROUND NAHA

A monorail *(operates 6am–11.30pm, ¥230–350)* crosses the city from the airport to the Shuri district, stopping at Kokusai-dori *(Kencho-mae and Makishi stops)*. City buses *(nos. 1 to 18)* cost ¥240 per journey. A taxi ride costs about ¥650.

BY BUS – **Asahibashi Bus Station** – One monorail stop southeast of Kokusai-dori. Buses to the different regions of the island.

BY CAR – Cars can be hired at the airport or in the city, from ¥6500 per day. **Nippon Rent-A-Car** *℘098-868-4554*, **Toyota Rent-A-Car** *℘098-857-0100*, **Orix Rent-A-Car Naha Airport** *℘098-859-3900/098-851-0543*.

BY GUIDED TOUR – Two bus companies offer day tours of the main tourist and cultural places of interest. **Naha Bus** *℘098-868-3750 (4 tours, duration 8hr–10hr, ¥ 4800–7200)*. **Okinawa Bus** *℘098-861-0083 (3 tours, duration 4hr–10hr, ¥4000–5500)*.

The Battle of Okinawa – There have been few more ferocious battles in history. The final phase of the war in the Pacific got underway when American troops landed on Okinawa on April 1, 1945. Although outnumbered, the Japanese had prepared their defenses well, creating a maze of underground tunnels and blockhouses. The slaughter was terrible, involving massive firepower, *kamikaze* attacks, hand-to-hand combat, and mopping-up operations with flame-throwers. The fighting lasted 82 days and claimed more than 230,000 lives, including 120,000 of the island's inhabitants. The Okinawans were not only bombarded by the Americans, they were also mistreated by the Japanese soldiers, forced to join the army as auxiliaries or to commit mass suicide so as not to fall into the hands of the victors.

The military burden – Although the rest of Japan regained its sovereignty in 1952, the US army retained control of Okinawa, establishing military bases on the island, which would become particularly active during the Korean and Vietnam Wars. In 1972, Okinawa was ceded back to Japan, but Okinawa-honto still has 75 percent of the American troops stationed in Japan, much to the displeasure of most islanders, who feel they get a raw deal from the Japanese central government.

SIGHTS

⌖*Regional Map.*

NAHA★ 那覇

⌖*Map, A2.*

The booming capital city of Naha is well on its way to becoming a modern

A Healthy Diet

One likely reason why Okinawans hold the world record for longevity is their low-fat diet, which helps to counter some effects of aging, and protect against cardiovascular disease and cancer. The Okinawan cuisine, considered medicinal by the islanders, consists mainly of rice, soy bean derivatives like tofu, a lot of vegetables, and sea produce, including seaweed, and green tea. The most popular local dish is *chanpuru*, a mixture of tofu, *goya* (a bitter melon, rich in vitamin C), and sautéed meat. *Umibudo*, or "sea grape" is a strange-tasting seaweed shaped like a miniature bunch of grapes. Pork is also common: in fact, every part of the pig is used, from the head to the trotters, in many different dishes including *rafuti*, a stew simmered in ginger, with sugar, soy sauce, and *awamori*, the powerful local rice-based liquor.

metropolis, with its towering skyscrapers and state-of-the-art monorail. The main street in downtown Naha is the long and lively **Kokusai-dori★** (pedestrian-only on Sundays), which stretches for 1mi/1.6km and is full of souvenir shops, military surplus stores, restaurants, bars, hotels, and shops selling traditional lacquerware. At the east end of the street, opposite the Mitsukoshi department store, is the **Makishi covered market** (🕐*open daily 10am–8pm*) nicknamed "the kitchen of Naha." Its stands, presided over by spry old ladies known as *anmaa*, display a multitude of colorful fish, vegetables, exotic fruit, and other ingredients typical of the island's cuisine, such as pig's head and dried snake.

Tsuboya District★ 壺屋

5min walk southeast of Kokusai-dori, at the end of the Heiwa-dori shopping arcade. A calm atmosphere prevails in this charming old quarter, with its cobbled streets, workshops, and small craft stores. It has been the center of **pottery** production in Okinawa for more than three centuries. The potters of Tsuboya traditionally produced large jars for storing water, *awamori* (the local rice-based liquor), or miso paste. Today, they mostly make small items for the tourist market: teacups, sake cups, and *shiisa*, the lion-dog figure that the islanders place on the roofs of their houses to ward off evil spirits. The district has a small **Pottery Museum** (🕐*open Tue–Sun, 10am–6pm; ⊛¥350*) explaining the history, techniques, and different styles of pottery, both glazed and unglazed.

The Birthplace of Karate

Karate, which today has 50 million followers, was developed in the former Kingdom of the Ryukyus, before spreading to Japan and then the rest of the world. The Okinawan fighting method *kara-te* (empty hand) was a martial art that developed in the 14C under the influence of Chinese boxing, which had been brought to the islands by merchants and sailors from continental Asia. At the beginning of the 17C, when the island was occupied by the Shimazu clan from Kyushu, the Okinawans were forbidden to bear arms. Left without a means of defense, they began perfecting their combat techniques in secret. From 1904, karate began to be taught in Okinawan schools and gradually emerged from the shadows. Today, it is practiced in the many *dojo* (training halls) on the island.

Find out more at the modern **Okinawa Karate Kaikan**, *which contains a small museum and interactive exhibits; kids especially will enjoy the chance to try karate techniques. Near the Japanese Naval Underground Headquarters; bus no. 33 or 46 to Tomigusuku-koen-mae (10min); museum* 🕐*open Thur–Tue 9am–6pm, ⊛¥310.*

Shuri-jo★ 首里城

1.9mi/3km northeast of Kokusai-dori.
Monorail to Shuri, then 15min walk,
or bus no. 1 or 14 from Kokusai-dori
(30min). oki-park.jp/shurijo.

A designated UNESCO World Heritage Site, from 1429 to 1879, Shuri-jo was the seat of the Ryukyuan kingdom before being annexed by Japan. This castle stood on a hill with a view of the East China Sea on one side, and the Pacific on the other. It comprised a complex of buildings, including fortifications, palaces, and temples, surrounded by terraced gardens. Combining Chinese and Japanese influences, it mixed elegant, pillared wooden pavilions with solid stone walls and a host of bastions, turrets, and tunnel-like gates cut into the thick granite. **Shurei-mon★** is particularly famous, as it appears on ¥2000 banknotes.

Razed to the ground during World War II, when it was used as the Japanese military headquarters, it was partly rebuilt at the beginning of the 1990s, only to suffer another **devastating fire in October 2019**. A crowdfunding campaign raised more than ¥372million (over US$3million) in just a week, showing the importance of the site to the local people. At the time of writing, it's unclear how long reconstruction will take, but it will be many years.

Shikina-en 識名園

1.2mi/2km to the east. Bus no. 5 or 14
(20min) to Shikina-en-mae. ◓*Open*
Thur–Tue: Apr–Sept 9am–6pm;
Oct–Mar 9am–5.30pm. ◠*¥400.*

Built toward the end of the 18C, this garden and its villa were used as a residence by the Ryukyuan Royal Family and their guests, including ambassadors from China. Destroyed during World War II, it was restored in 1975. The general layout of the garden is inspired by that of Japanese stroll gardens (◓*see p115*), with a lake in the middle. The villa, with its red-tiled roof, on the other hand, is typical of the local architecture, while a small stone bridge shows a Chinese influence.

THE SOUTH★

◓*Map, A2.*

The southern part of the island, heavily damaged by aerial bombardment, saw most of the fighting during the terrible battle of Okinawa. It was not only the location of the underground headquarters of the Japanese Navy, but also had a network of caves that were used as shelters by both Japanese soldiers and civilians.

Japanese Underground Naval Headquarters
旧海軍司令部壕

Tomigusuku town, Route 7, 2.5mi/4km
southwest of Naha. Bus no. 105 to
Kaigungo Irigushi (25min), then 10min
walk. ◓*Open daily 8.30am–5.30pm*
(Oct–Jun 5pm). ◠*¥450. kaigungou.*
ocvb.or.jp/english.

The Japanese Navy established its headquarters beneath the hill on which the former castle of Tomigusuku was built, digging out a vast labyrinth of underground corridors and rooms. Realizing defeat was imminent, Vice-Admiral Ota Minoru and his 4000 men committed mass suicide on June 13, 1945. Some of the walls still bear the marks of exploding grenades.

Peace Memorial Park★
平和祈念公園

Itoman, Route 331, 14mi/22km south
of Naha. Bus no. 89 to Itoman (40min),
then no. 82 to Heiwa-kinendo-iriguchi
(20min). ◓*Open daily 9am–5pm.* ◠*No*
charge. sp.heiwa-irei-okinawa.jp.

With its peaceful **view** over the south of the island, Mabuni Hill was the scene of the final stages in the Battle of Okinawa. Today it is a moving memorial park, containing a number of monuments in memory of the victims. Rows of marble tablets scattered over the lawns bear the names of the 238,429 people (Japanese and Americans, civilians, and combatants) who fell during this episode.

The **Peace Memorial Museum★** (◓*open daily 9am–5pm;* ◠*¥300)* traces the stages of the battle and presents the poignant testimonies of survivors. While many islanders perished in the Ameri-

The priestesses of Okinawa

The religion of the Ryukyu Islands was based on a belief in *onarigami*, which held that women have greater ability to communicate with the gods. Worship was in the hands of the *noro*, priestesses dressed in white (who may have originally been queens), and oracles were delivered by female shamans called *yuta*. Today many of the islands' older women still maintain ancestor worship, the foundation of the islands' religion, burning incense and saying daily prayers in front of the family altar (*buchidan*). The *yuta*, who practice both medicine and magic, may also be called on to perform a kind of exorcism: when a person has been deprived of their *mabui* (soul), the *yuta* aid recovery by invoking the ancestors.

islanders would communicate with the gods and make offerings. According to legend, it was at Sefa-utaki that the goddess Amamikiyo descended and gave birth to the Okinawa archipelago.

From the 15C, this was the principal place of worship for the Ryukyuan kings, who came here to celebrate the beginning of harvest. The rites were led by a high priestess known as Kikoe Ogimi, usually the king's sister or aunt. Altars are scattered amid the tropical forest. At the far end of the site, a triangular opening formed by two immense rocky walls leads to the most sacred part of the site facing the island of Kudaka, where the first divine couple settled.

THE CENTER

🐾*Map, A2.*

It is only when you follow Route 58 across the center of the island that you fully realize how much land (20 percent of the island) is occupied by American military bases and camps. On one side of the road, behind barbed wire, lie airstrips filled with the roar of F-18 Hornets and F-22 Raptors, and neat green lawns and equally neat little houses for the military families. On the other side stand the houses of the local Okinawans in cramped profusion. The surrounding towns are largely a succession of fast food joints, military surplus stores, shops, and seedy bars. The area farther north is a jumble of beach resorts and rather tacky tourist attractions.

can bombardment, many others were victims of the Japanese Army.

Himeyuri Monument – *1.6mi/2.5km west, on Route 331.* 🕐*Open daily 9am–5.30pm.* 🎫*No charge.* This monument is dedicated to the memory of 219 high-school girls who, having worked as nurses to the Japanese soldiers, committed suicide with their teachers in a cave to avoid capture by the Americans.

Sefa-utaki★ 斎場御嶽
Chinen Village, Route 331, 12.5mi/20km southeast of Naha. Bus no. 38 from Naha (50min). 🕐*Open daily 9am–6pm (Nov–Feb 5.30pm).* 🎫*¥300. okinawa-nanjo. jp/sefa/en.*
Part of the Related Properties of the Kingdom of Ryukyu UNESCO World Heritage Site, Sefa-utaki is of major importance to the indigenous religion of Okinawa as a place where worshippers could be closer to *Nirai Kanai*, the utopian paradise where the gods lived. *Utaki* is an Okinawan term for the sacred sites (groves, rocks, caves, etc.) where the

Nakagusuku-jo 中城城跡
Kitanakagusuku town, Route 330, 8mi/13km northeast of Naha. Bus no. 23 to Futenma (1hr), then taxi (10min). 🕐*Open daily 8.30am–5pm (May–Sept, 6pm).* 🎫*¥400. nakagusuku-jo.jp/en.*
Standing proudly on a hill 492ft/150m above the sea, this ruined castle was built by the Aji clan in the 14C, then enlarged by the local lord Gosamaru in the 15C before finally being destroyed by a rival lord, Awamari, in 1458. Only part of the huge perimeter walls remain, but they give a good idea of the size of the original building. From the top of the hill, there is a fine **view** of the island.

Nakamura-ke 中村家

10min walk from Nakagusuku-jo.
Open daily 9am–5.30pm. ¥500.
nakamurahouse.jp.

The residence of the Nakamuras, an important Okinawan farming family, dates from the early 18C. Protected from typhoons by a row of trees, it's the best-preserved traditional house on the island. It has thick limestone walls and a red-tiled roof on which stands a *shiisa* (the protective lion-dog figure), a stone pigsty, and grain stores raised off the ground to keep them safe from rodents.

THE NORTH★

Map, B1.

The most unspoilt part of the island, the north is a mixture of large beaches and hills covered in subtropical forest. Most sights of interest are concentrated in the lush peninsula of Motobu and its garland of islands.

Nakijin-jo 今帰仁城跡

Route 115, 13.7mi/22km north of Nago. From Nago, bus no. 65 or 66 (1hr).
Open daily 8am–6pm (May–Aug, 7pm). ¥400. nakijinjoseki.jp/en.

A few ruins on the top of a hill are all that is left of what, in the 14C, was the main fortress of the northern province of Hokuzan, ruled by the local Aji clan before the Ryukyu kingdom was united in 1429. Apart from a walk along the ramparts, not a great deal remains, but the site is noteworthy for its cherry trees, which blossom toward the end of January, and its magnificent **view** of the sea.

Ocean Expo Park★ 海洋博公園

Route 114, 11mi/18km north of Nago. From Naha, express bus no. 111 to Nago (1hr 40min), then bus no. 65 or 66 (1hr). oki-park.jp/kaiyohaku/en. Open daily: Mar–Sept 8.30am–7pm; Oct–Feb 8.30am–5.30pm. Garden: ¥760 (children no charge). Museum: ¥190 (children no charge).

A small electric bus (¥200) takes you to the various attractions of this huge park, built on the site of the 1975 World's Fair, whose theme was the oceans. Unfortu-nately, the aquarium has captive ceta-ceans and performances.

Tropical Dream Center – This lush botanical garden contains 2000 species of orchid and other tropical flowers and fruits in a series of greenhouses.

Oceanic Culture Museum – A small museum which displays objects (tools, masks, totems, instruments, canoes) from the islands of Polynesia, Melanesia, Micronesia, and Southeast Asia.

Emerald Beach★ – This superb beach, very popular at weekends with families, extends along the bay north of the park. It has showers, lockers, deckchairs, and umbrellas, and there are lifeguards.

Okinawa Churaumi Aquarium★★

– *Open 8.30am–8pm (Oct–Feb 6.30pm), last admission 1hr before clos-ing. ¥1,880; ¥1,250 (high school stu-dents); ¥620 6 and up; under 6 free (dis-counted admission after 4pm: ¥1,310; ¥870; ¥430).* This spectacular aquarium is the park's main point of interest. The second largest in the world after Georgia Aquarium in Atlanta, USA, it showcases the marine life of the Kuroshio Current that flows past the Archipelago. In the main tank, which holds 264,860cu ft/ 7,500cu m of water (the equivalent of three Olympic swimming pools), behind a screen of glass 23.6in/60cm thick, visitors can see whale sharks, manta rays, and many other fish. Dolphin shows are held at regular intervals.

Minna-jima★ 水納島

From Toguchi (Motobu), 2–12 ferries per day (late Jul–late Sept 8–12 ferries per day). 15min crossing. ¥1710 round trip. Within easy reach of the Motobu Peninsula, this tiny island may only be a mere 1.5sq mi/4sq km in area and populated by just a few fishing families, but it is famous for its beautiful **beach★** (showers and changing rooms) just by the jetty. Various water sports are on offer, including diving, or you can laze in the sun. A few stands serve snacks.

Ie-jima★ 伊江島

From Motobu, 4–10 ferries per day (most frequent Apr–May). 30min journey.
☎*¥1370 round trip. Bicycle rental avilable at the pier.*

🚲 A pretty island *(9sq mi/23sq km)* northwest of Motobu Peninsula, Ie-jima is perfect for biking. The north has rocky cliffs, the south a beach, the inland sugarcane, pineapples, and tobacco. From the central hill **Gusuku-yama**, *(564ft/172m)* is a splendid view of the whole island. In late April over a million water lilies bloom in the north.

THE NEARBY ISLANDS
🌀*Map, A2.*

Zamami-jima★★ 座間味島

From Tomari port in Naha, 2–4 ferries per day (fast service, 50min, ¥5970 round trip; slow service, 2hr, ¥4030 round trip). 🅸*Information Office* ☎*098-987-2277,* 🕐*open daily 9am–5pm. Bicycle and scooter rental at the port.* 18.5mi/30km southwest of Naha, this island paradise in the Kerama archipelago boasts some superb beaches lapped by turquoise waters, with huge coral reefs. It is also famous as a place where **humpbacked whales** can be seen. Boat trips to see them leave in the mornings *(Jan–Mar, 2hr 30min,* ☎*¥5000)*. **Furuzamami Beach★★**, some 15min walk to the east of the harbor, is well equipped, with snorkeling equipment available for hire and trips by sea kayaks also organized. Zamami village has several guesthouses for overnight stays.

ADDRESSES

🛏 STAY

NAHA

🛏 **Tatsuya Ryokan**
民宿たつや旅館・那覇店 – *1-9-21 Tsuji.* ☎*098-860-7422. tatsuyaryokan. com. 5 rooms. Dorms (women only) ¥1500 per person, doubles ¥7400.* ☐. 🍽. *10min from Asahibashi Bus Station, a pleasant, inexpensive family guesthouse. English spoken. Free wifi and bikes.*

🛏🛏 **Hotel JAL City Naha** ホテルJAL シティ那覇 – *1-3-70 Makishi.* ☎*098-866-2580. naha.jalcity.co.jp. 304 rooms. ¥18,650 ¥2400*☐. *A modern hotel on Kokusai-dori offering contemporary yet cozy comfort.*

CENTRAL REGION

🛏🛏 **Rizzan Sea-Park Hotel Tancha-Bay** リザンシーパークホテル谷茶ベイ – *Tancha Bay, Onna-son.* ☎*098-964-6611. rizzan.co.jp. 826 rooms. ¥10,650.* ☐. *A large resort hotel by sea: two pools, five restaurants, a spa, shops, and even a wedding chapel.*

NORTHERN REGION

🛏 **Vintage Centurion Resort Okinawa Churaumi** ロワジールホテル 沖縄美ら海 – *938 Ishikawa, Motobu-cho.* ☎*098-048-3631. centurion-hotel.com/okinawa-churaumi. 94 rooms. ¥7950. ¥2000*☐. *An affordable if slightly faded hotel complex facing the beach, with pool and activities.*

ZAMAMI-JIMA

🛏🛏 **Joy Joy Village** ジョイジョイヴィレッジ – *434-2 Zamami.* ☎*098-987-2445. keramajoyjoy.com/eg/villageguide. html. ¥11,450.* ☐. *Reservation required.* A small guesthouse with a diving center. Rooms with *tatami* mats and fans, aand a small garden. Will collect from the port.

🍴 EAT

SOUTHERN REGION

🛏 **Cafe Curcuma** カフェくるくま – *1190 Chinen, Nanjyo-shi.* ☎*098-949-1189. curcuma.cafe. Open daily: Apr–Sept 10am–8pm; Oct–Mar 10am–7pm.* 🍽. *A popular Asian restaurant on a hill with lovely garden and view. Salads, shrimp curries, pork with sesame, Thai chicken.*

NORTHERN REGION

🛏 **Pizza Cafe Kajinhou** ピザ喫茶花人逢 – *1153-2 Azayamazato, Motobu Town.* ☎*098-047-5537. kajinhou.com/english. Open Thu–Mon 11.30am–7pm. Menu in English.* In the mountains, on the Motobu peninsula, near Mukashiran Park. This beautiful traditional house has a terraced garden and stunning sea view. Pizzas, salads and coffee are on the menu.

SHOPPING

NAHA – **Kakuman** 角萬漆器 – *1-3-66 Makishi.* ☎*098-867-3709. kakuman.jp/en/ shop.html. Open daily 11am–7pm; closed over New Year and Thanksgiving.* On Kokusai-dori, the Ryukyus' oldest shop sells traditional Okinawan lacquerware.

Ishigaki-jima★★
石垣島

The gateway to the Yaeyama, the southernmost islands in Japan, Ishigaki-jima is a tropical paradise: an emerald sea, stunning coral reefs, beaches of pure white sand, and cultured black pearls. Unlike Okinawa-honto, the island was largely spared the fighting in 1945 and no American bases are located here. With its stone houses and old temples, it is the perfect place to explore the remains of the ancient culture of the Ryukyu. Head to the small nearby island of Taketomi, where the pace of life slows down even further and you can ride in a cart pulled by buffalo, and see traditional weaving looms, fishing nets drying in the sun, and water drawn from wells. Another island barely touched by civilization is Iriomote, with mangrove swamps worthy of the Amazon, and beaches of fine sand. Its mountains, with their impenetrable jungle, are home to the *yamaneko*, a leopard cat discovered here in 1967 and found nowhere else.

SIGHTS
Regional Map.

Ishigaki City 石垣市内
Map, B2.
The island's one outpost of modern civilization, this town is centered on its harbor and the two shopping malls behind the main thoroughfare. Everything is within walking distance.

Yaeyama Museum – *On Yui Road, near the post office.* *Open Tue–Sun, 9am–5pm.* *¥200.* This small museum has a modest collection of old ceramics, canoes, and examples of the traditional crafts of the islands, including weaving.
Miyara Donchi – *10min walk north of the port.* *Open Wed–Mon 9am–5pm.* *¥200.* Built in 1819, this house was the residence of the governor of the Yaey-

> ▶ **Population:** 48,100.
> 🛆 **Michelin Map:** Regions of Japan Map 9, Regional maps p625.
> ◖ **Location:** 280mi/450km from Okinawa-honto and 160mi/260km from Taiwan, the Yaeyama Archipelago consists of 15 islands, including Ishigaki-jima, the principal island, and Iriomote-jima, farther to the west. The city of Ishigaki, with its airport, is in the southwest of Ishigaki-jima.
> ♐ **Kids:** A buffalo cart ride on Iriomote or Taketomi.
> ◔ **Timing:** A stay of at least three days is ideal.
> ◉ **Don't miss:** Kabira Bay; a trip up the Urauchi River.

ama Islands. Surrounded by a garden, it is notable for its pyramid-shaped roof of red tiles.
Torin-ji – *On Yui Road. 15min walk northwest of the port.* *No charge.* This Rinzai Buddhist temple dates from 1614. Note the statues of the guardian kings at the entrance.
Tojin-baka – *3.5mi/6km northwest of the city, along the coast road.* *No charge.* This cemetery contains the graves of the Chinese laborers who found refuge on the island in 1852 after rebelling against the crew of the American ship taking them to California. Of the 380 fugitives, 128 were shot or committed suicide.

Kabira Bay★★★ 川平湾
Map, B2. 12.5mi/20km north of Ishigaki City. Bus (45min, ¥730) from the terminal located on the street just opposite the port.
One of the most beautiful and unspoilt places in Japan, this bay is a true haven, with transparent waters, a white sandy beach, and string of small islands. The reefs offshore have the largest concentration of corals in Japan—nearly 215 varieties. It is also famous for its cultured

USEFUL INFORMATION

Tourist Offices – At the airport, ☏0980-87-0468, visitishigaki.com, open daily 7.30am–9pm. In Ishigaki, the building opposite the library, ☏0980-82-2809, yaeyama.or.jp, open Mon–Fri 8.30am–5.30pm.

TRANSPORTATION
GETTING TO AND FROM ISHIGAKI-JIMA

BY PLANE – Ishigaki Airport, 9mi/15km north of the city (ishigaki-airport.co.jp/en). Buses (every 15min, journey time 45min, ¥550) or taxis. Daily flights by JTA, ANA, RAC, Solaseed Air to Naha; by JTA and ANA to Tokyo (3hr); by JTA, ANA and Peach to Osaka; by RAC to Miyako-jima.

GETTING AROUND ISHIGAKI-JIMA

Individually – From the port, buses to Kabira, Yonehara, and Shiraho (1-day pass, ¥1000, 5-day pass ¥2000). Car rental (Nippon, Nissan, Orix) at the airport, and scooter rental downtown. Most hotels offer bicycle rental.
In an organized group – Companies at the ferry terminal organize tours, including **Hirata Kanko** (☏0980-88-8835, hirata-group.co.jp/english, open daily 7.30am–6.30am). Tours around Ishigaki, Taketomi, and Iriomote.

---

black pearls. Bathing isn't possible, but you can take a trip in a glass-bottomed boat (30min, ☎¥1030).

Sukuji Beach★ – 1.2mi/2km west of Kabira. Forming a long crescent of fine golden sand, the beach is equipped with showers, changing rooms, and other facilities.

Manta Ray Scramble★★ – A few minutes by boat to the west of the Kabira peninsula, this is the best-known diving site in the region due to the huge manta rays that glide through its waters.

EXCURSIONS
🧭Regional Map.

Taketomi-jima★★ 竹富島

🧭Map, B2. 4.3mi/7km south of Ishigaki. Three ferry companies serve the island. Departures every 30min (10–15min crossing, ☎¥1150 round trip). Bicycle rental in the village.
A flat, oval island, only 2.3sq mi/6sq km in area, Taketomi is easily crossed on foot or by bike. Located in the middle of this peaceful retreat (population 360), the village is well-preserved and criss-crossed by small streets lined with low walls of coral stone, behind which are gardens bursting with hibiscus and bougainvillea.

The houses, of wood or stone, have long roofs of terra-cotta tiles typical of Okinawa, adorned with grimacing shiisa (lion-dogs) to ward off evil spirits. Stop at **Mingei-kan** (🕐open daily 9am–5pm, ☎no charge), where the minsa belts that young women used to weave for their future husbands are now made. The island has several fine beaches, notably **Kaiji-hama★** in the southwest. The sand here is known as "star sand" (hoshizuna), the grains being formed from the shells of microscopic, star-shaped marine organisms. 👥 Rides in small buffalo carts (30min, ☎¥1200, children ¥600) are also available; the buffalo know their routes so well that they're barely guided, and they're hosed down if they get uncomfortable in the heat.

Iriomote-jima★★ 西表島

🧭Map, A2. 19mi/31km southwest of Ishigaki. Ferries serve the island's two ferry piers: Ohara in the south (up to 12 ferries per day, 35–40min from Taketomi, ¥1690 one way; 45min from Ishigaki, ¥1830 one way), and Uehara in the north (45min crossing from Ishigaki, ¥2390 one way. Note, in case of cancellation of the route due to bad weather, there's a replacement bus service to Ohara). Buses, taxis, and rental of cars, scooters, and bicycles available.

© San Hoyano/Shutterstock

Buffalo cart, Taketomi-jima

Regular buses between Ohara and Uehara (4 per day, 1-day pass ¥1040). The main road goes only about halfway around the island, so some villages are only accessible by boat.

With a population of 2370 in an area of 112sq mi/289sq km, this mountainous island is one of the last truly wild regions in Japan—almost 90 percent is covered in dense tropical jungle and mangrove swamps. The coast is surrounded by the country's largest coral reef.

Apart from wonderful beaches and diving, the island also has many hiking trails, as well as rivers that are negotiable by boat or kayak. This natural sanctuary is home to some exotic fauna, such as the wild cat of Iriomote, an endemic species of which only about 100 remain.

Urauchi-gawa★ – Take a motorboat trip *(1hr, around ¥1900)* along 5mi/8km of this, the island's principal river, with mangrove trees at its mouth. Disembark and follow the trail (45min hike) to a beautiful waterfall in which you can bathe. Guided kayaking trips are also possible *(from ¥4000/2hr).*

Hoshizuna-no-hama★ – This fine beach located at the northwest point of the island is famous for its "star sand," made up from the shells of marine protozoa.

Yubu-jima – A small island off the east coast, with a botanical garden. Most people come for the crossing through shallow water from Iriomote-jima in a **cart pulled by buffalo** 👥 *(¥1730; includes entry to botanical garden).*

ADDRESSES

🛏 STAY

ISHIGAKI-JIMA

🛏 **Rakutenya Guesthouse** 民宿楽天屋 – *291 Okawa, Ishigaki-shi. ℘0980-83-8713. www3.big.or.jp/~erm8p3gi/english/english.html. 10 rooms. ¥7000.* 🍴. Rustic guesthouse in a delightful, old wooden building. *A/c is and extra ¥100/2hr.*

🛏 **Hotel East China Sea** ホテルイーストチャイナシー – *2-8 Misaki-cho. ℘0980-88-1155. courthotels.co.jp/eastchinasea. 79 rooms. ¥9700. ¥1350☕.* A comfortable business hotel in a centrally located skyscraper. The upper floors are quieter.

TAKETOMI-JIMA

🛏🛏🛏🛏 **Hoshinoya Taketomi** 星の屋竹富 – *Taketomi, Taketomi-cho. ℘050-3786-1144. hoshinoya.com/taketomijima/en. 48 rooms. ¥71,200. ¥4235☕, dinner also available. 2-night min. stay.* Impeccable luxury hotel, which looks more like an Okinawan village. Excellent food, cultural activities, and huge guest villas.

IRIOMOTE-JIMA

🛏🛏🛏 **Nilaina Resort** ニライナリゾート – *10-425 Uehara, Taketomi-cho. ℘0980-85-6400. nilaina.sakura.ne.jp/english. 3 rooms. ¥23,100.* ☕. Close to Hoshizuna beach, this stylish and intimate hotel has a diving center and organizes canoe trips.

🍴 EAT

ISHIGAKI-JIMA

🍴🍴 **Yamamoto** やまもと – *2-5-18 Hamasaki-cho, Ishigaki-shi. ℘0980-83-5641. Open Thu–Tue, from 5pm until all the meat has been used.* Opposite Shinei-koen, an ideal place to try Ishigaki beef, charcoal-grilled and perfectly tender.

INDEX

INDEX

J

K

INDEX

INDEX

INDEX

INDEX

INDEX

🏯 STAY

🍴EAT

MAPS AND PLANS

LEGEND
Understanding the symbols

Worth a special journey	Worth a detour	Interesting
★★★	★★	★

Hotels and Restaurants

Hotels
Up to ¥10,000
¥10,000–¥20,000
¥20,000–¥30,000
Over ¥30,000

Restaurants
Up to ¥1,500
¥1,500–¥3,000
¥3,000–¥8,000
Over ¥8,000

¥1050 — Price for breakfast
Breakfast included
On-site parking
Credit cards not accepted

Symbols in the text

Tourist information
Directions
Hours of operation
Period of closure
Especially for kids
Closed to the public
Entry fees
Also see
A bit of advice
Tours
Hiking trails
By bicycle
A2 B   Located on map

Maps

MONUMENTS AND SITES

Sightseeing route with departure point indicated
Ecclesiastical building
Synagogue
Mosque
Wayside cross - Fountain
Fortified walls - Tower - Gate
Historic house, castle - Ruins
Factory / Power plant - Dam
Viewpoint
Viewing table
Fort - Cave
Quarry - Mine

PRACTICAL INFORMATION

Tourist information
Parking - Park and Ride
Tramway - Subway
Railway - Coach station
Overhead cable car
Funicular - Rack railway
Tourist or Steam railway
Post - Covered market
Ferry services: Passengers and cars
Passengers only

ABBREVIATIONS AND SPECIAL SYMBOLS

i   Tourist information
B   Bank, Bureau de change
U   University
T   Theater
—   Metro station

Police station
Post office
Temple
Hot spring
Shop
Hospital

ADDITIONAL SYMBOLS

Motorway (unclassified)
Junction: complete, limited
Pedestrian street
Unsuitable for traffic, street subject to restrictions
Steps
Footpath
Access route number common to Michelin maps and town plans
Ferry (river and lake crossings)
Swing bridge

RECREATION

Outdoor, Indoor swimming pool
Stadium - Racecourse
Marina, Moorings
Trail refuge hut - Hiking trail
Outdoor leisure park/center
Theme/Amusement park
Wildlife park, Zoo
Gardens, park, arboretum
Aviary, bird sanctuary

Japanese Whisky

Some of the world's best and most coveted whisky comes from Japan.

Japan began producing whiskey around 1870, and its first commercial distillery Yamazaki was founded in 1924. Today Japan is a whisky powerhouse. The countries whiskeys range from inexpensive and mass-produced to rare and pricey collectors' bottles. And how do you order Japanese whisky in English? It's also Japanese whisky in Japanese (*Japanīzuuisukī*). **You can buy Japanese whisky in any supermarket or convenience store, including 7/11 and Family Mart.**

Whisky distilleries you can visit

- Fuji Gotemba Distillery in Shizuoka (*www.kirin.co.jp/entertainment/factory/english/whisky*)
- Hakushu Distillery in Yamanashi (*www.suntory.com/factory/hakushu*)
- Suntory Yamazaki Distillery in Osaka (*www.suntory.com/factory/yamazaki*)
- Mars Shinshu Distillery in Nagano (*www.hombo.co.jp/factory - no English site. Call +81 135-23-3131 to book a tour or use Google Translate to send an email through their website.*)
- Yoichi Distillery in Shiribeshi (*www.nikka.com/eng/distilleries*)

Must-try Japanese whiskys

- Akashi 5 Year Sherry Cask
- China Single Grain
- Hakushu 12
- Hakushu 18
- Hibiki 21
- Mars Maltage Cosmo
- Nikka Coffey Malt
- Nikka Date
- Suntory Whisky Toki
- Yamazaki 12

How to drink Japanese whisky

While you can certainly order whisky in Japan with or without water or ice, the most popular way it's enjoy is as a "highball" (haibōru). In a highball, whisky is mixed with club soda and water, and sometimes a slice of lemon, depending on the whisky. Highballs are lighter drinks, ideal for Japan's hot summers but also for sipping throughout a meal. You'll find them at restaurants and bars in every city, town, and village, and especially in *izakaya* (pubs). The Highball is so ubiquitous that a canned version is even sold in vending machines across the country.

THE**GREEN**GUIDE

France
- Alsace Lorraine Champagne
- Auvergne Rhone Valley
- Brittany
- Burgundy Jura
- Châteaux of the Loire
- Dordogne Berry Limousin
- France
- French Alps
- French Riviera
- Languedoc Roussillon Tarn Gorges
- Normandy
- Northern France and the Paris Region
- Paris
- Provence
- Wine Regions of France

North America
- Canada
- Chicago
- Montreal & Quebec City
- New England
- New York City
- San Francisco
- USA East
- USA West
- Washington, DC

British Isles
- Great Britain
- Ireland
- London
- Scotland

Rest of Europe
- Andalucia
- Austria
- Germany
- Grand Tour of Switzerland
- Greece
- Italy
- Portugal Madeira The Azores
- Rome
- Sicily
- Spain
- Switzerland
- Tuscany
- Venice and the Veneto
- Wine Trails of Italy

Asia
- Japan
- South Korea

Visit your preferred bookseller for Michelin's comprehensive range of maps and famous red-cover Hotel and Restaurant guides.

**YOUR OPINION IS ESSENTIAL
TO IMPROVING OUR PRODUCTS**

*Help us by answering the
questionnaire on our website:*
satisfaction.michelin.com

Michelin Travel Partner

Société par actions simplifiées au capital de 15 044 940 EUR
27 cours de l'Île Seguin - 92100 Boulogne Billancourt (France)
R.C.S. Nanterre 433 677 721

© Michelin Travel Partner
ISBN 978-2-067243-11-8
Printed: March 2020
Printed and bound in France : Imprimerie CHIRAT, 42540 Saint-Just-la-Pendue - N° 202002.0160